Advances in Information Systems Development

New Methods and Practice for the Networked Society

Volume 1

Advances in Information Systems Development

New Methods and Practice for the Networked Society

Volume 1

Edited by

Gabor Magyar and Gabor Knapp
Budapest University of Technology
Budapest, Hungary

Wita Wojtkowski and W. Gregory Wojtkowski
Boise State University
Boise, Idaho USA

Jože Zupančič
University of Maribor
Kranj, Slovenia

 Springer

Gabor Magyar
Budapest University of Technology
    and Economics
Budapest 1111
Muegyetem rkp. 1-3.
Hungary
magyar@mail.bme.hu

Gabor Knapp
Budapest University of Technology
    and Economics
Budapest 1111
Muegyetem rkp. 1-3.
Hungary
knapp@nava.hu

Wita Wojtkowski
Boise State University
1910 University Drive
Boise, Idaho 83725
USA
wwojtkow@boisestate.edu

W. Gregory Wojtkowski
Boise State University
1910 University Drive
Boise, Idaho 83725
USA
gwojtkow@boisestate.edu

Jože Zupančič
University of Maribor
Systems Development Laboratory
SI-6400 Presernova 11
Slovenia
joze.zupancic@fov.uni-mb.si

Proceedings of the 15th International Conference on Information Systems Development—New Methods and Practice for the Networked Society (ISD 2006), held in Budapest, Hungary, August 31–September 2, 2006.

Volume (1): Part 1 of a two-volume set.

ISBN-13 978-0-387-70760-0   e-ISBN-13 978-0-387-70761-7

Library of Congress Control Number: 2007929540

Printed on acid-free paper.

9 8 7 6 5 4 3 2 1

springer.com

Preface

This book is the outcome of the Fifteenth International Conference on Information Systems Development, ISD'2006, held in Budapest, Hungary between 31st August – 2nd September 2006. The theme of the 2006 conference was "New Methods and Practice for the Networked Society".

This theme expresses that we are living in a new era when practically all of our information resources are organized and managed in a networked environment. Information technology has reformed and restructured the workflows of companies and other organizations over the past several decades, and will continue to do so well into the future. This is particularly important now, as we see the emergence of complex networked information systems. "Being digital" by Nicholas Negroponte was the watchword at the dawn of the information society. "Being online" is now at the very heart of our everyday life. New postulates and requirements are stemming from this nature of society of today and tomorrow. The convergence of IT and infocommunication technologies has presented a challange for the ISD profession in terms of accomodating mobility, interoperability, the "always connected" state of information systems, the evolving distributed nature of information resources and the growing volume and diversity of information. IS development, both as a professional and academic discipline, has responded to this challenge through methodologies, tools and theory development. Progress in ISD comes from research as well as from practice. The aim of the Conference was to provide an international forum for the exchange of ideas and experiences between academia and industry, and to stimulate exploration of new solutions.

The ISD Conference evolved from the first Polish-Scandinavian Seminar on Current Trends in Information Systems Development Methodologies, held in Poland in 1988. It was a great honour and responsibility for us to organize the fifteenth event within this fine series of conferences.

Putting together a book of this magnitude requires the cooperation and assistance of many professionals with much expertise. We would like to express our gratitude to all the authors and participants for contributing to the conference that we believe to have been successful and memorable. The conference call for papers attracted a great number of very high quality papers. All papers were double-blind refereed by at least two independent reviewers and an Associate Editor. They provided detailed reviews on all papers submitted. We would like to thank the IPC members for their essential work.

Many thanks are due also to the assistance in organization of ISD 2006, especially to the Scientific Association for Infocommunications (HTE) and to the Conference Secretary, Mr. Sándor Szaszkó. We are also grateful to the National Office for Research and Technology (NKTH) for the financial support of the Conference.

Gabor Magyar,
Gabor Knapp
Conference co-Chairs,
ISD 2006

International Science Committee

Witold Abramowicz	Economic University	Poland
Gary Allen	University of Huddersfield	UK
Erling S. Andersen	Norwegian School of Management	Norway
Karin Axelsson	Linköping University	Sweden
Juris Borzovs	Riga Technical University	Latvia
Frada Burstein	Monash University	Australia
Rimantas Butleris	Kaunas University of Technology	Lithuania
Albertas Caplinskas	Institute of Mathematics and Informatics	Lithuania
Sven Carlsson	Lund University	Sweden
Dubravka Cecez-Kecmanovic	University of NSW	Australia
Antanas Cenys	Semiconductor Physics Institute	Lithuania
Rodney Clarke	University of Wollongong	Australia
Heitor Augustus Xavier Costa	Universidade Federal de Lavras	Brazil
Darren Dalcher	Middlesex University	UK
Gert-Jan de Verde	University of Nebraska at Omaha	USA
Vitalijus Denisovas	Klaipeda University	Lithuania
Dalé Dzemydiene	Law University	Lithuania
Jorgen Fischer Nilsson	Technical University of Denmark	Denmark
Julie Fisher	Monash University	Australia
Guy Fitzgerald	Brunel University	UK
Marko Forsell	SESCA Technologies Oy	Finland
Odd Fredriksson	Odd Fredriksson	Sweden
Chris Freyberg	Massey University	New Zealand
Edwin Gray	Glasgow Caledonian University	UK
Shirley Gregor	Australian National University	Australia
Janis Grundspenkis	Riga Technical University	Latvia
G. Harindranath	University of London	UK
Igor Hawryszkiewycz	University of Technology Sydney	Australia
Haav Hele-Mai	Institute of Cybernetics at Tallinn Technical University	Estonia
Alfred Helmerich	Research Institute for Applied Technology	Germany

Contents

A Revised Perspective on Documentation Practices in the Modern Organisation

J. Coady, R. Pooley

Heriot-Watt University, School of MACS, Riccarton, Edinburgh.

Abstract: There are a number of reasons for the use of various methodologies in the development of systems (Broady, Walters & Hartley (1994)), notably a reduction in user dissatisfaction and more effective communication between systems developers and users. These reduce the risk of a new system being presented to its users as a fait accompli. The use of an appropriate modelling paradigm can produce a better end product, improved consistency and the likelihood of improved user acceptance.

Formal methodologies may be appropriate for more technical systems where fewer human factors are involved; however, they may be too mechanistic to be effective in detailed, day-to-day organization of developers' activities. Traditional methodologies can still be valuable in IS development projects in order to maintain an image of control or to provide symbolic status (Nandhakumar & Avison (1999)).

Hard methods, such as structured and object-oriented approaches, (Bocij et al. (1999)) focus on the Computer Based Information Systems as a technical artifact, which must satisfy a set of well-defined user requirements. According to Chekland & Howell (1998), organisational change and improvement can only be successful when the organisational actors are engaged in that change. The IS is increasingly being viewed as a social artifact, and researchers such as Stapleton (2001) and Dewar et al. (2003) highlight the need for a revised perspective on ISD to deal with this development. Coady (2003) showed that, while there is a body of work which is concerned with the social aspects of creating a technical artifact, very little work has investigated documenting the IS as a social artifact.

This paper presents an empirical study; which identifies those practices that academia suggests are the current industrial standards, compares the perceived standards to current practice in the organisations involved in the research and develops conclusions suggesting better industrial practice.

1 Introduction

Early computerized information systems were typically implemented without the use of an explicit development methodology (Broady, Walters & Hartley (1994)). As a result of early era problems developers of the 60's and 70's learnt a number of lessons, which included the use of a life cycle, consisting of documentation, control and training, and that failings could be attributed to the narrowness of perspective of the analyst and the need for a real view of the organization. These lessons led to the development of many of the current methodologies (Broady, Walters & Hartley (1994)).

A system is an organized integrated unit that serves a common purpose, formed from diverse components (Ossenbrugen (1994)). There are many modelling notations available to analysts trying to simplify systems. Systems theory generally attempts to understand the nature of systems, which are large and complex. However, systems theory suggests that whatever methodology is adopted the analyst needs to look beyond the obvious boundaries and at the system as a whole. Information systems generically have human and computer elements and both aspects are inter-related. The technical aspects are closed and predictable, whereas the human aspects are often open and non-deterministic. The technological aspects are less complex than the human aspects in information systems, because the former are predictable in nature. Many information system methodologies only stress the technological aspects. This may lead to a solution, which does not work effectively, because often methodologies underestimate the importance and complexity of the human elements (Avison & Fitzgerald (1996)). This research study examines the problems of documenting systems and reviews the frameworks used within the firms studied for best practice in the light of what is known about IS documentation.

2 The need for a revised perspective of IS documentation

The concept of the learning organisation, as presented by Argyris & Schon (1996), is defined as a means to reflect upon, and re-evaluate the knowledge that is created by individuals within the organisational context. The organisation is changed as a result of this learning process. The learning process can be viewed as an ongoing sense making activity based on the collective knowledge of the individuals (Argyris (1976)). In this way the documentation of an organisation can help in the learning and development process and create a learning organisation by continuous re-evaluation and gathering of information.

According to Chekland & Howell (1998), organisational change and improvement can only be successful when the organisational actors are engaged in that change. By implication the area of IS documentation can also be affected by this change, whereby it is a necessity that the actors in a system are involved in the documentation and modelling process in order to ensure a compatible system. 90% of Information and Communication Technology (ICT) projects fail to meet their goals due to a misalignment of goals and organisational activities (Clegg et al. (1996)). IS documentation and development is supposed to consider organisational issues but too often IS is looked upon as a subsystem external or separate from the rest of the organisation. Bednar (1999) suggests a way of improving the disparate view of IS documentation and development is to view the organisation itself as an information system. By taking this view, IS becomes an inherent part of an organisation, including its actors, and its supporting processes, and not a separate entity, thus making it easier to see the relationships and making the documentation process easier and more standardised.

The computer industry is now over forty years old. During that time it has undergone enormous change, experiencing at least three completely new generations of hardware technology (Davis (1993)). Each new generation of computing has lead to wider and wider use of computer-based information systems (CBIS). CBIS are used to address an ever-increasing variety of problems in business, as was studied in this research. As the systems have become more and more sophisticated, researchers have recognised that the modern CBIS is something more than a passive, technical artifact (Stapleton (2001)). The evidence shows that information systems are social artifacts and an integral part of the organisation (Hirscheim & Newman (1989)).

Systems development theory has however maintained a focus upon the IS as a technical artifact, and the documentation reflects this. Many of the current best practice methodologies in the IS field do not support the social aspects of the IS, i.e. the actors and entities involved, rather seeing the IS as simply a technological solution. Development methodologies and their use are at the heart of the IS development process, yet to date, very little is known about how methodologies are used within the organisational context (Fitzgerald, Russo & Stolterman (2002)). These approaches develop a software machine, which satisfies a formalised set of information-use requirements.

This implies the need for a thorough review of the traditional documentation methodologies. As we progress in the technological aspects of IS, so too must we consider the ever-changing socio-technical aspects and document and develop systems to reflect these changes. Despite a long history and considerable research into methodologies and functional specifications for information systems documentation, researchers still continue to highlight the lack of knowledge concerning the development and hence documentation of information systems. Wynkoop & Russo (1995) claim that little is known about ISD and the use of the development methodologies. They state that there has been little evaluation of methodologies in use, or examination of the selection, development, adaptation or use of methodologies in practice. It is this lack of knowledge, which has important ramifications for research and practice (Stapleton (2001)).

3 The Research Study

The task of selecting a research method, which can appropriately address and test the research issues, is of vital importance. In many ways the research instrument is a microcosm of the thesis itself, implicitly or explicitly containing the key tenets of the study (Stapleton (2001)). Given the predominance of hard systems methods over soft methods in current ISD practice and university curriculum, a study was conducted which seeks to find out:

- Are responsibilities appropriately designated within IS documentation?
- Is IS documentation developed so as to address all areas in which it is used?
- Do people use diagrams extensively in IS documentation?

The starting point of a researcher's methodological choice within information systems is not so much a problem of how many methods to employ, or if those are of a quantitative or a qualitative nature, but the ability to identify the philosophical and theoretical assumptions which leads to the choice of the appropriate methodology (Garcia & Quek (1997)). Historically, information systems research inherited the natural sciences paradigm (Mumford 1991), and as a consequence, there are a number of underlying problems associated with information systems research (Cooper (1988)). The major criticism in the past was that research tends to be dominated by "scientific approaches" (Nissen (1985), Mumford (1991)). The information system is a social artifact (Stapleton (2001) and hence the identification of the requirements for the IS involves the IS community and user groups in a difficult relationship where the world must be subjectively interpreted and reinterpreted. This perspective sees the information systems design and development process as constituting discovery and rediscovery rather than logical analysis and design (Stapleton (2001)). The research methodology incorporated a combination of quantitative and qualitative data gathering techniques, as used elsewhere in similar information systems related studies (e.g. Stapleton (2001)). A Face-to-face interview with a semi-structured questionnaire was implemented, this also allowed for any inconsistencies, uncertainties to be clarified at will.

4 Findings

A total of 19 individuals were interviewed from the IT section of five organisations. The research was concerned with studying who documents, using both standardised and non-standardised approaches, within industries and if the documentation represents all areas in which it is used. It was also concerned with addressing the issue of diagrammatic notations within documentation, why documentation is used, if it is really useful, and hence it was important to gain access to the various levels of staff within the IT sector of the company, ranging from Analysts and Documentation Engineers, to Programmers and Management.

Traditional representation paradigms assume that IT-related notations are understood and a criterion of documentation is that all areas are modeled or represented in some way in the documentation. This study aims to get an overview of the documentation project at various levels within a number of different organisations. The research therefore focuses in detail on 5 organisations, with between 3 and 6 interviewees selected in each organisation. The virtual workplace was also a valued consideration for documentation in the focus of this research; an organisation was needed, which was working virtually. Virtual environments also need to be documented in order for people to be able to co-operate effectively. This study aims to compare the findings of the one virtual organisation and the 4 non-virtual organisations in its attempt to put forward a framework for best practice. The fieldwork was carried out over a period of 2 months. The timings were suited to the organisations needs and considerations were given to timing constraints and interview deadlines adhered to. The researcher approached five organisations based on the issues uncovered in the literary review, these five organisations being well known in their sector and having to adhere to stringent standards.

As 19 individuals were interviewed regarding an IT project they had recently undertaken, the range of projects and responses varied. These projects could be summarised into 3 major categories: firstly Type 1, the Automation of Information Streaming project, secondly, Type 2, an Advanced Supply Chain Integration System Implementation and thirdly, Type 3, the Augmentation of a Supply Chain Integration System

Table 1. Categories Breakdown of IS Project by Company

Company	A				B					C				D			E		
Person	1	2	3	4	1	2	3	4	5	1	2	3	4	1	2	3	1	2	3
Type 1				X	X			X	X	X		X		X	X		X	X	X
Type 2						X	X									X			
Type 3	X	X	X								X		X						

The Table below, Table 2, illustrates the comparison of each section to the ISD literature and shows whether the findings agree or disagree with the ISD literatures view. From the Table it is apparent that in some areas agreement in more prominent than in some other areas. The area of designation of responsibilities tends to agree with the ISD literature, which suggests that organisations stick to the traditional norms when creating documentation and finding representations of their work. As stated previously however, this can cause problems if the IS is viewed solely a technical artifact and the socio-technical factors are ignored.

Table 2. Comparison of Findings with Traditional ISD views

Section	Expected Traditional ISD View	Findings
2.1 Are responsibilities appropriately designated within IS documentation?	Yes	Yes
2.2 Is IS documentation developed so as to address all areas in which it is used?	Yes	No
2.3 Do people use diagrams extensively in IS documentation?	Yes	No

As we can see from Table 2, Section 2.2 and 2.3 tend to disagree with the traditional ISD literature views. Section 2.2 questions the reusability of documentation; in this study it was found that organisations did not reuse documentation to its full capacity, something that is suggested as a priority in the literature. The ISD literature suggests that it is through this reusing of documentation organisations can learn and provide a better IS. The purpose of documentation, as addressed in section 2.2, varies in organisations, which then leads to the issue of standardisation, also addressed in within a sub-section in section 2.2. It is possibly this lack of standardisation, and use of ad hoc methodologies, which leads to the variety in use of documentation and the perspectives on documentation within the firms studied. However it is clear that irrespective of standards and methodologies that the agreement with traditional ISD views that the problem solving capabilities of the documentation justify the effort taken to create the documentation. It can therefore be suggested that tailor made documentation for organisations can work effectively.

From the Table it seems that Section 2.3, which deals with the issues of Modelling and Diagrams, tends to disagree with the traditional ISD views. Diagrams are typically suggested as a means to simplify and explain in more detail in documentation, however this study has shown that companies are reluctant to use diagrams within documentation and where they are use are ad hoc, and personalised lacking in formal standards.

The findings of this study conclusively show the lack of standardisation within the organisations in this study. This research provides a platform for reviewing the key tenets of the documentation within industry and provides a platform towards creating a best practice procedure for documenting information systems.

5 Conclusion

This study reviewed the individuals involved in the documentation process within the various organisations. This investigation is an exploratory study into the documentation processes of organisations.

The literature suggests Soft Systems Methodology as an alternative approach to documenting information systems, as opposed to the structured methodologies, within organisations. The findings presented recommend that this is the case in most organisations, with firms tending to have an ad hoc approach to documentation, even where there are standards present. It is these ad hoc methodologies that work best for the interviewees within the organisations studied and people feel more comfortable using familiar methods they can design and manipulate themselves. It is these soft systems methodologies which go partly towards viewing the IS as a social artifact and can thus aid in the learning capabilities of an organisation. This increased learning power enables the organisations to create a more synergised and effective IS, with complete documentation. Fischer and Röben (2002) state that the learning which occurs when writing manuals is the most intense form of learning, and can aid in the implementation of the IS. It can also aid in the perceptions of documentation within the organisations and encourage individuals to participate more in the creation and use of the IS documentation. It can therefore be determined that the documentation of a company should be seen as a process which can aid the organisation, rather than simply an end product. It is only through discovery and rediscovery can the organisation learn effectively to produce a better IS.

Ultimately research itself is an iterative and learning process, and the conclusions drawn out here are broad. This research suggests the soft systems methodology as a best practice methodology. Despite the vagueness of soft systems methodologies, this work suggests that these methodologies can be used effectively for the documentation needs of an organisation if tailored to suit the organisation. Future research must examine the need for a tailored approach to documentation versus mass structured approaches to documentation as taught in academia.

As stated previously, individuals who feel involved in the analysis and documentation process, even onto the design and implementation phase, accept these changes more readily. They feel ownership of some part of the IS, and hence have a reasoning to overcome any fears they may have. The documentation process does not need to be enforced in such a way that resentment is caused, a possible formalising of the present informal methodologies used being a suggestion to ensure clearer benefits needs to be highlighted to industry regarding documentation and more user involvement is necessary in order to create useful documentation, which is generic enough to be applied throughout the organisation as a whole. This ensures transferability and re-usability of the documentation within the organisation. Green & Roseman (2002) suggest that the role of the person involved in the modelling process needs to be considered more deeply when evaluating the ontological completeness requirements of the system.

This research proposes a need to revise the traditional perception of IS documentation. This project is an attempt to see documentation in a different way and introduce a better perspective of IS documentation. New perspectives imply change, a process that is not always welcomed. This change needs to include the employees and not seen to have been directed from management levels above the individuals affected by this change. This is not only true in industry but also in academia, where programmes of learning need an updating.

References

Avison, D. & Fitzgerald, G. (1988). *Information Systems Development, Methodologies, Techniques and Tools,* London: Blackwell Scientific Publications.

Argyris, C. & Schon, D.A. (1996). *Organisational Learning II – Theory, Method and Practice.* Reading Mass: Addison Wesley.

Argyris, C. & Schon, D.A. (1976). *Organisational Learning.* Reading Mass: Addison Wesley.

Bednar, P. (1999). *Informatics – a working chaos for individuals and organisations. The impact of the notion of IS for System Analysis and Development (in Swedish).* Lund: Dept. of Information and Computer Science, Lund University.

Bocij, P., Chaffey, D., Greasley, A. & Hickie, S. (1999). *Business Information Systems: Technology, Development & Management*, Financial Times Pitman Publishing: London.

Broady, J., Walters, S. and Hartley, R. (1994). "A Review of Information Systems Development Methodologies (ISDMS)." *Library Management* 15(6), 5-19.

Checkland, P. & Holwell, S. (1998). *Information, Systems and Information Systems: Making Sense of The Field*, Wiley, Chichester, UK.

Clegg, C. et al. (1996). *The Performance on Information Technology and the Role of Human and Organizational Factors*, Report to the Economic and Social Research Council, UK, Systems Concepts Ltd., Vol. 2 (3). Accessed April 29, 2003 at http://www.system-concepts.com/stds/clegg.html

Coady, J. (2003). Information Systems Documentation: An Empirical Study of Current Practice in Irish Firms, Thesis for Degree of Master of Science of Waterford Institute of Technology.

Cooper, R. (1988). 'Review of management information systems research: a management support emphasis', *Information Processing and Management*, 24 (1).

Davis, A. (1993). *Software Requirements: Objects, Functions and States*, Prentice Hall: New Jersey.

Dewar, RG., Pooley, RJ., Lloyd, AD., Ure, J. & Cranmore, A. (2003). Enabling knowledge sharing in collaborative design using a socio-technical pattern language, 10th ISPE International Conference on Concurrent Engineering: Research and Applications, Madeira Island, Portugal, July 2003.

Fitzgerald, B., Russo, N. & Stolterman, E. (2002). *Information Systems Development: Methods in Action*. London: McGraw-Hill Education.

Fischer, M. & Röben, P. (2002). Organisational learning and knowledge sharing: The use, documentation and dissemination of work process knowledge, *Paper for The European Conference on Educational Research (ECER) for the European Educational Research Association (EERA)* ,LISBON, 11-14th September 2002.

Garcia, L. & Quek, F. (1997). 'Qualitative Research in Information systems: Time to be Subjective?', *Proceedings from the IFIP WG8.2 Working Conference on 'Information Systems & Qualitative Research'*, Philadelphia, USA.

Green, P. & Rosemann, M. (2002). 'Perceived Ontological Weakness of Process Modeling Techniques: Further Evidence', *Paper for The European Conference of Information Systems (ECIS)*, Poland, June $6^{th} - 8^{th}$ 2002.

Hirscheim, R.A. & Newman, M. (1991). 'Symbolism and Information Systems Development: Myth, Metaphor and Magic', *Information Systems Research*, 2/1, pp. 29-62.

Mumford, E. (1991). Information Systems Research-Leaking Craft or Visionary Vehicle? In *Information Systems Research: Contemporary Approaches and Emergent Traditions,* H.E. Nissen, H.K Klein, R. Hirschheim (Eds) North-Holland, Amsterdam.

Nandhakumar J. and Avison D. (1999). The fiction of methodological development: A field study of information systems development, *Information Technology and People*, 12, (2), 176-91.

Nissen, H. (1985). Acquiring knowledge of information systems - Research in a methodological quagmire. In E. Mumford, R. Hirschheim, G. Fitzgerald and A.T. Wood-Harper (Eds) *Research Methods in Information Systems*. North-Holland, Amsterdam.

Ossenbrugen, P.J. (1994). *Fundamental Principles of Systems Analysis and Decision Making,* 1-3, Wiley & Sons Inc., USA.

Stapleton, L. (2001). Information Systems Development: An Empirical Study in Irish Manufacturing Companies, Thesis for Degree of Doctor of Philosophy of National University of Ireland.

Wynkoop, J. & Russo, N. (1995). 'Systems Development Methodologies: Unanswered Questions', *Journal of Information Technology*, 10, pp. 65-73.

Towards a Dialectic Understanding of Enterprise Systems – Vendor Challenges and Contradictory Rhetoric

Stig Nordheim

Agder University College, P.O Box 422, N-4604 Kristiansand, Norway
Stig.Nordheim@hia.no

Abstract: Substantial Enterprise Systems (ES) research has focused on customers' implementation processes. This paper argues the need for a larger context to understand ES implementation. This context includes the fundamental challenge ES vendors are facing, how to satisfy unique needs with generic software. The designed solution to this challenge is analyzed, focusing on the two simple and yet fundamental concepts of commonality and variability. It is argued that the balance between commonality and variability may be viewed as a dialectic of design.

A study of ES vendors indicates that this dialectic of design is challenging. Finding an optimal balance between commonality and variability becomes an important design goal. This design challenge affects the customer directly. In the cases where variability is unable to meet the customer's requirements, a considerable pressure is applied by the vendor or implementation partner to make the customer adapt to the system. The study also demonstrates that leading ES vendors simultaneously promote both commonality and variability in their customer rhetoric, which may be viewed as dialectic. This rhetoric may even be considered paradoxical.

For customers the dialectic perspective on ES may shed light on the motivation behind the pressure applied by the vendor, and may prepare the customer for the contradictions likely to occur in the project and shakedown phases of ES implementations. For customers it is also important to understand the dialectic rhetoric in ES marketing, to be able to see through the dialectic rhetoric during the chartering phase.

1 Introduction

Enterprise Systems (ES) are commercial software packages that enable the integration of transaction-oriented data and business processes throughout an organization (Markus and Tanis, 2000). Two types of ES are studied here, Enterprise Resource Planning (ERP) and Enterprise Content Management (ECM).

ES represent an effort to apply generic software to meet the requirements of heterogeneous organizations. They may be viewed as a response to the challenge aptly formulated by Markus (1997): "the world around us is demanding that we find ways to satisfy unique needs with generic software and components". One may argue that the ES effort to satisfy unique needs with generic software implies a potential contradiction. This is a reasonable assumption as several studies have established the contradictory nature of ES implementations (Besson and Rowe, 2001; Robey et al., 2002; Soh et al., 2003; Wei et al., 2005).

A set of implementation choices may be viewed as a synthesis of the contradictory nature of ES implementations (Nordheim and Päivärinta 2006). Some generic ERP implementation choices are summarized by Luo and Strong (2004). These include three technical ERP customization options: module selection, table configuration and code modification.

This paper views the contradictory nature of ES implementations in a larger context, i.e. how ES vendors approach the challenge of solving the requirements of unique organizations with generic software solutions. The reason for focusing on such a larger context for ES implementations is two-fold. First of all, ES implementation involves a considerable knowledge transfer effort from the vendor to the customer (Lee and Lee, 2000). Secondly, according to Markus and Tanis (2000) misalignment issues and their resolutions in one phase may originate in previous project phases. An understanding of the vendor challenges may therefore be relevant for customers as a larger context for ES implementation.

There are two simple and yet fundamental design concepts used by ES vendors to address the challenge formulated by Markus (1997), namely the distinction between commonality and variability (C/V) (Leishman, 1999). Due to the contradictory nature of ES implementations, this paper takes a contradictory view of C/V in ES design, and raises the following question:

In a dialectic perspective, what are the ES vendor challenges related to the commonality/variability design issue, and what are the possible implications for ES customers?

Considerable ES research has focused on customer implementation issues, including dialectics (Besson and Rowe, 2001; Robey et al., 2002; Soh et al., 2003; Wei et al., 2005). Few studies have focused on ES vendors, one exception is Liang and Xue (2004).

First the concepts of commonality and variability (C/V) are presented, followed by the concepts of dialectics. An argument for a contradictory view of C/V is then presented. The empirical part is an interpretive study of nine ES vendors. The implications are discussed from an ES customer perspective, in relation to the ES implementation process and knowledge transfer.

1.1 Commonality and Variability in Enterprise Systems

Commonality and variability (C/V) is a characteristic of most software packages (Bühne et al., 2005). The general meaning of commonality is properties shared by all members of a group, and in software engineering commonality is expressed as "an assumption held uniformly across a given set of objects" (Coplien et al., 1998). Commonality is designed as properties shared by all customers of an ES.

Variability is generally understood as properties varying within members of a group, and may be viewed as "an assumption true of only some elements of a given set of objects" (Coplien et al., 1998). In a software engineering context, variabilities are "bound" by placing specific limits on each of the variabilities. One example of bounded variability may be a range of legal values for a parameter (Coplien et al., 1998). Variable properties are designed to be changed by different customers of an ES.

Within ES the designed commonality may include: common business processes, functions, workflows, screens, technical infrastructure layer, data models, and common default parameter settings (Leishman, 1999). As an example, SAP's variability includes the organization model, the process model, the function model, the data model and subsequent table settings, how applications and services are distributed across the computational tiers, and the user interface of screens and screen flows. It also includes interoperability with other programs, and the ABAP/4 programming environment (Leishman, 1999).

ES represent both bounded variability (e.g. configuration) and variability that is not bounded, (e.g. user exits and programming). For a customer it is interesting to note that bounded variability is associated with only slight maintenance efforts, whereas variability that is not bounded is associated with heavy maintenance efforts (Brehm et al., 2001). Customization is one example of variability that is not bounded, and to avoid code customization is a strategic critical success factor (Somers and Nelson, 2001).

Different vendors will, of course, reach very different decisions about the right balance between C/V (Davenport, 1998). This is also shown in the cases presented later.

1.2 Dialectics

Dialectics is a way of thinking, based on contradictions. A contradiction can be seen as a relation between two opposite aspects of a phenomenon, called thesis and antithesis; where antithesis is the negation of the thesis. The two aspects of a contradiction are intrinsically related, yet opposite and distinct from one another, and one aspect in a contradiction cannot be fully understood without considering the other (Van de Ven and Poole, 1995).

In dialectical theory, stability and change are explained by reference to the balance of power between the two opposing entities. A thesis (A) may be challenged by an antithesis (Not-A), and the resolution of the conflict becomes a synthesis (which is Not Not-A). By its very nature, the synthesis is a novel construction that departs from both the thesis and the antithesis. Dialectics is about dynamics, as dialectical theory is one way of explaining development and change (Van de Ven and Poole, 1995).

According to Dahlbom and Mathiassen (1993), contradictions can in some cases surface as trade-offs: "From a dialectical perspective, these trade-offs are manifestations of contradictions inherently related to the use and development of computer systems" (p63). Dialectic thinking is applied to the C/V concepts here, since dialectics contributes to the production of knowledge by an increased understanding of a phenomenon (Israel, 1979).

1.3 A dialectic view of C/V

Mechanisms for C/V are built into ES (Leishman, 1999), and commonality may be formulated as a thesis of ES design: "certain ES properties should not be subject to change". The thesis of commonality represents stability, and is true for a subset of the ES properties. The design idea behind commonality is that one should not change a certain property of the system, and one example is the ERP argument that the system contains "best practices" which should not be changed.

Variability may be formulated as an antithesis of ES design: "certain ES properties should be subject to change". The antithesis of variability represents change, and is true for a subset of the ES properties. The design idea behind variability is that one should be able to change a certain property of the system, as each customer is unique and requires a solution adapted to its requirements. Customers vary and their contexts may be different, therefore the system needs to have variable properties.

So for each ES property there is a design decision: whether the property should be subject to change or not. This design decision can therefore be viewed as contradictory, where one decision represents the opposite of the other (Figure 1).

"Property x should <u>not</u> be subject to change" (The thesis of Commonality)

⇕

"Property x should be subject to change" (The antithesis of Variability)

Fig. 1. The C/V design decision viewed in a dialectic perspective

If one accepts the thesis and antithesis as expressed in Figure 1, the C/V design decision of ES may be viewed in a dialectic way. An ES may then be viewed as a synthesis: some properties of the system can and should be subject to change, other properties of the system should not be subject to change. A design with 100% commonality would imply a rigid system, easy to install, but with an inflexibility that is completely unacceptable for a complex ES. A design with 100% variability would imply a total flexibility where every property had to be specified, a formidable installation effort and a completely meaningless situation for a complex ES. The synthesis is therefore a balance between commonality and variability, and represents the vendor's effort to satisfy unique customer needs with generic software. This study explores how the C/V balance is viewed by ES vendors, and possible consequences for ES customers.

2 Method

The study has been guided by the principle of the hermeneutic circle, combined with the principle of dialogical reasoning (Klein and Myers, 1999). Following an initial literature review, interviews were made with representatives from two ES vendors and one implementation partner. The two ES vendors were eZ Systems, one larger ECM vendor; and MultiPlus, a smaller ERP vendor. The implementation partner represented Agresso, a larger ERP vendor.

Six informants were interviewed, two for each system. They had 5-15 years' implementation experience. The interviews have been carried out by the author as qualitative, open interviews based on an interview guide. Dialectics was used as a "sensitizing concept" (Patton, 1990) to guide data collection and analysis. The interviews lasted ca 40 minutes each; they were audio-taped and transcribed. Using Atlas.ti for data analysis, the interviews were coded according to the following categories: commonality, variability, the C/V balance, adaptation of system and adaptation of organization.

The findings were followed up with a document analysis of vendor statements published on the web. Six dominant vendors were selected, to supplement the interview data. These included SAP, together with five major ECM vendors presented in the CMS report (CMS Watch, 2006) as providing enterprise platforms. Table 1 provides an overview of the data sources used.

Table 1. Data sources used in the study

Type of ES	Vendor	Type of data
ERP	Agresso	Interviews, transcribed and coded
	MultiPlus	Interviews, transcribed and coded
	SAP	Web documents
ECM	eZ Systems	Interviews, transcribed and coded
	FileNet	Web documents
	Vignette	Web documents
	Documentum	Web documents
	Interwoven	Web documents
	Stellent	Web documents

3. Cases

Two of the three cases where interviews were carried out, are described, since they provided interesting insights. The third case was a small ERP vendor, MultiPlus (www.multiplus.as). This case confirmed the findings from the two first cases, without adding new insights. Hence, it is left out of the description. The six vendors which were subject to document analysis are not described, only web references are given for these.

3.1 Agresso

Case number one is the Agresso ERP system (www.agresso.com), based in the Netherlands. With more than 2300 customers in 70 countries, Agresso offers solutions both to public and private sectors. Two interviews were carried out with the Agresso product manager at one of their main implementation partners in Norway. Another interview was with a hired consultant who was the project manager for a large Agresso implementation project. He had 15 years of experience with implementing Agresso for customers.

Commonality is heavily emphasized by Agresso. This is seen in their emphasis on complete solutions for public and private sectors. Variability is also emphasized, and is mainly provided by frameworks. Frameworks include customization and configuration tools. According to the informants, frameworks are only customized at national and business sector levels. At the customer level frameworks are in principle not customized, and the only variability mechanism recommended at customer level is configuration. Variability is also described as a "templated approach" to implementation (Agresso, 2005).

The Agresso product manager pointed out what he considered a puzzling phenomenon. On the one hand, Agresso provides a powerful customization tool that includes VBA interfaces (Visual Basic for Applications). On the other hand, Agresso emphasizes the importance of a limited configuration. According to the informant, this may indicate a rather ambiguous attitude to variability.

According to the informants, it appears that the more flexible the ES is in terms of configuration, the more customer pressure there is likely to be to configure rather than change the organization. Handling such pressure is considered a vital role of the consultant. From an implementation partner perspective, variability should not automatically imply an adaptation of the ES. The Agresso product manager advised against a mere ES configuration without a preceding organizational development process. As an illustration the Agresso implementation at the municipality of Oslo was cited, where the need for reports was reduced from around 1600 to 100.

3.2 eZ Systems

Case two is eZ Systems (http://ez.no/), an Open Source ECM vendor with 30-40 thousand downloads per month. eZ Systems' idea is to provide flexible solutions rather than "off-the-shelf" software. One of the informants has a split role between management of customer projects and programming, the other informant is responsible for all customer projects in the company.

Commonality is a kernel that is developed and controlled exclusively by eZ Systems. According to the informants, an implementation based on as much commonality as possible means better maintainability, higher quality and a cheaper solution.

There are two types of variability provided by eZ Systems' development framework; referred to as "supported" and "unsupported" variability by the informants. Supported variability consists of modifying HTML templates and configuration. Unsupported variability consists of interface programming, usually based on existing libraries. This variability is achieved by plug-ins into the kernel, and as the system evolves, plug-ins are extended without affecting the kernel.

Commenting on the C/V balance, the vendor's goal is to have as much configurability and as little programming as possible. The ideal is to empower non-programmers to establish complex solutions by simple configuration. A goal is to cover 95% of a customer's needs by configuration. Configuration constitutes the typical implementation effort, together with modifying HTML templates. There is hardly any programming in a typical implementation, although larger implementations are characterized by some programming.

The demarcation line between C/V is perceived by eZ Systems as an interesting design trade-off. As pointed out by one of the informants, if there is too much commonality compared to variability, the customer is being locked up due to lack of configuration options. But if there is too much variability compared to commonality, the customer will be confused due to the lack of standard functionality.

Consultancy on variability is part of eZ Systems' business model, and ranges from adapting templates for small businesses, to complex integration with legacy systems in large enterprises. Consultancy attempts to influence the customer, so that requirements can preferably be met by configurable variability.

3.3 SAP

This ERP vendor emphasizes commonality, that they provide complete solutions: "Building on the ground-breaking idea of standard enterprise software, we have become the leading provider of complete business solutions..." (SAP, 2003). In addition to a huge portfolio of software code, some commonality is represented by the so-called best business practices. These are claimed to be based on industry knowledge gained from nearly 19,000 customers in more than 20 industries (SAP, 2005).

SAP also emphasizes variability: "To deliver real value, your solutions have to be as unique as your business. That often means company-specific functionality and modifications – which can easily lead to spiraling costs. That's why we offer a range of dedicated custom-development services... This helps you get the most out of your investments in tailor-made solutions, while enhancing your competitive edge" (SAP, 2003b). One of the services of their more than 9000 SAP consultants is custom development (SAP, 2003b). There is also one example of reduced variability, the "mySAP All-in-One" solution, built to fit small customers. This is a pre-configured, industry-specific version (www.sap.com/solutions/sme/). SAP argues for its commonality by promoting best practices, and argues for its variability by promoting the services of its 9000 consultants to achieve unique customer solutions. SAP also promotes commonality and variability simultaneously: "Through extendability our customers can gain competitive advantage and have access to a cost-efficient mix of standard functionality and custom development" (SAP, 2003).

3.4 Five ECM Vendors

All the five ECM vendors studied (cf. Table 1) emphasize commonality, that they provide complete solutions. Commonality is also said to have the benefit of transforming the organization: "The true business value of Enterprise Content Management (ECM) emerges when it transforms an organization's operations to best meet the specific needs of its industry" (FileNet, 2006). Commonality is sometimes referred to as "out-of-the-box" software that allows customers to quickly create, update, manage and deploy virtually any type of electronic asset (Vignette, 2006).

All the five ECM vendors also emphasize the importance of variability, highlighting their adaptable and flexible software. Configuration, integration and consulting services are aspects of variability that are typically emphasized, and also custom code: "As with all business applications, certain business requirements may be entirely unique to a particular company or system environment. As a result, it often becomes necessary to construct custom code modules" (FileNet, 2006b). "ECM Documentum Consulting provides customers with highly customized solutions that support their unique combinations of platforms and applications... When business, process, or platform specifications dictate the extension of product or integration functionality beyond configurable capabilities, ECM Documentum consultants can apply programming expertise to ... tailor the platform to the specific business case or technical environment." (Documentum, 2006).

4 Discussion

According to Markus and Tanis' (2000) enterprise system experience life cycle, the origins of misalignment issues and their resolutions may be found in previous project phases. Following the principle of contextualization (Klein and Myers, 1999), it is reasonable to consider an even larger context of the ES experience; i.e. the origins of misalignment issues in ES implementations and their resolutions may be due to vendor challenges. This paper considers two simple concepts in this larger context, the C/V balance. This is at the heart of the ES attempt to satisfy unique needs with generic software. The C/V design decision (Figure 1) highlights an important design challenge for ES vendors, and provides concepts for discussing important issues at the heart of ES design. The main findings are summarized in Table 2.

Table 2. Summary of findings: ES vendor challenges related to C/V

Issue	Description
The C/V design challenge	ES vendors build C/V mechanisms and view the C/V balance a design challenge ("a dialectic of design").
Commonality	Commonality is emphasized by all the vendors studied, and

emphasis	ES are presented as complete solutions, e.g ERP best practices.
Variability emphasis	Variability is emphasized by all the vendors studied, that ES can fit unique customer needs. To provide sufficient variability is a vendor concern, especially configurability. For the customer it is crucial that the variability is supported by the vendor. Consulting services also promote variability.
Pressure related to variability	When variability (e.g configuration) can solve a requirement, customers apply pressure on the vendor to configure rather than adapt the organization. When variability can not solve a requirement, vendors apply pressure on the customers to modify their requirements to a configurable solution ("a dialectic of adaptation").
Both commonality and variability are promoted	Vendors simultaneously promote both commonality and variability aspects of ES in their marketing ("a dialectic rhetoric").

The C/V design challenge (Table 2) is to find an optimal balance between stability and change. In the eZ Systems case this is perceived as an interesting design trade-off. Such design trade-offs are indeed manifestations of contradictions inherently related to the development of the systems, as pointed out by Dahlbom and Mathiassen (1993). This C/V design challenge is here labelled "a dialectic of design", since dialectics is about dynamics (Ven de Ven and Poole, 1995), and the C/V demarcation line is dynamic. Viewed as a response to Markus' (1997) statement on how to find ways to satisfy unique needs with generic software, the dynamic C/V balance may be appreciated as a positive and important driving force for the development of ES. eZ Systems' goal to have as much configurability as possible is an example of a quest for increased variability, and SAP's "mySAP All-in-One" is an example of a quest for reduced variability. As ES vendors have chosen to balance C/V in different ways, the synthesis will presumably have to be dynamic, with no final solution.

The commonality emphasis of complete solutions is characteristic of ES, but they are hardly ready to be installed "out-of-the-box" as e.g Vignette (2006) claims. The variability emphasis of ES as "unique solutions", raises a question for customers: what kind of variability is promoted? Is it vendor-supported table configuration or unsupported code modification (cf. Luo and Strong, 2004)? To provide sufficient variability by configuration is a vendor concern. When consultancy is promoted, is this to remedy a lack of variability, or is consultancy necessary to handle the complexity of ES variability mechanisms?

The pressure related to variability (Table 2) means that the C/V demarcation line is important for the customer too. This raises a question concerning the knowledge transfer effort from vendor to customer during implementation (Lee and Lee, 2000). If vendors focused on the C/V demarcation line in their communication with customers, would knowledge transfer to the customer improve?

Further research should explore whether an explicit focus on the C/V demarcation line would facilitate knowledge transfer to the ES customer.

Both commonality and variability are promoted simultaneously, in what may be labelled a kind of "dialectic rhetoric" (Table 2). This is also done in practice, as with Agresso's dual emphasis on complete solutions and at the same time providing a powerful customization tool. Another example is SAP, promoting best practices, and yet promoting the services of more than 9000 consultants. ES consultancy has become a lucrative business that thrives on the challenge to satisfy unique needs with generic software.

The dialectic rhetoric raises a question about the dialectic view of the C/V design (Figure 1): that for each ES property there is an "either-or" decision. This contradicts the vendor rhetoric, where the sum of properties are presented as a "both-and". Which one is true? Is C/V a dichotomy or a continuum? This is a question of perspective. Considered at a detailed level, the C/V design decision is dialectic, each individual property is either subject to change or not (Figure 1). At an aggregate level however, the total set of properties may be viewed as a continuum, due to the large number of properties. The aggregate "both-and" perspective presented by the vendors, may be problematic for customers during the chartering phase of implementation. The ES chartering phase tends to be dominated by a deterministic vision (Besson and Rowe, 2001), and understanding some vendor rhetoric as contradictory "either-or", may enable the customer to see beyond the rhetoric. Further research is needed to establish how the dialectic rhetoric is perceived by customers, and whether it contributes to the chartering phase sense of technological determinism.

5. Conclusion

Based on two simple concepts, the C/V balance focuses on a key issue when unique needs are to be satisfied with generic ES software. To consider this larger context of the ES experience has the following implications. Viewing the underlying C/V design as a dialectic "either-or", may enable ES customers to see through the vendors' "both-and" rhetoric during the chartering phase. The C/V demarcation line also affects the customer directly. If variability is unable to meet the customer's requirements, a considerable pressure is likely to be applied by the vendor or implementation partner to make the customer adapt to the system. For customers therefore, it is important to view the C/V design as dialectic and focus on the scope of variability, thus to be prepared for contradictions likely to occur in the project and shakedown phases of ES implementations.

References

Agresso (2005) Whitepaper: "Implementation the easy way". www.agresso.com.

Besson, P. and F. Rowe (2001). "ERP project dynamics and enacted dialogue". SIGMIS Database 32(4): 47-66.

Brehm, L., Heinzl, A., Markus, M.L. (2001). "Tailoring ERP Systems: A Spectrum of Choices and their Implications". Proceedings of HICSS-34, Los Alamitos CA, IEEE.

Bühne, S., K. Lauenroth, et al. (2005). "Modelling Requirements Variability across Product Lines". 13th IEEE International Conference on Requirements Engineering, Paris, France, IEEE Computer Society.

CMS Watch (2006). http://www.cmswatch.com/CMS/Report/Vendors/

Coplien, J., Hoffman, D., and Weiss, D. (1998). "Commonality and Variability in Software Engineering". IEEE Software. 15(6): p. 37-45.

Dahlbom, B. and L. Mathiassen (1993). Computers in Context: The philosophy and practice of systems design. Cambridge, Mass., NCC Blackwell.

Davenport, T. H. (1998). "Putting the Enterprise into the Enterprise System." Harvard Business Review 76(4): 122-131.

Documentum (2006). http://www.documentum.com/consulting/custom_dev.htm

FileNet (2006). http://www.filenet.com/English/Industry_Solutions/index.asp

FileNet (2006b) Consulting Services. http://www.filenet.com/English/Customer_Center/Professional_Services/Consulting_Services/Consulting_Services/012050005.pdf

http://ez.no/

Israel, J. (1979). The Language of Dialectics and the Dialectics of Language. Copenhagen, Munksgaard.

Klein, H. K. and M. D. Myers (1999). "A Set of Principles for Conducting and Evaluating Interpretive Field Studies in Information Systems." MIS Quarterly 23(1): 67-93.

Lee, Z. and J. Lee (2000). "An ERP implementation case study from a knowledge transfer perspective." Journal of Information Technology 15: 281-288.

Leishman, D.A. (1999). Solution Customization. IBM Systems Journal, 38,1: 76-97.

Liang, H. and Y. Xue (2004). "Coping with ERP-related contextual issues in SMEs: a vendor's perspective." Journal of Strategic Information Systems 13: 399-415.

Luo, W. and D. M. Strong (2004). "A framework for evaluating ERP implementation choices." IEEE Transactions on Engineering Management 51(3): 322-333.

Markus, M. L. (1997). "The Qualitative Difference in IS Research and Practice". Proceedings of the IFIP TC 8 8.2 International Conference on Information Systems and Qualitative Research, Philadelphia. 11-27.

Markus, M. L. and C. Tanis (2000). "The Enterprise System Experience - From Adoption to Success". R. W. Zmud (ed.): Framing the domains of IT management: projecting the future through the past. Ohio, Pinnaflex: 173-207.

Nordheim, S. and T. Päivärinta (2006). "Implementing Enterprise Content Management: From Evolution through Strategy to Contradictions Out-of-the-Box." European Journal of Information Systems. In press.

Patton, M. Q. (1990). Qualitative evaluation and research methods. Newbury Park, Sage.

Robey, D., J. W. Ross, et al. (2002). "Learning to Implement Enterprise Systems: An Exploratory Study of the Dialectics of Change." Journal of Management Information Systems 19(1): 17-46.

SAP (2003). "SAP Makes Innovation Happen". SAP AG Brochure Material No. 50 065 210.

SAP (2003b). "SAP Customer Services Network". SAP AG Brochure Material No. 50 045 557.

SAP (2005). "Integrated Industry-Specific Enterprise Solutions For Midsize Businesses". AG Brochure Material No. 50 061 060.

Soh, C., S. K. Sia, et al. (2003). "Misalignments in ERP Implementation: A Dialectic Perspective." International Journal of Human-Computer Interaction 16(1): 81-100.

Somers, T. M. and K. Nelson (2001). "The impact of critical success factors across the stages of enterprise resource planning implementations". Proceedings of HICSS-34, Los Alamitos CA, IEEE.

Van de Ven, A. H. and M. S. Poole (1995). "Explaining development and change in organizations." Academy of Management Review 20(3): 510-540.

Vignette (2006) http://www.vignette.com/contentmanagement/0,2097,1-1-1928-4149-1966-4676,00.html

Wei, H.-L. H., E. T. G. E. Wang, et al. (2005). "Understanding misalignment and cascading change of ERP implementation: a stage view of process analysis." European Journal of Information Systems 14(4): 324-334.

Understanding Strategic *ISD* Project in Practice – An *ANT* Account of Success and Failure

Rebecca Abrahall[*], Dubravka Cecez-Kecmanovic[*], Karlheinz Kautz[**]

[*]School of Information Systems, Technology and Management, Faculty of Commerce and Economics, UNSW, Sydney, NSW 2052, Australia
dubravka@unsw.edu.au
[**]Copenhagen Business School, Department of Informatics, Howitzvej 60, DK-2000 Frederiksberg, Denamrk, and School of Information Systems, Technology and Management, Faculty of Commerce and Economics, UNSW, Sydney, NSW 2052, Australia, Karl.Kautz@cbs.dk

Abstract: This paper presents an interpretive case study of a strategic information system development (ISD) project in an insurance Company whose outcomes were perceived as both a success and a failure. By following actors – both human and non-human – involved in the strategic ISD project and the processes of inscribing and aligning interests within their actor-networks, the paper aims to unpack and provide a rich description of the contradictory nature of the socio-technical in such a project and the making of its success and failure. Guided by Actor Network Theory (ANT) the description traces the emergence of heterogeneous actor-networks and reveals how and why some interests did translate while others didn't into the IS designs, thereby producing the perceptions of success or failure.
Keywords: Strategic ISD, IS success, IS failure, Actor Network Theory, ISD as heterogeneous actor-networks

1 Introduction

The value and importance of strategic information systems (IS) – defined as systems that alter a firm's processes, products and/or services and change the way a firm competes in its industry – has long been recognized by industry practitioners and academics alike [5]. Many studies focusing specifically on strategic IS success or failure recognized the importance of social factors [8], implying a greater need for richer approaches to and deeper understanding of strategic ISD processes. The prescriptive solutions offered by the predominantly functionalist, positivist perspectives fail to offer a deeper understanding of complexities and subtleties involved in the strategic ISD processes in practice, especially perceptions of their successes and failures [8], [15]. Furthermore, it has been emphasised that in order to achieve deeper understanding both the socio-political and the technical nature of strategic ISD need to be investigated in an integrative way [2], [17], [13], [15].

Although a significant body of IS literature investigates social and technical issues, the bulk of this literature simplifies the ISD project environment into two segregated domains – the social and the technical. Many argue that such views are too simplistic to account for the complex nature of both IS strategising and ISD, calling for a more holistic research approach that better accounts for the inner-workings and intricacies of these vital business processes [23], [21], [3], [6], [15], [12]. But to do that we need to address the very nature of the social and the technical as they merge in ISD projects, which has been the subject of ongoing struggles in the IS literature [23].

In this paper we investigate a strategic ISD project in an insurance Company with the aim to i) provide a rich description of the socio-technical nature of such a project, and based on this description ii) improve understanding of the socio-technical interplay between actors and explain how this interplay impacts the perceived success and failure of the project. To achieve these objectives we use Actor-Network Theory (ANT) as a theoretical lens to investigate and explain the nature of socio-technical work and the interplay between human and non-human 'actors' throughout the strategic ISD project (see e.g. [4], [9], [10]). Following a brief description of some key concepts of ANT, we present research design and the interpretivist case study of the strategic ISD. The empirical data (interviews, researcher's notes and documentation) were then analysed and interpreted through the lens of ANT thus enabling deep insights into the socio-technical nature of ISD and the resulting perceptions of both success and failure of the system.

2 Theoretical Background: Some Key Concepts of ANT

By rejecting the traditional sociological view of the 'social' as a particular domain of reality used to provide explanations of science, technology and society, ANT aims to explain the social by tracing 'associations' among heterogeneous actors as they interact and form more or less durable wholes – actor-networks [4], [9], [10]. Also called the 'sociology of association', ANT assumes no a priori distinction between human and nonhuman actors, and sees them as active makers of actor-networks. ANT offers a uniform framework that accounts for micro, meso and macro levels of analysis, without privileging any [14]. ANT has been used in IS research to "study the social relations and processes by which [an IS] is fabricated, [considering] the facts and artefacts which mediate and reinforce those relationships" ([3], p. 200). Its central concern is to understand and theorise the role of technology and technological objects in making the social [6], thus enabling deeper understanding of ISD success and failure in strategic projects [8]. Examples of ANT research include Mitev's analysis of the new ticket reservation system at the French Railways [14]; Aanestad's investigation of the impacts of tele-medicine infrastructure in surgery [1]; and Walsham and Sahay's research into the adoption of GIS for district-level administration in India [24].

ANT is an emerging body of work and makes no a priori assumptions about the social world[1]. Some core ANT concepts, which remain constant throughout the body of literature, are summarised in Table 1. ANT is based on the core concepts of the actor. An actor is an entity – human, nonhuman or a combined hybrid object of the two – that can affect action in an actor-network. An actor-network is a heterogeneous network of aligned interests working toward the achievement of a common goal. The alignment of interests within an actor-network is formed through the enrolment of a body of allies (who become actors – both human and nonhuman) through a process of translating their interests to be congruent with those of the network [23]. This translation is achieved by inscribing actors' interests in the new system using 'scripts', which influence actors to assist an actor-network in the achievement of its goals. The act of inscribing actors with the necessary scripts is referred to as a program of action. Conversely, the act of challenging these programs of action is referred to as an anti-program of action [19]. These interests are inscribed into delegates, which are actors that stand in and speak on behalf of particular viewpoints that have previously been inscribed in them [24].

Table 1. Core concepts of ANT (adopted from [23], p. 468)

ANT concepts	Description
Actor or actant	Both human beings and nonhuman actors such as technological artifacts, documents, objects, etc.
Actor-Network	Heterogeneous network of aligned interests, including people, organisations and technology
Enrolment & Translation	Creating a body of allies, human and nonhuman, through a process of translating their interests to be aligned with the actor-network
Delegates & Inscription	Delegates are actors who 'stand in for' particular viewpoints which have been inscribed in them, e.g., software as a frozen organisational discourse
Irreversibility	The degree to which it is subsequently impossible to go back to a point where alternative possibilities exist
Black-Box	A frozen network element, often with properties of irreversibility
Immutable Mobile	Network element with strong properties of irreversibility and effects which transcend time and place, e.g., software standards

There are no prescriptive recommendations for the use of ANT as a research methodology. The following except from Walsham [23] is perhaps the best illustration and justification for the rationale behind ANT as a methodology:

> [ANT] is both a theory and a methodology combined...[as] it not only provides theoretical concepts as ways of viewing elements in the

---

[1] ANT has been criticised on several grounds (especially the symmetrical treatment of human and nonhuman objects). These criticisms will not be addressed in this paper, however a full analysis can be obtained from [23].

real world, it also suggests that it is exactly these elements which need to be traced in empirical work (p. 469).

Walsham and Sahay [24] noted that the aim of ANT is to examine the motivations and actions of actors in heterogeneous networks of aligned interests, by following these actors (and the work they do) through the actor-network. Underwood suggests that by following the actors of interest in a network and describing what we see as the key to revealing association s they make up the social, political, technical and contextual situations [20]. As a research methodology, we have chosen to enact the ANT methodology in this way, in order to trace actors through actor-networks, describing emergent situations using ANT terminology in order to understand, describe and ultimately reveal a rich description of a strategic ISD process and its outcomes.

3 Research Method

In enacting ANT methodology, we conducted an interpretive case study of a strategic ISD project – including a field study and a historical reconstruction of the project since its inceptions. Interpretive case study research was selected because it allows for tracing the associations and the construction of meaning through the direct engagement between the researcher and the actors – both human actors who experienced first-hand the situations being investigated and nonhuman actors involved in these situations. Secondly, achieving a rich understanding of the complex nature of a strategic ISD project necessitates that the study is conducted within its natural setting [22]. The case study was partially historically reconstructed as the key phase of the project studied was completed before the research started and some important actors left the Company.

The case selection required a strategic ISD project with an appropriate level of risk and complexity such that a degree of richness in data could be assured [16]. The selected Company that we call Olympia is the Australian arm of a large international insurance company. The project was unique in that it was an industry-first e-commerce system that transacted the Company's business insurance product direct to their brokers over the web. It was also interesting that the outcomes of the project were considered an outstanding success in the marketplace, however internally it was resented and considered a failure for not delivering required functionality and for being over-budget and over-time.

The case selected was auspicious in that one of the authors had previously worked at the Company over a six-month period as a member of the project team. The subsequent field study followed the actors: developers, managers, users as well as various technologies, plans, and documents. Empirical data gathered include i) transcripts of eleven interviews with two Architects, two Application Developers, Test Team Leader, Data Migration Developer, Senior Business Analyst, Business Expert– Underwriting, Business Project Manager, Senior Information Systems Executive, and Business Expert–Brokers; ii) project documentation (including historical documents); and iii) researcher's notes after the interviews and informal conversations with former colleagues.

The first stage of data analysis involved reading through printed copies of interview transcripts, notes and documents, highlighting interesting texts and tentatively classifying them under broad categories or 'codes' (open-coding). By following the actors – developers, analysts, managers, project plans, technology platform, strategic IS, etc., and by tracing their association and actor-networks' formation the analysis expanded, necessitating redefinition and (re)grouping of codes and sub-codes. Through an iterative process codes/sub-codes and related quotes were then arranged, on a 3x4m paper on a wall (dubbed the ANT wall) in a large office indicating various associations and actor-networks. Such a comprehensive visual representation of the findings enabled further exploration of the interplay between different human and nonhuman actors and dynamics of their associations within a bigger picture.

We approached theoretical interpretation by first identifying and making sense of key events and points in time throughout the project that for whatever reason were considered important to the actors and project outcomes. Through an iterative process of describing and examining the emergence of these events using ANT semiotics we traced the socio-technical associations, alignment of interests, inscription and translation, operating throughout the strategic ISD project.

4 The Case Company and its Industry Context

Olympia is (a pseudonym for) the Australian arm of a large multinational financial services institution, dealing primarily in general business and life insurance. In 2001, Olympia's General Insurance (GI) Business Division undertook to become the first insurance provider in Australia of web-based e-business services to their Broker Community (clients), selling their business insurance products online. Prior to the development of this Information System, named 'Olympia-Online', Olympia was not taken seriously, or seen as a major competitor in the Australian general insurance market. All e-business in the Australian Insurance Industry was conducted via 'BrokerLine', an outdated mainframe-based electronic platform, run by Telcom, an Australian telecommunications company. More so than any of their competitors, this platform was vital to Olympia since all its business is mediated through Brokers, and Olympia has no direct contact with individual customers in the general insurance domain.

In 2001 Telcom announced to the Insurance Industry that they were ceasing operation of the current e-business platform (BrokerLine) and all companies were required to move their business operations to 'Horizon', a new web-based platform. This situation is presented by an actor-network in Fig. 1 that shows the Telcom Company exercising influence on Australian insurance companies to transfer their business from BrokerLine over to Horizon and in doing so attempting alignment with the Broker community. Unlike Olympia, most insurance companies transacted their business both directly with individual business and via the brokers (indicated by their reciprocal alignment with both). This is why Olympia was particularly vulnerable to the change of the Telcom platform.

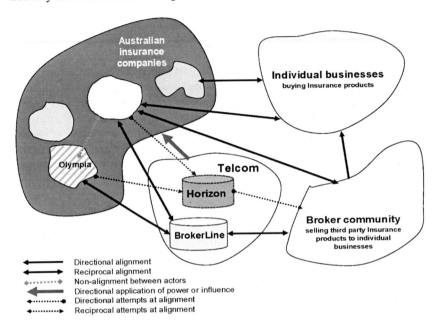

Fig. 1. An actor-network describing the situation in the Australian Insurance
Industry early-mid 2001

Fearing the loss of all their business, and simultaneously recognising the opportunities a new web-based platform afforded, Olympia's GI Business Division and Strategy and Planning Division went about putting together a business case for the development of a new web-based e-business system, Olympia-Online. By inscribing Olympia's interest and its new strategy into the Business Plan for Olympia-Online development and by charging Information Services Department with the responsibility to develop a concrete solution (a new information system to interface with the Horizon's web-based platform) GI Business Division and Strategy and Planning Division succeeded to enrol Information Services Department into the new actor-network. This inscription seems to be strong enough to motivate Information Services Department to attempt alignment with Horizon. With a prospect of becoming the only channel through which Olympia would interact with the brokers in order to sell its insurance products, Olympia-Online development became a key strategic IS project in the Company.

5 The Story of Olympia-Online Development

Olympia-Online was a new type of information system in the Insurance Industry of a magnitude never experienced by Olympia before. Their Information Services Department did not have the necessary skills or resources to conduct the development in house. To combat this, Olympia attempted to enrol an actor with the capabilities to develop Olympia-Online and ensure Olympia's alignment with Horizon. Based on the scripts (imperatives) expressed in the business case documentation, two companies attempted to forge an alignment with Olympia (mediated through the Information Services Architect). Azteka was unsuccessful as they said they were not able to deliver the proposed system within Olympia's desired timeframe (by September 2001). Reflex Technologies was successful as it did promise delivery within the desired timeframe and also offered a fixed-price contract. Developers from Reflex Technologies however developed a prototype based on the Emperor technology – a proprietary rules engine of which they were the sole reseller in Australia – in a very short time period. The prototype played the key role in enrolling Reflex Technologies into the Olympia-Online development actor-network. As a non-human actor the prototype gave an impression that the Emperor was an appropriate technology upon which the new system could be built. The contract signed July 2001 marked the beginning of the Olympia-Online development project which lasted for 12 instead of planned 3 months. This was later on referred to as Phase 1. After a year in operation the development continued mid 2003 until April 2005 as Phase 2. We now describe the Olympia-Online development project as it evolved through the phases.

5.1 Phase 1 Olympia-Online design

Phase 1 development began with some initial requirements-gathering sessions, run by business analysts from Reflex Technologies:

> We ran some formal requirements gathering sessions, first of all more in terms of use case development, just running scenarios to try and understand functionally what the product was supposed to do. (Alan, a Business Analyst)

Once development was underway and Reflex Technologies' developers engaged fully with Olympia's Information Services staff several problems emerged. As the project evolved, Reflex Technologies' developers recognised the actual breadth and depth of the problem at hand. Olympia's internal Information Services staff gradually became aware that Emperor was not the right engine for Olympia-Online's purpose, and was as such misaligned with Olympia-Online's initial objectives. In retrospect, the Senior Information Services Architect involved in commissioning Reflex Technologies noted that Reflex Technologies "didn't understand the problem at hand" and underestimated both its complexity, costs and the required development time. This was seen by the Information Services staff as the major reason for the seven months delay of the project.

The development of Olympia-Online emerged as a complex actor-network. It involved the integration between the existing Mainframe System, the new web-based application on Emperor, an interface with Horizon and PDF documentation development, which would be the customer's final output from the new system. The dynamics of this actor-network reflected the interactions among Reflex Technologies' developers completing the work that required Emperor, and Olympia Information Services staff responsible for all the integration between the Emperor component and the Mainframe resources. In addition, the interface development between the Olympia-Online and Horizon was being carried out by another third party, as was the development of PDF documentation.

That the work was eventually completed suggests that Olympia's interests were inscribed through a succession of translations into the Olympia-Online development actor-network. However the inscription was not strong enough to coordinate and channel the behaviour of actors so as to stabilize the actor-network. The Olympia-Online development actor-network involved eight actors, four of which were actor-networks themselves responsible for specific streams of development. Two other actors were overseeing this work – the Project Manager from Reflex Technologies and the Olympia Head Architect, who in their own words had "trouble ensuring the final system delivered the proposed system's original goals". Although they were officially in charge of Olympia-Online development their association with other actors was not strong enough to 'make others do things' ([9] p.107) and deliver the desired functionality.

Furthermore, GI Business Division, as a powerful actor, put pressure on Information Services. As the original deadline for Phase 1 completion past GI Business Division was anxious to announce to the brokers that the new system is ready for use. They promised that full functionality will be available by mid 2002, which upset Information Services personnel:

> [GI Business Division] shouldn't have gone out and promised that because there's no way in hell we can do it. We just had hundreds of defects outstanding, large parts of functionality not working... At the end of the day they convinced us, everybody put in a huge amount of effort and we sort of got it working with one or two brokers, full functionality, ah, I think somewhere in July [2002]. (George, an Information Services Architect)

However, despite 7 months delay, GI Business Division considered the implementation of Phase 1 Olympia-Online a success. This is based on the positive feedback from the brokers. The success was primarily due to Olympia recognising the power and value in aligning the Company with Telcom and the new Horizon platform. This alignment, combined with Olympia-Online's novelty value, which in turn was associated with being first-to-market with a web-based business insurance product, ensured the new system's success from a market perspective.

During the implementation and operation of Olympia-Online system Information Services staff experienced its poor technical quality, slow performance, frequent crashes and numerous defects. Its design was not modular and hence the system lacked the ability to be scaled to Olympia's future needs. As a result

Information Services staff had huge difficulties in maintaining Olympia-Online. They believed that Olympia-Online failures were caused primarily by the involvement of inappropriate actors – Reflex Technologies and Emperor. Emperor was originally designed for a different purpose and was not able to efficiently translate business rules into the rule engine.

However, Olympia's GI Business Division was unaware of the full extent of the system's technical instability, and thought the Olympia-Online system was an unqualified success. Based on this perceived success, GI Business Division, in discussions with Reflex Technologies, made the decision to purchase $1 million worth of Emperor software licensing such that the existing system could be rebuilt upon and more insurance products could be developed in the future. As Information Services did not enrol GI Business Division into the development actor-network, they were left out of this decision. GI Business Division, on the other hand, relied on their networks with brokers and Reflex Technologies. By purchasing the licence for Emperor they strengthened the actor-network with the Reflex Technologies and – perhaps inadvertently – translated their interests into Olympia-Online development actor-network. That Information Services, the only department that had the technical understanding and expertise, were neither involved nor consulted in this decision, had further implications for Olympia-Online re-development.

When the original Olympia-Online system became so unstable that its use could no longer be sustained, GI Business Division ultimately decided to redevelop Olympia-Online. However, since GI Business Division had already spent $1 million on licensing, redevelopment was planned again based on Emperor despite Information Services objections. This was then called Olympia-Online 'Phase 2' beginning mid 2003 and finishing in April 2005 when the system went alive.

5.2 Phase 2 Olympia-Online design

GI Business Division emphasised that their major goal of Phase 2 was to bring Olympia-Online development and knowledge in house, since it was key to Olympia's overall strategy and they wanted to prevent tacit knowledge and expertise from escaping the confines of the Company. This, goal, however, was not achievable since Olympia was reliant on Reflex Technologies' expertise during system development and design, as they were the only knowledge providers for Emperor in the market. Essentially, Emperor had become a delegate for Reflex Technologies' interests, and through the purchase of the Emperor license, Olympia had effectively enrolled itself in Reflex Technologies' actor-network, translating and aligning its own interests with those of the third party provider, as opposed to the other way around.

Phase 2 started with establishment of two new roles: the Business Project Manager responsible for ensuring internal business functionality of Olympia-Online and the IS Project Manager responsible for project completion on time and within budget. The third important actor was the Broker Business Experts (from GI) who presented the Broker Community's views. The Broker Business Expert managed to wield considerable influence on Olympia-Online development by translating the project objectives to be aligned with his own. This influence ensured the Phase 2 system was not implemented until a sufficient level of Broker Community functionality and quality had been delivered. He also made sure that the new system would be superior to both the existing system and other web-based products that competitors had recently developed in an attempt to attain parity with Olympia-Online.

This Broker Business Expert's high level of involvement resulted in the inscription of the Broker Community's interests in the new system, a strong alignment between the system and the Broker Community, and Olympia-Online's continued market success. This success in the market, however, is once again contrasted with internal failures.

The Business Project Manager appeared to be rather aloof and didn't engage in system development. As a result business requirements, including internally needed administrative functionality such as management and operational reporting, were not included in the Phase 2 Olympia-Online design. This means that GI's objectives were not inscribed in the new system.

Furthermore, the IS Project Manager's focus on time-line and budget control led to Olympia-Online design that was non-scaleable. Such a design would not enable adding easily new insurance products in the future. From this perspective the GI Business Division's interests were not aligned with or enrolled in the new Phase 2 development actor-network. This outcome is particularly disappointing for GI representatives, as they were promised the delivery of such functionality. A Senior Manager from within the GI Business Division expresses this frustration:

> [Phase 2] should have been *it*. So, well, you spend a considerable amount of money on Phase 1, you get to redo it in Phase 2 and it's disappointing when you hear you might have to do it again in Phase 3, to get what you actually thought you'd be getting in Phase 2.

This absence of core internal functionality has distanced the GI Business Division even further from the Olympia-Online development actor-network. Because they didn't see their interests inscribed they disaligned themselves from this actor-network. This might have long-term consequences for Olympia as further development of Olympia-Online was not planned while their competitors in the industry were building comparative systems.

6 Discussion and Conclusion

The ANT analysis of the strategic IS Olympia-Online development project reveals an open-ended structure of heterogeneous actor-networks which provide a rich description of its socio-technical nature. Such a description enables unpacking of the socio-technical interplay between the project actors, both human and non-human, which in turn explains how both success and failure of this strategic IS development were constructed. The key to success of Olympia-Online development was the ability of Information Services staff to align diverse interests of Olympia, the Broker Community and the new Telcom system Horizon and inscribe these interests into the Olympia-Online development actor-network. Especially by translating brokers' needs and interests into the design of Olympia-Online, or in other words, by inscribing these interests in 'durable materials' (Law, 1992), Olympia-Online implementation and subsequent use strengthened and stabilized this actor-network.

On the other hand, persistent technical problems faced during the development and the failure of Olympia-Online to deliver internal business functionality can be seen as resulting primarily from GI Business Division's simultaneous weak alignment with their own department of Information Services and strong alignment with Reflex Technology. Firstly, by enrolling Reflex Technology into the Phase 1 development actor-network GI Business Division enabled them to inscribe their interests through a succession of translations into Olympia-Online via their proprietary technology Emperor. Secondly, such inscription was highly strengthened by GI Business Division's decision to purchase the Emperor software licence. Alternatively, GI Business Division could have followed Information Services' recommendations not to continue further Olympia-Online development based on the Emperor engine. The concept of irreversibility of an aligned actor-network explains the impact of such a decision (Callon, 1991). As we have seen, purchasing of the Emperor software licence shaped and determined subsequent translations in the Olympia-Online development actor-network and caused significant technical problems and perceptions of the system technical failure with long-term implications.   This decision produced irreversibility of this actor-network as it became "impossible to go back to a point where that translation was only one amongst others" (Hanseth and Monteiro, 1998, p. 100).   The longer Olympia-Online development continued on Emperor technological platform the degree of irreversibility of its actor-network became higher. As a result technical problems persisted and complexity expanded taking more time and resources. While increasingly misaligned with Olympia-Online development actor-network GI Business Division perceived the project as failure from a project management perspective (over time and budget) and for not delivering the desired internal functionality.

By following the actors – human and nonhuman – and by tracing their associations as they created actor-networks of the strategic IS development project we described simultaneous making of its success and failure. Through a historical reconstruction of this project, we traced the emergence of heterogeneous actor-networks and revealed how and why some actors succeeded in translating their interests into the IS designs while others didn't. These processes of actor enrolments, translations and inscriptions of particular interests led to instability of some heterogeneous actor-networks and strengthening others, thereby producing the perceptions of failure and success.

References

1. Aanestad, M. (2003) The camera as an actor: design-in-use of telemedicine infrastructure in surger. Computer Supported Cooperative Work 12: 1-20
2. Avison, D., Jones, J., Powell, P. and Wilson, D. (2004) Using and validating the strategic alignment model. Journal of Strategic Information Systems 13: 223-246
3. Bloomfield, B.P., Coombs, R., Cooper, D.J. and Rea, D., (1992) Machines and manoeuvres: responsibility accounting and the construction of hospital information systems. Accounting, Management and Information Technology 2,4: 197-219
4. Callon, M. (1991) Techno-economic network and irreversibility. In: Law J. (ed) A Sociology of Monsters. Essays on Power, Technology and Domination, Routlegde, pp 132-164
5. Cavaye, A.L.M. and Cragg, P.B. (1993) Strategic information systems research: a review and research framework. Journal of Strategic Information Systems 2(2): 125-137
6. Doolin, B. and Lowe, A. (2002) To reveal is to critique: actor-network theory and critical information systems research'. Journal of Information Technology 17: 69-78
7. Hanseth, O. and Monteiro, E. (1998) Understanding Information Infrastructure (manuscript), http://heim.ifi.uio.no/~oleha/publications (accessed 18.04.06)
8. Hendry, J. (2000) Strategic decision making, discourse, and strategy as social practice. Journal of Management Studies 37,7: 955-977
9. Latour, B. (1991) Technology is society made durable. In: Law J. (Ed.) A Sociology of Monsters. Essays on Power, Technology and Domination, Routlegde, pp 103-131
10. Latour, B. (2005) Reassembling the Social: An Introduction to Actor-Network Theory, Oxford University Press
11. Law, J. (1992) Notes on the theory of the actor-network: ordering, strategy and heterogeneity. Systems Practice, 5, 4: 379-393
12. Luna-Reyes, L.F., Zhang, J., Gil-García, J.R. and Cresswell, A.M. (2005) Information systems development as emergent socio-technical change: a practice approach. European Journal of Information Systems 14: 93-105
13. Luftman, J. and Brier, T. (1999) Achieving and sustaining business-IT alignment. California Management Review 24,1: 109-122
14. Mitev, N.N. (1996) More than a failure? The computerized reservation systems at French Railways. Information Technology and People 9,40: 8-19
15. Myers, M. D. (1994) A disaster for everyone to see: an interpretive analysis of a failed IS project. Accounting, Management, and Information Technologies 4,4: 185-201

16. Neuman, W.L. (2006) Social Research Methods—Qualitative and Quantitative Approaches, 6th ed., Allyn and Bacon, Boston

17. Reich, B.H. and Benbasat, I. (2000) Factors that influence the social dimension of alignment between business and information technology objectives. MIS Quarterly 24,1: 81-113

18. Tatnall, A., and Gilding, A. (1999) Actor-network theory and information systems research. Proceedings of the 10th Australasian Conference on Information Systems, pp. 955-966

19. Underwood, J. (1998) Not another methodology: what ANT tells us about systems development, The 6th International Conference on Information Systems Methodologies, British Computer Society, Salford UK, accessed from http://www-staff.mcs.uts.edu.au/~jim/papers/ismeth.htm

20. Underwood, J. (2001). Negotiating the chasm in system development : some advice from ANT, Proceedings of the 12th Australasian Conference on Information Systems Coffs Harbour, NSW

21. Vidgen, R. and McMaster, T. (1997) Black boxes: non-human stakeholders and the translation of IT through mediation, Proceedings of the IFIP TC8 WG 8.2 International Conference on Information Systems and Qualitative Research, pp. 250-271

22. Walsham, G. (1995) The Emergence of interpretivism in IS research. Information Systems Research 6,4: 376-394

23. Walsham, G. (1997) Actor-network theory and IS research: current status and future prospects, Proceedings of the IFIP TC8 WG 8.2 International Conference on Information Systems and Qualitative Research, pp. 466-480

24. Walsham, G. and Sahay, S. (1999) GIS for district-level administration in India: problems and opportunities. MIS Quarterly 23,1: 39-65

How Can Organizations Achieve Competitive Advantages Using ERP Systems Through Managerial Processes?

Carl Erik Moe, Erik Fosser, Ole Henrik Leister, Mike Newman

Agder University College, Servicebox 422, 4604, Kristiansand, Norway

Abstract: Enterprise Resource Planning (ERP) systems have become a standard for collecting all business areas in one system. For some organizations it is a necessity for doing business, while others use it to outperform competitors. Prior research in the area of ERP systems and competitive advantage is dispersed and insufficient. Based on literature review and in-depth interviews at two Norwegian enterprises we have developed a framework which we believe gives insight into the areas managers should focus on when implementing ERP systems.

Our study supports the claim that ERP systems in themselves do not create a competitive advantage. Instead, they form an information basis which managers can utilize to outperform competitors. A good relationship between IT/IS managers and the rest of the management is crucial. The importance of top management support was highlighted and linking ERP and a data warehouse as a "bolt-on" was very beneficial in one of the enterprises.

1 Introduction

Enterprise Resource Planning (ERP) systems' aim to integrate all business processes into one enterprise wide solution by having one centralized database that all business areas have access to [21]. The integration facilitates information flow throughout the entire company [22]. It is possible to customize the ERP system to fit the original business processes. However this is usually not recommended because of the high cost and problems with system upgrades and maintenance difficulties [12]. Benefits from using ERP-systems are said to be revolutionizing [10]. However as our literature review shows, there are also stories of failures, cost overruns and problems with change management, hence it is of vital importance to understand how to achieve the promised benefits.

2 Prior research

Lengnick-Hall et al. [16] claims that ERP systems do not offer competitive advantages in themselves, but has to be coupled with social and intellectual capital within the firm. This is supported by others [14; 20; 23]. The overall benefit lies in the quality of *integrating* an organization's information flow and business processes [5]. By doing this the enterprise can optimize resources. However, others have argued that ERP can be part of making a competitive advantage in some situations [3].

Drawbacks with ERP systems have also been reported. Managers have not been aware of the difficulties in changing processes and organizational culture to fit the ERP system and struggled with change management [21; 18]. ERP systems may eliminate competitive advantages that organizations possessed before the implementation [3], due to the "common systems approach". Future needs of the enterprise can be hard to predict and further development of the ERP system is unknown to the buyer [18]. Drawbacks with lock-in of an organizations processes and principles into a specific software solution have been reported [15]. Shortcomings may lead to extensive switching costs, and it can be costly to combine the ERP system with other software products [22].

Not much research has been done on managerial processes concerning ERP systems and creating a competitive advantage [20; 3; 13]. More research has been done on the topic of implementation and realizing the benefits of ERP systems [9; 13]. A few studies has focused on mature systems up and running and achieving competitive advantage. This era has been called the "Post-Net" era [3] and "second wave" [6].

Kalling [14] focuses on how ERP systems and strategic management processes can lead to a competitive advantage. He suggests a framework to improve understanding of processes to achieve competitive advantage and uses the concept "bricolage" [7]. By this he means learning through trial and error and local tinkering. He argues that this may lead to improved work practices, new capabilities and therefore a strategic advantage. Many studies argue that it is important to have an open environment built on trust [16; 23]. The innovative organization which lies on top of the mechanistic ERP system should focus on open communication, consensus, alignment and flexibility [23]. The findings are dispersed and have sprung out of different school of thoughts. Most have never been tested empirically.

To structure our research, we developed a framework based on previous findings, shown in table 1, below. In our paper the resource-based view is used to define competitive advantage, the definition of resources [28] including broad aspects as brand names, in-house knowledge of technology, employment of skilled personnel etc. Mata et al. [20] concluded that managerial IT skills is the only attribute expected to create a competitive advantage. Powell and Dent-Micallef [23] found that flexible culture and supplier relationships are important. The results support the resource-based approach, and help to explain why some firms outperform others using the same ITs.

Table 1. Overview of significant prior research

Research domain	Our Research Topic	Prior Research
General	Common System Paradox	[3; 18; 16]
Competitive advantage	ERP systems and comp. advantage	[16; 3]
	The organizations' comp. advantage	[16; 3; 13; 14; 2]
	The managers' comp. advantage processes	[20; 1; 23; 16; 14]
Foundation for competitive advantage	The managers' knowledge of the organization and the ERP system	[1; 16]
	Training	Own curiosity
	Communication	[23; 20; 16]
	Cultures	[23; 15; 25; 21; 2]
	Business competent IT/IS dept.	[20; 13; 17]
	Top management support	[23; 22]
	Organizational structures and processes	[23; 16; 13; 25]
	Extraction of information	[16; 8]
	Creative usage of information	[16; 8]
	Extension of the ERP system	[26; 24; 4; 27; 19]
Processes	Future focus areas	[13; 14; 1]
	Plans for achieving comp. advantage	[14]
	Hurdles to achieve comp. advantage	[18; 14; 22; 21]

Based on the literature review we expect that ERP-systems can lead to competitive advantages, but that this depends on specific foundations in the organisation and on specific managerial processes. Our research question is therefore "What foundations and managerial processes can lead to competitive advantages when using ERP-systems?" To answer this we collected data at two organisations that were using the same ERP-system, and we will in the following briefly present our research approach before we present the results.

3 Research approach

We carried out 16 semi-structured interviews at the two organizations locations. As part of our triangulation we did an analysis of their IT/IS-strategies. The interviewees were asked to read through the "Interpretation and analysis" and the "Discussion" chapter for confirmation of our findings. Both companies are in the food industry. Foody had revenue of 485 millions NOK in 2004 and an IT budget of 4.5 million. Sllims revenue was 1.5 billions, and the IT budget was as much as 27.5 million. Foody had one department dealing with technology with only 3 employees, led by the director of finance. Sllim has both an IT and an IS department, both with their own manager.

4 Results and analysis

The chapter reports our main findings; table 2 below gives an overview.

4.1 General

All but one of the managers at Sllim said they were satisfied or very satisfied with their ERP system. The unsatisfied manager claimed that the system gave little support to his department's processes. At Foody five of the seven interviewed were satisfied with the ERP system. One was not satisfied and expressed it this way:

> *"The system is too hard to work with and navigate in. .... It is an A4 system, which force us to change to fit the system."*

The biggest benefit at both organisations was integration of data. This enabled them to streamline their value chain and internal processes across the entire business. The biggest drawback was that it was a bit too complex. Other drawbacks mentioned were that the sales module was not good enough, the system was too technical, and a lot of skills were needed to both use and manage it.

4.2 Competitive Advantage

At Sllim competitive advantage was something that had been discussed right from the start. Almost everyone stated that an ERP system could only give competitive advantage together with other systems or special competence. The director of IS explained that if their goal only was to maintain the status quo, they would be better off without the system. But when they added the data warehouse, they achieved an enormous data basis, which could give competitive advantage. At Foody they had difficulties in seeing potential for competitive advantage. The only two that really saw the advantage of the ERP system was the CIO and the director of finance. They explained what benefits the system could give, but had less focus on how they could differentiate themselves.

We wanted to know what different managers did to achieve a competitive advantage with basis in the system. We were especially interested in how they were able to arrange information, define structures and processes, customise the system, and manage employees. At Foody they mostly talked about improving. The answers we got at Sllim were reflective, but quite varied because of different areas of responsibility. The director of finance stated:

> *"I try to exploit the available tools in SAP, without investing money in new functionality. There are a lot of possibilities in the ERP systems, e.g. HR, ... to utilize our resources more efficiently."*

Other managers at Sllim focused on a tight cooperation with the business and tried to develop the business processes. Others again worked with parameter settings to optimize the system. The organization focused continually on training to enhance the user skills. They were also doing projects with suppliers and customers to extend their value chain. There was clearly focus on how to continuously develop and improve their work routines.

4.3 Foundation for Competitive Advantage

We wanted to know if the knowledge of the organization and the ERP system combined could be a source of competitive advantage. The two organizations are fairly different in this respect. Sllim rely on their IS department to improve their processes and to be innovative. The knowledge about both the organization and the ERP system are at its greatest in this department. The employees had worked in the company for a long time and knew the organization and the ERP system well.

At Foody they focused on the knowledge about the system and not the organization. Some thought they were finished with the implementation. The need for continual improvements, adjustments and the managers need for someone to push them were highlighted. The managing director confirmed that the combination of knowledge about the organization and the ERP system could be a source of competitive advantage. At the same time he was not very supportive concerning this.

Business competent IT/IS department is believed to be important. Sllim had a well established IS department with high focus on business knowledge as well as systems development. Dividing the IT and IS department helped them to avoid technical issues and focus on business development. The functional managers overwhelming trust in the IT/IS department impressed us. Their knowledge about the enterprise's processes and their strong determination to solve problems made them very effective. The IS department had tight communication with the users. Structured interviews to gather users opinions, was done once a year. Less structured communication was done continuously by walking around. At Foody the managers were divided concerning this issue. One indicated that their IT department had too much focus on technology instead of information systems as a whole. Another said that the IT department's knowledge was insufficient about his department's routines. However, the majority had a very different view.

We asked the individual managers how and if they encouraged their employees to utilize the information in the ERP system. The answers at Sllim were a bit diverse. Many reported that in some way they focused on extracting information and that the link to the data warehouse was very important. The data warehouse helped the employees to get structured reports that were used to further develop the organization. The director of IS explained that they focused on best practice and tried to transfer new, innovative knowledge to other departments. However, the ERP system was not set up to use information creatively. The job of the system was to deliver information to their data warehouse where all analysis was done.

Foody was concerned with how to extract information from the ERP system. When new ways of using the system was revealed, manuals were distributed to the various departments. The director of finance and other members of the original implementation team often developed intuitive user guides to help the employees get more out of the system. The director of production said they had a long way to go to use information creatively. Others argued that they were now in a "phase two" and could focus more on benefits.

The two organizations are at different levels, Sllim has had their ERP system for some time. They have created their own data warehouse which enables them to do comprehensive analysis and find creative improvements. Foody has not yet managed to stabilize their ERP system to develop their analytical skills. This topic of extension of the ERP system was mentioned by different managers during the interviews, at both enterprises. The bolt-ons could produce more firm specific advantages if configured properly. Sllim has had success with their data warehouse, whereas at Foody the managing director stated that *"we should probably have a data warehouse"*.

4.4 Processes

There had been limited focus on pre-analysis in both organizations. Still, Sllim had done more. The managers had some examples on what they did in the pre-phase of implementation. Not everything was done in the context of competitive advantage, however. Interviews were conducted to detect employees' need for support, and a number of requirements were identified from the entire organization. By tuning the system to the organization and the other way around, they achieved a good fit between system and organization. They had a "Phase II" of the implementation where they focused on how to exploit the extra efficiency gains of the system.

We wanted to know if the organizations had any plans or strategies on how competitive advantage could be achieved and if these were followed up and evaluated. This topic was discussed to identify their systematic approach to achieving a competitive advantage. It seemed that both organizations used their business strategies as pointers for what projects and processes they would initiate. They had however troubles with relating this to competitive advantage.

5 Discussion

How mature and stable the ERP system is, has impact on the level of utilization [22]. Markus and Tanis's [18] framework describes four phases in an ERP systems life cycle; the chartering phase, the project phase, the shakedown phase, and the onward and upward phase. Foody is still in the "shakedown" phase, whereas Sllim is in the "onward and upward" phase. The fact that the two enterprises were in different phases and that Sllim has been running their ERP-system for two more years than Foody has to be considered when we discuss the findings. But it was still a paradox that Foody had spent so little time on how the ERP system could give them a competitive advantage. Managers at Sllim have a more comprehensive and clearer strategy on how to succeed. This could also affect their level of adoption. The data warehouse gave them a competitive advantage and the ERP system was a part of this configuration. This is in line with [19] concerning data warehousing and [3; 14; 16] on information utilisation.

ERP implementations [14; 16] may eliminate competitive advantages an or-organization has. Features that made them unique and hard to imitate may be destroyed because of the adjustments to the system. At Foody, one situation may illustrate this effect. The director of production preferred an old customised system, it gave him all the information he needed and it was specially designed to fit his department's processes. Others told us that they were good at production, which confirms that the old system may be better suited for that department.

Mata et al. [20] described four important managerial skills to achieve a competitive advantage. These are IT managers' ability to: 1) understand business needs, 2) cooperate with other managers, 3) coordinate IT activities, and 4) anticipate future IT needs. Three of these skills were identified at Sllim, only one at Foody. We did not find evidence for the dual core structure, but it could be that it is used unconsciously. The dual core structure consists of an operational technical core and a strategic learning core [16]. At Sllim, they had opened for cross functional training. Users feeling they would benefit from extending their knowledge about surrounding departments' ERP processes could freely join. This can be seen as a path towards a dual core structure.

In both organizations the IT/IS department worked as a driver for ERP implementation and utilisation. The CIO and the director of finance at Foody were capable of being change agents. At Sllim, the IS department was really driving all other departments forward. One manager there told us that their competitive advantage consisted of an organizational culture compound with the ERP system which was not possible to copy, but he could not put words to it. It could be that he talked about a strategic important resource that fell under two of the conditions developed by Barney [2]; causal ambiguity and social complexity. This resource might be a tacit capability which was intertwined in social network and relationships [2].

Powell and Dent-Micallef [23] argues that supplier relations can create a competitive advantage. Managers at both companies talked about the importance of extending their value chains. One of the main reasons for implementing the ERP system at Foody was the possibility to exchange information with their biggest customer.

6 Summing up

Our study has confirmed some of the concepts from prior research. We confirmed that ERP systems do not give competitive advantage on their own, but can be the information basis for achieving an advantage. The few managerial skills mentioned in the literature have also been confirmed. What stood out as a beacon is the importance of a good relationship between the IT/IS manager and the rest of the management. The importance of top management support was confirmed. The management and organizational culture, and good supplier relations were also confirmed to some degree. The framework we developed can be important for further research. Below is a modified version of Table 1 with a summary of results and an overview of our contribution.

Table 2. Framework and findings

Research	Domain	Our Research Topic Support
General	Common System Paradox	No support
Competitive advantage	ERP systems and competitive advantage	ERP systems ability to create a competitive advantage had strong support in one
	The organizations' competitive advantage	organization and only weak support in the other
	The managers' competitive advantage processes	No evidence indicating that managers had a structured process
	The managers' knowledge of the organization and the ERP	Weak support for the learning loops described in the prior research, but it could be incorporated and hidden
	Training	in training.
	Communication	Opinions were highly dispersed and ranged from no support to strong support.
Foundation for competitive advantage	Cultures	Only a few highlighted the importance, but these few were strongly convinced.
	Business competent IT/IS department	Strong support
	Top management support	Strong support
	Organizational structures and processes	No or very weak support for the concept of the dual
	Extraction of information	core structure in both
	Creative usage of information	enterprises.
	Extension of the ERP system	Strong support for the importance of bolt-ons.
	Pre analysis	Some support for the importance of pre-analysis.
Processes	Future focus areas.	None of the organization had structured plans.

Research	Domain	Our Research Topic Support
	Plans for achieving competitive advantage	Both had focus areas and projects, but the link was not always visible.
	Hurdles to achieve competitive advantage	Hurdles described in prior research have been supported.

References

1. Andreu R, Ciborra C (1996) Organisational Learning and Core Capabilities Development: The Role of IT. J Strat Inf Sys. 5:2, 111-127
2. Barney JB (1991) Firm Resources and Sustained Competitive Advantage. J of Man 17:1, 99-120
3. Beard JW, Sumner M (2004) Seeking Strategic Advantage in the Post-Net Era: Viewing ERP Systems from the Resource-Based Perspective. J Strat Inf Sys 13:2, 129-150
4. Bendoly E, Kaefer F (2004) Business Technology Complementarities: Impacts of the Presence and Strategic Timing of ERP on B2B E-commerce Technologies Efficiencies. Int J Man Sci 32:5, 395-405
5. Brady JA, Monk EF, Wagner BJ (2001). Concepts in Enterprise Resource Planning. Thompson Learning, Boston
6. Brown CV, Vessey I (2003) Managing the Next Wave of Enterprise Systems: Leveraging Lessons from ERP. MIS Q Exec 2:1, 65-77
7. Ciborra C, Jelassi T (1994) Strategic Information Systems: A European Perspective. John Wiley and Sons Ltd., Chichester.
8. Daft RL (1978). A Dual Core Model of Organisational Innovation. Acad of Man J 21:2, 193-210
9. Davenport TH (1998) Putting the Enterprise Into the Enterprise System. HBR 76:4, 121-131
10. Davenport TH, Harris JG, Cantrell S (2002) The Return of Enterprise Solutions: The Director's Cut. Retr Oct 1st 2004, from http://www.accenture.com/xd/xd.asp?it=enwebandxd=_ins%5Cresearchreportabstract_174.xml.
11. Holland C, Light B, Kawalek, P (1999) Beyond Enterprise Resource Planning Projects: Innovative Strategies for Competitive Advantage. Proc 7th Eur Conf Inf Sys 1: 288-301
12. Kalling T (1999) Gaining Competitive Advantage through Information Technology: A Resource-Based Approach to the Creation and Employment of Strategic IT Resources. Lund Business Press, Lund
13. Kalling T (2003) ERP Systems and the Strategic Management Processes that Lead to Competitive Advantage. Inf Res Man J 16:4, 46-67

14. Kumar V, Maheshwari B, Kumar U (2003). An Investigation of Critical Management Issues in ERP Implementation: Empirical Evidence from Canadian Organizations. Technovation 23:10, 793-807
15. Lengnick-Hall CA, Lengnick-Hall ML, Abdinnour-Helm S (2004). The Role of Social and Intellectual Capital in Achieving Competitive Advantage through Enterprise Resource Planning (ERP) Systems. J Eng and Tech Man 21:4, 307-330
16. Markus ML, Benjamin RI (1996). Change Agentry – the Next IS Frontier. MIS Q 20:4, 385-407
17. Markus ML, Tanis C (2000). The Enterprise Systems Experience – From Adoption to Success, Zmud, R.W. (Ed.) Framing the Domains of IT Research: Glimpsing the Future through the Past. Pinnaflex Ed. Resources, Cincinnati.
18. Martin J (2000) A Fast Fix. Manufacturing Sys (MSI), 18:3, 88-94
19. Mata FJ, Fuerst WL, Barney JB (1995) Information Technology and Sustaining Competitive Advantage: A Resource-based Analysis. MIS Q 19:4, 487-505
20. O'Leary DE (2002) Enterprise Resource Planning Systems: Systems, Life Cycle, Electronic Commerce and Risk. Cambridge Univ. Press, Cambridge.
21. earlson KE, Saunders CS (2004) Managing and Using Information Systems (2nd ed.). Leyh Publishing LLC, New Caledonia.
22. Powell TC, Dent-Micallef A (1997) Information Technology as a Competitive advantage: The Role of Human, Business and Technology Resources. Strat Man J 18:5, 375-405
23. Rich N, Hines P (1997). Supply Chain Management and Time Based Competition: The Role of the Supplier Association. Int J Distr and Log Man 27:3-4, 210-225
24. Somers TM, Nelson KG (2003). The Impact of Strategy and Integration Mechanisms on Enterprise Systems Value: Empirical Evidence from Manufacturing Firms. Eur J Op Res 146:2, 215-228
25. Unal A (2000) Electronic Commerce and Multi-Enterprise Supply/Value/Business Chains. Inf Sci 127:1-2, 63-68
26. Vassiliadis P, Quix C, Vassiliou Y, Jarke M (2001) Data Warehouse Process. Man Inf Sys 26:3, 205-236
27. Wernerfelt B (1984) A Resource-based View of the Firm. Strat Man J 5:2, 171-180

Novel Approach to BCG Analysis in the Context of ERP System Implementation

Neven Vrček, Željko Dobrović, Dragutin Kermek

University of Zagreb, Faculty of Organization and Informatics, Pavlinska 2, Varaždin 42000, Croatia

1 Introduction

ERP systems have been the topic of interest for the researchers and practitioners for several decades. There are many success stories about their use and implementation [2, 42, 47], but also there are significant evidences of failures [16, 17, 18, 21, 35, 48, 49]. The controversy about them mostly arises from the fact that extremely high costs of licenses and implementation are not clearly related to the benefits of the enterprise [13, 15, 26, 28, 31, 45]. Also the measure of enterprise benefit has been vaguely defined with various performance indicators ranging from purely financial to complex composite performance measures [3, 14, 25, 29, 33, 34, 27, 37, 38, 41, 43, 46]. The reasons for low achievement of the desired goals have been found in various factors during implementation procedure, and there are several recommendations for better implementation approach (4, 6, 7, 50). It is generally accepted that every implementation requires strong organizational and management commitment (8, 20).

Standard ERP systems have been promoted as software solutions that are built on best business practices. According to the promoters, enterprises that buy them should embrace those built in business templates and achieve excellent business results. However, if enterprise has specific needs which are not part of standard ERP functionality, long lasting, expensive and complicated procedure of customization has to be carried out [5, 23, 24].

The link between competitive advantage and information system has been strong motivator for managers to buy ERP systems and force their implementation. However it is intuitively clear, that if something is commercially available to broad customer base, it cannot bring significant competitive advantage [36]. Many authors recognized that, and although there are certain positive indicators of business performance related to standard ERP systems, there is no strong evidence of such relationship [19, 44]. So what an enterprise or a non-profit organization can actually expect from an ERP system, and what benefits does it bring? It seems that certain organizations are better suited for ERP system implementation than the others [1, 30, 31].

Our results show that every serious attempt, which tries to answer this question, has to dig deep into business processes and find out what is their operational and strategic significance. Such comprehensive analysis requires significant time and strict methodology that enables unambiguous comparison between various organizations. This paper presents results of such approach. It is based on several years of research in various organizations that implemented or considered implementation of an ERP system. For that purpose authors developed methodology for strategic planning of information systems (SPIS). It was published in several scientific and professional articles and verified in relatively large number of commercial projects [10, 11, 12]. The methodology consists of a significant number of well known methods, but it combines them into structured and chained holistic process which gives deep insight into the business system and corresponding information system. By combining various methods under a common framework of methodology we obtain detailed and documented picture of an organization.

Table 1. Steps of SPIS methodology

Problem/step in IS design	Methods and techniques § -strategic, # -structured, □ -object oriented	Inputs and deliverables Inputs / Outputs	Usability Very powerful Powerful, Useful
1. Description of Business System (BS)	Interviewing	Missions and goals of current BS / Business strategy; Business processes (BP)	
2. Evaluation of the Impact of New IT on Business System	§ Balanced Scorecard § BCG-matrix § 5F-model § Value-chain model	BP / Performances of existing BS Business strategy / IS development priorities Business strategy / Information for top management BP / Basic (primary and support) business processes (BBP)	V P U V
3. Redefinition of Business Processes	# BSP decomposition # Life cycle analysis for the resources	BBP / New organizational units (OU) Basic system resources / Business processes portfolio	P P
4. Business System Reengineering	§ BPR § SWOT	Business Processes Portfolio / New business processes (NBP) Business Processes Portfolio / SWOT analysis for NBP	P V
5. Estimation of Critical Information	§ CFS analysis (Rockart) # EndsMeans analysis	NBP / Critical information for NBP NBP / Information for efficiency and effectivity improvement	P U
6. Optimization of New IS Architecture	# Matrix processes entities # Affinity analysis; Genetic algorithms	NBP / Business process relationships Business processes relationships / Clusters; Subsystems of IS	V P
7. Modeling of New Business Technology (BT)	# Work flow diagram (WFD) # Organizational flow diagram (OFD) # Activity flow diagram (AFD)	NBP / Responsibility for NBP New OU / Flows between new OU NBP / Activities for NBP	V P U
8. Modeling of New Business Processes, Supported by IT	# Data flow diagram (DFD) # Action diagram (AD)	NBP / NBP supported by IT (IS processes); Data flows; Business Data IS processes / Internal logic of IS processes	V P
9. Evaluation of New IS Effects	# Simulation modeling	IS processes / Guidelines for BP improvements	U
10. Business Data Modeling	# ERA model □ Object model	Business Data / ERA model Business data / Objects model	V P
11. Software Design	# HIPO diagram □ Transition diagram	IS processes / Logical design of program procedures (SW) Data flows / Events and transactions	V P
12. Detail Design of Programs and Procedures	# Action diagram □ Object scenario	Logical design of program procedures (SW) / Model of program logic Object model; Events and Transactions / Objects behavior	P P
13. Data Model Development	# Relational model; Normalization	ERA model / Relational model	V
14. Software Development	# CASE tools and 4GL □ OO CASE tools	Model of program logic; Relational model / Programs and procedures Object behavior / OO procedures	P P
15. Implementation of New IS	Case study; Business games	Programs and procedures / Performances of new IS	P
16. Evaluation of New BS Performances	# Balanced scorecard	Performances of existing BS; Performances of new IS / Measure of success	P

The SPIS has a number of methods, but some are applicable only in the case of the entirely new development cycle that brings new information system architecture. In the case of standard of the shelf software solutions, the methodology has been modified to produce combined information system that will be composed of standard and customized modules. One of the methods, which derived from such approach and proved extremely useful, is a combination of the Boston Consulting Group (BCG) matrix [39, 40] used in step 2 of the methodology, and the gap analysis performed during ERP system implementation. It shows the relationship between strategic relevance of the business processes and the level of support that is going to be achieved by standard software solution. Obtained results prove that in many cases strategic business processes are not supported at adequate level, and gained business results are sub-optimal [22]. Achieved outcomes are systemized and confirm initial hypothesis that standard ERP systems present low level of support for strategic business processes. Without detailed rethinking of the entire business paradigm, supported by really holistic and integral information system, competitive advantage will never be achieved.

2 Standard ERP system implementation methods

ERP vendors usually strongly promote their own approach to implementation of their products. Such examples are ORACLE AIM (Application Implementation Methodology) and SAP ASAP (Accelerated SAP). These implementation concepts have several advantages. They are:

1. Strictly focused and goal oriented to implementation of particular ERP system;
2. Based on standard documentation which enables easy transfer of knowledge and benchmarking of implementation projects;
3. Known by various ERP system consultants, which reduces dependence on certain implementation expert(s);
4. Verified on number of projects, which reduces the risk of successful implementation.

Therefore it is quite understandable that many enterprises, entering high risk and long lasting implementation projects, accept proposed implementation method without deep analysis how it applies to their own circumstances.

However standard implementation methods have serious downsides. Due to the fact that they are focused on software implementation and not on business improvement, they leave very little room for serious rethinking of business technology and business process reengineering. On the course of implementation, changes in business processes are usually proposed as a consequence of disproportion in functionality between ERP system and present work practice. Such forced business process reengineering adapts the enterprise to the ERP system without taking much care about actual business needs.

Standard step in every ERP implementation method is a gap analysis. Gap analysis denotes disproportions between current business processes in the organization and standard ERP system functionality. These disproportions are called gaps and might be solved in various manners, but there is usually very little attention paid to strategic importance of the declared gaps. Usually gap analysis is used to eliminate most obvious problems in implementation projects, and serious gaps, such as complete lack of support for certain business processes, are left to some subsequent projects. However results of the gap analysis are valuable source of information on which strategic impact of ERP system might be estimated.

3 BCG Matrix and Gap analysis

SPIS methodology is extremely detailed and requires strict modeling with description of business processes and data flows, before and after business process reengineering. Business processes are modeled through workflow, and activity diagrams. Workflow diagram presents distribution of processes within organizational units and data flows among them. Activity diagrams decompose each business process on activities performed by various jobs within organization. The consistency of the model is checked by the matrix of business processes and data classes. This matrix is entry value for affinity analysis algorithm, which gives logical grouping of processes with optimal modules and granularity of information system. In the case of standard ERP system, results of affinity analysis might be an early indicator of implementation problems. If grouping of business processes is different than grouping of standard ERP system modules, the level of required modifications might be significant.

At the final stage the model must be accepted by the management together with the plan for implementation of reengineered business technology with the new architecture of information system.

The early step of the methodology is the BCG analysis. This strategic method is important tool for valuating business processes in the context of their dependence regarding information technology and assessing the strategic significance of an information system. It is based on two-dimensional matrix showing four different types of management environments (see Figure 1).

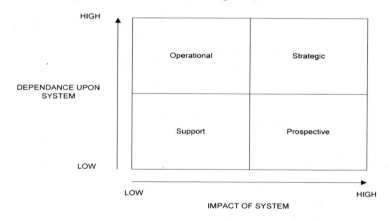

Fig. 1. Framework for assessment the strategic importance of an IT system

During analysis business processes are classified according to BCG matrix. Various business entities have different classifications of business processes according to the business sector or industry in which they operate and their strategic incentives. It is quite obvious that competitive advantage can be achieved by market differentiation which is obtained by excellence in strategic business processes. These processes must be supported by the information system to reach and maintain competitive edge. Therefore it is interesting to analyze how commercial of the shelf software packages relate to these processes and hence to the competitive advantage.

New in SPIS methodology is that, in this early step, results of BCG analysis are related to gap analysis. Gap analysis is used to analyze the level of support which will be given to the business processes by the standard functionality of ERP system. This analysis can not be performed on generic level but requires deep understanding of real ERP system functionality.

All ERP systems are developed on certain business templates and they have problems in situations where these templates are not suited to real organization which implements such standard software solution. These gaps might be solved by the change in the software, organization or, quite often, not at all. The question is how the existence of gaps relates to the competitive advantage of the enterprise and how are business processes that differentiate enterprise on the market supported by ERP system. This paper tries to find an answer by correlating BCG and gap analysis.

4 Materials and methods

The research was conducted in the period from 1996 to 2004. During that period the SPIS methodology was applied to nine large-scale projects. The projects, from which results presented in this paper were derived, took place in:

1. **Big international food industry (p1);**
   The company decided to improve business performance by introducing the ERP system. The decision for choice of an ERP vendor was based on benchmarking with similar industries on the market. The main motive for entering ERP project was cost control and costing mechanisms.
2. **Medium sized chemical and pharmaceutical enterprise (p2);**
   The enterprise was crossing the edge between medium and large company. Many business processes were not streamlined and management wanted to reduce chaotic reactions to market disruptions by using strict logic of the ERP system. The decision to choose standard ERP solution was mostly based on the desire to reach competition at every possible level as soon as possible.
3. **Big glass industry enterprise (p3);**
   The huge international consortium took over the enterprise and wanted to impose strict cost control, detailed and documented conduction of business processes and production planning integration with other member plants. The decision to use standard ERP system was imposed by the new owner and the fact that ERP system was consortium standard.
4. **Radio and video broadcasting enterprise (s1);**
   The enterprise was fully owned by the government and was preparing for the complete deregulation of the media and broadcasting market. By the decision of the national parliament the enterprise was separated from the

national television to offer video and audio signal broadcasting services on the market. Since it was highly dependent on the legacy information system, which was not any longer in its possession but was left to the national television, the enterprise was desperately trying to establish its own information system as soon as possible. Therefore it chose standard ERP solution, which seemed fast and promising solution for given price-performance constraints.

5. **National railway company – transportation of passengers (s2);**
The company was fully owned by the government and was part of the national railways. It was preparing for deregulation to become private owned, profit oriented enterprise for fast and convenient transportation of passengers. The management decided that one of the steps on this way was implementation of new information system. They found standard commercial ERP system to be most promising solution.

6. **National railway company – cargo transportation (s3);**
The company was fully owned by the government and was part of the national railways. It was preparing for deregulation and tried to cut down the costs and modernize itself to become serious competition to other means of cargo transportation. The management considered information system as very important tool to track and manage costs. Their choice was standard ERP system as fastest possible solution.

7. **National railway company – railroad infrastructure (s4);**
The company was fully owned by the government and was part of the national railways. In deregulated market it was still going to be owned by the government and would lease railroad infrastructure capacities to passenger and cargo transportation. Information system would be used primarily to support costs and planning of maintenance and development projects.

8. **National employment services (g1);**
The services operated in circumstances of high unemployment rate and constant pressure from various stakeholders. The management decided to modernize services and make it capable to face rising competition on job market. For that step it needed information system to consolidate data and monitor overall performance. On the course of the project several ERP systems were analyzed as possible support for business processes, but final results showed that new information system should be custom designed and management accepted proposal.

9. **National ministry of labor and social welfare (g2);**
The ministry operated in circumstances of high unemployment rate and tensed social relationships. It wanted to control high costs of its operations and rationalize social benefits system that was extremely expensive. To achieve these goals it urgently needed information system. During project several ERP systems were analyzed, but project strongly exposed arguments against standard off the shelf solution, which was accepted by the ministry.

All analyzed organizations intended to implement standard ERP solution or were in the process of decision whether to use standard or custom developed solution

Unfortunately in certain cases, decision for choice of the standard solution, was not based on deep business analysis and strategic planning, but mostly on desire to establish certain functionality of information system as soon as possible. Since such software solutions are usually marketed as support to best business practices, management also intended to improve business processes by changing them according to the requirements of software application. In these circumstances real strategic planning of information system was not possible. However, methods and techniques for strategic planning of information system, systemized in SPIS methodology, were applied in order to determine the real impact of standard solution on organization and its performance. Second goal of the described projects was to create architecture of complete information system composed of standard solution and custom developed modules, which should cover the whole organization and all the corresponding business processes.

In each of the projects, all relevant steps of SPIS methodology were applied. Methodology was modified to consider the fact that information system was not going to be completely developed but composed of standard and customized modules. Special emphasis was put on business process reengineering, and very significant work practice changes were proposed to maximize the influence of information system on business performance. Also the relationship was established between SPIS steps end ERP system implementation methods. Particular attention was directed towards gap analysis. Gap analysis revealed areas that were not supported by standard functionality of the ERP system. When related with other methods of strategic planning it could reveal complete new picture of the ERP system usefulness.

This paper describes relationship between gap and BCG analysis in abovementioned projects. BCG analysis groups business processes according to their strategic relevance and dependence on information technology. Combined with gap analysis, BCG matrix gives answer which business processes are supported by standard ERP modules and what is their strategic relevance. All organizations were thoroughly analyzed and business processes were classified according to the BCG criteria. The percentage of supported processes was calculated for each of the four BCG classes. Obtained results made possible comparison among analyzed organizations and sectors to which they belong.

Average duration of SPIS phase in abovementioned projects was approximately a year. The number of projects, in which results were collected, is not big enough to be statistically significant, but it certainly gives good insight to the fact that standard ERP systems quite often fail to support strategic and prospective business processes.

5 Results and discussion

The results of BCG analysis and gap analysis are presented in Table I and graphically in Figure 2. The table presents the percentage of all business processes in each of analyzed organizations supported by the standard functionality of an ERP system. The business processes are classified according to BCG criteria and organizations are grouped according to business sector to which they belong. Each analyzed organization has certain number of business processes in every quadrant of the BCG matrix and their classification was iterated several times and verified by the top management. During the gap analysis each process was checked against standard ERP functionality and the level of support was validated. Therefore in every quadrant of the BCG matrix two groups of business processes were obtained: supported and unsupported. The ratio of supported across overall number of business processes was calculated and is presented in Table 2.

The results of the research show that various groups of organizations are differently supported by standard functionality of the ERP systems. The best results are obtained in production industry. This is understandable because ERP systems have their origins in manufacturing systems. Also, variations between different business manufacturing systems are much less significant than in services oriented industry or public administration, so standard templates, on which ERP systems are based, fit relatively well. Differences between process oriented and discrete manufacturing systems might be quite significant but they are both well supported by most of the modern standard ERP packets. However, even in production domain, there is still much room for improvement and use of modern technologies in a manner that brings strategic advantage. The biggest support is on the level of supporting and operational business processes. These are usually financial, human resources, and standard production business processes. In production oriented organizational systems, strategic business processes are related to research and development, special features of production (e.g. integration of production equipment and information system) and warehousing. Prospective processes mainly deal with distribution of finished goods, operational maintenance and special features of supply chain management.

In services oriented organizations, standard ERP functionality gives much lover level of support. Again, better results are obtained at supportive and operational level, while strategic and prospective business processes are extremely poorly supported.

Public and governmental administration has low level of support at all four levels when compared to conventional production and services sector. This is quite understandable because their specifics are quite unique, especially for strategic and prospective level. Strategic and prospective processes of these organizations are related to improvement of their core business, which can hardly be found in standard ERP functionality. These are services to citizens (G2C), better communication with other governmental bodies (G2G) and various management issues that heavily relate on data analyses.

The results show that various sectors are not equally supported by standard ERP solutions and that in each sector level of support deteriorates towards strategic business processes. Without support for this kind of processes standard ERP system cannot bring strategic advantage to the organization. This is also true for prospective processes because they will never reach their full potential without proper use of ICT.

Table 2. Percentage of support that ERP system delivers to BCG classified business processes

	Production				Services					Public administration		
	p1	p2	p3	Avg.	s1	s2	s3	s4	Avg.	g1	g2	Avg.
Supporting	20	19	18.12	19.04	5.55	17.24	21.21	20	16	17.64	8.69	13.17
Operation	32	29.02	21.21	27.41	19.44	17.24	27.27	22.85	21.7	11.76	10.87	11.32
Strategic	17.14	16.03	14.13	15.77	13.88	0	12.12	8.57	8.64	0	6.52	3.26
Prospective	5.71	4.2	6.14	5.35	13.88	17.24	9.09	5.71	11.48	0	4.35	3.26

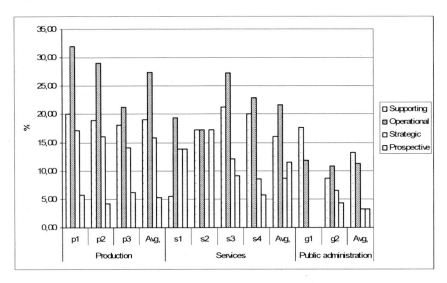

Fig. 2. Support of ERP system to BCG classes of business processes

6 Conclusion

Implementation of ERP system presents tremendous effort for the enterprise. Therefore it is normal that management, and organization as the whole, have high expectations from such modern software solutions. However long lasting implementation might lead to a disappointment if these expectations are not met. It might happen even in situations when implementation procedure was satisfying and all software modules were put in place. The reason for that comes from the fact that the key business processes were not supported by the standard software system. From the formal side such projects cannot be regarded as failures, but they simply do not bring competitive edge and adequate return of investment. They simply missed most important business processes.

Standard ERP system implementation methods do not pay enough attention to business process reengineering. They are too narrowly focused towards software implementation and deliberately avoid any broader context. Without severe rethinking of business work practice, significant changes in business processes, and detailed extension to integral information system such efforts are far from optimal.

Detailed business system analysis combined with strategic planning as in SPIS methodology gives comprehensive architecture of business processes and the architecture of information system, which should support them. Classification of these business processes with BCG matrix gives perspective of areas, which should be primarily supported to justify effort and investment. Special emphasis should be given to strategic business processes. These are processes, which give competitive advantage to the enterprise and differentiate it from the competition. Support for these processes cannot be bought off the shelf. ERP system must be implemented with clear vision of extensions that are going to be added to give new momentum to the enterprise.

Very important aspect is industry sector which is targeted by the implementation. Unfortunately ERP vendors enter all sectors promoting their software as silver bullet for all kinds of organizations. This is far from true. Results presented in this paper show that in government sector ERP system perform extremely poorly. However it is quite often that administration heavily invests in information technology and unfortunately frequently select ERP systems as solutions.

Therefore it can be concluded that ERP systems, although very expensive and complex, do not bring competitive advantage within boundaries of their standard functionality. Most often they are infrastructure on which specialized and strictly focused modules must be built. These modules will improve competitive edge and ERP system will give strength of integration, which will eventually lead to new business accomplishments or better services.

References

1. Abdinnour-Helm S, Lengnick-Hall ML, Lengnick-Hall CA (2003) Pre-implementation attitudes and organizational readiness for implementing an enterprise resource planning system. European Journal of Operational Research 146: 258–273
2. Al-Mashari M, Zairi M (2000) The effective application of SAP R/3: A proposed model of best practice. Logistics Information Management 13 (3): 56–166
3. Alpar P, Kim M (1990) A microeconomic approach to the measurement of information technology value. Journal of Management Information Systems 7(2): 55–69

4. Apperlrath H, Ritter J (2000) SAP R/3 Implementation: Method and Tools. Springer, Berlin
5. August-Wilhelm S, Habermann F (2000) Making ERP a success. Communications of the ACM 43(4): 57–61
6. Bancroft NH, Seip H, Sprengel A (1998) Implementing SAP R/3, 2nd edition, Manning Publications, Greenwich, CT
7. Bingi P, Sharma M, Godla J (1999) Critical issues affecting ERP implementation. Information Systems Management, 16(3): 7–14
8. Bradford M, Florin J (2003) Examining the role of innovation diffusion factors on the implementation success of enterprise resource planning systems. International Journal of Accounting Information Systems, 4: 205–225
9. Brumec J (1998) Strategic Planning of Information Systems. Journal of Information and Organizational Sciences, Vol. 23: 11–26
10. Brumec J, Dušak V, Vrček N (2001) The Strategic Approach to ERP System Design and Implementation. Journal of Information and Organizational Sciences, Vol. 24
11. Brumec J, Vrček N, Dušak V (2001) Framework for Strategic Planning of Information Systems. Proceedings of the 7th Americas Conference on Information Systems, Boston, MA, USA: 123–130
12. Brumec J, Vrček N (2002) Genetic Taxonomy: the Theoretical Source for IS Modelling Methods. Proceeding of ISRM2002 Conference, Las Vegas, NV, USA: 245–252
13. Brynjolfsson E, Hitt LM (1998) Beyond the productivity paradox. Communications of the ACM, 41(8): 49–55
14. Brynjolfsson E, Yang S (1996) Information technology and productivity: a review of the literature. Advanced Computing: 179–214
15. Brynjolfsson E (1993) The productivity paradox of information technology. Communications of the ACM, 26(12): 67–77
16. Chew W, Leonard-Barton D, Bohn R (1991) Beating Murphy's Law. Sloan Management Review: 5–16
17. Cliffe S (1999) ERP implementation. Harvard Business Review 77 (1): 16–17
18. Davenport TH (1998) Putting the enterprise into the enterprise system. Harvard Business Review 76(4): 121–132
19. Davenport TH (2000) Mission Critical: Realizing the Promise of Enterprise Systems. Harvard Business School Press, Boston: 56–62
20. Davis B, Wilder C (1998) False starts, strong finishes—companies are saving troubled IT projects by admitting their mistakes, stepping back, scaling back, and moving on, Information Week 30: 41–43
21. Diederich T (1998) Bankrupt firm blames SAP for failure. Computer World, August 28: 35-38
22. Drucker PF (1998) The coming of the new organization. Harvard Business Review, 66(1): 45–53
23. Everdingen Y, Hillegersberg J, Waarts E (2000) ERP adoption by European midsize companies. Communications of the ACM, 43(4): 27–31

24. Gefen D (2002) Nurturing clients' trust to encourage engagement success during the customization of ERP systems. Omega 30: 287–299, http://www.elsevier.com/locate/dsw
25. Grady MW (1991) Performance measurement: Implementing strategy, Management Accounting (June): 49–53
26. Grover V, Teng J, Segars AH, Fielder K (1998) The influence of information technology diffusion and business process change on perceived productivity: the IS executive's perspective. Information Management 34(3): 141–59
27. Gurbaxani V, Whang S (1991) The impact of information systems on organizations and markets. Communications of ACM 34(1): 59–73
28. Hayes DC, Hunton JE, Reck JL (2001) Market reaction to ERP implementation announcements. Journal of Information Systems, 15(1): 3–18
29. Hitt LM, Brynjolfsson E (1996) Productivity, business profitability, and consumer surplus: three different measures of information technology value. MIS Quarterly, 20(2): 121–42
30. Hong KK, Kim YG (2002) The critical success factors for ERP implementation: an organizational fit perspective. Information & Management 40: 25–40
31. Hunton JE, McEwen RA, Wier B (2003) Analysts' reactions to ERP announcements., Journal of Information Systems: 57–64
32. Hunton JE, Lippincott B, Reck J (2003) Enterprise resource planning systems: comparing firm performance of adopters and nonadopters. International Journal of Accounting Information Systems, 4: 165–184
33. Kaplan R, Norton D (1992) The Balanced Scorecard – Measures That Drive Performance. Harvard Business Rewiev, Vol. 70., No 1.: 71–80
34. Kayes J (2005) Implementing the IT Balanced Scorecard. Auerbach Publications, Bocca Raton, FL, USA
35. Langdoc S (1998) ERP reality check for scared CIOs. PC Week 15 (38): 88
36. Laughlin S (1999) An ERP game plan, Journal of Business Strategy, (January–February): 32–37
37. Lynn M, Madison R (2000) The role of ERP software revisited. Journal of Accountancy 190(1), (July): 104–105
38. Mahmood MA, Mann GJ (1993) Measuring the organizational impact of information technology investment: an exploratory study. Journal of Management Information Systems, 10(1): 97–122
39. McFarlan FW (1984) Information technology changes the way you compete. HBR, March/April
40. McFarlan FW, Cash JI (1989) Competing through Information Technology. Harvard Business School Press., Boston, USA
41. Mitra S, Chaya AK (1996) Analyzing cost-effectiveness of organizations: the impact of information technology spending. Journal of Management Information Systems, 13(2): 29–57

42. Motwani J, Mirchandani D, Madan M, Gunasekaran A (2002) Successful implementation of ERP projects: evidence from two case studies. International Journal of Production Economy, 75(1–2): 83–96
43. Peffers K, Dos Santos BL (1996) Performance effects of innovative IT applications over time. IEEE Transactions on Engineering Management, 43(4): pp. 381–92
44. Piturro M (1999) How midsize companies are buying ERP. Journal of Accountancy 188(3): 41–48
45. Poston R, Grabski S (2001) Financial impacts of enterprise resource planning implementations. International Journal of Accounting Information Systems, (2): 271–294
46. Ragowshy A, Ahituv N, Neumann S (1996) Identifying the value and importance of an information system. Information Management, 31: 89–102
47. Scheer A, Habermann F (2000) Making ERP a success. Communications of the ACM 43 (4): 57–61
48. Stein T (1997) Andersen consulting sued over R/3 installation. Information Week, (654), (October 27): 34
49. Umble EJ, Haft RR, Umble M (2003) Enterprise resource planning: Implementation procedures and critical success factors. European Journal of Operational Research, 146: pp. 241–257
50. Vincent A, Mabert L, Ashok Soni MA (2003) Enterprise resource planning: Managing the implementation process. European Journal of Operational Research 146: 302–314

Approach to Enterprise Knowledge Base Development

Saulius Gudas[*,**], Rasa Brundzaite[*]

[*]Vilnius University, Kaunas Faculty of Humanities, Muitines 8, LT-44280 Kaunas, Lithuania, {gudas, rasa.brundzaite}@vukhf.lt
[**]Kaunas University of Technology, Information Systems Department, Studentu 50, LT-51368 Kaunas, Lithuania, gudas@soften.ktu.lt

Abstract: Approach to Enterprise Knowledge Base development is based on the redefined concept of the knowledge-based enterprise and follows the Knowledge-based IS engineering paradigm. The Enterprise Knowledge component (Business, IT, Knowledge) is the core knowledge item of the presented approach. Enterprise Knowledge Space is formed for the analysis of the semantics and granularity of enterprise knowledge items. The UML class diagram of the Enterprise Knowledge Base is presented as a step towards practical development for the Enterprise Knowledge Base.

1 Introduction

Contemporary highly networked organizations use information technology (IT) extensively and need for an organizational memory accessible in the virtual environment. Well structured, validated and shared computerized part of the organizational memory is termed here as the Enterprise Knowledge Base (KB) and is intended to support management decision making, business and IT alignment as well as knowledge management (KM) and information systems (IS) development processes.

The knowledge-based theory of the firm considers knowledge as the most strategically significant resource of the firm [1, 2]. Information technologies play an important role in the knowledge-based view of the firm in sense that information systems can be used to synthesize, enhance, and expedite large scale intra- and inter-firm knowledge management [3]. There are a variety of KM models [4] and tools, but firms still face challenges when implementing IT systems for the support of KM [5]. Organizations require more systematic and formalized methods for the IT-based knowledge management implementation.

Enterprise KB is concerned as the obligatory component of the knowledge-based enterprise. The research starts with the identification of the core domains of the knowledge-based enterprise with the aim to clarify the role and the place of the Enterprise KB within the knowledge-based enterprise architecture.

In the chapter four the scope and boundaries of the enterprise knowledge are analyzed. In the chapter five the Enterprise Knowledge Space is defined with the aim to create practical method for Enterprise KB development. The basic components of the Enterprise KB are refined and represented by UML class diagram in the sixth chapter thus forming the background for the development of the Enterprise KB management system.

The presented models concern the knowledge management process in the knowledge-based enterprises. In the article the concept of the *knowledge-based enterprise* is used, which is based on the resource-based view of the firm [1,2], the conception of the *knowledge-based business*, provided by Zack [6] and follows the *knowledge-based information systems engineering* paradigm described by Gudas, Skersys, Lopata [7].

2 The Components of the Knowledge-Based Enterprise

The knowledge-based enterprise, regardless of whether its products are tangible or not, here is defined according the concept of knowledge-based organization, presented by M.H. Zack [6]; namely, the *knowledge-based enterprise*: a) recognizes knowledge as a key strategic resource, b) rethinks its business processes in the knowledge-oriented sense (i.e. "it takes knowledge into account in every aspect of its operation and treats every activity as a potentially knowledge-enhancing act." [6]), c) aligns its knowledge management activity with its strategy. Besides, in the article it is suggested, that knowledge-based enterprise uses Enterprise Knowledge Base (KB) together with explicitly modelled knowledge management activity as obligatory enterprise management and enterprise IS development component. This suggestion is derived from the knowledge-based IS engineering paradigm. Gudas, Lopata, Skersys [7] deal with the advanced IS engineering methods and tools and introduce the concept of the Enterprise Repository (Knowledge Base) as the main component for the intellectualization of the CASE tools as well as whole IS engineering process. The shared Enterprise Repository stores Enterprise Models and serves as the main knowledge source for the accomplishing IS engineering tasks as well as for automatic generation of IS models. Research, presented in this article, is directed toward extending the functionality of the Enterprise Repository for knowledge-based enterprise design, management and business-IT alignment tasks.

The concept of the knowledge-based enterprise is illustrated further by using Strategic Alignment Model (SAM) [8]. The content and role of Enterprise KB within the knowledge-based enterprise architecture is explored too.

In the knowledge management literature there are various KM definitions presented (listed by R. Maier [9]). Knowledge management can be considered as a strategic process of an enterprise and is intended to solve critical enterprise adaptability and competitiveness problems in the rapidly changing environment. The main goal of the knowledge management in enterprises is to create organizational context for effective creation, store, dissemination and use of organizational knowledge, which are essential for securing enterprise competitiveness against changing business environment and for setting environment towards a desirable direction. The newest vision of the most adaptive and responsive enterprise, based on IT, is expressed by Gartner Group [10] as the Real Time Enterprise (RTE). The RTE is the kind of the enterprise, which is able to gain the synergetic combination of IT, knowledge management and business strategy. Y. Malhotra [11] have analyzed the knowledge gaps which arise when implementing knowledge management in RTE and pointed out two main KM models: strategy-pull and technology-push, thus indicating two interrelated RTE domains: business (strategy) domain and technology domain. Henderson and Venkatraman [8] have also analysed business-IT alignment problem and proposed a Strategic Alignment Model (SAM) for business–IT alignment; the model was aimed to support the integration of information technology (IT) into business strategy by advocating alignment between and within four domains. In the SAM two interrelated aspects of computerized enterprise are defined: 1) Business domain and 2) IT domain; both domains are viewed in two levels of detail: 1) Infrastructure and processes level, 2) Strategic level. As a result of such decomposition four different domains were identified: Business strategy domain, Business infrastructure and processes domain, IT strategy domain and IT infrastructure and processes domain (see Fig.1).

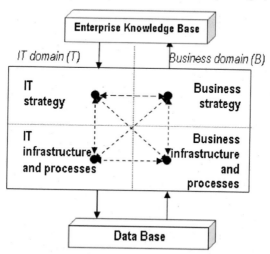

Fig. 1. Integration of enterprise components, related to knowledge management

Thus SAM model identifies major interactions between business and IT domain, which can be expressed as structural models.

Knowledge-centric enterprise, as any other contemporary organization, possibly uses the integrated data repositories which are presented in the SAM as the *Data Base* component (Fig.1).

In order to support alignment decision making between four domain, Strategic Alignment Model is complemented by one more additional structural element – *Enterprise Knowledge Base* element (see Fig.1), which supports enterprise knowledge management activities and allows continuous cross-domain alignment process for gaining the synergetic combination of both (business and IT) domains.

The scope and boundaries of the enterprise knowledge will be examined in the next chapter. First let us discuss the types of knowledge the Enterprise KB comprises.

Organizational memory comprises all the possible forms of organizational knowledge: tacit, explicit, computerized, not-computerized etc. [9].

There are a lot of possible facets for characterising knowledge [9] although it is important in this situation to analyse knowledge in the sense of its "objective" and "subjective" characteristics. According J.M Firestone [12], there are two kinds of knowledge: "Knowledge viewed as belief…", and "Knowledge viewed as validated models, theories, arguments, descriptions, problem statements etc."

In the area of IS engineering Enterprise KB is the source of knowledge about the problem domain (i.e. enterprise). Business-IT alignment is continuous decision making process and it also should be supported with reliable information and knowledge. Resuming it should be stated that Enterprise Knowledge Base stores the enterprise knowledge in the form of validated Enterprise Knowledge Models for business management and computerization.

According knowledge-based IS engineering paradigm [7, 13] enterprise knowledge models have to be validated according formalized enterprise model thus ensuring reliability of the acquired knowledge about problem domain.

So, Enterprise Knowledge Base is the reliable knowledge source for a support of business management decision making, business and IT alignment as well as for support of knowledge management and IS development processes.

3 Four Domains of the Knowledge-Based Enterprise

In SAM [8] two interrelated aspects of the enterprise are defined: 1) business domain and 2) IT domain. According the definition of the knowledge-based enterprise, another two important aspects of the enterprise can be identified: Knowledge domain and Data domain (Fig.1). All these four aspects forms four interrelated domains (see Fig.2), which have to be taken into account when transforming business into knowledge-based business.

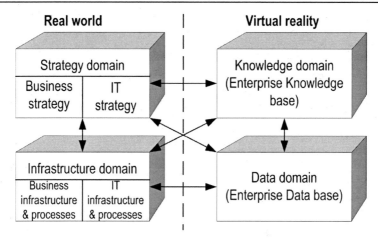

Fig. 2. Four domains of the knowledge-based enterprise

The peculiarity of the abstraction, presented in the Fig.2 is that it clearly separates the Knowledge domain and Data domain, in contrast to other conceptual enterprise models (e.g. presented in [14]).

Knowledge-based enterprise uses knowledge as a key strategic resource, as it was said before (see also Fig.2). It became evident that the *organizational knowledge (non-digital knowledge)* is human knowledge used (and hidden in the Fig. 2) in the *business* and *IT domains* as integral components of any enterprise.

Meanwhile *enterprise knowledge* (virtual, digital knowledge stored in the Enterprise KB) is obligatory component of knowledge-based enterprise, integrated with all enterprise domains. Accordingly three tiers Knowledge-based Enterprise Architecture (in the Fig.3), it includes Enterprise KB as key component, integrated with knowledge management systems.

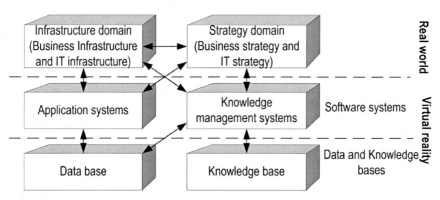

Fig. 3. Knowledge-based Enterprise Architecture

The following chapter is focused on the identification of the boundaries and actual content of the Enterprise Knowledge Base.

4 Modelling Views of the Enterprise Knowledge and Data

It should be pointed out two types of knowledge inherent to the knowledge-based enterprise.

First type of knowledge comprises all the organizational memory, which consists of various types of human knowledge, handled by managers daily to perform organizational activities as well as for management of these activities. This type of knowledge is referred to as *organizational knowledge*.

Another type of knowledge is a subset of knowledge stored in the Enterprise KB, and is named as *enterprise knowledge*. It comprises virtual (digital) knowledge about the problem domain, i.e. activities of knowledge-based enterprise.

From the abstraction shown in the Fig.2 it can be concluded that knowledge-based enterprise has four interrelated aspects: IT strategy and infrastructure (*T*), Business strategy and infrastructure (*B*), Enterprise knowledge (*K*) and Data. The major aspects of enterprise activities (*T, B, K*) are interrelated and comprises enterprise knowledge component (see Fig.4).

The enterprise knowledge component is associated with enterprise data repositories (data base) as well (see Fig.5).

The depicted (Figs.4,5) enterprise knowledge component structure represents a structural viewpoint to enterprise knowledge modelling: the Knowledge Base should include *integrated enterprise knowledge* (validated models, theories, arguments, descriptions, problem statements) about business strategy and infrastructure (*B*), IT strategy and infrastructure (*T*), and *enterprise modelling knowledge* (*K*).

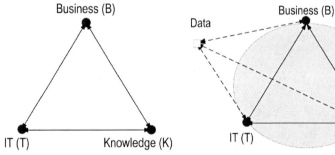
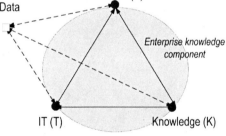

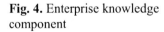

Fig. 4. Enterprise knowledge component

Fig. 5. Integration of enterprise knowledge and data

The detailed description of these three aspects of enterprise knowledge is the next chapter and illustrated in the Fig.6.

5 The Enterprise Knowledge Space

The next step is to identify the analysis levels of each enterprise knowledge aspect.

The Enterprise Knowledge Space *E (B, T, K)*, presented in Fig.6, is constructed for systematization of the enterprise knowledge research with the aim to find practical enterprise knowledge modelling method.

The contemporary organizational theories distinguish between four hierarchical levels in organizations: strategic management level, tactical management level, knowledge management level and operational management level [15].

On the basis of such a hierarchical system, we can define four adequate levels in organizational information management processes as well as technological processes management level. We have modified a slightly ordinary hierarchical structure by placing knowledge management in the second level of the management hierarchy, because of the overall nature of the knowledge management processes.

The enterprise knowledge space (Fig.6) was formed by fitting integrated knowledge component with the hierarchical information structure of the organization as mentioned above.

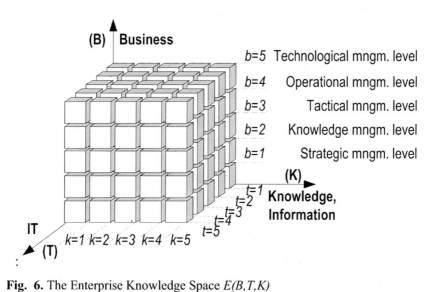

Fig. 6. The Enterprise Knowledge Space *E(B,T,K)*

Each item *e* in the enterprise knowledge space *E(B,T,K)* is identified according to three axes:

$$e(b;t;k) \in E, \quad \forall b,t,k \in \{1,...,5\}. \tag{5.1}$$

Each of the 125 items has its own semantics and identifies the element of enterprise knowledge, which integrates three aspects of the enterprise: business (*B*), information technology (*IT*) and knowledge (*K*) in 5 levels of detail (accordingly *b,t,k*).

Each index *b, t* and *k* can acquire values from following sets:

$\forall b \in$ {*b1=Strategic management level; b2= Knowledge management*   (5.2)
level; b3= Tactical management level; b4= Operational management
level; b5=Technological processes management level};

$\forall z \in${*z1=Ontological level; z2=Meta-metamodelling level;*
z3=Metamodelling level; z4=Conceptual modelling level;   (5.3)
z5=Business (knowledge, applied in business) level}.

$\forall t \in$ {*t1=User interface level; t2= Enterprise data (structures) level;*   (5.4)
t3=Business task logic level; t4=Network level; t5= IT infrastructure
level};

Knowledge axis (*K*) is divided into the 5 levels of detail (see Eq.4.3) according recommendations of the MDA [16]. And the third, IT axis is divided into five levels of detail (see Eq.4.4) on the ground of existing IT architecture principles.

The Enterprise Knowledge Space can be treated as a morphological box, which models various interactions between those three integrated enterprise aspects: business (*B*), information technology (*IT*) and organizational knowledge (*K*).

It is possible to abstract three two-dimensional spaces in the enterprise knowledge space: (*BxT*), (*BxK*), (*TxK*). Each of the two-dimensional spaces simulates the interactions of each two aspects from the Enterprise Knowledge Space. These two-dimensional models logically interrelate with such well-known models like Information System Architecture model by J.Zachman [17] and Multi-perspective enterprise modelling [18]. However, these models are quite different and the research of these two-dimensional models is outside the boundaries of our research.

6 The Major Classes of Enterprise Knowledge Base

The Enterprise Knowledge Model *M* is derived from formal description of Enterprise Knowledge Space.

The formal description of the Knowledge-based Enterprise Knowledge Model *M* can be expressed as the Cartesian product in the following way:

$$M = (T) \times (K) \times (B) \times (R) \qquad (6.1)$$

where *T* = information technology, *K* = knowledge, *B* = business process, *R* = business resources.

For the completeness of the model, *resources* (*R*) component was introduced into the model, as we consider knowledge as separate, but integrated enterprise aspect in contrary to the classical enterprise modelling methods which analyze knowledge alongside with other business resources.

This means, that each enterprise knowledge item m ($m \in M$) in Enterprise Knowledge Model M is related to the appropriate business process b ($b \in B$), knowledge k ($k \in K$), resources r ($r \in R$) and information technology t ($t \in T$). To put it in other terms, the enterprise knowledge model M item m is identified by a set of identifiers:

$$m(t;k;b;r;l) \in M \qquad\qquad (6.2)$$

where l ($l \in L$) is time period index.

The Enterprise Knowledge Model M is composed of interrelated items m and enables modelling a knowledge-based business, as it considers enterprise modelling knowledge (identifier k), business processes (identifier b), IT (identifier t), and their interactions. Each aspect (b,t,k) is modelled into the 5 levels of detail.

The enterprise knowledge modelling method and tool for practical business management needs can be developed on the basis of the Enterprise Knowledge Model.

In Fig.7 the class diagram (UML Class model) of the Enterprise Knowledge Model is presented.

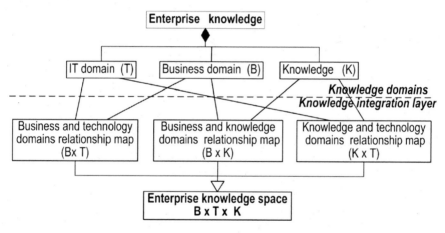

Fig. 7. Enterprise knowledge structure (subsets of knowledge), presented as UML class diagram

Consequently, Enterprise Knowledge Base contains integrated knowledge about three enterprise domains: business (B), information technology (T) and knowledge (K) as well as various relationships of these domains (represented as knowledge integration layer in Fig.7).

7 Conclusions

Several conceptual findings concerning knowledge management in the enterprise were made thus making background for the development the practical methods for the systematic implementation of the knowledge management elements in the enterprises and for the transformation into the knowledge-based enterprise.

Redefined concept of the knowledge-based enterprise led to the identification of its main architectural elements. The Enterprise Knowledge Base is concerned as main component of the knowledge based enterprise. The role and scope of the Enterprise Knowledge Base (KB) were specified as well as the interactions with other architectural elements.

The structuring of the knowledge-based enterprise according to the Strategic Alignment Model by Henderson and Venkatraman enabled the identification of four domains of the knowledge-based enterprise. According such as division of the knowledge-based enterprise, three components of the enterprise knowledge component were abstracted: business (B), enterprise knowledge (K) and information technologies (T).

For the explanation of the semantics of the enterprise knowledge according all three aspects, the Enterprise Knowledge Space was developed.

Formal description of the Enterprise Knowledge Space is assumed as the Enterprise Knowledge Model M, which forms background for the creation of practical method for the Enterprise KB development.

Finally, on the basis of the developed model Enterprise Knowledge Model M, the UML class diagram of the Enterprise Knowledge Base is presented as a step towards practical development for the Enterprise KB.

Enterprise KB integrates enterprise knowledge about three interrelated domains: business (B), enterprise knowledge (K) and information technologies (T), thus enabling support of the knowledge-based enterprise design as well as its IS engineering.

It is expected that the introduction of integrated enterprise knowledge base into the overall business management and development framework will improve on the enterprise's knowledge management, adaptability and flexibility.

References

1. Grant RM (1996) Toward a knowledge-based theory of the firm. In: Strategic Management J. 17, pp 109–122
2. Conner KR (1991) A historical comparison of resource-based theory and Five schools of thought within industrial organization economics: Do we have a new theory of the firm? In: J. Management 17(1), pp 121–154
3. Alavi M, Leidner, DE (2001) Review: Knowledge Management and Knowledge Management Systems, MIS Quarterly (25:1), March 2001, pp 107-136

4. Holsapple CW, Joshi KD (1999) Description and Analysis of Existing Knowledge Management Frameworks. In: Proceedings oh the 32nd Hawaii International Conference on System Sciences, 1999 vol. 1, pp 1072-1087, available at: http://csdl.computer.org/comp/proceedings/hicss/1999/0001/01/00011073.PDF

5. Malhotra Y.(2004) Why knowledge management systems fail. Enablers and constraints of knowledge management in human enterprises. Information Today Inc., Medford, NJ, pp 87-112, available at: www.brint.org/WhyKMSFail.htm

6. Zack MH (2003) Rethinking the knowledge-based organization. *Sloan management review*, vol. 44, no. 4, summer 2003, pp 67-71, available at: http://web.cba.neu.edu/~mzack/articles/kbo/kbo.htm

7. Gudas S, Skersys T, Lopata A (2004) Framework for knowledge-based IS engineering. In: Advances in Information Systems ADVIS'2004, T. Yakhno, Ed., Berlin: Springer-Verlag, 2004, pp 512-522

8. Henderson J, Venkatraman N (1990) Strategic alignment: A model for organization transformation via information technology. Massachusetts Institute of Technology, Working Paper 3223-90

9. Maier R (2004) Knowledge Management Systems: Information and Communication Technologies for Knowledge Management. Springer; 2nd ed

10. Now is the Time for Real-Time Enterprise (2002) Gartner Group, available at: http://www.gartner.com/pages/story.php.id.2632.s.8.jsp

11. Malhotra Y (2005) Integrating knowledge management technologies in organizational business processes: getting real time enterprises to deliver real business performance. In: Journal of Knowledge Management, vol. 9, no. 1, pp 7-28

12. Firestone JM (2001) Knowledge Management: A Framework for Analysis and Measurement. In: DsStar, vol.5, No.1, available at: http://www.taborcommunications.com/dsstar/01/0102/102505.html

13. Gudas S (2005) Žiniomis grindžiamos IS inžinerijos metodų principai [The principles of the Knowledge-based IS Engineering methods], In: IT'2006, pp 713-717

14. Iyer B, Gottlieb R (2004) The Four-Domain Architecture: An approach to support enterprise architecture design. IBM Systems Journal, vol. 43, no. 3

15. Laudon JP, Laudon KC (2002) Management Information Systems. Managing the Digital Firm (7th ed.). Prentice Hall

16. Hettinger MK (2003) Model-Driven Architecture, processes and methodology from the perspective of the "Modeling Discipline", In: MDA™ Implementers' Workshop Succeeding with Model Driven Systems

17. Zachman JA, Sowa JF (1992) Extending and Formalizing the Framework for Information Systems Architecture. In: IBM Systems Journal, vol. 31, no. 3

18. Ulrich F (2002) Multi-Perspective Enterprise Modeling (MEMO) – Conceptual Framework and Modeling Languages. In: 35-th Hawaii International Conference on System Sciences – 2002, available at: csdl.computer.org/comp/proceedings/hicss/2002/1435/03/14350072.pdf

Co-designing Models for Enterprises and Information Systems – A Case for Language Integration

Peter Rittgen

University College of Borås, 501 90 Borås, Sweden, peter.rittgen@hb.se

Abstract: To achieve a close alignment of information systems and enterprises their designs have to be interwoven to a mutually supportive pattern. This requires compatible languages for expressing the designs. We suggest a framework for integrating two hitherto distinct languages specialized for the respective domain, UML and SIMM. With the help of a case study we demonstrate that this integration does indeed support the co-design of an enterprise model and an information systems model.

1 Introduction

The term co-design can be understood in different ways. In the context of our study it refers to an idea that was elaborated in (Forsgren 2005). It has its roots in "systems thinking" as established by (Churchman 1968). His principal idea was that we can design an unlimited number of views on reality. They may differ in their granularity (level of detail), their perspective, their level of abstraction, and so on. But from Churchman's point of view this is not sufficient. We must also "calibrate" the viewing instrument (or measurement scale) to arrive at (or agree on) a view that is supposed to be "implemented". This collective process of designing views and moving towards a consensus view is called co-design. It has shaped the way we look at social systems in general and information systems in particular (Ackoff 1981; Checkland 1988; Mitroff and Mason 1981). But what are the implications of this idea when the objects of our design are models? We will return to this point later.

When we take a systematic approach to co-design we might ask what the co in co-design refers to. The most obvious answer is perhaps that a number of designers jointly develop a design. We speak in that case of the subjects **in** co-design. But the design process also has a number of customers, the ones we design for.

We call them the subjects **of** co-design. If we further broaden our view we might also discover that design is about objects, and again we can identify two dimensions, the objects **in** and **of** co-design. The objects **of** co-design are the things that we design, the results of the design process. But in the process we also need tools or artefacts, the objects **in** co-design.

Our study is primarily about the latter category, i.e. the tools or artefacts. In modeling, the primary tools are languages. But languages have a problematic double role in being both objects **in** and **of** co-design. We use a language to describe, for example an enterprise or an information system. In that sense the language is a tool **in** design. But at the same time, when using the language we discover it new, reinvent it and put it to a different use by reinterpreting existing concepts of the language and creating new ones. Each use situation therefore leads to a change of the language. In that sense the language is also an object **of** co-design.

If languages are shaped by their use, then different contexts of use will also yield different languages. An enterprise modeling language will turn out to be different from a modeling language for information systems because they are used for describing different things. But although an enterprise and an information system are not the same thing, they do share an intimate relationship: The information system (of an enterprise) is a subsystem of that enterprise.

Let us summarize these important points. Languages are both design tools and design objects. As tools for modeling enterprises and information systems they are used on two objects **of** co-design where one is a part of the other. This situation makes the co-design of enterprises and their information systems an intricate business. The separation of enterprise modeling and information systems modeling into different areas of concern has led to the development of completely different languages for the respective areas (see section 2). But a co-design of enterprises and information systems is only possible when the modeling languages for these areas are also co-designed. Both the current situation and the future scenario of co-designed languages are depicted in fig. 1.

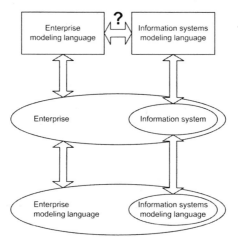

Fig. 1. Co-design of systems and languages

But how do we get started on such a process of co-designing languages? One approach would be to start at zero with "empty" languages, building both languages gradually from scratch in a co-design context, i.e. in projects that apply co-design thinking to develop an enterprise together with its information systems. But much of the time in this process would be spent on discovering concepts that already exist in current languages for enterprise modeling and information systems modeling. We therefore suggest another approach that avoids reinventing the wheel. We propose to investigate existing languages and to identify those concepts that could provide a "common ground" for language co-design. We call this process language integration. It consists of an analysis of the respective languages and their comparison (see section 2). Based on this we derive a framework for integration (see section 3) which we subsequently use for the co-design of business processes and information systems in the context of a case study (see section 4).

2 Language Analysis and Comparison

As candidate languages for our study we have chosen SIMM and UML. UML seemed a natural choice due to its high degree of standardization and its dominance in information systems modeling. Enterprise modeling, on the other hand, is less standardized and our choice of SIMM is hence less obvious. The justification for this particular method lies in a combination of a strong theoretical foundation and a significant empirical support. SIMM has its roots in Business Action Theory (Goldkuhl 1996, 1998; Goldkuhl and Lind 2004) and has undergone considerable empirical validation (Axelsson et al. 2000; Axelsson and Segerkvist 2001; Goldkuhl and Melin 2001; Haraldson and Lind 2005; Johansson and Axelsson 2004, 2005; Lind and Goldkuhl 1997; Lind et al. 2003; Melin and Axelsson 2004; Melin and Goldkuhl 1999).

The analysis of SIMM is based on the language specification (Röstlinger and Goldkuhl 2005). As SIMM is based on the ontology of Socio-Instrumental Pragmatism (SIP) (Goldkuhl 2002; Goldkuhl 2005) we have also made use of this information. Our analysis of UML is based on the UML 2.0 Superstructure Specification (OMG 2004) and the Infrastructure document (OMG 2006). In addition we make use of the ontological analyses of UML done in (Evermann and Wand 2001) and (Opdahl and Henderson-Sellers 2002). They employ the ontology by Bunge-Wand-Weber (BWW) which is an established tool for analyzing modelling languages. It is based on Mario Bunge's ontology (Bunge 1977, 1979) and was later adapted by Yair Wand and Ron Weber to the information systems field (Wand and Weber 1989, 1995; Weber 1997).

As an example of how language analysis and comparison are performed we look at three predominant concepts: Actors, actions and action objects.

2.1 Actors

In theories of social action an actor is always a human being. But SIP recognizes that there can be non-human agency. An artefact (e.g. a computing system) can perform actions and its actions can have a meaning in the social world. Artefacts can play the role of non-human agents, whereas actors are human agents. It is therefore that we speak of a "performer" in the context of SIMM, encompassing human and non-human performers.

In UML the concept of an actor is much broader and covers that of a performer in SIMM plus 'time' which is also an actor in UML (but not in SIMM). We might therefore map SIMM-performer to UML-actor. But in UML the concept of an actor is restricted to the particular context of use cases. Otherwise actions are considered to be performed by objects. This is due to the fact that the UML is primarily a design language for (software) artefacts. Another possible mapping is therefore the one from SIMM-performer to UML-object which allows for a proper translation of interaction graphs.

2.2 Actions

The concept of action exists in both SIMM and UML and the language descriptions agree largely. It is therefore valid to map SIMM-action to UML-action. It should be noted, though, that SIMM provides a more sophisticated concept of human action as purposeful, social action that is performed with the help of some instrument (artefact), whereas non-human action by artefacts is secondary. In UML these roles are reversed but there is no general conflict (only a shift in focus). SIMM also defines interaction as a special form of action directed towards another actor. Action objects involved in an interaction become interaction objects in that case (see 2.3). This has no effect on the nature of the objects themselves, though.

2.3 Action objects

The term action objects is an explicit concept of SIMM and it refers to objects that are involved in an action. As human action is purposeful it is performed to achieve some result(s). Action objects produced by an action can be such results. But action objects serve also as input for other actions. In the UML objects are a fundamental concept. They constitute a system and all behavior of that system consists basically of messages that are exchanged between objects and the objects' internal behavior. An UML-object can be the resource for another object and thereby play the role of a SIMM-action object. The mapping from SIMM-action object to UML-object is therefore valid. But in addition to that an UML-object can also be the performer of some action as discussed in 2.1.

3 Deriving the Integration Framework

We have extended the comparison described in section 3 to the remaining concepts. For this purpose we made use of the language specification (OMG 2004, 2006; Röstlinger and Goldkuhl 2005) but also of the more detailed information available from the ontological analyses (Evermann and Wand 2001; Goldkuhl 2002; Goldkuhl 2005; Opdahl and Henderson-Sellers 2002). By following this process we arrived at suitable matches for all SIMM concepts. The resulting mappings are shown in fig. 2 in the form SIMM concept → UML concept.

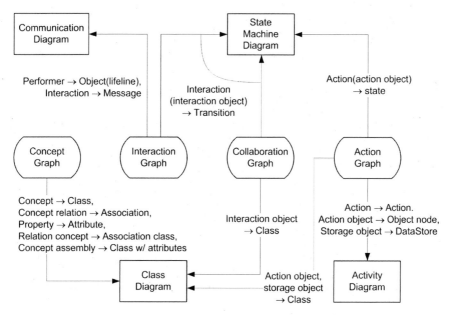

Fig. 2. The integration framework

But the mappings do not only help us in translating concepts from one language to another. The SIMM concepts are related to specific SIMM graphs and the UML concepts are related to certain UML diagrams. If we follow up these relations we can also establish a relation between SIMM graphs and UML diagrams, i.e. we can determine which information from which SIMM graphs we need to construct a certain UML diagram. In other words, we can derive a framework that supports the translation of SIMM models into UML models (see fig. 2).

To test the feasibility of this approach we used the framework in a project where we developed enterprise computing models in UML based on an enterprise model in SIMM. The following section reports on our experiences from that case study.

4 Co-designing Models: A Case Study

The case we investigated involved a retail chain in the home textile and home decoration industry. The logistics operation of that company had been outsourced to a third-party logistics provider. In the beginning of the project we performed an analysis of the business situation that led to an enterprise model that we documented with the help of the SIMM method. Two of the SIMM graphs serve as an example of this model, the interaction graph (fig. 3) and the action graph (fig. 4).

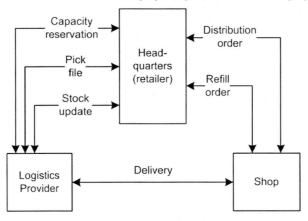

Fig. 3. Interaction graph

The main actors are the Logistics Provider (LogPro), the Headquarters of the retailer and a Shop. Fig. 3 shows the interactions between them with respect to order handling. It starts when Headquarters reserve capacity for handling a certain amount of items in advance of the actual order. LogPro allocates staff and space to provide for this capacity. The product assortment of the retailer consists of basic-range products and seasonal products. The latter are distributed to the Shop according to turnover quota (distribution order). This is triggered by Headquarters. Orders for basic-range products are initiated by the Shop. This happens when the Shop is running low on certain products (refill order). Headquarters forward both types of orders to LogPro in form of a pick list. LogPro performs delivery to the Shop. The confirmation can be accompanied by a complaint if items are missing or wrong ones have been sent. Periodically Headquarters ask for a stock update. This is necessary because they run their own warehouse management system which is not integrated with that of LogPro.

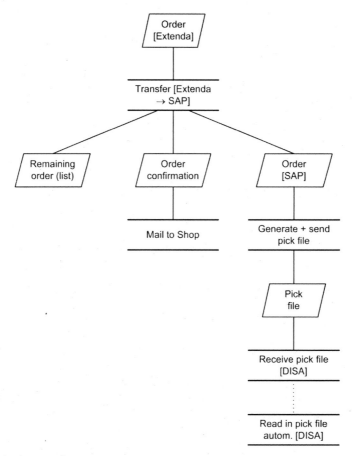

Fig. 4. Action graph

We take a closer look at one aspect of order processing, i.e. processing of the pick file. This routine requires the integration of different computing systems, the Extenda system of the Shop, the SAP system of Headquarters and the DISA system of LogPro. Fig. 4 shows an excerpt of the action graph for pick file processing. Based on the enterprise models we developed the UML models to support the design of respective enterprise computing systems. To give the reader an idea of this process we show the communication diagram (fig. 5) and the activity diagram (fig. 6) that have been derived from the interaction graph (fig. 3) and the action graph (fig. 4), respectively.

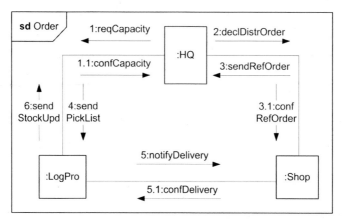

Fig. 5. Communication diagram

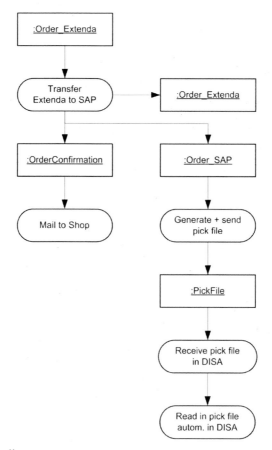

Fig. 6. Activity diagram

All in all the design involved one class diagram, six activity diagrams, one communication diagram and eight state machine diagrams. They were developed by one modeler in 68 hours. In a previous project of similar size the same modeler needed 92 hours without the help of the framework which was not yet developed at that time. These figures seem to indicate that the use of the framework has reduced the effort in that case by 35 %. But this has to be taken with a grain of salt as we cannot be sure that all other parameters were the same in both cases. Further empirical research in that area is therefore necessary.

5 Conclusion

The principal result of our investigation is that the ontological foundations of two particular languages for enterprise modeling and enterprise computing, respectively, exhibit a significant intersection. This common ground allows us to support the translation of enterprise models into computing models in a constructive way. This is done by mapping concepts of the "source language" (here: SIMM) to concepts of the "target language" (here: UML) and by specifying an integration framework that relates the graphs/diagrams of both languages to each other. The latter supports the translation of complete models, diagram by diagram.

We have applied this framework in a project that involved the development of both enterprise models and computing models. We found out that the time for developing the latter decreased by 35 % in relation to time time spent on a similar project without the support of the framework.

References

Ackoff RL (1981) Creating the corporate future. Wiley, New York.
Axelsson K, Goldkuhl G, Melin U (2000) Using Business Action Theory for dyadic analysis. Paper presented at the 10th Nordic Workshop on Interorganisational Research.
Axelsson K, Segerkvist P-A (2001) Interaction between actors and information systems in web-based imaginary organisations – Experiences from two case studies. Paper presented at the 1st Nordic Workshop on Electronic Commerce.
Bunge M (1977) Ontology I: The Furniture of the World. Reidel, Dordrecht.
Bunge M (1979) Ontology II: A World of Systems. Reidel, Dordrecht.
Checkland PB (1988) Soft systems methodology: An overview. Journal of Applied Systems Analysis 15:27-30.
Churchman CW (1968) The Systems Approach. Dell Publishing, New York.
Evermann J, Wand Y (2001) Towards Ontologically Based Semantics for UML Constructs. In: Kunii HS, Jajodia S, Sølvberg A (eds) ER 2001, 20th International Conference on Conceptual Modelling, Yokohama, Japan, November 27-30, 2001. Springer, Berlin, pp 354-367.

Forsgren O (2005) Churchmanian Co-design – Basic Ideas and Application Examples. Paper presented at the ISD 2005 - Information Systems Development, Karlstad, August 14-17, 2005.

Goldkuhl G (1996) Generic business frameworks and action modelling. In: Dignum F, Dietz J, Verharen E, Weigand H (eds) Communication Modeling - The Language/Action Perspective, Proceedings of the First International Workshop on Communication Modeling. Springer, Berlin.

Goldkuhl G (1998) The six phases of business processes - business communication and the exchange of value. Paper presented at the 12th biennial ITS conference "Beyond convergence" (ITS´98), Stockholm.

Goldkuhl G (2002) Anchoring scientific abstractions – ontological and linguistic determination following socio-instrumental pragmatism. Paper presented at the European Conference on Research Methods in Business and Management (ECRM 2002), April 29-30, 2002, Reading.

Goldkuhl G (2005) Socio-Instrumental Pragmatism: A Theoretical Synthesis for Pragmatic Conceptualisation in Information Systems. Paper presented at the 3rd International Conference on Action in Language, Organisations and Information Systems (ALOIS), University of Limerick.

Goldkuhl G, Lind M (2004) Developing e-interactions – A framework for business capabilities and exchanges. Paper presented at the 12th European Conference on Information Systems, June 14-16, 2004, Turku, Finland.

Goldkuhl G, Melin U (2001) Relationship Management vs Business Transactions: Business Interaction as Design of Business Interaction. Paper presented at the 10th International Annual IPSERA Conference, Jönköping International Business School.

Haraldson S, Lind M (2005) Broken patterns. Paper presented at the In Proceedings of the 10th International Conference on the Language Action Perspective, Kiruna, Sweden.

Johansson B-M, Axelsson K (2004) Communication media in distance selling – Business Interactions in a B2C Setting. Paper presented at the 12th European Conference in Information Systems (ECIS), Turku, Finland.

Johansson B-M, Axelsson K (2005) Analysing Communication Media and Actions – Extending and Evaluating the Business Action Matrix. Paper presented at the In Proceedings of the 13th European Conference on Information Systems, Regensburg, Germany.

Lind M, Goldkuhl G (1997) Reconstruction of different business processes - a theory and method driven analysis. Paper presented at the In Proccedings of the 2nd International Workshop on Language/Action Perspective (LAP97), Eindhoven University of Technology, The Netherlands.

Lind M, Hjalmarsson A, Olausson J (2003) Modelling interaction and co-ordination as business communication in a mail order setting. Paper presented at the 8th International Working Conference on the Language Action Perspective (LAP2003), Tilburg, The Netherlands.

Melin U, Axelsson K (2004) Emphasising Symmetry Issues in Business Interaction Analysis and IOS. Paper presented at the Sixth International Conference on Electronic Commerce, ICEC'04, Delft University of Technology, The Netherlands.

Melin U, Goldkuhl G (1999) Information Systems and Process Orientation - evaluation and change using Business Action Theory. In: Wojtkowski W (ed), Systems Development Methods for Databases, Enterprise Modeling, and Workflow Management. Kluwer Academic/Plenum, New York.

Mitroff II, Mason RO (1981) Creating a dialectical social science. Reidel, Dordrecht.

OMG (2004) UML 2.0 Superstructure Specification. Retrieved December 20, 2005, from http://www.uml.org/

OMG (2006) Unified Modeling Language: Infrastructure. Retrieved April 18, 2006, from http://www.uml.org/

Opdahl AL, Henderson-Sellers B (2002) Ontological Evaluation of the UML Using the Bunge-Wand-Weber Model. Software and Systems Modelling 1(1):43-67.

Röstlinger A, Goldkuhl G (2005) Grafnotation för SIMM metodkomponenter. VITS/IDA, Linköpings universitet, Linköping.

Wand Y, Weber R (1989) An Ontological Evaluation of Systems Analysis and Design Methods. In: Falkenberg ED, Lindgreen P (eds) Information Systems Concepts: An In-Depth Analysis. North-Holland, Amsterdam, pp 79-107.

Wand Y, Weber R (1995) On the deep structure of information systems. Information Systems Journal 5:203-223.

Weber R (1997) Ontological Foundations of Information Systems. Coopers & Lybrand and the Accounting Association of Australia and New Zealand, Melbourne.

The Integration of Functional Decomposition with UML Notation in Business Process Modelling

Adam Przybyłek

Gdańsk University, Department of Information Systems, 81-824 Sopot,
ul. Armii Krajowej 119/121, Poland
adam@univ.gda.pl

Abstract: Over the past decade business and software modelling have been carried out using different notations designed to fit the special needs of the respective tasks. This approach has introduced a gap between the software and business models, which has resulted in inconsistency. The objective of this paper is to propose a new approach to analysis of the business process using UML notation. UML is the most commonly used language in object-oriented software development. Moreover, it can be extended to the modelling of business processes. With this approach it is possible, in the same notation, to visualise a company's business processes, its information system requirements and the architecture of the relevant information system.

However, object-oriented decomposition is not well suited to business process modelling. In an object-oriented methodology the decomposition is achieved by objects on which operations are performed. The aspects of the process are hidden within the objects. In this case functional decomposition from structured methodology is a much better choice. Functional decomposition provides a high degree of abstraction, which is sufficient for business experts. It simplifies the analysis of business by breaking down (decomposing) the problem into the functional steps of which it is made up. The primary aim of this paper has been to integrate functional decomposition with UML notation in order to model business processes. A case study is presented as an illustration.

Keywords: business process modelling, process diagram, Eriksson-Penker Business Extensions, functional decomposition, UML

1 Introduction

In order to survive in today's global economy more and more enterprises are having to redesign their business processes. The competitive market creates the demand for high quality services at lower costs and with shorter cycle times. In such an environment business processes must be identified, described, understood and analysed to find inefficiencies which cause financial losses. One way to achieve this is by modelling. Business modelling is the first step towards defining a software system. It enables the company to look afresh at how to improve organisation and to discover the processes that can be solved automatically by software that will support the business. The outcome of business process modelling is to provide information system developers with the information system requirements. For information system development to be simplified the business model should be drawn up in an understandable notation by software engineers. UML is such a notation. In this paper I show that UML is suitable not only for IT professionals but also for the business community. As a result, UML enables all "stakeholders" to speak the same language. The next crucial issue in business modelling is dealing with the complexity of the business processes. The object-oriented methodology commonly used in software development deals with complexity in concepts of abstraction, encapsulation, generalisation and aggregation. However, object decomposition may not provide the best solution for business process analysis. Object decomposition perceives a system as a collection of collaborating objects, the object being the basic unit by which we organise knowledge. Thinking about a system in terms of messages passing (service requests) between objects is too low a level of abstraction. The natural approach for business people is to break down business processes into smaller sub-processes, as long as an elementary level is achieved that is simple enough to operate. This is called functional decomposition. My approach takes advantage of both UML notation and functional decomposition.

The remainder of this paper first provides a background for business process modelling and functional decomposition followed by a brief introduction to UML and the UML extension mechanism. The proposal, made by Eriksson-Penker Business Extensions and the author, to integrate it with functional decomposition is then examined, after which a case study is presented. The case study shows the application of the proposed approach in a business process model of a Polish institution of higher education in the private sector. The last section of the paper sets out the conclusions to be drawn.

2 Background

The aims of this section are to explain the concepts involved in the business process and to provide an overview of modelling from a business perspective. Then a well-known technique in software engineering, that of functional decomposition is introduced. This section also explains the need for a common language among software developers and business people. Subsequently the characteristics are described that make UML an adequate business modelling language.

2.1 The business process

Numerous definitions of the business process have been proposed in a variety of publications [19, 24, 4, 13, 11, 14]. The business process is a structured collection of activities that work together to produce an outcome in accordance with the business goals. The business process is typically cross-functional and cuts across departmental boundaries. Whether manual or automated, the process takes inputs, transforms them, adds significant value to them and provides outputs for its customers. The customer may be either internal or external to the business.

A resource is an object which can play a role in the realisation of a process. Resources can be classified as follows: input object, output object, supplying object and, controlling object [8]. The input objects are the resources needed to perform the process. These are usually transformed or consumed as part of the process. The input objects can also be refined by the process, in which case the process adds value to them. The output objects represent the accomplishment of the goals and are the result of the process. The output object may be a completely new object created during the processes or it may be a transformed input object. The output of one business process is often the input to another process. The process may also have connections with the supplying and controlling objects. The supplying objects carry information required by the process. Resources, such as people, that are responsible for executing the activities in the process are known as control objects.

Each business process has a goal that reflects business expectation of its outcome. All the processes collaborate to achieve the strategic goals of the business. The process may be defined at any level of viewing from enterprise-wide processes to a single task performed by a single person. The process can consist of lower level sub-processes. The lowest level of the process is referred to as the elementary business process (EBP), a process performed in one location at one time which leaves the business in a consistent state [11].

The main types of business process are core (primary) processes, support processes and management processes [8, 16]. The core processes are those that define the purpose of the existence of the organisation and contribute directly to the production of goods and services for the organisation's external customers. The support processes help to fulfil the services of the main processes. Their outcome is not visible to the external customer but is essential to the effective functioning of the business. These processes make the delivery of the core processes of an enterprise possible. The last category of process, the management process, describes the work of managers in support of the business processes. These processes affect the way the other processes are managed and the relationship of the business to its owners.

2.2 Business process modelling

Business processes are complex, dynamic and interconnected throughout an organisation, sometimes extending to its customers and deliverers. Modelling techniques have been created to deal with this complexity. The model demonstrates the relationships between processes and provides an understanding of how the business operates. Models allow irrelevant details to be eliminated so that the focus can be on important aspects of the business. The business model is a mechanism for capturing fundamental enterprise business knowledge and represents the essence of the business organisation. It describes at a high level of abstraction how the business is working today and how this might be improved upon tomorrow. The business model generates an overall picture of the business domain and enables the effects of changes to be identified before the changes have been implemented.

B. Baker writes [1] that there are three basic reasons for modelling a business: to re-engineer the business, to improve a business process or to automate a business process. The goal of business process re-engineering is radical re-organisation of an enterprise along the flow of work that generates the value sought by the customer [11, 14]. To achieve this goal the business processes must be revised, investigated and documented. This will enable the owners of the business processes to gain a better understanding of enterprise-wide operations. The next step is to find bottle-necks in current processes and to determine how to make necessary improvements so that the processes are more productive and cost-effective. The last reason for business modelling is to take decisions about which of the manual processes might be automated and conducted better by information systems. Automation of business processes is the primary use of information technology in organisations. It reduces human intervention and assembles software services to support the business. A clear map of the business processes at the beginning of a project helps to specify requirements for information systems and ensures that these systems meet the business needs when delivered.

2.3 Functional decomposition

The term "functional decomposition" was introduced with structured methodology and was the key concept in software engineering prior to object-oriented domination. The first stage in most of the system's life-cycles is business planning. Before analysts begin developing information systems they must understand the major business functions that the organisation needs to perform. It is then much easier to identify processes that occur within the business functions and the system that will ultimately support those processes [12].

A commonly used technique in business analysis is functional decomposition. This is a top-down analysis that views a business as a collection of functions. Each function can be decomposed into business processes, each of which may be progressively broken down into smaller sub-processes until the business has been specified in terms of EBPs. These can once again be broken down into actions.

The order in which these actions are performed and the flow control can be presented at an activity diagram, as explained in a later section.

2.4 Unified Modelling Language (UML)

Software development is known to be a complex task requiring the co-ordinated efforts of domain experts, business analysts, designers, programmers and testers. In the IT community UML notation is considered to be the industry's standard for object-oriented system development and is widely used all over the world. Different phases of the software development process require different numbers of diagrams, where each diagram emphasises a particular aspect of the system. UML 2.0 defines 13 types of diagrams which are divided into two categories: structure diagrams, and behaviour diagrams [26, 29]. All the diagrams put together create a complete picture of the system. For more detailed information about UML diagrams please refer to the information sources mentioned in the reference sections [26, 9, 21, 10, 29, 27, 28].

Nevertheless, there is no one standard in business modelling and various notations exist [13, 20, 18, 7, 6]. As emphasised in [1], however, there is a need to use the same notation throughout the entire life-cycle of a project. Such an approach provides a great advantage for all stakeholders, making the development process more efficient. By having the business experts and system developers using the same modelling concepts, the risk of costly errors related to misunderstanding of the models is significantly decreased. When the issues mentioned above are taken into account, UML is a good candidate as a business modelling tool [4, 20, 23, 17, 22, 25]. It provides a common notation that allows business people to express the design of their business processes in a way meaningful to them, while providing clear direction for information technology support.

UML was initially designed as a general-purpose visual modelling language used to specify, visualise, construct and document the artefacts of a software system [26]. However, its clear and easily comprehended notation makes UML understandable to non-technical stakeholders. A flexibility and extensibility metamodel enables UML to be extended into different areas of modelling, including business process modelling.

2.5 The UML extensibility mechanisms

No language could ever be adequate to express a specific subject across all domains. UML is designed to be open-ended, allowing users to customise and extend it to their own particular needs [2]. The UML extensibility mechanisms refer to stereotypes, constraints and tagged values [26, 9, 21]. A stereotype defines a new type of modelling element suitable for a specific problem. Each stereotype must be based on a certain existing type in the meta-model. A stereotype may be expressed as a label enclosed in guillemots «» or as an icon. Constraints represent restrictions that are applied to UML elements. A constraint is a text enclosed in curly brackets {}. Constraints may be expressed more formally using the Object Constraint Language (OCL). Tagged values are properties attached to UML elements as a name-value pair. Both the tag and the value are enclosed in curly brackets {tag = value}. The UML extension mechanism should be used in those cases in which the basic semantics of the language is insufficient.

3 Applying UML in business process modelling

This section presents two of the most useful diagrams in business process modelling: the activity diagram and the process diagram. The activity diagram is a useful tool for showing flow control in the outworking of a business process. The process diagram is part of the Eriksson-Penker Business Extensions and is suitable for gaining an overview of all the processes.

3.1 The activity diagram

The most important UML diagram from a business point of view is the activity diagram. This combines ideas from the event diagrams of Jim Odell, data flow diagrams and Petri nets and is the latest form of the flow chart. The flow chart, which treats a process as a collection of actions, is one of the most natural visualisations of a business process and makes the activity diagram suitable for the specification of business processes [20, 18, 6, 25, 3, 5, 15].

The activity diagram can describe complex business processes as well as elementary business processes. A functional decomposition approach organises activity diagrams in a hierarchical tree, depending on the complexity of the business under study. Each complex process is modelled as a sequence of activities that represents subprocesses. The elementary business process is modelled as a sequence of atomic actions. Too many activities on the same diagram will cause the diagram to become confusing. Functional decomposition provides a way of preventing confusion by creating diagrams at different levels of abstraction and organising them hierarchically. Activity from one diagram can be divided into actions in a lower level diagram.

Activities are presented as ovals and are governed by clearly defined control nodes such as decisions and merges (diamonds icon), forks and joins (solid horizontal line). When an activity is completed the control flow is passed to the next activity. A transition is modelled as a directed arrow from the source activity to the target activity. Objects may participate in the activity. They are either an input to or an output from the actions, or they can simply show that an object is affected by a specific activity [9]. Object flows are shown with a dashed line ending with an arrow. Partitions can be used to show in which part of an organisation the activity is performed. Moreover, the activity diagram can present more than one business process. However, if there is a need to give a broad picture of all the processes, the process diagram is a better solution. I also suggest using the process diagram instead of the activity diagram when objects involved in activity are crucial and there is a need to emphasise them.

3.2 The Eriksson-Penker Business Extensions

A number of techniques have emerged over the years to support business modelling, such as IDEF0, IDEF3, ARIS-EPC, BPMN, and Petri nets. These provide ways of expressing business processes in terms of activities and of arranging resources. None of them, however, is equipped to support the design of software. This creates a gap between business and software models and is a source of mistakes.

H.E. Eriksson and M. Penker have proposed extensions to UML that are intended as a basic framework for business modelling [24, 20]. These extensions can express a business process while at the same time providing consistency with a software model. Eriksson-Penker Business Extensions use four different views of a business: business vision, business process, business structure, and business behaviour. Each view focuses on a particular aspect of the business and is described through a number of diagrams and/or a textual document [8]. For the purpose of this paper only the process diagram, which is an element of the business process view, will be presented.

3.3 The process diagram

The process diagram is a specialisation of the UML activity diagram with a set of stereotypes that illustrates the interaction between the processes, the resources that participate in the processes and the goals of the processes. The process diagram describes how work is done within the business environment. The following stereotypes are used to define the process diagram: business process, resources, goals and rules.

The business process stereotype

The core business modelling element is represented by stereotyping an activity to a «process» or by a special icon. High-level processes may be divided into sub-processes placed inside the process element or on a separate lower level diagram. I suggest breaking down business processes until EBPs are achieved. Each EBP can then be specified on an activity diagram by internal actions. In this manner we obtain functional decomposition in UML notation.

Resource stereotype

The resource types are represented as classes. Resource instances are represented as objects. Input objects are usually placed on the left of the process and output objects are placed on the right. A result produced by one process can constitute input to another process. The supplying and controlling objects are placed below or above the process and can be linked to it by a dependency stereotyped adequately by «supply» and «control». Eriksson-Penker Business Extensions [8, 9] define the hierarchy of resource types (Figure 1). In the process diagram the resource type is indicated by the stereotype. The stereotype provides additional information about the resource. Abstract objects refer to intangible items. The "people resource" denotes human beings acting in the process.

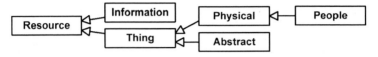

Fig. 1. Resource types

4 A case study

In this section, the demonstration that the proposed approach is capable of modelling business processes, is presented. For the purpose of the illustration, a business process model of an institution of higher education was developed. The research method applied to this organisation was open-ended interviewing. The persons who are most knowledgeable about the issue of interest were interviewed. Relying on the information collected from the interviews, a textual description to illustrate how the business is run was created. The first part of this section gives an overview of the main business processes, although the details are beyond the scope of this paper. The second part presents the relevant process and activity diagrams. Functional decomposition was applied to break the business processes into atomic actions.

4.1 Domain specification

The business domain modelled is a Polish institution of higher education in the private sector. The academic institution can be understood as a service provider, its main business function being the provision of higher education. This service is immaterial and students participate in it directly. The main business function is achieved by nine high level processes. The overview of each process is presented below as a textual description.

Analysis of business environment

Heads of departments are continuously tracking changes in the job market, to adjust what is offered to the needs of the educational market. IT magazines and internet portals are an essential source of this information. These members of staff are also watching the micro-environment, other colleges with which they are competing on the student market. The data for their analysis is gained from the internet web sites of other institutions of higher education. One of the main areas of interest is therefore what other educational institutions have on offer. The college's educational programme is drawn up on the basis of such data. The whole process is supervised by the Chancellor and verified by the school's position in the student market.

Marketing

The educational programme thus established has to reach a wide range of customers. In order to achieve this administrative staff create marketing materials tailored to the educational programme. These materials are disseminated through the press, radio and TV. Administrative workers additionally compile the contents of the website. Website creation is handled by an external company.

Human Resources Management

Heads of department have to select academic staff in the light of the educational programme offered. First the teaching of the academic courses is opened to those lecturers who were employed in the previous academic year and who were highly rated by students. Where new lecturers have to be employed, the background of candidates' research work is taken into consideration. Next payment is negotiated individually with each lecturer and the interest rate and staff profiles are accepted by the Chancellor. The assignment of lecturers to subjects is set out in a document known as the workload card, which must be signed by the Chancellor.

Teaching arrangements

Once classes have been assigned to the lecturers, the next step is the preparation of syllabuses. The lecturers can follow syllabuses that were used during the previous year and custom them to current scientific developments. The syllabuses must be approved by the Dean.

Ordering books

On the basis of the syllabuses, lecturers' advice and students' requests administrative staff draw up order forms for the books for the school library and monthly orders are sent to the publishers.

Timetabling

On the basis of the workload cards and classroom availability the timetable is drawn up by administrative staff, who contact the lecturers to find out when they are free to teach.

Conducting the classes

During the academic year lecturers conduct their classes according to the timetable. Consequently the students make educational progress.

Assessment of lecturers

After each semester the Assistant to the Dean ranks the lecturers on the basis of surveys, inspections and the attendance register. The surveys are conducted among the students by the Assistant to the Dean, the inspection is carried out by the Head of Department and the attendance register is kept by the porter.

Admission procedures

All candidates must submit to the Dean's Office an application form and a copy of their final school examination certificate. If the number of applicants exceeds the number of places available, the applicants undergo a process of evaluation based on their scores in their final school examination and an entrance examination. Applicants are notified of the exact time of their entrance examination and their qualifications are judged by the admission staff. If the number of applicants is lower than the number of places available, all applicants are accepted. Accepted applicants receive a letter asking them to pay their tuition fee, and the list of students admitted is drawn up according to the payment receipts.

4.2 Business process model

In this part the use of the activity and process diagrams to achieve functional decomposition was demonstrated. Figure 2 shows the business process in the organisation analysed in its entirety.

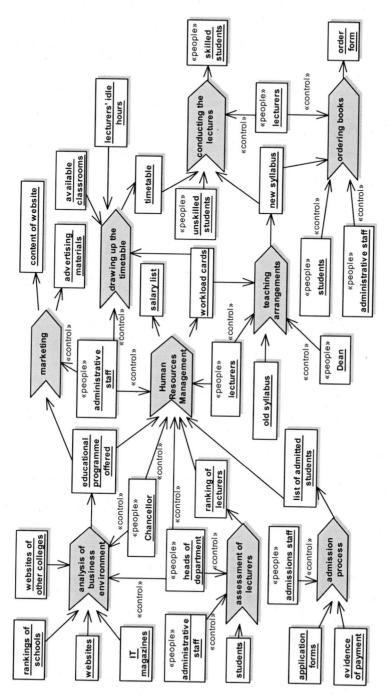

Fig. 2. Providing higher education

The goal of providing higher education is to prepare students to apply scientific knowledge and methods in their profession. The figure 2 conveys general information. The assessment of lecturers and admission procedures are given further attention. The admission of students to courses is an example of an EBP and so I have used an activity diagram to present it (Figure 3).

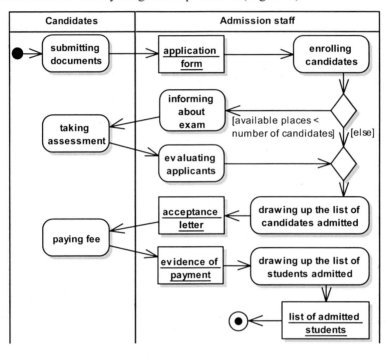

Fig. 3. Admission process

Figure 4 illustrates the four EBPs that make up the assessment of lecturers.

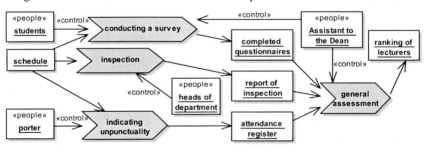

Fig. 4. Assessment of lecturers

In order to analyse the process of conducting the survey functional decomposition has been applied once again. The result is shown in Figure 5.

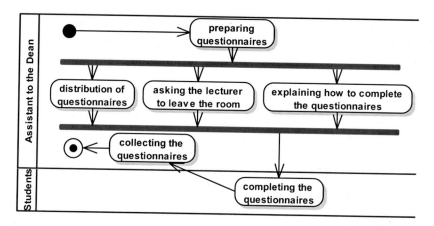

Fig. 5. The process of conducting the survey

In order to gain deeper understanding all business processes should be decomposed and shown in detail in the activity diagram.

5 Conclusion

Business modelling has appeared as a response to the need for describing a business in a formal way. The purpose of creating a formal model is to better understand, analyse, improve or replace a business process. In the last decade business practitioners have been overwhelmed with notations in diagramming business processes. These notations have been understandable for business people but have not been compatible with the notations used in software engineering.

The research contributes to business modelling in several ways. First of all, the proposed study introduces a new approach to business process modelling. It integrates a well-known strategy for dealing with complexity, that of functional decomposition, with a notation commonly used in software engineering, namely UML. The case study suggests that such integration is possible, but this should be confirmed empirically. Functional decomposition offers the analyst a mechanism to divide and conquer the complexity of business processes. The UML extension mechanisms allow UML to be fitted for specific needs. It is notation that can be used for business modelling just as it has come to be used for software modelling.

Secondly, the presented approach guarantees a smooth transition from business process analysis to system requirements, because the same notation is used for all models. This significantly decreases the time needed to transform the model from a business to a software model. Moreover, the availability of a common notation, aligning IT with the business community, improves communication among a project team. Good communication is a critical success factor in the development of information systems.

References

Baker B (2001) Business Modeling with UML: The Light at the End of the Tunnel. Rational Software

Booch G, Rumbaugh J, Jacobson I (1998) The Unified Modeling Language User Guide, Addison Wesley

Bruno G, Torchiano M, Agarwal R (2002) UML Enterprise Instance Models. CIT 2002

Castela N, Tribolet J, Silva A, Guerra A (2001) Business process modeling with UML. ICEIS 2001, pp 679-685

Desfray P (2004) Making a success of preliminary analysis using UML, Softeam

Dewalt C (1999) Business process modeling with UML. Johns Hopkins University Press

Eertink H, Janssen WPM, Oude Luttighuis PHWM, Teeuw WB, Vissers CA (1999) A Business Process Design Language. Lecture Notes In Computer Science, vol 1708, Springer

Eriksson HE, Penker M (2000) Business Modeling with UML: Business Patterns at Work. John Wiley & Sons, USA

Eriksson HE, Penker M, Lyons B, Fado D (2004) UML 2 Toolkit. Wiley Publishing, Inc., USA

Fowler M, Scott K (1999) UML Distilled – A Brief Guide to the Standard Object Modeling Language. 2nd ed., Reading, MA

Frost S, Allen P (1996) Business Process Modeling, SELECT Software Tools plc, Cheltenham

Harel D, Politi M (1998) Modeling Reactive Systems with Statecharts. McGraw-Hill, New York, USA

Havey M (2005) Essential Business Process Modeling. O'Reilly, USA

IBM Corporation (1996) Business Process Reengineering and Beyond, California

Loos P, Fettke P (2001) Towards an Integration of Business Process Modeling and Object-Oriented Software Development. Chemnitz Univeristy of Technology, Germany

May M (2003) Business Process Management. Pearson Education Limited, Great Britain

McLeod G (1998) Extending UML for Enterprise and Business Process Modeling. UML'98 - Beyond the Notation, First International Workshop, pp 195-204

Odeh M, Beeson I, Green S, Sa J (2002) Modelling Processes Using RAD and UML Activity Diagrams: an Exploratory Study. ACIT 2002

Omar A, Sawy EL (2001) Redesigning Enterprise for e-Business, McGraw-Hill

Ovidiu SN (2000) Business Modeling: UML vs. IDEF. Griffith University

Pender T (2003) UML Bible. John Wiley & Sons, USA

Podeswa H (2005) UML for the IT Business Analyst: A Practical Guide to Object-Oriented Requirements Gathering. Thomson Course Technology PTR, Canada

Sinogas P, Vasconcelos A, Caetano A, Neves J, Mendes R, Tribolet J (2001) Business processes extensions to UML profile for business modeling, Centro de Engenharia Organizacional, Lisbona. ICEIS 2001, pp 673-678

Sparks G (2000) An Introduction to UML: The Business Process Model. Sparx

Ståhl H, Jankko T, Oittinen P (2002) Modelling of publishing processing with UML. Helsinki University of Technology, Department of Automation and System Technology, Laboratory of Media Technology, Finland

UML 2.0 Superstructure Specification (2003) Object Management Group, Inc.

Wrycza S, Marcinkowski B (2005) UML 2 Teaching at Postgraduate Studies - Prerequisites and Practice, The Proceedings of ISECON 2005, vol 22, New Orlean

Wrycza S, Marcinkowski B (2005) Interaction Occurrences and Combined Fragments in System Dynamics Modelling with UML 2 Sequence Diagram art. (w:) (ed.) Nilsson G., Gustas R., Wojtkowski W., Wojtkowski G., Wrycza S., Zupancic J., ISD 2005 Proceedings of the Fourteenth International Conference on ISD, Karlstad University Studies, Karlstad, pp 59-68

Wrycza S, Marcinkowski B, Wyrzykowski K (2005) UML 2.0 in information systems modelling. Helion, Warsaw

The Framework for Adaptable Data Analysis System Design

Olegas Vasilecas, Aidas Smaizys

Department of Information Systems, Klaipeda University, Lithuania.
olegas@isl.vtu.lt, aidas@oil.lt.

1 Introduction

Enterprises today own large databases (DB) and widely use information systems (IS). IS used in business are mostly dedicated to various data input and analysis. The result of data analysis is information contained in specially designed reports, OLAP cubes, etc. Such information is used to track and evaluate the business situation according to the business strategy and tactics and determine conformance to the business policy and rules [10].

The decision making action is one of business system processes which follows rules too. Usually the operator of the information system is responsible for decision making and the part of business system is dedicated for data analysis processes to support such decisions [12]. The sources of data analysis rules are all the documents, legal requirements and laws [1], mutual agreements, business culture, limitations in various resources (people, software systems, hardware, etc.) and architecture, but most valuable of them are – experience and knowledge of the employees. Sometimes such knowledge or part of it is embedded into reports or stored in various knowledge bases in enterprises, but mostly it is lost after change of the staff.

According to the traditional system engineering the automation of business processes is done by transforming business rules (BR) into the functional requirements of platform independent information system and translating it into the specification of platform dependent software system (SS) [13]. The specifications are used later for coding of the final applications. Following such process the business rules are embedded into code and lost forever [1]. The same is with the analysis rules which are embedded in the traditional reporting and analysis SS. Part of the captured BR in functional requirements are data analysis rules already or are transformed into data analysis rules later. Although BR stated as requirements are stored and transformed statically and can not be changed later without all redesign cycle.

Another big flaw is pre-programmed in traditional design processes from the very beginning – it is different and mostly false interpretation of business rules stated as requirements or transformed into specifications by analysts or designers and into final software code by programmers. This entire staff directly involved in software application design and development is not involved in business directly. Such misinterpretations are replicated through all the design cycle and sometimes are not discovered even in testing phase, because of testing scenarios based on the same requirements. It can not be discovered even in already deployed software until some specific interference of various factors arises. It is very dangerous in large critical systems, because the corrections can not be done quickly and the whole redesign process is needed.

In this paper we discuss the possibility of use of the BR represented in XML for intelligent adaptive dynamic data analysis and representation of the information by automation of recurring decision making processes and describe the framework for such software system design. The paper states the goals of data analysis using BR approach and possible ways for solutions using XML transformations from business rules into dynamic executable MDX instructions used for data analysis and representation of the information.

The rest of the paper is composed as follows: Sect. 2 analyzes related work on system engineering methods used for data analysis, information processing and decision support, Sect. 3 describes enterprise material and information flow model, Sect. 4 proposes business rule based framework for adaptive data analysis system design, Sect. 5 presents experimental evaluation of the framework and the final section summarizes the proposed method.

2 Related works

The main difference between traditional data analysis methods and business rule driven is that the rule based data analysis involves business logics into data analysis processes using transformations of business rules into different artefacts in IS and SS instead of implementing them directly in the requirements or design specifications and SS code.

From the information system perspective, "...a business rule is a statement that defines or constrains some aspect of the business. It is intended to assert business structure, or to control or influence the behaviour of the business." [2] There are other business rule (BR) definitions as well [3, 5]. Business rules are derived from business policy formulated by business strategy and tactics defined in enterprise mission. Implementation of BR empowers to achieve the objectives [11] and goals setup by executive staff and stated in enterprise vision. Due to dynamics of its nature, business environment is changing frequently according to internal and external influences such as changes in law, new competition etc. Business requires immediate and adequate reaction to changes. Otherwise there is a big risk to fall off competition. This is the main reason not only for immediate analysis of the situation and decisions, but also for the need of continuous changes in business policy and business logics. Such changes challenge related changes in information and software systems.

To allow such functionality in the other papers [14, 15] we have discussed an approach to capture business rules separately and store them in some repository by creating rule model. In this rule model all the business rules, captured in business system, are later transformed into information processing (information analysis) rules in information system. Using such rule model information processing rules are still platform independent and have direct relations to the business rules and business objects and by tracking all the transformations they can be multiple re-used in different software systems. Even if not rule based – by transforming such rules into software procedures or other components in particular software system.

Data analysis is one of the main sources of information for prediction of business system changes, evaluation of influence, risk analysis and decisions. Information needed for decision support is derived from captured data using available knowledge. Knowledge can be represented by business rules as well. Data analysis results can be a reason for business changes and influence the change of all the business system or some part of it [11].

Summarising previous results, we can state that two main components for data analysis are needed – data and rules for evaluation and transformation of the data. Such rules operate in business environment as various instructions for data manipulation, business models, policies and laws, business conventions or are derived using knowledge and experience of the operator (human).

In [8, 9] the authors state that by selecting and combining the most suitable and economical web services, business processes can be assigned dynamically by observing the changing business conditions. We think the same way can be used for dynamic data analysis process generation according to the business situation. There are two different ways of data analysis process creation – design of different executable processes in software system, at the same time mapping different processes to different conditions stored in the software system rules and the other one – storing business rules and transformations needed for data analysis process generation and compiling the process, using stored transformations, on the fly according to the current business rule set loaded in the knowledge base of the system.

Experimenting with different methods of business rule representations we have discovered that the business rules represented in XML are easily transformed using specially designed XSLT transformation schema into data analysis SS code, queries and other artefacts according to the properties of rules or rule sets [15]. We have found very suitable use of such transformations for rule based data analysis.

Following proposed method of rule transformation using XSLT schema and according to the principles stated by C. J. Date [4] the rules can be represented in XML and combined into rule sets by rule sources and destinations. All rule sets should be stored in repository. Every new rule should be added to the existing rule set only after checking consistency of the rule set using inference engine first. Complete rule set is passed to the system and transformed into the SS code used for data analysis. On the other hand the changing business situation can create new facts added into the knowledge base of the inference engine making current rule set inconsistent and showing that the revision of the existing rules is needed. Using this approach it is possible to generate smart data analysis reports on-line and react to business system changes. Such reports would use rules for evaluating current business environment and act according to the situation. For example such smart report can display main summary of the business system parameters if there is good business situation (profit greater than 10%) and display detailed information (use slice and/or dice methods according to the OLAP systems, etc.) for such parameters below predefined in the business rules.

3 Enterprise information flow model

Summarising the information analyzed we have created business system material and information flow model (see Fig. 1). The proposed model represents information flow from the data source in material processing layer to the decision making and implementation of decisions. All the data carriers and transformation processes are grouped into four columns by origin according to the method described in [11].

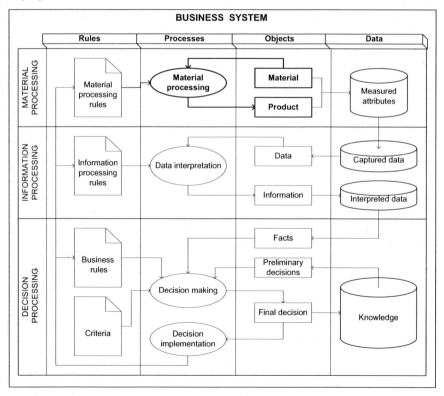

Fig. 1. Business system material and information flow model

In the first material processing layer we have displayed Material processing rules, Material processing process and the processing objects (initial material and final processing product). In business it represents some machinery equipment, for example equipment for production of the windows from the wood. In this case the measured attributes displayed will be the quality of the wood, size, price, etc. In the same way Material processing layer can be treated for services, too. In this case there should be service rules (discount, term) instead of material processing rules and the service process instead of material processing. The input and output objects in this case will be the initial and the final data or state of the maintained objects.

The second layer is dedicated for information processing. It is usually done in several information systems or at least hand written journals. It is represented in the model as captured data. Some captured data are usually used for data interpretation to get summarized information. It is usually done by creating reports (displayed as interpreted data) by predefined information processing rules implemented in the information systems usually using relational databases and SQL queries, but it can be done manually, too.

The third layer is dedicated for decision processing – decision making and implementation of decisions. According to the proposed model decisions are made using facts (information from interpreted data), BR (legal regulations, instructions, business policy, etc.), preliminary decisions based on the knowledge and selected decision criteria. The final decision is the source for new knowledge. The final decision usually is implemented changing material processing or information processing rules. The decision implementation by changing BR is possible, too, but it is out of our investigation scope.

The first two layers are usually easily automated using the present software engineering techniques. The software systems implemented in the business system are dedicated to support decisions of the management staff. However there is a lot of recurring decision tasks which should be automated. Due to the large uncertainty and frequent changes in business system it is still a very problematic and complicated task.

4 The framework

This section deals with automation of decisions according to the proposed enterprise information flow model (see Fig. 1), described in the previous section. For solution of such problem we propose the special software system architecture (see Fig. 2) and realization of the information interpretation and decision processes using special software system components.

First of all the automation of the data interpretation process is needed. Usually it is done by using DBMS built in services, although we have used data analysis services for execution of the MDX instructions dynamically created in the next layer [16].

In the second layer of the software subsystem according to the proposed framework the automation of the decision making and implementation processes is needed.

Decision implementation process is automated using transformations of the proved complete rule set, represented in XML and predefined XSLT transformation schema assigned to the fired preliminary decision, into executable MDX instruction later passed into data analysis service in the upper layer.

The preliminary decisions are validated using logical processing engine implemented in the inference subsystem. Decisions are validated according to the business situation represented by the facts received from interpreted data and predefined business rules. The decision selection process is implemented into the same inference subsystem and the additional criteria are used for selection of the rules which are placed for logical processing or for selection from several valid decisions.

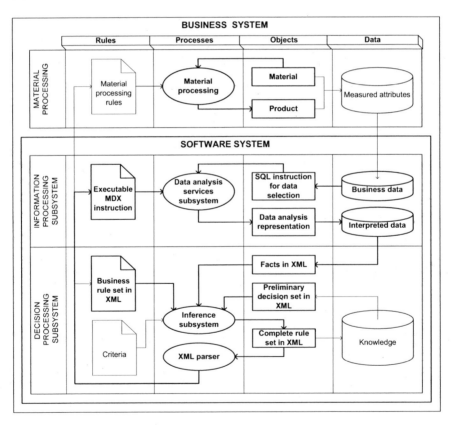

Fig. 2. Software system architecture for adaptable data analysis

According to the proposed framework and software system architecture execution of created MDX instruction the software system will produce the adaptive data analysis according to the current business situation (represented by facts) and business policy (represented as business rules) involved in the inference subsystem.

5 Experimental evaluation of the framework

The framework is still in the experimentation phase. We have made experiments by creating the prototype software system represented in the decision processing subsystem layer of the framework to examine possibility of dynamical creation of the MDX instructions for OLAP based data analysis cubes and pass it into upper information processing layer [16].

We have used the inference engine with backward chaining algorithm for logical processing in inference subsystem. We have selected backward chaining because it is useful in the situation where the quantity of data is potentially very large and we actually need only to prove the validity of the predefined preliminary decisions expressed as hypothetical preliminary decisions in the proposed framework. In case more than one hypothetical preliminary decision is involved, backward chaining attempts to verify each one independently.

We have represented Business rules in XML and transformed them according to the predefined XSLT transformation schema into predicates for use in inference engine and added automatically discovered facts, using predefined SQL queries, to the knowledge base of inference engine. According to the framework such facts represent current business system situation. The final OLAP cube is changed dynamically according to the inference results and is adapted to the current business situation.

During experimentation we have discovered that there are only few possibilities to influence decisions using OLAP cube transformations. Currently we can influence formatting and dimensions of data representation. For example, if the total revenue per moth is less than 10% - detail data are displayed for day-by-day analysis all around the stores; otherwise only summary data is proposed. However the use of inference subsystem and handling of the inference results makes a lot of problems not solved yet.

6 Conclusions and future work

The practical experimentations using proposed framework for adaptable data analysis software system architecture and design have led to the following conclusions:

- Business rules and facts about current business situation represented in XML can be processed in specially designed decision processing subsystem to choose predefined preliminary decision represented in XML.
- If business rules according to the selected preliminary decisions and selected facts make complete set they can be transformed using predefined transformation XSLT schemas to the executable MDX instruction for further use in adaptable data interpretation.
- The information derived from data analysis results can be translated into new facts and entered into the knowledge base of inference engine to evaluate the conformance of the current business system state according to the business policy expressed as business rules in repository and identify the source of inconsistency.
- Rule set and facts stored in the knowledge base of inference engine can be used for what-if analysis by modelling and adding new rules into rule set or adding new facts for examination. By checking consistency the influence of such business system changes can be examined.
- Business rule approach for rule based data analysis allows business rules to be stored separately by creating special SS infrastructure and allowing rapid business rule changes without changing SS code and redesigning all the entire IS. The proposed SS architecture allows reuse of the rule sets and transformations.

The proposed framework and SS architecture can be used for creation of the intelligent adaptable data analysis system. However, performance problems can arise when loading large rule sets into the knowledge base for inference. We expect such problems and limitations to be solved by evolving methods of logical derivations and new hardware.

References

1. Barbara von Hale. Business Rules Applied: Building Better Systems Using the Business Rules Approach. John Wiley & Sons, Inc., New York, 2001.
2. Business Rules Group. Defining Business Rules: What are they really? 3rd ed., 2002, URL: http://www.BusinessRulesGroup.org
3. Business Rules Group. Defining Business Rules: What is a Business Rule?, 2004, URL: http://www.BusinessRulesGroup.org/brgdefn.htm
4. Date C. J. What Not How: The Business Rules Approach to Application Development. Addison-Wesley Longman Inc., 2000.
5. Gladys S.W. Lam. Plainly Speaking: What Is a Rule? Business Rules Journal. May 2003, Vol. 4, No. 5.
   URL: http://www.BRCommunity.com/a2003/b149.html
6. Grosof B., Poon T. SweetDeal: Representing Agent Contracts with Exceptions using Semantic Web Rules, Ontologies, and Process Descriptions.

International Journal of Electronic Commerce, Accepted Journal paper, revised version of Nov. 19, 2003

7. Mahajan S. Building a Data Warehouse Using Oracle OLAP Tools. ACTA Journal, September 1997.

8. Orriens B., Yang J., and Papazoglou M. P. "Model driven service composition", in: Proceedings of the First International Conference on Service Oriented Computing, Trento, Italy, December 15-18, 2003.

9. Orriens B., Yang J., and Papazoglou M. P. "A Framework for Business Rule Driven Service Composition", Lecture Notes on Computer Science, Berlin: Springer-Verlag, 2003 [Proceedings of the 4th International Workshop on Conceptual Modeling Approaches for e-Business Dealing with Business Volatility, Chicago, United States, October 2003].

10. Prakash N., Srivastava S. Engineering Methods For Schema Transformation: Application to XML. IFIP TC8/WG8.1 Working Conference on Engineering Information Systems in the Internet Context, September 25-27, 2002, Kanazawa, Japan. Kluwer Academic publishers, pp. 153-175.

11. Rosca D., Greenspan, S., Wild, C.: Enterprise Modeling and Decision-Support for Automating the Business Rules Lifecycle, Automated Software Engineering, Vol. 9, n. 4, pp. 361, 44, 2002.

12. Ross R., Healy K. Organizing Business Plans. The Standard Model for Business Rule Motivation. Business Rules Group. 2000.

13. Ross R. Principles of the Business Rule Approach. Addison Wesley, 2003.

14. Vasilecas O., Smaizys A. Business rule based knowledge base integrated intelligent system framework. Information Sciences 2005, vol. 34, Vilnius. 2005, pp. 195-200.

15. Vasilecas O., Smaizys A. Business rule specification and transformation for rule based data analysis. Proceedings of 19th International Conference on Systems for Automation of Engineering and Research (SAER 2005), Varna, St. Konstantin resort. 2005, pp. 35-40.

16. Vasilecas O., Smaizys A. Business rule based data analysis for decision support and automation. Proceedings of 7th International Conference on Computer Systems and Technologies (CompSysTech 2006), Varna, 2006

A Comparative Review of Approaches for Database Schema Integration[1]

Aiste Aleksandraviciene, Rimantas Butleris

Department of Information Systems, Kaunas University of Technology, Studentu St 50–308, LT–51368, Kaunas, Lithuania, {aiste.aleksandraviciene, rimantas.butleris}@ktu.lt

1 Introduction

Any useful information system (IS) needs a conceptual schema, which produces an abstract, global view of all data, managed in the organization. Even though conceptual modeling represents only a small portion of the total information system development effort, its influence on the quality of the final result is probably greater than any other phase. Database (DB) schema is a major determinant of system development costs, system flexibility, integration with other systems and the ability of the system to meet user requirements [13]. This leads to the conclusion that conceptual data-base design is an essential activity of IS development [12].

Integration of local schemata is a popular way to compose correct and complete global database schema – the core of any IS. Schema integration has been a research area since the late 1970s [3] and many approaches to schema integration for various data models have been proposed [7].

This paper gives the results of comparative review performed on six database schema integration methods and models. For this study we used a modification of comparative analysis framework, proposed by Batini et al. [2]. This framework is based on the standpoint that any approach for schema integration is a mixture of four activities. Those are *pre-integration, comparison of schemas, conforming the schemas*, and finally *merging and restructuring*.

We used relatively old framework to define fundamental criterions applied to compare approaches for schema integration. However, we applied these criterions to new approaches mostly, so it was necessary to add certain new criteria that

---

[1] This work is supported by Lithuanian State Science and Studies Foundation according to Eureka programme project "IT-Europe" (Reg. No. 3473).

were not mentioned in the survey of Batini at al., i.e., cardinalities of corresponding schema elements and automation levels.

In this paper we focus on two contexts of using the term "schema integration". Those are *conceptual DB schema design* and *distributed DB management*. Although they are different enough, the overall philosophy of schema integration applies to both [14].

The comparative review proposed in this paper was strongly motivated. The results of this review were used to derive a set of desirable features for a special new algorithm suitable for entity-relationship (ER) schema integration in the context of conceptual DB schema design. These features summarize previously reviewed approaches.

In the next section we introduce the basic steps of our approach for conceptual DB schema design, including the above-mentioned algorithm. Six approaches used for the comparative review are introduced in Section 3, and the review itself is presented in Sections 4 and 5. Section 6 gives a set of expected features for ER schema integration algorithm we are going to develop. Conclusions and hints on future research are disclosed in Section 7.

2 Database Schema Design on the Basis of Data Flows

Conceptual DB schema design on the basis of data flows specification is a component of the functional requirements specification method named ODReS (Output-Driven Requirements Specification). Using this method the process of information system development starts with the analysis of requirements for outputs (e.g., reports, summaries) in order to define the limits of problem domain; then the inputs that form required outputs are analyzed. The use of outputs for requirement elicitation reduces the chances of misunderstandings of end-user requirements because the output information is the best for end-user to understand [5].

ODReS method relies on the standpoint that any organization is the sys-tem of incoming and outgoing information flows with links among them. On the basis of this standpoint data flows specification is composed. It is stored in a repository as relational metadata.

There are four steps of conceptual DB schema design on the basis of data flows specification [6]:

1. Specification of the structure of incoming information, referred to as *data resources*. This step produces a number of local schemata, one for each data resource. For conceptual modeling the ER model is used.
2. Specification of the links between data resources. In this step the relationships, reflecting semantic dependencies between elements from different local schemata, are defined. Set of these relationships, showing data transition between two data resources, is referred to as *data flow*.
3. Integration of local schemata, composed during the first step of conceptual DB schema design. In this step data flow structure is used to find out what local schemata can be merged. As data flow shows semantically dependant

elements between two local schemata, it is used as a basis for schema integration while defining corresponding fragments of component schemas. The activity of local schemata integration produces a global DB schema of information system. Generally the process of integration is iterative.
4. Verification of integrated schema using specification of the structure of required outputs.

It is obvious, that the fundamental principle of conceptual DB schema design described above is integration of local ER schemas (each composed for one data resource) using the structure of data flows. The first two phases of this decentralized bottom-up approach were presented in earlier publications [6, 8], and this paper is dedicated for the third one.

3 Approaches for Database Schema Integration

As it has been already mentioned, we applied the comparative review framework to six methods and models used for DB schema integration.

Table 1. Methods and Models of Comparative Review

Author/s	View integration	Database integration	Data model
Adam and Gangop-adhyay [1]	+		Conceptual dependency diagram
Bellström [3]	+		Enterprise model
Chao [7]		+	Object-oriented model
Lawrence [11]		+	Entity-relationship model
Navathe et al. [14]	+		Entity-category-relationship model
Sattler et al. [16]		+	Any model

It is evident from Table 1, that three of them are used for view integration, while the other three are applied when integrating databases. View integration is a task of conceptual DB schema design and database integration is a task of distributed DB management.

The basic input to schema integration process is a number of component schemata and a basic output is an integrated schema. Table 2 shows specific inputs and outputs for each schema integration method or model. View integration focuses on integrating all the local schemas into a global conceptual one, while database integration focus on providing a global view of all existing databases [3].

Table 2. Inputs and Outputs*

Author/s	Inputs	Outputs
Adam and Gangop-adhyay [1]	*n* database views	Global DB schema, transformed from global conceptual diagram
Bellström [3]	User-defined views	Conceptual DB schema
Chao [7]	Two component schemas	Integrated schema
Lawrence [11]	*n* local schemas of existing databases Relational semantic metadata Global dictionary	Global view *m* projections of global view for each user-group Global to local mappings
Navathe et al. [14]	*n* user views	Global DB schema Global to local mappings
Sattler et al. [16]	Local schemas of heterogeneous databases Global object types	Global view of DB federation Global to local mappings

* This table was filled using original terminology given by authors.

4 Process of Database Schema Integration

Any integration methodology is a mixture of the following activities [2]:

1. *Pre-integration.* An analysis of local schemata is carried out. The analysis made governs the choice of schemas to be integrated and the order of integration. A number of schemas to be integrated at a time and the amount of designer interaction are also decided in this step.
2. *Comparison of the schemas.* Schemas chosen for integration are compared to determine the correspondences among concepts and detect possible conflicts.
3. *Conforming the schemas.* In order to integrate schemas, the detected conflicts between them have to be resolved so that it was possible to merge them.
4. *Merging (a) and restructuring (b).* Schemas are merged in this step. The result of final or intermediate schema merging is analyzed and, if necessary, restructured in order to achieve several desirable qualities.

Table 3 shows how the steps of each approach cover these activities.

Table 3. Schema Integration Activities

Author/s	Step 1	Step 2	Step 3	Step 4a	Step 4b
Adam and Gangop-adhyay [1]	X ⟶	X ⟶	X ⟶	X	—

Bellström [3]	—	X ⟶	X ⟶	X ⟶	X
Chao [7]	—	X ⟶	X ⟶	X	—
Lawrence [11]	X ⟶	X ⟶	X ⟶	X ⟶	X
Navathe et al. [14]	X ⟶	X ⟶	X ⟶	X ⟶	X
Sattler et al. [15]	X ⟶	X ⟶	X ⟶	X	—

Note, that some approaches allow a feedback between two steps. Chao [7] provides a global loop from the end of the process to the initial comparison activity, meaning that there can be some correspondences that cannot be specified until the integrated schema is being constructed.

Navathe et al. [14] and Sattler et al. [16] provide an iterative execution of comparison and conforming steps before any merging is performed.

4.1 Pre-integration

In this step the decision on strategy for integration processing is made.

Strategies for schema integration processing are classified into *binary* and *n-ary* [2, 4].

Binary strategies allow the integration of two schemas at a time (n = 2). They are called *ladder* strategies, when a new component schema is integrated with an existing intermediate result at each step. A binary strategy is *balanced*, when the schemas are divided into pairs at the start and then are integrated in a symmetric fashion [2].

N-ary strategies allow integration of n schemas at a time (n > 2). An n-ary strategy is *one-shot* when n schemas are integrated in a single step, and it is *iterative* otherwise.

Table 4. Strategies for Integration Processing

Author/s	Strategy
Adam and Gangopadhyay [1]	Iterative n-ary
Bellström [3]	Binary, N/A
Chao [7]	Binary, ladder
Lawrence [11]	Binary, ladder
Navathe et al. [14]	One-shot n-ary
Sattler et al. [16]	Binary, N/A

As Table 4 shows, most of the analyzed approaches adopt binary strate-gies. As the complexity of integration increases with respect to the number of schemas integrated at a time, binary strategies simplify the activities of schema comparison and conforming. However, any binary schema integra-tion method typically requires more restructuring then any n-ary schema integration approach [1].

4.2 Comparison of Schemas

As is it evident from Table 3, all approaches of the comparative review provide the activity of schema comparison. Schema comparison is necessary for identifying corresponding elements and detecting conflicts.

A *conflict* between two representations of the same real-world object is every situation that gives rise to these representations not being identical.

Causes for Database Schema Diversity

There are three main causes for DB schema diversity:

1. The same real-world object can be seen from different levels of abstraction, or represented using different properties [10].
2. The same reality can be modeled using different combinations of data model constructs.
3. Incompatible design specifications (improper choices regarding names, types, integrity constraints, etc.).

Cardinality Cases of Corresponding Schema Elements

Suppose we have to compare two local schemas S_1 and S_2. Any element in S_1 can have one or more corresponding elements in S_2. Thus, we can use familiar relationship cardinalities to express four possible cardinality cases between corresponding elements of two different schemas. Those are exact case 1:1 and setoriented cases 1:N, N:1, and M:N [15]. Exact cardinality means that some element in S_1 corresponds to only one element in S_2. If there is a difference in representation of these elements (e.g. price in dol-lars vs. price in euros), a conflict occurs. Set-oriented cardinality 1:N means that some element in S_1 (e.g., attribute "Name") corresponds to multiple elements (e.g., attributes "FirstName" and "LastName") in S_2. There is always a conflict in such a situation. The same situation is in case of cardinality N:1. As cardinality case M:N is a combination of 1:N and N:1, it is the most sophisticated one.

Table 5. Cardinalities of Correspondences (at the element level)

Author/s	1:1	N:1	1:N	M:N
Adam and Gangopadhyay [1]	+			
Bellström [3]	+			
Chao [7]	+	+	+	+
Lawrence [11]	+	+	+	N/A
Navathe et al. [14]	+			
Sattler et al. [16]	+	+	+	

As it is evident from Table 5, all the analyzed approaches support the identification of correspondences with exact cardinalities, and only Chao [7] method can be used to define the full set of cardinality cases.

Types of Conflicts

As it was mentioned previously, various types of conflicts can occur among corresponding elements contained in two or more different sche-mas.

We identified three common types of conflicts: *naming*, *semantic*, and *structural*. Naming conflicts include homonyms and synonyms, while structural conflicts mainly deal with incompatible both schema- and data-level types, key equivalence and dependency conflicts. Semantic conflicts deal with semantic dependencies among two or more schema elements, expressed using modeling constructs of the same type (e.g., entities, classes, relations, attributes, etc.). A situation of exact semantic dependency is referred to as *equivalence* ($A \equiv B$), and it is not a conflict. But there are three situations of inexact semantic dependencies. Thus, there are three kinds of semantic conflicts: *containment* ($A \subseteq B$), *overlapping* ($A \cap B$), and *disjointness* ($A \cap B = \varnothing$). All of them can be detected using any of the reviewed approaches except the method, proposed by Bellström [3]; he does not mention semantic conflicts in his paper.

Table 6 shows, what kinds of naming and structural conflicts can be detected using reviewed methods and models.

Table 6. Naming and Structural Conflicts

Author/s	Naming	Structural
Adam and Gangop-adhyay [1]	Homonyms Synonyms	–
Bellström [3]	Homonyms Synonyms	Dependency conflicts Key conflicts
Chao [7]	Homonyms Synonyms	Domain type conflicts Object type conflicts (attribute-class)
Lawrence [11]	Homonyms Synonyms	Data level type conflicts Dependency conflicts Schema level type conflicts (attribute-entity, attribute-relationship, and entity-relationship)
Navathe et al. [14]	Homonyms Synonyms	Dependency conflicts (differences in roles, degree, and cardinalities) Key conflicts
Sattler et al. [16]	Homonyms Synonyms	Attribute conflicts Key (equivalence) conflicts Meta conflicts Table structure conflicts (overlapping fields)

4.3 Conforming the Schemas

Merging of schemas is possible, only if naming and structural conflicts are resolved. This is the essential condition for schema integration.

There is a plenty of suggestions, how to resolve naming conflicts. How-ever, we structural conflicts still remain an open issue. As Table 7 shows, most authors tend to agree with resolving homonym and synonym con-flicts by applying "rename" operations. Giving different names or prefix-ing eliminates homonyms. Unifying names eliminates synonyms. In some specific cases, if data model allows, synonyms can be excluded avoiding "rename" operations, e.g., in enterprise model a mutual inheritance is used.

Resolution technique used to resolve key conflicts is twofold: Bell-ström [3] recommends including both keys into the integrated schema, while Sattler et al. [16] suggest adopting only one of them.

Problems with incompatible schema level types are resolved by conver-sion from one type into the other, i.e., "upgrade" [7] and "convert" [11, 14] operations. Data level type conflicts are resolved using various conversion functions [16].

There is a whole methodology devoted mainly for resolving dependency conflicts in [14] and a newsworthy suggestion of Bellström [3] to adopt semantically weaker relationship in such case.

4.4 Merging and Restructuring

After the merging and restructuring is performed, the integration of schemas is completed and integrated schema is produced.

Such operations as "merge" [1], "create" [7, 14], and "integrate" [11] are applied in order to merge the same objects. Semantic conflicts are re-solved by using generalizations and/or specializations. Dissimilar objects are simply added to the integrated schema.

Integrated schema is analyzed and, if necessary, restructured to achieve desirable qualitative criterions [2]. Restructuring the integrated schema means eliminating redundancies, adding new components, etc.

Table 7. Operations for Schema Transformations

Author/s	Conforming	Merging and restructuring
Adam and Gangop-adhyay [1]	Rename	Add (dissimilar components) Generalize/specialize Merge
Bellström [3]	Prefix Adopt semantic weaker dependency	Create inheritance hierarchy Include both keys Set mutual inheritance
Chao [8]	Coerce Concatenate Rename	Compose Combine Create

	Upgrade	Create inheritance hierarchy
		Generalize
		Specialize
Lawrence [11]	Convert to entity	Add
	Convert to relationship	Change
	Standardize names	Integrate
Navathe et al. [14]	Convert entity to category	Add
	Rename	Create
		Generalize
		Remove redundant relationships
		Specialize
Sattler et al. [16]	Create a mapping table	Apply "Join" operator
	Transpose	Apply "Union" operator
	Use conversion functions	

5 Schema Integration Process: Manual or Automatic?

The automation level measures the ability of an approach to be automated. In general, there can be three levels of automation: *manual*, *semi-automatic*, and *automatic*. We examined the main activities of each approach against these criteria (see Table 8).

Table 8. Automation Levels

Author/s	Comparison	Integration	Reasoning
Adam and Gangopadhyay [1]	Semi-automatic	Semi-automatic	Integration rules (on the basis of Conceptual Dependency Theory).
Bellström [3]	Manual	Manual	Heuristic algorithms.
Chao [7]	Semi-automatic	Automatic (limited support)	– Correspondence assertions in form of predicates. – 5 integration rules: algorithmic steps containing primitive algebraic operators.
Lawrence [11]	Automatic	Automatic (limited support)	– Global dictionary (contains unique names of concepts represented in a global view). – RIM specifications (relational semantic metadata – a kind of export schema). – Mapping rules.
Navathe et al. [14]	Semi-automatic	Semi-automatic	– Hierarchal schema for relationship comparison against three criteria. – Integration rules.
Sattler et al. [16]	Automatic	Semi-automatic	– Interactive conflict detection and resolution, based on examples.

	– Advanced mechanisms for conflict resolution, supported by $F_{RA}QL$.

Referring to Table 8, it is evident, that none of the approaches provide fully automated both schema comparison and integration process.

6 Expected Features for a Future Approach

PROCESS OF DB SCHEMA DESIGN
ON THE BASIS OF DATA FLOWS

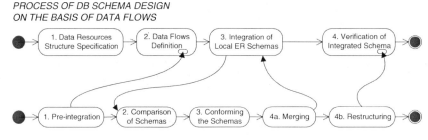

PROCESS OF SCHEMA INTEGRATION

Fig. 1. Links between the activities of two processes

Fig. 1 shows, how the activities of DB schema design, introduced in Sect. 2, are related to the basic activities of schema integration process. Definition of data flows includes pre-integration as sub-activity, because data flows, when defined, give the recommendations on grouping and sequencing schemas for integration. Integration of local ER schemas includes the activities of comparison, conforming, and merging the schemas. Finally the integrated schema is verified to check, if it is able to form all required outputs. If verification fails, restructuring is necessary.

Expected features for the future approach are given in Table 9. Note, that possible types of conflicts are determined by the boundaries of relational metadata structure.

Table 9. A Set of Expected Features for the Future Approach

Feature	Description
Context	Conceptual DB schema design (view integration)
Data model	ER model, Information Engineering (IE) notation [9]
Inputs	– *n* local schemata (one for each data resource)
	– *m* specifications of data flows structure
	– Data flows specification (relational metadata)
Output	Conceptual DB schema
Strategy	Binary, both ladder and balanced
Conflicts:	
Naming	Synonyms
Semantic	Containment, overlapping, disjointness

| *Structural* | – Attribute-entity conflicts |
| | – Key equivalence and dependency conflicts |

7 Conclusions

This survey is expected to be useful both to developers of new approaches for DB schema integration and to users who need to select from a variety of approaches. For the future research we are going to extend our survey with the analysis of ontology-based schema integration approaches. And we also plan to develop a semi-automated tool for bottom-up DB schema design, including ER schema integration.

References

1. Adam NR, Gangopadhyay A (1995) An N-ary View Integration Method Using Conceptual Dependencies. In: Proc. of 28th Hawaii Intl. Conf. on System Sciences. IEEE Computer Society, Washington, pp 391–397
2. Batini C, Lanzerini M, Navathe SB (1986) A Comparative Analysis of Methodologies for Database Schema Integration. ACM Computing Surveys 18(4):323–363
3. Bellström P (2004) Using Enterprise Modeling for Identification and Resolution of Homonym Conflicts in View Integration. In: Vasilecas O (ed) Information Systems Development: Advances in Theory, Practice and Education. Springer, pp 266-276
4. Boman B, Bubenko J, Johanesson P, Wangler B (1993) Models, Concepts, and Information: An Introduction to Conceptual Modelling for Information Systems Development. Royal Institute of Technology, Stockholm
5. Butkiene R, Butleris R, Danikauskas T (2002) The Approach of Consistency Checking of Functional Requirements Specification. In: Proc. of 6th World Multiconference on Systemics, Cybernetics and Informatics, vol XVIII. Orlando, pp 67–72
6. Butleris R, Danikauskas T (2004) Conceptual Data Model Using Functional Requirements Specification Method. In: Proc. of 16th Conference on Advanced Information Systems Engineering (CAiSE), vol 1. Riga Technical University, Riga, pp 221–232
7. Chao Ch-M (2001) Schema Integration between Object-Oriented Databases. Tamkang. Journal of Science and Engineering 4(1):37–44
8. Danikauskas T, Butleris T, Drąsutis S (2005) Graphical User Interface Development on the Basis of Data Flows Specification. In: Proc of 20th International Symposium on Computer and Information Sciences, LNCS 3733. Springe-Verlag, Berlin Heidelberg, pp 904-914

9. Halpin T (2002) Metaschemas for ER, ORM and UML Data Models: A Comparison. Journal of Database Management 13(2):20–29
10. Johannesson P (1993) Schema Integration, Schema Translation and Interoperability in Federated Information Systems. Ph.D. thesis, Stockholm University
11. Lawrence R (2001) Automatic Conflict Resolution to Integrate Relational Schema. Ph.D. thesis, University of Manitoba
12. Olivé A (2005) Conceptual Schema-Centric Development: A Grand Challenge for Information Systems Research. In: Pastor O, Cunha JF (eds) CAiSE '2005, LNCS 3520. Springer-Verlag, Berlin Heidelberg, pp 1–15
13. Moody DL, Shanks GG (2003) Improving the quality of data models: empirical validation of a quality management framework. Information systems 28:619–660
14. Navathe SB, Sashidhar T, Elmasri R (1984) Relationship Merging in Schema Integration. In: Proc. of 10th Intl. Conf. on VLDB. Singapore, pp 78–90
15. Rahm E, Bernstein PhA (2001) A survey of approaches to automatic schema matching. The VLDB Journal 10:334–350
16. Sattler KU, Conrad S, Saake G (2003) Interactive example-driven integration and reconciliation for accessing database federations. Information systems 28:393–414

Strategic Use of
Customer Relationship Management (CRM)
in Sports: The Rosenborg Case

Bjørn Furuholt[*], Nils Georg Skutle[**]

[*] School of Management, Agder University College, Kristiansand, Norway
E-mail: Bjorn.Furuholt@hia.no
[**] Buysec AS, Kongsberg, Norway

Abstract: Today's sports industry has turned into a billion industry on the same level as more traditional industries. Present-day information technology and Customer Relationship Management (CRM) has enabled companies to deal with vast numbers of customers and to establish one-to-one communication with each of them. Lately, sports clubs have also discovered the benefits of introducing CRM. A sports club's most important customers are its supporters. They are different from traditional customers in that they are characterized by a strong sense of loyalty to their favourite club. This article shows how one sports club, the Norwegian football club Rosenborg Ballklub (RBK), can use CRM as a strategic tool. Due to the limited material in this subject area, this is an explorative piece of work, based on examination of literature, in-depth interviews at RBK and collection of questionnaires from a selection of European football clubs.Our findings indicate that there are many similarities between a football club and a traditional company when CRM is introduced. In addition, for clubs, the CRM system must be adapted to the supporter role, and we propose the introduction of the concept Supporter Relationship Management in order to take better care of the strong ties between a club and its supporters.

1 Introduction

Professional team sports have become a billion industry where the biggest clubs in European top football have earnings that surpass €200 million [3]. This has led to the fact that the biggest teams operate more like large companies than traditional sports clubs and this increased professionalism has gradually spread to the smaller clubs across Europe.

A professional sports club's most important customers are its supporters. They provide direct income through buying tickets to matches and supporter gear as well as indirect earnings through sponsor and TV agreements, which are closely linked to how popular each club is. Gradually the clubs have entered "the digital world", which has paved the way for new channels to reach their supporters. and strengthen their relations with each individual person. This is what we call Customer Relationship Management (CRM).

There are few areas in information systems that have attracted as much attention as CRM in recent years. When it comes to the combination of CRM and sports, there are few articles with an academic starting point.

Rosenborg Ballklub (RBK) is Norway's biggest sports club regardless of sports type, when it comes to both success on the football field and financially. RBK started a CRM project for the 2005 season as the first sports club in Norway. Our research question is connected to this project and is formulated as follows: "How do we proceed to implement a successful CRM solution at RBK, and how can CRM be used strategically?" Primarily we will concentrate on sports specific circumstances, the use of CRM in relation to the club's supporters. When it comes to using CRM in relation to other customers, the clubs are not very different from traditional companies. In order to answer the question we have examined literature concerning general CRM implementations, carried out an investigation at a selection of European football clubs, and finally examined the situation in Norway and specific RBK conditions.

The paper is organized as follows. This introduction is followed by a review of relevant literature based on three main topics: sports and football economics, supporter loyalty, and CRM. Chapter three presents the methodology, whereas chapter four includes a survey of the findings from the questionnaire and the in-depth interviews at RBK. The findings are discussed in chapter five, and the article is rounded up with conclusions in chapter six.

2 Literature review

2.1 Football economics

Sports have evolved from a leisure time activity for amateurs in the beginning of the 20th century to the billion industry of today. This has resulted in the fact that clubs nowadays must to a great extent regard themselves as companies that operate in a competitive market. However, there are basic differences between the commercial mechanisms in professional team sports and traditional business activity. A company is successful if it can get rid of all competition and secure a monopoly situation. In sports, on the other hand, it would not be favourable for a team to reduce competition [4]. The reason is that added value in professional sports is inherently a joint achievement by the different teams in the league. Neale

[9] illustrates this by what he calls "the Louis Schmelling paradox". World champion Joe Louis' earnings were higher if there was an evenly matched contender available for him to fight than if the nearest contender was relatively weak. The same principle applies to professional team sports. This paradox goes against all logic in traditional economics where you strive for monopoly in order to eliminate the competitors. Neale [9] addresses this paradox by distinguishing between 'sporting' and 'economic' competition. Sporting competition is more profitable than sporting monopoly. When it comes to economic competition the different teams co-operate in order to create a joint product.

2.2 Supporter loyalty

Sports clubs are in a favourable position because their supporters are very loyal compared with traditional customers [13,16]. Loyalty can be understood as a two-dimensional concept with a psychological and behavioural dimension, and Backman and Cromton [1] developed a loyalty model, which takes these two dimensions into account. Based on Backman and Crompton's model Mahony et al. [8] developed a scale in order to measure the psychological commitment among supporters. This scale was used to place the supporters according to the four categories in Backman and Crompton's loyalty model: supporters with high loyalty, spurious loyalty, latent loyalty, and finally low or no loyalty.

Guilianotti [6] has made a taxonomy in which he, just like Mahoney, identifies four categories with ideal supporter types: supporter, fan, follower and flâneur. He employs two dimensions to differentiate between the different types: traditional/consumer dimension and hot/cool dimension that will say something about how strongly a supporter identifies with the club. If we compare Guilianotti's ideal types directly with Backman and Crompton's loyalty model, we learn that it does not quite add up. For instance we see that the supporter, who would be the ideal type with the strongest sense of loyalty to the club, end up in the category of latent loyalty. The fan, on the other hand, ends up in the category of high/genuine loyalty. Of this reason we will work out our own adjustment of these models, which will better demonstrate how the ideal types can fit in with several loyalty categories (figure 1).

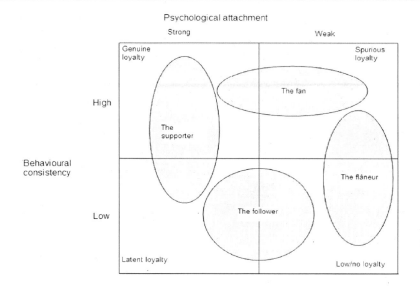

Fig. 1. The relation between ideal types and the loyalty model

This turns out to be more correct than a direct transfer because the supporter base in professional football clubs is consequently not a homogeneous group, but is made up of different types with individual motivations for supporting the club [6, 8, 11].

2.3 CRM

The concept of Customer Management has been around for as long as people have been trading goods and services and as the population has increased, it has become more and more difficult to keep track of customers [5]. Today's companies introduce Customer Relationship Management in order to make up for this. Zablah et al. [19, p.477] have gone through CRM literature and identified five different perspectives on CRM: process, strategy, philosophy, ability and technology. Based on this, they make an attempt at reaching a joint conceptualization of CRM. They consider the process to be the most fruitful perspective and arrive at the following definition of CRM:

"CRM is an ongoing process that involves the development and leveraging of marked intelligence for the purpose of building and maintaining a profit-maximising portfolio of customer relationships" [19, p. 480].

Unfortunately, a lot of CRM projects have failed and have by far kept their promise. The Gartner Group have found that 70% of all CRM projects result in loss or no improvement in the company's financial performance (stated in [12]). A series of articles discuss critical success factors and pitfalls that must be avoided in connection with CRM [e.g., 7, 10, 14, 15]. In these articles there are four areas that stand out as the most important areas: top management support, strategic thinking, organisational changes and management of these, and finally the role of technology in CRM.

CRM's strategic nature is an important argument for necessary top management support. The most important change the organisation must go through is to focus on the customer. Strong and sound change management is absolutely necessary if the organisational changes are to succeed. In investigations carried out in this area it turned out that lack of adequate change management was stated as the main reason that CRM projects failed in 87% of all the cases [7, 14].

The final area that needs special attention in a CRM project is technology. The biggest mistake companies make when it comes to technology is to place too much importance on it, and to think that a CRM solution will handle all customer relations and automatically make the organisation customer-oriented.

There has been little mention in academic literature of the use of CRM in the world of sports. It seems, however, to be a consensus that CRM and sports belong together [2, 17, 18]. There is no indication that success factors such as top management support, change management and strategic thinking become more or less important because we are talking about sports. What makes a customer at a sports club different from a traditional customer is that he considers himself as a supporter and not a customer. And, this important difference is what separates CRM in the sports industry from traditional CRM.

3 Methodology and data collection

Since CRM in football clubs is a relatively unexplored area, this article is exploratory by nature. RBK was chosen as a special case for further studies because it is the first Norwegian club to introduce CRM. The interviews made at RBK focused on three different aspects: What special circumstances are there in a football club? What special circumstances are there in a Norwegian football club? How can CRM fit in? Three semi-structured interviews were conducted, with the managing director, the marketing director and a project manager in the marketing department. The interviews were taped and then transcribed.

In addition a questionnaire, in English, was sent to 13 different clubs in Europe. These varied in size from top clubs such as AC Milan, to clubs of the same size as RBK such the Danish FC Copenhagen. The purpose of the questionnaire was to find out what kind of practice the various clubs had in relation to CRM and CRM strategy. By studying similarities between the clubs we wanted to bring up "best practices" in CRM usage in football clubs. The questionnaires were sent along with a cover letter from RBK, four were sent to the club's official address and nine were addressed to a contact person in the club, picked out together with RBK. We received six answers, all among the nine that were sent to specific contact persons. All contact persons were part of the clubs' top management. The questionnaires were completed by the respondents.

4 Findings

4.1 The clubs' responses to the questionnaire

We have categorized the six clubs, which returned the questionnaire, in three categories: top clubs (AC Milan, Juventus and Bayern München), intermediate clubs (Borussia Dortmund and PSV) and Scandinavian clubs (Djurgårdens IF from Sweden).

Four clubs, Bayern München, AC Milan, Borussia Dortmund and Juventus, stated that they had a CRM strategy. A common theme among these clubs is that they will develop stronger relationships with their supporters to get more satisfied customers. PSV is the only club that does not state any form of strategic thinking behind its CRM initiative. They consider CRM as a technical solution only.

The size of the CRM systems in the clubs varies from a simple web based solution at Djurgården to CRM as an integrated part of a large-scale Enterprise Resource Planning (ERP) system at Borussia Dortmund and Bayern München. Both clubs have systems that are specially adapted to the needs of a football club. In order to achieve the clubs' goals concerning customer satisfaction, the employees have access to updated customer information from several sources such as membership records, booking systems and online sales of supporter gear.

Based on the answers we can draw the conclusion that it is important for a CRM system to process customer data collected from several sources and put them together in an overall presentation of the customer. It is also clear from the answers that the system should be specially adapted for use in a football club.

AC Milan and Bayern München have run their CRM systems for a few years, and are a little ahead of the other clubs. These two clubs recognize the importance of the continuous development of both strategy and software in order to meet new challenges and possibilities.

Three points are mentioned when the clubs bring up advantages of CRM: improved customer information, efficiency and improved customer relationship. Our conclusion is that the most important advantage of CRM is improved customer data. When customer data are easily available, the clubs could increase the efficiency of their processes, both internally and towards customers.

Another important CRM system characteristic mentioned is the fact that it makes it possible for the clubs to tailor-make offers for the various customer segments. The number of categories varies from two at Juventus, to six at Bayern München and Borussia Dortmund and there are four main categories that stand out: ticket buyers, supporter gear buyers, sponsors and members.

It seems like none of the clubs have a carefully thought through a strategy for how to use CRM to get new supporters. CRM is first and foremost used to follow up existing supporters and for this they will primarily employ two methods. The active method is to use the CRM system to tailor information and offers and send it to the supporters by way of various information channels. In the passive variant, CRM is used to make personalized membership sites on the club's home page.

Some clubs, such as AC Milan and Bayern München appear to make use of both variants.

4.2 In-depth Rosenborg interviews

CRM can serve as a support for both the club's core product and the various by-products, and RBK hopes that CRM can contribute to improve customer communications and to coordinate marketing activities across customer groups.

Supporters are customers who are often very emotionally attached to their favourite club. This attachment to the club is clearly an advantage in a marketing perspective, but it is also a disadvantage. When supporters give so much to their club, they also expect that the club repays these affections at one level or the other. If supporters feel they are treated like ordinary customers, it may result in the opposite reaction of the desired effect.

European clubs operate in a much bigger market than RBK. In a CRM context this should not have any direct impact on neither the implementation nor the development of a strategy. It will, however, have an impact on the risk involved in such a project. As in the words of the managing director:

"... we are a lot more careful when investing, whereas Barcelona or United can with a greater degree of certainty get some return on the investment because it does not have to be that great. It is just that the number they serve is so much larger."

In other words, it seems like the risk associated with these kinds of projects is in inverse ratio to the size of the market.

Tradition is another difference between Norwegian and European clubs. All the while the Norwegian clubs based their economy on selling hot dogs or coffee during the break, the major European clubs have handled ten thousands of spectators for many years. This lack of professionalism in the organisation, may present a problem to the Norwegian clubs when they are about to introduce CRM. As for RBK this means that they must attach great importance to training as an important part of the investments. It appears from the interviews that RBK considers organisational factors as the greatest impediments to a successful CRM project:

"We are very old-fashioned when it comes to our work routines, and I believe this is one of the major challenges when it comes to getting full benefits from a CRM solution." – (Marketing manager.)

The challenge is to get the organisation to not only use the new technology, but get an understanding of its utility value as well. This applies to both the top management and the employees, and it underlines the assertion that RBK must focus on training as part of its CRM project.

5 Discussion

Based on the literature review we got four critical success factors to fully benefit from CRM: top management support, strategic thinking, change management and technology. In addition to these four important areas, a CRM project should also be an evolutionary project that is constantly under development. This implies that a CRM project does not necessarily have to involve the whole organisation at the same time. By choosing a smaller and focused CRM project the chance of success will be better [15].

Top management support triggers the whole process. When the CRM strategy falls into place, a change process in the organisation is started.

When it comes to technology, there is a different practice among the clubs, but none of the clubs in question, had systems that were delivered straight from the supplier's shelves, without any adjustments. In other words, it is not only the technology that affects the club, but the club affects the technology as well. This adjustment is not done once and for all, but it is a continuous improvement process.

RBK is in the first phase of its CRM project. They have not yet implemented a full CRM solution. They recognized the need for organizational changes, and they needed to increase the level of IT knowledge in the organisation. Therefore, in the case of RBK, training should be added as a fifth success factor. Risk was another point of interest to RBK and they must be certain of the project's profitability before the project starts up and thus a business case should be presented.

Based on the previously discussed success factors and the additional RBK factors (business case and training), we arrive at an implementation process model as presented in figure 2.

It is alleged that it is a waste of time and resources if you get started on a CRM project, which is not vital to the company's competitiveness [15]. RBK's core product is a competitive football team. CRM can not make Rosenborg play better football, but it may support the by-products and thereby give the club an improved financial foundation. We believe that RBK, in addition to CRM must introduce Supporter Relationship Management (SRM). SRM will be an integrated part of the club's CRM system and use the same underlying functionality. Whereas CRM takes care of the club's traditional customer relationships, the main function of SRM will be to take care of the club's relationship with the supporters.

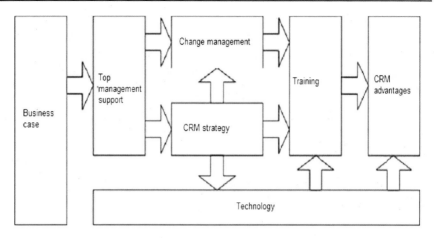

Fig. 2. CRM implementation process in a sports club

The results from the questionnaires demonstrate with total clarity that the supporter is the club's most important customer. One of the great advantages of SRM is that it makes it possible to have one-to-one communication with the supporter. RBK can differentiate between them based on their loyalty, and tailor marketing measures on the basis of the position of each supporter in the loyalty model, like newsletters and designated areas at the club's home page.

Richardson and O'Dwyer [13] found out that if supporters change loyalty, it occurs mainly among young people under the age of 10. This means that if a club is able to capture a young person's interest before someone else, it will most likely keep this supporter for the rest of his life. AC Milan has linked its CRM system to their activities that are aimed at young people because they recognize the importance of establishing a relationship with their supporters at an early stage.

In some cases the supporters are traditional customers for the club. They buy tickets and supporter gear. Some supporters may, however, spend very little money on the club. A traditional company with a traditional CRM system would spend little time and efforts on customers like that. However, a great deal of the club's market value is based on the outside world's conception of the size of the club's body of followers. Consequently, a SRM system must take these supporters into consideration as well and to keep them in the system as a reference for potential sponsors.

6 Conclusion

In this article we have shown that CRM can be used strategically in a football club. Based on the findings in the questionnaire responses we learn that the biggest clubs have a CRM strategy and that CRM is a prioritized area to these clubs. The two greatest advantages, which are stated by the clubs, are improved customer relationships and increased efficiency of internal processes. In order to consider

CRM as a strategic tool and to develop a CRM strategy you are dependent on top management support which is vital to a strategic foundation for CRM, and also important when carrying out the necessary organisational changes. The CRM project should also be concentrated only on areas that are crucial to the club's ability to compete. For football clubs this means that the chief concern is to focus on their supporters.

In addition, we point out how the supporters are different from traditional customers. This is something a CRM system in a football club must take into account. Guilianottis [6] ideal types of supporters combined with a survey of the club's different customers can be applied to segment supporters in a useful way, and we suggest that the Supporter Relationship Management (SRM) concept is introduced as well.

When it comes to RBK, two factors emerged, which were important in relation to CRM. One factor was the need to present a business case to map the risk involved in a CRM project, the other was the importance of training in an organisation that does not have the required level of IT competence. Rosenborg can make use of the findings in this paper in the planning of their continued CRM efforts. The most important findings are a survey of the critical success factors in a CRM implementation, a CRM implementation model (figure 2), and tools linked to the SRM concept.

This is an explorative piece of work, and the article is based on a limited selection of data. We therefore envisage several opportunities for further research, both through expanding the data basis with more clubs from more countries, and through following a specific project more closely over a longer period of time. In particular this can give us a better understanding of the implications of SRM in detail.

References

1. Backman SJ, Crompton JL (1991) Differentiating Between High, Spurious, Latent, and Low Loyalty Participants in Two Leisure Activities. Journal of Park and Recreation Administration 9(2)
2. Beal B (2004) CRM – it's a brand new ball game. SearchCRM.com, Available online at: http://searchcrm.techtarget.com/originalContent/0,289142,sid11_gci949574,00.html (Accessed on 03 May 2005)
3. Deloitte (2005) Football Money League: The Climbers And The Sliders. February 2005
4. Dobson S, Goddard J (2001) The Economics of Football. Cambridge University Press, Cambridge, UK
5. Goodhue DL, Wixom BH, Watson HJ (2002) Realizing Business Benefits Through CRM: Hitting the Right Target in the Right Way. MIS Quarterly Executive 1(2): 79-94

6. Guilianotti R (2002) Supporters, Followers, Fans and Flaneurs: A Taxonomy of Spectator Identities in Football. Journal of Sport & Social Issues 26(1): 25-46

7. Kale SH (2004) CRM Failure and the Seven Deadly Sins. Marketing Management 13(5): 42-46

8. Mahony DF, Madrigal R, Howard D (2000) Using the Psychological Commitment to Team (PCT) Scale to Segment Sport Consumers Based on Loyalty. Sport Marketing Quarterly 9(1): 15-25

9. Neale WC (1964) The peculiar economics of professional sports. Quarterly Journal of Economics 78: 1-14

10. Petersen GS (2004) Best Practices and Customer Relationship Management (CRM). Business Credit, January 2004: 48-49

11. Quick S (2000) Contemporary Sport Consumers: Some Implications of Linking Fan Typology With Key Spectator Variables. Sport Marketing Quarterly 9(3): 149-156

12. Reinartz WJ, Krafft M, Hoyer WD (2004) The Customer Relationship Management Process: Its Measurement and Impact on Performance. Journal of Marketing Research 41: 293-305

13. Richardson B, O'Dwyer E (2003) Football supporters and football team brands: A study in consumer brand loyalty. Irish Marketing Review 16(1): 43-53

14. Rigby DK, Reichheld FF, Schefter P (2002) Avoid the Four Perils of CRM. Harvard Business Review 80(2): 101-109

15. Rigby DK, Ledingham D (2004) CRM Done Right. Harvard Business Review 82(11): 118-129

16. Shank MD (2005) Sports Marketing. A Strategic Perspective. Prentice Hall, USA

17. Waltner C (2000) CRM: The New Game In Town For Professional Sports. informationweek.com. Available online at: http://www.informationweek.com/801/crm.htm (Accesssed on 03 May 2005)

18. Weinberger J (2004) Customers for Life. How to transform loyalty into commitment into revenue. CRM Magazine July 2004: 32-38

19. Zablah AR, Bellenger DN, Johnston WJ (2004) An evaluation of divergent perspectives on customer relationship management: Towards a common understanding of an emerging phenomenon. Industrial Marketing Management 33: 475-489

Towards Knowledge Management Oriented Information System: Supporting Research Activities at the Technical University

Marite Kirikova and Janis Grundspenkis

Department of Systems Theory and Design, Riga Technical University, 1 Kalku, Riga, LV-1658, Latvia; e-mail: marite.kirikova@cs.rtu.lv and janis.grundspenkis@cs.rtu.lv

1 Introduction

Recently in knowledge management and business process management communities attention has been focused at knowledge intensive processes (e.g., Verhooef and Qureshi 2005, Papavassiliou et al. 2003, Fedel and Tanniru 2005). There is no doubt that research is a knowledge intensive process as well. However, information systems (IS) support of the research work mainly addresses only two dimensions of scientific activities, namely (1) scientific data retrieval, processing and visualisation and (2) collaboration among scientists (Lincke et al. 1998, Yao 2003, Ludacher et al. 2005, Zhao et al. 2005). Other possibilities to support scientific work, e.g., university level knowledge management of research activities are less investigated and implemented (Hornbostel 2006).

Research activities in the university context should be considered not only from the point of view of generated knowledge and its value for science and industry, but also from the point of view of the value of this knowledge in education processes and attracting financial resources for university needs. In this paper we analyse research activities of the technical university from the process perspective using two process frameworks: (1) American Productivity and Quality Center (APQC) business process framework (APQC 2005) and (2) knowledge value chain (KVC) framework by Holsapple and Jones (2004, 2005). The purpose of the paper is to describe relationships between knowledge processes and business processes of research in terms of both functional and administrative dimensions, as well as to propose guidelines for the development of knowledge management based IS for supporting research activities in the university setting.

The context of university research activities is described in Section 2. Further, in Section 3, the related work in IS support for research activities is considered. In section 4 university research activities are described from the process perspective in the context of APQC and KVC frameworks. In section 5 the guidelines for IS support of research activities at the technical university are proposed. Section 6 consists of brief conclusions.

2 The context of research activities

According to Free Dictionary of Farlex, research is a primary activity of science, a combination of theory and experimentation directed towards finding scientific explanations of phenomena. It is commonly classified in two types: pure research [or basic research], involving theories with little apparent relevance to human concerns; and applied research, concerned with finding solutions to problems of social or commercial importance. The main difference between scientific activities of the technical university and institutions dealing with natural and social sciences is in tangibility of professional knowledge that impacts research activities (standards, certified methodologies, patents, etc.). On the other hand in many technical fields industry is a metrics oriented judge (Geisler 2002) of knowledge provided by the university, which is expected to comprise well integrated scientific and professional skills. The context of research activities at the technical university is illustrated in Fig. 1.

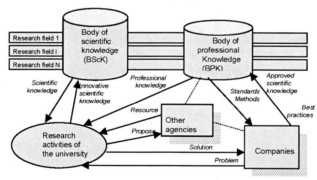

Fig. 1. A simplified scheme of the university research activieties context

As it is shown in Fig. 1, the research activities directly contribute to the body of scientific knowledge (BScK) and indirectly to the body of professional knowledge (BPK). Actually, each field of research has its own scientific and professional knowledge, but at the same time the cooperation of the branches is one of the main sources of innovative scientific and professional solutions. The research activities indirectly contribute to the body of professional knowledge and provide solutions for industrial problems. They are related to different agencies inside and outside the university in terms of resources and proposals. In more detail the research activities are illustrated in Fig. 2.

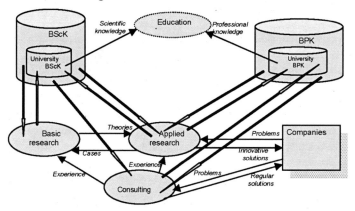

Fig. 2. Knowledge flows (simplified, shown by arrows) in the university research context

At the technical university basic (or pure) research and applied research as well as consultancy influence the bodies of university's scientific and professional knowledge and thus indirectly also the educational process of the university. Quite dense relationships between knowledge bodies, research processes and their external agencies (inside and outside of the university) suggest a necessity for knowledge oriented IS support for research work and its administration at the technical university (further in the text – university).

3 Related work

Necessity to support research work by advanced information technologies is well understood (Lincke 1998, Yao 2003, Ludascher 2005). One of the broadest frameworks for research support systems is given by Yao (2003), who groups information technology tools around seven phases of scientific research, namely: Idea generation, Problem definition, Procedure design/planning, Observation/experimentation, Data-analysis, Results interpretation, and Communication phases. The workflow system that consists of exploring support, retrieval support, reading support, analysing support, and writing support is suggested. The system should provide profile management, resource management and data/knowledge management facilities. It should consist of discipline independent component that supports general research process and domain specific components that support research in specific disciplines. Expert systems, machine learning, data mining, text mining, computer graphics, data visualisation and intelligent information agents are advocated as feasible tools for workflow system's implementation. The framework given in Yao (2003) is quite broad, but it does not show how exactly each phase of research process is supported and how supporting components may be organised in an integrated research support system. The main emphasis in the system is on information retrieval in the early phases of research, data analysis and writing.

Actually, most of research work support systems are devoted to the search of literature, scientific data processing, and scientific knowledge/data sharing. An interesting solution for creation, integration, reviewing and dissemination of domain specific knowledge is aimed by "NetAcademy" approach (Lincke et al. 1998), which uses system-immanent vocabulary allowing the mediation of knowledge through powerful search mechanisms on a semantic level. Information on tools for collaborative data processing and analysis is quite abundantly available (e.g., Watson 2001, Ludascher 2005). Universities can utilise such tools on personal, group, intra-university and inter-organisational levels.

Another branch of related work concerns knowledge management issues of research. The most common issue here, especially for basic research, is ontology oriented knowledge management that helps to handle scientific data (Zhao 2005). For applied research an important tool is collaborative multi-sector knowledge creation that requires a particular knowledge management culture (Rod 2005); and the phenomenon of university spin-offs (Shane 2004, Freeman 2004).

Knowledge management integrated with quality management is described in Rodriguez-Ortiz (2003). The paper states that "in an environment of competitiveness, productivity and quality, the investigation activity is no longer an area where researchers have a wide margin of performance to exploit their creativity, now the delivery schedules and the cost control are factors that have to be considered for success of a research project and the consequent customer of client satisfaction". Researcher's brain is considered as a non-traditional machine that produces the research result. Research project life cycle consists of four phases: Planning and definition, Execution, Delivery, and Evaluation. Knowledge management support for research projects includes the classification and storage of different project related documents such as designs, prototypes, studies, diagnosis, courses, methodologies, as well as proposals, contracts, quality plans, etc. This perspective of knowledge management of research will be discussed in more detail in Section 4.

The financial and non-economic metrics for evaluation of research are discussed in Geisler (2002).

An interesting issue that emerges in modelling of knowledge intensive processes is the possibility to separate knowledge management tasks and normal tasks (Papavassilio 2003). This is a challenge in university research activities context as in this case almost all tasks can be attributed to knowledge management. The analysis of this issue is outside the scope of the paper.

In general one can see that there are issues of research activities support that are well investigated and solution rich, e.g., scientific data processing, workflow support for data analysis, etc. However, in university context, research activities should be viewed taking into consideration knowledge flows between different research types and consultation as well as the impact of research activities on education (see Fig. 1 and Fig. 2 in Section 2). None of above mentioned papers handles these issues in an integrated manner. To move towards the system that can handle all knowledge flows relevant in the university context, in Section 4 we have employed the process perspective of research activities that enables us to deal with all issues of interest reflected in Fig. 1 and Fig. 2.

4 The process perspective of research activities

In this section we start with the process model of research activities. This model is used for further analysis of research activities in the light of APQC and KVC frameworks. At the end of the section we present a simplified conceptual scheme that can serve as a guide for the development of knowledge management oriented IS for research activities support.

4.1 The process model of research activities

The process model of research activities is based on seven-phase research process description of Yao (2003). This framework has been chosen because it itself is the result of analysis of several research activities frameworks. The basic processes and their inputs and outputs are shown in Fig. 3.

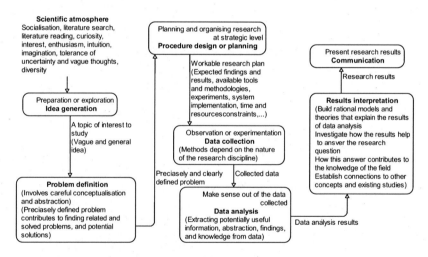

Fig. 3. Business process model of the university research activities

The model includes seven processes, namely Idea generation, Problem definition, Procedure design and planning, Data collection, Data-analysis, Results interpretation, and Communication. Ideally each of those processes as well as the important source of research – scientific atmosphere should be supported by knowledge oriented IS. It is necessary to emphasize that the "research atmosphere" is not always the ultimate trigger of research process (Rodriguez-Ortiz

2003). This refers to research projects invoked by problems proposed by companies, which need help of researchers as well as different calls for research proposals from other agencies (see Fig. 1). In those cases scientific idea and problem definition phases may be influenced by project intended project scope, schedule and metrics (Geisler 2002, Sergeant 2006). Therefore from the point of view of IS support it is reasonable to distinguish between Discovery oriented research and Project proposal oriented research.

4.2 Analysis of research using APQC framework

APQC framework (APQC 2005) is a benchmarking tool for process improvement provided by American Productivity and Quality Centre. The framework includes 12 processes described in high level of detail. They are divided in five operating processes and seven management and support processes. In Table 1 research processes are compared to APQC operating processes on a highest possible level of abstraction.

Table 1. Research processes and APQC operating processes

Research processes	APQC operating processes
Idea generation	Develop vision and strategy
Problem definition	Develop vision and strategy
Procedure design and planning	Design and develop products and services
Data collection	Design and develop products and services
Data analysis	Design and develop products and services
Results interpretation	Design and develop products and services
Communication	Market and sell products and services
	Deliver products and services
	Manage customer service

On the highest level of abstraction initial processes of research are more detailed than the APQC processes, because they show the specifics of scientific activities. On the other hand, research results communication is described by three APQC processes. Viewing research from the production perspective suggests also a high contribution to BPK, which is hardly given by basic research. Thus, IS supported consultation activities (Fig. 2) could compensate the peculiarities of basic research and bring balance between university BScK and BPK.

Correspondence between research processes and APQC operating processes suggest, which industry approved IS solutions could be chosen for each research process.

Management and support processes of APQC framework are as follows:

- Develop and manage human capital
- Manage information technology
- Manage financial resources
- Acquire, construct and manage property

- Manage environmental health and safety
- Manage external relationships
- Manage knowledge, improvement and change

Those processes and their IS solutions are relevant in research support on several levels: the level of individual projects, departmental level, university level, and inter-organisational level in partnership relations.

4.3 Analysis of research using KVC framework

KVC framework (Holsapple and Jones 2004, Holsapple and Jones 2005) presents five primary activities:

- Knowledge acquisition – acquiring knowledge from external sources and making it suitable for subsequent use
- Knowledge selection – selecting knowledge from internal sources and making it suitable for subsequent use
- Knowledge generation – producing knowledge either by discovery or derivation from existing knowledge
- Knowledge assimilation – altering the state of organisation's knowledge resources by distributing and storing acquired, selected or generated knowledge
- Knowledge emission - embedding knowledge into organisational outputs for release into the environment

In Table 2 research processes are compared to KVC operating processes on a highest possible level of abstraction.

Table 2. Research processes and KVC primary processes

Research processes	KVC primary processes
Idea generation	Acquisition, Selection, Generation, Assimilation
Problem definition	Acquisition, Selection, Generation, Assimilation
Procedure design and planning	Acquisition, Selection, Generation, Assimilation
Data collection	Acquisition, Selection, Generation, Assimilation
Data analysis	Acquisition, Selection, Generation, Assimilation
Results interpretation	Acquisition, Selection, Generation, Assimilation
Communication	Emission

The KVC framework does not impose any sequence of the primary activities. One can see in Table 2 that the research processes also do not impose the sequence for those activities (except of Emission, which corresponds to Communication). This suggests service orientation as the appropriate architecture for primary knowledge activities.

Table 2 proves high knowledge intensity of research processes and suggests wide spectrum of knowledge management oriented IS solutions for support of each research process.

The KVC framework presents also four secondary activities: namely, Knowledge measurement, Knowledge control, Knowledge coordination, Knowledge leadership. Those activities partly overlap with the management and support processes of APQC framework and in some extent may be used as organizers of primary activities services (Holsapple and Jones 2005). As KVC framework has been developed by analysing 200 variations of primary activities and 300 variations of secondary activities and is presented in a detailed way, it may serve as a tool for selection of particular knowledge activities for particular university needs.

4.4 Conceptual scheme of relationships between different knowledge bodies

Results of analysis of research from process perspective integrated with the findings of related research as well as features of the context of university research activities suggest the conceptual scheme reflected in Figure 4.

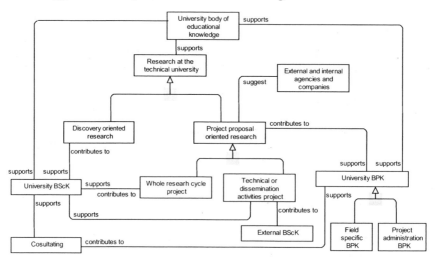

Fig. 4. Simplified conceptual scheme of relationships between different knowledge bodies relevant for research activities

A simplified conceptual scheme in Fig. 4 suggests three different types of research processes: discovery oriented research processes, project proposal oriented processes that generate new scientific knowledge and project proposal oriented processes that do not generate new scientific knowledge (usually those are projects where a university team serves as a technical developer of a particular object or as a disseminator of research results of other universities). The scheme includes also consulting as a supplementary type of research processes that uses scientific knowledge but contributes only to professional knowledge of the university. The scheme also suggests four interrelated bodies of university knowledge, namely BScK, Field specific BPK, Project management specific BPK and Body of educational knowledge. All these bodies of knowledge should be developed and maintained in terms of explicit codified knowledge and supported in terms of tacit knowledge. Thus the information system should support all three types of research, consulting, four types of knowledge repositories, as well as relationships between all entities mentioned and collaboration between researchers at different administrative levels.

5 IS development guidelines for support of research activities at the technical university

In this section we present several guidelines for IS development that are derived from research results presented in previous sections. After each guideline information about the issues, which have led to it, is given in brackets. The guidelines are as follows:

- IS development should be based on well understood research processes that are checked against necessities of knowledge production and knowledge value chain (Sections 4.2 and 4.3, related work (Geisler 2002, Rodriguez-Ortiz 2003)) in terms of supporting IS solutions
- IS should support knowledge management oriented culture (related research (Rod 2005))
- IS should support research atmosphere (Section 4.1)
- IS should support Discovery based and Project proposal based research, and Consultation (Sections 4.1 and 4.4)
- IS should consist of discipline independent component that supports general research process and domain specific components that support research in specific disciplines (related work (Yao 2003))
- IS should support four interrelated knowledge repositories (scientific, field specific professional, administrative professional, and educational) (Section 4.4) and tacit knowledge flows that support these repositories.
- IS should provide personalization support (related work (Yao 2003))
- IS should provide collaboration support (Section 3)
- IS should support metrics based evaluation procedures (KVC, APQC frameworks and related work (Geisler 2002, Rodriguez-Ortiz 2003))
- Primary activities of KVC framework and their support by IS components may be organized in service oriented architecture (because there are many to many relationships between research processes and primary activities (Section 4.3) as well as between primary activities and supporting IS components (Yao 2003))
- Hypothetically knowledge production activities and corresponding IS solutions should be organised in fractal architecture (as they have similar patterns at different levels of abstraction (Section 4)).

6 Conclusions

There are many solutions of IS support for research activities. Most efforts in this area have been directed to scientific data management and collaboration. However, in university environment, additional issues are to be considered when introducing IS for support of research activities, namely: the impact of research on education and industry oriented dimension of research activities. Consideration of these issues suggest knowledge management and process oriented approach of IS development where IS primarily supports all processes of knowledge production and invokes all knowledge activities that add value to scientific knowledge produced by research.

The guidelines given in this paper are the result of theoretical research and are intended to be tested in the development of the conception of IS support for research activities at the technical university.

Acknowledgment

Work on this paper is partly supported by research grant No. U7121 of Latvian Ministry of Education and Science and Riga Technical University.

References

APQC (2005) Process Classification Framework, APQC. Available at Http://www.apqc.org, accessed April 28, 2006.

Fadel KL and Tanniru M (2005) A knowledge centric framework for process redesign. In: SIGMIS-CPR'05, April 14-16, 2005, Atlanta Georgia, ACM 1-59593-011-6/05/0004, pp 49-58.

Freeman R, Tang K, Vohora A (2004) Taking Research to Market: How to Build and Invest in Successful University Spinouts, Euromoney Institutional Investor.

Geisler E (2002) What do we know about: R&D metrics in technology-driven organisations. Http://cims.ncsu.edu/documents/rdmetrics.pdf, accessed April 27, 2006.

Holsapple CW and Jones K (2005) Exploring secondary activities of the knowledge chain. Knowledge and Process Management, Vol. 12, No. 1, pp 3-31.

Holsapple CW and Jones K (2004) Exploring primary activities of the knowledge chain. Knowledge and Process Management, Vol. 11, No. 3, pp 155-174.

Hornbostel St (2006) From CRIS to CRIS: Integration and interoperability. Available at the website of Current Research Information Systems conference (CRIS 2006): Http://ct.eurocris.org/CRIS2006/, accessed June 28, 2006.

Lincke D-M, Shmidt B, Schubert P, Selz D (1998), The NetAcademy: A novel approach to domain-specific scientific knowledge accumulation dissemination and review, 1060-3425, IEEE

Ludacher B, Altintas I, Berkley Ch, Hoggins D, Jaeger E, Jones M, Lee EA, Tao J, Zhao Y (2005) Scientific workflow management and the Kepler system. Concurency and Computation: Practice and Experience, 2005, Wiley Inter-science DOI: 10.1002/cpe.994

Papavassiliou G, Ntiodis Sp, Abecker A, Mentzas Gr (2003) Supporting knowledge-intensive work in public administration processes. Knowledge and process Management, Volume 10, Number 3, pp 164-174, Wiley, 2003.

Rod MRM (2005) Collaborative multisector knowledge creation – the Institute of Health Economics. Available at Http://kmap2005,vuw.ac.nz/papers/, accessed April 27, 2006.

Rodriguez-Ortiz G (2003) Knowledge management and quality certification in research and development environment. In: Proceeding of the Fourth Mexican Conference on Computer Science (ENC'03), 0-7695-1915-6/03 IEEE.

Sergeant DM (2006) Using a virtual research environment to present CRIS grouped to support the real research users' research lifecycle. Available at the website of Current Research Information Systems conference (CRIS 2006): Http://ct.eurocris.org/CRIS2006/, accessed June 28, 2006.

Shane ScA (2004) Academic Entrepreneurship: University Spinoffs and Wealth Creation, Edward Elgar publishing.

Verhoef R and Qureshi S (2005) Collaborative infrastructures for mobilizing intellectual resources: Assessing intellectual bandwidth in a knowledge intensive organisation. In: Proceedings of the 38th Havaii International Conference on Systems Sciences, 0-7695-2268-8/05 2005 IEEE.

Yao YY (2003) A framework for Web-based research support systems. In: Proceedings of the 27th Annual International Computer Software and Application Conference (COMPSAC'03), 0730-3157/03, 2003, IEEE.

Zhao Zh, Belloum A, Sloot P, Hertzberger B (2005) Agent technology and scientific workflow management in an e-science environment. In Proceedings of the 17th IEEE International Conference on Tools with Artificial Intelligence (ICTAI'05), 1082-3409/05, IEEE.

An Architecture for Highly Available and Dynamically Upgradeable Web Services

Nearchos Paspallis and George A. Papadopoulos

Department of Computer Science, University of Cyprus 75 Kallipoleos
Street, P.O. Box 20537, CY-1678, Nicosia, Cyprus
{nearchos, george}@cs.ucy.ac.cy

Abstract: Developing distributed application architectures characterized by high availability
has always been a challenging and important task both for the academic and the industrial
communities. Additionally, the related requirement for dynamic upgradeability is usually
examined within the same context as it also aims for high availability. Although a number
of architectures and techniques have been proposed and developed for improving the
availability and upgradeability of traditional distributed systems, not many of them are
directly applicable to Web service-based architectures. Recently, Web services have
become the most popular paradigm for business-to-business and enterprise application
integration architectures, which makes their availability increasingly important. This paper
builds on existing high availability and dynamic upgradeability techniques which can be
applied to Web service-based systems. Based on them it describes an architecture which
enables high availability and dynamic upgradeability both for newly developed and for
prefabricated Web services.

Keywords: Dependable systems, Service engineering.

1 Introduction

Web services are the technology-of-choice for interoperability within non-homogeneous systems. They are briefly defined as *"self-contained, modular applications that have open, Internet-oriented, standards-based interfaces"* [3]. Although many expect that Web services will change the way enterprises interoperate with each other in the long-term, they have already proven themselves very useful in solving many of the interoperability problems that have troubled application integration efforts.

Today, one can observe more and more enterprises depending on their Web accessible services to a continuously increasing degree. Some of these services are critical and the enterprises invest a lot of effort and resources in maintaining them as highly available as possible. Examples of Web services requiring high levels of availability include medical, stock market, and airline ticket reservation applications.

While a number of techniques target at maintaining the high availability of a service in the exceptional case of a fault, additional effort is also required to maintain the accessibility of the service when it is undergoing a scheduled update. This is why systems designed for high availability usually provide mechanisms enabling dynamic (also known as live) software upgrades as well. Typical reasons for upgrading software include bug fixes, functionality enrichment and performance enhancements. Naturally, highly available services are expected to be upgradeable in a safe and consistent manner.

This paper studies techniques for achieving high availability of services offered over the Web and also techniques that allow dynamic upgrades of those services. Although some of these approaches could be applied to general distributed systems, this work concentrates on Web services and their underlying technologies (e.g. SOAP, WSDL, UDDI, etc).

In the next section, we examine the Web services technology from the availability and upgradeability point of view. Then, existing techniques for high availability and dynamic upgradeability are presented in section 3. Following that, a methodology for improving on the availability and upgradeability of Web services is proposed in section 4. The proposed method involves automatic generation of stubs and skeletons using the WSDL document. Furthermore the same section argues on the advantages and the disadvantages of this approach and, finally, section 5 summarizes the conclusions and points to future work.

2 Web services

Web services can be described as applications accessible over the Web [3]. More accurately the World Wide Web Consortium (W3C) describes them as: "...*software applications identified by URIs, whose interfaces and bindings are capable of being defined, described and discovered as XML artifacts. Web services support direct interactions with other software agents using XML-based messages exchanged via Internet-based protocols.*"

The promise of Web services is to serve as the foundation for a new generation of business-to-business (B2B) and enterprise application integration (EAI) architectures. Because Web services are both language and platform neutral, it is a common practice for enterprises to expose a selected subset of their functionality (of newly developed but also of legacy information systems) as Web services. This ability greatly contributes to the popularity of Web services in both B2B and EAI scenarios.

2.1 Highly available web services

In this paper the availability refers to a measure of the fault tolerance of a Web service. Consequently, high availability is defined as a goal that we try to achieve by employing a number of methods and techniques. Literally, availability is the percentage of time a Web service is available and functioning within its operational requirements. Obviously, to achieve high availability a service needs to maximize its uptime and minimize its downtime.

High availability is important for many enterprises because their system responsiveness is directly related to their customer satisfaction and, consequently, to their operations turnover. Also for many enterprises which are highly depended on Web services, their downtime is usually proportional to significant revenue losses. In many other applications such as medical information systems, high availability is inherently critical and extremely important.

The availability can be affected by factors such as connectivity (i.e. network availability) and server failures (i.e. hardware and software faults). Thus any solution aiming to provide reasonable protection against failures should cope with both factors.

Based on their definition, Web services need to be discoverable and also facilitate interactions with other systems by continuously allowing binding and interaction. Therefore, to ensure that Web services maintain high availability, their discovery and binding functionality need to be enhanced with appropriate mechanisms. The discovery of Web services is generally performed using service directories based on the UDDI standard, which are Web services themselves. Thus, improving on the availability of general services offered over the web, consequently benefits the discovery of Web services as well.

2.2 Dynamically upgradeable web services

With dynamic upgrades, we refer to the replacement of software components at runtime, with minimal (preferably zero) service interruption.

In the client-server paradigm, the upgrade can take place at either of the two sides, or at both. In most cases, client-side upgrades are more straightforward compared to server-side upgrades because they can take place in a controlled manner (i.e. the client can be instructed to suspend or drop any connections to the server or even completely shut an application down if necessary.) This eases the task of replacing some components or the whole application.

Contrary to this, upgrading server side components is significantly more challenging. Because no pre-determined downtime is known, clients initiate transactions with the service in an arbitrary way. In [9] Kramer *et al.* introduced the notion of quiescence, i.e. a period within which the component can be safely upgraded (e.g. replaced.) A component is said to be quiescent when the component itself and all components linked to it are in a passive state, i.e. seize initiating but continue serving transactions.

Dynamic upgrades are required for a number of reasons. These are classified as corrective, perfective and adaptive [11]. Corrective upgrades are used for fixing bugs (e.g. discovered after deploying the service). Perfective upgrades are used to enhance the product functionality and performance and, finally, adaptive changes are needed for adjusting services to a changing environment.

Dynamic upgradeability is important because it enables continuous service operation in the event of scheduled upgrades. Thus mechanisms for dynamic upgradeability are important (and quite often required) supplements to high availability architectures.

3 Related work

This section reviews existing high availability and dynamic upgradeability techniques with emphasis on those targeting server-side faults. While complex upgrade mechanisms have been proposed, a common approach employed by high availability architectures includes temporary redirection of the traffic before upgrading the server, and then redirection of the traffic back to the original server once that is completed.

It is worthwhile mentioning that different techniques operate at different layers of the system architecture. At the lowest layer some techniques use hardware replication, while at the highest layer other techniques simply embed the mechanisms required for high availability into the applications themselves.

There are a number of criteria that can be considered while evaluating architectures. Here, we concentrate on the transparency of the investigated techniques and their applicability to prefabricated Web services. By transparent we refer to those techniques which can be applied without requiring any major changes to existing infrastructures, i.e. those that can be directly applied to existing Web services.

3.1 Existing techniques

In [4] Birman *et al.* discuss methods for adding high availability to Web services. In addition, they also discuss how to enable autonomic behavior i.e. how to enable servers to automatically discover and configure themselves and then operate securely and reliably in an automated manner.

Their work uses extensions to the Web services model which aim to support standard services for monitoring the health of the system, self-diagnosis of faults, self-repair of applications and event reporting. The solution builds on existing technologies, such as WS-Transactions [6] and WS-Reliability [8] but it eliminates their need to save data to persistent memory or wait for failed components to restart.

This solution can act as a router component of a Web service platform, making it suitable for providing transparent high availability to existing applications.

However this approach does not define explicit methods to enable dynamic upgrades.

In [7] Cotroneo *et al.* propose an architecture which improves the availability of web-based services, such as Web servers, FTP servers, and video-on-demand servers. Their work examines the problem from a Quality of Service (QoS) perspective and specifically targets real-time systems. Their architecture provides application developers with an alternative API which can be used to access the network instead of the typical communication libraries.

Clearly, this approach is not transparent to the developers as the provided API is used instead of the standard UNIX network socket libraries. This solution operates at the network and the operating system layers and thus cannot be applied to other platforms.

In [12] Vilas *et al.* present a work where high availability is achieved at the Web service layer. Their proposed technique introduces the notion of Virtualization. This technique creates new virtual Web services and exposes them to the clients instead of the actual ones. At the back-end, the real Web services are invoked while they are internally managed in a cluster.

The authors of this work define three requirements: detecting faulty servers, providing maintenance mechanisms for the cluster and providing mechanisms for adding and removing servers in the cluster as needed.

Virtualization is a common technique with existing and popular applications in related fields such as in web servers. The way it works in the case of Web services is by grouping one or more services inside a unique wrapper which is then published as a single, standard Web service. The clients then use this virtual Web service as if they were contacting the real one.

This approach requires that the developer defines a Virtual Web Service (VWS,) and a VWSDL document. Also a VWS engine is required to enable clustering and high availability. Depending on the complexity of the application, the VWS engine can be as simple as some specialized code in the stub or as complex as a dedicated server. Furthermore, additional techniques are needed for forming and managing the cluster.

In addition to the other works presented in this section, this work does also not provide explicit mechanisms facilitating dynamic software upgrades. In [1] Ajmani provides a thorough and comprehensive list of software upgrade techniques for distributed systems. He starts his review from Bloom's work on reconfiguration in Argus [5] and continues with recent technologies used in modern systems (such as the Red Hat OS) and also by popular services (such as in Google's infrastructure).

3.2 Evaluating existing techniques

Although all the techniques presented in this section can directly or indirectly, improve the availability of Web services, no two of them are equal with respect to their development requirements. In principle, we are interested in techniques that can be applied in general situations without any specific requirements regarding the *programming languages*, *infrastructures*, or *hardware*.

Ideally, a solution would allow automatic deployment and management of Web services and transparently improve on their availability. Apparently, such a solution should be applicable to prefabricated Web services. Furthermore, it should allow dynamic upgrades of the deployed software, preferably with minimal, if not zero, interference to the service. To the best of our knowledge, none of the presented or existing techniques fully satisfies all these requirements. In the next section we propose an architecture that can provide the basis for delivering a solution which meets all these criteria.

4 An architecture for high availability and dynamic upgradeability

This section studies the requirements for a system offering both *high availability* and *dynamic upgradeability*. Then, it proposes an architecture which is designed to meet these requirements and transparently improve on both the availability and upgradeability characteristics of prefabricated Web services. Finally, this section concludes with a discussion on the drawbacks and the benefits of the proposed design.

4.1 Requirements for high availability and dynamic upgradeability

First, the high level requirements for architectures targeting high availability are detected and enumerated. These requirements are then further complemented with additional ones targeting dynamic upgradeability, as the latter is argued to be a key requirement for improving availability.

Mathematically, availability is simply defined as the ratio of time during which the service is considered to be satisfying to the service consumer. Of course, defining when a service is satisfying is not trivial and it requires further clarification. For example, in some cases a service response of a few minutes might be acceptable, while in others sub-second responses are essential.

Detect when the service responsiveness becomes unsatisfactory. The first requirement is to detect when the service responsiveness becomes unsatisfactory to the clients. A detection mechanism must be used to detect these events and inform the appropriate components. Once deviation outside the accepted operation range is detected, a procedure is initiated which aims to resume the service. Consequently, the second requirement is to carry out the necessary actions required to restore the service normal operation within the predefined boundaries.

Manage the availability infrastructure. The second requirement is the ability to manage the availability infrastructure. For example specific architectures might need to define the order of the servers in the failover list, modify the set of servers in the cluster, or change the monitoring attributes and characteristics. In this paper we focus on the first two requirements. More management requirements are expected to be considered in future work.

The high availability technologies can be classified into those that failover on the server side, and those that failover on the client side. In the first case the classic cluster-based solution is the obvious approach, herein referred to as intra-enterprise availability. In this case a cluster of servers appears as a single server, continuously offering the service at a predefined IP address, even in the event of single server failures. This is the common case, where the clients are completely unaware of any failures or possible actions that were taken to recover the system back to fully operational mode. Naturally, in this case the clients will not be able to recover from any network outages, regardless of the cluster health.

In the second case, the client is designed to be more adaptive with regards to availability. More specifically, if a service failure is detected (and not recovered within some predefined time) the client initiates a failover procedure to another service, possibly provided by a different enterprise. We refer to this technique as inter-enterprise availability.

The mechanism for discovering and selecting a Web service in this case can be similar to that of a typical UDDI registry. More than one UDDI registries can be contacted for better fault tolerance and for a richer options pool. Additionally, this method requires specialized mechanisms embedded in the client stub and additional logic might also be necessary to ensure that the failover involves a semantically and functionally equivalent Web service. The latter is a challenging issue because additional meta-information with regards to the service provider (e.g. pricing) might be needed when deciding on a suitable alternative service to failover to.

In the first case where the service usually runs on top of a server cluster, it is necessary to use a mechanism that continuously monitors the health of the individual servers of the cluster. In this way, any possible failures are detected before they get noticed by the clients. The failover can be performed using any of the existing methods proposed so far.

In the case of inter-enterprise availability, the detection and failover mechanisms must be embedded into the client-side. This method adds significant complexity into the clients, but has the advantage of surviving long-running network outages that prevent communication with the server side.

Support for dynamic upgrades. The last requirement we consider is the support for dynamic upgrades. By dynamic we refer to upgrades that take place at *runtime*, preferably without any service interruption. The upgrades can take place at any of the client, the server, or both sides. The following paragraphs examine the dynamic upgrade-related requirements in detail, building on results described in [2].

First a management mechanism that instructs the nodes when to upgrade must be defined. Consider for example the case where the upgrade of a service running on a cluster (i.e. for increased availability) is required. Apparently, not all the servers can be upgraded simultaneously because that would compromise the service's availability. A management mechanism can control how the servers are upgraded, so that a set of servers is consistently operational with an acceptable level of availability.

The second requirement is to provide a way to control when the servers are upgraded. Although the most straightforward solution would be to arbitrarily remove the node from the cluster and upgrade it (letting the availability infrastructure take care of the interrupted transactions) it is not an optimal one. A more appropriate solution would be one detecting an appropriate time-frame within which the upgrade would be possible without any service interruption and without breaking the consistency of the system.

The third requirement is to provide mechanisms that guarantee the normal operation of the system when nodes are running different versions of software. If, for example, the server is upgraded to support a different set of operations (e.g. specified by a different WSDL document), appropriate adaptation of the invocations is needed until the clients are also upgraded to the latest version.

The last requirement mandates a way to preserve the persistent state of servers from one version to another. If, for example, the client is in the middle of executing a long process consisting of multiple operations, it is important that the upgraded software preserves its state and continues with the next operation in the process after the upgrade is completed (rather than having to restart a large computation task). This applies to both the client and the server sides.

4.2. Smart-stubs and smart-skeletons

In order to satisfy all the requirements we have specified, we propose a skeleton architecture where components can be added and existing techniques be reused. This architecture supports prefabricated Web services and it builds on a minimal model described in [3] and depicted by Figure 1.

In this architecture the WSDL document is used as input to specialized compilers which generate client-side and server-side proxies, typically referred to as *stubs* and *skeletons*. A different compiler is required for each of the client and the server side. The application objects can then bind to the proxies and invoke the operation defined in the WSDL documents. These proxies enable distributed communication with the use of SOAP-based messages.

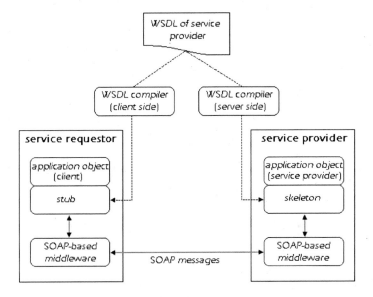

Fig. 1. Typical Web Service interaction: Based on the given WSDL document, appropriate proxy objects (i.e. the stub and the skeleton) are generated which are then used to facilitate the communication between the distributed objects by abstracting the remote objects as local

This approach extends the idea expressed in [10], where the authors argue that the reliance on machine readable metadata is probably one of the key defining aspects of Service Oriented Architectures (SOA). In this approach, the middleware exploits the additional metadata (in the form of availability directives and preferences) to enable seamless enhancements to the overall service availability.

The presented architecture requires the dynamic generation of intelligent proxies, namely smart-stubs and smart-skeletons. These proxy components directly accept invocations from the application objects in a fashion similar to the standard Web service paradigm. The proposed architecture is depicted by Figure 2. The grayed-out areas illustrate deviations from the original architecture.

In Figure 2, the HA-related properties are used to provide information describing different aspects of the high availability-related functionality such as connection time-out, preferred failover list, etc. These properties are then encoded into the generated smart-proxies.

Special compilers (i.e. HA-aware WSDL compilers) are used for the generation of smart-stubs and smart-skeletons. In addition to providing the functionality for SOAP–based communication these proxies contain additional functionality for dealing with rerouting, blocking and adapting SOAP messages.

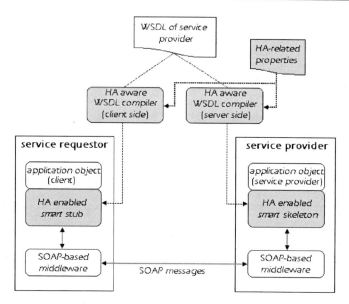

Fig. 2. Web Service interaction using smart-stubs and smart-skeletons: Based on a given set of properties describing the high availability requirements (or strategy), specialized WSDL compilers generate the smart-proxies (i.e. the smart-stub and the smart-skeleton). These objects act in a manner similar to that of the normal proxies, but additionally they incorporate specialized code which allows them to improve on the availability of the service, i.e. by enabling automatic failover and load-balancing

The smart-stubs and the smart-skeletons are thin, automatically generated proxy components. Their role is to implement the logic required to allow automatic and seamless rerouting of SOAP messages in order to ensure high availability in the event of faults. Additionally, their role includes blocking and adapting SOAP messages in order to enable seamless dynamic upgrades of software.

To make the processing and handling of the SOAP messages transparent to the end-users, these proxies intercept the communication on both the client and the server sides and appropriately reroute, block and adapt the communicated messages.

In addition to encoding the invocations to SOAP messages and marshalling or un-marshalling the data arguments, the smart-stubs provide additional logic for handling failures on the server side (e.g. by failing over to another server). Similarly, the smart-skeletons provide functionality for blocking messages while upgrading a Web service and also for adapting messages targeting a different version of the deployed object.

4.3 Satisfaction of the requirements by the architecture

The following paragraphs discuss how the general architecture, described here, satisfies the requirements that were detected in the previous section. First, in order to be able to discover when the service responsiveness becomes unsatisfactory, special client-side code is embedded in the smart-stub. This code allows the detection of faults and enables the failover to different service providers. Typically, this code is based on existing techniques which have a proven and trusted track in the area of fault-detection. In their simplest form these techniques usually depend on preset response-deadlines or on health monitoring systems which actively and periodically contact the servers (i.e. poke) to detect if they are responsive (i.e. healthy).

To manage the availability infrastructure the smart-proxies embed specialized functionality. Their management can be based either on static, predefined strategies encoded in the input data (i.e. in the HA-related properties), or it can based on a more dynamic and interactive scheme. The latter implies that the smart-proxies, which can serve as interception points, could be exploited to block, reroute and generally manage the operation of the Web-service from an availability point-of-view.

Additional logic might also be required to ensure the correctness of protocols such as the WS-Transaction. In particular, if the client decides to failover to another service provider while processing a business activity, specialized actions are required to ensure that suitable compensation operations are issued on the original service provider when it returns back online.

Last, dynamic upgradeability requires support by both the smart-stub and the smart-skeleton components. In particular they should both include code to address the additional, refined requirements that have been detected for enabling dynamic upgradeability.

For the management mechanism either an external, centralized coordination server should be used or special code should be embedded into the smart-stubs (or equivalently into the smart-skeletons.) Clearly, the first approach is more straight-forward from an implementation point-of-view. Embedding the code in the smart-proxies has the apparent advantage of making the system more self-reliant (but also more complicated). Finally, in simple scenarios where only a single client (or server) is upgraded, the management mechanism could be unnecessary.

For detecting when it is appropriate to perform an upgrade, specialized code should again be embedded in the implementation of the smart-stubs (or smart-skeletons). This requirement is usually related to the persistent state requirement. Suitable solutions exist which simultaneously address both. The latter usually requires that the upgraded applications provide mechanisms for enabling state persistence across different versions as well.

Finally, the concurrent support of different versions is addressed. If both the new and old versions of Web services define the same operations (i.e. they are described by the same WSDL document) then there is no need for any adaptation. If the two versions define different operations though, adaptors are required in the smart-proxies to map the old-version invocations to the corresponding operations of the new version. This is something that can be directly reused from existing solutions (i.e. designed to enable dynamic upgrades) and embedded into the smart-proxies.

Of course, this architecture is a high level overview of a skeleton system, purposely designed to intercept Web service communication at the point where invocations are applied. In this way the provided mechanisms have maximum control on the invocations and block the communication of SOAP-messages when necessary (e.g. when upgrading the Web service). Still, some issues remain to be addressed before this architecture fulfils the detected requirements.

5 Conclusions and future work

Custom solutions enabling high availability and dynamic upgradeability can be prohibitively complex and costly. In addition, they also require a combination of technologies and services such as *disaster recovery, consulting, assessment* and *management*. This paper concentrates on technical aspects of high availability and in particular on scenarios where Web service failover is used to maximize their availability. Additionally, it describes reusable techniques aiming at continuous availability during dynamic upgrades of Web services as such techniques are also required by any high availability framework.

The contributions of this paper are twofold. First, the need for availability and upgradeability is identified and existing techniques used to tackle the problem in Web service-based systems are presented. Second, a general architecture is presented which can provide the basis for systems aiming at high availability and dynamic upgradeability.

A main contribution of this architecture is that it improves on the availability of Web services, even in the event of inter-enterprise failover. As the failover mechanism entirely resides within the client this approach allows failing over to a Web service provided by a completely different entity. Also, the proposed architecture can be of benefit to prefabricated Web services as well as it only requires (re)compiling their WSDL documents to generate all that is required: the smart-stubs and the smart-skeletons. Because these smart-proxies are dynamically generated, the proposed architecture is also transparent to both the end-users, and the WSDL developers.

For the future, we plan to more elaborately define the structure and the functionality of the WSDL compilers as well as of the corresponding SOAP messages required by the protocols. Additionally, a prototype implementation is scheduled in order to evaluate the proposed architecture with the development of case study applications. Finally, related cluster management mechanisms will be examined and the use of UDDI directories for advertising and discovering alternative Web service providers will be more thoroughly studied.

6 Acknowledgements

This work was partly funded by the European Union as part of the IST MADAM project (6th Framework Programme, contract number 4169).

References

1. S. Ajmani, "A Review of Software Upgrade Techniques for Distributed Systems", *http://www.pmg.lcs.mit.edu/~ajmani/papers/review.pdf*, 2002.
2. [S. Ajmani, B. Liskov and L. Shrira, "Scheduling and Simulation: How to Upgrade Distributed Systems", *9th Workshop on Hot Topics in Operating Systems (HotOS 2003)*, USENIX 2003, Lihue (Kauai), Hawaii, USA, 2003, pp. 43-48.
3. G. Alonso, F. Casati, H. Kuno and V. Machiraju, "Web Services: Concepts, Architectures and Applications", *Springer-Verlag*, 2004.
4. K. P. Birman, R. V. Renesse and W. Vogels, "Adding High Availability and Autonomic Behavior to Web Services", *26th International Conference on Software Engineering (ICSE 2004)*, IEEE Computer Society 2004, Edinburgh, United Kingdom, 2004, pp. 17-26.
5. T. Bloom and M. Day, "Reconfiguration in Argus", *International Conference on Configurable Distributed Systems (CDS 1992)*, London, England, 1992, pp. 176-187.
6. W. Cox, F. Cabrera, G. Copeland, T. Freund, J. Klein, T. Storey and S. Thatte, "Web Services Transaction (WS-Transaction)", *http://dev2dev.bea.com/pub/a/2004/01/ws-transaction.html*, 2004.
7. D. Cotroneo, M. Gargiulo, S. Russo and G. Ventre, "Improving the Availability of web services", *22nd International Conference on Software Engineering (ICSE 2002)*, Orlando, Florida, USA, 2002, pp. 59-63.
8. C. Evans, D. Chappell, D. Bunting, G. Tharakan, H. Shimamura, J. Durand, J. Mischkinsky, K. Nihei, K. Iwasa, M. Chapman, M. Shimamura, N. Kassem, N. Yamamoto, S. Kunisetty, T. Hashimoto, T. Rutt and Y. Nomura, "Web Services Reliability (WS-Reliability) version 1.0", *http://www.oracle.com/technology/tech/webservices/htdocs/spec/WS-ReliabilityV1.0.pdf*, 2003.
9. J. Kramer and J. Magee, "The Evolving Philosophers Problem: Dynamic Change Management", *IEEE Transactions Software Engineering*, 16 (1990), pp. 1293-1306.
10. [N. K. Mukhi, R. Konuru and F. Curbera, "Cooperative Middleware Specialization for Service Oriented Architectures", *13th International World Wide Web Conference (WWW2004)*, New York, NY, USA, 2004, pp. 206-215.

11. [P. Oreizy, N. Medvidovic and R. N. Taylor, "Architecture-Based Runtime Software Evolution", *20th International Conference on Software Engineering (ICSE 1998)*, IEEE Computer Society, Kyoto, Japan, 1998, pp. 177-186.
12. J. F. Vilas, J. P. Arias and A. F. Vilas, "High Availability with Clusters of Web Services", *6th Asia-Pacific Web Conference (APWeb 2004)*, Springer-Verlag, Hangzhou, China, 2004, pp. 644-653.

Distributed Service Development in Personal Area Networks

Miklós Aurél Rónai, Kristóf Fodor, Gergely Biczók, Zoltán Turányi, and András Valkó

Ericsson Research, Traffic Lab, 1300 Budapest, 3., P.O. Box 107, Hungary, Miklos.Ronai@ericsson.com

Abstract: This paper presents the detailed description of the Middleware for Application Interconnection in Personal Area Networks (MAIPAN), which is designed to ease distributed service development for mobile and nomadic environment. This middleware provides a uniform computing environment for distributed applications that operate in dynamically changing personal area networks (PANs). MAIPAN hides the physical scatteredness and device configuration of the PAN and presents its capabilities as a single computer towards the applications. The solution provides easy set-up of PAN-wide applications utilizing multiple devices and allows transparent redirection of ongoing data flows when the configuration of the PAN changes. The proposed middleware interconnects services offered by applications running on different devices by creating virtual channels between the input and output outlets of the applications. Channels can be reconfigured when configuration or user needs change. In contrast to the approaches found in the literature, MAIPAN is a solution where session transfer, dynamic session management are tightly integrated with strong and intuitive access control security. A prototype implementation demonstrates the capabilities of the middleware.

1 Introduction

The ever-growing number of wireless terminals, such as smart phones, personal digital assistants (PDAs) and laptops, raises the need to set up, configure and re-configure personal area networks (PANs) in an easy and ergonomic way.

This paper describes in details the Middleware for Application Interconnection in Personal Area Networks (MAIPAN) that hides the individual devices participating in the PAN and presents the capabilities of applications running on the devices as if they were located on a single computer. This provides a standard "PAN programming platform", which allows the easy set-up of personal area networks and dynamic connection and disconnection of distributed applications running in the PAN. Application programmers using the uniform application programming interface (API) offered by the middleware can develop software without taking care of the various PAN configurations or PAN dynamics. They can assume certain capabilities, but disregard whether these capabilities are provided by one application running on one device or by a set of applications running on several devices. They only have to register the inputs and outputs of their applications in the middleware, and they do not have to take care of which kind of devices or applications will be connected to these outlets and will use their programs.

The presented middleware contains access control, flexible session management and transferable session control solutions. The middleware contains some intelligent functions, as well, which helps the user to control the PAN and improves human computer interaction (HCI). In theory all kind of solutions for service discovery, physical, link or networking layers can be used with MAIPAN. However, currently MAIPAN is implemented on top of TCP/IP.

The paper is organized as follows. Section 0 is about related work; in Section 0 the basic concepts and the middleware's architecture are outlined. The API is described in 0 and the internal operation of the middleware (e.g., message exchanges, control functions and access control mechanisms) is detailed in Section 0. Finally, Section 0 concludes the paper.

2 Related work

Middleware are essential part of pervasive and mobile computing environments. Mascolo et al. in 1 discussed why traditional middleware (such as CORBA 2) is not well suited for mobile environments and how a mobile computing middleware should be designed. Nowadays several projects are running in these research topics, some of them are presented in the followings.

The goal of the AURA project 3 is to provide each user with an invisible aura of computing and information services that persists regardless of location. The project Gaia 4 designs a middleware infrastructure to enable active spaces in which data and tasks are always accessible and are mapped dynamically to convenient resources present at the current location of the user. The Oxygen project 5 aims to develop very intelligent, user-friendly and easy-to-use mobile devices enabling users to communicate with the system naturally, using speech and gestures that describe their intent. In the frame of the Portolano project the one.world architecture 6 is designed, which is a comprehensive framework for building pervasive applications. The Cortex project 7 addresses the emergence of a new class of applications that operate independently of human control. The key objective of the EasyLiving 8 project is to create an intelligent home and work environment. The Speakeasy approach 9 focuses on the specification of minimal interfaces between devices using mobile agents and mobile code. The Virtual Device 10 concept considers all autonomous devices in the user's personal area network as one big virtual device having multiple input and output units, thus providing a coherent and surrounding interface to the user.

Similar to the Virtual Device concept, MAIPAN represents an entire personal area network as a single device to applications. On the other hand, MAIPAN represents a novel approach in its secure access control mechanism and the use of a transferable control role. MAIPAN access control ensures 1) seamless interworking of various devices of the same user, 2) protection of one user's devices from devices of another user, 3) still enabling controlled communication and lending between devices of different users. MAIPAN manages device access and configuration via a convenient central control entity, the dispatcher. MAIPAN is also unique in enabling the change of the dispatcher role, that is, the session control rights can be transferred between devices, from the old dispatcher to a new one.

The basic ideas of MAIPAN were introduced in 11 and the application programming interface is described in 12. Now, in this paper we provide a detailed description of MAIPAN's internal operation, including its structure, session creation, dynamic session management, session control transfer and access control functions.

3 MAIPAN – Middleware for Application Interconnection in Personal Area Networks

3.1 Basic concepts and definitions

MAIPAN distinguishes among devices, applications and services. The word "device" refers to the physical device and by "application" we refer to the software that offer the "services". For example, using these abstractions in case of a mouse we can say, that the mouse is a "device" where a "mouse application" is running, which offers a "mouse service".

MAIPAN is based on three concepts (**Fig. 1.**): pins, channels and sessions. Applications offering the services have input and output outlets, which are called pins—borrowing the expression from the integrated circuit world. Pins are the connection points of the applications to the middleware, so the middleware sees the applications in the PAN as a set of input and output pins. A pin has a predefined type, which shows the type of data that the pin can emit or absorb, that is, the type of information the application can handle (e.g., mouse movements, keystrokes). According to the needs new types can be defined any time. The dispatcher application is responsible to connect the pins with appropriate types.

To enable communication between pins, the middleware creates and reconfigures channels, which are point-to-point links that interconnect pins. The set of channels that are necessary to use a PAN service is called session.

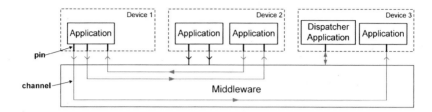

Fig. 1. MAIPAN session

3.2 Security and access control

Security and access control functions are defined and handled on device level. This means that access to services (i.e., access to application pins) are granted for devices, thus if a device gets the right to use a given service, then all applications running on this device will be able to access the service. If we assume that in the PAN there are small devices that offer one or two simple services (e.g., mouse, mp3 player), then in this case it is simpler to grant the access of services to devices instead to each application.

The dispatcher application running on a device, which plays the role of the control entity, can set up and reconfigure sessions. The control entity has to check and ask for the necessary access rights to enable the usage of a given service for the user. For instance, this main control entity can be a PDA, which has enough computing power to manage a PAN. All other devices participating in the PAN are called participants. In special cases, participants may delegate the access control rights to other devices, which will be referred to as managers.

3.3 Transferring sessions

In the PAN at least one device playing the role of the controller entity is needed. In case this device disappears all concerned sessions will be automatically torn down. To keep up such session MAIPAN offers the possibility to transfer a running session from the current control entity to another one.

For example, to make some music in a meeting room one of the users creates an mp3 playing session. This way the user's device becomes the control entity of the session. After a while, when the user wants to leave, she can transfer the session by telling to MAIPAN the identity of the new control entity, which can be for example another user's PDA.

3.4 Reconfiguring sessions

In case a participant disappears (e.g., the user leaves the room, or the device's battery is depleted), the concerned channels are automatically disconnected and the sessions have to be reconfigured. In the first step MAIPAN notifies the corresponding dispatcher(s) about the event. In the second step the dispatcher application(s) can decide which services to use instead of the disappeared ones. The dispatcher application can ask for user involvement, if there are multiple possibilities to replace the disappeared service(s), or it can decide on its own, if there is no or only one choice, or the user preferences are known. In the third step the dispatcher builds up the new channels or tears down the sessions concerned.

3.5 Architecture

Based on the concepts above we designed MAIPAN's architecture (see Figure 2). The aim of the *data plane* is to provide effective and secure data transport between applications, while the *control plane* is responsible for managing pins, channels, sessions and for handling security and access control.

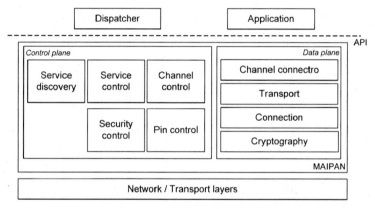

Fig. 2. Architecture of MAIPAN

3.6 Data plane

The application sends data through a pin to the middleware, where the channel connector layer redirects the data to the corresponding channel. The transport layer creates packets and provides functions such as flow control, reordering, automatic re-transmission, quality of service, etc., however these functions are not implemented, since the current version of the middleware is running over TCP/IP. The connection layer adds information to the packet, which is needed for the delivery: address of the source and destination device and the identifier of the channel. Finally, the cryptography layer calculates a message integrity check (MIC) value and encrypts the packet if necessary.

3.7 Control plane

The control plane contains the control functions which are necessary to manage the PAN. The service control part registers local services offered by the applications, handles their access rights and communicates with the service discovery protocol. The channel control creates and reconfigures sessions initiated by the dispatcher application. According to the needs of the dispatcher it asks the pin control parts of the participating devices to build up the channel between the pins. The pin control part instructs the channel connector layer to create a channel, activates the necessary transport functions for the given channel in the transport layer and sets the destination of the given channel in the connection layer. The security control part initiates and co-ordinates the authentication procedure between devices, manages the service access rights, and stores the necessary information for communication (e.g., security keys).

3.8 Implementation

MAIPAN is implemented in C on Linux 13. In this implementation the applications are connected to the middleware stack via inter-process-communication (IPC) message queues, where each pin is represented by an IPC queue. When-ever an application sends data to another application, the middleware gets the data from the IPC message queue, creates packets and sends the packet to the remote end point of the pin's channel using UDP/IPv4 for transporting. Channels are built up according to the instructions of the dispatcher application, which gets information about available services in the PAN from a simple service discovery protocol (SDP). This simple SDP is based on broadcast messages, however in theory any kind of SDP implementation could be applied.

In order to demonstrate the operation of the middleware—beside implementing the dispatcher—we created a fileserver/client application and attached an mp3 player to the system 14. This way we could set up a basic scenario, where the mp3 player could play an mp3 file located at a remote place.

4 Application programming interface

Application developers, who want to write PAN applications only and do not want to deal with PAN configuration, have to use just the service and pin registration functions of the API, which are described in the next section. Programmers, who are interested in configuring PANs and building dispatcher applications, can use all features of the API.

4.1 Service and pin registration

If an application wants to offer a service in the PAN, first it has to introduce the service to the middleware and register the input and output pins that are necessary for the use of the offered service. To do that the following message exchange is needed.

First the application sends a register service request message (Reg_Serv_Req) to the middleware. This message has to contain some service discovery protocol dependent information, which is automatically forwarded to the attached SDP. The middleware creates a new record for the service and a dedicated control channel for the application and returns an identifier, which will identify the service to the middleware in the future. Optionally the application can ask for a specific service identifier in the Reg_Serv_Req message. After this, the pins can be registered by sending a Reg_Pin_Req message for each pin. The message contains the following information: the type of the pin; whether the given pin is an input, an output or a bi-directional one; the minimum quality of service (QoS) parameters that the pin needs, such as reliability, reordering, flow control, encoding of transmitted data, etc., optionally a specific identifier for the pin.

Inside the middleware the service control forwards each pin registration request to the pin control, where the information on pins is stored. Furthermore it sets default access rights for the pins by informing the security control about the new pins. In case of successful registration, the service control acknowledges each pin registration request and returns an identifier, which will identify the pin on the given device. New pins can be registered at any time, when an application decides to do so.

Pins can be disconnected from the middleware by a Revoke_Pin_Req message, which has to contain the identifier of the pin. To disconnect services the Revoke_Serv_Req message is used, containing the identifier of the service. Revoking a service will delete all of its pins.

4.2 Gaining information about sessions, services and pins

With the Session_Info_Req message the dispatcher can query which sessions are the middleware aware of. In answer the middleware returns information on all sessions that were initiated locally and on sessions where local pins are involved. Information about services and pins can be gained with the Service_Info_Req sage. In the answer the middleware returns the locally registered services, the identifiers of the pins that belong to the services and the parameters of them. Moreover the middleware queries the SDP and forwards its answer to the application, as well.

4.3 Creating sessions

The dispatcher application can initiate the setup of sessions in the following way. First, it has to indicate that it wants to set up a session with the Create_Session_Req message. In the answer, the middleware sends an identifier for the session. After this, the dispatcher can start sending requests to interconnect pins with the Create_Channel_Req message. The control application sends as many requests as many channels it wants to establish in the given session. The message should contain the followings: the identifier of the session, the identifier of the device where the first pin is located, the identifier of the first pin, the identifier of the device where the second pin is located and the identifier of the second pin; and the quality of service (QoS) parameters that this connection needs.

Channels can be deleted with the Delete_Channel_Req message. The request contains the identifier of the session and the identifier of the channel that shall be deleted. To delete a session the Delete_Session_Req message can be used containing the identifier of the session.

4.4 Transferring sessions

The transfer of a session can be initiated by the current controller device with the Transfer_Session_Req message. The message shall contain the identifier of the session and the identifier of the new controller device. After a successful transfer the new controller will be responsible for the entire session.

4.5 Access control

The device, which is the owner of a service, can delegate its access decision right to other devices, by adding the MAIPAN ID of the device to the managers list of the given service. For this purpose the Add_Manager_Req message have to be used. As soon as the middleware receives the request to add a manager to a given service, it informs the chosen manager about the request. If the manager accepts the request, it will be added to the managers list of the service. To delete a manager the Del_Manager_Req message is used.

Each device has a white and a black lists about devices, that contain which devices are allowed and not allowed to communicate with. The white and black lists can be modified by the dispatcher application with the Set_Device_List_Req and Del_Device_List_Req messages, indicating whether the white or the black list has to be modified and which device has to be added or removed.

Also each service has a white and a black list about devices, which are allowed and which are not allowed to control the given service. The manager device stores these lists locally, so it is possible that there will be white and black lists for the same service both on the owner and on the manager, as well. The Add_Controller_Req or Del_Controller_Req messages can be sent to the middleware, indicating which service's list has to be changed and which device has to be added or removed.

4.6 Changing focus

The middleware provides facilities for connecting more pins to a given application's pin. Since data can flow only between two pins (by default towards the pin that was first connected to the source pin), similar to the X-Windows environment, the notion of "focus" arises, to determine which application receives the data flow. But unlike in X-Windows, mouse movements or the ALT+TAB key combination on the keyboard do not solve the problem, since there might be neither a mouse nor a keyboard that could be used for this purpose. In a PAN environment the concept of focus needs to be generalized and extended to handle such situations in an intuitive, ergonomic manner (e.g., placing a button on the Tetris-box, that switches between the monitors that are connected to the display output of the Tetris application). MAIPAN supports the focus change function, although, the solution of this ergonomic problem is out of scope here.

The dispatcher can initiate a focus change process with the Change_Pin_Focus_Req message. The request should contain the following information: the identifier of the session, the identifier of the device where the pin is located whose focus has to be changed, the identifier of the pin whose focus has to be changed, the identifier of the device where the pin is located which has to receive the focus and the identifier of the pin that has to receive the focus.

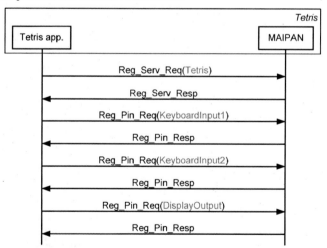

Fig. 3. Registering the Tetris

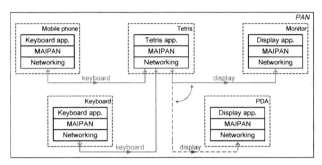

Fig. 4. Channels in the Tetris session

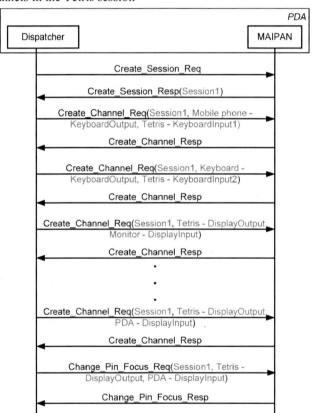

Fig. 5. Creating the Tetris session and changing focus

5 Internal operation and detailed architecture

A MAIPAN scenario can be, for example, the installation of software purchased in a MAIPAN-aware box, which is realized by adding the box to the user's PAN (see Fig. 3). Assume that the user wants to play a multi-player game with her friend in the room they are sitting. After the networking layer established the network connections, with the help of the service discovery protocol the user finds the Tetris game running on the MAIPAN-aware box. To "install" the software the user can instruct the MAIPAN dispatcher to connect one input of the Tetris-box to a PC keyboard, the other one to the keypad of her mobile phone, and the output of the Tetris-box to the large display located on the room's wall. In case the friends want to leave the room, the display output can be seamlessly redirected to the PDA's internal display—by instructing the dispatcher—, and they can continue gaming. Fig. 3 shows the channels that have to be created in the Tetris session: the arrows show the data flow between the devices, and the dashed arrow shows the configuration after the user switched from the monitor on the wall to the internal display of the PDA.

Let's see how it can be realized with the API of MAIPAN. To run the Tetris service, first the Tetris application has to register its pins to MAIPAN: two keyboard inputs and one display output is needed for the application to function properly. The message sequence of registering the Tetris service to MAIPAN can be seen in Figure 2. The mobile phone, the keyboard and the display applications has to register their services in similar way. Note that not every parameter is shown in the message sequence charts of this example.

To use the Tetris game the dispatcher application running on the PDA has to interconnect the keyboard output pin with one of the keyboard input pins of the Tetris, the mobile phone's keyboard output pin with the other keyboard input pin of the Tetris and the Tetris display output pin with the display input pin of the monitor. This message sequence can be seen in Fig. 4. From now on the game can be used by the two users.

After a while, when the users leave the room where the monitor is located, the display output of the Tetris game is redirected to the PDA's display input. This is done with the focus change function of the middleware. This message sequence is also shown in Fig. 4.

5.1 Addressing

Devices are distinguished using unique identifiers (MAIPAN ID). Devices also need a routing identifier (routing address), which is used by the routing layer to route the packets between devices (e.g., this identifier can be an IP address). The routing identifier may be changed in case network connections change, e.g., two

PANs merge or some devices appear or disappear. In contrast, unique identifiers never change.

5.2 Channel-end-point (CHEP) identifier

Channels are represented by their end-points. The identification of a channel end-point (CHEP) is twofold: it is identified by the unique identifier of the device where the end-point is located and by a CHEP identifier, which is unique on the given device. Thus channels are defined by four identifiers: two MAIPAN IDs and two CHEP IDs.

5.3 Authentication of devices

In case two devices want to communicate with each other, they have to initiate a procedure to establish a trust relationship. The exact mechanism of the authentication procedure is out of this paper's scope. However, some ideas are described in the following. The authentication procedure can be started, for example, with the following:

- The user enters a code on her own device, which is printed on the device she wants to use. With this code the devices will be able to establish a trust relationship avoiding a man-in-the-middle attack.
- The user points with her device's infra red (IrDA) port to the device she wants to use, the devices exchange some messages via IrDA and create a secure key for further communication.

After this procedure the devices can communicate in a secure way and has to know the following about each other:

- They know each other's unique identifier (MAIPAN ID).
- They are aware of each other's human-readable device name, e.g., pda111, mouse123, keyboard456.
- They know the current routing identifier of each other (routing address).
- They have either a symmetric key or asymmetric cryptographic keys, that they use to secure their communication. Every node has a different key with every single node. The key(s) may have expiration time, in case they expire new keys have to be generated and exchanged.

The communication keys are stored in the communication secrets registry, which is handled by the cryptography layer of the data plane. Other security information (e.g., certificates) are stored in the device identities registry, which is handled by the security control part.

5.4 Access control

The service control part registers services and stores the information about them in the services registry. The service access rights are stored in the service access rights registry, which is handled by the security control part. Three levels of service access rights have been defined. The highest level is the owner, which is the device the service is running on. The owner decides whether a controller can access the given service. If the controller is welcome, then the owner puts its unique identifier into the controllers' white list of the given service. If the controller is not welcome, then its identifier is put in the controllers black list. The owner can delegate its decision right to the managers by adding the identifier of the manager to the managers list of the service. If the right is delegated, the manager stores a white and a black list per service locally, about controllers that can or cannot use the given service. The third level is the controller level. Devices that are in the controllers' white list can use the service to build up sessions; devices that are in the black list cannot use the service. These lists can be modified by the dispatcher application, and thus by the user. Managers and controllers cannot delegate their rights farther to other devices.

There are also a devices white list and a black list in the device access rights registry handled by the security control part, where the allowed and forbidden devices are listed. If a device is in the black list, then its communication establishment request is always refused. The dispatcher application running on the device can modify the content of these lists. The lists are handled by the security control part.

It depends on the operating system and on its administrator, who is allowed to run a service over the middleware. The access rights set by the operating system determine, whether a user can start a control application or a service. The middleware trusts the operating system (OS), so there is no explicit trust relationship defined between the middleware and the services running on the same OS with the middleware.

Every information on local pins—including the properties (e.g., minimum QoS requirements, direction) and the status (e.g., connected, free)—are stored in the pins registry, which is handled by the pin control part.

5.5 Session setup

A session is created, when all necessary pins are interconnected by channels. Only the control entity knows which channels form the session, thus other devices are not aware of this logical grouping of channels.

In case the channel control receives a request from a local dispatcher to connect two pins, it has to set up a corresponding channel. First, the channel control starts to create two channel end-points at the participants by sending CREATE_CHEP_REQ messages to the pin controls of the two devices (see Figure 5). Upon receiving such a request, the pin control has to check whether the controller is allowed to access the given pin. This is done by checking the access rights registry or by asking the manager of the service with an ACCESS_QUERY_REQ message.

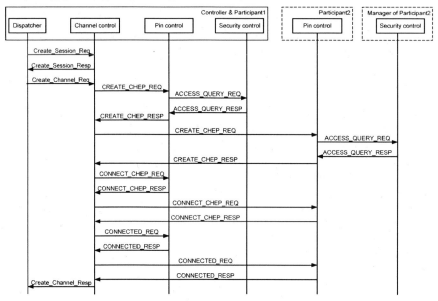

Fig. 6. Creating a channel

In case access is granted for the controller to use the given pin, the pin controller checks whether the pin is free. Connection of a new channel is only possible if the pin is not in use by another controller, or if it is in use, but the current user resigns of its usage. In the latter case an ACCESS_QUERY_REQ message is sent to the corresponding controller that uses the pin in order to determine whether it wants to resign the usage. If the controller resigns, then the new controller can use the given pin and the new channel end-point can be created.

In the second phase of setting up a channel, the two newly created channel end-points are connected to each other. This is done by sending a CONNECT_CHEP_REQ message to both participants, which contains the corresponding remote end-point of the channel and the required quality of service parameters. Thus, both participants will be aware of the channel's other end. Finally, the setup of the channel is registered in the managed channels registry of the channel control, and a CONNECTED_REQ message is sent to both participants indicating that the set-up of the channel was successful, the data transmission can be started.

In case a channel has to be connected to a pin that is already in use by the controller itself, the channel is not set up, but is registered by the initiator's channel control part as a non-active channel, i.e., a channel that does not have focus on.

MAIPAN devices, which participate in the same session, and which have not exchanged data with each other for a long time, send alive messages to indicate that they are still there. The timer of sending the alive message is reset every time, when a packet is sent to the device the timer corresponds to.

5.6 Transferring sessions

Transferring a session is done by the channel control in two steps. In the first step the new controller has to be informed about the session that has to be transferred. Thus a TRANSFER_SESSION_REQ message is sent from the old controller to the new controller, which contains the channels that belong to the session that has to be transferred.

Channel control parts cannot decide whether to accept or reject a request about transferring a session, so they have to ask the local dispatcher application. This is done by using a special notification message (EVENT).

In the second step the new controller has to rebuild the concerned channels. This is done by setting up a new session at the new controller, as shown in Figure 5. However, in this case the concerned pins are in use by the old controller, thus for each ACCESS_QUERY_REQ the old controller gives a positive answer and resigns the usage of the given pin to the new controller.

5.7 Changing focus

Although, from an application point of view, several channels can be bound to a pin at the same time, in fact at a given time only that channel is set up, which has the focus. The focus change can be initiated only by that controller whose channel currently has the focus.

The first step of the focus change is to disconnect the pin that will lose the focus. This is done by a CONNECT_CHEP_REQ message sent to the device whose pin has to be disconnected. This time the message does not contain the identifier of the CHEP to connect to, thus the CHEP at the receiver node will not have any CHEP pair and so the CHEP at the receiver will be disconnected. The second step is to create a new channel to the pin that receives the focus with CONNECT_CHEP_REQ messages.

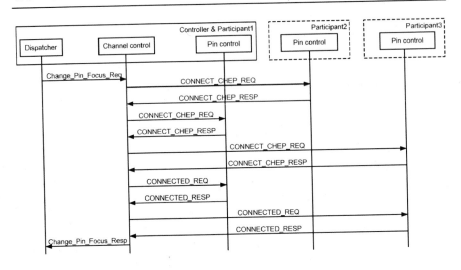

Fig. 7. Changing focus

Figure 6. shows an example, where the focus is changed at Participant1; the pin at Participant1 will be connected to a pin at Participant3 instead of its current connection to the pin at Participant2. In this case the channel between Participant1 and Participant2 will be deleted and a new channel between Participant1 and Participant3 will be created.

6 Conclusion

In this paper we described the internal operation of MAIPAN, a middleware for application interconnection in personal area networks. The essence of the middleware is to create a PAN programming platform, whereby hardware and software resources are interconnected, and the scatteredness of the PAN is hidden from the services. With MAIPAN distributed service development for mobile and nomadic environment can made easier.

MAIPAN represents a novel approach in its secure access control mechanism and the use of a central control entity. MAIPAN access control ensures 1) seamless interworking of various devices of the same user, 2) protection of one user's devices from devices of another user, 3) still enabling controlled communication and lending between devices of different users. MAIPAN manages device access and configuration via a convenient central control entity, the dispatcher. MAIPAN is also unique in enabling the change of the dispatcher role, that is, the session control rights can be transferred between devices, from the old dispatcher to a new one.

According to MAIPAN's access control scheme, access to services is granted for devices, thus if a device gets the right to use a given service, then all applications running on this device will be able to access the service. Dynamic session management handles the situation when a participant disappears. In this case MAIPAN notifies the dispatcher application, which than tries to automatically re-configure the session by involving new participants, or if there are multiple choices and the user preferences are not known, it may ask for user involvement. MAIPAN also provides session transfer, which is useful in the situation when the device that owns a running session has to leave. In this case, if the user wants to keep up the session after she left with her device, she can instruct MAIPAN via the dispatcher application to hand over the sessions from her device to another one.

In the future we plan to enhance the current implementation, create more applications running on top of the system and extend the architecture with various new functions to improve human computer interaction.

References

1. Cecilia Mascolo, Licia Capra and Wolfgang Emmerich: "Middleware for Mobile Computing (A Survey)", In Advanced Lectures in Networking. Editors E. Gregori, G. Anastasi, S. Basagni. Springer. LNCS 2497. 2002

2. Pope: "The CORBA Reference Guide : Understanding the Common Object Request Broker Architecture", Addison-Wesley, Jan. 1998.

3. D. Garlan, D. P. Siewiorek, A. Smailagic, P. Steenkiste: "Aura: Toward Distraction-Free Pervasive Computing", IEEE Pervasive Computing, 2002., http://www-2.cs.cmu.edu/ aura/

4. Gaia Project: "Active Spaces for Ubiquitous computing", http://gaia.cs.uiuc.edu/index.html

5. "MIT Project Oxygen", Online Documentation, http://oxygen.lcs.mit.edu/ publications/Oxygen.pdf

6. Robert Grimm, Janet Davis, Eric Lemar, Adam MacBeth, Steven Swanson, Thomas Anderson, Brian Bershad, Gaetano Borriello, Steven Gribble, and David Wetherall: "System support for pervasive applications", ACM Transactions on Computer Systems, 22(4):421-486, November 2004.

7. CORTEX Project: "CO-operating Real-time senTient objects: architecture and EXperimental evaluation"; http://cortex.di.fc.ul.pt/index.htm

8. Barry Brumitt, Brian Meyers, John Krumm, Amanda Kern, Steven Shafer: "EasyLiving: Technologies for Intelligent Environments", in Proc. of Handheld and Ubiquitous Computing Symposium, (Bristol, England), 2000.

9. W. K. Edwards, M. W. Newman, J. Sedivy, T. Smith: "Challenge: Recombinant Computing and the Speakeasy Approach", MobiCom'02, September 23-28, 2002, Atlanta, Georgia, USA.

10. Jonvik, T.E., Engelstad, P.E., Thanh, D.V.: "Dynamic PAN-Based Virtual Device", Proceedings of 2nd IASTED International Conference on

Communications, Internet and Information Technology (CIIT'2003), 17-19 Nov 2003

11. Miklós Aurél Rónai, Kristóf Fodor, Gergely Biczók, Zoltán Turányi, András Valkó: "MAIPAN: Middleware for Application Interconnection in Personal Area Networks", in proceedings of Mobiquitous 2005 conference, San Diego, CA, USA, July 17-21 2005

12. Miklós Aurél Rónai, Kristóf Fodor, Gergely Biczók, Zoltán Turányi, András Valkó: "The MAIPAN Middleware", in proceedings of Mobilfunktagung, Osnabrück, Germany, July 17-18 2006

13. Kristóf Fodor: "Implementation of a Protocol Stack for Personal Area Networks", Master's Thesis, Budapest University of Technology and Economics, June 2003

14. Balázs Kovács: "Design and Implementation of Distributed Applications in Ad Hoc Network Environment", Master's Thesis, Budapest University of Technology and Economics, May 2003

Using a SOA Paradigm to Integrate with ERP Systems

António Martins, Pedro Carrilho, Miguel Mira da Silva and Carlos Alves

Department of Computer Science, Instituto Superior Técnico, 1049-001 Lisbon, Portugal. antonio.jorge.martins@gmail.com, paqcarrilho@gmail.com, mms@tagus.ist.utl.pt, carlos.alves@outsystems.com

Abstract: Most Enterprise Resource Planner (ERP) systems already support a large part of the core organizational needs. However, other information systems need access to information stored on those ERP and, as a consequence, expensive "integrations" need to be developed between the ERP and those information systems. Sometimes, these integrations are even more expensive than the information systems themselves.

On the other hand, the Service-Oriented Architecture (SOA) paradigm has been helping businesses respond more quickly and cost effectively to information systems changes. In particular, SOA promotes reusability and interconnection of information systems – exactly what is needed for dealing with existing ERP systems.

We propose to apply the SOA paradigm to existing ERP systems so that building, changing and operating other information systems is not only faster and easier but mainly cheaper. This can be achieved by providing a tool that supports integration with ERP systems directly from other information systems without the need for ERP expertise or even write any code.

In order to demonstrate this proposal, we have implemented a tool to integrate with SAP systems from OutSystems, an Agile development framework, and evaluated this tool in a proof of concept. In the paper we present how this integration was achieved quickly and effectively without the need for any SAP expertise.

1 Introduction

As the business evolves, the applications must evolve to support them, thus requiring disposable and easy to build Enterprise Resource Planners (ERPs) and other applications that provide support for non-core processes and heterogeneous users. Evolution can only be achieved by ensuring that business processes can be changed nimbly, and this in turn is only possible when the existing applications are integrated flexibly to accommodate the required speed of change [15].

Service-oriented architecture (SOA) and Composite Applications Platforms are a solution to this problem. They allow interaction with business logic components and at the same time are deployable across a wide variety of user-defined environments, with faster deployment due to the Assembling policy [7, 8].

However, SOA environments are not usually used by ERPs. Some times this is due to the large amount of data that needs to be transferred, but mostly because ERPs owners companies prefer to provide their own solutions and modules to integrate with their ERP. SAP, for example, may require custom code that can reach up to 60% of the implementation time while on average, a costumer only uses 50% of the standard SAP code he paid for [14].

In this paper we propose to leverage an existing ERP using a SOA paradigm to integrate it with a Composite Application Platform (CAP). This way, new applications can be developed and changed quickly as also as easily integrated with the existing ERP, reducing the overall cost and project risk of ERP integration and extensibility [1, 3].

We have implemented this proposal for OutSystems HubEdition (a CAP) using SAP R/3. Developing a connector allowed the easy integration between the ERP and the CAP, enabling SAP access to OutSystems HubEdition service-oriented architecture. With this we enabled a CAP to have full integration with ERP modules and features [13].

Furthermore, we have evaluated the implementation using a real world case study (requisitions management application) and conclude that ERP can be effectively used in a SOA paradigm.

2 Service-Oriented Architecture (SOA)

To solve the interoperability problems, an effort was started to create standards for different systems to communicate in a well-known way, detached from any proprietary technology. Nowadays, Web Services are the most commonly used standard to perform this task [1, 10, 12].

Naturally, Web Services have evolved to become an implementation for an instance of a Service-Oriented Architecture (SOA), similar to the Distributed Component Object Model (DCOM) and the Common Object Request Broker Architecture (CORBA) [15].

OASIS (Organization for the Advancement of Structured Information Standards) [5] proposed a SOA reference model [15] and defined such architecture as a system of components that offer a service, which can be invoked by other components, in compliance with a service contract. According to OASIS, a Service Oriented Architecture (SOA) is a paradigm for organizing and using distributed capabilities that may be under the control of different ownership domains. In general, entities (people and organizations) create capabilities to solve or support a solution for the problems they face in the course of their business. It is natural to think of one person's needs being met by capabilities offered by someone else; or, in the world of distributed computing, one computer agent's requirements being met by a computer agent belonging to a different owner [5, 9].

2.1 Services-Oriented Development of Applications (SODA)

Gartner, on the other hand, has been working on the definition of a methodology [7, 8] capable of surpassing the obstacles of creating, changing and operating enterprise applications by using a SOA. Gartner calls this concept SODA, fitting it into the overall landscape of services-oriented architecture (SOA). SODA represents a key activity when making the transition to an SOA.

The definition of such a methodology involves the specification of the functional requirements that the tools must have, as the traditional application development tools are not suitable. This SODA methodology [7] has seven main aspects crucial for understanding the remaining of this paper:

1. **Design** - Establishment of how the requirements will be met or, in other words, definition of the application architecture. A SOA relies on loosely coupled and coarsely grained components, multi-channel access to services, process oriented design elements and early integration.
2. **Modelling** - Definition of the application's structure in some modelling language, with three distinct phases: business modelling, application modelling and technical modelling.
3. **Fabrication**- Creation of the core service components of the application and the necessary integrations. This means writing code.
4. **Assembly** - Aggregation of the service components, connection of their inputs and outputs and definition of its necessary translations. This can be done with visual editors.
5. **Orchestration** - Definition of the processes flow along the services and how information and logic will flow through a given process. This can be done with simple workflow managers.
6. **Automation** - Hiding complexity and removing the need to write code by generating it automatically to map the model on some executable component, such as .Net or Enterprise JavaBeans (EJB), enabling less tech-savvy developers to work rapidly.
7. **Variability and Rapid Change Maintenance** - Enabling changes to components that do not break the rest of the system. The variability of services should be encouraged and many small changes should be made continuously, rather than large changes sporadically. The variability of a system may be inversely proportional to its automation.

As stated, the emergence of Web services and service-oriented architecture is driving the formalization of a new style of development and tools. SODA promotes these concepts, inherent to building applications in a service-oriented world. Components become services and developers will require new integrated services environments (ISE) to build the next generation of software products.

2.2 Integrated Services Enviroment (ISE)

From these seven aspects that support the full life-cycle of applications, rises the notion of ISE that is, not only a technology stack to support service-oriented and composite applications, but also a suite of tools to sustain their development. The more it supports the seven aspects of SODA, the more complete it is. An ISE provides tools for their rapid development through composition and reusability that allow the applications to be easily changed. In addition, an ISE automates the deployment process, resulting in gains both in the development and the maintenance cycle. As a consequence, the development can be business-driven rather than technology-driven, meaning that can be focused on the business processes themselves and not on the technological details [4, 8, 10].

This paradigm also allows Agile developments [11] to be materialized in shorter cycles, allowing the feedback from real users to be incorporated in each new iteration, being immediately validated. Therefore, the application will rapidly converge to a solution which satisfies the user's needs, yielding higher success rates in projects.

2.3 Composite Applications

Composite applications are the end-products of a service-oriented architecture. They represent the business value a company derives from its SOA. Whether the composite application is designed for internal or partner use, it represents how any company can map business needs and processes to underlying information assets using SOA principles [12].

In computing, the term composite application expresses a perspective of software engineering that defines an application built by combining multiple services. A composite application consists of functionalities drawn from several different sources within the service oriented architecture (SOA). Their components may be individual web services, selected functions from other applications, or entire systems, whose outputs have been packaged as web services (often legacy systems). Composite applications often incorporate orchestration or "local" application logic to control how the composed services interact with each other to produce the new, derived functionality [3, 10].

A poorly designed composite application can endanger the performance and integrity of established production applications. A well-designed composite application can help enterprises reduce costs of IT services and improve time to market for new IT initiatives, needing careful design and planning to be built. A CA looks to the user like a regular new interactive application, yet in reality it may be only 10% new and 90% an assembly of pre-existing (purchased or in-house "legacy") components or data. The "glue" that brings a composite application together is always the integration technology. [12]

In this context, and with the growing awareness in mainstream enterprises of the opportunities offered by composite applications, users are expanding their traditional "buy vs. build" dilemma into a new "trilemma": buy, build or compose.

The compose option is not always available, and not all integration should be accomplished via only the composite application style. Yet, when the option is available, and once it is understood in its reality, composite applications emerge as a best-practice approach to modern software engineering.

3 Proposal

In this paper we propose an integration tool to use with an existing ERP and integrate it in flexible, disposable and highly configurable modules. This can be achieved using a Composite Application Platform (CAP) with SOA properties and Web-services. By creating an integration tool to link the existing parts - the ERP system and the composite platform - we have the better of both worlds.

We followed a Zero-Code approach for the integration tool [6]. This allows anyone without any SAP knowledge to create applications that reuse SAP modules without writing any code. The necessary data types are automatically converted as also as the necessary adapter code. This way the "integrator" just needs to focus on the components that he wants to integrate, and not on the specific implementation details.

Most of the above scenarios do not apply to enterprise applications. As SOA is network-centric, it requires complex monitoring and auditing of services. As services reusability and sharing are key characteristics of SOA, the number of consumer services, change management, and metering issues will be very high. These issues require a management infrastructure that may be too expensive for some projects.

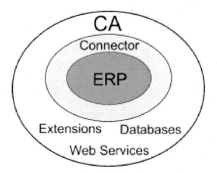

Fig. 1. ERP and Composite Application integration Architecture

This figure illustrates the essence of the ERP and Composite Application (CA) integration. Using the ERP and CA communications features, the connector can make a bridge between them. The connector is the essential integration key, because it enables ERP modules to be used by the CA accessing major SOA features. The connector maps the ERP specification to the Composite Application specification, allowing ERP access to the Composite Application. Although being the essence of the integration, the connector is also only an accelerator to the repetitive and time consuming tasks of the integration. The value of this architecture relies mostly on the CA features (mentioned before).

The presented architecture can be implemented over the majority of the existing ERPs, only requiring communication features like RPC or SOAP. In the next chapter our implementation is presented, for the mentioned architecture.

4 Implementation

Our implementation uses the SAP R/3 as ERP, the OutSystems HubEdition as the Composite Application, and the SAP Plugin for OutSystems Integration Studio as the connector.

Our connector is a plug-in for OutSystems Integration Studio, an application part of OutSystems HubEdition. OutSystems Integration Studio is an integrated visual environment where application designers can create connectors for integrating with existing enterprise systems such as SAP R/3, Navision, Siebel, etc., using agile properties (Figure 2).

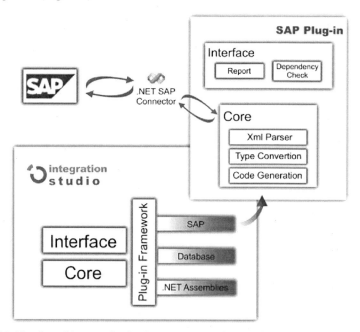

Fig. 2. SAP Plug-in architecture for OutSystems Integration Studio

Using the existing OutSystems Integration Studio plug-in framework, we created a four step wizard to guide all the integration process. We use SAP .NET Connector to connect to the SAP Server via RFC. A simple 4 step wizard (Figure 3)

guides developers through the process of identifying the SAP BAPIs (Business APIs) they wish to include.

The code to invoke each SAP BAPI is automatically created by Integration Studio, as well as the mapping of the SAP data types. This way integration with SAP can be achieved in a question of minutes, removing a traditional technological roadblock.

As mentioned, the great value of this approach is not solemnly in the connector, since there are already other connectors with similar behaviors such as SAP .NET Connector or SAP Java Connector. Only by using OutSystems HubEdition features it's possible to provide fast, cheap and reusable projects with SAP Integration. All this accomplished due to the SOA approach of OutSystems HubEdition.

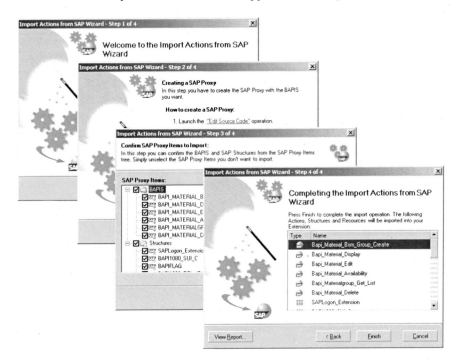

Fig. 3. SAP Plugin Wizard

5 Case Study

The best way to show the value of this approach is to provide a real world example. The solution showed in this example was implemented using a composite application.

5.1 Requisitions Management Example

The Challenge

With over 1.400 employees nationwide and a catalogue of more than 12.000 materials, the process of requisitions at ANA involved the whole company, literally generating tons of paper and requiring long manual approval cycles and error prone processes.

ANA intended to automate the requisitions process and make it available to all employees through its intranet, with the end objective of reducing overall time to request for materials, eliminate paper and reduce manual errors.

Online access was required for users to create requisitions directly from their workplace, using intuitive tools that required little training;

A simple process needed to be in place to ensure that Cost Center managers could approve requisitions easily and fast with little overhead.

The system had to integrate with SAP-MM, which was being implemented in parallel. The system had to go live in only 3 weeks, at the same time as the move into production of SAP-MM.

The Solution

- A composite application like OutSystems Hub Edition was used to create a centralized requisitions management system;
- The system has been integrated with SAP-MM to retrieve master data and trigger the creation of materials requisitions and stock reservations. The SAP integration has been achieved through an asynchronous interface to access master data periodically and a real-time interface to trigger actions directly in SAP;
- Requisitions are created by accessing the application through a regular web browser. The requisitions' front-end is available through ANA's intranet, accessible to all employees;
- When requisitions are created, Email notifications are automatically sent to the corresponding approvers. These Emails contains direct links to the online requisitions for fast access.

Once requisitions are approved, they become available to the Purchasing department, who validates them and ultimately can trigger their creation in SAP.

Company Information

ANA - Aeroportos de Portugal manages, operates and develops the Lisbon, Oporto, Faro, Ponta Delgada, Santa Maria, Horta and Flores airports, which in 2005 represented a total of 20 million passengers. Today the company has become a reference airport management group in terms of quality, profitability and ability to seize new opportunities.

6 Evaluation

Our proposal is similar to other connectors like SAP .NET Connector or SAP JCo. What these connectors don't have is the connection to a Composite Application Platform (CAP). Here relies the value to reuse and reduce integration costs, must of it due to the CAP properties, but nonetheless also provided by the connector.

A similar SOA approach also exists in SAP NetWeaver Composite Application Framework. SAP Netweaver is a technology stack comprising application server, portal and integration technology targeting the creation and extension of enterprise business processes related with ERP. Our approach is different since OutSystems Hub Edition Composite Application Platform tackles the process of rapidly creating, operating and changing user-centric enterprise applications that leverage any kind of existing enterprise systems in an agile way [11].

6.1 Proposal Advantages:

- Interact with business logic components in real-time, instead of moving data move back and forth between enterprise applications.
- Leverage Web services and the set of standards and technologies they comprise.
- Deployable across a wide variety of user-defined environments including rich, thin, mobile and portal clients.
- Create reusable business services so they can be quickly assembled and reassembled to provide new functionality for different business scenarios.
- Assembling - not coding - applications built from these business services to facilitate faster deployment.

Proposal disadvantages

The use of SOA requires additional design and development efforts and infrastructure, which translates into additional IT costs. Therefore SOA may not be a viable architecture for all cases [2].

For the following applications, SOA and Web Services may not be the recommended architecture:

- Stand-alone, non-distributed applications that do not require component or application integration; for example, a word processing application does not require request/response-based calls.
- Limited scope or short-lived applications; for example, an application that is built as an interim solution, not intended to provide functionality or reuse for future applications.
- Applications where one-way asynchronous communication is required, and where loose coupling is unnecessary and undesirable.

- A homogeneous application environment; for example, in an environment where all the applications are built using J2EE components. In this case it is not optimal to introduce XML over HTTP for inter-component communications instead of using Java remote method invocation (RMI).
- Applications that require rich, GUI-based functionality; for example, a map manipulation application with lots of geographical data manipulation is not suitable for service-based heavy data exchange.

Case Study

- The integration of the composite application like OutSystems Hub Edition with SAP-MM is exposed by Web Services that can be easily re-used in new applications without additional development costs;
- Only the Approver and Purchasing Controller profiles were formally trained. All remaining users fully mastered the requisitions front-end without any training;
- The SOA paradigm allows an agile development approach of a composite application like OutSystems Hub Edition. That way, new requirements and usability suggestions from users were quickly reflected in the requisitions system. Initially scattered organizational information is now centralized, complete and fully reusable in new applications and processes.

Integration: The system is fully integrated with SAP R/3, module MM. This integration is fully reusable by other applications without additional integration efforts, and has been achieved through the OutSystems Integration Studio SAP Plug-in.

Reach: The system is available to 1.400 users, distributed over 1.000 cost centers. Users create requisitions for up to 9 cost centers.

7. Conclusion

In this paper we have presented a proposal for a different approach to ERP integration. Through the work performed, the bases to integrate ERP components using the SOA paradigm are set.

Most organizations are service centered and not component centered. For that reason, SOA can be a major advantage since its development process and architecture are best suited for the present organizations reality.

Bearing in mind the disadvantages of this approach, we can still say that for many information systems this represents an improved solution. The connector is a valuable tool for reducing the costs and time of the integration process.

We also wanted to show that in many cases, it's better to surround legacy systems with a modern composite application, since they will still be used, but profiting with the SOA advantages. An example was given showing the advantage of using such approach to integrate and create reusable, change-ready business services.

8 Future Work

For future work, it would be interesting to collect more benchmarking data, so we would be able to say what is faster and cheaper to integrate, with a smaller level of detail. It would also be very interesting to compare several composite applications and agile methodologies, to confront different SOA architectures. With this profiling for the integration process, we would be able to recognize specific problems and implement the correspondent concrete solutions.

References

1. Adobe (2005) Service Oriented Architecture
2. D. Garlan, R. Allen, and J. Ockerbloom (1995) Architectural mismatch or why it's hard to build systems out of existing parts. Proceedings of International Conference on Software Engineering '95, Seattle
3. Dan Woods (2003) Packaged Composite Applications - An O'Reilly Field Guide to Enterprise Software, O'Reilly
4. Daryl C. Plummer, David W. McCoy, Charles Abrams (2006) Magic Quadrant for the Integrated Service Environment Market, Gartner
5. Duane Nickull, Francis McCabe and Mathew MacKenzie (2006) RM for SOA Public Review Document, OASIS
6. Emre Kiciman, Laurence Melloul, Armando Fox (2001) Towards Zero-Code Service Composition, Stanford University
7. Gartner (2003) Next-Generation AD Tools Will Bring SOA to the Mainstream
8. Gartner (2003) The Integrated Service Environment Market Magic Quadrant
9. IBM Corporation (2005) Service Oriented Architecture: Leveraging Data Integration within a Service Oriented Architecture
10. J. Calladine (2003) Giving Legs to the Legacy – Web Services Integration Within the Enterprise. BT Technology Journal, pp 22
11. M. Aydin, F. Harmsen, Slooten van K., R. Stegwee (2005) On the Adaptation of An Agile Information Systems Development Method. Journal of Database Management, Agile Analysis, Design, and Implementation 16, pp 20-24
12. Steve Benfield and Peter Fingar (2002) Managing Web Services, SOA Webservices Journal
13. WebMethods (2005) Business Integration ROI

14. WestTrax Applications (2004) The SAP ROI Debate: What Is The Real ROI From SAP?
15. Xin Peng, Wenyun Zhao and En Ye (2004) Research on Construction of EAI-Oriented Web Service Architecture. Lecture Notes in Computer Science

SOA-MDK: Towards a Method Development Kit for Service Oriented System Development

Balbir S. Barn, Hilary Dexter[1], Samia Oussena, Dan Sparks

Thames Valley University, Wellington St, Slough, SL1 1YG, UK
{Balbir.Barn, Samia.Oussena, Dan.Sparks}@tvu.ac.uk,
Hilary.Dexter@manchester.ac.uk

Abstract: This paper argues that appropriate modeling methods for service oriented development have not matured at the same pace as the technology because the conceptual underpinning that binds methods and technology has not been sufficiently articulated and developed. The paper describes a method for service oriented development based on an adaptation and enhancement of component based techniques. The use of reference models to widen the scope of the methodology is proposed. The method is described using a complex case study from Higher Education.
Keywords: Service Oriented Architecture, Components, Methods

1 Background

There is currently a convergence to so-called Service Oriented Architecture (SOA) for application design [13] for both new developments, releasing of existing IT software assets and for integration. Enterprise systems have attained a degree of technical integration in many cases but have not yet realized the benefits of full business integration that could be gained from seamless support of the business processes. A separate move towards a stronger focus on new systems development and application integration led by business process modeling is now being enabled by the developing SOA principles [13].

Service Oriented Architecture is a disruptive technology and has the potential to provide opportunities to rethink the way systems are created and evolved. Despite this, there is still a significant lack of methodology support for SOA. A substantial section of extant literature has largely focused on the technical issues and

---

[1] University of Manchester

software development practices required for SOA. Little effort is discernible in the earlier parts of the software lifecycle for SOA – in particular the analysis of systems specifically designed for SOA and the subsequent identification and specification of services using model based approaches. One example where the methodology issues have been addressed to some extent is the recent work by Erl [10] where there has been an effort to recognize that service-oriented analysis is an important element in the design of effective SOA. However, here, the focus has been to derive services from a business process orchestration specification. Certainly, progression into a full service specification – using a model driven approach [11] has not been sufficiently addressed.

Thus, designers when faced with the requirements to deliver applications based on service oriented architecture do not have ready access to specific methods and techniques to support key activities such as decomposition of applications into services which can then be integrated into one or more business processes.

This paper makes a contribution to methodology research by outlining an approach to service oriented architecture by drawing on the lessons learnt and the best practices from component based practices. A key feature of the approach taken is the application of model driven architecture principles within the context of reference models for providing a methodology framework for developing systems based on SOA and Component Based Development.

2 Case study

This section provides a short description of the context of the case study for which the business process modeling and subsequent application design was performed.

The e-Framework (http://www.e-framework.org) is an initiative by the U.K's Joint Information Services Committee (JISC) and Australia's Department of Education, Science and Training (DEST) to build a common approach to Service Oriented Architectures for education and research across a number of domain areas including course validation.

The Course Validation process is one of the most important business processes within Higher Education Institutions (HEIs) and between HEIs and other institutions. New courses and the continuation of existing courses are the direct outputs of this process. Activities within the validation process are knowledge centric and collaborative. Each instance of the process is a case and will focus typically on different subject domains and therefore require different knowledge bases and experts to support the process. The end result of the process is a course specification that addresses areas such as rationale, appropriateness, justification, marketing analysis, resources required, economic viability of the courses, and detailed descriptions of the courses in terms of outcomes, aims and objectives and so on.

In this research, the purpose of the COVARM project was to define and implement the course validation business process using SOA. Systems analysis was undertaken at four institutions using a case study approach. Visual models were constructed and evaluated and an approach to synthesizing the models from each institution into a single canonical model was developed and then applied. This approach includes rules for identifying variances between processes and is described in more detail elsewhere [4]. These models were used as input to the software design and implementation stages to develop a set of software services that allowed us to automate part the business process.

3 An approach to service oriented specification and implementation

The methodology for SOA is based on two key conceptual structures or frameworks – component based development and reference models. These underpinnings are described in this section.

3.1 Building on Component based development approaches

Component based methodologies and techniques have flourished because of the exposition of a robust conceptual understanding of a component reference model. Some of the earliest work on component based development was done by Texas Instruments as part of the strategic development roadmap for the then IEF™ application development toolset [15]. The IEF was an early example of a model driven architecture in that it supported model transformation and generation. This model completeness meant that any substantial new development was required to develop a meta model to support the toolset enhancement and accompanying methodology. Thus as part of the component enhancements to the IEF a Component Based Development (CBD) conceptual model was also produced. Sterling Software continued with this meta modeling strategy when they embarked on the first pure-play component specification toolset COOL:Spex™ [1,2] based on the Catalysis Method for component based development [9].

This paper also argues that there is a conceptual similarity between component based development and service oriented approaches to systems development. This conceptual similarity has been previously identified [3, 14]. Conceptual models for CBD have been articulated in a variety of CBD methods [2, 6, 7] and an overall model is succinctly summarized in Crnkovic et al [5]. Table 1 describes concepts from components and services and provides a mapping.

Table 1. Conceptual similarity between components and services

Component Concepts	Detail	Service Concepts
Component Spec	The implementation independent view of a component	Service defined within a WSDL package
Interface	The set of related operations supported by an interface	Service in WSDL package

Interface Type Model	The set of types that represent the information that an interface needs to remember. These types are used to specify parameter data typing and form the vocabulary of any pre-post specification pairs for an operation	Data Types contained with WSDL specification
Operation	A discrete piece of functionality offered by an interface	Operation (Port Type)
Pre Post Specification Pair	Declarative specification element of an operation – used for stating the before and after state of the Interface Information Model for an operation.	None – missing concept
Packaged Component (Implementation – code, compiled component, module, deployment descriptors)	A higher level of abstraction of the implemented component / service. This will include the code that implements the component, the compiled object code, packages making up a number of compiled files; deployment descriptors and the component executable that may be deployed on a platform.	External to service specification The WSDL file contains only the location information, the protocols for deployment.

A component specification can also include a semantic specification of operations (that is the pre-post declarations of an operation), it has no equivalence in a service specification. Also a component can conceptually support more than one interface; a service has only one interface (in WSDL 1.1).

3.2 Reference Models

The second aspect of the methodology approach taken in this paper is the use of reference models to provide a contextual framework. This section presents a discussion on reference models and states what is meant by a reference model in this paper. It is argued, that there is value in using reference models for methodology development.

Inspection of a number of existing reference models such as for workflow, topic maps and sharable e-learning content [16, 17, 18] points to emerging common themes. There is an effort made to define common terms; a well-defined framework for extending aspects of the specification; attempts to define a general, overarching structure for the domain; and a focus on interoperability and standardization. These aspects are the lingua franca for a reference model. If we then consider the software engineering community as a specific example, then in addition, a reference model specifies the logical structure of the external interfaces to other systems with enough precision to be practically realizable in an efficient manner while remaining deliberately independent of any particular implementation. The codification of the interface structure will also encourage the development of software tools to enable the development of systems that conform to a particular reference model. Thus the reference model will provide a strong (perhaps enforceable) steer on how systems for a particular domain (and with specific requirements on interoperability) should be implemented.

This discussion is concluded by formalizing a notion of a reference model as follows: *"A reference model is based on a small number of unifying concepts and is an abstraction of the key concepts, their relationships, and their interfaces both to each other and to the external environment. A reference model may be used as a basis for education and for explaining standards to a non-specialist and can be viewed as a framework for comparing architectures and operations of existing and future systems"*.

Reference model concepts can be further generalised to accommodate a bigger picture of service oriented architecture.

It is this bigger picture that informs the notion of a Methodology Development Kit for SOA (SOA-MDK) that is addressed in this paper. Work on reference models for open distributed computing (RM-ODP) has already defined the needs for different viewpoints. The diagram below (Figure 1) extends that notion of viewpoints to propose that a reference model for methodology – i.e. the SOA-MDK to support SOA needs to include multiple dimensions (architectural layers) and multiple perspectives on the layers.

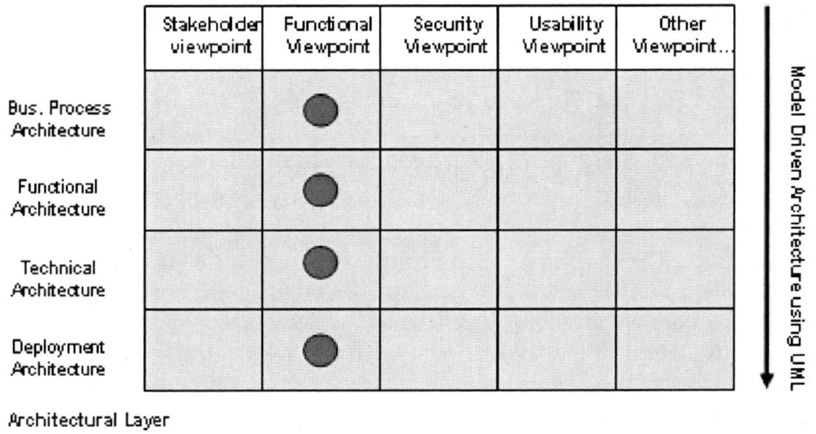

	Stakeholder viewpoint	Functional Viewpoint	Security Viewpoint	Usability Viewpoint	Other Viewpoint...	
Bus. Process Architecture		●				
Functional Architecture		●				
Technical Architecture		●				
Deployment Architecture		●				

Model Driven Architecture using UML

Architectural Layer

Fig. 1. Reference model framework

Thus the specification of a design of a SOA application is captured as a business process architectural description, refined into the a functional architecture expressed as a set of service specifications (the subject of the this paper) and then further refined into a technical architecture using Business Process Execution Language and finally a deployment architecture description of the location of services on specific computing hardware. Each of the architectural layers in turn, is described from specific viewpoints. The SOA-MDK viewpoint described in this paper focuses on the functional viewpoint – that is the capturing the functional requirements of the system from business process through to deployment. A key element of the approach is to focus on a model driven base utilising UML.

4 Method overview

The essence of our approach was a) to recognize and define the conceptual mappings between CBD and SOA, b) to extend and modify CBD methods to support SOA specific requirements and finally c) to ensure that a model based or model driven architectural perspective was rigorously applied from business process modeling through to service modeling using a reference modeling framework.

The key steps in the method for service oriented architecture are shown below in Fig. 2.

Fig. 2. Steps in the process

The activities shown are above are described briefly below.

Develop Process Models: Produce a business process model of the problem domain. Focus on activities, information flow and roles responsible for the activities.

Develop Information Models: Capture the domain concepts (types, attributes, associations and specialization relationships).Use this to define a precise vocabulary for the process models and any business rules and constraints

Factor Process Model: A process model can be come large and complex. It is useful to break down the process into a smaller set of sub-processes. We call these Event scenarios. One technique is to identify time – delay or information delay then group the activities that process a particular event as a sub-process. Rational Unified Process provides some guidelines on how to decompose processes – but there is no formality. Event Consequence Modeling is potentially a useful mechanism for factoring process models. In addition to constructing a sub-process model, the Event scenario is also supported by a textual narrative similar to a use case but with more "story". We have found that developers who were not part of the original business analysis team find these textual narratives particularly helpful.

Partition Information Model into Services: The information model is reviewed from a component perspective and a set of partitioning rules are applied [10] to create a set of components / services.

Allocate Activities to Services: Activities and sub-activities allocated to the services identified earlier. We propose using a variant of the Process/Entity Matrix from Information Engineering. Here, Activities are allocated to Services based on the information types impacted. For example, if an activity produces information which is captured by a particular information type – the service specification that contains that type will be location where the activity is allocated.

Specify service and Generate WSDL specifications: Each service comprises a number of operations. Each operation can be specified in terms of a pre and post conditions. The pre and posts are expressed in terms of types from the information model for the service. This is more or less identical to interface specification in Component Based Design. A good source of information for this and related techniques can be found in D'Souza and Wills' work on Catalysis [9]. Each service can have a WSDL (XML based) specification generated. This WSDL description is used for location and discovery and acts as implementation independent view of the service.

5 Case study example

In this section, we provide a description of how we applied the method outlined above to address the development of a number of services and their dependencies.

5.1 Develop domain models (Process Models and Information Models)

This stage entails a study of the both dynamic (process) and structural (data) information. Thus the stage requires the capture of roles/responsibilities (including teams), activities in the process, routes through the process, triggers, information consumed and produced by activities, constraints and interfaces with other information systems.

Each institution's course validation process was modeled as a UML Activity Diagram with activities (for each discernible task or action) grouped into assemblies (nested activities) corresponding to stages in the business process that were referred to as such by those responsible for setting procedure. Alongside the Activity Diagram of each institution's business process, a UML Class Diagram was created to capture the set of elements and roles in the course validation domain. This domain information model was kept at a high level of abstraction with only the key relationships between the elements included.

5.2 Factor Process Model

When a business process is a type of case process then an especially useful form of partitioning is to identify situations in the business process where there is delay in the process because there is a need for an external event to occur. When the event happens, there is consequence to the event which is set of activities that are triggered because the event occurred. There is a rich body of knowledge which supports the notion of business process understanding using this approach [8, 15].

The set of activities that are triggered can then be viewed as a sub-process of the overall business process. Such a sub-process or Event Scenario provides a better level of granularity for describing analysis scenarios for support the design and implementation stages of a software development process. An additional benefit using events to partition a business process is the direct modeling translation into BPEL specifications where there are modeling concepts for supporting events and their subsequent triggering of consequences of actions.

An Event Scenario comprising one or more activities is triggered by an event such as a time or data event. This scenario can then be analyzed by the software designer to identify operations on components. A scenario (subsetted from the overall process model) is shown below on Figure 3.

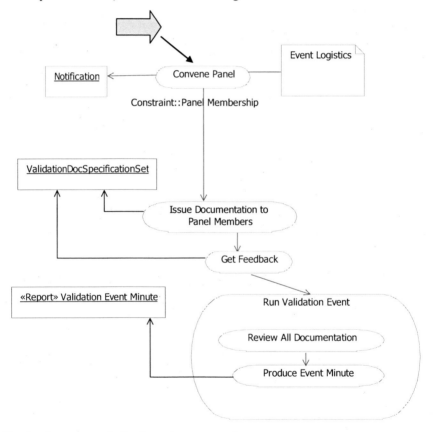

Fig. 3. Event scenario for "running an event"

5.3 Partition Information Models to Services

We propose that given the conceptual closeness between services and components, it is possible to utilize techniques from CBD. Thus, much of the service par-

titioning approach is obtained from the methods underpinning the component specification toolset – COOL:Spex. The approach is described in detail in [7]. In essence, the domain model or information model in our example is partitioned into "components" by firstly identifying types which are deemed to be core – that is business types or objects which are essential to the organization and then traversing associations to types that are detailing – that is providing additional details to the core type. This subsetting provides a natural component boundary. Each component identified is then allocated an interface type which will house the operations for the component.

5.4 Allocate Activities to Services

Once the components / services have been identified in this manner, the subprocess scenarios and their accompanying textual narratives are used to map activities from the process to an operation on a service. Service responsibility is based primarily on determining the types (information) being manipulated in the process and then allocating the service behaviour to the component/service that owns that type. The results of applying this technique to each of the sub-process scenarios is a set of components/services with behaviour allocated to them. A way of capturing the allocation of activities to a service is to use the so-called Process / Entity Matrix from Information Engineering [15]. A partial matrix is shown below (Table 2).

Table 2. Activity Allocations for the Event Scenario

Activity	Process Participant Information Service	Validation Document Service	Learning Product Specification Service	Event Coordination Service	Notification Service	Timetabling service
Identify appropriate panel members	■		■	■		
Notify potential panel members and recieve confimation/ unavailable responses				■	■	
Select best date and book event location				■		■
Send panel members event details and related documentation		■		■	■	

5.5 Specify Services

A service is defined by a set of operations and their parameters. These are stored in the component's information model i.e. the operations, the types and attributes of types used in the parameters of the operations. Once the component/service information model is fully specified, Rational Architect provides the generation of an XML view of the model i.e. the WSDL specification of the service.

6 Conclusion

The case study and modeling approach has demonstrated that there is sufficient conceptual equivalence between component based approaches and service oriented architecture to warrant the use of selected CBD methods. However, SOA does require an emphasis on a business process modeling and the research presented in this paper provides some enhancements to process modeling to ease the move from CBD to SOA. As we continue to develop services from new sub-process scenarios it is likely that we will refine our component partitioning strategy and the rules and good practice/guidelines for developers to support the strategy. The paper has also outlined a role for a reference model framework to provide a wider scope for methodology coverage. It is anticipated that further methodology development will address different areas of the reference framework. For example, quality of service is perceived to be an issue for service oriented architecture – so methodology to support specification of quality of service requirements from the business process architectural layer through to technical architecture i.e. the business process execution layer will be possible.

7 Acknowledgements

This work has been supported by funding from JISC – Joint Information Systems Committee http://www.jisc.ac.uk. Further details of the COVARM project are available at: http://covarm.tvu.ac.uk/covarm.

References

1.   Barn BS, Brown AW, Cheesman J (1998) Methods and Tools for Component Based Development. In Tools, p. 384, Technology of Object-Oriented Languages and Systems
2.   Barn BS, Brown AW (1999) Enterprise-Scale CBD: Building Complex Computer Systems From Components. In 9th International Conference on Software Technology and Engineering Practice (STEP'99), Pittsburgh, Pennsylvania, USA

3. Barn BS (2004) From Components to Web Services. Tutorial presented at ICEIS 2004, Portugal. (2004)
4. Barn BS, Dexter H, Oussena S. Petch J (2006) An Approach to Creating Reference Models for SOA from Multiple Processes. In: IADIS Conference on Applied Computing, Spain
5. Crnkovic I, Hnich B, Jonsson T, Kiziltan Z (2002) Specification, implementation, and deployment of components. Commun. ACM 45, 10, 35-40
6. Castek Ltd(2000) Component-based Development: The Concepts, Technology and Methodology. In Castek Ltd Company's white paper, available at http://www.castek.com
7. Cheesman J, Daniels J (2001) UML Components. Addison-Wesley
8. Cook S, Daniels J (1994) Designing Object Systems: Object-oriented Modelling with Syntropy. Prentice Hall
9. D'Souza DF, Wills AC (1999) Objects, Components, and Frameworks with UML: The Catalysis Approach. Object Technology Series. Addison Wesley, Reading Mass
10. Erl T (2005) Service Oriented Architecture – Concepts, Technology and Design, Prentice-Hall, USA
11. Frankel D (2004) Model Driven Architecture, OMG Press
12. Frankel D (2005) Business Process Trends. BPTrends http://www.bptrends. com/publicationfiles/07%2D05%20COL%20BP%20Platform%20%2D% 20Frankel%2Epdf
13. Ort E (2005) Service-Oriented Architecture and Web Services: Concepts, Technologies, and Tools. http://java.sun.com/developer/technicalArticles/ WebServices/soa2/index.html
14. Stojanovic Z, Dahanayake A, Henk S (2003) Agile Modeling and Design of Service-Oriented Component Architecture. First European Workshop on Object Orientation and Web Services. ECOOP 2003. http://www.cs. ucl.ac.uk/staff/g.piccinelli/eoows/documents/paperstojanovic.pdf
15. Texas Instruments Inc (1990) A guide to Information Engineering using the IEF™. TI Part Number: 2739756-0001.
16. Hollingsworth D (1995) The Workflow Reference Model; Workflow Management Coalition. http://www.wfmc.org/standards/docs/tc003v11.pdf
17. Durusau P, Newcomb S, Barta R. (2006) The topics map reference model. http://www.isotopicmaps.org/TMRM/TMRM-latest-clean.html
18. Advanced Distributed Learning (2004) Sharable Content Object Reference Model (SCORM) 2004 Public Draft. http://www.adlnet.gov/downloads/ 266.cfm

An Analysis of the Internal Structure and its Development of Virtual Organizations in the Grid

William Song* and Xiaoming Li**

*University of Durham, Durham, UK (Corresponding author)
**Peking University, Beijing, China (The paper is partly supported by the
w.w.song@durham.ac.uk

1 Introduction

For the last decade, the study on virtual organizations (VO) has gradually become an important research topic in the fields of the Grid [4]. A virtual organization can be seen as "a temporary alliance of contracted individuals or companies linked together by information and communication technologies, which assembles for the purpose of a specific business task" [6]. A virtual organization can be characterized as being a network of independent, geographically dispersed organizations. All partners in the network share the information and resources and the cooperation is based on common interest, trust, and interdependency. There is also a clear distinction between a strategic and an operational level of activity. As a characteristic of virtual organizations, interdependence is the cooperation and synergy between autonomous organizations, or between empowered departments or individuals within a single organization. Interdependence includes all types of associations: alliances, partnerships, value chains and outsourcing [7].

One of the key problems with virtual organizations in the context of the Grid is the lacking of a clear understanding of the internal structure of virtual organizations be-cause the resources are dispersed, type-vague (or we don't know their types), heterogeneous, semantically informal, and disorderly [15]. Most of the research efforts were put on semantic description and discovery of resources or services [8, 12] and se-mantic composition of services [1]. That these resources should be organized and work together to form a virtual organization and to fulfill a given task (expressed in a set of requirements) is not further studied. We think it is crucial to analyze a virtual organization, to find out its structure, and to express its behavior and working process [14].

Through analyzing the design of virtual organizations in our experiments, we see the importance of interdependence between organizations, but how to realize the interdependencies is not clear. We maintain the viewpoint that the interdependencies represent the coordination among the virtual organizations' components, which can themselves be (virtual) organizations. The components are motivated by the users' demands and requirements. We use the term task to represent a virtual organization component, or even we consider that a high level task represent a (sub-) virtual organization. Therefore, our task of the virtual organization design is to coordinate and integrate its tasks in a virtual organization.

While the tasks attempt to build up the virtual organization structure, we define services to represent the functions that are performed to meet the needs described by the tasks and to group the resources for the services. In this paper we attempt to ad-dress the problems of revealing the internal structure of VO in terms of tasks, ser-vices, and resources. As stated in [5] that the grid is considered to be a service-oriented approach, the virtual organizations should group and coordinate the grid services to flexibly serve the users' requirements.

The paper is organized as follows. In next section, we start with a simple semantic model to describe the components in VOs. We focus on the semantic description of tasks, by defining a metadata model for task description and an ontology model for tasks and services. Then we discuss the internal structure of VOs using the semantic model.

Workflow is the core process representation for VO, which bridges the tasks with services, and concerns their states and transformations. We discuss the workflow design and the VO formation in section 3. In section 4, we illustrate the task decomposition process and the workflow of VO through a demo system. Finally in section 5 we conclude the paper by discussing our research work for next steps.

2 Semantic model for VO and components

The core components in a VO are tasks and services. Tasks are considered to be the finalized representation of users' demands and requirements whereas services are the conceptual clustering of resources (being they logical or physical). Between tasks and services, a semantic matching process is, based on the properties of the tasks, to discover the most suitable services that satisfy the tasks. Once this semantic match is completed, the tasks and the services will bind together to form the VO workflow for the given objectives. In this section, we will discuss 1) what a semantic model is used to represent VO components; 2) what components to be semantically described; and 3) how to semantically represent the VO components.

Undoubtedly, semantics is extremely important in successfully building up a virtual organization and using it. In the following we address the semantic modeling problems in the users' requirements, the management of the stored resources, and the semantic uniform expressions of the virtual organization components. Firstly, user demands are often expressed in a very informal way. The proposed semantic description model should be able to describe the user demands in a formal manner with less semantic loss. Secondly, usually services and resources are already stored and de-scribed in the grid. However, their semantics is usually buried in their representation structures. The proposed semantic description model should be able to capture richer semantics out from the structures and the domain experts' expressions. Thirdly, the proposed model should be able to provide a uniform expression for them. The uniform expression requires the semantic description model to be sufficiently general to accommodate various modeling approaches of different semantic foci and precise enough to able to describe all most of the details.

2.1 Data models for tasks

As the number of components in the Grid is explosively growing, this complexity must be managed. Semantic modeling is an effective means to manage complexity in resource information construction. Semantic models help us to understand the Grid resources by simplifying some of details [3, 13]. Semantic modeling also helps us to represent main features and main structures of the Grid resources and their management and exchange. In this section, we consider two data models for tasks: Metadata model and ontology model.

2.1.1 Metadata model

In a virtual organization, tasks are the major components, which realize the end users requirements, construct workflows for the requirements, and discover and match services which then allocate and assembly the resources for the tasks. In other words, the tasks represent and formulate the users' demands and requirements at one end and deliver the basic services and consume the resources at the other end. It is obvious that the decomposition operation is a most fundamental one on the tasks. By applying the decomposition operation, the tasks form a tree structure, which supports to construct and schedule workflows for the virtual organization.

t-id:	#012
$<t_1, t_2>$:	t1:t2
description:	this task is to finding a suitable sort algorithm for sorting product prices.
service set:	{quick sort, bubble sort, ...}
roles:	triggers <#011, #01>, followers <#013, #121>
decomposition:	<#0121, #0122, #0123>
rules:	data type matching for <inputs, outputs>

Fig. 1. Example of the task to find a suitable sort algorithm for sorting product prices. Here the rules of the task mean that data type matching is required for the inputs and outputs.

A metadata model for a task, t, is defined to be a binary <t-id, t-attr>, where t-id is the internal representation of the task t and t-attr is a list of attributes, which are de-scribed as follows:

- $<t_{begin}, t_{end}>$: this is a pair of time units to indicate the beginning and the end of the task. So it delimits the life cycle of the task.
- Description: a natural language description of the task.
- Service set: a set of services from various servers. This set of services is discovered and suggested for the task to match.
- Roles: a number of actors that play various roles in performing the task, e.g., task trigger, task subject, etc.
- Rules: a set of rules, stipulating inputs to and outputs for the task to discover and match the services and resources.

In the following we illustrate the task metadata model with an example, see Fig. 1 above.

2.1.2 Ontology model

The ontology model is a special structure for a set of tasks, where only a special relationship between tasks is maintained, that is, the decomposition relationship. From the point of view of concepts, an ontology model is a tree, where all the nodes are concepts. There is one special node, called the root, which is the most general concept in the tree.

The purpose of defining an ontology model is to provide a referencing conceptual framework for a virtual organization, which we use to reason about, e.g., whether two concepts (e.g. Merge Sort and Quick Sort) belong to the same concept. The ontology model also supports tasks/service search, formulating search queries and service-task match.

Following is a widely accepted definition for the ontology. The ontology is defined to be a quintuple: concept (the concept itself), properties (all the relationships of the concept with other concepts and the attributes of the concept), axioms (rules and constraints on the concept), value domains and nominal (names or terms for the concept). However, based on our investigation on the application domain, we redefine the ontology to better accommodate the features of VO applications.

An ontology model for the tasks is defined as follows:

- Concept: a concept name is used to represent the concept of a task.
- Properties: a set of properties of the concept, e.g., execution time of the task.
- Constraints: the constraints on the concept of the tasks, e.g., disjoint (A, B), overlapping (A, B) where A and B are two concepts.
- Relationships: the semantic relations between two concepts, e.g., similar (A, B).
- Decomposition: this is a specific relationship between two tasks. This relationship results in a set of subtasks. In OWL-S [11], this relationship can be viewed to be similar to subClassOf, partOf. This forms an ontology tree for the concept of the tasks and services.

In the above example, we assume a hierarchical structure of the tasks for the virtual organization is available. This hierarchical structure is formed using domain knowledge. At the time of writing, we consult the domain experts for the decomposition patterns. The task hierarchical structured used in the above example is partially shown in Fig. 2.

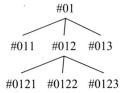

Fig. 2. In the hierarchical structure for the tasks used in the above example, the task #01 is decomposed into the subtasks #011, #012, and #013, and the task #012 is decomposed into #0121, #0122, and #0123

2.2 Services modeling

It is known to us, OWL-S provides an ontology language for web services. A description of a service covers its service profile, service process, and service grounding. The service profile provides various kinds of information about the service itself, such as contact information, service structure, inputs/outputs, and results. The service process describes the processes, which perform the tasks given by the service together with their data structures, as well as various conditions for the processes. The processes are of types: atomic and composite. The service grounding provides interfaces to the execution of services, including various parameters, input/output values, and process-related operations.

However, this kind of ontology description for web services has significant defects: Firstly, although an ontological description is provided the ontological structure for the service concepts is defined manually as there is not semantic framework is used for formally describing services. Secondly, service profile should be the place for accommodating semantic structural description for the service and the possible semantic relationships with other services. However, currently it provides only static, non-machine readable semantic information about the service. Thirdly, service process decomposition is not really the part of service ontology although it suggests that some (atomic) services may compose a composite service. Finally, atomic processes should be directly corresponding to grounding the interfaces. It would not be a se-mantic matching between the two. Rather, it should provide the names of processes, which match the names of functions (interfaces) on the ground (assuming that we had a service file library).

Therefore, we propose a semantic structure based, basic mechanism to implement a refinement structure for services ranging from high-level objective description for services to low level functional description for services. The representation model considers both the features at objectives level and concrete level. The proposed mechanism also implements a semantic matching, which bridges atomic ser-vices/processes with business and functional workflows.

A data model for a service, s, is defined to be a binary <s-id, s-attr>, where s-id is the internal representation of the task s and s-attr is a list of attributes, which are de-scribed as follows:

- Name: the name for the service.
- Input: a set of inputs and their types. The inputs to the service are from other services. The types of the inputs can help restricting the selection of services.
- Output: an output and its type. The output of the service is usually an input of the other service. The type also helps with the selection of services.
- Metadata: a set of data that describe the service, e.g., service description in natural language, service creator, service creation time, etc.
- Resource: a set of resources that is required for the service. We assume that for each service, a set of resources has already been decided, including their possible substitutes when some services fail to work.

In addition, we also assume that for a given domain a group of ontologies have been used for describing services. It is important to note the group of domain re-lated ontologies is critical for semantic matching between tasks and services.

2.3 VO workflow

In the previous definition for tasks, we have already pointed out that the decomposition operation on tasks will generate a tree structure for the tasks. Here we define a leaf task, denoted as t^a (atomic task), to be the task that cannot be further decomposed. Of course, it is difficult in the current task definition to judge whether a task can be further decomposed or not. Therefore we maintain a group of task decomposition patterns, which are created through consulting with the domain experts. Using the task decomposition patterns we know whether we can further decompose a task. In order to describe a workflow in a virtual organization, we consider a setting for a task. See Fig. 3.

Fig. 3. The setting for a task is on the left and the setting for a service on the right

Roughly a task has two incoming arrows and two outgoing arrows. One incoming arrow of the task is from its parent task if the task is not a root task, to indicate that the task is a compound of its parent task. Another incoming arrow of the task is from its sibling task(s), indicating that the task is directly after its siblings (this order can be in time sequence or functional sequence). One outgoing arrow of the task is to its direct next sibling task(s). Another outgoing arrow of the task is to its compound tasks if it is not a leaf task or to its matched service(s) if it is a leaf task.

Grid services, in this circumstance, are considered to be programs (or functions), which are defined to implement the tasks and allocate the resources available in the Grid. Like the setting of a task, a service has also two incoming arrows and two out-going arrows. See Fig. 3. One incoming arrow of a service is from its task. That is, a task is associated with a set of matched services (however, these services may not be available). We stipulate that at least one service is available to realize the task. An-other incoming arrow of the service is from its preceding service(s). More than one preceding services mean that the service has more than one input parameters. One outgoing arrow of the service is to its successor services. Another outgoing arrow of the service is to the set of resources. These resources are prepared for the service. For example, the task can be "to use quick-sort method to sort the data". The service that implements the task is a quick-sort program and the resources are the functions for the program, the CPU time, the memory, the prepared data, etc.

Now, we see that there is a one-to-one mapping from the leaf tasks to the services. Using the preceding and the successor relations between the leaf tasks, we can get the following an ordered sequence:

$$T_1 << T_2 << \ldots << T_n,$$

where T_i, $1<i<n$, is the ith leaf task in the leaf task set.

We call this sequence as the workflow of this virtual organization and the corresponding sequence of the services, $S_1 << S_2 << \ldots << S_n$, where S_i, $1<i<n$, is the ith service, as an implementation of the workflow.

3 Workflow design approaches and VO formation

The formation of VO has been proposed and discussed in [4]. A more detailed description of the VO formation process was given in [10], where it is considered that a VO system only exists for a temporary time needed for satisfaction of its purpose and therefore the process of a VO is defined as consisting of needs identification, formation of VO, operations, and dissolution in the context of electronic commerce. From the context of the Grid, we consider two more steps should be added to the above VO process, i.e., searching and matching the Grid resources and integration (or composite) of services.

In the following, we discuss the steps of VO development process in detail.

The first step is users' requirements and demands solicitation and identification. A VO is created to response to end users' demands. Usually such demands provide clear goals but unclear technical descriptions. Our tasks for the first step include soliciting users' demands and requirements and document them as detailed as possible. These demands and requirements are used to guide the technical development of the VO and validate the results produced from the VO. This step is at moment done by collaboration of domain experts and VO researchers and developers.

The second step, formalizing and modeling the requirements, is to analyze and model the requirements, and form a set of general tasks. Then the tasks are further decomposed into subtasks. The process of task decomposition continues until all the leave tasks are found and a sequence of (virtually executable) tasks is formed. This step is performed by the VO developers with the help from the domain experts. It is very important that the domain knowledge and ontologies will be included in the modeling results. The forming of the task hierarchy should be conformed to the application domain ontologies, which will be used for the later matching step.

The third step is searching for and matching services and resources. According to the description of the tasks, which includes a sequence of (leave) tasks, the task hierarchy, the ontologies for the tasks, and the task requirements (specifications), the VO development environment starts to search for the set of services together with the resources that best meet the description of the tasks. The efficiency and effectiveness of the match technology depends on the quality of the semantic description for tasks, the size of the service pool, and the matching algorithm.

Forming the VO is the fourth step, where to form a workflow from the refined tasks and the match services is the main activity. The workflow here embodies the business process of the virtual organization, as well as the execution of services and resources. The resulted VO is an optimal combination of the services and resources from the service pool (we assume in this paper that a service pool exists with all kinds of services available). Therefore, one service with a longer execution time may be better than the one with a shorter execution time when meeting better the task or making a less execution time in the matched sequence of services. This depends on the policies and mechanisms for both scheduling and allocating the services that make the plan for the VO [2].

The fifth step, negotiation, integration of services and the VO execution, indicates that the above steps are iterative. Negotiation and the users' interference may be required to adjust the task decomposition and service selection so that the users' goals and demands will be better satisfied. The service integration will be achieved as long as the predefined quality for the VO is met. Then the VO is run. But not all services and resources are necessarily ready for the VO execution. The scheduling mechanism for the VO system will fetch a service when it is required.

Dissolution is the final step, in which the VO execution system (a part of the VO development environment. The other part is the construction system) will gradually release the resources when they are not required by the VO. When all the tasks complete, all the services are freed and the VO system is dissolved.

We should note that the above-discussed process is a top-down approach for the VO development based on the assumption that the service and resource pool is al-ready available. Actually, we have been developing a bottom-up approach to constitute the service pool, where the concepts and methods of software reusability and the notion of software as a service [16] have laid a foundation to construct services from resources. In addition, we assume that, during the service construction process (e.g. using OWL-S as a specification language and protégé as an implementation tool), domain knowledge and ontologies have also been recorded as a knowledge base being a part of the service pool. In other words, we make a semantic rich, "UDDI" like service registry.

In a complete process of the VO implementation, the top-down and bottom-up approaches together produce workflow for VO.

4 An example for workflow formation

The semantic description model we proposed previously aims at providing a semantic based modeling approach to discover and formalize an internal structure of a virtual organization. This approach is also supporting component analysis for the virtual organization. This analysis will further supply mechanisms for reasoning about the task hierarchy, querying the services, and discovering the resources, as well as the virtual organization workflow design. In brief, a virtual organization can be illustrated in Fig. 4.

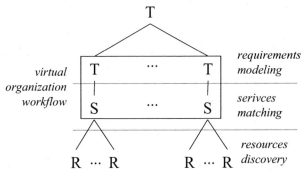

Fig. 4. The working structure of a virtual organization Here T, S, and R stand for task, service, and resource. The leaf tasks together with the services form the virtual organization workflow

Here a virtual organization starts from a high level task for general users' requirements and demands. The task is decomposed into subtasks, which are in turn further decomposed, and hence form a task hierarchy. The leaf tasks form the workflow of the virtual organization. The task hierarchy consists of the modeling for the users' requirements. The services which match the leaves tasks form an implementation of the workflow. The service sequence layer with the workflow represents the service de-sign and matching. The resources layer with the service sequence is the resource discovery and assembly.

In this section we use an example to illustrate our semantic description model for task decomposition and workflow. Suppose that the general task is "to sort out the product prices", denoted T0. The first decomposition makes T0 to have the com-pound tasks T11 ("sorting") and T12 ("product price data"). T11 is further decomposed into T211 ("sort methods") and T212 ("data"). T211 is then decomposed into T311 ("sort functions"). Now the task T311 cannot be further decomposed. It corresponds to a set of services: quick sort, bubble sort, selection sort, etc. Based on the performance required for the task, a suitable service, i.e., matched services, will be found. Part of the task hierarchy and the services are illustrated in Fig. 5.

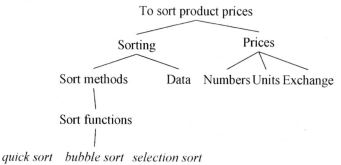

Fig. 5. The task hierarchy and the service set (in italics)

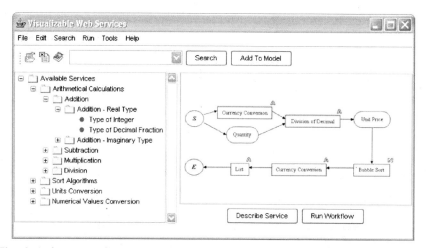

Fig. 6. A demonstration system to illustrate how the services from the task hierarchy above to form a workflow

In order to show the process of VO formation, we developed a demo system in Fig. 6. The field on the left provides a tree-structured task/service repository. All the available services in the repository, including both atomic services and composite services, are displayed there. The bar on the top is a search engine, for finding required services. A found service can be added to the modeling panel, which graphically illustrates the service composition process for a certain task. The tasks and ser-vices can be made up of atomic and non-atomic services. The panel also illustrates the flow of the task. By clicking the run button at the right bottom, the workflow is executed and shows the process of data transmission, from the starting node S to the ending node E. The description of a service can be displayed if clicking the description button.

Fig. 6 shows an example of the service of sorting the prices. The services, marked with A at its top right are atomic, marked by N, non-atomic. The function of currency conversion is to unify several kinds of currencies. After taking in the price and quantities, we can get unit prices after dividing the total price by the quantity. The unit prices will then be the input of the bubble sort. The whole flow terminates after converting the currencies back and list the result.

5 Conclusion

"Virtual organization" has become an important research issue in the areas of semantic grid computing, semantic web, e-Learning, e-Government, e-Business and so on. How to formally and semantically describe the components in a virtual organization and hence form a temporary and dynamic virtual organization is a big problem as there lacks a suitable semantic description model, which can be used to model the diverse and distributed components, including tasks, services, workflows, and resources. In this paper, we introduce a simple semantic description model for the tasks, and services, and resources in a virtual organization in order to reveal the internal structure of a virtual organization. The model includes a metadata sub-model for task property descriptions and an ontology sub-model for task conceptual descriptions. This semantic description model was proposed as the basis for the discussion of the internal structure of virtual organization and the development of virtual organization applications.

In the paper, we discuss the workflow design and the virtual organization formation in terms of these components previously described. Using a simple example in our demo system we illustrated the task-service work-flow with the internal structure for virtual organizations. Whether or not to decompose a service is still a question. As suggested in [9], to create service hierarchy will help to describe, reason, and discover, as well as maintain services. However, this depends on what kind of the internal structure we define for virtual organization. A few issues that we will explore in our future research work include:

- Formal model for virtual organization workflows. This will better support qualitative and quantitative analysis of business processes of domain applications and effective allocation and coordination of services and resources in the Grid.
- Design of a pattern template for the domain experts to formulating their domain knowledge. This is extremely important yet difficult to solve a problem as to discover the most suitable services for a domain application depends on accurate analysis and decomposition of the tasks.

References

1. Agarwal S, Handschuh S, Staab S (2005) Annotation, Composition and Invocation of Semantic Web Services, Journal of Web Semantics Vol. 2, Issue 1.
2. Alwagait E and Ghandeharizadeh S (2004) A Comparison of Alternative Web Service Allocation and Scheduling Policies, in Proceedings of IEEE SCC 2004: 319-326.
3. Conallen J (1999) Modeling Web Application Architectures with UML, Communications of the ACM, Vol. 42, No. 10, Oct. 1999.
4. De Roure D, Jennings NR, Shadbolt NR (2005) The Semantic Grid: Past, Present, and Future, Proceedings of the IEEE, Volume 93, Issue 3, March 2005, Pages 669-681, ISSN: 0018-9219
5. Goble C and De Roure D (2002b) The Semantic Web and Grid Computing, in Real World Semantic Web Applications, vol. 92, Frontiers in Artificial Intelligence and Apps., (eds. Kashyap and Shklar) IOS Press, 2002.
6. "ICENI Virtual Organisation Management", (2003) London e-Science Centre, UK, http://www.doc.ic.ac.uk/~asif/vom/index.html
7. Introna L, Moore H, Cushman M (1999) The Virtual Organisation – Technical or Social Innovation? Lessons from the Film Industry, Working Paper Series 72, Department of IS, London School of Economics and Political Science, UK.
8. Ludwig S and Reyhani S (2005) Semantic Approach to Service Discovery in a Frid Envi-ronment, *Journal of Web Semantics* Vol. 3 Issue 4.
9. Martin D, Paolucci M, McIlraith S (2004) Bringing Semantics to Web Services: The OWL-S Approach, *Proceedings of the First International Workshop on Semantic Web Services and Web Process Composition (SWSWPC 2004)*, July 6-9, 2004, San Diego, California, USA.
10. Oliveira et al (2003) Electronic Commerce and Virtual Organizations, http://paginas.fe.up.pt/~eol/PROJECTS/ec_vo.html
11. OWL-S (2004) http://www.daml.org/services/owl-s/1.1
12. Paolucci M, Sycara K, and Kawamuwa T (2003) Delivering Semantic Web Services, in Proceedings of WWW2003.
13. Song W (2003) Semantic Issues in the Grid computing and Web Services, in the Proceed-ings of International Conference on Management of e-Commerce and e-Government, Nanchang, China.
14. Song W and Li X (2005a) Semantic Modeling for Virtual Organization: A Case for Vir-tual Course, to appear in Advances in Information Systems Development - Bridging the Gap between Academia and Industry, (eds. Nilsson and Gustas), Springer.
15. Song W and Li X (2005b) A Conceptual Modeling Approach to Virtual Organizations in the Grid to appear in Proceedings of GCC2005 (eds. Zhuge and Fox), Springer LNCS 3795, pp. 382-393.
16. Turner M et al (2003) Turning up A Software into A Service, IEEE Computer, October 2003, pp. 38-44.

Mobile Systems Development: Exploring the Fit of XP

Ole Pedersen, Martin Lund Kristiansen, Marc Nyboe Kammersgaard, and
Jens Henrik Hosbond

oleslir@gmail.com, and {martinlk, prompt, joenne}@cs.aau.dk
Department of Computer Science, Aalborg University, Denmark

Abstract: Development of mobile software is surrounded by much uncertainty. Immature
software platforms on mobile clients, a highly competitive market calling for innovation,
efficiency and effectiveness in the development life cycle, and lacking end-user adoption
are just some of the realities facing development teams in the mobile software industry. By
taking a process view on development of mobile systems we seek to explore the strengths
and limitations of eXtreme Programming (XP) in the context of mobile software development. Following an experimental approach a mobile systems development project running
for four months is conducted. Experiences from the project are used for analysis and discussion of the fit of XP in mobile systems development. First, requirements for mobile systems development projects are proposed. Second, these are analysed and compared to the
prescribed principles suggested in XP.

In general, we find XP well-suited for mobile systems development projects. However,
based on our experiences and an analytical comparison we propose the following modifications to XP: Make an essential design to avoid the worst time waste during refactoring. For
faster development, reuse code components whenever possible. Test regularly on real devices, since the difference between emulators and real devices are significant. Take advantage of spikes. Do not use pair programming when spiking, and remember to write unit
tests for production code that was initially created during spikes. Monitor the user during
acceptance tests.

Keywords: Mobile systems development, systems development, eXtreme Programming,
XP

1 Introduction

Today most people carry around mobile devices, such as mobile phones, laptops,
PDAs, etc. The market for mobile devices has been growing the last many years.
In 2004 alone over 670 million mobile phones were sold worldwide (Gartner

2005). With this amount of people using mobile devices, developing software for these devices becomes increasingly interesting. This article focuses solely on software for mobile phones.

Currently there are a number of things that may be said to characterize software development for mobile devices – henceforth refereed to as mobile systems development (MSD). In this paper we take a closer look at the implications of common issues reflecting development of mobile software systems. These issues are: Rapid technology change, short time-to-market, high software quality, lacking end-user adoption, and immature software tools. Through the development of mobile application steered by the principles of eXtreme Programming (XP) we explore the pros and cons of an agile and product-driven approach to MSD – in this case XP. In addition, we suggest improvements to the principles of XP, increasing the fit of XP.

The paper is structured as follows: Section 2 describes the setting of the development project and briefly sketches the software application. In Section 3 a comparative fit is made between the requirements to MSD and the prescribed principles in XP. Section 4 discusses how to improve XP development method for enhancing the support for MSD, and Section 5 ends this paper with a conclusion.

2 Research Approach

This article is based on a MSD project that adheres to the XP principles described in 'Extreme Programming Explained' by Kent Beck (Beck 1999) and 'Extreme Software Engineering' by Steinberg and Palmer (Steinberg and Palmer 2004). The development project spans a 4 month period, where we effectively spend five weeks programming the software. These five weeks are divided into three iterations. The development team is comprised of six computer science students. The students are attending their sixth and eight semester at the University of Aalborg, respectively. The customer is a sixth semester Informatics student also from the University of Aalborg.

To document the development process we use a diary in which we each day write a short description of what project activity has been performed that day, and, most importantly, what has been experienced with regards to working with the XP principles. Each entry in the diary is written in the afternoon.

Diary writing is a qualitative data collection method that is useful when evaluating projects. It enables the diary writer to reflect upon his own actions and the development method that is used during a project. It also helps a team of developers to better understand the development method, and it makes it easier to remember the development process (Jepsen, Mathiassen et al. 1989; Patton 1990; Sá 2002). For creating and managing project diaries a simple web-based tool is applied.

2.1 The Mobile System

For exploring the fit of XP in a MSD context, we set out to develop an application for streaming music to mobile devices while moving about. The client application is executed on a Java-enabled mobile phone. On application start-up, the client automatically connects to the server and is immediately hereafter able to request MP3 streams. This enables the phone to function as an MP3 player with a virtually unlimited storage capacity, even though the phone actually only has a very limited amount of physical storage. In addition, the application allows the user to purchase music while wandering about supporting any instant and spontaneous music demand the user may have.

The server runs on a stationary computer that has an arbitrary number of MP3 files stored on disk. These files are available to clients for streaming, enabling devices to connect and listen to MP3 streams through a wireless network, provided that the network is fast enough (e.g. UMTS or GPRS Edge).

Tools The server is developed using the Java 2 Standard Edition (J2SE) platform with unit tests written in JUnit. The client is developed using the Java 2 Micro Edition (J2ME) and the Wireless Toolkit. We use the Sony Ericsson J2ME SDK 2.2.0 for emulating the Sony Ericsson K750i, a mobile phone with MP3 playback support through Java method calls. The unit tests for the client are written in J2MEUnit.

2.2 The Development Process

Throughout the development process we are true to the principles of XP as suggested by Kent Beck (1999) and Steinberg and Palmer (2004). In total 13 principles are used and together they represent the development process of the project. The 13 principles are: Whole Team, Metaphor, The Planning Game, Simple Design, Small Releases, Customer Tests, Pair Programming, Test-driven Development, Design Improvement, Collective Code Ownership, Continuous Integration, Sustainable Pace, and Coding Standards. For more in-depth coverage of these principles, see 'Extreme Software Engineering' by Steinberg and Palmer (2004).

3 Analysis

In this section we suggest a list of requirements that a systems development method should support in order for it to be applicable to MSD projects, and we explain how XP should fit these requirements. Thereafter we will describe our experiences of applying XP to a simulated MSD project.

3.1 MSD Requirements

In the introduction (Section 1) we described characteristics of the mobile market. Based on these requirements we suggest the following properties that a systems development method, that is suitable for MSD projects, should support: (1) High software quality, (2) short time-to-market, (3) frequently changing user requirements, (4) frequent technology changes, and (5) lacking standardization.

(1) Upgrading the software on mobile clients costs the wireless industry $8 billion a year (Fitchard 2003). Hence, maintaining a high level of software quality is important, because it is difficult to ensure that software updates reach the mobile devices that the users carry around with them. This implies that low software quality can lead to unhappy customers, since bug fixes are unlikely to reach the end-user. Furthermore, high expenses are associated with upgrading the software that comes pre-installed on devices.

(2) A short time-to-market requirement is most likely present in any MSD project (Aarnio 2002; Hosbond and Nielsen 2005). This is due to the mobile market being largely technology-driven (Vihinen and Tuunainen 2004). The companies that produce mobile devices compete against each other, all wanting to be the first to release a new gadget to the masses.

(3) It is important to be able to handle changing user requirements. The mobile market is characterized by not yet having software that standardizes how mobile software should look and behave. In other words, the customer do not yet know exactly what they want a piece of mobile software to do, nor do they know how the software should do it (Pescatore 2004).

(4) Mobile technologies are being introduced and replaced with an incredible speed (Krogstie, Lyytinen et al. 2003; Vihinen and Tuunainen 2004; Hosbond and Nielsen 2005). Consequently, it is important to decide how to handle technology that changes frequently.

(5) There is a lack of standardization in the mobile market. The available software platforms are all different and not necessarily compatible with one another, and the software development kits are immature and poorly documented (Arnason 2004; Atkins 2004).

3.2 MSD Requirements and XP support

Comparing the mentioned requirements for MSD with the principles of XP, it becomes clear that several of the principles support the requirements. Table 1 shows these relations.

High software quality should be attainable through Test-driven Development, Acceptance Testing, Pair Programming, Design Improvements, Continuous Integration, Simple Design, and Coding Standards.

The quality of software can be perceived in several ways, e.g. the quality of the actual code, the usability of the user interface, and the users' level of satisfaction when using the software. In this section we will perceive quality of software from a professional, computer scientific point of view, meaning quality of the actual code.

Table 1. MSD requirements and supporting XP principles

MSD requirements	XP principles
(1) High software quality	Test-driven Development, Acceptance Testing, Pair Programming, Design Improvements, Continuous Integration, Simple Design, and Coding Standards
(2) Short time-to-market	Simple Design, Small Releases, Whole Team, Test-driven Development, and Continuous Integration
(3) Frequently changing user requirements	Small Releases, Whole Team, and Simple Design
(4) Rapid technology chances	Simple Design and Test-driven Development
(5) Lacking standardization	Simple Design and Test-driven Development

Test-driven Development provides better code because the code is constantly tested using unit tests. Acceptance Testing helps the programmers provide the software that the customer wants. Pair Programming should also provide better code by utilizing the positive effects of teamwork. Pair Programming has been said to be a more efficient way of writing code and that it produces software that has both a better design as well as fewer bugs (Nosek 1998). Design Improvements provide better code by improving the code design whenever possible. Simple Design and Coding Standards should reinforce the readability of the code, which leads to fewer programming mistakes and therefore better code that is more stable.

Short time-to-market is ensured by using Simple Design, Small Releases, Whole Team, Test-driven Development, and Continuous Integration. Simple Design cuts down on excessive design activity and retains only what is necessary thus giving us a shorter time-to-market. Small Releases and Whole Team should provide faster development, since the customer is involved in the development process and tests the software frequently, ensuring that the development team is not wasting precious time working in a wrong direction. Test-driven Development ensures much faster testing by automating tests, eliminating the need for spending time on repeatedly doing thorough tests of the system. Continuous Integration arranges for the system to be running at all times, regardless of its level of implemented functionality. This also leads to shorter time-to-market, since a clash, where all individually developed components of the system are put together, will never arise. Had the latter not been the case, a lot of interface conflicts would be exposed at the time everything is put together, and comprehensive adjustments of the code would be necessary.

Frequently changing user requirements are handled in XP by Small Releases, Whole Team, and Simple Design. Small Releases and Whole Team involve the customer in the development process and ensure that the software is tested by the customer during the development project. This also ensures that new user requirements, established by the customer, are identified, and Simple Design makes it easier and faster to implement these new requirements. There is no bulky design document which must be held up to date, and the system is always a minimal implementation of the current requirements. All in all, XP should make it easier to introduce changes into the system (Kusiak and He 1998).

Rapid technology changes can be handled in different ways. If you choose to stick with the same technology all the way through a development project, you need to be sure that you have chosen the right technology for your particular project. This requires that you carefully consider all possibilities before deciding on a technology to deploy and start developing. XP as is provides no support for this. If instead you choose to make your code flexible with regards to handling technology changes, XP will support you by providing Simple Design and Test-driven Development. Simple Design makes it easier to adapt to new and emerging technologies, and Test-driven Development makes it easier to test the code after it has been extended to utilize new technologies.

Lacking standardization is supported in XP by using Simple Design and Test-driven Development, since these principles make it possible to make ongoing changes during a project.

4 Discussion

The mapping of XP principles onto MSD requirements in Table 1, provide a view of the supportive properties of XP for MSD. However, experiences collected through the project diaries and day-to-day conversations called for new ways of organizing essential activities in the project. The result is set of propositions for increasing the fit of XP to MSD. The propositions are listed in Table 2.

Table 2. Propositions for further XP support in MSD projects

Proposition	Description
Essential design	Make an essential design to keep wasted time to a minimum during refactoring.
Reuse software components	Reuse object-oriented code components when possible. Remember to construct unit tests.
Develop and test on physical devices	Test regularly on physical devices. If possible, give all programming pairs access to real devices while they are developing.
Spikes	Take advantage of spikes. Do not use pair programming when spiking, and remember to construct unit tests for the code obtained through spikes.
Monitor acceptance testing	By monitoring the user while he is testing the system, it becomes clear what works and what needs improvement.

Essential design

We find that doing Simple Design and Design Improvement has some undesirable effects on our development process. If you only do Small Designs, one task at a time, the system design in entirety will be created through an incremental process, consisting of patch after patch. You will end up with a cluttered design which will require a lot of refactoring to become structured. If the whole design needs to be decomposed and refatored, it will influence nearly all components in the system. While the components are being restructured, it is not possible for other programming pairs to work. If they do, they might end up writing code for classes and methods which may not exist when the refactoring process is complete.

The only solution to this problem is for the programmers to wait for the system to be refactored, before they continue their work. This is not a very productive way of working. To avoid the worst chunks of the refactoring, we need to somehow incorporate bigger designs. We should start out by constructing an overall design. The XP way of designing, is simply not enough for MSD projects. When designing, you must think beyond the current task. This is especially true in the initial phases of a project, where the entire core structure of the code is determined. If you do not follow this guideline, you will end up having to change many lines of code repeatedly.

When the development team and the customer are gathered in order to determine user stories for the first iteration, the development team should have a conversation with the customer about which user stories he thinks are absolutely essential for the software. An essential user story is one whose absence would render the software unusable. The number of essential user stories might be bigger than the first iteration allows for, but that can be dealt with. Let the customer split the user stories into two groups: (1) *essential user stories* and (2) *optional user stories*. If some of the user stories are hard to place in either group, simply place them in group (2).

Next it is time to design a minimal system that includes the essential user stories from group (1). This design includes back-end class structure, graphical user interface, and potential protocols.

The initial design should not be implemented at once. Instead it should be well-known by all developers, and they must have it in mind when they start writing code. Every time new code is written, it must be checked for coherence with the initial design. Designs needed during later iterations are constructed ad hoc in the beginning of each iteration.

Reuse software components

Object-oriented software development has the advantage that developers write software components, which can easily be reused. This should be taken advantage of in a MSD project, where time-to-market requirements are very important. Therefore, if reuse of components is ever possible, it should be exploited. We recommend writing unit tests for components that are reused. Without them you risk introducing bugs in your code during later refactoring, which can cost time when trying to remove them.

Develop and test on physical devices

Developing software using an emulator is often cheaper and easier than developing software using a physical device. There are even situations where developers require an emulator to be present, e.g. when the software that runs on a device is being developed alongside the actual device (hardware development). When developing software using only an emulator, you expect that emulator to function exactly as the real device will do when it becomes available. Unfortunately, we have experienced that this is not always the case. Emulators and real devices often differ, making the process of getting the software up and running on a real device cumbersome and time-consuming. This is not acceptable in MSD projects, due to low time-to-market requirements. If possible, developing and testing on real devices should be done regularly during a software development process, in order to avoid major obstacles when deploying the software on the real device. Preferably, all programming pairs should have access to a real device while they are developing and testing.

Spikes

Before a project sets out, there might be technologies a development team knows nothing about that will need to be investigated. If this is not done, problems that the team is not able to handle might present themselves during development. This is of particular interest when developing software for a market that has a lot of new technologies involved, and few experts since everything is new, cutting-edge technology (Lyytinen, Rose et al. 1998)

At times, when dealing with MSD, development teams must try out several things before reaching a solution that works. For instance, it takes some research finding out if a portable device will support MP3 playback. Spikes let you do this.

When a suitable solution to a problem is found, and the development team feels confident that the new code is ready to be integrated with the rest of the system, the team should do itself the favor of writing the test cases for the code. This should be done even though it is tempting not to, now that the implementation code has already been written. Writing the test will pay off if refactoring or extension is needed later on.

Lacking standardization and rapid technology changes in MSD projects may result in situations where the development team will have lacking experience. When the team is inexperienced with something, spikes are of particular interest. Spikes are already a part of XP, but they are particular interesting in MSD because of the rapid technology changes that characterize MSD.

Pair programming has many advantages. But there are still situations where pair programming is not that useful. A pair of programmers can get stuck, not knowing how to deal with the problem at hand, and the additional team members might not be able to help them out. If this happens, a spike should be conducted.

Conducting a spike does not necessarily require the team effort of two people. It requires surfing the internet looking for implementation examples and documentation as well as searching through literature. To do this, a programmer does not need a person sitting beside him, providing support. The pair can effectively split up and conduct each their spike. Alternatively, the second programmer can team up with another team member and continue doing pair programming.

Monitor acceptance testing

Monitoring the customer while he tests the software product at each of the small releases yields great results. It allows developers to see more easily what things the end-users will experience problems with and what works well. This is especially true for the user interface. When the developers notice the customer is having problems, they must take note of it. Afterward they can discuss with the customer how the problem should be handled. This form of primitive usability test should, however, not take the place of a professionally organized usability test. The on-site customer may already be more experienced with regards to the system than the end-user will be, and he will therefore be less likely to discover as many problems as an external user will.

5 Conclusion

Based on our analysis we can conclude that XP works as an obvious development method for MSD projects. This is confirmed by our experiment of coupling XP with MSD. Furthermore, we present a series of ideas that strive to make XP an even better candidate for future MSD projects. These include: Make an essential design, reuse software components, develop and test on real devices, focus on the importance of spikes, and monitor the user during acceptance tests.

References

Arnason, A. (2004). "The wireless evolution: A journey just begun." Rural telecommunications 23(5): 22.

Atkins, J. (2004). "New tools for new networks." Telecommunications 38(8): 16-20.

Beck, K. (1999). Extreme Programming Explained: Embrace Change, Addison-Wesley.

Fitchard, K. (2003). "Cutting Edge: Gene Wang." Wireless Review 20(8).

Gartner. (2005). "Gartner says strong fourth quarter sales led worldwide mobile phones sales to 30 percent growth in 2004." from http://www.gartner.com/press_releases/asset/_121402_11.html.

Hosbond, J. H. and P. A. Nielsen (2005). Mobile Systems Development: A Literature Review. IFIP 8.2 - Designing Ubiquitous Information Environments - Socio-technical Issues and Challenges, Cleveland, Ohio, IEEE.

Jepsen, L., L. Mathiassen, et al. (1989). "Back to thinking mode: diaries for the management of information systems development projects." Behaviour and information technology 8(3): 207-217.

Krogstie, J., K. Lyytinen, et al. (2003). Mobile information systems - research challenges of the conceptual and logical level. LNCS.

Kusiak, A. and D. He (1998). "Design for agility: A scheduling perspective." Robotics and computer-integrated manufacturing 14: 415-427.

Lyytinen, K., G. Rose, et al. (1998). "The brave new world of development in internetwork computing architecture (interNCA): or how distributed computing platforms will change systems development." Information systems journal 8: 241-253.

Nosek, J. (1998). "The case for collaborative programming." Communications of the ACM 41(3): 105-108.

Patton, M. (1990). How to use qualitative methods in evaluation. Newbury Park, Sage Publications.

Pescatore, P. (2004). "Mobile consumer applications will drive data traffic and revenues over next-generation mobile networks, says IDC." from http://www.idc.com/getdoc.jsp?containerId=pr2004_05_17_104704.

Sá, J. (2002). "Diary writing: An Interpretative research method of teaching and learning." Educational research and evaluation 8(2): 149-168.

Steinberg, D. and D. Palmer (2004). Extreme Software Engineering, Pearson Education.

Vihinen, J. and V. Tuunainen (2004). "Identifying the limitations and capabilities of m-commerce services in gsm networks." International journal of mobile communications 2(4): 329-324.

Aarnio, A. (2002). Adoption and use of mobile services: Empirical evidence from a Finnish survey. 35th Hawaii International Conference on Systems Sciences, Hawaii.

Implementation of Server on Grid System: A Super Computer Approach

Md. Ahsan Arefin, Md. Shiblee Sadik

Department of Computer Science and Engineering, Bangladesh University of Engineering and Technology (BUET), Dhaka - 1000, Bangladesh.
ahsan_arefin@yahoo.co.uk, mssadik73@gmail.com

1 Introduction

The idea of metacomputing is very promising as it enables the use of a network of many independent computers as if they were one large parallel machine, or virtual supercomputer for solving large-scale problems in science, engineering, and commerce [2][6]. With the exponential growth of global computer ownership, local networks and Internet connectivity, this concept has been taken to a global level popularly called as grid computing. This, coupled with the fact that desktop PCs (personal computers) in corporate and home environments are heavily underutilized – typically only one-tenth of processing power is used – has given rise to interest in harnessing these underutilized resources (e.g., CPU cycles) of desktop PCs connected over the Internet [7][9]. This new paradigm has been dubbed as Internet computing, which is also called by several different names including enterprise/desktop grid computing, peer-to-peer (P2P) computing, and public distributed computing. There is rapidly emerging interest in grid computing from commercial enterprises. A Microsoft Windows based grid computing infrastructure will play a critical role in the industry-wide adoption of grids due to the large-scale deployment of Windows within enterprises. This enables the harnessing of the unused computational power of desktop PCs and workstations to create a virtual supercomputing resource at a fraction of the cost of traditional supercomputers.

One important application of Grid Technology can be the implementation of a Server that processes the requests of multiple Clients and perform different database applications. Normally this type of Server running on a single PC takes large execution time and caused unwanted delay to the customers (Clients). But a super computer or any other multiprocessor computers can solve this problem. Typically super computers or the multi-processor computers are not available to all and also costly. But the flavor of super computer can be achieved easily through the Grid Technology by using the underutilized resources of the available computers in the world Internet. However, there is a distinct lack of service-oriented architecture-based grid computing software in this space. To overcome this limitation, we used a Windows-based grid computing framework called "Alchemi", implemented on the Microsoft .NET Platform. [9]

2 System Architecture

The System is implemented considering the demand of faster response and processing time of the Clients or Customers for any data Query. It can be shown using the following layered architecture in the Figure 1:

A Client, who wants some data of interest, performs a database Query sending a request to the Server Application. Server handles the Query and responses the Client as early as possible by performing all the queries of the connected Clients on different executors on the Grid System. This will reduce the response time and increase throughput for the individual customer and make him happy to reuse the Server for further queries and increase its popularity.

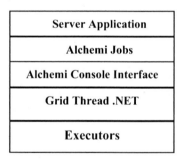

Fig. 1. Layered Architecture of Server on Grid System

2.1 Components of the System

Different types of nodes (or hosts) take part in desktop grid construction and application execution (see Figure: 2 below). Deploying a Manager node and deploying one or more Executor nodes configured to connect to the Manager construct an Alchemi desktop grid. One or more Clients can execute their applications on the cluster by connecting to the Manager through the Server. The operation of the Manager, Executor, Server, Client and Database nodes is described below.

Manager

The Manager provides services associated with managing execution of grid applications and their constituent threads. Executors register themselves with the Manager, which in turn monitors their status [6][9]. Threads received from the Server are placed in a pool and scheduled to be executed on the various available Executors. The Executors return completed threads to the Manager, which are subsequently collected by the respective Client. The Manager employs a role-based security model for authentication and authorization of secure activities. A list of permissions representing activities that need to be secured is maintained within the Manager. A list of groups (roles) is also maintained, each containing a set of permissions.

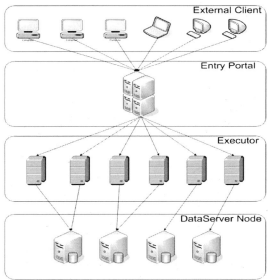

Fig. 2. Distributed Components and their Relations (Entry Portal = Manager + Server)

Executor

The Executor accepts threads from the Manager and executes them. An Executor can be configured to be dedicated, meaning the resource is centrally managed by the Manager, or non-dedicated, meaning that the resource is managed on a volunteer basis via a screen saver or explicitly by the user. In our application we used Dedicated Executors on each node. This provides two-way communication possible and exposes an interface so that the Manager may communicate with it directly. In this case, the Manager explicitly instructs the Executor to execute threads, resulting in centralized management of the resource where the Executor resides.

Server

The Server is a user written program that uses an API provided by the Alchemi developers. We used C# for our research application. The Server receives request from different Clients and performs different Database activities and some processing and calculation with the Data. The server can handle the request from multiple Clients and perform the request of all connected Clients in true parallel sense on different executors through the manager.

Client

Our Client is our User part and can be resided in any PC anywhere. We also implemented the Client using C#. In fact the Client part is totally isolated from the upper three parts, because it is not related to Alchemi rather it can be any Client written using any language whose only purpose is to connect to the Server and to send different request to the Server.

Database

The database we used here is a simple NATIONAL ADDRESS DATABASE (NAD). The format of the database is as follows (Table 1):

Table 1. The format of the database

NAD_ID	StreetNo	Street	Accuracy	DataUpID	Latitude	Longitude	StrCode
Province	PROV_ID	Town	TOWN_ID	TownCentY	TownCentX		Suburb
SUB_ID	SuburbCentY	SuburbCentX		StreetAvgY	StreetAvgX		StreetID
StreetName	StreetType						

The database contains about 2550000 Data. We placed the database on two (Better if more number of separate storage is used) different computers with high processing speed. Each storage conations different part of the database and responses to different queries. The Server decides which storage to use for executing the request from the Clients.

Database design is one of the trickiest parts of our System. The performance and speed of the Sever increase, if each executor uses different data storage nodes. This can happen in two ways:

- Using a replication of Database on different executor nodes.
- Another option is to use different part of the database on different executors. There parts should be independent and so are the queries.

2.2 Security of the System

Security plays a key role in an insecure environment such as the Internet. Two aspects of security addressed by Alchemi are: (a) allow users to perform authorized operations whether they are system related or resource related operations and (b) allow authorized or non-authorized users to contribute resources [4]. The problem of allowing users to only perform activities they are authorized to do is addressed using the role-based authorization model.

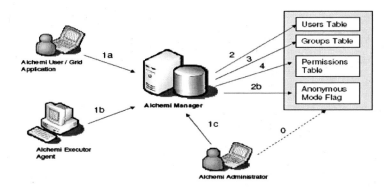

Fig. 3. Role Based Security System

Three roles are defined: User, Executors, and Administrators. We have used User role for our application

3 Implementation and Design

Let us make some review to get deeper feelings of the system. A large Database accessing and computation use large amount of CPU cycles, so now our approach is to build a powerful CPU with some idle Personal computers' CPU which are most of the time remain unused. Most of the times large numbers of Clients are connected to such a server, which access large amount of data and make same type of computation or little different type of computations those are mutually exclusive. We called this computation a job. These jobs are handled here parallely on this Grid Environment. The necessary Job model and the Thread model are described next with the sample codes.

3.1 Grid Thread Model

Minimizing the entry barrier to writing applications for a grid environment is one of Alchemi's key goals. This goal is served by an object-oriented programming environment via the Alchemi .NET API which can be used to write grid applications in any .NET-supported language.

```
public override void Start()
{
        try
        {
                m_startDateTime = DateTime.Now;
                SqlConnection thisConnection;
                SqlCommand thisCommand;
                SqlDataReader thisReader;
                thisConnection = QueryAnalyzer();
// QueryAnalyzer method creates the connection to the Appropriate Database
// for the Query
                thisConnection.Open();
                conn.Open();
                thisCommand = conn.CreateCommand();
                Console.WriteLine("Success");
                thisCommand.CommandText = m_strQuery;
                thisReader= thisCommand.ExecuteReader();
                while (thisReader.Read())
                {
                        this.m_inumber_of_row++;
                }
                Console.WriteLine("Thread {0} gets Row{1}",
                this.m_iThreadNo,this.m_inumber_of_row);
                thisReader.Close();
                thisConnection.Close();
                conn.Close();
        }
        catch (SqlException e)
        {
                Console.WriteLine(e.Message);
        }
}
```

Fig. 4. Code for Start Method (Remote Code)

"Remote code": code to be executed remotely i.e. on the grid (a grid thread and its dependencies), that is performing SQL query remotely on different Executors. And

"Local code": code to be executed locally (code responsible for creating and executing grid threads). This code is implemented here on the Server that is responsible for creating Grid Threads.

A concrete grid thread is implemented by writing a class that derives from GThread, overriding the void Start() method, and marking the Serializable class with the Serializable attribute. Code to be executed remotely is defined in the implementation of the overridden void Start() method. The sample code for this in the Figure 4:

The application itself (local code) creates instances of the custom grid thread, executes them on the grid and consumes each thread's results. It makes use of an instance of the GApplication class, which represents a grid application. The code is shown in Figure 5.

```
public void OnDataReceived(IAsyncResult asyn)
{
        SocketPacket socketData = (SocketPacket)asyn.AsyncState;
        try
        {
                int iRx = socketData.m_currentSocket.EndReceive (asyn);
                char[] chars = new char[iRx + 1];
                System.Text.Decoder d = Sys-
                tem.Text.Encoding.UTF8.GetDecoder();
                int charLen = d.GetChars(socketData.dataBuffer,0, iRx, chars,0);
                System.String szData = new System.String(chars);
                string msg = "" + socketData.m_clientNumber + ".";
                AppendToRichEditControl(msg + szData);
                string replyMsg = "Server Reply:" + szData.ToUpper();
                byte[] byData = System.Text.Encoding.ASCII.GetBytes(replyMsg);
                Socket workerSocket = (Socket)socketData.m_currentSocket;
                workerSocket.Send(byData);
                m_richTextBoxOut.Text += "Thread No " + m_iThreadCount+ "is
                addedn";
                m_appGrid.StartThread(newAlchemiThread(szData,m_iThreadCount
                ++));
                WaitForData(socketData.m_currentSocket, socket-
                Data.m_clientNumber);
        }
        catch (ObjectDisposedException)
        {
                System.Diagnostics.Debugger.Log(0,"1","\nOnDataReceived:Socket
                has been closed\n");
        }
        catch(SocketException se)
        {
                //Error message
        }
}
```

Fig. 5. Code for Creating Thread and Application (Local Code)

Instances of the GThread-derived class are asynchronously executed on the grid by adding them to the grid application. Upon completion of each thread, a 'thread finish' event is fired and a method subscribing to this event can consume the thread's results. Other events such as 'application finish' and 'thread failed' can also be subscribed to. This is shown in the Figure: 6.

3.2 Grid Job Model

Traditional grid implementations have offered a high-level, abstraction of the "virtual machine", where the smallest unit of parallel execution is a process.

```
private void initializaApplication()
{
    try
    {
        this.m_appGrid = new GApplication();
        GConnection connection = new
                GConnection("192.168.1.132",8888,"user","user");
        m_startTime = DateTime.Now;
        m_appGrid.Connection = connection;
        m_appGrid.Manifest.Add(new ModuleDepend-
        ency(typeof(AlchemiThread).Module));
        m_appGrid.ThreadFinish += new GThreadFinish(App_ThreadFinish);
        m_appGrid.ApplicationFinish += new GApplicationFin-
        ish(App_ApplicationFinish);
    }
    catch(Exception se)
    {
        MessageBox.Show(se.Message);
    }
}
private void App_ThreadFinish(GThread thread)
{
    AlchemiThread pnc = (AlchemiThread)thread;
    m_richTextBoxOut.Text += "\n"+"Total "+ pnc.m_iThreadNo +" Thread time
    ::"+(DateTime.Now - pnc.getStartTime());
}
private void App_ApplicationFinish()
{
    m_iThreadCount = 0;
    initializaApplication();
}
```

Fig. 6. Code for Finishing Thread and Application

By specifying a command, input files and output files. In Alchemi, such a work unit is termed 'job' with many jobs constituting a 'task'.

```
<task>
<manifest>
        <embedded_file name="Server.exe" location=" Server.exe" />
</manifest>
<job id="0">
        <input>
                < SQL_QUERY =" Select * from NAD where
        PROVINCE='GAUTENG' " />
        </input>
        <work run_command=" Server.exe SQL_QUERY > result1.txt" />
        <output>
                <embedded_file name="result1.txt"/>
        </output>
</job>
</task>
```

Fig. 7. Sample XML-Based Task Representation

Tasks and their constituent jobs are represented as XML files conforming to the Alchemi task and job schemas. Figure 7 shows a sample task representation that contains one job to execute the program against two input files

Before submitting the task to the Manager, references to the 'embedded' files are resolved and the files themselves are embedded into the task XML file as Base64-encoded text data. When finished jobs are retrieved from the Manager, the Base64-encoded contents of the 'embedded' files are decoded and written to disk.

It should be noted that tasks and jobs are represented internally as grid applications and grid threads respectively.

3.3 Complete Sequence Diagram

This scheduler is called GridApplication and these threads are called Grid Threads. The sequence diagram of the total system is some thing like in the Figure 8:

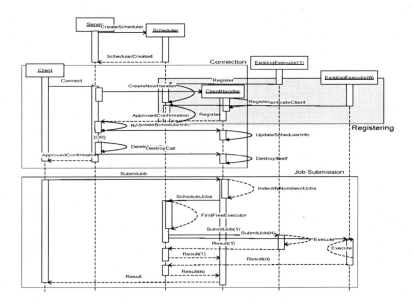

Fig. 8. Sequence Diagram (Connection and Submitting jobs)

This sequence diagram says that how these jobs are executed simultaneously on different PCs. That is any client can submit multiple jobs at a time, and the client handler will identify the No of Jobs and pass these jobs to the scheduler, and the scheduler will schedule them on different PCs. In the case of large Database access, individual executor will access the large database and compute the desired value, and the result will send back the result to the scheduler and the scheduler will send it to the ClientHandler.

4 Results and Performance

The experimental result shows a great wonder to us. We used Two PCs as Data storage nodes and compared the performance by changing the number of Executors and number of different Clients' requests. The result is shown in Table. 2

Table 2. Number of Executors Vs Execution Time

Submitted Jobs to the Server	Number of Executors	Cumulative CPU GHz	Time Min:Sec
10	1	1.694	5:14
10	2	3.189	2:28
10·	3	4.692	2:20
10	4	6.368	2:07

Here the Execution time is represented in the format of Min: Sec. The Graphical plot of Table 1 (Figure 9) shows the linear improvement of the Server's Execution time with the number of Executors.

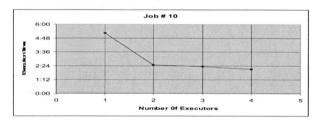

Fig. 9. Number of Executors Vs Execution Time

From this graph, we see that the performance increases much when 1 executor is replaced by the two, but the performance doesn't show a great improvement after that. This is because; we used two data storages in our experiment and each data storage can serve sequentially to the requests even though the requests are submitted to the DataServer parallely.

So the performance for three or higher executors will similarly improve much compared to the previous one if the data storage nodes can be increased with the increase of the executors

Our another experiments can prove this, shown in table: 3. Here the relation is being established between the number of Jobs and the Execution time and comparison is performed between one executor situation Vs two executors situation (see Figure 10). This really means a sense and we get the similar behavior as above if the number of executor is increased with the increases of data storage.

Table 3. Comparison for Different Number of Jobs

Submitted Jobs to the Server	Number of Executors	Cumulative CPU GHz	Time Min: Sec (Sec)
10	1	1.694	5:14 (314)
10	2	3.189	2:28 (148)
20	1	1.694	10:05 (605)
20	2	3.189	5:04 (304)
50	1	1.694	23:50 (1430)
50	2	3.189	9:45 (585)

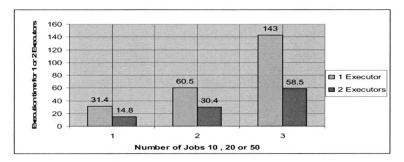

Fig. 10. Comparison for Different Number of Jobs

This can be represented mathematically as follows:
Let,

No of PC = n (all are same powerful)
No of Jobs assigned = x
And time for each job required = t
And the total time is = T
And scheduling time and networking overhead = t_s

Now, if only one CPU is available then the total time, $T = x*t$;

The network overhead can be neglected as today's fiber optics provides high speed and also neglecting the scheduling time, we can calculate as follows:
But, if n PCs are available then

$$\text{If } (n > x) \; T = t + t_s, \text{ if } (t_s \ll t) \text{ then } T \approx t$$

$$\text{If } (n < x) \; T = (x/n)*t + t_s \text{ if } (t_s \ll t) \text{ then } T \approx (x/n)*t$$

Thus by increasing the number of executors with the intelligent design of database, the execution time of a Server can reduce linearly that is proportion to the number of executors connected in the Grid System.

5 Conclusion

Our Server is just an application of Grid technology that can make our life very much easy. Though we have worked with only a small server version, our latent intension is to show that this technology can be widely used to implement any complex type of server even with low overhead.

References

1. D.H. Bailey, J. Borwein, P.B. Borwein, S. Plouffe, "The quest for Pi, Math. Intelligencer", pp. 50-57, 1997.
2. Ian Foster and Carl Kesselman, "Globus: A Metacomputing Infrastructure Toolkit", International Journal of Supercomputer Applications, 11(2): 115-128, 1997.
3. Peter Cappello, Bernd Christiansen, Mihai F. Ionescu, Michael O. Neary, Klaus E. Schauser, and Daniel Wu,Javelin "Internet-Based Parallel Computing Using Java", Proceedings of the 1997 ACM Workshop on Java for Science and Engineering Computation, June, 1997.
4. Yair Amir, Baruch Awerbuch, and Ryan S. Borgstrom, "The Java Market: Transforming the Internet into a Metacomputer", Technical Report CNDS-98-1, Johns Hopkins University, 1998.
5. Ian Foster and Carl Kesselman, "The Grid: Blueprint for a Future Computing Infrastructure", Mogan Kaufmann Publishers, USA, 1999.
6. Ian Foster, Carl Kesselman, and S. Tuecke, "The Anatomy of the Grid: Enabling Scalable Virtual Organizations", International Journal of Supercomputer Applications, 15(3), Sage Publications, USA, 2001.
7. Yufei Wang, Linlin Ge, Chris Rizos, Ravindra Babu, "Spatial Data Sharing On Grid", 2003.
8. Zaslavsky, I., Memon, A., Petropoulos, M., & Baru, C., "Online Querying of Heterogeneous Distributed Spatial Data on a Grid", 2003.
9. Akshay Luther, Rajkumar Buyya, Rajiv Ranjan, and Srikumar Venugopal, "Peer-to-Peer Grid Computing and a .NET-based Alchemi Framework", Conference on High Performance Computing: Paradigm and Infrastructure, Laurence Yang and Minyi Guo (eds), pg. 403-429 (Chapter 21), New Jersey, USA, June 2005.

Customizing Groupware for Different Collaborative Needs

Igor Hawryszkiewycz

Department of Information systems, University of Technology, Sydney, igorh@it.uts.edu.au

Abstract: Collaboration in organization now takes place in a large variety of cultural environments that have different purposes. Purposes can include relationship management, task management, team coordination or process management. Cultures can vary from highly structured process oriented organizations to mission oriented teams in result oriented organizations. This paper provides a framework for defining such environments and choosing strategies to satisfy needs. Such strategies can range from lightweight approaches to monitored processes. It then suggests that groupware systems should be able to adapt to different environments by providing collaborative services for that environment and describes the features needed to do so.

Keywords: Collaboration, Knowledge Sharing, Groupware

1 Introduction

There are many suggestions and examples as that in (Hansen, Nohria, Tierney, 1999) for consulting organizations where collaboration improves business processes. Such improvement is especially evident where people are required to deal with increasingly complex and knowledge intensive (Grant, 1996) situations that require a quick response. In all such cases there is a need to quickly gather information and bring together people who use their knowledge to assess the situation and propose responses. The general consensus is that organizations must become agile and quickly respond to such situations in creative and innovative ways. Agility and innovation in turn require ways to support people within the organization to collaborate and use their collective knowledge to quickly provide innovative solutions.

Design of collaborative business processes must go beyond the technical flows and functions but must consider wider issues especially fitting in with culture and less defined purpose. These factors are shown in Figure 3 and include culture, especially fostering teamwork, a clear definition of goal and process, as well as providing an infrastructure to simplify collaboration. The design thus becomes multi-dimensional but emphasizes collaboration between people, which is essential to create the new knowledge needed to respond to emerging situations.

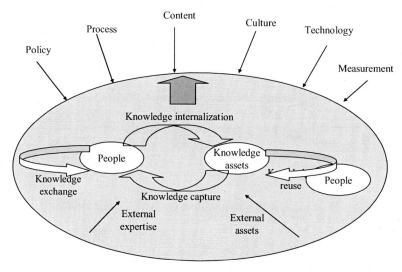

Fig. 1. Driving factors for Innovative organizations

The paper develops a design approach that enables organizations to assess the collaborative needs and ways to realize them. Collaborative technologies are important in such improvement as they support teamwork an essential component of managing any situation. This paper concentrates on collaborative technologies as they support teamwork and the exchange of knowledge and ways to integrate technologies with other driving factors shown in Figure 3. Our design approach emphasizes collaborative technology but considers the way it must be combined with the other factors shown in Figure 1. As one example are policy strategies that distinguish between personalized or codified (Hansen, Nohria, Tierney, 1999) use of information. The difference is that the former emphasizes the sharing of knowledge through personal exchanges whereas the latter sees knowledge more in codified form taking into account the work process.

2 Identifying the Issues

Design of collaborative systems is not a precise science as it is dependent on many qualitative factors including organizational culture, community practices and structure and the purpose of the collaboration. The design method must first identify and classify these factors before suggesting ways to provide technology support. The design dimensions are illustrated in Figure 2.

The major dimensions are:

Community size that ranges from open communities, small groups, through to interorganizational coordination,

The scope of the project, which may range from internal work, replying to a client request or managing an organization.

The purpose, which can range from maintaining relationships, task management, team coordination or process management,

The culture, which has been described by Hofstede (1980) who describes culture in terms of parameters such as power distance, dealing with uncertainty or individual rather collectivism,

Work practices particularly differentiating between different group structures, again distinguishing between structured, mission oriented or random groups.

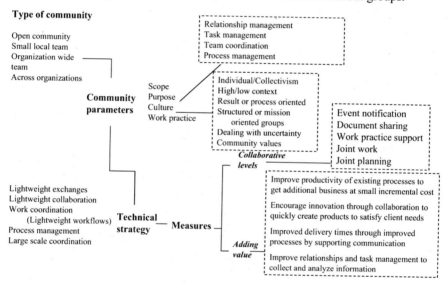

Fig. 2. The Design Dimensions

3 Defining the Technical Strategies

The strategies range from loose lightweight ones to highly structured. Lightweight in this case means little control exercised outside the people involved in the process.

Lightweight exchange primarily concerns exchange of messages between loosely connected individuals. It usually supports an environment where people stay in touch and share their responsibility but have no particular goal to achieve some outcome.

Lightweight coordination now includes the need to proceed to some outcome, although the outcome is decided as the process proceeds. Hence we now require ways to set up tasks, and assign responsibilities for them.

Work Coordination where the goal is more specific and usually requires the setting up of a plan and monitoring progress. The plan can be easily changed although the goal is usually remains the same.

Process management, where goals are now precisely defined and processes strictly followed.

The idea of lightweight exchange and collaboration was introduced by Whittaker (1999) to illustrate the kinds of technologies needed to establish and maintain productive relationships. Lightweight collaboration goes further where the exchange has some expected result as for example in (Anderson, and others, 2003) where a flexible workflow was developed for review processes in digital libraries. Lightweight in this sense means low entry barrier, flexible and web-based.

4 Choosing the Strategy

Design must to some extent satisfy the dimensions shown in Figure 2. This involves choosing the strategy, choosing the technologies to support the strategy, and providing the technologies to users through suitable interfaces. Furthermore design should be scalable and provide for evolution as often systems start with lightweight exchange but proceed to higher collaborative forms.

4.1 Relationship of Technical Strategy to Design Dimensions

Figures 3 and 4 illustrate a design decision framework. Figure 3 illustrates the relationship between the design dimensions and strategy. It shows that the choice is very subjective as it is not really possible to give a precise choice. It requires user analysis (Zhang, 2002) to determine the subjective features and then make an initial choice. As an example small groups working primarily as individuals in a large context where results are defined in general terms would probably select lightweight exchange. As the emphasis changes towards better defined results requiring collective input lightweight collaboration may be introduced. What is important is to provide technologies in ways that can support later strategic change.

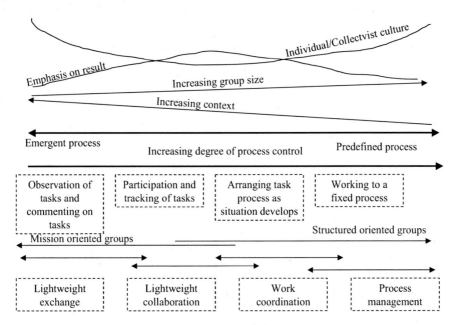

Fig. 3. Strategies and Environment

Figure 3 shows the gradual introduction of technologies that provide better ways of tracking the work.

4.2 Choosing Technologies

However adoption of collaborative technologies has not been wide and usually proceeded in an ad-hoc manner usually based on e-mail. At the same time there are few reports of effective use of leading technologies such as workspaces in business practices. Such failures often result from over reliance on technology as the major driver while ignoring its relationship to other driving factors. Most advanced technologies are used in emergency systems and in the military where technology is strongly integrated with process and peoples roles and responsibilities. Most business practices primarily using current practices such as e-mail, por-portals or in some cases discussion systems and rely on individuals to adopt technologies to suit their personal preferences.

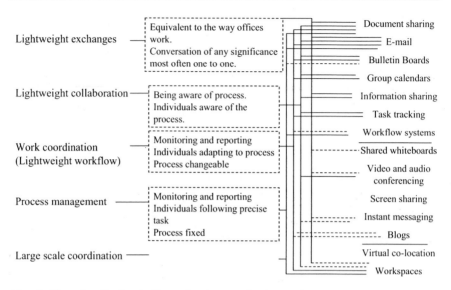

Fig. 4. Choosing Technologies to implement the Strategies

5 Measures

Measures are here divided into performance measures that can be readily measured and the less quantifiable outcome measures.

5.1 Measures of Collaboration

The collaboration levels used in this paper are shown in Table 1. These levels provide a way to gradually increase levels of sophistication as the interaction between people increases with each level. Table 1 describes each level and its characteristic, the technology needed as well as the knowledge needed to realize the level. The levels are:

- Event notification, where roles are informed of any changes that effect the roles.
- Document sharing, where documents are distributed between responsible roles,
- Work process support, which often defines monitoring levels of activity and sending reminders to collaborators,
- Joint work, where users work together in a synchronous manner, and
- Joint goal setting, where people jointly decide how they will work together.

    Usually collaboration starts with awareness, which simply concerns notifying people of changes that can impact on their work. Then document sharing is added to ensure that people are provided with information needed to carry out their responsibilities. Subsequent levels are more complex as they require more intense interaction to coordinate activities. Work process support, requires a precise definition of the way a collaborative process takes place. It includes the definition of responsibilities of identified roles. For example the process may define a way to develop a response to a customer request. The specific rules may define the expertise needed to define a solution, the risk assessment, budgetary evaluation, legal aspects and so on. The structure of documents may also be specifically defined. This process is clearly understood and followed. Joint work goes further in that many of the activities may be carried out synchronously thus reducing completion time. Joint goal setting is where involved units together plan and agree on their work processes. This level often requires support for asynchronous work as goal setting often includes resolving many imprecisely defined alternatives.

Table 1. Levels of Collaboration

Level	Characteristics of collaboration levels	Technologies needed	Knowledge requirements
Collaboration level 1 Awareness	Informing people about events related to their roles. Presenting the functional situation globally.	e-mail alerts. SMS messages. Visual displays. Information portals.	People responsibilities in the organization and their expertise and availability to direct alerts.
Collaboration level 2 Document Sharing	Sharing explicit information. Presenting to roles responsible for functional units.	e-mail, web portals	Information requirements of different roles.
Collaboration level 3 Work process support	Explicit definition of work activities and responsibilities. Definition of relationships between tasks. Group meeting.	e-mail Coordination and Workflow tools, Blogs, Video displays, Calendar systems.	Optimum team structures for identified situations. Location of experts. Ways to assign responsibilities.
Collaboration level 4 Joint work	Jointly create and develop artifacts.	Shared whiteboards. Workspaces.	Responsibilities of business units.
Collaboration level 5 Joint goal setting	Developing shared plans. Devise coordination strategies between functional units.	Synchronous video communication.	Organizational strategy and mission.

The choice depends on the where the best benefits are identified. For example collaboration is essential in supply chains. The goals here depend on the situation. Rodin (2006) for example emphasizes the need to maintain awareness between organizations in a supply chain to reduce delivery times in situations where customers change their requirements. This requires collaboration capability 1 across all steps of the chain to ensure that all steps are notified if there are unanticipated delays in one step. They can then take their own corrective actions. Alternately in more critical situation collaboration capability 2 may be needed to help users to quickly adjust activities across the entire supply chain.

6 Groupware support

Figure 4 provides the guidelines for the design of workspace systems. What one is looking for is ways to start with lightweight exchanges and gradually change the strategy. Figure 5 shows such evolution. It uses our LiveNet system to evolve collaboration to illustrate the development of interfaces to respond to a new competitor.

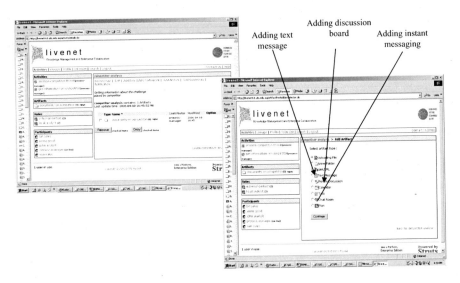

Fig. 5. Setting up lightweight exchanges

The first workspace in Figure 5 shows an initial folder containing information on the competitor. The second shows services that can be chosen to support lightweight exchange. It shows for example a chatroom that supports instant messaging as well as the ability post text messages and discussion boards.

Figure 6 illustrates progression to lightweight collaboration. The first workspace shows the workspace created for lightweight exchange using the services selected in Figure 5. The second interface shows the services that can be added to support collaboration.

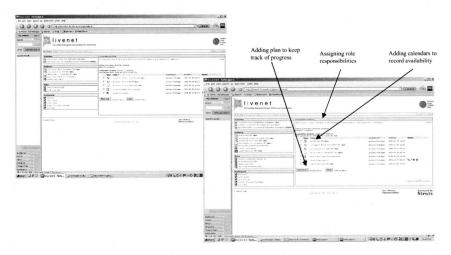

Adding plan to keep
track of progress

Assigning role
responsibilities

Adding calendars to
record availability

Fig. 6. Going on to lightweight collaboration

7 Summary

This paper developed a framework for choosing technical strategies to support collaborative work. It identified a number of strategies ranging from lightweight exchange to process management and the tools needed to support them. It also provided guidelines for choosing a strategy depending on organizational and cultural factors.

References

Anderson, K.M., Anderson, A., Wadhwani, w., Bartolo, L. (2003): "Metis: A lightweight, Flexible, and Web-based Workflow Services for Digital Libraries" Proceedings 3rd. ACM/IEEE conference on digital libraries, May 2003, pp. 98-109.

Cummings, J.N., Butler, B. and Kraut, R. (2002): "The Quality of OnLine Social Relationships" Communications of the ACM, Vol. 45, No. 1, July, 2002, pp. 103-111.

Grant, R.M. (1996): "Prospering in Dynamically-competitive Environments: Organizational Capability as Knowledge Integration" Organization Science, Vol. 7, No. 4, July, 1996, pp. 375-387.

Hansen, M.T., Nohria, N. and Tierney, T. (1999): "Whats your Strategy for Managing Knowledge" Harvard Business Review, March-April, 1999, pp. 106-116.

Hawryszkiewycz, I.T. (1996): "Support Services For Business Networking", in Proceedings IFIP96, Canberra, eds. E. Altman and N. Terashima, Chapman and Hall, London, ISBN 0-412-75560-2.

Hawryszkiewycz, I.T. (1997): "A Framework for Strategic Planning for Communications Support" Proceedings of The inaugural Conference of Informatics in Multinational Enterprises, Washington, October, 1997, pp. 141-151.

Hofstede, G. (1980): Culture's Consequences: "International Differences in Work-related values" Sage, Beverly Hills, California.

Rob Rodin Optimize Magazine http://www.optimizemag.com/issue/002/roi.htm (last accessed Jan 3, 2006).

Whittaker, S., Swanson, J., Kucan, J. and Sidner, C. (1999): "Telenotes: Managing lightweight interactions in the desktop".

Zhang, J., Patel, V., Johnson, K., Smith, J. (2002): "Designing Human Centered Distributed Information Systems", IEEE Intelligent Systems, September/ October, 2002, pp. 42-47.

Proposal for a System Based on the Universal Design Approach for Providing Tourism Information by Linking RFID and GIS

Akihiro Abe[*], Nobuyuki Maita[*], Yasunori Ooshida[**], Toru Kano[***]

[*] Faculty of Software & Information Science, Iwate Prefectural Universtity, Japan
[**] Morioka Support Plaza for Handicapped People, Japan
[***] Faculty of Social Welfare, Iwate Prefectural University, Japan

Abstract: In recent years, tourist regions have placed greater stress on the concept of Universal Design (UD), which takes into account the needs of a more diverse range of people, including senior citizens, the disabled, and foreign visitors. We have been conducting research and development on a system, based on the UD concept, for providing tourism information suited to various user characteristics. The system is designed for Hiraizumi, a tourist area which is aiming to register its historical cultural assets on the World Heritage List in 2008. This paper analyzes needs relating to Universal Design of tourist information, and describes system design and prototype development/evaluation efforts based on that analysis. Satisfactory results were obtained regarding the validity and implementation potential of our approach.

1 Introduction

In recent years, tourist regions have placed greater stress on the concept of Universal Design (UD), which takes into account the needs of a more diverse range of people, including senior citizens, the disabled, and foreign visitors [1]. As a concept which is broader than barrier-free design, UD aims to "design products, buildings and spaces so they can be used, as far as possible, by all people, regardless of age, sex or disability etc." The Hiraizumi region of Iwate Prefecture, Japan, is aiming to register its historical cultural assets (primarily Chusonji) on the World Heritage List in 2008 [2], but some have pointed out the issue of coping with the expected growth in the number of tourists after registration. There are limits on UD and guidance improvement of facilities and signs, and, media such as mobile phones are attracting attention as a means of overcoming this problem.

Research on information support for the mobility impaired covers a wide range -- from development of basic technologies to applications in the community -- and includes support for the visually impaired within train station premises [3], and searching for movement routes using barrier-free maps [4]. In Japan, community interest has grown in recent years due to the Project for Promoting Independent Movement of the Ministry of Land [5], Infrastructure and Transport, and this project is positioned as one of the key components of the u-Japan policy [6]. Based on these previous studies, we are taking Hiraizumi as an example, and focusing on more practical, empirical research into information-related UD which takes into account the need to shift to regional information. This should be useful for verifying the regional benefits and problems of an ubiquitous network deployed in a top-down fashion as national information policy.

In this research, R&D efforts focused on a system which combines RFID (Radio Frequency IDentification)[1] with a GIS (Geographical Information System). This system allows information needed in a tourist region to be provided in accordance with UD principles to various users via mobile phone. First, Section 2 analyzes the need for UD in providing information for tourist regions. Section 3 gives the basic design of the system based on results obtained from the analysis in Section 2. Section 4 describes prototype development and evaluation.

2 Analysis of the need for UD in providing information

In order to analyze tourist needs for information, we held two workshops to consider UD in tourist regions, and administered questionnaire surveys. The 33 subjects included able-bodied persons, as well as senior citizens, disabled persons and foreign nationals. The questionnaire asked about individual attributes such as respondent age and status (disabled or not), information needs and methods of providing information.

2.1 Needed information content

On the whole, there is a significant need for guidance information at historical sites, and relatively little need for souvenir and restaurant information.

Compared to able-bodied persons, the physically disabled have special needs for toilet information. This is because wheelchair users and persons with an ostomate require information describing the location of compatible toilets, width of each toilet entrance, and the area inside the toilet.

---

[1] RFID is used as a term referring to wireless tags and IC tags, and for convenience we use the term ID to refer to their identification codes. The term RFID system is used to refer to a system including RFIDs together with the read/write equipment needed for to read from or write to RFIDs.

The visually impaired responded that they need almost all kinds of information. This is because they cannot rely at all on vision, and the amount of information they can obtain from the environment is quite small compared to other people. Persons whose native language is Chinese pointed out that, in addition to linguistic factors, there are differences in ease of understanding due to differences in culture. More specifically, they find it difficult to understand years indicated by Japanese era titles like "Taisho" and "Showa". One way of addressing this problem is convert to years in the standard Western calendar, or to indicate years in a fashion suited each person's culture.

None of the subjects of the questionnaire were children, but in workshop discussions it was pointed out that there is little content for children to enjoy. Difficult to understand pamphlets and guide signs alone are not sufficient. It would be desirable to have materials incorporating pictographic symbols, Japanese descriptions with *furigana* (Japanese syllabary) added to the *kanji* (Chinese characters), and easier-to-understand text.

2.2 Methods of providing information

Some subjects were of the opinion that fixed kiosk terminals with a touch panel are easy to use, but on the whole, people favored the idea of acquiring information by mobile phone. The following are 3 important points which were expressed regarding information acquisition:

- Historic tourism involves enjoying the atmosphere of the tourist region. Immoderately placing guide signs everywhere because there is insufficient availability of information will ruin the scenery. Subjects also expressed a strong desire to preserve the scenery of the temple. Providing information using RFID makes this possible.
- Demand is high for terminals to provide audio and text information, like the guide receivers which are frequently seen at historical sites and tourism spots. When walking through a tourist region with a guide for a group trip, able-bodied persons, wheelchair users and the visually impaired move at different speeds, and thus cannot enjoy tourism at their own pace. If guidance information on historical sites can be easily retrieved using mobile phones (the most widely available terminals), it will help to resolve this problem.
- One potentially effective approach for people with physical limitations is to provide "push-type" information using active RFID which has a built-in battery and can communicate over longer distances. Although many people use mobile phones, most senior citizens find terminal operation complicated. Disabled persons may not be able to physically approach the location where information is being provided. Another possible application is to issue a warning when a visually impaired person approaches a dangerous location.

3 System design

3.1 Design principles

Fig. 1 shows the configuration the system should have, based on the results of need analysis in Section 2. With a built-in battery, reading can be done at a comparatively long distance of up to 10m. This can be achieved by providing active RFID (which is miniaturized to preserve scenery) at key indoor/outdoor tourism spots. This enables a tourist with an RFID mobile terminal to easily search for information suited to his or her own physical and language characteristics. Information needed by tourists includes not only guide information on historical sites, but also UD information on toilets and means of movement etc.In all cases, information should be provided in relation to geographical locations, and managed with the GIS.

A server is needed to link RFID and the GIS, and we decided to call this server ITAG (Integration server of e-Tag Applications and GISs). ITAG must be able to link up with multiple tourism GISs, such as commercial and public services. While ensuring adequate protection of privacy, the system must analyze the tourism behavior of tourists from RFID access logs, and have the ability to gather access logs for use in tourist region development as well.

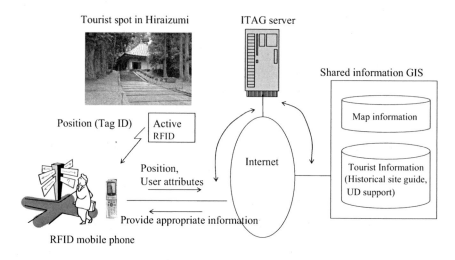

Fig. 1. Overview of system for providing tourism information

3.2 Definition of user requirements using a UD matrix

Based on the results of analyzing needs in Section 2, we define the requirements of a tourist information system based on UD principles. The requirements are organized from two sides -- information content and method of providing information -- using a UD matrix [7] for effectively extracting UD requirements and problems corresponding to the situation of each individual. User groups which bring together hypothetical users by their usage characteristics were established as fol-follows by referring to a standard user classification for a UD matrix.

1. No special consideration necessary
2. Wheelchair
3. Requires consideration of cultural differences
4. Requires consideration of ease of understanding
5. Cannot rely on vision
6. Requires consideration of vision
7. Requires consideration of hearing
8. Internal impairment
9. Consideration of advanced age

In analysis from the information content side, the requirements were organized using a matrix of the information categories required for each guide spot (historical site guide, facility management, transportation, pedestrian movement, toilets, rest areas, escape routes, and events) and the aforementioned user groups. In analysis from the standpoint of providing information, the requirements were organized using a matrix of the individual tasks involved in providing information by mobile phone (Open, Check status, Input, Select menu, Browse content, Close) and the aforementioned user groups (Fig. 2).

User Group / Individual Task	Wheelchairs	Consideration of cultural differences	Consideration of understanding	Cannot rely on vision	
Open	Easy to retrieve, with a strap etc.				
Check status		Can understand status in native language	Status is easy to understand	Can understand status with audio	
Input			Input method is easy to understand	Can perform input operation without relying on vision	

Fig. 2. UD matrix on providing information

3.3 ITAG basic architecture

Flow of server processing. Fig. 3 shows the basic architecture of ITAG. Fig. 4 shows the flow of processing up to obtaining GIS content from a tag ID acquired by the user with an RFID mobile phone. First, the tag ID and terminal-specific ID acquired by the user with the RFID reader of the terminal are sent to the IF module of the ITAG. If the authentication processing module completes authentication of the terminal-specific ID normally, a tag ID is sent to the data access module to specify the appropriate service, and if multiple selections are possible, a request for selection is sent to the user. When the user makes a selection, connection to the GIS server is secured via the data access module, and, as a result, the system searches out and stores information tied to the tag ID. The results of this processing are returned to the user via the IF module.

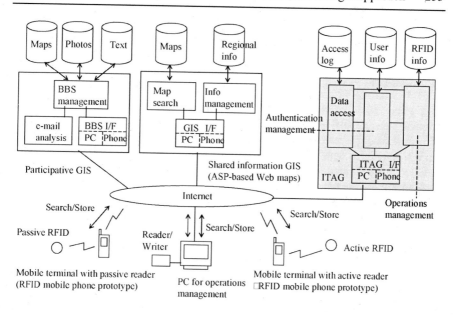

Fig. 3. System architecture

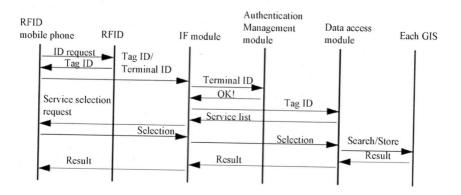

Fig. 4. Overview of processing at ITAG server

Authentication management module. For access from a mobile phone, authentication is performed using a terminal specific ID etc. If authentication processing is performed each time the ITAG server is accessed, users unfamiliar with character input using a mobile phone will be forced to go through extremely inconvenient input operation. Therefore, the system requests password input only for the first access, and then stores a terminal-specific ID for the authenticated user in the user management DB. This makes it unnecessary to perform input operation for the second and subsequent accesses. When an authenticated user is given privileges at a different level, the permitted privileges are stored together with the authenticated terminal-specific ID.

Data access module. The data access module is divided into tag analysis processing and DB processing. In tag analysis processing, processing is performed to properly select the GIS services related to the tag ID read with an RFID reader. GIS services corresponding to each tag ID are stored in the RFID management DB when the RFID is set up. If the services which can be used for each privilege are changed, the judgment of whether or not it is okay to provide information with the currently authenticated privileges is made after the service is determined. When further progress has been made in tag ID system standardization, a GIS server will be specified by accessing a global GIS server, but at the present stage, the aforementioned processing (including tag ID duplication management) must be performed on the ITAG server side.

In DB processing, logs of retrieval of management information to an RFID, or access to the GIS server, are stored in the access log DB. RFID management information is comprised of position information and information on services tied to an RFID. It is likely that the accessed tag ID, time, terminal-specific ID and GIS service are enough information for applications such as maintenance prediction for roadway structure management and analysis of tourism behavior by tourists.

Operations management module. Since a PC is used for operations management, it is necessary to have an operations management interface employing maps. When storing or updating RFID management information, it is necessary to specify the target RFID, but it is difficult for people to grasp the situation with just the numerical value for the RFID or GPS. Therefore, a management interface for the map base is essential as a means for managing the positions where RFIDs are installed.

4 Prototype development

4.1 System environment

First, we will describe the prototype development environment. As a mobile terminal environment employing RFID, we used an RFID reader equipped mobile phone test unit made by KDDI (hereafter called the "RFID mobile phone") (Table 1, Fig. 5,) [8]. RFID read control on the mobile phone side is written in Java. The ITAG was built on a work station of a university research laboratory. The OS is Solaris 9, the database is PostgreSQL and the server program was developed with PHP. As an RFID-linked GIS, we selected a citizen participation type GIS researched and developed by the authors and used for verification research in the context of various community activities [9][10], and a commercial ASP-based web map service.

Table 1. Specifications of RFID mobile phone prototype

Compatible electronic tag specifications	Individual specifications
Electronic tag frequency	315 [MHz]
Electronic tag ID bit length	64 – 128 [bit]
Electronic tag read distance	Approx. 10 [m] max
Operation count and time for electronic tag reading	Approx. 10 hours (Continuous operation time)
External dimensions of tag reader	38 [mm] × 80 [mm] × 10 [mm]
Remark	The tag ID value can be set from the application.

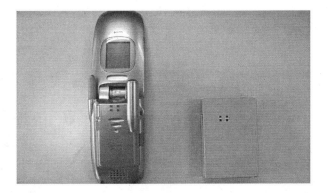

Fig. 5. RFID mobile phone prototype and active RFID

Next, we shall summarize the features of the implemented prototype. The system was designed to set user attributes relating to information acquisition using a Java application on the RFID mobile phone side (at left, Fig. 6). The attributes which can be set include: selection of language used (Japanese, English), wheelchair use, internal impairment and hearing impairment. When a user enters the transmission area of a tourism spot where an active RFID (Fig. 5, right side) is installed, the RFID mobile phone tag is received, and the mobile phone vibrates to alert the user of incoming information. When this happens, the user can select whether or not to acquire the content. If the user wishes to acquire the content, the tag ID indicating position and user attributes is passed to the GIS via the ITAG server. Content is generated on the GIS side by taking these values into account. For example, if the person is a wheelchair user, information on toilets nearest to the receiving spot is delivered to the user with data on the entrance width and a photo of the inside of the toilet (Fig. 6, right side). If the user desires, he or she can also acquire a map.

Fig. 6. Prototype screen

4.2 Field tests

We asked the Iwate Welfare GIS Promotion Study Group members, who include UD specialists and wheelchair users, to evaluate the prototype.

Installing active RFID. Key guide spots within the Chusonji Temple grounds were interspersed along an approximately 1km long approach path called "Tsuki-misaka" (moon viewing hill) surrounded by rows of cedar trees . Active RFIDs were installed on both sides of the approach path, while taking into consideration the tourist traffic lines, so that a communication distance of roughly 10m could be stably secured. Experiments were also conducted at a number of exhibition guide spots within the treasure hall, where the national treasures of Chusonji are exhibited, and we confirmed that it is possible to provide comparatively fine-grained area services by adjusting the strength of transmission from active RFID.

Using the RFID mobile phone. At the receive reader on the mobile phone side, the antenna is installed vertically on the right side of the phone body, and if this part is held down by the user's hand, it will have a significant effect on reception capability. This problem can be solved by, for example, having the user to move through the area with the terminal hanging from the neck by a strap, but this is not very desirable because it places constraints on utilization by the user.

Delay of information acquisition. It would be hard to notify a mobile phone from an active RFID when a visually impaired person mistakenly enters a dangerous area, because there is too long of a delay with the current system in acquiring information from the server. It may be possible to alert users of danger at the time of terminal reception by adding information to the tag ID.

Re-browsing of acquired information. Basically, content is acquired at the actual site, but since some users may wish to later use historical site guide information accessed at the actual site for history study, or for creating memories of their trip, some expressed the opinion that they would like to re-browse information acquired at the actual site after they return home from their trip. Various applications are possible in cases where RFID and dedicated terminals have been used in museums[11]. These services enable a user to later access information quired at the actual site from a PC using a designated login ID for a fixed time after returning home. We would like to incorporate ideas like this at Hiraizumi.

5 Conclusion

In this research, we proposed a system, based on UD principles, which makes it possible to supply tourism the information needed at Hiraizumi, in a form suited to the various characteristics of users. By conducting system design and prototype development/evaluation based on analysis of user needs, we were able to obtain satisfactory results with regard to the validity and feasibility of our approach. Based on these results, we plan to conduct a pilot program in key tourist areas of Hiraizumi in 2006. In this program, we plan to have actual tourists use the system for a fixed period of time, and thereby clarify the system requirements necessary for achieving practical use. At this time, the system will not be limited only to active RFID. We also plan to study approaches like combined use with passive RFID in stamp rallies for children, and intend to conduct a comprehensive verification of effective methods of using RFID in UD approaches to providing tourist information.

References

1. Principles of universal design. http://www.design.ncsu.edu/cud/
2. The cultural heritage of Hiraizumi toward world heritage inscription. http://www.pref.iwate.jp/~hp0907/english/index.html
3. Goto K, Matsubara H, Fukasawa N, Mizukami N (2003) A personalized information system for visually disabled people using mobile terminals in railway station environment. IPSJ Journal, vol 44, no 12, pp 3256-3268 (in Japanese)
4. Eguchi I, Igi S (2005) Geographic information system for pedestrian navigation with areas and routes accessibility. IPSJ Journal, vol 46, no 12, pp 2940-2951 (in Japanese)
5. Committee for promoting project to support moving independently.http://www.jiritsu-project.jp/
6. u-Japan policy. http://www.soumu.go.jp/menu_02/ict/u-japan_en/index.html
7. Yamazaki K, Yamaoka T, Okada A, Nomura A, Yanagida K (2001) Universal design practical guideline, 1st International Conference on Planning and Design, JP009-F01-06
8. KDDI news releases. http://www.kddi.com/english/corporate/news_release/2005/0302/index.html

9. Abe A, Sasaki T (2002) A bulletin board system using geographical location information for local community activities. Proc 2002 International Conference on Information and Management Sciences, pp 31-37
10. Abe A, Sasaki T, Odashima N (2003) GLI-BBS: A groupware based on geographical location information for field workers. Proc 5th International Conference on Enterprise Information Systems, vol 4, pp 3-9
11. His S, Fait H (2005) RFID enhances visitors' museum experience at the exploratorium, Communications of ACM, vol 48, no 9, pp 60-65

Industrial Automated Fingerprint-Based Identification System

Paulius Zubavicius, Antanas Cenys, Lukas Radvilavicius

Abstract: Fingerprints recognition is established technique for police agencies. Most of the companies and public organizations are using password or token such as magnetic or smart card based identity management systems. Security of these systems depends crucially on the proper behavior of the users since passwords and tokens can be easily transferred. Biometric identification has obvious advantages if security of the system is not always in the best interest of the users. Biometrical data of the fingerprint is the best way to identify the person taking into account efficiency, availability, reliability, time-constrains, etc. Technology advances in computing and optical scanners allow create low –cost small size fingerprint-based identification systems.

The paper describes principles of the industrial Automated Fingerprints Identification Systems (AFIS). Available technologies, algorithms, usage limitations are also provided. Implemented and functioning industrial AFIS system to register and analyze company's personnel working schedule is presented.

1 Introduction

Most organizations, companies and persons keep their confidential information in digital files and databases or/and paper files locked in safes. Only identified and authorized users should be able to modify and to have access to this information. Management of ID or more specifically electronic or eID is becoming a very significant part of the most of information systems. Shift from paper files to electronic files and databases resulted in the password based ID management and security systems as a standard. These systems are based on the identification by "what do you know" principle. Introduction of magnetic and smart cards as well as other type of electronic tokens added a possibility to identify person electronically by "what do you have" principle corresponding to traditional lock and key system.

These systems have, however, limitations since they could not guarantee the identification of the person. Both passwords and tokens can be stolen or voluntary transferred to another person. The only way to ensure identification of the person is to use biometric data unique for this person. This is identification by "who you are" principle. Biometrics-based authentication is emerging as an alternative method. It can overcome some of the limitations of the traditional automatic personal identification technologies because of dealing with physiological and/or behavioral characteristics, such as a fingerprint, signature, palmprint, iris, hand, voice or face [1]. This data can be used to authenticate a person's claim to a certain identity or establish a person's identity from a large database. The need for secure transaction processing using biometrics technology will be only growing in the future based on the rapid evolution of electronic commerce and other applications with increased emphasis on security [2].

The most developed and widely used biometric ID management systems are based on fingerprints recognition. Automated fingerprints identification systems (AFIS) can search for particular pattern in the large databases with more that 100 000 fingerprints as "one with many" identification. However, application of AFIS for "one-to-one" verification is faster and more common [3].

Until very recently fingerprint technologies were widely used in military, national security, police and similar institutions. Only now such technologies along with other biometric techniques are starting to be used it civil and commercial sectors. The main reasons for slow adoption in commercial systems were high costs and limited availability. Technology advances in technology and computing have changed the situation radically and nowadays fingerprint technology is becoming affordable even for small industrial ID management systems [3].

In the paper we present an implemented and functioning application of AFIS for registration and analysis of personnel's working schedule. The paper describes principles of the industrial Automated Fingerprints Identification Systems for this specific application, available technologies, algorithms, and usage limitations.

2 Biometric Identification

There are two different ways to resolve a person's identity: verification and identification. Verification is based on confirming or denying a person's claimed identity and answers question "Am I whom I claim I am?". In the case of identification one has to establish a person's identity answering the question "Who am I?". A biometric system is essentially a pattern recognition system allowing compare unique physiological or behavioral characteristic possessed by the user with prerecorded data. As such it can be used in both above approaches to identification [2]. The method how an individual is identified is very important, however, while designing a real world system.

Identification is "one-to-many" process of determining a person's identity by performing matches against multiple biometric templates. There are two types of identification systems: positive identification and negative identification. Positive identification systems are designed to find a match for a user's biometric information in a database of biometric information and answers the "Who am I?" question even though the response is not necessarily a name. It could be an employee's ID number, nickname or any other unique identifier. A prison release program where users do not enter an ID number or use a card would be an example of a typical positive identification system. Users then simply look at an iris capture device and are identified from an inmate database. The negative identification systems also compare one biometric template against many in the database. But, in fact, they are designed to ensure that a person is not present in a database in order to prevent people from enrolling twice in a system. It is often used in large-scale public benefits programs in which users enroll multiple times to gain benefits under different names [2].

The oldest method among all the biometric techniques is fingerprint-based identification which has been successfully used in numerous applications. Everyone has unique, immutable fingerprints which are made of a series of ridges and furrows on the surface. The pattern of ridges and furrows as well as the minutiae points determines the uniqueness of a fingerprint [4]. Minutiae points (Fig. 1) are local ridge characteristics that occur at either a ridge bifurcation or a ridge ending [5].

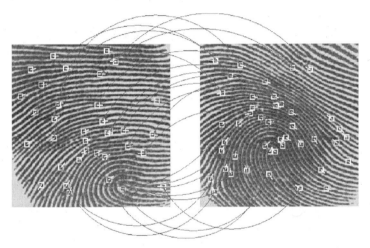

Fig. 1. Minutiae points

Fingerprint technology acquires the fingerprint pattern, but doesn't store the full image. Some particular data about the fingerprint is stored in a much smaller template or minutiae point data, requiring from 250-1000 bytes [6]. In the our particular system approximately 380 bytes of data are stored. The full fingerprint cannot be reconstructed from the fingerprint template and it is not stored after the data is extracted [4].

World-wide used fingerprint technology serves hundreds of thousands of people daily to access networks and PCs, enter restricted areas, and to authorize transactions. The technology is used broadly in a range of applications, primarily PC/Network Access, Physical Security/Time and Attendance, and Civil ID. Most deployments are "one-to-one" verification systems, but there are also a number of "one-to-few" deployments in which individuals are matched against modest databases, typically of 10-100 users. Large-scale "one-to-many" applications in which a user is identified from a large fingerprint database searches on databases of up to millions of fingerprints. Depending on computational power of Automated

Fingerprints Identification Systems (AFIS) these searches can be performed within only a few minutes [2].

3 Fingerprint Identification Based Employee Management System

Most of the companies and public organizations are using password or token such as magnetic or smart card based identity management systems. Security of these systems depends on the proper behavior of the users since passwords and tokens can be easily transferred. Such behavior can be expected only if it is in the own interest of the users to keep usernames, passwords, password cards and password generators safe. For example in internet banking systems users have access data to login and manage bank accounts. In case of loosing it users can have serious troubles or even loss of money.

In case of access control and employees management systems users can have serious incentives to give access data or tools to third party. Automated personnel management system described bellow is recording in/out time of employee. Since employees are obviously interested to have a right time records there is a place for cheating. Most of the automated access control systems use magnetic cards. Serious disadvantage of these systems is the possibility for user or employee to provide his card for another employee to make faked records. Moreover the same identification card can be used by several employees or several cards can be used by same person. There is no simple electronic system to exclude such possibility. This problem can be solved involving human control, however, this significantly increases costs and still one can have problems with human factor. Other tools used in automated identification process such as passwords, electronic tokens, smart cards, RFID tags are also transferable and sometimes can be even duplicated. Biometric and particularly fingerprint identification has obvious advantages.

Features of the different identification methods are summarized bellow in the Table 1:

Table 1. Features of the different identification methods.

Features	Password	Card	Human control	Finger print reader
Cheating possibility	+	+	+	-
Time consuming	+	-	-	-
Salary costs	-	-	+	-
Extra requirements	+	+	-	-
Falsification	-	+	-	-
Duplicate	+	+	-	-

The advantages of the fingerprint based identifications become evident while such identification is applied for work time accounting and control system at organization with more than 100 employees with variable schedule. Control of the work time of employees on a constant schedule is not difficult but often there are people working on a variable schedule including late hours, weekends, which is not easy to control. The magnetic card system is not effective since it does not guarantee person's identification.

We have developed and installed automated fingerprint-based personnel control system. The system works like timecard system and provides access control, work time accounting, fill time-board and etc. The system includes three components (see Fig. 2):

- Enrollment place
- Administrative place
- Data Base Server

The system is developed using Borland Delphi 7 IDE. All components run on separate PC's connected to TCP/IP network. The schematic layout of the components is shown in Fig. 2:

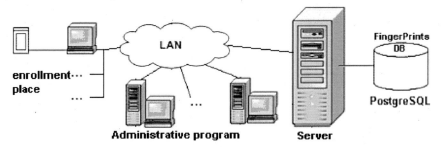

Fig. 2. The structure of the system.

3.1 Data Base Server

Fingerprints meta-data, employee's names, ID and related information is stored in the data base. The data base server is running "Gentoo" Linux OS because it's powerful and fast operating system for servers. PostgreSQL DBMS running in this server is an open source product. Data base is created in already existing DBMS and connected to a particular already running system. DBMS and data base have no identification function.

3.2 Administrative place

Administrative place is used to control the system and generate reports. It can be accessed and run remotely.

The main functions of this component are:

- Possibility to enter and edit employee's data in the database.

- Creation of both variable and constant working schedule.
- Reporting on employee lags.
- Reporting on working time, free days, vacations and so.

Other functions include:

- Possibility to edit real events if an employee made a mistake. It is available only for authorized employees.
- Possibility to know who is working at the moment and who is not.
- Each change or editing in scheduling is authorized.

3.3 Enrollment place

This component includes the hardware scanning fingerprints. The scanned fingerprint image is processed by the fingerprints hardware driver with the graphic algorithm. That we could get minutiae points' fingerprints identification and application takes these data from the hardware driver and places it in the data base according to the particular employee's ID (Fig. 3). Subsequently these data are applied for identification.

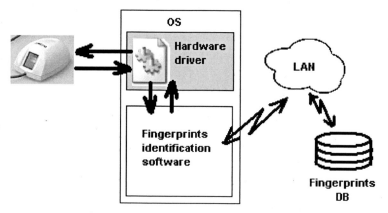

Fig. 3. The fingerprints identification.

All fingerprints data are read from the data base to dynamic array. The whole identification process including reading a fingerprint and comparing with the data in the dynamic array is shorter than one second. After the identification process in the data base is created record of employee's entry and escape. UML diagram of the working principle is presented in Fig. 4:

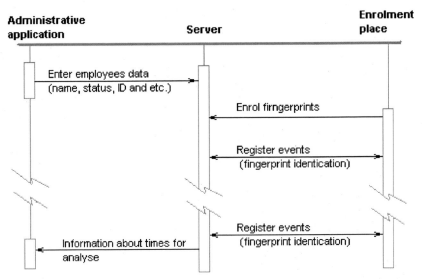

Fig. 4. Fingerprints system's UML diagram.

The employees are identificated each time they enter or leave a building. All the check-in's are recorded and compared to the pre-set schedule.

The system is installed and functions without any significant failures. Some times fingerprint reader fail, because fingerprint was damp or dusty. Employees with smaller fingers can have problem while reading fingerprint since reader does not get full image. These problems were eliminated adjusting fingerprint reader's quality and security parameters.

4 Conclusions

We have developed and installed functioning fingerprint-based system to automate the employees control process. It allows easily and conveniently monitor a real working time schedule and helps the executives to administrate the organization. The system is an example of successful application of biometric technology and integration of AFIS into the already existing and running control system.

References

1. **Biometric Consortium** (2005-12-28) Introduction to biometrics, http://www.biometrics.org/html/introduction.html;
2. **ROSISTEM** (2005-12-28) Biometrics, http://www.barcode.ro/tutorials/biometrics/;

3. **Sgt. David R. Ashbaugh**(2006-01-04). Automated Fingerprint Identification System (A.F.I.S.), http://www.ridgesandfurrows.homestead.com/afispage.html;
4. **Salil Prabhakar, Anil Jain** (2005-12-28) Fingerprint Identification, http://biometrics.cse.msu.edu/fingerprint.html;
5. **Dr. O.P. Jasuja** (2006-01-03) Poroscopy: a method of personal identification revisited, http://www.fingerprints.tk/;
6. **Sgt. David R. Ashbaugh** (2006-01-04). Friction Ridge Identification, http://www.ridgesandfurrows.homestead.com/identification.html;
7. **Jean-François Mainguet** (2005-12-28). Biometrics, http://perso.wanadoo.fr/fingerchip/biometrics/biometrics.htm;
8. **Security Database B.V.** (2006-01-04). Large Scale Automatic Biometric Identification System,http://www.securitydatabase.net/megamatcher.html;

Database Architectures: Current Trends and their Relationships to Requirements of Practice

Jaroslav Pokorný

Charles University, Faculty of Mathematics and Physics, Praha, Czech Republic, pokorny@ksi.ms.mff.cuni.cz

1 Introduction

Due to changes in the world of data, new demands on databases appear and consequently questions, where the databases field is and where it should be going. Abiteboul et al. [1] emphasize two main driving forces in database area: Internet and particular sciences, as the physics, biology, medicine, and engineering. These sciences produce large and complex data sets that require more advanced database support than current commercial systems provide. For example, BaBar database, containing nuclear data and considered as the biggest in the world, had more than 895 terabytes data stored in 847149 files on November 5, 2004. The system CORIE (Columbia River Estuary) produces in its simulations 5 gigabytes of forecast data each day [5]. Data volume doubles approximately every year and it is measured even in petabytes [8].

Another trend, existing since 60s, concerns industries responding to ever increasing environmental demands from customers, authorities, and governmental organizations. Also requirements on safety are increasing. In both cases the development tends towards an emergence of new monitoring systems. New functions are integrated into usual business information systems, governmental systems, and special systems, for example, digital "smart" home management systems.

Problems with processing data considered are well documented on example of environmental data. When users want to search and use environmental information, the following problems occur [17]:

1. Data does not exist or is insufficient; sometimes this may require synthesis or reproduction of data.
2. Data is not referenced by data suppliers and therefore hard to locate, or data is referenced under specific classification criteria that are domain-specific.

3. Data is hard to access; it is either private, or of a too high cost, or requiring costly pre-processing (for example, data must be re-entered manually from paper documentation) or format translation.
4. Accessed data sets are hard to use because they are inconsistent or non-compatible.
5. The quality of retrieved data is hard to assess; it is often hard to compare data produced using different scientific models because of a lack of documentation about the underlying computational processes.

Database community is focused on software architectures – *database management systems* (DBMS). The DBMS development is always driven by new applications, technological trends, and new synergy among associated fields, as well as by innovation in the field alone. Problems (1) - (5) are natural part of today's database research and development. New database technologies deployed in practice can overcome these problems.

DBMS development is influenced by a number of technological aspects. For a moment, we focus on scientific data. Sensor networks producing a part of this data consist of a large amount of cheap equipment, from which each is a data source measuring a quantitative quantity, for example, objects location or surrounding temperature. Processing such data usually distinguishes from that used in enterprise databases. Data occur in high-speed streams and queries over these streams need to be processed in online manner, which enables a response in real time. This data is moreover uncertain or imprecise, any measurements contain usual errors. Another aspect of this data includes unclear formulation of queries based on traditional techniques, as they occur, for example, in traditional databases. Often we are not able to formulate query in SQL even though we are convinced that it would be possible. In such situations apparently semantics are missing. To describe data semantics on the metadata level (formally, if possible) is more than desirable.

The purpose of the paper is to present main directions in development of database architectures reflecting an emergence of new data types and new kinds of their processing. In Section 2 we briefly describe a layered DBMS architecture as it was designed by Härder and Reuter [9] in the 80s. We consider it as referential, since any other development of databases meant to be successful in its realization. In Sections 3-7 we briefly discuss technologies and requirements of practice, which essentially influence today's database architectures; sensor data and sensor networks, processing data streams, considering uncertain and imprecise data, data mining and OLAP as well as wireless data broadcasting and mobile computing. Section 8 is already devoted to new database architectures. In Section 9 we generalize our considerations with the help of the notion of dataspace. Conclusions briefly summarize the ideas presented.

2 Multi-layered DBMS architecture

Everybody, who uses a relational database, is aware of the fact that tables occurring on the top of a database system are in some sense virtual. More specifically, they provide a logical data structure suitable for user-oriented processing data in a database. Tables are only one, most visible layer of a database system. Härder and Reuter [9] proposed a mapping model consisting from five abstraction layers. Table 1 adopted from [10] shows these five layers in detail. We can observe objects to be dealt with at each level and particular functions implementing mappings between two consecutive layers. For example, nonprocedural access in L5 layer provides tables and statements for their manipulation formulated usually in SQL. Layer L2 ensures dividing of linear address space of external memory into different types of pages. Among objects in layer L3 we can find data structures supporting indexing, for example, B-trees for strings and numbers or R-trees for spatial data. Going upwards, the objects and associated operations become more complex, also additional integrity constraints can appear.

Table 1. Description of the five-layered DBMS mapping hierarchy

	Level of abstraction	Objects	Auxiliary mapping data
L5	Nonprocedural access	Tables, views, rows	Logical schema description
L4	Record-oriented, navigational access	Records, sets, hierarchies, networks	Logical and physical schema description
L3	Record and access path management	Physical records, access paths	Free space tables, DB-key translation tables
L2	Propagation control	Segments, pages	Buffers, page tables
L1	File management	File, blocks	Directories

The concept a multi-layered architecture considers its ideal implementation with a machine, which has k layers. Although the number five is considered as a good compromise in the architecture, problems appear with its performance in practice. Simplification of layers complexness on one side increases run-time overhead on the other side. In consequence, various ways how to optimize DBMS performance are developed and the number of layers is for some system functions reduced.

Development of the L5 layer during last 10 years resulted in a specification of so-called *object-relational* (OR) *data model*. Its part is standardized in the standards SQL:1999 and SQL:2003. In the OR data model tables can have structured components of their rows, columns can be even of a user-defined type. Spatial data, time series or texts belong to this category. For some data types, for example VITA (video, image, text, audio), there is a standardized set of predicates and functions for manipulation of their instances. Such "extendible" approach resulted into so-called *universal DBMS* in the late 90s. The kernel of these database engines was extended by loosely-coupled additional modules (components) for each new data type. Vendors of leading DBMSs call these components *extenders*, *data blades*, and *cartridges*, respectively. Remind, that spatial and text components belong to the most successful results in this approach. Due to more complex data structures than rows of traditional relational tables, OR DBMS provide a chance for use in the field of storage and processing scientific data, where the structure ARRAY belongs among key data structures.

The possibility of user-defined types brought in implementation of DBMS architectures a lot of serious problems, particularly in case of conceptually wholly different data types, as e.g. VITA. For VITA types it is possible to use together maximally the layer L1, the other have to be implemented for each type separately. An open problem remains how to integrate these types into a common framework. Implementation of new access paths, like special types of indices, results usually in modification of the DBMS kernel, for example, SQL compiler, query optimizer, etc. Such changes are very expansive, time-consuming and tending to errors.

Each vendor uses to open the architecture of host system to some extent a different approach. Oracle cartridges are restricted to integration of secondary indices. In IBM DB2 extenders there is a framework for indexing new data types limited only to B-trees. It means that such indexing can bring an improvement of evaluation only for some types of queries. In other words, new functionality is supported, but only for a restricted class of user requirements.

It seems that the benefit of the universal database software is apparent mainly in case of requirements, which can be decomposed into relatively independent parts evaluated separately in the DBMS kernel and in the module, which implements a specific data type. Processing frameworks are either too complex or not flexible enough to cope with a wide range of user requirements on domain-specific access methods. In fact, a seamless integration can be hardly achieved with these attempts. Today's implementations of layered DBMS architectures are not sufficient for new requirements and fail in the case of universal DBMSs.

3 Sensor data and sensor networks

Among new ITC technologies the inexpensive micro sensor technology is number one in context of new requirements on databases. Sensors enable most objects to report messages about their attributes, as, for example, temperature, pressure, state or location, in real time. This information will support applications, whose main purpose is to monitor such attributes [3].

Sensor networks produce important data sources and create new requirements on data management. In fact, they become a new kind of a database engine, whose optimal use requires operations to be pushed as close to the data as possible. Generally, sensors and/or users can be even mobile.

A sensor information processing is establishing the most interesting database problems. Large data collections generated by sensors will be distributed through the world, and their data will come and go dynamically. Sensors can produce continual, possibly unlimited, data streams.

At first sight, sensor networks are similar to distributed databases extended by features related to real time. There is an important difference, that a degree of evaluation of data created in a sensor network is higher, than it is considered in distributed DBMS. This breaks the traditional information integration paradigm, since there is no practical way to extract and load data into a common database to each such occurrence. Strategies for query processing and optimization have to be redefined as well.

4 Data streams processing

Management of data coming from sensors based exclusively on traditional "store-and-query" model as it used in today's DBMSs usually can not effectively deal with volume and velocity of streaming data, whose values might exist a moment [3]:

- sensor nodes produce and deliver data continuously without receiving requests for that data,
- queries over collected data can be less frequent than data insertions,
- produced data has often to be processed in real-time because it can represent events, that need a rapid answer,
- queries run continuously because data streams never terminate, so, they can see system conditions changes during their execution,
- an entire stream can not be stored on disk, and
- if the data to be processed is not available, then operators must process data only when nodes make it available.

In consequence, *Data Stream Processing Systems* (DSPS) have been developed; see, for example, [6]. A *streams processor engine* for data processing is then an example of a new database architecture, that enables the execution of queries, computations, and actions on streaming data in real-time. Such engine should accept stream oriented, continuous queries formulated in the SQL. In DSPS, a data processing is done mostly in main memory, disk operations read and write are optional and can be in many cases handled asynchronously. For example, in Stream-Base DSPS, developed by Stonebraker [16] in 2005, it is possible to analyze 140,000 messages/s, while a leading relational DBMS could handle only 900 messages/s.

5 Approaching uncertain and imprecise data

In addition to data management issues of data streams, many other problems arise. Any measurement is usually a subject of errors. For example, location data for moving objects involves uncertainty concerning the current objects position. Individual sensors are not reliable; therefore wireless communication is also not reliable

Various approaches are used to provide more accurate estimation about object values, like fuzzy sets or Dempster-Shafer theory and other techniques of artificial intelligence [12].

Traditional DBMS were applied to processing enterprise data, which is typically represented by numbers and character strings. Data items are exact quantities - address, quantity on hand, delivery date, balance, and employment status. In consequence, current DBMS have no tools for processing approximate data and imprecise queries. Also sequences and images require approximate processing based on similarities, metrics, etc.

To increase data quality, new data models appear that preserve the origin of data and history of its processing, so-called *lineage* of objects and processes [4]. Data producers should include such data lineage (and authenticity) of information into metadata attached to basic (measured) data to ensure its best utilization. Other application of data lineage can be a system of personal data, where we want to preserve various document versions, related e-mails, etc.

6 Data mining and OLAP

Measured data needs to be analyzed in most cases, to obtain information necessary for decision making. A typical example is an environmental management. Comparing to simple forms of regularities or irregularities determined with statistical methods (OLAP), data mining methods can explore more complex hypotheses.

Historically, data mining focused on effective ways of discovering models of existing data sets. These models have to reveal some useful aspects of data, while obscuring details not useful for the intended application. Researchers developed algorithms, which perform operations as classification, clustering, discovering associate rules, and summarization. These techniques become new parts of products of main DBMS vendors and most of them are applicable in the field of scientific data. Unfortunately, many algorithms are super-linear (for example, for processing n points they are of complexity $O(n^2)$ or $O(n^3)$), which in case of collections mentioned in Section 1 can be unacceptable. A solution is, for example, approximate algorithms and use of parallelism.

Current interest in combination of data mining technologies and DBMS tends to discover new approaches how to store data sets which have to be mined to optimize data mining. The collection size is not issue of only scientific data. According to the Greg law, the volume of enterprise data doubles every 9 months. Data warehouses ranging in terabytes volumes are no exclusion now. Forrester [18] even estimates that most large enterprises have petabytes for data in all data repositories across the organization – and it is likely to grow to exabytes in the coming years.

Current research directions concerning mining stream data include:

- multi-dimensional OLAP for discovering unusual patterns;
- mining clusters and outliers for discovering unusual patterns; and

- single-pass classification methods for stream data mining.

7 Wireless broadcasting and mobile computing

Data broadcasting is an attractive alternative to approach "on demand", because it can broadcast data simultaneously to a large number of clients at a fixed cost. It is suitable for services based on an objects location, which exhibit strong temporal and spatial locality in that near clients in a certain time period, tend to seek the same kind of information [19].

Data to be broadcasted includes also sensor data. Sensors deployed in an environment can broadcast their data periodically or when an interested event happens. Unlike to traditional computing, client devices cannot make requests to sensors for the data. Instead, client devices just listen to the broadcast channels passively. Thus, the sensors have the initiative in communication. Sensors may broadcast data periodically, if they are measuring a continuous phenomenon producing data, or may broadcast data only when a particular event occurs, if they are detecting whether an RFID tag has come into range.

Higher-level sensors in a sensor network can pre-process low-level sensor data and then broadcast this derived information to client devices. Such processing can require modified database techniques to be successful.

It seems that location in spatio-temporal space becomes an important property of data and introduces a new dimension for data access methods. Traditional data access methods are not suitable in this case. The goal of current research is to re-define some well-known techniques, for example, processing space queries, into mobile environment with a special emphasise on data broadcasting.

8 Towards new database architectures

Database technology seems to be fundamental for deployment of technologies introduced in Sections 3-7 in context of new applications. Main benefits of the database approach should include: flexibility without complexity and ease of use. Database approach brings the opportunity to link all data together on a user level and simplify its analysis, for example with the help of technologies like data mining.

A common view on mentioned issues concerns the DBMS architecture. Today's DBMS provide practically universal architecture applicable to many various types of tasks, i.e. by words of Stonebraker and Çetinteme [15], "one size fits all". In new DBMS architectures rather separated database servers "made to measure" are expected, in accordance with requirements of particular applications. Besides traditional fields, as OLAP, data warehouses, and text retrieval, other candidates for separate engines are:

- data streams processing,

- sensor networks,
- scientific databases, and
- native XML databases.

We have tried to highlight some characteristics of the first three technologies. Considering native XML databases, solutions with a separate engine are popular today. In [10] Härder presents XTC architecture (XML Transaction Controller), which proves that native XML DBMS can be implemented in frame of five-layer architecture. There is also a possibility of so called hybrid engine. To integrate relational and XML data, IBM develops a new hybrid DB2, code-named Viper, enabling to work with a native XML store that is placed side by side with a relational data repository. On the top of both data stores sits one hybrid database engine. Similar solutions are used by many vendors, who combine a data warehouse and a usual transactional DBMS united by common parser. Such architecture can be inspiring for implementation of non-traditional data types.

Another approach evolves the idea of DBMS extendibility. Acker et al. [2] developed an Access Manager specification, a programming interface to several layers of a DBMS kernel. This enables the programmer to add new data structures to the DBMS with a minimum of effort.

There is also a third approach to achieve a flexibility of processing data in a database way: to produce a storage engine that is more configurable so that it can be tuned to the requirements of individual applications [14]. In principle, a solution must possess two features to cover the wide spectrum of today's application needs: modularity and configurability.

Modular DBMS must allow to the developer to use or exclude some subsystems depending on whether application needs them. DBMS must be configurable with respect to its operational environment: specific hardware, operation system and applications, which are using it.

9 From databases to dataspaces

All efforts on new DBMS architectures indicate, that current requirements on data management can not be dealt with storing the data into a database of one (in the best case relational) DBMS. There is a bias to place data rather into loosely coupled data sources, some of them are managed by a relational DBMS, but the other not at all. Data sources can be considered as members of a *dataspace*. Dataspaces are not another data integration approach. Data in a dataspace rather co-exists; semantic integration is not a necessary condition for operating parts of a system. Figure 1 adopted from [7] shows a categorization of existing data management solutions in two dimensions. "Administrative Proximity" indicates how close the various data sources are in terms of administrative control. "Semantic Integration" is a measure of how closely the schemas of the various data sources have been matched.

The notion of dataspace is a new abstraction described in [7]. A development of associated software – DataSpace Support Platform (DSSP) – is mentioned today as a main item of program in the field of data management, or as we often say, data engineering.

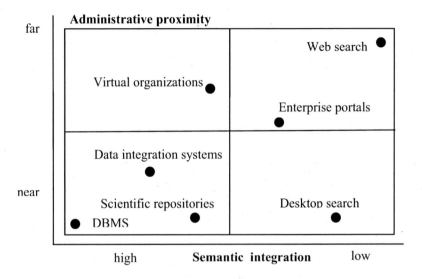

Fig. 1. A space of data management solutions

DSSP does not assume a total control on data in dataspace. It allows managing data by particular system under which belongs. It provides, however, new services over aggregations of these systems. DSSP includes a catalogue containing descriptions of *participants* (sources) in dataspace and *associations* among them. Participants are sources as, for example, relational databases, XML data repositories, text databases, web services, sensors producing data, etc. Dataspace assumes a possibility to model arbitrary association among participants, in extreme case a data exchange schema between sources. Often the relationship is simple, for example, one source is only a version of another. Integration in a dataspace is permanently evolved, on the base of demands; nevertheless data are still accessible, for example, in the simplest form via key words.

Querying includes both data and metadata, such as "Where I find something about ISD conference?", "Which sources have the attribute length?" Approximate answers are assumed, or "best effort" results in case of unavailability of sources. DSSP should also enable the user to come, if necessary, to the query language of the data source (if possible). It would be interesting to compare this proposal with semantic web, which is based on ontologies and URLs. In a dataspace we want achieve looser integration focusing rather into the depth of not necessarily web sources.

10 Conclusions

Certainly there are other criteria how to classify and evaluate new solutions in database architectures, than those discussed in the paper. We can mention, for example, the Service Oriented Database Architecture (SODA) developed by Microsoft and realized in SQL Server DBMS 2005 [11], technological solutions such as Asymmetric Massively Parallel Processing (AMPP) architecture or grid architectures.

We have seen that the trend of stand-alone database engines is rather against the previous effort to integrate all into one universal system. The concept of dataspace supports this direction. On the other hand, integration is considered rather on a global level, over data sources, based on metadata management. This feature is observable both in dataspaces and a semantic web. Possibly, the former considers integration more loosely, on demand, in comparing to the latter.

These observations are included also in challenges, which have been formulated by P. Selinger in [13]:

- re-examine DBMS architecture and invent ways to scale more and better, without sacrificing user-visible availability or performance,
- learn what managing content is all about, what is needed and create new models,
- treat metadata as and first class research.

In any case, databases architectures play a significant role in any data processing today. Everything indicates that the development of new database technologies has and will have consequences that influence future data-oriented systems.

11 Acknowledgement

This research was partially supported GACR grant 201/06/0756.

References

1. Abiteboul, S., et. al.: Lowell Database Research self-assessment. In: Communications of ACM, May 2005/Vol. 48, No. 5, 2005, pp. 111-118.
2. Acker, R., Pieringer, R., Bayer, R.: Towards Truly Extendible Database Systems. In: Proc. DEXA 2005 Conf., LNCS 3588, Springer-Verlag, 2005, pp. 596-605.
3. Amato, G., Caruso, A., Chessa, S., Masi V., Urpi, A.: State of the art and future directions in wireless sensor network's data management. 2004-TR-16, ISTI, 2004.
4. Bose, R., Frew, J.: Lineage Retrieval for Scientific Data Processing: A Survey. ACM Computing Surveys, Vol. 37, No. 1, 2005, pp. 1-28.

5. Bright, L., Maier, D.: Deriving and Managing Data Products in an Environmental Observation and Forecasting System. In: Proc. Conference on Innovative Data Systems Research (CIDR), January 2005, pp. 162-173.
6. Cherniack, M., Balakrishnan, B., Balazinska, M., Carney, D., Çetintemel, U., Xing, Y., Zdonik, S.: Scalable Distributed Stream Processing. In: Proc. of Conference on Innovative Data Systems Research (CIDR), January 2003.
7. Franklin, M., Halevy, A., Maier, D.: From Databases to Dataspaces: A New Abstraction for Information Management. ACM SIGMOD Rec., Dec. 2005.
8. Gray, J., Liu, D.T., Nieto-Santisteban, M., Szalay, A.S., DeWitt, D., Heber, G.: Scientific, Data Management in the Coming Decade. Microsoft Research, MSR-TR-2005-10, 2005.
9. Härder, T., Reuter, A.: Concepts for Implementing and Centralized Database Management System. In: Proc. Int. Computing Symposium on Application Systems Development, March 1983, Nürnberg, B.G. Teubner-Verlag, 1983, pp. 28-104.
10. Härder, T.: DBMS Architecture - Still an Open Problem. In: Proc. BTW, Karlsruhe, March 2005, pp. 2-28.
11. Kiely, D.: How SQL Server 2005 Enables Service-Oriented Database Architectures, 2006. Available: http://www.microsoft.com/technet/prodtechnol/sql/2005/sqlsoda.mspx#EHE
12. Ramamritham, K., Son, S. H., Dipippo, L.C.: Real-Time Databases and Data Services. Real-Time Systems, Kluwer AP, 28, 2004, pp. 179-215.
13. Selinger, P.: Five Data Challenges for Next Decade. Key note of ICDE conference, April 2005, Tokyo, Japan.
14. Seltzer, M. I.: Beyond Relational Databases. Databases, Vol. 3, No. 3, 2005, pp. 50-58.
15. Stonebraker, M., Çetintemel, U.: "One Size Fits All" An Idea Whose Time Has Come and Gone. In: Proc. Conf. ICDE, April 2005, Tokyo, pp. 2-11.
16. StreamBase Systems, Inc.: StreamBase™ 2.0, 2005. Available: http://www.streambase.com/index.html
17. Tomasic, A., Simon, E.: Improving Access to Environmental Data using Context Information. ACM SIGMOD Rec., Vol. 26, Issue 1, 1997, pp. 11-15.
18. Yuhanna, N., Gilpin, M.: Information Fabric: Enterprise Data Virtualization. Forrester, January 9, 2006.
19. Zheng, B., Lee, D.L.: Information Dissemination via Wireless Broadcast. In: Communications ACM, May 2005/Vol. 48, No. 5, pp. 105-110.

The IT Culture as an Obstacle to the Adoption of an ERP: Case of a High-Tech SME

Meissonier, R., Ph.D., Houzé, E., Ph.D, Belbaly, N., Ph.D.

GSCM, Montpellier Business School, France, 2300, Avenue des Moulins,
34185 Montpellier Cedex 4, CREGO, Montpellier University, France
Place Eugène Bataillon, Bâtiment 19, 34095 Montpellier Cedex 5, GSCM,
Montpellier Business School, France
2300, Avenue des Moulins, 34185 Montpellier Cedex

Abstract: The firm's IT experience is considered among the characteristics that influence the adoption of an ERP. Few authors assume that the firms IT experience act as a main risk factor for ERP implementation projects. In this paper, a literature review based on theories related to resistance and conflicts factors in ERP implementation is presented. Then we describe the outcomes that may be deducted from a high-tech SME which tried to adopt an ERP. We find in this case that IT expertise and culture turned out to be inhibitors of ERP adoption. In conclusion, we present a dual perspective on the firm's capability to implement an ERP.
Key words: ERP, resistance, conflicts, culture, IT expertise

1 Introduction

For more than 10 years, a lot of companies have implemented ERP's to update their information system and to benefit from an integrated functional infrastructure. In Information Systems research, these integrated applications have been the subject of many research projects mainly focused on large firms. In the present time, ERP software editors' are targeting more and more SMEs with adapted solutions in order to modernize their applications or even to allow them to be interfaced with the ones of their customers or suppliers. Among the characteristics considered as success factors in the ERP adoption, the experience of IT firm's projects hold the attention of many authors (Lapointe & Rivard, 2005; Akkermans & Van Helden 2002; Markus *et al.*, 2000; Grover *et al.*, 1995; Wilcocks & Griffths, 1994; Barki *et al.*, 1993). These studies put forward resistance to change as a main risk factor, where resistance to change is composed by the professional habits and culture of the employees.

The case study is dealing with a high-tech SME specialised in broadcast technology for media corporations (TV and radio channels). When the firm tried to adopt an ERP, its expertise in IT project management turned out to be an inhibitor because of the professional culture associated to this expertise.

The paper is organized as follow: First, a literature review based on ERP implementation theories related to resistance and conflicts factors is presented. Second, we analyse a high-tech SME case where the lessons that can be drawn are based on eight semi-directive interviews. Finally, the conclusion is focusing on the dual perspective of the firm's capability to implement an ERP.

2 Literature analysis

At the beginning of the 1990's, ERP (Enterprise Resource Planning) are the heart of the information systems of most of the companies. The investments made in this type of IT are often motivated by the rationalisation allowed by the integration of processes (Markus, 2000). These applications respond to a certain number of inconveniences discovered during the evaluation of information systems and originating principally from their heterogeneous and patchwork construction (Reix, 2004): problems related to the communication of data from different domains, to the difficulty of reaching synthesis status, to the high maintenance costs due to the heterogeneous nature of the application fleet or even to the difficulty involved in training users to the different application environments proposed. Among the advantages usually ignored regarding the ERP's, we can consider several elements that are involved in the logic of rationalization of the company information system and it's organization: the conception of a unique database, the deployment of standard processes through different company functions, the availability of reliable monitoring indicators, etc.

In management science, the literature on ERP can be divided into two types: one concentrated on conditions, *ex ante*, associated with ERP project success and failure factors and the other concentrating on the induced effects (Robey *et al.*, 2002). In our case, we consider that multiple exogenous and endogenous elements are likely to put the different project stages at risk (Markus, 2000). Based on the study of about 40 articles on the subject, we have identified no less than 22 different risk factors.

The case of the ERP's is probably one of the most complete illustrations regarding changes induced by the deployment of an information system. Their functional model consists into adopting and applying "business best practices" considered for the sector in which the firm competes. In other words, with an ERP, priority is given to the implementation of "standard modules" instead of specific developments. In that way, the adaptation of the application to the particularities of the firm is confined to the configuration of those modules (Davenport, 1998). A form of inflexibility is therefore put forward and some authors even go so far as to consider this operation mode as a new form of Taylorism (Gilbert & Leclair, 2004).

Leaving company particularities in the background and implementing pre-established process models is not without potential problems of resistance by employees. These problems can be specific to some individuals or may even grow into inter-personnel or inter-group conflicts (Barki & Hartwick, 2001). The efficiency of an ERP deployment project includes therefore a strong social character that must not be neglected for the risk of failure (Besson, 1999). Our analysis of the literature makes us identify two levels of resistance for the participants of ERP implementation: the first concerns the operational dimension and the second concerns social and political dimensions (Table 1). Hereafter, we will present the elements that compose these two dimensions.

1) *The conflicts regarding the definition of task execution.* Some frictions may arise in determining "best practices" that will be adopted when configuring the ERP (examples: the manner of establishing invoices or orders, data collection and coding of articles, the validation process of internal documents). Robey *et al.* (2002) reveals that the problem of the ERP is less based on the capacity of the company to manage change but more on the difficulty of users to understand the way they were supposed to complete their tasks. For Besson (1999), these conflicts may first raise internally in the form of the different processes confrontation or the same task involving several participants of the company. They can also appear externally by the alignment of the company policy with the "best practices" considered with the ERP implementation. In that case, conflicts are often illustrated by users claiming for a better consideration of the specificities of their needs (Besson, 1999; Markus & Tanis 2000; Larif & Lesorbe, 2004) and roundabout usages of ERP functions (Davenport, 1998; Markus & Tanis, 2000; Gilbert & Leclair, 2004).

2) *The competencies conflicts deals with* the expertise required for the completion of the task rather than the manner in which this will be completed. The job of accounting manager is one of the classic illustrations of professional changes induced by an integrated information system. While the job included, up to the appearance of the ERP, an intense work of collection, aggregation, synthesis of accounting and financial data, the job have moved to automated tasks supported by the ERP. The reduction of low added value tasks has led accounting manager to be more focused on analysis and consulting tasks.

3) *Value conflicts* concern the perceived objectives assigned in terms of value creation (Aubert *et al.*, 2002). For instance, in the hospital sector new processes imposed by the ERP were perceived like a market takeover attempt inconsistent with a public service mission (Besson, 1999; Ménard C. & Bernier C. (2004). In private sector companies this type of conflict may appear in different forms because of the firm finality profession. Among these, we could talk about the well-known "Moscow eye" to which these types of IT are often compared by users.

Table 1. Conflicts related to the implementation of an ERP

	Type of conflict	Examples of associated work
Operation dimension	Conflicts about the definition and the execution of tasks that the users must fulfill.	Robey et al., 2002; Markus & Tanis, 2000; Larif & Lesorbe, 2004
	Conflicts about the new professional skills	Robey et al., 2002; Markus & Tanis, 2000; Newman & Westrup, 2005
Socio-political dimension	Conflicts of values	Robey et al., 2002; Aubert et al., 2002; Menard & Bernier, 2004
	Conflict due to a loss of power	Hart & Saunders 1997; Watson et al., 1999; Jasperson et al., 2002.; Bancroft-Truner & Morley, 2002

4) *Power conflicts* concern the distribution of autonomy and the influence capability of participants. On one hand, ERP's can give key users more power by providing them real-time data processing ability (Davenport, 1998). On the other hand, they can increase the transversality of tasks and then reduce the independence of employees (Markus, 1983). As highlighted by Gilbert & Leclair (2004), in a classic management system, the individuals are not generally forced to give the information required by their collaborators, but they produce their own individual work. The organisation induced by the ERP brings a higher number of mutual instructions. The integration of the Information System thus represents a management vehicle of interdependencies (Rockart & Short, 1989) by which the user prescribes the conditions and the means of their colleagues.

Given the organizational upheavals induced by the deployment of an ERP, lot of research projects agree that a project of this type can not be correctly completed with few implication of the general management. The hierarchy must be a "sponsor" (Davenport, 1998; Markus & Tanis, 2000) of the project and make its "publicity" by assorting credible objectives (Goodman & Sproull, 1990). However, according to the threats perceived by the implementation of an Information System, the users may use their influence power to promote or even to inhibit the project (Beaudry & Pinsonneault, 2005). Indeed, power should not be perceived only as a vehicle of formal decision granted by an authority or by withholding resources. At the heart of an organization every actor has a reasonably large margin of freedom to gradually increase their power (Crozier & Friedberg, 1977). Those sociopolitical games illustrate the management problem induced by information systems.

Therefore, it is not surprising to observe that the experience of a company in the area of information technology project management is considered as a key competency (Wilcocks & Griffths, 1994; Akkermans & Van Helden, 2002) in the deployment of a sophisticated information system like ERP's. However, for Crozier & Friedberg (1977), key skills existing in an enterprise may also represent action enablers in such power games. In this case, individuals can use their recognized experiences as a vector of influence and as a force of persuasion to orient choices in the way of their personal interests. Consequently, the issue regarding the ambivalent character of the enterprise expertise in the domain of IT must be raised. To what extent can this expertise be used as positive enablers for the deployment of an ERP?

3 Case-study

NETIA, a French SME (located near Montpellier), is one of the leaders in broadcasting (40 countries covered). Its customers are TV channels and public radios like, BBC, ABC, Rai uno, Canal+, France Télévision, etc. Created in 1993, the company employs 70 persons spread over two sites in France and subsidiaries abroad (Amsterdam, Liege, Rome and New York). The firm is an IT service agency dealing with the deployment of audio and video data digital solutions. Besides development, its activity consists of implementation management (consulting, process analyse, engineering, training, maintenance and evolution).

The information system of Netia has been developed progressively by ad-hoc initiatives and requirements. These isolated and independent developments have involved a lack of data coherence as well as an excessive growth in the number of applications required to treat these developments. Consequently, a large part of the employee tasks was used to provide data in order to feed all of the parallel systems installed to response to local needs. For example, the control service has developed a set of Excel programs to partially deal with a divided use of the SAGE software used for the accountancy. Each process (the arrival of an order form, a delivery form, etc) corresponds to a data entry for one or more shared Excel files (on the server there is a file for the order forms, another for the clients, another for prospects, etc.) The operational structure of the information system consists therefore of Microsoft office files from which the data is manually extracted in order to produce management indicators required for the company control. Thus, the loss in productivity becomes apparent not only in the multiple repeated data entries due to the absence of information integration, but also by redundant procedures attempting to ensure a type of reliability by the systematic and repetitive cross referencing of data related to operations. The lack of integration of the information system is also highlighted by data access problems. Thus, the project coordinator can not know the status of the client order in progress without contacting directly the logistics service who must consult the SAGE application in order to respond. Given that the transaction history is dispersed throughout several isolated management applications, purchase tracking (in the case of client feedback or use of a guarantee) is difficult to retrace. Client invoicing is not automatically triggered by a delivery. Logistic managers must enter the information in an Excel file shared with the account department in order to know the state of the process, etc.

It is thus the ensemble of the administrative personnel who was asking of the deployment of an integrated information system to ensure a more coherent and efficient management of the tasks. We can at this point highlight the originality of this case, where the project is not requested by the management but directly by the users who are usually described in documentation about the ERPs as potential resistance vectors.

Two failed attempts at the integration of an information system have been made at Nétia. In 1998, a project to install an ERP was launched. The coordinator in charge of the project carried out an initial study that lasted more than six months and ended by the abort of the project. The second try have concerned a CRM application which was planned to be purchased in 2002. Tainted by an initial feeling of failure, this second attempt was also abandoned.

4 Research methodology

If Netia is expert in IT project management, from a client point of view, it turned out to be unable to apply its expertise to itself. Different reasons incited us to adopt an "action-research" methodology for this purpose:

- Because of the aborted previous projects, the company was eager of recommendations about IS project management from researcher point of view.
- The SME had a short budget concerning this project and could not afford buying the services of a consulting agency.
- In information systems research, "action-research" is turning out to be a more popular and accepted methodology (Baskerville & Myers, 2004).

Our interventions began the first semester of 2005 and the first step conceived with top managers was to identity the explicit and tacit conflicts explaining the ERP project rejection. We conducted 8 semi-directive interviews spread out over four months.

We identified the existing subcultures and examine in which ways these drove the company into dead-end situations. The interviews were divided among representative employees of the different professions (see Table 2).

The interview grid used (see appendix) has been conceived with reference to the risk factor lists of Markus *et al.* (2000), Akkermans & Van Helden (2002), Besson *et al.* (2002). To avoid some reluctance the interviews were realised in a one-to-one interaction and with an anonymous format of the responses collected. During a first part of the interviews the employee was asked to select on the grid, the factors he considered as explaining the rejection of the project. In a second part, we asked him to explain what happened and to develop his perceived dissents and tensions that occurred between employees for the ERP project. Each interview lasted around one and a half hour.

Table 2. Interviewees conducted

Initials	Service	Function
VB	Accounting	Management coordinator
AG	Computer	Computer Dept. Coordinator

	Dept.	
PV	Computer Dept.	Software developer
SR	Accounting	Supplier invoicing
SB	Accounting	Client invoicing, salaries
OC	Operations	Project Director
PD	Logistics	Logistics coordinator
XZ	Sales	Sales coordinator

5 Results and discussion

The interviews conducted allowed us to identify a deep opposition between the IT staff and the administrative staff (management control and logistics in particular) toward the ERP project.

5.1 A conflict of values

During the interviews, the developers put forward "the inconsistency of ERPs to the needs of Nétia" as the official reason of their reluctance. Nevertheless, other interviews allowed us to transcript the following declarations that highlight a conflict of values:

- Project coordinator statement: *"my analysis on the lack of evolution and integration of the Information System is: the IT staff is professional regarding computer based applications. So, they develop the tools they like and need without worrying about coherence. Thus we could not impose the development of others collaborative systems despite the overwhelming number of meetings!"*
- Management controller statement: *"When they* (the developers) *examined the interface and the application functions they were systematically pessimistic: I would have done better than that, in my opinion it's not great!"*
- Developer statement: *"I prefer open source tools".*

So, here the conflict of values concerns the adoption of a "ready to use application" like an ERP instead of pushing for an internally developed solution. In this context, it seems that the strong IT culture works against the acquisition of professional applications offered on the market. One of the management controllers said: « *If the developers were not at the heart of the company activity, we would not have had these problems.* » We can now draw links to this conflict of values between developers and user with the work of Ballé & Peaucelle (1972) which exposed that the culture of developers often collides with the logic of manager. Because managers are more concentrated on the completion of their work rather than on how the applications used to this purpose are constructed or should be constructed.

However, a second level of analysis reveals that this apparent situation hides a power conflict.

5.2 A power conflict

Developers represent a key competence asset for Nétia. Effectively, the broadcast software's developed by the company are not standard or straightforward applications that can be bought from a classical software editor. Composed by solutions invoiced for several K€, these programs ensure the storage, the management and broadcasting of audio and video programs. Therefore, very specific skills are required regarding sound, image and storage (on servers of several Terabytes), broadcasting by satellite, etc.

The developers in the company represent a reasonably rare workforce on the market and this gives them some power with regards to the hierarchy. Thus, they gained, overtime, strong independence in the completion of their tasks. *« I decide my own objectives! »* declared one of the developer coordinators interviewed. An administration coordinator described for us the holiday management example: *"The developers were use to freely organize their work depending on the tasks and on the assignments to be completed. They do not really respect the procedures for taking holidays. Holidays are taken without prior booking. Instead of filling out the relevant forms and having them validated by the hierarchy, the requests (when they are made) usually take the form of an informal conversation".* However, the implementation of an ERP implies the deployment of formal processes that are inconsistent with this type of *ad hoc* processes. Regarded as a control tool, such system represents a threat for the developer's independence that they gained.

For their part, the top managers have, until now, been passive and they have avoided imposing this unpopular solution to the computer personal. An administration coordinator stated: *"If we really wanted to impose a standard solution, we could. However, this would mean interfering with the developers. But they are the makers of the programs sold, so..."* Moreover, the fact that there has been no concrete or major prejudice due to the unreliability of the information system does not particularly motivate top managers to discuss more this situation. *«Regarding the successful implementation, the management favours the R&D, only the R&D. . . the rest, such as improving organization, is not considered as vital. »* The developer coordinator told us his feelings according to which this lack of attitude by the top management could be explained by *« a lack of awareness of the necessity to modernize the information systems »*. However, the same person declared not doing all the necessary in order to attract the attention of management for this point.

6 Conclusion

Nearly all of the work done on the resistance to change resulting from the possible deployment of an ERP was concentrated on the opposition of users to the operating mode of acquiring the ERP. Moreover, it is often considered important to involve the « key users » in the project team from the beginning. An important point about the case study is that the main inhibiting factor was not the users themselves (in this case they were asking for the ERP) but the developers who were opposed to the idea of using a package application made by another company. Certainly perceived as a potential threat to their independence, the preference for a "ready to use application" against a software editor could also be interpreted as raising doubts regarding their expertise. Even if the present information system results in reduced productivity, these losses appear not to be judged sufficient by management to proceed with the implementation of a new system to which the developer staff are opposed and thus risk social climate degradation.

The scientific and professional literature on IS is enthusiastic about work distinguishing *risk factor* and *success factors.* If those models could be useful in terms of project management, it is however convenient to avoid all determinist approaches and to adopt more contingent analysis that may reveal that IT expertise could in fact become weakness and vice versa. That's why the dual perspective on the firm's capability to ERP implementation is important to consider. In fact, the dual perspective opposes the IS research perspective that supports the IT experience as a success factor and our case study perspective which considers the IT experience as a risk factor. In IS research, most of the articles on ERP are considering the lack of IT experience as a *risk factor.* However, the case study highlights the organizational maturity in the IT field is not necessarily a *key success factor.* Adopting an ERP equally requires (perhaps above all) an experience in terms of information system outsourcing.

This article equally highlights the risks linked to a management style avoiding conflict management (Barki & Hartwick, 2001). If change must be achieved, then the coordinators must accept the inevitability of certain conflicts, try to channel expertise, and even impose arbitrary choices, rather than letting the organisation sinking into the abyss of power and influence games.

References

Akkermans H., Van Helden K. (2002), "Vicious and virtuous cycles in ERP implementation: a case study of interrelations between critical success factors", European Journal of Information Systems, vol. 11

Aubert B. A., Rivard S., Patry M. (2002), "Managing IT outsourcing risk: lessons learned", in R. Hirscheimm, A. Heinzl, J. Dibberns, Information Systems Outsourcing, Enduring Themes, Emergent Patterns and Future Directions, Springer, pp. 155-176

Ballé C., Peaucelle J.-L. (1972), Le pouvoir informatique dans l'entreprise, Les Éditions d'Organisation.

Bancroft-Truner & Morley (2002), "Organisational Politics is about to go positive", Training Journal, August

Baskerville R., Myers M. D. (2004), "Special issue on action research in information systems: Making IS research relevant to practice – foreword", MIS Quarterly, vol. 28, n°3

Barki H., Hartwick J. (2001), "Interpersonal Conflicts and Its Management in Information System Development", MIS Quarterly, vol. 25, n°2

Barki H., Rivard S., Talbot J. (1993), "Toward an Assessment of Software Development Risk", Journal of Management Information Systems, vol. 10, n°2

Besson P. (1999), "Les ERP à l'épreuve de l'organisation", Systèmes d'Information et Management, vol. 4, n°4

Besson P. (1999), "Les ERP à l'épreuve de l'organisation", Systèmes d'Information et Management, vol. 4, n°4

Beaudry A., Pinsonneault A. (2005), "Understanding User Responses to Information Technology: A Coping Model of User Adaptation", MIS Quarterly, vol. 29, n°3

Crozier M., Friedberg E. (1977), L'acteur et le système : les contraintes de l'action collective », Edition du Seuil

Davenport T. H. (1998), "Putting the Enterprise into the Enterprise System", Harvard Business Review, July – August

Gilbert P., Leclair P. (2004), « Les systèmes de gestion intégrés. Une modernité en trompe l'œil ? », Sciences de la société, n° 61

Grover V., Jeong S., R. Kettinger W. J., Teng J. T. C. (1995), "The implementation of Business Process Reengineering", Journal of Management Information Systems, vol. 12, n°1

Hart P. & Saunders C. (1997), "Power and Trust: Critical Factors in the Adoption and Use of Electronic Data Interchange", Organizational Science, vol. 8, n°1

Jasperson J. S., Carte T. A., Saunders C. S. (2002), "Power and Information Technology Research: A Metatriangulation Review", MIS Quarterly, vol. 26, n°4

Lapointe L., Rivard S. (2005), "A Multilevel Model Of Resistance To Information Technology Implementation", MIS Quarterly, vol. 29, n°3

Markus M. L. (1983), "Power, Politics and MIS Implementation", Communications of the ACM, vol. 26, n°6, June

Markus M. L., Axline S., Petrie D., Tanis C. (2000), "Learning from adopters' experiences with ERP: problems encountered and success achieved", Journal of Information Technology, vol. 15, n°4

Markus M. L., Tanis C. (2000), "The enterprise system experience: from adoption to success", in R. W. Zmud, Framing the domains of IT management: projecting the future through the past, Pinnaflex Educationnal Resources

Menard C. & Bernier C. (2004), « Le cas d'une mise en oeuvre ERP réussie aux centres hospitaliers de LaSalle et de Verdun: comprendre la démarche par laquelle s'installent les nouvelles façons de faire », Gestion, vol. 28, n°4

Newman M., Westrup C. (2005), "Making ERPs work: accountants and the introduction of ERP systems", European Journal of Information Systems, vol. 14, n°3

Reix R. (2004), Systèmes d'information et management des organisations, 4ème édition, Vuibert

Robey D., Ross J. W., Boudreau M.-C. (2002), "Learning to Implement Enterprise Systems: An Exploratory Study of the Dialectics of Change", Journal of Management Information Systems, vol. 19, n° 1

Rockart J. F. & Short J. E. (1989), "IT in the 1990s: Managing Organizational Interdependence", Sloan Management Review, vol. 30, n°2

Rowe (1999), « Cohérence, intégration informationnelle et changement: esquisse d'un programme de recherche à partir des Progiciels Intégrés de Gestion », Systèmes d'Information et Management, vol. 4, n°4

Watson E. E., Schneider H., Ourso E. J. (1999), "Using ERP Systems in Education", Communications of the Association for Information Systems, vol. 1, n°9

Willcocks L., Griffiths C. (1994), "Predicting risk of failure in large scale IT projects", Technology forecasting and social change, vol. 47, n°2

Appendix: Key factor grid

Project size	Number of users outside of the organization Number of users inside the organization Number of people in the implementation team Team diversity Number of hierarchy levels occupied by users Number of business units concerned
Lack of internal expertise in project management	Lack of expertise in the implementation of information management plan Lack of expertise in information technology organization Lack of experience and expertise in the contract management related organization Lack of inter-functional representation in the team Dependence on users
Organizational context	Insufficient resources Conflict intensity Lack of clarity in the definition of roles Organizational complexity and level of geographic dispersion Level of inter-service cooperation Level of the functional specialization Level of vertical centralization of decision taking Lack of engagement by the project team Lack of engagement by the higher management levels Level of organizational growth

An Analysis of Communication Technologies for Distributed Embedded Systems in Industrial Process Automation

Pavel Rusakov and Dmitry Mikoyelov

dmitrijs@klase.lv

1 Introduction

With the help of researchers of single-chip microprocessors, it is now possible to manufacture very small embedded devices and gather these in one network. In most cases, the network consists of various sensors, which communicate with the data gathering nodes, data processing nodes, data storage nodes and data visualization nodes (in case a human-machine interface is used to monitor such system). In general, each of such components can be a subsystem of a distributed system.

It is a fact that the current technologies quickly transform into outdated or obsolete ones. This inspires the development of new devices, sensors and systems, to research and manufacture a vast amount of new solutions every year. It is obvious that a distributed industrial process management and control system, which we are researching in this paper, cannot exist without outside connections. This means that we have to design such system having sensors and subsystems situated in different remote locations or vital parts of the industrial process. The problem of communication between these subsystems and the central system is raised.

Wired communications tend to bring a lot of problems and obstacles in building a flexible and fast-response system. Wireless network of subsystems tends to be the most flexible solution in most of the cases. In this paper, we are analyzing different wireless communication technologies, providing examples of implementations and present our conclusions on benefits and drawbacks of each of the modern technologies.

2 The characteristic features of communication technology analysis

In order to objectively compare the technologies used to build communication links between the remote subsystems of a distributed system, we have used the following values (Low, Moderate, High, and Very High {and Worldwide as an extremely high factor for range of service}):

1. **Reliability.** A factor that specifies the reliability of the system implementing the selected technology: the stability of the communication links, the guarantee of delivery of data, error-correction possibilities, etc.
2. **Adaptability.** A factor that specifies the possibility to modify or change (also improve) the configuration of the distributed subsystem network according to the new demands of the system.
3. **Scalability.** A factor that specifies the possibility to enlarge the quantity of subsystem in the distributed system without significant changes of the system structure, configuration or additional expenses.
4. **Complexity.** A factor that specifies the overall complexity of the system implementing the selected technology: how hard is to implement each layer of technology, including middleware communicating devices and similar.
5. **Costs.** A factor that specifies the cost of implementation of the system using the selected technology, which consists of two main components: installation costs, including all the hardware, software and middleware, and running costs (per-message, per-megabyte, per-minute) if applicable.
6. **Range.** A factor that specifies, how far can a distributed system span in space, if it is based on the selected technology. This factor is working with the natural ranges of service for the devices implementing the selected technology.

3 Wireless LAN technology

3.1 Advantage/disadvantage analysis

A wireless LAN is a local area network that uses electromagnetic waves (radio or infrared waves) as its carrier. It has a wireless access point, to give a network connection to all users in the surrounding area. Areas may range from a single room to an entire campus. The backbone network usually uses cables, with one or more wireless access points connecting the wireless users to the wired network [5]. There are various versions of WLAN standard IEEE 802.11: (Wi-Fi), an alternative ATM-like 5 GHz standardized technology, and faster standards: 54 Mbit/s 802.11a (5 GHz) and 802.11g (2.4 GHz) [5], [6], [7].

Wireless technologies can bring many benefits to industrial applications, one of them being the ability to reduce machine setup times by avoiding cabling. So far, however, wireless technologies have not gained widespread acceptance on the factory floor. One reason for this lack of acceptance is the difficulty in achieving the timely and successful transmission of packets over error-prone wireless channels.

In an industrial or factory floor setting, for example, the benefits of using wireless technologies are manifold. The cost and time needed for the installation and maintenance of the large number of cables (normally required) can be substantially reduced, thus making plant setup and reconfiguration easier. In terms of plant flexibility, stationary systems can be wirelessly coupled to any mobile subsystems or mobile robots that may exist in order to achieve a connectivity that would otherwise be impossible.

3.2 Possible schemes of subsystem communications

The easiest way to communicate two distributed system components (or subsystems) is a well-known *point-to-point* method. Here, two subsystems initiate a bidirectional connection. The second possibility is *point-to-multipoint* method. This approach has one base station or access point, which controls communication with all of the other wireless nodes in the distributed system.

In industrial settings, it can be hard to find a location for an access point that provides dependable communication with each endpoint. Moving an access point to improve communication with one endpoint will often degrade communication with other endpoints [11]. There is a major drawback in this solution, because it may be possible to wire together multiple access points in order to improve reliability, but the cost of additional wiring can defeat the original reasons for choosing a wireless solution.

The third possibility is *peer-to-peer method*. A subsystem can send and receive data frames, but in this kind of network organization, it functions as a router and can relay data for its neighbors. A packet of wireless data will find its way to its designated destination, passing through intermediate nodes with reliable communication links.

3.3 Use cases (case studies of possible system structures)

Let us review a water treatment facility as an example of successful implementation of WLAN industrial solution in building a distributed embedded data-acquiring device system. The example is based on Ember Corporation experience (Fig. 1).

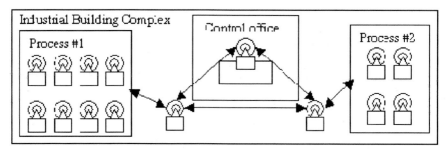

Fig. 1. Use case of Wireless LAN peer-to-peer method

Let us review the analysis of the system integration case:

- **Environment.** The environment includes significant wireless environment hurdles: thick reinforced walls, segmenting giant tanks of water with a lot of metal pipes between tanks.

- **The goal.** The goal is to connect the sensors in the pipe groups back to the control panel located in the control room on the third floor of the water filtration plant.

- **Benefits.** RS-485 serial bus wired to each sensor is replaced with wire-independent solution. Subsystems self-configured on power-up and began attempting to send data to the control room. Relaying subsystems between process parts improve the strength of signal.

- **Drawbacks.** Expensive middleware is needed in each subsystem due to relaying hardware. WLAN demands other technology if the parts of the system are deployed at significant distances. Using huge amount of relaying nodes is very inefficient.

4 GSM and GPRS technologies

4.1 Advantage/disadvantage analysis

The Global System for Mobile communications (GSM) is the most popular standard for mobile phones in the world. GSM phones are used by over a billion people across more than 200 countries [2]. GSM differs significantly from its predecessors in that both signaling and speech channels are digital.

GSM is a cellular network, which means that mobile phones connect to it by searching for cells in the immediate vicinity. GSM networks operate at various different radio frequencies: 900MHz and/or 1800MHz (USA and Canada: 850MHz and/or 1900MHz) [2], [4]. The technical fundamentals of the GSM system were defined in 1987. In 1998, the 3rd Generation Partnership Project (3GPP) was formed [3], [4].

General Packet Radio Service (GPRS) is a mobile data service available to users of GSM mobile phones. It provides moderate speed data transfer, by using unused TDMA channels in the GSM network. GPRS is integrated into GSM standards releases starting with Release 97 and onwards. First it was standardised by ETSI but now that effort has been handed onto the 3GPP [2]. The total available bandwidth can be immediately dedicated to those users who are actually sending at any given moment, providing higher utilisation where users only send or receive data intermittently [9]. GPRS originally supported (in theory) IP, PPP and X.25 connections [8].

GSM DATA is a technology that allows two subsystems to communicate bidirectionally. This approach needs the successful handshake operation to be performed between two GSM modems, until a tunnel between target subsystems will be made available for the information stream. The operation process of this approach is similar to that applied to analogue modems [1], [2]. The main benefit of communication links based on the GSM DATA is that large amounts of data can be transferred in both directions without limitations on session time or data amount. Unfortunately, one subsystem cannot communicate with more than one of remote subsystems. However, it is possible to make an operational environment for each of the distributed subsystems, which will close the connection to the remote subsystem after finishing the data transfer and initiate a new connection to the other remote subsystem. This approach is not suitable for distributed embedded systems with time-critical requirements to the initiation frequency of the inter-subsystem communication sessions.

The second GSM-based technology is *GSM SMS* (Short Message Service), which differs from GSM DATA or GPRS. SMS approach does not require the mobile entity including the subsystem to be active or to be within network range - messages will be held for a number of days until the phone is active and gets within the range. The main benefit of GSM SMS is that short messages have a validity period, which means that it is not expected to be delivered immediately. The message can wait in a mobile operator queue until receiving system can handle it. This approach is useful for such distributed systems that have remote subsystems, which are not constantly available in the network range. Unfortunately, time-critical systems do not allow this kind of lags in data delivery time. The second drawback is that the data sending may take up to 5 seconds. To override the sending and response timeout it is good to use a separate microcontroller for communication routines. Thus, SMS is not recommended in time-critical systems. Fortunately, most of the cases with gathered data transfers do not require extremely quick reactions and general process timing.

The *GSM GPRS* (General Packet Radio Service) technology significantly differs from other GSM technologies. Internet is used to transfer data, whereas the GPRS is the data protocol used for communications between remote subsystems. The GPRS offers high-speed data transfer from 56 up to 114 Kbps and continuous connection to the Internet for remote subsystems of the distributed embedded system. However, this technology brings serious difficulties in the inter-subsystem communication structure. For example, GPRS communication method, which needs an IP address for every subsystem, gives a possibility to connect to any other remote IP address, but impossible to connect to the system with mobile operator local IP address. It is possible to get a corporate IP (not random local) address range from the mobile operator. The second solution is presented in the next chapter.

4.2 Possible schemes of subsystem communications

Let us analyze the design of communication network between remote subsystems with GSM DATA. A possible implementation scheme of the method is based on authors' research in [8], [9], [10] and [12].

In case of implementation of GSM DATA approach, a *supervisor and monitoring* node should have a pool of GSM modems to support numerous connections simultaneously. In fact, this is a significantly weak point of GSM DATA approach. This drawback disappears in SMS or GPRS. We will analyze these issues later in the paper.

Next, let us proceed to the design of communication network between remote subsystems with GSM SMS. The scheme of possible implementation is similar to Fig. 3. However, GSM SMS approach brings significant benefits over GSM DATA, but still has its own drawbacks. For instance, an amount of data sent in a single data-message is limited to 140 bytes. But in the same time, GSM operator central is buffering all the messages and retries the delivery unless the *validity period* is not reached. Also, the central is informing if the message was delivered. Moreover, GSM module collects the received messages in special memory slots, until these can be processed and deleted. There is no way of receiving an erroneous message, meanwhile in GSM DATA the error-correction mechanisms must be implemented. Let us analyze a possible scheme of a data-acquisition subsystem whose task is to send requests for current data and receive responses from remote data-gathering subsystems (Fig. 2).

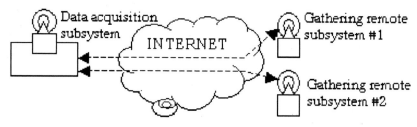

Fig. 2. Remote subsystem communication with GSM GPRS

There is a solution for building a connection between remote subsystems with the problem of dynamically assigned random IP addresses. The method involves an additional subsystem, which is a server with a real IP address, used to handle each session of the remote subsystem communication. The server is used to receive requests from remote subsystems, store and route the responses to the corresponding subsystem. Thus, the problem of data redirection is solved.

4.3 Use cases (case studies of possible system structures)

Let us overview the proposed distributed system, which is using embedded communication middleware in order to share current state of subsystems with the main monitoring station (Fig. 3).

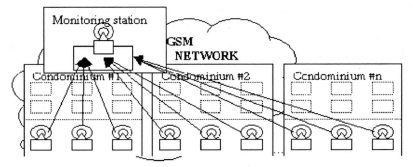

Fig. 3. GSM SMS case study: Monitoring and control of subsystems

The target of the system is automated centralized data acquiring from water flow meters (sensors; may be also electricity flow meters) located in each entrance of each condominium connected to the network of this distributed system. Low cost embedded devices (based on [1], but enriched with analogue to digital converters (ADC) in order to digitalize the analogue data coming from original sensors) are implemented in each subsystem.

- Gathering subsystem: water sensors connected to one data-collecting subsystems with an addition of middleware that sends several packages of data to the central monitoring station (one device for each entrance of the condominium).
- Monitoring subsystem: sends requests to remote data-collecting subsystems and gathers stores response (data-processing algorithms can be applied on the stored data).

In this case, we have a following distributed system:

- **Environment.** The environment consists of the main monitoring station and numerous condominiums scattered remotely around the main station. Each condominium has entrances serving all its water flow meters.
- **The goal.** The goal is to connect all the subsystems (condominiums) to the main station to organize a centralized stet monitoring and control of consumers' flow meters.
- **Benefits.** Cheap grouping of nearby entrances to one subsystem and linking these to the main station. Ability to monitor and control remote subsystems via the main station. Connection is spawned on demand, minimizing sending costs.

- **Drawbacks.** Connection to the main station requires subsequent charges for each short message. The charges are low, but contiguous. Message consists of a limited number of bytes (140).

For GPRS, the target distributed embedded system consists of remote subsystems. Consider that subsystems are situated in an industrial environment, where common communication methods cannot be applied: rough and heavily used terrain, high buildings and metallic or shielded constructions between the subsystems. Cables cannot be used, as well as direct infrared or similar links since serious obstacle or interference. GPRS greatly increases the flexibility of the distributed embedded system adding mobility to each subsystem. This means that each subsystem is not tied to its initial placeholder. This brings the ability of a subsystem to change its location continuously, without reconfiguration of communication. Moving objects (containers, robots). Thus, implementation of GSM/GPRS sets new grounds in process automation.

Let us consider system of several lighthouses, each using a generator, which charges accumulators used by the lamp. The generator has an electric starter and other controls, which allow the controlling subsystem to switch it on/off and read some state information. There is a system supervision server, which shows current states of the subsystems and sensor data. Also, a supervisor with a mobile phone can remotely monitor the system and change states of the subsystems by sending commands. There are two subsystems: "temperature monitoring" and "heating control", connected directly (close disposition). The remaining subsystems are communicating using GSM GPRS method, sending control messages only when it is necessary.

Let us review the analysis of the following system integration case:

- **Environment.** A distributed system consisting of a generator, which supplies power for charging accumulators used by some power consumer. Two subsystems, "temperature monitoring" and "heating control", are connected directly due to close disposition.
- **The goal.** The goal of the automation case is to connect all the subsystems (multiple lighthouses) to the main station to organize a centralized stet monitoring and control of each node.
- **Benefits.** Subsystems are communicating using GSM GPRS method, where the connection is permanent, ready to send data any time on demand. Data sending costs are applied only to the amounts of sent data. Ability to monitor, control, and charge remote subsystems via the main station interface. Connection is spawned only when needed, minimizing sending costs.
- **Drawbacks.** The charges for sending are very low due to small amounts of data, but still considerable.

5 Comparative analysis

The research involved the investigation of some selected scientific literature sources, personal research and contiguous practice in the field of automation of industrial processes and implementation of distributed embedded systems. The everyday research allowed gathering all the experience in one piece and covering as the topic of this paper. As GSM based solution in conjunction with wired network for local devices in the constraints of a single subsystem of a distributed embedded system (wired solution implementation depends on the given environment too much and thus is very case-specific; it is almost impossible to conclude on one perfect technology) resulted as the most flexible and effective of all the competitors, a set of universal middleware subsystem devices was established with a design of the first prototype (described in [8], [9], [10], [12] and [13]) of an embedded GSM SMS/GPRS based hardware/software solution to solve many cases in industrial process automation and beyond.

The analysis procedures performed in previous sections allow us to introduce the results of a comparison of the technologies in a form of two logically correlated tables (Table 1 and Table 2).

Table 1. Reliability, Adaptability, Scalability

Method	Reliability	Adaptability	Scalability
WLAN Point-to-Point	High	Low	None
WLAN Point-to-Multipoint	Low	Low	Moderate
WLAN Peer-to-Peer	High	High	Yes
GSM DATA	High	High	Moderate
GSM SMS	Very High	High	Yes
GPRS	High	High	Yes
GPRS (corporate)	Very High	Very High	Yes
GPRS SMS	Very High	High	Yes

Table 2. Complexity, Costs, Range

Method	Complexity	Costs	Range
WLAN Point-to-Point	Low	Low	Low (local)
WLAN Point-to-Multipoint	Moderate	Low	Low (local)
WLAN Peer-to-Peer	High	High	Low (local)
GSM DATA	Low	Moderate	Worldwide
GSM SMS	Low	Moderate	Worldwide
GPRS	Low	Moderate	Worldwide
GPRS (corporate)	Low	High	Worldwide
GPRS SMS	Low	Moderate	Worldwide

General outcome:

- GSM and GPRS solutions are the best choice where the industrial process profit can handle low, but still contiguous running costs (GSM: short messages, data calls; GPRS: data transmission).
- WLAN solutions are suitable for building industrial process automation distributed systems, where running costs are a crucial factor. Thus, system integrators have to avoid the obstacles that have to be faced in the process of implementation of these technologies. Nevertheless the Bluetooth technology is similar to WLAN, the possibility of its implementation in industrial distributed systems is very weak for now.

6 Conclusions

The main goal of industrial process automation is centralized monitoring and control centre. This increases the number of remote subsystems, which need communication middleware. The second goal of industrial process automation is reduction of industrial system maintenance costs. This includes getting the current status, updating firmware, and making changes to the action sequence the subsystem performs.

While some of our proposals (i.e. GSM-based solutions) require low, but obvious and contiguous running costs, these approaches bring benefits of flexible data gathering and secure connections. Meanwhile, approaches that do not require any running costs for data transmission (i.e. WLAN, Bluetooth) reduce the flexibility and bring a sensible instability of communication links or require static subsystem positions (movement from the installation point is very limited due to wire lengths) and high installation costs.

The systems implementing more than one technology are the best solution, where we implement different approaches, which suit each specific bottleneck of the distributed system. For example, local station sensors can be connected using WLAN, but each remote station can be connected with all the others using GPRS connections. At the same time, such systems require numerous middleware subsystems for interfacing different communication protocols and handle the integrity of the data in each point of the distributed system. Thus, hybrid solutions require significant time and resource consumption.

This work has been partly supported by the European Social Fund within the National Programme "Support for the carrying out doctoral study programm's and post-doctoral researches" project "Support for the development of doctoral studies at Riga Technical University.

References

1. 3GPP Consortium (1999) Network Architecture TS 23.002, http://www.3gpp. org/
2. ETSI (2005) The original GSM standard (GSM 07.05, GSM 07.07, GSM 03.40, GSM 03.38), http://www.etsi.org/
3. GSM Association (2005) GSM technology overview, http://www.gsmworld. com
4. GSM technical overview (2005) http://radio-electronics.com
5. IEEE 802.11 (1999) The original 1 Mbit/s and 2 Mbit/s, 2.4 GHz RF and IR standard
6. IEEE 802.11g (2003) 54 Mbit/s, 2.4 GHz standard (backwards compatible with b)
7. IEEE 802.11h (2004) Spectrum Managed 802.11a (5 GHz) for European compatibility
8. Mikoyelov D (2003) Microcontroller solutions for industrial process automation (Master's thesis), Riga Technical University
9. Mikoyelov D (2003) The development of operation environment for AVR microcontrollers (Engineer's thesis), Riga Technical University
10. Mikoyelov D (2006) An Implementation of Modern Communication Models in Process Automation, 40th Spring International Conference on Modelling and Simulation of Systems (MOSIS'06), Prerov, Czech Republic
11. Poor R, Hodges B (2002) Reliable Wireless Networks for Industrial Systems, Boston, USA, Ember Corporation
12. Rusakov P, Mikoyelov D (2005) Subsystem Communication in a Distributed Embedded System, 13th International Conference on Information Systems Development, Lithuania
13. Rusakov P, Mikoyelov D (2006) An Analysis of Distributed Embedded Systems in Industrial Process Automation, Design, Analysis, and Simulation of Distributed Systems 2006, Alabama, USA

How to Identify Objectives and Genres in E-Democracy Projects: Learning from an Action Case Study

Øystein Sæbø

Department of Information Systems, School of Management,
Agder University College, Kristiansand, Norway
Fax: +4738141029, Phone: +4738141626, E-mail: Oystein.Sabo@hia.no

Abstract: An increased number of public organisations engage in E-Democracy projects to improve their capability to communicate on democratic issues. Such efforts are complex due to lack of knowledge on how to develop information technology solutions to support the complex nature of the electronic communication taking place. In this paper a process is proposed, identifying objectives and genres in E-Democracy projects. The process addresses two major problems identified from the E-Democracy literature and a case study. Firstly, the purposes of E-Democracy projects are often unclear and somewhat naïvely understood. Secondly, it seemed difficult to enact technology to achieve the identified objectives. This paper first describes the suggested process and then focus on experiences from an action case study. The opportunity to link main ideas (phase 1) and genres (phase 2) showed importance in the discussion about what to develop in the action case project. Introducing E-Democracy models simplified a comparison between alternatives and initiated a discussion on the objectives before focusing directly on technology, which is found to be a weakness in other E-Democracy projects.

1 Introduction

E-Democracy refers to the use of information and communication technology (ICT) in political debates and decision-making processes, complementing or contrasting traditional means of communication. The idea of democracy leans fundamentally on effective communication and informed decision-making about public issues among citizens, politicians, officers and other stakeholders who may relate to the decisions (Habermas, 1996; Van Dijk, 2000). There is a need to address the connection between ICT and the electronic communication taking place in E-Democracy projects in more detail (Smith, 2000; Steyaert, 2000).

Experiences from a case study (Rose & Sæbø, 2005) identified two challenges related to the use of ICT in E-Democracy projects. First, the purpose of the E-Democracy project was poorly understood and not shared among major stakeholders in the project; the main objectives were not clear. Second, the connection between the objectives and the use of ICT were unclear. To address these challenges a process for identifying objectives and genres in E-Democracy projects was suggested (Sæbø, 2006). Introducing four E-Democracy models (Päivärinta & Sæbø, 2006) permits different expectations, motivations, and interests to be identified and investigated. The next challenge — how to enact the objectives to information technology — is addressed by linking knowledge on E-Democracy Models, Genre of communication and IT artefacts (Päivärinta & Sæbø, 2006). In this paper the process is first briefly described. Then the paper presents experiences from an action case study, allowing learning and reflection on the suggested process.

2 Theoretical background

The first problem, how to identify main objectives in E-Democracy projects (Rose & Sæbø, 2005), arose from analyses based on a Democracy Model framework (Bellamy, 2000). A democracy model describes a stereotypical form of democracy and outlines how it operates in practice. Literature on democratic models (Held, 1996; Lively, 1975; Van Dijk, 2000) uses varying characteristics to clarify differences among democratic ideas, making a detailed comparison of the competing models difficult. A review of this literature conducted by Päivärinta and Sæbø (2006) suggest a simplified comparison of various E-Democracy models based on two fundamental characteristics: inclusion in decisions and control of the agenda (Dahl, 1989). The four E-Democracy models are introduced in table 1.

Table 1. Models of E-Democracy (based on Päivärinta and Sæbø (2006))

	Partisan E-Democracy	Direct E-Democracy
Citizens set the agenda	Citizens express bottom-up opinions and critique on existing power structures. No explicit connection to the existing governmental or political decision-making processes is defined beforehand. Citizens set the agenda for public discussions but not for decision-making. ICT is introduced to obtain visibility for alternative political expressions uninterrupted by the political elite.	Citizens participate directly in decision-making processes. The citizens online affect the decisions to be made (mostly at the local level). Citizens set the agenda both for public discussion and decision-making. ICT is a crucial pre-condition for democracy to support coordination among decision-makers.

	Liberal E-Democracy	Deliberative E-Democracy
Government (politicians and officers) set(s) the agenda	Government serves citizens who participate in elections and related debates. Government would like to inform and be informed by the citizens without a clear connection to the decision-making process. ICT is introduced to improve the amount and quality of information exchange between government and citizens.	E-Democracy projects are used for targeted purposes involving citizens in the public decision-making processes. The citizens have a good reason to expect that their voices are being heard concerning a particular matter. ICT is developed for increased citizen participation and involvement in the decision-making processes.
	Citizens mainly implicitly included in decision-making processes.	Citizens have an explicitly defined role in decision-making processes.

The second problem, how to link objectives to ICT, is closely related to the first. Main objectives for E-Democracy projects can be identified from the suggested E-Democracy models. Genre theory is one way of studying the emergence of new media or sub-media (Ihlström, 2004) and is introduced here to explore detailed viewpoints on communication patterns for E-Democracy purposes. Finally, knowledge on information technology needs to be more explicit to the specific technology needed. Theories on IT-artefacts focus on the technology and its connection to tasks, structures and contexts. Knowledge of IT artefacts is connected to knowledge of genres and E-Democracy models and is used to explain the link between main objectives and ICT. A review based on the link between these three strands of research   (Sæbø & Päivärinta, 2006) identified technological forms for E-Democracy models. These are introduced in table 2.

Table 2. Communication genres for different democracy models

Form Partisan Democracy	Substance
Discussion forum	Channel for expressing opinions with little or no visibility under the prevailing political system
Chat system	Synchronous system for short messages
Information Portals	Provide either information on a particular view or as much neutral information as possible

Newsgroups/Usenet groups	Asynchronous discussions, allow longer threads when messages are not in real time
Mail-based discussions	Asynchronous, introducing push-technology by sending mail to participants
Weblogs	Broadcast a citizen's view

Liberal Democracy

Discussion forums	Information exchange among stakeholders without a clear connection to decision-making
Dialogue system	Citizens express their views as input to decisions made by politicians
Information broadcasting	Bring information from politicians to citizens
Governmental homepages	Inform citizens about timely issues
E-Debates between candidates	Broadcast debates between politicians
Information portals	One-stop access point for information achievements
Consultation	Government/politicians respond to citizen's questions
Candidate or campaigning websites	Promote a candidate or a case
Weblogs	Broadcast a politician's view

Deliberative Democracy

Discussion forum (issue-based), E-Docket	Initiating, drafting, and defining political issues
Dialogue system	Citizens express suggestions and ideas of issues
Invitation to submit suggestions	Citizens submit suggestions
(e-) Referendum	Inform decision-makers about citizens' view on a particular issue
Homepages	Inform and educate citizens about timely issues
On-line transmissions of meetings	Broadcast meeting for more transparent decision-making
Citizen panel/"jury"	Getting information from a sample of citizens concerning an issue
On-line questionnaire/Survey	Getting opinions from citizens on particular issue

E-voting/Membership ballot	Getting opinions from citizens/members of a community on particular issues
"Your question"	Citizens ask questions to politicians
Public opinion messages	Citizens express their opinions
Real-time chat, Group-to-group chat	Citizens and politicians discuss issues
Closed discussion forum	Party members can affect opinion within a party
Expert panel	Choosing appropriate background documentation for a targeted debate
Formal consultation report	Collecting viewpoints from targeted debate for decision-makers
Feedback about targeted discussions	Informing discussion participants how the discussion affects the decisions
Direct Democracy	
User Registration	To get rights to act in the community
Open discussion/idea forum	Citizens raise new issues and discuss them
Decision-making on issues to be debated	Decide which issues are to be debated and voted on further
Targeted debate forums	Discuss issues proposed for formal discussion
Background documentation	Inform users about timely issues and decisions taken
E-Voting	Decide how to act
Information about the party	FAQ, history, organization

2 A process for identifying objectives and genres in E-Democracy projects

The suggested process (Sæbø, 2006) has two major phases and addresses the criticised approach of concentrating on technology first without identifying strategies and purposes (Grönlund, 2003; Olsson, Sandstrom, & Dahlgren, 2003; Ranerup, 2000; Tops, Horrocks, & Hoff, 2000). The first phase concentrates on identifying objectives for the forthcoming projects. The second phase concentrates on how to enact technology to meet the identified objectives. Phase 1 results in an overview on what democracy model(s) to support. The identified genres (table 2) act as a starting point for the discussion on how to enact technology. Table 3 presents suggested activities for the process.

Table 3. Steps, participants, outcomes and suggested tools for the process

Steps	Participants	Outcomes	Suggested tools	Relation to theory
Phase 1: Identifying the purpose of the project				
Identifying major stakeholders	Project initiators	An overview of stakeholders to include in the process.	Interviews Mapping techniques Workshops	Precondition, no direct connection to the theories involved.
Analysing objectives and purposes	Stakeholders	Stakeholder's objectives are identified.	Interviews Workshops Surveys	Individuals' objectives are identified according to the four democracy models (table 1)
Consensus-building on main objectives	Stakeholders	Common understanding of objectives in the project.	Workshops Scenario building Interviews	Objectives are agreed on supporting one (or several) of the democracy models (table 1).
Phase 2: Enacting identified purposes into suggested genres				
Steps	Participants	Outcomes	Suggested tools	Relation to theory
Identifying technological opportunities	Stakeholders	An overview of different opportunities and reflection on the usefulness of different alternatives.	Prototyping Pilot testing Workshops Interviews	Technological opportunities are identified according to the genres (table 2) for the specified democracy model(s)

Developing a list of objectives and genres.	Project owners	Prioritized list objectives and potential genres to guide the forthcoming development process.	Workshops	An overview presenting the democracy models to support (table 1) connected to suggested genres (table 2)
			Interviews	

3 Exploring the suggested process in an action case study

To explore the process in a real-life context, an action case study was conducted in Kristiansand, a local municipality in Norway. The municipality decided to focus on the "Internet as a facilitator for increased political participation", and describes themselves as a municipality focusing explicitly on openness and dialogue.

Braa and Vidgen (1995) characterise action cases as "action components [that] reflect the potential for research to change organizations, resulting in changes to the social world. The case component reflects the understanding of findings in an organizational context". Action case studies are characterised by: short duration time, interventions in real-time, inclusion of case study elements to support understanding of the domain, emphasis on small (quasi)-experiments in real life-settings, reduced complexity, and focus on changes in a small scale (Braa, 1995). Thus the action case approach makes a good candidate for exploring the suggested process in a small-scale study.

The data sources include dialogues with major stakeholders, project documents, e-mail correspondences, and minutes from project meetings. Ten persons indicated by the executive officer in the project as holding key roles related to the forthcoming E-Democracy project were investigated. Six of them were politicians and four employees in the public administration.

4 Results

The intervention took the following two phases (table 4).

Table 4. Steps conducted in the action case study

Phase 1: Identifying the purpose of the project					
Steps	Participants	Outcomes	Tools	Relation to theory	Comments
Identifying major stakeholders	Stakehold appointed by the executive officer.	Twelve stakeholders identified: six politicians and six staff personnel.	E-mail correspond-ence Dialogue (by the executisve officer	*Precondition, no direct connection to the theories involved.*	Two of the staff personnel were not available for involvement in the project.
Analysing objectives	10 stakeholders	Stakeholder's objectives identified.	Dialogue	Support for Liberal and Deliberative democracy models identified	
Consensus-building on objectives	*10 stakeholders*	*(Not achieved in the action case)*	*No activity took place*	*No activity took place*	*No plenary activities took place, so the consensus building was mainly ignored.*
Phase 2: Enacting identified purposes into suggested technological forms					
Identifying technological opportunities	10 Stakeholders	Individuals' ideas on the use and usefulness of different technological opportunities	Dialogue	Technologi-cal forms supporting Liberal and Deliberative democracy models identified.	Opportunities discussed with each individual.

Developing a list of objectives and potential genres	Researcher	Temporary list of opportunities	Researcher's analysis	Main objectives and suggested genres presented (table 6).	The task is conducted by the researcher involved

4.1 Analysis phase 1: Identifying the objectives for the project

The first step — identifying major stakeholders — was conducted by the executive officer in the project. She appointed stakeholders based on their role in the project, earlier experiences on E-Democracy projects, and their availability for participation in the research project. The second step, analysing objectives, focused on the four different democracy models presented in table 1. The discussion surrounding the models was significant as participants began to reflect on the purposes of the project, but also on advantages and challenges for the different democracy models.

Discussing the Partisan Democracy model participants commented:

- Partisan democracy is not for us; it is not the municipality's concern.
- It is easy to get into an educator-role and disrupt the idea by becoming the initiator.
- You'll risk stealing the show if the municipality is interrupting (in Partisan democracies).… If the municipality interacts, don't you end up in another model?
- Is this the politician's concern? Isn't the main concern for the press and media?
- In Partisan democracy different organizations or stakeholder groups have the main responsibility. But I can't work as the responsible editor in the municipality if the responsibility is given away in that respect.
- Those who would like to go into action have to do it themselves. And everyone is able to develop a web-page if needed.

Key learning. The participants did not consider supporting Partisan democracy as the municipality's main responsibility. The participants are also worried about interrupting a free political discussion. The model as such is not seen as irrelevant, but it should be developed and maintained by actors outside the municipality, such as media and other stakeholder groups.

On the Direct democracy model participants commented:

- If you had small responsible units with money to spend, you might have had direct or deliberative democracy. But I don't believe in it, the representative democracy still needs to be the main model.
- In direct democracy, single subjects will obtain too much space. You'll lose the comprehensive overview needed in a democracy.

- Referendums require clear answers, yes or no or at least clear alternatives. And that is not the case in our society.
- A local area might vote on a specific topic, I don't disagree with that. In practice, on rare occasions a topic affects only a defined local area.
- Referendum is very difficult, almost impossible, to organise traditionally. It has to be on rare occasions and on specific topics.
- … (Direct democracy) costs a lot of money. And better decision-making is not to be achieved either.
- Referendum by Internet comes to a new opportunity. Maybe we can perform referendums easier, by voting for or against road tolls. But I don't accept a referendum for or against immigration, which is based on values I don't discuss. It is more a fight against selfishness we all have and is therefore more difficult.
- Referendums should be performed on major principal subjects. Electors have to know the opportunities and live with the consequences. By referendums, the people's will is represented, then politicians have to arrange their action according to it.

Key learning. The Direct democracy model achieved minor support. A missing tradition for referendums and high costs are seen as obstacles for this model. Referendums are not considered (by most of the participants) to interact sufficiently with the complexity needed in a modern democracy. The Internet may decrease the costs needed to perform referendums, but it does not change the challenge of achieving involvement by citizens.

On the Liberal democracy model, participants commented:

- Liberal democracy is unproblematic. It's a question on getting information in and out; the challenge then is the quality control on the information.
- I wish we had a huge element of Liberal as well as Deliberative democracy.
- I'm not sure if the decisions must always, at least in superior cases, be made by the county council. It is the only agency having the opportunity to keep a holistic view on the municipality, being willing to make painful decisions prioritizing one subject over another. I can't really see how that changes by the influence of Deliberative democracy.
- By the end of the day, politicians are making the decisions. Citizens are only adding contributions in the processes.
- The citizens' main contribution is to add good advice…. If there are many contributions concerning a subject, it's a sign of the importance of that subject, it's like taking the heat on citizens' concerns.
- I really don't know what a discussion forum should be except for securing publicity on single topics. It would have been interesting if some politicians stepped forward and said what they meant, but also what they wasn't sure of — please come and influence me! — that someone really asked to be influenced. But then they really have to be serious, to let themselves be influenced. The

problem in politics is that opinions are rarely individual; they are commonly decided for a party group.

- What's important for me as a decision-maker is to get as many contributions as possible, a wide range of viewpoints so that I can sort out the best and decide what to use later in the process.

Key learning. Liberal Democracy achieved support from many participants. The Liberal democratic idea of achieving more information without influencing the way decision-making is performed is seen as unproblematic by most of the participants. No promises are made on some kind of direct influence by citizens' participation. The Liberal model combines the opportunity to get input with the traditional representative democracy and is therefore seen by many as the only realistic opportunity.

On the Deliberative democracy model, participants commented:

- We need to strive for Deliberative democracy where it is possible. I can't see any other opportunity on the decreasing participation we now explore.
- I believe politicians would like to stay in the Liberal quadrant, being able to claim a comprehensive communication with the target group, but still making all the decisions themselves. That would not be very popular. To succeed, I think we need to get to the two models here (Direct and Deliberative Democracy). People don't want to engage without any influence. Then we fool them.
- I would like to see a shift from Liberal democracy towards more Deliberative democracy, in any case in a municipality like Kristiansand working exactly on such challenges.
- I think we should work more in the direction of Deliberative democracy, where it is possible. I can't see any other opportunity except the absence of Democracy, which may be present in general in our society.
- I would like politicians to give away some power on single topics, where it is possible. Sometimes you ask on stages where the opportunity to influence is absent, where inputs are only a finery. Then I think it's better not to ask.
- We have to go for the Deliberative model in the future. The party politics engage fewer and fewer people, so we have to develop new ways for citizens to influence and maintain the democracy.
- In an ideal world, the Deliberative model is the one to develop. But politicians are seeking power, that's why they become politicians. They would like to be seen as democratic, listening to others and so on, but I think there are some stable decision-oriented structures in the politicians that are difficult to change.

Key learning. The Deliberative democracy is by many seemed as an ideal model to support. Two main issues were discussed. Firstly, the tension between the model and the politicians' will to really be influenced by citizens is highlighted. If politicians are not willing to be influenced, solutions supporting Deliberative democracy should not be developed. Secondly, Deliberative democracy is by some seen as the only way to engage citizens. Citizens would like more than just the opportunity to speak; they are considered to look for some real influence.

The third step — Consensus-building on objectives and purposes — was not achieved in the action case study. The action case study faced restricted resources that did not allow consensus-building activities as part of the first stage, as suggested in the process (Table 3). The second stage is therefore based on individual views of how to enact technological forms with different models of democracy.

4.2 Analysis phase 2: Enacting objectives to E-Democracy genres

The analysis in stage 1 identified support the Liberal and the Deliberative E-Democracy models. On identifying technological opportunities in the Liberal democracy model, participants commented:

- You may develop layers of information on a web-page, including history, alternatives, and choices. The problem now is that the information is hard to get because of the complexity and tone in public documents. So technology may be used to introduce different topics more briefly and add links to more information on each subject.
- Instead of raising your hand and asking questions, people could send in their questions via sms', a communication form they actually know. Then it becomes like the TV-channels, with a window on the screen continually including new messages showing what the youth are engaged in.
- We would like to go for radio transmission from the county council meetings… Radio transmission seems to work perfectly well. The representatives do not seem to be interrupted at all. Examples in which politicians are videotaped illustrate how they became stiff in front of a camera.
- We need to develop a question and answer kind of service. But my hypothesis is that sending in an enquiry to a politician or a party office without getting a response feels like a slap in your face.
- We are currently redesigning an information portal. I believe the design of the portal will have great influence on the extent to which people would like to visit the page again.
- Many people retrieve information by e-mail who would not have the information elsewhere. I send out newsletters by e-mail to 30–40 people who, without e-mail, would have no opportunity to receive this information. It's extremely efficient.
- Personally I would like to have a blog where I write some thoughts about what I as a politician am doing right now. That would be great.
- We have discussed the opportunity to broadcast meetings with the opportunity to get instant feedback from citizens by having a computer on the table. I think

it will be too demanding for the elected since you have to be very concentrated to participate in a debate. It will become too intense.

- What is important in a Liberal democracy is the municipality's home page. Personally, I utilise the web to find old subjects and minutes, which I find very convenient.

Key learning. Technological forms for Liberal democracy focus on information exchange. The Internet is seen to enable a simplified presentation of information. Some of the participants find the governance-centric presentation of information to be a major obstacle to citizen participation. The Internet's opportunity to host citizen-centric information channels is therefore important. Other important issues are how to design the web-page, the efficiency of information distribution by e-mail or by blog, and the importance of offering communication channels that are known by the users.

On identifying technology for the Deliberative democracy model, participants commented:

- The only definite idea I have is the opportunity to make a closer connection between the Political Agenda (an archive of minutes and calendar of political meetings) where you'll find all the information needed and a discussion forum where you can take part in a discussion you are interested in. The integration between such services needs to be as tight as possible.
- In our party, we have an internet-part, an intranet-part, a closed internal discussion forum and an extra-net part for the national level. On the local level, we have continually ongoing communication among members, mainly based on e-mail. We would like to have the same communication with citizens, but have not yet either the priority nor the capability to include citizens as well.
- E-based debates between candidates are interesting, so far mostly utilised internally in the party. But they are utilised more and more by committees in the municipality.
- What are needed are simultaneous discussions taking place here and now, allowing for follow-up questions if needed. Without including such a service, our dialogue is useless. Dialogue is here and now. If I add a contribution to a politician, I also expect a quick answer. 10 minutes are ok, there might be more than me contributing, but 48 hours is not ok. For me, the Internet is nearly simultaneous.
- I find chat most convenient for deliberative democracy because you are then able to really discuss.

Key learning. Comments on how to enact Deliberative democracy focused much more on discussions than on information exchange. Participants also commented on the importance of simultaneous communication patterns if real discussions are to be supported.

Table 5 summarise the analysis made based on the action case study. The analysis is based on participants' support for two different models, the Liberal and the Deliberative.

Table 5. Summarized analysis of the action case project

Partisan Democracy	Direct Democracy
Restricted support from the participants. The model is not considered to be a main responsibility for the municipality.	Achieved only restricted support. Challenges such as representativity, costs and complexity of the decisions needed in a democracy are obstacles for utilising a Direct democracy model.
Liberal Democracy	**Deliberative Democracy**
Supported by participants. Unproblematic link between projects and the traditional democratic system. Quality of the information exchange is seen important.	Supported by participants. Challenging, but also more interesting for citizens than the Liberal model. Opportunities to discuss and influence are seen important.
Technological forms are characterised by ease of access, feedback on questions made, and opportunities for information broadcasting. Examples to evaluate further in the project are: Radio/TV transmission Question-and-answer services Information portals News mail Blogs Quality of the municipality's home-page	Technological forms are characterised by the opportunity to discuss, including feedback mechanisms showing the influence of the contributions, and the opportunity to participate in synchronous discussions. Examples to evaluate further in the project are: Discussion forums E-mail based discussions E-Debates between candidates and citizens Chat

4.3 Participants' reflection on the usefulness of the suggested process

The participants were asked to reflect on the perceived usefulness of the suggested process. They commented:

- I think it is necessary to look at what is needed to succeed. A presentation like this makes it possible to reflect on what is needed instead of just being positive to participate because it (the Internet) is a new way to communicate and therefore worthy by itself.
- I believe the models may bring up a lot of interesting ideas from politicians and act as a starting point for a discussion.
- It is really helpful to point out which direction this leads us, making visible the alternatives

- An overview like this on different opportunities is a nice tool in a decision-making process on where to go; it's a nice systemisation.
- It (the suggested process) is quite solid.... It has to be simplified for practical usefulness.
- It (the suggested process) is currently too complicated, but it helps me as an executive officer to better understand different opportunities.
- The problem is often that we start up with technical solutions before knowing what we would like to achieve, which I found to be meaningless. You need to look at what to achieve, different alternatives and thereafter choose the technical solution. Politicians need to get different opportunities plainly put, including cost accounting and what's expected from them on different alternatives.
- Immediately, it seems interesting to arrange a session for the city council where politicians themselves, based on this process, discuss what they would like to develop, simply a process of increasing awareness on what they like to achieve.
- There's a need for even more concretising of different alternatives. What are you achieving by a discussion forum, by a chat system? I don't know.
- Now we have this tool identifying opportunities by ICT, of course we have to use it (the suggested process) further in the process.

Key Learning. The suggested process was perceived useful by the participants involved in the project. This was underscored by the fact that all participants were able to immediately reflect on different democratic models and technological forms despite only a limited introduction. Participants find the idea of focusing on main purposes before discussing technology to be helpful in the developing process. The presentation was found by some to be too complicated, but despite of this still helpful. Participants address the need for being more concrete about the technology and costs connected to different alternatives.

5 Discussion

The main objectives of the project were identified by introducing the E-Democracy models. The dialogues illustrate the tension between the Liberal and the deliberative models. Some of the participants discussed the difference between the "realistic and unproblematic" Liberal model, and the "wanted, but much more challenging" Deliberative model. The process opens for a further discussion focusing particularly on these two models and their consequences.

The dialogues explored some strengths of the proposed process. Firstly, the immediate opportunity to link main ideas (phase 1) and connected genres (phase 2) showed a promising potential to guide the discussion on what to develop. The participants were able to discuss alternatives and express their viewpoints on what to achieve in the forthcoming project. Secondly, introducing the E-Democracy models simplified a comparison among alternatives and initiated a discussion on the objectives before focusing directly on technology, which is found to be a weakness in other E-Democracy projects (Grönlund, 2003; Marcella, Baxter & Moore, 2002; Rose & Sæbø, 2005).

Some challenges were also identified. The value of the suggested process may increase by being more definite on consequences, especially by estimating expected resources needed by different alternatives, such as time and competence requirements. Such knowledge is lacking because of restricted experience in utilising genres in E-Democracy projects. Further research is needed to explore consequences more in detail to further develop on the suggested process.

The suggested process could be taken into account by practitioners who may want to promote a certain kind of E-Democracy. A practitioner may identify first the assumptions of democracy in the development context in question and then the particular technological forms to be implemented in the system, such as those illustrated by the conducted action case.

By the suggested process, E-Democracy researchers can be specific in relation to the suggested framework whether the target of their research contributes to one particular E-Democracy model or a combination of various models. Furthermore, researchers can be specific when relating new knowledge to the field by identifying genres in light of the process. A new contribution can be identified as a genre instantiation supporting a specific E-Democracy model. Through such analyses, researchers can also inform the future practice of E-Democracy, offering lessons learned in a rather detailed manner.

6 Conclusion

This paper addresses the two identified problems (identifying main objectives and how to connect main objectives to genres) by introducing a two-step process. The conducted action case explored the process and gained insight on strengths and challenges. Supported by participants' reflections on the usefulness of the process I argue that the process shows importance by connecting main objectives and the use of ICT in E-Democracy projects. Participants were immediately empowered to discuss different objectives and connected genres after a brief introduction of the process.

More efforts need to be directed to further develop a dynamic experience base discussing particular E-Democracy genres, allowing for the growth of cumulative knowledge among researchers and practitioners. Particular technological forms should be investigated in more detail to find out more detailed lessons learned, including knowledge of resources needed.

Empirical research on E-Democracy has been a scattered field of experiments, lacking solid theoretical foundations, let alone cumulative knowledge to guide research and practice. The suggested process demonstrates how knowledge from established fields of research shows importance in the immature area of E-Democracy research. More research is needed to further explore and explain the ideas of communication genres when the development on new ICT and communication preferences offer new opportunities for future E-Democracy projects.

References

Bellamy, C. (2000). Modelling electronic democracy, Towards democratic discourses for an information age. In J. Hoff, I. Horrocks & P. Tops (Eds.), Democratic governance and new technology, technologically mediated innovations in political practice in Western Europe. London: Routledge.

Braa, K. (1995). Beyond Formal Quality in Information Systems Design, UiO, Oslo.

Dahl, R. A. (1989). Democracy and its critics. New Haven, Conn.: Yale University Press.

Grönlund, Å. (2003). Emerging electronic infrastructures - Exploring democratic components. Social Science Computer Review, 21(1), 55-72.

Habermas, J. (1996). Between facts and norms: contributions to a discourse theory of law and democracy. Cambridge, Mass.: MIT Press.

Held, D. (1996). Models of Democracy. Oxford: Blackwell.

Ihlström, C. (2004). The Evolution of a New(s) Genre. Unpublished Doctoral Dissertation, Göteborg University, Gothenburg.

Lively, J. (1975). Democracy. Oxford: Blackwell.

Marcella, R., Baxter, G., & Moore, N. (2002). An exploration of the effectiveness for the citizen of Web-based systems of communicating UK parliamentary and devolved assembly information. Journal of Government Information, 29(6), 371-391.

Olsson, T., Sandstrom, H., & Dahlgren, P. (2003). An Information Society for Everyone? Gazette: The International Journal for Communication Studies, 65(4-5), 347-363.

Päivärinta, T., & Sæbø, Ø. (2006). Models of E-Democracy. Communications of the Association for Information Systems, 17, 818-840.

Ranerup, A. (2000). On-line forums as an arena for political discussions. Lecture Notes in Computer Science, 1765, 209-223.

Rose, J., & Sæbø, Ø. (2005). Democracy Squared: designing on-line political communities to accommodate conflicting interests. Scandinavian Journal of Information Systems, 17(2).

Smith, C. (2000). British political parties: continuity and change in the information age. In J. Hoff, P. Tops & I. Horrocks (Eds.), Democratic governance and new technology: technologically mediated innovations in political practice in Western Europe (pp. 71-87). London: Routledge.

Steyaert, J. (2000). Local governments online and the role of the resident - Government shop versus electronic community. Social Science Computer Review, 18(1), 3-16.

Sæbø, Ø. (2006). A process for identifying objectives and technological forms in E-Democracy initiatives. Paper presented at the 12th Americas Conference on Information Systems, Acapulco, Mexico.

Sæbø, Ø., & Päivärinta, T. (2006). Defining the "E" in E-Democracy: a genre lens on IT artefacts. Paper presented at the 29th Information Systems Research Seminar in Scandinavia, Helsingoer, Denmark.

Tops, P., Horrocks, I., & Hoff, J. (2000). Tew technology and democratic renewal: the evidence assessed. In J. Hoff, I. Horrocks & P. Tops (Eds.), Democratic Governance and new technology. London: Routledge.

Van Dijk, J. (2000). Models of democracy and concepts of communication. In K. L. Hacker & J. Van Dijk (Eds.), Digital Democracy, Issues of theory and practice. London: Sage publications.

Replacing a Human Agent by an Automatic Reverse Directory Service

Géza Németh[*], Csaba Zainkó[*], Géza Kiss[*], Gábor Olaszy[*],
László Fekete[**], Domokos Tóth[**]

[*]Department of Telecommunications and Media Informatics, Budapest
University of Technology and Economics,
{nemeth, zainko, kgeza, olaszy}@tmit.bme.hu,
[**]T-Mobil Hungary Rt. {feketel, tothd}@t-mobile.hu

Abstract: Agents who answer the calls in a reverse directory service have to face a considerable challenge: they need to communicate proper names (such as the names of persons, companies and streets). Their pronunciation is frequently irregular and their spelling is not obvious. The authors developed a TTS specialized for this task, i.e. the reading of names and addresses in order to create an automatic reverse directory service. The novelty of our system compared to others developed earlier is that we employed a new reading mode and optimized the acoustic database based on an extensive analysis of Hungarian proper names. This resulted in high intelligibility and naturalness. Our system was launched as a service of T-Mobile Hungary. The specialized TTS can also be the basis of other applications in the future, such as location based services.

1 Introduction

In a reverse directory service, callers usually interact with an agent. After the caller enters a phone number, the agent tells him/her the name and the address corresponding to the number in the directory. In order to automate such a service, a TTS system is needed that is capable of handling most proper names (especially the names of persons, companies and addresses) correctly.

TTS systems developed for this purpose – we call them name and address readers – have been an important and commercially attractive application of synthetic speech. The Orator system, developed at Bellcore in 1990, was the first successful approach to solve this problem for US English [1]. In terms of other languages, Belhoula developed a solution to handle the variety in the structure of names in German in 1993. Unfortunately, it did not become a real-life application [2].

Eloquens, the Italian system developed at CSELT, was first tested by Telecom Italia in 1993 and, after gradual improvements, its quality increased significantly (MOS changed from 2.93 to 3.63) [3]. The main factor of the improvement was the development of a specialized acoustic database and synthesis method for this application and the continuous improvement of text analysis techniques.

For other languages (especially with less speakers), name and address readers have been developed only sporadically. An automatic Swedish reverse directory application was introduced by Telia in 1997 based on extensive text preprocessing (e.g. creation of a lexicon with 200k entries) and an MBROLA diphone acoustic database [4]. Callers were charged only the third of the service fee with human operators.

In Hungary, a TTS-based e-mail reader [5], became a successful service of T-Mobile Hungary. This was the motivation to develop a name and address reader to integrate into the reverse directory service of the mobile operator. Although the quality of the diphone-based PROFIVOX TTS [6] was satisfactory for e-mail reading, higher quality was required for the reverse directory application. The main reason is that e-mail reading has never been available with human operators while getting names and addresses from well-trained agents has been freely available for years (as a replacement for the legal obligation to provide printed versions to subscribers) so callers expect similar quality.

A high-quality name and address reader was developed in a cooperation. The voice of the system had to be the standard female announcer of T-Mobile Hungary and the quality had to be good enough to replace human operators. After successful field trials the system was launched at the beginning of 2004. It is fully automatic, i.e. there is no option to connect with a human operator. After a year of operation, user opinion polls were collected.

2 Structure of names and addresses

Our work was based on a database of app. 3 million wireline subscribers of 1997 out of app. 10 million Hungarian citizens where the association of names and addresses was mixed. A similarly constructed partial database of app. 2 million T-Mobile subscribers was used for validation and cross-checking. With respect to reading, names and addresses may be regarded independent so they will be discussed separately.

2.1 Features of Hungarian names

Hungarian names can be either person names or legal names (e.g. companies, organizations). Directory listings usually contain the whole name in a single record i.e. given, family and legal names as well as labels, titles and other signs might also appear in the record.

Person names may have several forms is Hungarian. In the simplest case there is a family name followed by a given name. There can be more family names and given names (like middle names in English). In case of married women, there are twelve possible forms (based on their and their husbands' family and given names). Placement of titles, such as 'Dr' further complicates the forming of ladies' names.

Hungarian given names are relatively easy to detect as they are selected from an official list of app. 1700 elements, published by the Hungarian Academy of Sciences.

Company names can be recognized from the abbreviation referring to the legal type of the company (e.g. 'Ltd'). In many cases, however, it is not the offical name that appears in the database. The real challenge is the reading of descriptions that do not have a standard way of reading, such as the company name '@rc Kft' (visual correspondence between a and @). To deal with this issue, in our categorization all names that contain other characters than letters and '-' are regarded legal names since they contain characters that are illegal in names of persons.

2.2 Features of Hungarian addresses

Addresses are also given in a single record. Their processing is simpler than names because the structure is relatively straightforward and the order of the elements is fixed (ZIP, city, street name, street type, number). The ZIP code and the city is always given, any of the other components might be missing or replaced (e.g. in case of a P.O. Box).

3 Database categories

Based on the initial analysis of 10k randomly selected database samples and taking into account the rules of Hungarian name creation, 35 name and address element categories have been defined. These define the sorts of elements used to build the name of a person, a legal name or an address. Such element categories are for example the ZIP code or the label for the first part of family names (e.g. 'Dr'). The elements for names of persons are the building blocks of maiden names also (the maiden name can be a part of a married woman's name).

4 Statistical name and address information

The directory contains 2.944.000 records, that were labeled by name and address categories in order to build the database that can provide the input for the TTS. 300.000 records were labeled manually to produce a training and test set. The rest was labeled with our automatic labeling tool. In case of uncertainties, the tool marks corresponding records with a special label. 2.627.000 person names and

285.000 legal names were found. 32.000 records could not be automatically classified. These results represent the first study of Hungarian proper names on such a large scale.

4.1 Given names

The database contained 1797 different given names. 183 of these were not on the Academy list and were regarded as foreign names. It was a surprise to see that the most frequent female name ('Mária') is only 23rd on the frequency ranking of all given names and there are only 3 others ('Éva', 'Katalin' and 'Erzsébet') in the most frequent 100. The reason might be the sociologic effect of phone numbers being mostly registered for the name of the husband, and also women frequently using their husband's name instead of their maiden name.

4.2 Family names

The large number of 103.850 different family names of the 2.627.000 proper names found in the database means that the variation of Hungarian family names is significant. Only 90% coverage of Hungarian family names may be reached by the most frequent 20k tokens.

4.3 Name prefixes and labels

Most of the 82 different name prefixes and titles appeared only in a few different positions. Many of them were single characters which have to be clearly separated from the other name elements during reading. This phenomenon has to be taken into account during prosodic planning. The vast majority of titles attached to name components are relatively simple but due to their variable position and possible joint appearance they also have a significant role in the final acoustic and prosodic design of the system.

4.4 Legal names

Approximately ¾ of legal names have a simple structure, suitable for reading. 10% of the examined items contain at least one given name. 10% contain mosaic words. 9% contain numbers and about 2.5% contain special signs.

4.5 Addresses

We compared the results of our address analysis in the directory to data obtained from the Hungarian Postal Service. The Post database lists 3562 different cities and towns while our database search yielded 3523. The number of new names was 29, mainly due to detailed local notation. There were about 16k different street names in the database. They were attached to 77 different street types (75% street, 15% road, 3% square, 7% other).

5 Recommendation for the spelling of Hungarian

During the course of the project it turned out that there is no formal standard of Hungarian spelling. In order to fill this gap a questionnaire of all Hungarian ASCII characters was created and 28 adults (university students and professionals with a university degree) were asked to describe how they would spell the given character. The proposals with the highest frequency were included in the final solution. Most of the reference words are given names (starting by a capital letter) the remaining are well known nouns. Special characters (@, &, #, etc.) are difficult to handle because a large part of the population has never even seen them. They can be regularly found in company names, however.

6 Prosodic analysis and design

Reading names and addresses requires a simpler prosodic structure than general TTS conversion. All sentences are statements. In case of reading the name, the carrier sentence ends with the variable part. The last word in the sentence is always a given name so if the most frequent given names are recorded in a sentence-final position, they can be used in most cases without any prosodic modification. In case of legal names, the name of the unit comes first and the final unit is always a legal name type. This implies that legal name types usually need no prosody adjustment. In case of reading the address, the ZIP code, the city, the street and number together and the further location parameters (e.g. building, floor, door) form separate phrases in the sentence.

7 The acoustic database

Results of the text and prosodic analysis were used to extend the acoustic database of the general purpose Profivox TTS system. The goal was to minimize the need for prosodic (especially pitch) modification and to maximize the use of longer units.

Family, company and street names are highly variable so they are usually generated by the concatenation of diphones and triphones. The most frequent 317 given names (>99% coverage) and all possible legal name types were recorded in a phrase-final position. 82 name prefixes and labels were also recorded in a sentence-final and medial position. In order to synthesize numbers (e.g. ZIP codes) with high quality, the number reader described in [7] was integrated and the number units were recorded. One thousand city names (covering >90% of all subscribers) were also recorded, uttered separately. About one hundred public-place definitions (e.g. street, road, floor, staircase) were also added in both sentence medial and final positions. Units for spelling were included as single statements. Altogether, the acoustic database contains about 12k variable length elements.

By analyzing the synthesis of 30k randomly selected addresses by our system, it turned out that the longer units (e.g. pre-recorded given names, spelling units) and triphones are the frequently applied acoustic elements. Diphones are used only occasionally. Pitch modification is rarely needed due to the careful selection of units and their consistent recording conditions. Prosody modification is usually limited to intensity and timing.

The database compiled for the name and address reading domain can be gradually extended to other domains such as car types, commercial locations, as new services will require.

8 Dialog strategies

Reading of names and addresses in a reverse directory service has to fulfill two contradicting requirements: efficient access to information and intelligible reading (so that the caller can also get to know the proper spelling, if needed).

Looking at the legal name examples of Section 2.1., it is clear that dictating them correctly may not be obvious, even for humans. The following dialogue structure was implemented after an iterative design process:

a) Input of 9 digit phone number by DTMF
b) search for the subscriber of the number in the database
c) if information is not available or secret, notification of the caller by a prerecorded prompt
d) if information is available

1. reading of name after a selection from the three name reading modes:
a)   general, continuous 'overview' reading mode
b)   syllabification mode (a special syllabification algorithm was developed for this purpose [8])
c) spelling mode

2. reading of address in all name reading modes The ZIP code and all other numbers are read by a number-reader [7]. Other elements are read by the specialized TTS.

With this approach, users may first receive a general 'overview' of the name and address information and can 'zoom' on details as required. The detailed modes provide a way for comprehending proper names efficiently that are irregular in some manner while keeping the menu structure very simple.

9 Evaluation

First, the TTS performance was tested. The testing corpus contained 100k randomly selected and 4k especially important directory records. These units were audibly checked by native listeners. The error rate (improper pronunciation) was less then 3%. Most of the errors were due to rare foreign words.

Initial user testing was also carried out. The general opinion was very positive. It was found that users appreciate the possibility to get detailed descriptions in the syllabification and spelling mode. Asking a human operator to do the same was embarrassing for them. The system was launched as a publicly available service, in fully automatic mode in February 2004.

9.1 User opinion polls after one year of operation

Operational complaints against the system were very limited. Most of the problems were caused by errors in the directory database. During the first 8 months of operation, 63% of the information requests used the overview, 18% the syllabification and 19% the spelling mode. These results show that all modes are exploited.

A formal opinion poll was also conducted by an independent market research company. The initial results reported here are based on the answers of 12 people. The poll is about to be carried out soon on a larger sample.

The subjects were customers who used the reverse directory service recently and were willing to answer questions. Four aspects of the system were rated on a scale from 1 (worst) to 5 (best), with the extremes labeled.

Generally, the users were highly satisfied with the service. The average score for speech quality was 4.58. The speech rate got 4.75, the correctness of the provided information 5.00, the dialog management 4.58. The overall score for the system was 4.92 on average – except one 4, everyone rated the system to 5.

Usage statistics also show a probably high user satisfaction: the number of calls per month did not significantly change since the automatic system replaced the human-based one.

10 Summary

A high-quality name and address reader was developed. The first analysis of names and addresses in Hungary on such a large scale was carried out. As a result, basic statistics about name and address distributions were computed and presented. A recommendation for the spelling of Hungarian was prepared. A syllabification module and a specialized TTS of names and addresses was also developed and a speech-based dialog system was designed. The reverse directory application was successfully introduced into service by T-Mobile Hungary in a fully automatic mode.

Acknowledgements

This research was supported by the Hungarian National Research and Development Program. The authors acknowledge the support of T-Mobile Hungary staff, especially Péter Pósafalvi and János Benke, in the integration of the new system into the existing infrastructure. Tamás Böhm contributed by reviewing the draft of the manuscript.

References

1. Spiegel, M. F., "Coping with Telephone Directories that Were Never Intended for Synthesis Applications", Proc. of ESCA-NATO/RSG 10 Tutorial and Workshop on Applications of Speech Technology, Lautrach, Germany, 1993, pp. 19-22
2. Belhoula, K., "A Concept for the Synthesis of Names", Proc. of ESCA-NATO/RSG 10 Tutorial and Workshop on Applications of Speech Technology, Lautrach, Germany, 1993, pp. 167-170
3. Nebbia, L., Quazza, S., and Salza, P. L., "A Specialised Speech Synthesis Technique for Application to Automatic Reverse Directory Service", Proc. of IVTTA '98, IEEE-ESCA Workshop on Interactive Voice Technology for Telecommunications Applications, Torino, Italy, 1998, pp. 223-228
4. Lundin, F. J., "The Swedish Automatic Reverse Directory Service", Proc. of IVTTA '98, IEEE-ESCA Workshop on Interactive Voice Technology for Telecommunications Applications, Torino, Italy, Sept, 1998, pp. 219-222
5. Németh, G., Zainkó, Cs., Fekete, L., Olaszy, G., Endrédi, G., Olaszi, P., Kiss, G., Kis, P., "The Design, Implementation and Operation of a Hungarian E-mail Reader", International Journal of Speech Technology, Kluwer, Vol. 3, No. 3/4, December 2000, pp. 217-236
6. Olaszy, G., Németh G., Olaszi, P., Kiss, G., Gordos, G., "PROFIVOX - A Hungarian Professional TTS System for Telecommunications Applications", International Journal of Speech Technology, Kluwer, Vol. 3, No. 3/4, December 2000, pp. 201-216
7. Olaszy, G. and Németh, G., "IVR for Banking and Residential Telephone Subscribers Using Stored Messages Combined with a New Number-to-Speech Synthesis Method", in D. Gardner-Bonneau ed., Human Factors and Interactive Voice Response Systems, Kluwer, 1999, pp. 237-255
8. Fék M., Németh G., Olaszy G., Gordos G.: "Megértést segítő részletező gépi névfelolvasás magyar nyelvre" (Automatic syllabification supporting understanding for Hungarian name-reading), Proc. of 2nd Hungarian Computational Linguistics Conference, Szeged, 2004, pp. 301-306

Topic Identification by the Combination of Fuzzy Thesaurus and Complexity Pursuit

Sándor Szaszkó*, László T. Kóczy*,†

*Budapest University of Technology and Economic, Hungary
†Széchenyi István University, Győr, Hungary

1 Introduction

An information retrieval system allows users to efficiently retrieve documents that are relevant to their current interests. The collection of documents from which the selected ones have to be retrieved might be extremely large and the use of terminology might be inconsistent.

Natural languages use many similar terms for the same or similar concepts. In order to most of the documents belonging to the same topic, special dictionaries have to be set up. A thesaurus is a collection of terms (words) which describe the same concept. With the use of the thesaurus we can discover connections among documents, which do not necessarily contain the same words, or retrieve relevant documents which do not necessarily include any of the query words.

Automated keyword search is the most widespread approach to this problem; however, it is easy to recognise that documents not containing the actual keyword(s), but maybe its their synonyms, or some terms with a closely related but more specific meaning, might be similarly relevant for the search. If the keyword in the query is Soft Computing (SC), documents on Fuzzy Systems, Neural Networks and similar topics will be unambiguously relevant, even if they do not mention the broader term (SC) explicitly a single time. Moreover, other parts of the same scientific community prefer to use the name Computational Intelligence with a rather similar meaning, so all documents related to the latter should be also retrieved.

In previous studies we suggested the use of hierarchical co-occurrence frequencies as indicators of the importance of individual words and groups of words in the contents of given documents 11011. This means that the occurrence frequencies of certain words in the title and sub-titles, the abstract and introduction or conclusion parts most of the documents might be characteristic for the occurrence frequencies of certain (other) words in the main body of the text. The frequency of word A in the title and word B in the text is called their hierarchical co-occurrence.

It is obvious that these frequencies are not probabilistic measures, as it is not the relative frequency of a certain word among all words of the document that directly measures its relevance. However these frequencies determine the possibility degrees of the documents in a somewhat indirect, certainly not linear and essentially non-additive way. In the next section a method for transforming the counted or estimated frequencies of occurrence into possibility measures (fuzzy membership degrees) will be presented.

There are several example for supporting IR by thesauri. 9 examine word cooccurring in a 40 word wide window. 7 and 8 construct thesauri by transposing the term-by-document marix. Applying fuzzy logic to automated information retrieval is not new. Some of the most important advances in this field are summarised in 6. In several points of this paper, reference will be made to concepts introduced in this work.

2 Keyword occurrence frequencies and possibility degrees

If analyzing a collection of documents related to a certain topic (e.g. folkloristic beliefs) it will be found that some of the words occur quite frequently in all or most of them, thus these words are of no significance with regards to the contents of any particular document. The words which are common in any natural language document are called stop words, while those, which might be significant in some context but have a role similar to that of the real stop words in a certain context will be called in this study relative stop words. In the context of folkloristic beliefs such a relative stop words are hard to identify. Because of this the set of relative stop words will become empty. These texts are usually rather short and they contain only relevant, often enigmatically short expressions – except the proper stop words.

By the omission of stop words (and relative stop words, if relevant) the set of significant words is obtained which m be used for a further analysis. Some of these words might be more important than the rest and might be chosen as the set of keywords. In a hierarchical co-occurrence approach the titles and sub-titles, etc. might be checked only for keyword occurrences, while the rest of the documents for any significant word. An example for classifying words into these four categories can be seen in Figure 1.

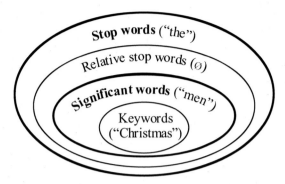

Fig. 1. Categories of words in documents

In the Fig. 1 the four categories of words can be seen: stop word like "the", relative stop words an empty set, and "men" as a general example for a significant word and finally, "Christmas" for a keyword, as beliefs connected to Christmas time form a large and important subgroup of our collection.

It is a crucially important issue how occurrence frequencies can be and are transformed into fuzzy membership degrees, which may be interpreted as important and relevant measures, satisfying the properties of possibilistic measures.

The following must be considered here. Membership degrees or fuzzy measures range from 0 to 1, where 0 expresses the total lack of importance, and 1 stands for absolute importance. Words occurring in a document very frequently are usually stop words (absolute or relative ones), and so they should be left out of consideration. For the remaining class of significant words it is generally true that higher occurrence frequencies indicate higher importance degrees as well. Although the connection between occurrence frequency (word count) and importance degree is strictly monotonic, it is certainly not proportional.

The critical domain is somewhere what can be defined as "a few occurrences", depending on the type and size of the document, generally somewhere between 2 and 20 word counts. It does not matter much whether a word occurs in a document 10 or 12 times, it is likely that this document will be rather important from the point of view of the query in both cases. On the other hand, one or two occurrences of a word might be coincidental or might indicate that the subject is touched upon only very superficially, while repeated mentioning (three or four or more) is an indicator that the word in question is an important word from the point of view of the document. With short documents like beliefs and superstitions these numbers might vary. Especially it can never be expected that words occur more than a few (two, tree or four) times.

The mapping from occurrence frequencies or counts to possibilistic membership degrees is thus generally a sigmoid function, with its steep part around the "critical" area of occurrences – the concrete values depending on the expected lengths and types of documents, and the category of environment (title, text, etc.). These sigmoids $\sigma(F)$ have to fulfill the conditions which are given in 5. In practice σ is not necessarily continuously differentiable, but its characteristics should be nevertheless "S-shaped".

3 Fuzzy Pre-processing of a Folkloristic Corpus

Hungary has a very rich folkloristic tradition and especially in the last century a successful work has been done to research and preserve this heritage. For instance, nowadays many young people learn the traditional dances of villages, in many cities there are parties with folk music and dance. The 3rd CIOFF World Folklorida, the "Olympia of Folk Art" took place in Hungary very recently, an obvious sign of international appreciation of this work.

Quite a few Hungarian cultural anthropologists were collecting beliefs and superstitions mainly in the 20th century. There are about 27 000 documents on paper in the National Museum. Unfortunately the classical techniques of anthropology are not able to process this amount of data and usually studies analyze only 6 to 10 documents. Of the above collection, there exists a digitized database of 2704 Hungarian belief texts, suitable for computerized analysis, which has been processed by principal component analysis12.

In order to distinguish the different dialects one word is spelled in different ways, sometimes even special characters are used to note the pronunciation down. The other problem is the use of old style language, a big part of the vocabulary of the corpus is not in use anymore. So first of all different appearances of the same words had to be collected into pre-process dictionary. In this way we also solved the problem of Hungarian language being an agglutinative language, it puts many different tags at the end of the words.

After all 1837 significant words remain in the pre-process dictionary. Special attention was paid for negation. Hungarian language puts *nem* (not) word before the verb for its negation, so if the software found the *nem* word in the text, it considered it together with the next word and it searched that whole string in the pre-process dictionary.

At this phase of the research we did not try to solve the problem of words with more than one meaning like *fog*, which can mean tooth and also to catch. The context has to be analyzed to select the actual meaning which is quite a complex task.

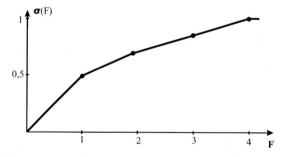

Fig. 2. Sigmoid curves used for the sort documents

The sigmoid function σ(F) used is shown in Figure 2. The documents are usually 2 to 5 lines longs, just very few of them exceed the size of half a page so even a single occurrence is quite significant. Thus in case of a single occurrence the membership degree is already 0.5. Less than 0.1% of the significant words appear more than 4 times, so in case a word occurs for times in a document the membership degree is 1.

By the end of the pre-processing matrix **M** was obtained whose size is 2704x1837, the words (W) and the documents (D) are listed at the edges. The fuzzy degrees stored in **M** show how much a given word is related to a document.

3.1 Word Frequency Degree

Let us define a degree in the following way:

$$I_w = \sum_{i=1}^{N} \sigma_{d_i W}$$

(1)

The Word Frequency Degree shows a given word how significant is in collection of the documents, in the whole corpus.

4 Establishing Fuzzy Pseudo-thesauruses by Co-occurrence

In order to define synonymy take the set of (all) concepts 6. The concepts may be abstract ones, which cannot be found in the real world. Now take the set of words. A word belongs to a concept with a fuzzy membership degree. One word may belong to several concepts and several words may belong to one concept.

Two words are synonyms if they belong to the very same concepts with the same degrees. The fuzzy thesaurus lists not just the synonyms, but also the degree of synonymy. For example if word A and word B belong to some concepts which are common, but they also belong to some different concept they are synonyms with a degree which is less than 1. If A and B are not related to any common concept they are synonyms with the degree of zero.

If we want to obtain this thesaurus there are two main questions:

1st: What to use instead of the set of concepts?

2nd How to choose degree of the synonymy when it is not 0 or 1?

There are not many possible answers for the first question if we want an automatic method to generate the thesaurus. We substitute the set of documents for the set of concepts. Because this is not a very good substitution the thesaurus obtained is called pseudo-thesaurus.

There are plenty of possibilities to define the degree of synonymy between pairs of words. In the next two subsections we will see that the obvious choices do not give good result, so in 4.3 a special weight factor is introduced.

4.1 Establishing the fuzzy pseudo-thesaurus step by step

Step 1: *Co-occurrence degree calculation*

$$\mu'_{ij}(D) = \min(\sigma_{W_iD}, \sigma_{W_jD})$$

$$\mu_{ij} = \frac{1}{C}\frac{1}{s}\sum_{z=1}^{N}\mu'_{ij}(D_z) \tag{2}$$

where C is a constant which keeps μ_{ij} in the range of [0,1], C is independent while s a weight may be dependent from i and j. The first idea how to choose C can be N, the number of the documents, but in this way the values of μ_{ij} are very small. We get more reasonable values if

$$C = \max_{i,j}\left(\frac{1}{s}\sum_{z=1}^{N}\mu'_{ij}(D_z)\right) \tag{3}$$

Step 2: *Suitable α-cut*
   If the number of the significant words is M, then the co-occurrence degrees (μ_{ij}) form a matrix size of $M \times M$, let call it **W**. The words are listed on both sides from 1 to M. Since $\mu_{ij} = \mu_{ji}$ this matrix **W** can be represented by an undirected graph.
   Choose a suitable α for which the *α-cut* leaves about 30 to 40 nodes in the graph. This is a representation of a pseudo-thesaurus.

Step 3: *Searching maximal cliques*
   An edge means that the connected two nodes representing words are "synonyms" in this broader term ("related" in the meaning). If a set of nodes are fully connected, than they are called a clique, and they are supposed to be related to the same broad concept.

Step 4: *Fuzzy clique*
   Many times among the found maximal cliques there are a few which have many common nodes. Since we chose α arbitrarily it is reasonable to check if these close cliques describe the same broad concept and they can be aggregated. We take the cliques which have just one different node and investigate these different nodes. If there is an edge between them on level $\alpha'=0.7\alpha$ cut we aggregate the cliques.

4.2 Weight s=1

Here the measure of co-occurrence is simply proportional with the sum of the co-occurrence. Column I_w shows in Table 1 that just very frequent words remained in the α-cut. The most frequent words of the corpus (number 18, "go" and 26, "do") have the most edges.

Table 1. List of words in case weight $s=1$

NR	HUN.	ENGLISH	I_w	NR	HUN.	ENGLISH	I_w
1	ad	giv(e)	74.7	18	megy	go, walk	218.4
2	asszony	woman, wif(e)	92.1	19	mise	(holy) mass	27.6
3	este	evening	103.3	20	mond	say	108.3
4	fent	Above	69.1	21	nap	day/Sun	172.3
5	fog	tooth/catch	123.5	22	ront	spoil, bewitch	48.7
6	férj	husband	66.1	23	sok	much, many	86.0
7	gyermek	Child	160.8	24	szent	saint (St.)	37.8
8	György	George	31.8	25	tehén	cow	97.1
9	haza	Home	42.8	26	tej	milk	61.3
10	3	3	83.7	27	tesz	do, put	177.8
11	ház	House	173.6	28	tojik	lay eggs	32.3
12	karácsony	Christmas	90.4	29	tyúk	hen	77.4
13	kicsi	small, little	110.9	30	víz	water	98.9
14	legény	young man, fel-low, lad	41.7	31	éjfél	midnight	40.5
				32	éjjel	night	87.2
15	Luca	Lucia (St.)	52.8	33	év	year	94.7
16	lány	girl, lass	142.4				
17	meghal	die	90.8				

Even though not all, but many of the edges give really meaningful pairs of words. The maximal cliques show some logic behind, but usually some very frequent words appears as an odd-one-out. (see Figure 3)

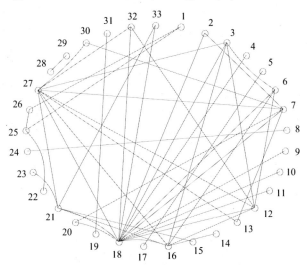

Fig. 3. Graph of a pseudo thesaurus, weight $s=1$

4.3 Weight $s=\max(I_{WA}, I_{WB})$

To avoid the dominancy of frequent words lets divide the co-occurrence measure, μ_{ij} by word frequency degree (I_w), which is greater from word j and word j. In this case $C=1$ because I_w is never smaller than the sum of μ'_{ij}-s.

The highest not empty α-cut has 90 nodes. For all words in the α-cut I_w=0.5, which means that all appear just once in the hole corpus. The relations found here have no significance because of the low occurrence.

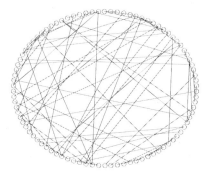

Fig. 4. Graph a of pseudo thesaurus, weight s= max(I_{WA} ,I_{WB})

4.4 Weight s=1+ (max(IWA ,I_{WB}))/20

By 4.1. and 4.2. we guess that weight s should be between 1 and max(I_{WA} ,I_{WB}). After several tests weight s=1+ (max(I_{WA} ,I_{WB}))/20 was proved to be the most efficient to identify concepts. As its can be seen in Table 2, these words represent a wider range of I_w values.

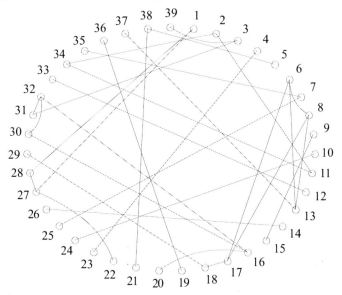

Fig. 5. Graph of a pseudo thesaurus, weight s=1+ (max(I_{WA} ,I_{WB}))/20

Table 2. List of words in case weight s=1+ (max(I_{WA} ,I_{WB}))/20

NR	HUN.	ENGLISH	I_w		NR	HUN.	ENGLISH	I_w
1	ad	giv(e)	74.7		22	ront	spoil, bewitch	48.7
2	bal	left	28.4		23	szarka	magpie	6.7
3	csibe	chicken	35.2		24	szent	saint, St.	37.8
4	csörög	clatter	5.5		25	szeplő	freckle	10.3
5	cédula	peace of paper	9.5		26	süt	bake	33.6
6	este	evening	103.3		27	tehén	cow	97.1
7	fecske	swallow	16.8		28	tej	milk	61.3
8	férj	husband	66.1		29	tesz	do, put	177.8
9	gyermek	child	160.8		30	tojik	lay eggs	32.3
10	György	George	31.8		31	tojás	egg	43.8
11	jobb	right	30.9		32	tyúk	hen	77.4
12	jön	come	91.1		33	vendég	guest	29.8
13	karácsony	Christmas	90.4		34	viszket	itch	25.5
14	kenyér	bread	51.4		35	Vér	blood	17.6
15	kicsi	small	110.9		36	éjfél	midnight	40.5
16	Luca	Lucia (St.)	52.8		37	éjjel	night	87.2
17	lány	girl, lass	142.4		38	ír	write	20.7
18	megy	go, walk	218.4		39	ültet	plant, seat	21.3
19	mise	(holy) mass	27.6					
20	nap	day, sun	172.3					
21	név	name	43.3					

The graph in Figure 5 is not dominated by any node, very frequent words like go, do, day (number 18, 29, 20) have not more than two edges. We managed to avoid that some very frequent words are connected to most of the other nodes like in Figure 3. It is logical that words with high are related to more concepts (this is why they are so frequent), but some of them should not be in most of the maximal cliques.

Table 3. Maximal cliques

giv(e) (1)	cow (27)	milk (28)
left (2)	right (11)	itch (34)
evening (6)	husband (8)	Christmas (13)
evening (6)	husband (8)	girl, lass (17)
Lucia (St.) (16)	lay eggs (30)	hen (32)

chicken (3)	egg (31)	bread (14)	bake (26)
chicken (3)	plant, seat (39)	Lucia (St.) (16)	day, sun (20)
clatter (4)	magpie (23)	girl, lass (17)	go, walk (18)
peace of paper (5)	write (38)	go, walk (18)	do, put (29)
swallow (7)	freckle (25)	(holy) mass (19)	mindnight (36)
swallow (7)	blood (35)	name (21)	write (38)
Child (9)	small (15)	Spoil, bewitch(22)	cow (27)
George (10)	Saint, St. (24)	egg (31)	hen (32)
come (12)	guest (33)		
charismas (13)	night (37)		

Table 3 lists the maximal cliques of the graph of Figure 5, these sets of word describe broad concepts which are important in this corpus. The 3rd an 4th line of the Table 3 differ just in the last word. Take a lover α-cut of Matrix **W**. We can find that already at α'=0.8α there is an edge between Christmas(13) and girl(17), so the two maximal cliques can be aggregated, they form the fuzzy maximal clique: evening(6), husband(8),Christmas(13) and girl(17). It is easy to imagine beliefs which are about how a girl can find a husband at Christmas Eve.

4.5 Two examples:

"Karácsony estélyén doboskát sütnek s a leány az elsôvel kiszalad és amely legénnyel találkozik legelôször az lesz a férje."

Christmas Eve "doboska" cakes are prepared and the daughter of the house runs out with the first piece and the young man whom she meets first will become her husband.

"Karácsony estélyén a lánynak egy öl fát kell felvenni és ha a számuk páros, akkor férjhez meg, ha páratlan, akkor nem megy."

Christmas Eve the girls should pick up a bunch of wood, if the number of pieces is even she will be married, if it is odd, she will not be married (namely, next year).

5 Establishing Pseudo-thesauruses by ICA

The idea of using Independent Component Analysis was initiated by 1, there Complexity Pursuit Algorithm was used to identify topics in chat flows. Complexity Pursuit Algorithm is an extended version of Independent Component Analysis, the advantage of CPA is that it is able to separate components from time series while it remains computationally simple.

CPA was tested also on our folkloristic corpus, since theoretically the algorithm could be to able separate important directions efficiently on data which does not contain time information. Experimental tests proved CPA unsuitable for finding meaningful associations on our test corpus, but the parent algorithm ICA showed interesting results. It can be stated and it can be shown that ICA was able to find at least as good words cliques as good ones were found in 1 by CPA.

5.1 Independent Component Analysis (ICA)

Our data model assumes that the observations x(t) are linear mixtures of some latent components:

$$\underline{x} = \underline{\underline{A}}\,\underline{s} \qquad (4)$$

where $\underline{x} = [x_1, x_2, ..., x_n]^T$ is the vector of observed random variables. In our case document containing words, $\underline{s} = [s_1, s_2, ..., s_m]$ is the vector of independently predictable latent components, and A is an unknown constant mixing matrix. The statistical independency of s_i is not strictly required.

s_i, the independent component is understood as independent topic in the corpus, so the later found s_i corresponding to set of words. These sets define the topics.

The task is solving equation (4) which has infinite number of solutions. We need to find a possible A matrix in which the entropy of the lines is minimal so it contains the most information. For finding the maximum non-Gaussian directions several comparison function can be used. Further details of the implementation of the algorithm can be found in 3.

5.2 Results

Since ICA uses a deep mathematical approach, the function of statistics in the connection between the resulting set of words and the parameters of the algorithm are quite hidden not like in the case of fuzzy pseudo-thesaurus, where the word frequency on the corpus has high correlation with the role of the word in the fuzzy clique. So in the case of using ICA we have not found special dominancy of some word, meaningful sets contain most of the words of the dictionary.

The following tables show sets of words identifying topics. The lists put together are results of ICA and fuzzy pseudo-thesaurus. The set are ordered in a way that is easy to recognize that the two methods are able to give very similar results.

Table 4. Four identical words in the result of two methods

ICA	Fuzzy		ICA	Fuzzy
witch	*witch*		drop	*children*
peel	*go*		*children*	small
go	*do*		small	say
do	*night*		*do*	*do*
night	water		*water*	*water*

Table 5. Three identical words in the result of two methods

ICA	Fuzzy		ICA	Fuzzy		ICA	Fuzzy		ICA	Fuzzy
chick	chick		go	give		draw	give		screw	screw
black	east		draw	keep		keep	keep		Georhge	dew
armpit	egg		keep	cow		cow	cow		Dew	pick
east			cow	milk		milk	milk		Go	
egg			milk			dug			Pick	

6 Conclusions and further study

Based on some further studies on textual document retrieval a method of automatic thesaurus generation has been proposed and an appropriate weight factor was introduced. The method was applied on a collection of Hungarian folkloristic beliefs. This way a pseudo-thesaurus was generated.

In the way of finding independent components of the terminus x document matrix a set of words were identified. Both kinds of set of words thus found in the thesaurus and ICA analysis were meaningful for the contents of the beliefs analyzed, and helped to understand the course topics of beliefs.

The fact that ICA and the fuzzy pseudo-thesaurus approach give many similar sets of words supposes that the two methods can be combined. We suggest that the topics identified in the fuzzy pseudo-thesaurus should be refined with sets of ICA.

Methods should be tested with different corpuses in order to identify and resolve side effects. In order to improve the usability of the topic identification the introduction of the topic's relevance measure is planned to be introduced.

References

1. E. Bingham, A. Kabán, M. Girolami, (2003) Topic Identification in Dynamical Text by Complexity Pursuit. Neural Networks Research Centre, Helsinki University of Technology
2. K. Chakrabarty, L. T. Kóczy, T. D. Gedeon (1999) Analysis of fuzzy relational charts in information retrieval *IETR99-01*, School of Computer Science and Engineering, University of New South Wales, Sydney
3. A. Hyvarinen (1999) Fast and robust fixed-point algorithms for independent component analysis, EEE Tr. on Neural Nw., 10(3),626–634
4. G. Klir, T. Folger (1998) Fuzzy Sets. Uncertainty and Information, Prentice-Hall, Englewood Cliofs, NJ
5. L. T. Kóczy, T. D. Gedeon and J. A. Kóczy (2002) Fuzzy tolerance relations and relational maps applied to information retrieval *Fuzzy Sets and Systems 126* 49–61
6. S. Miyamoto (1990) Fuzzy Sets in Information Retrieval and Cluster Analysis Kluwer, Dordrecht, 259p
7. Y. Qiu, H. Frei (1993) Comcept Based Query Expansion" SIGIR conf.
8. G Salton, C. Buckley (1990) Improving Retrieval performance by Relevance Feedback Jurnal of A. S. for Information Science, 288-297
9. H. Schütze, J. O. Pedersen (1997) A Cooccurrence-based Thesaurus and Two Application to Information Retrieval. Information Retrieval and Management, Vol. 33, 307-318
10. S. Szaszkó, L. T. Kóczy (2004) Identifying Concept in Folcloristic Corpus by Fuzzy Pseudo-thesaurus *Eurofuse* 2004, Warsaw, 522-532
11. S. Szaszkó, L. T. Kóczy (2004) What Lectures Note About, Identifying Concepts by Fuzzy Pseudo-thesaurus *EESTEC-IEEE Conference*, Italy
12. V. Voigt, M. Preminger, L. Ládi, S Darányi (1999) Automated motif identification in folklore text corpora. Folklore. Electronic Journal of Folklore   Vol. 12., Tartu, 1999 126-141 pp. Also available at: http://haldjas.folklore.ee/folklore/vol12/motif.htm

Long-term Preservation of Electronic Information – A study of Seven Swedish Governmental Organizations

Viveca Asproth

Mid Sweden University, SE-83125 Östersund
Viveca.Asproth@miun.se

Abstract: Information technology in combination with changes in organizational structures and forms for work has led to an increasing amount of information and also to totally new forms of information and records creation. Much of the information that earlier was produced on paper is now being produced in electronic form, for example as e-mail and in databases. A 10-year period is a long time when it comes to preserving electronic records. This is of course due to the rapid technological development, for example the problems with obsolete software and file formats. Vitale functions in society such as the social insurance and national registration have to be accessible for long periods of time. Without authentic, accessible, searchable, and reliable records these functions in society are in fact impossible to maintain. There still remain a lot of problems to solve before secure and efficient long-term preservation will be brought about. Digital preservation requires, in addition to the technological development, elaborated strategies, new workflows and organizational structures, standards and common metadata, new specific competences, and close co-operation across different professional fields. Though many problems still remain to be solved, governmental as well as business organizations are in an intermediate stage in the changeover to electronic records and have to deal with this situation. In this paper an empirical study of seven Swedish governmental departments is presented. The study was carried through with help of interviews and in some of the cases examination of complementary documentation. The result of the study shows the stage of changeover organizations are in, and the different strategies they use to handle the mixture of paper-bound documents, scanned documents, electronic records, databases, etc that comprise the information about one single commission or object and which has to be handled both in the short and the long run.

1 Introduction

Information technology in combination with changes in organizational structures and forms for work has led to an increasing amount of information and also to totally new forms of information and records creation. Much of the information that earlier was produced on paper is now being produced in electronic form, for example as e-mail and in databases. The Dutch archive theoretician Eric Ketelaar (1999) has invented the word "archivalisation" to describe the phenomenon that more and more seems to be worth to document and archive. This means that a considerably larger amount of information needs to be handled. Electronically generated and stored information is also exposed to change and manipulation in quite another way than paper-bound information.

A 10-year period is a long time when it comes to preserving electronic records. This is of course due to the rapid technological development, for example the problems with obsolete software and file formats. Goldstein (2004) stresses the need for a quick solution to the problem of archiving electronic information for the future. Further, he says that the major threat to archived material today is not the fire hazard but the rapid development of different file formats for documents, sound and images.

Vitale functions in society such as the social insurance and national registration have to be accessible for long periods of time. Without authentic, accessible, searchable, and reliable records these functions in society are in fact impossible to maintain. The technical development and transition to electronic media has led to that traditional methods have become obsolete or at least insufficient.

There still remain a lot of problems to solve before secure and efficient long-term preservation will be brought about. It seems that although much of the challenges associated with digital preservation is strategic, organizational, and structural and not only technical, the research concentrates at solving the technical issues. Digital preservation requires, in addition to the technological development, elaborated strategies, new workflows and organizational structures, standards and common metadata, new specific competences, and close co-operation across different professions from traditional preservation management to computing science. (Asproth, 2005)

Traditionally, preserving means keeping them unchanged; however, our digital environment has fundamentally changed our concept of preservation requirements. If we hold on to digital information without modifications, accessing the information will become increasingly more difficult, if not impossible.

This situation creates a fundamental paradox for digital preservation: On the one hand, we want to maintain digital information intact as it was created; on the other, we want to access this information dynamically and with the most advanced tools. (Chen, 2001)

Most of the governmental departments strives to become 24/7 agencies. Within 24/7 agencies, the whole idea is that exchange of information is done electronically. The Swedish Agency for Public Management have stated that without possibilities to manage and preserve e-records for long time, the development of working e-government services could be in danger (Statskontoret, 2003). Developing effective e-record management systems is proven to be difficult. For example in electronic healthcare, records have been difficult to access over time, and thereby the preservation issue has been difficult to solve, which makes development of e-record management systems difficult (Grimson, 2001).

Electronic records have proven to be difficult to preserve with maintained reliability and authenticity (Duranti, 2001a; Duranti, 2001b). Electronic records can be spread in separate databases with links between the separate parts. If records not fulfill the requirements of reliability and authenticity, they can not be used as evidence and not enable accountability (Thomassen, 2001).

Though many problems still remain to be solved, governmental as well as business organizations are in an intermediate stage in the changeover to electronic records and have to deal with this situation. In this paper an empirical study of seven Swedish governmental departments is presented.

2 The Study

The aim of the study was to investigate how different governmental departments managed electronic information both in a short and long run. As the organizations today handle both paper documents and electronic information, an overarching question is to see in which stage of changeover the organizations are in and which strategies they use to handle the mixture of paper document, scanned documents, electronic records, databases, etc.

2.1 Study object

The seven Swedish governmental departments that participated in the study were:

CSN

The national authority that handle the Swedish financial aid for students; i.e. loans and grants for studies.

The Swedish tax authority

Administration authority for all kinds of taxation, national registration and estate inventories

The Swedish Companies Registration Office (SCRO)

SCRO is a new government agency under the Ministry of Industry. Their operations are not financed by public funding and they therefore charge for the services they provide.

The Swedish Enforcement Administration and legislation

The authorities of the Enforcement Administration are responsible for the enforcement of both public and private claims. Public claims are debts to central and local authorities (taxes, VAT, excise duties, social security contributions but also for instance television licenses and parking fines). Private claims are based on judgments by general and administrative courts.

The National Government Employee Pensions Board (SPV)

Pension administration involves applying the rules of pension agreements and computing and paying out the different components of the pension.

The Swedish Social Insurance Administration

A new integrated government agency with responsibility for the Swedish social insurance system

County Council of Jämtland

The county council is responsible for several issues overarching the county, such as public transportation, culture and development of the county. However, the main task for county councils is medical and health care.

2.2 Method

The study was carried through with help of interviews and in examination of complementary documentation. The interviews were built up to follow an "object" or a commission from the initiation to the end and/or the filing for long term preservation. All additional information during the "objects" term of life was identified and questions about how different versions of the record was inquired. The "objects/commissions that were examined were:

CSN – one individual's loan from initiation to final repayment or removal from the cause list.

The Swedish tax authority – one individual's declaration for tax return to final assessment for income tax

The Swedish Companies Registration Office (SCRO) – one company from the start (though a company may come to an end it must not be sorted out)

The Swedish Enforcement Administration and legislation – one claim from the application to execution

The National Government Employee Pensions Board (SPV) – one individual's pension from saving to the person's death

The Swedish Social Insurance Administration – one individual's sick report from reporting to closing (fit declaration, pension, or death)

County Council of Jämtland – one individual's case record from birth or moving in.

2.3 Result

All of the studied objects were quite complicated and consisted of several steps and iterations. To exemplify a simplified picture of the information exchange for an individual's loan is shown in figure 1. Every step can be iterated several times. The example shows only a loan that is repaid in due time. What is not shown is if a person applies for respite for payment or refuses to pay, which causes separate decision processes and involves other authorities.

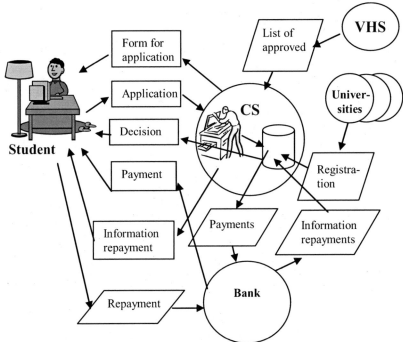

Fig. 1. Simplified picture of loans

The ambition of many governmental departments is to become 24/7 agencies. In table 1 can be seen how far the studied organizations have reached. Of the studied organization, four have e-services for some step in the process, though with varying shares of use. Two others plan to start e-services. The county council will not, for obvious reasons, supply any e-service for case records. All the studied organizations handle electronic records in the studied cases. They saved the electronic records in XML or other formats that is said to be appropriate for long-term preservation. Most of them also scanned paper documents and used them as electronic information. Much information is also stored as database records.

Table 1. E-service providing

Organization	E-service	E-records
CSN	Yes	Yes
Tax authority	Yes	Yes
SCRO	Yes, limited use	Yes
Enforcement Administration and legislation	Yes	Yes
SPV	No, planned	Yes
Social Insurance Administration	No, planned	Yes
County Council	No	Yes

The active times for the studied objects vary quite a lot, but mostly the information is active for decades (see table 2).

In some of the organizations is not all information preserved during that time, some sorting out is performed. Information that is sorted out is for example notes, e-mails, etc. As the amount of information is huge, just a selection is obliged to be preserved. However several of the organizations chose to save more than they were obliged to. Many of the organizations chose to save all the database records and did not sort out any of them. In some cases scanned documents were chosen to be the original and thus preserved. Other chose to print out the information and preserve paper documents. It deserves to be mentioned that electronic records has not existed for so long time and a feeling of uncertainty about how to do was expressed.

Table 2. Preservation for short and long term

Organization	Max active time	Long-term Preservation
CSN	Lifelong	A selection is preserved forever
Tax authority	5 years after declaration	A selection is preserved forever, in some special issues are all preserved
SCRO	"For ever"	Yes
Enforcement Administration and legislation	20 years	20 years
SPV	Lifelong	Yes
Social Insurance Administration	Several years	A selection is preserved forever
County Council	Lifelong	Yes

As information about an object or a commission is present for a long time an interesting question is whether different versions existed and was preserved. During the active time of the object several different documents were gathered. All documents were time stamped and thus it is possible to reconstruct different stages in the process. There are no assembled versions at different times. The information is rather accumulated over time. In the databases the records are dated, but there is far from any likeness of temporal databases. To be able to get a complete version of the information at a certain time an extensive selection and reconstruction of information is needed. Unlike paper-bound documents bits and pieces of information has to be put together to form a complete electronic record. As some information is paperbound and other is electronic a referential system is needed. Some organizations chose to have the references in a computer-based system. Other chose to create a folder with paperbound documents with a list of references to the electronic information.

Stove-piped organizations and systems, which have been predominant for a long time and still is very common in governmental organizations is showing weaknesses (O'Looney, 2002; Friday, 2003; Thakur & Satter, 1998; and Sundberg & Wallin, 2005). To manage more far-reaching commissions a stove-piped organization will be a hindrance. Some kind of business process reengineering would be preferable. Though the studied organizations are of a stove-piped character, they manage to act in a process-oriented way when it comes to manage the information about commissions.

3 Conclusion

The result of the study shows that all studied organizations are in some stage of changeover from paperbound information to electronic records. There is a lack of knowledge about how to handle the situation, but they have all developed different strategies to handle the mixture of paper documents, scanned documents, electronic records, and databases.

An increasing amount of electronic information is to be long-term preserved. There is very little knowledge about how this should be done. Guidelines must be developed and made available to those responsible for the preservation.

There is very little support in the systems for management of distributed information, information that is not only distributed in where it is stored, but also in what type of information it is. New tools, able to assemble the information in a transparent way, have to be developed.

References

Asproth. V. (2005) Information Technology Challenges for the Long-term Preservation of Electronic Information. International Journal for Public Information Systems, no 1, pp. 27-37.

Borglund, E. (2005).

Chen, Su-Shing (2001) The Paradox of Digital preservation, IEEE Computer, 34(3):24-28.

Duranti, L. (2001a) Concepts, Principles, and Methods for the Management of Electronic Records, The Information Society, vol. 17, pp. 271-279.

Duranti, L. (2001b) The impact of digital technology on archival science, Archival Science, vol. 1, pp. 39-55.

Friday, S. (2003) Organization Development for Facility Managers: Tracing the DNA of an FM Organization, Amacom Books.

Goldstein, H. (2004) The Infinite Archive, IEEE Spectrum, Vol. 41, p 74.

Grimson, J. (2001) Delivering the electronic healthcare record for the 21st century, International Journal of Medical Informatics, vol. 64, pp. 111-127.

Ketelaar, E. (1999) Archivalisation and archiving, in: Archives and manuscripts 27, pp. 54-61.

O'Looney, J. A. (2002). Wiring Governments. Challenges and Possibilities for Public Managers. Westport, CT: Quorum Books.

Statskontoret (2003) "Förstudierapport om framtidens lektroniska arkiv," 2003/67, 2003.

Sundberg, H., Wallin, P. (2005) Co-ordination of business and IT development processes – managing stovepiped organizations. International Journal for Public Information Systems, 2005:1, pp. 53-69.

Thomassen, T. (2001) A First Introduction to Archival Science, Archival Science, vol. 1, pp. 373-385.

The Managing and Complex Querying of the Digital Medical Images Collections

Liana Stanescu, Dumitru Dan Burdescu, Marius Brezovan

University of Craiova, Faculty of Automation, Computers and Electronics, stanescu_liana@software.ucv.ro, burdescu@topedge.com, brezovan_marius@software.ucv.ro

Abstract. The article presents a software tool working on-line with a multi-threaded client/server architecture that permits loading the images and alphanumeric data in a database either directly, or by processing a DICOM file. It also allows the simple text based query of the database and content-based query on color or color texture features at the level of the entire image or at the level of the regions. The software tool has a modularized architecture. The module for extracting the images and alphanumeric information from the DICOM files and the module for extracting image visual characteristics (color and color texture) and the color regions are on the server side and are implemented using Java technology. For the database the MySQL server is used, and the client interface which allows the execution of simple text based query and content-based visual query on color and color texture features is implemented using the JSP and Servlet technologies.

1 Introduction

With the development of the different technologies, in the medical field an impressive number of gray and color images is accumulated. A big part of these images comes from the medical devices satisfying the DICOM standard, providing a file with a standardized format that includes a multitude of alphanumeric information (the patient's name, the diagnosis, the time and date of the consult, the doctor's name, etc), and also one or several gray or color images, which can be compressed or not [4]. Other images come from digitizing the images stocked on different media (X-ray film, paper, etc). In the case of the existence of this large quantity of imagistic and alphanumeric data, a computerized management and their structuring in a database are necessary. The reasons are:

1. The DICOM file can't be visualized directly on the computer, it has to undergo a processing operation in order to extract the necessary information and to store in the database;
2. Creation of a database at the hospital level, its development at the regional and even national level in a distributed manner, allowing to keep track in time of the patient evolution; for example, a query on patient name can be launched, and all the necessary data (diagnosis, images) for each recorded consult is retrieved;
3. The database can be queried based on the image content and can be used in the processes of diagnosis, education and medical research;

The content-based visual query can take into consideration the entire image or only regions and this means establishing an image or a region as query in order to retrieve the images or regions from the database that are similar with the query [Smith JR 1997; Del Dimbo A 2001]. From the conversation with the doctors, the next situation appears frequently: the doctor visualizes a medical image, doesn't know exactly the diagnosis, but he is aware of the fact that he has seen something similar. The problem is that he doesn't have any possibility to search for something similar in the database. This problem can be solved setting that image as a query image. The content-based image query will provide the similar images from the database and it is very likely that among the retrieved images should be the searched image together with its diagnosis, observations, treatment. So the content-based visual query can be directly used in the diagnosis process. The visual characteristics (color, texture, shape) allow not only the retrieving of the patients having the same disease, but also the cases where the visual similitude exists, but the diagnosis differs, that can be useful in the medical research or medical education process.

There are few systems that are already integrated into the medical diagnosis process and the work for the application of the most suitable algorithms in image processing and features extraction continues [Muller H, Michoux N, Bandon D, Geissbuhler A 2004].

The most common type used for this kind of architecture is the client/server model [Djeraba C, Sebe N, Chang E 2006]. In this paper the multi-threaded client/server architecture of a software tool is presented. It permits the loading in a database of the images and alphanumeric data directly or by processing of the DICOM files and the querying of the database based on text or based on the image content represented by color or color texture features. The software system can run on different platforms (Unix, Windows, Linux), is developed using Java technologies, being robust, portable and extensible.

2 The Software Tool Architecture

In the case of the content-based visual query systems, it is desirable that the client interface, the database management system and the image processing module be executed on different computers. In the present case, using the JSP and Servlet technologies, the client will be able to access the service from anywhere using a Web browser and having an Internet connection. The database and the modules for DICOM files and image processing are executed on more powerful servers.

The general architecture of the software tools with modules and their connections appears in figure 1.

The software tool is designed using the client-server architecture. The module which processes the DICOM files by extracting the images and the alphanumeric data and the module which processes the images by extracting color, color textures features and color regions are on the server side and implemented in Java. The client graphical interface is implemented using Servlet and JSP technologies. Another module of the tool is the database server implemented using MySQL. The communication with the server is done by means of JDBC.

The communication protocol between the server and the client is a simple one:

- When DICOM file is uploaded, it is added first in the database (the client communicates directly with the database server by means of JDBC); the file is saved on the web server;
- The client sends to the server the unique ID of the file from the database; the server reads the file being processed, the alphanumeric data and the image(s) being extracted; the visual characteristics of the image are also extracted; the necessary information is saved in the database (DICOM file and image processing server and the database communicate by means of JDBC);
- The query requests are initiated by the clients and sent to the database server;

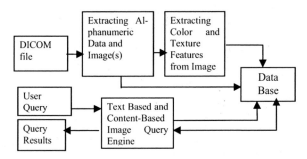

Fig. 1. The modules of the software tool

3 DICOM File Processing Server

It is the one of the most important module of the software tool and realizes the following functions:

- The processing of the DICOM standard files and extracting the alphanumeric data from tags and the image(s)
- Storing the generated data in the database

A DICOM file has the following structure [DICOM Homepage 2006]:

- A preamble of 128 bytes
- Prefix (4 bytes) where are stored the letters 'D', 'I', 'C', 'M' which represent the signature of the DICOM file
- Data Set that stores a set of information, such as: patient name, type of image, size of the image, etc.
- Pixels that compose the image (s) included into the DICOM file.

Extracting the data from the DICOM file can be made by taking into account every tag from the DICOM dictionary. This will be searched in the file and in case of finding it, the corresponding value will be extracted.

The steps of extracting information from DICOM files are:

- Verifying the existence of the 'D','I','C','M' characters
- Establishing the type of VR (ExplicitVR or ImplicitVR). This information is given by the UID (Unique Identifier), information stored in value field corresponding to the Transfer Syntax Tag.
- Establishing the Byte Ordering (BigEndian or LittleEndian). The information is also given by UID, stored in value field of the same Transfer Syntax Tag. The DICOM standard contains all the values that UID can have.
- Searching a tag in DICOM file according to the VR type and ByteOrdering
- Value extraction of the corresponding found tag.

Next it is described the problem of image extracting from the standard DICOM files. The images from DICOM files can be classified using several criteria [DICOM Homepage 2006]:

- The number of images stored in a file: single frame or multi frame.
- The number of bits per pixel: 8 bits, 12 bits, 16 bits or 24 bits.
- The Compression: without compression (raw) or with compression (RLE or JPEG).
- Photometric interpretation: gray scale images, color images, palette color images.

In the case of the images without compression, the extraction of pictures is made pixel by pixel, taking into account the number of bits stored for each pixel and the photometric interpretation (for monochrome images a pixel is stored using maximum 2 bytes and for color images, a pixel is stored using 3 bytes). In the images that use compression it is necessary a decompression algorithm before saving.

The pseudo code for retrieving the frames is:

```
Set variable number to 0
Loop until all frames are retrieved
        Set file dimension as Rows*Columns* (SamplePerPixel)
        Read all file dimension pixels from file starting with (Header Length +
        number* file dimension)
```

```
If MONOCHROME image
      Save as image
            Store image using GIF or JPEG image format
      Return
End If
If PALETTE COLOR image
            Get the Palette tables (one for red values, one for green values
            and one for blue values)
      Get Pixels color from the Palette.
            Save as image
            Store image using GIF or JPEG image format
      End If
If RGB image (24 bits)
            Get red, green and blue values
            Compute the color using the formula:
      ((255<<24) | ((0xff&r) << 16) |
      ((0xff&g)<< 8) | (0xff&b))
            Save as image
            Store image using GIF or JPEG image format
      End If
End Loop
```

4 Image Processing Server

It is another important module of the software tool and realizes the following functions:

- Extracting the visual characteristics (color and color textures) from images
- Detecting the color regions from images
- Storing the generated data in the database

Content extraction, indexing and retrieval of image and in general multimedia data continue to be one of the most challenging and fastest growing research domains. Primitive features (object motion, color, texture, shape) are generally extracted automatically and computed efficiently [Djeraba et al 2005; Hanjalic A, Sebe N, Chang E 2006; Lew M, Sebe N, Djeraba C, Jain R 2006].

The color is the visual feature immediately perceived on an image [Del Dimbo A 2001; Sebe N, Lew MS 2000; Smith JR 1997]. The color histograms represent the traditional method of describing the color properties of the images. They have the advantages of easy computation and up to certain point are insensitive to camera rotating, zooming, and changes in image resolution. In content-based visual query on color feature is important the used color space and the level of quantization, meaning the maximum number of colors. This software tool uses the representation of images in the HSV color space that has the properties of being complete, compact, natural and uniform and its quantization at 166 colors [Smith JR 1997]. The quantization algorithm generates a characteristics vector of maximum

166 values (that is stored in the database) and has the complexity O(width*height) where width and height represent the image dimensions [Burdescu D 1998].

Together with color, texture is a powerful characteristic of an image, present in nature and medical images, where a disease can be indicated by changes in the color and texture of a tissue. A series of methods have been studied to extract texture feature [Del Dimbo A 2001]. Among the most representatives methods of texture detection are the co-occurrence matrices and Gabor representations, implemented in this software tool [Del Dimbo A 2001; Palm C, Keysers D, Lehmann T, Spitzer K 2000]. There are many techniques used for texture extraction, but there isn't a certain method that can be considered the most appropriate, this depending on the application and the type of images taken into account.

In the case of the method based on co-occurrence matrices for the color images, one matrix was computed for each of the three channels R, G, B.

For an image f(x, y), the co-occurrence matrix $h_{d\phi}$ (i, j) is defined so that each entry (i, j) is equal to the number of times for that:

$f(x_1, y_1) = i$ and $f(x_2, y_2) = j$, where $(x_2, y_2) = (x_1, y_1) + (d\cos\phi, d\sin\phi)$ [Del Dimbo A 2001].

This leads to three quadratic matrices of dimension equal to the number of the color levels presented in an image (256 in this case) for each distance d and orientation ϕ. The classification of texture is based on the characteristics extracted from the co-occurrence matrix: energy, entropy, maximum probability, contrast, inverse difference moment and correlation [Del Dimbo A 2001]. The three vectors of texture characteristics extracted from the three co-occurrence matrices are created using the 6 characteristics computed for d=1 and ϕ=0. The texture representation in this case is done using a characteristics vector with 18 values stored in the database.

The functions that implement this method have the temporal complexity $O(m^2)$, where m is the maximum dimension of the image [Burdescu D 1998].

The computation of the Gabor characteristics for the image represented in the HS-complex space is similar to the one for the monochromatic Gabor characteristics, because the combination of color channels is done before filtering [Palm C et al 2000]:

$$C_{f,\varphi} = (\sum_{x,y} (FFT^{-1}\{P(u, v) \cdot M_{f,\varphi}(u, v)\}))^2 \qquad (1)$$

The Gabor characteristics vector is created using the value $C_{f,\varphi}$ computed for

3 scales and 4 orientations [Palm C et al 2000]:

$$f = (C_{0,0}, C_{0,1}, ..., C_{2,3}) \qquad (2)$$

So, the texture representation in this case is done using a characteristics vector with 12 values stored in the database.

The implemented Gabor filter procedure has a temporal complexity $O(n^2)$ where n is the maximum dimension of the image [Burdescu D 1998].

For detecting color regions it was chosen the color set back-projection algorithm, introduced initially by Swain and Ballard and then developed in the research projects at the Columbia University [Smith JR 1997]. The extraction system for color regions has four steps [Smith JR 1997]:

1. the image transformation, quantization and filtering (the transformation from the RGB color space to HSV color space and the quantization of the HSV color space at 166 colors; the binary color set with 166 values is computed-value 1 representing the present color and value 0 representing the missing color)
2. back-projection of binary color sets
3. the labeling of regions
4. the extraction of the region features

For each detected regions the color set that generated it, the area and the localization are stored. All the information is necessary further on in studying the evolution of the patients. The region localization is given by the minimal bounding rectangle (MBR). The region area is represented by the number of color pixels and can be smaller than the minimum bounding rectangle. Two original implementations of the color set back-projection algorithm are presented in [Burdescu D and Stanescu L 2005].

The application of an automated algorithm for detecting the color regions in medical images has two important utilizations:

1. in content-based region query on medical images collections, the specialist chooses one or more of the detected regions for querying the database, the purpose being the retrieval of images similar by color and texture; this can be useful for clarifying some uncertain diagnosis. This problem was studied in [Stanescu L and Burdescu D 2003] interesting results being presented.
2. during the evolution in time of the disease of patients that follow a certain treatment

5 The Database Server

The Entity-Relationship model for the structure of the database used by the software tool is presented in figure 2. The resulting tables are the following:

Tags table contains the following information:

1. tag – all the tags from DICOM Dictionary; for example: (0010, 0010);
2. the name of each tag; for example: Patient Name;
3. the Value Representation of each tag;
4. the Value Multiplicity of each tag;
5. the Version;

6. the Category of each tag; for example the information about the patient goes into Patient Category

Dicom_Files table contains:

- the unique identifier of the file;
- the path to that file;

Images table contains:

- the unique identifier of each image stored;
- the unique identifier of the DICOM file from where the image was extracted;
- the number of the frame (in case of DICOM file with multiple frames);
- the path and the name of the image;
- the color characteristics vector;
- the texture characteristics vector

Header table contains the values of the tags retrieved from DICOM files:

- the unique identifier of each entry in the table;
- the unique identifier of the DICOM file from where header information was retrieved;
- the tag;
- the extracted value;

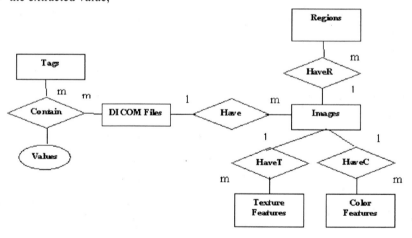

Fig. 2. The structure of the database

The Header table appears as a result of a m:m relationship between the tables Tags and Dicom_Files.

Regions table contains:

- the unique identifier of the detected region;
- colorset (the color set of the region);
- the coordinates of the upper left corner of the minimum bounding rectangle;
- the coordinates of the bottom right corner of the minimum bounding rectangle;
- the effective number of pixels corresponding to the considered color set, that is the surface of the region

6 The Client

The graphical interface plays an important role in the retrieving process. It must be, as much as possible, intuitively and friendly, permitting to the users that are not experts in the field, to navigate and search in the image collections. They don't need knowledge about image processing, about the mechanism of extracting visual characteristics, or about the measuring the images dissimilitude.

Also, the interface must permit the experts to improve the content-based query process using advanced settings of the parameters or combining the visual characteristics.

In the presented software tool, the client can issue four types of queries, namely:

- simple text-based queries;
- image queries based on color feature;
- image queries based on texture;
- region queries;

Some of the client functions are the following:

- The user can browse through the images;
- The user can design its own case by uploading DICOM files or images directly; these are processed and stored in the database;
- The user can search for images that are similar with the selected one on color or/and color texture features; also, the user can search for one or more regions similar with the query region taking into consideration sizes like color, area, absolute position. The user can set different values for the appropriate parameters.

For computing the distance between the color histograms of the query image and the target image, there have been taken into consideration the intersection of histograms, square distance between histograms and Euclidian distance [Smith JR 1997].

The reason why these three modalities for computing the images similitude were chosen is explained next. In the case of the medical images, the effectuated studies shown that the results were weaker than in the case of the nature images [Stanescu L and Burdescu D 2003]. None of the distances mentioned above caused much better results than the others, so that to motivate its choosing. In each case, relevant images for the query were retrieved with one of the distances and they were not retrieved by the others. It could be observed that in most cases, all the results retrieved by computing the three distances may be useful for not loosing relevant images for the query, consequently they complement one another.

In the case of the method based on co-occurrence matrices, the texture similitude between the query image Q and target image T is computed by the Euclidian metric.

In the case of the method based on Gabor filter, the similitude between the texture characteristics of the query image Q and the target image T is defined by the metric [Palm C et al 2000]:

$$D^2(Q,T) = \sum_f \sum_\varphi d_{f\varphi}(Q,T), where \; d_{f\varphi} = (f^Q - f^T)^2 \tag{3}$$

In the case of extracting color texture features two methods were also implemented, following the same above idea – the two resulting sets of images complement each other.

In figure 3 appears an example of user interface.

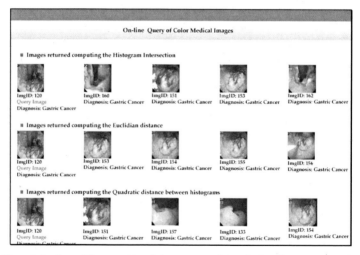

Fig. 3. User Interface: The results of the content-based visual query on color feature (three sets of results were computed)

7 Conclusion

The paper presents a Java based software tool with a multi-threaded client/server architecture and the following functions:

- The processing of the DICOM standard files provided by the medical tools in order to extract the alphanumeric data and images
- Storing the resulting data in a database
- Extracting the color feature from the image (the color histogram and the binary color set resulting from the HSV color space quantized at 166 colors)
- Extracting the color texture feature from the color images (using the co-occurrence matrices and the Gabor filters)
- detecting color regions and storing the new data in the database
- the simple text-based query of the database
- the content-based visual query of the database on color and color texture features
- the content-based region query of the database

The software tool is tested now by the medical personnel taking into consideration aspects like execution speed, retrieval quality and new necessary options.

References

Burdescu D (1998) Analiza complexitatii algoritmilor. Albastra, Cluj-Napoca

Burdescu D, Stanescu L, (2005) A New Algorithm For Content-Based Region Query in Multimedia Database. In: Lecture Notes in Computer Science 3588. Springer Verlag pp 124-133

Del Bimbo A (2001) Visual Information Retrieval. Morgan Kaufmann Publishers, San Francisco

DICOM Homepage (2006) http://medical.nema.org/

Djeraba C, Sebe N, Lew MS (2005) Systems and Architectures for Multimedia Information Retrieval. ACM Multimedia Systems Journal. 10(6) pp 457-463

Hanjalic A, Sebe N, Chang E (2006) Multimedia Content Analysis, Management, and Retrieval: Trends and Challenges. In: Proc. Electronic Imaging, SPIE'06, San Jose. USA

Lew M, Sebe N, Djeraba C, Jain R (2006) Content-based Multimedia Information Retrieval: State-of-the-art and Challenges. ACM Transactions on Multimedia Computing, Communication, and Applications. 2(1) pp 1-19

Muller H, Michoux N, Bandon D, Geissbuhler A (2004) A Review of Content_based Image Retrieval Systems in Medical Application – Clinical Benefits and Future Directions. Int J Med Inform. 73(1) pp 1-23

Palm C, Keysers D, Lehmann T, Spitzer K (2000) Gabor Filtering of Complex Hue/Saturation Images For Color Texture Classification. In: Proc. 5th Joint Conference on Onformation Science (JCIS2000) 2. Atlantic City, USA pp 45-49

Sebe N, Lew MS (2001) Texture Features for Content-based Retrieval. Principles of Visual Information Retrieval, Springer, ISBN 1-852333-381-2, pp 51-86

Sebe N, Lew MS (2000) Color Based Retrieval and Recognition. In: Proc. IEEE International Conference on Multimedia and Expo. New York. pp 311-314

Smith JR (1997) Integrated Spatial and Feature Image Systems: Retrieval, Compression and Analysis. Ph.D. thesis, Columbia University

Stanescu L, Burdescu D (2003) IMTEST-Software System For The Content-based Visual Retrieval Study. In: 14th International Conference On Control Systems And Computer Science. Bucuresti

Semantic Execution of BPEL Processes

Péter Martinek, Béla Szikora

Budapest University of Technology and Economics, Goldmann tér 3, Budapest, HU-1111

Abstract: Service Oriented Architecture (SOA) is an up-to-date software architecture, which is used in many areas of informatics today. There are lots of open standards and free tools which aim to realize the concepts of SOA.

This paper introduces an approach by using a given collection of open standards and tools to realize a semantically enriched SOA architecture. The main building blocks of the architecture, the Web services, will be extended by a semantic description. The resulting SOA architecture and the services themselves will be called semantically enriched. For orchestration we use the OWL-S [1] standard. The choreography will be described in BPEL. The semantically enriched Web services run on an OWL-S Virtual Machine, while the complex processes, described in BPEL [2] on a BPEL run-time. Between the OWL-S invoke and BPEL description a special, self-developed mediator service will be used.

In this paper we focus on the execution environment and the prerequisites to successfully build it, the publication of the service descriptions and discovery of the services will be only briefly introduced.

1 Introduction

Management of business processes is a key factor to enterprises today. Most of the business processes run through several different areas of information system functions, however the recently used business application systems (i.e: ERP, CRM, SCM, etc.) are rather isolated. Identifying the roles of partners and their functions on the processes can result in a process based integration scenario. These processes are mostly described by Business Process Execution Language (BPEL) which is a suitable open standard language to describe complex processes. The most important building elements of a complex process are as follows: **invoke** of services from information system, **assign** between variables come from the replies of the invoked services or constant values given by the designer itself and the **reply** of the results at the process endpoint. Although BPEL is a widely-used standard which is supported by reliable tools (designer with user-friendly graphical interface and run-time engines), designing a process is not an easy task to do. The builder of a process must know the specific services (more precisely: the location of the service descriptions) which will be invoked in the process run-time. Service registries can help to find the services by selecting the given categories (business entity, keywords, etc.) but searching according to the requested capability of the service is not properly solved yet. Enriching the services description with semantics and publish them in a searchable registry can solve the problem, as many paper has already been suggested. The attached semantic description carries information about service capabilities the input, output data of the service refers to a shared collection of concepts called ontology. This paper introduces an approach, which makes it possible to use existing BPEL tools combining them with the usage of OWL-S services and OWL-S run-time. We also show a small example which helps us to validate our approach.

2 Literature review

There are many research groups and publications which deal with (semantically enriched) SOA architecture today.

Large Scale Distributed Information System (LSDIS) group [3] at the University of Georgia has a SOA approach using BPEL for choreography as well, but the semantic descriptions of the Web services are in WSDL-S.

The Intelligent Software Agents Lab [4] at Carnegie Mellon deals with an SOA approach which is using OWL-S service description for choreography. They also developed tools for supporting the creation of the OWL-S description from a WSDL [7] basis and publicating them into a UDDI [8] registry. They, however, use the OWL-S to describe the processes as well, while we use BPEL for this purpose.

There are many tools and solutions to design and run standard BPEL processes, for example the Oralce Fusion Middleware [5] or the IBM Websphere [6]. But they don't provide the extension to describe the services in OWL-S and discovery them by their capabilities.

3 Adding semantics to services descriptions

The most widely-used standard to describe a Web service is the Web Service Description Language (WSDL). A WSDL description contains every necessary information to invoke the service, but it tells very little about how the service works. The extension of the description with this information happens in the so called annotation phase. The annotation starts with migrating the information found in the WSDL into an OWL-S skeleton. After that, the skeleton will be extended with the following: functional capabilities of the service will be described in the **profile**

part and the input and output data referring to the concepts in our ontology take place in the **grounding**.

Because the services come from different vendors and are described only with a WSDL, the input and output data of these native services must be transformed into and from the concepts of the ontology. By invoking a service, the inputs written according to the concepts of the ontology (in the OWL-S description) must be transformed into the input data type according the type of the input message contained in the WSDL. This is called **downcast transformation** because the direction of the transformation is from an abstract higher level (level of ontology concepts) towards a lower one (level of (complex) XSD [10] data-types. By catching the output of the invoked service usually we get a (complex) XSD data-type, which must be transformed into the concepts of the ontology. This is called **upcast transformation**. The transformations can be written for example in XSLT [11] and can also be stored in the grounding part of the OWL-S description. (There are many languages to describe data transformation, but XSLT have been chosen, because the selected OWL-S VM directly supports the usage of XSLT. See more in section 2.)

The OWL-S description also allow to put services into a given structure (sequence, junction, etc.) creating complex services this way. This can be done in the **process part** of the OWL-S description. In our approach we use BPEL engine for choreography purposes, because we believe, that BPEL engines are more reliable and robust for this task.

4 Invoking semantic services

There are existing tools to invoke semantic OWL-S services. In our approach we use the OWL-S Virtual Machine (VM) and API from the Project Mindswap by the University of Maryland [9]. The java code including the invoke of the OWL-S services can be extended as a standard Web service. This Web service has already a standard WSDL description, so it can be built into a BPEL process using a standard BPEL editor. The input and output data of these mediator Web services are not concepts of the ontology, so that transformations between complex XSD types defined in this WSDL and the individuals from the OWL-S description (input and output of OWL-S service) must be put here and done by this service. (This is a different kind of transformation than the XSLT mentioned in section 1. in up- and downcast transformations.) Because this service is placed between the BPEL runtime and the OWL-S VM it is called **mediator service**. The mediator service to each OWL-S service must be done during (or right after) the annotation phase. Because the concepts of our ontology are in a well known structure the generation of the up- and downcast transformation part of the mediator service can be largely automated.

5 Using Existing BPEL editor

After the services were successfully annotated they are ready to deploy and published in a registry. By using a suitable designer the services can be found according the semantic information during the design of the complex process. While the
discovery of the services happens according the OWL-S description, the building
in is made according the WSDL of the given mediator service. (Most of the standard BPEL editors rely on the WSDL description of Web services during the design of processes.) During the creation of the choreography (the complex process)
the assign of variables should be done as well. Because the BPEL editor works
only with the WSDL description of the mediator services, data can only be manipulated using the types from WSDLs. According to this building the right structure (with well-defined recognizable names) from the OWL [12] individuals in the
mediator service is essential. By creating an **assign** operation in the process, the
concepts of the ontology can be easily identified this way in spite of that the designing is practically made on other data types.

The approach for the overall execution environment is shown in Figure 1.

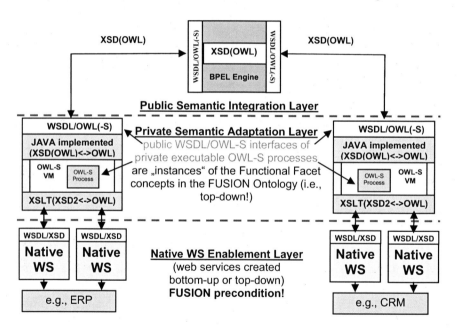

Fig. 1. The overall approach for the execution environment

6 Short Example

This section introduces short example which goal is the connection of two services. This means the realization of a process containing two Web services in a sequence. We consider implementing this process as a proof-of-concept that the approach is good enough to facilitate the specification of the execution environment and the overall solution. The Web services in the example were written in JAVA and published by the Eclipse environment as Web services. Testing of the Web services could be done easily by the Web service Explorer of Java, but other tools were used for testing as well, to make sure, that this solution (usage of Eclipse and Java implementation of Web services) fits to the current standards like SOAP, WSDL, etc.

The native WSDL services have been annotated according to our overall approach. The OWL-S descriptions were made by the Protégé OWL-S plugin. The descriptions of semantically annotated services contain the references to the standard WSDL grounding, plus the up- and downcast transformations between the native (WSDL) and the abstract ontology layer as well. To invoke these OWL-S services the Mindswap OWL-S API were used which is written in Java. It's input and output objects are standard Java objects but making automatically a Web service in Eclipse from them already gives us a native Web service with a standard Web service interface. The communication with the OWL-S services is done by OWL-individuals. By invoking an OWL-S service the input OWL individual must be sent to the OWL-S VM. By receiving the reply we get an OWL individual which we processed and transformed into a different Java object suitable for automatically transforming into a Web service reply. In our example these transformations were implemented hard-wired, which means, that two Web services were written for catching the Web service invoke from BPEL, doing these transformation, and invoke the OWL-S services. The overall BPEL process was designed according to the WSDL description of these Web services which acts as mediator between OWL-S and BPEL. In the BPEL we tried to use XML datatypes, which represents the concepts of the ontology (by using the same name, similar data-structure, etc.). In our simple example we needed to use only very simple assign operation (no XPath evaluations were needed, the input-output messages could be connected directly) between the two Web services, in a more sophisticated scenario we should use more complex assign operation, but it seems to be no problem from the point of our approach. The BPEL was designed and deployed by Active BPEL designer.

7 Summary

In the following points we summarize our results:

- Our approach deals with the proper annotation process of native (WSDL described) Web services. The OWL-S description contains references to the concepts of the Ontology for example the identification of the input and output of the Web service. The up- and downcast XSLT transformation code must be included in the same OWL-S description.

- OWL-S described annotated services are the building blocks of our processes, designed by the process designer.
- The invoking of the native Web services of the ERP and CRM systems is made by OWL-S Virtual Machine (we use the OWL-S API from the University of Maryland). This OWL-S API is responsible for running the up and downcast transformation as well.
- The execution of the process (which is an executable BPEL code) is done by the Active BPEL run-time engine. At the level of BPEL we use special XSD(OWL) data types (come from the WSDL of the mediator service) which are in a consistent connection with the concepts of the ontology.
- The mediator Web service (written in JAVA) is placed between the OWL-S VM and the BPEL run-time engine. This is responsible for catching the invokes from the BPEL, and transforming their input to the right OWL individual (according to the given OWL-S service which will be invoked) and catching the response from the OWL-S service and transforming them to the right XSD(OWL) type and forwarding it to the BPEL run-time.

The paper was supported by the **FUSION FP6-027385 Project**.

References

1. DARPA Agent Markup Language Working Group, "OWL-S: Semantic Markup for Web Services" at http://www.daml.org/services/owl-s/1.1/, 2004.11.
2. Business Process Execution Language for Web Services version 1.1" at http://www-128.ibm.com/developerworks/library/specification/ws-bpel/ 2003.03.
3. Large Scale Distributed Information Systems (LSDIS) group, at http://lsdis.cs.uga.edu/ viewed 10.07.2006.
4. Intelligent Software Agents Lab, at http://www.cs.cmu.edu/~softagents/ viewed 10.07.2006.
5. Oracle Fusion Middleware, at http://www.oracle.com/technology/ prod-ucts/middleware/index.html viewed 10.07.206.
6. IBM Websphere at http://www-306.ibm.com/software/websphere/ viewed 10.07.2006.
7. W3C, "Web Service Description Language, W3C Working Group Note" at http://www.w3.org/TR/wsdl, 2001.03.15.
8. OASIS, "UDDI, Advanced Web Services Discovery Standard" at http://www.uddi.org/specification.html, 2004.

9. Maryland Information and Network Dynamics Lab Semantic Web Agents Project, "OWL-S API", at http://www.mindswap.org/2004/owl-s/api/ viewed 10.07.2006.

10. W3C, "XML and XML Schema", at http://www.w3.org/XML/Schema viewed 10.07.2006.

11. [W3C, "XSL Transformation", at http://www.w3.org/TR/xslt viewed 10.07.2006.

12. W3C, "Web Ontology Language (OWL)" at http://www.w3.org/2004/OWL/ viewed 10.07.2006.

MEO Ontology Infrastructure

István Szakadát[*], Miklós Szőts[**], György Gyepesi[**]

[*]Budapest University of Technology and Economics, i@syi.hu,
[**]Applied Logic Laboratory, Budapest, {szots, gyepesi}@all.hu,

Abstract: MEO project (Hungarian Unified Ontology) started in 2005. The most important goals of the project were 1) building an upper level ontology, 2) developing a special application supported by ontological knowledge, and 3) planning, establishing and distributing an ontology infrastructure. All achievements of the project were intended to be freely accessible and usable according to the Creative Commons philosophy. In the first part of the paper we outline the ontology building process, briefly describe the most important ontological concepts, present and interpret our most important methodological decisions and our ontological commitments, and show the applied layered solution of the project: how the conceptual and the language layers can be separated and integrated. While the conceptual layer is always language independent, the language layer can contain any number of individual languages without restriction. In the second part of the paper we discuss the structure and the logic of MEO ontology, and present some interesting problems we had to solve in our project.

1 Introduction

The MEO project (Magyar Egységes Ontológia/Hungarian Unified Ontology) started in 2005. Based on a wide academic and industrial partnership with seven consortium members the project was sponsored by NKFP (a Hungarian governmental R&D Program). The most important goals of the project were:

1. building an upper level ontology,
2. developing a special application supported by domain level ontological knowledge in the field of the telecommunication call center activities,
3. planning, establishing and distributing an ontology infrastructure, and
4. forming a framework for cooperation, consensus management during ontology building processes.

Although in recent years the category of ontology has functioned as a relatively new buzzword, we put the emphasis on our third goal. In spite of the continuously increasing popularity of ontologies, it seemed to be evident to us, that our most important, current task is to learn how we can handle our ontologies, rather than build ontologies that we do not know how and for what purpose we can use. Of course, by the end of the project we shall build a top level and a domain ontology, but it will be more important to have a tool set (a special integrated, consistent ontology infrastructure component set), with the help of which we or anybody else can start a new ontology building process.

While the knowledge we build into our ontologies consists of words, expressions, concepts which are the results of constant human cooperation over the history of mankind, we decided at the beginning of the project that all achievements of the project would be freely accessible and usable by the public (in line with the Creative Commons philosophy we retain only the Attribution licence to all important achievements of the project). The project communication was fitted to our Creative Commons based commitment, and we launched a MEO session on the Hungarian ontology portal (ontologia.hu/meo), where we made all our project achievements (official project reports, working papers, models, manuals, ontology components etc.) freely accessible.

Of course we did not want to reinvent the wheel. From the beginning of the project it was obvious for us, that we would have to try to reuse all freely available resources. After composing the first version of our upper ontology, we compared our top level concepts to elements of possibly reusable upper level ontologies (like SUMO, WordNet, Dolce). For example we mapped SUMO's time and location concepts to the ones in MEO. Sometimes we adopted good solutions, useful concepts from SUMO and Dolce. But it was the area of ontology building methodology, which had really great influence on our project. We learnt a lot especially from the OntoClean methodology. Although we started to develop our own lexicon and ontology editor (MEOditor), a very popular, widely used ontology editor (Protégé) was also included into our suggested ontology infrastructure tool set. Our editor, of course, supports the two most important ontology related formal languages (OWL and DL), and we provided export/import utilities between MEOditor and Protégé as well.

2 Layered approach

In the MEO project we adopted a layered solution in order to ensure the language neutrality of the ontology. The task is obvious. An ontology – per definitionem – is language independent, but if we (human contributors) would like to use ontological knowledge, we necessarily need a language that is bound to it (a natural or an artificial language). In our MEO model we distinguished a language and a concept layer. We can build our ontologies within the concept layer – totally independently of any language, and in the language layer we can connect as many language dependent words, expressions to our concepts, as we wish. Due to this separation we can build our ontologies in a truly language independent way, and we do not have any language limits. An ontology can be built in any number of languages, and it can not present a problem if a certain language lacks a linguistic construction for a particular concept.

In the MEO model not only the language and the conceptual layers were separated, but we made another distinction as well. In the first phase of the project we could deal with our concepts only on a general level which meant that we divided our concept layer into two parts: a generic level and an instance level. The generic part, the so-called concept domain contains concepts (not instances), and in the other part of the model, what we called instance domain, we can build – in the future – our instance level knowledge base.

Based on the two dimensions briefly introduced in the previous paragraphs we show in Figure 1. how the different layers of the MEO model can be separated and integrated.

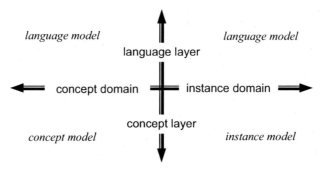

Fig. 1. Parts of MEO model

The language layer has its own model (a linguistic ontology). The elements of the language model provide a meta-ontology for our object level ontology. Although our model is valid at the levels of both spoken and written language, in our project we restricted our work to the written language domain.

The most important entities of the MEO linguistic ontology are:

- wordform
- morphological unit
- construction (similar to lexical unit)

Wordform is a simple string without any language binding. This is an entity where we need not differentiate the English word 'nap' (as an activity) from the ambiguous Hungarian word 'nap' (as a period (day) or a star (sun)). This level is needed because it is only here that we can assign word frequencies to the simple strings independently of the languages the wordforms may be found in. If we bind a language and a set of morphological features to a selected wordform, we can talk about a *morphological unit*. Based on this type of information we can predict the behavior of the wordform in sentences. But this grammatical information is not enough if we wish to know the sense of the selected wordform, so we need – on a third level – the entity of the *construction*. With a construction we can bind a cept (and its sense as well) and a wordform or morphological unit (a language specific utterance). Construction is very similar to the category of *lexical unit*, but the two notions are not identical. In our adopted linguistic theory lexical units are *construction constants*, but we need *construction functions* as well if we want to grasp all other types of linguistic phenomena (for example if we want to describe the productive derivation of words).

MEO has a strong commitment to construction grammar, which is not particularly widely used either in the ontology building community or in the field of linguistics. This is a unique feature of our project.

The next figure shows the most important linguistic relationships:

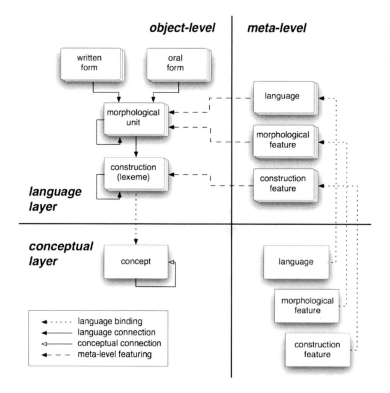

Fig. 2. Linguistic relationships of MEO

3 Concept model

The concept model is the most important part of the entire MEO model in the intersection of the concept layer and the concept domain. Within our model we needed to separate precisely the object level and the different meta-level concepts and concept areas. 1) At the most abstract level we have some mathematical concepts, of course, 2) we have an object level concept domain where we can build our ontological concepts, and 3) we have another meta-level area, where we separate and handle those meta-concepts that we need to describe our ontological concepts.

The function of the mathematical level having only three main categories is only to transform the concepts of ontology into the language of mathematical logic. We use the notion of *relationship* as is usual in mathematics, and we have two other subordinate categories, the notions of *first order relationship* and *higher order relationship* (with the usual interpretations).

Our basic meta-level entities are *meta-properties*, *meta-relations*, *operations* and *primitive types*. We declared and used the same primitive types that the programming world uses – these are roughly same the as the data types used in OWL. If it is necessary or simply useful, some meta-properties can be introduced into this meta-level of our model, such as rigid, semi-rigid or dependent in the Onto-Clean methodologies, but, of course, we can define any other types of meta-property. On this level we defined the most important relation properties (symmetric, asymmetric, transitive, intransitive etc.), and based on these properties and some consequences of them we can build and use a special relation property checking mechanism without using any complex inference system. On this meta-level of the MEO system meta-relations can be declared and used as well, such as the *generic* or *disjunction* relations (this term came from thesauri, and instead of 'generic relation' we could use a lot of other alternative terms like subclass, is-a-kind-of, AKO, subsumption etc.). The generic relation has a special and very important role in our model, we use it on various levels with the same interpretations, but between partly different entities (for example it is used between object-level concepts or between object-level concepts and mathematical entities). Finally, operations can be declared and implemented on this meta-level in order to create concepts from concepts with the help of operations on the object level. We introduced a lot of OWL and DL operators into the MEO model, such as union, intersection, complement, minimum or maximum cardinality, inverse, composition etc.

The main entity of the object level is the *concept*. The most important goal of the ontology building activity is creating new and new concepts, characterizing them with the help of different features, and establishing relations among the concepts. We differentiated three subtypes of concept, and declared *class concepts*, *relation concepts*, and *attributes*. The difference between class and relation concepts is obvious, we interpreted these categories as it is common in the database and programming world. Attribute is a relation-like concept, but attribute and relation differ from each other in their ranges. While the domain and the range of the relation concept can come from class concepts, in the case of attribute the range can come from primitive types. In this respect attribute overlaps the object level and meta-level area of our model. In our approach the three main subordinated concepts have totally equal status, and it is not so common in the ontology building community. Most ontologies concentrate on class concepts. Our ontology contains not only the concept of 'father' (which is a class concept), but the 'is father of' relation is considered as concept. In our universe there can be another relation type, a "*free*" *second order relation*. In this context 'free' means it can be freely declared and defined by the editors of the special ontology. A possible example for it can be the so-called evolutional development relation, with which we can describe the relationship between Horse and Przewalski's Horse in the taxonomy of animals. This relation is not generic one, because there is no connection between the real instances of the two concepts, and it can not be defined by a first order formula (in contrast to generic relation). It is a pure second order relation, since it can be interpreted between two concepts.

The different parts and the most important entities of the concept model are the following:

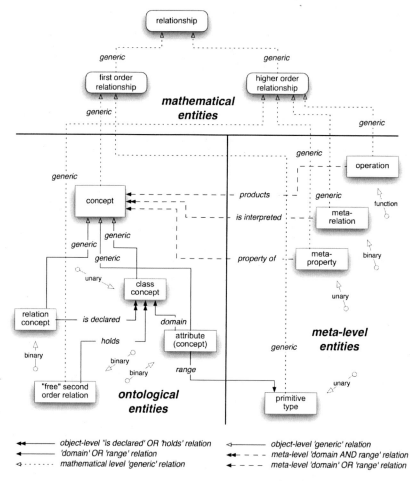

Fig. 3. Different parts and the most important entities of the concept

Under the highest level, most abstract conceptual entities, the model has some other concepts which can be used in all types of ontology. Very closely connected to the generic relation, we defined and applied the notions of *partition* and *hierarchy*. We declared a very important ontology building rule: in the object level area of the model, during the ontology building process we have to subordinate our new concepts to the already existing concepts in a given ontology. As we have three concepts subordinate to our main category (concept), all new concepts have to be subordinated to these (class, relation and attribute) concepts, and therefore potentially every ontology can have three disjunct hierarchies (generic relation based structures).

For each hierarchy we introduced a new concept type which we called *category*. Category (in our model) is a concept immediately subordinate to the root concept of the possible hierarchies. This notion (or more exactly this interpretation) came from the field of the classification systems and thesauri. In general 'category' is a widespread and overused term, but in our interpretation it has a definite, unambiguous meaning, and we can say, that categories are the first level concepts in the concept hierarchies.

4 Concepts and features

In the MEO project we tried to reuse a very old philosophical category first applied by Aristotle. When Aristotle described how we could create new concepts, how we could build taxonomies, he used the notion of *differentia specifica*. When we create a new concept with the help of the generic relationship we have to provide a feature, which unambiguously characterizes the new concept. This idea is very simple and seems to be very promising, although the well-known ontologies (or thesauri) did not adopt it. The probable explanation is again very simple. Providing new features every time we create new concepts would require much more effort. Based on this principle we should build a dual taxonomy, because we have to provide the same number of new features (differentia specifica) as the number of concepts we have. It is not an easy task.

In our project we did not require differentia specifica to be assigned to every new concept, but we incorporated this "featuring" possibility into our model. We can characterize our concepts in different ways. The attributes and the relation concepts can be described with the help of the well-known relation algebraic properties, such as symmetric, irreflexive, transitive etc. In the case of class concepts we can use meta-properties (the kind, for example, that OntoClean methodology introduced) in order to characterize our concepts. We can bind two other types of feature to class concepts and relation concepts. Essential features are those which are usually inherited via generic relation (although we have to provide exception handling capabilities as well, because inheritance is not a necessary requirement), while particular features are not inheritable. Figure 4 shows the most important connections between concepts and features.

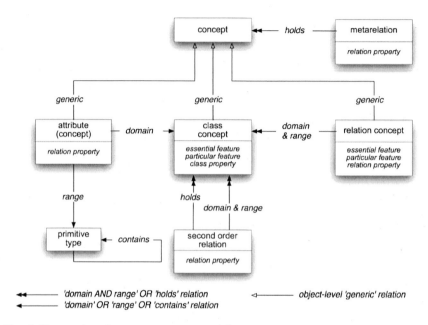

Fig. 4. Connections between concepts and features

5 MEO and OWL

Comparing the MEO concepts to the OWL concepts we can map the most important categories to each other. For example the MEO primitive type has the same meaning and role as the OWL Datatype, and we can MEO attribute to OWL DatatypeProperty, MEO relation concept to OWL ObjectProperty. MEO contains all DL constructors and relation properties which exist in OWL (except those concepts that have individual connections, for example OWL hasValue, because in the first phase we did not implement instance level system components). In MEO we can differentiate ObjectProperty (relation concept) and DatatypeProperty (attribute). Finally axioms are not allowed in OWL which can handle only comments (both exist in MEO), and the concept of feature is completely missing from OWL while it has a very important role in the MEO model.

6 Conclusions

In the MEO project we are building a top level and a domain ontology, but our main focus is on planning, building, using and distributing a robust, consistent ontology infrastructure. In order to ensure the real language independency of our ontologies, we clearly separated the language and the concept levels of our model, and we designed and implemented an integrated and institutionalized set of language management capabilities with which we can easily bind as many languages to our concepts as we wish. This objective and our implementation of it is, in our opinion, unique, we are not aware of any similar projects. While we have built our inner linguistic ontology, we based our work on construction grammar, which is, again, a less frequently used theoretical approach among the ontology building community. Of course, it is usual (maybe necessary), to have the entity of the concept stand in the centre of the model, but the fact, that we differentiated three subtypes of our main entity (concept) and evaluated these as three subordinated concepts with totally equal status is unusual and can be regarded as a novelty. And finally in contrast with the widely applied approach we attributed an important role to relation concepts, and we tried to provide an institutionalized role for features.

References

[Corcho et al. 2003]
Oscar Corcho, Mariano Fernández-López, Asunción Gómez-Pérez: Methodologies, tools and languages for building ontologies. Where is their meeting point?, in: Data & Knowledge Engineering, Vol. 46, 2003, pp 41-64.
[Green et al. 2001]
Green, Rebecca, Bean, C.A., Myaeng, S. Hyon, The Semantics of Relationships: An Interdisciplinary Perspective, Dordrecht: Kluwer, 2001.
[Guarino 2000]
Guarino, N., Welty, C., A Formal Ontology of Properties. Proceedings of 12th Int. Conf. on Knowledge Engineering and Knowledge Management Lecture Notes of Computer Science, Springer Verlag.
[Guarino 2001]
Guarino, N., Welty, C., Supporting ontological analysis of taxonomic relationships. Data & Knowledge Engineering 39 pp 51-74.
[Staab 2004]
Handbook of Ontologies eds. S. Staab, R. Studer, Springer Verlag.

A Semantic-Based Web Service Composition Framework

H-M. Haav*, T. Tammet**, V. Kadarpik*, K. Kindel*, M. Kääramees**

*Institute of Cybernetics at Tallinn University of Technology, Akadeemia 21, 12618 Tallinn, Estonia
**Institute of Computer Science of Tallinn University of Technology, Raja 15, 12618 Tallinn, Estonia

1 Introduction

There is widely recognized problem concerning WSDL-based descriptions of web-services that services are described syntactically not capturing enough meaning [Patil et al. 2004, Probst and Lutz 2004, Elenius et al. 2005]. In order to automate service discovery and composition several semantic heterogeneity problems should be solved.

Most of existing web services are described in WSDL -Web Service Definition Language [WSDL] that is standard protocol for service interface descriptions and SOAP – Simple Object Access Protocol [SOAP]. There is growing effort from the side of Semantic Web research community to make contributions to web service composition frameworks in the form of Semantic Web Services by using specification approaches like OWL-S [OWL-S] or industrial approach called BPEL4WS [BPEL4WS]. As the field of Semantic Web Services is in its early stage of development, then there is lack of practical tools for supporting developers in semantic web service modeling and composition.

Consequently, there is need for conceptual frameworks and tools enriching existing WSDL-based service descriptions with semantic domain-ontology based annotations and providing semantic-based automatic or semi-automatic web service composition for service developers.

The work presented in this paper is aimed at providing semantic-based web service composition framework and a set of supporting tools. The framework takes into account heterogeneity problems of data (input/output) semantics of web services and provides a solution for the problem by introducing domain ontology based annotations to web service WSDL descriptions.

In this paper, we consider only informational web services that do not change the world. This makes our task easier as we do not need to deal with the whole spectrum of semantics of web services, but concentrate only to data semantics. For example, we do not deal with problems of functional and execution semantics of web services as well as we do not consider preconditions and effects.

The main contribution of this paper is in providing framework for introducing domain ontologies describing the concepts of the web services domain, relating them to the data input and output of the web services in order to semantically enrich WSDL-based service descriptions, and providing automatic composition of web services by program synthesis.

A pilot application of the proposed conceptual framework is developed on the basis of Data Exchange Layer X-Road of Estonian State Information System gathering about 700 web-services [X-Road]. The system is implemented for the Linux platform as open source software and is available at [Rql]. As this paper is concentrated to providing the framework, then most of implementation details are omitted.

The rest of the paper is structured as follows. Section 2 presents overall architecture of proposed framework. Section 3 is devoted to semantic annotation of web service descriptions and section 4 describes a logic-based web service composition component of the framework. Section 5 is devoted to related works and section 6 concludes the paper.

2 Architecture of the framework

In this section, an overall picture of proposed framework for composing web services is given and explained (see Fig. 1). The architecture of the framework consists of 2 interrelated parts: web service annotation and logic-based web service composition components. Goal of the system is to automatically find a plan for service composition as an answer to the user request.

The most important processes of the framework are as follows:

1. Building web services domain ontology by using ontology editor Protégé 3.1.1 [Protégé 3.1.1] and creating corresponding OWL description of the ontology.
2. Annotating existing web services described in WSDL on the basis of created ontology by mapping concepts from ontology and labels of WSDL descriptions.
3. Taking as input the user requests for composition of new services. The user request is expressed on ontology level i.e. described in ontology terms.
4. Translating the user requests (queries), domain ontology descriptions in OWL as well as annotated WSDL descriptions of web services to the logic language ELM [Tammet 2004a] in order to make them understandable for the logic-based component of the system.

5. Performing reasoning tasks and composition of web services by program synthesis using the theorem prover RqlGandalf [Rql] that is extended version of Gandalf [Tammet 1997].
6. Extracting the result of program synthesis as a Python program corresponding to the required composite service.
7. Developing the composite service by refining and further implementing the synthesized Python program.

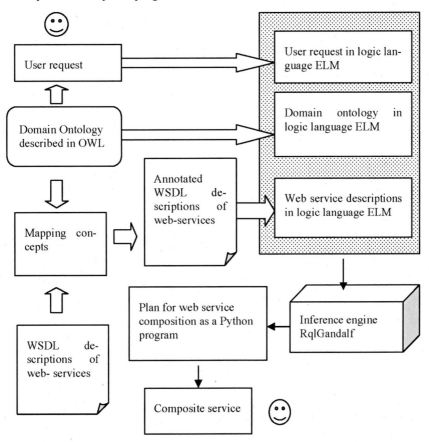

Fig. 1. Web-service annotation and composition framework

We now describe both components of the framework: web service annotation and logic-based web service composition components in more detail as follows.

3. Semantic annotation of web service descriptions

In this paper, we deal with data semantics of web services and do not consider other categories of semantics of web services like functional and execution semantics as identified in [Patil et al. 2004].

3.1 Data semantics of web services

According to our analysis done for Data Exchange Layer X-Road [X-Road], we identified semantic problems of data input and output descriptions of services captured in WSDL-based service descriptions. Similar observations can be found in [Probst and Lutz 2004] for GIS.

In this paper, we consider two types of semantic problems of WSDL-based service descriptions as follows:

1. Labels of input and output data types of services are different, but the descriptions denote the same thing or have the same meaning. It is clear that this type of semantic problem makes it hard to meaningfully compose new web services and makes it impossible to automatically compose web services.
2. Labels of input and output data types are the same, but the descriptions do not denote the same thing or do not have the same meaning. This heterogeneity can lead to incorrect composite web service, as the user or a program does not know that the identical labels in different services refer to different domain concept.

Annotating WSDL descriptions of service input and output with concepts from domain ontology can solve the semantic problems discussed above. This prevents that the services having conceptually not matching input and output are combined in a composite service. There is the third type of semantic problem related to data semantics also identified in [Probst and Lutz 2004] for GIS: type mismatch problem. In this paper, we do not deal with this problem; even we have identified this problem in X-Road web-service descriptions. In our approach, the user should resolve this for each case of type mismatch.

3.2 Semantic annotation

Our goal in developing service composition framework for X-road was to annotate existing web services already described in WSDL. We rely on manual annotation approach as most of developers, because research on automatic or semi-automatic annotation is in its early stage. Nevertheless, there are good examples like the Meteor-S framework for semi-automatic annotation of web services with ontologies [Patil et al. 2004], but these are not yet practical implementations.

According to our approach, a simple web based editing tool could be used for mapping input/output of web services WSDL descriptions to concepts from a domain ontology described in OWL. We used Protégé 3.1.1 ontology editing tool [Protégé 3.1.1] for creating domain specific ontologies and converting them to OWL. In the following we demonstrate our semantic annotation approach on the basis of an example from our pilot application.

3.3 Sample domain ontology

Let us consider small sample ontology from the state information system capturing concepts of citizen and enterprise. Most of web-services of the state information system are related to the first concept. Citizen concept has the following properties: ID-code, First_name, Last_name, Citizenship, and Place_of_birth. Citizen concept has 2 subconcepts as Estonian_citizens and Foreigners. Enterprise concept has the following properties: Reg_no, Name, Field_of_business, and Owner. Enterprise concept has also 2 subclasses: State_owned and Private.

3.4 Sample web services

Let us suppose that we have the following sample set of individual web services available as follows:

1. Web service GetPersonalData finds all personal data of a citizen by citizen's identification code. Its input data type has label *idcode* and its output is complex type having the following sequence of elements in the corresponding WSDL file: *idcode, fname, lname, citizenship, place_birth.*
2. Web service GetCompany finds among other output fields a registration number of a company by business field of this company. Its input parameter has label *businessfield* and one of its output fields is denoted by label *reg-code* in the corresponding WSDL file.
3. Web service GetOwner finds identification code of a person, who is owner a company by given registration code of a company. Its input parameter has label *comp_reg_no* and its output is denoted by label *owner_id_code* in the corresponding WSDL file.

3.5 Annotation of service descriptions

Web services are described using WSDL and annotated using the ontology as represented above. As input for the annotation process are ontology description in OWL (produced by Protégé) and web services input and output parameters' descriptions from WSDL file. We need to annotate only input/output of web services, as our service composition component needs this conceptual information for composition process.

For example, *idcode* as the input parameter name of the service GetPersonalData should be mapped to the attribute ID-code of the concept Citizen in the ontology above. The output of the same service should be mapped as follows: label *citizenship* to the attribute (slot) Citizenship of the concept Citizen in the ontology, label *fname* to the concept *First_name*, etc. Corresponding similar mappings should be done for input/output of other web services as well. The described above process of semantic ontology based annotation of web services described by WSDL files is semi-automatic. Using annotation editor, the user can load WSDL file to be mapped to suitable domain ontology.

Another approach might be to build the editor into Protégé as in [Elenius et al. 2005], where in contrast to our approach; OWL description of domain ontology is enhanced by instances that refer to corresponding elements (syntactic names of input/output) from WSDL descriptions.

4 A logic-based web-service composition component

4.1 Composition of web services by program synthesis

Our logic-based web-service composition approach is based on general scheme of automated deduction and program synthesis [Green 1969, Manna and Waldinger 1980]. According to that, we formulate an axiomatic theory of the application domain including background knowledge. In this theory, domain ontology concepts and their properties are expressed by axioms. Each web service is expressed by a set of axioms that describes the service. The query (request) is expressed as a theorem in the language of application domain theory. Usually, the theorem expresses the existence of the entity (e.g. a citizenship, a name, etc) that the query is asking to find by given entity or entities. Using an automated theorem prover, it is proved that the theorem follows from the axioms of the application domain theory. The proof should be sufficiently constructive, so that from proving the existence of a desired entity we can construct a program of finding it.

As the automated theorem prover we use FOL theorem prover Gandalf [Tammet 1997] extended for synthesis of programs in order to be suitable for web service composition tasks [Rql]. The core method employed by the system is the classical combination of the resolution method with the ans-predicate mechanism; see [Green 1969, Tammet 1995]. The system is looking for suitable instantiations of the variable(s) in the query. These variables will be the arguments of the special ans-predicate. A clause containing only the ans-predicates is considered to be an empty clause, with the arguments of the ans predicate representing the solution to the query.

The simplistic usage of the ans-predicate will not be sufficient for program synthesis. We will need additional rules and mechanisms. The four main extensions built into the core prover are as follows:

1. Built-in strings, dates and arithmetic.
2. A PROLOG-like mechanism for deriving different alternative answers.
3. A derivation rule for eagerly disambiguating clauses containing several answerliterals.

4. A derivation rule for converting logical conditions into term-level conditions. For example, if we have a clause —A|ans(s), then we can derive ans(if (A, s)) as a new clause, provided that A is computable. Resolution proof search extended by such rules may give us a result in the form of a term. Next, this term should be compiled to an executable program.

Our compilation stage consists of two phases as follows. First step is the loop-lifting conversion modifying the term. Second step constitutes compilation of the modified term to an executable Python function. We have decided to use Python for practical usability, and we are also avoiding comprehension and lambda-terms in the Python program.

An important methodological decision we have taken is to avoid any forms of explicit induction. We describe lists using special function symbols, which will eventually be translated to loop constructions. Similarly, we avoid error handling in logic. The synthesized programs will handle possible error situations instead.

4.2 Methodology

As any other logic-based system, our system also can accept different input specification languages and convert them to logic for reasoning purposes. We have developed a user-friendly rule language ELM [Tammet 2004a] to be used and understood by developers (users). This language is built on the top of core language ECL [Tammet 2004b], which is basically first order logic extended with several data types like numbers, string, dates, etc. and operations on them. ECL is an input language for the theorem prover Gandalf.

According to our framework, user requests (queries), domain ontology descriptions in OWL as well as a part of annotated WSDL descriptions of web services are converted to ELM language (see Fig.1) in order to make them understandable by logic-based component of our system.

For capturing ontological information we need OWL to ELM converter and for getting descriptions of input and output data types of web services we need extractor of this information from annotated WSDL descriptions and converting the latter to ELM language.

Our intention is that the end user operates on the level of domain ontology concepts and places his/her requests on this level.

In the next section, we give main principles of conversion of domain knowledge represented in OWL and annotated WSDL to logic language in order to form domain theory for program synthesis. Due to limited scope of the paper we need to omit exact definitions of transformations from OWL to ELM.

4.3 Transformations to the logic language ELM

The ELM language [Tammet 2004a] is a sugared version of extended FOL. Extensions to FOL allow writing predefined computable functions, sentences in SQL and several nonmonotonic and (weak) epistemic operators, as well as select data sources to be used in queries.

In this chapter, not full syntax of ELM is presented, but it is described without any formal definitions of syntax or semantics in the scope needed for explaining examples. The formal definitions for the language can be found in [Tammet 2004a].

Taking into account features of ELM we now demonstrate translations from OWL to ELM and from annotated WSDL to ELM. In the latter case, only part of WSDL description is needed for logical reasoning.

Translating OWL ontologies to ELM

Translation of OWL ontologies to FOL axioms is not new as correspondence between OWL and Description Logic (DL) is well known [Baader et al. 2003] as well as translation from DL to FOL [Borgida 1996]. As ELM language is extended FOL, then the translation of OWL ontologies to ELM can be done in standard way.

In the following examples, OWL ontology from section 3 is translated to ELM in order to demonstrate our transformation principles.

- **Representation of classes.** We use unary predicates for representing classes. In the ELM language we may write, "X is something" to say that X is something (in standard logical notation, something(X)), where X is either OWL individual name or ELM variable. Variables are denoted by symbol "?" in ELM language. OWL classes *Citizen* and *Enterprise* are translated to the following unary predicates: *?P is citizen, ?E is enterprise*
  Each OWL instance is then translated to literal fact like
  > *John is foreigner* or *Jaan is citizen* or *IBM is enterprise*

- **Representation of properties.** Each OWL property R is translated to binary predicate R(X,Y). For example, if OWL class *Enterprise* has a property businessfield, then this is translated to the following ELM sentence: *?F is businessfield of enterprise*

- **Representation of subsumption relationships.** Each subclass/superclass (subsumption) relationship is translated to the following rule in the form: *Each predicate1 is predicate2*
  For example, *Each estonian_citizen is citizen*

- **Representation of queries.** User requests (queries) are given on ontology level and translated to ELM as following sentence: *Find var_1,...,var_N where sentence?*, where *var_1,...,var_N* are variables and *sentence* is an ELM sentence.
  For example, our sample request is translated to the following ELM sentence:
  > *find ?S where banking is businessfield of ?C*
  > *and ?O is owner of ?C and ?S is citizenship of ?O*

Web service description in logic language

In order to translate web service descriptions to ELM language annotated WSDL to ELM translations are needed. Not entire WSDL description is converted to ELM, but necessary information about data input and output of the service and corresponding service name are extracted from the WSDL file and converted to a sentence in logic based language ELM.

For example, previously given web services are expressed in ELM language as follows.

If a web service returns as output a structure, then for each ouput field of the web service the following type of sentence is created as for example for GetPersonalData returning a structure containing different data fields of personal data according to the properties of the concept of citizen.

if ?I is ID_code of ?P then

getfield(citizenship,call(GetPersonalData,?I)) is citizenship of ?P.

If a web service has only one output field as GetOwner, then the following typical sentence is generated.

if ?R is Reg_no of ?C then

call(GetOwner,?R) is ID_code of ?P.

The web service GetCompany returns a list of companies operating in a given business field. As Reg_no is one output field of GetCompany, then the following sentence is created.

if ?F is businessfield of ?C then

foreach(L,getfield(Reg_no,L),call(GetCompany,?F)) is Reg_no of ?C.

In general, this type of sentence is generated for each output field.

4.4 Composition of web services

Given web services domain ontology and web services descriptions in ELM language, the logic-based component of our framework translates these to internal logic language of FOL theorem prover Gandalf (i.e. to extended FOL). The resulting theory is passed to Gandalf, where it can be used for reasoning tasks and for composition of web services by program synthesis as discussed in the beginning of this section. We now show the web service composition on the basis of our running example.

Let us suppose that the user (service developer) requests to compose a new service that finds a citizenship of owner(s) of an enterprise by given business field of an enterprise. This request is simplified but rather similar to what is used in real application. In order to satisfy the request the composite web service should be created as follows.

If the user is submitting the query to find citizenship of owner(s) of an enterprise, which business field is banking, then this query is translated to the following sentence in the logic language ELM:

find ?S where banking is businessfield of ?C
and ?O is owner of ?C and ?S is citizenship of ?O

The system tries to find an answer to this query and synthesizes a program that implements corresponding web service. The resulting program is generated in Pyhton programming language as follows:

```
def query( ):
    result=[ ]
    data=call("GetCompany","banking")
    for i in data:
        result=result+\
        [getfield("citizenship",call("GetPersonalData",call("GetOwner", i)))]
    return result
```

The result is a list of citizenships of owners of enterprises, which operate in banking field. This automatically obtained program code is presented to the developer of web services in order to aid him/her in the web service composition process. This code needs further refinements, but in principle, having individual web services available, it can invoke them in the sequence given by the synthesized program.

4.5 Implementation

A proof of concept implementation of the web service composition framework is done as a part of the larger system of development of web-based applications called Rql technology [Rql]. The technology consists of 2 main parts: the application server Xstone for creating 3-layered systems and the RqlGandalf solver. The middleware server Xstone connects to Oracle, PostgreSQL databases and the RqlGandalf solver. In addition, the Rql technology includes browser-based interface creating toolkit for Xstone. The whole system can be downloaded from [Rql]. It is written for Linux in C and licensed under GPL.

5 Related Works

Semantic markup of web services has been proposed by many projects and initiatives like WSDL-S [WSDL-S], WSMO [WSMO], OWL-S [OWL-S], METEOR-S [Patil et al. 2004]. Semantically most expressive is OWL-S, but OWL-S profile model duplicates input and output descriptions embodied in the WSDL used for grounding of OWL-S descriptions. It is also bound to only one ontology language OWL. OWL-S being web service ontology does not really solve the data semantics problems discussed in the beginning of this paper as it is intended to semantically describe all aspects of web services including composition. Data semantics problems in OWL-S should be solved on the WSDL level that leads us in any case to WSDL annotation. These are reasons why our approach is rather close to WSDL-S. Comparing to WSDL-S, our semantic annotation approach is not as general as WSDL-S proposal. We have used very pragmatic solution of annotating only input/output of web services in order to provide (semi)-automatic web service composition framework for service developers. Our approach is independent on the service description language in its logic based service composition part.

Regarding to automation of web service composition, the approaches proposed fall into two main categories based on workflow models or on AI planning. Our work is tightly related to AI planning approaches based on automated program synthesis that relies on strong theorem proving technology. In [Waldinger 2001, Waldinger and Shrager 2006] available services and user requirements are described in FOL, and then constructive proofs are generated with SNARK theorem prover. Nevertheless, our approach differs from their approach in that they do not consider web services and do not relate their approach to web services description standards. We also enhanced FOL theorem prover in order to meet requirements of synthesis of web services.

Other logical approaches are used for web service composition in [Rao et al. 2004, Ponnekanti 2002, Sirin et al. 2004]. In [Rao et al. 2004] linear logic (LL) is used. For external presentation of web services they use semantic web service language DAML-S and for composition process they translate web services into extralogical axioms and proofs in LL. Service composition tool SWORD [Ponnekanti 2002] generates composite service plans by using rule-based plan generation implemented in Java. [Sirin et al. 2004] have developed semi-automatic service composition prototype, which consists of two basic components: a composer and an inference engine. First user selects the service he/she is interested in, and then inference engine finds all the other services that can supply appropriate data for selected service input.

6 Conclusions

The paper presented a conceptual framework for semantic-based web service composition that consists of 2 interrelated components: semantic-based web services annotation and logic-based web services composition components. We have shown how WSDL descriptions of existing web services have been annotated on the basis of introduced domain ontologies and converted to logic based language for logic-based service composition. We have demonstrated how FOL theorem prover RqlGandalf has been used for automatic composition (synthesis) of annotated web services.

Many of theoretical and practical aspects of the program synthesis are still open. Our system is not always capable of synthesizing a program, nor is it capable of selecting a best variant from several different synthesized programs. This constitutes our future work.

7 Acknowledgements

This work was partially funded by Enterprise Estonia funding within R&D project RQL "Rule-based databases for creation of web services" and ESF grant 5766. We thank anonymous referees for their comments.

References

Baader F, Calvanese D, McGuinness D, Nardi D, Patel-Schneider P (Eds) (2003) The Description Logic Handbook, Cambridge University Press

Borgida A (1996) On the relative expressiveness of description logics and predicate logics, Artificial Intelligence, 82(1-2): 353-367.

BPEL4WS, Available from: http://www-128.ibm.com/developerworks/library/ws-bpel

Elenius D, Denker G, Martin D, et al (2005) The OWL-S Editor- A Development Tool for Semantic Web Services, Gomez-Perez, A., and Euzenat, J. (Eds) Proceedings of ESWC 2005, LNCS 3532, Springer-Verlag, pp 78-92.

Green C (1969) Application of theorem-proving for problem solving. In Proceedings of 1st International Joint Conference on Artificial Intelligence, pp 219-239.

Manna Z, Waldinger R (1980) A Deductive Approach to Program Synthesis, ACM Transactions on Programming, Languages, and Systems.2: 90-121.

OWL, Web Ontology Language. Semantics and Abstract Syntax. W3W Working Draft 31 March 2003. Available from: http://www.w3.org/TR/owl-semantics/

OWL-S, Web Ontology Language for Web Services. Available from: http://www.daml.org/services/

Patil A, Oundhakar S, Sheth A, Verma K (2004) METEOR-S Web service Annotation Framework, Proceedings of WWW Conference 2004, ACM, New York, pp 553-562.

Ponnekanti SR, Fox A (2002) SWORD: A Developer Toolkit for Web Service Composition, Proceedings of Eleventh World Wide Web Conference (WWW2002, Web Engineering Track), Honolulu, Hawaii

Probst F, Lutz M (2004) Giving Meaning to GI Web Services, J. Hu (Ed), Proceedings of Second International Workshop on Web Services: Modeling, Architecture and Infrastructure, Porto, INSTICC Press, pp 23-35.

Protégé 3.1.1, Protégé OWL Editor. Available from: http://protege.stanford.edu

Rao J, Küngas P, Matskin M (2004) Logic-based Web Services Composition: from Service Description to Process Model, Proceedings of the 2004 IEEE International Conference on Web Services, ICWS'2004, San Diego, California, USA, July 6-9, 2004, IEEE Computer Society Press, pp 446-453.

Rql, Rule-based systems for creation of web services. Available from: http://deepthought.ttu.ee/it/xstone/

Sirin E, Parsia B, Wu D, Hendler J, Nau D (2004) HTN planning for web service composition using SHOP2. Journal of Web Semantics, 1(4): 377-396.

SOAP, Available from: http://www.w3.org/TR/soap12-part0

Tammet T (1995) Completeness of Resolution for Definite Answers. Journal of Logic and Computation 5(4): 449–471.

Tammet T (1997) Gandalf. Journal of Automated Reasoning 18(2): 199-204.

Tammet T (2004a) Extended Logical Markup language (ELM) Model and Syntax Specification. Available from: http://deepthought.ttu.ee/it/elm/elm.html

Tammet T (2004b) Extended Common Logic (ECL) Model and Syntax Specification. Available from: http://deepthought.ttu.ee/it/elm/ecl.html

Waldinger R (2001) Web Agents Cooperating Deductively, Rash, J.L. et al (Eds): Proceedings of FAABS 2000, LNAI 1871, Spriger-Verlag, pp 250-262.

Waldinger R, Shrager J (2006) Deductive Discovery and Composition of Resources, Proceedings of RoW2006: Reasoning on the Web, Edinburgh, Scotland

WSDL, Available from: http://www.w3.org/TR/wsdl

WSDLS, WSDL-S: Adding semantics to WSDL - White paper. Available from: http://lsdis.cs.uga.edu/library/download/wsdl-s.pdf

WSMO, Web Service Modeling Ontology. Available from: http://www.wsmo.org/

X-Road, Data Exchange Layer X-Road. Available from: http://www.ria.ee/27309

Community-Based Partnerships in the Design of Information Systems: The Case of the Knowledge Commons

Natalie Pang, Henry Linger, Don Schauder

{natalie.pang, henry.linger, don.schauder}@infotech.monash.edu.au

Abstract: Using the case of a cultural institution in Australia, the paper introduces the context and application of the knowledge commons, a vision in cultural institutions and in doing so, argue for the case of community centred approach to design based on structurational and action research principles for cultural communities. The paper argues for the application of design principles and in studying how these principles may be enacted in cultural institutions; it argues for potential of empowering and sustaining communities.

1 Introduction

In cultural institutions, such as museums, galleries and libraries amongst others, a knowledge commons represents the process of creating and sharing public knowledge. In this public domain the design of information systems is characterised by changing structures of ownerships that raises issues of power, the intentionality of tasks (between individuals, groups, organisation, and the context of the societal system) and the control and flexibility expressed in the design. This allows a focus on the users changing perceptions of the information systems and the relationship between the variety of actors within the design process and their relationship to the information system design.

The importance of understanding users was first articulated by Norman and Draper (1986) who coined the term user centred design (UCD) that 'emphasizes that the purpose of the system is to serve the user, not to use a specific technology, not to be an elegant piece of programming. The needs of the users should dominate the design of the interface, and the needs of the interface should dominate the design of the rest of the system' (Norman, 1986). In this sense, the interface functions more than just a medium between the computer and the user; it also acts as a type of intermediary communicator, negotiating understandings and meanings between the computer and user. For cultural institutions, an information system is an emergent property of a dynamic ecosystem and the design process must incorporate a cultural vision and accommodate community engagement based on structurational and action research principles.

This paper explores how UCD principles are enacted in the process of creating and sharing public knowledge in cultural institutions. This involves the investigation of UCD concepts and their application to the ongoing development of cultural institutions as multi-stakeholder partnerships. We examine the discourses around user-centred design as an approach for the design of the information system and extend these to accommodate the specific requirements of the knowledge commons. The link between the design of information systems and its place in the knowledge commons is discussed from insights gained from the case of a unique relationship between a women on farms' community and a museum. From these insights we argue to extend UCD as a community-based participatory design approach for the purpose of contributing to the construction and sustainability of the knowledge commons in cultural institutions. The paper demonstrates how this approach to the design of technological applications and systems serves as a dynamic influence in facilitating the knowledge commons in cultural institutions and their communities.

For this study we seek to define 'museum' but this is not intended to be an exhaustive definition. According to the International Council of Museums (ICOM), a museum is 'a non-profit making, permanent institution in the service of society and of its development, and open to the public, which acquires, conserves, researches, communicates and exhibits, for purposes of study, education and enjoyment, material evidence of people and their environment.'

2 User-Centred Design: A Complex of Disciplines

A premise underlying UCD is that the dynamic interplay of user needs and feedback and translating these needs into some practical specification of requirements for an information system cannot be satisfied in a linear, non-recursive methodology of design. The difficulty users have in communicating ideas or concepts (Bonner, 2002) ensures that capturing user needs is time-consuming and costly. The iterative view of UCD implies that there can never be an "ideal" information system for the community to use (Fraser, 2002; Head, 1999; Cockton, 2004). But perhaps this is not a problem to be solved but an opportunity for information systems requirements to reflect the continuous negotiations between cultural institutions and communities.

Perhaps one of the most famous representations in thinking about designing around users came from Norman's (1988) groundbreaking ideas in 'The Psychology of Everyday Things' reflecting a paradigm shift in information systems design. It is not our intention to critique information systems design methods but to focus on how the user is incorporated into the design process.

The main contributions to UCD advocated by well known researchers in this area are summarised in Table 1. This table is not intended to be an exhaustive, but highlights some of the most significant contributions towards the study of UCD since 1983. Many of the works in Table 1 result in methodological instruments that are applied to users who are assessed individually, seated in front of their computers.

Our focus on designing with the user, instead of designing for the user, allows participatory design to be interpreted as UCD. This interpretation involves the collective participation of all stakeholders including communities. Moreover, participation in the design process is not seen as a once-off assessment of stakeholder and community needs, but as ongoing dialogues that are both explicit and implicit.

Author(s)	Main area(s)	Contribution
Carroll, J (2000)	Scenario based design and claims analysis	Introduced the idea of iterative design through the task-artifact cycle, and user-centred design strategies in scenario based design and claims analysis. Carroll (2000) stresses the importance of maintaining a continuous focus on situations of and consequences for human work and activity to promote learning and the structure and dynamics of problem domains, thus seeing usage situations from different perspectives. His work is significant in the field of process-oriented design modelling.
Nielsen, J (1993)	Ten usability heuristics	Main contribution in using heuristic principles as a method for usability evaluation, to be used in any stage of a development process.
Schneiderman, B (1992)	Nassi-Shneiderman diagrams, and the 'Eight golden rules of interface design'	The nassi-shneiderman diagram was co-developed by Shneiderman and Nassi, a graphical design representation for structured programming: breaking large tasks into smaller subtasks, until only simple statements remain. The main contribution of this work is a top-down approach of design. This work is rarely used nowadays, as modifications usually require the whole diagram to be drawn. His other main contribution in the field lies in propagating rules of interface design, similar in nature to Nielsen's usability heuristics.
Norman, D (1988)	The Psychology of Everyday Things	Norman was perhaps one of the earliest to apply insights from the field of psychology and industrial product design and apply them to the design of user interfaces. He also introduced the model of interaction, a framework to explain human interactions with systems.
Card, Moran and Newell (1983)	GOMS	The GOMS (goals, operators, methods, selection rules) method is a model used for task analysis to analyse and predict total time for user task performance. Alongside with this purpose, GOMS also makes clear a hierarchy of goals and sub-goals of users.

Table 1. Key contributions in UCD

2.1 The User in Design

A historical analysis of the role of the 'user' highlights the shifts in the perceptions and roles of the user in design. The term UCD is widely used, but there appears to be only a basic consensus as to its meanings and implications: user needs should inform the information systems design process. Although organisations express their own UCD philosophies in different ways, all would claim a focus on the functional needs of users. Karat and Karat (2003) acknowledge the diversity of interpretations of UCD, but note that they are all agreed in distancing themselves from Taylorist principles of techno-centric, mass production in information systems design methodologies. Beyond these clear points of agreement there is a broad consensus in the UCD world that reality is 'mutable', there are 'no certain truths', and 'knowledge is constructed through communally created knowledge and action'. Gulliksen et al. (2003) further reinforces this alarming observation in that 'the concept of user-centred...design has no agreed upon definition'. Much of the research in UCD is driven by a concern that the lack of consensus is obscuring the concept of UCD, turning it into a concept with no pragmatic meaning. This gives rise to misunderstandings about the effectiveness of UCD.

A significant contributed to the conceptual development of UCD has been the establishment of ISO 13407, an international standard established in 1999. The standard aims to provide 'guidance on human-centred design activities throughout the life cycle of computer-based interactive systems' (Jokela et al., 2003). Almost as if agreeing to the observation that there is simply too much variety in UCD methods and techniques, ISO 13407 is set up for 'those managing design processes' (Jokela et al., 2003) and does cover methods and techniques.

The user as 'a user'

The term UCD, as introduced by Norman and Draper (1986), account for many of the contributions outlined in Table 1, where key research areas have included cognitive engineering and psychology, interaction models between the individual user and computer, the development of heuristics, and so on. These activities typically involve testing by seating users in front of individual computers with testing being conducted on individuals or groups. Another significant activity lies in gathering of user requirements. Requirements are usually collated from the assessments of needs collected through meeting with representatives from the recognized user communities.

While such efforts are worthwhile, it challenges the UCD concept by characterising the user as a 'victim' to be 'rescued' (Spinuzzi, 2003). Such an interpretation can be drawn from UCD literature that concentrates on the adeptness of designers, developers, usability specialists and managers to capture the needs of users effectively. But these approaches go no further than providing effective interfaces and systems to 'rescue' end users. Such passivity results in a lack of understanding about the decisions facing community groups, and the barriers and challenges involved (Merkel et al., 2004).

From user to participant

A principle advocated in participatory design (PD) is that UCD involves the collective participation of all stakeholders (Schuler and Namioka, 1993) and is distinguished from other UCD approaches in its philosophy of inclusion of the user as early as the conceptual stage of design. PD approach is beyond designing around the interface as it views users as participants in the design process and shifting responsibilities, such as prototyping, to the users (Gulliksen et al., 2003). The developments in PD have much to thank the Scandinavian efforts in their advocacy for extensive user involvement in design (Gulliksen et al., 2003; Taxen, 2004). Taxen (2004) noted that the motivation in the majority of the early PD projects in Scandinavia was an agenda of empowering workers when technologies were introduced in the workplace. This empowerment and transposition of power and responsibilities is a significant aspect of the design process that is central to community based design as argued below.

Community-centred design

According to Preece (2000), the community-centred design is both participatory and evolutionary. The design of socio-technical environments is the main focus in community-centred design, with the emphasis on social interactions between humans mediated by technology instead of human-computer interactions. Here the social elements that influence the use of technology and interactions amongst users are addressed (DePaula, 2003).

Arguably, community-centred design is included in the domain of socio-computing, a recent research area concerned with the influence of technology on socio interactions and vice versa (DePaula, 2003). Socio-computing has been viewed through the lens of structuration theory (Giddens, 1986), adapted in the context of design (Pang and Schauder, in press; Pang et al., 2006). Structuration theory is used as a framework for design in this discussion because of its ability to recognise both the duality of structure and emergence of use that is a typical outcome of this design process as has been appropriately highlighted in the literature (Pang and Schauder, in press; Pang et al., 2006; Orlikowski and Robey, 1991; DePaula, 2003). In addition to structuration theory, the community-centred design process is also an interventionist approach that is informed action research principles. The combination of structuration theory and action research principles ensure that community centred design (CCD) empowers communities and leads to the co-ownership, co-construction, and co-production of dynamic design, systems, and information resources. These are the outcomes that are the focus of cultural production in the knowledge commons that cultural institutions seek.

The knowledge commons

The idea of a commons is not new – in fact it has been around as long as the first human cooperation. Men hunting together for food, and sharing their skills and eventually, their produce, the commons, is rooted in communities of social trust and cooperation (Bollier, 2004). Derived from the historical commons, the commons defined by Benkler (2003) are 'institutional spaces, in which we can practice a particular type of freedom; freedom from the constraints we normally accept as necessary preconditions of functional markets'. The term has also been used to refer to the infusion of digital technologies and resources to be used freely (MacWhinnie, 2003; Hales et al., 2000; Beagle, 1999; Bailey and Tierney, 2002; Bollier, 2004; Cowgill et al., 2001; Lukasik, 2000). Moritz (2004) defines the knowledge commons as 'zones of free and equitable use for data, information and knowledge' consisting of physical, logical and content layers of resources (Bollier, 2004).

It should be highlighted that several understandings of the 'commons' have emerged with the popular ones being the information commons, the learning commons, and the knowledge commons. The information commons emphasises the free and equitable use of information resources, while the learning commons (an increasingly popular concept used by libraries) infuses services, resources and technologies in spaces to promote learning. The focus of the learning commons is on the open nature of processes to capture revelations from information and knowledge; to learn, in other words.

In this paper we focus on the knowledge commons that is envisioned to include not only information resources, but also indigenous knowledge and processes and communities that concern themselves with the production of knowledge. Such a purpose implies that these communities come together not only for the creation and sharing of information resources, but also involves processes, explicit or implicit, that facilitate the communities' production of knowledge. This conceptualisation of the knowledge commons is critical as information, as a scarcity, could be deplete while knowledge, as a resource, 'has the characteristic of not being degraded when used, but rather to increase in value' (Drucker, c.f. Hellstrom, 2003). This also recognises that communities in the knowledge commons are dynamic and their creation and sharing of knowledge can be influenced by their very dynamism.

A key principle of the knowledge commons lies in the perception of people; they are seen not just as users, or even participants, but also as creators and co-producers. The relationship between the UCD approach and the knowledge commons lies in the commonality they share in the inclusion of dialogue from the community: individual voices, group reflections and influences from institutions and the larger society. The implication for UCD is that design consists less in products than in processes that engage all participants in reflective practice and continuous learning expressed in negotiated action outcomes.

In this paper we looks at the knowledge commons in the context of cultural institutions. These institutions seek to protect, preserve and construct collective resources, and in doing so, make resources freely available to their communities. Today, these institutions are constantly challenged with privatisation and market forces seeking to dominate even the information and resources they are protecting and creating. One example is the licenses-limited access to electronic periodicals and journals. The core role of cultural institutions, their raison d'etre, has not changed but the means by which this role is discharged has changed radically.

Charles Leadbeater recently said that if we neglect the public platforms of our society then we are neglecting a vital part of what makes us a society (Leadbeater, 2006). Cultural institutions form a large part of this public platform. In addition, on this platform they ensure the creation, sustainability, preservation, and convergence of communities and their cultures.

Through a discussion of a museum case study and its relationship with a community, we demonstrate how cultural institutions create and sustain a knowledge commons in the community, in zones of free and equitable access and use, amidst technological and environmental changes, using as a starting point and a continuing motif, a collaborative endeavour in design.

Addressing contexts through tasks

In considering community centred design, there needs to be a framework for considering various interactions of communities. Thus tasks need to be considered beyond the traditional methods of HCI (human-computer interaction) that focus on the work level task. In our framework we are particularly interested in addressing the contexts of tasks to reveal the real problems and needs. At the same time, our the focus on communities and the commons necessitates that UCD issues are elucidated at both the individual and group levels. The concept of community is bound up with various kinds of group affiliations or belonging by individuals. Consequently, CCD needs to reflects an understanding that individuals belong to multiple communities.

The focus for a renewed vision of UCD, CCD, is on the interaction between the individual and the group, and the community culture generated by this interplay against the backdrop of wider social structuring processes within the knowledge commons. Linger (2002) arrived at a model, Figure 1 below, that extends the task-based approach to Knowledge Management (Burstein and Linger, 2003; 2005) across individual to societal levels of analysis and engagement. The formulation of this model is influenced by the Information Continuum Model (ICM) (Schauder et al., 2005) that is constructed on key structurational concepts from Giddens as applied to the creation, capture, organisation and pluralisation of information at the levels of individuals, groups, organisations, and societies (Schauder et al., 2005).

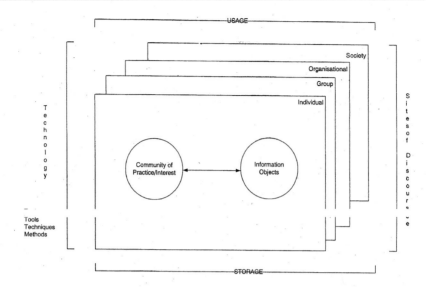

Fig. 1. The Linger model (Linger, 2002; Pang and Schauder, in press)

Conceptualising this model in the context of CCD highlights the following:
Communities and information objects

Referring to the 'common resources' within the knowledge commons, information objects are defined as the public resources cultural institutions seek to provide for communities. Depending on the cultural institution, this may include literary works, digital resources, spaces, moving pictures and other multimedia, community information, and so on. These information objects come about through the construction and reconstruction of cultures by communities. They have both structural and agency relationships with communities, and vice versa.
Layers/levels of interactions

The interactions between communities and information objects are contextualised using 4 layers of interpretations. This is an extremely important as information objects that have not been contextualised have no agency attributes. Within the *individual* layer, the individual makes sense of her own self-knowledge and engages in private projects. This is an important construction of knowledge that is later shape, and in turn be shaped by, other layers of interpretations.

With this construction of knowledge, the individual contributes to the production of knowledge within the community, the *group* layer in Linger's model. This is in turn shaped by organisational influences that impact on the communities and their interactions with information objects. However, the organisation are also significantly influenced by the very dynamics of the interactions at the community level. The fourth and overarching layer lies in societal interpretations that shape the organisation while at the same time are collectively shaped by the organisation and its partners.

These layers of interpretations relates also to two ends of a spectrum of information systems. On one end is the storage of information objects and the other relates to the usage of information objects in the context of the knowledge commons. For the purpose of this study, the usage-end of the spectrum is the focus of our study.

Concluding remarks

Tasks in communities are considered against these layers of interactions, and are considered through the lens of cultural institutions. Having this in mind, it must be noted that the four levels of interactions (and tasks): individual; group; organisational; and societal; are not dichotomies but dynamically related within their contexts. The mapping of tasks in design must be cognisant of these levels and take into account the interplay between communities and information objects.

In the knowledge commons, community members create, access, contributes to, and own resources in the commons. In this context, the perspectives of users are not those of traditional users but those of co-producers of knowledge and participants in activities that are meaningful to the communities they belong to. To understand the transformations of cultural institutions our study proposes an approach that is at the intersection of the proposed view of UCD, as CCD, and the knowledge commons.

3 Community-Based Design: A Case-Based Program of Research

In recent times case study research designs have increasingly been argued for their value and ability to investigate contexts within which research questions are raised (Kaplan and Maxwell, 1994; De Vaus, 2001; Yin, 1994). In contrast to experimental design, this study requires and desires little control over parameters as the contexts of information use is the focus of the study. Below we present the case study a farm women's community in Victoria as an example of community centred design.

3.1 The Women on Farms Gathering Community

The **community** and its interactions evolve around annual gatherings held in various locations in the rural areas of Victoria, an Australian State. These gatherings are organised for the purpose of sharing stories amongst farm women, empowering the women in the communities in the process. Although the first gathering was held as early as 1990, the involvement of the Museum of Victoria, as a cultural institution, was not significant until 2001. At the Beechworth gathering that year, objects and the women's stories were brought together as a collection as history boards. With the design and display of these history boards, the community was immediately aware of a collection that is unique to them, and an imminent task at hand. A central, neutral institution that could curate the collection would also ensure the sustainability of it. There was also a larger motivation: this relationship will protect the culture and resources of the community from being lost over time. The Museum was contacted for this purpose.

According to the earlier definition of a museum by ICOM, museums conserve, research, and communicate 'material evidence of people and their environment.' In a narrow sense, this implies physical artefacts that museums collect, hold or exhibit – but museology have also introduced new ways of thinking about these artefacts (Dale, 2003) to include also the stories that are directly related to the physical and material artefacts. This also allows collections to be curated in a participatory sense, having the stories of people to provide diverse and richer accounts of artefacts in the collection. Through these interactions the community and the museum come together to create a knowledge commons that promotes the open sharing of stories, on artefacts that are agreed by the community to be important and symbolic.

Since then the collection grew over time and across a broader geographic area, and the engagement within the community and between the community and the Museum evolved. These deepening interactions highlighted the need for a medium to communicate and exhibit the collection to the community as well as more broadly to members of the public. This led to the formulation of a digital approach to develop the WoFG collection. A detailed analysis of the tasks was conducted leading to the development of a specific approach to define the requirements of the collection. This approach took into account the broader contexts of the partnership between the community and the Museum along with the four layers of interaction (from individual to society).

Because the WoFG was a self-initiated 'grass-root' endeavour, the Gatherings were viewed by the Museum as a particularly valued partnership as they provided unique experiential knowledge, instantiated both in objects and stories. The involvement of the Museum as a cultural institution was intentionally kept as an equal partnership ensuring appropriate engagement with the WoFG community. It is important to note that this effort came from both sides – the institution and the community. Such guiding principles were largely based on participatory action research philosophies that saw the community as a knowledgeable partner, the researchers as collaborators, with a primary goal to contribute to the betterment of the community in its context (Nyden, 1997; McKay and Marshall, 2001).

Researchers and developers involved in the project were engaged in discussion groups and meetings between the Museum and the community. The generation of functional requirements for the information system was therefore largely inspired through observations and first-hand engagement with the partnership between the cultural institution and the community. Thereafter, these functional requirements were developed into technical specifications with developers after considering the various levels and layers of interactions. The information system was designed around the information objects (the stories of women, symbolic icons, banners, oral history recordings, videos, photographs, and other memorabilia relating to the lives of Victorian farm women) and interaction with these object for individuals, in the sharing of stories between individuals (community/group) and for the role of the Museum as a cultural institution charged with the protection of public knowledge within the knowledge commons. This design was also shaped by the broader society, highlighting the duality that exists in these interactions, as indicated by structuration theory.

It is possible that the aggregation of individual needs, when assessed separately, might lead to the same design arrived at when the community's needs are negotiated collectively. However, there would seem to be a better balance of power in the latter approach, effectively transposing the user from an object (the user as a 'victim' to 'rescued') to that of active participant in the design process (an actor). Such an interpretation can be drawn from UCD literature that concentrates on the adeptness of designers and developers, (including usability specialists and managers) to capture the needs of users effectively. Such approaches only provide effective interfaces and systems to 'rescue' end users. This was highlighted by a participant at the beginning of the study who feared IT researchers even if they brought gifts. This attitude might be construed as an unwillingness to be 'rescued' in this way. Lottkowitz (2005) wrote: "I don't mean to caste aspersions on IT researchers as such, but frequently there's a lack of sensitivity about the different needs in rural communities, and ways to get research 'out there' in a credible fashion." She also commented: "... I have a sense from the early discussions about this project that it needs to be women focused and driven, and IT is not always friendly for many women in the communities ..."

Yet it is notable that this same participant has championed an e-bulletin for the groups involved in the project. She recognises the irony of her commitment to that system alongside her scepticism about the involvement of IT researchers. This 'us and them' tension is a manifestation of the kind of problem in information systems design practice that our proposed community-based, adaptive approach to UCD seeks to address. Such comments reinforce a view that while there is a lack of fear about using technologies in rural communities; at a deeper level there is a fear and cynicism about the approaches adopted by technology developers and researchers.

4 Conclusion and Future Work

The proposed community-centred design approach was implemented using action research principles in a case study of a women's community and its partnership with a cultural institution. Although the actual development of the information system was completed within six months, the functional and technical specifications were generated through an emergent process using the approach proposed in this paper. Other case studies using the community centred design approach are being conducted that focus on different cultural institutions and different communities to explore other aspects of the framework presented in this paper. On completion of these studies, there is considerable interest to apply this approach to other institutional domains, such as political organisations.

5 Acknowledgements

We would like to also thank Ms Liza Dale-Hallett and members of the Women on Farms Heritage Group for their participation and inputs for this study. The research project has been supported by these Monash University research grants: "Cultivating memory in the Victorian women on farms gathering heritage collection: a digital approach"; "Community building: the power of public library networks"; and "Towards a knowledge commons: modeling a transformation of library services and information resources provision in the vocational education sector".

References

Bailey, R. and Tierney, B. (2002) Information commons redux: concept, evolution, and transcending the tragedy of the commons. *The Journal of Academic Librarianship*, 28 (5), 277-286.

Beagle, D. (1999) Conceptualising an information commons. *The Journal of Academic Librarianship*, 25 (2), 82-89.

Benkler, Y. (2003). The political economy of commons. UPGRADE*: European Journal for the Informatics Professional*, 4(3), pp 6-9.

Bollier, D. (2003). The Rediscovery of the Commons. *UPGRADE: European Journal for the Informatics Professional*, 4(3), pp 10-12.

Bollier, D. (2004). Why we must talk about the information commons. *Law Library Journal*, 96(2), pp 267-282.

Bonner, J. V. H. and Porter, J. M. (2002). Envisioning future needs: From pragmatics to pleasure. In Green, W. S. and Jordan, P. W. (Eds.), *Pleasure with Products: Beyond Usability* (pp 151-158). London: Taylor & Francis.

Burstein, F. and Linger, H. (2003) Supporting Post-Fordist Work Practices: A Knowledge Management Framework for Supporting Knowledge Work. *Information Technology & People Special Issue on Organizational Implications of Knowledge Management Systems*. 16(3). pp 289-305.

Burstein, F. and Linger, H. (2005). "Task-Based Knowledge Management." In Schwartz, D. (ed.) *Encyclopedia of Knowledge Management*. Idea Group Reference.

Card, S. K., Moran, T. P. and Newell, A. (1983) *The psychology of human-computer interaction,* Lawrence Erlbaum, New Jersey.

Carroll, J. M. (2000). *Making use: scenario-based design of human-computer interactions*. Cambridge: MIT Press.

Cockton, G. (2004) From quality in use to value in the world. In *Proceedings of the Conference on Human Factors in Computing Systems (CHI)* (pp 1287-1290). Austria: ACM.

Cowgill, A., Beam, J. and Wess, L. (2001) Implementing an information commons in a university library. *The Journal of Academic Librarianship*, 27 (6), 432-439.

Dale, L. 2003 Stories and storytelling: a cultural partnership between Museum Victoria and the Victorian Women on Farms Gathering In *Proceedings of the Setting the Agenda for Rural Women: Research Directions* (70-87). Wagga Wagga: Centre for Rural Social Research.

De Vaus, D. A. (2001) Research design in social research, Sage, London.

DePaula, R. 2003 A new era in human computer interaction: the challenges of technology as a social proxy In *Proceedings of the CLICH 2003 - Building Bridges among Individuals and Communities* (219-222). Rio de Janeiro, Brazil

Fraser, J. (2002) The culture of usability. *New Architect*, Vol. 7, pp. 26-30.

Giddens, A. (1986) *The constitution of society*, Berkeley, University of California Press.

Gulliksen, J., Göransson, B., Boivie, I., Blomkvist, S., Persson, J. and Cajander, A. (2003) Key principles for user-centred systems design. *Behaviour & Information Technology,* 22 (6), 397-409.

Hales, S., Rea, D. and Siegler, M. 2000 Creating a technology desk in an information commons In *Proceedings of the SIGUCCS Conference on User Services* Richmond, Virginia, USA: ACM.

Head, A. J. (1999) Web redemption and the promise of usability. *Online,* 23(6) 20-32.

Hellstrom, T. (2003) Governing the virtual academic commons. *Research Policy,* 32 391-401.

Jokela, T., Iivari, N., Matero, J. and Karukka, M. 2003 The standard of user-centred design and the standard definition of usability: analyzing ISO 13407 against ISO 9241-11 In *Proceedings of the Latin American conference on human-computer interaction* (53-60). Rio de Janeiro, Brazil: ACM Press.

Kaplan, B. and Maxwell, J. A. (1994). Qualitative research methods for evaluating computer information systems In *Evaluating health care information systems: methods and applications*(Eds, Anderson, J. G., Aydin, C. E. and Jay, S. J.) Sage Thousand Oaks, California, pp. 45-68.

Karat, J. and Karat C. M. (2003) The evolution of user-centered focus in the human-computer interaction field. *IBM Systems Journal*, 42 (4) 532-541.

Leadbeater, C. (2006) Libraries and the creative economy. *Symposium: Libraries of the 21ˢᵗ Century*, State Library of Victoria, 23 February 2006.

Linger (2002) *Conceptualising IMS* [diagram]. Unpublished – used with permission.

Lottkowitz, Anna (2005) *Email to Marian Quartly,* 23 May – used with permission.

Lukasik, S. J. (2000). Protecting the global information commons, *Telecommunications Policy*, 24(2000), pp 519-531.

MacWhinnie, L. A. (2003) The information commons: the academic library of the future. *Libraries and the Academy*, 3 (2), 241-257.

Merkel, C., B, Xiao, L., Farooq, U., Ganoe, C. H., Lee, R., Carroll, J. M. and Rosson, M. B. 2004 Participatory design in community computing contexts: tales from the field In *Proceedings of the Participatory design conference* Toronto, Canada: ACM Press.

Moritz, T. D. (2004) Conservation partnerships in the commons? Sharing data and information, experience and knowledge, as the essence of partnerships. *Museum International*, 56 (4), 24-31.

Nielsen, J. (1993) *Usability engineering*, Academic Press, Boston.

Norman, D. (1988) *The psychology of everyday things*. Basic Books Inc: New York.

Norman, D. A. (1986). Cognitive engineering In *User centred systems design* (Eds, Norman, D. A. and Draper, S. W.) Lawrence Erlbaum Associates Inc, Hillsdale, New Jersey.

Norman, D. A. and Draper, S. W. (Eds.) (1986) *User centred systems design,* Lawrence Erlbaum Associates Inc, Hillsdale, New Jersey.

Orlikowski, W. J. and Robey, D. (1991) Information technology and the structuring of organizations. *Information Systems Research*, 2 (2) 143-169.

Pang, N. and Schauder, D. (In press). User-centred design and the culture of knowledge creating communities: a theoretical assessment. In *Proceedings of the 8th Australian Conference on Knowledge Management and Intelligent Decision Support*, 5-6 Dec 2005, Melbourne.

Pang, N., Schauder, D., Quartly, M and Dale-Hallett, L. (2006). User-centred design, e-research, and adaptive capacity in cultural institutions: the case of the Women on Farms Gathering Collection. In *Proceedings of the Asia-Pacific Conference on Library and Information Education and Practice*, 3-6 April 2006, Singapore.

Preece, J. (2000) *Online communities: designing usability, supporting sociability,* John Wiley & Son Inc, New York.

Schauder, D., Johanson, G. and Stillman, L. (2005) Sustaining a community network: the information continuum, e-democracy and the case of VICNET, *Journal of Community Informatics* 1(2) 79-102.

Schneiderman, B. (1992) *Designing the user interface: strategies for effective human-computer interaction (2nd edition),* Addison-Wesley, Reading, Mass.

Schuler, D. and Namioka, A. (Eds.) (1993) *Participatory design: principles and practices,* Lawrence Erlbaum Associates, Hillsdale, New Jersey.

Spinuzzi, C. (2003) *Tracing genres through organizations: a sociocultural approach to information design.* Cambridge: MIT Press.

Taxen, G. 2004 Introducing participatory design in museums In *Proceedings of the 8th Biennal Participatory Design Conference* (204-213). Toronto, Canada.

Yin, R. K. (1994) *Case study research: design and methods,* Sage, Thousand Oaks, California.

ICT Solution and Network Capabilities Development: The Role of the Codification Process in the KMP Experience

Pierre-Jean Barlatier, Catherine Thomas

GREDEG Sophia Antipolis UMR 6227 UNSA-CNRS, France
barlatier@gredeg.cnrs.fr, thomas@gredeg.cnrs.fr

Abstract: The objective of this paper is to explore the contributions of a codification process to the analysis of knowledge creation mechanisms within a network of firms. The idea is to provide a theoretical framework on knowledge creation dynamics within a network through the notion of network capabilities, and to analyse the impact of a codification process on the development and the strengthening of these capabilities. The illustration of this work in progress is located in the scientific park of Sophia Antipolis (Alpes-Maritimes, France), focusing on the Telecom Valley® association which gathers the main actors of the sophipolitan Telecom cluster. Our empirical study is conducted as a part of a research contract, the Knowledge Management Platform (KMP) project. The aim of this contract is to build a semantic web service of competencies in order to enhance exchange and combination dynamics of knowledge within the Telecom cluster thanks to the codification of tacit knowledge. We have centred our analysis on the codification process conducted within the Telecom Valley® network during the conception of the KMP project. The KMP experience shows the main role of the codification process in the enhancement of the organizational knowledge creation mechanisms of the Telecom Valley® network.

1 Introduction

According to Kogut and Zander (1992), and Nahapiet and Ghoshal (1998), organizational knowledge creation is above all a process of social exchange and combination, and absorption of knowledge. It reveals therefore the need to rely more and more on the exchange and the combination of external resources with partnerships and alliances, and conduct firms to open themselves on the outside. Following Håkansson (1993) and Kogut (2000), an organizational form able to offer the benefit of both specialization and variety generation exists: the network. Hence, the network capacities to create, accumulate and transfer collective knowledge are named "network capabilities" (Foss 1999 and Kogut 2000). Based on the previous analysis of Nahapiet and Ghoshal (1998) on social capital, this paper provides theoretical refinements of the concept of network capabilities as well as the role of these capabilities on the knowledge creation dynamics within a network. Thus, we intend to cross network capabilities and codification approaches through the design of an ICT tool, and analyse the impact of a codification process on the enhancement of these network capabilities. In order to do so, we are carrying out a case study located in the scientific park of Sophia Antipolis (Alpes-Maritimes, France). A major association of this park, the Telecom Valley® (TV), aims to build a web service of competencies in order to enhance exchange and combination dynamics of knowledge within the Telecom cluster.

This paper is composed by three different parts:

We identify and analyse in a first part the impact of networks on organizational knowledge creation processes, by studying the different dimensions of network capabilities.

We present in a second part the empirical study of the KMP project within the TV network. We analyse therefore the specific knowledge codification process offered by KMP.

Finally, the third part illustrates the reciprocal influences and interactions between network capabilities, the codification process and knowledge creation dynamics within a Telecom cluster.

2 Knowledge-creation mechanisms within networks

After emphasizing the importance of the social relations in the knowledge creation process, we analyze the network capabilities concept thanks to Nahapiet and Ghoshal's (1998) works.

2.1 Organizational knowledge-creation processes

According to Kogut and Zander (1992), Nahapiet and Ghoshal (1998) and Shawney and Prandelli (2000), organizational knowledge creation is above all a social process. Their work shows that organizational knowledge-creation processes are in accordance with a sociological approach "an emerging, dynamic and diffuse process" where "new knowledge is the output of a synergistic interplay between individual contributions and social interaction" (Shawney and Prandelli 2000: 28). Thus, we can point out that this conception is close to the one advanced by Nahapiet and Ghoshal (1998) who maintain that organizational knowledge creation based on two key mechanisms: exchange and combination.

However, Nahapiet and Ghoshal (1998) have identified four required conditions in order to make exchange and combination as knowledge-creation mechanisms effective: (i) the opportunity to make exchange and / or combination may exist; (ii) the actors must be able to anticipate the value created by the exchange / combination processes; (iii) they must be motivated; and (iv) they must be able to combine knowledge and resources.

Combination and exchange are therefore complex social processes that reflect the interlocking of knowledge forms in an organization able to create and share knowledge, to coordinate, structure, and communicate. The thesis defended by Nahapiet and Ghoshal (1998) is that the social substratum (and the social capital concept in particular) makes the development and the creation of organizational knowledge easier by affecting the necessary conditions in order to enhance the combination and exchange processes. In this perspective, the setting up of a network of firms thanks to spatial and / or technological proximities creates exchange opportunities. A network's efficiency is measured notably with its capacity to transfer information quickly (role of information provider and distributor), but above all in its capacity to lay out various competencies and professions. Beyond information traffic it poses a problem of comprehension (receptivity, adaptability) that can not be solved by a purely technological approach and requires the establishment of a common language.

The network is thus an efficient means for firms for acquiring external resources like knowledge (Håkansson 1993), and these capacities to create, accumulate and transfer collective knowledge are named "network capabilities" (Foss 1999 and Kogut 2000). Hence the idea of combinatorial diversity proposed by Kogut (2000) and Håkansson (1993) lies on the hypothesis of actors' knowledge bases complementarities and network capabilities.

2.2 Network capabilities: what are they?

Network capabilities are seen as beneficial factors that lie outside the individual firm, referring to "...what collectivities of firms – networks – know about the production of goods and services, the organization of this production (network capabilities), and how they learn about it (collective learning)" (Foss 1999: 3); or emerging factors from interactions of individual firm's capabilities and collective learning phenomenon: "network capabilities... are not specific to a firm, but represent joint gains to coordination and learning" (Kogut 2000: 406). According to Foss (1999), network capabilities are accumulated over time and experience.

Thus, network capabilities create value thanks to synergy effects between complementary assets and competencies. The various definitions of this concept proposed in the literature are all referring to coordination and learning gains. Kogut's works (2000) emphasize two dimensions of network capabilities: the structure and the identity. This author highlights then the role of the identity on the generation of rules of coordination.

These works suggest the key role played by network capabilities on the knowledge creation process. However, their definition is still fuzzy and not operational. Since organizational knowledge creation is a fundamentally social process, we suggest thus to explore the social dimensions of networks to refine network capabilities' concept. In order to do so, we propose, as Nahapiet and Ghoshal (1998) have made with the social capital concept, to start with a reflection on the notion of embeddedness developed by Granovetter (1985). Indeed, Granovetter thinks that every social collective (such as a network) is embedded in relational and structural relationships. The relational embeddedness represents the quality of the dyadic relations of the network, the kind of personal relationships that actors have developed between them through the story of their interactions emphasizing then trust relations and cooperative norms. The structural embeddedness represents the general properties of the network as a whole, such as the network configuration and the nature of its ties. Nahapiet and Ghoshal (1998) have added a third dimension, the cognitive one, based on shared representations and meaning systems. Then we propose an enrichment of the concept of network capabilities considering the structural, relational and cognitive dimensions suggested by Nahapiet and Ghoshal (1998), as well as their interactions with the knowledge creation process (Fig.1). This model presents a double interest, first it improves our comprehension of network capabilities, and second, it outlines their role in the creation of organizational knowledge.

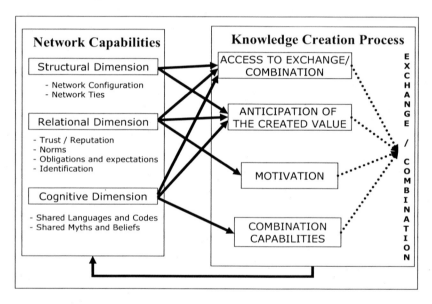

Fig. 1. The Theoretical Model.

We propose to use this model in order to design and implement an ICT solution of knowledge management within a network of firms. Indeed, if ICT enhance actors' connections, they can not substitute for the social substratum inherent to organizational knowledge creation processes. This analysis suggests thus that an ICT solution of knowledge creation should not only enhance information exchanges but has to foster network capabilities by integrating these three dimensions.

3 The KMP Project : the building of a KM solution shared by a community of firms and institutions

The illustration of this study is located in the scientific park of Sophia Antipolis (Alpes-Maritimes, France). Sophia Antipolis, is "one of the most highly publicized technology parks which combine establishments of multinational corporations, small and medium-sized firms, and large public research centers and universities, under the auspices of public regional authorities" (Castells and Hall 1994: 85). We present in a first part our empirical study: the KMP project. In a second part, we detail the uses-based methodology used in the conception process of the KMP solution.

3.1 The Empirical Material: The KMP Project

A non profit business-driven association, Telecom Valley® (TV, founded in 1991 by eight leading actors in telecommunications industry), has initiated in 2002 a project of inter-firm knowledge management, the "Knowledge Management Platform" (KMP). The objective of this project is to propose an innovative Solution including a map of competencies of TV's actors in order to enhance exchange and combination of knowledge within the Sophia Antipolis Telecom cluster. The goal here is to obtain a better identification of actors and projects while facilitating the cooperation and the creation of a shared language between its members. KMP is an experimentation of an ICT infrastructure, a semantic web service of competencies. An abstract representation of competencies based on five points (action, deliverable, business activity, beneficiary and key resources) has been proposed (Rouby and Thomas 2004). These categories constitute an abstract level of codification allowing the creation of codes. These codes ensure the detection of competencies and their comparison depending on actor's interests and vision. Hence these actors can consider appropriate combinations of their choice. These first points for representing competencies are still being used and absorbed by actors. They constitute the first codes shared by the network and the first bricks for building the shared language. This shared language is based on the elaboration of specifics ontologies for each category of codes. An ontology "is an object capturing the expressions of intensions and the theory accounting for the aspects of the reality selected for their relevance in the envisage applications scenarios" (Gandon 2001). Hence, its role is to define worlds constituting the area in which the knowledge will be represented by the actors involved.

An important outcome of the KMP codification process is to convey the nature of the diversity of existing competencies, in other words, their similarity and complementarity, according to Richardson's terminology (1972). Similarity in KMP is related to competencies sharing the same 'action' and 'resources' whereas complementarity is about competencies found within the same 'business activity' that could probably be combined if they belong to different organizations.

The KMP codification process includes various stages: models building, language creation and message writing. These stages are not sequential but iterative, implying the co-evolution of several forms of knowledge (tacit, articulated and codified). The "step by step" approach, developed by the uses-based methodology, allows a progressive implication of actors in order to sustain a process of adoption / adaptation in the prototype building and for generating trust in the codification process.

3.3 A Uses-directed methodology

This study has been conducted through the commitment of researchers in management in the KMP project. Our tasks were to find managerial models in order allow the conception and the implementation of the web service. As we have intervened on and during the research process, we are in the framework of an intervention research (Argyris 1970). Within the framework of our intervention research a high position is granted to the web service's conception which is fully integrated in the researchers-actors interactions process.

The aim of this research revealed an open issue without clearly specified outlines, which has justified the hallmark of the RNRT (French Telecom Research Network) since 2002 to 2005, as an exploratory project. Hence, a multidisciplinary approach was essential to the understanding of Knowledge Management practices. Consequently, the KMP project involved researchers from socio-economic sciences (GREDEG), cognitive sciences (INRIA), telecommunications (ENST) and practitioners and users (TV) for a total force of 187 men / month for a three years period. The conception of the solution is based on "uses scenarios" which occur at the same time upstream from the tool for its conception and downstream for its evaluation. Uses scenarios describe the inter-organizations recurrent interactions models which define in observable and behaviouristic terms the essence of actor's roles and their communication strategies about their competencies.

In addition, uses-based methodology implies a co-conception of the tool and a co-evolution of conception and uses. An iteration of conception/experimentation loops is then necessary, given that every loop is the occasion of enrichment to each step. The project is at the moment in its fourth loop, the first one took place in 2001-2002, during its conception.

4 Results and Discussion

The analysis reveals two distinctive categories of results, one considering the impact of the KMP solution on the different dimensions of network capabilities and another one revealing the enrichment of these mutual influences by highlighting the dynamic interactions between network capabilities' dimensions, codification processes and knowledge creation conditions.

4.1 Impact of the development of network capabilities dimensions on knowledge creation conditions

Given the recent (and still limited) implementation of the KMP prototype, we are able to identify four main kinds of ties that illustrate the relations between the impacts of the codification process on the several network capabilities' dimensions and their consequences on knowledge creation conditions.

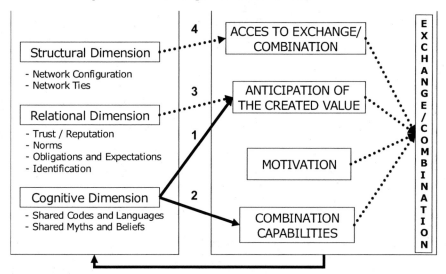

Fig. 2. KMP's impact on network capabilities and knowledge-creation conditions.

The ties 1 and 2 (Fig. 2) emphasize the influence of the cognitive dimension on the anticipation of the created value by cooperation and the combination capabilities. The main effect of KMP comes from the creation of shared languages and codes such as ontologies of competencies. Indeed, we have noticed, that the representation of the "sophipolitan territory" allowed by the use of complementarity / similarity notions, has made possible the identification of competencies poles (similar competencies) and value chains (complementary competencies). This identification was largely appropriated by network actors, leading therefore to two main results:

- Every club and association that aimed to enhance synergies within the whole sophipolitan cluster has been mapped. Indeed, some were classified as aiming to foster complementarities (more market oriented) and others as aiming to foster similarities (more oriented towards technological innovation). This was presented during the "Club's Day" event by members of KMP's steering committee and has solved many problems of roles and legitimacy of clubs and associations. Hence, the diffusion of KMP methodology beyond the telecom cluster shows the important needs in terms of representation and of development of combinative capabilities;

- Moreover, this mapping methodology based on the "similarity /
complementarity" concepts have also been adopted and reused by the PACA
region in order to present a national project about competitiveness poles, the
"SCS" pole (Secured Communicating Solutions). Hence, these concepts have
really structured the presentation of cooperation projects within the pole,
showing then their impact on network's combinative capabilities and
anticipation of created value. This ability to manage these concepts appears to
be a source of competitive advantage, as in this specific high velocity industry,
increasing technological knowledge requires the capability to reduce
mismatches between the production and demand sides (Antonelli et al. 2001).

Thus, we have observed KMP's various effects on the network's cognitive dimension, providing notably shared languages and codes such as ontologies and
common space representations that develop actor's abilities to anticipate created
value (tie 1 in Fig. 2). Hence, these specific communication codes represent, according to Kogut and Zander (1992), an asset source of value creation. In addition,
we can also quote another significant effect, regarding the software engineering
and consulting "pilot" firms involved in the KMP process of codification. Indeed,
during the process of construction of ontologies in which they have played an active role, these pilot firms have realized that they can gain more in being partners
than being fierce competitors. Most of them have today the project to develop
partnerships about joints solutions, aiming to reach more and bigger customers,
within and outside Sophia Antipolis. They even think about creating a new association, composed exclusively with software engineering and consulting firms.
Therefore, we have effectively here another concrete example of the impact of
KMP on the cognitive dimension, and its consequences on conditions of knowledge creation such as anticipation (the will to cooperate, tie 1 in Fig. 2) and combination capabilities (creation of a new association and mutual projects, tie 2 in
Fig. 2).

The third tie (Fig. 2) shows the main impact of KMP on the relational dimension. This comes from the process of codification of obligations and expectations
as well as norms of cooperation, taken from the identification of "best practices"
in matter of cooperation, revealed by executives of biggest firms (i.e. biggest customers) of the network. Indeed, during this codification process, we have seen that
largest companies were looking for partners and / or subcontractors that present
not only required technological competencies but also managerial and organizational competencies such as project-team management, total quality management,
etc.; another request was to include several "levels of accessibility" about information, in order to have the possibility to give more detailed information to privileged partners if one needs to. Expectations about these managerial skills allow
them to better anticipate the value created (tie 3 in Fig. 2). TV has always been
concerned about membership rules, and some have progressively emerged, before
KMP, through various prizes such as the CLIPSAT Trophy (rewarding the best
ranked sub-contractor of TV) or the "Innovation Prize" (rewarding the most original project in the Telecommunications domain or related services). The codification of these rules of cooperation has quickly appeared as a *sine qua non* condition

to the realisation of KMP. They are capital in the success of an inter-firm knowl-edge management solution which aims to develop partnership dynamics. TV has even modified its CLIPSAT Trophy, adding requirements about the accuracy, the authenticity and the pertinence of the companies' description and updating of or-ganizational competencies in the KMP base. Through KMP, TV has implemented strong membership rules, in trying to elaborate a professional code of ethics and subcontracting, which enhances trust relations and reputation effects that have a positive impact on anticipation of value through exchanges (tie 3 in Fig. 2). KMP has also developed the identification process within the network thanks to mana-gerial models displayed during the codification process. This shared representation allowed the sharing of "similarity" and "complementarity" concepts taken from Richardson's (1972) works on cooperation. In this case, "similarity" represents competencies sharing the same resources and the same actions; "complementar-ity" represents competencies aiming to a same supply system. The common repre-sentation and the introduction of these concepts enhanced actor's capabilities to anticipate the created value through partnerships, as they were able to select the best cooperation opportunities and perspectives (tie 3 in Fig. 2).

The fourth tie (Fig. 2) shows the main impact of KMP on the structural dimen-sion. Indeed, the use of KMP makes easier the identification of new contacts for network actors as well as external ones, and makes these potential partners also easily reachable. We quote, for instance, a user from a company [X], which has experienced the KMP solution and has voluntarily shared his experience with us in sending the following e-mail: "*I have a selective request: 'company [X]' is look-ing for on-board applications editors/integrators on symbian tel. or java environ-ment which are located in the 'Alpes-Maritimes' department. I have found in the KMP base 'company [Y]' in IT Services, Solutions and Applications Providers. Do you know about other companies?*" As a consequence, the KMP web service, in allowing the multiplication of inter-organizational links, develops exchange and combination opportunities within the network, and *de facto*, intensifies the dynam-ics of partnership (tie 4 in Fig. 2). We can however notice that these new ties are initially weak.

Globally, we can observe from these results that they confirm in a way Na-hapiet and Ghoshal's perspectives about the effects of the different dimensions on knowledge creation conditions. But as a second kind of results, our empirical ex-perience allows us the detection of multidimensional effects on organizational knowledge creation conditions.

4.2 The enrichment of multidimensional, dynamic interactions

We have seen that the implementation of the KMP web service of competencies has developed network capabilities dimensions and knowledge creation condi-tions. But beyond the "simple" dynamics we have shown, the KMP codification process and the construction of managerial models have generated complex, mul-tidimensional dynamics that have affected at a same time network capabilities, or-ganizational knowledge creation conditions and the coherence of the TV network.

Indeed, the Telecom value chain has provided a collective representation to every TV's actor that had as main consequence a collective realization of the network boundaries, mass effects and actor's games of interests. This awareness of TV's current situation by its own actors has rapidly triggered off a dynamic of change, because they have quickly detected the network's shortcomings for innovation and have found reasons of their collective inertia. This gave then indications about the current level of coherence of the Telecom cluster, which had an impact as well on demand and profile choice of newcomers and on trajectories of members' strategic diversification, i.e. their games of interests. For instance, we can notice the recent request of a small network of firms (Multimed) working in multimedia and content, located outside Sophia Antipolis but in the PACA region, which wants to join TV after having heard about the KMP experience. A few years ago, they wouldn't have applied for a TV membership, as they are geographically and technologically quite far from TV members, lacking information and anticipation abilities. Today, thanks to the Telecom value chain model, this potential newcomer is able to detect opportunities *via* the KMP showcase, and TV has now increased its possibilities of selecting the right newcomers, of widening the network's knowledge base, of determining their specialization trajectories, etc.

Hence, this representation provided by the codification process and the collective self-consciousness about network shortcomings has had a great impact on both cognitive and relational dimensions of the network, i.e. its identity. This collective comprehension of TV's identity has provoked an "organizational closure" of the network, because TV's actors were, at this point, able to define precisely the boundaries of the network, and consequently, its knowledge base. This closure is then paradoxically the source for appropriates perspectives of network's openness, and is today a key element of the network's coherence management.

Consequently, this led to a significant impact on both relational and cognitive dimension of network capabilities, creating thus a genuine collective "savoir-voir" (cognitive dimension) that influences mainly access and motivation conditions, as showed in Figure 3:

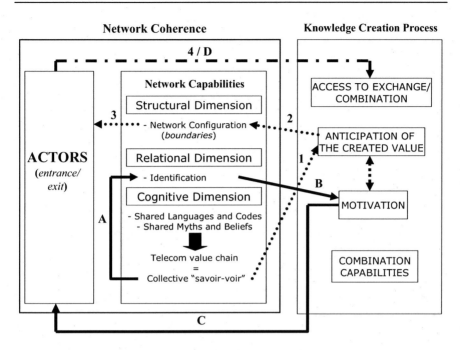

Fig. 3. Multidimensional interactions and knowledge creation conditions.

In this Figure, we can see that the collective "savoir-voir" resulting from the cognitive appropriation of the value chain model by the actors leads to an example of complex dynamics:

- Indeed, by mapping current exchanges, the value chain revealed profitable future opportunities that increased anticipation abilities (tie 1 in Fig. 3), leading to the necessity to open network frontiers and to alter then its configuration (tie 2 in Fig. 3) in order to let new external actors enter (tie 3 in Fig. 3);

- Simultaneously, the value chain model, by determining network boundaries, has developed identification abilities of network actors, that can henceforth benefit from a clear representation of themselves within the network (tie A in Fig. 3), enhancing consequently their own motivation to develop exchanges in order to influence, to master their position within the network (tie B in Fig. 3). This can lead also to the entrance of new actors or the exit of current ones (tie C in Fig. 3).

Then, we have seen two different dynamics engendered by the codification process that have impacted network capabilities dimensions, leading simultaneously (or not) to the necessity of altering its coherence (by the entrance of new actors or exist of current ones) in order to develop negotiated opportunities, i.e. access to exchange and combination (ties 4 / D in Fig. 3), primordial condition for knowledge creation (in particular in a long time perspective). Thus, this codification provides TV a major opportunity to manage its own dialectic heterogeneity /

specialization, i.e. its coherence. We can also highlight that codification processes have reduced cognitive dissonances within TV actors, i.e. enhanced their cognitive proximity, which *in fine* has allowed TV to develop its coherence, while widening its geographical proximity (to the PACA region) and its technological proximity (multimedia and content).

5 Conclusion

In this paper, we have proposed an enrichment of the concept of network capabilities as well as a reflection on their role on organizational knowledge creation, based on Nahapiet and Ghoshal's theoretical works (1998) about social capital. Then we have shown, through an empirical study based on the design and implementation of a web service of competencies, the role of the codification process on the strengthening of network capabilities.

This study has allowed the expanding and the generalization of theoretical propositions in Yin's sense (1989): indeed, this experimentation allowed the refining of simple relations between social dimensions and knowledge creation conditions theoretically identified by Nahapiet and Ghoshal (1998), with partly validating them empirically. Nevertheless, we have outlined the existence of complex, multidimensional dynamics, where the codification process has appeared as being predominant. Hence, we have noticed that the representation of a network's common space through codification processes engendered by the creation of an ICT solution have had a massive impact on both relational and cognitive network's dimensions. As a result, a collective "savoir-voir" has emerged and has definitely developed the network's identity, provoking then an "organizational closure" that has paradoxically given to the network the possibility to open itself from the outside without harming its coherence. This opening has consequently transformed the network's structure by the attraction / searching of new actors and the alteration of the nature of its ties.

References

Antonelli C., Gaffard J.L., Quéré M., 2001. "Interactive learning and technological knowledge: the localized character of innovation processes", "Nouvelle économie" Conference. Sceaux (France), May 17-18.

Argyris C., 1970. Intervention Theory and Method, A Behavioral Science View. Reading MA, Addison Wesley.

Barlatier P.-J., 2003. "Knowledge creation within a localized network of firms in the Telecom industry: the role of communities", XIXth EGOS Conference. Copenhagen (Denmark), Jul. 3-5.

Castells M., Hall P., 1994. Technopoles of the World, the making of 21st Century Industrial Complexes. Routledge London.

Foss N.J., 1999. Networks, Capabilities, and Competitive advantage. Scandinavian Journal of Management, Vol. 15. 1-15.

Gandon F., 2001. "Engineering an Ontology for a Multi-agents Corporate Memory System." INRIA Research Report, INRIA, France -, http://www.inria.fr/rrrt/rr-4396.html

Granovetter M., 1985. Economic Action and Social Structure: the Problem of Embeddedness, American Journal of Sociology, n°91: 481-510.

Håkansson H., 1993. Networks as a mechanism to develop resources, In Beije P., Groenewegen J., Nuys O. 1993, Networking in Dutch Industries, Garant, 207-223.

Kogut, B., 2000. The Network as Knowledge: Generative Rules and the Emergence of Structure. Strategic Management Journal, 21: 405-425.

Kogut, B., Zander, U. 1992. Knowledge of the firm, combinative capabilities, and the replication of technology. Organization Science, 383-97.

Nahapiet J., Ghoshal S., 1998. "Social Capital, Intellectual Capital, and the Organizational Advantage", Academy of Management Review, Vol. 23, 242-266.

Richardson G.B., 1972. The Organisation of Industry. The Economic Journal, September: 883-896.

Rouby E., Thomas C., 2004. La codification des compétences organisationnelles : l'épreuve des faits, Revue française de Gestion, mars/avril, n°149, 51-68.

Shawney M., Prandelli E., 2000. Communities of Creation: Managing Distributed Innovation In Turbulent Markets. California Management Review, Vol. 42, N°4: 24-54.

Yin R.K., 1989. Case Study Research: Design and Methods, London, Sage.

Ontology as an Information Base for a Family of Domain Oriented Portal Solutions

Michal Barla, Peter Bartalos, Peter Sivák, Kristián Szobi, Michal Tvarožek, Roman Filkorn

Institute of Informatics and Software Engineering, Faculty of Informatics and Information Technologies,
Slovak university of Technology in Bratislava, Slovakia.
{barla,bartalos,tvarozek,filkorn}@fiit.stuba.sk, szobi@chello.sk,
psivak@mail.t-com.sk

Abstract: Ontologies are becoming increasingly accepted as a form for information representation of distributed web-based information and its processing. In our paper we build a web-based application around an ontology, which serves both as a data base and metadata source used in processing of the data. We propose techniques and methods that exploit this metadata to provide an easy and flexible implementation of the CRUD pattern. We identify patterns in the ontological representation of domain entities and transform them into web-based forms for data management. Based on this flexible framework we can model variations to adapt the application for specific sub-domains.

1 Introduction

A significant amount of resources has already been invested into the development of web-based applications that use ontologies for data storage [6]. Among other advantages, ontologies support the execution of semantic queries on an ontological database, explicit and inherent access to metadata and reasoning based on the formal representation of both the data and metadata.

By definition, an ontology is an explicit formal specification of a shared conceptualization (of a domain) [4]. Ontological languages provide means for the basic modeling of concepts such as classes, relations and various properties. Based on the corresponding language constructs, domain specific concepts can be defined and their semantics specified. Consequently, the model of a domain consists of both concepts defined by ontological languages, which are reused in other domain models and domain-specific concepts unique to a particular domain or set of domains.

If we create a model of a specific domain represented by an ontology, this model will necessarily have to be changed at some time in the future to compensate for changing requirements. Ontologies are especially suited for such change and provide flexible means of data storage.

However, the flexible data storage provided by ontologies would be of limited use unless applications are flexible enough to accommodate a similar degree of change. Otherwise, for any change in the ontology, the corresponding application code would have to be manually updated, which is unpractical for real-world applications.

Thus the apparent flexibility of ontologies results in the need for flexible applications. If we consider forms as the main mean of communication between portal and its users we come to the need for flexible form generation tools. These would be based not only on data stored in ontologies but also on additional (meta)data, which would be needed because domain ontologies shall not contain the information about the desired visual data representation, preserving their generality and delegating application-specific information to other sources.

2 Proposed approach

In our approach, we take advantage of the native availability of metadata in ontologies, which make the data self-descriptive and allows for effective searching in the stored data. Based on the assumption that an ontology may represent a formal model of an information domain, we propose the use of such metadata to build a domain oriented web portal solution for a particular domain.

In order to process ontologically structured data by the state of the art GUI frameworks, we implement mapping tools that transform data between its graph representation and an object-oriented representation. Consequently, we define the mapping of modeling concepts between these two modeling paradigms.

To design a flexible framework, we identify patterns as repeating structures (sets of concepts and their relations) in ontological representations and define consecutive data and processing around these patterns. We assume that similar patterns are shared between ontologies with the patterns themselves being defined using different types of ontological concepts - classes, relations between them, properties, instances and restrictions.

We map identified patterns onto sets of visual elements (graphical user iterface widgets) that correspond to the data stored in a specific ontology. Based on this approach we implement the CRUD pattern (Create-Retrieve-Update-Delete) for a particular entity in a domain ontology.

Since the metadata available in ontologies are not always sufficient to fully create a satisfactory user interface, we define additional metadata, which describe the arrangement of visual components on web-based forms.

Finally, we automatically generate the forms corresponding to ontological concepts, where first the respective ontological patterns are identified. Next, the proper graphical representation is determined and lastly the form descriptions are saved and used during operation.

3 Object--ontology mapping

The creation of an object-oriented representation of ontological concepts introduces new challenges due to the fundamental differences of both representations. These come from the differences between description logic and object-oriented systems and lie primarily in the completeness and satisfiability. Ontologies have a significantly higher expressivity compared to object-oriented approaches [3].

We automatically generate a set of Java bean classes, each corresponding to an integral part of an entity described by the ontology. We represent literals by a simple data type field of the appropriate type and each object property by a separate Java bean.

In order to process these Java beans and store the values in an ontological repository, we need to generate additional metadata for the mapping between objects and classes and properties (RDF graphs) of the ontology. These metadata allow us to bind the ontological class to Java bean fields and include the name of the Java bean, the names of its fields, information about the corresponding OWL properties (e.g. multiplicity, data type) and the type of the object in the RDF triple (object type or a data type - literal).

The mapping itself is performed by a pair of graph-to-bean and bean-to-graph transformers (analogical to O/R mapping in relational databases [2]). These transformers work the graph representation of RDF and use reflection to invoke *get* and *set* methods on the generated Java bean objects.

The transformation process is performed recursively, in each step performs mapping between one object and an integral part of the RDF graph, i.e. object property. Finally, a simple Java bean field is mapped to an RDF triple and vice versa, with the name of the field being used to determine the corresponding ontological property. Thus a simple data type field corresponds to a literal in the ontology and an object property corresponds to an instance of the respective Java bean class.

4 Pattern types

We identified two distinct types of patterns that can be applied at different levels of abstraction and are thus useful for a broad set of ontologies:

- *Widget patterns*, which are based on basic ontological language concepts and correspond to relatively simple configurations in ontologies.

- *Visual patterns*, which define the higher-level visual style of forms, the layout of individual widgets and other form controls (close to user interface design).

To achieve independence from the used ontology we base our metadata processing on basic ontological language concepts. Moreover, we specify a model for the representation of variability in information sub-domains, e.g. specializing the structure and behavior of an instance of the CRUD pattern of a domain entity for some specified subset of users.

4.1 Widget patterns

Widget patterns focus on the structure of classes, subclasses, properties and possible restrictions. They determine the widgets used in a form to edit instances of classes.

4.2 Simple widget patterns

Primitive datatype properties

Patterns for *primitive datatype* properties include all properties, whose ranges are literals (string, integer, float, date, boolean etc.). The graphical representation of these patterns is straightforward - the *rdfs:label* of each property is displayed next to the input field for its value. This would generally be a dropdown list for Boolean values (true, false, undefined), a calendar for date values and a *textbox* for text strings. It is more convenient to use *textarea* input field for longer strings as it increases the readability of the form. To distinguish cases where a normal *textbox* and where a *textarea* should be used, we can either define additional metadata about desired form template or we can compare the average length of existing instances to a predefined threshold.

If the respective property has multiple cardinality, the above elements would be placed inside a special control called *repeater*, which enables users to add/remove more values by means of additional buttons for these actions.

Same-range object properties

Patterns for *same-range object properties* identify classes that have several object properties with multiple cardinality and the same range (class or a union of classes). In this case, the fields for the range are displayed only once and an additional component is used to distinguish the specific property that is being edited. Such a component can be either a dropdown list or a set of radio buttons. All these components are wrapped in a repeater to allow multiple values to be added.

For example, the *Prerequisite* class form the Job Offer domain ontology of the NAZOU [5] project. Each prerequisite has two multiple properties: the *Requires* and *Prefers* which have as their range a union of experience and qualification classifications. Thus, the visual representation provides a radio button to select between the *requires* and *prefers* properties while the rest of the widget is common for both properties and is used to assign experience and qualification prerequisites for job candidates.

Enumerations

Patterns for *enumerations* identify object properties, whose range is a class fully defined by its instances. It should not be possible to add new or edit existing instances. Enumerated classes are defined in the ontology itself, e.g. a class representing the days of the week or various time periods (hour, day, month etc.).

Several graphical representations of this pattern exist. If the cardinality of an object property whose range is an enumerated class is single then it can be represented by a dropdown list of its instances. If the cardinality is multiple, the mentioned dropdown list can be wrapped in a repeater or instances can be represented by a multi-choice *listbox*.

Besides enumerated classes, also classes which allow users to create new instances or choose an existing one can be identified. This information must be stored in the metadata for the appropriate class. In this case all fields necessary to create an instance would be displayed and a *dropdown list* or *listbox* with existing instances would be added as mentioned above.

4.3 Tree hierarchies

Since hierarchies offer a wide range of values, they must be structured in a way that allows users to easily understand and choose amongst them. For example, when users want to choose a country where a company is based, it might be convenient for them to first choose a continent, then a country on that continent, etc.

In ontology, there are two basic ways to represent tree hierarchies. The standard property *rdfs:subclassOf* between classes which represents an *is a* relation and/or custom defined properties between instances can be used, which define relationships between nodes in the tree hierarchy.

One can assume that if a class in an ontology has a property which is transitive and points to instances of the same class (its range and domain are the same), then it is used to represent some form of hierarchy. The job offer ontology of the NAZOU project [5] defined two properties in this way: the *isPartOf* property and the *consistsOf* property, which were mutually inverse and allowed for navigation in a hierarchy of regions.

Additional characteristic of a class is the number of levels of its subclasses and also whether or not a class is fully defined by its subclasses. A class is fully defined by its (direct) subclasses if every individual belonging to that class must belong to at least one of its (direct) subclasses.

If a class is fully defined by its subclasses and only has direct subclasses, we represent it by a dropdown list component that contains labels of these subclasses. Figure 1 and 2 shows the example of the *jo:Benefit* class. Its graphical representation is a simple dropdown list and since *jo:Benefit* is a multiple object property of another class (*jo:JobOffer*), it is wrapped in a repeater (bottom).

In this way, users choose the type of instance they want to create. If the class is not fully defined, the dropdown list will also contain the label of the parent class to enable users to create an instance of it instead of its subclasses.

If there is more than one level of subclasses, their presentation should enable users to browse them. If there are only a small number of classes, it is suitable to display them in a dropdown list as in the previous case and indicate the hierarchy by adding a symbol before the actual name of each class (for instance one dot for each level of hierarchy). This approach might not be suitable to display complex and deep hierarchies, where it is better to create a component which simulates the navigation in a tree. E.g. a *listbox*, which contains all classes of the same level and is redrawn with the classes of the next level when the user chooses one value.

The current location in the tree would be indicated next to the component and users would have the ability to return to a higher level in the hierarchy (e.g. a button, hyperlinks in the path).

The same approach can be applied to a hierarchy created by transitive properties between instances. Whether the user can choose a class or instance which is not a leaf of a tree hierarchy is determined from additional metadata about the class. Metadata are also used when both classes and instances are used to define a hierarchy.

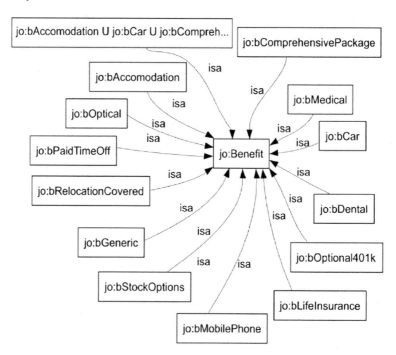

Fig. 1. Example of class *jo:Benefit* that is fully defined by its direct subclasses.

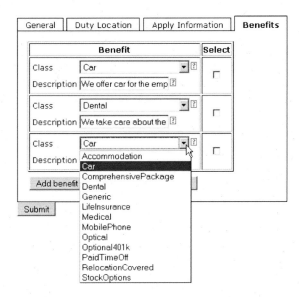

Fig. 2. Visual representation of benefits.

4.4 Visual patterns

Visual patterns describe the concepts of sub forms and identify the typical structure, when a class has an object property pointing to another class (which can also have object properties). So, if class A has an object property pointing to class B, there are several possibilities how to represent it in a form for class A:

- Dedicating an area of the form for the properties of class B, usually bounded by a rectangle. This representation is suitable when class B has only few datatype properties.
- Dedicating a special part of the screen to display any object property of class A and creating a button for each object property of class B. Users choose the property, they want to edit by clicking the appropriate button. If a user clicks on a button of a property in class B, the content of the dedicated part would be redrawn and would contain the form for the editing of the instance of class B.
- Creating a button for each object property of class A. If a user clicks a button for class B, a pop-up window would be shown, where the object property could be edited. This solution is not desirable since pop-ups are usually annoying and are often filtered by web browsers.
- Using a tabbed interface, where each tab would represent one object property of class A. Selecting a tab for class B makes it editable. If class B also contained other object properties, a second row of tabs would be available.

5 Form Generation: Mapping patterns to form controls

The basic principle of dynamic form generation lies in the use of data stored in the ontology along with the appropriate metadata to identify ontological patterns. Patterns are used to define a binding between the data in an ontology and their graphical representation to create forms for specific classes and form controls for specific properties.

Since one pattern can have more than one graphical representation, additional metadata must be used to choose the most appropriate one.

Form generation is a recursive process which begins from the given identifier of a class from an ontology for which the form should be generated and continues via its object-type properties. During form generation, the visual description and the data model of the form must be generated. Furthermore, the corresponding implementation related objects such as Java classes (e.g., Java beans), which store form data must also be generated as well as mapping rules between these classes and the respective ontology. These mapping rules are used by the previously mentioned graph-to-bean and bean-to-graph transformers.

The proposed method matches the structure of each class to patterns described in the previous section. This determines whether the process of form generation is recursively applied to object properties of the class or is terminated by defining a set of simple widgets for display. The matching itself is done by examining the conformance of a selected class to a sequence of patterns in predefined order.

5.1 Form layout

The previously described *widget patterns* map the structure of an ontology to the form controls but do not describe the layout of the form. Although we already discussed the visual representation of object properties between classes (*Visual patterns*), none of the proposed solutions (e.g., tabbed interface) provide information about ordering of the visualization. Moreover, these representations do not allow the personalization of forms preventing us from creating various specialized form templates which fit the needs of individual users. These include hiding of unnecessary form elements or pre-filling forms with default data.

Another problem is that ontologies normally do not contain application-specific information, e.g. whether users are only allowed to choose from existing instances or have to create new ones. Finally, ontologies may contain concepts that should not be displayed on specific forms at all.

Since the lack of flexible form layout support would degrade the proposed solution we defined an additional ontology (fig. 3) which contains information about the order of form tabs and their titles as well as the order of the class properties displayed in these tabs. Additional metadata define whether users are allowed to create new instances of certain classes or are only allowed to choose from existing ones, or the combination of both. The ontology can also describe predefined values for specific fields thus allowing for the creation of forms which are more user-friendly compared to forms generated by generic ontology editors such as Protégé (http://protege.stanford.edu).

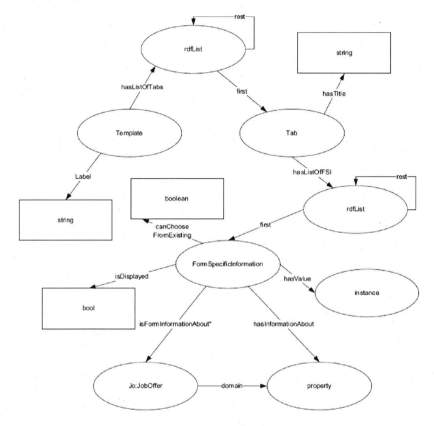

Fig. 3. Meta-model of a form layout information.

The model in fig. 3 shows that our solution supports the reuse of its parts since one Tab instance can be used in multiple lists and one *FormSpecificInformation* instance can be used in multiple tabs. This allows for quick customization of a form template, where some parts of a form can be reused and new layout can be defined for the rest of the form.

The fact that the model is directly connected to a domain ontology (class jo:JobOffer in our case) allows for easy personalization of a form template to meet the needs of organizations and individuals. If a system determines that a user always fills in the same value in a field (e.g., duty location or qualification prerequisites) it can create a template for this user which does have these fields pre-filled with the appropriate values (instances in the ontology). On the other hand, if the user is constantly ignoring some field of the template (e.g., level of management or salary bonus) the system can hide these fields from the template while still allowing their use if user explicitly requests the complete form.

The identification of the template that is used for a specific user is stored in a user model which is used for adaptation throughout the whole system if we consider the CRUD pattern as a part of a larger system.

6 Conclusions

We briefly described one of the current trends – the drive towards web applications built around the semantic web principles and technologies. We also explored the problems introduced by the dependency of portal systems on ontologies as means for information storage.

We proposed dynamic form generation as a possible approach which would accommodate changes in ontologies by increasing the flexibility of web portals. We identified and described several patterns in ontologies and their mapping to form controls. With this knowledge we designed an algorithm that dynamically generates form descriptions from ontologies, which can be used by portal solutions to display and process forms for instances from these ontologies. We find this approach suitable for easy creation of flexible forms for portal solutions with similar tasks. Typical usage is in the domain of offers (job offers, realty offers, vacation offers etc.) and in solutions where CRUD pattern is to be realized by system's users.

To verify the feasibility of proposed solution, we created a job offer portal that uses the job offer domain ontology developed as a part of the NAZOU project [5]. The portal enables users to input and publish job offers by filling in various aspects of the respective job offers in appropriately generated web-based forms.

Future work might include the identification of more complex patterns in ontologies and their mapping to form controls. Exploring the possibilities offered by adaptive hypermedia technologies and their relevance to dynamic form generation is another promising direction of research.

Acknowledgement

This work was partially supported by the State programme of research and development "Establishing of Information Society" under the contract No. 1025/04 and by the Scientific Grant Agency of Slovak Republic, grant No. VG1/3102/06.

References

1. Aldred L, Dumas M, Heravizadeh M, Hofstede A (2002) Ontology Markup for Web Forms Generation. In: Workshop on Real World RDF and Semantic Web Applications

2. Ambler S W (2006) Mapping Objects to Relational Databases: O/R Mapping In Detail. http://www.agiledata.org/essays/mappingObjects.html

3. Battle S, Jiménez D, Kalyanpur A, Padget J (2004) Automatic Mapping of OWL Ontologies into Java. In: Frank Maurer and GÄunther Ruhe (eds) Proc. of the Sixteenth International Conference on Software Engineering & Knowledge Engineering (SEKE'2004)

4. Benjamins V R, Fensel D, Studer R (1998) Knowledge engineering : Principles and methods. Data and Knowledge Engineering, 25(1-2): 161-197

5. Bieliková M, Návrat P, Rozinajová V (2005) Methods and Tools for Acquiring and Presenting Information and Knowledge in the Web. In: Proc. of International Conference on Computer Systems and Technologies CompSysTech'2005. Varna, Bulgaria

6. Dong J S (2004) Software modeling techniques and the semantic Web In: Proc. of 26th International Conference on Software Engineering (ICSE'04), pp. 724-725, IEEE

7. Obrst L (2003) Ontologies for semantically interoperable systems. In: Proceedings of the twelfth international conference on Information and knowledge management (CIKM '03). CM Press 366{369, New Orleans, LA, USA

Business Rules in Clinical Trials

Olegas Vasilecas, Evaldas Lebedys

Vilnius Gediminas Technical University, Vilnius, Lithuania,
olegas@isl.vtu.lt, evaldas@isl.vtu.lt

Abstract: The paper focuses on the scope of the clinical trials. As clinical trials are rigorously controlled, it is important to have a well-designed control mechanism for clinical trials quality assurance. Each clinical trial is executed according to a set of rules. All the rules for a particular clinical trial are described in different source documents and are not stated explicitly. While rules for particular trial are not organized as a whole, it complicates the control of the trial. The need for accurate recording and processing of patient data is fundamental to any clinical trial. If data stored in the clinical trial database are incorrect, conclusions of the analyses will also inevitably be incorrect. The need of a central storage for rules in particular trial is obvious. The clinical trial business rules repository may be used to reuse the knowledge gathered in one clinical for further trials. The paper presents a method for business rules retrieval from UML models and the employment of proposed in conduct of clinical trials. The analysis of business rules approach principles application in clinical trials is presented.

1 Introduction

Clinical trials are people based studies aimed on new drugs or treatment procedures testing. Clinical trials are conducted to find out whether the new drug or treatment is safe and effective. Clinical trials are performed in all areas of medicine. All clinical trial procedures are documented in detail, because conduct of clinical trial is supervised by local and international authorities. All steps of a particular clinical trial are executed in accordance to specific explicitly expressed rules. Management of these rules is essential in each trial, because it influences the quality of the trial. The appliance of business rules approach in clinical trials is already the subject of researches [4], but the job already done is focused on the clinical trial protocol design improvement. Business rules in clinical trial applications cannot be used to do any changes in the data automatically [7]. Business rules affecting a particular trail are from these types of rule sources:

- clinical trial related documents – clinical trial protocol, clinical trial data validation procedure description, special sponsors requirements, etc.;
- documents representing generic requirements for clinical trials – standard operating procedures for clinical trial design and management, Declaration of Helsinki, the Guideline for Good Clinical Practice, local laws, code of ethics, etc.

Business rules specified in generic requirements for clinical trials are general
and stand for many clinical trials. Business rules stated in clinical trial related rule
sources differ in different clinical trials because trials are performed with different
purposes, are executed in different countries. However, some rules stated in clinical trial related documents may be used as generic rules with slight variation. For
example, the rules for validation of adult patient vitals examination data are similar in various clinical trials. A global view on rules in clinical trials gives an impression that a major part of rules for each trial is general and these rules with
nonessential changes may be applied in other clinical trials.

The paper is organised as follows. Section 1 introduces the paper. Section 2
gives a brief overview on clinical trials. Section 3 proposes the way to improve
clinical trial design. Section 4 discusses modelling of clinical trials using UML.
Section 5 shows the way to retrieve business rules from UML models and presents
the prototype of application for business rules management. Section 6 concludes
the paper.

2 Clinical trials

When the purpose of the trial is defined, the document used to justify the design
and describe the trial procedures in detail is prepared. This document is called a
clinical trial protocol. A protocol is the document containing the information relating to the purpose, eligibility criteria, design and conduct of the trial [1], [8]. A
protocol also specifies what activities are to be performed in a trial, what measurements are to be evaluated, how the study will be coordinated, etc. [1]. Generally, protocols define all aspects of the proceeding of a particular clinical trial.
Thus, it is a crucial document, and if incomplete, disorganised or incorrect, can
prejudice the whole study [3].

The analysis of data gathered during the clinical trial is as important as protocol
design, because the obtained results are fundamental to subsequent activities. The
main purpose of having well designed forms is to make patient evaluations suitable for statistical analysis, but before performing the analysis all data has to be
collected, processed and checked [1].

It is obvious that the means for data collection and analysis in clinical trials
have to be precise, qualitative, verified and validated. These requirements also
stand for the applications used in clinical trials for data interchange, data entry,
data clarification, data records tracking, etc. The lack of the system for gathering
and managing all the requirements for particular trial complicates the control of
quality. Requirements for particular clinical trial may be expressed as business

rules. The use of business rules approach principles may facilitate the control of the quality. This is especially applicable to clinical trial applications, as these applications are rules centred. Trial related knowledge and know-how knowledge stored in business rules repository gives a broad view on a whole of all requirements. The question how to gather all the rules in to one repository arises here. We propose to use the model of a clinical trial to gather all the rules in to rules repository. The modelling of a clinical trial may slightly prolong clinical trial design and may require additional resources, but it is definitely advantaged. First of all a graphical model of a clinical trials gives a broad view on the organisation and the procedures of a clinical trial. Besides, clinical trial model is suitable to capture trial related rules. The following sections discuss the use of clinical trial models in detail.

3 Improvement of clinical trial design

Mostly the model of the clinical trial is not created during the design of the clinical trial. As a result of the clinical trial design a clinical trial protocol is produced. The clinical trial protocol presents all the information needed for the conduct of the clinical trial, but the information is represented in natural language. Additional charts and diagrams may be included in clinical trial protocols, but these do not present the conduct of trial as a whole and in detail. The use of natural language for clinical trial description has both negative and positive aspects:

- the positive aspect of the use of natural language is clarity of the protocol for everyone interested in the clinical trial. In other words the protocol is understandable, easy readable and does not require any special knowledge;
- the negative aspect of the use of natural language is ambiguity of natural language. Natural language is informal and can be interpreted. As clinical trial protocol is the primary document for the conduct of clinical trial it is desirable to have unambiguous specification of all trial procedures.

The use of some formal or semi formal modelling language for clinical trial modelling may allow reduce the ambiguity of the protocol. But as there are special requirements for the clinical trial protocol and it has to be approved before the start of the trial, it is impossible to present a model of the trial instead of clinical trial protocol to the responsible authorities. Thus a model of a clinical trial cannot replace protocol. A model of a trial may be prepared in parallel with the construction of protocol instead of replacing the clinical trial protocol with the model of the trial. It would be even better to start the design of the trial from the model, but it may be impossible, because the design of the model may prolong the design of the study. Therefore the trial should be modelled using any formal or semi formal language to represent the procedures of the trial in a graphic way in parallel with the design of the protocol or just after the clinical trial protocol is created.

4 The model of a clinical trial

There are many modelling languages suitable to represent different aspects of systems – UML, IDEF, conceptual graphs, etc [11]. As UML became the most popular modelling language for any kind of systems in recent years, we analyse the use UML for clinical trial modelling in this paper. The Unified Modelling Language is a visual language for specifying, constructing and documenting the artefacts of systems. It is a general-purpose modelling language that can be used with all major object and component methods, and that can be applied to all application domains (e.g., health, finance, telecom, aerospace) [5]. UML diagrams can be classified into three different classes [6]:

- diagrams describing the roles and obligations of system users generally (Use Case diagrams). In the clinical trial models these diagrams should represent the roles and obligations of the clinical trial team members and participants. For example, the right to revoke the patients informed consent or the obligation of investigator to record medical history in the Case Report Form can be represented in the UML Use Case diagrams;
- diagrams describing structural system aspects (class and object diagrams). In the clinical trial model class diagrams should be used to represent the organisation of a trial in detail. For example, each examination, visit, laboratory assessment, etc., should be represented as classes with attributes and operations. Class model may be used to create the structure of the database for the clinical trial data;
- diagrams describing the internal and external behaviour of system (state transition diagrams, sequence and collaboration diagrams). In the clinical trial models these diagrams should be used to represent the sequence of actions in each step of a clinical trial. For example, the proceeding of screening visit can be described in sequence or collaboration diagrams and the states of the patient diary can be represented in state transition diagrams.

UML models are not fully formal [10]. Some information represented in UML diagrams can be interpreted, but generally UML models are suitable for automation of systems development. Business rules representing requirements for clinical trial can be retrieved from UML models and placed in the business rules repository. We highlight the following main advantages of UML usage for clinical trial research:

- UML model would give a broad graphical view on the whole trial. This would improve quality control and documentation of clinical trial procedures;
- Duties and responsibilities of clinical trail team members represented in UML Use Case models would simplify preparation of operational manuals for investigators and other team members;
- The organisation of clinical trial structural components represented in UML Class diagrams, can be for clinical trial database design;

- Representation of all requirements for valid clinical trial data in one model would give a broad view on all rules for data validation.

The results of our previous research showed that UML models could be used to retrieve business rules from UML models. The types of business rules that can be retrieved from UML models we discussed in detail in [9] and they are not analysed in this paper in detail. Further we shortly present the results of he experiment performed to check the reliability of proposed.

5 Retrieval of clinical trial rules

In this section a few sample diagrams are presented to show how different aspects of clinical trials can be represented using UML. We were using Sybase® PowerDesigner® 9.0 for modelling of a clinical trial.

A Use Case model representing the roles and obligations of Investigator and patient at Visit1 is shown in Figure 1. The sample Use Case model is presented only in the scope of Visit 1.

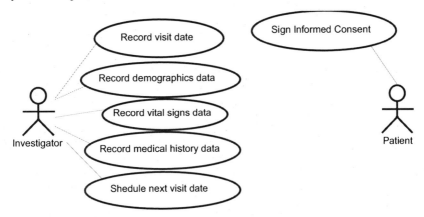

Fig. 1. Use case model representing the roles of Investigator and patient on Visit 1

Figure 2 shows the sequence of actions for Visit 1. Sequence diagram contains rules such as "Data can be collected only after the Informed consent is signed by the patient".

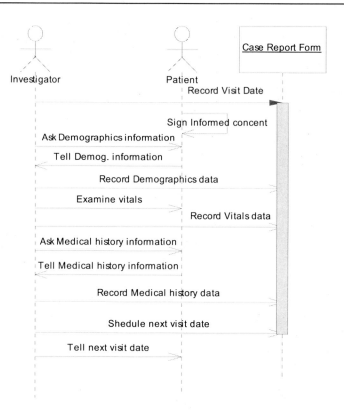

Fig. 2. Sequence diagram representing the sequence of actions to be performed on Visit 1

Figure 3 presents class diagram representing the organisation of objects involved in Visit 1 and their relationships. Class diagram contains rules describing the relationships between classes, class properties constraints. In Figure 3, for example, the rule "At least one medical history record has to be recorded for each patient" is represented as relationship between classes "Medical history" and "Visit 1".

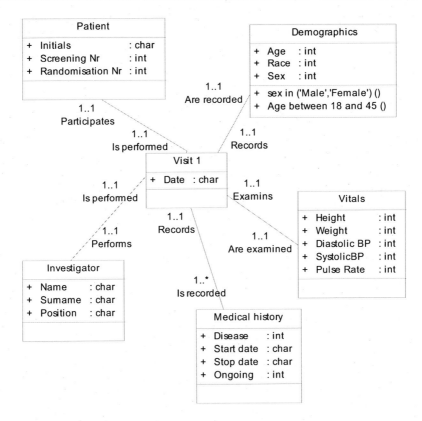

Fig. 3. Class diagram representing the organisation of Visit 1

The prototype application was developed to retrieve business rules from UML models and place in the business rules repository. At this stage of research the prototype application operates only with Use Case diagrams. Retrieval of business rules from other UML diagrams is being implemented.

Created model is stored in XML file. Data are copied from XML file to temporal storage for model analysis. The search for business rules represented in the use case model can be performed directly in XML file, but in order to accelerate the process of business rules search, the data is copied to temporal storage and indexed. Figure 4 presents a general architectural view of the software prototype.

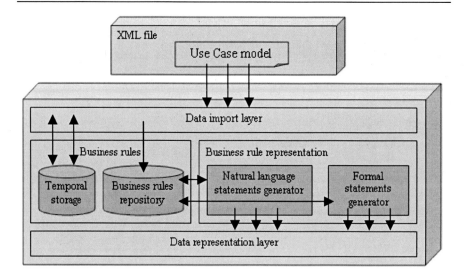

Fig. 4. The architectural view of the experimental tool

The following components of business rules are looked for and copied to temporal storage: actors, use cases, relationships between actors and use cases, stereotypes of relationships. Figure 5 presents a part of the business rules repository structure for storage of rules represented in UML use case diagrams. Table "Actors" is used to store the information of actors represented in use case model. The purpose of table "Use Cases" is to store the information of use cases represented in the use case model of the business system of interest. The information of business systems actor's roles and obligations is stored in the table "Obligations". Table "Predicates" contains the information of predicates, which are formed, on the basis of actor's roles and obligations data. The relationships between business rules components are stored in table "Use_Case_Rule". The information stored in this table is used to express business rules formally and informally. Formal business rules expressions are stored in the table "Formal_UseCase_Rule". Business rules expressed in natural language are stored in table "UseCase_Rule_Text".

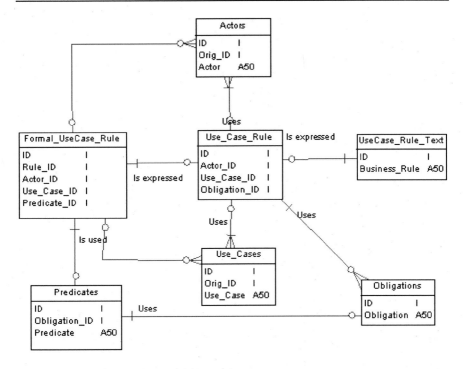

Fig. 5. A part of the business rules repository

Stereotypes of relationships are used to specify the roles of actors. Business rules components are connected and business rules are composed in the following step. The roles of business actors are used to form business rules expressions. Business rules stored in the repository can be expressed in natural language. Figure 6 presents a list of business rules retrieved from Use Case model.

It is natural that the clinical trial protocol does not contain all the requirements for clinical trial conduct, because too much detail clinical trial protocol may exceed the normal ranges of the protocol pages amount. More requirements for particular trial are general and may not be recorded in any document, but these requirements are still active. These requirements come from know-how knowledge. For example, the requirement that each visit date recorded in the CRF has to be correct is obvious, but therefore it has to be checked to avoid human mistakes. Additional trial related requirements described in other documents for management of clinical trial have to be entered into repository manually.

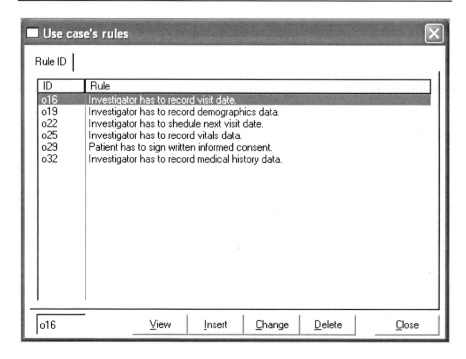

Fig. 6. A list of rules retrieved from Use case model

6 Conclusions

Analysis showed that clinical trials are very important and have to be conducted assuring the quality and precision, because investigations are performed on humans. As there are many requirements for conduct of clinical trials, it is difficult to maintain the quality of the trial. We proposed to use UML for clinical trial modelling in the paper. The benefits of UML model of clinical trial were explored and presented. Analysis and the results of the experiment showed that the design and conduct of a clinical trial could be improved using UML for trial modelling. The future work will concentrate on the implementation of retrieval of business rules from all UML diagrams and development of user interface for additional rules management.

References

1. Ablett S. An introduction to clinical trials. United Kingdom Children's Cancer Center study Group, 2004. URL: http://www.ukccsg UKCCSG Data Centre, [retrieved on 2006.04.05].

2. American Cancer Society. Clinical Trials: What You Need to Know, 2004. URL: http://www.cancer.org/docroot/ETO/content/ETO_6_3_Clinical_Trials_-_Patient_Participation.asp, retrieved on 2006.04.12.
3. Modgil S, Hammond P, Wyatt J C, Potts V. Developing A Knowledge-based Tool for Authoring Clinical Trial Protocols. First European Workshop on computer-based support for clinical guidance and protocols (EWGLP 2000). IOS Press, Amsterdam, Leipzig, Germany, 2000.
4. Nammunil K, Pickering C, Modgil S, Montgomery A and others. Design-a-Trial: A Rule-Based Decision Support System for Clinical Trial Design. Knowledge Based Systems, 17/2-4, 2000, p. 121-129.
5. Object Management Group (OMG). Unified Modeling Language (UML) Specification: Infrastructure version 2.0. URL: http://www.omg.org/docs/formal/05-07-05.pdf, retrieved on 2006.04.14.
6. Shen W, Compton K, Huggins J K. A Toolset for Supporting UML Static and Dynamic Model Checking. In proceedings of the 26th International Computer Software and Applications Conference (COMPSAC 2002), Prolonging Software Life: Development and Redevelopment, Oxford, England, IEEE Computer Society, 2002: p. 147-152.
7. U.S. Department of Health and Human Services, Food and Drug Administration. Guidance for Industry. Computerised systems used in Clinical Trials. Draft guidance, 2004. URL: http://www.fda.gov/Cder/guidance/6032dft.htm, retrieved on 2006.04.17.
8. U.S. Department of Health and Human Services, Food and Drug Administration. Guidance for Industry. E6 Good Clinical Practice: Consolidated Guidance,1996. URL: http://www.va.gov/chrr/regulatory/vrb/files_forms/GoodClinicalPractices.pdf, retrieved on 2006.03.11.
9. Vasilecas O, Lebedys E, Laucius J. Formal methods for representation of business rules specified using UML. // In: R. Simutis (eds.). Proceedings of the International Conference "Information Technologies for business - 2005", Kaunas: Technologija, p. 41-47, 2005.
10. Vasilecas O, Lebedys E. Business rules repository for business rules represented using UML // In R. Rachev, A. Smrikarov (Eds.). Proc. of the International Conference on Computer Systems and Technologies "CompSysTech, 05", Varna, Bulgaria, 16-17 June. 2004, p. II.5-1 – II.5-6.
11. Vasilecas O, Lebedys E. Repository for Business Rules Represented in UML Diagrams // Izvestia of the Belarusian Engineering Academy, 2005, Vol. 1 (19)/2, p. 187-192.

On Some Inferences Based on Stratified Forward Chaining: An Application to E-Government

El-Hassan Bezzazi

IREENAT, University of Lille 2, France bezzazi@univ-lille2.fr

1 Introduction

This paper is twofold. It introduces first an expert system shell whose inference engine is based on stratified forward chaining presented in detail in the paper [1]. The stratified forward chaining (hereafter *sfc*) was proposed as a generalization for the inheritance networks with exception since it allows more than one antecedent in the premises part of a rule. In [2] *sfc* was tuned to what was called specific stratified forward chaining. Precisely, rules which have more literals in their body are said to be more specific than those with a subset of these literals in their body under some conditions. This way, more specific rules can easily be added to the rulebase and will prevail over more general ones in case they have conflicting conclusions. Expert systems built with this tool are rule based and the user interface is web based. The chaining *sfc* allows to manage the application of conflicting rules (i.e. those whose conclusions are opposed) according to the same intuition as the one in inheritance networks and which is expressed by the rule of preemption [5]. The practical use of *sfc* is presented through the three chaining methods: forward chaining, backward chaining and mixed chaining. Our current aim is to make use of these inference mechanisms to help the user in his interaction with public administration to identify in an efficient way the relevant information he needs. For example, when a user applies for some administrative document, the system would help him know the required documents [3]. This is done through a question-response dialog to determine the user profile. This kind of dialog exempts the user from spending time for extracting the relevant information out of the general available documentation. On the other hand, the fact that the user-system interaction is mainly based on yes/no questions makes it particularly well suited for mobile government, when using mobile phones which have, in general, small screens. The GPL programming language PHP [4] was used to implement the inference engines in our prototype. In its second part, this paper considers also a special kind of inference built on *sfc* called deontic inference. The rationale behind this kind of inference is the possible presence of deontic rules which may impose a change in the base of current facts to make it comply with the obligations they prescribe. The paper is organized as follows. In section 2 we present the language used for knowledge representation and in a rather informal way the specific stratified forward chaining. In sections 3 and 4 we define respectively the stratified backward chaining *sbc* and the stratified mixed chaining *smc* which comply with *sfc*. An example of dialog using *smc*. Section 5 begins the second part of this paper by introducing deontic rules and deontic inference as well as a measure to evaluate how far or how close is a situation described by a set of literals to the ideal situation computed by deontic inference. In section 6 we discuss a more general characterization for deontic inference. In section 7 we give some examples of deontic rules and inferences.

2 Knowledge representation, Cautious union and specific stratified forward chaining

A literal is an atom or an atom preceded by ! which represents negation, it is then a negative literal. Currently, an atom is simply a symbol but atoms with more structure such as comparisons could be easily incorporated in the system. The shape of a rule is: $l_1 l_2 ... l_n > l_m$ where $l_1 l_2 ... l_n$ and l_m are literals. Literals are separated by one space or more in the body of the rule and the conclusion is a single literal.

A knowledge base is identified by a name and has a base of rules and a base of facts. The function *lit* identifies and puts in the set *literals* the literals which appear in the knowledge base.

The function *clean* removes from a set of literals all opposing literals. The function *cu* is a non commutative operation that carries out the cautious union of two sets of literals by adding to the first set only those literals in the second set which do not have their opposites in the first set and cleaning the resulting set. $clean(L) = L - \{l, !l : l, !l \in L'\}$, $cu(L) = clean(L \cup \{l \in L' : !l \notin L\})$

The stratification of a rulebase is carried out by the function s. The stratification mechanism consists in computing for each literal of the rulebase its stratum. The stratum of a literal is, roughly speaking, the biggest number of one-step forward chaining that infers it [1]. The stratum of a rule is the biggest stratum of its body. Note that a stratified rulebase is necessarily acyclic when thought of as a graph. We give, in what follows, an informal description for this inference based on two partial orders p_1 and p_2. A rulebase is said to be stratified by the mapping $s : lit(R) \longrightarrow [1, n]$ if and only if for any rule in R, $l_1, ..., l_n > l_m$ we have $s(l_i) < s(l_m)$ and there is no other such mapping $s' : lit(R) \longrightarrow [1, n']$ with $n' < n$. This stratification induces a partial ordering on R defined by $r \, p_1 \, r'$ iff

$max(s(body(r))) < max(s(body(r')))$. Let p_2 be the partial ordering that specific-ity defines, $r\,p_2\,r'$ if and only if $body(r') \subseteq body(r)$ and $r\,\not p_1 r'$. We combine these two orders to define a new partial order p_p as $r\,p_p\,r'$ iff $r\,p_1\,r'$ and $r'\not p_1 r$. In other words, $r\,p_p\,r'$ iff $r\,p_1\,r'$ and either r is more specific than r' or they do not compare to each other. Let p_t be any total ordering on R which is consistent with p_p, *i.e*, if $r\,p_p\,r'$ then $r\,p_t\,r'$. Specific *sfc* inference, starting from a rulebase $R = r_1,...,r_n$ with $r_1\,p_t\,...\,p_t\,r_n$ and a set of initial facts L, pro-ceeds as follows: Among these totally ordered rules we look for the first rule r which can be fired by L, *i.e.* such that $body(r) \subseteq L$. If such a rule does not exist, the process is done, otherwise the process continues with the new totally ordered rulebase $R - \{r\}$ and the set of facts $L \cup \{head(r)\}$. Notable properties for *sfc* are, given two sets of literals L, L':

- Non-monotony *i.e.*, in general $sfc(L) \not\subseteq sfc(L \cup L')$
- $L \subseteq sfc(L)$
- If L is consistent then so is $sfc(L)$

The function *sfc* computes the literals inferred using stratified forward chain-ing and retains at the same time the rules which were applied with relevance in the inference, i.e. the rules which were applied and whose conclusion was actually kept (and not rejected during the cautious union by the opposite literal previously inferred). The relevant rules will help us define in the sequel the stratified back-ward chaining.

3 Stratified Backward Chaining

Backward chaining is a bottom up method used in expert systems. It starts with a literal called a goal to see, in case it is not an initial fact, if there are rules that sup-port it and so on for the literals in the body of these rules which become sub-goals to be confirmed. The goal is confirmed when all the ultimate sub-goals are among the initial facts. Because of the fact that this method is goal-driven, it will not use all the rules that would have been used to check a given goal by forward chaining. However, attention must be paid to possible cycles that may exist in the rulebase to guarantee the termination of the process. Fortunately, this would never be the case as far as we are dealing with stratified rulebases. This is the classical defini-tion of backward chaining with respect to classical forward chaining. The defini-tion we are about to give now of backward chaining which we will call stratified backward chaining (*sbc* in short) is made with respect to *sfc*. Unlike the definition of classical backward chaining which does not use forward chaining, *sbc* does use *sfc*. Indeed *sfc* allows the selection of the relevant rules *i.e.* those which conclusions are inferred with respect to *sfc* and the initial facts. Besides stratified backward chaining uses two functions *sbc* and *prove* which are executed according to a cross recursion (they call mutually each other). In fact, the function *sbc* selects among the relevant rules those which are especially relevant for the goal being processed.

Consider the following fragment of a rulebase which describe documents required to apply for a passport. There is an exception which is stated in case the application is made for a modification, fore example a new born child to be added into the passport. In this case the stamp, denoted by doc_7, is no more required.

renewal > passport_application;
passport_modification > passport_application;
passport_a pplication > documents;
documents > doc_1;

....

documents > doc_9;
passport_modification > !doc_7;

If we take as initial facts the only fact passport_modification and as a goal the fact doc_7, the classical backward chaining will conclude on a success whereas we would rather like it to conclude on a failure in accordance with sfc. The solution consists in checking before concluding on a success with the classical backward chaining that the rules which made it possible to deduce the goal are relevant for sfc.

Function prove(list_of_goals)
if(list_of_goals is empty) then return(true);
else if (sbc(head(list_o f_goals))) return(prove(tail(list_o f_goals)));
else return(false);

function sbc(goal,list_of_relevant_rules)
if (goal in current_facts) then success=true
else if (list_of_relevant_rules is empty) then success=false;
else if (goal!=conclusion(r))
then success=(sbc(goal,tail(list_of_relevant_rules)));
else if (prove(premises(r))) then success=true;
else success=(sbc(goal,tail(list_of_relevant_rules)));
return(success)

list_of_relevant_rules is the set of relevant rules in the rulebase for sfc.
current_facts stocks the facts entered by the user and which initially constitute the facts base.

Fact: Given a stratified rulebase, $sbc(goal, list\_of\_relevant\_rules)$ returns a success if and only if $goal \in sfc(current\_facts)$.

4 Stratified Mixed Chaining

Mixed chaining is an inference method using the forward chaining to infer new facts and backward chaining to confirm facts possibly by questioning the user. The stratified mixed chaining carried out by the function *smc* that we present here combines the forward and backward stratified chaining. In general, it works through a dialog with the user during its execution. The dialog relates exclusively to the truth value of certain facts among the initial facts. It is the function *backward_all* which chooses the facts to be questioned on. The function *sfc* is called in the processing of the form submitted as the answer to each question. It is interesting to notice here that the forms sent to the user during this dialog save at the same time the execution environment of the function *smc*. Indeed, the fact that the http protocol is stateless, the html page sent to the user carries as hidden fields all the data necessary to save the recursion context. Questions are put only about positive literals i.e. if it is a negative literal on which the user must be questioned, the question will be put rather on the opposite literal which then gives the answer for the literal in question. The questioning to be sent to the user through an html form is prepared by the function *to_ask_user*.

```
function smc(list_of_rules,goal)
n = 0;
dialog = false;
while(n < number_o f_rulesand!dialog);
r = list_o f_rules[n];if(conclusion(r) = goal)
if((backward_all(premises(r)))) return(true);
n = n + 1;
return(false);


function backward_all(list_of_goals)
dialog = false;
if(list_of_goals is empty) return(true);
elsefact = head(list_of_goals);
if (fact in result) return (backward_all(tail(list_of_goals));
else if (inverse(fact) in result) return(false);
else if (initial(fact) and not (asked(fact) or asked(inverse(fact))))
to_ask_user(fact);
sfc();
dialog = true;
else if(smc(fact)) return (backward_all(tail(list_of_goals)));
else return(false);
```

number_of_rules is the number of rules in the rulebase.
dialog is a boolean variable used to simulate the mutual recursion.
result stocks the facts deduced with the function *sfc*.
initial returns true if the literal occurs only in the premises false otherwise.
asked returns true for a literal which the user was asked about during runtime.

Fact: Consider a session of *smc* which has concluded either on a success or not and let answers denote the set of literals added to current_facts through the session dialog by the user's answers. Given a stratified rulebase, *smc(goal)* returns a success if and only if *goal* ∈ *sfc(current_facts* ∪ *answers)*.

We give here an example of a dialog which the reader will be able to test at the web address: http://droit.univ-lille2.fr/eadministration/exp.php worked out of government texts. The rule   renewal out-of-date<2 childs childs<=4 > validity-5-years must be read as follows. If the case is about a renewal of an out-of-date passport since less than two years and that the children must be recorded there and that their number does not exceed four then the validity duration of the passport will be of five years.

emergency > !stamp_60;
emergency > stamp_30;
emergency > validity_6_months;
emergency > documents;
renewal out_of_date<2 childs childs<=4 > documents;
renewal out_of_date<2 childs childs<=4 > docs_childs;
renewal out_of_date<2 childs childs<=4 > valid_5_years;
renewal out_of_date<2 childs !childs<=4 > documents;
renewal out_of_date<2 childs !childs<=4 > docs_childs;
renewal out_of_date<2 childs !childs<=4 > demand_elders;
renewal out_of_date<2 childs !childs<=4 > valid_5_years;
renewal out_of_date<2 !childs > documents;
renewal out_of_date<2 !childs > validity_10_years;
renewal !out_of_date<2 > first_demand;
modification > documents;
modification > !stamp_60;
modification > current_validity;
documents > form;
documents > 2_photos;
documents > stamp_60;
documents > proof_residence;
documents > identity;

The following rules are used to define the final facts among which the inferred facts should be chosen for the answer.
form > goal; 2_photos > goal;
stamp_60 > goal; stamp_30 > goal;
proof_residence > goal;
identity > goal;
first_demand > goal; demand_elder > goal;
documents_childs > goal;
valid_10_years > goal; valid_5_years > goal;
valid_6_months > goal;
current_validity > goal;

Example of session:
emergency ?
no
renewal ?
no
out_of_date<2 ?
yes
childs ?
yes
childs<4 ?
yes

5 Deontic Rules

Deontic logic is a logic for reasoning about ideal and actual behaviour [11]. Applications of deontic logic can go beyond legal analysis and legal automation to cover other domains like the specification of security policies and fault tolerant systems [10]. Traditionally, this logic is developed as a modal logic with, essentially, a modal operator o to define obligation which can be used in its turn to define permission and prohibition. However Instead of using such an operator and in order to stay at a propositional level, we enrich the language by considering a new kind of literals which are intended, if inferred, to describe an obligation to be respected. These literals, we shall call deontic literals, are of the form $o(l)$ or $!o(l)$ where l is a descriptive literal, $i.e.$ a literal defined as in section 2. Let O be the set of deontic literals and Lit_D the set of obligated literals $i.e.$ $l \in Lit_D$ if and only if $o(l) \in O$. The function ω returns the obligated literal of a deontic literal $i.e.$ $\omega(o(l)) = l$ and the function o returns the deontic literals of a set of literals, $o(L) = L \cap O$. An operation of cautious union cu' is defined for two sets of deontic literals L_D, L'_D in the following way. $cu'(L_D, L'_D)$ adds to the first set L_D only those literals in L_D which do not have their opposites in the first set or which do not oblige a literal whose opposite is obliged in L_D.

A deontic rule is a rule where the body is made out of descriptive literals and the conclusion is a deontic literal. Therefore, we shall deal from now on with two kinds of rulebases: A descriptive rulebase R and a deontic rulebase D. Note that the set of rules $R \cup D$ is stratified since R is stratified and the heads of the newly added rules never occur in the rules body.

5.1 Deontic inference and Legal sets

Given a set of literals L, we define elementary deontic inference through sfc $edi(L, R \cup D) = sfc(L, R \cup D)$. In the sequel, we shall drop the parameter $R \cup D$ from both $edi(L, R \cup D)$ and $sfc(L, R \cup D)$ in order not to encumber the notation. The result of this inference is a set of literals L' which may contain deontic literals. A set of descriptive literals L is said to be legal or equivalently D-consistent when $sfc(L)$ does not contain a positive deontic literal which is violated by one of its descriptive literals or conflicted by a contrary obligation: L is legal if and only if $o(l) \in sfc(L) \Rightarrow !l \notin sfc(L) \wedge o(!l) \notin sfc(L)$. A set of literals which is not legal is called illegal. inference from an illegal set L yields an illegal set L' since $L \subset L'$. An elementary legalization $\lambda(L)$ for L is an update of L by replacing l with $!l$ whenever $l \in L$ and $o(!l) \in sfc(L)$, in other words $\lambda(L) = cu(\omega(o(sfc(L))), L)$.

The legalization of an illegal set L consists in a succession of elementary legalizations. In order to be able to cumulate along this process the deontic literals in accordance with their cautious union, we need to keep track of them.

$$\begin{cases} \lambda^{(0)}(L) = L, \Delta^0 = \varnothing \\ \lambda^{(n+1)}(L) = cu(\omega(\Delta^{(n+1)}), \lambda^{(n)}(L)), \Delta^{(n+1)} = cu'(\Delta^{(n)}, o(sfc(L))) \end{cases}$$

Since the set Lit of all literals is finite, the sequence $\{\lambda^{(n)}(L)\}_n \in N$ is such that there is necessarily an integer i satisfying $\lambda^{(i)}(L) = \lambda^{(i')}(L)$ for some $i' > i$. Let k and k' be the smallest integers satisfying $\lambda^{(k)}(L) = \lambda^{(k')}(L)$ with $k' > k$. Two cases are to be distinguished:

1) The case where $k = k'$ which means that the sequence $\{\lambda^{(n)}(L)\}_{n \in N}$ is stationary. We define then the deontic inference of L to be $di(L) = edi(\lambda^{(k)}(L))$

2) The case where $k \neq k'$ which means that the sequence $\{\lambda^{(n)}(L)\}_{n \in N}$ is cyclic.

This will be considered as an inconsistency and the deontic inference is undefined $di(L) = \perp$. This means that the set of deontic rules D does not provide the means for handling the case described by L.

Deontic inference defined this way incorporate defeasible reasoning thanks to stratified forward chaining which operates at the descriptive level as well as at the deontic level. The issue of dealing with conflicting and conditional obligations in deontic logic at the light of non-monotonic reasoning has been discussed in several papers [6][8][9]. In particular, in [8] the author recommends the use of an already existing non-monotonic logic with a deontic logic instead of a built-in non-monotonic deontic logic and in [9], the author underlines the difference between an obligation which is defeated and an obligation which is violated. The elementary legalization plays a crucial role in deontic inference. it takes the deontic output of *sfc* and reuses it to correct the input, possibly altering it by replacing some of its literals by their opposites, to make it comply to the obligations of the rulebase. Making a difference between the declarative statements and the norms is an approach already singled out in [7] where the set of conditional norms is seen as a black box which transforms the input into output following some basic rules.

5.2 Legality Degrees

Let us consider now the case where $di(L) \neq \perp$. $di(L)$ describes the ideal situation to which L must comply whereas $sfc(L)$ describes the actual situation. The similarity between the actual situation and the ideal situation can be evaluated with well known similarity measures for finite sets such as the Jaccard measure. We define the degree of legality of a set of literal L with respect to the rulebases R and D as

$$\delta(L) = \frac{|\,sfc(L) \cap di(L)\,|}{|\,sfc(L) \cup di(L)\,|}$$

5.3 A more general characterization for legal sets

Let L, R, D, Lit be respectively a set of literals, a descriptive rulebase, a deontic rulebase and the set of all literals appearing in these sets. Let Lit_D be the set of obligated literals *i.e.* $l \in Lit_D$ if and only if $o(l) \in Lit$. The issue we investigate in this section is, given a consistent set of literals L, in case it is not legal, which legal sets of literals, if any, could be proposed as "legalizations" for it. A model for L with respect to $R \cup D$ is defined as being any consistent set $L = cu(L_D, L)$ of literals with $L_D \subseteq Lit_D$ such that:

(1) $sfc(L)$ is D-consistent and

(2) for any $l \in L_D$ there is $L_l \subseteq L_D$ such that $l \in \omega(sfc(L_l))$ where $L_l = cu(L_l, L)$

Let L be a consistent set of descriptive literals. The legalized set obtained by deontic inference when defined is a model for L.

Proof. The legalized set is $L = \lambda^{(k+1)}(L) = cu(\omega(\Delta^{(k+1)}), \lambda^{(k)}(L))$ for some $k \in N$. We put $L_D = \Delta^{(k+1)} = cu'(\Delta^{(k)}, o(sfc(L)))$. L is D-consistent since it is the legalization of L by di. On the other hand, property (2) is satisfied since the sequence $(\Delta)_{i\in[0,k]}$ is an increasing chain. Ω

Consider the following rulebases:
a>o(c);
a>o(!c);
There is no model for $\{a\}$.
a>o(!b);
b>o(!a) ;
$\{a,!b\},\{!a,b\}\,and\,\{!a,!b\}$ are models for $\{a,b\}$. Indeed, the last one for example is the result for $cu(\{!a,!b\},\{a,b\})$, on the other hand $sfc(\{!a,!b\})=\{!a,!b\}$ and $!a\in sfc(\{!a,b\})=\{!a,b,o(!a)\}$ and $!b \in sfc(\{a,!b\}) = \{a,!b,o(!b)\}$

5.4 Examples

We comment in this paragraph some examples on the use of deontic inference and legal sets.

No smoking

Consider a building where smoking is forbidden. However, smoking is allowed in the room number 4 of this building.
room4 > building;
building > o(!smoking);
room4 > !(o(!smoking));
smoking > pollution;
The sets {room4, smoking}, {room4, !smoking}, {building, !smoking} and {room4, building, smoking} are legal sets. The set{building, smoking} is an illegal set and its legalization yields {building, !smoking}.

Consider the set $L = \{building, smoking\}$. $sfc(L)$ is not D-consistent. Consider the set $L = cu(!smoking, L) = \{building, !smoking\}$.

$sfc(L) = \{building, !smoking, o(!smoking)\}$ is D-consistent.

Privacy

Let bob_privacy denote personal data of Bob. Agency A is not allowed to have access to Bob privacy unless Bob is okay. If it happens that Agency A did have access to Bob privacy, it is committed not to communicate it to others. Note that as long as the information cannot be erased from his mind, there must be a rule in the rulebase asserting that no obligation can be made to change this state. Corrective actions as sanctions may be prescribed in this case. This is an example of the so-called contrary-to-duty norms in deontic logic where violation of some obligations must be tolerated in favour of other appropriate obligations which become operative.

Agency_A > o(!bob_privacy);
agency_A bob_okay > !o(!bob_privacy);
agency_A bob_privacy > !o(!bob_privacy);
agency_A bob_privacy > o(!communicate);
agency_A bob_privacy !bob_okay > o(sanction);

Cyclic

A simple example of a cyclic case is the following one where D states that light must be on if it was off and the switch pressed and similarly must be off if it was on and the switch pressed.

!light press > o(light);
light press > o(!light);

Considering $L = \{light, press\}$ as our starting set of literals, the legalisation of L by the first elementary deontic inference gives $\{!light, press\}$, the following step gives $\{light, press\}$ which shows the starting of a cyclic inference. This is explained by the fact that the literal press hides some crucial information to put the light on or off. Actually it should be replaced by two literals $press_0$ and $press_1$ for stating respectively the facts of putting off and putting on the light. There is no model for L. This example shows a need to enrich the language by the concept of action to deal with discrete event systems.

6 Conclusion

The first purpose of this paper was to introduce an effective implementation of inference engines based on a non-monotonic logic. Our system enjoys of the conceptual simplicity of systems based on propositional logics. As a matter of fact the examples given in the literature to introduce and motivate the concerns of non-monotonic logics are mainly written in a propositional language, this is why we restrict our definitions to propositional logics in addition to the fact that interesting classical expert systems based on propositional logics do exist and are effectively used. However, we project to investigate on the use of a kind of first order predicate logics as in Prolog clauses for writing the knowledge base rules. A methodology should also be investigated to help define the specificity of rules with respect to each other during the rulebase construction. The second part of this paper investigated the use of deontic literals to handle normative statements. It was noticed that a set of literals may have several sets as candidates for its legalization in the interpretation structure and that the legalization preferred in some cases by deontic inference was severe in comparison to other possible legalizations. This issue must be investigated further in order to make the interpretation more adequate for a possible completeness theorem to hold. Another promising issue is to consider the concept of action in the language as long as the system encompasses the concept of change in the inferred literals.

References

1. Bezzazi, E-H, Revision and Update based on Stratified Forward Chaining in Frontiers in Belief Revision, edited by Mary-Anne Williams and Hans Rott, 2001 Kluwer Academic Publishers. (2001) 315–332
2. Bezzazi, E-H, Specific Stratified Forward Chaining, Proceedings of the International Conference on Artificial Intelligence, Las Vegas, Nevada, USA, (2000) 1455–1460
3. Bezzazi, E-H, Workflows et Systèmes experts dans l'administration électronique, Communication au Colloque International Administration électonique et qualité des préstations administratives, Lille, France, 11/19/2004
4. The official site of PHP: http://www.php.net
5. Horty, J., Thomason, R., Touretzky, D., A skeptical theory of inheritancein nonmonotonic networks, Artificial Intelligence, (1990) 311–348
6. Horty, J., Nonmonotonic foundations for deontic logic, In Nute, D., ed., Defeasible Deontic Logic. Kluwer. 17–44
7. Makinson D., Van Der Torre L., Input-output logics, Journal of Philosophical Logic, vol. 29, 2000, p. 383–408
8. Prakken, H., Two Approaches to the Formalisation of Defeasible Deontic Reasoning, Studia Logica 57 (1), pp. 73–90, 1996
9. Van Der Torre L., Violated obligations in a defeasible deontic logic, In A.Cohn (ed.), Proceedings of the Eleventh European Conference on Artificial Intelligence (ECAI'94), pages 371–375, John Wiley & Sons, 1994
10. Wieringa R.J., MeyerJ.-J.Ch., Applications of Deontic Logic in Computer Science: A concise Overview, In Deontic Logic in Computer Science, pp 17–40, John Wiley & Sons, Chichester, England, 1993
11. Von Wright G.H., An Essay in Deontic Logic and the General Theory of Action, Acta Philosophica Fennica, Fasc. 21. North-Holland, 1968

Requirements Determination for Knowledge Management Systems in Information Technology Outsourcing Relationships

Dolphy M. Abraham

College of Business Administration, Loyola Marymount University, 1 LMU Drive, MS-8385, Los Angeles, CA 90045, USA

Abstract: This paper discusses ongoing research studying requirements determination for knowledge management (KM) systems across organizational boundaries. The domain of information technology outsourcing (ITO) relationships is used as the example in this discussion. Business networks, such as, outsourcing arrangements for information technology management or business process management have become a routine arrangement. Data and knowledge sharing becomes a vital aspect of operating and managing such business networks. Consequently, the role of knowledge management becomes more important as business networks become more prevalent. Knowledge management, in the context of business partnerships or networks, is the set of processes necessary to facilitate sharing of information and process knowledge. KM processes also direct the information and knowledge sharing in a way that supports each organization's objectives.

The relationship between the client and service provider in an ITO engagement is unique with respect to the types of processes, information technology infrastructure, geographical location, terms of the contract and individual managers involved. The study of ITO engagements also points out that information and knowledge sharing is critical during the various stages of the engagement. At the start of the ITO engagement, the service provider is dependent on the client for process knowledge relating to the tasks under the contract. During the contract period and at the end, the client is dependant on the service provider to learn about changes in the business environment observed by the service provider's staff. Each of these dependencies involves the use of the appropriate systems or procedures to share the relevant information and process knowledge. These systems and procedures also have to contend with local social and business cultures in the various locations of the client and service provider organizations. This paper identifies the key issues that affect requirements determination for KM systems that support the various stages of ITO relationships.

1 Introduction

Knowledge Management is the organizational process for acquiring, organizing and communicating the knowledge of individual employees so that the work of the organization becomes more effective (Alavi and Leidner 1999). Knowledge Management (KM) is an increasingly important process in business organizations because "managing human intellect – and converting it into useful products and services – is fast becoming the critical executive skill of the age" (Quinn et al. 1998). Grover and Davenport (2001) state that KM becomes "an integral business function" when organizations "realize that competitiveness hinges on effective management of intellectual resources." Grover and Davenport (2001) also argue that knowledge management works best when it is carried out by all the employees of the organization and not just KM specialists.

Business organizations frequently partner with other firms to complement their core competencies. To collaborate effectively, partner firms have to communicate with each other information about business processes as well as share ideas of how to design or improve business processes. This phenomenon of knowledge sharing across organizational boundaries is called interorganizational learning (Argote 1999). Knowledge management is the set of processes necessary to facilitate interorganizational learning and direct it in a way that supports the organization's overall objectives.

Business networks, such as, IT outsourcing and business process outsourcing to multiple service providers have become a routine option in both product-oriented and service-oriented industries. Data and knowledge sharing becomes a vital aspect of operating and managing such business networks. Consequently, the role of knowledge management becomes more important as business networks become more prevalent.

We propose a framework that will help plan the requirements for systems that support knowledge management activity in inter-organizational relationships. The framework addresses a key need for organizations as they seek to manage their operations in a manner different from traditional methods. As organizations rely increasingly on partners to carry out some of the business processes, the ability to share not only operational data but also process knowledge between partners becomes a critical capability. By helping determine the requirements for knowledge management systems, the proposed framework will support the successful implementation of outsourcing relationships.

2 Prior Research

Prior research in KM originates in the area of organizational learning. Subsequently the area of knowledge management developed as information technology (IT) tools to support document and content sharing became widely available. We first discuss prior research into KM processes within organizations followed by the experience with KM initiatives across organizational boundaries as well as management issues that arise in IT outsourcing relationships.

2.1 Knowledge Management Processes within Organizations

Software applications called Knowledge Management Systems (KMS) are tools used to support the Knowledge Management process by providing document repositories, employee directories showing areas of expertise, discussion groups and information retrieval tools (Davenport et al. 1998). Where such applications have been deployed, it has been noted that many such initiatives have failed due to several factors including neglect of people management issues, and because KM initiatives are seen as information technology (IT) projects rather than initiatives that deal with changes in organizational processes (Storey and Barnett 2000). In order to implement KM practices in infrastructure management, it is necessary to understand the processes involved in knowledge management. Abraham (2000) posits that the steps in capturing and using knowledge in an organization consist of the following processes linked as shown in Figure 1.

- Collection or acquisition of content
- Organization or filtering of the document repository
- Analysis of the repository
- Utilization of the contents for subsequent work processes

Collection or *acquisition* of content involves the accumulation of content from all relevant business processes in any form that can be documented. This can include formal (or finished) documents, working papers or notes, e-mail messages, archives of instant messages, etc. The accumulation of various types of content into a comprehensive archive that can be searched by all authorized users facilitates the search for prior work product. Each type of document can be categorized by project, incident, or the employees involved. Meta-information in the form of categories and keywords facilitate the task of retrieval. Such archives can also include links to external sites where appropriate.

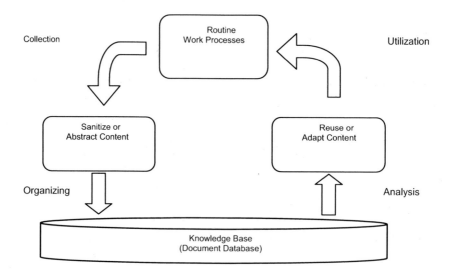

Fig. 1. Linking the KM Processes within an Organization

Organizing or *filtering* helps to make the archived content more usable. As the volume of content in the repository increases, it becomes necessary to make the task of searching through the collection more effective. Database capabilities become necessary to manage the documents. The meta-information that was developed while the documents were accumulated help to structure the document database. Information about domain specific and organization specific processes can also help to structure the document database. Other ways in which documents can be categorized include nature of usability (reusable, adaptable, training material, etc.) and usage patterns (stage of project, users, organizational unit, etc.).

Analysis of the repository helps determine relationships between content items. For instance, it is possible that multiple projects use similar skills, information or processes. As organizations become larger it becomes more difficult for project teams to coordinate with each other. By analyzing document content from across the organization and creating a lexicon of work-related terms or concepts, it becomes possible to add value to the document database. The analysis will help identify relationships between documents and also identify different types of relationships (common skills, personnel, or resources). Items throughout the repository can be analyzed and it is conceivable that links to sources outside the document database can be added based on terms in the lexicon.

Utilization is how the organization derives benefit from the KM process. Making use of the content from the document database is the initial step. Making the use of documents from the repository a standard step in any project needs to become the practice in the organization. By incorporating the use of the accumulated knowledge a part of the routine work process ensures that all employees understand the value of the KMS and how it can be used on a daily basis.

In order to implement this set of processes it is necessary to understand the organizational culture and how it will impact the KM initiative. It is necessary to plan properly and implement the system in layers so that capabilities become available when users are ready to make use of them (Abraham and Seal 2001). Financial and performance metrics are needed to evaluate the KM initiative. (Abraham et al. 2004).

Managing both documented and undocumented (tacit) knowledge is critical (Polanyi, 1967). Managing the documented knowledge involves determining which formal documents must be shared and the mechanisms that must be set up to make them accessible. Identifying any existing mechanisms for information and idea sharing within an organization as well as between organizations will help determine the processes used to share tacit knowledge. The current practices must be extended to enable decision makers within the organization as well as those at interdependent infrastructures to learn from prior incidents. The framework must also enable an individual decision maker to get in contact with another individual who may have situation-specific knowledge. Nidumolu et al. (2001) report that "in order to be successful," (KM initiatives) "need to be sensitive to features of the context of generation, location and application of knowledge." The operating procedures, technology and information systems and organizational culture will collectively impact KM efforts in infrastructure management.

2.2 Knowledge Management across Organizational Boundaries

Prior work in the area of interorganizational learning (IOL) includes studying the role of information technology to support interorganizational learning. Scott (2000) studied the process of and reasons for information technology (IT) support for interorganizational learning. Studying the disk drive industry, Scott identified the need for interorganizational learning to help "cope with the complexity of new products and the capital intensity" in the industry. The model developed as a result of the study helps explain the role of IT in lower and higher levels of interorganizational learning. Gottschalk (2001) surveyed law firms in Norway to determine the predictors of information technology support for interorganizational learning. Firm cooperation and knowledge cooperation were identified as significant predictors. Inter-organizational trust was another factor that affected the use of IT to support interorganizational knowledge management.

Other studies have focused on organizational factors that affect knowledge management across organizational boundaries. Abou-Zeid (2002) studied the factors that impact knowledge transfer between subsidiaries in multi-national corporations. A condition necessary for successful knowledge transfer between subsidiaries was identified to be the explication of the value systems of the subsidiaries involved in the knowledge transfer. A list of organizational values was used to develop an ideal organizational value profile for inter-organizational knowledge transfer. Learning-by-hiring was another strategy for acquiring knowledge studied by Song et al. (2003). Studying the patenting activities of engineers who moved from U.S. to non-U.S. firms, they suggest that "learning-by-hiring can be useful when hired engineers are used for exploring technologically distant knowledge rather than reinforcing existing firm expertise, and also for extending the hiring firm's geographic reach. Hansen (2002) introduces the concept of knowledge networks. His study showed that project teams obtained more knowledge and completed projects faster when the knowledge transfer utilized shorter paths between organizational units. He identified the need for additional research studying the impact of connections between organizational units and the relationship between knowledge content in different organizational units.

2.3 Information Technology Outsourcing

Information Technology Outsourcing (ITO) is broadly defined as a process undertaken by an organization to contract-out or to sell the organization's IT assets, staff and/or activities to a third party supplier who in exchange provides and manages IT assets and services for monetary return over an agreed period of time (Kern et al. 2002). In this contractual relationship the outside vendor assumes responsibility of one or more IT functions, but alternative functions may require alternative processes.

Variations on ITO engagements can include technical staff placed within the client organization to application development with staff located locally or at remote locations, and even dedicated offshore development centers. Offshore Development Centers (ODC) are comprised of a facility and staff dedicated for a client's IT project requirements and are a virtual extension of client's development environment. The ODC team of developers and project managers links up to client's offices and machines via dedicated links and thereby works in the same environment as the client's IT team.

To make the decision about outsourcing it is necessary to understand the factors that affect ITO engagements. These include globalization and the factors that impact globalization. The presence of IT infrastructure especially high-bandwidth network infrastructure is a necessary component for offshore engagements. Regulations and community activism are also factors likely to influence companies faced with the decision to outsource IT processes.

Once the decision to outsource has been made, the success of the engagement is dependent on multiple risk factors (Kirkwood, 2005), including:

- Conflict resolution mechanisms
- Control over the engagement including control over intellectual property and human resources
- Communication mechanisms between managers, between locations, and across management layers
- Management and measurement methodologies including service level agreements, governance structures, and meeting schedules.

Process and governance design becomes the means by which risks can be managed during the life of the engagement. Many managers in client organizations believe that the outsourcing vendor should have processes in place for service delivery and support, removing the need for internal process development. It is vitally important, however, for process and governance design to be driven by the client organization itself in order to ensure alignment with the IT services that support core processes (Kirkwood, 2005). Effective governance procedures require timely sharing of information related to the performance of the service provider.

The study of ITO engagements also points out that information and knowledge sharing is critical during various other stages of the engagement. At the start of the ITO engagement, the service provider is dependent on the client for process knowledge relating to the tasks under the contract. During the contract period and at the end, the client is dependant on the service provider to learn about changes in the business environment observed by the service provider's staff. Each of these dependencies involves the use of the appropriate systems or procedures to share the relevant information and process knowledge. These systems and procedures also have to contend with local social and business cultures in the various locations of the client and service provider organizations (Abraham et al. 2005).

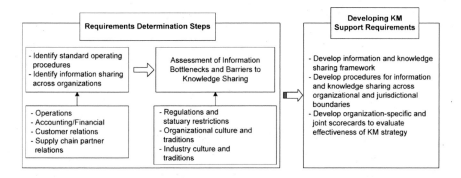

Fig. 2. Requirements Determination for Interorganizational KM Systems

3 Requirements Determination for Inter-organizational KM Systems

Unlike traditional systems analysis processes, determining requirements for KM systems being used in an inter-organizational setting necessitates multiple levels of analysis. There is a need for business process analysis followed by the more detailed analysis of systems requirements. In the context of IT outsourcing relationships, this implies the need to understand the higher level processes first before studying the detailed information and process knowledge that is shared between the service provider and the client.

The first task is a business process analysis of organizational partnerships focusing on the information and knowledge sharing mechanisms already in place. In addition it is necessary to understand the standard operating procedures in place at both the service provider and client organizations. These processes are likely to be those that are prescribed in the outsourcing contract and are part of the operating arrangement. In a sense, this analysis identifies the procedures that generate information and process knowledge that need to be communicated and the planned communication mechanisms between the two organizations.

This task starts with an assessment of operating procedures and the corresponding information systems and procedures associated with tasks that span organizational boundaries as well as tasks within one organization that have a significant impact on the other organization(s) in the partnership. Such systems and procedures would be situated in the day-to-day operations and management of each company, including accounting and financial, customer relations, and outsourcing contract arrangements. The information systems involved with the delivery of the primary product or service would also be part of this analysis. The purpose is to determine how these existing systems are used in a knowledge management role. The questions that will be addressed include how information is shared across the organization in each company and the interaction between decision makers across the organization. In addition, the analysis will help determine the existing formal and informal procedures used within each organization to learn from prior experience.

The second task as part of the analysis involves identifying the factors that affect sharing of information and process knowledge. This task involves determining how the organization culture and traditions affect the practice of knowledge sharing. Regulations and jurisdictional variations of regulations as well as industry practices that impact knowledge sharing will be studied. These factors affect information and knowledge sharing across the organizations in a partnership or network. Regulations and industry practices also impact how managers in each organization use information from other organizations. This analysis will help identify interdependencies between the companies in decision-making processes.

A critical factor in this step of the analysis is in understanding the impact of cultural differences especially those related to the countries in which the two companies have their primary locations. Understanding the cultural factor helps in adapting KM processes to each partner organization's expectations of how information sharing needs to be carried out.

Based on the analysis of the current state across multiple organizations and partnerships, the knowledge management support strategy can be developed. The primary component of the strategy is a general framework that can be used to plan and execute KM initiatives. This includes the processes and systems support necessary to facilitate the sharing of information and process knowledge between the service provider and the outsourcing client. These processes have to be specified to account for the interaction across corporate boundaries and needs to take into consideration the location, language differences and cultural differences between the two organizations.

To manage the KM initiatives, it is also necessary to identify metrics that can be used to measure the use and effectiveness of the KM processes across the organizations in the partnership. These metrics will help evaluate processes within a single organization as well as process that span multiple organizations.

4 Next Steps

The proposed framework will help develop systems to support knowledge management across organizational boundaries. The next step in this project will involve using this framework in real-life outsourcing relationships to test the applicability of the framework to actual settings. This will be attempted in the context of multiple outsourcing projects involving service providers and client organizations located in different countries. In parallel, outsourcing partnerships between companies in the same country will be used to apply the framework. The application of the framework in cross-border settings will be compared with IT outsourcing relationships within one country to identify factors that are specific to cross border relationships.

The expectation is that the final framework following refinements based on real-life testing will enable organizations to create effective KM systems that enhance the quality of outsourcing relationships.

References

Abou-Zeid, E., (2002) An Ontology-based Approach to Inter-organizational Knowledge Transfer, *Journal of Global Information Technology Management*, Vol. 5, No. 3, pp. 32-47.

Abraham, D.M. (2000) An Information Systems Framework for the Development and Deployment of a Knowledge Management Infrastructure, *Proceedings of the INFORMS/KORMS International Conference*, pp. 1280-1284, Seoul, Korea, June 2000.

Abraham, D.M., Brownstein, E., Dai, W., Golper, S., Luolamo, T., Merter, Y., Moalej, A., and Ruvalcaba, C. (2005), Planning Successful I.T. Outsourcing Engagements: Lessons Learned from East Asian Service Providers, *Proceedings of the First International Conference on Managing Globally Distributed Work*, pp. 267-272, Bangalore, India, December 2005.

Abraham, Dolphy M., Fuentes, C. and Abraham, Dulcy M., Evaluating Web-Based Bidding in Construction: Using Simulation as an Evaluation Tool, *International Journal of Electronic Business*. Vol. 2, No. 2, pp. 121-141, March-April 2004.

Abraham, D.M. and Seal, K.C. (2001) CLASIC: Collaborative Layered System using Intranet Capabilities, *Logistics Information Management*, Vol. 14, No. 1&2, pp. 99-106.

Alavi, M. and Leidner, D.E. (1999), Knowledge Management Systems: Issues, Challenges and Benefits, *Communications of the AIS*, Vol.1.

Argote, L. (1999) Organizational Learning: Creating, Retaining and Transferring Knowledge, Kluwer, Norwell, MA.

Davenport, T.H. De Long, D.W. and Beers, M.C. (1998) Successful Knowledge Management Projects, *Sloan Management Review*, Winter, pp. 43-57.

Gottschalk, P. (2001) Predictors of Information Technology Support for Interorganizational Knowledge Management: Lessons learned from Law Firms in Norway, *Knowledge and Process Management*, Vol. 8, No. 3, pp. 186-194.

Grover, V. and Davenport, T.H. (2001) General Perspectives on Knowledge Management: Fostering a Research Agenda, *Journal of Management Information Systems*, Vol. 18, No. 1, Summer 2001, pp. 5-21.

Hansen, M.T. (2002) Knowledge Networks: Explaining Effective Knowledge Sharing in Multiunit Companies, *Organization Science*, Vol. 13, No. 3, pp. 232-248.

Kern, T., Willcocks, L. P., Heck, E. V. (2002), The Winner's Curse in IT Outsourcing: Strategies for Avoiding Relational Trauma, California Management Review, Vol. 44, No. 2, pp. 47-69.

Kirkwood, S. (2005), Intelligent Outsourcing: Applying ITIL Process Governance and Architecture to Outsourced IT Operations, International Network Services.

Nidumolu, S.R., Subramani, M. and Aldrich, Alan, (2001) Situated Learning and the Situated Knowledge Web: Exploring the ground beneath Knowledge Management, Journal of Management Information Systems, Summer, Vol. 18, No. 1, pp. 115-150.

Polanyi, M. (1967) The Tacit Dimension, Doubleday, Garden City, NY.

Quinn, J.B., Anderson, P. and Finkelstein, S. (1998), Managing Professional Intellect: Making the Most of the Best, *Harvard Business Review of Knowledge Management*, HBS Press, pp. 181-205.

Scott, J. E., (2000) Facilitating Interorganizational Learning with Information Technology, *Journal of Management Information Systems*, Fall 2000, Vol. 17, No. 2, pp. 81-113.

Song, J., Almeida, P. and Wu, G. (2003) Learning-by-Hiring: When is Mobility More Likely to Facilitate Interfirm Knowledge Transfer? *Management Science*, Vol. 49, No. 4, pp. 351-365.

Storey, J. and Barnett, E., (2000) Knowledge Management Initiatives: Learning from Failure, *Journal of Knowledge Management*, Vol. 4. No. 3.

Using Concept Maps in Adaptive Knowledge Assessment

Alla Anohina, Vita Graudina, Janis Grundspenkis

Riga Technical University, Kalku street 1, Riga, Latvia, LV 1658
{alla.anohina; vita.graudina; janis.grundspenkis}@cs.rtu.lv

Abstract: The paper presents a novel approach regarding adaptive knowledge assessment using concept maps. Adaptive knowledge assessment adapts assessment tasks to the ability and knowledge level of a particular learner and makes a corresponding system more powerful and valuable. The already developed prototype of an intelligent knowledge assessment system based on multiagent paradigm and concept maps is described, but mainly the paper focuses on the support of adaptive assessment regarding the further enhancement of the system.
Keywords: computer-assisted assessment, concept maps, intelligent assessment system, adaptive assessment

1 Introduction

Computer-assisted assessment of learner's knowledge is not a novel term in computer science and education. The most widespread systems are ones based on various tests where correct answers are pre-defined. The main drawback of such systems is a level of intellectual behavior, which can be assessed. As a rule it is not above the fourth level in the well-known Bloom's taxonomy [4]. Only a few computer-assisted assessment systems, which assess higher levels of intellectual abilities and skills, have been developed. They are based on strongly subject dependent tasks such as essays or free-text responses. These systems use methods of natural language processing and, therefore, are extremely complicated.

The paper offers a reasonable compromise replacing tests by concept maps, which allow to assess higher order skills and simultaneously do not require natural language processing. So, in rather simple systems the idea of adaptive knowledge assessment may be implemented.

The remainder of this paper is organized as follows. Section 2 briefly discusses computer-assisted assessment. Section 3 gives an overview of different assessment tasks based on concept maps. The developed multiagent concept map based intelligent assessment system is described in Section 4. Section 5 introduces computer adaptive assessment. The possibilities to use concept maps in adaptive knowledge assessment using the developed system are discussed in Section 6. Finally, conclusions are presented and some directions for future work are outlined.

2 Computer-assisted assessments

According to [9] the term "computer-assisted assessment" refers to the use of computers in assessment, encompassing delivering, marking and analysis of assignments or examinations, as well as collation and analysis of data gathered from optical mark readers. The most widespread computer-assisted assessment systems are ones based on objective tests [5, 24] that offer a learner a set of questions, answers on which are pre-defined [9]. The mostly used question types are multiple choice questions, multiple response questions, graphical hotspot questions, fill in blanks, text/numerical input questions, etc.

Computer-assisted assessment typically is included in virtual learning environments, e.g. Blackboard (http://www.blackboard.com) or WebCT (http://www.webct.com), or it can be implemented in the form of a specialized assessment system. In the last case there is a set of available tools both from institutional and commercial developers [24]. CASTLE (http://www.le.ac.uk/castle), TRIADS (http://www.derby.ac.uk/assess/newdemo/mainmenu.html), and TAL (http://www.tal.bris.ac.uk) are examples of software developed within the framework of institutional projects. Commercial tools are Hot Potatoes (http://hotpot.uvic.ca), Respondus (http://www.respondus.com), WebQuiz XP (http://eng.smartlite.it/en2/products/webquiz/index.asp), Questionmark™ Perception™ (http://www.questionmark.com/us/home.htm), and others. The analysis of these products allows to define the following functional capabilities of computer-assisted assessment systems: templates for creation of questions, full functionality related to the management of questions (creation, removing, editing, etc.), planning of knowledge assessment activities, defining of feedback, reporting on the performance of both learners and questions, creation and support of question banks, extensive possibilities of question randomizing (different questions at each attempt of a test, different questions for each learner, etc.), various question delivery modes (without returns to already answered questions, re-answering of questions and moving through them, etc.), multimedia integration into questions, and others.

Computer-assisted assessment provides a number of advantages [10, 14, 16, 18, 24]: greater flexibility regarding place and time of assessment, potential for providing assessments for large number of learners efficiently, instant feedback to learners, extensive feedback to teachers, reduced errors in comparison with human marking, decreased time needed for supervising and marking of assessments, and potential for frequent assessments. Besides the advantages computer-assisted assessment systems have also drawbacks [10, 14, 18, 24]: some types of questions cannot be marked automatically as computer-assisted assessment is suited to those questions which require a limited response, unsupervised computer-assisted assessment sessions present a risk of plagiarism and illegal use of other materials, and some learners may have poor skills of information technologies usage.

However, the main drawback of such systems is a level of intellectual behavior, which can be assessed. According to [5, 16], it is not above the fourth level in the well-known Bloom's taxonomy [4], which includes three levels of lower order skills (Knowledge, Comprehension, and Application), and three levels of higher order skills (Analysis, Synthesis, and Evaluation). However, in [9] this assertion is called to be erroneous, but it is pointed out that designing test questions to assess higher order skills can be time consuming and requires skill and creativity.

Tasks such as essays or free-text responses which allow a learner to offer original answers and his/her judgments and assess higher order skills demand more complex structure and functional mechanisms of systems. Such systems are based on artificial intelligence, for example, e-rater [6], c-rater [15], Auto-marking [23], Atenea [20], and others. Unfortunately, essays and free-text responses are strongly subject and language dependent, and, as a consequence, a corresponding assessment system is narrowly focused. From the authors' viewpoint the concept mapping approach offers reasonable balance between requirements to assess higher levels of knowledge and complexity of an assessment system.

3 Concept mapping for knowledge assessment

Concept mapping can be used "to externalize and make explicit the conceptual knowledge that student holds in a knowledge domain" [7]. Concept maps are graphs, which include concepts as nodes and relations between them as arcs. Sometimes so called linking phrases are used. Usually concept maps are represented as a hierarchy with most general concepts at the top of the map and the more specific concepts placed at the lowest levels [17]. Concept maps can have different topologies, too [26].

Assessment based on concept maps can be characterized in terms of: 1) a task that invites a learner to provide evidence bearing on his/her knowledge structure in a domain, 2) a format for the learner's response, and 3) a scoring system to evaluate learner's concept map [21].

In order of issued task and required answer format, it is possible to provide learners with various levels of task difficulties, as well as assess different knowledge levels. One of the ways to deal with different degrees of difficultness is to issue tasks with different degree of directedness [22]. Directedness is connected with information provided to learners. Tasks vary from high-directed to low-directed. High-directed concept map tasks provide learners with concepts, connecting lines, linking phrases, and a map structure. In contrast, in a low-directed concept map task learners are free to decide which concepts and how many of them should be included and how they will be related in their maps. In other words, tasks can be divided in a subset of "fill-in tasks" where learners are provided with a blank structure of a map and lists of concepts and linking phrases, and in a subset of "construct a map tasks" where learners are free to make their choices.

"Fill-in tasks" can be different, too (Table 1). First, they vary on what is provided for learners (concept list, and/or linking phrases list), do they need to define something by themselves or do they need to use linking phrases at all. Second, they vary on how a pre-defined concept map structure is provided: does it contains already some filled concepts and/or linking phrases, or it is empty. "Construct a map tasks" can have the same variety as "fill-in tasks" and also constraints on a number of concepts needed to use in the concept map, and on a structure (should it be strictly hierarchical or have some cycles).

Difficultness degree can be provided also with different number of concepts. Assessments based on "construct a map tasks" more accurately evaluate differences in learners' knowledge structures and elicit more high-order cognitive processes [26].

Table 1. Fill-in tasks

Task	Is provided		Need to define	
	Concepts list	Linking phrases list	Concepts	Linking phrases
A	X	X		
B	X			X
C	X			
D		X	X	
E			X	X
F			X	

4 The intelligent knowledge assessment system

The first prototype of an intelligent assessment system based on concept maps and multiagent paradigm has been developed and tested [2]. Its main purpose is to allow a teacher put into practice the notion of process oriented learning when learners' knowledge is assessed continuously during a learning course. At the moment the system supports only one task: filling of a concept map structure. Two types of links are used. Important conceptual links show that relationships between the corresponding concepts are considered as important knowledge in a given learning course. Less important conceptual links specify desirable knowledge. The linking phrases and direction are not used in the developed prototype.

The system consists of three modules. The administrator module allows to manage data about learners and groups of learners, teachers and learning courses. The teacher's module supports a teacher in the development of concept maps and in examining of learners' final score. The learner's module includes tools for filling of concept maps provided by a teacher and for viewing feedback after his/her solution submission. The modules interact sharing a database which stores data about teachers and their learning courses, learners and groups of learners, teacher-created and learner-completed concept maps, learners' final score and system's users (Fig. 1).

The system's functionality and its client/server architecture are described in details in [2]. Use case diagrams of construction of a new concept map by a teacher and examining of learners' results, as well as concept map filling by a learner are given in [3].

The system supports the following scenario. A teacher divides a learning course into some stages. Using the developed system the teacher prepares concept maps for each stage in the following way. Concepts taught to learners at the first stage are included in the first concept map of the learning course. At the second stage learners acquire new concepts which the teacher adds to

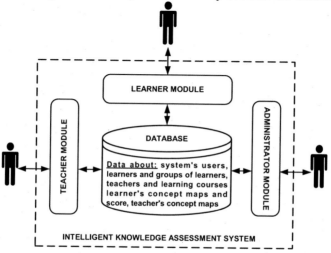

Fig. 1. The architecture of the system

concept map of the first stage without changing the relationships among already existing concepts. Thus, a concept map of each stage is an extension of a concept map of the previous stage. A concept map of the last stage displays all concepts in the learning course and relationships between them. During knowledge assessment learners get a structure of a concept map, which corresponds to the learning stage. At the first stage it is an empty structure with very few initial concepts defined by the teacher. In the subsequent stages new concepts are included in addition with those, which a learner already has correctly inserted during the previous stages. After finishing the concept map, the learner confirms his/her solution and the system compares concept maps of the learner and the teacher on the basis of five patterns described below. The final score and the learner's concept map are stored in the database. The learner receives feedback about correctness of his/her solution. At any time the teacher has an opportunity to examine a concept map completed by the learner and his/her score. Figure 2 displays the described scenario.

The system is a multiagent system, which consists of an intelligent agent for assessment of learners' knowledge level and a group of human agents, i.e. learners who are communicating with this agent. The intelligent assessment agent is a core of the system and its unique feature. It makes the basis of the learner's module and includes the communication, knowledge evaluation, interaction registering, and expert agents described in [2].

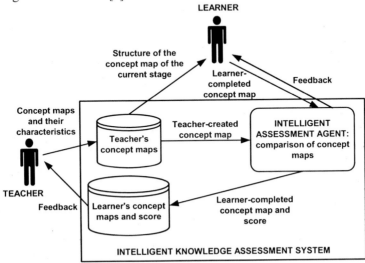

Fig. 2. The scenario of the system's operation

The intelligent assessment agent is responsible for the comparison of teacher's and learner's concept maps using an algorithm sensitive to arrangement of concepts. The main assumption is that the learner's understanding of relationships between concepts has the primary value, while the type of a link and a place of concepts within the structure of a concept map are the secondary things. Five patterns of learner solutions can be recognized by the agent (Fig. 3):

Pattern 1. The learner has related concepts as they are connected within a standard map of the teacher. In this case the learner receives 5 points regarding every important link and 2 points for less important link. Fig. 3b shows that the learner has related concepts A and E which fully matches the same relationship in the teacher-created concept map (Fig. 3a).

Pattern 2. The learner has defined a relationship, which does not exist in a concept map of the teacher. In this case he/she does not receive any points. In Fig. 3c it is shown that the learner has related concepts A and H, but such relationship does not exist in the teacher-created map (Fig. 3a).

Pattern 3. The learner's defined relationship exists in a standard map, the type of a link is correct, but at least one of concepts is placed in an incorrect place. The learner receives 80% from maximum score for that link. Fig. 3d shows that the learner has defined relationship between concepts B and D, which also exists in the teacher's map (Fig. 3a). Both concepts are placed in the incorrect places although the type of the link is correct.

Pattern 4. The learner's defined relationship exists in a standard map, the type of a link is wrong, and at least one of concepts is placed in an incorrect place. The learner receives 50% from maximum score for the correct link. This pattern is displayed in Fig. 3e. Comparing the learner defined relationship between A and F with teacher's one (Fig. 3a) it is easy to see that concept F is placed in an incorrect place, as well as type of the link between concepts is less important instead of important link.

Pattern 5. A concept is placed in a wrong place, but its place is not important. The learner receives maximum score for a corresponding link. Fig. 3f displays that the learner has exchanged concepts M and L by places comparing with the teacher-created concept map (Fig. 3a).

The developed system has been tested in four learning courses and seventy four students were involved (the testing example is described in [2]). The students positively evaluated the chosen approach to knowledge assessment, as well as functionality and user interface of the system (questions and student answers are given in [1]). They also stated desire to use such assessment technique in courses that will follow.

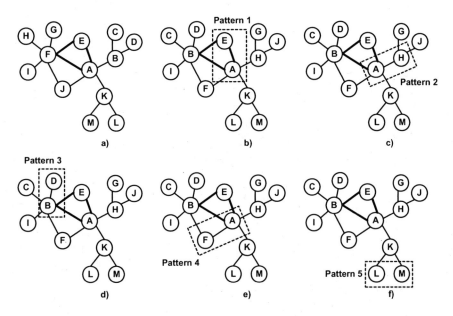

Fig. 3. Patterns for learner's solution evaluation with the intelligent assessment agent: a) a teacher-created concept map; b) – f) patterns within a learner-created concept map

The idea to computerized concept mapping is not new at all. A number of commercial and non-commercial graphical software packages and tools already exist, for example, AXON Idea Processor (web.singnet.com.sg/~axon2000/), Inspiration (www.inspiration.com), IHMC CmapTools (cmap.ihmc.us), which provide such functions as concept map construction, navigation and sharing, and can be used as a useful learning tool. These products do not assess created concept maps. This task can be solved by such tools as COMPASS [12] and the system described in [8]. The developed system has two discriminative features in comparison to them. Both known systems consider assessment as a discrete event, while the system described in this paper supports process oriented learning and allows the teacher to extend the initially created concept map for the new stage of assessment. The second unique feature is an algorithm that compares the teacher's and learner's concept maps and is sensitive to the arrangement and coherence of concepts. The third feature that is under development at the moment is concept map adaptive knowledge assessment described below in this paper.

5 Computer adaptive assessment

Computer adaptive assessment adapts tests to knowledge level of each learner [19], in the following way [25]. A learner receives an assessment item of average difficulty. If he/she does not answer this item or gives an incorrect answer, a less difficult item is presented. Otherwise, he/she gets a more difficult item. This process continues until the predetermined test termination criteria have been met. Therefore, learners with a low knowledge level do not respond to very difficult items, but learners at a high achievement level are not required to answer too simple items. Adaptive assessment provides more accurate conclusions about the actual knowledge level of each learner [19].

This kind of assessment is supported by some software products mentioned in Section 2, e.g., Questionmark™ Perception™ and TRIADS. There is also some research in this area. PASS module [11] is based on adaptive testing and adaptive questions techniques, and can be integrated in an Adaptive Educational Hypermedia System in order to provide personalized assessment selecting the appropriate question for a learner according to the questions' parameters, the assessment parameters, and the current learner's knowledge level. E-TESTER [13] automatically creates questions based on e-learning content provided to a learner.

6 Concept map based adaptive knowledge assessment

Functionality of the developed system can be essentially improved by providing adaptability of offered tasks to knowledge level of a learner. At the moment the same structure of a concept map and initial concepts are presented to all learners irrespective of a level of achievements of a particular learner. The idea of computer adaptive assessment allows to identify at least two possibilities. The first assumes to change the system's behavior when a learner fills the structure of a concept map. The system should monitor each learner's performance during the task. If it determines that the learner has some difficulties, it should intervene by filling some empty places with correct concepts. This process continues until only a few empty places will remain or the learner will complete the task. Despite of simplicity of the approach there are several unsolved issues:

- What methods will allow the system to determine when the learner has met difficulties? Whether the system should take into account how long the learner does nothing before inserting the next concept? Whether the system should track multiple movings of the same concept?
- What principle will the system use to put correct concepts into empty places?
- What number of empty places can serve as a criterion of the termination of system interventions?
- What should the system do with concepts which the learner has incorrectly inserted into structure of a concept map?

The second approach assumes enrichment of the system by tasks of various types. In this case adaptability can be implemented using the following scenario. At the first assessment stage all learners receive the task of the lowest directedness. If the system determines that a learner has some difficulties, it increases a degree of directedness. This process continues until the learner completes the task or reaches the highest degree of directedness. At the next stage the learner receives the task of directedness which he/she has achieved in the previous assessment. The level of task directedness can be increased in case if the learner has successfully completed the task in the previous assessment without lowering the directedness. Of course, it is necessary to store achieved degree of task directedness in a profile of the learner. There are uninvestigated aspects. First of all, it is necessary to find methods which will allow the system to determine that the learner has met some difficulties. The next problem is the large set of concept map based tasks ranging from "fill-in tasks" to "construct a map tasks" (Section 3). All of them cannot be implemented due to huge amount of needed work. Thus, it is necessary to select a subset of tasks. Last, but not least, is the development of the user interface which should offer new tools when the directedness degree of the task will increase.

7 Conclusions and future work

The paper focuses on computer adaptive assessment which main advantage is opportunity to present learners with tasks appropriate to their knowledge level. Concept maps can be successfully used as a core of adaptive assessment systems. Authors believe that usage of concept maps provides possibility to issue tasks with different level of difficultness and to assess fourth and fifth levels of knowledge according with Bloom's taxonomy. At the moment the analysis of the described possibilities concerning adaptive assessment using concept maps is at its early stage.

8 Acknowledgment

This work has been partly supported by the European Social Fund within the National Program "Support for the carrying out doctoral study program's and post-doctoral researches" project "Support for the development of doctoral studies at Riga Technical University".
The main results are outcomes of the research project "Concept maps and ontology based intelligent system for student knowledge self-assessment and process oriented knowledge control".

References

1. Anohina A, Graudina V, Grundspenkis J (2006) Intelligent system for learners' knowledge self-assessment and process oriented knowledge control based on concept maps and ontologies (accepted for Annual Proceedings of Vidzeme University College)
2. Anohina A, Grundspenkis J (2006) Prototype of multiagent knowledge assessment system for support of process oriented learning (accepted for the Proc. of the 7th Int. Baltic Conf. on DB&IS)
3. Anohina A, Stale G, Pozdnyakov D (2006) Intelligent system for student knowledge assessment (accepted for Proceedings of Riga Technical Univ.)
4. Bloom BS (1956) Taxonomy of educational objectives. Handbook I: The cognitive domain. David McKay Co Inc., New York
5. Bull J Introduction to computer-assisted assessment. Available at: http://asp2.wlv.ac.uk/celt/download.asp?fileid=44& detailsid=200008
6. Burstein J, Leacock C, Swartz R (2001) Automated evaluation of essays and short answers. In: Proc. of the 5th Int. Computer Assisted Assessment Conf., pp 41-45
7. Canas A (2003) A summary of literature pertaining to the use of concept mapping techniques and technologies for education and performance support
8. Chang KE, Sung YT, Chen SF (2001) Learning through computer-based concept mapping with scaffolding aid. J. Computer Assisted Learning, vol. 17: 21-33
9. Computer-assisted Assessment (CAA) Centre - http://www.caacentre.ac.uk
10. E-assessment. Available at: http://en.wikipedia.org/wiki/E-assessment

11. Gouli E, Papanikolaou KA, Grigoriadou M (2002) Personalizing assessment in adaptive educational hypermedia systems. In: Proc. of the 2nd Int. Conf. on Adaptive Hypermedia and Adaptive Web-Based Systems. Springer-Verlag, London, UK, pp 153-163
12. Gouli E, Gogoulou A, Papanikolaou K, Grigoriadou M (2004) COMPASS: an adaptive Web-based concept map assessment tool. Proc. of the 1st Int. Conf. on Concept Mapping
13. Guetl C, Dreher H, Williams R (2005) E-TESTER: A computer-based tool for auto-generated question and answer assessment. In: Proc. of the E-Learn 2005-World Conf. on E-Learning in Corporate, Government, Healthcare, and Higher Education, vol. 2005, no. 1, pp 2929-2936
14. Lambert G (2004) What is computer aided assessment and how can I use it in my teaching? (Briefing paper) Canterbury Christ Church University College
15. Leacock C, Chodorow M (2003) C-rater: scoring of short-answer questions. Computers and the Humanities, 37(4): 389-405
16. Mogey N, Watt H (1996) Chapter 10: The use of computers in the assessment of student learning. In: Stoner G (ed) Implementing Learning Technology. Learning Technology Dissemination Initiative, pp 50-57
17. Novak JD, Canas AJ (2006) The theory underlying concept maps and how to construct them. Technical Report IHCM CmapTools 2006-1
18. Oliver A (2000) Computer aided assessment - the pros and cons. Available at: http://www.herts.ac.uk/ltdu/learning/caa_procon.htm
19. Papanastasiou E (2003) Computer-adaptive testing in science education. In: Proc. of the 6th Int. Conf. on Computer Based Learning in Science, pp 965-971
20. Pérez D, Alfonseca E, Rodríguez P (2004) Application of the BLEU method for evaluating free-text answers in an e-learning environment. In: Proc. of the 4th Int. Language Resources and Evaluation Conf
21. Ruiz-Primo MA, Shavelson RJ (1996) Problems and issues in the use of concept maps in science assessment. J. Res. Sci. Teaching 33(6): 569-600
22. Ruiz-Primo MA (2004) Examining concept maps as an assessment tool. In: Proc. of the 1st Conf. in Concept Mapping
23. Sukkarieh JZ, Pulman SG, Raikes N (2003) Auto-marking: using computational linguistics to score short, free text responses. In: Proc. of the 29th Conf. of the Int. Association for Educational Assessment
24. Using computer assisted assessment to support student learning. The Social Policy and Social Work subject centre with the Higher Education Academy (SWAP) – http://www.swap.ac.uk/elearning/develop6.asp
25. What is CAA? (2005) Castle Rock Research Corp.- http://www.castlerockresearch.com/caa/Default.aspx
26. Yin Y, Vanides J, Ruiz-Primo MA, Ayala CC, Shavelson RJ (2005) Comparison of two concept-mapping techniques: implications for scoring, interpretation, and use. J. Res. Sci. Teaching, vol. 42, no. 2: 166-184

Term Clustering and Confidence Measurement in Document Clustering

Kristóf Csorba and István Vajk

Department of Automation Technology and Economics,
kristof@aut.bme.hu, vajk@aut.bme.hu

1 Introduction

Document clustering is the classification of documents into several groups based on a given classification criteria, like the topic similarity. In a supervised learning scenario, the system extracts features from labeled examples and learns to identify documents of the same categories. A large family of methods is based on vector spaces, where documents are represented by vectors in a space of features, like occurrences of the various terms. Every used term (not a stopword and not too rare) is assigned to a feature and the coordinate of the document along this dimension is a function of the occurrence of the term in the documents. A frequently used weighting scheme family is the TFIDF (term-frequency, inverse document frequency) scheme [1].

This paper presents a novel technique for the clustering of documents in scenarios, where there is no strict need to cluster all the documents, and the system is allowed to return some results declared as unsure. This way we achieve a much cleaner result by rejecting the classification of documents with ambiguous topic. The rejection is decided based on a confidence value described in this paper. This has an advantage for the term filtering as well, because some documents are allowed to get ambiguous because of the removal of the majority of its terms.

Our clustering technique uses a vector space model, so we start the procedure by creating the document term matrix (X) with column vectors representing the documents and row vectors standing for the various terms. The values of X are in this case the occurrence numbers of the terms in the given documents.

[4] showed that the roles of documents and terms can be swapped regarding the clustering: we can not only cluster the documents in the space of terms, but the

terms can be clustered in the space of the documents as well. The information bottleneck method aims to perform the document clustering in a more compact feature space. This is achieved by the clustering of the features by preserving as much information for the document clustering as possible. That means features with similar influence on the clustering result are merged.

In this case the information bottleneck method means the employment of a term clustering step before the document clustering, to create term clusters. This way the documents are classified in the space of the term clusters instead of single terms. This is a very strong dimensionality reduction, as only a much smaller number of term clusters in needed for the correct classification, than the number of available individual terms, even after traditional term filtering.

Further parts of this paper are organized as follows: Section 2. describes the novel algorithm for creating term clusters, Section 3. presents how the document clustering works with the term clusters created, and how confidence is measured. Section 4. presents experimental results and finally conclusions are made in Section 5.

2 New term cluster creation method

In the literature the term clustering of the double clustering is usually performed by an unsupervised clustering algorithm [1]. K-means is often used together with the cosine distance measure for this purpose.

Our novel method aims to perform a supervised term clustering together with a strong term filtering. It selects for every target cluster the terms, which allow the best classification of the documents. The term clusters are created iteratively until there is a need for additional ones. The terms not used in any of these term clusters are discarded and not used in the later part of the clustering procedure. Not surprisingly the terms in the first term clusters are the most topic specific terms of the given topics. After every document class has been covered by one term, additional term clusters can be created to increase the number of successfully clustered documents. This is important because all the documents not containing any of these most important terms are mapped into a null—vector in the new feature space and cannot be assigned to any of the document clusters.

The term cluster creation algorithm uses the frequently used clustering performance measures precision, recall and their harmonic average, the F-measure. These are defined as follows: let us suppose we have to select the elements of a document class as good as possible. The result is a document cluster, which contains documents from the given class, and some misclassified ones from other classes. Precision is the amount of correctly selected documents among all selected document. Recall is the rate of correctly selected documents among all documents in the target class. These two measures are usually used together, as none of them is enough on its own: maximal precision can be achieved by selecting one single document from the target class, as there will not be any misclassifications. On the other hand a maximal recall can be achieved by selecting every document. That ensures the selection of every document in the target class, but leads to many misclassified documents as well. For this reason, F-measure is defined as their harmonic middle to enable optimizations based on both criteria.

2.1 The two steps of term cluster creation

The term cluster creation procedure consists of two main steps: the building and the reduction steps. The building step collects the terms which identify the target document class with the highest precision. The reduction step eliminates the redundancies. Overview of the procedure is shown in Fig. 1.

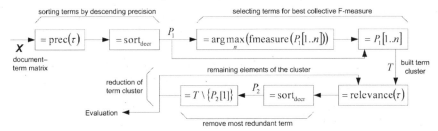

Fig. 1. The term cluster creation procedure.

In the term cluster creation a term is treated to select a document if it occurs in it. Term cluster building for a given document class starts with sorting the terms by descending precision for the selection of the documents of the given class. It then iteratively adds the terms in this order (Fig. 2.)

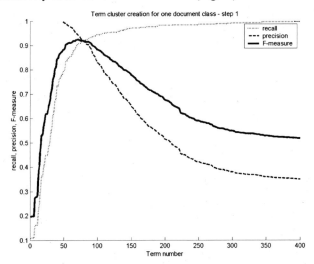

Fig. 2. First step of term cluster creation.

After adding the terms occurring only in the documents of the target class, the precision will begin to decrease. It will still increase the recall of course, because the term cluster will select more and more documents. This leads to a maximum of the F-measure, after which the recall increment cannot compensate the falling precision. Terms are added to the term cluster till this point.

At this point the term cluster may contain terms, which select the same documents. The aim of the second step is to remove such redundancies. The redundancy of a term τ is measured by the change rate of the precision if the term is removed from the term cluster.

$$redundancy(\tau) = \frac{recall(T \setminus \tau)}{recall(\tau)}, \tag{2.1.1}$$

where T is the set of terms in the term cluster.

The redundancies have to be recalculated after every term removal, but as the figure shows, we can expect relative many terms with high redundancy. The second step removes iteratively the terms by selecting always the one with the highest redundancy in a greedy way (Fig. 3.).

As term removal continues, the recall of the remaining term cluster decreases. If it reaches a predefined minimal recall value, the reduction step terminates. The lower the minimal recall limit is, the more terms can be removed from the term cluster.

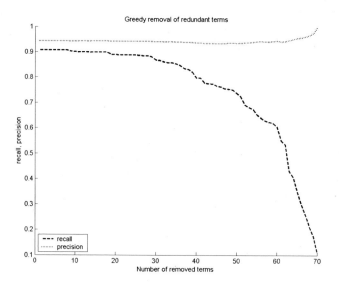

Fig. 3. Second step of term cluster creation.

The term clusters from the document clustering are created after each other for the different target document classes with the same, predefined minimal recall limit. As every term can occur in at least one term cluster, after a cluster has been created, all the terms in it are removed from the set of available terms. Theoretically the term clusters can be created after each other until every term is assigned to a cluster.

2.2 Term clusters for multiple document classes

If we have some document classes with relative near topics, we may expect some terms to occur in more document classes. If a term can select documents from two classes, it can still be useful to separate these two classes from the others. This means we can create term clusters for two document classes as well.

Our method first creates a term cluster for every document class. These are called the basic term clusters. After that the remaining terms are used to build the additional clusters. In every iteration we create a term cluster for every document class and document class pair. Among these temporarily term clusters only the one with the highest F-measure is used as a term cluster in the clustering system.

3 Document clustering and confidence

Once the term clusters are created, they can be used to assign documents to document clusters. Starting from the document term matrix X, a document term-cluster matrix Y has to be calculated by applying the clustering of the terms. This is done by merging of the row vectors in X belonging into the same term cluster into a single row vector in Y:

$$Y_{\theta,\bullet} = \sum_{\tau \in T_\theta} X_{\tau,\bullet} \,,$$

(3.1)

where T_θ is the set of terms in the θ-th term cluster. The same operation can be expressed with a matrix multiplication by defining

$$C_{\theta,\tau} = \begin{cases} 1 \; iff \; \tau \in T\theta \\ 0 \; else \end{cases},$$

(3.2)

where τ is the term index. In this case, $Y=CX$. The document clusters can be defined as a linear combination of the term clusters. The matrix Q contains the weights of the term clusters for the document classes similar to Y for the term clustering. This enables the calculation of Z, the basis of the decision as $Z=QY$.

During the supervised learning of the clustering system we have to assign a weight for every (document class; term cluster) pair. The later a term cluster was created, the more good separating terms were already assigned to a previous cluster, which leads to a lower quality term cluster.

$$Q_{\lambda,\theta} = \begin{cases} \dfrac{1}{\left(\max(d,\theta)-d+1\right)^2} & \textit{iff } \lambda \in \Lambda_\theta \\ 0 & \textit{else} \end{cases}$$

(3.3)

where d is the number of document classes and Λ_θ is the set of document classes, for which the term cluster with index θ was created. This means that for a given document class λ the Q matrix has nonzero weight for the term clusters, which were created to cover this document class. As the index of the term cluster increases, the quality is expected to decrease and so the weight gets smaller.

3.1 Decision making an its confidence

The matrix Z can be treated to contain scores for every (document; document cluster) pair. Each document is assigned to the document cluster, for which its score is maximal. That means the document δ is assigned to the document class λ for which

$$\lambda(\delta) = \arg\max_\lambda \left\{ Z_{\lambda,\delta} \right\}$$

(3.1.1)

The confidence of this decision can be expressed by the ratio of the maximal and the second maximal score from Z:

$$conf(\delta) = \frac{Z_{\lambda(\delta),\delta}}{\max_{\lambda \neq \lambda(\delta)} \left\{ Z_{\lambda,\delta} \right\}}$$

(3.1.2)

As the confidence value can be infinite, if only one document class gets non-zero score, we are going to maximize the values to 5 in the following figures.

Fig. 4. and Fig. 5. present the histogram of confidence, if we use only the basic term clusters. If we define a minimal confidence limit, under which we declare the result to be ambiguous, we can avoid some of the false classifications and move them to the unsure category. There are still confident, but false results, which is caused by their infinite confidence. That means, that unfortunately they contain only a few terms used in the term sets, but all of these terms belong to another topic cluster, which leads to a zero score for the correct cluster.

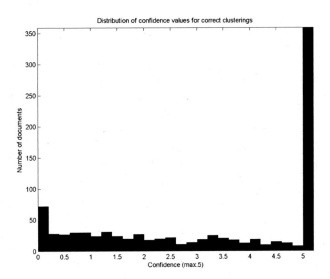

Fig. 4. Example confidence histogram for correctly classified cases.

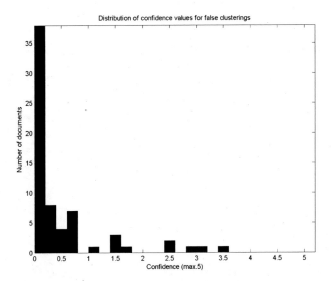

Fig. 5. Example for confidence histogram for misclassified cases.

If there are more term clusters (with even lower separation abilities), the confidences are often lower, but the confidence of the misclassifications is hardly always below 2. That means we can declare results with confidence below 2 to be ambiguous in the current case. This filtering will move most of the false results into the unsure category. The confidence measure shows a behavior one would expect.

3.2 Cascading of classifiers

If we can build a classifier with a training set, which is capable to decide, which results are sure and which are ambiguous, we can easily route the unsure results into a new classifier, which is trained specialized for the ambiguous cases of the previous stage. In this way, we get a cascade of classifiers as shown in Fig. 6.

To train such a cascade the training document set has to be directed into the input of the first classifier. Every document labeled as unsure by this stage can be forwarded into the next classifier. This composition is an effective way for further improvement of the classification quality, because the individual elements can be optimized for maximum precision: the rate of undecided cases gets much less important, which allows to pay less attention to the recall.

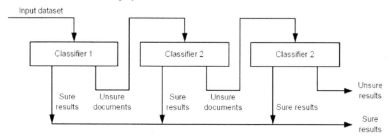

Fig. 6. Cascade of classifiers.

4 Experiments

The experiments presented in the followings were performed on a part of the commonly used dataset 20Newsgroups [2]. The dataset contains news in 20 categories with 1000, usually short documents each. For our evaluation purposes 3 categories were used: "alt.atheism", "comp.graphics" and "rec.autos". The set of 3000 documents were divided into a training set with 2000 documents and a testing set with 1000 documents.

First we examined the basic term sets created by the algorithm for the three document clusters. Some of the terms are shown in Table 1. They are definitely important terms of the given topics.

Table 1. Terms in the three basic term clusters

atheism, Christianity, church, Bible, Christians, moral, objective, belief, morality, Christian, religion, notion, beliefs, atheist, murder, context, gods
viewer, TIFF, processing, shareware, polygon, GIF, JPEG, formats, VESA, pixel, VGA, Windows, Mac, pixels, rendering, format, PC
insurance, vehicle, radar, mph, gear, detector, suspension, GM, lights

Using the two minimal recall limits 0.6 and 0.8 we compared the precision of the term clusters the algorithm created. Fig. 7 shows the results. The lower minimal recall limit enables the removal of more terms from the clusters. This increases the precision. Beside this effect, lower limit removes more terms which leads to more possible term clusters from the given set of all terms.

Using only the first t term clusters we can control the number of used terms. As this increases, precision increases slightly, because the few misclassified documents are moved into the category of ambiguous results. The increment in performance is shown in Fig. 8. The number of terms begins with the total term number of the base term clusters, as before creating these, the overall performance of the system cannot be measured.

Although the increment of the precision is very useful, it leads to a strong decrement in the rate of sure results, because using more terms to calculate scores decreases the confidence values.

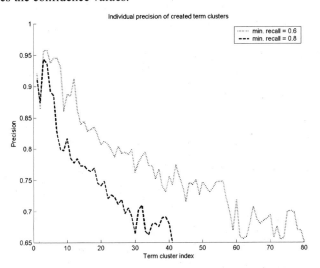

Fig. 7. Precision of the created term clusters for various minimal recall limits.

Using classification units created with high minimal recall and confidence limits, the performance of a cascade was analyzed. Fig. 9. shows the number of correctly, false and unsure assigned documents. The number of correct classifications increases clearly in the beginning, but more than 3 elements in the cascade seem not to be useful. Most of the unsure documents in the beginning are classified correctly by the second and third stages and only a few documents are assigned to the false topic.

A disadvantage of the cascade is the increasing number of used terms, as the second and third stages in the measurement above use nearly 400 terms together, although the first element used only 60. The reason for the increasing term need is the fact, that the documents reaching the second stage cannot be classified with the most frequent high-precision terms anymore. Rarer terms need to be used, from which the system needs more for a confident classification.

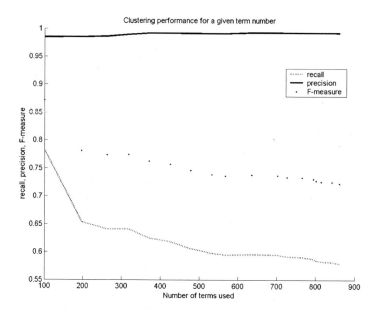

Fig. 8. Clustering performance with a given term number.

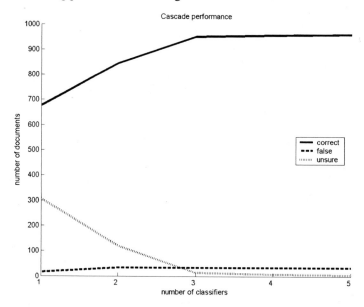

Fig. 9. Performance of a cascade of classifiers.

5 Conclusions

We have presented a novel term clustering and term filtering technique, which aims to cover the document classes in a greedy way by selecting the terms with the highest precision and after achieving the maximal F-measure, it removes redundant terms to minimize the term cluster size. Combined with the confidence measurement in the document clustering procedure, an effective way was shown for the document clustering in situations, where the entire document set does not have to be clustered, because a 30-40% ambiguous result is acceptable. This is often the case in text retrieval systems, where as much as possible documents have to be retrieved, but discarding of the ambiguous documents is still better than risking the false classification.

If the current application does not allow discarding the unsure documents, the base technique is still applicable by cascading multiple classifiers. Every element of a cascade becomes the unsure results of the previous stage as input. This way every cascade element will be specialized to different document types. This allows a high precision clustering, but the more elements we use in a cascade, the more terms are needed for the whole procedure.

6 Acknowledgments

This work has been fund of the Hungarian Academy of Sciences for control research and the Hungarian National Research Fund (grant number T042741).

References

1. Singhal (2001) Modern information retrieval: A brief overview. In: IEEE Data Engineering Bulletin, vol. 24, no. 4, pp. 35–43.
2. K. Lang (1995) Newsweeder: Learning to filter netnews. In: ICML, pp. 331–339.
3. L. Li and W. Chou (2002) Improving latent semantic indexing based classifier with information gain. In: tech. rep., May 16 2002.
4. N. Slonim and N. Tishby (2000) Document clustering using word clusters via the information bottleneck method. In: Proceedings of the 23rd Annual International ACM SIGIR Conference on Research and Development in Information Retrieval, Clustering, pp. 208–215.

Automation of the Ontology Axioms Transformation into Information Processing Rules Model

Olegas Vasilecas, Diana Bugaite

Department of Information Systems, Vilnius Gediminas Technical University, Lithuania. Olegas.Vasilecas@fm.vtu.lt, diana@isl.vtu.lt

1 Introduction

The business rule approach is used in information systems to represent domain knowledge and to maintain rules systems efficiently in volatile business environment. But firstly, it is necessary to determine the business rules and ensure that the rules are appropriate. The important requirement for developing of the rules model is to reduce efforts, costs and time. This requirement can be implemented by the explicit use of enterprise knowledge for generation of rules, which can be implemented as modern DBMSs triggers.

In computer science, ontologies are used to represent real-world domain knowledge. Therefore, knowledge represented by ontology can be used for generation of rules. Moreover, ontology expressed in a formal way [1] can be transformed into rules model automatically.

In this paper, a method for representing knowledge by ontology transformation into the rule model is presented. The method is based on transforming ontology axioms into information processing rules.

2 Related Work

A definition of a business rule (BR) depends on the context in which it is used. From the business system perspective, a BR is a statement that defines or constrains some aspects of a particular business. At the business system level, BRs are expressed in a declarative manner. [2].

From the perspective of information systems (IS), a BR is a statement, which defines the major rules of information processing using a rule-based language [3].

At the execution level (or software systems level), rules are statements that are transferred to the executable rules, like active DBMS triggers.

Information-processing rules are used in ISs to process the required information correctly. These information-processing rules are derived from BRs, which are taken from the business system level. In practice, information-processing rules are implemented by executable rules. Information-processing rules should be expressed as ECA (event-condition-action) rules to be implemented by executable rules, like active DBMS SQL triggers.

Therefore it is necessary to determine and elicit rules from the application domain and develop ECA rules.

One of the possible ways to solve the defined problems is the use of the domain ontology.

The term 'ontology' is borrowed from philosophy, where Ontology means a systematic account of Existence. In computer science, the definition of ontology is rather confusing. By [4] all definitions of the term 'ontology' attempt to explain what an ontology is from three different aspects: the content of an ontology, the form of an ontology and the purpose of an ontology.

Gruber defined ontology as a specification of a conceptualisation [5]. This definition explains the content of ontology, but it is confusing because it does not explain what a conceptualisation is. According to Genesereth, a conceptualisation includes the objects and their relations which an agent presumes to exist in the world. The process of a conceptualisation is the process of mapping an object or a relation in the world to a representation in our mind. [4]

Ontology defines the basic terms and their relationships comprising the vocabulary of an application domain and the axioms for constraining the relationships among terms [2]. This definition explains what an ontology looks like [4].

In the simplest case, an ontology describes a hierarchy of concepts related by particular relationships (like, is-a, part-of, e.g.). In more sophisticated cases, constraints are added to restrict the value space of concepts and relationships. They, for example, express cardinality, possible length (like, maxLength, minLength...)... In most sophisticated cases, suitable axioms are added in order to express complex relationships between concepts and to constrain their intended interpretation [1].

Ontologies are being built today for many reasons. The reason of creating an ontology depends on research field and an application area where it is going to be used. In this paper, ontology is used for its transformation into the rules model.

3 On Ontology Axioms Transformation into Business Rules

In the application domain or ontology, to which the BRs belong, they are not always expressed in terms of ECA rules. Some of these BRs have explicit or implicit condition and action parts. The missing condition can always be substituted with a default condition state as TRUE. Some BRs may have no explicit action since they can state what kind of transition from one data state to another is not admissible. [6]. But the majority of these BRs do not define explicitly or implicitly the event. There are three possible ways to trigger rules: automatically trigger all rules every time when any related event occurs, trigger rules manually when somebody decides it is necessary, specify necessary events and link them to actual rules. In this research, the third way was used for rules triggering, since the specification of the events and their linking to actual rules enable the system automatically react to the defined events and perform the defined operations, e.g. trigger rules automatically. Moreover, it is not necessary to execute all rules when some event occurs. Only related rules are executed.

Obviously, it is confusing to form information-processing rules of ECA form and consequently implement them by executable rules.

Since BRs are captured in ontology by axioms and constraints of relationships among terms [2], ontology axioms (and ontology as a whole) represented in a formal way can be transformed into BRs (and into conceptual schema) automatically. Moreover, it facilitates BRs transformation into consequent information-processing and executable rules.

The general schema of axioms transformation into BRs is presented in the Fig. 1. It is independent of implementation.

Axioms don't stand alone in ontology. Since axioms define constraints on terms, terms are used to specify axioms. Therefore, those terms and their relationships should be transformed into (conceptual) schema in parallel with transformation of axioms into BRs. For the sake of simplicity ontology axioms transformation into BRs is analysed only.

Axioms define the state in which the domain should be. E.g., axioms can have clearly defined action and, sometimes, condition. Events are not defined in axioms. Therefore, it is necessary to develop some rules to transform ontology axioms and events into ECA rules.

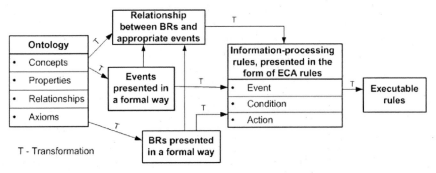

Fig. 1. Transformation of ontology axioms into ECA rules and consequent executable rules.

By [7, 8, 9, 10, 11] events are defined by terms used in ontology vocabulary.

Terms can be used to link axioms with appropriate events, since ontology axioms and events are defined by terms used in ontology vocabulary.

4 A Case Study of Ontology Axioms Transformation into Rules Model

The ontology for a particular business enterprise was created using Protégé-2000 ontology development tool to support the statement of the authors that ontology axioms and events can be transformed into information-processing rules and consequent executable rules. We chose Protégé-2000 to develop the ontology because it allows the open source software to be installed locally. A free version of the software provides all features and capabilities required for the present research as well as being user-friendly. [12]

The axioms are implemented in Protégé-2000 ontology by the Protégé Axiom Language (PAL) constraints. PAL is a superset of the first-order logic which is used for writing strong logical constraints [13].

PAL provides a set of special-purpose frames to hold the constraints. PAL constraints are presented as instances of the *:PAL-CONSTRAINT* class. The class has the following slots [14]:

- *:PAL-name*, which holds a label for the constraint;
- *:PAL-documentation*, which holds a natural language description of the constraint;
- *:PAL-range*, which holds the definition of local and global variables that appear in the statement;
- *:PAL-statement*, which holds the sentence of the constraint.

The main part of the PAL constraint is the *PAL-statement*, which can be mapped to the BR and consequently to the ECA rule.

The EZPal Tab plug-in is used to facilitate acquisition of PAL constraints without having to understand the language itself. Using a library of templates based on reusable patterns of previously encoded axioms, the interface allows users to compose constraints using a "fill-in-the-blanks" approach. [15].

Examples of definition of axiom using the EZPal Tab are the following:

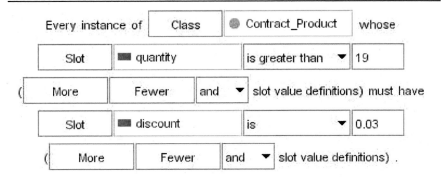

Fig. 2. An example of axiom creation using the EZPal templates.

The non-formal interpretation of the axiom is:

The discount of a contract product depends on quantity of units of a contract product customer buys per time.
If quantity is greater then 19, discount is 3 %.

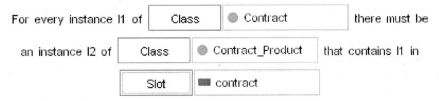

Fig. 3. An example of axiom creation using the EZPal templates.

The non-formal interpretation of the axiom is:

Every Contract must have a Contract_Product.

PAL constraints and SQL triggers were analysed in details to automate constraints transformation into SQL triggers. The schema of PAL constraints transformation into SQL triggers is presented in Fig. 4.

The main parts of PAL constraints (denoted by grey clouds) are transformed into the main parts of SQL triggers (denoted by grey clouds). 'PAL-documentation', 'PAL-name' and 'PAL-range' are transformed into SQL 'Comment', 'trigger_name', 'table | view' without significant changes. 'if statement or condition' and 'action or possible state' are transformed into 'sql_statement'.

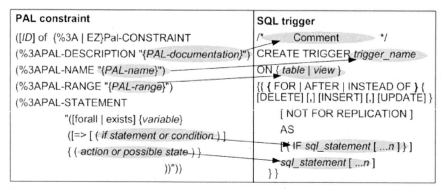

Fig. 4. The detailed schema of automatic transformation of ontology axioms into SQL triggers.

An event of a trigger (DELETE, INSERT, UPDATE) should be taken from defined events in ontology.

The relationships between axioms and events are determined by classes, used to define particular axioms and events. An example of the event is the following:

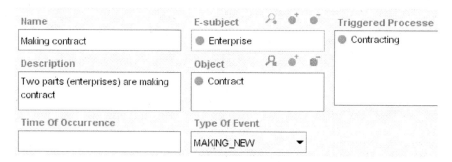

Fig. 5. An example of the event 'Making contract'.

The event 'Making contract' (Fig. 5) and the axiom 'contract-must-have-contract-product' (Fig. 3) use the same class 'Contract' in their definitions. Moreover, the axiom 'contract-must-have-contract-product' is directly related with the axiom 'discount-3-percent' (Fig. 2). Therefore, the following ECA rule can be generated:

When '*Making contract*', if '*quantity*' of a '*Contract_product*' '*is greater than 19*', then '*discount*' of a '*Contract_product*' '*is 3 %*'.

The plug-in for automatic transformation of constraints is under development now. The consequent plug-in for ontology transformation into the conceptual model is described in [16], since both axioms don't stand alone in ontology and constraints don't stand alone in conceptual model.

The next step of the research is to develop the necessary plug-in and full case study employing the proposed concepts and ideas of the proposed method.

5 Conclusions and Future Work

The analysis of the related works on knowledge-based information system development using the domain ontology shows that the business rules are part of knowledge represented by the ontology. Business rules are captured in ontology by axioms and relationships-constraints of the terms.

The method for ontology transformation into business rules, which are implemented by information-processing rules, was offered. We argue that the ontology axioms can be used to create a set of information-processing rules. They can be transformed into ECA rules and then to active DBMS triggers. Such transformation is possible, since ontology axioms can be mapped into active DBMS SQL triggers.

The experiment shows that the suggested approach can be used to transform ontology axioms described in a formal way into SQL triggers. For this transformation, a suitable tool – Protégé-2000 – was chosen.

PAL constraints can be transformed into ECA rules only manually at the moment. The plug-in for automatic transformation of constraints is under development now.

The next step in our research should be developing prototype and the refinement of the suggested method.

References

1. Guarino N (1998) Formal Ontology and Information Systems. In: FOIS'98, Trento, Italy, 1998. Amsterdam, IOS Press, pp 3-15
2. Bugaite D, Vasilecas O (2006) Ontology-Based Elicitation of Business Rules. In: Nilsson AG et al. (eds.) Advances in Information Systems Development, Springer, Sweden, pp 795-806
3. Lebedys E, Vasilecas O (2004) Analysis of business rules modelling languages. In: IT'2004, Lithuania, Technologija, pp 487-494
4. Yang X (2001) Ontologies and How to Build Them. (March, 2006): http://www.ics.uci.edu/~xwy/publications/area-exam.ps
5. Gruber T (2004) What is an Ontology? (March, 2004): http://www-ksl.stanford.edu/kst/what-is-an-ontology.html
6. Valatkaite I, Vasilecas O (2004) On Business Rules Approach to the Information Systems Development. In: Linger H et al. (eds.) Proc. of ISD'2003, Australia, Kluwer Academic/Plenum Publishers, pp 199-208
7. Cilia M, Bornhovd C, Buchmann AP (2005) Event Handling for the Universal Enterprise. Information Technology and Management - Special Issue on Universal Enterprise Integration, 5(1): 123-148
8. Chen H, Perich F, et al. (2004) SOUPA: Standard Ontology for Ubiquitous and Pervasive Applications. In: Proc. of the First Annual International Conference on Mobile and Ubiquitous Systems: Networking and

Services, Boston, (March, 2006): http://ebiquity.umbc.edu/get/a/publication/
105.pdf.

9. Event Ontology. KendraBase - server 3 (March, 2006):
http://base4.kendra.org.uk/event_ontology.

10. eBiquity Event Ontology :: Classes and Properties. SchenaWeb (March,
2006): http://www.schemaweb.info/schema/SchemaInfo.aspx?id=114.

11. Chen H (2004) SOUPA Ontology 2004-06, Semantic web in ubicomp,
(March, 2006): http://pervasive.semanticweb.org/soupa-2004-06.html.

12. Jakkilinki R, Sharda N, Georgievski M (2005) Developing an Ontology
for Teaching Multimedia Design and Planning. (September, 2005):
http://sci.vu.edu.au/~nalin/MUDPYOntologyPreprintV2.pdf.

13. Grosso W (2002) The Protégé Axiom Language and Toolset ("PAL").
(September, 2005): http://protege.stanford.edu/plugins/paltabs/pal-
documentation/index.html.

14. PAL Conceptual Framework (2005) (February, 2005): http://protege.stanford.
edu/plugins/paltabs/pal-documentation/lang_framework.html.

15. Hou J (2005) EZPal Tab, Stanford University (March, 2006):
http://protege.stanford.edu/plugins/ezpal/.

16. Vasilecas O, Bugaite D, Trinkunas J (appear) (2006) On Approach for
Enterprise Ontology Transformation into Conceptual Model. In: Rachev
B, Smirkarov A (eds.): Proc. of the International Conference on Computer Systems and Technologies "CompSysTech'06", Varna, Bulgaria, pp
281-289

Using Common Process Patterns for Semantic Web Service Composition

Xiaofeng Du, William Song, Malcolm Munro

Durham University, South Road, Durham, DH1 3LE, UK, {xiaofeng.du, w.w.song, malcolm.munro}@durham.ac.uk

Abstract: The web service composition has become an activity research area to improve the usability of web services. By composing web services, enterprise can rapidly deliver cheaper and better business services to their customers. However, how to efficiently select and compose required services is a challenge. The challenge is caused by the gap between customer requirement and service description because the current service description technology lacks abstraction and has no semantics. Many research works on service composition are integrating semantics to solve the service description problem, but they have not sufficiently addressed abstraction. In this paper we propose an approach, named common process pattern, which can improve the efficiency of service discovery and composition. A common process pattern instance abstractly describes a set of services and their relationships based on a commonly used business process. Because of the abstraction provided by this approach, a common process pattern instance's description can be much closer to a customer requirement than a technical service description. Therefore, the service discovery becomes easier.

1 Introduction

Web service composition has become a major research area [3] whose outcome can support efficient and effective business integration so that the enterprises can rapidly deliver better business services to their customers with low cost. How the existing services can be efficiently selected and composed to fulfil the customer requests is a challenge. One of the aspects causing the difficulty is the gap between customer requirement and service description. A customer requirement is normally abstract and business oriented, but a description of a service is concrete and technology oriented. The customers considered here are general business customers who have little or no technical knowledge about the actual services, e.g. parameters type and communication protocols described in a WSDL [2] file. So it is very unlikely to get a customer's request like "*call an air ticket booking service with input parameter: String 'airport code', integer 'number of ticket', String 'outgoing date', and String 'return date' and followed by a hotel booking service with input parameter: String 'location', integer 'number of people', String 'start date', and integer 'number of days'"*. Rather they may state the request like "*I want to go to New York on 1ˢᵗ of March for a week*". Customers are only interested in the abstract business services which the company can provide for them, not the concrete services used to achieve these business services. Therefore, a mapping from the abstract business services to the concrete services is crucial for efficient service composition and fulfilling customer requirements with low cost. Martin et al. [8] introduced a semantic language, named OWL-S, to add a semantic layer on the top of WSDL service description and provide syntax to describe high level composite processes. However, the OWL-S is still insufficient to bridge the gap because it does not address enough abstraction in the service description. In this paper we propose a pattern based approach to overcome the abstraction problem of service description in order to bridge the gap between the customer requirement and concrete service description.

The main contributions of this paper are the following:

- Introduces a common process pattern approach.
- Builds up a stable abstract description layer on the top of existing services in order to solve the service availability problem in the open Internet service pool.
- Extends the OWL-S language to describe abstract services and common process pattern and implements a prototype to implement the common process pattern.

The rest of the paper is organized as follows. Section 2 discusses the generic approach to service composition and requirement decomposition. Section 3 presents the common process pattern approach together with its definition and description language, and how it can fit into the business model. Section 4 discusses how to implement the common process pattern by using our prototype. Some related work is discussed in section 5. Finally, Section 6 presents the conclusions and future work.

2 Generic Approach

The generic approach (Top-down approach) for mapping the customer request to the concrete services uses knowledge decomposition process which is similar as people solving a problem using their existing knowledge. A customer requirement can be decomposed into several tasks and each task can be further decomposed into subtasks until each of the subtasks is primitive task [5] which can be possibly accomplished by an existing service.

Once the requirement decomposition is done, the business processes rules and AI planning techniques [5] [13] can be applied to form those tasks into a workflow. The dataflow among tasks is based on the data dependency of the required services and the control flow is based on the business processes rules. The services for achieving the tasks in the workflow are located dynamically by using the semantic matching methods [9] based on the specified requirements and goals of each task. Figure 1 illustrates a request decomposition process and a possible workflow after the request decomposition. The dashed lines represent the data flow among the concrete services.

From previous discussion we can summarise some problems exposed by the top-down approach.

- After the request decomposition, the requirements for each task are specified so implicitly that the automatic service discovery is very hard to achieve.
- Due to the uncertainty of customer requirements, it is not guaranteed that the required services can be found because such a required service may not exist at all.
- The workflow formation at runtime is difficult, so is the semantics of input/output parameters to be determined at run time [7]. For example, an address has been provided by a directory service, but it is very confused for a delivery service to decide whether this address is a "from address" or "to address" at runtime. One solution could be that all kind of addresses are explicitly specified in an ontology, and then this ontology will be extremely large.
- Some common requirements and widely used non-primitive tasks have to be repeatedly decomposed into primitive tasks.

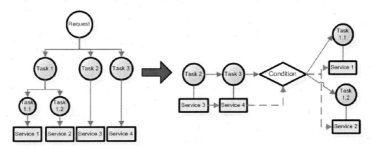

Fig. 1. Request decomposition process and a possible workflow.

3 Common Process Pattern

To address the problems discussed in the previous section, this paper introduces an approach which is a combination of the generic top-down approach with a bottom-up approach, termed Common Process Pattern (CPP). A CPP instance is an abstract representation of a solution for a common business process. It contains

abstract specifications to explicitly specify how the business process can be performed and what kinds of services are required. It is generated using the bottom-
up approach which is started with existing web services rather than customer
requirements. The existing services can be composed together based on the service
properties analysis and semantic relationships between services. Many composite
services can be generated from a large service pool, but some of them may not be
useful or meaningful. Then the top-down approach can be applied here to evaluate
whether the new composite services are useful for fulfilling customer requirements. If a composite service can achieve a customer requirement or a non-
primitive task, it can be considered as useful because thereafter the requirement or
non-primitive task does not need to be decomposed anymore. Then the useful
composite service can be abstracted into a CPP instance, which can be described
using an extended OWL-S semantic language, for future reuse. Figure 2 illustrates
the CPP instance generation process.

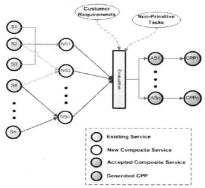

Fig. 2. CPP Generation Process, combination of top-down and bottom-up
approaches.

3.1 Motivation and context

A CPP instance can be considered as an abstract composite service. The difference
between a CPP instance and a composite service is that the CPP instance only
defines how the services can be composed together, i.e. the workflow structure including control flow and dataflow, and the explicit specifications of required services. It does not link to any concrete service. When a CPP instance is executed,
the required services are dynamically linked. This technique can prevent the risks
brought about by the unavailability of hard coded services in a composite service.
Because the CPP instance is generated using bottom-up approach, it is guaranteed
that each CPP instance is executable because all the required services exist. Although some existing services may be not available temporarily at runtime, other
services with the same type can be found and used as replacement if we assume
the service pool is large enough. The usability of the CPP instance is also guaran-

teed because it has been evaluated by current customer requirements or non-primitive tasks using the top-down approach.

In general a pattern is "the abstraction from a concrete form which keeps recurring in specific non-arbitrary contexts" [11]. The key characteristics of a pattern are abstraction and recurrence. Although this definition is used to define the pattern for object-oriented design, it is still suitable to define the characteristics of other kinds of pattern. Refer to the CPP approach introduced in this paper, a CPP instance can represent a solution for recurring business processes and give the abstract description of the solution and requirement for this recurring business process. An image of a CPP instance is illustrated in figure 3. The circle holes in the diagram represent the missing service that need to be filled in. The thin dashed lines represent the data flow between services and the control structure. The clouds represent the requirements specification for each required service. Because a CPP instance is defined as an abstract composite service, see section 3.2, it can act as a building block to build up other CPP instances. This is also a key feature of CPP approach because it enables CPP instances to build up a hierarchical structure in order to fit for different abstraction levels.

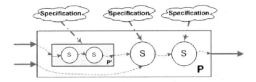

Fig. 3. An Image of the CPP Approach.

A four layers business model proposed by Song [15] shows how an enterprise is operated, see figure 4. The CPP approach can be nicely fitted into this model. It can help to ease the construction of the workflow. A CPP instance describes how a complex task can be achieved by existing resources. Thereafter, that complex task does not need to be further decomposed anymore. The CPP approach also can bring concrete web service descriptions much closer to customer requirements by building up a hierarchical structure of CPP instances to fit for different levels of business requirements.

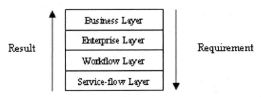

Fig. 4. Four layers business model, the arrows represent the directions of the requirement and the result.

3.2 Formal definition

Before the definition for a CPP instance is given, some basic definitions for concrete web service and abstract web service are given.

Definition 1: Based on the model introduced by OWL-S [8], a concrete service can be represented as: $CS = <Des, I, O, preCon, postCon, T, Grding>$

Where:

Des: A description of the service.

$I = \{I_1, I_2, ..., I_n\}$: A set of inputs.

$O = \{O_1, O_2, ..., O_n\}$: A set of outputs.

$preCon = \{preCon_1, preCon_2, ..., preCon_n\}$: A set of pre-conditions.

$postCon = \{postCon_1, postCon_2, ..., postCon_n\}$: A set of post-conditions.

T: The type of the service.

$Grding$: The service grounding to bind the service with WSDL.

An abstract service can be considered as a specification for a set of concrete services. If a concrete service appears in this set, then this concrete service is a realization of an abstract service [10]. The service grounding is not applicable to an abstract service because an abstract service cannot be invoked directly.

Definition 2: An abstract service AS can be represented as:
$AS = <Des, IS, OS, preCon, postCon, TS>$
Where:

Des: A description of the abstract service.

$IS = \{IS_1, IS_2, ..., IS_n\}$: A set of specifications of inputs.

$OS = \{OS_1, OS_2, ..., OS_n\}$: A set of specifications of outputs.

$preCon = \{preCon_1, preCon_2, ..., preCon_n\}$: A set of pre-conditions.

$postCon = \{postCon_1, postCon_2, ..., postCon_n\}$: A set of post-conditions.

TS: A specification of the service type.

A CPP instance can be considered as an abstract composite service and its definition is similar to the composite service definition, but some modifications have to be made in order to represent the abstraction.

Definition 3: A composite service can be defined as:
$CptS = <Des, I, O, preCon, postCon, CS, T, DS, CtrlS>$
Where:

Des: A description of the composite service.

$I = \{I_1, I_2, ..., I_n\}$: A set of inputs.

$O = \{O_1, O_2, ..., O_n\}$: A set of outputs.

$preCon = \{preCon_1, preCon_2, ..., preCon_n\}$: A set of preconditions.

$postCon = \{postCon_1, postCon_2, ..., postCon_n\}$: A set of post-conditions.

$CS = \{CS_1, CS_2, ..., CS_n\}$: A set of concrete services used for composing the composite service.

T: The type of the composite service.

$DS = \{(o,i) \mid o \in CS.O \wedge i \in CS.I\}$: DS represents the data flow which is a set of arcs, where each arc connects one service's output to the other service's input. $CS.I$ and $CS.O$ are sets of inputs and outputs of CS.

$CtrlS = <stmt, cdt>$: $CtrlS$ represents the control structure, where $stmt$ is a set of control statements and cdt is a set of conditions.

Definition 4: A CPP instance (an abstract composite service) can be defined as:
$P = <Des, I, O, preCon, postCon, AS, T, DS, CtrlS>$
Where:

Des: A description of the composite service.

$I = \{I_1, I_2, ..., I_n\}$: A set of inputs.

$O = \{O_1, O_2, ..., O_n\}$: A set of outputs.

$preCon = \{preCon_1, preCon_2, ..., preCon_n\}$: A set of preconditions.

$postCon = \{postCon_1, postCon_2, ..., postCon_n\}$: A set of post-conditions.

$AS = \{AS_1, AS_2, ..., AS_n\}$: A set of abstract services.

T: The type of the pattern.

$DS = \{(o,i) \mid o \in AS.O \wedge i \in AS.I\}$: DS represents the data flow which is a set of arcs, where each arc connects one service's output to the other service's input. $AS.I$ and $AS.O$ are sets of inputs and outputs of AS.

$CtrlS = <stmt, cdt>$: $CtrlS$ represents the control structure, where $stmt$ is a set of control statements and cdt is a set of conditions.

The above definition illustrates that the difference between a composite service and a CPP instance is that the CPP instance only defines a set of abstract services rather than a set of concrete services in order to achieve dynamic service discovery and invocation at runtime.

To describe how the inputs and outputs of a CPP instance are related to its internal services, a directed partial graph G_p (V_p, E_p) is used to represent the internal structure of a CPP instance and the connections with outside environment, see figure 5, where

1. V_p: is a set of internal abstract services.
2. E_p: is a set of arcs indicating the data relationships between internal services and internal and external services.
3. $V_p \subset V \wedge E_p \subseteq E$, where there is a whole directed graph G (V, E)

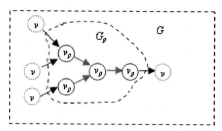

Fig. 5. Partial Directed Graph, black arcs represent inputs and outputs.

The inputs of a CPP instance can be represented as P_{input} which is a set of arcs that satisfy $P_{input} = \{(v, v_p) \mid v \notin V_p \wedge v_p \in V_p \wedge (v, v_p) \in E_p\}$

The outputs of a CPP instance can be represented as P_{output} which is a set of arcs that satisfy $P_{output} = \{(v_p, v) \mid v \notin V_p \wedge v_p \in V_p \wedge (v_p, v) \in E_p\}$

3.3 Description

As discussed previously, a CPP instance is an abstract composite service, thus a semantic language which can address composite service is required to describe a CPP instance. In order to properly describe a CPP instance, we propose a language which extends OWL-S. The upper ontology of OWL-S [8] has been extended to address the abstract composite services and patterns, see figure 6. In the following paragraphs we show how to use the extended OWL-S to describe a CPP instance.

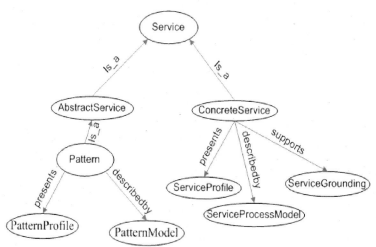

Fig. 6. Extended OWL-S upper ontology.

Suppose we have a CPP instance for the task: calculating the volume of a cylinder. In this CPP instance we specified two required services for achieving the task. One is to calculate circular area and the other is to calculate multiplication of two values. *PatternProfile* is used to describe a CPP instance's functional and non-functional attributes as well as the types of the services which used to build it. A piece of code fragment of *PatternProfile* for describing the cylinder volume CPP is listed in figure 7. Note that the profile does not provide any inputs or outputs details for the required services. The reason for this is because the required services for building the pattern are only used to be invoked within the CPP instance. The details of required services are only described in *PatternModel* for automatic discovery purpose.

```
...
<rdf:Description rdf:resource="http://localhost/PatternExample.ows#CylinderVolumePattern">
    <rdf:type rdf:resource="http://localhost/ServiceOntology.ows#VolumePattern"/>
    <patternProfile:subService>
        <rdf:Bag> <rdf:Description rdf:resource="http://localhost/PatternExample.ows#CircularArea">
                <rdf:type rdf:resource="http://localhost/ServiceOntology.ows#AreaCalculation"/>
            </rdf:Description>
            <rdf:Description rdf:resource="http://localhost/PatternExample.ows#Multiplication">
                <rdf:type rdf:resource="http://localhost/ServiceOntology.ows#BasicCalculation"/>
    </rdf:Description> </rdf:Bag> </rdf:Description>
<patternProfile:hasInput rdf:resource="http://localhost/PatternExample.ows#PI"/>
<patternProfile:hasInput rdf:resource="http://localhost/PatternExample.ows#Radius"/>
<patternProfile:hasInput rdf:resource="http://localhost/PatternExample.ows#Height"/>
<patternProfile:hasOutput rdf:resource="http://localhost/PatternExample.ows#Volume"/>
...
```

Fig. 7. PatternProfile sample code.

PatternModel is an extended *ServiceProcessModel*. Compared with the original *ServiceProcessModel*, the *PatternModel* is specifically used to describe composition of services rather than processes. The process information is ignored here because the services are considered as whole abstract units to join the composition. The properties and syntax used to describe a composite process have been inherited from the *ServceProcessModel*. The code fragments in figure 8 illustrate how the *PatternModel* is used to describe the composition relationships between services. We can see that the mulitplicatio service in step2 uses the circular area service's output in the previous step as one of its inputs to calculate the final result for the cylinder volume.

ServiceGrounding only applies to concrete services rather than abstract services, so it is not part of CPP description.

```
...
<patternModel:Perform rdf:ID="Step2_Volume">
    <patternModel:subService rdf:resource="#Multiplication"/>
    <patternModel:hasdataFrom>
        <patternModel:InputBinding>
            <patternModel:toParam rdf:resource="#Multiplication_Input1"/>
            <patternModel:valueSource> <patternModel:ValueOf>
                    <patternModel:theVar rdf:resource="#Area_Output"/>
                    <patternModel:fromSubService rdf:resource="#Step1_Area"/>
            </patternModel:ValueOf> </patternModel:valueSource> </patternModel:InputBinding>   ·
        ...
    </patternModel:hasdataFrom>
</patternModel:Perform> ...
```

Fig. 8. PatternModel sample code.

4 Implementation of the Common Process Pattern

To realize the CPP approach, a web based web service composition prototype has been developed. The main functions of this prototype include service browsing, build composite service, service flow execution, and generating extended OWL-S description for describing CPP instances. This prototype makes creating a CPP instance as easy as drawing a flowchart diagram. When the user try to connect two services together during the composition process, the prototype will give help information about whether these two services are compatible to be linked together. When a CPP instance is executed in the prototype, service matchmaking will be performed and all the required services are dynamically located based on the specifications. Due to the length limitation of the paper we have omitted the description of the matchmaking method, see [14] for details.

4.1 System architecture of the prototype

The system architecture of the prototype consists of four components: user interface (UI), service flow execution engine (SFEE), service searching engine (SSE), and semantic service pool (SSP), see figure 9.

The semantic service pool (SSP) component consists of three layers. The first layer is the WSDL described service pool. The services in the service pool could be from anywhere on the Internet. The second layer is the OWL-S description layer to add semantics into the WSDL service description. The third layer is the service ontology layer which organises the services in the service pool into a conceptual hierarchical structure.

The service search engine (SSE) component searches the OWL-S described service pool and locates the relevant services based on the requirements passed by the user interface or service flow execution engine. The SSE ranks the search results and returns it back to the user interface or the service flow execution engine. Normally the top ranking service is likely to be the service required by user or service flow execution engine, and the services with the lower ranking could be the alternative choice.

The service flow execution engine (SFEE) component executes the service flow created by the user and returns the executions result back to the user. The execution is based on the service flow control structure and the data dependency among services. Because the services within the service flow are abstract services which only have requirements specification, the service flow execution engine has to locate the concrete services through the SSE to execute the service flow.

The user interface (UI) component provides some utilities for a user to compose and run a service flow. It also provides an ontological display of service pool and a SSE interface for user to locate the required services.

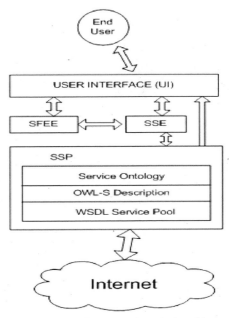

Fig. 9. System Architecture, arrows illustrate the relationship among components.

5 Related Work

Reuse is a major research area in software engineering field. Developers and designers realise how much effort and resource can be saved by enhancing the reuse
technology. Therefore, many research works are focusing on reuse technology and
pattern is one of the approaches. Gamma et al. [4] first identified the recurring
elements in the object-oriented design and programming. Through three categories, they introduced 23 design patterns for design and constructing object-
oriented program. Although these patterns are limited to use on object-oriented
programming, the ideas of the pattern approach has been established.

Aalst et al. [1] worked on patterns for workflow construction. In order to address the complex workflow functionality, they provided 10 patterns and grouped
them by four aspects, such as task synchronisation, common control structures,
multiple instances of an activity, and state problems. All of these patterns are independent from the workflow language and workflow management system. These
patterns focus on the low level workflow construction and execution and provide
the common solutions for constructing workflow and monitoring workflow execution, but they cannot provide solutions for high level business process model.

Sirin et al. [12] presented a workflow template technique for dynamic web service composition. A workflow template is a generalised workflow and the activities within the workflow template are abstract. The idea of using abstract activity
is to discover and substitute services at runtime. They use an extended OWL-S
language to describe the abstract process and the matchmaking algorithm devel-

oped by Paolucci et al. [9] to match suitable service process with an abstract process. An extended HTN [13] planning formalism, HTN-DL, is used to describe how to generate the composition of web services. However, they did not address clearly how the workflow template can be created and used. Also the matchmaking algorithm makes it hard to locate a proper service.IBM [6] has provides several business patterns used to describe the relationship between the users, the business organizations or applications, and the data to be accessed. The patterns they provided are very high level patterns, such as self-service pattern (User to Business), information aggregation pattern (User to Data), collaboration pattern (User to User), and extended enterprise pattern (Business to Business). Those patterns provide solutions for the whole business rather than a common business process.

6 Conclusion and Future Works

Web service composition is important for reducing the developing time and cost of business services. An efficient and effective way to realize the composition is essential. In this paper, we proposed a CPP approach, to reduce the complexity of the process of service composition and requirement and task decomposition. A CPP instance contains abstract explicit specifications for each required service, so the concrete services can be located and invoked dynamically based on these specifications. Using bottom-up approach to build the pattern grantees that each of the CPP instances is executable.

Through the service composition research work, we realize that only integrate semantics into the service description cannot sufficiently address a service, the contextual information is also important for identifying services. In the future work, we will propose a contextual based semantic model to better describe services and a searching method based on this model to more accurately locate required services.

References

1. Aalst, W.M.P. van der, Hofstede, A.H.M. ter, Kiepuszewski, B., and Barros, A.P. (2003) Workflow Patterns, *Distributed and Parallel Databases*, Kluwer Academic Publishers, 14(1): pp. 5-51

2. Christensen, E., Curbera, F., Meredith, G., and Weerawarana, S. (2001) Web Services Description Language (WSDL) 1.1,http://www.w3.org/TR/wsdl

3. Dustdar, S. and Schreiner, W. (2005) A Survey on Web Services Composition, Int. J. *Web and Grid Services*, Inderscience , Vol. 1, No. 1, pp.1–30.

4. Gamma, E., Helm, R., Johnson, R., and Vlissides, J. (1995) Design Patterns: Elements of Reusable Object-Oriented Software, Addison-Wesley Professional.
5. Ghallab, M., Nau, D., and Traverso, P. (2004) Automated Planning: Theory and Practice, Morgan Kaufmann, pp. 229-262.
6. Keen, M., Acharya, A., Bishop, S.n, Hopkins, A., Milinski, S., Nott, C., Robinson, R., Adams, J., and Verschueren, P. (2004) Patterns: Implementing an SOA Using an Enterprise Service Bus, IBM Redbook First Edition (July 2004), http://www.redbooks.ibm.com/abstracts/sg246346. html
7. Kumar, A., Srivastava, B., and Mittal, S. (2005) Information Modelling for End to End Composition of Semantic Web Services, in Proceedings of *4th International Semantic Web Conference (ISWC)*, 6-10 November 2005, Galway, Ireland.
8. Martin, D., Burstein, M., Hobbs, J., Lassila, O., McDermott, D., McIlraith, S., Narayanan, S., Paolucci, M., Parsia, B., Payne, T., Sirin, E., Srinivasan, N., and Sycara, K. (2004) OWL-S: Semantic Mark-up for Web Services, http://www.daml.org/services/owl-s/1.0/owl-s.html
9. Paolucci, M., Kawamura, T., Payne, T. R., and Sycara, K. (2002) Semantic Matching of Web Services Capabilities in Proceedings of the 1st *International Semantic Web Conference (ISWC)*, 9-12th June 2002, Sardinia, Italy.
10. Preist, C. (2004) A Conceptual Architecture for Semantic Web Services, In Proceedings of Third *International Semantic Web Conference*, Nov. 2004, Hiroshima, Japan, pp. 395-409.
11. Riehle, D. and Zullighoven H. (1996) Understanding and Using Patterns in Software Development, *Theory and Practice of Object Systems*, John Wiley & Sons, 2(1):3-13.
12. Sirin, E., Parsia, B., and Hendler, J. (2005) Template-based Composition of Semantic Web Services, 1st *International Symposium on Agents and the Semantic Web*, AAAI Fall Symposium Series Arlington, Virginia, USA 4th - 6th November, 2005.
13. Sirin, E., Parsia, B.,Wu, D., Hendler, J., and Nau, D. (2004) HTN planning for web service Composition using SHOP2, *Journal of Web Semantics*, Elsevier, 1(4), pp. 377–396.
14. W. Song (2006) A Semantic Modelling Approach to Automatic Services Analysis and Composition, to appear in the IASTED *International Conference on Web Technologies, Applications, and Services (WTAS)*, Calgary, Canada, 17-19 July.
15. W. Song (2006) Business Process and Integration Model: an Approach to Guide Constructing Service Flows, to appear in the IASTED International Conference on Web Technologies, Applications, and Services (WTAS), Calgary, Canada, 17-19 July.

Categories Extraction for Reuse in Semantic Applications and Profile Based Recommendation Service*

Vytautas Taujanskas *, Rimantas Butleris **

* Department of Information Systems, Kaunas University of Technology, Studentu St. 50-308, LT-51368 Kaunas, Lithuania
** Department of Informatics, Vilnius University Kaunas Faculty of Humanities, Naugardo g. 2, LT-44280, Kaunas, Lithuania

1 Semantic web – the new level of service

Consequent formalization of requirements for intelligent web came after the chaos with static, then afterwards with dynamic web resources. The semantic web is an extension of the current web, where information has well-defined meaning, better enabling computers and people to work in cooperation [**Hiba! A hivatkozási forrás nem található.**]. Abstract requirements [**Hiba! A hivatkozási forrás nem található.**] for information formalization became specific technologies [**Hiba! A hivatkozási forrás nem található.,Hiba! A hivatkozási forrás nem található.**] aimed to implement the vision of semantic web.

The rise of web 2.0 hype [**Hiba! A hivatkozási forrás nem található.**] is confirmed by the formation of critical mass of semantic applications. However, some of so-called web 2.0 applications take advantage of popularity and do not provide intelligent solutions. But the overall setting indicates the need of qualitatively new level of service, which could provide better functionality in *semantics*, *usability* and *collaboration*.

System must locate meaningful information resources on the Web and combine them in meaningful ways to perform tasks [**Hiba! A hivatkozási forrás nem található.**]. The process of locating or creating meaningful information should be

---

* The work is supported by Lithuanian State Science and Studies Foundation according to Eureka programme project "IT-Europe" (Reg. No 3473).

transparent to the end user. Various tools are needed to enrich data by integrating resources, dispersed across the web. The system itself must be intelligent to collect users' behavior patterns and to derive findings, which could be used to perform tasks.

This article is aimed to design web system according to the new generation of web application principles and to adapt the system for managing Lithuanian content. The study of internet activities of the Lithuanian users is performed in order to select the specific content for the system.

Collaboration functionality was taken into account, when designing the application. Collaboration is employed to build profile-based recommendations. The use of intelligent solutions, aggregation and other principles of the semantic web allowed us to reach the result by modeling service of recommendations.

2 Case study of local user

The idea of recommendation based system evolved in the context of research of semantic web technologies. The authors considered the idea of integrating personal data of Lithuanian web user. Case study of popular Lithuanian websites[1] was done to refine considerations about content.

Lithuania's online society has big variety of communication means: news portals (4 of 20 positions), lots of friendship services (5 of 20 positions) and places for communities, interested in some special knowledge domain (4 of 20 positions). The development of latter part of websites confirms the local formation of crowd wisdom [**Hiba! A hivatkozási forrás nem található.**] of some particular content categories (automobiles, family).

Widespread usage of friendship and communication services show popularity of communication systems. Though quality of functional characteristics of these systems in Lithuania, such as usability and intelligent way of presenting data, is quite low [**Hiba! A hivatkozási forrás nem található.,Hiba! A hivatkozási forrás nem található.**]. Most systems look like simple directories: they are defined in a rigid way, not discovered, are single-mode instead of multi-modal, connect users by means of shared artifacts [**Hiba! A hivatkozási forrás nem található.**]. Actually most of the systems do not have shared artifacts, just serve as directories for friends' contacts.

Summarizing main features Lithuanian internet user we can conclude, that he likes to read the news, shows trust to specialized communities and uses communication portals [**Hiba! A hivatkozási forrás nem található.**].

Therefore we intend to provide following functionality for our system:

- aggregate news content by using semantic technologies,
- implement user profiling functionality for extracting groups of likings (or wisdom) by using social networks,

---

[1] Lithuania's Top 20 2006 websites: http://www.ebiz.lt/article.php3/7/7993/0

- provide functionality of collaboration among the group members inside social networks.

3 Strategies for implementation

According to the functionality, as described above, the type of data of our system is defined as *Content*. As we choose data from news portal, the *Content* data element is the news article. Every *Content* instance is assigned to one or more *Categories* (Fig. 1). The *Categories* are used to define *User*.

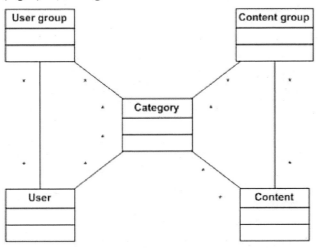

Fig. 1. Logic diagram for recommendation system

Associations among all entities in figure 1 have many-to-many multiplicity. Physical realization will use association class to reduce this complexity. However, *User* profile can be described by using multiple *Categories*, and *Category* can be used for multiple descriptions of *Users* likings. We use the same logic for describing *User groups'* likings, as the *Users* are assigned to *Users groups* according to related likings, described by *Categories*. Singular *User* can be assigned to multiple *User groups* according to likings match.

Analogical logic is used for defining *Content group, Content, Category relations*.

In this way, system can be divided into following modules:

- *Content* provider. This module is aimed to ensure content supply and provide functionality of simple categorization (as it is described in section 0 3.1 Providing the content). This part fills-in the *Content* and *Category* entities.

- Categorization module. This module provides more intelligent and accurate categorization functionality by filling *Category* entity. This process is described in section 0 3.2 Categories for user profiles building.

- *User* profiler. This module defines user profile according to actions of user in the system. For example, most preferred categories are used to describe user likings. In the next stage of using the system other types of information can be aggregated, such as extracted user data from popular portals, mentioned in section 0 2 Case study of local user.

- Recommendation service. This module analyzes data provided in the *User* profile description, links it to the other users of *User group*. Service has to provide related Content according to *Categories* profile description. *Content Categories* are used to define *Content groups* and provide dynamic flow of *Content*. The strategies for recommendations are described in section 0 3.3 Recommendations as a part of collaborations.

3.1 Providing the content

The main problem of building recommendation system is content aggregation. We chose to redirect the received content, which is available through RSS (Rich Site Summary/ Really Simple Syndication) or other format feeds [**Hiba! A hivatkozási forrás nem található.**]. The most popular Lithuanian news portals provide separate feeds for different categories (daily, business, sports, entertainment, lifestyle and subcategories). That helps us to define initial categorization as presented in figure 2. During initial launch of system we chose the strategy of providing simple categories management, by using easily extracted, though maybe not so accurate categories.

More complex categorization can be done by analyzing data provided in the feed. For example, one of content providers displays categories name in brackets before title *element* in each *item*. For getting better results the authors of [**Hiba! A hivatkozási forrás nem található.**] analyze various types of sources: meta-data, URL.

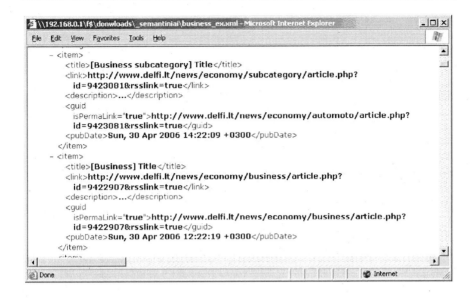

Fig. 2. News feed example

Other necessary data, which is not available in feeds, can be parsed using XPath queries for DOM [2] (Document Object Model). At the time of writing the article only one of 4 most popular Lithuanian news portals (section 0 2 Case study of local user) did not provide feeding service. XPath queries can be used to supplement feed with link, name and category of the content.

For successful functioning of the system, the need of tracking content structure changes is indicated. This functionality is planned for later implementations and should include auto disabling of erroneous scripts for building feed.

3.2 Categories for user profiles building

However, in order to provide better service of categorization and, therefore, better description of user likings, the system needs more intelligent category building solutions. For this purpose the reusable solutions [3] for analysis of English texts can be used. For analysis of Lithuanian texts the ready-to-use solutions do not exist yet. Lithuanian language is inflective and therefore it implies specific morphological and ambiguity removing issues to be solved.

Category building function can be assigned to system users themselves [**Hiba! A hivatkozási forrás nem található.**], but this approach incurs risk of lack of user input for qualitative categorization, caused by quickly changing content.

---

[2] http://www.w3c.org/DOM
[3] http://www.topicalizer.com

One more available method is automatic categorization [**Hiba! A hivatkozási forrás nem található.**] based on machine learning with preset [4] or emerging categories.

The lack of functionality for Lithuanian language, similar to WordNet [**Hiba! A hivatkozási forrás nem található.**], limits application of semantic relation queries to this language. Some useful relations shown in table 1 could be used for analyzing categories: generalization, association building and others.

Table 1. Semantic relations available in WordNet

Relation	Definition	Example
Hypernym	from concepts to subordinate;	breakfast -> meal
Has-Member	from groups to their members;	faculty -> professor
Member-Of	from members to their groups;	copilot -> crew
Has-Part	from wholes to parts;	table -> leg
Part-Of	from parts to wholes;	course -> meal
Antonym	opposites;	leader -> follower
Homonym	same form, but different meaning	bank: river bank, financial institution
Polysemy	same form, related meaning	bank: blood bank, financial institution)
Synonymy:	different form, same meaning	singer, vocalist

However there are some solutions, available for morphological [**Hiba! A hivatkozási forrás nem található.**] and ambiguities removing [**Hiba! A hivatkozási forrás nem található.**] features of Lithuanian language. The motivation to put these solutions on the web guides us to use machine-based categorization or simple frequent mean words list describing the article.

Implementation of publications categorization and multiple user aware system could allow us to examine available information and employ it for collaborative filtering.

3.3 Recommendations as a part of collaborations

Collaborative filtering is the method, used to predict interests of a user by collecting similar information from other users. The main assumption of this approach states, that the group of users which used to like the same thing will like the same thing in the future. In the [**Hiba! A hivatkozási forrás nem található.**] we use this approach to define user groups in social networks.

Collaboration, as a part of social network installed in the system, is provided by commercial and non-commercial systems AmphetaRate, LastFm and etc [5].

---

[4] http://www.dmoz.org/World/Lietuvių/

[5] www.amazon.com, www.last.fm, www.stumbleupon.com and http://amphetarate.newsfairy.com/

AmphetaRate focuses on the items found on dynamic feeds. It uses Bayesian statistics [**Hiba! A hivatkozási forrás nem található.**] method for choosing the items which could possibly be liked by the user. Generally, the Bayesian approach is used for spam filters, and AmphetaRate uses it for ratings. Another RSS rating approach, used in AmphetaRate and also in other collaborative systems, is called collaborative filtering [**Hiba! A hivatkozási forrás nem található.**] (often abbreviated as ACF). Functionality installed in AmphetaRate includes:

- Person related ratings. Rating estimation depends on ratings of the user.
- Employs the social factor to define relations. as it uses people to determine relations.
- Provides fortunate discoveries by accident.

Authors of [**Hiba! A hivatkozási forrás nem található.**] provide comprehensive research of recommendation systems. They separate three classes of such systems:

- Content-based recommendations, where the user is recommended according to the items which he preferred in the past.
- Collaborative recommendations, where the user is recommended according to the items, which were liked by people with similar tastes and preferences in the past.
- Hybrid approaches, which combine both of above.

The research enumerates possible extensions of recommender systems capabilities, which could take into account *more comprehensive understanding of the user*, analysis of user's transactional, navigational web usage patterns and other available data.

The system should be non-intrusive, as it could measure the amount of time, spent by the user for reading an item, and also should be accurate for the noise. One way of exploring the *non-intrusiveness* is determining the optimal number of ratings. Other way is to develop marginal cost model (instead of the fixed cost) and to provide the cost/benefit analysis. Authors [**Hiba! A hivatkozási forrás nem található.**] propose active learning methods to address this issue.

Interesting flexibility approach is proposed, where RQL (Recommendation Query Language) is used to resolve the flexibility issue. Despite of the method, used to solve it, it should *provide recommendation not for the particular items, but for brands or categories of items to the corresponding segments of users.*

4 Conclusions

The system, which aggregates information from the web and analyzes it by adding recommendations functionality, is proposed. In order to select sources for aggregation the local internet user analysis is made. Categorization functionality is added for description of content and user profile. Initial categories extraction is implemented by multi-way analysis of incoming data feeds. More intelligent solutions adapted to Lithuanian language are substantiated for later use.

Recommendation system contains available categories and uses them to describe user's profile. Automatic extraction of categories has advantage over tagging, as it can ensure non-intrusiveness, which is essential aspect.

More extensive user oriented analysis should be done by providing other data aggregation (i.e. friendship directories) or transactional actions recording. Rating is liable for correct recommendations as well.

References

1. Adomavicius G, Tuzhilin A (2005) Toward the next generation of recommender systems: a survey of the state-of-the-art and possible extensions. IEEE Transactions on Knowledge and Data Engineering, vol 17, issue 6, ISSN: 1041-4347, pp 734 – 749
2. Bayesian statistics. http://en.wikipedia.org/wiki/Bayesian_statistics
3. Berners-Lee T, Hendler J, Lassila O (2001) The Semantic Web. Scientific American. http://www.scientificamerican.com/article.cfm?articleID=00048144-10D2-1C70-84A9809EC588EF21&catID=2
4. Boyd DM (2004) Friendster and publicly articulated social networking. In CHI '04 Extended Abstracts on Human Factors in Computing Systems, ACM Press, New York, NY, pp 1279-1282
5. Decker S, Melnik S, van Harmelen F, Fensel D, Klein M, Broekstra J, Erdmann M, Horrocks I (2000) The Semantic Web: the roles of XML and RDF. Internet Computing, IEEE, vol 4, no 5, ISSN: 1089-7801, pp 63–73
6. Fisher D (2003) Social Networks for End Users. Survey Paper for Advancement to Candidacy. University of California, Irvine. http://www.bsos.umd.edu/gvpt/CITE-IT/Documents/Fisher 2003 Soc Ntwks for End Users.pdf
7. Gupta KM, Aha DW, Marsh E, Maney T (2002) An architecture for engineering sublanguage WordNets. In Proceedings of the First International Conference On Global WordNet, pp 207-215
8. Mika P (2005) Flink: Semantic Web Technology for the Extraction and Analysis of Social Networks. Journal of Web Semantics, vol 3, no 2, pp 211–223
9. Ohmukai I, Hamasaki M, Takeda H (2005) A Proposal of Community-based Folksonomy with RDF Metadata. In Proceedings of the ISWC 2005 Workshop on End User Semantic Web Interaction (2005), published on CEUR-WS
10. O'Reilly T (2005) What is Web 2.0. http://www.oreilly.com/go/web2

11. Rimkute E, Grybinaite A (2004) The most frequent types of the morphological ambiguity of the Lithuanian language and the automatical disambiguation of them (in Lithuanian). Kalbu studijos, vol 5, pp 74 – 78

12. Sebastiani F (2002) Text categorization in general - a survey paper: Machine Learning in Automated Text Categorization. ACM Computing Surveys, vol 34, no 1, pp 1 – 47

13. Surowiecki J (2005) The Wisdom of Crowds. Anchor, ISBN:0385721706

14. Svatek V, Berka P, Kavalec M, Kosek J, Vavra V (2003) Discovering Company Descriptions on the Web by Multiway Analysis. Springer-Verlag, Advances in Soft Computing series, ISBN 3-540-00843-8, pp 111 – 118

15. Tepper M (2003) The rise of social software. netWorker, vol 7, no 3, ISSN:1091-3556, pp 18–23

16. Tutkutė L, Taujanskas V (2006) Forming recommendations in semantic web (in Lithuanian). Information technologies for business and study 2006. vol 1, pp 178–183

17. Ungar L, Foster D (1998) Clustering Methods for Collaborative Filtering. In Proceedings of the AAAI-98 Workshop on Recommender Systems, AAAI Press, pp 112 – 125

18. Uschold M (2003) Where are the semantics in the semantic web? AI Magazine, vol 24, issue 3, ISSN:0738-4602, pp 25 – 36

19. Wusteman J (2004) RSS: the latest feed. Library Hi Tech, vol 22, no 4, MCB University Press, ISSN 0737-8831, pp 404 – 413

20. W3C. Semantic web activity. http://www.w3.org/2001/sw/

21. W3C. SPARQL Query Language for RDF. http://www.w3.org/TR/rdf-sparql-query/

22. Zinkevicius V (2000) Morphological analysis with Lemuoklis (in Lithuanian). Darbai ir Dienos, vol 24, pp 245 – 273

Knowledge and Decision-Making within Software Projects

*Birinder Sandhawalia, **Darren Dalcher

*School of Computing Science, Middlesex University, Trent Park, Bramley Road, London N14 4YZ, UK. b.sandhawalia@mdx.ac.uk
**School of Computing Science, Middlesex University, Trent Park, Bramley Road, London N14 4YZ, UK. d.dalcher@mdx.ac.uk

Abstract: The effective use of knowledge results in better decision-making within projects. Moreover, the unpredictable nature of software projects and the need for effective communication within project teams requires a framework for social interaction and feedback that results in better decision-making. This paper analyses the creation and capture of knowledge within software development projects and discusses the central role of decision making in the development process, and how the effective use of knowledge helps improve decision-making. The paper views how the knowledge generated and decisions made within a software project can be provided greater visibility and communicated effectively, and to achieve this, presents a framework to facilitate social interaction and feedback during the development process.

1 Introduction

The use of knowledge is expected to result in better decision-making, innovation and competitive advantage within organisations and projects. While organisations are permanent structures that emphasise functional structure, projects are temporary endeavours that are predicated on a deadline and the ultimate delivery of an artifact, product, service or quantified business value or benefit. As part of their normal operations, organisations capture knowledge in repeatable situations that are relatively straight-forward and make-sense. Projects, by definition, are focused on change. They function in an uncertain and ambiguous environment, and need to be flexible and adaptive. The temporary nature of projects and their deadline driven schedules require a decision-making process that lies at the core of the project processes to ensure that they are executed smoothly. Projects need reflection, practitioner's experience, and the ability to build on acquired knowledge.

Software development projects are life-cycle driven and are organised around teams that are assembled specifically for the limited duration of the project. The software development process relies on the knowledge and creativity of individuals and teams, and the formation of these teams requires the involvement and participation of all team members in the development process. There is also an increasing need to involve users early in the software development life-cycle since designing software requires extracting detailed knowledge of the users. Effective communication is the basis for discussion between users and developers during the requirements definition process that is essential to provide an understanding of the software requirements. However, problems of communication occur due to the diversity of professional expertise and organisational roles that confer users' different views and expectations of the system to be developed.

The unpredictable nature of software projects and the need for effective communication within project teams necessitates a framework for social interaction and feedback that results in better decision-making. This paper analyses the creation and capture of knowledge within software development projects. The paper discusses the central role of decision making in the development process and how the effective use of knowledge helps to improve decision-making during the development process. The knowledge created and decisions implemented need to be effectively communicated across the entire process. Social interaction and feedback are key factors that facilitate the effective use of knowledge within software projects. The paper views how the knowledge and decisions implemented can be provided greater visibility within the projects and communicated effectively, and also presents a framework to facilitate social interaction and feedback during the development process.

2 Knowledge

Knowledge is the capacity for effective action. Alavi and Leidner (1999) define knowledge as 'a justified personal belief that increases an individual's capacity to take effective action.' While 'personal' implies the contextual nature of knowledge, action requires competencies and know-how, and implies the dynamic nature of knowledge. Knowledge is fluid and formally structured, and it exists within people, processes, structures and routines, (Davenport and Prusak 1998). Polanyi (1967) suggests that knowledge exists as tacit and explicit. Tacit knowledge comprises an individual's mental models, and while it is personal and in the mind of an individual, it is also context specific and difficult to articulate, formalise and verbalise, and is therefore hard to communicate and share. The factors that influence an individual's mental model include the individual's education, expertise, past experiences, perceptions, biases, prejudices and environment. Explicit knowledge can be easily articulated and codified and therefore transmitted and communicated. Polanyi (1967) contends that human beings acquire knowledge by actively creating and organising their own experiences and sums it up by stating that "we can know more than we can tell."

The importance of knowledge is increasing as organisations recognise that they posses knowledge and increasingly learn to view this knowledge as a valuable and strategic asset. Knowledge assets include knowledge which resides within the individuals, systems, processes, documents and structures of the organisation. Davenport and Prusak (1998) recommend that to remain competitive, organisations must efficiently and effectively create, capture, locate and share their organisations knowledge and expertise, and have the ability to bring that knowledge to bear on problems and opportunities.

2.1 Knowledge Management

The American Productivity and Quality Center (1996) defines knowledge management as "a conscious strategy of getting the right knowledge to the right people at the right time and helping people share and put information into action in ways that strive to improve organisational performance." Knowledge management, therefore, requires that it is imperative to identify what knowledge needs to be managed, how, when, where, by whom, and for whom. Consequently, the key elements of KM are collecting and organising the knowledge, making it available through knowledge infrastructure, and then using the knowledge to improve decision making and gain competitive advantage. Alavi and Leidner (1999) refer to knowledge management as a systematic and organisationally specified process for acquiring, organising and communicating both tacit and explicit knowledge of employees so that other employees may make use of it to be more effective and productive in their work and decision-making while improving product and process innovation.

3 Decision Making

Decision making is a crucial part of organisational as well as personal activity. Simon (1977) states that decision making comprises four principal phases which are: finding occasions for making a decision, finding possible courses of action, choosing among courses of action, and evaluating past choices. Simon suggests that the four phases be called intelligence, design, choice and review activities. The intelligence activity involves searching the environment for conditions calling for decision, while the design activity comprises inventing, developing and analysing possible courses of action. The choice activity entails selecting a particular course of action from those available, and the review activity assesses the choices made. The four phases are similar to those suggested by Nutt (1989) who states that the decision making process requires exploring possibilities, assessing options, testing assumptions and learning. As KM attempts to make available 'the right knowledge to the right person at the right time', it improves the processes of exploring possibilities, assessing options and testing assumptions.

Simon (1977) further distinguishes between programmed and non-programmed decisions. Well-structured, repetitive and routine decisions are programmed so that a definite procedure for handling them exists, while non-programmed decisions are novel, unstructured and unusually consequential. Programmed decisions are addressed by routine standard operating procedures, while non-programmed decisions require human judgment, insight and intuition. Therefore while programmed decisions would benefit from the explicit knowledge of an organisation, non-programmed decisions require creativity and rely upon the tacit knowledge of the individuals.

Knowledge provides the context and insights required to improve the quality of information used in the decision making process, as knowledge is considered to be authenticated information viewed with context. Knowledge improves the ability to respond to the sub-merged problems and issues and helps in identifying and evaluating several courses of action before committing to one while exploring possibilities. Knowledge enhances the ability to identify factors that influence estimates used to value the merits of alternative courses of action while assessing options. Knowledge is also useful to examine the value attached to each option or alternative while testing assumptions. Reflecting upon the outcome of the decisions made and identifying missed opportunities results in learning and provides important insights that lead to the creation of further knowledge. This dynamic creation of knowledge, where knowledge created is the basis for further knowledge creation, is made possible through feedback and interaction of knowledge (Nonaka and Takeuchi (1995). The knowledge created provides the basis to explore further possibilities, set objectives, and identify ways to respond thereby resulting in more effective decision-making within organisations and projects.

4 Projects

Compared to organisations which are permanent structures and have routines, projects are temporary by nature and their implementation requires creative actions, practitioner's experience, and the ability to apply knowledge to development problems. Projects are designed to achieve specific objectives within a predetermined time frame, budget and resources. Projects involve planning for non-routine tasks to be conducted in several phases, and can be characterised as unique, goal-oriented and complex undertakings steeped in uncertainty, which aim to produce a meaningful product or service in order to satisfy a need, (Dalcher 2003). Davis (1951) defines a project as "any undertaking that has definite final objectives representing specified values to be used in the satisfaction of some need or desire." The Project Management Institute (PMI) makes a distinction between ordinary work and projects by emphasising the temporary and unique nature of projects (PMBOK 2000).

Bredillet (2004) states that for the past forty years projects and their management have become a well-accepted and strategic way to manage organisations. According to him, projects as strategic processes modify the conditions of the organisation and its environment. Meredith and Mantel (1995) describe three basic types of project organisations:

- projects as a functional section of a larger organisation
- pure project organisations where a project is accommodated in a separate, largely self-contained section that is disbanded when the project is completed or disbanded
- organisations where projects are run on matrix basis in which control rests with a project manager but the majority of human and other resources are borrowed from different sections of the larger organisation

Knowledge is required to implement the project in relation to the type of project organisation. Koskinen (2004) suggests a metaphor of a project tree to visualise the entire knowledge required by a project organisation and states that the types of knowledge that a project may require are tacit, explicit, additive or substitutive. Koskinen refers to additive and substitutive knowledge as knowledge that is new to the project and is either invented internally or acquired from external sources. This is similar to Bredillet's (2004) view that project teams need to know what knowledge is available to complete the project based on past experience, and what knowledge needs to be acquired or will emerge as a result of the unique nature of the project tasks, especially within software projects.

4.1 Software Projects

Software projects are life cycle driven and follow the sequence of going from concept through definition and development, to testing and delivery. However, unlike other projects, the requirements of software projects are subject to frequent change. As a product, software can be changed, and it is therefore assumed that this change is possible at even the later stages of the development process. Such change and uncertainty make software projects more unpredictable than other projects, and are therefore organised around teams, relying upon the knowledge and creativity of the individuals and the teams.

Myers (1985) states that more than half the cost of complex software development is attributable to decisions made in the 'upstream' portion of the development process, namely, requirements specification and design. Traditional software development models like waterfall and spiral follow a sequential approach where the 'upstream' and 'downstream' aspects of development are clearly distinguishable. However, modern approaches like agile methods are more emergent and evolutionary, and rely on frequent feedback and interaction between and within self-organised teams while attempting to address change and uncertainty in the requirements. Self-organised teams comprise a group of peers who posses a sense of ownership and share responsibility for managing their own work, which includes problem-solving and continuous improvement of work processes. Gruenfeld et al (1996) and Politis (2003) are both of the view that self-organised teams create and share new knowledge, resulting in improved decision making and, furthering the ability of the teams to deliver the best possible solutions. Knowledge is the raw material required for decision making within software design teams and for complex projects, knowledge from multiple technical and functional domains is required (Curtis et al 1988). Walz et al (1993) state that ideally, software development teams are staffed so that both the levels and distribution of knowledge within them match those required for the successful completion of the project. Software development processes require that the individual activities are co-ordinated towards the team activities, focusing on the different areas and stages of the developmental process. The software development process involves eliciting the user requirements and software satisfying the requirements is then designed, built, tested and delivered.

Process models for software development depict sequential, incremental, prototyping or evolutionary approaches. Developmental models help simplify and reduce the complexity within software projects by providing a perspective to organise the different stages or phases of the development process. However, as stated by Myers (1985), decisions made early in the software development process have an effect in the later stages of the process. Software projects involve dealing with trade-offs between characteristics, preferences and quantities, while maintaining a balance between requirements, expectations, perceptions, opportunities and risks. Therefore software projects require a framework that enables the use of knowledge to facilitate decision making within the process to achieve the desired outcome. The next section presents a model that provides the framework for decision making within the developmental process.

5 The Dynamic Feedback Model

Complex and uncertain software development situations require a model that can account for the knowledge needed to plan and implement decisions within the development process. An example of such a model is the Dynamic Feedback Model (DFM) that underlines the relationships and interactions between the entities by depicting the feedback loops operating between them. The model, as depicted in Figure 1, focuses on four different functional areas that are intertwined throughout software development. The DFM models the relationships in a non-linear fashion amongst the functional areas and allows a continuous view of the development process. The four areas are management, technical, quality and decision making.

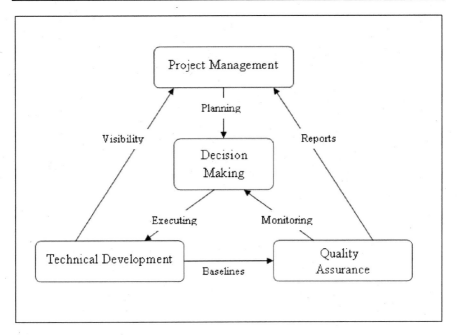

Fig. 1. Dynamic Feedback Model

5.1 Functional Areas

The management area involves the planning, control and management of the software development process. It also pertains to the strategy and operation of the project. Key concerns revolve around identifying performance gaps, assessing progress, and allocating resources to accomplish tasks. As technical development and knowledge creation are on going activities, the management area also takes on a continuous view. It does not limit its focus to delivering a product, but to the continuous need for generating and maintaining an on-going flow of knowledge required for continuous development.

The technical area deals with the creation and continuous improvement of the software system. The area recognises the changing needs and perceptions of the development process. The activity in this area includes evolution and maintenance of the software, while also maintaining its functionality and utility. Experimentation, learning and discovery take place as the software goes from inception to evolution. The development and design of the software form the basis for interaction between team members, and the knowledge created through the interaction provides the raw material for decision making within the process.

The quality area is perceived as a dynamic dimension, which continuously responds to perceived mismatches and opportunities reflected in the environment. It is concerned with assuring the quality of the product developed and the process used to develop it. Being an area of assessment, it provides the basis for learning.

The decision making area lies at the core of the model as software development is described as a decision making process (Dym and Little 2000). This area attempts to balance knowledge, uncertainty and ambiguity with a view to maximise the expected returns on an on-going basis. Knowledge acquired from implementing decisions is used within the process either as background knowledge available to support future decisions, or as a formalised part of an integral body of knowledge which can be used to optimise the decision making process. Decision making helps manage opportunity and risk and therefore this area can also be considered the risk management area. Risk assessment and planning are key activities within this area, which also ensures the implementation of decisions and the monitoring of their execution on a continuous basis. The knowledge and information required for the implementation, execution and monitoring of decisions is provided by the interaction and feedback loops of the model.

5.2 Feedback Loops

The DFM is in essence a set of interactions and feedback loops governing and controlling the development of software form a continuous perspective. The decision making perspective of the DFM ensures that rational and reasoned choices are made from the alternatives available during the development process.

The basic loop in the dynamic system is the planning-control-visibility loop. This loop helps to plan and control the production, evolution and growth of the software in association with project management and decision making. The loop enables the continuous generation of new information as well as feedback knowledge. The use of this knowledge is crucial in changing plans to adapt to reality and opportunities, modifying the decisions and re-examining the assumptions. The visibility of this basic feedback loop provides a continuous process to ensure the system remains relevant with regard to its objectives.

The configuration control loop links control, baseline and monitoring that provide the link between monitoring and controlling. Monitoring provides feedback on the strategies implemented, and is the link between decision making and quality. The monitoring loop is a closed–loop system providing feedback to the decision making area and ensuring effective control of the decisions made in technical development while relying upon quality assurance techniques and feedback mechanisms to evaluate progress and quality.

The reporting planning loop provides visibility to the project management area regarding the opportunities and mismatches present in the quality area and also provided by the implementation and execution of the decisions made.

The above mentioned loops depict relationships between the different functional areas. The DFM can therefore be used as a framework for understanding the dynamic nature of the interactions between entities in software development. The model moves away from linear thinking and offers a continuous perspective for understanding and implementing relationships, and the role these relationships play in decision making. The model achieves this through the on-going feedback and interactions of the loops, which present the framework to provide knowledge required for decision making. The following section examines the feedback and interactions between the different phases of software development.

5.3 The DFM Process

The phases of the software development process can broadly be categorised as problem definition, requirements analysis, design, implementation and maintenance. The DFM views knowledge as a key asset in the development of software and focuses on its feedback within the functional areas of development. In doing so, the DFM encourages thinking about software development in terms of the different phases and their interactions. The feedbacks within the functional areas of the DFM are depicted in Figure 2, and the use of knowledge for decision making within the various activities of software projects are discussed there-after.

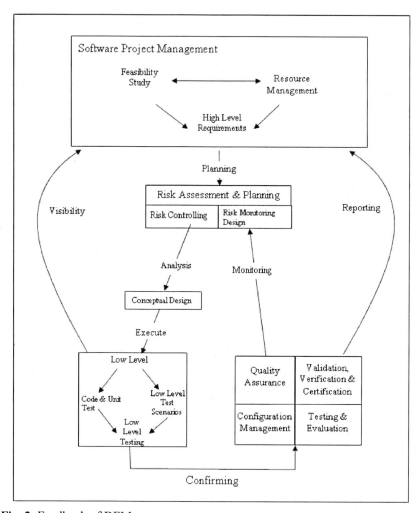

Fig. 2. Feedback of DFM

The project management area facilitates project planning and execution, and is also where the user requirements are elicited and the problem defined. Planning involves resource management where the skills and competencies required to execute the project are identified and teams are formed. Proper requirements analysis and specification are critical for the success of the project, as most defects found during testing originate in requirements. In order to understand the customer requirements, the developers require insight into the domain of the business system and the technical concepts of the system to be developed. Knowledge is created while understanding the requirements by the interaction of the different team members, and also between the users and the developers. This knowledge provides the perspective for decisions made to implement the project. The project management area is where negotiation takes place between the users and developers of the software. Johnson (1993) defines negotiation as a process in which individuals or groups seek to reach goals by making agreements with each other. Software development requires that users are involved in the development of the software. A clear understanding is needed between the users and developers to build the software, and this understanding is established through dialogue and negotiation. The formalisation of such an understanding usually results in the form of proposals and contracts. The feasibility of the project and the cost involved in executing the project are the basis for the proposals and contracts. The project management area addresses the need to assess the feasibility of the project and its cost analysis.

Based upon the decisions made and the outcome of planning within the project management area, an analysis of the impact the project will have on the business and technical environment is made along with the possible risks involved in implementing the project. The analysis views the goals, scope and functionality of the system being developed and how they fit or respond to the existing processes with which they are required to interact. Risk assessment and planning are conducted and feature the two traditional components of risk identification and prioritisation. Identification tries to envision all situations that might have a negative impact on the project, while prioritisation involves analysing the possible effects and consequences of the risk in case it actually occurs. The project also requires crucial decisions to be made in the design stage. High level design is the phase of the life cycle that provides a logical view of the development of the user requirements. Design involves a high level of abstraction of the solution, through which requirements are translated into a 'blueprint' for constructing the software, and provides the architecture of the application and its database design. Decision making at this stage of the process helps transform the requirements into a set of software functions and a physical database structure. Scenarios are developed to test the acceptability of the design with relation to the requirements.

The technical activities of design, code generation and testing are performed in the technical area. The area includes the detailed design phase where the high level design is converted into modules and programs. A unit test plan is created for the conditions for which each program is to be tested. The required programs are coded or translated into the programming language, and the programs are tested using the unit test plans. The technical area ensures that the integration plan is implemented according to the environments identified for integration. The area also ensures the maintenance, functionality and utility of the software apart from its creation and evolution. The decisions made in this area relate to the technical activities and provide confirmation of the design and suitability of the requirements. The decisions made are verified during system testing within the quality assurance area.

Pressman (1997) states that quality assurance consists of the auditing and reporting functions of management, and that its goal is to provide management with the data necessary to be informed and assured about product quality. The quality assurance area involves system testing which validates that the software developed meets the requirement specification. This phase identifies the defects that are exposed by testing the entire system. A series of tests are performed together, each with a different purpose, to verify that the system has been properly integrated and performs its functionality and satisfies the requirements. The quality assurance area thus provides verification of the decisions made and tasks performed in the technical area while confirming the decisions made during the design phase, and validating the requirements.

The different phases of the process are validated and given visibility by the feedback loops. Controlling the execution of decisions generates knowledge (Dalcher 2003a). The feedback loops globalise this knowledge within the process and ensure that knowledge is available for decision making. The decisions made in the decision making area during design and risk analysis receive confirmation during technical development and quality assurance. Technical development provides the project management area visibility of the software being developed to meet the requirements. Quality assurance further reports and validates to project management the decisions made during design and technical development. The project management area is able to assess the feedback and incorporate it in planning to help address some of the change and uncertainty inherent within the software development process

6 Conclusions

The DFM model provides a decision-making perspective and the execution of decisions helps create new knowledge. The knowledge created further helps support decision making which lies at the core of the DFM process. Knowledge is globalised to the functional areas of the process through feedback loops. The loops represent the knowledge intensive activities which connect decision making to other phases of development process.

The DFM adopts a long-term perspective of software development that enables it to address the issues of uncertainty and ambiguity, and therefore benefit from the decisions made and knowledge created during the development process. The long-term perspective also enables the DFM to look beyond a single project and use the knowledge generated towards improvements in future software projects. The DFM is receptive to changes in the environment and tackles them by feeding acquired knowledge back into the decision making process. As software development becomes more integrated in management practices the importance of continuous learning, knowledge, and skill acquisition as underpinned by the DFM will remain central to improved control, visibility and management. The availability of a long-term view justifies the adoption of multiple perspectives, the reuse of knowledge and the utilisation of a decision making perspective, which underpin feedback and improvement. The DFM provides a framework that facilitates social interaction and feedback, which further enhance the use of knowledge for decision making within the software development process.

References

1. Alavi M and Leidner DE (1999) 'Knowledge Management Systems: Issues, Challenges and Benefits,' Communications of the Association for Information Systems, Vol 1, Article 7.
2. American Productivity and Quality Center (APQC) (1996), Knowledge Management: Consortium Benchmarking Study Final Report; Available from http://www.store.apqc.org/reports/Summary/know-mng.pdf
3. Bredillet CN (2004) 'Projects are Producing the Knowledge which are Producing the Projects......' Proceedings of IPMA, Budapest.
4. Curtis B, Krasner H, and Iscoe N (1988) 'A Field Study for the Software Design Process for Large Systems,' Communications of the ACM., Vol 31, No 11, pp 68-87.
5. Dalcher D (2003) Computing Project Management, Middlesex University Press, London.
6. Dalcher D (2003a) 'Software Development for Dynamic Systems.' Developments in Metainformatics. LNCS, Springer Verlag, Peter J Nurnberg (ed): pp 58-75.
7. Davenport TH and Prusak L (1998) 'Working Knowledge,' Harvard Business School Press, Boston.
8. Davis RC (1999) 'The Fundamentals of Top Management,' New York: Harper and Brothers, 1951, (quoted in Cleland DI. Project Management: Strategic Design and Implementation, 3rd ed. New York: McGraw-Hill, p-3.
9. Dym C L and Little P (2000) 'Engineering Design: A Project Based Introduction.' John Wiley, New York.
10. Gruenfeld DH, Mannix EA, Williams KY, and Neale MA, (1996) 'Group Composition and Decision Making: How Member Familiarity and Information Distribution Affect Process and Performance,' Organisational Behaviour and Human Decision Process, Vol 67, pp 1-15.
11. Johnson RA (1993) 'Negotiation Basics,' Sage Publications, Inc.
12. Koskinen KU (2004) 'Knowledge Management to Improve Project Communication and Implementation,' Project Management Journal, Vol 35, No 1, pp 13-19.
13. Meredith JR and Mantel JS (1995) 'Project Management: A Managerial Approach,' Wiley, New York.
14. Myers W (1985) 'MCC: Planning the Revolution in Software,' IEEE Software.
15. Nonaka I and Takeuchi H (1995) 'The Knowledge Creating Company: How Japanese Companies Create the Dynamics of Innovation,' Oxford University Press, New York.
16. Nutt PC (1989) 'Making Tough Decisions,' Jossey-Bass Inc.
17. Polanyi M (1967) 'The Tacit Dimension,' Routledge and Keon Paul, London.

18. Politis JD (2003) 'The Connection between Trust and Knowledge Management: What are its Implications for Team Performance,' Journal of Knowledge Management, Vol 7, No 5, pp 55-66.
19. Pressman RS (1997) 'Software Engineering – A Practitioner's Approach,' The McGraw-Hill Companies, Inc.
20. Simon H A (1977) 'The New Science of Management Decision,' Prentice-Hall, Inc.
21. Walz DB, Elam JJ and Curtis B (1993) 'Inside a Software Design Team: Knowledge Acquisition, Sharing and Integration,' Communications of the ACM, Vol 36, No 10, pp 63-77.

Index

Printed in the United States of America

PREFACE TO THE SECOND ENLARGED EDITION

THE COLUMBIA GRANGER'S® GUIDE TO POETRY ANTHOLOGIES is the only such guide in the English language, and this second edition is twice as large as it was when it was first published in 1991. It is based on the seventh, eighth, ninth, and tenth editions of THE COLUMBIA GRANGER'S® INDEX TO POETRY. Librarians and researchers use that index for a variety of purposes, among them to find a poem whose title, first line, author, or subject they know. There they have access to well over a hundred thousand poems in nearly eight hundred anthologies, so it is quite likely that searchers will succeed in their quest.

One feature of THE COLUMBIA GRANGER'S® INDEX that has been very popular with librarians is the choice by its editors and consultants of the anthologoies they consider particularly commendable. Such notation led naturally to the present guide. Why not go beyond the starring of a few anthologies and provide a full description and evaluation of all the anthologies indexed in recent editions of THE COLUMBIA GRANGER'S® INDEX? Which are the noteworthy anthologies of American poetry? What are the distinct virtues of the several anthologies of women's poetry? of poetry for children? of Chinese poetry in translation? No book offers this service at present. This one fills that need and will be as useful in its own way as THE COLUMBIA GRANGER'S® INDEX has proved to be throughout this century.

What makes an exceptional anthology? We used the same criteria that librarians use when they review reference books: comprehensiveness; ease of use; authority of editor and publisher; presence of such trappings as introduction, notes, indexes, and biographical information; and, always underlying everything, the excellence of the poems chosen.

A fairly accurate indication of the purpose, scope, and proposed audience of an anthology can be found in its introduction. One can readily recognize the serious approach to the selection of poems from an introduction that makes interesting points about them and quotes from them to support the observations. We have found numerous introductions that are exceptionally interesting in themselves and also make one want to read the poems they are introducing. We comment on them and quote from them whenever we feel they help us summarize an opinion.

We point out the method of organization adopted by the editor or editors. Is it chronological? topical? alphabetical by author? Much can be conveyed about an anthology by these simple descriptions. Does the book have illustrations? Is there prose with the poetry? Is the purpose of the anthology mainly for students and teachers, or is it designed for all kinds of poetry readers? We have covered all such essential features of the anthologies in the seventh, eighth, ninth, and tenth editions of THE COLUMBIA GRANGER'S® INDEX TO POETRY.

How original is an anthology? It may be the first anthology of a particular type of American poetry; another may be the first collection to identify a group of young poets, a "movement"; another may be the first anthology of a nation's poetry in translation. Evaluating such collections is more difficult than evaluating anthologies the bulk of whose poetry is known.

This brings up the question of balance. In an anthology that, for example, claims to include the best of English poetry, one looks for a preponderance of works endorsed by historical opinion, as well as for some adventurous discoveries made by the compilers. The goal is to strike an effective balance between classical, generally praised work and fresh, new additions to the canon.

Clear examples of the artful maneuvering between old and new choices can be found in most of the Norton introductory series, as well as in the numerous Faber and Faber and Oxford University Press offerings. Furthermore, there are scores of collections from small presses that succeed in supplying noncanonical poetry, primarily because they accept the challenge of extending the public's artistic horizons. In all cases, our judgments reflect the criteria used by librarians and critics to evaluate books of nonfiction.

For the second edition of this work, Esther Crain was responsible for writing the descriptions and evaluations of the three hundred anthologies first indexed in the eighth and tenth editions of THE COLUMBIA GRANGER'S® INDEX. Max Winter wrote the descriptions and evaluations of anthologies in the seventh edition. We are very pleased that their work now provides comprehensive coverage of the best anthologies indexed between 1970 and 1993.

We hope that in THE COLUMBIA GRANGER'S® GUIDE TO POETRY ANTHOLOGIES we have defined the standards that will help potential readers and buyers make informed choices.

AFRICAN POETRY

The Heinemann Book of African Poetry in English. *Adewale Maja-Pearce, ed.* **(1990) Heinemann. 224p., pap.**

Of the relatively small number of anthologies of African poetry anthologies published in recent years, this one is among the best. It is a slender, neatly arranged, simple volume, featuring poets from across the African continent, particularly from South Africa, Kenya, and Nigeria. Twenty-two poets are included, arranged chronologically and spanning the past thirty years. The poems are generally brief, intense with vivid, beautiful images. Much of the verse deals with the political and social changes that have raged through Africa for the past several decades. The excellent introduction states that many of these poets have been jailed for their work and many live in exile. Despite the troubling themes, however, each poet reveals a deep loyalty to Africa. This is a fine introductory volume of African verse. None of the poems are translations, and the collection does not claim to represent any particular movement or culture.

The Negritude Poets; an Anthology of Translations from the French. *Ellen Conroy Kennedy, ed.* **(1989) Thunder's Mouth Press. 284p., pap.**

This medium-sized anthology, with a foreword by Maya Angelou, offers a talented sampling of the major, yet relatively unknown, African and Caribbean poets of the twentieth century. Translated from French, the volume features twenty-seven poets native to Guadeloupe, Senegal, Cameroon, and other historically French nations. The term *negritude* was coined to describe indigenous black poets writing in French; these poets largely, but not exclusively, deal with subjects central to developing nations. But the anthology is not bound to any political or social themes, so poems about colonialism and racism share space with the universal themes of romantic love and natural beauty. The poets come from many backgrounds — some born into tribal royalty and educated in French mission schools, others currently exiled from their ravaged countries. An informative introduction explains the social and cultural differences between negritude writers and their American counterparts. Arranged by geographic region, the anthology features distinctive, hard-to-find poetry, and to initiate further study there is a helpful bibliography for each section.

The Penguin Book of South African Verse. *Jack Cope and Uys Krige,* **eds. (1968) Penguin Books. 332p., o.p.**

The compilers note that "poetry is something of an obsession in South Africa." They go on to trace the development of the form from the earliest known peoples through the current generations. One learns, for example, that Afrikaans literature begins only in the twentieth century, strongly influenced by nineteenth-century English and Dutch poets. The compilers edit *Vandag,* a magazine in which many of these poems first appeared, including numerous ones by women poets. The strife in South Africa over the years has resulted in a severe curb on certain poets. Many, for this reason and others, went into exile. Of more than a dozen in this category, among the most famous are Roy Campbell and William Plomer. For those who stayed, "there has been little inclination towards experiment for its own sake. Men and women of all races write verse in English — and the language as a medium has collected undertones of protest." Those poems not in English are translated by the compilers, and these are primarily in the Afrikaans section, where some fifteen poets are found. The other two sections, with about double that number of voices, are devoted to English and African works.

The Penguin Book of Southern African Verse. *Stephen Gray, ed.* **(1989) Penguin Books. 402p., o.p.**

The poets in this fine volume come mainly from the provinces of South Africa, although some hail from such independent nations as Zimbabwe, Angola, and Mozambique. About 120 poets are represented by a few selections each, from Zulu battle songs to Kipling's verse on the Boer War to several modern poems by both whites and blacks on the racial strife of the region. Arranged chronologically beginning with seventeenth-century verse, the volume contains mainly poems from the twentieth century, written largely when the Southern African nations were still colonies of Britain, Portugal, and France. A fair number of dirges and elegies are here. The diversity of voices in this anthology makes it fascinating to read, with high-quality, or at least stimulating, verse. Compiled to introduce contemporary readers to the poetic traditions of this rich, multilingual region, the volume is a fine collection of

African poetic voices; many are in translation. There is no index, but notes on the poets are included.

Poems from Black Africa. *Langston Hughes, ed.* (1963) Indiana University Press. 160p., o.p.

Edited by a distinguished American poet, this is a successful effort to explain black Africa to the English-speaking world. The majority of the English-, French-, and Portuguese-speaking poets are not, even today, that well known. Hughes was not creating celebrities; he was delivering their concerned messages. The collection, from the anonymous "oral traditionals" to the modern age, is, as he says, "a rediscovery of self, a turning within for values to live by, rather than a striking outward in revenge for past wrongs." Also, Africa is made up of many peoples and many histories, all of which move along different paths. The translations, where necessary, are excellent. Most of the poems can be enjoyed as much as songs and vivid portraits of people and places as they can be seen as examples of "a poet's endeavor to recover for his race a normal self pride."

When My Brothers Come Home; Poems from Central and Southern Africa. *Frank Mkalawile Chipasula, ed.* (1985) Wesleyan University Press. 280p.

A Malawian poet and editor gathers together the work of fifty-one poets. Each is represented by four or five typical poems. The countries include Angola, Botswana, Malawi, Mozambique, Namibia, South Africa, Zambia, and Zimbabwe. The greatest number of poets, fourteen, are from South Africa; the fewest from Botswana (one) and Namibia and Zambia (two each). All the poems were written in English with the exception of poems from Angola and Mozambique, former colonies of Portugal. These appear in translation. Explaining the content of his particular choices, the editor says, "This is not a mere extension of Western literary traditions; instead, it reflects in its major themes and attitudes the contentious relationship between Europe and Africa. The major recurrent themes are Negritude; protest against colonial domination and apartheid; anger and bitterness over oppression . . . [and] love, hope, the beauty of the land, and the pathos of the human condition." Each poet is introduced with a brief biographical and bibliographical sketch.

AFRICAN-AMERICAN POETRY

African-American Poetry of the Nineteenth Century; an Anthology.
Joan R. Sherman, ed. **(1992) University of Illinois Press. 506p., pap.,
o.p.**

This is a fascinating historical collection of black poetry that, unlike
the poetry that emerged at the time of the Harlem Renaissance, never
earned lasting popularity. The thirty-five poets included were fairly
prominent in pre-Civil War, Civil War, and Reconstruction years, each
having published at least one volume of verse or with poetry that appeared in black journals of the nineteenth century. Poets with talent and
ability that ranges from mediocre to technically skillful, they are represented by poems that reflect the themes and mood of the era —
abolitionism, social issues, or religion. Arranged chronologically by the
year of the poem, the editor has included one to two pages of biographical information on each poet. There are several fine books of contemporary black poetry; but this emphasizes the literary heritage of black
Americans. Highly recommended for all readers, and indexed by title,
poet, and subject.

American Negro Poetry. *Arna Bontemps, ed.* **(Rev. ed., 1974) Hill and
Wang. 252p., pap., o.p.**

A highly selective, yet totally representative collection of modern
American black poetry and poets. The editor-poet collaborated with
Langston Hughes in a similar work, *The Poetry of the Negro,* that goes back
to the eighteenth century for inspiration. Drawing from the Harlem
Renaissance of the Twenties for more than half of the anthology,
Bontemps then turned to some lesser-known voices of the 1940's and
1950's. Among the poets are Paul Laurence Dunbar, Hughes, and Arna
Bontemps himself. Later come Gwendolyn Brooks, then LeRoi Jones,
and Julia Fields. Most of the poetry reflects the racial struggles of the
black people and the longing and need for freedom, respect, and economic advancement. Two unexpected prose writers are Richard Wright
and Frank Yerby, both respectable poets, although Yerby appears con-

siderably less sure of himself than most of the other poets in the anthology.

Black American Literature: Poetry. *Darwin T. Turner, ed.* **(1969) Charles E. Merrill. 132p.**

This is a very slim, representative collection, offering a competent but general sampling of twenty-three black American poets, spanning three decades with enormous diversity in theme and style. The volume opens with such traditional poets as Phyllis Wheatley and Paul Laurence Dunbar and concludes with more contemporary poets — Don E. Lee and Etheridge Knight; in between are such distinguished favorites as Langston Hughes and Gwendolyn Brooks. The eighty-one poems are strong but written with a range of depth and expression. Brief biographical and critical information prefaces each writer. When published, this anthology was a competent record of the black poetic voice, from a conservative beginning that rarely dealt with race to the angry, experimental, acclaimed poetry of the 1960's.

Black Out Loud; an Anthology of Modern Black Poems by Black Americans. *Arnold Adoff, ed.* **(1970) Macmillan. 86p., o.p.**

This collection was compiled to introduce African-American children to modern black poetry. Included are sixty-seven poems by such poets as Gwendolyn Brooks, Amiri Baraka, Nikki Giovanni, and Langston Hughes, with the quality of the poetry ranging from excellent to mediocre. Most of the poems were written during the civil rights era, at a tumultuous time for America's black neighborhoods, and reflect intense joy and pride as well as bitterness and anger. The anthology is divided into six sections, each addressing a different facet of black life: family, white America, creativity, and heroes, among others. Some of the poems, filled with jarring images, have the look and feel of musical lyrics rather than metered, subdued verse. But there are several powerful poems in this collection by both well-known and more obscure writers, particularly Dudley Randall and Conrad Kent Rivers. Compiled by black poet Arnold Adoff, the poems in this volume are mainly short and lyrical (even more illustrious when read aloud), aiming to capture the mood and voice of black America.

The Black Poets. *Dudley Randall, ed.* **(1971) Bantam Books. 355p., pap.**

In the introduction to *The Poetry of Black America*, Gwendolyn Brooks calls fellow poet Dudley Randall "poet-publisher-anthologist-father figure, and platform provider." The description is apt. Concentrating on poets "turning away from white models and returning to their roots," Randall salutes black poetry under several broad headings. He begins with folk poetry, including folk seculars and spirituals, a fitting reminder of how much we owe to these early composers and poets. Where would American culture be today without, for example, "John Henry" or "Deep River"? Signed verses, which Randall labels "literary poetry," make up most of the collection. Such "forerunners" as Paul Laurence Dunbar soon give way to the "Harlem Renaissance" and finally in the 1960's to such poets as Nikki Giovanni, Ishmael Reed, and James Randall. Unlike larger anthologies, this one is limited to the better-known poets. The result is highly selective, yet highly satisfying. In its way, it represents the heart of the heart of the country.

Black Sister; Poetry by Black American Women, 1746–1980. *Erlene Stetson, ed.* **(1981) Indiana University Press. 312p. $22.50; pap.**

Most anthologies of black American poetry include the work of women, but often, because of constraints of space, represent them with only one poem each. Here, the various talents of black American women are more fully displayed. Beginning with eighteenth- and nineteenth-century poets, we have four poems by Phillis Wheatley, seven each by Frances E. W. Harper and Henrietta Cordelia Ray. The twentieth-century poets include Angelina Weld Grimké, Alice Dunbar-Nelson, Helene Johnson, Margaret Walker, Mari Evans, and the great Gwendolyn Brooks; younger poets are Sonia Sanchez, Lucille Clifton, and Ntozake Shange. This is a collection of the highest quality. All the poets who appear here are well worth the time of the general reader.

The Book of American Negro Poetry. *James Weldon Johnson, ed.* **(Rev. ed., 1931) Harcourt Brace Jovanovich. 300p., pap.**

First published in 1922, this was immediately considered an important collection. The revised edition introduced readers to a new group of poets, including Countee Cullen, Sterling Brown, and, of course, Langston Hughes. The preface was changed, but Johnson's view of black poetry was essentially unaltered in 1931. He had faith in the intellectual capacity of his poets, in the messages they had to deliver. He included all points of view, even those one suspects he may not have entirely agreed with. The result is one of the more satisfactory collections, even though by now it is much dated. Limiting himself to poets in the United States, Johnson included a few who were less than expert at their craft. But even here the message was often so powerful that it overcame the roughness of style. Johnson was a true poet, selecting other vibrant poets to add to the clamor for black artistic recognition and understanding. He achieved his goal.

The Books of American Negro Spirituals, including the Book of American Negro Spirituals and the Second Book of American Negro Spirituals. *James Weldon Johnson and J. Rosamond Johnson, eds.* (1925) 1926) Viking. 187, 189p.

Although the spirituals included in this two-volume set are more song than poetry, they are nonetheless powerful, often deeply revealing examples of folk verse. Attributed to no author and not specifically dated, these 120 spirituals have been reproduced on the pages in traditional African-American dialect and with careful attention to preserving the original rhythms. They vary considerably in tone and subject, typically evoking the hardships of slavery and a steady faith in God. Full musical notation is included for each spiritual. Some, like "Swing Low Sweet Chariot" and "Deep River," will be known to many readers. The material is neat and accessible, indexed by title only. James Weldon Johnson has written a thorough, interesting introduction to the anthology. He provides a historical setting for the development of Negro spirituals, explaining the relation between African rhythms and the songs passed down among slaves. His introduction is unambiguous without being condescending, and the anthology demonstrates that the black spiritual is an American folk-art form that is skillful and unique.

Caroling Dusk; an Anthology of Verse by Negro Poets. *Countee Cullen, ed.* (1927) Harper & Brothers. 237p., o.p.

An early effort to pay tribute to black poets, this collection was strongest in its focus on many younger poets who have since become basic to American poetry and culture. But it also included some fairly poor choices, particularly one Albert Rice. But this came from the daring spirit of the compiler who wanted to represent not only well-known writers, but also relative beginners. Cullen published several volumes of his own work in the 1920's and 1930's that apparently suffered from many of the same artistic faults as his choices in this collection. This is more of historical/literary interest than a good place to turn for representative black poets. It is a more useful reference work for libraries, but not of real value to general readers today.

Celebrations; a New Anthology of Black American Poetry. *Arnold Adoff, ed.* **(1977) Follett. 285p., o.p.**

This anthology, prepared by a teacher in the New York public schools, is aimed primarily at students. It can, however, also be appreciated by anyone who is interested in current black poetry. Some eighty-five writers, male and female, are represented by two hundred forty poems. All were written in this century, and many are by highly regarded black writers. These include Robert Hayden, Sterling A. Brown, Dudley Randall, Gwendolyn Brooks, Ishmael Reed, Amiri Baraka, and Audre Lorde. The poems are arranged thematically into such sections as "Young Soul," "True Love," and "Myself When I Am Real." The taste of the compiler is reliable and challenging.

Collected Black Women's Poetry. Vols. I–IV. *Joan R. Sherman, ed.* **(1988) Oxford University Press.**

This work in four volumes, from The Schomburg Library of Nineteenth Century Black Women Writers, reprints some historically interesting writing, often in the format in which it first appeared, right down to the title-page. The collection begins in the nineteenth century, with particular focus on the years 1890 to 1910. Literary historians call this the "Black Woman's Era." Only a handful of poets are represented in the four volumes, and nine of them were published in the last decade of the nineteenth and first decade of the twentieth century. Christian idealism and morality dominate many of the poems, although there is an occasional reference to contemporary racial problems. Most of the poets have obvious technical ability, but unfortunately, aside from the short introductions, there are few notes to help one interpret the obscure material covered by the majority of the writers. The result is an anthology of historical value, and of great interest to professionals, but of limited interest to most other readers.

Forerunners, The; Black Poets in America. *Woodie King, Jr., ed.* (1975) **Howard University Press. 126p.**

The "forerunners" are the poets who "carried the baton of poetic tradition from the Renaissance in the forties and fifties and created the foundation for the writers of the sixties and seventies." Arrangement of the sixteen poets is alphabetical — a poor choice as it does not place the poets in time. But there is a nice touch: after brief biographical notes for the poets, each one has written a paragraph or two about his or her views on the black poet. Sometimes (particularly in the case of Gwendolyn Brooks or Arna Bontemps), this gives the reader a better understanding of the whole movement and also of the individual voice. The strength of this anthology, one of many welcome collections of black verse, lies in the excellence of the selection. These are the best authors, and there is just enough of their poetry to be the best of the best. This is a grand place to start on a trip through African-American literature.

Golden Slippers; an Anthology of Negro Poetry for Young Readers. *Arna Bontemps, ed.* (1941) **Harper. 220p., o.p.**

The poems in this pocket-sized volume may seem cute and complacent compared to the hard-edged verse by black authors in some contemporary children's anthologies. Published more than fifty years ago, the rhymes and short poems here have timeless charm. There is great diversity in the voices represented, from the urban themes of Langston Hughes and Countee Cullen to the Southern blues lyrics of William Christopher Handy. The verse is simple, evocative, and lyrical. Some of the poems are lullabies, some are spirituals like "Swing Low, Sweet Chariot" that children will know — all grouped in such categories as "Waking Up" and "Big Cities," with biographical information, illustrations, and a first-line index. Here is high-quality verse, but today's children and their parents may find some of it anachronistic.

I Am the Darker Brother; an Anthology of Modern Poems by Negro Americans. *Arnold Adoff, ed.* (1968) **Macmillan. 128p.**

The subtitle is slightly misleading by this time, since the poems are no longer particularly modern, but they are, as the editor states, "easily available to both Negroes and whites." Beginning with Langston Hughes's familiar "Me and the Mule," the sixty short poems are arranged under six broad, rather ambiguous, subject headings. The indexes to first lines and to authors are more helpful. There are short biographical sketches for each of the thirty writers included. Hughes is most copiously represented with seven poems, followed closely by Robert Hayden and Conrad Kent Rivers. Other excellent poets whose work will be found here include Gwendolyn Brooks, Margaret Walker, and Raynold Patterson. Many of the others were born at the close of the nineteenth or beginning of the twentieth century. The selection is of a high order and fulfills the purpose of introducing younger people (grades seven and up) to black poets. Effective line drawings add to the pleasure of the volume.

Jump Bad; a New Chicago Anthology. *Gwendolyn Brooks, ed.* **(1971) Broadside Press. 190p., pap.**

The famous black poet Gwendolyn Brooks offers a collection of a dozen Chicago black voices, all of whom share youth (at the time of publication most of them were in their twenties). They were "involved in an exciting labor, a challenging labor; admitting that it is not likely all blacks will immediately convert to Swahili, they are blackening English. Some of the results are effective and stirring . . . True black writers speak as blacks, about blacks, to blacks." There are several prose pieces in this volume, and the reader is advised to read Don Lee's "Black Critic" and "Black Writing" for excellent background material on the attitudes and hopes of most of the poets in the collection. Each of the poets is represented by four or five pieces. By now, much of the poetry seems dated but is still of social interest and remains a basic reference for anyone studying the thought of the late 1960's and early 1970's.

The New Black Poetry. *Clarence Major, ed.* **(1969) International Publishers. 156p.**

Among the accomplished anthologies that feature black poetry, this is one of the most angry and militant. This is accomplished poetry by talented poets, but too often this slim collection sacrifices talent for "social black consciousness." Al Young, Ishmael Reed, Audre Lord, and Etheridge Knight stand out among the poets, and there are dozens of others whose poetry is equally raw, rhythmic, and effective. Most of the poets were born just after the Second World War, and many of them express anger without any design or form to their work. Major, who includes his own verse here, offers brief biographical information on each writer, as well as a lengthy preface. The anthology records in strong terms the emotions and personal statements of its contributors. There are more solid collections that present a broader range of contemporary black poets and of ideologies and skill.

New Black Voices; an Anthology of Contemporary Afro-American Literature. *Abraham Chapman, ed.* **(1972) Mentor. 606p., pap.**

This solid anthology is divided into four categories: black fiction, black poetry, criticism of black literary and social issues, and documents written by black leaders and officials. The poetry and fiction are the most compelling — angry free verse and evocative lyrics of traditional themes and of class struggles, prejudice, and urban life. Amiri Baraka, Victor Hernandez Cruz, Nikki Giovanni, and Al Young are among the better-known writers. Johnetta Cole, James Baldwin, and Malcolm X are among those featured in the documentary section. The long introduction on the state of black literature and art seems outdated after more than two decades, but the compilation is strong and skilled. Brief biographical information is given.

New Negro Poets U.S.A. *Langston Hughes, ed.* **(1964) Indiana University Press. 127p., o.p.**

Though the word *Negro* is outdated now, this anthology stands as a slender collection of the foremost black poets writing during postwar, civil rights America. Standard anthologized poets such as Nikki Giovanni, Dudley Randall, and LeRoi Jones (now Amiri Baraka) are among the best. But many of the other thirty-seven poets are no less noteworthy. Arranged alphabetically by poet, the volume is divided into five sections, with "Protest" and "Personal, Reflective Statements" containing the most evocative verse. The poets write with anger and pride at being an invisible underclass, but also with great sensitivity of the great joy and warmth in their lives. Gwendolyn Brooks penned a short foreword, explaining that these poets are bound to a double standard: "They have to write poetry, and they have to remember that they are Negroes." Although many anthologies of black poetry exist, this volume is particularly recommended for the general or younger reader — each poem is blunt and powerful.

The Poetry of Black America; Anthology of the 20th Century. *Arnold Adoff, ed.* **(1973) Harper & Row. 552p.**

Among the collections of black poetry this is outstanding. As Gwendolyn Brooks explains in the introduction, "The collection opens with elder heralds and songmakers . . . but what surprises, of a less anthologized nature, are available." For if W. E. B. DuBois and Paul Laurence Dunbar are represented well, so are the poets of what Brooks calls "intensified anger, fed by amazed observation and voracious reading." A decade or so later some of these unknown writers were found in almost all collections, others dropped out of sight, and still others enjoy a small, but loyal audience. This sharp presentation of black poetry gives the reader an amazingly varied view of life, of history, and, of course, of fine artistry. There are about one hundred and fifty poets represented, usually with at least a half dozen poems. The short biographical notes show an amazing number born in the 1920's and 1930's, with few coming from the years before. Noticeably, there is a fine share of outstanding women poets. This basic anthology should be revised to include the poets of the 1970's, 1980's, and 1990's. It is recommended for all libraries.

The Poetry of the Negro, 1746–1970. *Langston Hughes and Arna Bontemps, eds.* **(Rev. ed., 1970) Doubleday. 645p., o.p.**

Here, black poetry is considered in its manifestations not only in the United States, but in such related areas as the Caribbean. Its most questionable section consists of poems by whites writing about blacks. It is not that the whites are critical; on the contrary, most are sympathetic. But should they be included in a book devoted to black poets? At any rate, one hundred sixty poets offer here a cross section of their work. While the translations of some of the poems are excellent, the selection of some of the individual poets is doubtful. The percentage of excellent poetry is probably no more and no less than in any ambitious anthology of this type, i.e., one that tries to cover so many years with representative poets and poetry from each era.

Shadowed Dreams; Women's Poetry of the Harlem Renaissance. *Maureen Honey, ed.* **(1989) Rutgers University Press. 238p., pap.**

The years between the end of the First World War and the Great Depression were the Harlem Renaissance years, although often only men have been identified as the artistic figures of that movement. This anthology uncovers dozens of mostly middle-class, educated black women who wrote about the ordinary and extraordinary moments in their lives. The poets are largely obscure, and their level of ability varies greatly. Their verse is a composite of extremes — frank and intricate, sometimes beautiful, and deceptively simple. All, however, are worth reading, if only for the historical perspectives of a class of women often left behind in history books. The verse is arranged in four parts by theme — "Protest," "Heritage," "Love and Passion," and "Nature." A long introduction provides historical and biographical information about the poets and the era in which they wrote. This is highly recommended for all readers.

3000 Years of Black Poetry. *Alan Lomax and Raoul Abdul, eds.* **(1970) Dodd, Mead. 263p., pap., o.p.**

One of the fathers of folk song and poetry collecting, Lomax exerted a strong influence here. The collection opens with primitive songs from black Africa, followed by "Black Ravens of the Arab World." It is only on page sixty-five that individual European names are tied to poems, and then only for about ten pages. After Spanish, Russian, and French black poetry, the reader is introduced to the Creole of Latin America and the Caribbean. Modern African and American poetry make up the last third of the book, and only sixty pages are given to such well-known black poets as Paul Laurence Dunbar, Langston Hughes, and Gwendolyn Brooks. The anthology captures the spirit and the culture of a people from almost the beginning of history to the present, although the search for continuity is sometimes stretched. To call Ahkenaton a black is to open an argument about the role of Egypt in history that has yet to be settled. Where this collection does triumph is in the selection and the wide scope of its poets and their writings. A major work.

AMERICAN POETRY
Comprehensive Collections

America Forever New; a Book of Poems. *Sara Brewton and John E. Brewton, comps.* **(1968) Thomas Y. Crowell. 270p., o.p.**

This attempt to capture American themes divides the poetry into subsections concerned with the land itself, with the immigrants who came here and the different concepts of liberty they brought with them, with the diversity of the continent, including portraits of American cities, and with the overriding sense of progress in America. Some wonderful poets have been included in the various sections: Carl Sandburg, Emily Dickinson, Robert Frost, Richard Wilbur. But there are also many trivial poems included, and they tend to diminish the treatment of the subject. One can still enjoy, however, the outpourings of the real artists that this land produced.

America in Poetry. *Charles Sullivan, ed.* **(1988) Harry N. Abrams. 207p.**

Handsome, glowing illustrations are the hallmark of this unusual book of poetry about America. The poems, limited as they are by the narrow subject matter, are of varying quality, but the illustrations are of the highest caliber: paintings by Edouard Manet and Winslow Homer, Currier and Ives lithographs, watercolors by John Marin, and pastels by James McNeill Whistler. All the drawings and paintings concern aspects of American life over the ages, and the poems intensify those visual representations. The poems are often by very good poets: Emily Dickinson, Edgar Allan Poe, John Hollander, Carl Sandburg. But many other less-renowned and less-talented poets are also featured, diminishing somewhat the aesthetic appeal of a book that movingly and beautifully attempts to give a sense of what America has been like over the past two centuries.

America Is Not All Traffic Lights; Poems of the Midwest. *Alice Fleming, ed.* **(1976) Little, Brown. 68p., o.p.**

In this anthology's brief foreword, Alice Fleming states that she wishes to "offer a unique insight into what Middle America means to those who see it with a poet's vision and can describe it with a poet's gifts." Indeed, she has included such great midwestern poets as Carl Sandburg, James Wright, Gwendolyn Brooks, and Donald Hall. Although moody and certainly evocative of the midwest, the thirty-two poems chosen are not necessarily these poets' greatest works. Also, the poems are not placed in a recognizable order or indexed. *America Is Not All Traffic Lights* includes fourteen sensitive photographs of midwestern scenes.

American Poetry. *Gay Wilson Allen, Walter B. Rideout, and James K. Robinson, eds.* **(1965) Harper & Row. 1274p., pap., o.p.**

This big anthology is an excellent guide to the major American poets. Forty-nine poets are here, from Anne Bradstreet and Edward Taylor in colonial Massachusetts to such contemporary poets as W. S. Merwin, W. D. Snodgrass, and Wendell Berry. In between are Whitman, Dickinson, Sandburg, and Crane, along with several lesser-known, praiseworthy writers. These poets have created or pioneered a distinctly American type of poetry: Whitman's celebratory songs or e. e. cummings's sly, untraditional verse. The poets are arranged chronologically, and the poems are generally the signature poems of each writer. The editors explain that this anthology was compiled to provide students with a general survey of American poetry that does not sacrifice depth for breadth or leave out competent, more obscure poets. There are no surprises in this literary history of American poetry. It is a helpful record of its styles, movements, and forms.

Anthology of American Poetry. *George Gesner, ed.* **(1983) Avenel Books. 735p., o.p.**

The table of contents begins with "Poets of America" and chronologically lists the major, traditional figures from Anne Bradstreet and Philip Freneau to Theodore Roethke and John Updike, but there is no indication of what poems are to be found under their names. Next comes a list of a half dozen broad subjects with poems listed, but no indication of authors. Before each poet's entry there is a brief biographical sketch, and the choice of poems centers around typical American themes. So, this is more than your average anthology of American poets. It is a collection totally dedicated to American ideas, landscapes, history, personalities. From the first entry, "The flesh and the spirit" to the last, "A visit from St.Nicholas," it is totally, completely, and without question the American dream in poems. As such, it is a marvelous work for schools and many individuals, but those with a more adventuresome nature will wish to turn to other, less parochial works.

The Best Loved Poems of the American People. *Hazel Felleman, ed.* **(1936) Doubleday. 670p., pap.**

Conservative almost to a fault, this anthology includes the basic choices of not only the editor but of laypersons who contributed ideas about what to include. The compiler spent fifteen years on *The New York Times Book Review* answering "queries" put to the section by readers. Many of the poems in this anthology are based upon those same queries, i.e., requests by readers for the reprinting of favorite poems. The choices, too often, are precisely the kind of poems that one finds in the newspapers and that tends to age quickly. Many of the old standards are included, but probably the best use of this book now is in the library where it is a good guide to once much-loved but now forgotten poems.

Early American Poetry; Selections from Bradstreet, Taylor, Dwight, Freneau, and Bryant. *Jane Donahue Eberwein, ed.* **(1978) University of Wisconsin Press. 383p., pap.**

In the preface, the editor says of this fine anthology, "It examines the changing patterns of literature through the work of five poets, each representative of a period in America's cultural development but distinctive as well, speaking in a personal voice on a variety of themes." This volume is not just a collection of verse. Rather, it is a meticulous, in-depth critical study of the colonial and early national periods in American literature. Arranged chronologically, the five poets are represented by dozens of popular and less familiar selections, each illustrating the range and diversity of the poet's skill. Several pages of historical and biographical criticism precede each poet's work, in addition to annotations of the more obscure poetic references. Indexed by poet, title, and first line, this anthology is not for the casual reader looking for an overview of early American verse. It is, however, an excellent, thorough volume for readers interested in the verse of five major poets and the impact this verse had on establishing an American poetic tradition.

The Gift Outright; America to Her Poets. *Helen Plotz, ed.* (1977) **Greenwillow Books. 204p., o.p.**

Helen Plotz, a noted anthologist, hit upon a fertile theme: the response of poets to America and things American. She divides her subject into the topical categories of: "Columbus," "Indians," "Settlers," "Regions" and "History," as well as "The Idea of America." She then chooses poems from the earliest writings on this continent to the most modern, to demonstrate these themes. The poets featured include Philip Freneau, Henry Wadsworth Longfellow, and Ralph Waldo Emerson from older times, to Adrienne Rich, Muriel Rukeyser, and Lawrence Ferlinghetti from modern times. The poems, organized as they are around these potent national classifications, are most compelling, and the great variety of authors included in this rather slim volume is a testament to the editor's assiduous search to illustrate these subjects. These poems are not only fascinating for revealing the impact the concept of America had on writers over the centuries, but also, since they are poems of the highest quality, for providing a great deal of aesthetic enjoyment and intellectual stimulation.

The Little Treasury of American Poetry. *Oscar Williams, ed.* (1948) **Scribner's. 860p., o.p.**

This was the first member of a family of pocket-sized volumes that later included *A Little Treasury of British Poetry* and *A Little Treasury of Modern Poetry*. Its arrangement is chronological, beginning with "American Indian Poetry" and "The Chief Poets from Colonial Times to the Present" and ending with "Poetry of the Forties." Anne Bradstreet has four entries, beginning with her "The flesh and the spirit." Close to one hundred pages are given to Walt Whitman, while Emily Dickinson, Richard Eberhart, and W. H. Auden have between twelve and twenty-five pages. The choice of the balance of the poets ranges from good to excellent, and the reader has a splendid overall view of American poetry up to the mid-1940's. There are some fascinating, now much-dated, photographs of the poets and an index of authors and titles. In the introduction, Williams observes that the growth of American poetry "may lead us to expect even more exciting work in the future." He was correct, as a glance at the anthologies of American poetry after his time will demonstrate.

The Mentor Book of Major American Poets. *Oscar Williams and Edwin Honig, eds.* **(1962) New American Library. 535p.**

The strength of this fine, reissued anthology is its careful, comprehensive treatment of twenty major American poets. Arranged chronologically by poet, the volume begins with colonial writer Edward Taylor and continues through Emerson and Longfellow, concluding with the best-known works of Frost, Millay, and Auden. Prolific poets are favored for inclusion, and most are represented by dozens of selections. This volume is an excellent anthology for students because it introduces the poets in great detail and at a slow pace. Its one drawback is the absence of any of the accomplished poets who have gained recognition since it was first issued. The editors have also included biographical information on the poets and a long introduction detailing the development of the American poetry canon. Indexed by title, poet, and first line.

The New Oxford Book of American Verse. *Richard Ellmann, ed.* **(1976) Oxford University Press. 1,076p.**

Its great size and its editor's good taste make this volume unsurpassable as a survey of American poetry from its earliest days to the present time. A massive anthology, it provides long sections on all the major American poets, as well as shorter sections on minor ones. There are well over fifty poets here, stretching from the early years of the Republic to contemporary times. Among the writers given particular emphasis are Ralph Waldo Emerson, Walt Whitman, Emily Dickinson, and Robert Frost. The poems by these writers and by the others who are featured are superb. All of T. S. Eliot's "The Wasteland" is printed, as are extended selections from Ezra Pound's "Cantos." More modern writers included are Richard Wilbur, Adrienne Rich, Denise Levertov, and A. R. Ammons. There is an appropriate balance between the past and recent generations.

The New Pocket Anthology of American Verse from Colonial Days to the Present. *Oscar Williams, ed.* **(1966) World. 670p., o.p.**

Pocket-sized but full of great poems, this anthology covers American verse from colonial beginnings to the post-Second World War generation. Included are such traditionally anthologized poets as Anne Bradstreet, Poe, Dickinson, Whitman, and Pound. There is a very strong emphasis on contemporary poets, many of whom have gained great distinction since the volume was published: W. S. Merwin, Elizabeth

Bishop, and William Stafford, among others. The poets are arranged alphabetically, with younger poets juxtaposed with older, classic writers; readers will be interested to contrast styles and themes. More than one hundred poets are represented by their most enduring verse. This collection is broad in scope and as strong as any American poetry anthology. The "newer" poets here aren't as new as they once were, but they are skillful and talented, and this collection clearly demonstrates their talent. Indexed by author and title.

The Other Side of a Poem. *Barbara Mattes Abercrombie, ed.*

See under Young Adult Poetry

The Oxford Book of American Verse. *F. O. Matthiessen, ed.* **(1950) Oxford University Press. 1,130p.**

A renowned collection, this displays ideal selective judgment. The distinguished editor-critic begins with America's first poet, Anne Bradstreet (1612–72) and moves through the centuries to close with Robert Lowell. The sixty influential voices represent the canon, although here and there are important poems rarely found in collections. The rule "fewer poets, with more space for each" creates a compelling profile of American poetry. Space allotted to each poet varies, but the usual number is twenty to twenty-five poems for each. There is an evocative, critical introduction that provides an excellent overview of poets and poetry. The standard of printing is up to the usual Oxford high quality, and there are supporting indexes. The dominant theme is one of intelligence and sensibility in poetic discourse. An ideal choice for high school, public, and academic libraries, as well as for the average reader.

Patriotic Poems America Loves. *Jean Anne Vincent, ed.* **(1968) Doubleday. 240p., o.p.**

Here are those favorite American standbys every schoolchild learns: "America the Beautiful," "The Star-spangled Banner," "The Battle Hymn of the Republic," and "Paul Revere's Ride," among others — 121 poems and songs about famous American battles, historic figures, and landmarks. Poets have written about everything from Pocahontas to the Battle of Ticonderoga to the assassinations of Abraham Lincoln and John F. Kennedy. Arranged chronologically by dates of the events, the poems are generally quite accomplished, although perhaps sometimes a little overzealous. Most of the poets are obscure, but among the more prominent are Stephen Vincent Benét, Bret Harte, and Herman Melville. This anthology is a lyrical history lesson, couched in patriotic, popular poems. Indexed by author, title, and first line.

Poems of American History. *Burton Egbert Stevenson, ed.* (Rev. ed., 1922) Houghton Mifflin. 704p.

There are some good poems about American history here, as well as numerous mediocre ballads and refrains that sing America's glory. It is a fine collection for library reference shelves, particularly for locating a difficult-to-find, lesser-known title, but it is a poor choice for today's individual reader because most of the poems are so badly dated. Lesser-known events and personalities are stressed over and over again, and much of the poetry is poor. Conversely, one can say the collection truly reflects American attitudes at the turn of the century, when the first edition was published.

The Poet in America, 1650 to the Present. *Albert Gelpi, ed.* (1973) D. C. Heath. 825p., o.p.

The Poet in America is a reliable text of American poetry, spanning more than 300 years of literary and political history. It begins with a brief introduction that contextualizes the major authors in the book (including Anne Bradstreet, Edward Taylor, William Cullen Bryant, Walt Whitman, William Carlos Williams, and Theodore Roethke). The work is divided into four sections: "Colonial Beginnings," "American Romantic Poetry," "The American Poetic Renaissance," and "The Contemporary Scene." Because this text was published in 1973, "The Contemporary Scene" contains only poets popular in the 1970's. Otherwise, this anthology aptly illustrates the variety of styles evident in American poetry from its beginnings onward with such works as Whitman's "Song of Myself," Longfellow's "Song of Hiawatha," Frost's "Mending Wall," and Stevens's "Idea of Order at Key West." Works are indexed by author, title, and first line.

Salt and Bitter and Good; Three Centuries of English and American Women Poets. *Cora Kaplan, ed.*

See under WOMEN'S POETRY AND FEMINIST POETRY

Six American Poets; an Anthology. *Joel Conarroe, ed.* **(1991) Random House. 281p.**

Rather than skim over three hundred years of American poetry, this volume concentrates on six poets who are generally acknowledged to be among the nation's greatest: Whitman, Dickinson, Wallace Stevens, William Carlos Williams, Frost, and Langston Hughes. The anthology is designed for the general reader as an introduction to these poets, offering a thorough tour of their work as well as biographical and critical information to supplement the poems. The poets are arranged chronologically, represented by dozens of their best-known selections along with some lesser-known gems. The quality of verse is high, from Whitman's sonorous free verse to the jazzy lyrics of Hughes. *Six American Poets* is fairly inclusive and provides valuable information on the structural and thematic differences among the six poets. The arrangement is lucid and accessible. Indexed by title and first line.

The Treasury of American Poetry. *Nancy Sullivan, ed.* **(1978) Doubleday. 838p.**

Born before Shakespeare died, Anne Bradstreet was among America's early settlers and was considered its first major poet. Here readers are introduced to the special tone that made her truly American and not simply reflecting English style. It is the quest for the American voice that inspires this large and, for the most part, traditional collection. There are some one hundred poets represented. About three hundred pages are devoted to poets before the twentieth century, while the remainder (beginning with Edward Arlington Robinson and Robert Frost) are distinctly modern. William Carlos Williams is given fourteen pages, while Ezra Pound has eleven and T.S. Eliot nineteen. With the end of the Second World War, the number of pages for each poet averages seven or eight, thus permitting a wide selection of poets and poetry for the last half of the century. The book is a good source of well-known verse with a wide choice of poets.

Yankee Doodles; a Book of American Verse. *Ted Malone, ed.*

See under BALLADS AND SONGS

See also AFRICAN-AMERICAN POETRY; ENGLISH AND AMERICAN POETRY: COMPREHENSIVE COLLECTIONS; POETRY: STUDY AND TEACHING

AMERICAN POETRY
17th, 18th, 19th Centuries

An American Anthology, 1787–1900. *Edmund Clarence Stedman, ed.* **(1900) Houghton Mifflin. 878p.**

Anyone who wishes to find out what their grandparents or parents thought was the best in American poetry need only turn to this historical collection. As American as the flag, the choices were made by a banker and critic who wrote a history of the New York Stock Exchange. But Stedman was a literary figure, too, and gathered together the works of Poe and Whitman. Although he died in 1908, his idea of high quality poetry helped mold public opinion through the Second World War. Today his anthology is primarily a place to turn to for old favorites from Philip Freneau (b.1752) to Bryant, Longfellow, Whitman, all of whom published before 1900. Fifty-eight pages near the end contain short biographical sketches of all the poets. This is an extremely helpful feature, as many are now forgotten. For example, how many can recall the work of Francis Miles Finch, Mary Bradley, or Sarah Piatt? One suspects that the majority of the four hundred authors in the book are now little more than vague figures from a time past. But the anthology is invaluable for its social and historical implications and for any study of the history of American poetry.

American Poetry: The Nineteenth Century. Vols. I–II. *John Hollander, ed.* **(1993) The Library of America. 1099p., 1050p.**

This compact, tight two-volume set is a comprehensive and traditional anthology that will very well serve those who wish a fuller picture of American literature. So impersonal that it does not even have an introduction, the set is arranged chronologically, the first book spanning the period from Freneau to Whitman, the second from Melville to Stickney, with the addition of Native American poetry, folk songs, and spirituals. The selections are indexed by title and first line, and each volume has a section of biographies. The addition of fairly large sections of Native American and other folk songs sets these books apart from other conventional anthologies.

American Verse of the Nineteenth Century. *Richard Gray, ed.* (1973) **Rowman and Littlefield; published in Great Britain by J. M. Dent. 234p., o.p.**

Richard Gray, in his introduction to *American Verse of the Nineteenth Century*, discusses the importance of "self-definition and self-discovery" in American poetry of the nineteenth century by addressing the works of a few of the included poets (for example, Freneau, Emerson, Longfellow, Poe, Whittier, and Dickinson). The 130 well-crafted and introspective poems anthologized are, on the whole, those valuable to an understanding of each poet's work — such poems as Poe's "To Helen" and Whitman's "Song of Myself." Gray has grouped poems by author and arranged authors chronologically, with a biographical note preceding each poet's work. There are ample footnotes and an index of first lines at the end of the volume. This thorough, smartly constructed research tool should be useful for the student of nineteenth-century American literature.

American Women Poets of the Nineteenth Century. *Cheryl Walker, ed.*

See under   WOMEN'S POETRY AND FEMINIST POETRY

Cowboy Poetry; a Gathering. *Hal Cannon, ed.* (1985) **Gibbs M. Smith. 201p.**

This pocket-sized collection, able to fit in a saddle bag, "begins with the classic poems that have proven their vitality by their longevity." The first entry is "The Cowboy's Soliloquy," which was first published in 1885 but "was undoubtedly sung and recited long before that." Notes accompany the verse, usually a line or two to a poem. About two-thirds of the book is devoted to contemporary poets. The folklorist/compiler hopes to set the record straight about the real life of the cowboy by puncturing its stereotyped picture. He allows the cowboys to speak for themselves "as they celebrate the huge sky, the rodeo, busting broncos, the cattle drive . . . the land, and the life and the times of the people who continue, spiritedly, to live that cowboy life." The book ends with a brief bibliography. There is neither an author nor a title index. The idea is marvelous, but its realization, especially in the modern period, is far from ideal. The collection often stumbles into sentimentality, with exactly the sort of stereotypical bravado the compiler has been trying to avoid. There are pleasant black and white drawings by Carrie Henrie.

Kissing the Rod; an Anthology of Seventeenth-Century Women's Verse. *Germaine Greer, Susan Hastings, Jeslyn Medoff, and Melinda Sansone, eds.*

See under   WOMEN'S POETRY AND FEMINIST POETRY

The New Oxford Book of Seventeenth Century Verse. *Alistair Fowler, ed.*

See under   ENGLISH POETRY: 1500–1700 — EARLY MODERN ENGLISH

101 Patriotic Poems. (1986) Contemporary Books. 138p., o.p.

No compiler is identified. No introduction or preface is supplied, and there is no table of contents, so it is difficult to see the plan, if any, of the poems' arrangement. One must, none the less, celebrate the effort, particularly as the well-known authors (from Patrick Henry to Martin Luther King) are balanced by those less celebrated. There are one hundred and one poems, beginning, suitably enough, with Shelley's "Tribute to America." The reader then moves on to Robert Bridges's "A Toast to Our Native Land" and from there to John Pierpont's "The Fourth of July." A number of the poets are English, with Sir Walter Scott's "Breathes There a Man" just preceding the final entry, Martin Luther King's "I Have a Dream" speech. Few of the poems are more than a few stanzas in length, and almost all have a recurring drumbeat rhythm. It is the stuff that children recite and memorize. At the end there is an index of authors and of titles.

The Oxford Book of Victorian Verse. *Arthur Quiller-Couch, ed.*

See under   ENGLISH AND AMERICAN POETRY: COMPREHENSIVE COLLECTIONS

Poems of the Old West; a Rocky Mountain Anthology. *Levette J. Davidson, ed.*

See under   BALLADS AND SONGS

Seventeenth-Century American Poetry. *Harrison T. Meserole, ed.* **(1968) Doubleday. 540p., o.p.**

Anyone who is familiar with the historical background of American poetry knows that a woman, Anne Bradstreet (c.1612–1672), was our first great poet. Her verse "The Flesh and the Spirit" is an American classic. It is, of course, here along with twelve other outstanding poems. In the collection's chronological arrangement, she is followed by Michael Wigglesworth (1631–1705). His poem "A Song of Emptiness to Fill Up the Empty Pages Following" fairly well sets the tone for his work. It opens with the line "Vain, frail, short lived, and miserable Man." He, too, is a major poet, as is Edward Taylor. After these three follow the "Minor Writers" (fourteen, plus entries from The Bay Psalm Book) and "Other Representative Writers" (about three dozen). Thanks to this arrangement, the collection may be read in two ways. For the best writers of the age, simply stay with the three opening poets. For an overview of what it meant to be a poet in seventeenth-century America and what the concerns of the average individual were, turn to the body of the book. Whichever way you choose, do not miss the splendid introduction. There are biographical sketches, and authors and titles of poems are indexed.

AMERICAN POETRY
20th Century

The Actualist Anthology. *Morty Sklar and Darrell Gray, eds.* (1977) **Spirit That Moves Us Press. 144p., pap.**

The Actualist Movement, according to editors Morty Sklar and Darrell Gray, began in 1970 in Iowa City. Although the anthology's introduction does not clearly define Actualism, the fourteen poets included here (among whom Anselm Hollo, George Mattingly, and Allan Kornblum are notable) do seem to rejoice in the surprise element of daily life. Their 150 poems are fun, spontaneous, and realistic; subject matter ranges from cell transplants to the art of poetry. The works are grouped by author, with a photograph and an author's note preceding each section. No set principle seems to guide the placement of authors or works within the anthology and the book lacks an index. Although its focus may be too specific to be useful to the average student, the volume provides a good cross section of a small part of recent American poetry.

The American Poetry Anthology. *Daniel Halpern, ed.* (1975) **Avon Books. 506p., pap.**

The editor of *Antaeus* and *The Antaeus Anthology* has a sure sense of modernity, and it is never better displayed than in this collection of the work of seventy-five poets, all of whom were born after 1934. While many of the poets have more or less disappeared or are no longer that representative of modern times, their voices were an excellent guide to the period between the Korean and the Vietnam wars. There are amazingly different configurations of interests. Here one may find the absurdist alongside the humorist and the realist. Most of the poets seem rather naive. The sounds of youth and the preoccupations with trivial experiences dominate. An exception may be the women, from Louise Glück to Diane Wakoski. They have interests that today seem much broader in scope than some of their contemporary men. James Tate and Charles Simic are among the survivors from this period, and their poetry demonstrates why they were able to escape the 1960's. An important collection about an important period in American history, this should be in many libraries. Individual readers will prefer anthologies of a wider scope.

American Poetry since 1970; Up Late. *Andrei Codrescu, ed.* **(2d ed., 1989) Four Walls Eight Windows. 623p., pap.**

Codrescu explains in his introduction that this anthology offers a different version of American poetic history, featuring more poets whom he terms "activist," as opposed to "academic." Most of the 110 authors featured here will be familiar to readers who have followed poetry for the past three decades. They include Ed Sanders and Ted Berrigan, who gained fame in the 1960's, as well as Ishmael Reed, Bill Knott, and Mei-Mei Berssenbrugge, who are at the height of their careers. This second edition has dropped a few selections to make room for new poems and some new poets. Many of the poems, ranging in quality from excellent to average, take on a familiar cynicism and ghoulish humor in the face of various injustices. They deal largely with political and social issues; many are composed in experimental or free-verse form. Codrescu includes a final section of brief biographical information on each poet. This large volume is recommended for readers who want a quick representation of the state of mainstream contemporary poetry in America. These are the poets who win literary prizes, hold professorships at universities, and are highly visible in the world of modern American poetry. Arranged chronologically by poet and indexed by title and author.

The Ardis Anthology of New American Poetry. *David Rigsbee and Ellendea Proffer, eds.* **(1977) Ardis. 368p., o.p.**

This useful, comprehensive anthology accurately displays the new voices and styles present in American poetry of the late 1970's. Many of the poets featured had published one book (at most) when the anthology went to press; several have since achieved success, including Lynn Sukenick, Cynthia MacDonald, Gary Soto, William Logan, Thomas Lux, and Ellen Bryant Voigt. The anthology emphasizes writing rather than writers: the editors state, in an introductory note, "This is an anthology of poems, not poets." The works included address primarily personal subjects: death, marriage, love, divorce, memory, anger, family relations, and human preoccupations. The images from everyday life reflected in the poems are clearly intended to make poetry more accessible to the common reader. Peter Meinke's "Chicken Unlimited" suggests that a super-sized box of fried chicken bonds the poet to his children; Thomas Lux's "Green Prose" pokes fun at poets obsessed with nature by suggesting that they write with green ink. The editors have placed their index at the book's front, with a sensitive collection of author photographs and illuminating biographies at the end.

Bear Crossings: an Anthology of North American Poets. *Anne Newman and Julie Suk, eds.*

See under Animal and Bird Poetry

Blood to Remember; American Poets on the Holocaust. *Charles Fishman, ed.* **(1991) Texas Tech University Press. 426p.**

These haunting, stark poems were compiled, according to the editor, so that no one would ever forget the horror of the Holocaust. Of almost 250 poems, many include graphic depictions of concentration camps, terror on the streets of Jewish ghettos, and vivid descriptions of Nazi guards. Some of the verse is more subtle and personal, honoring murdered relatives and families torn apart. Such well-known poets as Anthony Hecht, Marvin Bell, Denise Levertov, and David Ignatow are included. But many obscure or unknown writers are also featured, often translated from German and Yiddish. Here are poems of all lengths and styles, some written just after the war, some written more recently. Notes on the poems and poets are particularly interesting. Highly recommended for the quality of verse and the straightforward arrangement, although this volume may not be for everyone. Indexed by poet, title, and translator.

The Bread Loaf Anthology of Contemporary American Poetry. *Robert Pack, Sydney Lea, and Jay Parini, eds.* **(1985) University Press of New England. 348p., pap.**

"This book derives its title from the Bread Loaf Writers' Conference of Middlebury College in Vermont, which for sixty years has offered American poets a gathering place and . . . encouragement for the writing and reading of poetry." Beyond that necessary criterion for inclusion, a poet must have published at least two books since 1980. Most important, "none of these poems has yet been published in individual collections." The rigorous rules of inclusion eliminate amateurs, although here and there among the nearly 100 poets there are some less than persuasive voices. On the whole, though, who can argue with A. R. Ammons, John Ashbery (to begin the alphabet), or with Richard Wilbur and Charles Wright (to end it)? Men outnumber women about four to one. Each poet has an average of two to four entries, and they move from "Long Island" (Marvin Bell), to the "Abyss" (X. J. Kennedy), to Ellen Voigt's "Landscape, Dense with Trees." If one word were needed to summarize the poetry, it would be "professional," almost to a fault. This works well enough for the truly gifted, but it is a trifle dry for some others. Still, as a cross section of relatively modern American verse, it is a winner.

Brother Songs; a Male Anthology of Poetry. *Jim Perlman, ed.* **(1979) Holy Cow! Press. 118p.**

Brother Songs: A Male Anthology of Poetry is divided into four sections: "Poems about Fathers," "Poems for Sons," "Poems about Brothers," "Poems for Friends and Lovers." This anthology shows the importance of male relationships and "maleness" in contemporary American poetry. Although modern poets are represented, the editor does not include enough material by each poet to show adequately the effect of such relationships on a poet's life and work — which in effect would better show the significance of the male relationship within current American poetry. The poems published are profound and reflective. Robert Bly, David Ignatow, William Stafford, Charles Wright, Donald Hall, and Philip Levine are among the major poets here represented. A poet may appear in more than one section; heavily published poets appear often. Finding work by a specific author may be difficult: the work has no index. This anthology is inspired by a worthy sentiment but would have been improved by better organization.

California Bicentennial Poets Anthology. *A. D. Winans, ed.* **(1976) Second Coming Press. 217p., pap.**

A. D. Winans seems to have had confused intentions in compiling this anthology. He states in his one-page introduction, "The poems in this anthology speak of love, hate, beauty, violence, hope, and despair . . . . These poets are today's poets . . . . This bicentennial anthology is dedicated to them, and the likes of them, throughout the U.S. and the world." This anthology is indeed a collection of notable California poets, but it does not display qualities of California poetry to distinguish it from other poetry. Lawrence Ferlinghetti, Allen Ginsberg, Philip Levine, Gary Soto, and Brother Antoninus are among the poets in this volume, and each writer's coverage is proportional to his success when the book was published. There are occasional photographs of authors, and the volume has contributors' notes at the end, but no index. This is an interesting but uninformative volume.

Contemporary American & Australian Poetry. *Thomas Shapcott, ed.*

See under WORLD POETRY

Contemporary American Poetry. *Donald Hall, ed.* **(1972) Penguin Books. 280p.**

All of the poets included in this pocket-sized volume gained distinction after the Second World War, breaking the literary tradition established by T. S. Eliot and the New Critics a generation earlier. Hall, himself a distinguished poet, here arranged the poets chronologically, beginning with William Stafford and Dudley Randall and ending with Sylvia Plath, X. J. Kennedy, and Etheridge Knight. Thirty-nine poets are represented by almost two hundred poems, among them the most structurally precise and distinctive of each writer's work. Hall praises the verse's "new kind of imagination," explaining that only in the twentieth century did a particularly American tradition of poetry emerge. This volume accurately reflects the shape of modern poetry between the late 1940's and early 1960's. It bypasses many stylistic movements and colloquial trends, such as the Beat movement, and instead presents a range of superior poetry of all types. Although no longer considered truly contemporary, this is still an excellent anthology for anyone interested in the foremost poets of the fifteen years or so following the Second World War.

Contemporary American Poetry. *A. Poulin, Jr., ed.* **(4th ed., 1985) Houghton Mifflin. 728p.**

Teacher and poet, Poulin offers here a collection of poets whom he believes every American student should know. The format is in the familiar university style, but it goes beyond a typical textbook and may be enjoyed by anyone, in or out of college. The fifty poets are offered in alphabetical order, and for each there is a selection of representative work. A full-page photograph of each of the poets precedes their dozen or so poems. There is an extensive section of "Notes on the poets" that provides some one hundred pages of biography, bibliography, and criticism. This is followed by an essay, "Contemporary American Poetry; the Radical Tradition," that in many texts would be the introduction. It is just fine here because it presupposes that by this point the student will have read many of the poems and at least be familiar with the ground the editor is covering. Almost all of the poets are widely published, and there are few exceptions to the high quality of their work.

The Contemporary American Poets; American Poetry since 1940.
Mark Strand, ed. **(1969) World. 390p., pap.**

Poet and compiler, Strand observes, "It is one of the points of this anthology to demonstrate the variety of American poetry since 1940 and, in those cases where careers extend from that time, to demonstrate their development." Poets who published before 1940 are not included. Arrangement is alphabetical by poet, with A. R. Ammons and John Ashbery at the beginning and, some one hundred poets later, Charles Wright and James Wright. There are brief biographies and indexes of titles and first lines. Twenty-five years later, it is fascinating to look back to when this collection was published and see just how astute Strand was in his choices. Most of today's famous poets who were writing then are included. Some few simply disappeared in the 1970's and 1980's, but these are the exception. Strand is also to be commended for his wise choice of poems, some of which are by now minor classics or are well worth recalling.

Contemporary Northwest Writing; a Collection of Poetry and Fiction.
Roy Carlson, ed. **(1979) Oregon State University Press. 199p., pap.**

Roy Carlson's anthology of poetry and fiction begins with an interpretative history of literature in the Northwest, followed by brief commentaries on all of the writers included in the book. *Contemporary Northwest Writing* features the work of twelve poets and six fiction writers, all of whom were residents of the Northwest at the time of publication; the 108 poems are distributed equally among their respective authors (Gary Snyder, William Stafford, Theodore Roethke, and Richard Hugo, among others). Many of the poems, although they do address the Northwestern landscape, cannot be considered distinctly "northwestern." Poems are arranged chronologically by poet; the book lacks an index. The anthology's extensive bibliography will be helpful to poetry student and common reader alike.

Contemporary Poetry in America. *Miller Williams, ed.* **(1973) Random House. 189p., pap., o.p.**

Miller Williams's large-format anthology is an expansive collection of 340 poems by ninety-six American poets from the three decades following the Second World War. Although it ignores the New York school and contains far more male than female poets, readers will find this work a basically trustworthy survey of poetry from those decades. Included here are such notable poets as Allen Ginsberg, Robert Bly, James Dickey, Charles Bukowski, John Hollander, and Sylvia Plath. When authors did not provide their own biographies, the editor supplied introductory biographical summaries. The editor has included strong work by each poet; the busy, full layout is peppered with (in most cases) poorly reproduced photographs of authors. The book is usefully indexed.

Contemporary Southern Poetry. *Guy Owen and Mary C. Williams, eds.* **(1979) Louisiana State University Press. 203p., o.p.**

The editors of this anthology begin their introduction by supplying three characteristics of southern poetry after the Second World War: rural subjects, conservatism in matters of form, and the use of distinctly southern dialects. The collected poems are all readable and accessible, taking a personal approach to topics as different as hermits, faith healing, and William Wordsworth. Such poets as James Dickey, A. R. Ammons, and Miller Williams have been widely anthologized, while other poets present here are possibly more well known in the southern portion of the United States. The 150 poems selected here have not been indexed, but they have been arranged alphabetically by their 61 authors — who, incidentally, come from assorted racial and cultural backgrounds within the South. Also, the editors supply brief biographies of each author at the end of the book.

A Controversy of Poets. *Paris Leary and Robert Kelly, eds.* **(1965) Anchor Books. 567p., o.p.**

According to the editors, both distinguished poets, this pocket-sized anthology was meant to "turn the attention of the reader to the contemporary poem, away from movements, schools or regional considerations." They protest the labels critics tend to slap on writers and want the reader to choose what he likes on his own. And because they have included so many first-rate poets and fine selections, readers will have much to choose from. All of the poets here were young when this volume was published, just beginning long, distinguished careers — John Ashbery, Adrienne Rich, W. S. Merwin, and Richard Wilbur, to name only a few. The anthology is arranged alphabetically; short biographies are included, sometimes by the poets themselves. Both editors have written short afterwords, but no critical information is given. Their intent is to show the range of styles and forms of mid-century poetry, offering quality verse and no gimmicks.

The Criterion Book of Modern American Verse. *W. H. Auden, ed.* **(1956) Criterion Books. 336p., o.p.**

W. H. Auden's complex, fascinating introduction is as impressive as the poetry selected for this accomplished volume. He analyzes the social and academic development of the American poetic tradition, setting a historical tone for the anthology. Eighty-one prominent poets from the twentieth century are included, represented by their best poems. Almost all of the poets will be familiar to modern readers. The volume begins with Stephen Crane and Edgar Lee Masters, continues with such frequently anthologized writers as Sandburg, Pound, and Aiken, and concludes with modern poets Anthony Hecht and Richard Wilbur. Arranged chronologically by author and indexed by first line and title, poems vary in size, form, and subject. Recommended for readers looking for a solid, inclusive volume of the best American poets of the first half of the century, this anthology traces American poetry since it began to develop its own unique form.

Divided Light: Father & Son Poems; a Twentieth-Century American Anthology. *Jason Shinder, ed.* **(1983) Sheep Meadow Press. 293p., pap.**

Concentrated around the subject of fathers and sons, these poems are written by men about their relationships with their most significant male progenitors and progeny. The selection of poems is both astute and discriminating. The authors are of uniformly high caliber, and the poems are among the best of their work. All pieces were written in the twentieth century by Americans, and this narrow focus increases the depth of the exploration, since our distinctive society is plumbed for its insights into a particularly emotional topic. The material is arranged chronologically and features the work of Stanley Kunitz, Theodore Roethke, Robert Lowell, and Michael Harper, among many others. The variety in the handling of the subject matter is remarkable, moving from the beauty of Richard Wilbur's evocation of his father's artistic temperament, to Donald Hall's bittersweet reflection on the mortality conferred upon him by his baby boy. This anthology provides sharp insights into the artistically fertile ground of father and son relationships.

Do Not Go Gentle; Poetry and Prose from behind the Walls. *Michael Hogan, ed.* **(1977) Blue Moon Press. 85p., pap.**

The poems in this anthology are the products of a workshop conducted at the Arizona State Prison from 1973 to 1975 by Richard Skelton, a professor at the University of Arizona. The workshop served both as a generator of artistic activity and as an emotional and creative outlet. These seventy-five poems, often shockingly direct, communicate convicts' thoughts and emotions; they address subjects from love to nature to happiness. All but two of the 16 poets were alive at the time of publication. Michael Hogan, anthology editor and former member of the workshop, has organized the book poorly: poets are not arranged in any discernable order and there is no index. Also, Hogan supplies no biographical information. The anthology makes interesting reading, though, for its depiction of a little-known portion of this country's population: prisoners.

Don't Forget to Fly; a Cycle of Modern Poems. *Paul B. Janeczko, ed.* **(1981) Bradbury Press. 133p., o.p.**

Unfortunately for curious readers, this volume includes no biographical information, no index of first lines, and most important, no introduction. Although we shall never know what Janeczko intended when he chose these poems for an anthology, it is still an interesting collection. The 130 poems, from those of Walt Whitman to e. e. cummings to Al Young, do not seem to have any uniting theme. Here are also frequently anthologized favorites by Ogden Nash, Randall Jarrell, Adrienne Rich, and Lucille Clifton, all strong examples of each poet's skill. Oddly, the anthology is arranged by subject, sometimes with very few poems in a section, and those not always clearly related. Grouped together, for example, are "Old Men," by Ogden Nash, "The Two Old Gentlemen" by Robert Wallace, and "The Old Men," by Charles Reznikoff. But the categories are never listed in the table of contents. Janeczko has included splendid poems about everything from amputations, cars, and insomnia to children and suicide. For all readers, from the casually interested to the more discriminating, this is a strong, haphazard, somewhat mysterious collection.

An Ear to the Ground; an Anthology of Contemporary American Poetry. *Marie Harris and Kathleen Aguero, eds.* **(1989) University of Georgia Press. 334p., pap.**

Containing a wide variety of mediocre to exceptional poetry, this is one of many new anthologies that seeks to present minority and women writers they feel have been ignored by the white literary establishment. Among the 103 compelling, accomplished poets featured are Etheridge Knight, Gwendolyn Brooks, and Quincy Troupe. But most are obscure to general readers and write poetry that tends to take on a self-importance that far exceeds their skill. Political, social, and personal anger is the overwhelming theme, and the selections representing each poet also deal with cultural assertions that grow tedious with repetition. The verse is contemporary, all written within the past 20 years, and part of the multicultural movement in American literature today. Arranged alphabetically by author, this volume includes some fine work but falls short of its undertaking.

Ecstatic Occasions, Expedient Forms; 65 Leading Contemporary Poets Select and Comment on Their Poems. *David Lehman, ed.* **(1987) Collier Books/Macmillan. 256p., o.p.**

Deriving from a reasonable supposition that poems develop their particular forms because of impulses on the part of their creators, this volume pursues this premise by asking a number of contemporary poets to provide a poem along with a statement on the decisions they made as they wrote it. The result proves fascinating indeed to all those who are interested in the art and craft of poetry. The poets who contributed to this anthology include A. R. Ammons, John Ashbery, Amy Clampitt, Robert Creeley, Marilyn Hacker, Brad Leithauser, James Merrill, Louis Simpson, Mona Van Duyn, and Richard Wilbur, to name only some of the distinguished authors included. Their commentary on the poems tends to be brief, ranging from one half page to two pages in length, but reveals much about the poets' decisions and their creative process.

Editor's Choice: Literature & Graphics from the U.S. Small Press, 1965–1977. *Morty Sklar and Jim Mulac, eds.* **(1980) Spirit That Moves Us Press. 501p., pap.**

The editors state, in their well-considered introduction, that their objectives are to collect poetry that combines craft and raw emotion, to publicize work printed by small presses (such as Ally Press, Curbstone

Press, or Dustbooks), and to suggest a new direction for modern writing. They have divided the book into four sections: "Poetry," "Fiction," "Essays," and "Graphics." Poetry occupies the first half of the book, while prose and visual art fill the second half. The anthology includes some foreign and U.S. poets who had gained a following before the volume's publication (Rilke, Holub, Lorca) or who have prospered since 1980 (Stafford, Bukowski), along with lesser-known poets who have remained lesser-known. The sixty-nine poems collected here are generally mediocre works or lesser works by great authors. Although the book ends with brief biographies and descriptions of various small presses, it has no index.

The Face of Poetry; 101 Poets in Two Significant Decades — the 60's and the 70's. *LaVerne Harrell Clark and Mary MacArthur, eds.* **(1979) Heidelberg Graphics. 302p., pap., o.p.**

The Face of Poetry contains no introduction — only a foreword by Richard Eberhart. The editors introduce these poets to readers through photographs instead. The book contains 101 poets, including such writers as Mark Strand, Charles Simic, and Donald Hall, arranged alphabetically and accompanied by a photograph taken by LaVerne Clark. The poems are, on the whole, representative of each poet's style, but there is only one poem for each poet. This anthology is an interesting document, although not a prime source of information about contemporary poetry.

15 Chicago Poets. *Richard Friedman, Peter Kostakis, and Darlene Pearlstein, eds.* **(1976) Yellow Press. 128p., pap.**

Although some of the 100 poems in *15 Chicago Poets* refer to Chicago, the only common characteristic that makes the poets "Chicagoan" is their residency in the city in the mid-1970's. Readers should find several familiar names here: Gwendolyn Brooks, Ted Berrigan, Maxine Chernoff, and Alice Notley, to name a few. The poems are dynamic and highly readable, about subjects ranging from fishbowls to x-rays to trust. The editors have aided readers by including photographs and biographies before each poet's section. Sections are arranged alphabetically by poet; the work, however, has no index. The inclusion of more works by each poet would have given readers a stronger sense of the nature of Chicago poetry.

Fifty Contemporary Poets; the Creative Process. *Alberta T. Turner, ed.*
(1977) David McKay. 355p.

This anthology recommends itself by concentrating less on the actual
poetry and more on the poet's accompanying notes about how the poem
came to be written. It is an interesting experiment that works overall
because most of the poets manage to avoid sounding too literary or
condescending. But readers who are bored by the idea of a poet explaining his own poem as if lecturing to a class should beware. Fifty
poems are analyzed, selected and criticized by such poets as Hayden
Curruth, Marvin Bell, Norman Dubie, and Charles Wright. Turner provides a lengthy introduction about the nature of the poetic process, but
this generalization tends to make long-winded reading. The highly in-
dividualized and mysterious poetic "process" can be understood only
with difficulty, and this anthology is recommended mainly for fans of the
included poets or for those who like to read writing about writing. The
poems are skillful, but the accompanying explanations will probably interest only familiar readers.

Fifty Years of American Poetry; Anniversary Volume for the Academy
of American Poets. Introduction by Robert Penn Warren. (1984) Harry
N. Abrams. 260p.

Here one celebrates fifty years of the Academy of American Poets,
which should not be confused with the Poetry Society of America (which
earlier celebrated its fiftieth anniversary with *The Golden Year*). Warren
explains that one hundred and twenty-six poets are represented, each of
whom is an award winner. "A glance at the table of contents will show
that no one school, bailiwick, method, or category of poetry has dominated the interest of the Academy." True. Where else would one find
Edgar Lee Masters and Ezra Pound award winners in the same year? In
another fifty years one may ask who is Oliver St. John Gogarty, Edward
Markham, or Kenneth Rexroth, but today they are well enough appreciated to be found in these pages. This is a profile of different approaches to verse, of truly different voices and opinions; an excellent
choice for the individual reader who wants a broad impression of American poetry from 1924 to 1984.

Flowering after Frost; the Anthology of Contemporary New England Poetry. *Michael McMahon, ed.* **(1975) Branden Press. 120p., o.p.**

This anthology collects within one volume the work of twenty-two New England poets who achieved success after the death of Robert Frost. Among the writers anthologized here, Lyn Lifshin, Wesley McNair, and David Kherdian remain prominent; the 125 included poems address such diverse topics as marriage, killing turkeys, and meteorology. The book contains no index, and poets such as Robert Lowell, who clearly "flowered after Frost" and were prolific at the time of this volume's publication, have been omitted. This anthology will give readers a taste of 1970's New England poetry, but it is by no means a complete collection.

The Generation of 2000; Contemporary American Poets. *William Heyen, ed.* **(1984) Ontario Review Press. 364p., pap.**

"Contemporary," one learns from the introduction, refers to poets born between 1932 and 1949. The thirty-one poets are well established, and all have an audience reached, for the most part, through the little magazines. About one third are more widely published and are now well known to the general public, e.g., the late Raymond Carver, Wendell Berry, Louise Glück, Albert Goldbarth, Joyce Carol Oates, and Charles Simic. The one thing they share in common is excellence. Even the less well-known poets speak with authority, and they are a delight to read. This may be owing to the age constraints set by the compiler, but the fact remains that few of the poets are really weak. Each of the selections is preceded by a biographical sketch and a photograph. Of particular interest is the statement each poet offers about his or her poetry, often with quite specific notes about the poems that follow.

A Geography of Poets; an Anthology of the New Poetry. *Edward Field, ed.* **(1981) Bantam Books. 560p., o.p.**

Compiled in response to the "cultural decentralization" of poetry since the 1960's, this pocket-sized volume divides modern poetry into ten geographical groupings. More than two hundred poets obviously write from a diversity of viewpoints and styles. From the Northwest comes Tess Gallagher and William Stafford; from the Northeast comes Hayden Curruth and Charles Simic, and among those from New York City are John Ashbery and Adrienne Rich. Each poet is well represented by accomplished examples of his or her talent. In his perceptive introduction, Field chronicles the postwar development of American poetry, pointing out that most of these poets came of age in response to the dissolution of the "new criticism" of the 1940's and with the sudden appearance of over two thousand small presses and literary magazines devoted to new writers. Field also includes detailed indexes of small presses, special library collections of poetry, and poetry centers across the country. This is a strong anthology, successfully displaying the talent of modern poets and providing an informative introduction by a distinguished poet himself. One could argue that the differences in style and structure among today's poets have less to do with geography and more to do with their casual "anything goes" mindset, with much bad poetry being passed off by professors and editors as "innovative."

The Golden Year. *Melville Cane, John Farrar, and Louise Nicholl, eds.* **(1960) Fine Editions Press. 368p.**

To celebrate its fiftieth anniversary, the Poetry Society of America invited members to submit no more than three poems for consideration. The result is this volume. It "includes at least one poem by every member submitting." There are over three hundred poets represented, but the collection is rather uneven. Witter Bynner, for example, is the only really well-known poet in letters "A" and "B." Louis Ginsberg is included, but not his somewhat better-known son; Robert Frost is represented by three poems (not his best), and numerous lesser-known figures find their way into the pages. The work resembles in no small way the Stedman *American Anthology*, which also pays tribute to poets who are better known to history than to current readers. This collection is of value to anyone wishing to discover poets of the years between the Second World War and 1960 but will be of marginal interest to others. (See also the similar volume, *Fifty Years of American Poetry*.)

A Green Place; Modern Poems. *William Jay Smith, comp.* **(1982) Delacorte Press/Seymour Lawrence. 225p., o.p.**

The well-known translator and editor William Jay Smith surveys the artistic scene and decides upon the more representative and better poets of the current half century. The choices are not that eccentric, and most of the poets included, as well as their poems, are good to excellent. One would have to go far to find a more inclusive anthology of truly modern poets. There are both the well known and some whom only Smith and a select few seem to read. More the pity, as many of the less celebrated figures have more imaginative verse. There are few disappointments, and much to celebrate. The artistic drawings by Jacques Hnizdovsky complement the poems.

The Harvard Book of Contemporary American Poetry. *Helen Vendler,* **ed. (1985) Belknap Press. 440p.**

A better title might be *The Helen Vendler Book of Contemporary American Poetry,* for she is so well known, particularly as an intellectual critic for *The New Yorker* and *The New York Review of Books*. She shares the distinction of being both a scholar and a popular poetry reviewer, an author and a fine teacher. Furthermore, she has a strong following among people who read poetry, not just among professors of the subject. Her choices, with the possible exception of a few younger poets, are hardly a surprise. She begins with the classic, short pieces of Wallace Stevens, moves on to Langston Hughes and Theodore Roethke, and some thirty poets later, she ends with Rita Dove, a questionable choice. Still, one can't help but admire Vendler's ability to pick winners before they are famous. There is no finer introduction to modern American poetry than this splendid collection.

Heartland II; Poets of the Midwest. *Lucien Stryk, ed.* **(1975) Northern Illinois University Press. 255p., pap.**

Lucien Stryk states in his twenty-eight–page historical and analytical introduction to this anthology of midwestern poets that he intends in this book, and intended in its first edition, to "give a full sense of the region." Many of its 213 works (by eighty poets) have an abrupt, dramatic tone that evokes the midwestern landscape. Some of the notable poets included are Stanley Plumly, Dave Smith, Marvin Bell, and Jim Harrison; the editor has included short biographical notes at the beginning of each poet's section. Some poets are more generously represented than others, possibly reflecting their relative success in 1975. The anthology lacks an index, but it should still prove a useful resource for the common reader or student of poetry.

In the American Tree. *Ron Silliman, ed.* **(1986) National Poetry Foundation. 628p.**

Much poetry is meant to be read aloud. Not here. "A latent tradition of poetics not centered on speech," is the course followed by the compiler. Furthermore, little attention is given to questions about excellence of composition. "It is now plain," Mr. Silliman explains, "that any debate over who is, or is not, a better writer, or what is, or is not, a more legitimate writing is, for the most part, a surrogate social struggle." The most important consideration does not regard quality, but the reader who is being addressed in the poem. "How does the writing participate in the constitution of this audience, and is it effective in doing so?" It is all a debate, of course, and the compiler is more than aware of the struggle. He divides the sixty or so modern poets geographically, i.e., West and then East, believing this accounts for "very different orientations toward such issues as form and prose style." A third part, "Second Front," is more thematic "and is intended to show how the concurrent discourse on poetics which has been so much a part of this debate relates to, and illuminates, the writing." Each contributor has a brief biographical sketch, helpful because few are that well known. Conversely, almost all are familiar to little magazine fans.

"Language" Poetries; an Anthology. *Douglas Messerli, ed.* **(1987) New Directions. 184p.**

The mysterious title of this book refers to a little known movement in poetry called "language poems." In his introduction, Douglas Messerli strains to provide an adequate definition and in doing so explores the history of the movement and suggests basically that these poets attempt to speak in dense and opaque terms rather than try to achieve lucidity or transparentness of expression. If the definition leaves the reader a bit bewildered, then the reading of the poems might help in showing exactly what these poets have achieved. Twenty poets are included, each represented by several works. One can't say that they will appeal to lovers of conventional poetry, but those who are interested in adventurous, modern forms will find them worth studying.

The Longman Anthology of Contemporary American Poetry. *Stuart Friebert and David Young, eds.* **(2d ed., 1989) Longman. 629p., pap.**

'Contemporary" poetry in the second edition of this lively, diverse anthology means poetry dating from the 1910's to the 1980's, with most of the entries balanced around the decades since the Second World War. More than fifty poets are generously represented, with one or two pages of biographical and critical information preceding their work. The verse is arranged chronologically by poet in five parts. These are among the most distinguished poets of the century, poets who have rightly earned a place in the American poetry canon; many of their names should be familiar to readers of modern poetry: Thomas Lux, Robert Bly, John

Ashbery, and Sylvia Plath, among others. More than a third of the poems are new to this edition. The editors of this highly recommended volume emphasize the poets rather than just a few samples of their work; they also ignore movements or schools of poetry in favor of individual diversity. A great range of verse is featured, from that of Wallace Stevens to Rita Dove's, making a fine representative collection of the major poets of the twentieth century.

The Made Thing; an Anthology of Contemporary Southern Poetry. Leon Stokesbury, ed. (1987) University of Arkansas Press. 326p.

Here "contemporary" refers to poets who have published major works in the past thirty years. Here "Southern" means poets who "were either born and raised in the South or who have lived in the South at least since they began publishing their mature work." Beyond that, the only rule for inclusion or exclusion is quality as judged by the compiler. The seventy or so poets are arranged alphabetically with up to four poems each. A photograph and a brief biographical sketch open each selection. There are several points shared by the group beyond their point of origin. Most are teachers, and many have advanced degrees. Most are men. Most write about the historical South, and one is "struck by how much of the poetry is centered around a profound relationship to the natural world." Finally, "Southern poets are in general somewhat conservative in their approach to form." The most famous poets here are Wendell Berry, James Dickey, Donald Justice, Robert Penn Warren, and Charles Wright. But the real delight of the collection is to discover the numerous poets who deserve more recognition.

Mark in Time; Portraits & Poetry / San Francisco. *Nick Harvey and Robert E. Johnson, eds.* (1971) Glide Publications. 189p., o.p.

Several of the eighty active San Francisco poets of the early 70's, pictured and anthologized in *Mark in Time,* are famous in the 90's, with good reason (Allen Ginsberg, Josephine Miles, Kenneth Rexroth, and Thom Gunn, for example). Nick Harvey and Robert E. Johnson have chosen one or two poems by each poet. The poet's work is accompanied by a contemporary, page-size, black-and-white photograph. The poems vary in style and quality; some seem carefully crafted (among them, those of Rexroth and William Everson), others seem to float by the force of inspiration (Ginsberg, Nina Serrano). Autobiographical notes end the anthology. This well-designed book provides an entertaining look at somewhat earlier San Francisco poetry.

Mid-Century American Poets. *John Ciardi, ed.* **(1950) Twayne Publishers. 300p., o.p.**

Most of these poets were considered innovative in 1950; today, all can rightly claim their place in the American poetry canon. Fifteen poets are featured generously (including Ciardi). Richard Wilbur, Theodore Roethke, Randall Jarrell, and Delmore Schwartz are among the best known. Each poet is preceded by several pages of self-critical evaluation (apparently in response to an interviewer's questions about the process of poetic creation). This introductory information offers an unpretentious glimpse into the poet's own sensibilities. The poetry is ambitious, well crafted, and evocative, and it is rewarding to know that most of these writers have gone on to write even greater poetry. The sharp, critical introduction by Ciardi is worth reading for his analysis of the legacy of American poetry left by nineteenth-century writers. This volume was intended to introduce a new tradition of American poets and to take a look at the state of American poetry at the mid-century mark.

Modern American Poetry. *Louis Untermeyer, ed.* **(8th rev. ed., 1962) Harcourt, Brace. 701p., o.p.**

Louis Untermeyer was an anthologist other poets admired for the acuteness of his critical judgment. This volume, though only of average size, packs in more great American poems written from Walt Whitman up through the early 1960's than any comparable collection. The major poets are given very generous room for their work: Whitman has almost fifty pages; Emily Dickinson has almost fifty poems included; and Edwin Arlington Robinson has more than thirty poems. Robert Frost, Wallace Stevens, William Carlos Williams, and Elinor Wylie are also accorded a good deal of space. All of T. S. Eliot's "The Waste Land" is there, along with fine poems by Theodore Roethke, Elizabeth Bishop, Delmore Schwartz, Randall Jarrell, and Robert Lowell. Untermeyer's taste for good poems makes this volume a continual pleasure. It is an excellent place to start for those who have only a mild interest in poetry, for they will be met with the finest of poems by the most eminent writers. Also helpful are the rather lengthy biographical and critical introductions that precede each poet. This is a first-rate anthology.

Modern Poetry of Western America. *Clinton F. Larson and William Stafford, eds.* **(1975) Brigham Young University Press. 234p., pap., o.p.**

This anthology gathers together the work of forty living and dead poets of Western America, including Robinson Jeffers, Ivor Winters, Richard Hugo, Gary Snyder, and Sandra McPherson. There is no unifying characteristic to these 205 poems, short of their creators' residence in the West. One can note, however, many references to the Western landscape and, as well, a contemplative tone, as when Ivor Winters writes, "What end impersonal . . . will yet assuage / This final drouth of penitential tears?" or when Richard Hugo writes, "Dead are buried here because the dead / will always be obscure. . . ." Poems are arranged chronologically by poet and indexed by author, title, and first line; contributors' notes are included at the end. This anthology provides an accurate view of a specific sector of American poetry.

The Morrow Anthology of Younger American Poets. *Dave Smith and David Bottoms, eds.* **(1985) Quill. 784p.**

Although some ten years have gone by since this selection was published, most of the poets included are still relatively young. Diane Ackerman, for example, is such a poet, as are Albert Goldbarth, Michael Blumenthal, Robert Pinsky, William Matthews, and close to a hundred others. It should be mentioned that both poet/editors are included. Bottoms has only nine pages, while Smith has fourteen. All styles and types of poetry are included, but the particular emphasis is on the lyrical. Most of the writers born after 1940 are more involved with home life and with personal and economic difficulties than with metaphysical problems. In other words, there is little to shock or startle, but much to consider. There is some splendid verse that is as good as anything written during this century. See, for example, the aforementioned Ackerman and Goldbarth. Anthony Hecht has written an imaginative and informative introduction. He observes that daily activities are a major concern, with poets celebrating a librarian, a filmmaker, a lawyer, and even a sheepherder. The small photographs and brief biographies of each of the poets add to the book's appeal.

Naked Poetry; Recent American Poetry in Open Forms. *Stephen Berg and Robert Mesey, eds.* **(1969) Bobbs-Merrill. 392p., pap.**

Despite its racy title, this is a serious book concerned with new poetic forms — open forms or nontraditional verse. The names of the poets will all be familiar to readers of modern poetry: Kenneth Rexroth, Theodore Roethke, William Stafford, John Berryman, Robert Lowell, Denise Levertov, Allen Ginsberg, W. S. Merwin. Even Sylvia Plath is included. Each poet is introduced through a photograph and some biographical information, and then follows a long section of poetry, ranging from ten to forty pages or so. The poets are among the most powerful of their generation, and the selection is sensitive to the strengths of the individual artists. This volume offers the reader a clear insight into the new movement of poetry writing in the 1950's and 1960's. The search for new poetic forms and experimentation with the placement of poems on the page is well recorded. At the end of their selections of poetry, the authors include some notes on the new formal elements.

The New American Poetry, 1945–1960. *Donald M. Allen, ed.* **(1960) Grove Press. 454p., o.p.**

From 1945 to 1960 and after, Charles Olson, Allen Ginsberg, and Robert Duncan were among the major names in American poetry. They paralleled the periods of abstract and expressionistic art that were unique to America. They celebrated the new jazz, the new contemporary culture, and the new America that came out of the Second World War. The three, along with forty-one other poets and over two hundred poems, are by now less revolutionary and more a part of literary history, but their collective view of the world still influences much American thought. One is sad not to find Allen Ginsberg's "Howl" here, but there are few other oversights. There may be, in fact, too much Gregory Corso and not enough John Ashbery or Kenneth Koch. Be that as it may, this remains the standard anthology for anyone wishing to understand the period. Note, too, at the end of the volume the fascinating statements on poetry by the contributors, as well as biographical notes and a short bibliography that includes several little magazines and recordings.

New American Poets of the 80s. *Jack Myers and Roger Weingarten, eds.*
(1984) Wampeter Press. 435p., pap.

Who are the new American poets of the 80's? Two of the sixty-five
presented here are the compilers. The others are either well known
(Russell Edson, Carolyn Forché, Tess Gallagher, Albert Goldbarth) or,
not infrequently, rarely found these days in the little magazines or elsewhere. The selection process, made in the early 80's, proved to be extremely accurate in pinpointing some developing talents. For the most
part, the poets, in alphabetical order with four or five poems each, were
then between thirty and forty-five years of age. Each had to have produced at least one book. The compilers succeeded in their goal: there is
hardly a poem in the work that is not worth considering. "We hope we
have made our selections with an objective eye toward an eclecticism
regarding styles, concerns, and forms." While "younger" is hardly applicable to many of the poets today, this anthology serves as a backdrop
for their later, often more ambitious and polished, poetry.

New American Poets of the '90s. *Jack Myers and Roger Weingarten, eds.*
(1991) David R. Godine. 443p., o.p.

Many of these ninety-five poets earned distinction before the 90's, but
some are still obscure despite the prediction of this volume. Jorie Graham, Chase Twitchell, and Naomi Shihab Nye are among the most recognizable; many others have had some success in the literary magazine
and journal world. Selections are arranged alphabetically by poet, and
much of the poetry reads like any contemporary literary journal —
reflective, personal poetry written in unmetered format. Although the
poems vary in length, the verse suffers from a sameness, a problem in
many contemporary anthologies. Too many of the poems are indistinguishable from each other. The editor has competently picked promising
or established poets, but the difficulty of distinguishing one from another makes this volume less engaging than it should be. The verse, alas,
is not always, in the words of the editor, "provocative, timely, important,
and accessible." Still, it is generally well crafted and earnest, and merits
examination by readers who are unfamiliar with modern American poetry.

A New Geography of Poets. *Edward Field, Gerald Locklin, and Charles Stetler, eds.* **(1992) University of Arkansas Press. 324p.**

This anthology follows the format of the earlier *Geography of Poets*, in which poets are arranged alphabetically within the region of the country they write from. The writers featured here will be familiar to any reader of contemporary literary journals: William Stafford, Fred Chappell, Amy Clampitt, and Charles Bukowski are placed, respectively, in the Northwest, the South, New York City, and Southern California. Seven sections accommodate 183 poets. The geographical arrangement is meant to highlight the provincial differences in contemporary American poetry, such as differences in vernacular speech and cultural traditions — even in landscape. Much of the verse is sensual and evocative, and the overall quality is high. Apart from physical descriptions or names mentioned in it, however, one might be hard-pressed to identify which region a poem is supposed to represent. There are differences between many of the poems that the geographical format of the book only masks. With respect to region, American poetry is largely homogenized, although individual poets may retain their distinctive voices nonetheless. Indexed by poet and title.

The New Naked Poetry; Recent American Poetry in Open Forms. *Stephen Berg and Robert Mesey, eds.* **(1976) Bobbs-Merrill. 478p., o.p.**

This is a follow up of the same editors' *Naked Poetry.* Published seven years later, it follows the format of the earlier edition, i.e., the poet is represented by a dozen or so poems, and then there is a "Statement," of the poet's explanation of the work, or of his or her life, or of poetry in general. Statements are normally a page or two in length but may be no more than a single paragraph. Dead poets have largely been deleted from this revision. The twenty-six modern American voices in the book range from Gary Snyder and William Stafford to Denise Levertov and Adrienne Rich. Brief biographical sketches are given for each poet, as well as some fascinating photographs. (Some seven years later it is interesting to compare the faces with those in the earlier edition.) The "open form," about which the collection is built, is briefly explained, but here the editors ask the reader to return to the first edition for a fuller explanation. Briefly, "The metaphor is of the living and growing thing. The rhythm and shape of the flower cannot be made clear as separate from or meaning anything different." An excellent collection.

New Poems by American Poets. *Rolfe Humphries, ed.* **(1953) Ballantine Books. 179p.**

New Poems by American Poets, #2. *Rolfe Humphries, ed.* **(1957) Ballantine Books. 179p.**

Both of these volumes are compact and competent, but not outstanding, anthologies that feature poets who emerged in the 1950's. The first volume includes such writers as Theodore Roethke, Galway Kinnell, Richard Wilbur, and Padraic Colum. There are some half dozen new poets in the second volume. Both collections are arranged alphabetically, both include a range of styles, themes, and forms, and both emphasize a fair number of poets who have lapsed into obscurity. Much of the verse is better than average, and some excellent; brief biographical information is given for each poet. These two anthologies are recommended for their uncomplicated arrangement and the editor's selections; they wisely make no claim to represent an era or capture any particular voice of a generation.

New Poetry of the American West. *Peter Wild and Frank Graziano, eds.* **(1982) Logbridge-Rhodes. 104p., o.p.**

The editors, quoting Mary Hunter Austin, write in their introduction that the best regional literature "has come up through the land, shaped by the author's own adjustments to it." This slender anthology contains poems that competently reflect the feeling for the American West — not the cowboys and gold mining of another age, but the natural beauty and sometimes discomforting vastness of the region. The eight featured poets have achieved prominence within the last thirty-five years, with William Stafford and John Haines among the best known today. Arranged alphabetically, the poets write accomplished, often moving, verse. In the introduction the editors explain that each of the included writers has "earned his voice by coming up through a West which, in turn, has been rediscovered and reaffirmed by his voice." But surely more than eight writers have been able to accomplish this; unfortunately there is not enough poetry here.

New Voices in American Poetry: an Anthology. *David Allan Evans, ed.* **(1973) Winthrop Publishers. 265p., o.p.**

This anthology of American poetry of the 1970's should be valuable in a library's collection because it includes poets with varying styles: Mark Strand's lyricism, Thomas Lux's spare drama, and Charles Simic's macabre clarity. It attempts to give personal glimpses of each poet through photographs and biographical notes, and there are helpful paragraphs in which poets trace the steps in the creation of one or two of their poems. In this unbiased reflection of the diverse poetry of the period, Evans allows readers the freedom of their own evaluation. In the introduction Donald Justice writes, "Our poetry is either still divided into camps, or it is all one country. . . . I think that this anthology comes down strongly on the one-country side of the argument." Poems are arranged in alphabetical order by poet; there is no index.

New York: Poems. *Howard Moss, ed.* **(1980) Avon Books. 345p., o.p.**

Anyone who lives in or frequently visits New York City should feel a special attraction to this anthology. Moss, a poet whose works are included here, has selected more than two hundred poems that capture the mystery, energy, and sensuality of this often-derided city. Such longtime New York poets as Walt Whitman, e. e. cummings, Allen Ginsberg, and Langston Hughes join other natives and residents in poeticizing the city. The skillful poems address a wide range of subjects — running the annual marathon, Fifth Avenue parades, a West Village street, and the roaches invading a cocktail party. Arranged alphabetically by poet, the verse is reflective and lively, evoking legendary neighborhoods, buildings, and streets. In his introduction Moss writes about the "transitions" constantly occurring within the city that create its varying moods and rhythms. The range of the poetry captures "moments of pure feeling . . . histories of desperation or hope; notetakings of the phenomenal; musings on loneliness; outcries of the body; commentaries of the intellect." Moss has compiled an excellent, evocative anthology for New Yorkers and others alike.

The Next World; Poems by Third World Americans. *Joseph Bruchac, ed.* **(1978) Crossing Press. 238p., o.p.**

The 200 poems in this anthology grew out of two workshops — one in Wisconsin and one in Ellensburg, Washington — that focused on writing by American poets from Third World backgrounds (Puerto Rican, Filipino, Native American, Japanese-American, Chicano, Chinese-American, and African-American). Poems are arranged alphabetically by poet, with an author photograph and biographical note. Such an anthology helps to assert minority identities in America. These evocative, angry poems range in style from the blunt realism of Ntozake Shange to the clamor and excitement of Pancho Aguila. Many of the poems reflect the speech patterns and dialects of Third World communities in America. The anthology does not have an index.

19 New American Poets of the Golden Gate. *Philip Dow, ed.* **(1984) Harcourt Brace Jovanovich. 468p., o.p.**

The alluring conception behind this book is to present a sample of the work of several poets writing in northern California today, letting them provide their own introductions to their lives and poetry. The result is a warm, informal introduction to the accomplishments of several lesser-known, and such quite famous, authors as Al Young, Robert Pinsky, and Susan Griffin. The standard of the work varies, but its intention to acquaint readers with contemporary voices and forms in poetry is fresh and serious. The writing is in no way provincial, and the concerns transcend state borders. Each author is represented by about a dozen poems that demonstrate his or her strengths in some detail. Handsome photographs of the writers further personalize the biographical introductions.

The Pittsburgh Book of Contemporary American Poetry. *Ed Ochester and Peter Oresick, eds.* **(1993) University of Pittsburgh Press. 397p., pap.**

Editors Ed Ochester and Peter Oresick have put together a thoughtful sampler of the 45 poets of the esteemed Pitt Poetry Series currently in print. There are such familiar names in the anthology as Gary Gildner, Etheridge Knight, and Paul Zimmer, but for the most part it consists of relatively unknown poets. The work of each poet is given generous consideration, approximately 300 hundred lines worth, and is accompanied by a short biography at the back of the book and by a photograph. Both sexes are equally represented, as are a variety of cultural and ethnic backgrounds, lending credence to the editors' statement that the anthology is "as valid a cross-section of contemporary American poetry as we know." Ochester and Oresick's selections are excellent — the poetry is compelling throughout, making a fine showcase for the talents of the Pitt poets. The anthology aptly illustrates why the series itself has garnered such wide respect over the course of its twenty-five-year existence.

The Poet Upstairs; a Washington Anthology. *Octave Stevenson, ed.* **(1979) Washington Writers' Publishing House. 180p., o.p.**

There is no introduction to *The Poet Upstairs,* but the back cover explains that "over 100 poets of varying backgrounds have been chosen to represent the wealth, variety and excellence of the poetry currently being written in the nation's capital." Many of the 177 poems collected here contain unexpected leaps and dynamic images that will attract most readers of contemporary poetry. They have, however, nothing to do with Washington, D.C. Many of the poets had previously appeared only in literary magazines. Works are arranged alphabetically by author; Stevenson has given us no indexes. This is indeed a strange collection, but it provides an interesting view of one region of American poetry of the late 1970's.

Poetry Hawaii; a Contemporary Anthology. *Frank Stewart and John Unterecker, eds.* **(1979) University Press of Hawaii. 157p., pap.**

The 114 cool and sensitive poems in *Poetry Hawaii* were written by fifty-five poets who either were born in Hawaii or were resident long enough to make them "Hawaii poets" in the editors' estimation. John Unterecker assigns two qualities to these works in his introduction: "an acknowledgment of the special value that islanders almost always assign mountain, sea, and sky" and "a kind of tentativeness, as if the poet does not have all the answers." W. S. Merwin, John Logan, and Alfons Corn are among the noted poets who found their way into this collection. The editors, both successful poets, have also included themselves. The biographical sketches at the end are full of useful information, but there is no index. The anthology's oblong shape and attractive layout, along with the black-and-white author photographs, add to its appeal. This book adequately samples the work of poets popular during the late 1970's in Hawaii.

The Poet's Choice. *George E. Murphy, Jr., ed.* **(1980) Tendril. 176p., pap.**

Murphy points out that an artist is not always the best judge of his or her own work. This anthology contains, however, the personal favorites of 100 American poets. The writers themselves are of varying stature, ranging from popular poets Richard Wilbur and Mark Strand to lesser-known writers such as Marieve Rugo and Russell Edson. How is their taste? In general, these poets have chosen solidly constructed poems of their own that will engage both casual reader and poetry enthusiast. The book (one poem for each author) is arranged alphabetically by poet. There is no index. This slim volume should provide an unusual insight into the nature of each poet's work.

Poets West; Contemporary Poems from the Eleven Western States. *Lawrence P. Spingarn, ed.* **(1975) Perivale Press. 162p., pap.**

The poets in *Poets West* range from well-known Mark Strand and Philip Levine to the lesser-known George Hitchcock and Robert Huff; these authors reside in the western United States. The tone of most of the poetry is casual and honest. These 124 poets depict life as they see it, withholding no details. Some of the 140 poems are sexually explicit, while others depict violence in a shockingly straightforward manner. The works also address such subjects as nature, competition, and Van Gogh. There is a section of biographies but no index. Spingarn has gathered together a variety of western poets from the 1970's and has arranged their works for contrast, so that readers will be constantly excited.

The Portable Beat Reader. *Ann Charters, ed.* **(1992) Viking Penguin. 642p.**

Although not everybody would consider Bob Dylan's "Blowin' in the Wind" Beat poetry, this collection is still among the most thorough and eclectic of any anthology featuring Beat writers. Particularly interesting is the structure of this volume. Divided into six sections, the editor arranges the verse chronologically and geographically, first introducing the major, earlier New York Beat poets and then moving on to the San Francisco scene. (The book is indexed by authors and their works.) There is a chapter featuring one or two selections from minor poets of the time. Major figures like Kerouac, Ginsberg, and Burroughs are most heavily represented — up to eight selections that include some fiction pieces. Others include Amiri Baraka, Ed Sanders, Tuli Kupferberg, and Brenda Frazer. A separate section of the volume features thoughts on the Beat scene from more recent writers, and a final section includes excerpts from the Beat poets' thoughts on themselves. Recommended mostly for readers already familiar with Beat poetry and the movement, this is a probing, compelling volume. The selections are from each poet's best-known work, for instance, from Ginsberg's "Howl" and Mailer's "The White Negro."

The Postmoderns; the New American Poetry Revised. *Donald Allen and George F. Butterick, eds.* **(1982) Grove Press. 436p., pap.**

Who are the postmoderns? According to the compiler the thirty-eight Americans here represented can claim that title because, first, they tend to be experimental and avoid the traditional, second, they emerged in the 1950's and came into their own in the 1960's and 1970's, and third, they were and are published in literary reviews and little magazines. Finally, but not least, "The body of them are writers who were given their wider recognition through the first edition of this anthology, titled plainly *The New American Poetry,* and published in 1960." (See *The New American Poetry.*) Arrangement is by the poets' birthdates. Charles Olson (b. 1910) is followed by William Everson, Robert Duncan, Lawrence Ferlinghetti, and Barbara Guest — all born before 1921. The poets born in the nineteen thirties end the collection, and they make up the greatest single group. Most are fairly well known and include Jerome Rothenberg, Michael McClure, Diane DiPrima, Amiri Baraka, Ed Sanders, and Ann Waldman. Each poet is represented with four or five poems. There are excellent biographical/bibliographical notes.

Preferences; 51 American Poets Choose Poems from Their Own Work and from the Past. *Richard Howard, ed.* **(1974) Viking Press. 323p., o.p.**

What fun! The appeal of this volume is multifarious: there are informal, clear photographs of all the poets; their poems are beautifully printed on large format pages; they revealingly select "in their own work and in the work of the past, a pair of poems . . . which they saw fit to put together." And then there is a substantial commentary on their choices by the distinguished writer and poet Richard Howard. He attempts to delve into the minds of the poets to explain their choices; he frequently quotes from interviews and essays that shed light on their decisions. He also comments on the essence of the two poems selected. In general, then, the reader has something of the pleasure of attending fifty poetry readings by distinguished authors offering their own kind of personal commentary. A. R. Ammons chose his own "Gravelly Run," along with Ralph Waldo Emerson's "The Snow-storm"; W. H. Auden chose "In Due Season," along with Thomas Campion's "What Faire Pompe"; Adrienne Rich chose "The Afterwake" and Gerard Manley Hopkins's "Patience, Hard Thing!" The pleasures in this volume are hard to beat.

Psyche: The Feminine Poetic Consciousness; an Anthology of Modern American Women Poets. *Barbara Segnitz and Carol Rainey, eds.*

See under Women's Poetry and Feminist Poetry

Rising Tides; 20th Century American Women Poets. *Laura Chester and Sharon Barba, eds.*

See under Women's Poetry

Settling America; the Ethnic Expression of 14 Contemporary Poets. *David Kherdian, ed.* (1974) Macmillan. 126p., o.p.

The fourteen poets in *Settling America* realistically represent the range of cultures that gives the American population its eclectic character. Poets commenting on their heritage in this anthology include Gergory Corso (from an Italian background), Lawson Fusao Inada (of Japanese descent), Stephen Stepanchev (born in Yugoslavia), and Kherdian himself (born to Armenian parents). The editor introduces each poet with a brief biography and a statement by the poet about what his poetry means to him. The poems, while usually not well-known, clearly and intelligently describe their authors' experiences as Americans with roots in other cultures. Gregory Corso writes, for example, of the "all too real mafia streets" and the ten black cadillacs in a dead baby's funeral procession. Stepanchev reminds himself that the pain he suffers when a loved one returns to Romania "is some sort of punishment." This anthology is full of well-chosen, evocative works indexed by title and first line. Kherdian has also provided a short glossary of unfamiliar terms.

70 on the 70's; a Decade's History in Verse. *Robert McGovern and Richard Snyder, eds.* (1981) Ashland Poetry Press. 97p., o.p.

The idea of a poetry anthology revolving around the news topics of a particular decade might seem interesting, except when the quality of poems is as poor as that displayed here. This extremely slim volume features trite, flat verse about Patty Hearst, Three Mile Island, the Attica prison uprising, and the death of Janis Joplin, among other memorable events. Almost a hundred poems are presented, and most have little literary value. Even the poems by such accomplished writers as Howard Nemerov and X. J. Kennedy are mediocre in comparison to the richness of their other works. McGovern and Snyder provide a short introduction, in addition to their own poetry. The volume is divided into two sections:

one dealing with events and the other consisting of verse about the prominent people who died in this decade. In short, some of the poetry in this volume is tolerable, but too much of it is downright bad.

Singular Voices; American Poetry Today. *Stephen Berg, ed.* **(1985) Avon Books. 326p., o.p.**

The thirty poets are in alphabetical order, and at the time of publication were all living and most of them famous. There is only one poem by each poet, followed by criticism of that piece by the poet. "Faced with their own poems . . . the poets were driven to talk about the difficulties of creation and interpretation and just plain understanding, and to come up with fresh personal ways to guide the reader." There is a widely different approach by each of the writers, and, as the compiler claims, this is "an unpredictable cache of poems and essays." It is a wonderful place for both the beginner and the trained expert to dip into for ideas and criticism. Most of the poems take up a page or less, followed by two to four pages of critique. The volume ends with brief biographical sketches of the poets, among whom one will find Robert Bly, Hayden Carruth, James Dickey, Tess Gallagher, Louise Glück, Donald Hall, Maxine Kumin, Stanley Kunitz, Denise Levertov, Czeslaw Milosz, Louis Simpson, W. D. Snodgrass, William Stafford, Robert Penn Warren, and Richard Wilbur. Here is an ideal book for learning about poetry that is equally good as a bedside reader.

Social Poetry of the 1930s; a Selection. *Jack Salzman and Leo Zanderer*

See under POLITICAL POETRY

Strong Measures; Contemporary American Poetry in Traditional Forms. *Philip Dacey and David Jauss, eds.* **(1986) Harper & Row. 492p.**

This anthology works from the provocative premise that there are substantial, pertinent poems being written today in the verse forms of the past. The compilers have combed the best of contemporary poetry to ferret out these modern poems in traditional forms. The introduction is a long, thoughtful consideration of verse forms and their use by contemporary authors. Such devices as disguising the form, alternating between formal and free verse, and creating hybrid forms are considered. The poets whose works are featured range from John Berryman and Elizabeth Bishop to Amy Clampitt, X. J. Kennedy, and Mona Van Duyn. Many of the poets are women, all are American. The compilers have fine taste in poetry, and all the poems make for rewarding reading. Almost two hundred poets are included, many of them represented by more than one poem. Here is a superb overview of some of the strong poetry written in America in recent decades.

Take Hold! an Anthology of Pulitzer Prize Winning Poems. *Lee Bennett Hopkins, ed.* **(1974) Thomas Nelson. 96p., o.p.**

This book should entertain both trivia enthusiasts and lovers of good poetry. It contains the work of Pulitzer Prize winners from 1918 to 1974 — a roster of poets that includes Auden, Amy Lowell, Millay, Frost, and Merwin. Lee Bennett Hopkins gives his choice of the authors' best poems, along with detailed biographies. The works chosen are not necessarily those most commonly associated with these authors, but their quality will disappoint no one. Hopkins presents the sixty-nine poems chronologically by poet and indexes them by author, title, and first line. Also helpful is a short history of the Pulitzer Prize for Poetry and a table of award dates and winners. Skeptics sometimes doubt the validity of the Pulitzer Prize or consider it of minor importance when judging a writer's oeuvre. This anthology should restore their confidence in the taste and intelligence of the awards committee.

The Third Coast; Contemporary Michigan Poetry. *Conrad Hilberry, Herbert Scott, and James Tipton, eds.; Preface by David Wagoner.* **(1976) Wayne State University Press. 296p., pap., o.p.**

As David Wagoner writes in his preface, the thirty poets in this book are "unsettled, uncomplacent, still willing to search for the untried possibilities of poetry, to be daring, willing to take the chance of appearing or sounding odd for the sake of discovery." Indeed, the 180 poems approach their large subjects — love, nature, isolation — from skewed perspectives. In "Palmistry for Blind Mariners," Judith Minty describes palmistry as if it were a form of navigation. Herbert Scott, in "The Fear of Groceries," sees his children amid the confusion of the word "fishes" with the word "peaches." James Tipton, in "America, the Elephant," presents a short history of the elephant's role in American culture. The editors provide photographs and brief biographies for each of the authors. Poems are indexed by title and first line. This book will be a lucky find for any reader interested in Michigan's poetry.

Traveling America with Today's Poets. *David Kherdian, ed.* **(1977) Macmillan. 154p., o.p.**

In his preface the editor of this slender volume writes that "whether native or tourist, each of the poets in this book is grounded differently to his or her place." This anthology shows both the provincialism and the diversity of many different Americas, focusing on dialects, moods, and geographical characteristics. Better known of almost a hundred poets are Al Young, Charles Bukowski, and Lucille Clifton; most are fairly obscure. None are "provincial" poets, although their poems reflect cultural differences brought about by geographic separations. Arranged by state, the volume begins in New York, goes through New England, crosses over to the West, and then finishes back in the South and Mid-Atlantic states. Most of the verse was written after the Second World War. These are not deep poems; they are enjoyable because they are earthy rather than probing — poems on such diverse subjects as Massachusetts clam diggers and New Mexico's Indian burial grounds. Indexed by poet, title, and first line.

Twentieth-Century American Poetry. *Conrad Aiken, ed.* **(1963) Random House. 552p., o.p.**

Aiken explains in his introduction that this volume was compiled in order to expose British readers to great American poetry; it is also a strong, representative anthology for American students and readers. Eighty-one writers are represented by hundreds of their most famous poems. Indeed, the poems and authors here are among the greatest of this (and some from the preceding) century. Beginning with Dickinson, Robinson, and Frost and concluding with Galway Kinnell and Ann Sexton, the poets are listed in chronological order. Aiken has penned a short preface, and indexes of poets and first lines are included. The collection's strength lies in the quality of the verse and in the traditional, unpretentious format. There are no surprises!

Under 35; the New Generation of American Poets. *Nicholas Christopher, ed.* **(1989) Anchor Books. 240p., pap., o.p.**

Most of the thirty-seven poets here are fairly accomplished — many already published in literary journals and holding positions on writing faculties at prestigious universities. Most of the general audience this volume is aimed at, however, will probably not recognize their names, despite the promising talent and seriousness evident in their work. Geographically they are a diverse group, but all came of age in the 1960's and seem to share a common view of the world. Their poems have a tone of distrust and cynicism, and are often ambiguous. Arranged alphabetically by author, they vary in quality, although all are by competent and illustrious poets. Brief biographical notes are provided, but the poems themselves are not annotated — the only drawback in this volume of sometimes enigmatic poetry. This anthology is well crafted and accessible, one of many collections by young writers who should not be overlooked by readers searching for fresh voices and new talent.

The Vintage Book of Contemporary American Poetry. *J. D. McClatchy, ed.* **(1990) Vintage Books. 560p.**

"Contemporary" here means poets who came of age largely in the generations before and after the Second World War: Robert Lowell, Allen Ginsberg, Adrienne Rich, and Howard Nemerov, among others. Despite the fact that many of the sixty-five poets gained fame years ago, most are still writing and influencing the newer, less well-known poets included with them. These poets hail from across the country; no specific "movement" or school captures their range of talent and sensibility. They are represented by as many as seven poems to best illustrate their skill. Arranged more or less chronologically by poet, the anthology is attractive and neat, aimed for general readers interested in the major poets who loosely define an "American" style and tradition. Although lacking indexes and the usual biographical notes on each poet, this is still a solid collection, a worthy showcase of twentieth-century American verse.

Visions of America by the Poets of Our Time. *David Kherdian, ed.* **(1973) Macmillan. 92p., o.p.**

The thirty-five poets in this collection all flourished in the 1950's. They envision America in various ways. Ferlinghetti remembers his days as a barefoot Brooklyn kid, playing in the summer heat in the cool spray of firemen's hoses. Charles Bukowski describes painting his doves of peace during shooting season. Edward Dorn places a cowboy beneath a "brick-orange" moon. Kherdian writes in his introduction that the poets of Williams's generation used the "common language all of us speak and from which all of us make our lives." One can read these fifty-nine poems, arranged in sections called "Growing Up," "In America," and "And Its Cities," as easily as one would read letters. They are easily found, too, because Kherdian indexes them by author, title, and first line. Although he could probably have given more information about the generation of writers that fills most of the book, he has still collected a group of rich and evocative poems that paint lasting pictures of American life.

The Voice That Is Great within Us; American Poetry of the Twentieth Century. *Hayden Carruth, ed.* **(1970) Bantam Books. 722p., pap.**

One of America's leading poets put this collection together, and unlike many poet/compilers, he limits his own entries to five "short-shorts" he wrote while compiling the book. These brief works are "offered simply as a token . . . of fellowship with all poets." For each of the one hundred thirty-six poets represented, there is a brief biographical sketch and list of major works. The poets are arranged chronologically, from 1900 to 1970. Robert Frost leads off with sixteen poems, about the average for major writers in this collection. Younger and minor poets have three or four pieces. No one is missed, and the selection from modern and contemporary American verse is among the best now available. Carruth employs three primary selection criteria: he reprints only works he thinks are the best, and not those that are merely famous; translations are excluded, as are excerpts from long or extensively annotated poems; and, finally, the choices are dictated "by my own feeling" of quality. The single drawback is the lack of either an author or title index.

Washington and the Poet. *Francis Coleman Rosenberger, ed.* **(1977) University Press of Virginia. 79p.**

Some of the fifty poems in *Washington and the Poet* are intelligent hymns to the capital city, while others address national political themes. Still others describe such specific events as the first President's crossing of the Potomac, a march against the Vietnam War in 1965, and the Watergate controversy. Styles range, as well, from the eloquent to the verbose in Stanley Kunitz, from the pithy to the ponderous in Robert Bly. Poems have been arranged chronologically by author. Rosenberger has not indexed the anthology, but he has included short biographies. This book will fill the need for either patriotic verse or a simple evocation of a unique American city.

AMERICAN POETRY
20th Century (Periodical)

The Antaeus Anthology. *Daniel Halpern, ed.* **(1986) Bantam Books. 615p., pap.**

Antaeus, a distinguished literary journal, has been published since 1969. This anthology is a gathering of some of the most remarkable poems published in the journal in its first twenty years. Among the extraordinary selections are verses that W. H. Auden wrote for the musical *Man of La Mancha.* These lyrics, based on the Don Quixote story but never performed, are printed here in their entirety. Many foreign poets are included in this volume: Paul Celan, Anna Akhmatova, Osip Mandelstam, and Czeslaw Milosz, to mention only a few. Some of the great American poets featured include John Berryman, Marianne Moore, "H. D." (Hilda Doolittle), and William Carlos Williams. English poets are in abundance: Philip Larkin, Peter Porter, John Fowles, and Roy Fuller. This is an extraordinarily fine compilation of modern poems, made particularly rich by the interplay of English, American, and foreign voices.Because the taste of the editor is outstanding, the reader can be assured of finding poetry of the highest quality. Many new forms are on display, including poems written in paragraphs of prose.Individual poems are printed on separate pages, so they retain the dignified look they originally had in the journal.

Anthology of Magazine Verse and Yearbook of American Poetry, 1981 Edition. *Alan F. Pater, ed.* **(1981) Monitor Book Company. 640p., o.p.**

This volume, the second in a series begun in 1980, republishes the best and most diverse poetry from a variety of contemporary magazines and literary journals. Although the editor chose the selections largely on the basis of artistic merit, they range from skillful to mediocre. Many prestigious modern journals are represented by such distinguished poets as Marvin Bell, X. J. Kennedy, and Daniel Halpern, but most of the writers have sprung anonymously from eclectic little magazines. There are indexes of title, author, and first line, with an extra section listing the addresses of many literary journals, awards, and writers' organizations.

This last list is helpful for fledgling poets trying to publish their work. For general readers, the volume is a mixed bag. Those who read one or more contemporary literary magazines already have an idea of the type of poetry lauded by critics today; they will not need this volume. In addition, each anthology in the series reprints only some of the poems published in a given year, so that it may not even help a reader look up a specific poem. But to anyone without time to keep up with journals and interested in the state of modern poetry, this anthology is recommended.

The Before Columbus Foundation Poetry Anthology; Selections from the American Book Awards, 1980–1990. *J. J. Phillips, Ishmael Reed, Gundars Strads, and Shawn Wong, eds.* **(1992) W. W. Norton. 429p.**

This anthology, which has a companion volume of prose, features chiefly "multicultural" poetry: women, blacks, latinos, gays, and other traditionally underrepresented groups in the canon of American poetry. Readers who do not like to mix the politics of the multicultural debate with literature should be forewarned. Although many solid, distinguished poets of all backgrounds are included here, most of the poets are not as talented as the editors deem them to be. Several of the forty-six poets are anthologized elsewhere, particularly Allen Ginsberg, Ai, Amiri Baraka, and Etheridge Knight. Unsurprisingly, many of the poems deal with race, prejudice, and ethnic consciousness; many experiment with form, style, and genre. Arranging them alphabetically, the editors have included about a page of biographical and critical information about each poet. A final section of the book lists all the winners of American Book Awards in the past decade. Judged solely on the merits of the poetry, this is a promising volume. But the nagging politics of the multicultural debate may cause some readers to approach this anthology with apprehension.

The Best American Poetry, 1988. *John Ashbery, ed.* **(1988) Collier Books/Macmillan. 249p., o.p.**

This book performs a twofold function. It prints what it deems to be the best of American poetry published in the past year (in this case 1988), with remarks on the poems by the poets themselves. These comments are similar to ones poets make at poetry readings: they illuminate some aspect of the work or detail its inception. There is also some biographical information about each poet. Many of the finest poets in America are included: Joseph Brodsky, Donald Hall, James Merrill, Richard Wilbur, Seamus Heaney, and May Swenson. But there are seventy-five poets represented, many of whom were published in magazines, and most of them are completely unknown to the general reading public. Many of the contributors are women. In general the selective judgment of the editors is first rate; this is a fine way to acquaint oneself with the poetry published in America today.

The Best American Poetry, 1989. *Donald Hall, ed.* (1989) Macmillan. 293p., pap.

This series aims to emphasize the diversity of American poetry "and honor excellence regardless of what form it takes, or what idiom it favors, or from what region of the country it comes." Skip the long introduction and go right to the poetry, which may not always reflect the diversity the editors looked for but is, nonetheless, of high quality. The seventy-five poems are arranged alphabetically by poet, neatly and attractively. The verse varies widely in theme, form, and skill — many are first-rate, others a few levels below. What some of the poems lack in polish they make up for in sensitivity and depth. Many of the poets will be recognized by readers of contemporary verse: among them, Charles Simic, William Stafford, Robert Bly, and Amy Clampitt. Although some readers may find any volume with a title claiming to be "the best of" dubious, these really are worth more than a passing look. Brief biographical information is given about the poets.

The Best American Poetry, 1990. *Jorie Graham, ed.* (1990) Macmillan. 283p.

This collection is part of an annual series containing the "best" poetry of the year, culled from popular to fairly obscure magazines and literary journals during the previous year. Although readers should beware of any volume claiming to contain the best of anything, this is an imaginative, skillful anthology. The seventy-five poets are among the most distinguished of modern times, arranged alphabetically and represented usually by a single selection. They range from spiritual to political and encompass a variety of movements and themes. Differences in poetic ability vary, however: some poets lack the depth that would make their work stand out in years to come, and many of the poems are indistinguishable from other selections — and probably from those of the preceding year as well. But overall this is a competent volume that contains some real gems. Brief biographical information on the poets is included.

The Best American Poetry, 1993. *Louise Glück, ed.* **(1993) Macmillan. 277p., pap.**

The Best American Poetry series is a valuable and important force in modern poetry. Every year a major poet is chosen to edit the collection, and this poet selects from the year's poetry publication. This 1993 collection includes some major poets: John Ashbery, Denise Levertov, Thomas Lux, and Charles Simic, among a wide and interesting group. This is definitely a book that will appeal to those who enjoy modern poetry. Louise Glück describes these poems in this way: "There were voices that stood out, like the voice at the dinner table whose next sentence you strain to hear. . . ." There are enlightening biographical notes and comments on their work by the poets. There is also an index of the entire fine series.

From A to Z; 200 Contemporary American Poets. *David Ray, ed.* **(1981) Ohio University Press. 259p., o.p.**

The poetry of this diverse, mostly talented group of modern poets originally appeared in the University of Missouri literary review *New Letters*. Of the many poets included, some are well established, post-Second World War writers such as Maxine Kumin, Robert Bly, David Ignatow, and Daniel Halpern; others are of questionable talent, authors of short, impulsive verse. To its credit, the anthology represents a wide variety of styles and regions; it is neatly arranged alphabetically, from A. R. Ammons to Richard Wright. Some authors are accompanied by photographs or sketches. Unfortunately, no biographical information is provided on the more obscure poets. David Ray's brief introduction is primarily about the state of contemporary American poetry — particularly the often misunderstood relationship between poet and critic. This is a useful anthology for those unfamiliar with the diversity and complexity of modern poetry, but it lacks the depth provided by other contemporary anthologies of contemporary poetry. The collection offers few surprises.

The Hopwood Anthology; Five Decades of American Poetry. *Harry Thomas and Steven Lavine, eds.* **(1981) University of Michigan Press. 155p., o.p.**

All of the thirty-two poets included in this volume are recipients of Hopwood Awards — prestigious cash prizes offered by the University of Michigan since the 1930's to promising young writers. Although few will be recognized by general readers, their poems are evocative and complex, representing a diversity of styles and influences. Among the recipients who have achieved national prominence are X. J. Kennedy, Robert Hayden, and Frank O'Hara. Short biographies of each poet show that none of the recipients fell short of expectations. The editors' brief preface, written by a University of Michigan professor and a 1979 Hopwood recipient, explains that the anthology was prepared by asking the poets to submit their newer poems as well as older favorites. The result is a strong balance of verse from the 1930's to the late 1970's. This is a small volume of accomplished poetry, arranged chronologically and neatly compiled with general readers in mind; those looking for a sampling of talented twentieth-century poets will not be disappointed.

Keener Sounds; Selected Poems from the Georgia Review. *Stanley W. Lindberg and Stephen Corey, eds.* (1987) University of Georgia Press. 224p.

One of America's outstanding literary reviews, the *Georgia Review* is edited by Lindberg. Published since 1947, the quarterly has gained distinction for its fiction and graphics. There are lengthy essays on poetry and usually fine selections of poetry. But while the poetry is worthy of consideration, it does not measure up to the fiction the review has published over the years. With that reservation, one must applaud the collection for offering one hundred fourteen new and older poets, for suggesting both new and older ways of approaching poetic subjects. John Ashbery, Maxine Kumin, Howard Nemerov, and David Wagoner are certainly among America's strongest poetic voices; conversely, there are as many lesser-known poets with, all too often, lesser talents. There are some English poets, but most are American. The brief biographies of the contributors read like a roll call of modern poetry. This is an important anthology.

Leaving the Bough; Fifty American Poets of the 80s. *Roger Gaess, ed.* (1982) International Publishers. 168p., o.p.

The editor states in his introduction that this anthology "attempts to present an entire range of human experience — the overall impression of what it's like to be alive in the America of today and of the recent past." This is a lofty goal. The anthology features the work of fifty contemporary poets, mostly of moderate skill, from small literary magazines and presses. Such well known poets as Ai, Alice Walker, and Mei-Mei Berssenbrugge highlight the collection. Arranged alphabetically, they are a diverse group, representing a variety of styles, structures, and influences; they have nothing in common but their dates of publication. Gaess's introduction condemns the established, academic poets who, he claims, carry an "anti-emotional prejudice" and whose "knowledge has largely been acquired from books rather than experience." Whether or not academic poets and commercial publishing houses should be so condemned is not the point. This collection is an interesting sampling of the poetry published outside the major academic and established publishing world (i.e., New York). There are other anthologies that exhibit the talent of struggling poets in a less pretentious way.

The New Yorker Book of Poems. *The New Yorker editors, comps.* **(1969) Viking Press; paperback ed. of 1974 published by William Morrow. 835p.**

Limited to entries from the pages of *The New Yorker*, this excellent collection covers poets who appeared there from the first issue in 1929 through 1969. There are nine hundred poems by almost every famous and minor poet of America, England, and Europe. The subject matter alone is a profile of the hopes and anxieties of the world at mid-century. Byron Buck can write about a "Song from a Two Desk Office," while W. H. Auden is equally serious about "Installing an American Kitchen in Lower Austria." At another level, Daniel Berrigan explains why "Somewhere the Equation Breaks Down," and Delmore Schwartz is eloquent "During December's Death." Less satisfactory is the arrangement, which the editors note "may strike the reader as an odd way." Indeed! The poems are printed alphabetically by title, although there is an author index. It is a pointless organization, but that hardly detracts from the brilliance of the volume. It is a book that can be by the bedside for a lifetime. Highly recommended for all.

The Ploughshares Poetry Reader. *Joyce Peseroff, ed.* **(1986) Ploughshares Books. 335p.**

Ploughshares is a little magazine with a big voice in contemporary American literature, publishing as it does some of the finest writers at work today. This anthology is a selection of the best poetry to appear in *Ploughshares* since its inception in 1971. The work of over a hundred poets appears here, many of them very familiar to readers of modern poetry: Denise Levertov, Philip Levine, Derek Mahon, Robert Lowell, James Merrill, W. D. Snodgrass, Mona Van Duyn, and Richard Wilbur, each represented by one to three poems. There are numerous lesser-known poets, all of whom are worth reading. The standard of writing here is very high; many of the poets are women. All the poems were written in English, and there is great variety; from an evocation of Noah's thoughts concerning the flood in "A Life-Giving," by Brad Leithauser, to "Letters from a Father," documenting an elderly man's turning from the pain of old age to the pleasures of nature, by Mona Van Duyn.

The Poetry Anthology, 1912–1977. *Daryl Hine and Joseph Parisi, eds.* **(1978) Houghton Mifflin. 555p.**

Limited to work that appeared in *Poetry* magazine, here are samples from sixty-five years of modern poetry writing, beginning with Ezra Pound and ending with a somewhat less well-known but fine poet, Sandra M. Gilbert. In between, under seven time divisions, we are presented with the work of almost everyone from A. R. Ammons to Louis Zukofsky. Even the lesser-known authors are carefully selected, not for their names, but for their contributions, to create a particularly strong record of what can be termed "new" voices, at least for the time. Ezra Pound, W. B. Yeats, and Vachel Lindsay have now joined the traditionalists, but such later entrants as John Ashbery and Frank O'Hara have a time to go before they can be completely understood or become a part of everyday culture. Note, too, that the introduction is a brief history of that great magazine, *Poetry,* and its founder, Harriet Monroe. One of the editors of the anthology, Daryl Hine, was editor of the journal from 1969 through 1977.

See also   ENGLISH AND AMERICAN POETRY: COMPREHENSIVE COLLECTIONS; NATIVE AMERICAN POETRY

ANIMAL AND BIRD POETRY

Bear Crossings; an Anthology of North American Poets. *Anne Newman and Julie Suk, eds.* (1978) New South. 127p.

The editors of this anthology posit in their foreword that the bear is a common metaphorical image in contemporary American poetry and a symbol for the human species itself. Although the suggestion might be feasible, *Bear Crossings* is by no means representative of the full breadth of modern American poetry. The editors have published "bear poems" by great and minor writers, ranging from William Carlos Williams to feminist Adrienne Rich to an anonymous Navajo poet. They have, as well, allotted to each writer a poem that accurately represents the poet's style. The anthology is arranged in five sections, each reflecting a different side of the bear's spirit — and, by extension, the human spirit: immortality, imagination, extremes of emotion, alienation, and survival instincts. These rather ambiguous categories, compounded with the lack of an index, make this interesting volume a less than convenient reference tool.

A Book of Animal Poems. *William Cole, ed.*

See under   CHILDREN'S POETRY

Cat Will Rhyme with Hat; a Book of Poems. *Jean Chapman, ed.* (1986) Scribner's. 80p.

The copy on the book's jacket explains it all. This "rich and varied collection of poems will delight cat lovers, moving them both to laughter and to tears. The poems are grouped in eight sections, each celebrating an aspect of cat charm or behavior." The sections have such titles as "The Trouble with a Kitten," "I Am the Cat," and "Tip the Saucer of the Moon." The better-known tributes are by such writers as T. S. Eliot, Ogden Nash, W. B. Yeats, and Wordsworth. Even the selective "anonymous" poems have a degree of charm. Those who are less than thrilled by a cat will still give honor to the eighth-century scribe who opens his work with the marvelous line, "I and Pangur Ban, my cat. . . ." The compiler is an Australian, young adult author who loves cats. The collection is for any person of any age who loves cats. Others may prefer to pass.

Fellow Mortals; an Anthology of Animal Verse. *Roy Fuller, comp.* **(1981) Macdonald and Evans. 274p.**

An English poet and novelist, Roy Fuller opens his tribute to animals with the "Creation of the Animals" from *Paradise Lost* and verses from Job and Isaiah in the King James version of the Bible. The arrangement after that is chronological, beginning with Henry Constable and, some one hundred poets and about twice as many poems later, ending with Ruth Pitter's "The Bat." There is a witty introduction and an index of first lines and extracts, but no other notes or guides. Fuller lets the poets speak for themselves. In his explanation of the collection, he makes several points. First, the chronological arrangement is because "I was interested in man's changing attitude to animals that the historical arrangement would be bound to reveal." Next, the cutoff for the birthdates of the poets is 1900, which, he says, "admits the modern sensibility, but does not allow it to dominate." That corresponds with the *raison d'être* of the book: "The growth of compassion for brute creation, as here revealed, must be accounted a considerable virtue, especially over a period when man has done much damage to his own kind. . . . It is man who has fallen, not the beasts."

Good Dog Poems. *William Cole, ed.* **(1981) Scribner's. 142p., o.p.**

Dogs being man's best friends, it is only fitting that they have their own poetry anthology. This slim, attractive volume is intended for younger readers but is charming enough for any dog lover. Here are more than eighty poems about the virtues of canines — in war, at home, on vacation — probably everywhere man can take his beloved pet for work and companionship. These poems are grouped into sections according to age and breed: for example, there are sections devoted to puppies, old dogs, mutts, and purebreds. Most of the poets extolling the benefits of dogs are distinguished modern or classical writers — Byron, Robert Frost, Dorothy Parker, Robinson Jeffers. Their verse may be sentimental or witty, tributes to their own beloved pets. The anthology presents decent poems bound to please all readers and accompanied by illustrations. Indexed by poet, title, and first line.

Mice Are Rather Nice; Poems about Mice. *Vardine Moore, ed.* **(1981) Atheneum. 76p., o.p.**

The editor writes in her introduction that mice appear "in poems from Mother Goose to Shakespeare." If this is so, she probably could have included more than the fifty poems found here. Illustrated with pleasant line drawings, this anthology collects mouse poems written by such varied authors as Walter de la Mare, Edith Sitwell, and William Stafford. Among the more famous poems are Burns's "To a Mouse" and the Mother Goose verse "A Frog He Would a-Wooin' Go." These generally funny, lively poems are indexed by author and first line; they should provide pleasant reading for younger readers and lovers of animal poetry.

101 Favorite Cat Poems. *Sara L. Whittier, ed.* **(1991) Contemporary Books. 153p., o.p.**

This slim anthology contains a brief sample of evocative, animated poems about cats: dumb cats, cats as metaphors for life, dead cats, reflections on specific feline breeds. Here are Chaucer, Arnold, Yeats, and T. S. Eliot and contemporary poets Elizabeth Bishop, Ted Hughes, and Ogden Nash; most are English-speaking writers who employ a variety of mood and tone. Among the best poems are probably some truly depressing ones by Baudelaire, with his usual themes of loneliness and love. The poems are arranged in no specific order, an unpretentious plan that highlights the fine verse rather than fancy artwork or critical essays. Recommended for cat lovers and poetry lovers alike, this volume lacks a table of contents but it is indexed by title, author, and translator.

The Oxford Book of Animal Poems. *Michael Harrison and Christopher Stuart-Clark, eds.* **(1992) Oxford University Press. 157p.**

Another delightful, vivid anthology about animals and suitable for young children, *The Oxford Book of Animal Poems* could be a tour of the world's greatest forests, jungles, and plains. The 130 poems are by a variety of writers and include such distinguished poets as Spenser, Blake, and Hardy and many modern accomplished poets of the stature of Theodore Roethke, Ted Hughes, and Randall Jarrell. Their poems, some brief, some fairly long, are populated with eagles and owls, swans and horses, camels and crocodiles. Arranged by continent, the verse is evocative and lyrical, beautiful when read silently or aloud. Accompanying the poems are enchanting illustrations, many of them in color.

Harrison and Stuart-Clark have produced another masterful children's collection that needs no introduction. The verse speaks for itself: illustrious, adventuresome, and moody. Indexed by animal, author, title, first line, and artist.

The Penguin Book of Bird Poetry. *Peggy Munsterberg, ed.* (1984) **Penguin Books; first published by Allen Lane (1980). 361p., o.p.**

A peculiar feature sets this volume apart from almost all other anthologies. The subject is, of course, unusual, but even more so is the fact that almost a third of the book is devoted to an introduction. There may be a more thorough study of bird poetry elsewhere, but it is hard to believe. Ms. Munsterberg offers the reader not only the chronologically arranged poems, but a brilliant essay on how the bird has been celebrated by poets from the ninth century up to William Butler Yeats. Almost sixty poems at the close are from the anonymous oral tradition, without a time frame or an author, but familiar to many as nursery rhymes. The book ends with a selected bibliography (surely one of the most detailed for this subject anywhere), a glossary of bird names, an index of birds, an index of poets, and an index of first lines. The focus is on English poets, but the compiler points out that of the one hundred twenty species of birds treated in the poems, most can be found in America. Still, "if Americans have a complaint, it is not the question of names, it is the fact that among the species which we do not have are three of the most prominent birds in poetry." They are the cuckoo, the skylark, and the nightingale. In its poetic observations on birds, this anthology is truly unique and is recommended for both libraries and individuals.

The Poetry of Birds. *Samuel Carr, ed.* (1976) **Taplinger. 88p., o.p.**

For centuries poets have admired and glorified birds, and it would only make sense for someone to compile an anthology of these celebratory poems. This slender volume includes a good selection of poems from a wide range of authors and times. Included are Milton's "Creation of Birds," from *Paradise Lost*; "The Bullfinches," by Thomas Hardy; "The Mocking-Bird," by Walt Whitman; and forty-one other poems about parrots, nightingales, peacocks, eagles — the inspiration of poets for thousands of years. Shakespeare, Yeats, Pope, and Robert Frost are also here. Each page contains beautiful black-and-white illustrations, as well as reproductions of classic paintings in which people are posed with birds or birds are majestically painted by themselves. This is an attractive, pleasing volume for bird lovers. No condemnations of birds, just praise and exultation.

The Poetry of Cats. *Samuel Carr, ed.* **(1974) Viking Press. 96p., o.p.**

Cats may not turn up in verse as often as horses or dogs, but there are enough poems written for or about cats to justify their own poetry. In this slender collection, about fifty poems of varying styles, forms, and length are featured. Some of them are accompanied by accomplished paintings or sketches of cats in various stages of play and hunt. The poems are by such diverse distinguished writers as Chaucer, Swift, Wordsworth, Baudelaire, and T. S. Eliot. Some of the selections are rather emotional dedications to beloved pets, others are simple, coy musings on the mysterious feline. Listed by title and author, this collection is breezy and lighthearted, filled with entertaining poems for young readers, general readers, and, of course, cat lovers.

The Poetry of Horses. *William Cole, ed.* **(1979) Scribner's. 180p., o.p.**

As well as dogs, cats, and birds, horses are frequently the subject of odes and elegies. This is a collection of mostly simple, touching poems about all kinds of horses, from racers to workhorses to horses of war and battle. Poets as diverse as Shakespeare, Whitman, Frost, and Kipling are featured, although most of them are more obscure and more contemporary. Arranged according to theme, the volume includes poetry as varied as biblical passages, long story poems, and brief, humorous rhymes about silly horse-antics. Some are about a single, beloved pet, others are tributes to the entire species. This is a slim, charming volume to delight younger readers or horse lovers of all ages; readers will not find the meaning of life on these pages but are sure to be entertained with vivid, charming verse. Indexed by poet, title, and first line.

The Sophisticated Cat; a Gathering of Stories, Poems, and Miscellaneous Writings about Cats. *Joyce Carol Oates and Daniel Halpern, eds.* **(1992) Penguin Books. 396p.**

Here is the quintessential anthology true cat lovers have been waiting for, crammed not only with poems about cats but also with stories, essays, and fables detailing the antics of the world's most popular pet. The literature is divided by theme and year into eleven chapters, including "Cat Stories by the Masters," which contains stories by Chekhov, Balzac, Saki, and Poe. Other chapters feature works by authors ranging from Yeats to

Aesop to Ben Franklin to Adlai Stevenson (among the more surprising writers). Here are 31 stories, 15 essays, and 59 poems, some celebrating cats, others looking upon them with scathing cynicism. All are first-rate reflections that should win the approval of cat lover and of general poetry reader alike — unless, of course, the subject drives the reader crazy first. Listed only by table of contents, with two introductions by the two editors.

A Zooful of Animals. *William Cole, ed.*

See under   CHILDREN'S POETRY

ARABIC POETRY

Arabic & Persian Poems. *Omar S. Pound, ed. and tr.* **(1970) New Directions Books. 80p.**

The only glimpse of Arabic or Persian verse most English-language readers see comes from Fitzgerald's translation of Omar Khayyam's "Rubáiyát." This slender anthology was compiled to address the dearth of Arabic and Persian poetry available to general readers. Included here are thirty-six fluid, lyrical poems written between the sixth and the thirteenth centuries, at the peak of the Arabic and Persian poetic tradition. Arranged alphabetically, the twenty-seven poets are among the most skillful in their language. Perhaps the most helpful section, particularly to readers with no familiarity in Arabic or Persian literature or history, are the two introductions that offer critical and historic information about the Arab nations and Persia at the time these poems were created. Although there are no indexes, biographical notes are provided on each poet. Without being too didactic, Pound offers a steady, informative volume of illustrious verse. Readers may not fall immediately in love with Arabic or Persian poetry, but they will clearly see the differences and variations when compared to English or European verse.

Modern Arabic Poetry; an Anthology. *Salma Khadra Jayyusi, ed.* **(1987) Columbia University Press. 498p.**

Prepared under the Project for Translation from Arabic Literature, this is a valuable collection for anyone attempting to understand the Arab world, particularly so because the compiler, a distinguished poet and critic, is a leading expert on the Arab nations as well. While the focus is on poetry written in the twentieth century, primarily from the latter half of the century, the influence of earlier work is evident, as is the constant struggle for identity in, and reconciliation with, the modern world. If a window is opened for even the most avid poetry reader on a dark part of poetry, it is due in no small part to the superior system of translation. All of the poems are translated twice, the final version representing a consensus between the literal version and that creatively rendered by English-language poets. The list of the poet translators (each with a short biographical sketch at the end of the volume) includes John Heath-Stubbs, W. S. Merwin, Christopher Middleton, Anthony Thwaite, and Richard Wilbur. The introduction, which explains the content, form, and history of the poems, is a forty-page essay worth reading for its own merits.

Modern Poetry of the Arab World. *Abdullah al-Udhari, ed. and tr.* **(1986) Penguin Books. 154p., pap., o.p.**

Poet, teacher, translator, and editor, Abdullah al-Udhari is in an excellent position to present modern Arabic poetry to the West. He does not disappoint. Much, if not all, of the poetry is within the reach and understanding of the average reader. While the table of contents offers short biographical sketches of each of the twenty-two poets and the compiler's eight-page introduction is of some help, there are few notes. The poems must stand by themselves. This can be difficult when the secondary meaning of some verse, e.g., "Traffic Lights," by Mu'in Besseisso, or Mahmoud Darwish's "I have witnessed the massacre," is puzzling. At the same time, these two poems, as well as the hundred or so others, can be appreciated for the sheer beauty of movement, content, and style. "The strength of the Arab poet," the compiler writes, "is that he writes about the misery and tragedy of individuals who suffer. . . . The poet proclaims the individual and promotes Arab dignity." The translations are fluid, and the collection gives the outsider an excellent view of Arab thought and modern history. Indexes of titles and first lines are supplied.

ASIAN-AMERICAN POETRY

Breaking Silence; an Anthology of Contemporary Asian American Poets. *Joseph Bruchac, ed.* **(1983) Greenfield Review Press. 295p., o.p.**

The technological success of the Japanese, the remarkable business skills of Asians in America, and the power of their children to excel in schools have forced Americans to view Asians more favorably in a reappraisal of the exotic and sinister former stereotype. Drawing upon numerous little magazines, the editor (a little magazine publisher himself) offers the work of 50 poets, some of their poems being original to this collection. "My choices were subjective," Bruchac explains. "I picked the poems I liked best with an eye for variety and giving each poet enough space to give the reader a good taste of his or her work." The procedure for the first poet, Mei-Mei Berssenbrugge, is typical. Her entry opens with her picture and a brief biographical sketch, followed by a selection of her poetry. "Silence" is indeed now broken, and the murmurs to the explosions indicate a way of looking at life and at America rarely found elsewhere. It is a view that is as perceptive and imaginative as it is intelligent and disciplined. While few of the poets' names are that well known, their ideas and their dreams are known to all. Highly recommended for most libraries and for all people who enjoy poetry.

The Open Boat; Poems from Asian America. *Garrett Hongo, ed.* **(1993) Doubleday. 303p.**

A few of the poets featured in this engaging anthology have published relatively successful novels or volumes of poetry in America — Maxine Hong Kingston and Mei-Mei Berssenbrugge, for example. But most of the thirty-one poets will probably be obscure to readers, even though their poetry is often accomplished and skillful. It is a relatively young group of poets, all born after the Second World War, generally growing up with dual American and Asian identities, with roots in India, China, the Philippines, and elsewhere in Asia. Arranged alphabetically by author, with selections in contemporary style and form ranging from metered to free verse, the poetry attempts to combine the features of both cultures: rooted in American style but with themes of cultural identity and family security. Despite an introduction that spends too much time identifying Asian stereotypes, this is a sensitive anthology that readers unfamiliar with contemporary Asian-American poetry will find well worth looking into. It is too brief a volume to be a definitive Asian-American overview, but it does contain the work of some fine contemporary poets.

AUSTRALASIAN POETRY

An Anthology of Twentieth-Century New Zealand Poetry. *Vincent O'Sullivan, comp.* **(3d ed., 1987) Oxford University Press, 460p., pap.**

The compiler claims to have selected the poems for this volume on the basis of excellence. This may be the ideal, but when one is limiting the collection to a country the size of New Zealand (approximatley one quarter the population of New York City), choices based on history and the natural development of the literature are inevitable and correct. There are not that many really outstanding poets when one is drawing from a base of about two million people, and the reader will probably fail to recognize more than two or three. Most of the poets are good, but not that good. Arrangement is chronological, with the vast number of entries coming from the late twentieth century. This anthology would be a good reference source in libraries and be of unquestioned interest to New Zealanders, but it is of quite limited value to others.

The Collins Book of Australian Poetry. *Rodney Hall, comp.* **(1981, 1984) Fontana/Collins. 460p., o.p.**

Suitably enough, the Australian saga opens with a Wonguri-Mandjigai song about the birth and death of the moon. The Aborigine's highly rhythmic, ritual poem is followed by some hundred and fifty "most alive of Australian poems." The work is in chronological order and ends in the mid 1980's. The compiler admits there have been literary influences on the poetry from the Pacific as well as from Britain and America, but he sees the Australian voice as distinctive. Any one poet's "poems interact and grow from one another. . . . If the poems have a secondary life, I would suggest it is not so much that of authorial ambition and achievement, as a special history of Australia." For example, Rhyll McMaster outlines the "Profiles of My Father" and also discourses on water tanks so suggestively as to give the outsider as potent a picture of the country as any travel book. The liveliness, the zest of most of the poetry is caught in the work of Henry Lawson, one of scores of poets who sing about the trials and the joys of early settlement. In "Will Yer Write It Down for

Me?" he opens the story with "In the parlour of the shanty where the lives have all gone wrong" and ends it with "Takes his pen in tears and triumph, and he writes it down for them." The nineteenth-century poet's biography, along with those of all the entrants, is given in loving detail at the end of the volume. This is a marvelous collection.

Contemporary American & Australian Poetry. *Thomas Shapcott, ed.*

See under WORLD POETRY

The Faber Book of Modern Australian Verse. *Vincent Buckley, ed.* **(1991) Faber and Faber. 275p.**

Probably none of the forty-seven poets included in this volume will be recognized by the general American audience. But the work of these poets is worth reading for the clear, ordered forms and lush, descriptive imagery. "Modern" here dates from the early parts of the century to about 1980, with most of the writers gaining recognition after the Second World War and in the 1950's. All are English-speaking writers; there are no translations from aboriginal languagues. The poets are arranged chronologically, and unfortunately no biographical information is given. A fine introduction traces the development of the genuine yet little-known Australian literary tradition. Indexed by poet, title, and first line, this is a very traditional anthology, offering a good sample of Australian poetry to the unfamiliar foreign reader.

The First Paperback Poets Anthology. *Roger McDonald, ed.* **(1974) University of Queensland Press. 195p., o.p.**

Roger McDonald has edited, in *The First Paperback Poets Anthology,* a collection of extremely observant, contemplative poems. Among the more noted poets included are Thomas Shapcott, Rodney Hall, David Malouf, and R. A. Simpson. The book itself is not a paperback, but these 100 poems were selected from 22 paperback poetry volumes published by the University of Queensland Press between 1969 and 1974. A one-page editor's note describes the evolution of this anthology and the series that produced it. The collection contains no index but does include biographical notes at its end; often, other poets in the anthology have written these biographies. Within the body of the book, arrangement is alphabetical by poet. This work should prove an enjoyable look at the Australian poetry of its period.

The Golden Apples of the Sun; Twentieth Century Australian Poetry. *Chris Wallace-Crabbe, ed.* **(1980) Melbourne University Press. 243p., o.p.**

Chris Wallace-Crabbe states, in the introduction to this anthology, "I wanted to use the poetry which interested me the most deeply rather than seeking to represent careers or bodies of work." He places Christopher Brennan's "The Wanderer" at the beginning of twentieth-century Australian poetry and then shifts to a discussion of the issues and concerns of that country's recent verse. To the editor the poems are analogous to the apples of the title. Wallace-Crabbe has collected 144 poems by 63 writers — many of whom are noted contemporary Australian poets. Peter Porter, John Tranter, Les A. Murray, and David Malouf are among the poets included here. These chronologically arranged works, varying in quality, range in tone from mournful to spirited. The anthology ends with brief contributors' notes and an index of first lines. The general reader or student of world poetry should enjoy this collection.

A Map of Australian Verse. *James McAuley, ed.* **(1975) Oxford University Press. 342p., o.p.**

In his foreword, James McAuley likens the approach of his anthology to that of an earlier volume, John Press's *A Map of Modern English Verse.* He begins with work from the end of the nineteenth century and progresses forward to the year of publication. A brief General Introduction touches upon many of the included poets. McAuley says of contemporary Australian poetry, "It is mainly through dissatisfaction with this endemic conservatism [of past Australian poetry] that some younger poets want to make a fresh start." He provides commentary by Australian and other poets, along with a select bibliography. The book is divided into 14 sections, many containing the work of a single poet (such as Christopher Brennan, A. D. Hope, and McAuley himself), others addressing specific periods ("Continuity and Change in the Fifties" or "The Sixties and After"). Each section includes a brief critical introduction (and notes), followed by several contemplative and pleasurable poems representing a poet's best work; the selections provide a clear view of each poet or period. There is a general index. This well-constructed text should be useful for the general reader or beginning student of Australian poetry.

The New Oxford Book of Australian Verse. *Les A. Murray, ed.* **(Enl. ed., 1991) Oxford University Press. 399p., pap., o.p.**

In his foreword, the editor of this surprisingly eclectic anthology states that the poems were included for their "liveliness and readability." All of the verse lives up to that claim, from the homesick poems of early European settlers to Aboriginal mourning songs and highly polished contemporary verse. More than two hundred poets spanning three centuries are featured, each represented by two or three selections. Arranged chronologically by author and indexed by first line and by author and title, the verse advances from moderately skillful to quite accomplished, but by the late twentieth century it loses some of the flavor and idiosyncrasies particular to an Australian "feel." Although the anthology lacks biographical information or notes on the poems that would be helpful for general readers, this volume is still recommended for its broad sampling of Australian poetry; it is planned not as a student's text but as an anthology for more general readers.

The Oxford Book of Contemporary New Zealand Poetry. *Fleur Adcock, ed.* **(1982) Oxford University Press. 146p.**

The typical reader probably knows very little about New Zealand's poetry. This collection may not shed great light on New Zealand's poetic tradition, but the quality and range of the poetry are impressive. The twenty-one poets were published primarily in small New Zealand literary magazines in the 1970's or later. The poetry is usually free form, neither particularly innovative nor overly rigid in form and syntax. There is skillful composition in this slim collection that makes for some beautiful verse. The poetry is unconscious and genuine, glancing into a culture strange to most modern readers. Indexed by title and first line with a glossary of indigenous terms.

The Penguin Book of New Zealand Verse. *Ian Wedde and Harvey McQueen, eds.* **(1985) Penguin Books. 575p., pap., o.p.**

This anthology begins with almost one hundred pages of Maori traditional poetry, drawn primarily from the nineteenth century and by memory from many centuries before that. There is a fine introduction to the Maori verse that does much to set the scene for what follows. Edward Tregear (1846–1931) is first in line of the credited poets, and he draws upon that same tradition for his art. The remaining eighty or so poets are presented in chronological order by date of birth, ending with Elizabeth Nannestad (b. 1956). There is a select bibliography for each of the poets, but no biographical data is provided. And while there are a few notes, these are primarily for the Maori verse. As with other collections of this type, the real problem is the uneven talent of so many of the poets. At the same time, one must be grateful for the overview it offers the student and, of course, the sense of pride it affords the New Zealander.

Poetry in Australia. Vol. I: From the Ballads to Brennan; Vol. II: Modern Australian Verse. *T. Inglis Moore, comp. Vol. I; Douglas Stewart, comp. Vol. II.* (1965) University of California Press. 313p., 246p., o.p.

In 1965, this was the definitive edition of Australian verse. The strength of the set is the first volume that has an exceptionally strong section of folk songs and ballads, as well as "bush ballads and popular verse." The volume ends with the end of the nineteenth and the beginning of the twentieth century. In addition to the ballads, there are some fifty credited poets. The pleasant surprises are the writers from "the colonial age," and a few of those writing in the nineties. All of them receive short biographical sketches, as do the poets in the second volume. In retrospect, the choices for the twentieth century are sometimes less than rewarding, although even the poorest give one a new appreciation of the land and its people. One notes the relative lack of introspective verse and the heavy debt owed the earlier ballads and verse. Both volumes are to be treasured for the popular, folksy entries that remind us that poetry first and foremost is something from and for the people. This was never more true than in this collection.

AUSTRIAN POETRY

Contemporary Austrian Poetry; an Anthology. *Beth Bjorklund, ed. and tr.* **(1986) Fairleigh Dickinson University Press. 328p.**

In his "Meditation at Seventy," senior poet Rudolf Henz admits to having been less than a social activist during his life. At the same time, he was committed to composing "book after book, line after line, for five decades." That might be the theme of the present collection, which covers almost the same amount of time for the fifty-five poets represented here. Representing a cross section of modern Austria, the assembled poets range in age from thirty-nine to eighty-seven. Probably not more than a handful are that well known outside of their own country. Initiated by h. c. artmann (a poet who frowns on upper case letters), the so-called "Vienna Group" is often found in English language journals. This and other equally fascinating movements are traced in the witty introduction by the translator and compiler.

BALLADS AND SONGS

American Folk Poetry; an Anthology. *Duncan Emrich, ed.* **(1974) Little, Brown. 831p.**

Year in and year out this is a favorite, much-consulted work at home and in the library. It is as basic as any collection of folk poetry can be. Although the editor points out that "folk poetry should not and cannot be judged on the aesthetic scales used to weigh the poetry of great literature," he suggests that it offers some strong challenges. The irony is that most of the poems are by the ubiquitous "anonymous." They are such a part of daily life that the original author has been long forgotten, a Homer without a name. Yes, Homer is brought to mind when one reads the magnificent section on "Wars and Other Disasters." The numerous pages dedicated to children's songs and verses do justice to anything in the literature. Combining song and verse, the eight separate sections are often subdivided. One imaginative subsection includes types of work: sailing, lumbering, coal mining. The massive volume, and it weighs several pounds, ends with a well-constructed bibliography and an index of titles and first lines. Highly recommended for anyone with the slightest curiosity about folk poetry, and a must for the library.

The American Songbag. *Carl Sandburg, comp.* **(1927) Harcourt, Brace. 495p., pap.**

There are songs (both words and music) galore in this collection by the well-known poet Carl Sandburg. He has divided the songs into "Dramas and Portraits," "The Ould Sod," "Minstrel Songs," "Tarnished Love Tales or Colonial and Revolutionary Antiques," "Frankie and Her Man," "Pioneer Memories," "Kentucky Blazing Star," and so forth. You will find such wonderful creations as "Foggy, Foggy Dew" and "The Erie Canal" among the two hundred and eighty songs, ballads, and ditties that Americans have been singing down the centuries. Many of these tunes and lyrics will be new to the reader, for most of them are by now obscure, but they should prove of interest to those who would like to pick them out on the piano or guitar. And it is delightful to come across a famous song like "Sweet Betsy from Pike" with all nine stanzas printed. Sandburg comments briefly before each of these songs, filling in its background and responding to its charms. With their personal tone, the notes make an appealing songbook even more attractive.

As I Walked Out One Evening; a Book of Ballads. *Helen Plotz, ed.* **(1976) Greenwillow Books. 265p., o.p.**

Helen Plotz, in *As I Walked Out One Evening*, wishes to focus on the thematic and plot elements of ballads. She has grouped them into such categories as "Narratives," "War," "Work," and "Love." "The Twa Corbies," "John Henry," "As I Walked Out in the Streets of Laredo," and "Yankee Doodle" are among the more famous ballads included. In several cases, alternative versions have been supplied. Although the collection is by no means exhaustive, Plotz has tried to include as many well-known ballads as possible. The works are not accompanied by background information; songs from the Middle Ages are mixed with ballads by poets as modern as Kenneth Rexroth and Donald Hall. The anthology is indexed by author, title, and first line.

The Ballad Book. *MacEdward Leach, ed.* **(1975) Harper. 842p., o.p.**

This rich anthology includes more than two hundred English, Scottish, and American ballads, many of them variations of the same tale. These superb, eclectic examples of folk verse are arranged chronologically in two sections, one listing distinctly American verse and the other containing British ballads with their American and Danish variants. All are fascinating, anonymous tales, popular from medieval days to the time of the industrial revolution. Leach has included a lengthy, informative introduction in which he explains the origins of ballads, the structure of the verse, and the importance of the ballad as a literary form in early American history. He provides a thorough analysis of the style and structure of the ballad as a literary form meant to be heard rather than read. Unfortunately he includes no music because, as he argues, "no system of musical notation that I am aware of can indicate accurately the music of the ballads." This anthology presents much information about a literary genre not often given the recognition it deserves. General readers will find the tales evocative and fascinating, as will readers more familiar with folklore and the stories handed down over the centuries.

Best Loved Poems of the American West. *John J. Gregg and Barbara T. Gregg, eds.* **(1980) Doubleday. 515p., o.p.**

Containing such poems as "Starving to Death on a Government Claim" and "My Sweetie's a Mule in the Mine," this collection is witty and refreshing. The editors explain in their introduction that they tried to include a wide range of poetry about the West and its legendary inhabitants. Without sacrificing depth and quality, they have successfully gathered fascinating verse about cowboys, railroads, Native Americans, and desolate terrain. Many of the poems are well known, written by such prominent poets as Ambrose Bierce, Willa Cather, Lucius Harwood Foote, Mark Twain, and Bret Harte. Most of the 141 poets are, however, relatively unknown. The poems are divided into groups, some devoted to people of the West ("Heroes and Villains" and "Poems of the People"); others are arranged by territory ("California: the Golden Gate" and "Desert Songs"); they were written from cowboy, settler, and Native American viewpoints. They are illustrative and lyrical, chronicling the West's importance to the growth of a young nation. This collection of poems that capture the mood of a long-lost era is highly recommended for anyone interested in the literary history of nineteenth-century western America.

Best Loved Songs and Hymns. *James Morehead and Albert Morehead, eds.* **(1965) Funk & Wagnalls. 405p., o.p.**

Although this anthology was published almost thirty years ago, the songs in it are still favorites. The collection is organized by type of song: patriotic; sentimental; sea, western, and folk; hymns; Christmas carols; and spirituals. Included are such famous songs as "On Top of Old Smoky," "Come All Ye Faithful," "Rock of Ages," "She'll Be Comin' 'round the Mountain," "Home on the Range," "La Cucaracha," "Loch Lomond," and "Drink to Me Only with Thine Eyes." Each of the 200 songs in this book is accompanied by an informative introduction, author and composition date, musical notation, and guitar chord diagrams where applicable. Each page is enclosed in an attractive floral border, and the lyrics are easily read in the book's large format. The editors have included many popular foreign songs, often with an English translation. The index includes first lines, titles, and author names. *Best Loved Songs and Hymns* will be useful for the student of popular culture or for anyone who simply wishes to sing.

Best Loved Songs of the American People. *Denes Agay, ed.* **(1975) Doubleday. 403p., pap., o.p.**

Anyone looking for a thorough collection of American folk songs, ballads, love songs, and minstrel songs will be satisfied by this anthology. Large and heavy, it contains close to two hundred songs fondly remembered by some and altogether forgotten by others. The most popular ones are all here, with full musical notation provided: "When Johnny Comes Marching Home," "The Blue Tail Fly," "Carry Me Back to Old Virginny," and "On Top of Old Smokey," among others. Many of the melodies are known to schoolchildren, and readers will see that some folk rock songs of the 1960's and 1970's are actually variants of these old ballads. The volume is arranged chronologically by song and divided into five chapters, such as "Old Colony Times and the New Nation" and "From Tin Pan Alley to Main Street." Brief historical information is provided for each song, as well as an index of titles and first lines. The introduction states that new musical arrangements are here to facilitate modern playing and singing, and some small spelling adjustments were also made when the editor felt the overall character of the song would not be affected. This volume makes available authentic American songs that people have enjoyed for years.

The Blues Line; a Collection of Blues Lyrics. *Eric Sackheim, ed.* **(1969) Grossman Publishers. 500p., o.p.**

The blues have fully entered mainstream popularity, and so anthologies of blues lyrics have proliferated. This volume is one of the most comprehensive available. Although not accompanied by musical notation, this large, heavy text presents 270 examples of old-time blues lyrics by such musicians as Robert Johnson, John Lee Hooker, and Bessie Smith. The songs are arranged largely by region and year — for example, "Mississippi: the Delta" and "The '40's and '50's." The lyrics are rhythmic, exciting, and subdued; one can imagine the smoky room and almost hear the music. Many of the songs are followed by illustrations of the artists, and a list of sketches precedes the text. According to Sackheim, these songs were sung mostly by black singers and recorded on 78 rpm records from the 1920's through the 1950's. The lyrics were reproduced from listening to the records, and there may be some phonetic errors. But on the whole readers will find this to be one of the most accessible and representative, although by no means exhaustive, collections of blues lyrics available.

The Books of American Negro Spirituals, including the Book of American Negro Spirituals and the Second Book of American Negro Spirituals. *James Weldon Johnson and J. Rosamond Johnson, eds.*

See under AFRICAN-AMERICAN POETRY

Breathes There the Man; Heroic Ballads & Songs of the English-Speaking Peoples. *Frank S. Meyer, ed.* **(1973) Open Court. 281p., o.p.**

Although *Breathes There the Man* contains famous heroic verses by such authors as Whitman, Byron, and Longfellow, it is not sufficiently balanced to be very useful to the average student. Almost half of the book is concerned with American history: "America: The War of Independence," "America: The War of 1812," "America: The War Between the States," and "America: Other Poems." The rest of the book is given to shorter sections: "England," "Scotland," "Ireland," and the miscellaneous "Poems of Other Lands." Meyer does not sufficiently represent the United Kingdom, which has certainly more wars in its history than America. Also, the term "English-Speaking Peoples" includes such countries as Australia and New Zealand, which Meyer omits completely. The book has an adequate index but a sketchy table of contents. The student of American history may find this anthology useful, but readers with broader needs must look elsewhere.

The Common Muse; an Anthology of Popular British Ballad Poetry, XVth–XXth Century. *Vivian de Sola Pinto and Allan Edwin Rodway, eds.* **(1957) Philosophical Library. 470p.**

Ballads are one of the most enduring and entertaining of all poetic forms, and this anthology is a collection of several hundred popular British ballads written from the fifteenth through the twentieth centuries. The organizing principle, after a long and scholarly introduction, is to divide the poems into general and amatory ballads. The former might be about history; social criticism; manners and fashion; soldiers, sailors, highwaymen, and poachers; portents and prodigies; crime and punishment; concluding with religion. The amatory section is divided into rural, urban, vocational, clerical, marital, and wise and foolish virgins. Those categories seem to encompass more or less everything an author would want to write about, and these ballads make for very varied and rewarding reading. They should please those who are interested in the history of poetry, as well as readers who are looking for entertaining, accessible poems with strong, lilting, musical underpinnings. Occasionally an author is identified, but most often the author is unknown.

Cowboy Songs and Other Frontier Ballads. *Alan Lomax and John A. Lomax, eds.* **(1967) Macmillan. 431p., o.p.**

This is a large, lively collection of folk ballads, conveying the exciting lawlessness and the stark desolation of the nineteenth-century American West. Grouped into chapters with such titles as "Up the Trail," "Campfire and Bunkhouse," and "Son of a Gun," the songs picture rambling cowhands, open trails, lonely nights, and vast frontiers. Few of the more than two hundred ballads have been traced to an author, but this anonymity adds to the fascination of cowboy legends. In the collector's note, Lomax explains that he included the best lines from various versions of the same tale, and that the ballads will reveal to readers "a truer conception of what [the cowboy] really was" as opposed to "those who know him only through highly colored romances." After reading the verse aloud, it is easy to imagine generations of settlers reciting songs, creating new lyrics over campfires. Musical composition accompanies many of the ballads. This anthology is equally enjoyable for readers interested in a vivid, historical record of the American frontier and for those interested in vibrant, lyrical verse.

English and Scottish Ballads. *Robert Graves, ed.* **(1957) William Heinemann. 163p., pap.**

A frontispiece of a facsimile page from The Roxburghe Ballads (an eighteenth-century collection of broadsheets), complete with a dramatic woodcut of St. George fighting a dragon, gives an accurate, historical feel to the poems. Ballads, according to a dictionary definition that Robert Graves includes in his long, scholarly introduction to this wonderful book, are "simple, spirited poems in short stanzas, in which a popular story is graphically told." The works in this collection date from the early fourteenth to the middle of the seventeenth century, the great age for the composition of ballads. Graves reports that ballads were sung to the music of a harp or viol to entertain people as they ate or drank. Their material came originally out of old, pagan witch cults, and many of the allusions can be traced to those occult roots. Ballads recounted the exploits of Robin Hood, a particularly popular figure whose adventures showed up in fifty different works, a few of them included in this collection. Other well-known ballads are "Lord Rendal" and "Barbara Allen." All these poems are beautifully wrought and a pleasure to read.

They are here accessible to the ordinary reader and still provide the same enjoyment they afforded those long centuries ago.

English and Scottish Popular Ballads. *Helen Child Sargent and George Lyman Kittredge, eds., from the collection of Francis James Child.* **(1904, 1932, reissued, 1947) Houghton Mifflin. 730p.**

Thanks to his systematic collection of folk ballads, Francis Child is remembered today as America's earliest advocate of the importance of these works. His largest undertaking was the eight-volume collection of *English and Scottish Ballads,* one of the most extensive in existence. This was revised and reedited by a contemporary, equally famous, professor at Harvard, and Child's daughter. The present volume represents each of the three hundred and five basic ballads in one or more versions. Short notes conclude the volume. (Scholars must turn to the original work for the exhaustive collations, elaborate bibliographies, notes, etc.) The introduction, although written almost one hundred years ago, remains one of the best overall histories of the ballad, in abbreviated form. This is by George Lyman Kittredge, a master of the well-turned phrase and one of Harvard's greatest teachers. "Mary Hamilton" is typical enough of how the material is handled. There is a brief explanation of the ballad's history, then two versions. While all of this may be too much for the average reader, the fact remains that it is still the one place to turn for the definitive rendition of a popular work.

The Faber Book of Ballads. *Matthew Hodgart, ed.* **(1965) Faber and Faber. 267p., pap., o.p.**

Easy to understand, thrilling to read, "a ballad is a song that comments on life by telling a story in a popular style," to quote the introduction to this comprehensive collection of ballads. The editor has divided ballads into various categories: "Traditional," "Robin Hood and Border Ballads," "Scots Eighteenth Century," "Folksong and Lyric," "Broadside Ballads," "Irish," and finally, "Australian and American." So, here you will find "John Henry" and "Barbara Allen," as well as "Sir Patrick Spens," "Edward," "Finnegan's Wake," and "Lord Randal." There is enormous variety in this collection, and the quality of the verse is very high indeed. Being outside the Great Tradition of English literature, they speak for "the people," and they continue, very powerfully, to speak to them as well. The introduction helpfully places the ballads within their historical contexts. Here they stand, accessible, emotional, literary experiences for anyone who can read.

Favorite Songs of the Nineties; Complete Original Sheet Music for 89 Songs. *Robert A. Fremont, ed.* **(1973) Dover. 401p.**

The 1890's were a legendary time in American cultural development, and these songs evoke whichever sobriquet one wishes to ascribe to the era: the "gay" nineties, the "naughty" nineties, or, as the introduction puts it, the "gaudy" nineties. These are songs that people still enjoy playing and singing, such favorites as "A Bicycle Built for Two," "The Sidewalks of New York," and "You're a Grand Old Flag." Arranged alphabetically by song, they have been reproduced in their original sheet-music form, with musical notation and illustrations. The introduction interestingly details the rise of mass-produced sheet music and the recordings that began in this decade. This is a solid, entertaining volume of the popular sentimental hits of that period. Some readers will be amused to read and sing along; for others it will provide a historical trip back to a time when pop music was just beginning; for anyone interested in the sociology of American musical development, this collection is one of the best.

Folksinger's Wordbook. *Irwin Silber and Fred Silber, eds.* **(1973) Oak Publications. 430p.**

This large, spiral-bound songbook provides the lyrics to over 1,000 folk and traditional songs representing a diversity of styles, geographical regions, and political ideologies. Many come from folk and protest movements of the 1940's through the 1960's; some were inspired by the Bible, some are blues lyrics, and still others were coined by sailors, soldiers, and prisoners in America's early years. Rather than print full musical notation as other songbooks do, this one includes only guitar chords. The poems are grouped by subject. There is a bibliography for readers looking for sheet music to these songs. The book seems planned for contemporary American folk musicians, although the lyrics can be read as poetry of grassroots counterculture movements and disenfranchised Americans.

The Illustrated Border Ballads. *John Marsden, ed.* **(1990) University of Texas Press. 192p.**

This anthology is an illustrious, specialized, tall volume, also featuring a glossary, extensive notes, and a detailed map of the English-Scottish border where these ballads originated in the sixteenth century. The collection consists of only sixteen ballads — each several pages long. They are evocative and entertaining either as verse or as historical records of a long-gone culture. Each ballad is enhanced by splendid photographs and paintings of the surrounding countryside and battlegrounds, juxtaposing the beauty of these narratives with the beauty of the land. A fascinating introduction and notes throughout the text explain the history of the border country and the oral tradition these ballads were born of. Middle English words are translated for the reader's benefit. This is highly recommended for ballad fans and readers who enjoy a rousing story, and the editor has enthusiastically collected these ballads in a volume to be treasured. Indexed by title, poet, illustration, and subject.

The Jazz Poetry Anthology. *Sascha Feinstein and Yusef Komunyakaa,* **eds. (1991) Indiana University Press. 293p.**

The fusion of jazz and poetry became popular in the 1950's, according to the editor of this spirited, eclectic volume. Jazz purists denounced the movement, but readers of this collection will see that some energetic, expressive verse was produced by 133 mostly well-known poets such as Amiri Baraka, Marvin Bell, and Sonia Sanchez. Each author is represented by one or two selections, and a "musical index" matches the poem with the jazz musician who influenced its creation. The anthology begins with lyrics of early jazz from the early part of the century, but it concentrates mainly on later writers and musicians, both American and international. No musical notation is included, however; all of the verse was inspired by jazz, but not necessarily set to jazz music. Lively and vivid, this collection should be read not just for the poetry but for the history of jazz it inadvertently provides. This is a treasure for music fanatics and general readers alike.

Modern Ballads and Story Poems. *Charles Causley, ed.* **(1965) Franklin Watts; also published in Great Britain as Rising Early by Brockhampton Press (1964). 128p., o.p.**

The English poet Charles Causley limits "modern" to only some forty poems and ballads. The slim volume indicates the popularity of the form. Among the group is almost every well-known poet of the twentieth century: W. H. Auden, Robert Frost, John Betjeman, Ted Hughes, Edith Sitwell, Stevie Smith. What is fascinating about the selection is its focus. It takes a dim view of modern life, and while there are dashes of humor to relieve the tension, the topics move grimly from suffering and death to love and hatred. The compiler, in a fine introduction, fully explains his focus and his choices. He tells the reader to be watchful "for all kinds of ironic understatements." There is help not only by Mr. Causley, but by the poets themselves who sometimes explain the background of their work at the end of the poem. There are fine drawings by Anne Netherwood.

One Hundred English Folksongs. *Cecil J. Sharp, ed.* **(1975) Dover. 235p.**

Like the many other Dover song collections, this is well organized, and full of songs whose tunes are known to most people even if the words have been forgotten. Here are songs that describe the lives of sailors, farmers, shepherds, and highwaymen. From a period spanning several centuries, the songs have long been ignored, although lately, with a folk revival still in swing, their popularity is on the rise. Some well-known favorites are here — "Scarborough Fair" and "The Twelve Days of Christmas" among them — but most will be unknown to most readers. A thorough introduction provides historical background for most of them, explaining how different versions of these songs have emerged over centuries; all are accompanied by full musical notation. Indexed by title, this is a fine volume of long-lost yet timeless English folksongs.

The Oxford Book of Ballads. *James Kinsley, ed.* **(1969) Oxford University Press. 711p., pap.**

In 1911 Sir Arthur Quiller-Couch published a similar work to this. Professor Kinsley has taken over the project, revised many of the ballads, and made additions. About half the ballads in the earlier edition have been dropped. The present volume includes about eighty-five with music to which the ballads are sung; almost fifty of these are new to Kinsley's edition. The entries are limited to traditional ballads of England and Scotland. They are "ballads which are related in theme or in mood." Here can be found riding ballads of the Scottish Border, Biblical ballads, tales of romance, among others. The compiler has rejected the printing of numerous versions of the same ballad and uses only the one he thinks is close to the oral tradition. All and all, this is the most authoritative collection of its type available.

The Oxford Book of English Traditional Verse. *Frederick Woods, ed.* **(1983) Oxford University Press. 424p.**

Complementing *The Oxford Book of Ballads,* this volume focuses on song lyrics that are part of the English oral tradition. Many of the lyrics, of course, are known and sung today. The scope is wide, and the compiler moves from the earliest English songs to a section of relatively contemporary verse familiar to anyone who appreciates the twentieth-century craze for folk songs. The "verse" is limited solely to song lyrics. The book is divided into such large subject headings as "The Pain of Love." The compiler leaves it to other collections to record sea chanties and familiar ballads and rhymes that are not traditional folk lyrics. While an argument persists over whether or not current or earlier versions of a song should be given, the compiler favors the latter; he also makes the point that "the words can be detached without damage" from the music. Lack of music may be considered a fault by some.

The Oxford Book of Sea Songs. *Roy Palmer, ed.*

See under   SEA POETRY

The Penguin Book of Ballads. *Geoffrey Grigson, ed.* **(1975) Penguin Books. 374p., pap., o.p.**

Grigson's introduction takes a critical look at the state of the ballad in contemporary society. He traces its progress from medieval times, when it was a primary source of entertainment in the court and by the fireside, to present times, when it is important in the classroom. This anthology presents 124 ballads for study and pleasure. While many of the songs, such as "Willy the Weeper" and "Waltzing Matilda," are part of a singing tradition, they may also be read and interpreted as stories or poems. Most of these lays are by unknown bards, but the anthology includes, for instance, songs by Auden and Kipling. The poems are arranged chronologically and indexed by title; Grigson has also included a brief section of scholarly notes. This is a useful text and a good source for ballad lyrics.

Poems of the Old West; a Rocky Mountain Anthology. *Levette J. Davidson, ed.* **(1951) University of Denver Press. 240p.**

This anthology is valuable not as a collection of brilliant poems but as a window into a colorful period of American history. The verse may often be sentimental and hackneyed, but it is always entertaining and interesting. The hundreds of poems — or more accurately, songs — are grouped among subjects with such titles as "The Great Outdoors" and "Indians, Scouts and Soldiers." These are traditional cowboy and settler ballads, telling stories of frontier life, brave soldiers, and desolate landscape. Biographical information is included on the poets, but there is only a title index at the end, and no table of contents identifies where chapters begin. This is a minor inconvenience, however, in a rich, unpretentious anthology, as strong as any collection of poems about the Old West.

Popular Songs of Nineteenth Century America; Complete Original Sheet Music for 64 Songs. *Richard Jackson, ed.* **(1976) Dover; published in Great Britain by Constable. 290p.**

In his introduction Jackson writes, "Not only do the popular songs of another era call to mind certain actual historic events, they can give us important hints as to the preoccupations and ways of thinking of the people who wrote them and the people who bought them and performed them." These songs have all been reproduced in their original sheet-music design and evoke the pioneers, the railroad workers, Civil War battles, and plantation life of the early nineteenth century. Almost all of the songs are popular American classics: "The Battle Cry of Freedom," "Adeste Fideles," "Oh My Darling Clementine," and "The Yellow Rose of Texas," among others. Arranged chronologically by song, the volume also has a section of brief historical information on the origins of each song. There are many Stephen Foster tunes most Americans will be familiar with. Jackson has written an informative introduction on the history of these purely American tunes.

The Richard Dyer-Bennet Folk Song Book. *Richard Dyer-Bennet, ed.* **(1971) Simon and Schuster. 176p., o.p.**

Richard Dyer-Bennet was a renowned folk-song performer when his book was published. The collection will be of interest to folk-song fans and, more importantly, Richard Dyer-Bennet fans. (All of the songs are available on his records.) "Waltzing Matilda," "The Foggy, Foggy Dew," and "Frog Went a-Courting" are among the entries in this collection. Dyer-Bennet presents the lyrics of the fifty songs as completely as possible, providing musical notation and chords for guitar accompaniment. He introduces and attempts to date most of the ballads — a considerable task, given sung tradition. Songs are indexed by first line and illustrated with tasteful line drawings. Although a bit brief, this anthology will still be useful as a source of great ballads.

The Ring of Words; an Anthology of Song Texts. *Philip L. Miller, ed.* **(1963) W. W. Norton. 518p.**

In introducing *The Ring of Words*, Philip Miller explains that "of the few attempts that have been made to write the history of the song, not one has approached the subject as a combined art, with poetry as the inspiration of music." This anthology of art songs works, then, to revive a sense of the dynamic relationship between music and poetry. *The Ring of Words* presents the poetically vibrant texts of over 250 art songs, many canonical and some obscure, from Germany, France, Russia, Italy, Spain, Norway, and Sweden, and arranges them by author within the country. Miller facilitates the reader's engagement with the songs by providing a substantial and rich introductory essay. He presents clear translations alongside the texts and situates the songs within their historical and musical contexts, presenting them as poems with strong literary qualities. There is no musical notation in the anthology to help the reader experience the dynamic qualities of the lyrics. There is an index of composers who have at some time set the poems to music, in addition to a not-very-helpful index of titles and first lines.

Shantymen and Shantyboys; Songs of the Sailor and Lumberman. *William Main Doerflinger, ed.* **(1951) Macmillan. 374p., o.p.**

The hundreds of songs and ballads in this anthology were recorded after years of popularity aboard windjammers and schooners and in forests and logging camps in the Pacific Northwest. Originating in the mid-nineteenth century, these are robust, romantic poems created in the isolation of the sea and the American frontier. They are grouped in sections with such titles as "Minstrelsy of Murder," "Satirists of the Sawdust Country," and "Deep Water Songs." Each section is prefaced by extensive historical information about the era from which these songs date, in addition to Doerflinger's longer, informative introduction. Musical notation and notes are provided for each song. The volume also contains a diagram of a nineteenth-century ship, and there is biographical information on the famous singers who helped keep these songs from oblivion. This spirited anthology is highly recommended for general readers and for those looking for a unique collection of American folk ballads. Indexed by title.

Songs of Work and Protest. *Edith Fowke and Joe Glazer, eds.* **(1973) Dover Publications. 209p., pap.**

Included in this 209-page collection are one hundred songs that chronicle the organized-labor movement and worker struggles mainly of the industrial age. The songs will seem familiar to most readers, telling the stories of coal miners, union strikes, racial prejudice, and contempt for the rich man. Most of the songs have obscure origins, and roughly a third chart the modern American labor movement. A few, however, date back to European medieval times and provide an interesting perspective for the modern songs. Divided loosely under 11 subheadings such as, "The Rich Man and the Poor Man," and "Solidarity Forever," these are powerful songs of both intense bitterness and great joy. Full musical notation is provided for each song, as well as a title and first-line index. In the introduction, the editors state that the book has two goals: "to provide a good selection of songs that can be sung by trade unions and other interested groups, and to show how these songs reflect mankind's struggle for a better life." Most readers will probably be moved by their intensity.

A Treasury of American Song. *Olin Downes and Elie Siegmeister, eds.* **(1943) Knopf. 408p., o.p.**

In their introduction the editors write that "the songs in this treasury are those of the multitudes and generations who have made America." This large collection gathers together hundreds of songs, ballads, and blues lyrics — sung and composed by pilgrims, cowboys, and sharecroppers, to name just a few. Full musical notation accompanies the familiar lyrics, which include such popular favorites as "Old Joe Clarke," "Frankie and Johnny," "Jeanie with the Light Brown Hair," and "Oh Susanna!" They are grouped into categories, indexed by title, and arranged chronologically, beginning with songs of Colonial times and concluding with Broadway melodies of the 1930's and 1940's. The editors' interesting introduction details the impact and influence of the ethnic traditions obvious in these songs.

The Viking Book of Folk Ballads of the English-Speaking World. *Albert B. Friedman, ed.* **(1956) Viking. 473p., o.p.**

Friedman in his introduction writes that "originally and naturally ballads were preserved in the memory of peoples whose culture was traditional, word-of-mouth, preserved without benefit of pen and ink." Cultures from different eras come alive in this rich collection of songs and ballads that ranges from African-American rhythms to lonely cowboy songs and grisly tales of Scottish murders — ballads with religious, historical, and romantic themes, some of which will be known to many. Arranged by such subjects as "Accidents and Disasters" and "Tabloid Crime," this anthology features a large number of tragic and gruesome ballads. All are preceded by historical notes on their derivations and era of popularity, and Friedman's introduction is full of information on the nature and history of the ballad as a literary form. This is a first-rate text of entertaining and lively stories. Indexed by title and first line.

Yankee Doodles; a Book of American Verse. *Ted Malone, ed.* **(1943) McGraw-Hill; edition of 1948, published by Garden City Publishing, had title The All-American Book of Verse. 246p., o.p.**

This is a volume of patriotic, folksy American verse, or "Yankee Doodles," as the editor calls them. The hundreds of selections are divided into sections largely by such themes as "whimsy," "satire," and "philosophy," although the philosophical musings are by no means too profound to be entertaining. Dozens of distinguished American satirists and poets are featured, including Longfellow, Nash, Whitman, and Sandburg, to name just a few, but most of the verse is by poets or ordinary Americans whose names have fallen into obscurity, and this latter work is among the most interesting. Here is a collection of homilies, songs, and provincial voices to fascinate and stimulate. Some of the verse is profound, much of it is from the point of view of the common man, and some is just mawkish. But this is Americana, if not great poetry — although the reader will be able to find such classics as "A Visit from St. Nicholas," "The Star-spangled Banner," and "Frankie and Johnny." Indexed by title.

CANADIAN POETRY

Canadian Poetry in English. *Bliss Carman, Lorne Pierce, and V. B. Rhodenizer, eds.* (Rev. and enl. ed., 1954) Ryerson Press. 456p., o.p.

Covering Canadian poetry from the earliest times to slightly after the Second World War, this collection offers almost two hundred poets, all of whom wrote in English although not a few are from French backgrounds. The collection is particularly strong in late nineteenth-century and early twentieth-century work, and, as the compilers point out, it is only a "reasonably critical" work. Verses are included that may not have earned critical acclaim but are familiar to almost all Canadians. In addition, the original compiler, Bliss Carman, is a traditionalist who took a dim view of modern trends in poetry. The result is a collection with wide appeal for people who normally do not read poetry, or, at the most, equate it with old time favorites that are recited in school and sometimes at home. Thanks to the short biographical sketches before each of the poet's work, one can glimpse many of the lesser-known writers from one coast of Canada to the other. Carman is here, as is Pauline Johnson, Duncan Scott, and numerous earlier favorites. The nineteenth century is filled with male poets, but by the beginning of the twentieth such women as Elizabeth Brewster and Miriam Waddington came into prominence, usually for the best.

Modern Canadian Verse. *A. J. M. Smith, ed.* (1967) Oxford University Press. 426p., o.p.

What sets this apart from other Canadian collections is that it is "in English and French." Here is one of the few anthologies to take notice of the major French-speaking poets in Canada, many of whom suffer from not being translated into English. The French-language poems are scattered throughout the volume. It is worth emphasizing that there are no translations here; it is assumed that the reader has a command of the French language. "Modern" in 1967 meant that all but a few of the poets were living. By now, some have died, at least those in the first part of this chronologically ordered book. The scope of the collection is explained briefly by the compiler: "This aims at variety, and it seeks to be representative — not of the average but of the best." There is no argument with this short explanation. One might have appreciated notes about the contributors, but it was decided to let the poets and the poems speak for themselves.

New American and Canadian Poetry. *John Gill, ed.* **(1971) Beacon Press. 280p., pap., o.p.**

Among the outstanding Canadian poets in this collection are Margaret Atwood, Irving Layton, and Patrick Lane. Americans include Marge Piercy, Dick Lourie and J. D. Reed. But few of the thirty or so poets are that well known. The compiler is a famous little magazine editor, and he has selected poets who are regulars in the little journals and not that frequently published in the larger literary magazines. The result is a limited success. The majority of poets and poems are well worth considering, but a few seem to be there primarily because they are personal enthusiasms of Gill. It is hard, however, to argue with a veteran editor's choices. What is interesting more than twenty years later is how few of the "new" voices became veterans. Ironically, Atwood, among the best known of the names, is now a major novelist as well as a substantial poet. There are some striking photographs of the poets and longer than usual biographical notes.

The New Oxford Book of Canadian Verse in English. *Margaret Atwood, comp.* **(1982) Oxford University Press. 477p., o.p.**

Chosen by Margaret Atwood, the highly acclaimed Canadian novelist and poet, these verses cover the time of the earliest settlements in the sixteenth century to the present day. Many authors will be new to the general reader, but some like Earle Birney, Malcolm Lowry, and Michael Ondaatje, to say nothing of Robert Service, are better known. Atwood also includes many women in her collection, noting that Canada has had a higher proportion of fine female poets than either England or the United States. Many of the older works in this anthology are primarily of historical interest, conveying a picture of life in a newly settled land and the feelings that such an experience engenders. Later poems make a stronger aesthetic claim on our attention, and over half of the volume is devoted to modern works. Atwood provides an astute introduction in which she relates the poets from different generations to one another and to the reading public.

The Oxford Book of Canadian Verse in English and French. *A. J. M. Smith, ed.* **(1960) Oxford University Press. 445p., o.p.**

Including the works of almost one hundred poets who wrote in either English or French, this anthology begins its journey through Canadian literature in the early nineteenth century. Most of the poets will be new to general readers, but many of them are represented by at least two poems, giving the reader a sense of their general interests and how they treat their subjects. The French-language poems are not translated, so to fully appreciate this collection one must be able to read French. But even if the reader is limited to the poems written in English, there is still a great deal of material here. The editor points out, in a lengthy and perceptive introduction, that Canadian poetry has long been split by two quite contradictory goals: one is to communicate "whatever is unique or local in Canadian life," while the other is to register what Canadians have in common with people of other, more established cultural traditions. Both those aims can be seen in this anthology.

The Penguin Book of Canadian Verse. *Ralph Gustafson, ed.* **(1967) Penguin Books. 282p., o.p.**

The main premise of this anthology is that Canadian poetry is wholly distinct from its American and British counterparts. Many of the earlier poets emulate the themes and techniques of other English-speaking writers, but a certain Canadian sensibility is evident, particularly among the later poets. More than seventy poets are generously represented; they come from all regions of Canada and from different generations, from the beginning of the nineteenth century to the 1950's and 1960's. There are poems about Canadian independence, romantic verse in the tradition of Thoreau and Emerson, and poems with social and political themes, including protest poems written after the World Wars. The quality of the verse varies greatly. Arranged chronologically, with biographical notes and author and title indexes.

The Wind Has Wings; Poems from Canada. *Mary Alice Downie and Barbara Robertson, eds.* **(1968) Oxford University Press. 96p.**

The poems in this fine collection are all by Canadian poets, most of whom are probably unknown in the United States. They are written in a diversity of styles, from songs and psalms to elegies and longer story poems, their tones and themes often evoking the harsh, yet beautiful, Canadian landscape and the solitude and solemnity of both French and

English Canadians. Some translations from Eskimo, Yiddish, and French have also been included. Brief, lyrical, well-written selections dominate the collection. The poems may be only descriptions of Indian summer or rattlesnakes, but both older children and adults will be moved by this volume of simple, sensual poems that does not aim to represent the whole Canadian consciousness.

CHILDREN'S POETRY

Amazing Monsters; Verses to Thrill and Chill. *Robert Fisher, ed.* **(1982) Faber and Faber. 95p.**

This book is nothing if it is not fun. The poems are all about monsters of a most horrible variety, things that are slimy or are always behind you, dongs with luminous noses, or serpents that insist on singing. The names of some of the poets of these awful creatures will be familiar: Edward Lear, Lewis Carroll, Theodore Roethke, or J. R. R. Tolkien. Others are less well known. These poems seem ideal for reading aloud to children who want to be gently scared, but they are also a good deal of fun for adults who enjoy images of dreadful figures such as dragons, dinkey-birds, gruesomes, malfeasances, or even wendigos. The monsters are amusing as well as amazing, and the poems are generally of a fairly high caliber, as if that mattered when dealing with such unsettling topics as things that go bump in the night.

The Batsford Book of Light Verse for Children. *Gavin Ewart, ed.* **(1978) B. T. Batsford. 160p., o.p.**

The Batsford Book of Light Verse for Children gives the reader a sense of the nature and scope of light verse (although the term is never really adequately defined). Gavin Ewart explains in his introduction that he has taken most of the book's traditional nursery rhymes from an older anthology, Iona and Peter Opie's *Oxford Nursery Rhyme Book*. The authors of the anthology's ninety-seven poems range from Robert Herrick (who is, as Ewart points out, probably beyond the grasp of younger children) to Stevie Smith. The poems are arranged in four basic categories — "Stories," "Songs and So On," "Animals," "People" — and listed in the table of contents. Included are such lively poems as Browning's "The Pied Piper of Hamelin," "London Bridge," and Hilaire Belloc's "The Crocodile."

The Book of a Thousand Poems; a Family Treasury. *J. Murray Macbain, ed.* **(1983) Peter Bedrick Books. 630p.**

Another anthology of verse for young children, this differs from its competitors in several ways. First, the compiler includes the familiar with the not-so-familiar and laces it with poems of adventure. Second, the compilation is as much for the parent or teacher helping the child learn to speak and read as it is for the youngster who enjoys it. Macbain's thoughts on the use of poetry in the development of the child are set forth in the introduction. Third, there is a good section in the introduction on "suggestions for practical use" that demonstrates how the poems may be employed in the classroom. The collection itself is divided into thirteen topical sections. There is a classified list of subjects at the end of the volume, as well as indexes of first lines and authors. Essentially, the value of this anthology is to bring together in one place the classics of children's verse; it is good reference work for librarians.

A Book of Animal Poems. *William Cole, ed.* **(1973) Viking. 288p., pap., o.p.**

This is an enchanting and delightful anthology of children's poetry. The almost 150 poets include many well-known adult favorites: Shakespeare, Whitman, Yeats, Robert Frost. And there are modern and lesser-known poets and such light-verse favorites as Ogden Nash and Walter de la Mare. The collection is arranged in animal categories, with a final "All Animals Together" section for poems with multiple characters. Dogs, cats, insects, horses, and wild animals all have their own chapters. Much of the emphasis is on contemporary verse, although enough classic selections balance the text. Usually lyrical and silly, they are not very long, just the right size for younger children to enjoy and read over and over. Some take on a more grisly tone, such as the infamous "Are You Digging on My Grave," by Hardy. But children will enjoy them all, along with the sketches accompanying some of them. Indexed by title and poet.

Catch Your Breath; a Book of Shivery Poems. *Lilian Moore and Lawrence Webster, eds.* **(1973) Garrard Publishing. 64p., o.p.**

Catch Your Breath should frighten young readers — but they should not consider it the ultimate source for a good scare. Editors Lilian Moore and Lawrence Webster have included nursery rhymes and anonymous poems; short, macabre works by lesser-known poets; and verses by

Langston Hughes, Carl Sandburg, and John Ciardi. Poems are indexed by author. The forty-two poems have been grouped in the following categories: "Queer and Eerie," "Real and Scary," "Shiver and Smile," "A Witch Story," "The Shivers of Halloween," "The Creepiness of Creatures," and "Suddenly Strange." Although these frightening poems make engaging reading, the collection is too brief to be all-inclusive.

A Child's Treasury of Verse. *Eleanor Doan, ed.* **(1977) Zondervan. 207p., o.p.**

Although the 400 poems in *A Child's Treasury of Verse* include such favorites as Carroll's "Jabberwocky," Longfellow's "The Village Blacksmith," and selections from the biblical "Song of Solomon," many of the works printed here are too light to provide prolonged enjoyment. Eleanor Doan has anthologized poems by poets of the stature of Shakespeare, Keats, and Tennyson, as well as verses by children — but she has omitted many notable recent poets (for example, Eliot and Kenneth Koch) who have also written works suitable for younger readers. The poems are organized under such numerous headings as "Adventure," "Growing Up," and "Talking To God"; Doan has indexed the works by title, first line, author, and source. The layout is extremely crowded and cluttered with illustrations; the introduction is too short to be useful.

Come Hither. *Walter de la Mare, comp.* **(3rd ed., 1957) Knopf. 777p., o.p.**

Many consider this the best introduction to English poetry for young people. As such, it is a standard item in many libraries and is familiar to parents and their children. The selection is excellent. The comments by the poet-compiler are to the point and easy to understand. The more-than-seven-hundred poems are as familiar as anything in the language, and the poets are all the old faithfuls. There is little truly modern English or American verse, but what is selected is truly representative. Most of the focus is on English poetry, particularly poets who appeal to children from age six through their teens. The subtitle is perfectly correct in its statement that this is "a collection of rhymes and poems for the young of all ages." The decorations by Warren Chappell are appropriate, although not overly imaginative. The format is bulky, but attractive.

Ducks and Dragons; Poems for Children. *Gene Kemp, ed.* **(1980) Faber & Faber. 124p., o.p.**

The seventy-three short poems in this anthology, as editor Gene Kemp states in his one-page introduction, are meant to be read to children at "odd moments, in little spaces in the day, just right for fitting a poem into." He has included many poems in English from varying sources and periods, organized into such distinct sections as "Seasons," "Fantastical," and "A Finger of Fear." Kemp has included such modern poets as Yeats, Hughes, and Roethke, along with poems by Chaucer and Shakespeare and numerous anonymous authors. Although certainly simple and intended for younger readers, the poems are enjoyable to readers of all ages; Kemp has indexed them by author and first line. The book includes black-and-white line drawings.

Dusk to Dawn; Poems of Night. *Helen Hill, Agnes Perkins, and Alethea Helbig, eds.* **(1981) Thomas Y. Crowell. 49p., o.p.**

All children find nighttime special, enchanting, and more than a little spooky. This slender anthology has poems that describe all that goes on in the night while much of the world is asleep. There are only thirty-five here, written by such contemporary poets as e. e. cummings, Archibald MacLeish, Langston Hughes, and Randall Jarrell. The poems are rich with images from the child's world — with animals or other children as the central characters. Almost all the poems are shorter than sonnets, and they represent a variety of styles and forms. Indexed by title, poet, and first line, the poems are presented attractively and accompanied by illustrations. This is a small collection of vivid poems, irresistible for children to read by themselves or to have read aloud.

Every Child's Book of Verse. *Sarah Chokla Gross, ed.* **(1968) Franklin Watts. 302p., o.p.**

Much of Sarah Chokla Gross's four-page introduction to this anthology explains that she chose the 340 poems most accessible at the time of publication, omitting subjects unfamiliar to the book's modern readers. The poems are by a variety of authors, from Russian poet Cornei Chukovsky to W. S. Gilbert to Robert Graves. The editor has organized the verses into such categories as "Signs of Love," "Birds," and "What's to Eat?" The work is amply indexed, but the editor's listing of poems at the beginnings of a section — rather than in a table of contents — is distracting. Red and green line illustrations enhance the visual appearance of the book, which young readers will enjoy even if they do not use it extensively.

Everybody Ought to Know. *Ogden Nash, ed.* (1961) **J. B. Lippincott. 186p., o.p.**

These poems, gathered together and clearly intended for children, are yet witty and enjoyable enough for all readers. Nash, who includes some of his own light verse, also features almost eighty English-speaking poets, among them Shakespeare, Coleridge, Dickinson, T. S. Eliot, and Whitman. The poems Nash feels "everybody ought to know" are typically short and refreshing, many under four lines, and accompanied by simple illustrations. Frost's "The Road Not Taken" and Hardy's "The Darkling Thrush," among the most "adult" of the poems, are here along with Edward Lear's "The Jumblies" and other traditional staples of children's verse. The anthology is breezy and entertaining, full of some well-known but mostly lesser-known poems. Indexed by title and author. Younger readers who have outgrown many of the children's light-verse collections will be pleased by this one.

The Faber Book of Children's Verse. *Janet Adam Smith, comp.* (1953) **Faber and Faber. 412p., pap.**

The selection here is incredible. My hat goes off to the compiler since she obviously thinks that children can read more sophisticated poetry than their parents! And, why not? If children are not challenged, then they will never have a sense of what they could respond to. And that is exactly what it takes to understand many of these poems: motivation and education. The editor has aimed her poetry at children from the ages of eight to fourteen. Some poems are sure to appeal to the younger set: some marvels and riddles, poems about fairies and nymphs, and such tales as the "Pied Piper of Hamelin," by Robert Browning. Much of the material is, however, for the older group of children, and a very bright group they had better be, if they are to comprehend these very advanced verses: John Keats's "On First Looking Into Chapman's Homer," Shelley's "Ozymandias," and Milton's "On the University Carrier." Nonetheless, with warnings that these poems will bewilder and confuse most children, they are still an outstanding collection for gifted children and adults who are interested in fine poetry.

A First Poetry Book. *John Foster, comp.* **(1979) Oxford University Press. 128p.**

Robert Louis Stevenson, Hilaire Belloc, and Ogden Nash are the most notable poets included in John Foster's anthology, but many of the volume's writers are little known. The 100 poems in *A First Poetry Book* are playful and make enjoyable reading but are not necessarily remarkable or familiar. Foster has arranged the poems randomly and indexed them by first line. The book's dynamic layout and colorful illustrations should stimulate a child's eye. The editor has not included an introduction; perhaps he thought it unnecessary.

Gladly Learn and Gladly Teach; Poems of the School Experience. *Helen Plotz, ed.* **(1981) Greenwillow Books. 144p., o.p.**

The ninety-eight poems in this anthology are divided into four sections: adults reflecting on their school experiences, the troubles of restless students and plodding textbooks, tributes to teachers, and verse on the pleasures of learning. It is a fine collection of poems about nostalgia for school days and about longing for the carefree days of youth. Among the eighty poets are Frost, Coleridge, Tennyson, and Whitman, all remembering some aspect of their school days with a fond, sometimes tenderly endearing, tone (and luckily, recalling those days with wit). The poetry is diverse in form and style, some of it in English translation. Planned for readers of all ages, this collection will probably be most popular with younger schoolchildren and reminiscing adults. Indexed by title, author, and first line.

Golden Slippers; an Anthology of Negro Poetry for Young Readers. *Arna Bontemps, ed.*

See under AFRICAN-AMERICAN POETRY

Good Dog Poems. *William Cole, ed.*

See under ANIMAL AND BIRD POETRY

The Home Book of Verse for Young Folks. *Burton Egbert Stevenson, ed.* **(1929) Holt, Rinehart and Winston. 676p., o.p.**

This is a fine collection of light, endearing poetry for children. But today's parent, as well as today's child, may find some of the verse outdated by today's standards. Among the hundreds of poems are accomplished, classic pieces by Shelley, Longfellow, and Whitman, but the vast majority are simple rhymes and homilies by more obscure poets, echoing Victorian morals and the theme of childhood innocence. The chapters have such titles as "The Duty of Children," "Fairyland," and "The Happy Warrior." The many nursery rhymes, Christmas carols, and adventure poems will perhaps be the most entertaining to young readers. Indexed by author, title, and first line.

I Like You, If You Like Me; Poems of Friendship. *Myra Cohn Livingston, ed.* **(1987) Macmillan. 143p.**

This volume is aimed at young people who are especially interested in the concept of friendship and would like to see how poets have charted this somewhat treacherous terrain. There are over ninety poems included, by poets from Wang Wei, writing in eighth-century China, to Shel Silverstein, who is writing today. These are likeable, simple poems, very lilting in some cases and sharply descriptive in others, selected to appeal primarily to younger readers. The book is divided into such categories as "Lonesome: All Alone," "Would You Come and Be My Friend?" "The Friendly Beasts," and "One Good Friendship." This treatment is decidedly focused on adolescents and younger children who should appreciate poetry about a subject so close to their hearts.

I Saw Esau; the Schoolchild's Pocket Book. *Iona Opie and Peter Opie, eds.* **(1947; American reissue, 1992) Candlewick Press; original edition published 1947 by Williams and Northgate. 160p.**

Several solid anthologies of children's poetry are available, but this volume may be the most entertaining and fun. First published in 1947 with the subtitle "traditional rhymes of youth," this small, compact collection now features new, enchanting illustrations by Maurice Sendak. His many drawings complement the short poems and add a dreamy, carefree touch to hundreds of captivating rhymes. Arranged in 31 short divisions according to subject, the poems range from silly rhymes to enchanting lyrics, all meant to be read aloud. Also included after the text are brief notes on the poems themselves — references to real people and historical derivations. This is a charming, mischievous volume of children's rhymes and verse, better for preschoolers and younger children than for older children who may *say* these babyish and old-fashioned rhymes are not for their sophisticated tastes!

Imaginary Gardens; American Poetry and Art for Young People. *Charles Sullivan, ed.* **(1989) Harry N. Abrams. 111p.**

This generous quarto volume is another lovely, animated anthology for children — reading like a tour among the most enchanting rhymes and accomplished artwork of the past two centuries. There are eighty-six poems, mostly brief lyrics and rhymes, complemented by spirited illustrations, most of them in color and compelling enough to hold a child's interest. Many of the poets are distinguished American writers, although, in general, their lesser-known work is featured — Dickinson, Whitman, Sandburg, and Howard Nemerov, among others. Usually the poems are paired with a painting, drawing, or photograph; for example, Millay's simple "Afternoon on a Hill" is paired with Wyeth's "Christina's World" and Longfellow's "The Children's Hour" with an Edward D. Boit painting. The pairing works well, matching tone and mood of poem and art. There is an index of authors and titles but no chapters or sections and none of the critical or explanatory notes frequently found in "adult" anthologies. Rather, this is a breezy, exciting collection, colorful and sensory, with an eclectic enough mix of the classic and contemporary to capture the imaginations of children of any age.

In the Witch's Kitchen; Poems for Halloween. *John E. Brewton, Lorraine A. Blackburn, and George M. Blackburn III, comps.* **(1980) Thomas Y. Crowell. 88p., o.p.**

The compilers of this anthology of Halloween poems have included forty-five short, lively poems for younger readers. The various English-language authors include Jack Prelutsky, Shel Silverstein, X. J. Kennedy, and Theodore Roethke. The poems are grouped by such subjects as witches, skeletons, and goblins. Most of these lesser-known poems are enjoyable; often, the poems contain deeper messages on the nature of fear. Playful illustrations enhance the visual appearance of the anthology. The book has indexes of authors, titles, and first lines, but no introduction. Although not necessarily a source book of scary poems, this anthology should prove a worthwhile read for younger readers.

Listen, Children, Listen; an Anthology of Poems for the Very Young. *Myra Cohn Livingston, ed.* **(1972) Harcourt Brace Jovanovich. 96p., o.p.**

This anthology of seventy poems for younger readers includes William Blake's "The Piper" and T. S. Eliot's "The Song of the Jellicles." Also anthologized are Shakespeare, Roethke, Tolkien, and Yeats. These lesser-known poems are consistently enchanting. Myra Cohn Livingston has gathered great poets within one small book, along with forms ranging from limericks to ballads to carols. Subjects include fairies, the moon, staircases, and animals, but the book has neither an imposed structure nor an introduction. Livingston has indexed the work by author and title. Readers will appreciate the tasteful line illustrations.

Love Is like the Lion's Tooth; an Anthology of Love Poems. *Frances McCullough, ed.*

See under LOVE POETRY

Messages; a Book of Poems. *Naomi Lewis, comp.* **(1985) Faber and Faber. 255p.**

Critic and writer Naomi Lewis draws upon contemporary poetry to offer young people (ages ten to fifteen) the best of the modern poets. The particular gift of the compiler is to select lesser-known poets from the twentieth century and earlier who will appeal to a young audience. Arrangement is by broad subjects that range from "A pen, a paintbrush, a guitar" to "Children's country" and "Difficult relations." Among the poets in the section on "A host of furious fancies" are Stevie Smith, Harold Monro, Louis MacNeice, and the compiler herself. Each part has about a dozen poems. There are indexes of authors and first lines.

The Moon Is Shining Bright as Day; an Anthology of Goodhumored Verse. *Ogden Nash, ed.* **(1953) J. B. Lippincott. 178p.**

One of America's greatest satirical poets, Ogden Nash proves to have been equally humorous and good natured. "When the suggestion was made that I assemble a collection of not-too-serious poems for boys and girls, I easily fell in with it. . . . As a man moves into his fifties [i.e., in 1953] he becomes increasingly aware of the reading that illuminated his childhood, and the temptation to pass a good thing along is irresistible. That is why there are few rare specimens in this collection, which has been gathered from the daisies rather than the orchids." The six sections have such wildly imaginative titles as "Has anybody seen my mouse" and "Yonder see the morning blink." Three indexes of titles, first lines, and authors bring the selection together for the user and librarian. But for the child such order is hardly required. The poems flow into one another. Every major and minor poet seems to be included, from Hilaire Belloc to William Wordsworth. There are few blunders in choice of either poets or poetry. Nash is represented by a half dozen works, including his immortal "The Wapiti." It can be quoted in full: "There goes the Wapiti, Hippity-hoppity!" That fairly well sets the tone for the book, which can be read by the first reader or the sophisticated high school student, or by any adult with a sense of wonder and humor.

Mother Goose Nursery Rhymes. *Arthur Rackham, ed.* **(1975; reprint of 1913 ed.) Viking Press. 153p., o.p.**

Arthur Rackham writes that the verses included here (and the versions printed) were his personal favorites when younger, and he has provided remarkable color and black-and-white illustrations for the 166 poems in this anthology. Children will find such familiar Mother Goose rhymes as "Solomon Grundy," "One, two, buckle my shoe," and "Hark, hark, the dogs do bark." The poems are printed in large type, two or three to a page. Some of the verses are attributed to Mother Goose, others have come down from unknown sources. Rackham makes brief reference to this difference in his introduction. These popular, lovable verses are indexed by first line. The book's wonderful illustrations are easily as memorable as the poems themselves.

New Coasts & Strange Harbors; Discovering Poems. *Helen Hill and Agnes Perkins, eds.* **(1974) Thomas Y. Crowell. 283p., o.p.**

All of these poems are short, evocative and lyrical; what they lack in depth they make up for in sensual richness. Grouped according to the subject of the poem, for example "Nightmares," "When I Was a Child," and "Of Song and Dance," they are dreamy and vivid, suited for both adults and younger readers alike. Most of the poets are fairly contemporary: e.e. cummings, Sylvia Plath, Marianne Moore, and Theodore Roethke are among the best known. The foreword briefly summarizes the purpose of the anthology as the attempt to persuade readers that poetry need not always be read for esoteric meanings. Instead, they hope young people will realize that the poems "might give them pleasure, either because the poets had expressed familiar or half-recognized feelings more surely than the readers could themselves, or because the poems suggested new and strange ways of looking at the world around them." The anthology neatly collects poems that accomplish this end.

A New Treasury of Children's Poetry; Old Favorites and New Discoveries. *Joanna Cole, comp.* **(1984) Doubleday. 224p., pap.**

A children's author and winner of numerous "Notable Books" awards from the American Library Association, Joanna Cole knows well what poems young children like to read and have read to them. She begins with "First poems of childhood" and introduces the reader to such favorites as A. A. Milne's "Hoppity" and James Kirkup's unusual "Baby's drinking song." With that stage passed, she moves on to "People and portraits" and seven other sections that focus on things children enjoy. Here are animals, silly poems, play poetry, holidays, and a "Different way of seeing." For example, she introduces us to Charles Malam's "Steam shovel" and Mary O'Neill's "What is black?" The content is wildly varied. "I have not tried to make an objective collection, including all of the classic and contemporary poems that children ought to know. Instead I have chosen poetry that made me stop, feeling full of the brightness of the images or the joyousness of the rhythm or the recognition of a hidden feeling." The compiler's promises are more than fulfilled in this charming collection.

A New Treasury of Poetry. *Neil Philip, ed.* **(1990) Stewart, Tabori, and Chang. 256p.**

This tall, engaging anthology contains a large collection of lovely, classic poems, intelligible enough for children to appreciate but also amusing and provocative. Poems are loosely divided by subject into eight sections with such titles as "Seasons and Holidays," "Birds and Beasts," "Sing a Song of Seasons," and "Once Upon a Time." This last section contains story poems as imaginative as those in any collection of children's verse. All the poets are English-speaking: Stevenson, Frost, Blake, T. S. Eliot, and some contemporary authors are among the 120 poets included. Many of the selections are classics adults will remember and enjoy. But this volume, with its attention to senses and everyday scenes, will become a favorite among children who love to read or be read to. Indexed by poet, title, and first line.

Of Quarks, Quasars, and Other Quirks; Quizzical Poems for the Supersonic Age. *Sara Brewton, John E. Brewton, and John Brewton Blackburn, eds.* **(1977) Thomas Y. Crowell. 113p.**

The poems in this slender, entertaining volume revolve around science — or, in the case of several of the selections, anti-science. There are seven sections, chapters with such titles as "Blast Off" and "Where the Neuter Computer Goes Click," and the poems may be just as silly or sly. Here are works by such distinguished writers as Hilaire Belloc, Maxine Kumin, John Updike, and, of course, Ogden Nash. Many of the brief poems conjure up images of spacecraft or atomic energy. Some poke fun at the idea of "progress," and some assume the guise of nursery rhymes to cloak satire. Most are more silly than clever, and younger children should enjoy this mix of the breezy and the wise. Indexed by title, author, and first line.

Oh, Such Foolishness! *William Cole, ed.* **(1978) J. B. Lippincott. 96p.**

The sixty poems in this book, which use such words as "wiggley-woggley," "horseplayziness," and "panteater," have no purpose deeper than a simple laugh. Shel Silverstein, Spike Milligan, and James Reeves are among the authors included; the book contains little-known non-sense rhymes as well. They address all kinds of subjects, from wasps to a mythical creature called the Hidebehind to big-game hunting, and all are well-indexed. Noted illustrator Tomie de Paola provides light-hearted drawings to go with the simply designed text. Readers in search of well-known silly poems (by such authors as Edward Lear or Gelett Burgess) should look elsewhere.

Once upon a Rhyme; 101 Poems for Young Children. *Sara Corrin and Stephen Corrin, eds.* **(1982) Faber and Faber. 157p., o.p.**

Here one finds both American and English poems, mainly modern, and ideally suited for children in grades one to seven. The poems are arranged under such catchy subjects as "Wind and weather," "Odd and funny," and "Viewpoints." This allows the reader to go from mood to mood, place to place. There are poems about animals, fabulous creatures, fireworks, locomotives. The poets range from the famous and nearly famous to the virtually unknown. All seem to have a good grasp of what entertains the child. There are black and white illustrations on almost every page, but here and there one finds garish color plates — all by artist Jill Bennett. This works well enough with lesser known works, but not when the illustrator is asked to pinch hit for Milne or Lear. The poetry is compiled for children, not for adults, and the book could be just the right one to buy a child.

The Oxford Book of Children's Verse. *Iona Opie and Peter Opie, eds.* (1973) Oxford University Press. 407p.

Celebrated scholars of children's literature, Iona and Peter Opie have assembled here "verses that have been written for children, or written with children prominently in mind, which either were cherished in their own day, or which have stood the test of time. Its object is thus to make available in one place the classics of children's poetry: that small satchelful of verse whose existence constitutes one of the pleasing advantages of being born to the English tongue." Most of the authors are British, but a few Americans are also in evidence. Here one can find Robert Southey's poem "The Old Man's Comforts and How He Gained Them," which Lewis Carroll parodied so triumphantly in "You are old, Father William." Several other superb Carroll poems are also reprinted. The anthology is arranged in chronological order, beginning with medieval poetry and works from the sixteenth century and concluding with twentieth-century verse. There are poems by John Bunyan, Isaac Watts, William Blake, Charles and Mary Lamb, and Robert Louis Stevenson, to name only a few of the famous authors. Many of the contributors are now unknown. This book is essential reading for families with small children. The poems should delight youngsters and provide as much pleasure for adults.

The Oxford Book of Children's Verse in America. *Donald Hall, ed.* (1985) Oxford University Press. 319p.

A fine companion to *The Oxford Book of Children's Verse,* which features English poems, and *The Oxford Nursery Rhyme Book,* this collection concentrates on poems for children written in America in the English language. But the editor does not end there: he also includes poems that were not intended particularly for children, and yet were avidly consumed by them. So, although this volume begins with two alphabets from *The New England Primer of 1727 and 1768* and carries on with Clement Moore's "A Visit from St. Nicholas," it also features Edgar Allan Poe's "Annabel Lee" and "The Raven," poems not usually thought of as youth-oriented. In the same way, many of Emily Dickinson's poems are reprinted here. But, the anthology is essentially indebted to poems from the pages of children's magazines over the past hundred and fifty years.

There is a lot of Henry Wadsworth Longfellow, many poems by little-known poets, and from modern times we find Ogden Nash, Countee Cullen, Theodore Roethke, and X. J. Kennedy. Children should find this book extremely satisfying.

The Oxford Book of Story Poems. *Michael Harrison and Christopher Stuart-Clark, eds.* **(1990) Oxford University Press. 175p.**

This vibrant anthology has a mixture of distinguished, "adult" poems and sillier, entertaining children's rhymes, most accompanied by colorful or intricate illustrations. From Tennyson, Robert Browning, and Lewis Carroll to the contemporary poetry of X. J. Kennedy and J. R. R. Tolkien, the classic verse of more than fifty poets is included. The poems range from simple verses to reflective poems of a depth and length not usually found in children's volumes. They are arranged in no particular order but are indexed by theme, author, artist, title, and first line. Highly recommended for the splendid artwork and the fine quality of its poetry, this volume should appeal to both younger and older children. There are mysteries and ballads, poems on people and animals and sometimes on nothing at all in particular. But all tell a story, and all will entertain any child who enjoys reading and imagining worlds unfamiliar to his own.

The Oxford Nursery Rhyme Book. *Iona Opie and Peter Opie, comps.* **(1955) Oxford University Press. 224p.**

There are over eight hundred rhymes and ditties in this volume, enough to entertain even the most truculent child or the most nostalgic adult. The compilers have included "infant jingles, riddles, catches, tongue-trippers, baby games, toe names, maxims, alphabets, counting rhymes, prayers, and lullabies." Here you will find "Jack Sprat," "Tommy Tucker," "Jack Horner," "Ding, Dong Bell," "Goosey Gander," and hundreds more. The contents are divided into helpful sections: "Baby Games and Lullabies," "First Favorites," "Little Songs," "People," "A Little Learning," "Awakening," "Wonders," "Riddles, Tricks, and Trippers," and "Ballads and Songs." Throughout, excellent, old woodcuts illustrate the verses. Especially appealing are the ones for "The Tragical Death of A, Apple Pie; who was cut in pieces, and eaten by twenty-six gentlemen, with whom all little people ought to be very well acquainted." An alphabet follows. This book is delightful reading both for adults and for children and is unsurpassed as a resource book for parents or childminders.

Piping Down the Valleys Wild; Poetry for the Young of All Ages.
Nancy Larrick, ed. **(1968) Delacorte Press. 248p.**

The title, to be sure, is the first line in William Blake's famous "The Piper." The poem concludes with the fitting lines "And I write my happy songs/Every child may joy to hear." The sure sense of high quality makes this an outstanding collection for children. A. A. Milne is represented with "Puppy and I." Right after the child walks off with the puppy, Gwendolyn Brooks introduces us to "Pete at the Zoo." In the second of sixteen sections one meets Laura E. Richards and her "The Giraffe and the Woman," and a few pages on comes the unforgettable "Purple Cow." There are masses of animals pounding through these pages. When they are not on center stage, there is the sound of concrete mixers, and "Bam, bam, bam" a poem by Eve Merriam. One must not forget the clowns, gnomes, friendly witches, scarecrows, and, of course, Christopher Robin at "Buckingham Palace." All of the poems can be read aloud and were chosen precisely for that quality. This marvelous, imaginative collection is a total success.

Pocket Poems; Selected for a Journey. *Paul B. Janeczko, ed.* **(1985) Bradbury Press. 138p., o.p.**

In this simple, pocket-sized collection no poem is longer than sixteen lines. All are about adventures children will find entertaining — imaginative poems involving tree houses, rocking chairs, or long rides on Amtrak. Of course not all are about a "journey" in the traditional sense; some deal with loss, mourning, and renewal. Poets as distinguished and diverse as John Updike, Ogden Nash, William Carlos Williams, and Maya Angelou are here, although most of the poets are largely unknown. Children will find this an easy, enjoyable collection of evocative, upbeat poems. The volume lacks an introduction and biographical notes.

Poems for Children and Other People. *George Hornby, ed.* **(Rev. ed., 1975) Crown Publishers. 110p., o.p.**

The 203 poems in *Poems for Children and Other People* may be of primary interest to children but will also appeal to adults. Hornby places the work of the most acclaimed poets of the English language — Coleridge, Shakespeare, Joyce, Whitman, Dickinson — alongside the poems of such children's writers as Eugene Field and Edward Lear. The works presented here are highly accessible but still sophisticated. They include Shakespeare's "The quality of mercy is not strain'd" speech and Byron's

"She Walks in Beauty," as well as Lewis Carroll's "Jabberwocky" and Edward Lear's "The Owl and the Pussycat." The book has been printed in a large format and is well-indexed and illustrated with photographs of sculptures from the English Cybis workshop. The book is as much a showcase for the sculptures as a collection of children's poetry. Parents and children will consider this anthology an attractive, intelligent, entertaining read.

Poems for Young Children. *Caroline Royds, comp.* **(1986) Doubleday. 45p.**

This is a brief, delightful collection for pre-school and early grade-school children. There are forty-five poems, most of which are familiar. Here one finds Mother Goose and Robert Frost side by side with A. A. Milne and e. e. cummings. There are pastel illustrations on every page and enough space around the poem so it stands out and can be easily read. Inga Moore's illustrations are excellent; they do as much for the work as the poems themselves. Every subject and mood is covered from tears and laughter to animals and the thrills of bed time. The poems are found in countless other similar anthologies, but the wise, limited choices and the marvelous layout make this an ideal book for young children — and certainly for parents reading to those children.

Poems to Read Aloud. *Edward Hodnett, ed.* **(Rev. ed., 1967) W. W. Norton. 390p., o.p.**

What makes a poem ideal to read aloud? Until the time of mass education and mass distribution of books and magazines in the late nineteenth century, almost all poems were delivered orally. At least this was the case with popular verses that hoped to gain more than a limited recognition at court or among the elite, and even here the poets and their followers prided themselves on memory and rhetorical skills. Things changed, and today, while poetry reading is no longer even as popular as it was in the late 1960's, it has a strong following at two or three levels. First, there are the poetry readings by established and aspiring poets. Second, a certain amount of memory is required for literature courses. And finally, a few people love to get together and rattle off poems which have a particular meaning for them and their friends. Of course, there are other reasons to value poetry readings, but with the general public in mind the compiler of this volume has brought together the best-loved poems in England and America. Shakespeare has the greatest number of entries, but other songs, sonnets, and readable verse by W. H. Auden, Thomas Campion, Emily Dickinson, John Donné, Rudyard Kipling, and William Wordsworth, to name a few, are here in abundance. They all contribute to a fine, specialized approach to poetry.

The Poetry of Horses. *William Cole, ed.*

See under   ANIMAL AND BIRD POETRY

The Poet's Tales; a New Book of Story Poems. *William Cole, ed.* **(1971) World Publishing. 320p., o.p.**

In constructing this collection of narrative verses, William Cole has valued effective storytelling more than poetic ability. In fact, he admits in his introduction that "most of the poetry in this book isn't great poetry." The verses, nevertheless, tell good stories. Arranged in eight sections, such as "Love Stories," "Adventures and Disasters," and "At Sea," they include songs of the caliber of "Waltzing Matilda," "The Man on the Flying Trapeze," and "The Twa Corbies." Among the authors are Conrad Aiken, Walter de la Mare, John Masefield, William Stafford, and Eleanor Farjeon; Cole has also included some poems by anonymous authors and traditional ballads. The book is well indexed, and captivating line illustrations appear throughout. This book is a reliable source for poems that tell tales — from the famous to the obscure.

The Random House Book of Poetry for Children. *Jack Prelutsky, ed.* **(1983) Random House. 248p.**

A poet himself, the compiler begins each of the numerous sections in this volume with a poem written especially for it. In addition, there are almost six hundred other poems, most of which are modern. Topics range from dogs and cats to the seasons, home, children, nonsense, wordplay, ghosts, and almost anything else of interest to the reader. Furthermore, there are almost as many illustrations, usually quite small, by Arnold Lobel, that fit in nicely with the poems. Most of the emphasis is on fun, humor, and the delights of being a child in an adult world. Some serious and thoughtful poems are included, such as Lilian Moore's "Foghorns" and the work of Christopher Morley and Walter de la Mare. Many of the entries are from such great artists as Shakespeare, William Blake, and Emily Dickinson. There is a useful subject index. The collection is one of the best available for elementary school children.

Read-Aloud Rhymes for the Very Young. *Jack Prelutsky, comp.* **(1986) Knopf. 98p.**

In the familiar over-sized, picture-book format, the compiler, assisted by illustrator Marc Brown, brings together nursery rhymes and poetry for those aged five years and under. All of the poems are chosen to be read aloud. Children "are great listening machines," and Prelutsky, also the editor of *The Random House Book of Poetry* (annotated here), has collected more than two hundred little poems to "feed little people with little attention spans to help both grow." The poems are set against the background of the colorful illustrations, and a child might enjoy looking as much as listening and, eventually, reading. An index of titles, an index of authors, and an index of first lines help the parent and librarian, but the average child will need no assistance in going through this colorful book. Most of the authors (the majority of whom are women), though familiar to young people and parents, are not in the mainstream of American poetry. Exceptions include Gwendolyn Brooks, Marchette Chute, Nikki Giovanni, and Maxine Kumin.

The Real Mother Goose. *Blanche Fisher Wright, Illust.* **(1944) Checkerboard Press. 128p.**

Adults and young children alike will be charmed by this tall, slender collection that features the classic, beloved rhymes of youth. These include "Cock Robin," "Little Boy Blue," "Miss Muffet," "Old King Cole," and three hundred other traditional favorites. The verse is not arranged in any particular order and is complemented by colorful drawings and vivid illustrations. Especially welcome in a children's anthology is the large print and size of the text; they will have no trouble picking it up and reading on their own. The anthology is standard, time tested, and enchanting — with an old-fashioned tone of innocence and simplicity. Originally published almost fifty years ago, this volume continues to demonstrate its appeal. Indexed by first line and title.

Ring Out, Wild Bells; Poems about Holidays and Seasons. *Bennett Hopkins, ed.*

See under HOLIDAY POETRY

A Rocket in My Pocket; the Rhymes and Chants of Young Americans.
Carl Withers, ed. **(1948) Henry Holt. 214p., pap.**

Although the vernacular speech of American children has changed since the publication of this anthology, it is still a fun, enchanting volume for the very youngest audiences. More than a hundred songs and verses are divided into sections by theme and form — "Tongue Twisters," "Riddles," and "Spelling Rhymes" among them. Here are brief lyrics, songs, silly rhymes, and other forms of children's speech and games. Most of the rhymes are under six lines and evoke holidays, playground games, and familiar animals. The editor comments soundly that "in the field of verbal nonsense American children are extremely inventive." Adults may recognize some of these chants, older children will be amazed at what used to pass for clever verse. This collection is innocent and fun. Indexed by first line or first word.

Round about Eight. *Geoffrey Palmer and Noel Lloyd, eds.* **(1972) Frederick Warne. 127p., o.p.**

There are two predecessors of *Round about Eight*. One is *One, Two, Three, Four*. The other is *Fives, Sixes and Sevens*. The books in the series are intended for the age groups in their titles. The 118 poems gathered here are neither overwhelmingly moralistic nor annoyingly shallow. They range from sad to silly without losing their imaginative charm. Coming from such poets as Edith Sitwell, Walt Whitman, Stevie Smith, and Oliver St. John Gogarty, the works selected are well known and representative — for example, William Blake's "The Lamb" and Louis MacNeice's "Glass Falling." Some poems by eight-year-old children are included but are not clearly indicated as such. Numerous one-color illustrations animate each page. The poems, unfortunately, are not indexed, but the book should, nevertheless, give young readers hours of quality pleasure.

Saturday's Children; Poems of Work. *Helen Plotz, comp.* **(1982) Greenwillow Books. 174p., o.p.**

Divided into four sections, here is a successful effort to explain work to children through poems. The compiler's succinct introduction nicely covers the points she is illustrating through the selections. The divisions include poetry about rural work, industrial labor, women's work, and working in general. There is a subsection on unemployment and another on child labor. There are two primary points about this unusual collection. First, there is a wide variety of poetry by outstanding poets. Among those represented are Anthony Hecht, May Sarton, Richard Wilbur, and Langston Hughes. While much of the emphasis is on modern poetry, there are representative voices, such as Robert Louis Stevenson, from earlier years. Second, the poetry is used to demonstrate sometimes willful misconceptions about work and to explain derogatory comments about working-class people.

Shrieks at Midnight; Macabre Poems, Eerie and Humorous. *Sara Brewton and John E. Brewton, eds.* **(1969) Thomas Y. Crowell. 177p., o.p.**

The preface tells us that the 159 poems featured here are about "death and doom, ghosts and ghouls, bare bones and shiverous beasts." It is indeed an entertaining collection of verse more humorous than grave; it is definitely not an anthology for everyone, particularly for some younger children. Limericks, folk legends, and longer narratives are here, with the parody of Poe called "Cannibalee" one of the best selections; all are grouped loosely by subject into chapters. There are even several epitaphs for more ghoulish readers to enjoy. Such prominent poets as A. E. Housman, Walter de la Mare, Bret Harte, and Ogden Nash are included, although most of the poets are more obscure or anonymous. Indexed by author, title, and first line, it is a collection for children who wish every day were Halloween.

Sing a Song of Popcorn; Every Child's Book of Poems. *Beatrice Schenk de Regniers, Eva Moore, Mary Michaels White, and Jan Carr, eds.* **(1988) Scholastic. 142p.**

This is an outstanding volume of rhymes and songs for children, made exceptional by the beautiful and vivid illustrations throughout the oversized text. Verse by such noted adult and children's writers as Shel Silverstein, Edward Lear, Ogden Nash, and Emily Dickinson are all featured, along with other poems by prominent or more obscure authors. They are arranged according to theme — for example, sensory poems, rhymes, or scary poems. The verse is colorful and upbeat, usually lightly humorous, although some poems, indeed, are more probing. Brief biographical information on the illustrators and indexes by author, title, and first line round out this highly recommended collection. It is filled with vibrant, entertaining poems and top-notch illustrations that all children will find enchanting.

Speak Roughly to Your Little Boy. *Myra Cohn Livingston, ed.* **(1971) Harcourt Brace Jovanovich. 180p., o.p.**

Most children's anthologies contain poems about holidays and school days; this one features traditionally "adult" verse and the parodies that mimic it. Well over a hundred original poems and their parodies are collected, with accompanying black-and-white sketches that will charm both adults and children. Most of the original poems are well known — "Upon Julia's Clothes," "Ozymandias," and "Annabel Lee." The parody following Poe's elegy is entitled "The Cannibal Flea," which pretty much signifies the playful, mischievous tone of the volume. The parody or burlesque follows the original. There are helpful annotations, and the poems are indexed by title, author, and first line — surprising features in a children's anthology. This is a volume sure to amuse older children, who will never again complain that poetry cannot be entertaining and witty.

Sprints and Distances; Sports in Poetry and the Poetry in Sport. *Lillian Morrison, comp.*

See under SPORTS POETRY

Straight On Till Morning; Poems of the Imaginary World. *Helen Hill, Agnes Perkins and Alethea Helbig, comps.* **(1977) Thomas Y. Crowell. 150p., o.p.**

A collection of nearly one hundred poems, nicely illustrated with black and white drawings by Ted Lewin, this anthology concentrates on the child's world of imagination. "Two things have been important in our choice of poems: content and style." The content is for a child of five to about twelve years of age, and the style "is as various as the people who wrote the poems." There are the standard subject divisions. This time the eight sections range from "Funny and fabulous friends" to "Once there was and was not. . ." This is usual enough for children's collections, but what is unusual is the choice of poets. Few of them write exclusively for young people, and almost all are well known to adults. The list of authors is, in fact, a roll call of modern American poetry, with a bow to some equally famous English poets. Among those featured are: Hilaire Belloc, e. e. cummings, Robert Frost, Nikki Giovanni, Donald Hall, Ted Hughes, Randall Jarrell, Kenneth Patchen, Theodore Roethke, May Swenson, and William Carlos Williams. This is an outstanding collection of poems.

Sung under the Silver Umbrella. *Association for Childhood Education International editors, comps.* **(1935) Macmillan. 211p., o.p.**

Many of the poems in this children's anthology were written by such "adult" poets as Emily Dickinson, Walter de la Mare, Tennyson, and Carl Sandburg. The quality of verse is high and still entertaining for young readers. More than two hundred poems, varying in length and style, are grouped loosely by theme — Christmas, nighttime, animal poems. Padraic Colum in his eloquent foreword addresses the historical tradition of children's literature, from Mother Goose rhymes to Christina Rossetti. Although the anthology was published in 1935, the verse retains a timeless simplicity and innocence, charming and captivating enough for modern children to identify with.

Talking like the Rain; a First Book of Poems. *X. J. Kennedy and Dorothy M. Kennedy, eds.* **(1992) Little Brown. 96p.**

Like many of the best children's anthologies, this volume emphasizes the illustrations — colorful, evocative paintings and sketches that heighten the action and description of the story in each poem. It is a tall, slender book, attractive and vibrant enough to catch the eye of any young reader. The poems are divided into nine sections based on such subjects as "Play," which contains poems about dressing up or running around dirty. "Just for Fun" has slick rhymes and silly chants; "Magic and Wonder" consists of imaginative story poems. Both adult and children's poets are to be found here, among them Stevenson, Dickinson, Christina Rossetti, and Langston Hughes. The 123 poems by sixty poets are presented alongside pastel scenes children will fall in love with. Highly recommended for the quality of the verse and for its lighthearted arrangement, this is a volume parents and children will delight in. Indexed by author and title.

Talking to the Sun; an Illustrated Anthology of Poems for Young People. *Kenneth Koch and Kate Farrell, eds.* **(1985) Metropolitan Museum of Art/Henry Holt. 112p.**

This oversized poetry anthology for children celebrates the pleasures in, and close ties between, art and poetry. The goal is achieved by illustrating each poem with a work from the Metropolitan Museum of Art. Most are paintings in full color and range in size from a small insert to a full page. The makeup is extremely well thought out, and the whole is an invitation not only to the child, but to the adult. Koch, who is famous for his work with young people in various writing programs, explains that the poems were chosen first, and then the art was selected to go along with them. Some, although not all, of the poems are prefaced by a word or two to make the child think about the poem and the work of art. The book opens with an almost full-page picture of a Tiffany stained-glass window. The poem to accompany it is "Hymn to the Sun" from the African Fang people. Across the page is another African poem and a Russian painting of a sunset. The world view of poetry and art is carried throughout the collection's ten distinct sections. Here may be found the work of Robert Bly and Robert Frost, there, an American folksong or the Japanese poet Basho. The art is just as diverse. A remarkably imaginative book for children of all ages.

These Small Stones. *Norma Farber and Myra Cohn Livingston, comps.* **(1987) Harper & Row. 84p.**

Compiled for children in grades three to seven, the collection celebrates "small things of the real and imagined world." The slim volume is divided into six sections, each with about ten short poems. "In My Hand" may concern a match, a jumping bean, marbles. A crab, a ladybug, or other little things make up the part about "On the Ground." In "In the Air" the readers find fireflies, birds, and even mosquitoes. And so it goes to the end, where there are useful indexes of first lines and titles. A subject index would have been helpful. The poets are wisely chosen, and while a few wrote only for children, the majority wrote for the child in everyone. Among these are Federico García Lorca, Emily Dickinson, Edward Lear, Pablo Neruda, Theodore Roethke, and other outstanding voices of the late nineteenth and twentieth centuries. Norma Farber died before the little book was published, but she is represented with two poems, as is her fellow editor. Thanks to the splendid selection and emphasis on easy-to-understand, shorter works, this is an ideal collection for both children and adults. Most of the verse begs to be read aloud.

They've Discovered a Head in the Box for the Bread and Other Laughable Limericks. *John E. Brewton and Lorraine A. Blackburn, eds.* **(1978) Thomas Y. Crowell. 129 p.**

This entertaining anthology collects more than two hundred limericks, from ridiculous rhymes about the town of Limerick to the clever "There once was a . . ." — favorites of young and old readers. Such well-known satirical writers as Mark Twain, Ogden Nash, and Roy Blount, Jr., are here, along with other more obscure or anonymous writers. The volume is arranged by concerns and situations children daily experience: etiquette, school, animals, love. Two final sections are particularly creative: one of tongue-twisting, tricky limericks and the other of limericks with the last line omitted so that children can supply their own endings. Children will delight in the ease, charm, and admitted silliness of this little book. Indexed by author, title, and first line.

This Delicious Day. *Paul B. Janeczko, comp.* (1987) Orchard Books. 82p.

Almost every year or so this compiler issues a new anthology for children and young people. This is one of his latest. As is his custom, there is no introduction, nor any word of explanation about its content or its purpose. In this case the title explains the scope. The sixty-five poems by almost as many poets are exclusively concerned with daily activity, primarily in the out-of-doors. The collection begins with Richard Snyder's "O I Have Dined on This Delicious Day," moves on to X. J. Kennedy's "A Certain Sandpiper," and winds down with Doris Hardie's "Song for Susannah: A Lullaby." Few of the poems are more than one or two stanzas, and all are within the easy understanding of a child. The poems are uniformly good, but no more than half a dozen would be of equal interest to adults. Happy exceptions are the work of X. J. Kennedy and a few other well-known writers such as Theodore Roethke and Philip Whalen. Mr. Janeczko is represented with a passable parody. A pleasant, but not altogether necessary book for children.

This Same Sky; a Collection of Poems from around the World. *Naomi Shihab Nye, ed.* (1992) Four Winds Press. 212p.

The poems in this lively anthology come from places as varied as American Samoa, Mexico, and the former Yugoslavia. No American point of view is represented. Instead, this volume concentrates on the poetic voices of nations all over the globe, particularly of countries not traditionally represented in American textbooks or anthologies. The 161 poems featured usually evoke the landscape or physical beauty of a particular culture and explore family relations or customs. The verse is loosely arranged in sections such as "Loss," "Dreams," and "Portraits of People." The tone and depth of the poems are just right for not-so-young children — intelligently written without being silly. Brief biographical information and a map of the featured nations are also included in this well-organized, evocative collection of fine poetry.

Time for Poetry. *May Hill Arbuthnot, ed.* (1959) Scott, Foresman. 512p., o.p.

This anthology of children's verse is intended for teachers hoping to encourage young students to enjoy poetry. The introduction includes ways to offer poetry to children that they will find palatable — for instance, bringing out the melody and rhythm in poetry by reading it aloud. Although the idea of "teaching" poetry to children may seem counterproductive or old-fashioned to many adults, here is an entertaining collection of simple, lyrical verse young readers and listeners will enjoy. Divided into sections with such titles as "How Ridiculous" and "Traveling We Go," the hundreds of short poems are lovely and delightfully silly, evocative of a child's world. They include verse by, among others, Christina Rossetti, Edward Lear, and Robert Louis Stevenson, as well as classic Mother Goose rhymes. All are enchanting, and probably more so if read aloud. This anthology, perhaps anachronistic at first, is well suited for all children. Indexed by author, title, and first line.

Untune the Sky; Poems of Music and Dance. *Helen Plotz, comp.* (1957) Thomas Y. Crowell. 162p., o.p.

Still another fine collection by the ubiquitous Helen Plotz, this, like her other anthologies, is directed to an audience of young people. William Carlos Williams sets the stage with verse from "The Desert Music." Two dozen other poems celebrate various musical instruments. As is her custom, the compiler includes writing from around the world, from all periods, and insists on the best works, whether they be by Plato, Po Chü-i, or a nursery rhyme. Psalm 100 is among the verses in the second section in "Singing Over the Earth," and W. H. Auden begins the section "One God Is God of Both" with his famous poem "The Composer." Dance is less frequently the subject of poems, but the compiler meets the challenge with fewer, but still quite good, poems, such as the delightful "I cannot dance upon my toes," by Emily Dickinson. As with her other collections, this is highly recommended for children and for anyone who delights in poetry and the arts.

Who Has Seen the Wind? an Illustrated Collection of Poetry for Young People. *Kathryn Sky-Peck, ed.* (1991) Museum of Fine Arts, Boston. 63p.

The selection of poetry here is excellent children's fare. Care has been taken by editor Kathryn Sky-Peck to choose poems that will appeal to a child's mind without pandering to it. Among the poets here included are

Ogden Nash, William Blake, Emily Dickinson, and Robert Frost. Each poem is accompanied by an illustration, all of which are from the Museum of Fine Arts in Boston. The illustrations are certainly striking, but the heavy reliance upon American artists lends the book an austerity that may not be as attractive to a child's eye as to an adult's (for example, John Singer Sargent's "The Daughters of Edward Boit"). There are, however, some colorful and animated works of the impressionists, and the book is, on the whole, very beautiful. A challenge for children, but certainly an educating and enjoyable one.

Why Am I Grown So Cold? Poems of the Unknowable. *Myra Cohn Livingston, ed.* **(1982) Atheneum. 269p.**

In twelve sections, the compiler brings together one hundred and fifty poems to thrill and chill the child. Here are ghosts, devils, monsters, witches, and an aura of mystery. Ms. Livingston is widely known as an editor of poetry collections. Here she explains that "humankind has always been intrigued by the possible presence of ghosts and spirits. . . . Poetry abounds in tales of enchantment; its very words, rhythms, and sound create their own mystery." One may question the notion that "science has explanations for many phenomena, but it has yet to unravel many mysteries." Still, who is to argue with the poetic choices, serious or not, on the part of the compiler. She is to be congratulated for drawing upon the world's best poets, from Robert Frost and Thomas Hardy to Alexander Pushkin and Ezra Pound. This is the strength of an otherwise less-than-inspired reason for an anthology. One may debate what she thinks excites children, but who is to deny the strength of the poets and their work.

The Wind Has Wings; Poems from Canada. *Mary Alice Downie and Barbara Robertson, eds.*

See under CANADIAN POETRY

The Year Around; Poems for Children. *Alice I. Hazeltine and Elva S. Smith, eds.* **(1956) Abingdon Press. 192p., o.p.**

This is an especially captivating anthology of poems for children that uses holidays and seasons as its main theme. Each of the poems conjures up the excitement and contradictions of a different time of year: spring rains and blooming flowers, July's warmth and thunder, and Christmas gift-giving and religious traditions. Many of the poems were written by

well-known children's poets; others are traditional poems, simple and
rhythmic enough for younger readers, and listeners, to enjoy. The verse
is arranged in sections that begin with spring and March and end with
poems about Valentine's Day and Washington's birthday. They differ in
form and style but are typically melodic and lyrical; the tone is
celebratory, inspiring, and innocent. This is a collection suitable for very
young and older children alike. Indexed by author and title.

A Zooful of Animals. *William Cole, ed.* **(1992) Houghton Mifflin. 88p.**

Of Cole's many poetry anthologies for children, this tall slim volume
is probably his most accomplished. Brief by typical standards (containing
only 44 poems), the collection is spirited, inviting, and illustrious. There
are selections by almost forty fine contemporary poets: Theodore
Roethke, Ted Hughes, and X. J. Kennedy are here, along with many
lesser-known writers. Each poem is complemented by colorful illustrations children will find exciting. Arranged in no particular order, the
poems are usually simple rhymes or silly lyrics about the zoo or the
animals in the zoo: gift wrapping elephants, the mask of the raccoon, or
the unique warning of a skunk. Best for youngest children learning to
read or who enjoy being read to, this anthology combines familiar scenes
with vibrant illustrations that will enchant them even more. Highly recommended for its entertaining verse and arrangement.

See also HOLIDAY POETRY; YOUNG ADULT POETRY

CHINESE POETRY

Among the Flowers; the Hua-chien Chi. *Lois Fusek, tr.* **(1982) Columbia University Press. 240p.**

The translator explains that this is "a collection of five hundred *tz'u* lyrics compiled by Chao Ch'ung-tso (fl. mid-tenth century), a minor official of the later Shu dynasty (934–965). . . . The lyrics are dedicated mainly to the celebration of love. . . . The world depicted is the world of the courtesan and the singing girl, the beautiful 'flowers.' " Unfortunately, economics dictated a reproduction of the typewritten script, and there is nothing beautiful about the format. There is the usual, and in this case much appreciated, scholarly apparatus. While a trifle technical, the introduction sets the scene for the eighteen poets. What is known of them is given in biographical notes, and there is a useful glossary, bibliography, index of tune titles, and general index. It is difficult to evaluate the translations objectively. The sense of intent is nicely captured: although one suspects the loss of joy and the misery of the period, the *tz'u* are an attempt "to find, in beauty and pleasure, an end to pain." One regrets the absence of difficult-to-capture cultural supports. The lesson, as with anonymous early Egyptian poetry, is that love is a universal of time and place.

The Book of Songs; the Ancient Chinese Classic of Poetry. *Arthur Waley, tr.* **(1960) Grove Press. 358p., pap., o.p.**

Written, sung, and recited between 800 and 600 B.C., the two hundred and ninety songs were used for ceremonial purposes as well as for moral instruction. In this respect they are similar to the Japanese *Manyoshu* and the Greek *Anthology*, all of which is clearly explained in the introduction and in additional notes and appendices. Waley usually follows a song with a brief explanation, as well as with an occasional note. Much of this is not necessary. The songs rarely need any background information for the reader to appreciate them, particularly as they are divided into such subject areas as courtship, marriage, hunting, friendship. By now almost as famous as the verses he translated and explained, Waley's comments are great fun. For example, why are clothes and articles of personal adornment so often mentioned? Waley is not sure, but he suspects it is because clothes "may be regarded simply as an indication of personal status." He then proceeds to give an example or two of what he means, and while much of this is obvious, it is true that Waley comes close to being able to "recreate all the mental associations of people in China three thousand years ago."

The Columbia Book of Chinese Poetry from Early Times to the Thirteenth Century. *Burton Watson, ed. and tr.* (1984) Columbia University Press. 385p.

Focusing on daily activity, "The book of Odes" sings of farming, building, love, war, and the natural interests of all people at all points in history. The odes probably were recited and later written down around 1000 to 600 B.C. These are the earliest entries of twelve sections that move through the principal dynasties of Chinese history to the 13th-century Yuan period. (After that, see the companion volume: *The Columbia Book of Later Chinese Poetry*). Poet Gary Snyder pays them the ultimate compliment: "The gathering of translations is the surest, the clearest, most comprehensive presentation of Chinese poetry yet. Burton Watson's life-long dedication to Chinese literature becomes a gift to us all." The antiquity, the remarkable continuity of Chinese poetry makes it impossible to do more than sample the virtually unbroken line of creativity. Limitations placed upon the selections in this volume are dutifully and clearly explained in the informative introduction. Watson is particularly helpful in his discussion of recurring themes and characteristics of the poems. And, when that is done, one is left with a marvelous reading experience. "The Chinese," the compiler explains, "have customarily looked upon poetry as the chief glory of their literary tradition." This anthology explains why.

The Columbia Book of Later Chinese Poetry. *Jonathan Chaves, ed. and tr.* (1986) Columbia University Press. 490p.

The companion volume to *The Columbia Book of Chinese Poetry*, this covers the period 1279 to 1911 (the Yuan, Ming, and the almost endless Ch'ing dynasties). Most of the focus is on the Ming period, and less on the shorter Yuan dynasty. The balance is perfect, not only between periods but in the choice of poets in terms of both quality and representativeness. The translations are equally excellent, and if one considers the ten scroll samples, typography, and general make-up, the book is a tribute to the poets and the translator/compiler. An introduction explains the various dynasties to the layperson. Before each of the sections of poetry is a brief biographical sketch of the poet. The compiler says: "I have omitted a number of major figures either because I could not find an appropriate way to translate them effectively or because they were simply not to my taste. On the other hand I have included some fairly obscure poets who I think deserve to be better known." The formula is close to perfect, particularly for the individual who may know little or nothing of Chinese poetry — and certainly for the reference librarian seeking translations of Chinese poets.

The Isle Full of Noises; Modern Chinese Poetry from Taiwan. *Dominic Cheung, ed. and tr.* **(1987) Columbia University Press. 265p.**

"The background of the development of modern Chinese poetry in Taiwan is quite complicated," the compiler explains. "Poets bearing a strong Chinese sentiment were writing in Japanese; other poets, strongly committed to the Taiwanese identity, were writing in Japanese and Chinese." This brief quote from a thirty-page, scholarly introduction helps explain the title from, of course, "The Tempest," and particularly the line which follows, "Sometimes a thousand twangling instruments will hum about mine ears." Trying to sort out the instruments, the compiler opens with Yang Mu (1940), gives a brief biographical sketch, places his poetry on the island, and offers a generous sampling of his work. The process is followed with some thirty other poets in chronological order. An appendix includes names and titles of poems in Chinese, with English equivalents.

Literature of the Hundred Flowers. Volume II: Poetry and Fiction. *Hualing Nieh, ed.* **(1981) Columbia University Press. 615p.**

This large collection is part of the two-volume Modern Asian Literature Series, with the first volume containing essays on literature that date from the early years of the Communist regime in China. This second volume is much larger and actually contains the literature, in translation, that is debated in the first volume. The text is divided into a poetry section and a fiction section, each containing critical essays and articles from the "Hundred Flowers" movement of 1950's China. The poetry section features about eighty poems, and the fiction section includes excerpts and entire stories and fables. The selections are arranged by author. This is not a volume with which to introduce Chinese literature to the general reader. The analysis is scholarly, and readers are assumed to know something about the "Hundred Flowers" movement. The anthology features distinguished writing, which is complemented by in-depth intellectual and political information. The poems are subtle, satirical, and lyrical; the fiction sharp, terse, and lush. A final section contains notes on the writers. This is quite a stunning text, especially in the light of restrictions imposed on artistic expression by the Communist regime.

One Hundred More Poems from the Chinese; Love and the Turning Year. *Kenneth Rexroth, ed. and tr.* **(1970) New Directions. 140p.**

This brief anthology offers an introduction to the richness and beauty of Chinese poetry. Like Rexroth's other volumes of translated verse, this is an attractive, well-crafted collection. Sixty-one poets — from 32 B.C. to the eighteenth century — are included. The verse is terse, controlled, and especially poignant. Many are love poems, or meditations on nature. Rexroth wisely avoids including poems with extensive references to Chinese historical events or figures, making this an excellent beginner's volume and sparing any need for annotations. Arranged alphabetically by poet, Rexroth includes extensive notes on the poets, some of whom are women and several of whom are anonymous. This anthology is highly recommended for readers looking for a first volume of Chinese poetry. It may not be as inclusive as others, but it offers a sampling of the Chinese poetic tradition.

Poems of the Late T'ang. *Arthur Charles Graham, ed. and tr.* **(1977) Penguin Books. 173p., pap.**

This slim anthology contains the illusory and delicate verse of seven revered poets of the T'ang dynasty — regarded as a time of great poetic transformation and artistic change in China. Writing roughly between the eighth and ninth centuries — a time of "new sensibility" for Chinese writers, according to the editor — these poets are considered to be among the most brilliant in China's long tradition of exceptional artists. Each poet is represented by several selections, and short critical and biographical information is provided on each. Most English-language readers will notice the great variation among the poets' styles and forms, as well as the complexity and depth of the verse. Some of the poems are dedicated to love, while some are bitter and cynical. The editor has included a long section on the process of translating Chinese poetry, particularly the intricate verse from the T'ang period. The absence of indexes is a drawback to this well-constructed anthology.

A Splintered Mirror; Chinese Poetry from the Democracy Movement.
Donald Finkel and Carolyn Kizer, eds. **(1991) North Point Press. 101p.**

Haunting and ambiguous at times, the poems in this slender anthology chronicle the recent Chinese struggle for democracy. All of the poets were born after the First World War, and the bulk of their verse was written in the last few decades. They are well known to the Chinese but probably obscure to general American readers. Their passion for the movement is fascinating; the six men and one woman have all been arrested, and all but two now live outside of China. Their fifty-seven poems are mostly lyrical, articulate, and brief. They chart the personal aspect of the democracy movement, revealing the tremendous anger and gloom in their lives. Arranged by poet, the volume also includes brief biographical information. It is a beautiful, attractive collection for all readers. It is regrettable that there are not more collections like this: thought provoking, skillful, and dense with imagery.

Sunflower Splendor; Three Thousand Years of Chinese Poetry. *Wu-chi Liu and Irving Yucheng Lo, eds.* **(1975) Indiana University Press. 635p., pap.**

The aim of this comprehensive collection is twofold — to provide an adequate sense of the continuity present in "an unbroken three-thousand-year-old tradition," while at the same time emphasizing, through the contribution of more than fifty different translators, the formal, metrical, and stylistic variegation of that tradition. The poems are grouped in five major periods that comprise Chinese poetic history from the 12th century B.C. to modern times. An introduction gives a brief account of the important evolutionary changes that mark the boundaries of these periods and provides a general explanation of the specific linguistic, thematic, and sociopolitical contrasts between Chinese poetic tradition and that of the West. Supplementary material is extensive and includes two bibliographies, background information on poets and poems, and an appendix of Chinese dynasties and historical periods. While an index of first lines is lacking, an author index is provided, as is a list of tune titles and their translations.

Waiting for the Unicorn; Poems and Lyrics of China's Last Dynasty, 1644–1911. *Irving Yucheng Lo and William Schultz, eds.* **(1986) Indiana University Press. (1986) 425p.**

The Ch'ing Dynasty (the last Chinese dynasty) includes a wide diversity in politics, art, and poetry. Considering the length of the reign of the Manchus, it is little wonder there is so much difference from age to age, poet to poet. At the same time, there are no new genres, but more dominant modes of thought and aesthetics. And, as the editors observe, there is a great degree of historical-mindedness and "preference for dealing with the concrete, as evidenced by the growth of realism and popularity of both narrative and . . . poems on objects." Arranged chronologically, the almost seventy-five poets wrote from the mid-1660's to the turn of the twentieth century. Each is represented with anywhere from four to a dozen poems. To help set the stage, there is a biographical background sketch for each, which not only tells about the poet, but about the period, content, and style. (There are some delightful examples of calligraphy, usually accompanying a scroll painting or drawing.) The translations are good to excellent. The scores of translators are dutifully given credit after the selected bibliography. Liang Ch'i-ch'ao wrote: "Trying to stay the departing spring is of no avail." True, but at least a gallant effort is made to show the essence of numerous springs. The success of the effort is impressive.

Women Poets of China; the Orchid Boat. *Kenneth Rexroth and Ling Chung, eds. and trs.* **(1972) McGraw-Hill; also published 1972 by Seabury Press as The Orchid Boat. 150p.**

Of the small number of anthologies devoted to Chinese women poets, this one is among the best for unfamiliar readers. Slender and well organized like other Rexroth anthologies, the fifty-four poets are represented by no more than seven selections each. The poems are mystical, meditative, and sometimes angry. Generally translated into free verse, they range from powerful love songs and cries of loneliness to thoughts on the modern Communist government. Extensive notes on the writers are included, helpful for readers who may be puzzled by the historical references in the verse. It is interesting to see that these women, writing from 300 B.C. into the years following the Second World War, occupied all levels of society, from privileged daughters of officials to concubines and prostitutes. Arranged chronologically by poet, but with no index, the collection does include a table of Chinese historical periods and a well-written introduction about the rich but generally unacknowledged position of Chinese women in the literary tradition.

Zen Poems of China & Japan; the Crane's Bill. *Lucien Stryk, Takashi Ikemoto, and Taigan Takayama, trs.* **(1973) Grove Press. 143p., pap.**

This slim volume offers the layperson a fine introduction to Chinese and Japanese poetry. While the focus is on Zen, the style and content is more broadly Asiatic, and the selections will give the Western reader an excellent notion of thought in that part of the world. Beyond this, the hundred and fifty translated poems are moving in themselves. Few are difficult to comprehend, although they may be considerably more subtle than a first reading would indicate. The verse is divided into three broad subject categories: "Enlightenment," "Death," and "General." There is a well-written introduction that will help the general reader understand the history of Zen as well as its essentials and how it is related to Zen poetry. The foreword and preface also explain the four basic moods of Zen: sabi, wabi, aware, and yugen. These are nicely defined, and the examples given for each render them relatively clear. There are notes at the end of the volume that enlighten the reader about basic cultural situations, foreign terms, etc. As there is a note for virtually each poem, the poetry is always lucid.

DEATH POETRY

Death in Literature. *Robert F. Weir, ed.* **(1980) Columbia University Press. 451p., o.p.**

Unlike the *Oxford Book of Death,* which it closely resembles, this is confined to the subject as it is represented in literature. The amount of duplication is less than one might think, and anyone who turns to one will want to use the other. They nicely complement each other. Here the selections range from 2300 B.C. to A.D. 1979, and a variety of cultures are tapped. Literature of India, China, Japan, Greece, Nigeria, Lebanon, Russia, Germany, England, France, Spain, Ireland, and the United States provide material. Each of the eleven sections has a separate introduction of two to four pages. "Many of these introductions contain brief descriptions of literary works which are used to illustrate a sectional theme and supplement the selections." In addition, there are often brief remarks about individual pieces. The emphasis falls much more on excerpts from prose than on poetry. In fact, the poetry is limited to rather obvious choices from such poets as Donne, Milton, and Dylan Thomas. This, too, is the case with the *Oxford Book of Death,* so one might conclude that there is still room for another anthology devoted entirely to poetry about death. A small point — the names of the numerous translators are not given after the work, and one has to turn to the acknowledgments to discover a vital piece of information.

In the Midst of Winter; Selections from the Literature of Mourning. *Mary Jane Moffat, ed.* **(1992) Vintage Books. 274p., pap.**

The editor explains that "this book is a gathering from world literature of the words of those who have survived the death of someone they love." Not weighed down by sentimentality, these well-written poems (and prose excerpts) are bare, personal, and deeply emotional. Writers as diverse as Catullus, Emily Dickinson, and Mark Twain are here along with such twentieth-century authors as Anne Sexton, James Agee, and C. S. Lewis. The theme is simple: separation after death. But each poem tells a different story. The writing is in three chapters named after the seasons of the year, with such subheadings as "The Grief of Children" and "Widows and Widowers." Moffat has also included excerpts from letters and journals that address the death of a loved one, and she has annotated the poems. Here is a collection of solemn, deeply revealing poetry that rarely becomes mawkish.

The Oxford Book of Death. *D. J. Enright, ed.* **(1987) Oxford University Press. 352p.**

Poet, novelist, and critic, D. J. Enright makes an obvious point early in his brief introduction: "In this line . . . the compiler could easily and even pleasurably persist in his task until death should part the one from the other." This unusual collection is thus conceived as a book for everyone. Ironically, death seems to be a theme where writers show "themselves more lively" than in many other situations. The anthology is divided into fourteen complementary sections, from definitions of death to views and attitudes about it. Side by side with graveyards and funerals, one finds the subjects of resurrection and immortality, as well as the hereafter. Fittingly, the collection concludes with a section of "Epitaphs, Requiems and Last Words." About half of the book is devoted to poetry, the other half to prose. In the "Definitions" section, for example, one finds a page-long introduction by Enright—a practice he follows throughout the volume. A poem by Shelley follows, and several exemplary passages from longer works by the Venerable Bede, Stevie Smith, and others. The bits and pieces sometimes seem like long quotations from a commonplace book. The last lines in the anthology are the last words of Goronwy Rees: "What shall I do next?" After this marvelous collection it is hard to think of anyone doing anything more brilliant on the subject.

DUTCH POETRY

Dutch Interior; Postwar Poetry of the Netherlands and Flanders. *James S. Holmes and William Jay Smith, eds.* **(1984) Columbia University Press. 326p.**

Recalling the genre paintings of the seventeenth century, here the Dutch interiors are equally rich, complete with the same hidden ironies, messages, and interpretations. For example, Adriaan Morriën begins "Gastronomy" with: "She is the finest banquet you could eat:/ from top to toe fried liver, beefsteak, kidneys, / sweet & sour like a none-too-large gherkin." Then there is Gerrit Komrij, another of the forty-five voices here, whose poem "An Afternoon" resembles a Jan Steen interior. What is quite remarkable is that all of the poets began publishing after the mid-1940's; as the introduction points out, "There was no truly modern poetry in Dutch." But there was, and is, a tremendous *avant garde* that had the courage to draw upon old themes while avoiding the familiar prosodic forms. This is experimental poetry whose song should be better known outside of the Netherlands and Flanders. Arrangement is by "Prelude to Experiment" (five poets); "The Fifties" (fifteen poets); "The Sixties"; and "The Seventies: Neo-reality and a Return to Form." There are able translations, a bibliography, and excellent notes on the poets.

ENGLISH POETRY
Comprehensive Collections

A Book of English Poetry. *G. B. Harrison, ed.* **(1950) Penguin. 416p., pap.**

This is a volume of broadly representative, stellar verse, intended to chronicle the progression of English poetry from the fourteenth century to the nineteenth, from Chaucer to Matthew Arnold, including selections of sonnets, poems, and lyrics from plays and longer epic poems. Arranged chronologically by author, the poets are among the greatest writers in English literary history. The size of the collection dictates more of an overview and less of a comprehensive study; there are no biographical notes and no dating of the poems. It is a fine collection, solid and unpretentious, but a no-frills one.

British Women Writers. *Dale Spender and Janet Todd, eds.*

See under WOMEN'S POETRY AND FEMINIST POETRY

English Lyric Poems, 1500–1900. *C. Day Lewis, ed.* **(1961) Appleton-Century-Crofts. 249p., pap.**

This anthology covers a long time span: 1500–1900. The table of contents divides the selections into: songs, story lyrics, lyrical poems, and devotional lyrics. Within the sections, the poems are arranged chronologically. This is quite a lovely organizing scheme, since the poems can be read with others of their genre, as well as with other works by the same author and his compeers. Thus, in the "Song" section, many of Shakespeare's poems are followed by those of Thomas Campion and Robert Herrick. The section entitled "Story Lyrics" includes over two dozen anonymous folk songs and ballads. Among the "Lyrical Poems" are works by Emily Brontë, Blake, Thomas Hardy, and W. B. Yeats. Most poets are represented by up to three of their works; it is the rare poet who is accorded more space, but this provides a good overview of some of the finest poems written in Great Britain and Ireland in the four centuries surveyed.

English Poetry; a Poetic Record, from Chaucer to Yeats. *David Hopkins, ed.* (1990) Routledge. 269p., pap.

This slim volume is not an anthology of poetry in the usual sense. Instead it is a collection of poems and critiques of distinguished poets by other distinguished poets — with the criticism written in verse and in prose. The book has two main sections. The first section contains general reflections on poetry and the art of poetry, arranged chronologically by poet; the second, larger section, also arranged chronologically, here by subject-poet, has criticisms on the work of poets from Chaucer to Yeats. More than sixty-six poets are addressed, some in long essays and some in short, often nasty, quips. All types of poets and verse are covered. This may sound confusing, but, in fact, here is a fascinating volume, filled with responses by poets to other poets, often contemporaries — for example, Coleridge on Wordsworth. The poetry is annotated in great detail, and the works are in general the best known of each poet. Both the general and the more specialized reader should find this a rare, uncensored look at what great poets think of each other's work. Indexed by author and such topics as theme, subject, and form.

Everyman's Book of English Verse. *John Wain, ed.* (1981) J. M. Dent. 672p.

Everyman is an English series that pioneered pocket-book sized reprints of the classics. The present anthology is from the same publisher. Here, alas, the number of pages matches its weight; there is simply too much of everything, with little or no real focus. The compiler is a well-known author and critic whose introduction is skillfully written and indicates an unusual sensibility. Of his selection, he says, "It is an act of homage," adding, "an utterance of thanksgiving for the richness and beauty of English poetry." He catalogues what is different about his choices. First, there "is a mass of lesser-known verse . . . including the anonymous, the scurrilous, the randy and the rollicking." Fine, but this is better done in other collections that are limited to humor and satire. Second, Victorian nonsense poets are included. But this is not unusual. Third, bits are taken out of long poems. One can take strong exception to that editorial choice. The collection opens with the Anglo-Saxons, which the editor thinks unusual. It is, in fact, common in most collections of this type. It then moves chronologically to end with Seamus Heaney and Brian Patten. There are over five hundred numbered entries and about one third that many poets. Indexes of authors, titles, and first lines are provided. As far as it goes, this is a standard, much too bulky, collection of standard English verse. Good enough, but there are other better, more focused collections.

Everyman's Book of Evergreen Verse. *David Herbert, ed.* **(1984) J. M. Dent. 387p., pap., o.p.**

This neatly arranged anthology is another good collection of classic British poetry, capable, but not outstanding, in its presentation and selections. Spanning 900 years of literary tradition, it begins with the usual anonymous ballads and Chaucerian excerpts, continues with several Shakespeare selections and some American poems, and concludes with Dylan Thomas and Henry Reed. There are no surprises, and perhaps its most commendable feature is the collection of excerpts from Shakespeare's plays; rather than rely on his sonnets, the volume includes parts of sixteen plays and other poems. The hundreds of other selections are fairly standard, recommending the volume as an introductory text. There is no criticism, introduction, or supplementary information about the poets — just classic verse. Indexed by author, first line, and title, but without a table of contents.

The Faber Book of English History in Verse. *Kenneth Baker, ed.* **(1988) Faber and Faber. 448p., o.p.**

The premise of this anthology has great merit and is carried out quite successfully. Here is a swift, compact collection of poems that tell the story of England, from pre-Norman times to the House of Windsor in the early twentieth century. Chronicling this history are vibrant ballads, songs, and excerpts from plays that retell dozens of events in English history. More than three hundred poems, covering four hundred years of history, are collected here — most of them by relatively well-known English poets. Shakespeare and T. S. Eliot are prominently featured, along with many less well-known or anonymous poets. The poems are divided into eight chronological eras of English history and then further listed under the monarch who reigned when the events occurred. This is a unique, fascinating volume, highly recommended for readers of English literature as well as for beginning students. The battles, rulers, commerce, and politics of England are described in beautiful, vivid poems — all of which have gained a place in the English literary canon. Indexed by title and first line.

The Faber Book of Reflective Verse. *Geoffrey Grigson, ed.* (1984) Faber and Faber. 238p., o.p.

Geoffrey Grigson declares at the beginning of this book that he hopes readers will not be upset at finding a good many familiar verses in this collection of works that are " 'poetical' in the sense of being solemn, peaceful, musical, and correspondent to the solemn and peaceful mood rather than the excited or ecstatic mood. . . ." Since it seems clear that many lovers of poetry relish particularly the insights they gain from writing that is reflective in nature, then this volume should find its strong admirers. The poems are arranged in no clearly discernable order, but seem to be placed next to others of similar subject matter. The solemn topics revolve around the seasons, death, sleep, ignominy, failure, and, in the words of Samuel Johnson, "the vanity of human wishes" (the poem that corresponds to that heading being inexplicably omitted). Authors represented herein include Matthew Arnold, William Cowper, John Donne, Shakespeare, Tennyson, and Wordsworth. Very few modern poets show up, and again one wonders why. Surely solemnity has not disappeared from the poetic vocabulary. The most recent authors cited are Louis MacNeice and W. H. Auden. This is surely the most appropriate anthology to turn to when you are in a melancholy mood and wish to intensify it.

The Family Poetry Book; 100 Favorite Poems. *Foreword by Felicity Kendal.* (1990) Michael Joseph. 208p.

The poems in this collection are chosen the top ten favorites of prominent British writers and theatrical and political figures. These 100 poems are arranged by popularity, with "To His Coy Mistress," "Ode to a Nightingale," and "The Love Song of J. Alfred Prufrock," ranked first, second, and third, respectively. Those three poems should give a good sense of the type of verse featured here — all British classics of high quality, renowned poems that span the length of English literary history. Forty-five poets are featured in an attractive volume, and a final section prints the top-ten lists of all those who participated in the survey. In her forward to this nicely sized, competent collection of best-loved poems, Kendal states that she intends for the book to "be picked up by those who like to come across an old friend, well-remembered or half-forgotten, or equally to make a new one." This is a little old-fashioned and sentimental and has nothing to do with "family" except that these poems are among the most familiar. But it works. Indexed by poet and first line.

Fifteen Poets: Chaucer to Arnold. *H. S. Bennett and others, eds.* **(1941) Oxford University Press. 503p., o.p.**

The best explanation of content and purpose is found in the three-paragraph preface: this collection "contains a substantial sample — about 1,000 lines by each poet — of the best work of the great masters of English poetry from Chaucer to Matthew Arnold. . . . The selections are preceded by short essays of appreciation by various hands, and by summaries of the poets' lives." This is almost to hide the glory of the collection. Who, then, does the introductions? W. H. Auden offers four pages on Byron; F. L. Lucas has six pages of tribute to Wordsworth; C. S. Lewis salutes Edmund Spenser; and E. C. Blunden comments on the skills of Shelley. Even those who are not well known, those who may be less at home with poetry than others, manage to offer original ideas about the poet and his poems. It is a unique collection with many insights, and it does, as the preface hopes, "serve as a link between the normal type of anthology, in which a large number of poets are each represented by a small amount of verse, and the Complete Works of the poets." A helpful feature is a glossary of names that explains who everyone is in the poems from Abbethdin to Zoroaster. Unfortunately, there are no indexes of authors, first lines, or poems; one must work through the table of contents.

First Lines; Poems Written in Youth, from Herbert to Heaney. *Jon Stallworthy, ed.* **(1987) Carcanet. 119p., pap.**

Inspired by the question of when or why or how does a writer begin to write poems, the editor compiled some of the first efforts of well-known poets. They make for fascinating reading. Each author is briefly introduced, and the circumstances surrounding his first work are sketched. The poems follow in a spacious, attractive layout. Here we find George Herbert's sonnets written to his mother while he was at Cambridge University. He was only sixteen years old at the time. William Chatterton, who died at the age of eighteen had, of necessity, to get an early start, and his poem "Sly Dick," a satirical work, was written when he was only eleven. Blake composed a song that was reputedly written when he was only thirteen years old, but the editor queries that age, for the work does indeed appear to bear the marks of greater maturity. Elizabeth Barrett Browning's first lines also date from the age of thirteen, and Edgar Allan Poe's poem "To Helen" was composed when he was either fifteen or sixteen. This is altogether an astonishing volume! Some of the modern authors whose earliest work is included are Sir John

Betjeman, Louis MacNeice, W. H. Auden, Dylan Thomas, Sylvia Plath, and Philip Larkin. Engrossing as the poems themselves are, the informative notes that precede them, offering documentation and biographical context, make the works even more fascinating.

Five Hundred Years of English Poetry: Chaucer to Arnold. *Barbara Lloyd-Evans, ed.* **(1989) Peter Bedrick Books. 1,200p., pap.**

This very large anthology is attractive, comprehensive, and highly recommended for all readers — except those looking for solid emphasis on Shakespeare, who has been omitted entirely here, since, the editor explains, it would be too difficult to represent his genius in the space available. Unfortunately, the omission does weaken the text, despite the wealth of other great poets. The volume follows standard English-poetry arrangement, beginning with Chaucer, Spenser, and Donne and concluding with Tennyson, Robert Browning, and Arnold. Twenty-two great English poets are featured, represented by famous and less familiar works. Each poet is preceded by brief biographical information, and the poetry concludes with extensive notes on specific lines. A glossary of terms, names, and devices, as well as biblical terms and a lucid guide to versification, will be particularly helpful. Despite the absence of Shakespeare that gives the text a feeling of incompleteness, this is a fine volume. Indexed by first line.

Golden Treasury of the Best Songs and Lyrical Poems in the English Language. *Francis Turner Palgrave, comp.* **(1929) Oxford University Press. 555p.**

Working with Tennyson, to whom he dedicated the first edition in 1861, Palgrave set the course for acceptable English poetry through the rest of the nineteenth and well into the twentieth century. Even today the original selection, despite numerous modifications and additions, is better known to laypersons than almost any other anthology. There are better ones. Many are more comprehensive and offer necessary guidance in terms of meaning and style, but Palgrave (as the collection usually is called) dominates. The notable omissions in the 1861 edition long ago were added, particularly the seventeenth-century poets. Palgrave still is honored for being among the first to appreciate the delights of Wordsworth, and if he gave too much space to Tennyson he also had the courage to include "anonymous," which at that time had been considered less than acceptable in many homes. Today Palgrave is a figure who has earned a place in every library in America.

Golden Treasury of the Best Songs & Lyrical Poems in the English Language. *Francis Turner Palgrave, comp. With a fifth book selected by John Press.* **(Updated ed., by Christopher Ricks, 1991) Oxford University Press. 526p., pap.**

This deservedly famous anthology claims to be different from the others in that it aims "to include in it all the best original Lyric pieces and Songs in our language... and none beside the best." What is, therefore, effectively excluded is narrative verse and didactic poetry. The poems are arranged chronologically by period. Book One includes works from Sir Thomas Wyatt to Shakespeare; Book Two, George Herbert to Milton; Book Three, Thomas Gray to Burns; and so forth. The final book is selected by John Press, who brings in the work of the latter part of the nineteenth and twentieth centuries. The result of such a concentration on lyrical writing is that the poems tend to be passionate and deeply personal. The editors succeed in reprinting only the work of the best poets, so the collection is filled with riches. On any page, readers will find poems to engage them on many levels: intellectual, emotional, and aesthetic. For this edition, Christopher Ricks has reinstated (and clearly identified) the poems dropped earlier by Palgrave from the 1861 edition. And he has quietly appended, "so as not to come between a reader and the poems themselves," a section of his own clearly written helpful notes — a long desired critical addition to this wonderful collection.

A Little Treasury of British Poetry. *Oscar Williams, ed.* **(1951) Scribner's. 874p., o.p.**

Set between the little treasuries of American and modern poetry, this follows the same format as its cousins. It is bulky, pocket-sized, and concludes with small photographs of the poets. The arrangement is chronological and in two parts — poets from 1500 to 1900 and poets from 1900 to 1950. Coverage, as in the other anthologies, is excellent in that all of the major, and not a few minor, poets are represented by characteristic, usually well-known poems. As might be expected, more space is given to Shakespeare than anyone else, but Williams strikes a sound balance between the figures and their work. One might confidently read this from cover to cover and end up an expert on British poetry, even without benefit of notes or commentary by the compiler. Williams believes in letting the poems speak for themselves, and he offers no help — besides a well-written introduction — to either the beginner or expert. He does point out his natural bias: "two fifths of the pages herein [are devoted] to the verse of the past fifty years. . . . This anthology is being published for living readers." And with that he justifies what may or may not be a good choice, but his own.

The London Book of English Verse. *Herbert Read and Bonamy Dobrée,* **eds. (2d, rev. ed., 1952) Eyre & Spottiswoode. 891p., o.p.**

This is a large, formal anthology of "every English poet of importance," according to the editors — a comprehensive volume, highly recommended for its depth and the quality of selections. All the great English poets are included, from Chaucer to T. S. Eliot. The editors have carefully excluded much sentimental and romantic verse in favor of less lyrical selections and then grouped the poems according to the type of verse. There are, for example, sections devoted to descriptive, lyrical, and "moralistic" verse, and to "the symphonic poem." This is a collection for readers looking for a comprehensive volume that emphasizes the form of the poem. Notes on the poems and indexes by author and first line are included.

The Mentor Book of Major British Poets. *Oscar Williams, ed.* **(1963) New American Library. 576p., pap.**

Like its American poetry counterpart, this collection of important British poetry concentrates on just a handful of the greatest poets of the past two hundred years, from the Romantics to writers of the mid-twentieth century. Here is the most accomplished verse by Blake, Wordsworth, Robert Browning, Yeats, and Dylan Thomas, among other distinguished poets. Arranged chronologically by poet, the works are buoyant and celebratory, a presentation of timeless classics in a convenient sturdy anthology. A fine introduction assigns these poems their proper place in the history of British literature. Williams takes time, for instance, to explain that T. S. Eliot's publishers denied him permission to include Eliot's verse — a small indication of how much poetry meant to Williams and of his concern for his reader.

The New Oxford Book of English Verse, 1250–1950. *Helen Gardner,* **ed. (1972) Oxford University Press. 974p.**

A huge expanse of time is covered in this anthology; it takes in the full range of English, nondramatic poetry written primarily by British authors. This sensitive, discerning volume opens with an anonymous poem "Cuckoo Song," with its famous beginning, "Summer is y-comen in, / Loude sing, cuckoo!" and ends with poetry by Dylan Thomas. In between, all the major poets are given ample space to display some of their most glorious works. Gardner allots Blake eight pages, Pope twelve, and John Donne eighteen, but Edmund Spenser has been allowed thirty so some of his long poems can be printed. The same is true for T. S. Eliot, whose "The Love Song of J. Alfred Prufrock," "The Waste Land," and "Little Gidding" are printed in full, along with a few short poems. The poets are arranged chronologically by their date of birth. Among the scores of poets included, several are women, most notably Aphra Behn, Emily Brontë, Elizabeth Barrett Browning, Christina Rossetti, Kathleen Raine, and Stevie Smith.

100 British Poets. *Selden Rodman, ed.* **(1974) New American Library. 345p., o.p.**

Rodman's selection of poems for this anthology was based less upon the judgments of past critics than upon his own taste as a reader. While poems like Matthew Arnold's "Dover Beach" or John Donne's "The Extasie" have been considered great works for many years, many of the other works have garnered little acclaim. The 221 poems are arranged in chronological order by poet, from the unknown author of "Beowulf" to John Lennon; unfortunately, there is no index. At the volume's end, Rodman includes a section of lively biographical notes; although they often leave out factual data, they nevertheless help readers to understand Rodman's selection principle. This anthology is a good sampling of British poetry from its beginnings to the 1970's.

The Oxford Anthology of English Literature. Vols. I–II (see note at end). *Frank Kermode and John Hollander, general eds.* **(1973) Oxford University Press. 2,376p., 2,238p.**

By anyone's reckoning, these would be judged massive volumes. Their purpose, in the words of their editors, is "to provide students with a selective canon of the entire range of English literature from the beginnings to recent time. . . ." This, assuredly, is what they accomplish. The poems are organized in chronological stages, and they are amply introduced. "Beowulf," for example, is given eight pages of introductory comment. Furthermore, there are many helpful notes to aid the reader. Many plays written in verse are reprinted in full, including, in the medieval section, *The Wakefield Second Shepherd's Play*, a mystery play on religious themes, and *Everyman*, a morality play. The editors have printed the music for those ballads they chose to include — a delightful addition. There is a great deal of Edmund Spenser's *The Faerie Queen*, and dozens of poems by Shakespeare, John Donne, Ben Jonson, and Pope. Later, in the second volume, Blake and the Romantic poets are much in evidence, followed by Thomas Hardy, W. B. Yeats, D. H. Lawrence, and T. S. Eliot. The volume concludes with works by Philip Larkin, Ted Hughes, and Geoffrey Hill. Once again, as with the *Norton Anthology of English Literature,* reading this seriously is comparable to taking a University course in English literature.

NOTE: This work is also published as six paperback volumes: Medieval English Literature, *J. B. Trapp, ed.;* The Literature of Renaissance England, *John Hollander and Frank Kermode, eds.;* The Restoration and the Eighteenth Century, *Martin Price, ed.;* Romantic Poetry and Prose, *Harold Bloom and Lionel Trilling, eds.;* Victorian Prose and Poetry, *Lionel Trilling and Harold Bloom, eds.;* Modern British Literature, *Frank Kermode and John Hollander, eds.*

An Oxford Anthology of English Poetry. *Howard Foster Lowry and Willard Thorp, eds.* (2d ed., 1956) Oxford University Press. 1,356p., o.p.

This is a weighty, solid, excellent survey from Oxford — too early, however, to have included many of the skilled English poets who emerged after the Second World War. The first edition of this work featured poems up to the turn of the century; for this second edition, the editors have included such later poets as Hardy, Housman, and T. S. Eliot. Featured writers range from Chaucer to Dylan Thomas, represented by their most distinguished, best-known poems. The editors have refrained from extensive criticism to allow more space for the poetry, and their chosen poems reflect the historical tone of the past five centuries in England. The collection is arranged alphabetically by poet and with both helpful notes on the verse and biographical information; it is indexed by title, author, and first line.

The Oxford Book of English Verse, 1250–1918. *Sir Arthur Quiller-Couch, ed.* (New ed., rev. and enl., 1939) Oxford University Press. 1,083p., o.p.

The editor's ambitious task here was to gather into two volumes the best of English verse from the thirteenth century through the First World War. He begins firmly within the British Isles, but toward the end of his project he includes a good deal of American poetry. Many of the great poems are included in this anthology, but they are all of a lyrical or epigrammatic nature. No epic works are included, and there are few shortened versions of long poems. For the most part, each author is given a relatively small space in which to make an impression on the reader. Occasionally authors, like Edmund Spenser, for instance, are given more. Others so favored are Michael Drayton, Shakespeare, and Milton. Since this anthology has so long a period to explore, most authors are represented cursorily, although there are generous selections from Wordsworth, Keats, and Shelley. In general, this is a worthwhile anthology of fine poetry.

The Oxford Book of Short Poems. *P. J. Kavanagh and James Michie, eds.* (1985) Oxford University Press. 307p., pap.

The short poems that the title refers to are very short — less than fourteen lines. The two poets set out to explore "what poets and poems have been overlooked or treated ungenerously, and what short poems, even if they have been anthologized, have had their effect muffled by their longer companions." Although arranged chronologically from the thirteenth century to the present, the compilers admit to certain imbalances in their selection. First, the eighteenth century put great emphasis on long poems, and there are few short ones of note from that great era. Second, the tones alter, sometimes drastically, from period to period. "The vernacular, unembarrassed directness of the earliest lyrics drifts . . . into the tight grip of reason, reasonableness and sounds." Third, confidence in the short poem is restored in the twentieth century through the genius of the great masters: Thomas Hardy, W. B. Yeats, and Robert Frost. The pleasure in the collection resides in the variety of moods, subjects, and tones. Consider, for example, Thomas Beedome (d. 1641) and his four-line tribute to Sir Francis Drake: "Drake, who the world hast conquered like a scroll, / Who saw'st the Arctic and Antarctic Pole, / If men were silent, stars would make thee known: / Phoebus forgets not his companion." The compilers call this "sudden perfection," and fortunately there is much more of the same in this unique, fine collection.

The Penguin Book of Ballads. *Geoffrey Grigson, ed.*

See under BALLADS AND SONGS

Poetry for Pleasure; a Choice of Poetry and Verse on a Variety of Themes. *Ian Parsons, ed.* **(1977) W. W. Norton. 352p., o.p.**

The editor of this diverse collection makes it clear in his preface that these poems do not represent any specific style, era, or theme. Rather, they are meant only for pleasurable reading. In this, the collection is a success, with verse from the sixteenth century to about the beginning of the twentieth and including a wide range of prominent and lesser-known English poets. The arrangement is by subject, progressing from child-hood themes to more reflective, "adult" works. There are hundreds of selections, from cute rhymes and songs in the first part of the book to narratives and ballads later on. One of the most delightful sections is that of epitaphs and epigrams, humorous and witty and not commonly anthologized. This is an entertaining, often probing, volume to browse in, but it lacks structure and guidance. Indexed by title and first line.

Poets and the English Scene. *Elinor Parker, ed.* **(1975) Scribner's. 118p., o.p.**

This anthology's fifty-five poems — by authors such as Wordsworth, Lionel Johnson, and Hardy — are accompanied by some lovely photographs of the English countryside and by brief prose commentaries. Elinor Parker has divided this book into sections, each a different geographical region of England. Many of the poems (Wordsworth's "Lines Composed a Few Miles Above Tintern Abbey" and Matthew Arnold's "Dover Beach") involve English landscapes, if only on a superficial level. The editors abridge many of the chosen works to focus upon passages dealing directly with British topography; these abridgments may frustrate the reader who wishes to read the poems in full. Parker includes indexes of first lines, titles, and authors, as well as a glossary.

Seven Centuries of Poetry: Chaucer to Dylan Thomas. *A. N. Jeffares, ed.* **(1955) Longmans, Green. 463p.**

This work signified a struggle against specialization. As the compiler explained: "We now have an emphasis upon the value of examining several writers in some detail. A greater depth of knowledge and more original power of criticism" are needed. To that end, the anthology begins with anonymous Old English poems and moves through the centuries to conclude with Dylan Thomas. The selection is limited exclusively to English poets. Within that limitation, the scope is broad; the compiler has succeeded in overcoming the difficulty of narrowness. Unfortunately, after a five-page introduction, there are no notes, no explanations, no biographical sketches, nothing but the well-known poets and their work. While no one can fault the collection itself, there is some doubt that a work of this kind is of any real value to anyone who can find better, more complete, and more informative collections of English poetry.

Six Centuries of Verse. *Anthony Thwaite, ed.* **(1984) Thames Methuen. 290p., pap.**

Based on a television series about English poetry, the "six centuries" in the title refer to the period from Chaucer to the late twentieth century. And that is how the book is divided. There are fourteen time periods, with Chaucer, Shakespeare, Milton, and Wordsworth given separate sections. Other poets are grouped under such headings as "Romantics and Realists, 1790–1920." "This book is an attempt to give a guided tour of English poetry . . . rather than a literary history or a straightforward anthology, although it has elements of both." Written as a companion to a television series, it is no accident that the text has more illustrations than usual. It is all for the good. For example, in the "Medieval to Elizabethan, 1400–1600" section one finds reproductions of contemporary woodcuts or paintings (in black and white) on almost every page. The text of the television series is fitted nicely before and after each of the poems. The result is an illustrated, friendly introduction to the basics of poetry for students and laypersons alike. Biographical and bibliographical notes round out a fine approach.

The Treasury of English Poetry. *Mark Caldwell and Walter Kendrick, eds.* **(1984) Doubleday. 734p., o.p.**

This is not the largest or the most bulky of numerous collections of this type, but it has a definite advantage over others. The compilers try to print the poems in their entirety, and not in part as is too often the case in other anthologies of such wide scope. Also, all of the Old English poems are translated into modern English for the student and the general reader of the collection. "Our selections are ample enough to portray the unique qualities of the more than a hundred English, Irish, Scottish, and Welsh poets we include." The work has the most famous and best loved of English poems in their complete form. The only real exceptions are Milton's *Paradise Lost* and Chaucer's *Canterbury Tales*. Unfortunately, while the brief introduction is useful, there are no supporting notes or any specific information about the poets, a major drawback in a compilation primarily for students. Conversely, the excellent selection and the decision to include numerous lesser-known poems gives this a dimension that makes it well worth considering.

Victorian Parlour Poetry; an Annotated Anthology. *Michael R. Turner, ed.*

See under   ENGLISH AND AMERICAN POETRY: COMPREHENSIVE COLLECTIONS

See also   POETRY: STUDY AND TEACHING

ENGLISH POETRY
c. 450–1500 — Old English, Middle English

The Anglo-Saxon World; an Anthology. *Kevin Crossley-Holland, ed.* **(1982) Oxford University Press. 308p.**

According to the editor, this anthology aims to "introduce the Anglo-Saxons in their own words — their chronicles, laws and letters, charters and charms, and above all their magnificent poems." The literature is divided among such chapters as "Heroic Poems," "Allegory," and "Exploration," each section prefaced by a brief, informative introduction. The selections in this book, besides being fine literature, are also historically fascinating. "Beowulf" is reprinted in its entirety, but most of the other selections will be less well known to modern readers. Here are fifty regular poems, as well as other more obscure selections, including a section excerpted from a medical journal on how to take care of poisonous spider bites or "woman's chatter." Many of the selections chart the rise of Christianity among Anglo-Saxons. This is a wonderful anthology for Anglo-Saxon enthusiasts. It contains exciting, narrative epics, and other representative works, but it is also a fine text for students of history looking for a glimpse into the origins of modern British culture.

An Anthology of Old English Poetry. *Charles W. Kennedy, tr.* **(1960) Oxford University Press. 174p., pap., o.p.**

Divided into nine categories, generically rather than chronologically, the collection opens with elegies and dramatic lyrics, moves on to "Beowulf," and closes with historical battle poems. The translator remarks, "It has been my endeavor to translate selections into a modern verse faithful to the Old English text, and, as far as linguistic changes permit, suggestive of the alliterative rhythms of the Anglo-Saxon originals." As these poems were all in the oral tradition or in written form before the Norman Conquest they are, literally, in a foreign language. Just how much so is spelled out nicely in the brief, yet scholarly and well-written, introduction. Anyone not familiar with the verse should begin here and then move gradually into the collection. One may take exception to some of the translations, particularly the famous poem

"The Wanderer," but in other sections, most evidently "Beowulf," the translation is exceptional. As the translator points out, "In this body of Old English poetry much is excellent; a part is timeless." As such, this is a special collection that should be treasured by anyone who loves poetry.

English Verse, 1300–1500. *John Burrow, ed.*

See under POETRY: STUDY AND TEACHING

Medieval English Lyrics; a Critical Anthology. *R. T. Davies, ed.* (1964) **Northwestern University Press. 384p., o.p.**

Beginning in the mid-12th century and ending with Thomas Wyatt's "What I Once Was" in the early sixteenth century, here are nearly two hundred poems that reflect thought, aesthetics, politics, and, in general, the history of medieval times. The compiler has chosen to reprint the verses in modernized spelling and punctuation. Also, he has supplied each poem with a title of his own invention. This, he notes, "will probably offend everybody," but there is no need for an apology. The spirit of the sometimes fugitive verse is captured, and where there is need for additional explanation, it is appropriately given in footnotes. There are also notes near the end of the work. The introduction gives a full account of how the poems were translated, changed, and otherwise edited. Despite the care given to spelling changes, reading these poems may be difficult for anyone but the student or dedicated layperson, particularly in the earliest works. At the same time, the verse is so delightful, so expressive of what for many is a black hole in the history of poetry, that it is well worth the effort.

Middle English Lyrics; Authoritative Texts, Critical and Historical Backgrounds, Perspectives on Six Poems. *Maxwell S. Luria and Richard L. Hoffman, eds.* (1974) **W. W. Norton. 360p., pap.**

This intricate, fascinating anthology mixes Middle English lyrics and criticism. The critical essays and analysis may even be too technical at times for any but the specialized reader. Here are hundreds of lyrics, mostly less well known, often anonymous, but also some by Chaucer and Lydgate. The poems are grouped loosely by such themes as "I Sing a Maiden" and "A God and Yet a Man?" Subsequent text contains critical essays that fully discuss the poems and deal with such topics as theme and historical context. This is a scholarly anthology for those seriously interested in Middle English lyrics. Indexed by first line.

The Oxford Book of Late Medieval Verse and Prose. *Douglas Gray, ed.* **(1985) Clarendon Press. 586p.**

There are twenty sections in this volume, beginning with a combination of prose and poetry drawn from early chronicles. These offer glimpses of life at the end of the fifteenth and start of the sixteenth century. Next come representative letters, and from then on there is a counterpoint of prose and poetry by an individual author (John Lydgate to John Skelton) and subject sections that include both forms. The concluding hundred or so pages include extensive commentaries, a glossary, and the standard indexes. There are many kinds of writing, many opinions, many styles, and many skills. It is hardly a work to encourage browsing by laypersons, but those who are curious, along with scholars and students, will find much here to enliven the time and impart a sense of what it meant to move from the medieval period to the "modern" stage.

The Oxford Book of Medieval English Verse. *Celia Sisam and Kenneth Sisam, eds.* **(1970) Oxford University Press. 617p., o.p.**

In their brief preface the editors write that they "have tried to show the range of interest offered by medieval verse rather than to select for poetic quality alone." They go on to explain that more space has been given to secular verse because of the diversity existing in secular poems, and they have included a collection of proverbs and song fragments popular between the twelfth and sixteenth centuries. Only twenty poets are featured here (Chaucer may be the only one most readers will recognize), arranged chronologically, with dozens of their short poems, ballads, and longer epic pieces. The anthology has a clear first-line index. The Sisams' informative introduction will make this a compelling volume.

ENGLISH POETRY
1500–1700 — Early Modern English

The Anchor Anthology of Seventeenth Century Verse. Vols. I–II. *Louis L. Martz, ed. Vol. I; Richard S. Sylvester, ed. Vol. II.* **(1969) Doubleday; Vol. I reissued 1973 by W. W. Norton as English Seventeenth-Century Verse, Vol. I. 525p., 684p., o.p.**

These two large, commendable volumes present the major and minor seventeenth-century English poets, as well as extensive critical information about the literary history of that century. The first volume features nine poets, from Robert Southwell and John Donne to Henry Vaughan. The long introduction chiefly analyzes the metaphysical and meditative genres that were popular during the early years of the century. The second volume features twenty poets, from Ben Jonson and Michael Drayton to Dryden, Suckling, and Herrick. The introduction to the second volume contrasts the themes and structure of the early and later seventeenth-century poetry. Both volumes are arranged chronologically by author, well-indexed, and both are inclusive, thorough, and solid, treating each poet and his work with great reverence. Recommended for students and general readers, these volumes are among the best that cover the major English poets of the seventeenth century, as well as more obscure writers who are often not included in broader poetry surveys.

The Anchor Anthology of Sixteenth Century Verse. *Richard S. Sylvester, ed.* **(1974) Doubleday/Anchor Books; also published 1984 by W. W. Norton as English Sixteenth-Century Verse. 623p.**

Designed for students but useful for all readers, this thorough collection comprises almost two hundred poems by nineteen English poets of the sixteenth century. All the poems are presented in their original spellings and punctuation, culled by the editor from first editions. Beginning with John Skelton and arranged chronologically, the collection includes such major British poets as Edmund Spenser and Christopher Marlowe as well as some, including Sir Thomas Wyatt, George Gascoigne, and Thomas Campion, who are less frequently anthologized . At the back of the volume, a long section features the work of eight sonneteers who wrote toward the end of the century. Sylvester includes a well-written introduction to complement the verse, providing historical background and analyzing the metrical development of sixteenth-century poetry. Most interesting, however, is his condemnation of those critics who describe the poetry of this century as of an "empty stage." Sylvester successfully provides the greatest selection of verse for those poets who were most prominent then, offering an anthology that serves both as a broad overview and as an in-depth study.

Ben Jonson and the Cavalier Poets. *Hugh Maclean, ed.* **(1974) W. W. Norton. 591p., pap.**

One of the aims of this volume of seventeenth-century English verse is to make available to modern readers a large canon of poetry that has not received the critical attention it is due. Although history may not always remember these "minor" poets, this anthology does an excellent job of reintroducing them to general audiences. Most general readers will be familiar with Jonson, but sixteen other major poets of the time are also featured, including Richard Lovelace, Henry Vaughan, and Thomas Carew. They are represented by hundreds of selections, including mock epics, satirical verse, and love poems. Interestingly, several poems are addressed to Jonson, revealing the influence he had over writers of the time. Determining whether these poems are undervalued by literary historians is the reader's job, but it must be said that they are worth exploring. This volume provides a solid overview, but of paramount importance are the almost 200 pages of critical evaluation by poets who include Jonson, William Hazlitt, and T. S. Eliot. These critical essays will be fascinating to those already familiar with the Cavalier poets, but those who are not acquainted with these overshadowed artists will find the entire volume a worthy, lucid introduction.

The Cavalier Poets. *Robin Skelton, ed.* **(1970) Oxford University Press. 291p., o.p.**

The Cavalier poets, according to Skelton's complex introduction, are those "minor" poets who flourished under the reign of Charles I and Charles II and were concerned with the conflict between social pleasures and an "impulse toward solitude." More specifically, they are mostly lesser-known poets writing between 1625 and 1689 (popularly regarded as "amateur entertainers") because they lived after the Renaissance and before the Jacobean period; here is a clear picture of the poetry of the period, perceived against a background of the historical events of that

turbulent century. According to Skelton, the most widely known poets of
the Cavalier years are probably Milton and Dryden, although they are
often mistakenly associated with other movements. Many of the sixty-
four poets included here are familiar, particularly Richard Lovelace,
Thomas Carew, Sir John Suckling, and Andrew Marvell. They are arranged alphabetically, and Skelton provides brief biographical information on each writer. The format is both lucid and attractive, planned for
more discriminating readers but accessible to all. On all counts this is an
excellent anthology, highly recommended for the quality of poetry and
for Skelton's sharp, analytical introduction.

Cavalier Poets: Selected Poems. *Thomas Clayton, ed.* **(1978) Oxford
University Press. 364p., pap., o.p.**

Never was a group of poets more suitably named. The Cavaliers were
the legendary lyric voices of the court of King Charles I. Before his
untimely execution, they surrounded him with some of the best verse in
the English language. Robert Herrick, for example, opens this marvelous
collection with "The Argument of His Book." He sets the stage for the
other three: Thomas Carew, John Suckling, and Richard Lovelace.
Herrick begins with the now famous lines, "I sing of brooks, of blossoms,
birds, and bowers; / Of April, May, of June, and July flowers." And
Lovelace draws the anthology to a conclusion with the end of Charles,
the end of an age, and the end of the poets: "Sir, now unravelled is the
Golden Fleece." In between is what the jacket copy for once correctly
describes as "quintessentially romantic, graceful, courtly, and sometimes
roguish verse." There is a scholarly introduction; footnotes to help explain allusions, personalities, and historical events; a chronological table;
a good bibliography; as well as a glossary and index. A work like this does
more to explain the glory and delights of poetry than almost anything
else in the English language. A must for all libraries, and for many
individual bookshelves.

Elizabethan Lyrics. *Norman Ault, ed.* **(3d ed., 1949) William Sloane
Associates; paperback ed. published 1960 by G. P. Putnam's. 560p.**

In close to six hundred and fifty poems, the editor dramatically illustrates why the Elizabethan lyric was and, to a lesser extent, remains so
popular. As they were written to be recited, sung, and thoroughly enjoyed by the populace, they are a far cry from the metaphysical and
philosophical poems of the same period. Recognizing their unique contribution to popular culture, the editor arranges them according to the

date when each poem first became known to the public. "The plan renders it possible to follow step by step the development of the lyric, and its many fashions and phases, throughout the period." What makes these verses so lovely and bewitching is their essential beauty and, quite often, their high sense of humor. Written to be sung, intoned, or spoken, they sparkle with the life of the times. Fortunately for the average reader, the editor has employed modern spelling and modern punctuation. From time to time, where the original spelling is needed for a sense of rhythm and meaning, there are explanatory notes. "Forget not yet . . ." opens the volume. It is a suitable beginning — and an end. Anyone who takes the time to read in this collection will "forget not yet."

Elizabethan Sonnets. *Maurice Evans, ed.* **(1977) J. M. Dent. 238p.**

In the first sentence of his twenty-five–page historical introduction, Maurice Evans defines the primary subject matter of the 350–400 poems in *Elizabethan Sonnets:* "the fulfillment and the frustration of passion." He then presents works by fourteen Elizabethan sonneteers, among whom are Sidney (the whole of "Astrophel and Stella"), Spenser, and Drayton; their verses are indexed by first line at the end of the anthology. Although Evans has preserved these sonnets as printed in their original sixteenth- and seventeenth-century folio editions and provided extensive scholarly footnotes at the book's end, he provides no biographical information about the poet — information that would have been helpful about the more obscure writers. The editor omits Shakespeare's work because it is easily found in other sources. The poems included here are highly readable but not especially memorable.

English Renaissance Poetry; a Collection of Shorter Poems from Skelton to Jonson. *John Williams, ed.* **(2d ed., 1990) University of Arkansas Press. 416p.**

This anthology of English Renaissance poets — one of the many reflecting a new interest in the lesser-known poets of the time — concentrates on the short-poem form popular during these years. Shakespeare, Donne, and Jonson are here, as well as twenty-one other distinguished poets. There are generous selections for each, with separate prefaces and biographical information preceding each author. Arranged chronologically by poet and indexed by title and first line, this is a measured, thorough look at one of the most profound eras of English poetry. The editor's illustration of the genius and diversity of the age is excellent. Rather than shrug off the poetry as "metaphysical" or treat the lesser-known poets as appendixes to the age of Shakespeare, the editor includes some first-rate critical information on the era and treats each poet with equal care. Highly recommended for students and those readers interested in the poets of this age.

English Satiric Poetry: Dryden to Byron. *James Kinsley and James T. Boulton, eds.* **(1966) University of South Carolina Press; first published in Great Britain by Edward Arnold Publishers (1966). 208p., o.p.**

While *English Satiric Poetry* is, in many ways, a helpful text, it has definite deficiencies. It begins with a learned introduction that supplies readers with a history of satire during the period covered (c.1690–1810). The editors state that English satirical poetry of this period "not only vitalised many literary genres but became in itself a major kind of poetry." The body of the book proceeds, in chronological order, from Dryden's "MacFlecknoe" to Byron's "The Vision of Judgment," and includes such poets as Burns, Goldsmith, and Johnson. A paragraph about author and work precedes each entry. Although one can get a sense of eighteenth-century satire by reading the eighteen examples here printed, the editors could have made their collection more valuable by including more than one poem by each poet. Also, the anthology may be difficult to use because authors' names are not printed at the top of each page and there is no index.

George Herbert and the Seventeenth-Century Religious Poets. *Mario Di Cesare, ed.* **(1978) W. W. Norton. 401p., pap.**

This careful anthology is divided into two main parts: one contains the verse of five distinguished poets and the other offers twenty-six critical essays on those five poets by well-known writers and noted modern critics. Herbert, Marvell, Crashaw, Vaughan, and Thomas Traherne are featured, each represented by several selections and with extensive notes on the verse. All of the verse selections are religious in theme and intricate in form and style. The essays are well written and fascinating, particularly those of T. S. Eliot and Aldous Huxley on George Herbert, as are Coleridge's letters on Herbert. The editor successfully outlines Herbert's importance as a religious poet (eschewing the commonly used term *metaphysical poet*) and his influence on three centuries of literature in English. This is a thorough, scholarly volume intended for readers interested in critical interpretation. Brief biographical information precedes each poet's work.

Jacobean and Caroline Poetry; an Anthology. *T. G. S. Cain, ed.* (1981) **Methuen. 334p.**

The poetry of 1600–1660 is the subject of many college courses, and "the primary aim of this anthology is to offer an annotated selection substantial enough for it to be used as the only primary text in a course on early seventeenth-century poetry." Arrangement is chronological, and the first of two parts consists of substantial selections from ten leading poets of the period, including Michael Drayton, John Donne, Andrew Marvell, and Henry Vaughan. The second shorter section covers minor poets, although the compiler insists this is really "a miscellany in which poems have been chosen either for intrinsic merit or in a very few cases for the light they shed on intellectual attitudes of the period." For the student, each of the major poets is introduced by a one-page essay, but there are no essays for the second part; such notes as there are focus primarily on the ten poets. Recommendations for further reading and an index of first lines concludes the volume.

Kissing the Rod; an Anthology of Seventeenth-Century Women's Verse. *Germaine Greer, Susan Hastings, Jeslyn Medoff, and Melinda Sansone, eds.*

See under WOMEN'S POETRY AND FEMINIST POETRY

Metaphysical Lyrics & Poems of the Seventeenth Century: Donne to Butler. *Herbert J. Grierson, ed.* (1921) **Oxford University Press. 302p., o.p.**

This is a close second to Hugh Kenner's collection entitled *Seventeenth Century Poetry: The Schools of Donne and Jonson.* It suffers from being somewhat outdated. Published in 1921, it lacks the benefits of later scholarship. The number of choices is not so great, and the arrangement by three broad subject headings, rather than by poets, is awkward. It also lacks an author index. In spite of that, the volume has positive features. First and foremost, compared to Kenner and others, the introduction is more informative and certainly more graciously written. The notes, too, are fuller and respond to the shortcomings of some readers' historical knowledge. And while there are fewer poems than in Kenner, they are more representative and are ones likely to have meaning for the average student or reader. Finally, but not least significant, the format, and particularly the typeface, beautifully suit the subject.

The Metaphysical Poets. *Helen Gardner, ed.* **(1957) Penguin Books; reprinted by Oxford University Press, 1961. 310p.**

Kenner, Grierson, Gardner, and Willy — all, with certain authorial inclusions and exclusions, edited versions of the metaphysical poets. Gardner differs from the other compilers in that she moves beyond the usually accepted seventeenth-century time limit to include such previous and subsequent poets as Milton and Sir Walter Ralegh. In her biographical notes she carefully explains why these others qualify as metaphysical poets outside the seventeenth century. With occasional modifications, the original spelling is maintained. There are too few explanatory footnotes and only a selective reading list. The felicitous introduction is not as far reaching as Grierson's, but in terms of clarity and definitions it is an improvement over her other rivals. Except for the broader scope, the selection pretty well follows the standard choices found in the other works.

The Metaphysical Poets. *Margaret Willy* **(1971) University of South Carolina Press; first published in Great Britain by Edward Arnold Publishers. 149p., o.p.**

Willy explains that this anthology stems from a renewal of interest in the metaphysical poets; she associates the intellectual and social revolutions of Renaissance Europe with the changes occurring in America during the first seventy years of the twentieth century. Willy has divided the book into "Poems of Love and Death" and "Divine Poems." Included are such great metaphysical poets as Donne ("The Canonization"), Herbert ("The Collar"), and Marvell ("To His Coy Mistress") but only single works by such minor poets as Walter Ralegh or William Davenant to give a sense of their artistic accomplishment. The editor provides a biographical and analytical paragraph for each poet and in some cases discusses individual poems. Writers are arranged chronologically within each section; the book has no index.

The New Oxford Book of Seventeenth Century Verse. *Alistair Fowler, ed.* **(1991) Oxford University Press. 831p.**

It must have been agonizing to pick the selections to represent one of the greatest periods of English-speaking literary history. But the quality and depth of verse printed here is exceptional; most are classics, but some lesser-known pieces by Donne, Herrick, Jonson, and other religious poets are also included. In total, 197 poets are generously represented. The volume is arranged chronologically by author, beginning with Michael Drayton and ending with Pope. Unlike other poetry surveys of the same era, this collection offers many female writers and some colonial American poets, few of whom are usually anthologized with their contemporary English male counterparts. Several varieties of style and form are noted, from sonnets to songs to epigrams. Highly recommended for its breadth, variety, and accessible arrangement, this anthology is an excellent choice particularly for students. The editor wants to be sure readers understand that the seventeenth century was not just a time of the Metaphysical poets and of Jonsonian followers.

The New Oxford Book of Sixteenth Century Verse. *Emrys Jones, ed.* (1991) Oxford University Press. 769p.

Solid and comprehensive, this Oxford anthology aims to show that the sixteenth-century literary tradition is richer and more diverse than historians usually maintain. Eighty-three distinguished and lesser-known poets, from Skelton to the early Ben Jonson, are represented by over five hundred poems. Some excerpts from Shakespearean drama are also included, as well as epigrams, satire, religious verse, and classical translations. The anthology is arranged chronologically by poet, the amount of poetry almost overwhelming and with the selections representing Spenser and Shakespeare alone enough to fill an entire volume. But its size and breadth serve the reader well. A fine introduction explains that "sixteenth century verse is much more untidy" than previously noted. Any reader of this highly recommended volume will see that the Elizabethan age is far more than love poems and lyrics. Indexed by author and first line.

The Oxford Book of Seventeenth Century Verse. *H. J. C. Grierson and G. Bullough, eds.* (1934) Oxford University Press. 974p., o.p.

This heavy volume pays homage to the masters of seventeenth-century English verse. John Donne is accorded sixty pages or so, Ben Jonson and Robert Herrick over thirty pages each, Dryden fifty pages, and Milton a whopping one hundred. Interspersed among these great writers are scores of lesser ones. So readers can steep themselves in the work of the masters, as well as acquaint themselves with such other fine writers of the period as Andrew Marvell. It is interesting to see their work alongside that of the dominating figures of the age. The selections tend to be of the highest order. There are hundreds of short, lyric poems, as well as extended extracts from such long works as Milton's "Paradise Lost." In general, this anthology is an excellent introduction to this exciting, passionate age.

The Oxford Book of Sixteenth Century Verse. *E. K. Chambers, comp.* **(1932) Oxford University Press. 905p., o.p.**

With the end of medieval poetry and the beginning of the sixteenth century, who is on the doorstep waiting for the new age? "The Nutbrown Maid," of course, and she suitably begins this standard anthology. After a few more ballads, one is introduced to John Skelton, "the only authentic voice that comes to us from the first quarter of the sixteenth century." Authentic or not (the point is controversial), until the Elizabethan age much verse was written, to be charitable, by "minor" poets who were little more than court hangers-on in quest of patronage. Reading the short, informative introduction, one sees why Elizabethan poetry is so popular, even today. It is "characteristically light hearted," and shows a "thorough going zest in earthy things." There was a sober side to it as well, and room, too, for the disillusionment of Greville and "the quietism of Dyer." Within the nine hundred pages is a glutton's sampling of all sides of the sixteenth century. Note that the spelling, capitalization, and punctuation are modernized.

Seventeenth Century Poetry: The Schools of Donne and Jonson. *Hugh Kenner, ed.* **(1964) Holt, Rinehart and Winston. 460p., o.p.**

Traditionalists seem particularly fond of the age of Donne and Jonson, and the distinguished editor is no exception. It is the age of gossip and metaphysics, two related aspects of the human spirit. "For more generally," Kenner explains, "it was a time of great active intelligence, intelligence working its way down into the very capillaries of a poem; and it ended when, by the time of the Restoration, the nature of the intellective process itself had been revalued." Opening with a generous sampling of Donne (1572–1631), Kenner moves on to the Donne circle, i.e., Lord Herbert of Cherbury, Aurelian Townshend, Richard Corbett, and Henry King. Then come the one whom he dubs "the divine poet," George Herbert (1593–1633), and his successors, Richard Crashaw, Henry Vaughan, and Thomas Traherne. Then Cavalier poets take center stage with Robert Herrick and Thomas Carew. The collection ends with the Restoration of Charles II and the poetry of Andrew Marvell. Since this is primarily a student's anthology, the editor chooses to retain original spellings, and while there are some footnotes, there are really not enough to clarify the more obscure poems for the modern reader. Each poet has the usual biographical/historical introduction. The selection is generally good, if traditional. This works nicely for most of the poets, but not for all, particularly Richard Lovelace. (See *Cavalier Poets; Selected Poems* for better choices in this period.)

Seventeenth-Century Verse and Prose. Vol. I: 1600–1660; Vol. II: 1660–1700. *Helen C. White, Ruth C. Wallerstein, and Ricardo Quintana, eds.* (1951, 1952) Macmillan. 498p., 472p., o.p.

Dividing the seventeenth century between Charles I and Cromwell in Vol. I and the Restoration into the Stuart reign in Vol. II, the authors follow traditional lines. There are several unusual points. First, the scope is much broader than general collections of this type, particularly since a good half is prose. Second, the scholarly introductions that open each volume and precede the different sections are written with the student and layperson in mind. They make a difficult period, a group of some-times abstruse writers, easier to appreciate. Third, the choices for each of the authors is more extensive than usually found in similar compilations. And then there are the usual aids from an index of authors and an index of titles and first lines. Note, too, the useful bibliography in each of the volumes. Although the work is intended for college courses, it is an ideal reference work for medium to large libraries and a fine introduction to the seventeenth century for both beginner and expert.

Silver Poets of the Sixteenth Century. *Gerald Bullett, ed.* (1947) J. M. Dent. 428p.

The Everyman Library editions are famous for bringing prose and poetry to the ubiquitous everyman at a reasonable price. While the list is not growing as quickly as it did in earlier years, and while the cost of a volume has gone up dramatically, the present work is an excellent illus-tration of the series — as well, of course, as being a fine collection of sixteenth-century poetry. The editor sets the stage: "The word silver in the title of this volume, where minor might perhaps have been expected . . . marks the critical survey of English poetry." Wyatt, Sidney, Ralegh, Davies, the Earl of Surrey are represented with three subject areas each, and there are the usual glossary, index to first lines, and background material on Elizabethan thought and publishing. (Best of all, in this day of giant volumes, the slim work fits nicely into the hand, if not always the small pocket). Typically, one finds for Wyatt sonnets, translation from Petrarch, songs, and satires. The drawback is the complete absence of notes. The uninformed may be at sea, literally, when it comes to appreciating the imagery and figures in Ralegh's "The Ocean's Love to Cynthia."

Tudor Verse Satire. *K. W. Gransden, ed.* (1970) Athlone Press. 182p., o.p.

The thirty-five satirical verses in this book are wry and acute, poking intelligent fun at human weaknesses and pretensions. K. W. Gransden includes Spenser, Donne, and Jonson, along with several lesser-known satirists of the English Renaissance. Jonson's "To Penshurst" exploits the resemblance between a mansion and its residents. Spenser's "Mother Hubbard's Tale" retells an old fable, using such animals as foxes, mules, and lambs to symbolize human traits. Poems are arranged chronologically by poet. Gransden provides ample scholarly notes and a twenty-nine–page historical and analytical introduction. The book lacks an index, but its select number of poets and poems may make indexing unnecessary.

ENGLISH POETRY
18th Century

Eighteenth-Century English Verse. *Dennis Davison, ed.* **(1988) Penguin Books. 321p., pap., o.p.**

This intelligent collection is a strong text for beginners, filled with the classics of the century, with a fascinating introduction to put the verse in a historical and literary context. The poetry is grouped into such broad subjects as love, work, and nature. Most of the 163 poems are by lesser-known poets, although Pope, Blake, Cowper, and Swift are well represented. These and the more obscure selections easily acquaint readers with the odes, hymns, narratives, and satires of the eighteenth century. In his introduction, Davison explains how the shift from religious to rational thought altered the course of history and how that shift changed the tone and theme of poetry. Most of the selections are complete, although longer works, such as "The Rape of the Lock," are excerpted. Modern readers will be interested in the great variety of verse here, much of it about mundane events or situations, chronicled in serious and careful detail, some of it witty observations of human nature. Biographical information is included, and the anthology is indexed by author and title.

Eighteenth Century Women Poets; an Oxford Anthology. *Roger Lonsdale, ed.*

See under WOMEN'S POETRY AND FEMINIST POETRY

English Poetry, 1700–1780; Contemporaries of Swift and Johnson. *David W. Lindsay, ed.* **(1974) Rowman and Littlefield. 239p., o.p.**

David W. Lindsay's anthology is a sound, scholarly reference work. The editor's introduction incorporates almost all of the twenty-one included poets in an interpretative history of English poetry from 1700 to 1780. The well-designed text presents authors in chronological order. Particularly helpful are the biographies and notes at the book's end, as well as an index of first lines. Lindsay's introduction does not, however, discuss thoroughly the relation or influence of Swift and Johnson to these authors. The book would greatly benefit from the inclusion of more than one major poem by each of the featured poets.

English Satiric Poetry: Dryden to Byron. *James Kinsley and James T. Boulton, eds.*

See under ENGLISH POETRY: 1500–1700 — EARLY MODERN ENGLISH

Late Augustan Poetry. *Patricia Meyer Spacks, ed.* **(1973) Prentice-Hall. 678p., o.p.**

This is a comprehensive collection of eighteen Augustan poets, focusing in the early and final sections on more obscure writers and in the middle section on such well-known poets as Christopher Smart, Oliver Goldsmith, and William Cowper. Most of the poets have several selections, with each poet preceded by biographical information and criticism. The editor characterizes their work as much more ambitious in theme and form than that of earlier poets, as the achievements of the Augustans themselves are often overshadowed by those of the Romantics who followed them. She considers the best of them "madmen" — an interesting description. With beautiful sonnets, odes, hymns, and elegies not always found in other collections, and with fine critical introductions, this is a highly recommended volume.

The Late Augustans; Longer Poems of the Later Eighteenth Century. *Donald Davie, ed.* **(1958) Heinemann. 130p., o.p.**

The nine poems that constitute this slender collection are among the most compelling and accomplished of the eighteenth century. The Augustan period in English literature, according to Davie, has long been regarded as a time of "complacency" by literary historians; Davie has selected these poems to show that the strength of the Augustan poets has been underestimated. Among the selections are Samuel Johnson's "Vanity of Human Wishes," Thomas Gray's "Elegy Written in a Country Churchyard," and William Wordsworth's "The Old Cumberland Beggar." Christopher Smart, Oliver Goldsmith, and William Cowper are also represented. The poems are often long and are structurally fascinating. In a separate section Davie has included helpful notes on poem and poet, explicating references and words that may trouble contemporary readers. His long, thorough introduction is a compelling historical commentary. These are complex poems, not all for every reader, but they are an excellent introduction for those interested in the poetry of a very special period in English literary history.

Major British Poets of the Romantic Period. *William Heath, ed.* (1973) Macmillan. 1140p.

William Heath's standard textbook presents a comprehensive overview of the Romantic movement in English poetry by gathering together 542 major works of Blake, Wordsworth, Coleridge, Shelley, Keats, and Byron. In a brief introduction, Heath discusses the Romantic movement in its historical and artistic context, stating that the Romantics' efforts were "directed towards reconciling their sense of what the world might become if the energy of human potential were realized according to their hopes and visions, with the awareness that the meaning and value of this energy seemed to be changing. . . ." Each poet has his own historical and analytical introduction, which includes a select bibliography and an outline of important events in the artist's life; the editor has also placed explanatory paragraphs before some poems. Terms and place names are identified in footnotes, and poems are indexed by title and first line. This anthology also includes such important prose works as Shelley's "Defense of Poetry," Coleridge's "Biographia Literaria," and the correspondence between Keats and Byron.

The New Oxford Book of Eighteenth Century Verse. *Roger Lonsdale, ed.* (1984) Oxford University Press. 870p.

The beauty of this collection lies in its wide-netted culling of all sorts of poetry from the eighteenth century. While such great and well-known poets as Pope, Blake, Burns, and Thomas Gray are given ample space, dozens of less well-known poets are also included. Among these, several are women whose way into anthologies was all too often firmly blocked. So, many discoveries await the reader. One, surely, is the wide-ranging subject matter of the verse. Another, since the voices here are so diverse, is a clear sense of exactly what life and writing in the eighteenth century were really like. In his learned introduction, Roger Lonsdale contrasts the stated ideals of eighteenth century poetic verse — "lucidity, elegance, refinement" — with the broader sense of the period's fuller, more varied artistic output.

The Oxford Book of Eighteenth Century Verse. *David Nichol Smith, ed.*
(1926) Oxford University Press. 727p., o.p.

This is an anthology of the most distinguished poets of eighteenth-
century Britain, comprising hundreds of well-known and lesser-known
poems. Opening with Daniel Defoe and Jonathan Swift, the volume includes Pope, Wordsworth, Robert Southey, and well over a hundred
other poets. The selections are characteristic of the poets' style and subject. Nichol Smith has arranged a competent overview that encompasses
the variety of poetic traditions that spanned the century, from Swift's
satire to Coleridge's satirical ballads. Poets are presented chronologically
by the date of their most important work. There are no surprises in this
anthology — no critical analysis of the eighteenth century as a whole, no
claim to being the exclusive authority on its variety of styles and subjects.
Today's critical appreciation and personal choices might dictate a different configuration of eighteenth-century poetry, but this splendid collection offers almost five hundred brilliant, time-honored poems for both
students and more general readers. Indexed by poet and first line.

The Oxford Book of Regency Verse 1798–1837. *H. S. Milford, ed.*

See under   English and American Poetry: Comprehensive Collections

ENGLISH POETRY
19th Century

British Poetry, 1880–1920; Edwardian Voices. *Paul L. Wiley and Harold Orel, eds.* (1969) Appleton-Century-Crofts. 681p., o.p.

This heavy volume concentrates on a specific moment in British poetry; it begins with the end of the Victorian era (and includes Thomas Hardy and A. E. Housman), and it ends at the conclusion of the First World War. Authors of Hardy's caliber are accorded almost thirty pages, and readers can get a fine sense of their achievements in verse. In the second section, "The Decadent Movement," there are poems by Oscar Wilde, Arthur Symons, Ernest Dowson, and William Henley, none of them among the great writers of English verse. Robert Louis Stevenson and Rudyard Kipling are featured. This more or less indicates the arrangement of the rest of the book: several mediocre voices along with fine poets. Among the other excellent writers who are given considerable space are Gerard Manley Hopkins, W. B. Yeats, Rupert Brooke, D. H. Lawrence, Sigfried Sassoon, and Wilfred Owen. The great poets' treatment of the First World War makes for memorable verse.

A Choice of English Romantic Poetry. *Stephen Spender, ed.* (1947) Dial Press. 384p.

Often called a romantic poet himself, Stephen Spender is in a splendid position to choose from the best of the English romantics. And he does. His choices are limited to a few familiar major figures — Blake, Wordsworth, Samuel Taylor Coleridge, Byron, Shelley, Keats, Tennyson, and Emily Brontë — with brief sections on minor figures. None of these was exclusively a romantic poet, and Spender's contribution is to guide the reader from one poem to another within the boundaries of the romantic landscape. He makes the point, too, that there is a great difference between the romanticism of the early nineteenth century and of other periods. "The Romantics," he explains, "emphasize one aspect of imagination: inventive fantasy. They lack the imaginative power that has a firm grasp of objectivity and of systems of thought." Spender is correct in saying some readers may be upset at his choosing segments of long poems, although the passages are complete in themselves. At the same time he has selected what he terms the "best plums" of romantic poetry.

The Dark Tower; Nineteenth Century Narrative Poems. *Dairine Coffey, ed.* **(1967) Atheneum. 169p., o.p.**

There are fourteen narrative poems in this vibrant anthology, and each tells a story, with the romance of elopement in Keats's "Eve of St. Agnes," love and murder in Hardy's "The Sacrilege," and Shelley's mythological tale "Arethusa" among the most chilling. The tales are dramatic, diverse, and evocative, culled from a time, according to the editor, when poetry was often read as prose. Long works by Byron, Matthew Arnold, Christina Rossetti, Robert Browning, Elizabeth Browning, and Oscar Wilde are also featured. Arranged chronologically by poet, each poem is treated as a chapter in itself, giving readers the sense that these are poems to be read slowly and thoroughly, as one might read a fully developed novel or short story. There are brief notes by the editor on the verse.

English Romantic Poetry and Prose. *Russell Noyes, ed.* **(1956) Oxford University Press. 1,324p.**

A huge, comprehensive volume, this, in the words of its editor, is "useful for the selections of fifty-four representative English Romantic writers." The reader is also supplied with a helpful introductory essay devoted to major aspects of English romanticism, including its historical and literary roots, its overriding emotional postures, and its concomitant philosophies. The anthology begins with writers from the early eighteenth century and includes Thomas Gray, William Cowper, Burns, Blake, Wordsworth, Samuel Taylor Coleridge, Byron, Shelley, and Keats. There are extensive selections from these greatest exponents of English romanticism. Anyone interested in this celebrated movement could not hope for a more helpful, generous, sampling of its intense, lyrical poetry. This volume presents its finest achievements.

English Satiric Poetry: Dryden to Byron. *James Kinsley and James T. Boulton, eds.*

See under ENGLISH POETRY: 1500–1700 — EARLY MODERN ENGLISH

English Verse, 1830–1890. *Bernard Richards, ed.*

See under   Poetry: Study and Teaching

The Everyman Book of Victorian Verse; the Post-Romantics. *Donald Thomas, ed.* **(1992) J. M. Dent. 284p., pap.**

No one will question that these forty-five poems belong in an anthology of Victorian poetry. Among the masterpieces Donald Thomas has chosen are Arnold's "Dover Beach," Tennyson's "Locksley Hall," and an excerpt from Browning's "Sordello" — no chaff here. Most of the selections come from these three authors; four by Clough and three by Swinburne round out the collection, which is striking in its exclusivity. Arguments could be made for including more Swinburne (where are "Ave atque Vale" and "Tristram of Lyonesse"?) or some Christina Rossetti, but then it would be a different, less concentrated anthology. The ample introduction provides an overview of the Victorian period in literature and its relationship to the Romantic movement that preceded it, and each of the major poets is discussed in some depth. Poems are arranged in five sections, by author. Thomas introduces each poem with a note, in some cases a full page or more, in which he epitomizes the work, points out literary allusions, or places it in a historical context. He includes more than seven pages of bibliography but no index, although the selections are few enough that the table of contents should suffice.

Everyman's Book of Victorian Verse. *J. R. Watson, ed.* **(1982) J. M. Dent. 373p.**

The subject of verse written during the reign of Queen Victoria is divided here into Early Victorian (1837–1851), Mid-Victorian (1851–1867), High Victorian (1867–1885), and Fin de Siècle (1885–1901). This arrangement allows the reader to see how the Victorian style developed and finally drew to a close. The editor has selected what he found to be the most interesting and timeless poems written in this era, and he has included work by little-known poets as well as by the famous ones. The editor, a scholar of the Victorian age, wishes to reawaken the public's appreciation for Victorian verse, and in this anthology, he goes a long way to doing so. There are many discoveries to be made: Anne Brontë's lovely, lyrical poems, along with those of her sister Emily; Robert Browning's considerable achievements in narrative verse; Tennyson's poems; and later the works of Gerard Manley Hopkins and Thomas

Hardy. There are scores of lesser-known poets whose moving work should also absorb the reader.

Major British Poets of the Romantic Period. *William Heath, ed.*

See under ENGLISH POETRY: 18TH CENTURY

The New Oxford Book of Victorian Verse. *Christopher Ricks, ed.* **(1987) Oxford University Press. 654p.**

Christopher Ricks, the eminent critic, explores in his introduction the meaning the connotations of the word "Victorian." He traces its image of flawed creativity to the early deaths of the three great writers of the second generation of Romantic poets, Byron, Shelley, and Keats. The Victorians, nevertheless, had their own literary geniuses, and Ricks presents them in all their glory, awarding Tennyson and Robert Browning over forty pages each, and selecting many poems by Emily Brontë, William Barnes, and Elizabeth Barrett Browning. Other poets given considerable compass are Christina Rossetti, Gerard Manley Hopkins, Lewis Carroll, Rudyard Kipling, and Thomas Hardy. Lesser-known poets are included along with these authors, although they are given less space. In general, this anthology provides a broad, accurate, and absorbing picture of the precise accomplishments and limitations of the often-maligned Victorian poets. And it offers readers several entire, long masterpieces: Christina Rossetti's "Goblin Market," Lewis Carroll's "The Hunting of the Snark," and Edward Fitzgerald's "Rubaiyat of Omar Khayyam."

19th Century British Minor Poets. *W. H. Auden, ed.* **(1966) Delacorte Press. 383p., o.p.**

Designated "minor" poets by Auden, many of the esteemed writers in this fine, handsome volume have more than earned distinction in the nineteenth-century poetic hierarchy — Sir Walter Scott, Edward Lear, Dante Gabriel Rossetti, Elizabeth Barrett Browning, and A. E. Housman, to name a few. Most, of course, will be relatively unknown to general American readers. Arranged chronologically, each poet is generously represented. Auden has chosen a wide range of styles, themes, and forms for this anthology, many exemplified by the light or comic verse so often ignored by literary critics. There is an introduction and brief biographical information on the poets, and Auden also has included several timelines detailing historic developments of the century in science, politics, and literature.

One Hundred and One Classics of Victorian Verse. *Ellen J. Greenfield, ed.* (1992) Contemporary Books. 187p.

This slender anthology is recommended for any Victorian poetry enthusiast who wants a very general collection of favorites. All of the great poets are here: Robert Browning, Elizabeth Barrett Browning, Tennyson, Yeats, and Arnold, among others. They are represented by 101 of their best-known poems, all arranged attractively in this compact volume. Here are sensitive and tender poems from one of the most accomplished ages of poetry; they exemplify "visual elegance," as the editor explains in her introduction. She also offers some interesting background information on this era — enough to convey a sense of its historical and aesthetic legacy. There is biographical information on the poets, but the poems are not indexed.

The Oxford Book of Nineteenth-Century English Verse. *John Hayward, ed.* (1964; reprinted, with corrections, 1965) Oxford University Press. 970p., o.p.

Among these six hundred poems by more than eighty-five poets who lived and wrote in the nineteenth century can be found many of the masterpieces of English Romantic verse. Here, all the writers are in fact British, and all the great ones are in evidence: Blake, Wordsworth, Samuel Taylor Coleridge, Byron, Shelley, and Keats. Later writers include Tennyson and Robert Browning, as well as Christina Rossetti and Thomas Hardy. All of these major authors are accorded a great deal of space, some more than fifty pages in which to demonstrate their talent and their range. The editor has chosen wisely among the vast number of poems of each writer, and this volume is a pleasure to read for anyone with a taste for English Romantic poetry. There are excerpts from such long works as Byron's "Childe Harold's Pilgrimage" and Wordsworth's "The Prelude," all of "The Hunting of the Snark," by Lewis Carroll, and "The Rime of the Ancient Mariner," by Samuel Taylor Coleridge, and hundreds of lyrical poems. Admirers of the Brontë sisters will find examples of the verse of Charlotte and Emily.

The Oxford Book of Regency Verse, 1798–1837. *H. S. Milford, ed.*

See under ENGLISH AND AMERICAN POETRY: COMPREHENSIVE COLLECTIONS

The Oxford Book of Victorian Verse. *Arthur Quiller-Couch, ed.*

See under   ENGLISH AND AMERICAN POETRY: COMPREHENSIVE COLLECTIONS

Poems of Faith and Doubt; the Victorian Age. *R. L. Brett, ed.*

See under   RELIGIOUS POETRY

The Poorhouse Fugitives; Self-Taught Poets and Poetry in Victorian Britain. *Brian Maidment, ed.* **(1987) Carcanet. 374p.**

One must have an understanding of, or at least an interest in, the development of England during the Industrial Revolution to appreciate fully this unusual collection of poems by self-taught English artisans. It is true the compiler includes extensive notes and gives background information before each of the six sections and subsections, but even with that, the reader needs to be concerned with, say, "poems of social indignation" or the city of Manchester or the ideals of the Chartists. Made even more difficult by a variety of dialects, the collection is not for the general reader. Nevertheless, the compiler is to be applauded for a truly outstanding profile of Victorian writers who may be labelled poets of humble birth, uneducated poets, industrial poets, regional poets, or even "auto-didacts." Little or none of the poetry will be recognized, because the editor has tried to avoid well-known anthology pieces and local favorites. Instead he concentrates on works that have "never been reprinted since their original publication." For example, under the heading "Chartist Lyrics" one finds five poets giving us such poems as "When the world is burning" or "The song of the low." Of particular value is the prose section with the self-explanatory title "The Difficulties of Appearing in Print."

Victorian Literature: Poetry. *Donald J. Gray and G. B. Tennyson, eds.* **(1976) Macmillan. 1,060p.**

This multi-faceted, comprehensive volume was intended to "illustrate the central canon of poetry published in Great Britain between 1830 and 1900." It is a standard survey, full of wonderful, traditional poems and lesser-known gems. The verse is in sections, each chronologically arranged by poet but some sections based as well on theme or form — sections such as religious poetry, parlour poetry, and popular "common" songs. Poetry from later (and more obscure) Wordsworth to early Hardy is featured to exhibit the variety in the poetry of the Victorian age; most of the popular poets were not churning out only long narratives and dramatic verse. This collection of lyrics, comical verse, hymns, and other poetic forms will "expand" our expectations of Victorian literature. A final, fascinating section presents essays by famous poets on their literary counterparts — for example, Robert Browning on Shelley. This is a large book, a book for students and for connoisseurs of nineteenth-century poetry, one not to be missed. Indexed by author, title, and first line, and with a first-rate introduction.

Victorian Poetry: "The City of Dreadful Night" and Other Poems. *N. P. Messenger and J. R. Watson, eds.* (1974) Rowan and Littlefield; published in Great Britain by J. M. Dent. 242p., o.p.

This anthology features only those Victorian poets often considered secondary to Tennyson, Browning, Arnold, and Hopkins, and so it is not intended for beginning students of Victorian verse. Messenger and Watson in their lengthy introduction do not defend their omission of those four poets, the quality of whose work is matched in most cases by that of the poetry found here. The editors have selected great works, including Rossetti's "Goblin Market" and parts of Elizabeth Barrett Browning's "Sonnets to the Portuguese." They arrange the 100 verses chronologically by poet and introduce each with a brief biography. There is a section of scholarly notes and an index of first lines.

Victorian Verse. *George MacBeth, ed.* (1986) Penguin Books; first published 1969 as The Penguin Book of Victorian Verse. 440p., pap.

Rather than reduce Victorian poetry to a collection of repressed or sentimental narratives, as many critics have, the editor of this anthology explains that the narrative form is actually an effective cover for poets to explore a variety of illicit topics. MacBeth's critical introduction is accomplished, but the quality and diversity of the poetry is the main attraction. More than sixty-two poets are featured here, well-known masters and several obscure writers. Usually the author's best-known poems are presented. Arranged chronologically by poet, the verse is of high quality, with the lucid, introductory arrangement making this a good text for beginning students. The selections, and MacBeth's critical introduction, clearly demonstrate that the Victorian era was a golden age in English poetry, as diverse and rich as any other period. Indexed by author and first line.

Women Romantic Poets, 1785–1832; an Anthology. *Jennifer Breen, ed.* **(1992) J. M. Dent. 182p.**

The only female Romantic writer usually studied in introductory English classes is Mary Shelley; scant attention is paid to less well-known women writers of that era. This anthology counters that by featuring twenty-six women poets who wrote the bulk of their work during the later part of the Romantic age. None of these poets will be familiar to general readers (Mary Shelley is not included in the volume). All have different degrees of skill and talent. Many of their poems deal with nature and death — familiar Romantic topics — but also with family life and lovers. The poets use a variety of forms, particularly sonnets, odes, and songs. A great many speak out against woman's lack of freedom, so it could be argued that these are very early feminist poems, forerunners of themes still commonly found in modern verse. The volume is arranged chronologically by poet. This is a fine collection of poetry, recommended as a supplementary view of the Romantic age. Indexed by author, first line, and title.

ENGLISH POETRY
20th Century

The Chatto Book of Modern Poetry, 1915-1955. *C. Day Lewis and John Lehmann, eds.* **(1966) Chatto & Windus. 288p., pap.**

This is a distinguished anthology of British verse whose early twentieth-century British writers include Hardy, Yeats, and D. H. Lawrence, as well as such lesser-known, praiseworthy poets as Helen Spalding and Norman MacCaig. The poems are arranged chronologically by author and indexed by author and first line; each poet is generously represented. Younger poets of the time are not here, and Day Lewis and Lehmann, themselves prominent poets whose work is included, have wisely limited the poetry to writers anthologized elsewhere. They have concentrated on poets who emerged in Britain during the First World War and after the Second World War — poets no longer modern, but representative of a clear departure from the form and style of their predecessors.

Here & Human; an Anthology of Contemporary Verse. *F. E. S. Finn, comp.* **(1976) John Murray. 148p., o.p.**

This anthology, compiled by F. E. S. Finn, presents samples of the work of eight leading British poets of the mid-1970's: Patricia Beer, Arthur J. Bull, D. J. Enright, Seamus Heaney, Robert Morgan, Leslie Norris, Vernon Scannell, and Anthony Thwaite. Each poet includes an introduction to his section; while some introductions provide biographical information, others resemble personal statements describing each writer's artistic vision. The book itself has neither introduction nor index; poets are arranged in alphabetical order. The anthology's poems have a variety of tones, ranging from the dramatic and intense poetry of Patricia Beer and Robert Morgan to the more meditative work of Seamus Heaney and Leslie Norris. *Here & Human* presents a solid overview of British poetry of the 1970's; one just wishes it were more extensive.

Modern British Poetry. *Louis Untermeyer, ed.* (7th rev. ed., 1962) Harcourt, Brace. 500p., o.p.

By the 1960's Louis Untermeyer had split his *Modern American & British Poetry* into two distinct volumes. As with all of his collections, here one finds a bias toward the traditional and the conservative, but always excellent, poetry. There are few, if any, of the wilder voices in English poetry, particularly those that came up after the Second World War. At the same time, the tried and true, from C. Day Lewis to W. H. Auden and Stephen Spender are given considerable space to reveal their unique talents. And there is the joy of the collection. There may not be that many poets, but their representative poems indicate their various moods, styles, and stages of development. As a result one can find almost any favorite, well-known poem by well-known British poets. In an informative preface, the compiler not only gives a bit of background on each poet, but places him or her in the history and development of the English scene. More complete information on the life of the poets is given generously before each of their sections.

The New British Poetry, 1968–88. *Gillian Allnutt, Fred D'Aguiar, Ken Edwards, and Eric Mottram, eds.* (1989) Grafton Books. 361p., pap.

This anthology is divided into four distinct sections that chronicle different categories of British poetry: black British poetry, feminist poetry, the work of young poets, and experimental-format poetry. Each of the four editors was responsible for a section, and each has penned a brief introduction to the included works. There are eighty-four poets of varying ability arranged alphabetically within each section. Some of the poets have a natural, rich voice, while others seem to use poetry primarily to send a message. The editors want to show how groundbreaking these poems are. Overall, the verse is fairly competent, the voices real and vibrant, but it is hardly "groundbreaking," as the editors hoped. Ignoring traditional forms and restraint does not necessarily mean a poet's work merits distinction. There is brief biographical information at the end of the book.

The New British Poets; an Anthology. *Kenneth Rexroth, ed.* (1949) New Directions. 312p., o.p.

Any anthology with the word "new" in its title will sooner or later no longer be new by anyone's standards. All of the poets here became prominent in Britain before 1950. Several have maintained their distinction, others have fallen into relative obscurity. Dylan Thomas, W. R. Rogers, Denise Levertov, and Vernon Watkins are still frequently anthologized, while most of the other sixty-seven poets fall into the second category — although not necessarily for lack of talent. All are highly skilled. Arranged alphabetically by author and with biographical notes, the anthology suffers, nevertheless, from the lack of an index or useful table of contents. Rexroth offers some interesting criticism, not about the poets themselves, but of the schools and labels critics assign to them. This is a strong, interesting anthology of first-rate, intricate poetry.

The Oxford Book of Twentieth-Century English Verse. *Philip Larkin, ed.* **(1973) Oxford University Press. 641p.**

Philip Larkin is widely viewed as one of the most perceptive voices in contemporary British poetry, if not indeed in the English-speaking world. His choice of English verse is, therefore, fascinating to see. He confines himself to poets who wrote and/or lived in Britain for a significant part of their careers, so there are few American writers in this very English collection of verse. Larkin first devotes a great deal of space to a poet he holds in the highest esteem, Thomas Hardy, allowing him a full twenty-five pages. Kipling, W. B. Yeats, T. S. Eliot, and W. H. Auden are also given copious space in which to demonstrate the scope of their talent. Virtually all of the other poets are given much less room, but the selection of their poems is made with great care and taste. Larkin includes only six pages of his own poems, so modest and so devoted is he to presenting a wide variety of modern voices, many of whom are less well known and many of whom are women. Over two hundred poets are introduced to the reader, all of them worth reading. A fine sense of the active, dedicated, twentieth-century English poet is resoundingly established.

Poetry with an Edge. *Neil Astley, ed.* **(1988) Bloodaxe Books. 320p.**

The fifty-six poets represented in this accomplished anthology have all had or will soon have volumes of poetry published by a British press called Bloodaxe. As of now, however, most have not yet gained the recognition they seem to deserve. Some are already well known — Martin Bell, Denise Levertov, and Brendan Kennelly. Most are young, born after the Second World War; their poems evoke the English vernacular, customs, and landscape in metered and free verse. The poems are arranged chronologically by poet, with brief biographical information and photographs of the poets included. There's a charming wit to the verse, and the poems are relatively free of political and social pleas. The sense of depth here present is uncommon in modern anthologies, and because of this depth, the collection is recommended for all readers. It is not overly esoteric, but neither is it shallow. The editor does not profess to feature the best British poetry, just a sampling of capable, skilled writers unknown to Americans.

Portraits of Poets. *Sebastian Barker, ed.* **(1986) Carcanet. 124p., pap.**

Limited to the English "senior poets of our time," i.e., born between 1897 and 1939, this is a combination of brilliant individual photo-portraits of the writers and representative, previously published poems. Possibly an important figure was missed by Barker, but he is hard to identify. Some of the longer works are excerpted, but primarily the whole poem is printed. What the reader has is a photographic album and an anthology of poetry in one book. Both the photographs and the poems are first rate. The camera work is formal, but highly imaginative. The pictures are particularly impressive because they are taken where the poet is most at home, whether that be in a study or in a locale related to a particular poem. There is as much variety in the photographs as there are attitudes among the poets. The result is a brilliant portrait gallery of many of England's leading poets.

Some Contemporary Poets of Britain and Ireland; an Anthology. *Michael Schmidt, ed.* **(1983) Carcanet. 184p.**

The editor explains that these poems resemble in form those of the literary tradition established in the Victorian age. These newer poets of Britain and Ireland exhibit fair skill and imagination, worthy of a look by interested contemporary readers. Eighteen somewhat obscure poets are here, poets whose main themes are more existentialist than personal, dealing more with man's finding his place in the world than with romantic love. The work is arranged chronologically by poet, most writing in the 1960's and 1970's and representing no one movement or school of writing — poets of talent and curiosity who write orderly and measured verse. There is a section of biographical notes.

23 Modern British Poets. *John Matthias* **(1971) Swallow Press, 338p., o.p.**

23 Modern British Poets conveys the vitality of British poetry during the 1960's and 1970's. The editors include sections of David Jones's "Anathemata"; a poem by George MacBeth called "The Twelve Hotels," which is actually a narrative of the poet's travels through Europe; and John Daniel's "Phrases for Everyday Use by the British in India," which is just that. Peter Jay writes in his critical introduction that the book "does, while steering clear of received critical opinion and remaining catholic in taste, bring out the variety of British modernist poetry." These 118 poems are forceful, and learned and sophisticated without being inaccessible. They are arranged in rough chronological order and, unfortunately, not indexed. John Matthias has enhanced the table of contents by adding biographical notes to the authors' sections. If you want poetry that handles ponderous issues — war, poverty, history — with grace and charm, this is the book to read.

A Various Art. *Andrew Crozier and Tim Longville, eds.* **(1987) Carcanet. 377p., o.p.**

Few of the seventeen contemporary English poets in this volume will be familiar to American readers. Many have gained minimal attention although they have published poetry since the 1960's. In the editors' view, the anthology represents what is "most interesting, valuable, and distinguished in the work of a generation of English poets now entering its maturity." Unfortunately the poems do not always live up to that promising claim. Some are good indeed, while others are merely experimental in form and devoid of deeper significance. Some are not even poems in the true sense, but one of the "prose poems" that have become popular in recent years. The poems are arranged chronologically by poet, but the volume concentrates on too few poets. The poems are not dated, and there are no biographical notes and no indexing.

ENGLISH AND AMERICAN POETRY
Comprehensive Collections

Ancients and Moderns; an Anthology of Poetry. *Stewart A. Baker, ed.*
(1971) Harper & Row. 352p., o.p.

This anthology should prove useful in many ways. Its thirty-five–page
introduction solidly defines such crucial terms and phrases as "poem,"
"words," "rhythm and meter," and "symbol." Present here are thirty-
eight poets, from John Donne to Denise Levertov; poets are arranged
chronologically within this well-designed volume. The works chosen are
among these poets' best; students will find here Wallace Stevens's "Idea
of Order at Key West," Coleridge's "Kubla Khan," and Donne's "Love's
Alchemy," among others. Possibly because of the limitations of space, the
editor's choice of poems by each author seems scarcely sufficient. In
addition, the anthology has no index. In general, however, *Ancients and
Moderns* should give the student of literature a good sense of each poet's
style and artistic achievement.

Beginnings in Poetry. *William J. Martz, ed.* **(1965) Scott, Foresman.
494p., pap., o.p.**

The editor intends this slender anthology to "present a view of poetry
and some handy tools of analysis in company with good poems." The
anthology is highly recommended as an introductory text for poetry students. The thirty-three distinguished British and American poets are
represented by their best-known poems. Arranged chronologically, they
include Shakespeare, Donne, and Jonson, but also Snodgrass, Bly, and
Dickey. Special effort has been made to feature contemporary American
writers. Styles and forms include sonnets, songs, farces, and satires, and
a comprehensive, stimulating essay on style and technique heads the
text. There are footnotes, biographical information, and indexes by subject, type of poem, verse type, and humor.

Best Loved Story Poems. *Walter E. Thwing, ed.* (1941) Garden City. 754p., o.p.

It's all here, from "The Shooting of Dan McGrew" to "Horatius at the Bridge" and "The Owl and the Pussy-Cat." Now these may not always be the work of "great poets" as the compiler claims, but they certainly are familiar. The criteria, besides familiarity, that are used for selection are twofold. The poems must originate in America or England, and they have to be contemporary with, or after, Shakespeare. A glance at the eleven bold subject areas indicates that most of the glory is from the late nineteenth and early twentieth centuries, before MTV and rock and the modern song poem. Even the subject divisions are related to the natural bravado of a day past, e.g., "Courage and Adventure," "Faith and Repentance," and "History and Legend." Fittingly enough, this last subject area opens with Tennyson's "The Revenge" and shuts down with Robert Browning's "Incident of the French Camp." This is not the type of anthology many people will have around, but it is a grand choice for libraries. It has the old favorites, it has the beloved themes, and it offers a shadow of days long past.

The Brand-X Anthology of Poetry. *William Zaranka, ed.* (1981) Apple-Wood Books. 358p., o.p.

Despite the title and the compiler's effort "to present an alternative to the traditional literary corpse," this collection follows traditional lines. Arrangement is chronological, beginning with Chaucer and moving through the Renaissance, the Cavalier poets, the eighteenth century and so on, ending primarily with Americans born after 1930. What makes this effort different, but not all that different, are comments along the way by Zaranka, a professor at The University of Denver. Unfortunately, he is prone to punning and writing in a style that worked well enough for Ezra Pound's brand of pedagogy, but is a repetitive reminder of "Brand-X" types of crankiness. He calls the Middle Ages, for example, "The Middle-Aged" and opens this section with a characteristic phrase: "no survey of Middle-Aged literature could call itself complete without at least some mention of the great Hell's Anglo-Anne Sexton poet." Fortunately, the choice of numerous poets and poetry overcomes this foolishness, and the result is a passable collection of use to libraries. Individuals should look elsewhere.

Burning with a Vision; Poetry of Science and the Fantastic. *Robert Frazier, ed.* **(1984) Owlswick Press. 139p.**

Science and the fantastic: a fascinating topic for poetry! Here we have poems on such subjects as "Computative Oak," by Ruth Berman, "Cytogenetics Lab," by Lucille Day, "The Pterodactyl," by Philip Jose Farmer, and "The Aging of Clones," by Andrew Joron and Robert Frazier. These poems, written in a variety of contemporary styles — some traditional forms, some prose poems, others in open forms — are not as impenetrable as they first may sound. And they are certainly up to date in their concerns. This is the place to look for a bisection of art with science. Most of the poets are little known to the general public, but some names are familiar: Diane Ackerman, Loren Eiseley, Ursula K. Le Guin, and D. M. Thomas, for example. But, as the editor states in the introduction, "In this volume, you will encounter poetry that speaks directly of science; that deals with it in an indirect manner; that employs its language for uncommon effect on a common situation . . ." and where else are you likely to find that in abundance? This is new poetic territory. It must be said, however, that the quality of the poetry varies.

The Chatto Book of Cabbages and Kings; Lists in Literature. *Francis Spufford, ed.* **(1989) Chatto and Windus. 313p.**

For all those lists fanatics who also read poetry, this anthology is for you. Actually, to feature well-known poems and prose excerpts that contain some kind of internal list is an irresistible concept. Hundreds of selections — mostly by English-speaking writers, but some translations as well — are collected: works by the ancient Greeks, nursery rhymes, Hemingway, the Bible. Many forms are included, particularly a large number of excerpts from epics and narratives. The verse is divided into nine chapters, roughly by subject, with such titles as "Feasts," "The Lists of the Heart," and "Comic Elaborations." The selections are all of high quality, mostly classic pieces, and in many cases readers may not even notice the list present. The editor has here expanded the definition of list so that readers will realize any sequence of events can be construed as a list. Who ever knew so many lists were featured in great literature! This is a fine volume that could be improved only with a better index. Indexed by author only.

Chief Modern Poets of England and America. *Gerald DeWitt Sanders, John Herbert Nelson, and M. L. Rosenthal, eds.* **(4th ed., 1964) Macmillan. 964p.**

This collection is divided into three sections: "Modern British Poets," "Modern American Poets," and an index of authors, titles, and first lines. The editors include such significant British authors as Hardy, Yeats, Lawrence, Auden, and Spender; they represent American poetry in work by poets such as Williams, Pound, MacLeish, Sandburg, and Wilbur. The anthology includes ample and enjoyable selections from each poet, with more space given, of course, to those the editors consider of greater stature. The work is enhanced by biographies at the end of each major section. The anthology's weaknesses lie in the editors' ten-page introduction, which contains more opinion than helpful information, and in its pagination, which begins anew with each section.

The Classic Hundred; All-Time Favorite Poems. *William Harmon, ed.* **(1990) Columbia University Press. 250p., pap.**

Like Harmon's 1992 collection in *The Top 500 Poems*, this volume is a showcase for the hundred poems that have been most frequently anthologized. And again, like the larger collection, this one features an intelligent arrangement, unambiguous notes, and a wide range of stellar verse. All of the greatest poets of the English language are featured, with Blake's "The Tiger" topping the list; poems are arranged in order of their popularity. Poetry lovers will enjoy seeing how their favorites rank. Clear, informative, critical information precedes each selection. Harmon has a gift for explaining technical and thematic information, making this a perfect introductory volume for general readers. It is also recommended as one of the best collections for knowledgeable readers who are looking for an attractive, simple collection of poetic favorites.

The College Anthology of British and American Verse. *A. Kent Hieatt and William Park, eds.* **(1964) Allyn and Bacon. 631p., o.p.**

Containing such highly skilled contemporary poets as Anne Sexton and W. D. Snodgrass, this volume's strength is in its fine collection of classic English and American poetry. There are ninety-five poets, arranged chronologically, along with the same ballads and anonymous Middle English lyrics that head off most surveys. There are, however, features to distinguish this from other surveys: this one contains no excerpts and its interesting, well-written critical essays are in unpedantic langauge, easy for a student to understand. Among the chronological subdivisions, the editors have curiously grouped Dickinson, Hopkins, Yeats, and Hardy in a section entitled "The Moderns." This oddity aside, the anthology is to be recommended as solid and competent. Indexed by poet, title, and first line.

Common Ground; an Anthology. *Marghanita Laski, ed.* **(1989) Carcanet. 295p.**

The purpose of this anthology seems to be to collect in one concise volume the "common ground" that defines the basis of the poetic tradition in English. More than 120 poets are generously represented here with undisputedly some of the greatest poems of the language. The verse is divided into sections based on such subjects as love, dreams, animals, political events, and death. Intended as a primer to answer a growing ignorance of these poems among readers, the anthology is neat, accessible, and satisfying. It is not quite a real introduction to poetry; it contains no critical information and the arrangement is not that of a survey text. And it is not technically a "best of" volume, because the editor has made her personal choices. But it is an accessible, solid collection of favorites. Indexed by poet, title, and first line.

The Everyman Book of Narrative Verse. *David Herbert, ed.* **(1990) J. M. Dent. 315p.**

Readers unfamiliar with narrative verse will be surprised by the range of this thorough anthology. There are poems with serious tone or of lighter mood, adventure stories, reflective commentaries, metered poems, free verse, or almost any other form. The sixty-five poets span seven centuries, from Chaucer to Keats to Poe to Frost. Most of the poems will be familiar to the general reader, among them "Frankie and Johnny," "The Rime of the Ancient Mariner," and "The Rape of the Lock." They are arranged chronologically by poem. This is a highly recommended collection of narratives — a compendium of boisterous, imaginative, splendid poems. Indexed by title and first line.

The Faber Book of English Verse. *John Hayward, ed.* **(1958) Faber and Faber. 483p., o.p.**

This Faber volume is a fine, comprehensive anthology of familiar first-rate poetry. More than four hundred years of English and American verse is represented, from the sixteenth century with Elizabethan greats to well into the twentieth century, closing with Auden, T. S. Eliot, and Dylan Thomas. The poets are arranged chronologically, with a goodly number of American voices that includes William Cullen Bryant and e. e. cummings, among others. Longer poems have been reduced to manageable extracts to include the widest scope of poetry in the most economical text. There are no surprises in this collection; the absence of pretentious analysis and its comfortable arrangement recommend it as an introductory collection. Indexed by author and first line.

The Faber Popular Reciter. *Kingsley Amis, ed.* (1978) Faber and Faber. 256p.

Breathes there a reader so young, who never to herself hath said — "No more reciting!" With due respect to Sir Walter Scott and hundreds of others, Amis has collected a number of poems and verses that are standard material for recitation, primarily in the primary through high school grades. Most of them are so well known as to be the objects of parodies, and almost all are less than appropriate for the average collection of excellent poetry. Here the focus is entirely on verse, no matter how banal, no matter how bad, that the school child must learn by heart. True, from page to page one does find evocations of anguish, love, hate, and something more than the constant, repetitive rhythm of the words, but this is not as frequent as that familiar beat. Kipling's "Boots-boots-boots-boots-movin' up an' down" is a typical entry. In the introduction, Amis, an English novelist, points out how all of these verses bring back memories, some delightful, others chilling. Today, for better or for worse, few school children master any of these poems, and Amis believes they are missing a great experience. No matter, the old favorites are all here, and it is a grand collection for that reason alone.

The Family Album of Favorite Poems. *P. Edward Ernest, ed.* (1959) Grosset & Dunlap. 538p., o.p.

The title speaks for itself, particularly as there is no introduction to better gauge the potential audience. The few line drawings depicting typical scenes of family life set off the sixteen sections of traditional poetry. Actually, with the exception of some shining lights (from Robert Browning and John Donne to T. S. Eliot and W. B. Yeats), most of the poets are now little read except in anthologies of this type. Here, however, the compiler has gathered together numerous old "chestnuts" that may be recited by secondary school students or asked for in libraries. Favorites such as Edgar A. Guest's "Just Folks" will never win a prize as great poetry, but at one time it was on the lips of millions of people as the ideal type of poem for the ideal family. The titles of the sections pretty well set the tone: "Life Is Real, Life Is Earnest"; "Mother nature, father time"; and "The Children's Hour." There are useful indexes of authors, first lines, and titles.

The Family Book of Best Loved Poems. *David L. George, ed.* (1952) **Doubleday. 485p., pap.**

The purpose, scope, and audience is clearly stated in the first sentence of the introduction. The compiler wishes "to provide for all members of the family a satisfying collection of poems which have long endeared themselves to every American home." Some lesser-known works are introduced, too, but "in all cases the sentiment of the poem rather than the fame of the poet has been the deciding factor in determining its selection." Here sentiment is neatly arranged in sections from "Love" to "Faith and Inspiration" to "Frontier Days." The menu is so well known as to need little or no explanation, and there are few, if any, surprises. Poets are limited to English and American voices, primarily of the late nineteenth and early twentieth centuries. The tried and true receive the most space. Whether it is Elizabeth Barrett Browning or Robert Browning, whether it is Longfellow or Tennyson, one will find most of their well-known verses included. But since sentiment is the evaluative guide, there are some less than satisfying poems by writers now forgotten. The collection promises familiar verse for the family, but it may be mildly faulted for considering all families equally innocent and unsophisticated.

The Gambit Book of Popular Verse. *Geoffrey Grigson, ed.* (1971) **Gambit; also published in Great Britain as The Faber Book of Popular Verse. 376p., o.p.**

In his introduction, Geoffrey Grigson defines popular verse as that which is "not 'literary,' it is not egoistic or private, or . . . obscure." He mentions as well that its appeal is immediate. His book is divided into thematic sections: "Childhood, Some Children's Rhymes, and Game Rhymes"; "The Seasons"; "Living Things";"Nonsense and Mystification"; "Love"; and so forth. The poems,which are mostly anonymous, satisfied a large public in the past and are just as appealing today. There are riddles in verse that should delight youngsters, as well as adults who relish puzzles. Perhaps some of the most enjoyable moments are when one comes unexpectedly across lyrics to tunes one knows: "The Foggy, Foggy Dew," for example, or "I Know Where I'm Going."

The Gift of Great Poetry. *Lucien Stryk, ed.* **(1992) Regnery Gateway. 271p.**

This anthology, edited by American poet Lucien Stryk, is a brief collection of great verse in English. It does not have the breadth and critical information that a survey volume offers, and only one selection for each poet is included. But this is still an effective anthology, less an introductory text and more an abbreviated collection of the best English poetry. The 130 poems lead off with anonymous Middle-English ballads, continue through most of the standard anthologized poets, and conclude with Dylan Thomas's "Do Not Go Gentle into That Good Night." Several lesser-known Metaphysical and Cavalier poets are also included. Selections are arranged chronologically. Here are no surprises. This is a sampling of the best works by English-speaking poets of the past thousand years, recommended for younger readers as well as for poetry enthusiasts looking for an attractive, accessible volume of their favorite verse. Indexed by first line.

The Golden Treasury of Longer Poems. *Ernest Rhys, ed.* **(1949) E. P. Dutton. 405p., o.p.**

This anthology contains the most distinguished longer work of such poets as Chaucer, Milton, Keats, and D. H. Lawrence. Here are "The Knight's Tale," "An Essay on Man," "Christabel," and sixty other poems, most of them well known to even the most general reader; the lesser-known poems represent eras and genres that historians have frequently passed over. Arranged chronologically by poem, they exemplify the styles, themes, and techniques of seven centuries — narratives, ballads, odes. There are no annotations, footnotes, indexes, dates, or critical information to recommend the anthology to any but the most general audience.

The Harper Anthology of Poetry. *John Frederick Nims, ed.* **(1981) Harper & Row. 842p.**

This volume has the look of a textbook in English and American poetry: it is thick, each poet is briefly introduced, there are brief definitions of obscure words and voluminous notes on the more esoteric poems. This approach will prove very helpful to general readers who wish to extend their knowledge of poetry. The editor discusses his enchantment with poetry in the introduction, and that sentiment is present throughout the volume and proves to be contagious. The collection begins with anonymous poems written before 1400, runs through the time of Chaucer, John Skelton, Edmund Spenser, Shakespeare, Donne, Robert Herrick, Milton, and onward. After the Romantic poets, we find Emily Dickinson, Thomas Hardy, Robert Frost, Wallace Stevens, William Carlos Williams, and then the contemporary poets. All in all, the works of more than two hundred poets are on display. This is a very civilized anthology: the selection of poems is extremely tasteful, with the most important works in English represented. The contemporary poets are allocated ample space to lay serious claim to a reader's attention.

The Heath Introduction to Literature. *Alice C. Landy, ed.*

See under   POETRY: STUDY AND TEACHING

The Home Book of Modern Verse. *Burton Egbert Stevenson, ed.* **(9th ed., 1953) Henry Holt. 1,124p., o.p.**

The editor in his introduction to this very big anthology writes that he originally wanted to compile "the most comprehensive collection of English and American verse ever brought together in one volume." Although admitting later that this goal was far too ambitious, he may have come close. In this book of more than a thousand pages, hundreds of poems are grouped in seven sections, from "Poems of Youth and Age" to "Poems of Love," "Poems of Nature," and the inevitable "Poems of Sorrow, Death and Immortality." The collection generally features the work of acclaimed English-speaking poets, from James Joyce to Vachel Lindsay, although it also includes many lesser-known provincial poets, the undiscovered gems of this volume. Overall, and in spite of its grand scope, this is a fascinating collection of traditional verse collected for general readers. Many of the poets have distinct historical and cultural perspectives from the past century, but it is rewarding just to thumb through the pages and read what these lesser-known poets thought about urban migration and the First World War.

I Have No Gun But I Can Spit; an Anthology of Satirical and Abusive Verse. *Kenneth Baker, ed.*

See under   HUMOROUS AND NONSENSE VERSE

Immortal Poems of the English Language. *Oscar Williams, ed.* (1952) **Simon & Schuster. 637p., pap.**

This is one of the best general collections of British and American verse, with almost five hundred poems by the most accomplished poets, from Chaucer to Dylan Thomas. They are presented chronologically by author in a compact, uncluttered volume. Many are short songs, anonymous ballads, and excerpts from plays, and Williams includes several long poems in their entirety. In his brief introduction, Williams writes that "a poem, if it is a good one, is inexhaustible; we want to read it over and over, wherever we may be." Indeed, this is a collection for every poetry lover — convenient, straightforward, and comprehensive — up to 1952, that is! Indexed by author, title, and first line.

Introduction to Literature: Poems. *Lynn Altenbernd and Leslie L. Lewis, eds.*

See under   Poetry: Study and Teaching

Introduction to the Poem. *Robert W. Boynton and Maynard Mack, eds.*

See under   Poetry: Study and Teaching

The Liberating Form; a Handbook-Anthology of English and American Poetry. *Bert C. Bach, William A. Sessions, and William Walling, eds.*

See under   Poetry: Study and Teaching

A Little Treasury of Modern Poetry, English and American. *Oscar Williams, ed.* (3d ed., 1970) **Scribner's. 937p., o.p.**

This pocket-sized collection is as familiar to the average reader as any work in this guide. Williams had an uncanny skill for intelligently selecting precisely the type of poet and poetry that appeals to the average reader — as well, of course, as to students of Poetry 101 in hundreds of colleges and universities. The anthology is a standard for library browsing and reference. It is not hard to see why it is so popular. The format is easy to handle, and the pages are loaded with the familiar, tried and true. As one might expect, "modern" begins with Thomas Hardy and a selection of about a dozen of his poems. This is the average number for the major writers, with half again as many for the lesser figures. American and English authors are mixed together in chronological order. It is hard to name one major poet who was writing up to the time of this edition who is not represented. The introduction, notes, and related aspects of the book make it a fine companion for one and all.

Master Poems of the English Language. *Oscar Williams, ed.* (1966) **Trident Press. 1,072p., o.p.**

Judged by its size and title, this huge anthology could very well include a thousand poems written in English over the past 1,500 years. Instead, it presents just over a hundred carefully selected poems, each followed by several pages of criticism by a prominent critic or poet. For example, Lionel Trilling provides a 21-page analysis of Wordsworth's "Intimations Ode," and William Stafford wrote five pages on Keats's "Eve of St. Agnes." Shakespeare's sonnets and Shelley's "Adonais," among a few others, merit two critiques. Arranged chronologically by poet and indexed by title and first line, the poems are undoubtedly masterpieces, and the critiques are comprehensive and highly intricate. In the preface, an editor working with Williams at the time of his death writes that Williams had hoped to compile the greatest poems with the best modern criticism. This fascinating anthology, well suited to readers familiar with classic poetry and the complexities of modern criticism, accomplishes his aim.

A New Canon of English Poetry. *James Reeves and Martin Seymour-Smith, eds.* (1967) **Barnes & Noble. 326p., o.p.**

The editors of this fine anthology have included hundreds of English and American poems that they feel have, over the centuries, been neglected by historians and undervalued by critics. Shakespeare, Dickinson, and Blake are all included, but the editors have published their less familiar, but not less skilled, verse. Here are sixty poets, beginning with the fifteenth-century verse of John Skelton and concluding with nineteenth-century Trumbull Stickney. In between are familiar poets whose poetry is not widely anthologized. The poets are arranged chronologically, and there is an interesting section that features lyrics from Elizabethan and Jacobean songbooks. Notes to some of the poems are included, and there is an index of titles and first lines. This is a neat, attractive anthology, designed to supplement other standard anthologies.

The Norton Anthology of Literature by Women; the Tradition in English. *Sandra M. Gilbert and Susan Guber, eds.*

See under WOMEN'S POETRY AND FEMINIST POETRY

The Norton Introduction to Poetry. *J. Paul Hunter, ed.*

See under POETRY: STUDY AND TEACHING

One Hundred and One Famous Poems. *Ray J. Cook, comp.* (Rev. ed., 1958) Reilly & Lee; reprinted by Contemporary Books (1981) 186p., o.p.

Suitably enough, this well-known, much publicized collection of popular poetry opens with Longfellow's "The Builders." This tribute to the joys of capitalism and individualism runs like a theme throughout the whole work. The volume ends with a prose supplement that includes the "Gettysburg Address," "The Ten Commandments," the "Magna Carta," Patrick Henry's speech "The War Inevitable," and "The Declaration of Independence." It celebrates the glories of nationalism and the singular pleasures of what William Watson calls "the things that are more excellent." And those things are what the editor describes in a three-paragraph preface: "There are souls, in these noise-tired times, that turn aside into unfrequented lanes, where the deep woods have harbored the fragrances of many a blossoming season. . . . It is the purpose of this little volume to enrich, ennoble, encourage." No one can argue with the sentiment, but sentimentality is another thing. The book is unfortunately, sentimental to a fault, although, to be sure, there are some excellent poems, each accompanied by a photograph of the poet. It is historically interesting, but that is about all anyone can say for this collection.

100 Poems by 100 Poets; an Anthology. *Harold Pinter, Geoffrey Godbert, and Anthony Astbury, comps.* (1986) Grove Press. 176p.

Playwright Harold Pinter explains that "this book took final shape on a train journey to Cornwall. Anthony Astbury, Geoffrey Godbert and myself . . . consider each poem here to be representative of the poet's finest work." On the twelve-hour train trip, the three argued fiercely about what was to be included since they were limiting themselves to one poem per poet. Entries are not necessarily the most famous works. The distinguished jury decided to reprint all poems in full, to include only those written in English, and to exclude living poets. The latter decision may have been a consideration of copyright, but Pinter claims it was made "since we needed to make our choice from the total corpus of each poet's work." The poets are arranged in alphabetical order, ranging chronologically from John Skelton (1460–1529) to Sylvia Plath. It is an awe-inspiring gathering. Almost every poet belongs to the "classics" roll call, but not all of the poems; there are numerous, marvelous surprises. This is a nearly perfect collection for anyone who loves poetry.

Other Men's Flowers. *A. P. Wavell, ed.* (1990) Jonathan Cape. 448p.

This current volume is an anniversary edition of a popular anthology of British and American poetry first published in 1944. It was originally compiled as a collection of the poems that sustained the editor's father as a soldier in the Second World War. The earlier edition remains virtually intact, with only a few new poems and a second introduction added. The poetry is divided into nine sections according to theme, with such titles as "Music, Mystery, and Magic," "The Lighter Side," and "Love and All That." Nearly three hundred poems are arranged for browsing rather than as a student's text or teaching guide. Yeats, Shakespeare, Kipling, Hardy, and Wilde figure prominently. The notes about the poems that frequently conclude each selection add to the friendly, familiar tone of the collection. Recommended for general readers, the volume also contains a final section of brief poems and eulogies commemorating those who died in battle. Indexed by title and poet.

The Oxford Anthology of English Poetry. Vols. I–II. *John Wain, ed.* (1990) Oxford University Press. 659p., 770p.

These anthologies are competent, thorough Oxford volumes of English poetry, perfect for students and general readers who are looking for comprehensive yet up-to-date texts. The first volume covers the mid-sixteenth century to just before the Romantics, while the second picks up with William Blake and continues to the modern verse of lesser-known poets. Included are 206 poets, many commonly left out of other introductory texts. English here means language rather than nationality, so many American, Irish, and Welsh writers are also represented. Arranged chronologically by author, in standard anthology format and well indexed, this volume is highly recommended for its inclusion of both classic poets and promising contemporary writers. Some readers may object to the two-volume format, but it is sleek and well crafted and not cumbersome.

The Oxford Book of Narrative Verse. *Iona Opie and Peter Opie, eds.* **(1983) Oxford University Press. 407p.**

Narrative poems have a particular charm: they combine the delights of verse with the plots of fiction. All too often, anthologists are unable to include narrative poems in their collections because of their length. This volume adjusts the balance and prints dozens of narrative poems, most of them in their entirety, beginning with some of the tales of Geoffrey Chaucer and concluding with a poem by W. H. Auden. Some of the choices of the astute editors are predictable, for example, Pope's "The Rape of the Lock," and Samuel Taylor Coleridge's "The Rime of the Ancient Mariner." Others are lesser-known works, such as Christina Rossetti's "Goblin Market" and William Plomer's "Atheling Grange: or, the Apotheosis of Lotte Nussbaum." All these works comprise an important part of the poetic tradition in England and America, and they deserve to be readily available to readers. They are particularly good for reading aloud, and some of the works, such as Dryden's "Cymon and Iphigenia" or Burns's "Tam o'Shanter" could provide a taste that whets the appetite for more of the author's works. Humor can also be found in this collection, e.g., Lewis Carroll's "The Hunting of the Snark," as well as a great deal of drama. This is a most absorbing collection.

The Oxford Book of Regency Verse, 1798–1837. *H. S. Milford, ed.* **(1928) Oxford University Press; edition of 1935 had title The Oxford Book of English Verse of the Romantic Period, 1798–1837. 888p., o.p.**

This fine anthology is the link between the poetry in *The Oxford Book of Eighteenth Century Verse* and that in *The Oxford Book of Victorian Verse*, verse that falls between *Lyrical Ballads* of Wordsworth and Coleridge and the golden age of Tennyson and Robert Browning. These eighty-four English and American poets are arranged chronologically. Here is familiar, classic verse — Shelley, Byron, Keats, Blake, Scott, Bryant, and Poe, among others — as well as the work of minor poets of the time, many all but forgotten by modern anthologists. There is a brief preface and author and first-line indexes.

The Oxford Book of Victorian Verse. *Arthur Quiller-Couch, ed.* **(1971) Oxford University Press. 1,023p., o.p.**

This is a large, definitive anthology — a new edition of a classic volume from 1912 — that considers "Victorian" any poet born or writing in the nineteenth century. Thus, the 273 English and American poets range from William Cullen Bryant and Hartley Coleridge to James Joyce and George Santayana. In between are such widely anthologized Victorian poets as Elizabeth Barrett Browning, Robert Browning, Thomas Hardy, Matthew Arnold, and W. B. Yeats. Much of the volume contains rarely published, almost forgotten poets and presents them alongside Keats, Poe, and Swinburne. These poets are particularly interesting simply because they have been almost forgotten, writers of ballads, sonnets, and odes of all sizes. Arranged chronologically, each poet is represented by a range of popular and lesser-known verse. Quiller-Couch, himself a distinguished poet (and included in this volume), explains in his brief introduction that he hoped to provide a text that presented classic poems of his "Victorian" age alongside overlooked, competent poetry. Like all large anthologies, this one is planned for a broad audience, and readers looking for a diverse sampling of Victorian poetry will be pleased with the neat arrangement of these sentimental favorites; those looking for the depth of a more focused volume will also be pleased.

The Pleasure of Poetry: From His Daily Mirror Column. *Kingsley Amis, ed.* **(1990) Cassell Publishers. 245p.**

Amis edited an English newspaper that adopted the custom of printing one poem each day, along with brief notes on the poem or poet. The success of this feature was so overwhelming and responses by the readers so great that Amis decided to collect those poems in one volume — this anthology. The premise of making great poetry accessible to all is commendable, and the anthology itself succeeds in featuring fine, accomplished verse. Mostly the poems are by British poets, although a few Americans have slipped in. The 245 poems are divided into sections based on the months of the year, repeating the order in which they appeared in the newspaper. These poems include everything from Shakespeare to drinking songs, lacking any pretentiousness of style or preference for one era over another. This is a highly recommended hodgepodge of poetry, presented in a clear, standard manner with the sole aim of making fine verse available to general readers. Indexed by first line and author.

The Pleasures of Poetry. *Donald Hall, ed.*

See under   POETRY: STUDY AND TEACHING

Poems That Touch the Heart. *A. L. Alexander, ed.* (1956) Doubleday. 403p.

Compiled in the hope that readers will "discover something that truly warms and touches the heart," this anthology has hundreds of homilies, sentimental verses, and sometimes downright mawkish stories — inspirational poems of the kind that show up on refrigerator doors and calendar corners. Occasionally the verse of a Longfellow or a Pope appears, but most of these poems are by obscure authors. These brief entries celebrate friendship, matrimony, pleasant thoughts, and family relations. Many have a preachy tone or are a sentimental treatment of a harmless theme. Planned for readers who may have suffered hardship or who are trying to overcome sadness or grief, these simple poems may strike a sympathetic chord, or they may be just too saccharine, too pedantic, even for the suffering. Indexed by author, title, and first line.

Poems for Children and Other People. *George Hornby, ed.*

See under   CHILDREN'S POETRY

Poetry for Peace of Mind. *Alison Wyrley Birch, ed.* (1978) Doubleday. 232p., o.p.

This anthology is a collection of 220 poems meant to solve various emotional problems. Each section of the book addresses a different state: "Depression," "Grief," "Fear," "Fatigue." The poems in each section will, presumably, change the reader's mood. Birch has certainly chosen suitable poems and poets for her purpose. Fatigue can be treated with a dose of Shakespeare ("Shall I compare thee to a summer's day?") or W. B. Yeats ("When You Are Old"). For depression, read Edwin Markham's "Victory in Defeat" and Thomas Hardy's "The Darkling Thrush." The prose accompanying the poetry is encouraging but oversimple. The introduction explains that the book grew out of experimental seminars in hospitals around the country. An otherwise pleasant epilogue includes the rather daunting sentence, "Man is language." Poems are indexed by title, first line, and author. Small line illustrations at the beginning of each section give the book a pleasant appearance. Enjoy!

Poetry for Pleasure; the Hallmark Book of Poetry. *Hallmark Cards editors, comps.* **(1960) Doubleday. 470p., o.p.**

Readers who associate Hallmark only with sentimental greeting cards will be pleasantly surprised by this anthology, a collection of poetry by writers as diverse as Catullus, Shakespeare, and Lawrence Ferlinghetti. The poems are divided by subject with such borderline-insipid titles as "New Voices," "Life Sketches," and "In the American Grain." But readers should not let this (or the banal introduction and haphazard arrangement of the poems within each chapter) deter them from serious browsing. All themes, forms, and styles are represented, mostly by well-known English-speaking poets — although some translations and verse by lesser-known authors are also included. This is not a student's text or a trend-setting volume, but a diverse collection to read in at leisure and for pleasure. Indexed by poet, title, and first line.

Poetry; Points of Departure. *Henry Taylor, ed.*

See under   POETRY: STUDY AND TEACHING

Poetry Worth Remembering; an Anthology of Poetry. *Roy W. Watson, comp.* **(1986) Brunswick. 274p., o.p.**

Depending on individual taste any poem is worth remembering. How, then, does the compiler decide what he thinks is memorable? A nine-line preface offers little help. "The purpose of this book is to show the beauty, the depth of thought and creativity of both men and women in their poetic writings . . . this book explores, along with other meanings, the realities of life and the mysteries of death." In other words, it is a collection of traditional, middle-of-the-esthetic-road, verse — in no apparent arrangement. There is an index of poets and a table of contents arranged alphabetically by title. Many of the poems are from collections published at the turn of the century. This anthology is useful primarily for featuring many little-known poets. (The basic writers are found in abundance in other better-edited and better-organized collections.) Here, for example, is Phillips Brooks, Maimee Lee Brown, and George W. Bungay, along with Horatius Bonar and Noah Barker. The only readily recognizable poets in the "B's" are Robert Browning and William Cullen Bryant. Surprisingly, this collection was published in 1986 not 1906!

Poets of the English Language. Vols. I–V. *W. H. Auden and Norman Holmes Pearson, eds.* (1950) Viking Press. Vols. I–III, V: o.p.; Vol. IV, "Romantic Poets." pap.

This is one of the most famous collections of the twentieth century. Working with a Yale professor, Auden wrote the introductions to each volume. Pearson's initial selection of poems was reviewed and approved by Auden. The publisher has divided what is normally a single-volume work into five separate, pocket-sized books. In terms of format and convenience, much can be said for the decision. The problem for libraries may be, of course, keeping the five together.For the layperson the separate volumes are a definite plus. One can pick up English poetry at five distinctive points, beginning with the medieval and Renaissance poets and ending with the Victorians and Edwardians. The selections of American and British verse from 1400 to1914 hold numerous surprises; there is pleasure in finding the unusual choice. If Matthew Arnold and Walt Whitman are well represented, so are Herman Melville, Coventry Patmore, and Lionel Johnson — all in the fifth and final volume. Arrangement throughout is chronological, and each volume is indexed with biographical notes. A "Calendar of British and American Poetry" opens each book, in which parallel historical dates are given in relation to the poems.The special delight of the collection is in Auden's astute, personal involvement. His intellectual appraisals and explanations establish the poets and poems as only a great poet could. The volumes should be treasured for Auden's far-reaching, polished literary introductions. Highly recommended for libraries and for individuals.

Quest for Reality; an Anthology of Short Poems in English. *Yvor Winters and Kenneth Fields, eds.* (1969) Swallow Press. 200p.

Most of the nearly two hundred poems by forty-eight poets share three things. First, they are short — a half to two pages in length. Second, only the sixteenth and seventeenth centuries are included, with a few nineteenth-century entries, followed by numerous poets from the twentieth-century American scene. Third, their selection is based on "a high degree of concentration which aims at understanding and revealing the particular subject as fully as possible." The eccentric criteria allow for few real surprises before the twentieth century. After that, when one turns to Edgar Bowers, Catherine Davis, Alan Stephens, Helen Pinkerton, and Charles Gullans (all born in the late 1920's), there is a suspicion that Winters trusted more to highly personal taste than to concerned judgment. While a useful library source for hard-to-find modern poets, the volume is of quite limited value to laypersons.

The Rattle Bag; an Anthology of Poetry. *Seamus Heaney and Ted Hughes, comps.* **(1982) Faber and Faber. 498p., pap.**

Compiled by two of the best poets writing in English today, "this anthology amassed itself like a cairn." The familiar are in the same mixed, or rattle, bag as the poems from the by-ways. At the same time, the focus is on the average reader, young or old, who is looking to experts for guidance to the best in American and British poetry since Ben Jonson. There is a dash of European, Latin American, and other poetry, but the primary emphasis remains on English and American verse. Both compilers show a strong preference for twentieth-century work. It is arranged, as the title suggests, in no particular order. Poems are in alphabetical order by title or first line because any other arrangement "would have robbed the order of the poems of an unexpectedness. . . . To have done it thematically would have made it feel too much like a textbook. To have done it chronologically would have left whole centuries unrepresented." There is a brief glossary and a listing of poets and their poems. The introduction is exactly two short paragraphs; the compilers preferred the anthology to speak for itself. And it does. When published it received high acclaim as "a standard which other anthologies will find it difficult to equal." There is no argument with that evaluation.

Roofs of Gold; Poems to Read Aloud. *Padraic Colum, ed.* **(1964) Macmillan. 179p., o.p.**

The editor of this rich, entertaining anthology explains that he chose these poems because of their "visualness, striking imagery, picturesqueness, action, and humor." Indeed, any of the verses here fit that description. Many of the poems are well-known classics: "Kubla Khan," "To a Skylark," and "Annabel Lee," for example. The poets include Shakespeare, Keats, Frost, and T. S. Eliot, representing centuries of the best verse in English. Their verse demonstrates a great diversity of styles, forms, and themes. Colum, an established poet in his own right, includes selections of his own work. Here are beautiful, vibrant poems, treasures to be read aloud. Colum has included brief, helpful notes on some of the poems. Indexed by author and first line.

The Roses Race around Her Name; Poems from Fathers to Daughters. *Jonathan Cott, ed.* (1974) Stonehill. 145p., o.p.

Near the end of his introduction Cott observes that "the poems in this anthology continually remind us of the possibilities of the unassailable integrity in the encounter of two human beings subsisting in a consubstantial relationship of acceptance, sympathy, and devotion. . . ." The introduction explores the heights of affection attainable by inspired fathers. These seventy loving verses come from every imaginable period; Robert Herrick, James Joyce, Robert Creeley, and William Wordsworth are among the poets displaying their fatherly love in this collection. Cott has included Theodore Roethke's "Elegy for Jane (My Student, Thrown by a Horse)" and William Blake's "Little Girl Lost," along with many lesser-known works by great authors. The book places poems to "Imaginary Daughters" and "Poems to Daughters" in separate sections of uneven length, with, of course, many more poems in the latter section. Cott has not indexed the works. *The Roses Race around Her Name* is not an exhaustive collection, but it provides an introduction to a very specific genre.

Seven Centuries of Verse, English & American, from the Early English Lyrics to the Present Day. *A. J. M. Smith, ed.* (1957) Scribner's. 778p., o.p.

This anthology, a survey of poetry in English for college students, is an excellent, sweeping volume for general readers as well. The emphasis is on hundreds of major poets and their most famous poems, although the editor has left out on purpose some longer, frequently anthologized works in order to widen his choice of writers. Arranged chronologically by poet, the text includes all the classic poetry from Chaucer, Milton, and Shakespeare right through to Robert Frost, Edna St. Vincent Millay, and Dylan Thomas. The volume begins with a large section of anonymous ballads and early lyrics and ends with an intelligent collection of essays about the poetry of Jonson, Shelley, T. S. Eliot, and others. There is a section on the mechanical and stylistic aspects of verse as well as definitions of common poetic terms that students may encounter as they study poetry. One large index includes title, author, and first-line references. This is a strong, distinguished anthology.

Seven Traditional, Seven Modern Poets. *Hulon Willis, ed.* **(1971) Chandler. 318p., o.p.**

This anthology compares Shakespeare, Blake, Keats, Robert Browning, Housman, Robinson, and Frost with Yeats, Stevens, Eliot, Cummings, Roethke, Thomas, and Robert Lowell, in an effort to "provide material for in-depth study of both traditional and modern poetry." Hulon Willis seems to forget that in-depth study of either "traditional" or "modern" poetry would require more work (at least 260 poems) by more poets. Also, he fails to define adequately either "traditional" or "modern" poetry. These problems aside, the anthology contains Blake's "The Chimney Sweeper," Eliot's "Gerontion," Stevens's "Disillusionment of Ten O'Clock," and Housman's "To an Athlete Dying Young," among other notable works. Poems are arranged chronologically by poet within the volume's two main categories. Willis also supplies informative, accessible biographies for each author and an index of titles and first lines. Students may not learn as much from this book as the editor would hope, but they will find classic poems by distinguished poets.

Six Centuries of Great Poetry. *Robert Penn Warren and Albert Erskine, eds.* **(1955) Dell. 544p., pap., o.p.**

This small anthology collects hundreds of the best-loved and most familiar classics of English and American verse from Chaucer to Yeats. In between are poets often skipped over in surveys — John Skelton, Robert Herrick, Wilfred Owen, and other "minor" poets. The arrangement is chronological by poet. Because there are no excerpts from longer works, poets like Pope and Johnson have been omitted. No biographical information about the poets has been included. Otherwise, this is a good, solid volume of verse—up to 1955. Indexed by title and first line.

Sometime the Cow Kick Your Head; the Biennial of Light Verse & Witty Poems (Light Year '88/89). *Robert Wallace, ed.* **Bits Press. 1988. 235p.**

Good light verse is a perennial delight, and good light verse of contemporary vintage is often hard to find. Is it being written, and, if so, where can it be found? That difficult question is addressed in this series of annuals/biennials by an editor who clearly relishes his task of accumulating the best entertaining, witty, amusing, and frolicsome verse currently being written. Gavin Ewart, the British poet, opens this collection with a gloomy view of "Country Matters" that begins, "The badgers are boring, the trees are so trivial, / they both have me snoring — for I am convivial." It is not a perspective of which Wordsworth would have approved. Most of the poets will be new to readers, although, along with the acclaimed Ewart, there are Roy Blount, Jr., John Updike, Donald Hall, William Stafford, and the always witty X. J. Kennedy. Women are generously represented, with, among many others, famous poets like May Swenson and Marge Piercy. After an introduction that discourses upon the state of the art of light verse, the poems are arranged along thematic lines. This is a collection to revel in, to read out loud to friends, and generally to smile and chuckle over. The quality of the verse is high, and the humor never palls. The enigmatic title, by the way, derives from a poem by Andrew J. Grossman that starts, "Sometime the cow kick your head / Sometimes she just moo / Even the cow don't know / What she going to do." You, if you are smart, will find a copy of this superior anthology. Recommended for all libraries.

The Sonnet; an Anthology. *Robert M. Bender and Charles L. Squier, eds.* (1987) Washington Square Press. 428p., pap.

Prepared as a textbook for college classes, this is "a comprehensive anthology of British and American sonnets from the Renaissance to the present." The editors first bring on stage Thomas Wyatt (1503–1542), the earliest of the English Renaissance poets. There is the usual, expected brief background information on the poet and his poetry and then a half dozen works selected from his more typical, well-known verse. The pattern is carried right through to the modern period. There is an index of authors, titles, and first lines and a brief (perhaps too brief) explanation of the sonnet and its place in history. It is hard to think of a poet composing in the English language who is left out. Conversely, there are too many minor voices and probably too much is attempted for one volume. While the selection is good, the volume disappoints in its failure to offer many surprises in the development of the form. Still, as a basic, representative text it is hard to beat.

Sounds and Silences; Poems for Performing. *Robert W. Boynton and Maynard Mack, eds.* (1975) Hayden Book Company. 114p., o.p.

The editors of *Sounds and Silences* take a very casual attitude toward the teaching of poetry. They write, "We're not pushing for 'appreciation of the classics'; our feeling is simply that those we have chosen will hit you where you live." Its three sections are named "Twenty-five Short Poems," "Forty-nine More Poems," and "Ways In" (a section of stimulating questions and commentary). The poems in this book come from all over the literary map. Gwendolyn Brooks's "We Real Cool," William Carlos Williams's "This Is Just to Say," and Lawrence Ferlinghetti's "The Pennycandystore beyond the El" are placed beside Oliver Goldsmith's "An Elegy on the Death of a Mad Dog," Lewis Carroll's "Father William," and Oliver Wendell Holmes's "The Deacon's Masterpiece." The poems are not indexed. Boynton and Mack want students to become familiar with them through repeated readings, until the relationship of the reader to the poem resembles that of a musician to a piece of music. Just such a study of the included works could be very rewarding.

The Speaker's Treasury of 400 Quotable Poems. *Croft M. Pentz, ed.* **(1963) Zondervan. 159p., o.p.**

Although there is no indication of it in the title, this anthology emphasizes short, tendentious poems full of biblical names and evoking God. The verse is arranged in sections with such titles as "Smoking-Drinking," "The Devil," "Salvation-Conversion," and "God's Touch." Most of the verses are by obscure or unnamed authors, and no dates place them in time. At best the poetry is almost mediocre: full of clichés, and lacking in wit and depth. In short, these are four hundred cheerful lessons in behavior aimed at younger children and teenagers and disguised as poetry. They *are* quotable, and there is nothing wrong with them as such; they are just not very distinguished.

The Symbolist Poem; the Development of the English Tradition. *Edward Engelberg, ed.* **(1967) E. P. Dutton. 350p., o.p.**

In his introduction, Engelberg defines the symbolist poem as that which uses language to "evoke and to suggest, rather than to describe or declare." This type of verse is different from symbolic poetry, he explains, because "while all poetry may be symbolic, by definition, not all poetry is fashioned into a symbolic system; and the word symbolist must be carefully distinguished from symbolic." If all this sounds a little technical, skip the introduction and read the poems. Divided into such sections as "Symbolist and Decadent Poetry" and "French Symbolist Poetry in Translation," the more than two hundred poems here are by mostly well-known writers, Coleridge, Dickinson, Baudelaire, and Wallace Stevens, among others. The selections are strong but probably not new to avid readers. The last chapter of this volume contains interesting critical essays on such poets as Yeats, Keats, and Dante Rossetti, written by Arthur Symons, T. S. Eliot, Yeats, and others. Engelberg's deft and intricate understanding of poetry enables him to provide a useful intro-duction. This pocket-sized anthology will be of interest to poetry enthu-siasts who don't object to labels and categories.

The Top 500 Poems. *William Harmon, ed.* **(1992) Columbia University Press. 1,132p.**

Comprehensive yet accessible, this anthology is exactly what it says it is: a collection of the five hundred most frequently anthologized English-language poems. These include the great sonnets, ballads, narratives, and lyrics — spanning 750 years and by the greatest poets, Shakespeare, Donne, and Blake among them. The book includes 160 poets, some of them lesser-known British writers of past centuries as well as several contemporary American writers. Arranged chronologically by poet, this volume is a tour of the best verse written in English; scholars would find it hard to argue that a more deserving poem had been excluded. Brief notes and explanations appear at the beginning and end of the selec-tions, a great aid to the student and to the general reader the book is intended for. Highly recommended for not resorting to a pedantic or authoritative tone, this anthology also includes a ranking of the poems anthologized most often (Blake's "The Tiger" is Number One). Indexed by poet, title, and first line.

A Treasury of Great Poems, English and American. *Louis Untermeyer, ed.* **(Rev. and enl. ed., 1955) Simon and Schuster. 1,286p., o.p.**

This is a huge volume that auspiciously begins with personal remarks by poets about poetry. It is evident from the start that the well-known editor is someone who cares deeply about the subject to which he is introducing the reader. The anthology opens with selections from the Bible. Treating the Bible as literature, the "Song of Songs" is included, along with selections from "The Book of Job" and other passages from the Old and New Testament that are of interest to students of literature. The anthology then proceeds chronologically through "Foundations of English Spirit," featuring the works of Chaucer, "The Popular Ballad," "Early Songs of Unknown Authorship," and so on, through the fifteenth and sixteenth centuries. There are long sections devoted to Shakespeare's sonnets and passages from his plays, many poems from John Donne, Robert Herrick, George Herbert, Milton, Andrew Marvell, Blake, and the Romantic poets. In the section "Challenge to Tradition," American poets begin to appear: Walt Whitman, Herman Melville, Emily Dickinson. Finally, in the twentieth century, there are selections from A. E. Housman, Edwin Arlington Robinson, Robert Frost, and Marianne Moore, concluding with the work of Robert Lowell, May Swenson, and Richard Wilbur. This is a very readable, very accessible, excellent collection. Each author has a biographical introduction, and throughout the book there are running, perceptive comments on the essence of the various poems and their place in the literary scene.

A Treasury of the Familiar. *Ralph L. Woods, ed.* **(1942) Macmillan. 751p.**

A Second Treasury of the Familiar. *Ralph L. Woods, ed.* **(1950) Macmillan. 722p., o.p.**

A Third Treasury of the Familiar. *Ralph L. Woods, ed.* **(1970) Macmillan. 682p., o.p.**

These three separate anthologies contain a hodgepodge of poems, lyrics, and pieces of prose with no common thread except that the editor liked them. The hundreds of selections have been frequently anthologized or are most likely in the average American's memory. The arrangement in all three volumes is haphazard. In the first volume, for example, Tennyson is followed by a biblical passage, "Miniver Cheevy," an anonymous 19th-century folk ballad, and the Boy Scout Oath. There are no chapters, no chronological or alphabetical order. The forewords are glib and tell very little about the anthology itself. Luckily, all volumes contain good indexes based on title, author, and familiar lines. Here is an eclectic diversity of literature, difficult to characterize; the selections are time-honored, cherished, known and loved by many. These are good anthologies, then, for readers to browse in.

Tygers of Wrath; Poems of Hate, Anger, and Invective. *X. J. Kennedy, ed.* **(1981) University of Georgia Press. 282p.**

The epigraph that adorns this book is taken from Blake's *Proverbs of Hell:* "The tygers of wrath are wiser / than the horses of instruction." It is clear that X. J. Kennedy is taking his project seriously. Wrath, hatred, anger, and invective are in full supply here, vividly portrayed by authors both old and modern. Many more men are in evidence, which may say something either about the sexes or about their writing habits. The poems are divided by subject: "In Praise of Hate," "Nearest but Not Dearest," "Sexual Skirmishes," "Personal Animosities," "Collective Detestations," "Nobles, Statesmen, Prelates, and Top Brass," "Poets, Critics and

Scholars," "Offending Race of Humankind," and "Damned Abstractions." There are enough subject categories for any poet to work out his bile. And, for readers with darker sides to their personalities, these poems can provide some group support. The poets are largely first rate: T. S. Eliot, William Carlos Williams, Pope, Sylvia Plath, John Donne, Philip Larkin, Emily Dickinson, to name a few. This is a foully engrossing volume of verse.

Victorian Parlour Poetry; an Annotated Anthology. *Michael R. Turner, ed.* **(1992) Dover Publications; originally published in 1969 by The Viking Press as Parlour Poetry; a Casquet of Gems. 325p., pap.**

The idea of "parlour" poetry may seem strange, but, in fact, as the introduction to this lively anthology explains, sentimental ballads, narratives, and story poems used to be enthusiastically read at gatherings in people's homes. Here are more than a hundred long, melodramatic pieces, most of them probably unfamiliar to modern readers. Many, however, were written by such well-known poets as Longfellow, Tennyson, Poe, and Kipling. A few of their most famous works are included, but the bulk of the volume is made up of forgotten poems that at one time had achieved great acclaim. The poems are grouped under such sections as shipwrecks and castaways, poems of tragic deaths, and poems narrated by poor but noble orphans. The achievement of this anthology is not in collecting brilliant poetry (much of this is laughably pious and bad) but in gathering mawkish, trite verse about noble characters and patriotic events. This is a gem of an anthology, not to be missed by readers wondering what was popular and acclaimed by ordinary readers back in the Victorian era. Indexed by poet, title, and first line, with a first-rate introduction.

The Viking Book of Poetry of the English-Speaking World. Vols. I–II. *Richard Aldington, ed.* **(Rev., Mid-Century ed., 1958) Viking Press. 1,297p., o.p.**

This is one of the best, most inclusive anthologies of poetry in English — of value to students, general readers, and anyone looking for an overview of classic British and American verse. More than twelve hundred poems by at least three hundred writers are collected in these two volumes. Arranged chronologically by poet, the first volume begins with Beowulf and the second ends with Robert Lowell and Richard Wilbur. In between are all the standard anthologized great poets and many more obscure writers who, although distinguished in their day, have lost favor with some scholars and anthology editors. The collection is indexed by first line, author, and title and contains a detailed, informative introduction by Aldington. He provides a survey of English and American literary history, particularly the development of poetic forms and semantics. Aldington has taken great care that diverse forms, styles, and tones are represented and has ensured that excerpted works are clearly marked as such. His concern and love for poetry in English is evident, making this a superb, thorough collection.

Voices of Poetry. *Allen Kirschner, ed.* **(1970) Dell. 207p., o.p.**

The six sections of *Voices of Poetry* represent the different human voices that may generate poems: "The Poet in Meditation," "The Poet in Love," "The Poet in Revolt," "The Poet in Despair," "The Poet in Nature," "The Poet in Exultation." While Kirschner's guiding thesis that "all poetry is but the projection of a human voice" is credible, his final product falls short of his ambitions. It is hard to imagine that the Thomas Hardy who writes "The Darkling Thrush" is a despairing poet, not a meditative one, or that William Cullen Bryant is overjoyed and in exultation when he writes, in "Thanatopsis," that "To him who in the love of Nature holds / Communion with her visible forms, she speaks / A various language. . . ." The categories are, as is evident, extremely ambiguous. Kirschner should be given credit for providing biographies and an index of authors, titles, and first lines. He has gathered many famous and well-loved poems in one volume, but its brevity (only 150 poems) and misguided organization diminish its usefulness.

The Winged Horse Anthology. *Joseph Auslander and Frank Ernest Hill, eds.* **(1929) Doubleday. 669p., o.p.**

This anthology intends to be a volume suggestive of the greatest poetry ever written in English. Published in 1929, it accomplishes this goal—up to 1929. Middle English ballads, lyrical passages from Shakespeare's plays, and the then "modern" verse of A. E. Housman and Walt Whitman are among the hundreds of poems included. Arranged chronologically by author, the volume is straightforward, representing several centuries of verse, but, to its credit, adequate space has been given in the text to poets making their mark in the early part of this century. The editors explain in their introduction that they have omitted some frequently anthologized verse, but most of the poems will be recognized by more general readers. Students of English and American literature may find such a representative anthology helpful, and all will find the included minor poets interesting. Indexed by author, title, and first line, this volume is a substantial, accomplished collection.

The World's Best Loved Poems. *James Gilchrist Lawson, comp.* **(1927) Harper & Row. 455p., o.p.**

Considering the fact that this was published over sixty years ago, it is not a criticism to say that the collection concentrates on popular verse that is often more sentimental than worthy, more filled with moral and religious lessons than with vivid portraits of individuals or situations. Sensibility, if not always sense, rules the compiler's choices. The collection is an effort "to gather into one volume the choicest of the world's most helpful short religious and popular poems. . . . Many of the pieces were selected not from the standpoint of highest literary merit, but because of their appeal to the human heart." The arrangement is by subject, beginning with "Autumn" and working through the alphabet to "Worry." There are indexes of first lines, titles, and authors to bring some order to the compiler's selection. Particularly striking is the index of authors; few are known today. This is a reference work for the library where hard-to-find, little-known poets may be a problem to locate.

See also POETRY: STUDY AND TEACHING

ENGLISH AND AMERICAN POETRY
20th Century

Chief Modern Poets of England and America. *Gerald DeWitt Sanders, John Herbert Nelson, and M. L. Rosenthal, eds.*

See under ENGLISH AND AMERICAN POETRY: COMPREHENSIVE COLLECTIONS

The Direction of Poetry; an Anthology of Rhymed and Metered Verse Written in the English Language since 1975. *Robert Richman, ed.* (1988) Houghton Mifflin. 168p.

Tradition is the key word in this anthology. While all of the poems are modern — and nothing here was written before 1975 — they all share the traditional form of rhyme and meter. The seventy-six poets are of various ages, but the majority are young and not that well known. They come primarily from America and Britain, but others call Australia, Canada, and the West Indies home. As the compiler says, this collection "celebrates the work of a particular group of poets — the most important group to have emerged in the last fifteen years." One may argue with the characterization of "most important," but there is no argument with the quality of the selection. This seems particularly evident among such older poets as Elizabeth Bishop, John Fuller, and X. J. Kennedy. Somehow their training and their experience make the work of the senior members more memorable. At the same time, the fascination of the collection lies in sampling the traditional forms through the eyes of the truly young, less well-known writers. This is a collection that will have wide appeal.

Dylan Thomas's Choice; an Anthology of Verse Spoken by Dylan Thomas. *Ralph Maud and Aneirin Talfan Davies, eds.* (1963) New Directions. 182p., o.p.

Included in this volume are more than a hundred poems by many British and American poets, either broadcast by Dylan Thomas on Welsh radio in the 1950's or found hand-copied among his belongings after he died. Among these poems are selections by Yeats, Thomas Hardy, and Robert Graves. Fifty-six other poets, many Welsh contemporaries of Thomas, round out the diverse collection. These are poems that come alive particularly when the words are spoken; the anthology is a fine one for anyone looking for verse to read aloud. It will also satisfy Thomas enthusiasts interested in any poetry that influenced him. The introduction by Maud and Davies reverently details Thomas's love of reading poetry aloud. The poems are arranged alphabetically and indexed by first line. Dylan Thomas had a rich, powerful voice and enjoyed giving readings of other poets' work, and in this anthology his favorite poems have been collected for others to enjoy and to read with the same passion.

English and American Surrealist Poetry. *Edward B. Germain, ed.* **(1978) Penguin Books. 348p., o.p.**

The strange dreamlike quality of surrealism is here captured in verse. The many poems celebrate the delights of surrealism in film, art, and artistic living. The fantastic imagery is everywhere, and many of the poems must be read several times for meaning — if, indeed, there is any meaning at all, other than the poet and the poem. The combinations and juxtapositions may not be every reader's idea of good poetry, but it is, at the very least, challenging. For a good explanation of surrealism and poetry see Germain's introduction. People, he explains, who dismiss surrealism outright are missing an important step, taking the work at its literal meaning. "If the poet writes: A horse galloped on a tomato, that is exactly what he means." And here he illustrates his point with a poem by David Gascoyne. Not all of the poets and poetry are quite so difficult. There is the work of Dylan Thomas, for example, who may be in unfamiliar company, but is there. Most of the surrealists gave up writing before the Second World War. The anthology is a reminder of a fascinating long-gone age.

The Faber Book of Modern Verse. *Michael Roberts, ed.* **(4th ed., revised by Peter Porter, 1982) Faber and Faber. 416p., pap.**

This is a compelling anthology of modern verse. There are ample selections from many of the great modern poets, and the choice of their works is outstanding. Furthermore the range of the poets covered is liberal: American as well as English authors are included, and many contemporary poets are among those worthy of representing the modern canon. Among the present-day poets whose verse is printed alongside

the works of Gerard Manley Hopkins, W. B. Yeats, T. S. Eliot, Ezra
Pound, and Marianne Moore are Geoffrey Hill, Ted Hughes, John
Ashbery, and Seamus Heaney. The reader can turn to this volume to
look seriously at the various, difficult, and marvelous accomplishments of
poets in the modern age, for much of their very best work is on display
here. A few omissions however seem strange: there is no sign of Robert
Frost, and of the twenty-four contemporary poets added by the current
editor, only one is a woman — Sylvia Plath.

The Faber Book of Twentieth Century Verse. *John Heath-Stubbs and*
David Wright, eds. **(3d ed., 1975) Faber and Faber. 348p.**

No matter what the titles of the scores of poetry anthologies, the
majority in part, or in full, embrace the twentieth century. There is no
shortage, then, of twentieth-century verse collections. Why, then, another compilation? As this one has gone into several editions and sold
rather well, there must be an explanation. It is not the arrangement,
which is the perfunctory A to Z by author. It is not the wide selection of
individual poems. There are normally no more than two to four for each
of about one hundred and twenty-five poets. (And there are some questionable choices of scope. W. H. Auden has five poems, Philip Larkin
one, and Robert Graves seven, outnumbered only by Ezra Pound). It
may be the unusual choice of minor poets. For example, in how many
collections does one find Lascelles Abercrombie or Anne Finch matched
poem for poem with Ted Hughes and Sylvia Plath? Still, all the major
twentieth-century figures are in evidence. So, in general, the collection is
about as diverse as any. The varied styles and preoccupations of the
writers establish "the expression of the common imaginative experience
of the age."

Mindscapes; Poems for the Modern World. *Richard Peck, ed.* **(1971)**
Delacorte Press. 165p., o.p.

Richard Peck's introduction to this anthology discusses the shift in
modern poetry outwards, away from the self and into everyday life. He
writes that his book "is designed to emphasize communication through
a collection of poems, mostly modern, that deal in encounters with a real,
hectic, unpretty, and recognizable world." Peck has organized the eighty-
five poems in this book in eleven sections whose titles, such as "A Paw on
the Sill," "A Design of White Bones," and "The Brick Bench Outside the
House," all come from the poems themselves. With the exception of
César Vallejo, all the poets, including Whitman, Auden, Housman, and

Williams, write in English. Readers should find these works personal and well-crafted. Poems are indexed by author and first line. This disappointingly brief anthology should be valuable to the student and general reader.

Modern American & British Poetry. *Louis Untermeyer, ed., in consultation with Karl Shapiro and Richard Wilbur.* **(Rev., shorter ed., 1955) Harcourt, Brace. 697p., o.p.**

Karl Shapiro and Richard Wilbur each have eight or nine poems in this standard collection. They have a discerning hand, too, in the other selections for this edition, which was considerably updated from earlier ones. There are many more first-rate, modern (up to 1950) poets in both the British and American sections. Guided by the two younger poets, Louis Untermeyer, the father of numerous collections, was wise enough to delete some earlier, less inspired poetry. At any rate, the 1955 edition remains very basic, in that all major, and many minor poets, are included. This selection truly is representative of the twentieth century, including works by Emily Dickinson and Gerard Manley Hopkins who really came to be appreciated only in this century. The choices are exceptionally fine. Here one finds the best of American poets Robert Lowell, James Merrill, Randall Jarrell, Robert Frost, and, from the British side, W. H. Auden, Louis MacNeice, Stephen Spender, to name a few. One can readily pick up countless volumes to carry the reader from 1950 to the present day.

Modern Poetry, American and British. *Kimon Friar and John Malcolm Brinnin, eds.* **(1951) Appleton-Century-Crofts. 580p., o.p.**

Although an anthology featuring Gerard Manley Hopkins can hardly be viewed as modern today, this large volume stands as a superb survey of mostly twentieth-century poets. Such writers as W. H. Auden, T. S. Eliot, Robert Frost, and Dylan Thomas share the pages with lesser-known, equally competent poets of all forms and schools. The eighty-four poets are well represented and arranged chronologically beginning with Emily Dickinson and ending with James Merrill. The poems are the authors' most skillful verse, although this may mean that the same poems are widely anthologized. Fortunately, the editors have fairly successfully eliminated the over-anthologized poems and provided other equally accomplished, well-crafted verse. On all counts, this is still a highly recommended volume for students and poetry readers who may be unfa-

miliar with such signature poems as Crane's "To Brooklyn Bridge,"
Hardy's "The Darkling Thrush," or Yeats's "Sailing to Byzantium."

The Modern Poets; an American-British Anthology. *John Malcolm*
Brinnin and Bill Read, eds. **(1963) McGraw-Hill; revised edition of 1970**
has title Twentieth-Century Poetry, American and British (1900–1970).
427p., o.p.

The editors of this anthology write in their brief introduction that
they hoped to compile a volume of "poems that give pleasure." They
have succeeded, choosing eloquent, vibrant poems mainly from post-
Second World War writers. W. H. Auden, e. e. cummings, Donald Hall,
Sylvia Plath, and seventy-eight others are represented. The selections are
usually among the best known by each author. A photograph of each
poet accompanies short biographical information and informal commentary; there is a title index and bibliographical information. Without pretension or heavy-handed criticism, Brinnin and Read have compiled a
fine anthology; all of the poets here contribute significantly to this
century's literary canon.

Modern Verse in English, 1900–1950. *David Cecil and Allen Tate, eds.*
(1967) Macmillan. 688p., o.p.

Although the title indicates that the verse spans only 1900 to 1950,
some earlier writers have crept into this volume, including Emily
Dickinson and Gerard Manley Hopkins. This small misrepresentation
aside, the anthology features the most familiar poems of many frequently anthologized British and American poets of the first half of this
century. Readers will be familiar with most of the poets here, beginning
with Hardy and Robinson and concluding with Nemerov and Robert
Lowell. Arranged chronologically, a large number of the poets are post-
Second World War writers, although today probably not as "modern" as
the title implies. This is a thorough, well-crafted anthology, with helpful
indexes and biographical information, a fine introductory volume to recent poetry. Because of the broad scope of the poets and the variety of
styles and movements included, the editors wisely make no attempt at
any analysis in their introduction. Instead, Cecil and Tate have each
written an introduction — one for British and one for American
poetry — to discuss the changes in poetry during the first half of this
century.

The New Modern Poetry; British and American Poetry since World War II. *M. L. Rosenthal, ed.* **(1967) Macmillan. 289p., o.p.**

More than a hundred "new" poets are featured here, each represented by praiseworthy and distinguished poems. Most of the included poets have achieved a lasting prominence in twentieth-century British and American literature — William Stafford, W. D. Snodgrass, John Berryman, and Allen Ginsberg, among others. They represent no particular style or form, and Rosenthal wisely avoids characterizing this generation of poets as "confessional" or "beat." The quality of the writing is first rate, the alphabetical arrangement of the poems is intelligent, and there are indexes by author, title, and first line. Of the anthologies of poetry by post-Second World War writers, this is rated high for its clarity, unambiguous introduction, and the quality of its poetry.

New Poets of England and America. *Donald Hall, Robert Pack, and Louis Simpson, eds.* **(1957) Meridian Books. 351p., o.p.**

Selected by what were then three young poets (all widely published today), this includes almost all famous American and English poets writing from the 1930's to the mid 1950's. But the emphasis is on "new," so the regulars from Pound to Cummings are not included. Instead the reader is given representative samplings of some of the best work of Robert Lowell, Richard Wilbur, Kingsley Amis, to name a few. The pattern was to be followed again in the even better *New Poets of England and America: Second Selection*. In both anthologies, the work is divided into two sections: English and American; in both anthologies, the English seem to fare better, if not in the amount of space, then in the quality of the verse. But only in this earlier edition can one find a marvelous, sometimes sarcastic introduction by Robert Frost. Both works are indispensable for an understanding of modern poetry.

New Poets of England and America. *Donald Hall and Robert Pack, eds.* **(Second selection, 1962) World. 384p., o.p.**

Anyone over forty years of age was not considered for this project, for that was the definition of "new" in 1962 when the well-known collection was published. Based on the earlier successful edition, it is neatly divided into two sections. Hall edited the English side and opens with: "People are writing some very good poems in England these days. Not many American critics will admit it." He goes on to support his argument with Kingsley Amis, Thom Gunn, Geoffrey Hill, Ted Hughes, Philip Larkin, and about two dozen other worthies. There are only one or two women in the group, a group which over the years has gratified most readers. Robert Pack edited the American side, with James Dickey, Anthony Hecht, John Hollander, Philip Levine, among other poets. In retrospect, the English poets do look superior to the Americans. One would venture to guess that more English poets are better known to readers than are the Americans. Suitably enough, some of the best Americans are such women as Sylvia Plath, Denise Levertov, Adrienne Rich, and Anne Sexton. There are short biographical notes, but no first line, subject, or title indexes.

The Oxford Book of Contemporary Verse, 1945–1980. *D. J. Enright, comp.* **(1980) Oxford University Press. 299p., o.p.**

Poet and critic, D. J. Enright selects those he considers the leading English, American, and Commonwealth poets for the period from 1945 to 1980. Arrangement is chronological by birth date, with Stevie Smith (b. 1902) leading off the group of about forty-five poets. Douglas Dunn (b. 1942) is the last to be included. About five lines of biographical data are given for each of the poets in the Table of Contents, and there are indexes of first lines and authors. In making his selection, Enright says he went out of his way to achieve geographical representation. Other principles of selection are explained in the thirteen-page introduction. Half a dozen or a dozen poems are given for each of the authors. The value of the choices is obvious, since a decade later almost all of the poets are still highly regarded, still often quoted. Some, such as Stevie Smith and Philip Larkin, are dead, but most are still alive. Among these are the compiler himself, Kingsley Amis, Roy Fuller, Seamus Heaney, Ted Hughes, and Richard Wilbur. While women are included, they are in the minority. Still, the poems are among the best written by contemporary poets up to 1980, and the introduction, a short essay on the delights of poetry, should not be missed.

The Oxford Book of Modern Verse, 1892–1935. *William Butler Yeats, ed.* **(1936) Oxford University Press. 454p., o.p.**

The great Irish poet William Butler Yeats was asked in 1936 to choose the best poetry from his generation, and this volume is the result of his search. A few poets have been excluded because they would not give their permission to be anthologized (e.g., Robert Graves and Laura Riding), and others were scantily represented because their fees were too high (e.g., Ezra Pound), but for the most part the selection is startlingly good. The poems by T. S. Eliot that Yeats chose are impeccable, what is included from Ezra Pound is also of the first rank, and it is particularly interesting, of course, to see what Yeats selected from his own vast oeuvre. Many of the other poets are little known today, but their writing bears inspection, for it reveals the convention from which the most modern poets revolted. Among other well-known authors whose work is included are Thomas Hardy, C. Day Lewis, W. H. Auden, and Louis MacNeice. The poets are frequently represented by more than one work, so the reader is able to grasp something of the range of their poetry. Yeats supplies an introduction in which he details the many strands that went into the making of modern poetry.

The Paris Review Anthology. *George Plimpton, ed.* **(1990) W. W. Norton. 686p.**

Since its inception in 1953, *The Paris Review* has typically featured the best modern poetry, enhancing the status of established poets and introducing new ones to readers. This anthology successfully represents the best of the high-quality poetry and fiction that has appeared in *The Paris Review* over the past four decades. The poetry is divided into five sections, each covering seven years of the journal's history. Each section has a short preface by Plimpton introducing the included writers. Most of the text consists of poetry, although some fiction excerpts are included. The list of writers reads like a *Who's Who* of contemporary literature: Philip Roth, Robert Bly, X. J. Kennedy, Bill Knott, and Jorge Luis Borges, among others. Each poet's most compelling, imaginative work is featured, making this a strong, highly recommended volume for all readers. Plimpton has wisely omitted poems that were widely circulated and reprinted in other anthologies. Biographical information on the authors is included.

Poems since 1900; an Anthology of British and American Verse in the Twentieth Century. *Colin Falck and Ian Hamilton, eds.* **(1975) Macdonald and Jane's. 176p., o.p.**

Poems since 1900 is a collection of 150 accessible English-language poems. Falck and Hamilton omit the more arcane modernist works (such as Pound's *Cantos* and Eliot's "The Wasteland"), criticizing their authors for believing that "poetry should be difficult and provide students with work to do." They prefer poems that are "ways into life, not ways out of it." The editors have included such poets as Lowell, Hardy, Auden, Ted Hughes, and Philip Larkin. Their work, as they address love, loss, history, war, and other significant subjects, is somber but readable. These well-known poems, including Eliot's "The Love Song of J. Alfred Prufrock" and Yeats's "The Second Coming," are arranged chronologically by poet and indexed by first line. This book will introduce readers to modern, intelligent poetry about experiences and hopes and human feelings.

The Poet Dreaming in the Artist's House; Contemporary Poems about the Visual Arts. *Emilie Buchwald and Ruth Roston, eds.* (1984) Milkweed Editions. 142p.

Borrowing the title from a Howard Nemerov poem, this volume presents poems about art, describing famous artists, specific works in general, and the nature of art as a function of life. The poetry of such accomplished contemporary writers as Howard Nemerov, Denise Levertov, David Wagoner, and Patricia Hampl stands out among that of lesser-known poets. The quality of the poems is generally good; most are as evocative and sensual as the paintings or sculptures they attempt to capture in words. The poems are accompanied by vivid, surreal sketches. In their preface Roston and Buchwald, both of them poets who include their own work here, write that "these poems affirm for us the fact that the impulse to make art and to write poems rises out of the same desire to sing 'the secret history of the mind.' " This anthology successfully links visual art and poetic art in an attractive, slender volume.

The Poetry Anthology, 1912–1977. *Daryl Hine and Joseph Parisi, eds.*

See under AMERICAN POETRY: 20TH CENTURY (PERIODICAL)

Sounds and Silences; Poetry for Now. *Richard Peck, ed.* (1970) Dell. 178p., o.p.

According to Richard Peck, the poets in this anthology "write to communicate what being alive in the mid-twentieth century is like." They communicate through the use of imagery from daily life: subways, boxes, marmalade, frog ponds, yachts. Among the authors recreating the modern experience are Dylan Thomas, Paul McCartney, Leonard Cohen, Pete Seeger, Carl Sandburg, e. e. cummings, and William Carlos Williams. Peck has blended well-worn verses (Auden's "The Unknown Citizen" and Yeats's "An Irish Airman Foresees His Death," for example) with popular songs (such as Lennon and McCartney's "Lucy in the Sky with Diamonds" and Woody Guthrie's "I've Got to Know'), trying to show that poetry may appear outside of the classroom and be an experience more valuable than a good grade. The 100 poems in this book are organized into such topical categories as "Love," "War," "Identities," and "The Childhood." *Sounds and Silences* will introduce you to the various forms and purposes of poetry in the twentieth century.

FINNISH POETRY

Salt of Pleasure: Twentieth-Century Finnish Poetry. *Aili Jarvenpa, tr.* **(1983) New Rivers Press. 240p., pap., o.p.**

Thanks to numerous black-and-white photographs (by Oliver and Robert Jarvenpa) that set the mood, crystal clear translations, and a brief sketch of each poet, this is an easy, delightful collection to read. There probably is not one person in a thousand who would recognize more than one or two of the poets, at least if they are not Finnish Americans, as is the translator/compiler. The twenty-six poets "have been selected as representative of the best in twentieth-century Finnish poetry." Eino Leino (1878–1926) begins with "Äijö's Song": "He was Äijö, born alone / began alone / died alone, / sat on the edge of the cloud, / watched the world go by." A lyric poet of considerable influence, his style and intellectual interests are reflected by many of the others. If there is any universal theme it is, as the introduction notes, "the reflective melancholy." There is a surprising lack of Russian influence and of war poetry in the collection. The quality of the work is high, and anyone who appreciates nature will find pleasure in these pages.

FRENCH POETRY

The Defiant Muse; French Feminist Poems from the Middle Ages to the Present. *Domna C. Stanton, ed.*

See under WOMEN'S POETRY AND FEMINIST POETRY

The Poetry of Surrealism; an Anthology. *Michael Benedikt, ed. and tr.* **(1974) Little, Brown. 375p., pap., o.p.**

This is similar to the *Random House Book of Twentieth-Century French Poetry,* but its focus and emphasis differ. Benedikt, as the title indicates, is involved only with modern French poets who have something to do with surrealism. Here, the elusive quality of the surreal is explored in the introduction, but it comes down to a single, simple statement: "Man is in a crisis." The compiler then calls upon some fifteen poets to elucidate. In the Random House collection there are twice that number of voices, a third again as many pages, and original French as well as the English translations. A number of poets and poems duplicate what is found in Benedikt. And while the compiler is a fine translator, his translations are not always as satisfactory as those found in the Random House work. So, for an individual, either book would suffice; for libraries, the Random House collection might be preferable, with its separate scope, a separate focus, and translations and poetry not found in the other.

Proensa; an Anthology of Troubadour Poetry. *Paul Blackburn, comp. and tr.; George Economou, ed.* **(1986) Paragon House. 325p.**

Troubadours were singer-poets who performed throughout the south of France in medieval times. Their poems date from the twelfth through the thirteenth centuries, and they sang of courtly and profane love. Paul Blackburn elected to make the poetry sing again, to a modern, English-speaking audience, and so he translated the poets in a richly passionate and contemporary style. He preserves the essence of the old verses, but gives them fresher structures and graceful, English phrasing. The result is that these aged poems are easy to read and empathize with, as they render the emotions of a long, lost society comprehensibly to a modern audience. Thus, the troubles of Bertran de Born, writing in the late twelfth century, with the performance demands of his Count, seem easy to understand. Blackburn's translations, which took over ten years to complete, serve the cause of this ancient Provençal poetry by allowing modern readers to appreciate its artistic excellence and variety.

The Random House Book of Twentieth-Century French Poetry. *Paul Auster, ed.* **(1982) Random House. 638p., pap.**

While Auster successfully conveys the glory of French verse, he fails on one count. The book is much too large. While the reference value of such bulk is fine for a library (and, as such, highly recommended), it is a bad choice for the individual who may wish to read in comfort. The number of poets is appropriate, but there are too many selections from lesser-known, less-talented people. With that, one must commend Auster for insisting on a bilingual edition and excellent translators. For example, the volume opens, as it should, with Apollinaire. "Zone" is in French on the left hand side. The translation into English on the other side is by Samuel Beckett. And within this single poet's work, one also finds translations by Richard Wilbur, Dudley Fitts, W. S. Merwin, and others. The cast of translators is as impressive as the translations and, in some of the later poets' work, even better than the original. There are adequate notes on the poets and a list of translators, but despite the size of the volume no alphabetical listings of poems, poets, or first lines. Auster's own translations and his introduction support his reputation.

The Women Troubadours. *Meg Bogin, ed.*

See under   WOMEN'S POETRY AND FEMINIST POETRY

GAY AND LESBIAN POETRY

Gay & Lesbian Poetry in Our Time; an Anthology. *Carl Morse and Joan Larkin, eds.* (1988) St. Martin's Press. 463p.

Here are more than ninety poets and over two hundred poems that testify to the gay and lesbian movement, primarily in the United States. Although the volume is large, the compilers limited their choices to poetry written after 1950. For the most part, the selection is good, and the work represents a fair cross-section of the movement's advocates. As of 1988, it is the best collection of its type. From page to page, one moves from psychological and mystical preoccupations to the everyday problems and delights of the poets. The writers are among the best, from W. H. Auden and James Baldwin to Adrienne Rich and Allen Ginsburg. The alphabetical arrangement of poets scatters the better-known among the less common.A definite attraction is the offering of leading poets from the black, native American, Asian-American, and Hispanic communities.There are some excellent photographs of the poets. As one might expect, AIDS plays a role in many of the poems, but none excels that of Thom Gunn's "Lament" for a lost friend.

The Penguin Book of Homosexual Verse. *Stephen Coote, ed.* (1983) Penguin Books. 410p., pap.

Published five years prior to *Gay & Lesbian Poetry in Our Time,* this book includes many of the same poets and poetry, but the selection is more historical, going back to Homer, Sappho, and Pindar. As the compiler points out, the collection "ranges in time and place from classical Athens to contemporary New York." Furthermore, not all of the poets celebrate the gay life. In fact "in tone and content [the poems range] from celebration to satire." The editor offers a brief, yet thorough, well-written introduction to the history of homosexual poetry and love. Gay and homosexual are used interchangeably, although "homosexual was chosen for the title because it can be employed relatively neutrally." Most of the poems are written in the Western tradition, and there are numerous translations, with due credit to the translators. Approximately half of the poems are from the late nineteenth and twentieth centuries, and the majority of poets are represented by one or two poems. The exceptions, with at least a half dozen entries each, are C. P. Cavafy, A. E. Housman, Shakespeare, and epigrams from the Greek Anthology.

GERMAN POETRY

An Anthology of World Poetry. *Mark Van Doren, ed.*

See under WORLD POETRY

The Defiant Muse; German Feminist Poems from the Middle Ages to the Present. *Susan L. Cocalis, ed.*

See under WOMEN'S POETRY AND FEMINIST POETRY

German Poetry from the Beginnings to 1750. *Ingrid Walsøe-Engel, ed.* (1992) Continuum. 338p., pap.

Beginning with religious verse of the tenth century and concluding with odes and songs of the eighteenth century, this anthology features the lyrical, beautiful poetry of German writers. The fifty-three poets include Walther von der Vogelweide, Martin Luther, Hans Sachs, and Wolfram von Eschenbach, among others, and are represented by hundreds of selections translated by several different scholars. Arranged chronologically by poet, the anthology also features many German "minnesongs" — a German poetic form that enjoyed great popularity in the thirteenth century. Included here are love songs, war songs, and many religious hymns. The lengthy foreword is particularly interesting, providing a critical and historical background on the development of German poetry and the unfortunate loss of pre-Christian tribal writings. Biographical information on the poets accompanies a helpful title- and first-line index, rounding out a strong volume for readers interested in an overview of the early German poetic tradition.

The Oxford Book of Verse in English Translation. *Charles Tomlinson, ed.*

See under WORLD POETRY

GREEK POETRY
Classical

The Greek Anthology and Other Ancient Epigrams. *Peter Jay, ed.*
(1981) Penguin Books. 447p., pap.

Peter Jay has done much more than compile sensitive translations of
epigrams from the Greek Anthology. He has provided a critical apparatus that includes a glossary, appendices, maps, scholarly notes on individual poems, a bibliography, a précis of the life and work of each
Greek poet represented here, and an informative introduction to the
whole volume. Although he occasionally gets bogged down in his effort
to distinguish between ancient and modern definitions of *lyric, elegiac,*
and *epigram*, the discussion succeeds in preparing the reader for a poetic
style that does not always conform to modern tastes. About 850 of the
original 4,000 epigrams have been selected. For a few of them more than
one translation is given. Departing from the traditional order, in which
the epigrams are arranged loosely by subject, Jay has divided them into
ten chronological periods, from the pre-Classical to the later Byzantine,
and within each period has grouped them by author. Poems are indexed
by author and by their number in a standard manuscript source. Among
the 40 translators are many distinguished poets, including Richmond
Lattimore, W. S. Merwin, Ezra Pound, and Kenneth Rexroth.

Hellenistic Poetry; an Anthology. *Barbara Hughes Fowler, ed.* **(1990)**
University of Wisconsin Press. 357p.

The editor states in her preface that this volume was intended to
introduce comprehensible Greek poetry to general readers and students.
Indeed, it is a strong beginner's anthology, complete with helpful indexes and a first-rate introduction to understanding ancient poems. Obscure works were excluded in order to feature verse that represents the
variety of forms expressed in Hellenistic poetry and to give the reader a
greater sense of what distinguishes Hellenistic poetry from other Greek
verse. Thirty-nine selections are presented in translation, most grouped
according to the eight featured poets. There are also carefully reconstructed, detailed maps of Greece, in addition to a helpful glossary of

proper names and references. Fowler's introduction provides a thorough analysis of the Hellenistic culture and period, and she explains the great impact these poets have had on such English writers such as Milton, Shelley, and Yeats. This handsome anthology succeeds as a fine introduction to Hellenistic verse, with clear, vivid translations.

The Infinite Moment; Poems from the Ancient Greek. *Sam Hamill, ed.* **(1992) New Directions. 108p.**

This is a competent, yet inadequate, volume of Greek poetry in translation. The verse the editor has included is quite beautiful, but because the anthology is so brief, with an average of 20 poems in each section, readers looking for a larger sampling of ancient Greek verse should look elsewhere. The text is divided into seven chapters — chapters for Sappho, Alcaeus, Anacreon, and Paulus Silentarius, and three featuring lesser-known poets and categorized by form, such as the epigram. Some of the verse, particularly that of Sappho, is highly sensual, while that of Alcaeus deals with political rather than personal themes. Overall, the poems are dreamy, mystical, and lyrical. Because the ancient Greeks have a rich literary tradition and distinctive forms of poetry, readers may be disappointed that this slim volume does not more fully illustrate that heritage. Hamill provides no index but a short foreword and an afterword offer some insight into the verse.

Poems from the Greek Anthology. *Kenneth Rexroth, ed. and tr.* **(1962) University of Michigan Press. 111p.**

This volume is a brief collection of more than a hundred short, lyrical Greek poems in English translation. It is an adequate collection, despite its lack of indexes, critical information, or even a table of contents. In a sparse, uncluttered way, the volume introduces some beautiful poems. Sappho and Plato may be among the most well known, but probably only readers already familiar with Greek verse will recognize the majority of the poets featured here. Arranged alphabetically by poet, all the poems are a page or shorter, and some only three or four lines. Rexroth acknowledges in his foreword that he has knowingly published translations that may irk traditional scholars. Also, he has included a few "lyric fragments" in Latin, as an "extra dividend" for readers. This anthology is merely a small representation of brilliant Greek lyrics; students and general readers may find more comprehensive volumes of equal or greater merit.

GREEK POETRY
Modern

Voices of Modern Greece. *Edmund Keeley and Philip Sherrard, trs. and eds.* **(1981) Princeton University Press. 204p.**

The voices are five major Greek poets, Constantine P. Cavafy (1863–1933), Angelos Sikelianos (1884–1951), George Seferis (1900–1971), Odysseus Elytis (b. 1911), and Nikos Gatsos (b. 1914). The translations, by the compilers, seem to capture the meaning and usually the spirit of the verse. Only here and there do the poems seem a bit flat, a trifle too hampered by literal translation. Of some help are the notes that establish the background of the works and pinpoint individuals mentioned in the poems. There is also a section that gives the biographies of each poet. An index of first lines completes the volume. Numerous poems were published earlier, and this is a splendid opportunity to have them gathered into a single volume, together with an author's later work. The selection is, in the words of the editors, "composed of translations of what seem to us to come over most successfully into English and at the same time to be representative of the best poetry of the original poets." A worthy goal and one they successfully achieved.

HEBREW AND YIDDISH POETRY

American Yiddish Poetry. *Benjamin Harshaw and Barbara Harshaw,* *eds.* **(1986) University of California Press. 815p.**

In this bilingual anthology the compilers rightfully set out to save seven Yiddish poets from neglect or oblivion. These are Americans who wrote in the twentieth century, who published in Yiddish newspapers and magazines, whose verse appeared in books long out of print. Most were born at the close of the nineteenth century, and the majority are now dead. They had a major influence on Jewish thought in America, and some of them went beyond the community to speak to the world. Most of them, however, gained little recognition outside their immediate circle. And they deserve an audience that will weigh their individual and collective contributions. There are excellent translations, notes, brief introductions, and, not least significant, a sixty-five-page introductory essay, "American Poetry in Yiddish."

Israeli Poetry; a Contemporary Anthology. *Warren Bargad and Stanley* *F. Chyet, comps. and trs.* **(1986) Indiana University Press. 273p.**

Hebrew, in the words of these editors, was assuredly "never a dead language." It has always been used for religious purposes and sometimes for secular literary ones as well. Since the founding of the state of Israel, there has been a flowering of creative writing in Hebrew. The poetry that has been collected in this anthology treats the past forty years of literary achievement in Israel. The contributors are arranged chronologically, and each of the eleven poets is accorded a good deal of space. Perhaps the most famous of the authors is Yehuda Amichai, but all of them are outstanding. Two are women. Each poet is introduced through generous biographical notes. The forms of the works vary; there are traditional forms, prose poems, and open forms. These are excellent poems, but they would be more accessible with notes explaining some of the foreign words.

Modern Hebrew Poetry. *Bernhard Frank, ed. and tr.* **(1980) University of Iowa Press. 176p.**

Compared to *Voices within the Ark; the Modern Jewish Poets,* which came out the same year, this is about one sixth the size and limited only to Hebrew poetry. Most of the poets are in both volumes. The poems however, are not the same, and where the individual or library has one, the other will be wanted. If a choice must be made, this collection has generally superior translations. And yet, it is worth emphasizing, the scope is so much narrower that comparison is hardly fair. There are some sixty poets present. The greatest number of entries are for Israel Efrat, Yehudah Amikhai, and Itamar Ya'oz-kest. Pinkhas Sadeh has a single poem. The introduction contains a history of modern Hebrew poetry, with its place in the Hebrew tradition.

Modern Hebrew Poetry; a Bilingual Anthology. *Ruth Finer Mintz, ed. and tr.* **(1966) University of California Press. 371p.**

The editor of this volume has translated the works of twenty-eight European and Israeli poets into English, preserving the original Hebrew-language versions on opposite pages. "Modern" here stretches back to the turn of the century, before Israel was technically a nation, and includes poetry written up to the date of publication. In total, 121 poems are featured, ranging from ballads and prayers to contemporary free-form verse. Much of the poetry is rich and lyrical, evoking the Hebrew Bible and other sacred texts — although the poetry is not "biblical" in any sense. In translating the poems, Mintz explains that, because of the differences in the structure of English and Hebrew, she has had to omit poems whose emotional tension and cadence would be compromised. A lengthy introduction provides historical and critical analysis on the development and distinctiveness of Hebrew poetry. In addition, notes about the authors and poems are particularly insightful. Most English-language readers will be unfamiliar with the poets and their verse, but this anthology serves as a strong, stimulating introduction.

The Penguin Book of Modern Yiddish Verse. *Irving Howe, Ruth R. Wisse, and Khone Shmeruk, eds.* **(1987) Viking Press. 719p.**

A bilingual anthology, this is particularly useful for those who read Yiddish; it also a fascinating anthology for English readers who are interested in Yiddish culture. While it covers a variety of Yiddish verse written in the past hundred years, it features the works of such major poets as Jacob Glatstein, Moyshe-Leyb Halpern, and Abraham Sutzkever. The translations are by such fine writers as Cynthia Ozick and John Hollander. A learned introduction by the editors details the socio-political context in which the poems were created, and biographical notes introduce each of the writers. This book is an eye-opener for readers with only a vague knowledge of Yiddish cultural achievements. The poems evoke a vivid sense of life in the European and American ghettos, intense religious experiences, celebrations of the family, and sophisticated ruminations on art. The variety of poets is great, and their responses to their own and surrounding communities are highly individual and compelling.

A Treasury of Jewish Poetry. *Nathan Ausubel and Maryann Ausubel, eds.* **(1957) Crown Publishers. 471p., o.p.**

Both secular and religious Jewish poetry is included in this standard, although by now somewhat dated, anthology. The material moves from the biblical period to the modern, and while the focus is on Jewish poets, their themes do not necessarily concern Jewish subjects. This wide scope allows the compilers to say in the introduction that the content is much broader than in similar collections. "Jewish poetry consists of all poetry created by Jews." On the whole, the choices from this wide field are excellent, and most of the outstanding poets of all times are included. Post-Second World War writers, possibly for lack of space, are not as well represented as they might be, but this is made up for by the emphasis on poets throughout the ages. There are biographical sketches of each of the authors, and an index of titles and first lines. The introduction is a model of scholarship, as are the numerous translations throughout the whole volume.

Voices within the Ark; the Modern Jewish Poets. *Howard Schwartz and Anthony Rudolf, eds.* **(1980) Avon Books. 1,210p., pap.**

The problem is familiar and can be stated as a question: If one limits a collection of verse to "modern" poets and then imposes a further, narrower limitation, is it possible to find that many good voices? Here the focus is on "modern Jewish" poets, and the net is cast wide to include those writing in Hebrew (over seventy-five), Yiddish (another forty or so), English, and "other languages." The latter two categories take up almost eight hundred pages. Poets are arranged alphabetically under each category, and for each there is a reasonably detailed biographical sketch. The translations seem excellent. Each section has separate, perceptive introductions that are models of their kind, providing the setting for the poetry. It is difficult to find a Jewish poet writing between 1920 and 1980 who is not included. To return to the opening question, more selectivity is needed. There are absolutely marvelous poems in this volume, but the majority are, to say the least, minor. The major poets are found in greater depth in other collections. It is, nevertheless, a must for libraries and for individuals because of its target audience.

HISPANIC-AMERICAN POETRY

After Aztlan; Latino Poets of the Nineties. *Ray González, ed.* (1992)
David R. Godine. 258p., pap.

The introduction to this competent anthology stresses the differences among the thirty-four poets included here, but many of them tend, in fact, to sound alike. They have composed vivid poetry, largely with themes of cultural identity and racial oppression. Several forms and styles are included. Most of the poets, all of whom are Americans from different Latino backgrounds, particularly Puerto Rican and Mexican, will be unknown to average readers. They write illustrious verse that draws upon mythology and urban influences and incorporates spirituality and family themes. Arranged alphabetically by poet, the verse is accomplished and vivid, particularly effective when read aloud. Although no anthology can summarize an entire culture and no one poet stands out as genius, this volume is highly recommended as a solid view of modern Latino poets and the vivacious poetry they have produced. There is brief biographical information about each poet at the back of the book.

Contemporary Chicana Poetry; a Critical Approach to an Emerging Literature. *Marta Ester Sánchez, ed.* (1985) **University of California Press. 375p., pap.**

There is a great deal of prose in this volume, since it is an attempt to introduce its readership to an emerging poetry. At the outset, in "Setting the Context," the editor discusses the precarious topics of gender, ethnicity, and silence in Chicana poetry today. She then goes on to explore the work of Alma Villanueva, Lorna Dee Cervantes, Lucha Corpi, and Bernice Zamora. Along the way, many poems by each of these writers are quoted, and the appendix includes still more poems. The analyses are sophisticated and require a good deal of knowledge about poetic techniques and explication. But the introduction to societal codes and norms will prove helpful to those who want an understanding of contemporary Chicana poetry. And the poems themselves are a striking choice from a group of poets who are not heard from very often by the general reading public. All of these poets are women, and they represent a fairly wide range of Chicana writing today.

The Defiant Muse; Hispanic Feminist Poems from the Middle Agesto the Present. *Angel Flores and Kate Flores, eds.*

See under   Women's Poetry and Feminist Poetry

Fiesta in Aztlan; Anthology of Chicano Poetry. *Toni Empringham, ed.* **(1981) Capra Press. 128p., o.p.**

In only three bilingual sections, the poets celebrate the life of the Chicano. "La Familia" has eight poems, from Teresa Acosta's "My mother pieced quilts" to Margarita Reyes's "The old man who is gone now." The next section is called "The Streets of the Barrio" and is by far the finest in the collection. Here eight poets tell what it is like to live in their own community. Luis Rodriguez sums it up in prose: "Here in the barrios we can open up, be ourselves, and be funny in a Chicano sort of way. . . . True there is death and violence here, but there is much more life." "El Mundo," the final section, is the longest, and its fifteen poets consider everything from a "Dopefiends Trip" to "The Spanish Girls" and "Visions of Mexico While at a Writing Symposium in Port Townsend, Washington." There are biographical sketches of the poets, and a splendid introduction by the compiler who also translated the poetry. He explains the title: Chicanos "live in Aztlan, the name given by the Aztecs to their place of origin, the land to the north, which they left to found their great empire near Mexico City. For Chicanos, Aztlan represents their homeland."

Inventing a Word; an Anthology of Twentieth-Century Puerto Rican Poetry. *Julio Marzán, ed.* **(1980) Columbia University Press. 183p.**

This bilingual edition includes twenty-three poets who represent "a continuation into the twentieth century of two poetic traditions — each with distinct attitudes toward language, culture, and politics that have competitively co-existed in Puerto Rican literature since the emergence of Puerto Rican consciousness in the nineteenth century." One would be hard pressed to find a better history of that development than in the articulate, scholarly introduction by the compiler. The poems, ably translated by the same compiler, represent a variety of styles. Final choice, as is often the case with translations, is based on which of the poems can be understood in English. "To be sure, deciding on this basis resulted in some notable omissions, especially of the purist and avant-garde poetry.... These omitted poems sounded either old fashioned or generally unexciting in translation." There are brief biographical notes, but no index.

See also LATIN-AMERICAN POETRY

HOLIDAY POETRY

Callooh! Callay! Holiday Poems for Young Readers. *Myra Cohn Livingston, ed.* (1978) Atheneum. 131p., o.p.

The eighty holiday poems in Myra Cohn Livingston's *Callooh! Callay!* are arranged by holiday — "Thanksgiving," "Christmas," and "Mother's Day," for example. The poems, all pleasant and evocative of specific holidays, are by various authors: anonymous Chinese, Native American, and English poets; such earlier poets as Whitman and Tennyson; modern poets Langston Hughes, e. e. cummings, and X. J. Kennedy; and such non-Western authors as Russian poet Alexandr Blok and Chinese poet Su T'Ung Po. The book, however, lacks poems about such non-Christian holidays as Chanukkah or Kwanzaa. Although children may enjoy reading the poems in this book, they will not learn much about the world's holidays.

The Naked Astronaut; Poems on Birth and Birthdays. *René Graziani, ed.* (1983) Faber and Faber. 380p., o.p.

The quest for a subject that has not already been the theme of a poetry anthology drives editors to compile guides such as this one. Sometimes they do quite nicely. This is a case in point. "To the best of my knowledge, the subject of birth and birthdays has not been anthologized before." Here is a pleasing collection, divided by broad subjects from "Birth and Good Wishes" to "Variations." The first has the greatest number of poems, closely followed by "Poet's Anniversaries," where Walt Whitman writes about his seventy-first year and Howard Nemerov celebrates his fifteenth birthday. In general, the poets and the poems are outstanding and would be so in any collection, no matter what its theme. There are an index of first lines and a brief glossary.

O Frabjous Day; Poetry for Holidays and Special Occasions. *Myra Cohn Livingston, ed.* **(1977) Atheneum. 205p., o.p.**

Each basic American holiday is celebrated with a half dozen poems by almost as many poets. Most of the entries are from the moderns, i.e., those born no later than the end of the nineteenth century. And most of the poets are standard voices, from T. S. Eliot to Ted Berrigan and William Carlos Williams. The compiler is to be congratulated on three counts. First, there are some exceptional voices from other lands, other times, and these include a Chinese ninth-century poet and the noble Roman Sedulius Scottus. Second, while centered on American culture, there are holidays — particularly Halloween, Easter, and birthdays — where the English and others are brought into the collection. Third, the selection itself represents an unusual, imaginative grasp of the meaning of our holidays, and while much of this is suitable for children, it can be enjoyed as well by adults. The holidays include, other than those previously mentioned, New Year, Valentine's Day, Lincoln's and Washington's birthdays, Memorial Day, Fourth of July, Columbus Day, Thanksgiving, Christmas, and other religious holidays. An odd section: Assassination Poems, which includes poetry about the death of John F. Kennedy, Lincoln, Malcolm X, etc. There are brief notes on a few of the poems, followed by indexes of authors, titles, first lines, and translators.

Our Holidays in Poetry. *Mildred P. Harrington and Josephine H. Thomas, comps.* **(1929) H. W. Wilson. 479p.**

Some sixty years ago, this book was first published. It has been a hit ever since. Teachers, librarians, students, and parents all love it because of the three hundred and fifty poems that enhance the experiences of various holidays. The poems are listed alphabetically by title under eight headings: Abraham Lincoln, George Washington, Easter, Arbor Day, Mother's Day, Memorial Day, Thanksgiving, and Christmas. About forty poems are given for each event. Published in a period when holidays were significant, there is no effort to commemorate sports, local customs, or commercial kinds of diversions. The poems are old-fashioned and safe. Quality varies considerably, although no one could ever accuse the compilers of being inconsistent about tying poems to holidays. Annette Wynne's "The Pilgrims Came," for example, is side by side with several Psalms, Robert Herrick, and Robert Bridges. In the index of authors the first entry is Henry Abbey with "What Do We Plant When We Plant the Tree," followed directly by Joseph Addison. Quite jolly, without preten-

sion, the collection serves its purpose well and faithfully. It is likely to be
around for at least sixty more years.

The Oxford Book of Christmas Poems. *Michael Harrison and
Christopher Stuart-Clark, eds.* **(1983) Oxford University Press. 160p.**

This is a splendid anthology for young people and adults. Any collection with such a title needs no introduction, and the compilers agree.
They open immediately with the poems and some one hundred and sixty
pages later close with an index of titles and first lines. The poems are
arranged under four major subject headings: "The sky turns dark, the
years grow old"; "This was the moment when before turned into after";
"Glad Christmas comes, and every hearth makes room to bid him welcome now"; "Open you the east door and let the New Year in." All of the
headings, of course, are from poems — normally the first in each section.
There are colorful illustrations throughout the slim volume, and while
almost all of the poems will appeal to adults, the line drawings seem
particularly suited to younger readers. Most of the poets are well known,
having found fame in the latter part of the nineteenth or in the twentieth
century, and almost all are exclusively English and American voices.
There are a few traditional poems, although the majority are by such
people as Louis MacNeice, W. H. Auden, Spike Milligan, and John
Betjeman.

Poems for Seasons and Celebrations. *William Cole, ed.* **(1961) World.
191p., o.p.**

Children will enjoy this collection of poems that evokes all the enchantment of such seasons and holidays as Christmas, summer, October,
and Halloween. The poems are lyrical and vivid, by poets as distinguished as Frank O'Connor, e. e. cummings, Robert Frost, and William
Blake. Indexed by title and author, the verse is presented attractively,
with illustrations accompanying some of the selections. Divided by subject, the poems in this volume cover everything from Ground-Hog Day
and the Fourth of July to New Year's Eve. Some of the verse may feel
too young and innocent for older children to enjoy, but all of it has a
special, magical quality that will delight younger readers, whether they
are reading alone or being read to.

Poems for the Great Days. *Thomas Curtis Clark and Robert Earle Clark, eds.* (1948) Abingdon-Cokesbury Press. 245p.

It is hard to tell for whom this volume of holiday poems is planned. The verse is simple and joyous, almost childlike in its simplicity; there are no colorful illustrations, no evocative subtitles, just a collection of three hundred poems, most from the mid-nineteenth to the mid-twentieth century. Poets include Christina Rossetti, Whitman, Wilde, and Tennyson. The verse is arranged according to the calendar, beginning with New Year's Day and Lincoln's Birthday and ending with Thanksgiving and Christmas, but this anthology omits many important days — Halloween and the Jewish holidays, for instance. These are poems some older readers may remember from school assemblies, recitations with patriotic or strong Christian themes. There are no dates or notes on the diversity of the year's events, and no biographical information. Indexed by author, title, and first line.

Poems of Christmas. *Myra Cohn Livingston, ed.* (1980) Atheneum. 172p.

The well-known anthologist turns her hand to Christmas and produces a good selection of poems for ten-year-olds to teenagers. Many of the verses will be equally attractive to adults. There are eight subject sections with about one hundred poets from various eras. The majority are American and English, and there is a strong influence of late nineteenth- and early twentieth-century voices. While W. H. Auden, Gwendolyn Brooks, T. S. Eliot, Robert Frost, and W. B. Yeats are strong entries, one wonders about some of the company they keep — Clement Clarke Moore and Edwin Morgan, to name only two of dozens of poets whose only apparent claim to prominence lay in writing about holidays. Nevertheless, it works well enough. The modest and mediocre fit nicely into the pattern of the theme, and the handful of genuine poetic voices are a pleasant change. The book is compiled primarily for children and to illustrate the joys of a single holiday. Indexes of titles, authors, and first lines, are provided.

Ring Out, Wild Bells; Poems about Holidays and Seasons. *Lee Bennett Hopkins, ed.* (1992) Harcourt Brace Jovanovich. 80p.

This slender children's volume should be noted for its poetry as well as for its color and black-and-white illustrations. Arranged chronologically by season and holiday, it begins with New Year's Day and Ground Hog Day and continues through the calendar, ending with Christmas,

Hanukkah, and the winter solstice. Seventy-five poems are featured in this tall book, complemented by artwork children will find enchanting. Christina Rossetti, Robert Frost, Carl Sandburg, and X. J. Kennedy are among the best known of the featured poets; many of the more contemporary authors are obscure. The verse is generally brief and joyful, finding pleasure in the holidays and illustrating all the things children see and experience during holiday times. Recommended for younger children, this is the kind of volume they will want to have with them as they grow older. Indexed by author, title, and first line.

Sing a Song of Seasons; Poems about Holidays, Vacation Days, and Days to Go to School. *Sara Brewton and John E. Brewton, eds.* **(1955) Macmillan. 200p., o.p.**

This anthology will enchant young readers and probably also remind their elders of the excitement children feel during special holiday and vacation times. The poems include many classics loved by older audiences — Frost's "Stopping by Woods on a Snowy Evening" and Blake's "Infant Joy," among many others. Yet much of the delightful, simple verse was written by poets just for children, works by Robert Louis Stevenson, Christina Rossetti, and Eleanor Farjeon. The poems are arranged by the cycle of the seasons and by holidays throughout the year, beginning with poems about morning, autumn, and birthdays and concluding with summer and the end of school. This anthology is unpretentious and uplifting, capturing the simple joys of catching bugs and dressing up for Halloween — captivating verse with a celebratory, innocent feel.

HUMOROUS AND NONSENSE VERSE

A Century of Humorous Verse, 1850–1950. *Roger Lancelyn Green, ed.* (1959) E. P. Dutton. 289p.

There are enough selections in this anthology to tickle anyone's funny bone, but what might be the best of the lot are located in the appendixes at the end of the book. There, all but buried, is a superb, plentiful collection of limericks by known and unknown authors, along with some wonderful rootless rhymes and stray verses. Otherwise, in the core of the book, one can find lively and amusing examples of comic verse written by Kipling, Lewis Carroll, Edward Lear, and Ogden Nash, to mention the most famous. There are also scores of currently unknown poets who are, as often as not, quite adept at satire, parody, and nonsense. Also included are the delightful poems "The Ballard of Private Chadd," by A. A. Milne, "Aunt Tabitha," by Oliver Wendell Holmes, and "The Bath," by G. K. Chesterton. This book is most entertaining to dip into for small, comic breaks in the day; it helps provide therapeutic moments of helpless laughter.

The Chatto Book of Nonsense Poetry. *Hugh Haughton, ed.* (1988) Chatto & Windus. 530p.

After browsing through this delightful anthology, readers will be amazed at the wide range of poets who have written "nonsense" or light, comical verse. Collected in this thick volume are obscure tenth-century French poets, such English Renaissance writers as Donne, Jonson, and Dryden, later poets Millay and Yeats, and even such rock singers as Bob Dylan and David Byrne. Hundreds of poems by about forty poets are here, many in translation and some in their original language. They are arranged chronologically by poet, from medieval times to the late twentieth century. All forms and styles are featured, and generally they are silly, clever, and brief. The anthology is primarily for adults. Too often, collections of light verse take on a childlike tone or are directed at children as a way of introducing them to poetry, but the strength of this volume is its amazing, wide choice of selections that delve deeper than the ubiquitous Ogden Nash poems. Indexed by author, title, and first line.

The Devil's Book of Verse; Masters of the Poison Pen from Ancient Times to the Present Day. *Richard Conniff, ed.; Foreword by Willard R. Espy.* **(1983) Dodd, Mead. 269p., o.p.**

This is one of the most refreshing anthologies in recent years, with witty, misanthropic verse by both well-known and anonymous writers. Rarely is an anthology so wonderfully brazen in its denunciation of mankind as this one, edited by Richard Conniff (who also contributes two poems). Conniff includes writers from Catullus to Shelley to Dorothy Parker — some known for caustic verse, some not, but all unapologetically vicious in their observations. Neatly arranged under such subject headings as "War is Heaven" and "The Joy of Living," the poems are candidly nasty. Yet it is the well-written nastiness that makes this anthology so delightful; the tone of the poems ranges from silly to bitter, and all are superbly crafted. Conniff has an ear for powerfully satirical verse, and his introduction and the foreword by Willard R. Espy make for equally enjoyable reading. Conniff writes that the attraction to nasty verse is probably obvious to "anyone who has ever been advised by an ice cream counter girl that 'This is the first day of the rest of your life.' " — a sentiment only a misanthrope could fail to appreciate.

The Faber Book of Comic Verse. *Michael Roberts and Janet Adam Smith, eds.* **(Rev. ed., 1974; paperback ed., 1978) Faber and Faber. 400p., o.p.**

This volume concentrates on nonsense, parody, and satire and covers a span of four centuries of comic writing. It arranges the material chronologically and, within time periods, topically. Therefore, it is easy to spot such highlights as hilarious epitaphs and epigrams. In addition, there is a fairly good selection from such top writers as Edward Lear, and Lewis Carroll. The book is regrettably weighed down by much undistinguished verse — neither very funny nor very fine — and its coverage of modern comic poetry is sparse. It provides, nevertheless, a sense of the range of humorous and satirical verse in English and includes such popular forms as the limerick and many works by the productive anonymous writers of the sixteenth through the twentieth centuries. Most poets are represented by just one or two poems.

The Faber Book of Epigrams and Epitaphs. *Geoffrey Grigson, ed.* (1977) Faber and Faber. 291p., o.p.

Reading too many of these poems at one sitting could put you off epigrams for life, but if taken in judicious doses these are really succulent, small morsels. Epigrams and epitaphs have a long, distinguished history, dating back to ancient Greece and Rome. Epigrams tend to be short, sharp poems that praise or disparage someone or some thing; epitaphs comment, sometimes grimly or amusingly, on the dead. This collection, with its lucid introduction by Geoffrey Grigson, sets forth the epigrams and epitaphs of such major writers as Martial, Blake, Robert Herrick, Pope, and Emily Dickinson, alongside dozens of anonymous writers. Many of these poems are funny, lightly humorous, or rude and wounding; others are clearly philosophical. Whatever the reader's taste or temperament, there will be poems here to suit — poems of outrage, poems of spite, poems of acclaim, poems of gratitude. Also included is John Gay's wonderful epitaph for himself, summing up everything a sardonic spirit has to say about life.

The Faber Book of Nonsense Verse. *Geoffrey Grigson, ed.* (1979) Faber and Faber. 352p.

In his introduction, Geoffrey Grigson explores the meanings of nonsense verse, and concludes, "Whatever the kind or the mixture, the nonsense poem — if it works — refreshes us by surprise, by invention, or by commenting, in what is said or how it is said, on sense taking itself too seriously or being pompous, or in fashion." There are some real surprises here: the original "Pop Goes the Weasel," which was a popular song in the Victorian era, and many wonderful limericks. The great stars of this collection are, predictably, Lewis Carroll and Edward Lear. The former has dozens of his nonsense poems reprinted, including the long and celebrated "The Hunting of the Snark." You will also find "Jabberwocky," "The White Knight's Ballad," and "Father William" among the many entries. Edward Lear's "The Owl and the Pussycat" and "The Dong with a Luminous Nose" are included. Among the more remarkable modern poets found here are Stevie Smith and T. S. Eliot. The overall quality of the book varies: many of the poems are undistinguished, but most of them are amusing. The anonymous verses are printed in roughly chronological order.

The Faber Book of Parodies. *Simon Brett, ed.* **(1984) Faber and Faber. 383p., pap.**

At least half of this collection is prose, but there is more than enough poetry to justify its inclusion in a collection of poetry anthologies. Arrangement is alphabetical by the author being parodied. Usually there are one or two parodies for each of the writers. The book opens, for example, with a parody on Douglas Adams's "The Scriptwriter's Guide to Galaxy" by Andrew Marshall and David Renwick. Ronald Mason, John Flood, and Russell Davies poke affectionate fun at three of W. H. Auden's poems, and Ezra Pound is among those who poke fun at W. B. Yeats. Who are the writers most likely to be parodied? If the number of listings is any guide, Shakespeare comes first, followed by Swinburne, Tennyson, and Wordsworth. Most of the take-offs tend, incidentally, to concern English writers, by about nine to one. Among the Americans present are Ernest Hemingway (with parodies by Raymond Chandler and Henry Hetherington), Damon Runyon, J. D. Salinger, and Mickey Spillane. A good number of the parodies are by equally famous writers, from Robert Benchley and Kenneth Tynan to Ezra Pound and Lewis Carroll. One learns some surprising things, e.g., Carroll's famous verse "Father William" was inspired by a deadly serious poem with similar lines from the pen of Robert Southey.

The Fireside Book of Humorous Poetry. *William Cole, ed.* **(1959) Simon and Schuster. 522p., o.p.**

This heavy volume of humorous poetry is a mixed bag: some of the verses are largely forgettable and others are excellent. The poems are thematically arranged: "The Other Animals," "Eccentrics and Individualists," "Edibles, Potables and Smokeables," and "Juveniles" are the first four sections, and there are fifteen others. The best poets, whose work keeps recurring throughout the anthology, are W. S. Gilbert, with some of the excellent lyrics from his operettas, Lewis Carroll, with, most notably, "The Walrus and the Carpenter," and Ogden Nash with many entries. Some superior segments of the book are those about animals and the section of witty verse forms such as epigrams and clerihews. Other authors who are well represented are Hilaire Belloc and Dorothy Parker. There should be some humor here for every reader's taste, but unfortunately the finest writers are surrounded by too many mediocre ones.

I Have No Gun But I Can Spit; an Anthology of Satirical and Abusive Verse. *Kenneth Baker, ed.* **(1980) Faber and Faber. 185p., pap.**

Anyone charmed by the W. H. Auden verse that lends its title to this collection will enjoy this spirited anthology. Slender and brief, the volume is arranged in fourteen categories with titles such as "Money the She-Devil," ". . . And Hate My Next Door Neighbour," and "Behold the Politician." Most of the poems were written by distinguished British and American poets of the past three centuries and include such masters of satire as Jonathan Swift and Ogden Nash. Several poems are taken, however, from less-expected sources, including the Bible and Monty Python. In his fine introduction, the editor explains that he compiled this volume because there are so few anthologies devoted to intense hatred and abuse. The verse here is brash, biting, and often downright nasty, but it is entertaining and well written, sure to be enjoyed by all readers. There are poet and first-line indexes.

Innocent Merriment; an Anthology of Light Verse. *Franklin P. Adams, ed.* **(1942) McGraw-Hill. 523p., o.p.**

The editor states in his introduction that he compiled this collection in order to give light verse the credit due from critics who routinely disparage it. The playful tone of this introduction permeates the volume, making it worthwhile and entertaining. Almost five hundred poems of widely varying length are presented. They represent a variety of periods, styles, and writers, including Dorothy Parker, Stephen Vincent Benét, Alexander Pope, and Oliver Wendell Holmes. The poems are divided into sections based on subject or form — for example, "Burlesque Parody" and "Song and Story." Most of the poems could, however, cross over into any of the sections. The poems here are not particularly vicious or belligerent, but most are wry and cleverly amusing. This anthology collects a wide range of light poems by well-known and not-so-well-known authors, presenting their verse without frills or pretension. Indexed by title, poet, and first line.

The New Oxford Book of English Light Verse. *Kingsley Amis, ed.* **(1978) Oxford University Press. 347p.**

Compiled by the celebrated writer Kingsley Amis, this volume of comical, wry, and satirical poetry is arranged in chronological order, from Shakespeare to the present day, and includes both the work of acknowledged poets and savory contributions from anonymous authors. (If Virginia Woolf was right in claiming that Anonymous usually was a woman, then women are well represented in this collection. Otherwise, they are in very short supply.) The standard of the light verse is high, with substantial sections devoted to the work of Byron, Lewis Carroll, and Philip Larkin. The limericks Amis has chosen are bawdy and extremely funny. The spirit soars with this collection; the verse is unreservedly delightful. In a thoughtful introduction, Amis defines "light verse" and makes clear his differences with W. H. Auden, the previous compiler of this volume. Auden's selections tended to have a more revolutionary intent, Amis's are resoundingly apolitical. His purpose is to provide the kind of verse that people love to read, and he has gathered together an outstanding collection of just that kind of poetry.

A Nonsense Anthology. *Carolyn Wells, comp.* **(1930) Scribner's; paperback edition of 1958 published by Dover. 300p., pap.**

"On a topographical map of literature," writes the compiler in her introduction, "nonsense would be represented by a small and sparsely settled country, neglected by the average tourist." Well, that was probably true back in 1930, but by 1989 there have been at least a dozen popular collections of nonsense and humorous verse published. This anthology has the distinction of being one of the first and is still one of the best. Here one finds the familiar, venerable poets from Lewis Carroll and "Jabberwocky" to Edward Lear and his "Limericks." Of the seventy or so poets, the majority are English. Happy exceptions include Gelett Burgess, with "The Purple Cow" and seven other equally delightful poems. Many of the experts at fun are well-known serious poets, but some are remembered today only for their nonsense verse, Francis Stokes's "Blue Moonshine" and George Canning's "The Old Gentleman." There are indexes of authors, first lines, and titles. The arrangement is by such rather arbitrary categories as "High Sentiments" and "Resounding Trivialities," but the verse ought not to require any order at all.

The Norton Book of Light Verse. *Russell Baker, ed.* **(1986) W. W. Norton. 447p.**

Chosen by the exemplary satirist Russell Baker, more than four hundred entertaining poems are here arranged thematically, covering such topics as "Twentieth Century Blues," "Some Fun with the Mother Tongue," "Love," and "Words to Live By." The definition of light verse is broad enough to include bleakly sardonic, wisely bemused, and blithely humorous works. A delectable selection, the volume features excellent poems by first-rate writers, as well as good deal of delicious fluff. Unfortunately, the editor also prints lyrics from songs, and although undoubtedly clever, their infectious music is sadly lacking. (Noel Coward and Cole Porter are the most obviously abused; others, like W. S. Gilbert, survive the translation of mere words into print.) English and American, male and female, well-known and minor poets from the nineteenth and twentieth centuries are in evidence. This is a superior survey, one every library should own.

The Oxford Book of American Light Verse. *William Harmon, ed.* (1979) Oxford University Press. 540p.

From Colonial times to the present, the compiler assembles a group of masters of light, humorous verse. Among those included are Ogden Nash, X. J. Kennedy, Walt Whitman, and many anonymous and little-known poets. Among the best are those who were unintentionally humorous. These are so bad that they are good. Examples range from the Rev. Thomas Holley Chivers to Julia A. Moore, the "Sweet Singer of Michigan." Compared to Kingsley Amis's *New Oxford Book of English Light Verse* (see above), this is a bit tame. The difference between the two is most marked in subject matter. The English tend to consider class, intellectual games, and politics fair targets, while Americans put greater emphasis on common daily activities. Given that distinction, the American light verse book is to be recommended for its frequently witty, sometimes satirical, and even ribald, approach to life.

The Oxford Book of Light Verse. *W. H. Auden, ed.* (1938) Oxford University Press. 552p., pap., o.p.

Similarly to the more ambitious *Poets of the English Language*, this volume has the distinction and interest of having been compiled by W. H. Auden. The choices illustrate the poet's infatuation with style and shades of satire. The order of the poems is chronological, and "the impossibility of adequately modernizing poems of the Middle English period has made it necessary to reproduce in their original forms all poems up to the early sixteenth century." After that the poems are modernized in spelling and punctuation. Many of the early entries are anonymous ballads, but by the time of Chaucer, there is a spattering of named authors. Auden unfortunately chose not to include any of his own better nonsense verses, but all the other fine writers are here, from Edward Lear and Lewis Carroll to John Betjeman, who winds down the collection. Light verse is not easy to describe or delimit, but Auden explains it neatly in his brief introduction. His choices support his considered definition, and one should remember that "light" does not necessarily mean popular or pleasing. There are numerous examples of ready wit, such as Sassoon's devastating "The General" or the more famous "Verses on the Death of Dr. Swift Written by Himself: Nov. 1731" that were equally suitable when he died some fifteen years later.

The Oxford Book of Satirical Verse. *Geoffrey Grigson, comp.* **(1980) Oxford University Press. 454p., pap., o.p.**

Ernest Hemingway is not associated with poetry, but here he is represented with one satirical scatological verse of six short lines. Pope, Dryden, and Swift, who knew a bit more about satirical comment, are given seven to twelve times as much space, as are such later poets as Byron and Hilaire Belloc. The eighty or so masters of the art are disparate in time and in fame, but they share one common trait: the ability to swing a punitive, often scathing, blow at the ego. The juxtaposition of the varying talents is unceasingly fascinating. Failures or successes at conventional verse, these writers are all articulate in satire, even if they have only one entry as in the case of Hemingway, Kingsley Amis, Clive James, and, yes, Philip Larkin. Perhaps the weakness of an otherwise fine collection is the failure to give over space to the moderns, such as Larkin, who really deserve more than one entry. Modest Geoffrey Grigson fails to include any of his own fine poetry, and he does little service to American writers. He clearly favors the English. The chronological arrangement (from the fifteenth through the twentieth centuries) has its points, but would it not have been better to arrange the poems by broad subject? The brief introduction contains an excellent definition of "satire."

Parodies; an Anthology from Chaucer to Beerbohm — and After. *Dwight Macdonald, ed.* **(1960) Modern Library. 575p., pap.**

An outstanding social and literary critic, Macdonald loved parody. "I enjoy it as an intuitive kind of literary criticism. . . . It is Method acting, since a successful parodist must live himself, imaginatively, into his parodee. . . . I like its bookish flavor because I like books, and parody is a kind of literary shop talk." The parodists move through literary history, from Chaucer to Jane Austen to Cyril Connolly. The authors parodied are sometimes also the parodists, but this is unusual. Macdonald acknowledges that parody ages faster than any other literary genre because the reader must be familiar with the material being parodied. Twentieth-century readers may be particularly deficient with respect to literary references. In addition, "the objections to breadth in parody are that it is not sporting to hunt with a machine gun. . . . Most of what passes for parody is actually so broad as to be mere burlesque." The compiler fortunately avoids both what can no longer be understood or appreciated and the broad, meaningless parody. Probably more than two thirds of the collection is poetry, but there is such noteworthy prose as Baron Corvo's "Reviews of Unwritten Books" and E. B. White's "Across the Street and into the Grill," the latter a takeoff on Ernest Hemingway. There are four logical sections, followed by an excellent appendix in which Macdonald gives a fuller explanation of the parody form.

Pegasus Descending; a Book of the Best Bad Verse. *James Camp, X. J. Kennedy, and Keith Waldrop, eds.* **(1971) Macmillan. 238p., o.p.**

Collecting the best of the worst poetry can be a daunting task, but the editors of this lively, little anthology have come up with some gems. Grouped under such subjects as "Death," "Food and Drink," and "Social Comment," the hundreds of poems are all bad in their own unique way. Some are long-winded and pompous, others mawkish, sly, and terribly amateurish. All are funny, even the tombstone epitaphs and the entire section devoted to truly awful opening lines. Most of the verse is by obscure writers, although featured here are some by such well-known poets as Robert Browning, Hopkins, Hardy, and Emerson. Critical notes and biographical information are provided for each poem, and the collection has an index of authors and titles. This collection is lighthearted and amusing, except perhaps to the poets who may inadvertently find their work herein.

The Penguin Book of Light Verse. *Gavin Ewart, ed.* **(1980) Penguin Books. 639p., pap., o.p.**

This anthology presents an excellent — and funny — overview of the history of light verse. From bawdy, anonymous riddles to the wry, satirical poetry of T. S. Eliot, Nash, and Updike, this volume is a real treasure — more than 350 poems are featured by 150 poets, many of them prominent writers not known for their humorous poetry. Some of the selections are scathing replies to "serious" poems such as "Dover Beach" and "Who is Sylvia?"; others are sexual and political commentaries, or brief put-downs and quips. The poetry is arranged chronologically by author. Superb well-known and more obscure verse by Donne, Byron, Browning, Pope, and other masters of "serious" poetry make this anthology a gem. The selections are often laugh-out-loud funny, a breezy read for all. Indexed by poet, title, and first line.

The Penguin Book of Limericks. *E. O. Parrott, ed.* **(1983) Penguin Books. 304p., pap.**

This anthology is unquestionably one of the finest limerick collections, with about eight hundred serious, amusing, sly, and naughty examples. They are grouped by such themes as sex, politics, literary pursuits, and the meaning of life. There are sections of tongue-twisters, "double limericks," "limeraiku," unrhymed limericks, and the like, and there are even limericks on limericks, to illustrate how seriously the genre is treated in this collection. A great many are ascribed to distinguished writers of the last 150 years, but many are anonymous efforts, passed down for centuries. A very fine, long introduction on the history of the limerick and the history of limerick criticism introduces this stellar collection. Indexed by author and title.

Pith and Vinegar; an Anthology of Short Humorous Poetry. *William Cole, ed.* **(1969) Simon & Schuster. 158p., o.p.**

This is a slender collection of silly rhymes and satirical, often dark, verse. It is divided into sections by such themes as "Love Is," "Sex and Such," and "The Things of Nature." Some chapters are entirely of brief epigrams or clever epithets. Humorous versifiers include Ogden Nash, Hilaire Belloc, and X. J. Kennedy, among others, all writing to amuse and delight. The poems are all short, always entertaining. Unfortunately, there is no table of contents and only an index of authors. Otherwise, the anthology is recommended for all readers who enjoy short, funny poetry.

Poems One Line & Longer. *William Cole, ed.* **(1973) Grossman. 182p., o.p.**

Cole explains in his introduction that one-line poems are only a small part of the anthology, that the bulk of the volume is devoted to poems "shorter than sonnets." He has collected more than three hundred brief poems from diverse modern writers of many nationalities. Most of the poets will be familiar to readers: A. R. Ammons and Theodore Roethke, for example, among contemporary poets, and Dickinson, Blake, and Pope among the classics. More than two hundred poets write about everything from animals to love and sexual fulfillment. Indexed by author and first line, the poems are loosely arranged by theme. Cole, a poet who includes his own verse here, has compiled a volume that shows that an epigram can be as skillful as an epic. He explains that some of the verse may not have been intended as one-line poems. Whatever its intention, the verse accomplishes what it sets out to do, which is to entertain readers.

Sometime the Cow Kick Your Head; the Biennial of Light Verse & Witty Poems (Light Year '88/89). *Robert Wallace, ed.*

See under ENGLISH AND AMERICAN POETRY: COMPREHENSIVE COLLECTIONS

Unauthorized Versions; Poems and Their Parodies. *Kenneth Baker, ed.* **(1990) Faber and Faber. 446p.**

Anthologies that parody other poems are always refreshing — able to entertain readers in a way "serious" poetry seldom can. This sometimes scathing, always amusing anthology contains hundreds of classic, well-known poems and arranges their parodies on the opposite page. Among the most enjoyable: "All Things Bright and Beautiful" becomes, thanks to Monty Python, "All Things Dull and Ugly." An excerpt from Byron's "Childe Harold's Pilgrimage" becomes "The Sea Responds to Byron." Other well-spoofed poems include "To His Coy Mistress," "Ozymandias," and "Elegy Written in a Country Churchyard." Some twentieth-century poets and pop figures are also targets, although the majority are spoofs of classic works. The editor acknowledges that many of the parodies do not fit the traditional definition of parody; rather they attack the author or movement the poem is associated with. In any case, they entertain and delight in a wonderful way, and readers could not ask for more fun in a volume of excellent poetry. Indexed by poet and parodist.

What Cheer; an Anthology of American and British Humorous and Witty Verse. *David McCord, ed.* **(1945) Coward-McCann. 515p., o.p.**

The selections in this anthology range from satirical, wry poems to simple, amusing rhymes that have no other intent but to entertain. There are more than six hundred entries, grouped loosely by subject — "The Unfair Sex," for example, and "The Human Race" and "Limericks." A separate, shorter section of the volume contains the "editor's choice" of particularly witty verse, with accompanying historical and bibliographical commentary. Much of the verse is brief, and the tone of each selection varies from slightly humorous to downright nasty. Readers who specialize in caustic verse will appreciate the "Tombstone and Twilight" section. McCord distinguishes the verse he has selected for this volume from regular "light verse," which he dismisses as merely charming and facile. He seems to have had fun putting this volume together, and readers will enjoy not just the verse but his playful tone as well. Indexed by poet, title, and first line.

HUNGARIAN POETRY

The Face of Creation; Contemporary Hungarian Poetry. *Jascha Kessler,*
tr. **(1988) Coffee House Press. 190p., pap.**

In contrast to the earlier volume, *Modern Hungarian Poetry,* this work
has been translated by only one compiler. There are about half as many
writers included, and, of these, only a handful are found in the companion volume. The comparison is inevitable because Kessler worked
with the editor of the earlier collection to arrive at his choices. The
translations, though, are his alone. Each of the selections is prefaced with
a brief biographical sketch of the author and a black-and-white photograph. István Vas, Sándor Csoóri, and Márton Kalász are most heavily
represented, with a dozen or so poems each. All are found with different
works in the aforementioned *Modern Hungarian Poetry.* Essentially, then,
purchasing one necessitates the purchase of both collections. It is hard to
think of interested individuals or libraries who would not require both.

Modern Hungarian Poetry. *Miklós Vajda, ed.* **(1977) Columbia
University Press. 290p.**

"The background of some of the best poems in this collection is nothing less than five hundred years of unjust and debilitating history ...,"
the compiler explains. As editor of *The New Hungarian Quarterly,* Vajda
breaks through the past, even across the Iron Curtain, and brings the
general reader forty-one poets from Lajos Kassák (1887–1967) to half a
dozen who were born slightly before or during the Second World War.
William Jay Smith assisted with the translations, as did Ted Hughes,
Edwin Morgan, Daniel Hoffman, and a dozen other prominent poets. As
commendable as it may be for poets to translate other poets, the question
remains of just how faithful they are to the original. Reviews indicate
they dutifully respect the Hungarian voices, and some critics believe this
volume to be the best of its type. Unfortunately, several of the best poets
are overlooked. "This anthology was designed to survey postwar ... contemporary Hungarian poetry ... selected from the pages of *The New
Hungarian Quarterly.* Those poets who did not live to see the end of

World War II are not included." For example, Miklos Radnoti, who died at age 33, was a Hungarian Jew whose last poems were found on his body after the war, in a mass grave. There is no sign of Miklos Radnoti. A pity. See also above, the companion volume, *Face of Creation*.

INDIAN POETRY

The Golden Tradition; an Anthology of Urdu Poetry. *Ahmed Ali, ed. and tr.* (1973) Columbia University Press. 286p., o.p.

Urdu originated in the twelfth and thirteenth centuries in India's western sectors, but it was not until the seventeenth century that Urdu poetry assumed its present form. Sufficient background is given about the language and the poets by the compiler and translator in the scholarly, well-written introduction that comprises the first hundred pages of the collection. The poems open with eight poets of the eighteenth century and close with seven of the nineteenth. For each of the poets there is a two-to-four-page introduction that not only gives biographical data, but sets the poetry in its place within the history of the form. A brief glossary and index conclude the anthology. As for the translations, they are exact and remain as faithful to the original as possible. "I have left the translations, like the originals, unexplained, so that each reader can interpret the poet in accordance with his own sensibility." A wise decision. The collection is a delight for both expert and layperson.

Poems of Love and War from the Eight Anthologies and the Ten Long Poems of Classical Tamil. *A. K. Ramanujan, comp. and tr.* (1985) Columbia University Press. 335p.

Spoken by over fifty million people, Tamil is one of the two classical Indian languages of Tamilnadu State (formerly Madras), in southeastern India. It is spoken, too, in Sri Lanka, Malaysia, and the Fiji Islands. The Ten Long Poems and the Eight Anthologies reflect early classical Tamil literature (c.100 B.C.–A.D. 250). Selections are given from each, along with a detailed commentary on Tamil poetry and poetics. The poems, which came to be known as Cankam poems, vary in length from three to over eight hundred lines. Many are anonymous, while nearly half were by sixteen poets, of whom Kapilar and Ammuvanar are among the most famous. The work is in four sections, with a seventy-five page explanatory "Afterword." The book opens with Akam Poems, i.e., love poems. Next comes Puram Poems, i.e., poems of war, kings, and death. "The third and fourth sections consist of a small sample of late classical poems (c. fifth to sixth century) . . . [that] offers some comic, earthy, even bawdy poems. . . . It also includes an unusual poem on the bull fight contests of the time." The last section is a long hymn to Visnu. The translation captures the tone of the poems, and even someone who is totally unfamiliar with their background will be charmed and thrilled by much of the verse.

The Penguin Book of Modern Urdu Poetry. *Mahmood Jamal, ed. and tr.* **(1986) Penguin Books. 170p., pap., o.p.**

A poet and critic brings together seventeen poets who write in Urdu, the language that developed in northwestern India and traces its roots back to the twelfth century. "One of the peculiarities of Urdu is that, in spite of its being one of the most widely spoken languages of the subcontinent, it has no home in any province." In Pakistan it is a national language, but only a small percentage consider it a work-a-day tongue. At the same time the India cinema, which is widely attended, has come to make Urdu its "official" tongue. This, and much more about the history and modern use of Urdu, is discussed in the fascinating introduction. The editor then goes onto explain briefly his translation techniques and opens with a poet who lived from 1911 to 1984. A short biographical sketch introduces him, and there is one for each poet in the book. Many of them were jailed for civil disobedience, and much of the subject matter concerns human rights. "All of this attention from rulers is an indication of the importance of Urdu poets." Unfortunately, there are neither author nor poetry indexes.

Songs of the Saints of India. *John Stratton Hawley, ed.* **(1988) Oxford University Press. 244p.**

"The verses of the great poets of medieval north India stand at the fount of the Hindi language, and many would say that they also represent its greatest flowering. Unlike the poems of Chaucer or Donne, which occupy a somewhat similar place in the history of the English language, these Hindi verses are as lively and familiar to Indians today as they were four hundred years ago." This astonishing information derives from the introduction to this volume of verse. The songs of the saints are short, they deal with the various Hindu gods and a vast variety of human emotions and experiences. They are both exotic and beautiful and are clearly understandable to Western readers. Each of the six saints (Ravidas, Kabir, Nanak, Surdas, Mirabai, and Tulsidas) is given a separate chapter, and each is accorded a careful, substantial introduction that serves as biography and poetic analysis. The lovely poems help to bridge some of the cultural gap that exists between Western experience and Eastern realities. Furthermore, they reveal a part of poetic history that is unknown to most modern readers outside India.

IRISH POETRY

An Anthology of Irish Literature. *David H. Greene, ed.* (1954) Modern Library. 602p., o.p.

Random House's familiar Modern Library series preceded the famous portables by Viking (e.g., *The Portable Medieval Reader, Greek Reader, Cervantes*). This is a perfect example of the form. The six hundred pages are literally pocket sized and strike a sound balance between prose and poetry. "The Viking Terror" (seventh or eighth century) is translated from the Gaelic and opens the compact volume. The verse of Louis MacNeice and W. R. Rodgers winds it down, before the bibliographical notes and the index. Myth, sagas, and romance fill the first two hundred pages, while late-nineteenth- and early-twentieth-century prose and poetry take up the remainder. The translations are as lively as the choices of poems and poets: Shaw, W. B. Yeats, "Æ," Synge, O'Casey, for example, are all here with representative pieces. The publishing date has obviously eliminated any of the brilliant voices since 1954, but with that caveat, one would be hard pressed to find a better collection of Irish writing.

An Anthology of Irish Verse; the Poetry of Ireland from Mythological Times to the Present. *Padraic Colum, ed.* (1948) Liveright. 425p., o.p.

This anthology distinguishes between the Irish Gaelic and Anglo-Irish literary traditions of Ireland. It is also concerned more with the racial distinctiveness of Ireland than with chronology and notoriety, and this concern is reflected in the arrangement and selection of the verse. Divided into eight sections, entitled, for example, "The Celtic World and the Realm of the Faery" and "Poems of Place and Poems of Exile," more than two hundred poems represent all facets of Irish life, from farmers and kings to women, wars, and mythological gods. Many of the poems were written anonymously or by little-known poets of past centuries. Prominent Irish voices, those of Yeats, O'Connor, and Joyce, are also represented, primarily in the final section of post-1920 verse. Short biographies on the poets are also included, as well as author and first-line indexes. The scope of this volume is enormous, and Colum, himself a prominent Irish poet, has produced a distinguished collection. There is nothing fancy about this anthology. Rather, it offers a fascinating, neatly compiled glimpse into two separate Irish poetic traditions.

Bitter Harvest; an Anthology of Contemporary Irish Verse. *John Montague, ed.* (1989) Scribner's. 211p.

The deep-rooted poetic tradition in Ireland that blossomed in the last century has brought about sharper, more politicized verse in these past few decades, according to the introduction of this compelling collection. Such masters as Seamus Heaney, Thomas Kinsella, and Paul Muldoon are featured here, along with forty-two other highly skilled poets, almost all writing within the later half of the century. Much of the verse is fraught with tension and images that mirror the current strife between the North and the South. Some are elegies and memorials; some are beautiful recreations of life in a war-torn land. Arranged chronologically by author and aimed at the general audience as well as at more informed readers, the anthology includes indexes of authors, translators, titles, and first lines. This anthology holds its own with other volumes of modern Irish verse, successfully using the strife of internal war as its theme and including some true gems to illustrate that theme.

The Book of Irish Verse; an Anthology of Irish Poetry from the Sixth Century to the Present. *John Montague, ed.* (1974) Macmillan; also published as The Faber Book of Irish Verse. 400p., o.p.

The poet and compiler John Montague (b. 1929) gives himself four entries in this collection, and the number is about the same for everyone else. The exceptions are Swift, Merriman, W. B. Yeats, Synge, and Kavanagh, where the number of poems ranges from eight to a dozen. Also, under the broad classifications of "Old Mythologies," "A Way of Life," "A Monastic Church," "Women in Love," "Courtly Love," "The Bards Mourn," and "Songs from the Irish," there are more Irish poems than are usually found in one place. The first sixth- to seventeenth-century poets, often anonymous, account for about a quarter of the volume. Add some dozen poets from the seventeenth and eighteenth centuries and about the same number from the nineteenth, and one is half way through the collection. Properly, and historically, the memorable modern poets from W. B. Yeats to Seamus Heaney make up about half of the volume. The limited number of selections illustrates the problem with any work that tries to cover so much time and so many poets.

Contemporary Irish Poetry; an Anthology. *Anthony Bradley, ed.* **(New and rev. ed., 1988) University of California Press. 526p.**

As the compiler points out, "the range of accomplishment in contemporary Irish poetry is great . . . and my choice of individual poems cannot please everyone." Yes, but it surely comes close. He has included all of the major modern Irish poets, among them Louis MacNeice and Samuel Beckett, as well as Seamus Heaney and Derek Mahon. The fifty or so poets leave almost no one out, and if the compiler errs, it is in including too many; their relative importance, at least in his view, is indicated by the number of poems selected from each writer. He finds John Montague a leader, for example, with more poems than either Heaney or Mahon. Choices like that are open to argument, but the point is that the compiler is here trying to show what he thinks is best, what is more representative. In his witty introduction he points out that when it gets right down to it, the selection must be personal. Each poet has a photograph and a brief biographical sketch. Eavan Boland ("It's a woman's world") is among the women poets, but they are so few they can be counted almost on one hand. There are useful notes and good indexes.

The Faber Book of Contemporary Irish Poetry. *Paul Muldoon, ed.* **(1986) Faber and Faber. 415p.**

This thick volume contains the works of only a handful of famous modern Irish poets, ten to be exact. As a result, many of their verses are printed, and the reader can have a clear sense of their artistic style and attainment. All but two of the poets are alive today. Aside from the deceased Patrick Kavanagh and Louis MacNeice, there are Thomas Kinsella, John Montague, Michael Longley, Seamus Heaney, Derek Mahon, Paul Durcan, Tom Paulin, and one woman, Medbh McGuckian. The decision to print the work of only a few poets means that the quality can be kept extremely high. Ireland, to paraphrase one critic quoted in the Prologue, is the place that pure poetry comes from. Certainly, the poems in this collection are among the finest of contemporary verse. They can be read for the pleasure they provide on their own, or they can be seen as the current flourishing of a perennial literary talent in the Irish.

The Inherited Boundaries; Younger Poets of the Republic of Ireland. *Sebastian Barry, ed.* **(1986) Dolmen Press. 192p.**

This slender, unpretentious anthology was compiled to show that the Republic of Ireland produces a great variety of voices rather than one collective poetic sensibility. Only seven poets, all born in the 1950's and all published, are featured here, each represented by dozens of selections. But they are poets of great skill and versatility with narratives and elegies and the more experimental forms. The poetry is very contemporary, with an excellent, informative introduction that explores the poetic traditions of both Irelands as well as the lack of exposure given to the Republic's obviously skilled poets. The volume lacks indexes and biographical information on the poets that might have been helpful for readers unfamiliar with Irish verse. But this is still a fine collection of beautiful poetry, dense with compelling images and themes.

Ireland in Poetry. *Charles Sullivan, ed.* **(1990) Harry N. Abrams. 208p.**

This beautiful anthology might also be called "Ireland in Art," for at least half of the volume is devoted to evocative photographs, sketches, paintings, and wood carvings depicting the Irish cities and countryside. Over 150 poems by half as many poets are placed among the artwork — poems by such masters as Joyce, Auden, Yeats, and Swift, as well as by lesser-known poets. The verse is divided loosely into four parts titled "The Country of Ireland," "The History of Ireland," "The People of Ireland," and "The Future of Ireland." Most of the art is by prominent Irish artists, but you can also find work by Albrecht Dürer and Norman Rockwell. The overriding theme of the volume is the transformation of Ireland from a provincial nation steeped in tradition to a nation slowly embracing the modern world. Many poems chronicle past glories as well as present troubles. This collection is recommended not for its scope or literary history but for its sense of the spirit and history of Ireland. Indexed by artist, author, and poem.

Irish Poetry after Yeats: Seven Poets. *Maurice Harmon, ed.* **(1979) Little, Brown. 231p., pap., o.p.**

The seven poets are Austin Clarke, Patrick Kavanagh, Denis Devlin, Richard Murphy, Thomas Kinsella, John Montague, and Seamus Heaney. Arrangement is chronological according to the birth of the poet. A fair sampling of work is offered, although, rightly, there are more generous selections for the more important poets such as Kinsella and

Heaney. Ten years on, one might have composed a different list, but essentially the choices here represent one man's view of the progress of Irish verse. There is a twenty-one-page introduction in which each of the poets is considered and his gifts weighed. The judgments are discerning and generally accurate, although one might argue here and there not only with the poet selected but the reasons given for his place in the ranks. (There are no women included, an oversight not attributable to a lack of talented Irish women.) Each of the selections is prefaced with an indifferent black and white photograph of the poet. There is a lackluster bibliography, but no index. The collection has little new to offer except the odd poem not found in other anthologies.

Irish Poets, 1924–1974. *David Marcus, ed.* (1975) Pan Books. 203p., o.p.

David Marcus's collection gathers the work of many Irish poets born in and after 1924. He excludes such poets as Yeats and Parnell, both born before 1924, because he would have had to limit the works of younger Irish poets. He cites the importance of the end of civil war and of the British presence in Ireland. The 170 poems included are solemn and contemplative, often addressing political or religious themes. Among the fifty-nine poets are Thomas Kinsella, Eavan Boland, and Paul Muldoon. The volume's introduction is only two pages long, and the book has no index. Marcus has arranged poets chronologically. Although short, this anthology will provide readers with an honest view of Irish poetry of its time.

Kings, Lords, & Commons. *Frank O'Connor, ed. and tr.* (1959) Knopf.

Acclaimed Irish writer Frank O'Connor edited and translated this slim volume from Old Irish, with help from W. B. Yeats. Spanning 1,200 years, the lyrical, smoothly translated verse is arranged in three chronological sections beginning at A.D. 600. Each section reflects the historical and cultural changes of the era. For example, "Saints and Soldiers" covers A.D. 600 to 1200 and its poems detail the religious upheaval of the time, as Ireland was moving from paganism to Christianity. "Lords and Scholars" deals with the rise of the monarchy, "Peasants and Dreamers" with the hopes of the impoverished underclass. Most of the poems are rich with references to Irish pagan myths and the great legendary battles in early Irish history. Beside these proud elegies are beautiful, eloquent poems on the timeless themes of love, nature, and mourning. O'Connor provides a brief introduction to each poem, indicating the translations that have directly influenced certain modern poems. This is a fascinating anthology, recommended for readers looking for a glimpse into old Ireland or at the beginnings of a long, proud, literary history.

New Irish Poets. *Devin A. Garrity, ed.* (1948) Devin-Adair. 210p., o.p.

The built-in danger of using such terms as "modern" and "new," particularly in a collection of poetry, is evident here. Almost 50 years later, the "new" Irish poets are not so bold, not so young, and, unfortunately, not so well remembered. Of the thirty-seven voices, only a half dozen or so will be immediately recognized, and only half again of these might find their way into a 1990's book of "new" or "modern" Irish verse. So this collection is primarily of historical interest, and a good place to find otherwise difficult-to-locate early Irish poets. By "early," one means those born near the turn of the century or just before the outbreak of the First World War. Delightful features are the down-home photographs of the authors and the brief, yet cleverly written, biographical notes. After this time, how good are the poems? The romantic verse is fairly weak, although the detailed, concrete poems about the history of Ireland are still good. This is a fine reference source in a library, although of limited value to the average reader.

The New Oxford Book of Irish Verse. *Thomas Kinsella, ed. and tr.* (1986) Oxford University Press. 422p.

This anthology's poems stretch back in time to before the sixth century, so astonishingly long is the history of Ireland's poetry. The very early works are frequently by unknown authors or by those connected with the Christian Church. Although, as Thomas Kinsella suggests in his introduction, some of these early works also look back, in their "incantatory character," to a close association with pre-Christian art. Christian themes took root in the following centuries, to give way only later to bardic poetry and love poetry. Famous Irish authors of the eighteenth century are afforded considerable space, authors such as Swift, Goldsmith, and Sheridan. Folk poems and songs are included as well, along with ballads. Among the modern poets well represented are W. B. Yeats, Samuel Beckett, and Seamus Heaney. This selection of Irish poetry is of the highest order. The range of the poems is vast and serves to give the reader a clear feeling for the depth of creativity that welled up in Irish poets over the centuries. A lucid introduction by Kinsella helps place the poems in their historical context, and notes on each of the poets explicate the significance of their poetry.

1000 Years of Irish Poetry; the Gaelic and Anglo-Irish Poets from Pagan Times to the Present. *Kathleen Hoagland, ed.* **(1975) Devin-Adair. 833p.**

This anthology is both an overview and a detailed study of the rich Irish poetic legacy. Divided into four sections — "Ancient Irish Poetry," "Modern Irish Poetry," "Anonymous Street Ballads," and "Anglo-Irish Poetry" — the volume encompasses a wide range of styles and subjects. Much of the poetry covers such particularly Irish concerns as English oppression, Celtic rituals, and the Catholic Church. More than two hundred poets are generously represented by hundreds of sonnets, ballads, and elegies. Yeats, Swift, Joyce, and O'Connor share space with gifted poets unknown to most readers. The arrangement is neat and clear, with helpful indexes and brief biographical information prefacing each poet. Hoagland's introduction is lively, deft, and informative. She explores the literary history of ancient Ireland and explains the strong tradition of Irish poetry and its development during the centuries of British rule. The poems tell the story. This collection is highly recommended for the quality and diversity of the verse, as well as for the historical perspective it offers.

The Oxford Book of Irish Verse, XVIIth Century–XXth Century. *Donagh MacDonagh and Lennox Robinson, eds.* **(1958) Oxford University Press. 343p., o.p.**

The seventeenth to twentieth centuries were years of subjugation and turmoil for Ireland, but also a prolific time for Irish poets. More than a hundred Irish poets are represented here, beginning with Swift, Goldsmith, and Thomas Moore and ending with contemporary poets Roy McFadden and Thomas Kinsella. In between are the other great Irish poets — O'Connor, Edward Fitzgerald, and James Joyce, for example. And the editors also include many who, though distinguished in Ireland, may not be as well known to American readers. They have chosen poets who are Irish by birth, descent or *adoption* — a handful of poets, such as Emily Brontë, may not generally be considered as typically "Irish" writers. Much of the verse was translated from Irish. In his introduction MacDonagh outlines the changes and emergence of a particularly Irish literary voice; this broad anthology is a fine showcase for that proud, Irish distinctiveness. Indexed by author and first line, with biographical and critical information provided.

The Penguin Book of Contemporary Irish Poetry. *Peter Fallon and Derek Mahon, eds.* **(1990) Penguin Books. 462p., pap.**

From among the large number of Irish poetry anthologies, this volume is highly recommended for both students and general readers. It is arranged in standard anthology form, with a slightly more comprehensive look at the major figures of post-Second World War Irish literature. The volume begins with poets Thomas Kinsella, John Montague, and Seamus Heaney and ends with more obscure but equally competent writers yet to establish themselves outside their native country. There are thirty-five poets, represented by their most accomplished work and arranged chronologically. Most of the verse was written in English, although there are a few translations. Some distinguished poets of the postwar years were left out because the editors felt they represented a different generation. The verse included here is first rate: some narrative, some lyrical, concentrating less on social and political themes, but all fascinating and evocative and illustrating the beauty and intricacy of the Irish language. Biographical notes and an index of first lines are included.

The Penguin Book of Irish Verse. *Brendan Kennelly, ed.* **(1981) Penguin Books. 470p., pap.**

The strength of this anthology of Irish poetry is its sturdiness and the competence of its editor. Nothing here to astound readers already familiar with Irish poetry, just a dependable guide to it. The poetry is divided among three sections: "Gaelic Translated," which contains many anonymous ballads of the seventh and eighth centuries; "Anglo-Irish," which includes Swift and Wilde; and "Yeats and After," which marks the beginning of the modern poetic age in Ireland. This last section is probably the strongest, featuring many twentieth-century writers — Padraic Colum, C. Day Lewis, Seamus Heaney, and Thomas Kinsella are all here. The poets are arranged chronologically within each section. This volume is recommended for its balance of classic and modern poets; it successfully illustrates the rich tradition of Irish poetry. Indexed by title and first line.

Poems from Ireland. *William Cole. ed.* (1972) Thomas Y. Crowell Company. 237p., o.p.

Readers will be familiar with some of the 84 authors in William Cole's anthology: Yeats, Thomas Kinsella, Louis MacNeice; others (such as Kuno Meyer, James Clarence Mangan, and F. R. Higgins) are important within Irish literary history but not extensively anthologized. The 176 poems collected here are generally of high quality; in well-crafted verse these poets candidly address such subjects as death, Catholicism, the supernatural, and fishing. The book begins with a casual yet informative history of Irish literature up to the 1970's. Cole has arranged poems alphabetically by author, and there are indexes of authors, titles, and first lines, along with brief biographies of the poets. This fairly short book will not disappoint readers in search of a brief overview of the country's verse.

Poets from the North of Ireland. *Frank Ormsby, ed.* (New ed., 1990) Blackstaff Press. 336p., pap.

Twenty-seven poets and hundreds of their poems are featured in this fine collection, including such renowned writers as Seamus Heaney and W. R. Rodgers. Most of the poets will be obscure to general readers, although their work is first-rate. Each poet is represented by as many as thirteen selections, with the poets arranged chronologically. Ormsby, who includes some of his own verse here, has penned a fascinating introduction in which he explains how the conflicts of Northern Ireland breed imaginative, reformist writers in an area long considered a "cultural Siberia" by other English-speaking nations. Many of the poems deal with political and social strife, although most draw upon the timeless themes of nature, beauty, and love. Haunting and lyrical, this anthology is recommended for both general and more specialized readers. These poems represent the best of contemporary Northern Irish writers and draw on the rich Irish poetic tradition. The book is indexed by title and first line, with biographical information provided for each poet.

Some Contemporary Poets of Britain and Ireland; an Anthology. *Michael Schmidt, ed.*

See under ENGLISH POETRY: 20TH CENTURY

Treasury of Irish Religious Verse. *Patrick Murray, ed.*

See under   RELIGIOUS POETRY

ITALIAN POETRY

The Defiant Muse; Italian Feminist Poems from the Middle Ages to the Present. *Beverly Allen, Muriel Kittel, and Keala Jane Jewell, eds.*

See under WOMEN'S POETRY AND FEMINIST POETRY

The New Italian Poetry, 1945 to the Present; a Bilingual Anthology. *Lawrence R. Smith, ed. and tr.* **(1981) University of California Press. 486p.**

The "present" referred to in the title, is 1980. The "new" is divided into: (1) realism, with seven poets, the earliest being Franco Fortini (b. 1917); (2) hermeticism, with only Andrea Zanzotto and Luciano Erba (both born in the early 1920's); (3) experimentation, with four diverse poets; and, finally, (4) avant-grade, with eight voices. Each poet is represented by a half dozen or so choices, although three or four wrote such long poems that there are excerpts from these. The translations are uniformly excellent, but the translator seems to be more comfortable with the poems in the last section. Each poet is introduced with a short biographical/literary sketch. The bilingual arrangement is excellent, as are the layout and the typography. Unfortunately, the publisher chose not to include standard indexes, and a search of the table of contents is required to find a given poem or poet.

New Italian Poets. *Dana Gioia and Michael Palma, eds.* **(1991) Story Line Press. 385p., pap.**

In order to ensure greater depth to the volume, the editors chose to focus on ten contemporary young writers rather than try to represent the entire breadth of modern Italian poetry. This focus makes for a first-rate anthology, particularly since many readers are unlikely to be familiar with Italian verse, old or new. All of the poets have been writing since the 1950's and are major figures in the modern Italian literary tradition. They represent a wide spectrum of literary influences, themes, and styles; some poets work with rhyme and meter, others write long odes.

Many evoke the beauty of the Mediterranean landscape, and some incorporate political or social themes. Each is represented by between two and nineteen selections, and helpful critical notes precede each poet's work. The verse is arranged chronologically, with the original poem on the page facing its English translation. The editors have written an informative, clear introduction, intended for readers looking at modern Italian poetry for the first time. These readers will not be disappointed. The anthology is lucid and diverse, with poems that blend modern techniques and themes with Italian literary traditions.

Poems from Italy. *William Jay Smith and Dana Gioia, eds.* (1985) New Rivers. 456p., pap.

The Italian poem on the left, the translation into English on the right — everyone is familiar with a bilingual format. This is a model of its kind. The poet William Jay Smith and his collaborator chose only work that could be translated into English and still retain its beauty. And for translators, they went to the best. Smith and Gioia translated a dozen between them, but in addition one finds the work of Byron, Shelley, Robert Lowell, William Arrowsmith, Gavin Ewart, Richard Wilbur, and just about every major poet/translator from the nineteenth and twentieth centuries. The result is a true, lyrical collection that begins with Saint Francis of Assisi and moves chronologically to the twentieth century and Pier Paolo Pasolini and Rocco Scotellaro. Almost two thirds of the poems were written before 1700, because of the nearly "eight centuries of poetry represented here, the greatest work is clearly from the earlier period, especially the Renaissance." And "in presenting the twentieth century we have concentrated on established writers." There is no better bilingual anthology of Italian poetry available.

JAPANESE POETRY

From the Country of Eight Islands; an Anthology of Japanese Poetry.
Hiroaki Sato and Burton Watson, eds. and trs. **(1981) Columbia University Press. 652p., pap.**

The earliest poems in this brilliant collection are from the Kojiki (Record of Ancient Matters), compiled early in the eighth century. Another oral-based collection is the Manyoshu, which began about the same time but was compiled over a period of centuries. This, in the words of the editors, "marks the real beginning of the tradition of Japanese poetry and contains poems so powerful in artistic and emotional appeal that they have seldom if ever been surpassed in later periods." Matsuo Basho (1644–1694) is a challenge to that statement in that his poems have great significance for us today, as do the poems of Ryokan (1758–1831), or, for that matter, Takahashi Mutsuo (b. 1937), the last poet in the collection. The development of the sophisticated tradition is traced through the major poets from the eighth to the middle of the twentieth century. In addition to a generous group of poems from each writer or school, the compilers provide a historical introduction that is essential to anyone who wishes to appreciate the background of the poetry. There are brief biographical sketches of the poets and a useful, select bibliography. The translations are outstanding, and they were understandably the winner of the P.E.N. Translation Prize for the year.

Japanese Literature in Chinese. Vol. I: Poetry and Prose in Chinese by Japanese Writers of the Early Period; Vol. II: Poetry and Prose in Chinese by Japanese Writers of the Later Period. *Burton Watson, tr.* **(1975, 1976) Columbia University Press. 134p., 196p.**

It is all a trifle esoteric, but one must quickly appreciate that beyond the imposing titles of these two volumes is exceptionally lyrical and historically fascinating poetry. The compiler explains that these are poems composed by Japanese writers, but in a foreign language, i.e., Chinese. Some connoisseurs are critical of what they see as essentially imitative work. Still, the consensus is that this poetry successfully "transcends the insularity of Japan," particularly before the opening of the country in the nineteenth century. The earliest poet is Prince Otomo, who reigned only a brief seven months in the seventh century. Some 300 pages away, in the second volume, the enthusiasm for Chinese comes to a natural conclusion with the novelist Natsume Soseki (1867–1916). Each section of poems is prefaced by helpful background notes on the time and the poets. There are numerous other guide posts to help the reader who may be as bewildered by the genre as by the period and the poets. The collection is a journey well worth taking.

The Manyoshu. *Foreword by Donald Keene.* **(1965) Columbia University Press. 502p., o.p.**

This is the best translation available of one thousand poems from the major Japanese poets who wrote from the pre-Omni and Omni Periods (A.D. 400–673) to the Nara Period (A.D. 710–840). The book is divided into three primary parts. First, there is a lengthy introduction explaining the period, the poets, and the poetry to Westerners who are probably unaware of what the verse represents or its background. Second, there is the body of the work in translation, followed by the text in *romaji*, i.e., mainly modern Japanese. (The complicated translation procedures are explained in the introduction.) Finally there are biographical notes, chronologies, and an index. All of this, helped in no small way by frequent explanatory footnotes, is extremely useful in explaining the full meaning of the poems. The poems are verse, as one poet put it, "on which I never tire to look!"

The Penguin Book of Japanese Verse. *Geoffrey Bownas and Anthony Thwaite, trs.; Introduction by Geoffrey Bownas.* **(1964) Penguin Books. 245p., pap.**

Emperor Onin reigned from about A.D. 270 to 312. The last poet, born in 1931, Tanikawa Shuntaro treats of "Growing Up." Between the two are seventeen centuries, some one hundred and seventy-five poets, and diverse shifts in the sensibility and imagery that capture the elusive Japanese culture. Even today, the Emperor's poetry prize "attracts tens of thousands of entries." The Japanese "delight in their poetry, write for a public, and are not hesitant to stand up and recite it." This enthusiasm translates into subject matter and a style that is easy to appreciate and normally appeals where Western poetry may fail. It is a paradox that while the content seems almost transparent, the layers of meaning often are beyond the American or European comprehension. Tanka and haiku are, for example, simplicity itself. But what does it all really signify? One returns time and time again to the puzzle. Here the brief notes and the scholarly introduction may help, if only in a general way: the reader must choose the appropriate meaning. The translations are uniformally excellent, and the selections are equally good. This is the standard collection for anyone in the West involved with Japanese poetry.

Waiting for the Wind; Thirty-six Poets of Japan's Late Medieval Age. *Steven D. Carter, tr. and ed.* **(1989) Columbia University Press. 354p.**

The title is as esoteric as the verse, which was composed between 1250 and 1500. The form is the classical *uta,* a "thirty-one syllable lyric that was the major genre of court poetry throughout its history." According to the editor, all of the poets of this period "enriched the poetic heritage in ways that influenced later poets writing in newer genres now fairly familiar to Western readers — including Sogi (1421–1502) and other poets of linked verse, and the haiku poets Basho (1644–1694) and Buson (1716–1783)." The collection includes just over four hundred poems, all in the *uta* form. There are thirty-six poets, of which only four are women. This, again according to the compiler, "is a reflection of the social realities of the medieval period." No one who is interested in the poetic form or the history of its development should miss the extremely well-written introduction. The translations seem equally good. The content puzzles from time to time, but on the whole it consists of topics familiar to everyone. There are biographical sketches of each of the poets and frequent notes to help the reader along the way.

Women Poets of Japan. *Kenneth Rexroth and Ikuko Atsumi, eds.* **(1977) New Directions Books; also published 1977 by The Seabury Press as The Burning Heart. 184p., pap.**

This is a slender, beautiful volume featuring 76 Japanese female poets — probably one of the most attractive anthologies on its subject for American readers. Extending from the seventh century to the contemporary twentieth century, the verse exemplifies traditional Japanese poetry: terse, delicate in form, and subtle. Arranged chronologically, the poets' names are lettered in calligraphy, giving the volume a mysterious, ancient feel. None of the poets will be familiar to general English-language readers, although most readers are familiar with the haiku form, here used by several of the poets. They are fascinating poems, dense with the imagery and emotion of Japanese women's lives over 14 centuries. The editors have included brief biographical sketches of each poet and also an interesting, well-written historical analysis of Japanese poetry. This analysis contains critical information on each poet's style and development and a table of Japanese historic periods. This is a first-rate anthology, perfect as an introduction to Japanese poetry for unfamiliar readers.

KOREAN POETRY

Anthology of Contemporary Korean Poetry. *Koh Chang-soo, comp.* **(1987) Seoul International. 130p.**

If the reader wishes to become acquainted with Korean poets who are writing today, this is surely the place to do it. There are six poets represented in this anthology, including the editor. They would appear to be in the mainstream of contemporary Korean literature. The poems all tend to be in the lyric mode, and some have an enchanting delicacy about them. Nature imagery plays a large part in their composition. There is something old-fashioned about their tone, perhaps attributable to the translation. The images are frequently sharp and poignant, symbolic of a more rarefied age than ours. For readers who are curious about contemporary Asian poetry, this anthology makes a welcome addition to their libraries.

LARGE-TYPE ANTHOLOGIES

Best Loved Poems in Large Print. *Virginia S. Reiser, ed.* **(1983) G. K. Hall. 585p.**

There are two primary aspects of this collection. The first, obvious from the title, is that this is a large-print book, and all of the poems are in sixteen-point Times Roman, or about twice the size of the type found in most books. Second, the authors, generally from the nineteenth and early twentieth centuries, are famous, but utterly traditional. This is hardly the place to look for the unusual. The exceptions include Marianne Moore, Wallace Stevens, William Carlos Williams, and W. B. Yeats, but for each poet of this caliber there is an Edwin Markham, Joyce Kilmer, and William Cullen Bryant. So while the compiler is to be congratulated for a major service, one takes some exception with her conventional choices. This volume is fine, of course, if the reader is not too familiar with poetry. The arrangement is by broad subjects, and within each of these the poets are presented chronologically. For example, the part devoted to "Love and Friendship" opens with an anonymous work, moves on to Edmund Spenser and Sir Philip Sidney and concludes with Conrad Aiken, Edna St. Vincent Millay, and Hart Crane. This is a collection that should be in every library and in not a few homes.

Favorite Poems in Large Print. *Virginia S. Reiser, ed.* **(1981) G. K. Hall. 462p.**

This is similar to the compiler's later (1983) collection, *Best Loved Poems in Large Print.* It is arranged by such sections as "Stories and Ballads" and "Nature and the Seasons." Under each of the ten headings are about two dozen poems. The selection is traditional, and, if anything, the collection suffers from the assumption that people who need large print (in this case sixteen point) may not be overly sophisticated. While traditional poetry is fine, a few more modern, avant-garde poets would have been appreciated. The volume is limited, also, to English and American writers, from Edward Lear and Lewis Carroll to Eugene Field and Gelett Burgess (all in the "Humor" section). Where things are a bit more serious, as in the grab-bag section of "Various Themes," the compiler comes up with the estimable Donne, Keats, Emily Dickinson, Amy Lowell, W. B. Yeats, Edna St. Vincent Millay, and Robert Frost.

Poems by Favorite Poets in Large Print. *Leslie Lewis, ed.* (1992) **G. K. Hall. 449p.**

This anthology, generally indistinguishable from English and American anthologies published for general readers, is part of a series of poetry anthologies published in large print. The poems are outstanding, although standard choices. Arranged chronologically by poet, the collection begins with six selections from Shakespeare and ends with two from Robert Lowell. In between, fifty-three classic British and American poets are represented. Most works are represented in full, although some longer works have been reduced to excerpts. Still, readers of large-print books will not feel cheated. The choices are excellent, the arrangement intelligent; the collection is indexed by author, title, and first line. Indeed, nothing in this volume will set it apart from other fine anthologies except the print size.

LATIN POETRY

An Anthology of World Poetry. *Mark Van Doren, ed.*

See under WORLD POETRY

More Latin Lyrics: From Virgil to Milton. *Dame Felicitas Corrigan, ed.;*
Helen Waddell, tr. **(1977) W. W. Norton. 392p.**

This volume charts the course of Latin poetry in Europe for over
1,600 years, featuring translations by Helen Waddell of poems chosen
not so much for the quality of their poetry, but for "their courage and
poignancy; indeed in their bare existence." This statement reflects the
passionate tone of this first-rate anthology, one that includes poems in
original Latin, with English translations and editorial notes on the verse
and poets (all well-indexed). The translator's critical notes precede each
selection. These are informative, lively, and wonderfully literate in their
own right. In total, 30 well-known and more obscure poets are featured,
usually represented by several selections each. This volume has two distinctive audiences: one that has no previous knowledge of Latin poetry
and one that wants crisp, new translations of Horace, Boethius, and
Thomas Aquinas. Both audiences will be pleased with this anthology. It
is accessible and unintimidating for a beginning student, yet erudite
enough for more demanding readers. Clean, precise translations of poems with the common theme of "the defiance of man against material
circumstance" are the main strength in this collection.

The Oxford Book of Verse in English Translation. *Charles Tomlinson,*
ed.

See under WORLD POETRY

LATIN-AMERICAN POETRY

An Anthology of Twentieth-Century Brazilian Poetry. *Elizabeth Bishop and Emanuel Brasil, eds.* (1972) Wesleyan University Press. 181p., pap.

An exceptionally beautiful and fascinating volume of poetry, this is edited and introduced by Emanuel Brasil and the outstanding American poet Elizabeth Bishop. They open the anthology by discussing the remarkably high position poetry has among the Brazilian elite: the term "poet" is an honor to bestow on a person and has nothing to do with literature. Consequently, poetry is taken very seriously by educated Brazilians. The selection of poetry presented here is by fourteen prominent authors who wrote from the 1920's to the 1970's. The translators of their work are also of the first rank, poets like Richard Wilbur, Elizabeth Bishop herself, Barbara Howes, June Jordan, and W. S. Merwin, to name only some. The poetry is printed both in Portuguese and English in a most handsome format. This is verse that allows the reader to expand his or her vision of the world by entering into the creative experience of poets whose culture is foreign and strange but whose artistry is marvelously developed.

Mexican Poetry; an Anthology. *Octavio Paz, comp.; Samuel Beckett, tr.* (1985) Grove Press. 215p.

There may be more famous poets in literature today than Paz and Beckett, but none so imaginative and so important in shaping twentieth-century thought. While one usually thinks of Beckett as a French-Irish playwright and novelist, not a translator of Spanish, the surprise is pleasant and rewarding. He is a master of translation and responsible for the success of this important volume in introducing the spirit and content of Mexican verse to non-Spanish-speaking readers. Applause, too, to the compiler who had the good sense to arrange the collection in chronological order so that one can fully appreciate the development of Mexican poetry. The book opens with Francisco de Terrazas (1525–1600), who was praised by Cervantes. It concludes with Alfonso Reyes, "regarded as one of the great contemporary writers in Spanish." The forty or so poets are represented by two to ten poems each. Not to be missed are the scholarly introduction by C. M. Bowra and Paz's fascinating history of Mexican poetry. The anthology was first published by agreement between Unesco and the government of Mexico.

The Penguin Book of Caribbean Verse in English. *Paula Burnett, ed.* **(1986) Penguin Books. 446p., pap.**

The scene is set in a forty five-page introduction that details the development of verse in the Caribbean from the oral tradition to the current literary scene. About one quarter of the volume is given to songs, Rastafarian chants, and related material, often by such individual musicians as Bob Marley. This volume is remarkably comprehensive. In the section on the literary tradition, there are close to a hundred poets with four to five poems each. Their content moves from the religious and the agrarian interests of the population to satire and topical poetry. A striking aspect of the poetic form is explained by the editor: "There is almost no major poet of the English-speaking Caribbean who does not have the vernacular as one of the languages of his poetry. . . . The word is still intimately bound up with the music." At the same time, the early poets reflect the prevalent European tastes, following well-established literary models. This can be traced in the chronological arrangement, beginning with Nathaniel Weekes and James Grainger, eighteenth-century poets. The collection is particularly valuable because of the editor's insights and the fact that there has been no substantial anthology of Caribbean poetry for more than a decade. There are a good biographical section, explanatory notes, and a glossary.

Peru: The New Poetry. *David Tipton, ed.* **(1977) Red Dust. 173p.**

Here is the best of Peruvian poetry from about 1959 to 1970. All of the translations are by the compiler and Maureen Ahern. The selection covers all styles and schools of poetry. It is quite amazing to realize how much truly good writing can come out of a single Latin American country in a relatively short period of time. Much of it is shaped by the social-realists and the purists. The former use poems as "a direct weapon in the service of Marxism." The latter seek "verbal and stylistic perfection . . . their poetry claiming to be a song to beauty." There are some fifteen poets represented, with an average of a dozen or so poems each. The volume concludes with a section of statements, "On the Situation of the Writer in Peru," including one by Antonio Cisneros. Biographical notes indicate that most of the poets were born in the 1930's and 1940's.

Volcán; Poems from Central America. *Alejandro Murguía and Barbara Paschke, eds.* **(1983) City Lights Books. 160p., pap.**

When these poems were written, many were banned by their governments. The exception was Nicaragua, but even here there was some check on total freedom of expression. How, then, did the poems from Mexico, Honduras, El Salvador, Guatemala, and Nicaragua reach us in this slim collection? According to the editors, "the poems were often copied by hand and smuggled" into the various countries. Of the thirty-nine poets represented, each grouped under their country of origin, not all had such dramatic lives. The list of credits indicates that at least a few had published their work in literary periodicals, but this is not to deny the danger involved in their work. The effort to bridge the political, cultural gap between the United States and Central America is helped in no small way by the fact that this is a bilingual edition, Spanish on one page and the English translation facing it. While there are numerous poems about love, home, and family, the primary focus is on war, exile, and death. It is neither pretty nor always monumental, but it is real.

See also HISPANIC-AMERICAN POETRY.

LOVE POETRY

Art & Love; an Illustrated Anthology of Love Poetry. *Kate Farrell, ed.* **(1990) Metropolitan Museum of Art. 176p.**

This anthology collects 169 distinguished and less-well-known poems about love and pairs each one with artwork from New York's Metropolitan Museum of Art. The volume contains an eclectic mix of artistic styles and cultures, bound only by the broad theme of love. For example, Nicolas Maes's painting "The Lacemaker" complements Charles Bukowski, while verse by Chinese poet Po Chü-i is paired with Picasso's "Bacchanalia." Skeptical readers need not worry that this is just a clever repackaging of commonly anthologized love poems; it is an exceptionally rich volume, both literally and visually. Poetry as diverse as Chinese haiku and contemporary American unmetered verse is featured with Hellenic sculpture and European surrealism. The poems are categorized by such different types of love as familial, romantic, and lost love. The text features many classic poets — Shakespeare, Andrew Marvel, and Elizabeth Browning, among others. The corresponding artworks are meant to "illuminate" the poems, and all is beautifully indexed. By pairing obscure art with well-known poems and vice versa, the editor has produced an attractive, diverse treasury.

A Book of Love Poetry. *Jon Stallworthy, ed.* **(1974) Oxford University Press; also published in Great Britain as The Penguin Book of Love Poetry. 393p.**

All varieties of love are reflected in the poems in this anthology: respectful declarations, vulgar intentions, glorious proposals, adamant denials. The poets come from many different cultures: seventh-century India, ancient Greece, eighteenth-century England, nineteenth-century France. The subject of love has been divided thematically into: "Intimations," "Declarations," "Persuasions," "Celebrations," "Aberrations," "Separations," "Desolations," and "Reverberations," or more or less everything anyone could think of saying about the topic of love. It is interesting to look at these verses in the company of others on their general subject, especially as those observations span the centuries. The authors are all of high quality, with many well-known names set alongside exotic ones from other times and places. John Donne has several entries, as do Robert Burns, Robert Browning, and Christina Rossetti. There is a great deal of food for thought in this volume, and since love is of continual interest, readers should be delighted by the fresh treatment it receives from the scores of writers included.

The Chatto Book of Love Poetry. *John Fuller, ed.* **(1990) Chatto & Windus. 374p.**

The poems in this generous volume cover the last four centuries, although some anonymous thirteenth-century selections are also included. Such great English-speaking poets as Robert Browning, Yeats, Byron, and Dickinson are featured, along with some distinguished contemporary writers. The verse ranges from devoted love sonnets to brief, ribald rhymes. Indeed, the charm of this volume could be its haphazard arrangement of poems of different tones and forms — two-line verses will precede long narrative epics, and smutty lyrics will share the page with somber character portraits. The poems themselves are all of high quality. Many have been widely anthologized. Some, particularly the funnier ones, will be greatly appreciated in this age of melodramatic poetry. The editor omitted listing the date of the poem or the poet's name by the selections in the text, making it very difficult for readers to know who wrote what or when it was written. Otherwise, this is an accomplished volume with a not-too-serious tone.

Dancing the Tightrope; New Love Poems by Women. *Barbara Burford, Lindsay MacRae, and Sylvia Paskin, eds.* **(1988) Peter Bedrick Books. 112p.**

This collection, with its fresh perspective on love, was put together by an eclectic group of women: Barbara Burford is a black woman in her forties who has published short stories and poems; Lindsay MacRae is a poet in her twenties and has worked as a journalist and scriptwriter; and Sylvia Paskin is a writer and lecturer on film, literature, and feminism. The poets in this collection are largely unknown to the general reading public. Besides Burford and MacRae, there are Janet Dube, Fran Landesman, Sue May, and thirty other poets. The only familiar name is that of Medbh McGuckian, an acclaimed Irish poet. Some of the writers are performance poets, and most of them now have their homes in London although several were born abroad. As for the poems themselves, they are a mixed bag: they emphasize sexual love between women and women and between women and men. The best are by Medbh McGuckian, and they are very fine indeed. The others, in rather artless verse, tend to be revealing glimpses into personal moments of their lives. This will be of interest mainly to those who wish to keep up with the periphery of women's writing.

English Love Poems. *John Betjeman and Geoffrey Taylor, comps.* (1957; paperback ed., 1964) Faber and Faber. 220p., pap., o.p.

Compiled by the estimable poets John Betjeman and Geoffrey Taylor, this volume owes its originality to their rereading the poetical work of a poet — without consulting other anthologies — to find the poems that best express the "different moods of love." As a result, this collection includes a good deal of fresh, rarely encountered poetry: the lyrics, for example, of Philip Ayres and Barnabe Barnes, as well as the more expected selections from Donne and John Gay. This is a tasteful compilation, the verse of high quality and great sophistication. It is arranged chronologically, with each poet represented by up to four poems. At the end of the volume, there are short notes on some of the poets and the poems. They are extremely interesting and sometimes illuminating, noting, for example, that the poet "Michael Field" was actually two women, a writer and her niece who collaborated intimately on all their work. There is excellent poetry in this collection, even for those who think that love is a sentimental subject.

Erotic Poetry; the Lyrics, Ballads, Idyls, and Epics of Love — Classical to Contemporary. *William Cole, ed.* (1963) Random House. 501p., o.p.

This is a book of high-quality verse. In his Foreword, well-known poet Stephen Spender suggests that the topics of erotic poetry such as "nakedness, love-making, and sex" are "simply part of the common human condition available to literature." That surely is a sensible stance, but the editor, William Cole, unfortunately subdivides his volume into aggressively playful categories like "Of Women: Virgins & Harlots, Teasers & Losers: the Controversial Sex Is Considered in Its Fascinating and Maddening Variety." Another section concerns "Incitement and Desire: Spurrings of Honest Lust and the Varieties of Sublimation." There is a sense of humor at work here, but the attitude of the editor is openly sexist, an attribute not necessarily true of the poems themselves. These range over an extraordinarily long period of time, from Juvenal's excerpt from "The Sixth Satire" to Ted Hughes's "Secretary." The selection of poems is discerning and astute. Female poets are occasionally heard on the subject of eroticism, but only rarely. The perspective is decidedly male. Poets from other countries are heard: Baudelaire and Mallarmé, as well as Petronius Arbiter. It is interesting to see what serious poets have written on the subject of sex, and here we find the voices of Edmund Spenser, Kingsley Amis, Robert Burns, and Delmore Schwartz — very different voices, some openly sexual, some quite raunchy, others merely sensual.

The Gambit Book of Love Poems. *Geoffrey Grigson, ed.* **(1973) Gambit; originally published in Great Britain by Faber and Faber as The Faber Book of Love Poems. 407p.**

In an attempt to infuse freshness into a familiar theme, the editor has cleverly arranged his poems into sections that correspond to the various stages of love: "Love Expected," "Love Begun," "The Plagues of Loving," "Love Continued," "Absences, Doubts, Divisions," and, finally, "Love Renounced and Love in Death." That pretty much covers all possible attitudes. The editor remarks that there are two essential kinds of love poems: in-love poems and poems about love. They are both in evidence here, but the former are given more prominence, since they are the more dramatic. Dozens of these poems have been written by anonymous authors over the centuries, and they are joined by the creations of William Barnes, Baudelaire, Blake, Donne, Robert Graves, Robert Herrick, Walter Savage Landor, Thomas Hardy, George Meredith, and many others, including Christina Rossetti and Shakespeare. There are not too many women in this collection, possibly because the emphasis is on poets from other centuries. The quality of the verses is generally very high; the emotion of love seems to have worked its own magic on the writers.

Love. *Walter de la Mare, ed.* **(1946) William Morrow. 822p., o.p.**

Compiled by poet Walter de la Mare, this huge collection contains more than seven hundred poems, all about love: love of nature, family, friendship, first love, godly love, love after death, and about every other situation that arouses the human heart. Shakespeare, Christina Rossetti, Hardy, Keats, and Donne are all here, with several poems each, listed along with hundreds of the world's most renowned or more obscure English-speaking poets. Many of the verses are eloquent and sensuous, although they also tend toward more sentimentality than the contemporary reader may be used to. They are neatly arranged and carefully indexed, helpful in an anthology of this size and scope. De la Mare's introduction, thorough and well-written, is nonetheless sprawling and anachronistic. He provides a careful analysis of love throughout history (including an interesting bit about Freudian interpretations of love) and theorizes about the natural differences between men and women that draw the sexes together. Some may be put off by the chivalrous tone of this anthology, but overall it is a sweeping collection of moving, beautiful verse.

Love Is like the Lion's Tooth; an Anthology of Love Poems. *Frances McCullough, ed.* **(1984) Harper & Row. 80p., o.p.**

Unlike other love poetry anthologies, this one is short and makes no effort to be inclusive. Its actual subject is passion, and its poems are aimed specifically at younger readers, so there tends to be a simplicity about them. Some of the most interesting of these verses are foreign ones, translated from the Azande (of the Congo), from Hungarian, Russian, Japanese. There are famous love poems by Petronius Arbiter, e. e. cummings, and W. H. Auden. But many of these poems are rarely collected and will be new to most readers, especially adolescents. Their quality tends to be high, so this is a reliable collection to give to young readers to expose them to fine literature. It is a subject that surely will interest them, and its treatment is refined.

Love Poems from Spain & Spanish America. *Perry Higman, ed. and tr.* **(1986) City Lights Books. 243p.**

A bilingual anthology with splendid translations, this is a survey of love lyrics in Spanish. The collection opens with anonymous ballads of the sixteenth century and moves alphabetically to Xavier Villaurrutia. Each of the poets is given a brief biographical sketch and placed within the history of Spanish verse. The majority of poems, generally two or three for each poet, are from Spain, although Spanish America is represented by both known and lesser-known figures. Among the poets well known to non-Spanish-speaking readers are Juan Ramón Jiménez, Lope de Vega, Federico García Lorca, Pablo Neruda, César Vallejo, and Jorge Luis Borges. While one might suspect the single theme would soon run its course and there would be a great deal of repetition, this is hardly the case. Each poet and each poem offers a distinct, imaginative response to love. The variations on the theme are quite astonishing, perhaps because of the music of the Romance language or perhaps because of the particular feelings of the poet. The result is a marvelous collection that can be enjoyed by anyone, including young people.

Love's Aspects; the World's Great Love Poems. *Jean Garrigue, comp.; Introduction by Nancy Sullivan.* **(1975) Doubleday. 413p., o.p.**

In the brief, poetic introduction to this volume, Nancy Sullivan notes, "The present anthology is divided into twelve sections representing the rising and falling action of the seasons of the year, the twelve hours from the high noon of love to its darkest midnight, or the twelve months of the year which symbolize in a similar pattern the rising and falling of love's cycle." The 355 poems included here are by authors from all over the world — Paul Éluard, Federico García Lorca, D. H. Lawrence, and Wallace Stevens. The quality of the poems varies: for example, Andrew Marvell's "To His Coy Mistress" and W. B. Yeats's "Adam's Curse" are eloquent expressions of romantic sentiments; others are more flowery than memorable. Illustrations by noted American painter Nell Blaine enliven the book's appearance without distracting readers from the poems themselves. The book is well indexed. Readers will find here a comprehensive look at the world's love poetry.

Loving: Poetry and Art. *Charles Sullivan, ed.* **(1992) Harry N. Abrams. 160p.**

Slender and colorful, this anthology combines one hundred songs and poems and pairs them with almost as many different pieces of art, all celebrating different types of love: romantic love, familial love, burning passion, and the love of beautiful objects. Arranged in chapters by theme, the selections are often from such frequently anthologized poets as Blake, Shakespeare, Dickinson, and Yeats. Artists include Mattisse, Rodin, Michelangelo, and Warhol. Most of the verse is English and the artwork Western, with one poem and corresponding artwork on a page. The range of art and literature is what sets this apart from similar anthologies. Instead of concentrating solely on classics of art and literature, the editor makes some unorthodox choices, including songs by John Lennon, a Calvin and Hobbes cartoon, and Keith Haring sketches. Although some readers may not call some of these examples art, the anthology is still recommended for its beautiful design and the personal nature of the art and verse. Indexed by poet, title, and first line.

Scottish Love Poems: a Personal Anthology. *Antonia Fraser, ed.*

See under SCOTTISH POETRY

Under All Silences; Shades of Love. *Ruth Gordon, comp.* **(1987) Harper & Row. 78p.**

According to the compiler, "these poems illuminate the many shadings of love, from its first inception to meetings, discovery, passion, knowledge, and beyond — its place in the timelessness of the cosmic world." The purpose is not an easy one to realize, at least for junior high and high school students who may be more familiar with MTV's version of love than that of Osip Mandelstam, Rainer Maria Rilke, or Paul Verlaine. A wise person, the compiler also includes such popular writers as Joan Baez, Ewan MacColl, and May Sarton. They rub shoulders with both signed and anonymous verse from Egypt, Japan, India, and Greece. All periods, all countries, all situations seem to be dutifully considered. In the jacket copy, Gordon explains: "I am a librarian, but I don't try to teach poetry anymore — it's all too personal." Personal or not, the choice of poems is beyond reproof. Any adult will enjoy them as much, if not more, than the young people who are the target audience.

An Uninhibited Treasury of Erotic Poetry. *Louis Untermeyer, ed.* **(1963) Dial Press. 580p., o.p.**

"Erotic" has many different meanings. In this volume erotic means sensual and lustful, sometimes ribald, but never smutty or lewd. Readers looking for titillation must go elsewhere. The volume could, in fact, be a collection of love poems, because the overwhelming majority of the poems are about courtship and longing — with a little lust thrown in. Such favorites as Marvell's "To His Coy Mistress" and Jonson's "To Celia" are here. The poets are represented by their most erotic work; some are generally categorized as sensual writers, others are not often anthologized as such. Arranged chronologically, the volume moves from classical Greek and Roman times to the Middle Ages and the English Renaissance through the Victorian years to conclude with twentieth-century erotic verse.

The Virago Book of Love Poetry. *Wendy Mulford, ed., with Helen Kidd, Julia Mishkin, and Sandi Russell.* (1990) Virago Press. 288p., o.p.

According to the editor this volume was intended to "stretch the definition of the love poem" as far as possible. Although on the whole it is not innovative or outstanding, the volume does have an unusually large number of love poems fraught with bitterness and disgust, as well as some overtly lesbian poems. The work of more than two hundred women poets is collected here. They write as lovers, as the objects of devotion, as angry spouses, and they write of the love of God, of children, and of friends. The poets come from all over the literary map, from ancient Sumeria to contemporary America, and include such diverse writers as Sappho, Dickinson, Queen Elizabeth I, and Margaret Atwood. The verse is divided into six chapters loosely arranged by such titles as "Go Home and Put My Man Out" and "Your Name on My Tongue." These can give a good indication of the tone of the book and pretty much defines the anger and sensuality that pervades many of the poems. They are usually well written; many are well known and often anthologized. An anthology of love poems from a women's perspective, it could never be called romantic. Indexed by poet and first line.

MEDICAL AND SICKNESS POETRY

Poems from the Medical World. *Howard Sergeant, ed.* **(1980) MTP Press. 179p.**

This collection of 136 poems about medical topics is divided into such ambiguous categories as "Eyes That Shine," "Doctors, Clinics, and Surgeries," and "The Healer Walks with Burning Hands." Most of these section titles are derived from poems within them. The anthology includes Keats, Abraham Cowley, and Oliver Goldsmith, but such poets are outnumbered by twentieth-century writers (Dannie Abse, U. A. Fanthorpe, and Ronald Mann, among others) whose lives have been dominated, in some cases, by medicine rather than by literature. The works are direct but not always artful; poems by recent authors often pale beside such verses as Keats's "Ode on Melancholy" or Thomas Lovell Beddoes's "Resurrection Song." This work contains contributor biographies and an index of authors.

Poets for Life; Seventy-Six Poets Respond to AIDS. *Michael Klein, ed.* **(1989) Crown Publishers. 243p., pap.**

The poems in this anthology are often grave, sometimes extraordinarily powerful in their portrayal of a killer disease. Seventy-six poets contributed 116 poems of varying depth, style, and skill. All of the poems are about AIDS — from the perspective of lovers, relatives, friends, and the suffering victims. Among the more prominent poets included here are Marvin Bell, William Dickey, and Allen Ginsberg; producer Joseph Papp has written one of four short introductory essays. Some of the poems are disquieting elegies, some are political messages. Arranged alphabetically by author, the anthology also includes biographical information on the poets. According to Klein's introduction, the majority of these poems were written especially for this volume, and the purpose of the volume is to "celebrate the profound human tragedy of AIDS." Because of its harrowing focus, this collection is not for everyone. There is not much to celebrate about this disease, but this anthology does convey varying degrees of grief and anger.

Toward Solomon's Mountain; the Experience of Disability in Poetry.
Joseph L. Baird and Deborah S. Workman, eds. (1986) **Temple University**
Press. 151p.

The editors ask a rhetorical question: "Why, one might ask, why an
entire volume of poetry devoted to this particular subject," i.e., to the
experience of disability. The thirty-five poets, most of whom suffer some
type of health problem, answer the question in several ways. The most
captivating is with a tone of black humor and its disregard for traditional
tears and moaning. There is great self detachment and a wide variety of
approaches to encounters with ill health. Neil Marcus, for example, offers "Zotz," a shorthand method of writing. It is an expression that is
heroic and humorous. While few of the poets' names will be known to
readers, the topics are familiar to anyone. The high level of writing, the
hard-won conquest of pain is related in cool lines and phrases. The thematic index gives one a good idea of subject matter. The first section
covers aging, with five poems. Longer sections are devoted to alienation,
anger, day-to-day realities, irony, and synthesis. Although this is a special
book for a special reader, it reaches out as well to a general audience.

Unending Dialogue; Voices from an AIDS Poetry Workshop. *Rachel*
Hadas, ed. (1993) **Faber and Faber. 150p.**

These poems are the result of a New York City poetry workshop for
people with AIDS — none of whom had written poetry before.
Expectedly, the poems are often rudimentary or amateurish; readers
looking for highly polished work must seek elsewhere. But the lack of
polish is overshadowed by the stark fear and anger emanating from these
poems. The book is divided into three sections titled "The Lights Must
Never Go Out," "AIDS and the Art of Living," and "Out of Your Nakedness, Out of My Nakedness" — indications of the level of sensitivity
and melodrama found here. Sixty-one poems and "prose poems" are
included, largely detailing a procession of hospitals and dying friends
and revealing glimpses into the contemporary gay male culture. A long
introduction explains how the poetry workshop came about and what the
editor's expectations for it are. The editor includes explanations for some
of the poems, perhaps unnecessarily: sometimes there is more power in
ambiguity.

NATIVE-AMERICAN POETRY

Carriers of the Dream Wheel; Contemporary Native American Poetry.
Duane Niatum, ed. **(1975) Harper & Row. 300p., o.p.**

The oral tradition dominates these pages. Some twenty Native American (i.e., American Indian) poets draw upon that tradition to explore their past and their present. Unfortunately, all of the poetry is by modern Indians, all written in English. This is within the scope set by the compiler, yet one longs for the roots of that oral tradition, for the voices out of the earlier years. The talents here are uneven, although in the deepest sense they all are reflective of a history that for too many years was forgotten or badly skewed by white American opinion and romance. The editor himself is among the best of the group, followed by Liz Sohappy Bahe, Wendy Rose, and Ray A. Young Bear. Note that few of these names find their way into standard anthologies. Most of the poems were originally published in little magazines or by university presses, neither having the wide audience of commercial publishers. Fortunately, this collection rights a wrong.

A Gathering of Spirit; Writing and Art by North American Indian Women. *Beth Brant, ed.* **(1984) Sinister Wisdom Books. 240p.**

A special issue of the little magazine *Sinister Wisdom,* this was issued as a separate book in 1984. The work of accepted, well-known poets from Alaska and America are included, as well as Native American verse from less-familiar writers. The balance is excellent, and what some of the less-accomplished poets may lack in style and authority they make up for in content. Often these humbler voices have much to say about the life and times of a typical Native American woman and her family. But there is more to the collection than poetry. The editor includes telling photographs, drawings, letters, excerpts from novels, and diary entries — just about anything which will complete the picture of their life. There is little about the famous battles with the whites and more on the daily experiences of the poets and writers. Topics move from the adjustments to urban life to the feelings of a child and a prisoner. There are few better collections on this subject.

Harper's Anthology of 20th Century Native American Poetry. *Duane Niatum, ed.* (1988) Harper & Row. 396p., o.p.

While there are several collections of Native American poetry, this is the most comprehensive and the most current. In many ways it complements the same publisher's *Carriers of the Dream Wheel,* 1975, which was also compiled by Duane Niatum. He has brought together the work of "thirty-six poets who attest to the health of both the Native American spirit and American literature.... These poets constitute a powerful force . . . one far older, given the oral tradition, than the present republic." One should read the preface and the eighteen-page history, by Brian Swann, to appreciate the work that has gone into this anthology. The result is splendid. Beginning with Frank Prewett (1893–1962) and ending with A. Sadongei (b. 1959), the poets are arranged in chronological order. There are some famous voices, including that of the compiler and Ray A. Young Bear and, of course, Louise Erdrich. Brief biographies of each poet are found at the end of the book, as are notes and indexes to titles and first lines.

New and Old Voices of Wah'Kon-Tah; Contemporary Native American Poetry. *Robert K. Dodge and Joseph B. McCullough, eds.* (1985) International Publishers. 144p.

These verses are impressive in their simplicity and directness. They come out of a long tradition of storytelling and poetry developed by Native Americans over many centuries. Since their poetry has been largely ignored by the greater reading public, these works seem especially fresh. The nature imagery in them is extraordinary: the people and the land are strongly interactive. These are poems by Indians and about Indians. Most of the names will be new to general readers; the only really famous poet is Ted Berrigan, who hasn't been particularly associated with Native American culture. The subject matter here is decidedly varied, ranging from going to a dance that ends in a murderous, drunken brawl to a contemplation of Machu Picchu, in Peru. There is a strong sense of being drawn into the visions and experiences of an alien culture, one that is too infrequently taken seriously by the greater American public.

Shaking the Pumpkin; Traditional Poetry of the Indian North Americans. *Jerome Rothenberg, ed.* **(Rev. ed., 1986) Alfred van der Marck Editions. 424p., o.p.**

The title is derived from twelve songs from the Seneca Indians. The poems, which resemble modern concrete poetry in form, are "to welcome the society of the mystic animals." There are extensive "commentaries" at the conclusion to guide the reader. The translation of the visual pattern is typical throughout of a strong effort to match in English not only the words but also the spirit of the poetry. The poet / compiler translates many of the verses himself, but he is helped by a battery of experts, many of whom are themselves poets. Arrangement is by arbitrary sections, with particular attention to religious categories: "I try to establish contexts for the poems where possible or useful, and to carry forward discussions of Indian and tribal poetry, philosophy, or history as lightly touched on in this introduction." Coverage, as the subtitle suggests, is broad. There is verse from the Maya as well as from the Aztec, Navajo, and Eskimo. In truth, the whole of North America is represented. The result is, by and large, the best of the numerous books of Native-American poetry, at least in scope and in subject. If only one book in this subject area is possible, this is the choice.

Songs from This Earth on Turtle's Back; Contemporary American Indian Poetry. *Joseph Bruchac, ed.* **(1983) Greenfield Review Press. 295p., pap.**

Entering the era of the powerful, green political parties, this is an ideal guide. Representing slightly over one and a half million Native Americans, the poets have a great deal to offer all human beings "who believe in the Earth, in the survival of living things, in the survival of the spirit. Let us listen carefully to their words." Similar in scope to Duane Niatum's *Carriers of the Dream Wheel,* this collection offers different poems of many of the same writers in that 1975 anthology. It has the advantage, too, of offering twice again as many poets, many from a later period. Each of the photographs of the sixty or so poets is followed by a brief autobiographical sketch and usually three to five poems. Many of these have appeared earlier in little magazines or in small press books that tend not to be found either in home or library. The arrangement is in alphabetical order, by author. While much of this is, as Laura Tohe puts it, "living among cedar and sagebrush," it has a message that will involve anyone who bothers to step outside: Treat the earth well and it will care for you.

That's What She Said; Contemporary Poetry and Fiction by Native American Women. *Rayna Green, ed.*

See under   WOMEN'S POETRY AND FEMINIST POETRY

Voices of the Rainbow; Contemporary Poetry by American Indians. *Kenneth Rosen, ed.* **(1975) Viking Press. 232p., pap.**

Similar in purpose and scope to two other anthologies, *Songs from This Earth* and *Carriers of the Dream Wheel,* this one features many of the same poets. There are twenty-one Native American voices in the collection. Aside from the "contemporary" aspect of its scope, the editor explains: "My criteria for selection has been simple. If the reader listens carefully, can he or she hear, clearly and directly, the voice of the poet. . . . While I prefer to think of American Indian literature as an integral part of American literature in general, I recognize in these poems a pervasive feeling for the spiritual which resides in the palpable, a common feeling for the land, the climate, the specific place, which infuses this poetry. . . ." Little more can or need to be said about the essence of these creative writers.

NATURE POETRY

Art & Nature; an Illustrated Anthology of Nature Poetry. *Kate Farrell, ed.* **(1992) Metropolitan Museum of Art. 175p.**

Drawing from a wide variety of viewpoints, cultures, and poetic styles, this anthology has found a common bond in the universal lore of nature. Poems included range from discourses on elephant love to romantic or seasonal verse; they celebrate aspects of the plant and animal kingdoms, natural scenery, and the changing seasons. *Art & Nature* concisely lays out the wonders of the world around us and provides the reader with a fantastical vision of it. The verses have been paired with art from The Metropolitan Museum of Art to help bring the poems to life in the reader's imagination. *Art & Nature* is divided into four sections: Spring, Summer, Fall, Winter — the poems working their way through the year; poems that do not correspond to a specific season have been placed according to the whims of the editor. Each illustration, needless to say, is carefully identified. The book is indexed by author, title, and first line, and also by artist. As the editor points out, this book is an opportunity to enjoy art, nature, and poetry all in the same place.

A Book of Nature Poems. *William Cole, comp.* **(1969) Viking Press. 256p., o.p.**

From Dickens and Coleridge to Frost and Updike, these are personal views of nature that are notable for evoking every season over a number of centuries. The poets celebrate the delights of flowers and trees, night and day, rain and wind, and other aspects of nature seen by the imaginative eye. All of the well-known poets and poems are included, with a particular focus on the modern period. At the same time, Cole includes such lesser-known voices as William Barnes and other early English poets. The black and white illustrations by Robert Parker add little to the collection, but they may help set a mood. Here is a discriminating, fascinating anthology that considers virtually all facets of the natural world. For example, in the index of titles, the first poem is "Afternoon: Amagansett Beach," by John Hall Wheelock; near the end are Robert

Frost's "Young Birch" and a Gaelic verse "Welcome to the Moon." It is difficult to think of an aspect of nature not covered.

Earth Prayers from around the World; 365 Prayers, Poems, and Invocations for Honoring the Earth. *Elizabeth Roberts and Elias Amidon, eds.* **(1991) Harper Collins. 451p., pap.**

In their introduction the editors explain that "these prayers seek to heal the division that has grown between us and the rest of nature." A little later they write that "when the human spirit is understood in this sense, as the mode of consciousness in which we are connected to the planet as a whole, it becomes clear that our entire life is an Earth Prayer." Although it seems too simplistic to be true, the editors are earnest. Hundreds of prayers, poems, and chants are arranged in chapters with such titles as "The Ecological Self," "Healing the Whole," and "Meditations." The volume features verse from many different cultures and religions, particularly Native American and Buddhist. Many, however, are poems by such noted English-speaking poets as Allen Ginsberg, W. S. Merwin, and Walt Whitman, whose works here are about the ecological decline of the Earth or man's abuse of the land. The quality of the verse varies, and reading the anthology grows a little tiresome because most of the selections repeat the same theme without any variation in tone or form. On the other hand, readers interested in the environmental movement or Native American verse will find this anthology just the thing. Indexed by first line with a "Calendar of Earth Prayers" at the end.

Four Seasons, Five Senses. *Elinor Parker, ed.* **(1974) Charles Scribner's Sons. 132p., o.p.**

Elinor Parker has collected a set of nature poems by renowned authors—Shakespeare, Keats, Coleridge, Longfellow, Tennyson, and Dylan Thomas (the most recent poet). The ninety-nine works included are arranged according to the four seasons. Line illustrations at the beginning of each season enliven the appearance of the book. Parker has indexed poems by author, title, and first line, but the anthology has neither introduction nor table of contents.

Moods of the Sea; Masterworks of Sea Poetry. *George C. Solley and Eric Steinbaugh, comps.*

See under SEA POETRY

Moonstruck; an Anthology of Lunar Poetry. *Robert Phillips, ed.* (1974) **Vanguard Press. 181p., o.p.**

"Before there was man there was the moon." So begins this eclectic collection of verse about the moon. The poems spotlight man's shifting perspective of the moon — from ancient Greece to the Middle Ages to the modern, post-Apollo years. Distinguished poets such as Sappho, Byron, Joyce, and Auden are included. A special effort has been made by the editor to feature the more obscure, equally skilled contemporary verse of Allen Ginsberg, W. D. Snodgrass, and Maxine Kumin, among others. Divided into such subjects as "Orb of Love," "Fables of the Moon," and "After Apollo," the poems represent a wide range of styles, lengths, and forms. Some are mythological, some psychological, and some are simple romantic love poems. All are interesting and evocative — even creepy at times — and paint a lively picture of the heavens. Indexed by title, author, and first line, the poems include several in translation.

The Oxford Book of Garden Verse. *John Dixon Hunt, ed.* (1993) **Oxford University Press. 341p.**

With the enthusiast's habit of expanding his own interest to encompass all things, the editor of this anthology has compiled a collection whose scope is small, gardens, but whose raison d'être is rather grandiose: "One recurring theme is how essentially ambiguous the garden can be: haven and safe retreat . . . a triumphant creation, but also harboring its own destruction. . . ." If the editor tends to wax lyrical in the introduction, however, this same expansiveness works well in the anthology's organization. The poems are in chronological order, not by theme, with footnotes by the editor giving occasional definitions and historic facts. There are two indexes, by first line and author. This is an anthology for people who enjoy reading about gardens — musings from many different eras. Those with a less horticultural taste should probably eschew this rather precious anthology.

The Poetry of Flowers. *Samuel Carr, ed.* (1977) **Taplinger. 88p., o.p.**

In his introduction to *The Poetry of Flowers,* Carr writes that the flower poetry of such poets as Milton, Donne, and Blake is often clearly about a subject far removed from the plant itself. For readers, "the ostensible subject loses focus in the universal context of its setting." Carr intends to collect flower poems that make poetry from the mere physical appearance of a bluebell, a marigold, or a poppy, rather than using flowers as primary metaphors within profound discourses. There are fifty-one poems in this anthology by poets as varied as St. Matthew, Samuel Taylor Coleridge, and John Masefield; included are Tennyson's "Flower in the Crannied Wall," Wordsworth's "Daffodils," and Blake's "Ah Sunflower!" There is no index. The anthology contains floral illustrations by Monet, Renoir, and Van Gogh, among other renowned artists, and, in including these works, the editor has risked eclipsing the poems beside them! One wishes this lovely book were more extensive.

Pop/Rock Songs of the Earth. *Jerry L. Walker, ed.* **(1972) Scholastic Magazines. 96p., o.p.**

Pop/Rock Songs of the Earth aspires to be nothing more than a collection of twenty-five popular songs from the 1960's and 1970's with ecological or conservational themes. It includes, indeed, such favorites as Bob Dylan's "A Hard Rain's a-Gonna Fall," "Across the Universe," by John Lennon and Paul McCartney, and J. C. Fogerty's "Have You Ever Seen the Rain?" While these songs may address nature in a superficial way, their deeper meanings often have nothing to do with natural themes. "A Hard Rain's a-Gonna Fall," for example, is more a prophecy of the downfall of society and a final judgment than a statement about the environment, although it does abound with natural imagery. Jerry L. Walker has omitted musical notation, implying that readers are to consider these songs as poems. They were meant, however, to be sung rather than read; stripped of their music, they pale in comparison to literary poetry. The book has a table of contents but no index. Songs are accompanied by black-and-white photographs of the groups and musicians who made them popular. This anthology is neither a satisfying collection of poetry nor an exhaustive source of pop songs about the natural world, but it may be useful to readers in search of song lyrics.

See also ANIMAL AND BIRD POETRY; SEA POETRY

POETRY
Study and Teaching

American Poetry and Prose. *Norman Foerster, Norman S. Grabo, Russel B. Nye, E. Fred Carlisle, and Robert Falk, eds.* **(5th ed., 1970) Houghton Mifflin. 3 vols., pap., o.p.**

This three-volume textbook offers a comprehensive view of American poets and prose writers from the Colonial period through the 1960's. Each volume is divided into several parts. For example, the second volume concludes the "Romantic Movement" begun in the first volume and goes on to "Realism" and "Naturalism." Each chronological period is subdivided by genre. Approximately two thirds of each volume is given over to prose. The periods are introduced by detailed historical, social, and literary essays, with the revised edition strongly emphasizing the literary aspect. In addition, there are suitable introductory statements about the authors and their work. The selection is well balanced, and the compilers note that authority and readability are important criteria in their choices. The design is pleasing, and the three-volume format replaces the unwieldy, cumbersome earlier single volume. This is not the work many people will turn to for entertainment, but it is a useful collection for libraries looking for the best work of hard-to-locate poets and prose writers.

English Verse, 1300–1500. *John Burrow, ed.* **(1977) Longman. 397p., pap.**

Because this volume is fully annotated, it will be a help to the student or perplexed reader of Middle English verse; it was intended as a teaching guide to the lyrics and ballads of Chaucer, John Lydgate, William Dunbar, and other minor poets of the period. Arranged chronologically by poet and poem (in the case of anonymous verse), this anthology represents the work of nine English and Scottish poets, a seemingly small number, but remember that there are copious annotations to help understand the language and some of the more obscure terms. A chronological table charting the literary and historic milestones of the era is provided, as well as a splendid introduction that explains the development of the poetic forms and devices that have become standard in our modern literature. Indexed by title and first line.

English Verse, 1830–1890. *Bernard Richards, ed.* **(1980) Longman. 543p., pap.**

This well-structured volume of Victorian poems is one of a series of Longman anthologies of annotated English and Scottish poetry. The collection has an informative introduction, a chronological table of historical and literary events in Britain, and helpful biographical and critical information on each poet. The eighteen poets are arranged chronologically, beginning with John Clare and William Barnes and concluding with Hardy, Hopkins, and Francis Thompson. In between are selections by Robert Browning, Elizabeth Barrett Browning, and Emily Brontë, among others — generally, their best-known work, the gems of Victorian literature. Indexed by title and first line.

Exploring Poetry. *M. L. Rosenthal and A. J. M. Smith, eds.* **(2d ed., 1973) Macmillan, 531p., o.p.**

This reliable anthology, containing 320 poems, would clearly be useful for the student of literature who wishes to learn about poetry. The collection includes a variety of such great poets as Homer, Eliot, Yeats, Wilbur, Levertov, and Jones. Poets who have achieved critical acclaim appear more often than lesser-known authors. Each of the book's nine sections examines a different facet of poetry (for example, "Poetry as Symbol and Evocation," "Tradition and the Sense of the Present," "Poetry as Narrative and Drama"). Each section has an explanatory introduction by the editors (both respected literary critics) explicating several poems in the section; larger sections are divided into smaller units — each with its own brief introduction. All of the included works are time tested; they are listed in the table of contents and indexed by author, title, first line, and topic.

Familiar Poems, Annotated. *Isaac Asimov, ed.* **(1977) Doubleday. 272p., o.p.**

In this unusual anthology, Asimov explains the mysterious names, places, and events described in thirty-six famous poems, including "Alexander's Feast" and "Miniver Cheevy." The poems have nothing in common stylistically or thematically, but they all contain references not familiar to the modern reader — who will, nevertheless, probably be familiar with the poems themselves. Asimov admits that some of them are even wretched, although he does not disclose which he feels have earned that distinction. They are arranged by the date of the action in the poem. Thus, "Ozymandias" opens the volume not because Shelley is the oldest author but because the events in that poem occurred around 1250 B.C. "The Battle Hymn of the Republic," "The Star-spangled Banner," "Fire and Ice," and "The Pied Piper of Hamelin" are among those annotated. The notes are clear and succinct, explaining obscure references — to the Bible, for example, and to long-forgotten wars.

Fifty Contemporary Poets; the Creative Process. *Alberta T. Turner, ed.*

See under   AMERICAN POETRY: 20TH CENTURY

Fine Frenzy; Enduring Themes in Poetry. *Robert Baylor and Brenda Stokes, eds.* **(2d ed., 1978) McGraw-Hill. 417p., o.p.**

The organizing principle behind this volume is one that explores such potent poetic themes as "Exuberance," "Love," "Mutability," "Marriage," "Illusion/Reality," and "Art and Aesthetics." The selection of poems, covering the work of English and American writers from Chaucer to the present, is uniformly high. The reader is able to examine fine poems by more than one writer dealing with the same general topic. While serving as a good introduction for those who are reading poetry seriously for the first time, this volume also contains enough little-known material for the more seasoned poetry lover. The thematic positioning of the poems also increases its potential value: if someone is curious about the way poetry addresses various themes, he or she could turn to this volume and be enlightened. A concluding essay on prosody is helpful for the general reader, and a glossary provides succinct definitions of poetic and figurative terms.

The Heath Introduction to Literature. *Alice S. Landy, ed.* **(4th ed., 1992) D. C. Heath. 1,142p., pap.**

Don't let the number of pages here scare you away. This is one of the best introductory anthologies for students and beginning readers, rating high on accessibility, arrangement, quality and range of the poems, and critical questions and supplementary information. Collected in this one volume are short stories, complete plays, and 150 poems, all arranged neatly in their own sections and then further subdivided within these sections, usually according to theme and form. The great writers of English literature are all represented, with an emphasis on the nineteenth century and on contemporary and minority writers. The questions following each poet's work are neither too unchallenging nor so analytical as to drive away unfamiliar readers. This anthology is understandable, accessible, and comprehensive. Its only drawback may be the disproportionate emphasis on modern writers, but students should enjoy and appreciate this collection because of its variety of styles and voices. Indexed by title, author, and first line.

The Heath Introduction to Poetry. *Joseph DeRoche, ed.* **(4th ed., 1992) D. C. Heath. 561p., pap.**

This fourth edition of *The Heath Introduction to Poetry* is the latest to be indexed in *Granger's Index to Poetry*. New poems have been included in this student's text of the most influential and skilled verse since the Middle Ages; others have been dropped for this edition. Many of the selections are well-known classics, often seen in other surveys. The text begins with Beowulf and Chaucer, quickly moving to Shakespeare and then to the Romantics and Victorians. Much of the text features contemporary poetry, so students must look elsewhere for a more thorough sampling of classics. The 134 poets are usually represented by just a few of their best-known verses. They are roughly arranged chronologically by poet, with special attention given to Shakespeare's sonnets and to Edna St. Vincent Millay, Whitman, and Dickinson. Each section has a brief, clear introduction; extensive footnotes on more obscure poems are provided; there are indexes of terms, authors, and titles. As a student's survey this is a fine volume, especially for high school classes. It lacks the usual critical essays featured in many introductory volumes, allowing the poetry to stand for itself.

How Does a Poem Mean? *John Ciardi and Miller Williams, eds.* **(2d ed., 1975) Houghton Mifflin. 408p.**

In eight chapters that range from "The Image and the Poem" to "The Words of Poetry," the distinguished poet and critic John Ciardi explains the art form to the layperson. (As translator, Williams serves to balance Ciardi's opinions, but it is primarily the poet whose voice is heard throughout the guide.) The technique they employ is simplicity itself. A poem is given in full, then followed by one, two, or three pages of comment about its meaning and how it illustrates a certain poetic principle. In chapter seven, "The Poem in Motion," "Buick," by Karl Shapiro, precedes an analysis that, among other things, includes a basic explanation of iambic pentameter and the trochee — always with Shapiro's poem as witness and example. The illustrative selections cover all periods, all styles, all countries. The result is an exemplary teaching device and a constant source of pleasure. The rare combination reminds one of Wallace Stevens's "Anecdote of the Jar," which is considered here under the topic "Rippling Pools." This guide, like the jar, takes "dominion everywhere." Highly recommended for home and library.

Introducing Poems. *Linda W. Wagner and C. David Mead, eds.* (1976) Harper & Row. 368p., o.p.

The editors' discussion of such major components of poetry as imagery, metaphor, and sound pattern is lengthy and oversimple. In one instance we read, "Although some poems may be rather long, comprised of interlocking segments, poems usually tend to be short because the poet aims at capturing the heart of an emotion . . . in one moment" — a suspicious statement, given the large number of lengthy poems in the anthology itself, poems such as Eliot's "The Love Song of J. Alfred Prufrock" and Frost's "The Death of the Hired Man." The volume's 268 well-known poems are by such authors as Su T'ung Po, Neruda, Christina Rossetti, and Edwin Arlington Robinson, as well as numerous anonymous English and native American poets. The editors have included favorites by all writers. Works are grouped into six categories: "The Self," "The Circle of Love," "Community," "The Other World," "Nature," and "Poetry"; sample explications of two poems by Robert Hayden and Galway Kinnell end the book. There is a helpful glossary of terms and an index of authors and titles.

Introduction to Literature: Poems. *Lynn Altenbernd and Leslie L. Lewis, eds.* (3d ed., 1975) Macmillan. 89p., pap.

This third edition of Macmillan's *Introduction to Literature: Poems* contains almost 800 English-language poems, from the anonymous "Sumer is Icumen In" to Laurence Lieberman's "Homage to Austin Warren." The editors have arranged poets chronologically. Altenbernd and Lewis begin their thirty-seven-page introduction by defining poetry as "imaginative discourse that gives powerful expression to experience, ideas, and emotion in heightened, patterned language"; they then discuss its nature, language, form, and content. The book is indexed by author, title, and literary term (as defined and discussed in the introduction).

An Introduction to Poetry. *X. J. Kennedy, ed.* **(6th ed., 1986) Little, Brown. 480p., pap.**

X. J. Kennedy is one of America's most lively and imaginative poets. He happens to be, too, an excellent teacher. The combination is reflected in this basic guide to poetry. It is one of the best available and should be found in all libraries and in many personal collections. In the Preface, opening with the question "What is poetry," Kennedy explores the answer and addresses such other common questions as "Who needs it?" Speaking to the average college student, the compiler then moves on to examples of the best poems in the English language. The guide is in three sections. The first explores the quality of verse from "Listening to a Voice" and "Reading a Poem" to "Symbol," "Evaluating a Poem," and "Poems for the Eye." Here, as throughout, each part opens with an explanatory section, gives some examples, and after each poem poses four or five questions. Where there are no questions, there often are brief notes. The second part is called simply "Anthology: Poetry" and is an alphabetical arrangement of over one hundred poets, from John Ashbery and W. H. Auden to W. B. Yeats. A subsection, "Anthology: Criticism," has brief prose remarks by a dozen or so poets and critics, including Samuel Johnson and Barbara Herrnstein Smith. The "Supplement" is primarily an aid to writing a paper about poetry and, finally, provides information on the mechanics of writing a poem. Selection, comments, and focus are first rate. The anthology cannot be praised too highly.

An Introduction to Poetry. *Louis Simpson, ed.* **(3d ed., 1986) St. Martin's Press. 640p.**

One of the strong points of this anthology is its extremely complete glossary of poetic terms. In addition, it provides a guide to understanding poetry in a series of introductory essays. These cover the significant aspects of poetic composition: metaphor, rhythm, sound, and meter. The introductory remarks are fairly brief and are followed by a long, very well-selected anthology of poems dating from Chaucer in the fourteenth century to the contemporary poets. The editor confines himself to poetry written in English, but he chooses from poetry of all centuries. There are long selections from Edmund Spenser, Shakespeare, Donne, Pope, Byron, Keats, and Emily Dickinson, among scores of others. The editor's judgment in selecting poems is outstanding. People who love poetry will find many of their favorite poems here. And for those who are not especially familiar with the genre, this is an excellent volume to dip into and sample some of the great poetic achievements in English in the past seven centuries. After the brief introduction the readers are, however, on their own: the poets are not individually introduced nor are their poems individually discussed.

Introduction to the Poem. *Robert W. Boynton and Maynard Mack, eds.* (Rev. 2d ed., 1973) Hayden Book Company. 221p., pap.

Boynton and Mack have divided this anthology into five sections: "The Poem as Subject," "The Poem as a Dramatic Situation," "The Poem as a Pattern of Rhythm and Sound," "Devices of Compression," and "Additional Poems Chronologically Arranged." The ambiguous fifth section, called a collection of "poems for further reading" in the preface, includes such well-loved poems as Dickinson's "I heard a fly buzz when I died" and Yeats's "The Wild Swans at Coole" — which could well have been included elsewhere in the book. The anthology draws mainly from an expected poetic canon. In addition, the editors have provided no information to distinguish this edition from the earlier one. Each section contains an explanatory introduction; each poem is accompanied by several study questions. Although not particularly memorable, *Introduction to the Poem* is a careful and useful text.

Invitation to Poetry; a Round of Poems from John Skelton to Dylan Thomas. *Lloyd Frankenberg, ed.* (1956) Doubleday. 414p., o.p.

The approach taken by this anthologist is a congenial one, particularly for those who are just beginning to experience the joy of reading poetry. He prints a variety of poems and then writes a series of comments upon those works. For example, after "Kubla Khan," by Samuel Taylor Coleridge, he provides approximately four pages of observations about the history of the poem, his aesthetic response to the verse, the sounds of the poem, and, finally, the possible meaning of the poem. He is quite sensitive to issues of tone and quite unauthoritarian about his judgments. In fact, many of his comments are questions to stimulate the reader to think about what has just been read. Not all of his comments are long, but they are always intelligent and probing. They help to shed light on poems as diverse as a sonnet by Shakespeare and a lyric by e. e. cummings. His choice of poems is astute, his selections evenly divided among the sixteenth, seventeenth, eighteenth, nineteenth, and twentieth centuries.

The Liberating Form; a Handbook-Anthology of English and American Poetry. *Bert C. Bach, William A. Sessions, and William Walling, eds.* (1972) Dodd, Mead. 403p., o.p.

In their introduction to *The Liberating Form*, the editors state that it is an anthology intended for teachers and students alike. It should prove most useful for college students. The editors never completely explain the organizational principle of their volume. Its ten sections are devoted to such poetic forms as ballads, couplets, and Spenserian stanzas. The poets range from Shakespeare and anonymous English balladeers to such twentieth-century poets as Allen Tate and Theodore Roethke. The poems are generally classics — Wordsworth's "Lines Composed a Few Miles above Tintern Abbey," Donne's "The Flea," Roethke's "Papa's Waltz." The editors provide stimulating study questions for some of the poems and detailed analyses for others; the work has author, title, and critical term indexes. One table of contents lists poems, a second arranges the book by poetic form. This is a useful reference and study tool.

The Longman Anthology of Contemporary American Poetry. *Stuart Friebert and David Young, eds.*

See under   AMERICAN POETRY: 20TH CENTURY

Messages; a Thematic Anthology of Poetry. *X. J. Kennedy, ed.* (1973) Little, Brown. 386p., o.p.

This thematic anthology is divided into twelve sections: "The Nature of Poetry"; "Cities"; "Environments"; "Life Styles"; "Identity of a Woman"; "Peoples"; "Nightmare and Apocalypse"; "Journeys"; "Magic"; "Solitude"; "Loving"; and "Enduring." Weirdly, the poems are printed without giving the names of the authors; those are provided at the very back of the book. The Preface explains that this is done so the reader can make up his or her own mind about the worth of a poem without being influenced by the reputation of the writer. This seems a precious arrangement, but the selection of poems is, nonetheless, very good. At the end of the volume, there are also a section on the lives of the poets and a glossary of poetic terms that is short but helpful. Many modern writers are included in this anthology, and the thematic arrangement makes for an interesting context in which to read their poems. There are also selections from writers of Shakespeare's time to the present, but the emphasis seems to be on twentieth-century verse.

Middle English Lyrics, Authoritative Texts, Critical and Historical Backgrounds, Perspectives on Six Poems. *Maxwell S. Luria, ed.*

See under ENGLISH POETRY: C. 450–1500 — OLD ENGLISH, MIDDLE ENGLISH

Modern Poems; an Introduction to Poetry. *Richard Ellmann and Robert O'Clair, eds.* **(1976) W. W. Norton. 526p., pap.**

An acclaimed biographer of Joyce and Wilde, Richard Ellmann joins forces with a professor of English to introduce college students to a wide range of modern poetry. The poems move "from the easily accessible to the more difficult." The guide opens with a remarkably well-written and clear introduction on "Reading Poems." Some fifty pages in length, it considers everything from imagery to figurative language, usually with examples. Walt Whitman is the first poet. He is introduced by a biographical and literary sketch, a practice common for all of the poets included. There then follows a half dozen poems. Where necessary, there is a footnote to explain a particular situation, word, or phrase. A brief essay, "Modern Poetry in English," a bibliography, and an index close the anthology. There are some one hundred poets included. As the book draws close to the 1970's the number of poems for each writer decreases to about two or three. Still, these are representative. There is a fair balance between American and English poets, although the Americans rightly take up more space, and there are more of them included. While this is not as ambitious or as useful as such related works as X. J. Kennedy's *Introduction to Poetry* or Brooks and Warren, *Understanding Poetry,* it is extremely good for the modern authors. See also below *The Norton Anthology of Modern Poetry.*

The Norton Anthology of American Literature. Vols. I–II. *Nina Baym and others, eds.* **(2d ed., 1985) W. W. Norton. 2,535p., 2,652p.**

These two massive volumes (each is over 2,500 pages) are a "collaboration between editors and teachers" involved in educating college students about American literature. The format, size aside, is familiar. There are six divisions in the two volumes. Each is introduced by a preface of five to ten pages, followed by examples from the work of the leading American authors. Each author is given a page or so of introduction, and there are short, useful footnotes to explain situations, persons, or places in the selections. Most of the focus is on prose, not poetry. For example, in the second volume one is given an overview of American

Literature, 1865–1914, followed by the writings of Samuel Clemens and about twenty more writers, not one of whom is a poet. While there are several poets in the next chronological part, it is only at the end that more than three hundred and fifty pages are devoted to "American Poetry 1945–." Indeed, the major poets are given a good deal of space throughout, but essentially the two volumes concentrate on prose. The collection cannot be recommended either to the library or to the individual as a selection of poetry. Still, it is a marvelous overview of American writing.

The Norton Anthology of English Literature. Vols. I–II. *M. H. Abrams, general ed.* **(5th ed., 1986) W. W. Norton. 2,616p., 2,578p.**

An extremely comprehensive survey, this anthology comprises two enormous volumes. Volume I covers "The Middle Ages," "The Sixteenth Century," "The Seventeenth Century," and "The Restoration and the Eighteenth Century." In the second volume we find "The Romantic Period," "The Victorian Age," and "The Twentieth Century." Each of the individual periods is treated in great depth. From the Middle Ages, for example, there is a long selection of Old English poetry, including "Beowulf" and Caedmon's "Hymn." That is followed by long selections from Chaucer's *The Canterbury Tales,* several of which are included in full. From the seventeenth century, there is a multitude of poems by John Donne, Ben Jonson, Milton, Andrew Marvell, and Robert Herrick. Each century is treated with the same meticulous attention to the great figures and many minor figures who comprise the genius of the age. This is an excellent survey. Those who read it seriously can participate, in essence, in a university course in English literature.

The Norton Anthology of Literature by Women; the Tradition in English. *Sandra M. Gilbert and Susan Guber, eds.*

See under   WOMEN'S POETRY AND FEMINIST POETRY

The Norton Anthology of Modern Poetry. *Richard Ellmann and Robert O'Clair, eds.* **(2d ed., 1988) W. W. Norton. 1,863p., pap.**

Among the numerous Norton anthologies, this is one of the best. The reason is twofold. First, the editor, Richard Ellmann (ably assisted by Robert O'Clair) insisted on rigorous selection practices, and he provided copious notes to help the student. (Ellmann died only a few months before the second edition was published.) Second, there is more here than in other collections of this type — more poems, more explanation, more biographical material, and close to two thousand pages representing every major poet writing in English in the twentieth century. If only one anthology of modern poetry were to be purchased, this would be the first choice. The selection begins with the late nineteenth century and Walt Whitman, Emily Dickinson, Gerard Manley Hopkins, and Thomas Hardy. Cathy Song (b. 1955) is the last writer included. Her name reminds the reader that the compilers "have provided a generous selection of poets less celebrated but still of commanding interest."

The Norton Anthology of Poetry. *Alexander W. Allison and others, eds.* **(3d ed., 1983) W. W. Norton. 1,452p., pap.**

Among numerous Norton anthologies, this is one of the most famous and most comprehensive. In close to fifteen hundred closely packed pages, the compilers "provide readers with a wide and deep sampling of the best poetry written in the English language, from early medieval times to the present day." The first four poems are anonymous lyrics from the thirteenth and fourteenth centuries. Some two hundred poets and more than a thousand poems later the anthology ends with three poems by Leslie Silko (b. 1948). There is a clear, twenty-page explanation of versification at the end of the volume, as well as an index of authors, titles, and first lines. What makes this edition outstanding for all readers, and a useful guide for college students, are the numerous notes. These may range from two or three for a poem, to long, in-depth comments. The beginning reader will, therefore, have no difficulty understanding esoteric persons, places, and metaphors. Most commendable is the discriminating choice of new poets, women poets, and African-American poets. In addition, "there is a significant increase in poems written in English in other countries." All and all, this is an ideal collection for individuals and libraries alike.

The Norton Anthology of World Masterpieces. Vols. I–II. *Maynard Mack, general ed.* **(5th ed., 1985) W. W. Norton. 2,052p., 2,165p.**

These whopping volumes could probably help readers develop muscles in their arms as well as improve their minds. There is a massive amount of poetry here: the work of Homer, in long excerpts from *The Iliad* and *The Odyssey;* and entire verse plays, such as *Agamemnon,* by Aeschylus, *Oedipus the King,* by Sophocles, *Medea,* by Euripides, and Aristophanes' *Lysistrata.* Then there are the poems of the Latin poet Catullus, Virgil's *Aeneid,* and selections from Ovid's *Metamorphoses.* All of

these were from the section "Masterpieces of the Ancient World." There
follows "Masterpieces of the Middle Ages," with some of Dante's *The
Divine Comedy*. In "Masterpieces of the Renaissance," there is Petrarch's
verse and essays by Montaigne and Cervantes, and so on and so on, until
we come to the contemporary writings of Samuel Beckett. Throughout
the ages, prose is featured along with poetry, and there is a great effort
to recognize extraordinary writing on all the continents. This anthology
could serve as a textbook for many college courses. The poetry it provides is of the highest quality.

The Norton Introduction to Literature: Poetry. *J. Paul Hunter, ed.*
(1973) W. W. Norton. 573p., o.p.

The Norton Introduction to Literature: Poetry is intended for use as a
textbook; it contains such classics as Milton's "Lycidas," Arnold's "Dover
Beach," and Thomas's "Fern Hill." Among the other authors included
are Blake, Sir Walter Ralegh, Tennyson, Richard Wilbur, Theodore
Roethke, and Imamu Amiri Baraka. The editor has provided a foreword,
a "preface to poetry," and an informative appendix that addresses such
poetic elements as argument, audience, and figurative language. The
book's 600 poems have been divided into three sections: "The Poem in
Focus: Subject and Tone," "The Middle Distance: Craft, Form, and
Kind," and "The Larger Frame: Poems in Contexts." Poems are indexed
by author, title, and first line. This anthology provides an overview of the
nature of poetry, although it contains less explanatory material than do
some other educational anthologies.

The Norton Introduction to Poetry. *J. Paul Hunter, ed.* **(4th ed., 1991)**
W. W. Norton; first edition had title The Norton Introduction to
Literature: Poetry. 578p.

This fourth edition of *The Norton Introduction to Poetry*, with eighty-
nine new poems replacing those dropped from the third edition, concentrates on contemporary and twentieth-century poets — a substantial
number of those being women and minorities. The volume also offers a
sampling of classics from Keats, Dickinson, Shakespeare, and
Wordsworth, but the emphasis here is on the contemporary writers students will not generally find in introductory texts. More than four hundred poems are arranged in five main sections to facilitate the study of
the tone, setting, verse form, or other technical aspects of the verse. The
strength and originality of each individual poem is emphasized. The
quality of the poetry varies, some of it in experimental form and of

unorthodox length. What makes this slender anthology among the best of the introductory texts, however, are the diversity of poetic style and the helpful, clear, critical remarks. Biographical information is included at the back, and the volume is indexed by poet, title, and first line.

The Pleasures of Poetry. *Donald Hall, ed.* **(1971) Harper & Row. 338p., o.p.**

The text of *The Pleasures of Poetry* is intended to "introduce poetry to the beginner" and "concentrates on . . . feelings that begin in the mouth and that end in resolutions of wit, or in discoveries of inward life." Almost half of the book consists of Hall's explorations of such issues as "Image and Metaphor," "Pleasure and the Words of Poems," and "The Noises Poems Make." Hall discusses poetry inventively, describing it as "a pleasure, like making love." A section called "Ten Great Poets" consists of work by Shakespeare, Donne, Milton, Pope, Blake, Keats, Tennyson, Whitman, Yeats, and Roethke. A section called "One Hundred Poems" contains poems by such poets as Marvell, Eliot, and Bly. The final section, "Five Lyrics by the Beatles," simply contains the words to five Beatles hits. In his preface Hall acknowledges the highly arbitrary nature of these categories. Despite these organizational decisions, few students will be disappointed by the book's 186 poems or its instructional value.

Poems on Poetry; the Mirror's Garland. *Robert Wallace and James G. Taaffe, eds.* **(1965) E. P. Dutton. 328p., o.p.**

The editors of this compact anthology feel that "poems are the only true definition of poetry's indefinable and changing nature." Here they have put together an anthology to chronicle this changing nature. Older poems have been left out in favor of contemporary verse, and the punctuation in the remaining older poems has been normalized. The hundreds of poems chart "the maker" of the poem and "the making and the made." Featured poets include Frost, Dickinson, Keats, X. J. Kennedy, Sylvia Plath, and Howard Nemerov; half of the poems are by contemporary writers. The verse is lively, imaginative, and diverse. This is a solid anthology; the editors have selected superior poetry, having sought out poems "that are not only statements about poetry but imaginatively successful poems in their own right." There is an author and title index.

Poetry. *Jill P. Baumgaertner, ed.* **(1990) Harcourt, Brace, Jovanovich. 703p., pap.**

This large teaching anthology is representative and neatly constructed — perfect as an introduction to understanding poetry but maybe too didactic for more sophisticated readers. Created for the college-age audience, the volume is divided into two sections. The first features 148 mostly modern, distinguished English and American poets, arranged alphabetically, with a large proportion of minority and female writers represented by selections of their best-known writings. The second section contains eleven chapters concerned with explaining the structure and sensibility of verse — chapters with titles such as "Elements of Poetry" and "Becoming a Discriminating Reader." A hundred famous, mostly classic, poems are analyzed for form and rhythm in this section. In addition, a glossary of poetic terms and author, title, and first-line indexes are included. This is a solid text of largely contemporary poets that should be helpful to teachers trying to make poetry interesting to younger students who tend to look at poetry as an out-of-style bore. On the other hand, many college-level students and general readers may find the pedantic tone too elementary, too ready to assume that poetry is an alien form that one has to "learn" to understand and appreciate.

Poetry, an Introduction and Anthology. *Edward Proffitt* **(1981) Houghton Mifflin. 463p., pap.**

At the end of the section entitled "To the Student," Proffitt demonstrates a desire to "reach you on a personal level and . . . show you that poetry is a form of knowledge." The book is divided into educational and "anthology" sections. The seven parts following the introduction address such facets of the poet's craft as "Abstraction, Concretion, Imagery," "Rhyme Schemes and Formal Designs," and "Rhythm and Meter." The text consists of individual poem explications and study questions; often, Proffitt has students write poems that focus on the dominant issue in each section. It is an exercise that, as he acknowledges, he has adapted from the educational works of Kenneth Koch. The poets selected are well loved, the poems apt teaching examples. Among the poems he explicates in his first, educational, section are Roethke's "My Papa's Waltz," Stevens's "Domination of Black," Frost's "Fire and Ice," and Blake's "The Sick Rose." The poems in the anthology section, also classics, are divided into sections that correspond to the chapters in the instructive section. One wishes that these works followed the chapters themselves. There is a glossary and an extensive index. Here is a valuable textbook and a fine collection of poems.

Poetry in English; an Anthology. *M. L. Rosenthal, general ed.* **(1987) Oxford University Press. 1,196p., pap.**

In another massive volume for the college student, there are six sections with seven editors, including the general editor. Only one is from England, Beryl Rowland, of York University, who was editor of "The Middle Ages." Canadian and United States scholars are about evenly spread over the five other parts: the Sixteenth Century; the Seventeenth Century; the Restoration and Eighteenth Century; the Nineteenth Century; and the Twentieth Century, divided between the Early Moderns and the Late Moderns. The final section is devoted to explaining versification. Editorial annotations, which are frequent in the earlier sections and less so later on, appear at the bottom of each page. Preceding each poet is a short biographical and literary/historical sketch by the editor of the section. In terms of balance, one hundred and twenty-five pages are devoted to the Middle Ages, while the twentieth century opens with Thomas Hardy and closes nearly four hundred pages later with Seamus Heaney. The explanation of poetic form, i.e., versification, is extremely clear and should be of great assistance to layperson and student alike. It is a working volume that will be of great value to librarians and to others seeking representative verse of well-known poets. Of particular value are Rosenthal's remarks about the Early Moderns.

Poetry, Past and Present. *Frank Brady and Martin Price, eds.* **(1974) Harcourt Brace Jovanovich. 527p., pap.**

Professor of English, a literary critic, and editor, Brady brings a thorough understanding of the needs of college students to a basic introduction to poetry. The detailed introduction explores the critical aspects of English and American poetry. The text is written in an extremely clear, easy-to-understand fashion. It serves as a good explanation of the subject not only for students, but for involved laypersons. The techniques and theories of poetry are considered, as are the various elements that set off an acceptable piece of work from mere sentimental verse. There is the usual detailed glossary. Of particular interest is the thematic and generic table of contents that should help the beginner find a way through more than four hundred poems. Arrangement is chronological, from Chaucer to Sylvia Plath. The hundred and fifteen poets are pri-

marily English, but there are enough of the American masters to make
this a suitable introduction to American-English poetry.

Poetry; Points of Departure. *Henry Taylor, ed.* **(1974) Winthrop. 345p.,
o.p.**

Poetry; Points of Departure is divided into an instructional section and
an anthology section. Taylor has separated the first half into such topical
chapters as "Approaching Poems," "Form, Sound, and Structure," and
"Imagery and Figures." He addresses each topic through lucid discussion
of pertinent poems. A glossary at the book's end supports the instructional sections. The poems in the anthology section are grouped by
subject — for example, "The National Habit: Politics" and "One Name is
Pain: Sports." Among the poets are Thomas Campion, Wordsworth,
Robert Frost, Swift, and Gwendolyn Brooks. The editor includes famous
works (Yeats's "Leda and the Swan," for example, and Wordsworth's
"Composed upon Westminster Bridge, September 3, 1802") with lesser-
known poems of equal quality, indexing them by author and title.

Poet's Choice. *Paul Engle and Joseph Langland, eds.* **(1962) Dial Press.
303p., o.p.**

The editors of this anthology asked 100 prominent, primarily American poets to contribute a favorite poem they had previously published
and explain why it is special to them. The result is a volume that offers
vivid contemporary verse as well as insight on each poet. The diversity
of the poets ranges from Robert Frost, William Carlos Williams, and
Robinson Jeffers to X. J. Kennedy, W. D. Snodgrass, and Anne Sexton,
whose chosen selections are usually unknown. The poets' comments are
brief and varied: some have chosen a particular poem because they feel
it may best represent their work; many explain that the poem reminds
them of a certain memorable period or person in their life. In the short
introduction, Engle and Langland observe that "the poet has one great
and rewarding advantage over other practicing artists. When he speaks
of his own work, he does so in the same medium, language, in which he
wrote." Built around this concept, the editors have put together a fine,
reflective volume.

Poetspeak: In Their Work, about Their Work. *Paul B. Janeczko, ed.*

See under YOUNG ADULT POETRY

The Practical Imagination; an Introduction to Poetry. *Northrop Frye, Sheridan Baker, and George Perkins, eds.* **(1983) Harper & Row. 500p., pap.**

While essentially a college textbook, the collection, with its numerous notes, comments, and data on the various poets, will be of considerable interest to the involved layperson. It covers the forms and varieties of poetry "moving from the simple elements to the more subtle and complex, with principles explained and questions provided to guide the students' progress." After a brief background introduction on the aesthetic pleasure and the sound and meaning of poetry, the compilers open with a discussion of the lyric and narrative forms. The short but informative text preceding each section and many of the poems themselves help make the point over and over again that such concepts as symbols, allegory, and metaphor can be understood and appreciated with a little study. The compilers avoid the simplistic, but they are able to convey some difficult lessons in relatively easy to understand terms. Coverage is generous of American and English poets from early anonymous works through to Wordsworth, W. B. Yeats, Philip Larkin, and e. e. cummings.

Sleeping on the Wing; an Anthology of Modern Poetry with Essays on Reading and Writing. *Kenneth Koch and Kate Farrell.* **(1981) Random House. 313p.**

While serving as an anthology of modern poetry, this book performs the further function of introducing readers to the genre of poetry. After an introduction in which such ideas as how to read and talk about poems are considered, the work of twenty-three poets is printed, each being allotted from four to ten pages. These poets range from Walt Whitman, Emily Dickinson, and Gerard Manley Hopkins to Ezra Pound, John Ashbery, and Amiri Baraka. After each of their sections of poems, there is an essay on their work written by the editors. These essays tend to be fairly brief, sometimes only a page in length; they also include a poetry-writing exercise for the reader to undertake. One of the delightful aspects of the essays is their precise, sincere appreciation of the particular genius of each poet. This sense of devoted admiration is contagious. Still, the very simple nature of the essays probably makes them more appropriate for younger audiences in high school and college.

Sound and Sense; an Introduction to Poetry. *Laurence Perrine and Thomas R. Arp, eds.* **(8th ed., 1992) Harcourt Brace Jovanovich. 342p., pap., o.p.**

For several decades a popular introduction to poetry for college and advanced high school students, this is an exploration of poetic concepts as well as an anthology of poetry. Throughout, there is a clear sense of what constitutes fine writing and the choice of poetry reflects that high degree of critical judgment. Poets whose work is featured in great detail include Emily Dickinson, A. E. Housman, and Robert Frost. Following each of the poems in the general text, there are questions to provoke the reader to consider particular aspects of the poem. They tend to be sharp, probing inquiries about the essential nature of the work. The elements of poetry that are covered through brief discussions of the concepts, with close examinations of individual poems, are: denotation and connotation, imagery, figurative language (including metaphor, personification, metonymy, symbol, allegory, paradox, overstatement, understatement, and irony), allusions, meaning and idea, tone, musical devices, rhythm and meter, and so forth. The thoroughness of the approach and the excellence of the poems that are explicated make this a fine introductory textbook for those starting out on a quest to understand poetry. In this Eighth edition about a third of the poems have been replaced with different selections. A glossary of poetic terms is included.

Time for Poetry. *May Hill Arbuthnot, ed.*

See under   Children's Poetry

To Read a Poem. *Donald Hall, ed.* **(2d ed, 1992) Harcourt Brace Jovanovich. 411p., pap.**

In his introduction, Hall explains that he is concerned with esthetic emphasis in this collection, and that he intends to "examine the way poetry works." His approach may be too pedantic for the high school or college student this volume is aimed at. The quality of the poetry is excellent, but the organization and lack of emphasis on older poets might make it unattractive to teachers of survey courses. The verse is divided into explanatory sections with such titles as "Images," "The Sound of Poetry," and "Symbols and Allusions." A section concentrates on the work of five poets — Keats, Dickinson, Frost, Roethke, and Adrienne Rich — and the main section of the book contains almost two hundred superior poems. Brief biographical information precedes the work of the poets in the main section. Here is first-rate verse by some of the best English-speaking poets, but the emphasis on teaching the esthetics of poetry and analyzing the aspects of verse may turn away the very students Hall so earnestly wants to interest. Indexed by poet, title, first line, and critical or mechanical terms.

Twentieth-Century Poetry, American and British (1900–1970). *John Malcolm Brinnin and Bill Read, eds.* **(Rev. ed., 1970) McGraw Hill (Text edition entitled The Modern Poets). 515p., o.p.**

Not another textbook for college students? Yes, and while the selection is much the same as that found in other anthologies, it is blessed with some distinguishing features. First, the compilers have attempted to include pleasurable poetry, eliminating that which is "dense, tough, and technically adventurous." Second, and this does set it apart, there are "informal commentaries" at the end of each section whenever they are needed to explain the poem and the poet. There are also the customary, brief biographical sketches for each writer. Third, and the most charming aspect of the whole collection, there are full-page, black-and-white photographs of the poets by Rollie McKenna that are highly individualistic and worth the price of the volume. There are no better portraits of Wallace Stevens, Vernon Watkins, James Merrill, Marge Piercy, and scores of others in the collection. More than a hundred poets are represented by from three to ten poems each. There are a good bibliography and an index.

Twice Ten; an Introduction to Poetry. *Chad Walsh and Eva T. Walsh, eds.* **(1976) John Wiley & Sons. 435p., o.p.**

This textbook contains 250 poems by twenty poets. For Donne, Dickinson, Yeats, Browning, Blake, Frost, Williams, Ginsberg, Auden, and Stevens, the Walshes have supplied detailed biographies, discussions of major works, and selections of poems without discussion. The editors hope that careful study of these writers will facilitate the study of other poets. The ten additional poets, with brief biographies and no discussion, are Eliot, Cummings, Thomas, Brooks, Rich, Ammons, Keats, Marvell, Housman, and Crane. The editors have picked a reasonable, basic core of ten poets — who would YOU pick? — but their guiding principle is still shaky; they explain neither their choice (other than personal preference) nor the basis for the oversimple belief that the study of these ten poets will make all other poets more accessible. They have chosen such often-read poems as Browning's "Andrea del Sarto," Dickinson's "Because I would not stop for Death," and Donne's "The Sunne Rising." The book contains a glossary of poetic terms but no index; its weakness lies less with its content than with its rationale.

Understanding Poetry. *Cleanth Brooks and Robert Penn Warren, eds.* (4th ed., 1976) Holt, Rinehart and Winston. 602p., o.p.

Many authorities correctly believe this to be the best single, modern guide to poetry for student and layperson alike. Prepared as a textbook, with a justifiably famous "letter to the teacher" in the first (1938) edition, it is the skilled work of two famous critics, poets, and, yes, teachers. "This book has been conceived on the assumption that if poetry is worth teaching at all it is worth teaching as poetry." The guide is divided into such broad sections as "Dramatic Situation" and "Theme, Meaning, and Dramatic Structure." Each section has a foreword that explains the particular aspect of poetry. The editors then cite examples from Shakespeare, Robert Lowell, and almost every famous American and English poet to emphasize their point. Approximately a quarter to a third of the poems are analyzed within the sections. Questions to stimulate further study sometimes are included. The analyses presented in the early part of the book are relatively simple, as are the poems. They grow progressively more difficult and sophisticated as the book progresses. The arrangement is based on "aspects of poetic communication, and on pedagogical expediency." In the course of numerous editions, the compilers have added comments that dutifully explain their slight changes in direction, as well as their additions and deletions. These are based as much upon changes in critical judgment as upon the expressed needs of students and teachers. There may be other places for the close study of poetry, at least for beginners and laypersons, but none is as celebrated, or as free of the burden of jargon. An absolute must in libraries and for many individuals. For a similar approach, see *How Does a Poem Mean?*

The Uses of Poetry. *Agnes Stein, ed.* (1975) Holt, Rinehart, and Winston. 410p., o.p.

Each of the four sections of *The Uses of Poetry* begins with a casual discussion of a few poems pertinent to that section — "To Sing or Cry with Emotion," "To Play," "To Protest," and "To Tell a Story." The editor then adds poems to each section, without discussing them. Some of the book's 375 poems will be familiar — for example, Keats's "Ode to a Nightingale," Thomas's "Poem in October," and Ferlinghetti's "Constantly Risking Absurdity"; others were less well known in 1975. Stein has indexed works by author and title, and she has a separate index for poetic terms, concepts, and names of theorists discussed in the text. With the substantial basis it provides, this anthology allows students to instruct themselves in the nature of poetry.

Western Wind; an Introduction to Poetry. *John Frederick Nims, ed.* **(3d ed., 1992) Random House. 639p., pap.**

The last two hundred pages of this introduction to poetry are an anthology that begins with some of the earliest English ballads and ends with contemporary writing. The choice includes many of the master-pieces of poetic discourse, with great poems by Donne, Milton, and Blake. The contemporary authors range from Gary Snyder to Li-Young Lee. This collection of poems is preceded by a stimulating introduction organized around the senses, the emotions, words, sounds, rhythms, and the mind. As the editor suggests: "The book begins, as our lives do, with sense impressions and the emotions they arouse. It then proceeds to the words with which the poet, like the rest of us, has to express such images and emotions. It goes on to consider the qualities of these words as poets use them: their sounds as well as their meanings, the rhythms they as-sume, the forms . . . in which they find expression." This methodical approach reaps real benefits when it comes to analyzing such difficult or puzzling poems as Wallace Stevens's "The Emperor of Ice Cream." Nims's leading questions (under his heading "Exercises and Diversions" and his canny definitions and illustrations of poetic terms help to expli-cate his own and many other compositions. This third edition has been slightly modified and updated by the addition of about seventy new po-ems. And there is a section of color reproductions to illustrate that "po-etry is not an isolated art." As an introductory text, this is highly rec-ommended.

Words in Flight; an Introduction to Poetry. *Richard Abcarian, ed.* **(1972) Wadsworth Publishing. 267p., o.p.**

Abcarian is obviously sensitive to the needs of the poetry student and to poetry itself. He writes in his introduction, "This anthology is based on the assumption that poetry does well on its own, that the joy, excitement, and power of poetry we talk so much about are more likely to be expe-rienced by the student the less we talk about them. . . ." The poetry found here does do well on its own; it includes Yeats's "Lapis Lazuli," Browning's "My Last Duchess," and Leonard Cohen's "Suzanne." Abcarian groups the poems into such general topical categories as "Poetry and the Fine Arts," "The Words of Poetry," and "Poetry, Sound, and Music." The book ends with a short section of drafts of poets' masterpieces, including Blake's "The Tiger," Yeats's "The Second Coming," and Spender's "An Elementary School Classroom in a Slum" — all intended to show that even great artists make mistakes. Poems are indexed by author, title, and first line. Enjoy!

POLISH POETRY

Postwar Polish Poetry; an Anthology. *Czeslaw Milosz, ed.* (3d ed., enl., 1983) University of California Press. 192p.

Three points distinguish this unusual collection. First, it is selected and edited by one of the century's greatest poets, Nobel Prize-winning Czeslaw Milosz. Six of his poems are reprinted here. (Zbigniew Herbert, on the other hand, whom he greatly admires, is represented by at least twice as many works.) Second, the translations, primarily by the compiler, are as sensitive as they are reflective of Polish thinking since the Second World War. Third, Milosz includes only poems that he believes are adaptable to English translations. And, finally, the third revised edition has several poems that he "translated especially for the occasion." Aside from the poets mentioned, among the twenty-five others are Aleksander Wat, Witold Gombrowicz, and Anna Swirszczynska. Each poet is presented with a brief biographical sketch and the compiler's evaluation of his or her place in the history of modern Polish literature. The work's "mixture of macabre and humorous elements, its preoccupation less with the ego than with dramas of history . . ." give it wide appeal for any Western reader. A highly recommended collection for individuals and libraries.

POLITICAL POETRY

Anthology of Poems on Affairs of State; Augustan Satirical Verse, 1660–1714. *George de F. Lord, ed.* **(1975) Yale University Press. 800p., o.p.**

How many people read the political poems of the Augustan period? Today, not many. The verses are limited to the purview of scholars and specialists. More the pity. The lines originally were written as lampoons and satires for popular consumption. The subjects ranged from kings and queens to actresses and "orange wenches and leaders of the court, as well as more momentous matters of state." Thanks to these verses, we now know more about the loves of Charles II than about the secretive foreign policy of the day. Even Charles's friends had to admit the king had more than a few personal weaknesses! In order to give the proper background to the individual poets and their works, each is introduced by a short essay and often an engraved portrait. Each and every line that might give the reader pause is explained in easy to follow footnotes. Given these numerous crutches, one has the pleasure not only of splendid poetry but also of an actual history lesson. In fact, the primary arrangement is by historical topic, from church affairs to Defoe's and Swift's comments on the Act of Union.

The Faber Book of Political Verse. *Tom Paulin, ed.* **(1986) Faber and Faber. 482p.**

Dante is the first on the poetical platform, with his biting appraisal of Count Ugolino. He is followed by Thomas Wyatt, Milton, Swift, Wordsworth, Walt Whitman, and Robert Lowell. In between are close to a hundred other poets, the majority English or American. But one does find selections from Osip Mandelstam, Hans Enzensberger, and other outstanding Russian, German, and Italian poets. The book makes two points. First, a considerable amount of verse can be classified as political. Second, as Tom Paulin points out in his introduction, there are at least seven distinct types of such verse: popular, monarchist, Puritan-Republican, Irish, Scottish, American, and the anti-political. It is to be expected that Milton is given more space than almost any other poet. (Paulin has a strong preference for the Puritan-Republican tradition). Others who are judged almost as important, at least in terms of space, include Blake, Wordsworth, and W. H. Auden. A surprise is Arthur Hugh Clough, who the compiler believes is a much neglected voice, and quite up to the best work of the others. The collection spans six centuries, and its scope cannot be faulted. It is the best single place to turn to for representative political verse.

Poems of Protest Old and New. *Arnold Kenseth, ed.* **(1968) Macmillan. 140p., o.p.**

This slender, provocative anthology focuses on the premise that the poet, and man in general, is by nature a protester. The poems speak out specifically on particular subjects like newspaper empires and child labor and on universal themes like death, war, and taxes. Featured here are ninety-eight very different, mostly well-known, writers, including Aeschylus, Shakespeare, Dickinson, and e. e. cummings. The poems vary in tone and style as much as they vary by subject. Some are angry, jarring, shorter poems, while others are winding and graceful. All, however, manage to state their messages with skill and strength. The arrangement of the poems is especially interesting, with poems of similar themes often appearing on opposite pages. Brief biographies on each poet are also included. Kenseth's introduction, primarily about the universality of the protest poem, is lucid and reflective. This anthology succeeds because it concentrates more on quality than on presenting any political or social slant. "Protest" in modern society has become synonymous with sit-ins, picket lines, and boycotts, but this anthology avoids such stereotyping and is able to offer a stirring collection. Highly recommended for readers looking for a first-rate volume of poetry, one that ultimately shows that the more things change the more they stay the same.

Social Poetry of the 1930s, a Selection. *Jack Salzman and Leo Zanderer* **(1978) Burt Franklin. 334p., o.p.**

According to the editors' introduction, most of the poets in *Social Poetry of the 1930s* have been ignored by literary historians. Muriel Rukeyser, Kenneth Fearing, and Kenneth Patchen, all poets included here, have since become well known. If the others have been overlooked, it's a pity. Although they might wax sentimental at times, many of these 180 poems convey compassion through the confident use of strong imagery — for example, Funaroff's "men with bared feet in the grass" (in

"Unemployed: 2 A.M."), Rukeyser's "the whole green South is shadowed dark" (in "City of Monuments"), and Norman MacLeod's blue machinery and fire in a milltown. Salzman and Zanderer have arranged the poets alphabetically; they include biographies but no index. This anthology will, at the very least, give an impression of the state of the world during the 1930's. It just may also raise the reader's social consciousness.

Songs of Work and Protest. *Edith Fowke and Joe Glazer, eds.*

See under   Ballads and Songs

RELIGIOUS POETRY

Adam among the Television Trees; an Anthology of Verse by Contemporary Christian Poets. *Virginia R. Mollenkott, ed.* (1971) Word Books. 215p., o.p.

The purpose of this work is to show the lay reader the developments in religious poetry since Auden and R. S. Thomas. Virginia R. Mollenkott writes in her introduction that recent Christian poetry "will give us the experience of what it feels like to be a certain Christian individual in moments of joy or doubt or rebellion or disgust or what-have-you. . . ." She then relates Christian poetry of the 1970's to religious poetry of the past and justifies her omission of well-established poets from the collection by saying that such poets as Eliot, Merton, and C. S. Lewis are readily accessible in other sources. There are 201 poems by forty-one lesser-known poets, among whom Collette Inez and Peter Meinke have been successful in recent years, but most of the poems in the anthology are of questionable quality. The work is indexed by theme, author and title, and first line. It provides an informative glance at the Christian poetry of its time.

American Hymns Old and New. Vols. I–II. *Albert Christ-Janer, Charles W. Hughes, and Carleton Sprague Smith, eds.* (1980) Columbia University Press.

A magnificent reference work, this is in two volumes. The first, as the preface points out, is "a generous selection of hymns with suitable tunes." The music covers four centuries of American religious song. The second volume is in two major sections. The first two hundred and eighty pages offer advanced scholarly commentaries on the individual hymns. The equally fascinating second part prints "biographies of authors and composers." A bibliography winds it all up. The first volume begins in the seventeenth century where there is a brief, general introduction to the century, and shorter prefaces for each subdivision: psalters; English devotional verse; devotional verse of the Dutch, Germans, and Italians. The same general pattern is followed throughout, concluding with the

twentieth century and a brief section on "commissioned hymns." There
are five indexes, including tunes, meters, and Bible verses. In the second
volume the notes on the hymns are arranged alphabetically by their first
lines and are abundantly documented. This definitive work is an absolute
must for libraries and for many individuals.

An Anthology of Catholic Poets. *Shane Leslie, ed.* **(Rev. ed., 1952)
Macmillan; later published by The Newman Press. 378p., o.p.**

A highly personal selection, here are Catholic poets and Catholic verse
from almost the beginning of the Church to the early part of the twentieth century. Arranged in an orderly fashion by subject and time, the
collection represents poets who are spiritually, and sometimes aggressively, devoted to the Roman faith. In the main, though, the work is
more a collection of Catholic poets than Catholic themes. As a consequence, most of the verse may be read and appreciated by anyone who
enjoys imaginative, intellectual poetry. The introduction should be read
for its marvelous survey of Catholic poets and for the personal insights
of the compiler. Most of the poetry is limited to Great Britain and Ireland, with few modern writers included. The scope, then, is restricted as
much by time as by place and subject. Note that in the revised edition the
compiler has added Hilaire Belloc and G. K. Chesterton. Lack of title
and author indexes is a bother.

The Best Loved Religious Poems. *James Gilchrist Lawson, comp.* **(1933)
Fleming H. Revell. 253p., o.p.**

With confidence the compiler observes that "this is probably the most
complete anthology of favorite Christian poems yet offered to the public." Some 50 years later the claim is no longer true. Still, the collection
has been in print for many years and has a regular following. There are
close to 500 poems, for the most part brief. Selection is based "not on
literary merit, but because of popularity and heart appeal." The arrangement is by religious, even sentimental, subject headings. We find atone-
ment, brotherhood, giving, humility, heart purity, satisfaction, security,
and the like. Hymns, oddly enough, are limited to a single page. The
index of authors indicates the compiler was true to his own conviction:
Most of the work "offered to the public" is from religious newspapers
and "several hundred monthly church magazines," and, in consequence,
the authors are less than household names. "Anonymous" and the Bible,
as might be expected, have by far the most entries, followed by Annie
Johnson Flint, Frances Ridley Havergal, and John Oxenham. Elizabeth

Barrett Browning, Bunyan, Kipling, and Tennyson are limited to one or two poems each. This may or may not "help in deepening the spiritual life and character of its readers."

A Book of Religious Verse. *Helen Gardner, ed.* (1973) Oxford University Press; first printed in Great Britain as The Faber Book of Religious Verse. 377p., o.p.

Helen Gardner's *Book of Religious Verse* will not disappoint the curious student or casual reader; Gardner has included meditative religious works by Herbert, Milton, Marvell, Hardy, Browning, Yeats, and Eliot, among others. The book should prove useful in any home or school library; present here are such well-known poems as John Donne's "Batter my heart, three-personed God" and Gerard Manley Hopkins's "God's Grandeur." In attempting to give each poet equal space in the anthology, Gardner has failed to give enough space to poets who have written extensively about religion (Milton and Donne, for example). The work is arranged chronologically, is indexed, and provides helpful biographies. The anthology fairly represents varying religious sentiments, from despair to passionate devotion.

Chapters into Verse; Poetry in English, Inspired by the Bible. Vol. I: Genesis to Malachi; Vol. II: Gospels to Revelation. *Robert Atwan and Laurance Wieder, eds.* (1993) Oxford University Press. 481p., 391p.

The organizing principle of this anthology is novel, useful, and intelligently executed. Invoking Matthew Arnold ("Hellenism and Hebraism") and Ezra Pound ("Muses and Moses"), the editors in their introduction write that English-language poetry has two great heritages, classical and scriptural, and that the latter now tends to receive short shrift. *Chapters into Verse* is an attempt to redress that imbalance. More than 700 poems inspired by the Bible have been selected and keyed to the appropriate chapter and verse. They are arranged in biblical order, from Genesis 1:1 to Revelation 22:20, and are preceded by a quotation from the relevant passage in the King James Version of the Bible. The value of this format, as the editors note, is that it "places the dialogue between individual poet and sacred text in plain view." Volume I covers the Hebrew Bible, Volume II the New Testament. In a few instances, such as Pound's "Ballad of the Goodly Fere," the biblical passage to which the editors tie a poem seems less than inevitable. Poems are indexed by title, first line, and author.

Contemporary Religious Poetry. *Paul Ramsey, ed.* **(1987) Paulist Press. 227p., pap.**

It is hard to predict which contemporary American poets would show up in a book of religious poetry. As it happens, several of the authors here are well known. There are Amiri Baraka, John Berryman, T. S. Eliot (a more obvious choice), X. J. Kennedy, Frank O'Hara, Theodore Roethke, Richard Wilbur, and William Carlos Williams, to name only the most famous. The editor has divided his anthology into such subjects as "Against the Wind of Time," "By Light and Sorrow," "Epigrams and Light Verse and Kin." This proves a very fruitful arrangement. It allows small poems to be read with others that are concerned with the same subject matter. In this volume are poems written from the 1950's to the 1980's. Although all the verses have religious themes, the religion is not always Christian: Jewish poets, Muslim poets, and others are included. It is interesting to see how contemporary authors handle a topic virtually as old as poetry itself, although somewhat eclipsed in recent years.

The Earth Is the Lord's; Poems of the Spirit. *Helen Plotz, comp.* **(1965) Thomas Y. Crowell. 224p., o.p.**

Despite the somewhat simplistic introduction, the well-known compiler succeeds again in offering an intelligent, imaginative, and wide-ranging collection of poetry for young people. The theme is evident, but the scope goes beyond Judaeo-Christian themes. Even a cursory examination of the five sections, all of which are oddly named, indicates the scope of the collection. For example, under "Praise Doubt" or "The Vision Splendid," or "Our Daily Bread" one discovers short entries from Joseph Addison, Martin Luther, and Henry Vaughan. There are adequate translations of Pindar, The Book of the Dead, a Dahomean song, and Zen parables. Plotz rightly conceives of an eternal God with a world vision. True, the vast majority of poems do concern the Christian religion, but they are so well chosen as to seem, as one poet puts it, to be "rising into sunlight / out of soil and darkness." The result is a close-to-perfect summary of religious verse for readers of all ages and backgrounds.

Eerdmans Book of Christian Poetry. *Pat Alexander and Veronica Zundel,* *eds.* **(1981) William B. Eerdmans. 125p., o.p.**

In the quick introduction to this short anthology the editors explain that "it is the content of the poems themselves, not the Christian standing or theology of the poets, which has determined the selection." Therefore, although some of the authors may not describe their poetry as particularly Christian, the poems portray God or Christian traditions in a celebratory manner. Some of the poems, curiously, may only have a passing mention of God, which makes one wonder exactly how these poems were chosen. The anthology is arranged chronologically, beginning with Caedmon, the seventh-century herdsman whom Alexander dubs "the father of English verse," and ending with such modern writers as Madeleine L'Engle. In between are many of the greatest English and American writers: Edmund Spenser, William Blake, Emily Dickinson, and C. S. Lewis. Most of the later twentieth-century poets, however, are fairly obscure. Sketches and photographs complement most of the poets, as well as brief biographical information and, when it applies, information about their religious beliefs. This anthology succeeds because the poetry chosen for the volume is true poetry, even if the collection seems incomplete and off balance.

The Enlightened Heart; an Anthology of Sacred Poetry. *Stephen Mitchell, ed.* **(1989) Harper & Row. 171p.**

This fascinating, slim anthology collects the undisputed greatest examples of religious, spiritual, and mystical verse from a wide range of cultures and religions. Full reproductions and excerpts from the Upanishads, Psalms, the Odes of Solomon, and the poetry of Yeats are among the selections featured here. But there is also a variety of religious verse from such other cultures as Native American, Japanese, Chinese, and Arabic. The 123 selections are arranged chronologically. This book easily could have been ten times as large, and although it offers a representation of spiritual verse, it lacks the extensive background information and the notes that would be helpful. But it can be recommended as a brief collection of fine verse, arranged accessibly and unpretentiously.

The Golden Book of Catholic Poetry. *Alfred Noyes, ed.* (1946) J. B. Lippincott. 440p., o.p.

The hundreds of gentle, largely celebratory poems here all have traditional Catholic themes or espouse Catholic doctrine. Many are about Jesus Christ or Mary; others are self-reflective, and some are not conspicuously religious. The collection begins with selections from Saint Francis of Assisi, Dante, and Chaucer and ends with Christina Rossetti and Walter de la Mare. Much of the poetry is by more obscure, though by no means untalented, twentieth-century authors. Here is accomplished devotional verse, some of it structurally and thematically brilliant. Indexed by author and title, these rich, compelling poems are divided into poems by Catholics (a fair number of whom belong to religious orders) and "tributary" poems by non-Catholics.

I Sing of a Maiden; the Mary Book of Verse. *Sister M. Thérèse, ed.* (1947) Macmillan. 459p., o.p.

Each of the poems in this unique collection celebrates the Virgin Mary. Drawn from sources ranging from the Bible to twentieth-century literature, the poems reflect different ways Mary has been portrayed in literature. Most of the poems were originally written in English, although there are some translations. Here are psalms, anonymous Latin lyrics, verse by Donne, Coleridge, Oscar Wilde, T. S. Eliot, and lesser-known twentieth-century writers. Arranged chronologically by poet, they encompass all styles and forms, from short elegies to long, devotional epics. Biographical information is given for each poet, and the book is indexed by title and author. Many of the poems are selections from longer works. In her intricate introduction, the editor summarizes how poets have regarded Mary over time, tracing the development of different Christian theologies and denominations.

In Love with Love; 100 of the Greatest Mystical Poems. *Anne Fremantle and Christopher Fremantle, eds.* (1978) Paulist Press. 170p., o.p.

Included in this slender collection are ninety-one spiritual, mystical poems, many from such religious texts as the Hebrew Bible and the Vedas. Some of the poems are centuries-old works of Chinese, Arabic, and Indian poets, works probably not generally familiar to most readers. The majority, however, were written by such great English-speaking and European poets and philosophers as Milton, Donne, Dickinson, Goethe, Hesse, and Auden, all deeply spiritual, exulting in a devotion to God and questioning man's place in the universe. Arranged chronologically, with a short introduction and brief biographical information where appropriate. The scope of this anthology is broad, the focus deeply compelling, the tone joyful.

The New Oxford Book of Christian Verse. *Donald Davie, ed.* **(1981) Oxford University Press. 320p.**

This anthology in no way skimps on artistic quality. In fact, in his introduction, Donald Davie remarks that he chose to exclude any kind of devotional poetry that could only be called mere verse and not poetry. The writers whose work is particularly featured include the great hymn writers, Isaac Watts, Charles Wesley, and William Cowper. The other authors, too, adhere to the Christian dogma in their poetry, the anonymous poets who wrote from the seventh through the sixteenth centuries, as well as Donne, George Herbert, Milton, Anne Bradstreet, and Henry Vaughan. Emily Dickinson is also on hand with several poems of a Christian nature. Modern poets include Sir John Betjeman, W. H. Auden, and Elizabeth Jennings. This anthology should prove extremely satisfying to those readers concerned with Christian faith; it provides some of the finest literary expressions of religious experience.

News of the Universe; Poems of Twofold Consciousness. *Robert Bly, comp.* **(1980) Sierra Club Books. 305p.**

One of America's leading poets here gathers together poetry that reaches out beyond the self and human ecology to the very heart of nature and the universe. The hundred and fifty poems are arranged in six parts, but it is the last section in which Bly addresses himself to the modern individual in quest of "an interior unity." Each of the sections includes a splendid introduction, followed by the poems. The "Old Position" leads off — the time when people had little or no appreciation of nature and its way. There were exceptions, of course, and these are the quoted poets — Gotthold Lessing, Pope, Milton, and Swift. "The Attack on the Old Position," one finds, is a much longer section, with such writers as Blake and Walt Whitman. Throughout the volume numerous poems are translated by Bly, as expert a translator as he is a poet; the work is thus given an added dimension. This is evident particularly in the final section where he translates poems from numerous cultures: "I've included Eskimo, Ojibway, Zuni poems here, early Anglo-Saxon poetry, and some medieval ballads." There is an index of authors and poems.

The Oxford Book of Christian Verse. *Lord David Cecil, ed.* (1940)
Oxford University Press. 560p., o.p.

Cecil's informative introduction enriches this superb anthology. He
writes about the theological tradition in British literature, from the devotional poets to philosophic writers to hymn poets, and examples of all
are featured here; their poems represent "significant expression of
Christian feeling." Masterpieces by Chaucer, Spenser, Shakespeare,
Donne, and Coleridge are included, as well as many meditative poems by
lesser-known writers. Arranged chronologically by author, the anthology
concludes with poems from the early twentieth century, with T. S. Eliot
among the youngest of the poets. Cecil explains that he avoided being
influenced by an author's personal faith when selecting the poets for this
volume, although he claims that he did choose verse that is consistent
with conventional Christian teachings. Solid and comprehensive, this collection will satisfy even the most discriminating reader. Indexed by author and first line.

The Penguin Book of English Christian Verse. *Peter Levi, ed.* (1984)
Penguin Books. 379p.

The editor of this fine anthology writes in his introduction that verse
featured here had to be "a poem by any Christian which touches on
Christian themes or throws a Christian light on some common experience." If this seems fairly ambiguous, the editor acknowledges that too.
Rather than produce a collection loosely based on that vague definition,
he has compiled a beautiful, diverse collection of deeply spiritual but also
disturbing poetry. All of the greatest poets writing in English are here,
arranged chronologically from John Skelton through such religious poets as Milton and Donne up to the twentieth century with Dylan Thomas
and Theodore Roethke. More than eight hundred poets are represented
in a volume whose emphasis is on quality. The editor states that many
hymns were excluded because, although they espoused Christian ideals,
they were not very good poetry. This collection includes a broad selection of splendid, reflective, sometimes moody verse.

Poems of Faith and Doubt; the Victorian Age. *R. L. Brett, ed.* **(1970) University of South Carolina Press; first published in Great Britain by Edward Arnold Publishers (1965). 191p., o.p.**

Brett begins his enlightening introduction to *Poems of Faith and Doubt* by pointing out that Victorians are often "accused of smugness, complacency and hypocrisy in matters of religion." He objects to this accusation, discussing each of the writers represented here (including Lionel Johnson, Tennyson, Arnold, Swinburne) in order to trace the development of religious thought in Victorian England. He has selected thirty-two poems, including Tennyson's "Locksley Hall" and Johnson's "The Dark Angel," that address religious issues seriously and with integrity. Subjects range from memories of close friends to the weakening of English nationalism. Poets and works are arranged in rough chronological order but are not indexed. The religious faith of the Victorian was particularly assailed by doubts and difficulties, and these poems sympathetically and clearly represent the despair and hope, the doubt and faith of his religious experience.

Poems of Inspiration from the Masters. *James R. Mills, comp.* **(1979) Fleming H. Revell. 173p., o.p.**

In his two-page verbose and sermonic introduction, Mills expresses hope that readers "will surely discern the incandescent word of God in this book. . . . That reaction was my criterion as I selected poetry for inclusion." Although Mills's instincts have guided him to such great poems as Blake's "Jerusalem" and Milton's "On His Blindness," his editorial decisions seem odd in other ways. He includes nothing by Gerard Manley Hopkins and little by Emily Dickinson, who wrote countless poems about her relationship with God. The book's 120 works are indexed by author, first line, and title but are organized into rather ambiguous thematic categories, such as "The Man of God," "O Worship the King," and "Around the Feet of God." This anthology, while it may be an interesting expression of individual taste, is not an entirely reliable source of great religious poetry.

A Poet's Bible. *David Rosenberg, tr.* **(1991) Hyperion. 410p.**

This collection of modernized translations from the Hebrew scriptures has been written with a markedly personal touch. The translator's intent is to personalize and rework biblical texts, to make them more emotionally accessible, as poetry written by poets. Whereas the King

James version of Psalm 130 begins, "Out of the depths have I cried unto thee, O Lord," Rosenberg begins with the haunting lament: "I am drowning / deep in myself, Lord / I am crying." The book is divided into three lyrically titled sections: "The Body's Call," which includes the Psalms and the Song of Solomon; "The Inner Call," which includes Jonah and Isaiah; and "The Story's Call," which includes Ruth and Esther. Each section has an introduction that gives background on the ascribed author of the text and the time it was written. The translations are inventive and elegant — the translator was aware of the influence of such modern poets as Emily Dickinson and Gertrude Stein. This is a book for someone who wants to look more closely at the Bible in less traditional ways; it is probably not so well suited for traditionalists, however, since its emphasis is on deconstruction and demystification.

Shivering Babe, Victorious Lord; the Nativity in Poetry and Art. *Linda Ching Sledge, ed.* **(1981) Eerdmans. 188p.**

This is a strikingly beautiful, illustrious anthology, filled with mostly joyful poems and classic paintings that depict the infancy of Jesus and his impact on the ordinary people around him. Divided chronologically into sections, the anthology begins with anonymous verse of the Middle Ages and continues through Renaissance poems and paintings of Michelangelo, followed by such eighteenth-century romantics as William Blake and nineteenth-century carols and hymns; it ends with twentieth-century poems by T. S. Eliot and Robert Lowell. Here are sixty-one poems with paintings by such masters as Raphael, Dürer, Picasso, and Botticelli. Woven between the verse and paintings are extensive historical notes and criticism. The first-rate verse and art show how images of Christ have changed with the times. Some of the poets are not conventional Christians, and they create a richer, diverse picture of Jesus and his influence. This is a first-rate, fascinating, compelling volume.

Tongues of Fire; an Anthology of Religious and Poetic Experience. *Karen Armstrong, ed.* **(1987) Penguin Books. 352p., pap., o.p.**

The title comes from an English television series that explored the relationship between poetry and religion. While most of the focus is on Christianity, the divisions of the book (and, indeed, the series) try to emphasize ideas and emotions rather than particular religious groups. The collection is divided into ten sections. In each, one finds standard, and not so standard, poets and poems that celebrate and explain the topic. "Sex and Religion" has eighteen poets and about as many poems.

The balance is much the same in the other sections. One finds the work primarily of English poets — Donne, Blake, Milton, Thomas Hardy, and Robert Browning are typical. On the other hand, there are the words of Czeslaw Milosz (one of the poets who helped with the series), Ibnu 'l-'Arabí, and Teresa of Avila. So, while it would be wrong to say an exact balance has been struck between faiths, at least they are represented. Each section opens with a brief introduction that attempts to show the relation between the poetry and the subject, a device that is sometimes a bit simplistic. On the whole the collection is for the generalist.

The Treasury of Christian Poetry. *Lorraine Eitel, comp., with others.* (1982) Fleming H. Revell. 182p., o.p.

A number of distinguished poets set apart this collection of popular religious verse. Among those present, and not that often found in competing collections, are W. H. Auden, Ezra Pound, and W. B. Yeats. One also finds, of course, such earlier poets as Ben Jonson and John Donne. The better-known writers are represented by some of their lesser-known poetry. Be that as it may, the poems are first rate and show a side of the poet that may be unfamiliar. The standard Christian verses are counterbalanced by the not-so-standard, and usually much better, poems. The compilers arrange the works under broad subject headings that are sometimes less than descriptive. There is a combined author-title index, and the compiler says all of the works may be delivered orally — a matter of opinion — but in no way does it detract from a superior religious anthology.

Treasury of Irish Religious Verse. *Patrick Murray, ed.* (1986) Crossroad Publishing. 295p., o.p.

According to tradition, some hundreds of years before Christ the Irish poet Amergin composed the first Irish poem, "Leabhar Gabhala," or "Book of Invasions." This collection opens with an excerpt from that work called "The Mystery." (Actually, this might well be the title for the entire anthology that, after a chronological presentation, concludes a good two thousand years later with Seamus Heaney's "St. Francis and the Birds.") After one or two anonymous poems, the work takes a leap forward with a poem attributed to St. Patrick in the fifth century. After that, there is no holding back the Irish bards who sing more of nature and the ordeal of loss in relation to Christianity than of religious experiences as such. Little of these early verses remains, so it is no accident that most of the book is involved with the eighteenth, nineteenth, and particularly the twentieth centuries. Many of "the later poems recall the dark days of persecution and suppression." This sometimes results in inartistic verses, as the compiler observes, but they do show the anguish of the times as no other writers do and for that reason are valued. There are brief notes on the authors and a most useful index of themes.

A Treasury of Poems for Worship and Devotion. *Charles L. Wallis, ed.* **(1959) Harper. 378p., o.p.**

Here are over four hundred poems written by several hundred poets, most of them unknown to the general reader or scholar. Their work is organized by such Christian religious themes as "To God the Father," "The Varied Ministries of Nature," and "Petitions of Doubt and Protest." This book is clearly aimed at a religious audience, one that wishes to increase spiritual experience through the power of poetry. This volume ignores the interest of more secular readers by printing only excerpts from longer poems by such accomplished poets as Robert Browning and William Cowper. For the full flavor of their handling of religious experience, one must consult their collected works. If a reader desires to sink into a pool of potentially popular, overly simple, and aesthetically unchallenging religious verse, then this treasury will fill the need. A more sophisticated approach to religious utterance can be found elsewhere, such as in *The New Oxford Book of Christian Verse.*

The Treasury of Religious Verse. *Donald T. Kauffman, ed.* **(1962) Fleming H. Revell. 371p., o.p.**

"Religious" verse here means Christian — poems that exult in God, honor Jesus Christ, or generally celebrate Christian theology. It is a diverse collection dominated by mostly spiritual, uplifting poetry, some excerpted from longer works, and some of it simple, jesting verse. Many of the greatest English-speaking poets are here, among more obscure or anonymous writers. The poetry is divided into chapters with such titles as "God of Glory" and "The Life of the Spirit." Some of the verse is simple in its message of God's goodness, some poems are more complex. And there are curious choices: Lincoln's "Gettysburg Address" and Benjamin Franklin's "Epitaph," for example. The editor has included the standard indexes of authors, titles, and first lines, with separate indexes of subjects and "special days and occasions."

The World's Great Religious Poetry. *Caroline Miles Hill, ed.* **(1954) Macmillan. 836p., o.p.**

First published in 1923, here is a standard work that groups the poems of primarily Christian poets under broad subject headings. One finds suitable verse arranged by period, from Pre-Christian to Medieval and modern, as well as by such topics as "Trees" and "Animals." The editor admits in earlier editions that "this collection . . . is not all great [literature] and it makes strange combinations and sequences." Hymns, for example, may be side by side with the poetry of Lord Byron. And Gustavus Adolphus's "Battle Hymn" and "O Mother Dear, Jerusalem," are here alongside Sara Teasdale. Work from the nineteenth and twentieth centuries dominates, although one finds the basic Christian poetry from earlier periods. Very little space is given to other faiths. This is the last place to turn for a true picture of the "world's great religions." Still, as far as it goes it is an adequate aid for individuals and librarians attempting to locate hard to find songs, poems, and poets. There is an index of titles, authors, and first lines.

RUSSIAN POETRY

An Age Ago; a Selection of Nineteenth-Century Russian Poetry. *Alan Myers, comp. and tr.; Foreword and biographical notes by Joseph Brodsky.* **(1988) Farrar, Straus and Giroux. 171p.**

Aside from the eleven poets represented here, no one should miss the foreword and the impressive biographical notes by Joseph Brodsky. The Nobel Prize-winning poet writes a revealing essay on the nineteenth-century poets. "Most belonged to the class of impoverished gentry — the class which is almost solely responsible for the emergence of literature everywhere. . . . Looking through the little window of this anthology onto the nineteenth century, we should try to see it for what it was, for what it felt about itself." And that is made much easier by the careful selection and the sensitive translations. Certainly, most readers will instantly recognize Pushkin and Lermontov, but few will have read such excellent renditions of their poems into English. Brodsky sets the stage for such lesser-known writers as A. A. Fet, "a lyrical poet of the highest acumen." In no other collection will the reader better see what has come to be known as the steam engine that carried Russian writers into the twentieth century.

The Oxford Book of Verse in English Translation. *Charles Tomlinson, ed.*

See under WORLD POETRY

SCOTTISH POETRY

An Anthology of Scottish Women Poets. *Catherine Kerrigan, ed.; Meg Bateman, tr.* **(1991) Edinburgh University Press. 363p.**

This book reveals a whole area of women's poetry that might otherwise be ignored. It is an attempt to show the range of women's poetry in Scotland — poems in Gaelic (with the translations), ballads, and a section called Scots and Anglo-Scots, arranged chronologically. The anthology effectively presents the wide range of women's writing in Scotland; it is full of poems that will appeal to traditional or more modern tastes.

A Book of Scottish Verse. *Maurice Lindsay and R. L. Mackie, eds.* **(1983) St. Martin's Press. 476p., o.p.**

This anthology, updated from an earlier edition to feature more twentieth-century and contemporary Scottish poets, is an excellent collection of the ballads, elegies, and lyrical poems that largely define Scottish poetry. Arranged chronologically, the volume opens with anonymous verse and ballads from the fifteenth and sixteenth centuries, including several selections from such distinguished poets as Robert Burns and Sir Walter Scott, and concludes with modern writers influenced by the Scottish Renaissance movement. The text is arranged neatly and attractively, with an index of first lines. The preface explains that the volume is intended for general readers and students to help them understand the impressive tradition of Scottish language and literature. In his stimulating introduction, Lindsay (one of the poets in the collection) describes the Scottish literary heritage and the importance of language and tradition to the Scottish people.

The Faber Book of Twentieth-Century Scottish Poetry. *Douglas Dunn, ed.* **(1992) Faber and Faber. 419p.**

The introduction to this anthology gives an historical overview of Scottish poetry, not allowing it to be subsumed under the heading of English poetry. This distinction and the emphasis on nationalism set the tenor for the book. The collection is arranged chronologically, with marginal translations of Scottish words when necessary. When a poem is translated from Scots Gaelic, both versions are included. This is a thick, comprehensive book, with an index of poets and titles. It contains some astonishingly lyrical works, worthwhile reading material whether or not you are interested specifically in Scottish poetry.

The Golden Treasury of Scottish Poetry. *Hugh MacDiarmid, ed.* (1941) **Macmillan. 410p., o.p.**

The great poet Robert Burns, the ballad form, and the talented anonymous writers are the best-known features in the wide field of Scottish poetry. All three sometimes need explanation, and to that end this anthology supplies a useful glossary and a lengthy introduction. The collection draws upon the whole history of the land. Translated from the Gaelic, for example, "The Path of Old Spells" is an early entry in the book. Here the choice is a prose translation that makes more sense of the verse but fails to convey the elementary power of the poetry. Be that as it may, no one can fault the collection for lack of proper choices. Everything is here, even "Auld Lang Syne," which opens rather than ends the anthology. Among the ballads, "The Bonny Earl o' Moray" may be the most familiar, but a real treat is "Rare Willie Drowned in Yarrow." And so it goes. The familiar rub shoulders with the lesser known, and often the latter is the more exciting, the more vibrant. This is true as well of poets who may have only one or two poetic claims to fame. If they are not of the caliber of Burns, they still are distinctive voices. Along the way one acquires a marvelous profile of Scottish history.

Made in Scotland. *Robert Garioch, ed.* (1974) **Carcanet. 94p., o.p.**

Garioch states in his introduction that the fourteen poets in this anthology (including Robin Fulton, Tom Buchan, and Paul Mills) had not been published earlier by a major publisher. Few of the writers have been extensively published since. Some of these poems are in Scots, others are in English; the editor has carefully footnoted the Scots poems, explaining words or phrases unknown to the common reader. Many of the poems are rather sentimental; they often address in an unoriginal manner such well-worn themes as love, the moon, and relatives. On the other hand, the heavily imagistic work of such poets as Fulton and Mills makes refreshing reading. Poets are chronologically arranged. The book ends with brief biographical notes, but it has no index. This anthology provides a brief look at Scottish poetry of the 1970's.

Modern Scottish Poetry; an Anthology of the Scottish Renaissance, 1925–1975. *Maurice Lindsay, ed.* **(3d ed., 1976) Carcanet. 248p., o.p.**

Maurice Lindsay's thorough introduction to *Modern Scottish Poetry* summarizes the history of the Scottish Renaissance, calling "Hugh MacDiarmid" its inspiration. Lindsay also differentiates among the first, second, and present editions of this volume, explaining that he has added such crucial older poets as Pittendrigh MacGillivray, Violet Jacob, and Marion Angus, as well as some important contemporary poets. Also present in this edition are Norman MacCaig, G. S. Fraser, Iain Crichton Smith, and numerous other well-known Scottish authors. Most of the book's 250 poems are in English, although some are in Scots and a few in Gaelic. The Scots verses may be difficult to analyze because Lindsay has not translated all of their Scots words. Poems are arranged chronologically by poet; the work has no index. Some poems are a little sentimental, the majority are essentially enjoyable. This is an anthology for either the student of twentieth-century Scottish poetry or the general reader.

The Oxford Book of Scottish Verse. *John MacQueen and Tom Scott, comps.* **(1966) Oxford University Press. 633p.**

According to the compilers, the purpose of this collection "is to lay the greater emphasis on verse written in Scots as opposed to English." This is done in an anthology that begins in the thirteenth and moves to the mid-twentieth century. The poems are arranged chronologically by author, and the focus in on poetry of literary, rather than social or historical, importance. The editors often give readers some help by defining and explaining Scottish words. When published, it was the best one-volume anthology of its type, and over the years there have been no serious competitors. If there is any criticism to be made, it is in the decision to devote almost a quarter of the book to poets born since 1880. There seems to be an overemphasis on the Scottish Renaissance; there are, on the other hand, solid offerings of all the great figures, no matter what century they were born in.

Poems of the Scottish Hills; an Anthology. *Hamish Brown, comp.* **(1982) Aberdeen University Press. 202p.**

A famous fisherman, Norman MacCaig, writes in the foreword of the feeling of freedom found in "the natural, physical world." It is that part of Scotland the compiler, who climbs mountains and writes poems, celebrates in this collection. "This is a collection for the hill goer's pack rather than a literary or historical study. . . . Come to it as we do to the hill, with rambling opportunism." Divided into sections, the two hundred or so poems tend to be short and deeply involved with the out-of-doors. In "Questions and Answers," which leads off the book, one finds Archie Mitchell's "Hills of the Middle Distance," Leen Volwerk's "Bog," and Kathleen Raine's "The Wilderness." So while the setting is Scotland, most of the poems can apply in spirit to other parts of the globe. Few of the poets are that well established, but if the names lack familiarity, there is no lack of skill and enthusiasm. Most of the writers are modern and Scottish, but a few are from other sections of the United Kingdom.

The Scottish Collection of Verse to 1800. *Eileen Dunlop and Antony Kamm, eds.* **(1985) Richard Drew. 256p., pap., o.p.**

This lively collection features five centuries of Scottish poetry, from early, illustrious ballads to the accomplished verse of Robert Burns. In between are selections by many lesser-known poets and balladeers writing in Scots and English (there are also some translations from Gaelic). The 140 poems are grouped by such subjects as war, nature, sea, and, of course, death. All the poems are eloquent, rhythmic, and gracefully written. The Scottish literary tradition is clearly evident in this exceptional, compact anthology. The volume does not aim to be inclusive but to suggest the wealth of Scottish poetry. Recommended as an introductory volume for unfamiliar readers, the anthology would probably be more helpful if it were arranged chronologically. Nonetheless, here is a strong collection with notes on some of the old Scots words and concise, informative prefaces to each of the chapters. Many of these epitaphs, love songs, laments, and narratives may be hard to follow because of the Middle Scots language, but the notes should help troubled readers. Indexed by poet, first line, and title.

Scottish Love Poems: a Personal Anthology. *Antonia Fraser, ed.* **(1975) Penguin Books; first published by Canongate Publishing (1975). 255p., pap.**

Antonia Fraser writes that the "purpose of this anthology is first and foremost to give pleasure." Indeed, the love poems in her anthology will please and surprise you. Written by poets as diverse as Burns, "Hugh MacDiarmid," G. S. Fraser, Byron, and Iain Crichton Smith, many of the 183 verses approach love directly through choice impressions: the smell of roses, a white and unbroken bed, the circle of a lover's arms. In fact,

some of these poems have become famous for their subtle explicitness —
Burns's "Comin' thro' the Rye," Byron's "So We'll Go No More a' Rov-
ing," and Sir Walter Scott's "Nora's Vow." Far from being flowery or
sentimental, most of the works are brief, romantic, and poignant. Fraser
has separated them into categories concerned with such aspects of love
as "Obsessions," "Marriages," "Longing and Waiting," and "Love in
Abeyance." She indexes the works by author and title. Here is a rich little
collection to rouse the emotions, whether you're a Scot or nae.

SEA POETRY

American Sea Songs and Chanteys. *Frank Shay, ed.* (1948) W. W. Norton; 1924 edition published by Doubleday, Doran, with title Iron Men and Wooden Ships. 217p.

The spirited sea chanteys collected here were composed and sung by sailors during the eighteenth and nineteenth centuries. All the elements of traditional sea lore are vividly brought to life — clipper ships, pirates, Colonial and English industrial ports, and the wives waiting back home. Each of the eighty chanteys is accompanied by musical notation and a brief comment on its origin and influence. There are a helpful introduction about the development of sea songs and a title index. The chanteys themselves are simple and entertaining: sometimes wild, sometimes sad, but always evocative of a long-lost, legendary life, one where songs were important diversions.

Echoes of the Sea. *Elinor Parker, ed.* (1977) Charles Scribner's Sons. 134p., o.p.

Elinor Parker has collected poems by many renowned authors, including Tennyson, Yeats, Byron, Lawrence, Spenser, and Shakespeare. The 100 poems selected, while evocative of the sea, are not necessarily great works. The two-page preface tells readers more about the editor's preference than about the anthology itself; Parker pauses only to call her collection "very personal." She has indexed the book by author, title, and first line and divides the volume into several clear sections, such as "Sea Serpents," "Shells," and "Swimmers." The book is a pleasant read, with occasional illustrations enlivening the text.

The Eternal Sea; an Anthology of Sea Poetry. *W. M. Williamson, ed.* (1946) Coward-McCann. 565p.

This extensive volume of sea poetry is planned for lovers of literature of quality as much as for lovers of the sea. More than three hundred poems by such poets as Shakespeare, Chaucer, Shelley, and Whitman are here, as well as many lesser-known writers of the past five centuries. The verse is loosely divided into such chapters as "Homeward Bound — Making Port," "Pirates and Buccaneers," and "The Building of the Ship." Some of the poems are a writer's definitive ode to the sea, some are portraits of the sailors and fishermen who spend their lives on the ocean. The editor has included a brief introduction and indexes by author, title, and first line. These are compelling, awe-inspired poems, sometimes joyful, sometimes mysterious, and sometimes downright sad.

Moods of the Sea; Masterworks of Sea Poetry. *George C. Solley and Eric Steinbaugh, comps.* **(1981) Naval Institute Press. 300p.**

Originally the quest was to find a book of sea poems for use in the classroom at the Naval Academy. Nothing suitable could be found, and the compilers decided to edit one. It follows several guidelines. First, it includes standard sea poems of England and America, ranging widely from different periods and in different styles. Few long poems are offered complete; many are excerpted. The editors were careful not to include too many poems from such well-known poets of the sea as Herman Melville and John Masefield. The only translations are those from classical sources, such as Chapman's version of Homer's *Odyssey*. Arrangement is thematic, suggested by the poems themselves. The sections are: "Sounds of the Sea"; "Man and the Sea"; "Tales of the Sea"; "The Laughter of the Waves"; "Legends of the Sea"; and "The Sea as Metaphor." There are helpful notes and an index to authors, poems, and first lines. "Each section contains poetry arranged roughly in chronological sequence." It is difficult to imagine a sea poem not here included. A superior collection for the individual and for libraries.

The Oxford Book of Sea Songs. *Roy Palmer, ed.* **(1986) Oxford University Press. 343p.**

About half of the approximately hundred and fifty songs in the collection have the primary music score. The others often state "sung to the tune of _____ ." "Sir Walter Raleigh Sailing in the Lowlands" is, for example, sung "To the tune of 'The Sailing in the Lowlands.'" This superior gathering of songs is "chiefly from England, but also from Ireland, Scotland, Wales, Canada, New Zealand, Australia, and America." They are arranged roughly in chronological order, which is often "dictated by the subject matter, a specific battle or shipwreck, for example, which took place on a particular date." Often at the conclusion of the entry, there is a detailed note supplying historical background information. There are also numerous footnotes explaining obscure words or phrases, as well as a separate glossary of nautical terms. The compiler's introduction discusses the history of the genre. He explains, too, why so often the music is lacking, remarking that "the words of a song without music are very like dry bones."

Rhyming in the Rigging; Poems of the Sea. *Lahaina Harry, ed.* **(1978) Ox Bow Press. 174p.**

The 105 poems in *Rhyming in the Rigging* evoke varying aspects of the sea. In Matthew Arnold's "Dover Beach," for example, the sea is used as a metaphor, which means that readers learn more about its symbolic depth and calm than its physical appearance. In Longfellow's "The Wreck of the Hesperus," on the other hand, the poet stresses the force and turbulence of the ocean's waves to increase the tragedy of his story. Harry has included also Coleridge's "The Rhyme of the Ancient Mariner," Carroll's "The Walrus and the Carpenter," and Poe's "Annabel Lee." The works, by poets as venerable as Shakespeare and as modern as O'Hara, are indexed by author and title. Harry could have improved the anthology by including more poems and providing an historical introduction.

The Ring of Words; an Anthology of Song Texts. *Philip L. Miller, ed.*

See under   BALLADS AND SONGS

Shantymen and Shantyboys; Songs of the Sailor and Lumberman. *William Main Doerflinger, ed.*

See under   BALLADS AND SONGS

SERBIAN POETRY

The Horse Has Six Legs; an Anthology of Serbian Poetry. *Charles Simic, ed. and tr.* **(1992) Graywolf Press. 222p., pap.**

The Serbian poetry featured in this attractive volume differs from American poetry; it fuses mythology and imagination to create beautiful, sensory verses. Simic, a distinguished poet in his own right, includes the work of eighteen poets, in addition to a section of "women's songs," which are verses passed down orally through generations. Arranged chronologically by poet (but not indexed), the verse begins with that of early twentieth-century poets and continues through the work of poets who have reached prominence in the past few decades. Brief biographical information precedes the work of each poet. Many of the poets live outside of Eastern Europe, and they tend to avoid overt political or social themes in favor of the depth of more timeless subjects. Simic offers a brief introduction to the history of Serbian literary tradition. This is a rich, distinctive volume, but readers looking for a more historical and representative or critical anthology should look elsewhere. Simic admits this is no definitive collection, as it features only poems that have touched him enough to inspire a translation. Still, as an introductory volume to poetry not widely anthologized in this country, it is highly recommended.

SPORTS POETRY

American Sports Poems. *R. R. Knudson and May Swenson, comps.* **(1988) Orchard Books. 226p.**

Drawing upon the sports which are best known to young people, the compilers have collected poems that demonstrate the thrills of both the players and the spectators. Baseball, running, football, swimming, basketball, and gymnastics are a few of the popular sports considered. There are short notes at the end of the volume that give information on the particular sport and the poet. There is an occasional interpretation, but on the whole the poems are left to speak directly to young people through high school. Among the contributions are numerous favorites by Ogden Nash and Shel Silverstein, for example. May Swenson's image of a rodeo is one of the best, as is Howard Nemerov's "Watching Football on TV." Among the other poems are John Updike's "Ex-Basketball Player," Lucille Clifton's "Jackie Robinson," and Arnold Adoff's "Wrestling the Beast." A totally satisfying collection that can be enjoyed by adults as well.

Sports Poems. *R. R. Knudson and P. K. Ebert, eds.* **(1971) Dell. 181p., o.p.**

Sports Poems begins with a witty introduction that tries to solidify a connection between sports and poetry. Mr. Knudson has divided these 120 poems about different sports into three categories but has not indexed them. "Major Sports" includes poems about football, baseball, and basketball, while "Minor Sports" covers fishing, hunting, boxing, and soccer; the poems in "Losers/Winners" address athletic competition. The "minor" games, for the purposes of this book, obviously had less mass appeal than those considered "major" — although it may seem strange, in an anthology published in 1971, to label soccer and boxing minor sports. In any case, some well-loved poets and sports figures appear in these pages. Andrei Voznesensky writes about soccer, Robert Frost about rabbit hunting, and James Dickey (himself a quarterback in college) about scoring a touchdown. Knudson and Ebert include as well a selection from Wordsworth's "The Prelude," Williams's "The Yachts," and Housman's "To an Athlete Dying Young." Most of the poems here were written in English in the twentieth century. The anthology is not extensive enough to be an all-purpose source of verse about sports, but it should suit less-demanding readers.

Sprints and Distances; Sports in Poetry and the Poetry in Sport. *Lillian Morrison, comp.* **(1965) Thomas Y. Crowell. 212p., o.p.**

What a good idea! Collecting sports verse, particularly with an eye towards involving younger people, seems clearly justified. Still, the compiler does briefly make a case for the relationship between sport and poetry. The unique approach covers any and all periods, poets, and areas, so long as they deal with sports. Furthermore, the editor warns, "Nor are all the poems in praise of sport. Some are critical, some satiric." The real measure for inclusion is quality and the appeal to young sports persons. (At the same time, as with most poetry collections for the younger reader, there is little verse that will not be enjoyed by an adult.) The primary concern of most sport poets is the race, and much of the book is given over to runners and field sports. Still, there is plenty of space for fishing, swimming, skating, and baseball, among others. There is a most useful index by sport. Yeats considers the fisherman, Euripides the poor athletes, and Kipling the delights of skating. Anonymous is here in force, as are numerous other poets whose only real claim to fame is a single poem. No matter, the overall selection is close to perfect for the subject.

This Sporting Life. *Emilie Buchwald and Ruth Roston, eds.* **(1987) Milkweed Editions. 176p., pap.**

The arrangement is almost ideal for the reader who enjoys participating in or watching sports. Each section's half dozen to a dozen poems are devoted to specific sports. They are: "Life Is Water: Swimming, Diving, Canoeing, Sailing"; "Climbing the Air: Rock Climbing . . . to Parachuting"; "Tennis and Squash"; "Play Ball — Baseball, Basketball, Football"; "Running, Jogging, Skating, Skiing"; "Blood Sports: Hunting, Fishing, Boxing, Wrestling." After that are three broad sections that are catchalls: "Coaches"; "Playing the Game"; and "This Sporting Life." All of the poets are contemporary Americans. Among the more famous are Maxine Kumin, Thomas Lux, Richard Hugo, James Wright, Donald Hall, and Robert Bly. The eighty or so other names may be familiar only to those who are avid poetry readers, particularly in little magazines.

Most, as the compilers claim, "give vivid language to wordless experience." The collection is as suitable for young people as it is for adults.

Wetting Our Lines Together; an Anthology of Recent North American Fishing Poems. *Allen Hoey, Cynthia Hoey, and Daniel J. Moriarty, eds.* **(1982) Tamarack Editions. 185p., o.p.**

There may not be many anthologies devoted to fishing poetry, but this volume of more than one hundred poems shows that there are many poets who write about their fishing experiences. Every possible fishing tale must be collected here, from fishing for the first time, deep-water fishing, fishing with fathers, sons, friends, and lovers, to the natural beauty of a trout-filled river and fishing at night. The verse is sometimes illustrious, often meditative, and rich with imagery of the water and feelings of solitude. Much of it is free verse, with a provincial feel to the language and the subject. Most of the poets are less well known, although Raymond Carver and Galway Kinnell have here expressed themselves on the sport. The poets are arranged alphabetically, but there is no biographical information and the poems themselves are undated, although they do seem fairly contemporary. Highly recommended to those who enjoy fishing and to those who enjoy evocative poetry.

TRAVEL POETRY

The Faber Book of Poems and Places. *Geoffrey Grigson, ed.* **(1980) Faber and Faber. 387p., pap.**

The distinguished poet and critic Geoffrey Grigson looks back on "poems and places" and offers the reader a delightful view of his sense of reality and of imagination, often inseparably linked. The introduction is only three pages long, but it pinpoints the scope of the anthology: "I have chosen verse about places in England, Wales, Scotland and Ireland, and the Channel Islands, into all of which our emotion flows outward, to be returned to us gladly or reflectively as well." In addition, Italy and France are considered, as are French poems about the English and their country. "I know little of comparable Italian poetry." The content is arranged by locality, and begins with a prologue and then moves to "The South." There are sections on London, Oxford, Cambridge, the Lake Country, Scotland, and Ireland, and about forty pages of translated French and Italian verse. The poets are predominantly English, from the eighteenth and nineteenth centuries. There are few modern voices — air flight seems to have done away with much of the mystery of places, particularly in Europe. Some useful notes and references are included, as well as an index of first lines.

The Oxford Book of Travel Verse. *Kevin Crossley-Holland, ed.* **(1986) Oxford University Press. 423p.**

Under the heading "En Route," one begins to travel with Sir Richard Grenville (1541–1591). Midway through his poem, he explains the joys and profits of travel, this time by sea, with the line "I must abroad to try my lot." The other one hundred or so poet/travelers are of a similar mind. Arranged geographically, the poets take to the high roads of Europe (by far the favorite route) and of Africa, Asia, Oceania, and North and South America. All of the voices are British, including Scottish and Welsh poets "and those Irish writers not averse to union with their English peers in an anthology of this kind." The poets write from direct experience. Every travel poem paints a sometimes glorious, sometimes quite terrible picture of the places where the poet has wandered. Within each of the primary sections and subsections, the dozen or so poems are arranged chronologically. One of the earliest (c. 1425) is an anonymous poem about Iberia. A comparative youngster, Frank Ormsby (b. 1947), is of the contemporary school. Threading their way through the descriptions are every emotion, from humor and joy to grief and longing. The selection is representative of the best travel poetry, as least as practiced by English writers, and can be recommended as a companion volume to Geoffrey Grigson's *Faber Book of Poems and Places.*

VAMPIRE POETRY

The Vampire in Verse; an Anthology. *Steven Moore, ed.* **(1985) Dracula Press. 196p., pap.**

If the subject matter here needs an explanation, it should be noted that the press that published this slim volume is an important part of the "Count Dracula Fan Club." The publisher has issued numerous related works, from *Dracula Made Easy* to the current volume. The intentions and aims of the society are much the same as the one evidenced in this collection — "good fun." The compilation celebrates the fact that many poets, and not a few of them excellent, have fallen under the vampire spell. Goethe, for example, is represented here by "The Bride of Corinth," and Byron, Keats, Théophile Gautier, Baudelaire, and even James Joyce and Rudyard Kipling are included. There are about fifty poets with approximately the same number of poems. They are arranged in chronological order and with a few exceptions are primarily American and English. One should note, too, that while much of the verse is fun, "I have avoided all light verse." In fact, especially during the Romantic period, many of the poems are deadly serious; only by the time of the twentieth century is the vampire more amusing. There is also a strong component of sublimated sex and violence, nicely explained in the copious notes.

WAR POETRY

Articles of War; a Collection of American Poetry about World War II.
Leon Stokesbury, ed. **(1990) University of Arkansas Press. 229p.**

The editor of this slender, sensitive anthology states that he compiled these poems in order to "expose the reader to the full evolving spectrum of American poems about World War II over this last half century." The verse is arranged by poet — fifty-three, who are represented by 119 poems of many styles and forms. The poets are divided in roughly three parts: those writing when the war began, those too young to experience the war first-hand, and, in the main section of the book, those who participated in the war either in battle or on the home front. From Robinson Jeffers to W. D. Snodgrass and Donald Hall, the verse is reflective, compelling, and often chilling. Short biographical information is provided, as well as indexes by title and author. Recommended for readers too young to have viewed the war except from a history book, these poems are wide enough in scope to be about Pearl Harbor and the bomb, but personal enough to detail mail call and foxholes.

Chaos of the Night; Women's Poetry and Verse of the Second World War. *Catherine W. Reilly, ed.* **(1984) Virago Press. 150p., pap., o.p.**

When one thinks of "war poets," women writers may not spring immediately to mind. In fact, when the editor of this volume explored prestigious anthologies of war poetry, she found that women were strikingly under represented. In this volume, she seeks to redress a wrong. This collection focuses on women's responses to the Second World War in Great Britain, where they were intimately involved in battles that sent shells crashing through their houses or into their Armed Forces. Some of the authors of these poems are familiar: Ruth Pitter, Edith Sitwell, Stevie Smith, and Sylvia Townsend Warner are some of the most famous, but most of the eighty-seven poets whose verses appear here are unknown. Their work was discovered by the editor in the course of her researches at the Bodleian Library at Oxford, where the holdings provided her with material neglected by other anthologies. These poems are fascinating, eye-opening accounts of women's reactions to the utter turmoil and intense suffering of a war brought to their doorsteps.

Men Who March Away; Poems of the First World War. *I. M. Parsons, ed.* **(1965) Viking Press. 192p., o.p.**

Can the horrors of battle ever be caught in poetry? Besides Homer and the later epic poets, the answer is a resounding NO. There are numerous gallant efforts, and some of the near successes in this volume captured the terrors and emotions of the trenches in the First World War. Yet, for anyone who has been under fire, the poem is only a shadow of the reality. Obviously the compiler of this volume would not agree, although numerous front-line poets are the first to admit that only a proximity to the dreadful truth of war is all that is possible. The poems dealing with casualties actually do attain higher proportions of poetic truth than do other sections. The editor points out that "Ivor Gurney's 'To his love' [and] F. W. Harvey's 'Prisoners' . . . are cases in point. But the established names inevitably predominate. Here are Rosenberg's terrifying 'Dead Man's Dump,' Robert Graves's 'Last Post,' Sorley's sonnets, Sassoon's 'The Death Bed,' and the great poems of Owen's maturity." The compiler's divisions, from "Visions of Glory" to "The Dead" and "Aftermath," trace the evolution of thought about the First World War. As such, the volume is a tribute to the power of poets to capture the emotions of common people in the hurricane of war.

Never Such Innocence; a New Anthology of Great War Verse. *Martin Stephen, ed.* **(1988) Buchan and Enright. 358p., pap.**

The "great war" in the title refers to the First World War, although it could also refer to the quality of the selections included here. This is a thorough, provocative collection that includes many poems seen in other war anthologies, but there are also many that are more obscure. All were collected from magazines and journals of the time, echoing the sentiments of the war by participants and those at home. Rather than try to include only flawless poetry, the editor has sacrificed skill in technique for authentic, gripping verse. The hundreds of poems are divided by theme: early days, the home front, and even a section on natural poetic metaphors for war. Here are 128 poets, among them the best-known war poets as well as a few who did not gain fame until the war was over. An informative introduction precedes each section, and there are critical notes throughout the book. Well organized and unambiguous, this volume is recommended for all readers. Indexed by title, first line, and author, with short biographical notes.

The Oxford Book of War Poetry. *Jon Stallworthy, ed.* **(1984) Oxford University Press. 358p., o.p.**

In his introduction, Jon Stallworthy writes that "there can be no area of human experience that has generated a wider range of powerful feeling than war." His selection of poems effectively bears out that contention. Stallworthy traces the significance of war over the centuries in the different societies that nurtured the authors, and he comments on their lives and accomplishments. He has chosen works from many different countries and times (including a few from ancient Greece and Rome, as well as later ones from France, Germany, and Russia), but modern poems are primarily English and American. Stallworthy arranges the verses in chronological order according to the wars that inspired their creation. His taste and judgment are splendid: the range of poems is broad, their quality fine, and he has included a few works by women. But the emphasis on the theme of war is so relentless — and not really so varied — that the reader must be truly fascinated by the subject for these verses not to pall.

Peace and War; a Collection of Poems. *Michael Harrison and Christopher Stuart-Clark, eds.* **(1989) Oxford University Press. 208p.**

This volume features classic, beautiful verse by distinguished poets: Aeschylus, Shakespeare, Milton, Whitman, and Frost, for example. The focus here, unlike that of other anthologies that concentrate on a particular war or era, is on wars from biblical to modern times. The breadth is enormous but the subjects are timeless: loss of loved ones, waiting in a foxhole for impending death, the politics and leaders deciding the fate of the people. More than two hundred poems are featured here, arranged according to theme and indexed by title and first line. The works vary in form and style; some are quite brief, some longer, some elegiac. The book's tone is, overall, one of condemnation, reluctantly accepting the travesty and inevitability of war. Although the volume seems directed at younger readers and students, it is recommended for all. Indexed by title and first line.

The Penguin Book of First World War Poetry. *Jon Silkin, ed.* **(1979) Penguin Books. 258p., pap.**

A comprehensive, polished introduction prefaces this collection of First World War verse, analyzing war poetry over the centuries and appraising the verse featured here. The cream of the volume is, of course, the poetry. Verse by such distinguished writers as Hardy, Sassoon, Kipling, and e. e. cummings is included with that of lesser-known writers. Particularly fascinating are the poems by soldiers and those active at the front. There are also some translations. This is a fine, well-organized anthology, arranged chronologically by poet, presenting gripping, elegiac verse. It would have been helpful to know the dates of the poems to determine whether a poem was written during the war or immediately after it. This is a highly recommended collection. Indexed by poet, title, first line, and translator.

The Poetry of Survival; Post-War Poets of Central and Eastern Europe. *Daniel Weissbort, ed.* **(1991) Anvil Press Poetry. 384p.**

The poems here are sometimes stark, gripping descriptions of life during the Hitler era and its constant warfare, and of life after the war ended, with the task of piecing together torn families and cities. Arranged alphabetically by poet, some of the poems are personal, some political; all are poignant and authentic testimonies in varying style and form. Here are twenty-eight well-represented poets. Readers will not recognize many of them, except for Bertolt Brecht perhaps; few have gained great recognition outside their native countries. The poets' themes are the same although their treatment of the horrors of war differs. This a compelling anthology, but because of the starkness of its verse it may not be for all readers. An excellent introduction details the qualities that make these poets — the first generation to emerge after the Second World War — unique and worth reading. There is no index, but an appendix lists each poet's published works.

Poetry of the World Wars. *Michael Foss, ed.* **(1990) Peter Bedrick Books. 192p.**

This accomplished, haunting anthology is divided neatly into three parts: poetry written during the First World War, in the years after it, and then during or about the Second World War. The chapter titles, such as "Call to Arms," "Come, Death . . ." and "Interlude, Our World in Stupor Lies," indicate to readers that this is hardly a light, pro-war volume. Instead it is among the most solemn of the many anthologies of war poetry, with an overall tone of revulsion and condemnation. Included are 151 poems by sixty-five great British and American poets — among them D. H. Lawrence, e. e. cummings, Kipling, Hardy, Dylan Thomas, and Randall Jarrell. Their verse deals mostly with the personal side of war: the everyday routine of soldiers, the lament of families waiting at home, and especially the soldier's awaiting his fate. Chilling, bleak, and well written, this is a highly recommended volume for all readers. Indexed by author and first line.

Scars upon My Heart; Women's Poetry and Verse of the First World War. *Catherine W. Reilly, ed.* **(1981) Virago Press. 144p., o.p.**

These elegies are poignant reminders of the losses English women suffered in the First World War, and of the losses of all women in all wars throughout time. The verse varies in skill as much as it does in form and length, but the emotions conveyed are strong and genuine. Amy Lowell, Eleanor Farjeon, and Dame Edith Sitwell are among the most prominent poets; most of the others will not be generally known to modern readers, although their first-rate verse chronicles the losses of husbands, brothers, lovers, and sons. They condemn the war but not their loved ones who perished or suffered. The preface, written by Judith Kazantzis, provides an interesting critique of the proliferation of women's verse during war years, faulting war poetry by male writers for not giving enough weight to the pain war inflicts on women. The anthology includes biographical information on the poets and a first-line index. The verse is saddening, often angry, and always provocative.

War and the Poet; an Anthology of Poetry Expressing Man's Attitudes to War from Ancient Times to the Present. *Richard Eberhart and Selden Rodman, eds.* **(1945) Devin-Adair. 240p.**

Published in the time of war, this selection of poems is exceptional in its scope. Most anthologies are limited to a single period, a single war, or certainly to English-speaking poets. Here, United States Navy officer (Eberhart) and Army of the United States sergeant (Rodman) begin with the Asiatic campaigns of Thutmose III (about 1450 B.C.). The first fifty or so pages, in fact, deal with military matters before the Dark Ages. Part II carries the poetry up to the First World War, and the final section highlights verse from the Second World War, as well as anti-war poetry. Both of the compilers are, of course, well-known poets as well as war veterans. Their choices reflect "man's varying reactions to war through the centuries." There are a few odd choices. Basho, for example, normally associated with seventeenth-century Japanese poetry of peace, has a three-line poem. Among the scores of poets, there are only one or two women, including Emily Dickinson. There are subjective notes about each of the poets and an index to first lines.

The War Poets; an Anthology of the War Poetry of the 20th Century. *Oscar Williams, ed.* **(1945) John Day. 485p., o.p.**

With regard to the title, one can now say that its extent is not quite the twentieth century. When this was edited, the century was only half over; the Korean and Vietnam wars and other concentrated intense ideological battles were yet to rage. The editor can hardly be faulted for an accident of time; and, even nearer the end of the same century it is still hard to locate poetry that does justice to the years after the Second World War. Given, then, the limitation of time, the editor has done all readers a great service. He has included Sgt. Randall Jarrell's familiar "The Death of the Ball Turret Gunner" and poems by Wilfred Owen, Rupert Brooke, and Vernon Watkins. Divisions are by the two World Wars and, more imaginatively, by "Poems by the Men in the Armed Forces of England and America" and "War Poems by the Civilian Poets," one of which Williams counts himself. The unique approach is reason enough to consider the volume, but what is better is the selection of poems rarely reprinted, little known, and deserving of wider attention. One may argue with his conclusion that "our war poetry as a whole is perhaps the document of our time that will outlive all the rest," but one must applaud this different and, for the most part, compelling anthology.

Women on War; Essential Voices for the Nuclear Age. *Daniela Gioseffi, ed.*

See under WOMEN'S POETRY AND FEMINIST POETRY

WELSH POETRY

Anglo-Welsh Poetry, 1480–1980. *Raymond Garlick and Roland Mathias, eds.* (1984) Poetry Wales Press. 377p.

The editors point out in their introduction that none of the poems here are translations from Welsh; all were written by Welsh authors in English. Spanning five centuries, the featured poets include Henry Vaughan, Vernon Watkins, and Dylan Thomas, among the best-known of the 124 who are represented by hundreds of poems of all forms and styles, including ballads, narratives, and elegies. All are beautifully rendered, illustrious poems evoking Welsh history, politics, and culture. Arranged chronologically by poet and indexed by title and first line, the poetry is prefaced by a lengthy, careful introduction that offers critical and historical information about the Welsh poetic tradition, particularly in terms of other English-language cultures. Highly recommended for general readers and students, the volume features delicate yet powerful verse.

The Oxford Book of Welsh Verse in English. *Gwyn Jones, ed.* (1977) Oxford University Press, 313p.

Gwyn Jones's introduction to *The Oxford Book of Welsh Verse in English* supplies a concise history of Welsh poetry from the "professionalizing of the poetic art" of the early minstrels to such later "richly gifted men" as Dylan Thomas, R. S. Thomas, and Wilfred Owen. Many of the 238 poems here are rich with the names of places, persons, and events important to Welsh history. Jones has amply represented each poet, so that one can distinguish between the various voices represented in this volume — for example, the resolute voice of Dylan Thomas, the nostalgic tone of Vernon Watkins, the cool narrative of Leslie Norris. Poems are arranged in chronological order by poet. The book is indexed by author, translator, and first line; Jones has included scholarly notes. This anthology provides a comprehensive overview of Welsh poetry from its beginnings to the present day.

WOMEN'S POETRY AND FEMINIST POETRY

Ain't I a Woman! a Book of Women's Poetry from around the World.
Illona Linthwaite, ed. **(1988) Peter Bedrick Books. 195p.**

There are contrasting literary styles in this volume of poetry, written by women about their lives. The material is organized thematically according to the essential events that make up most women's lives: childhood, love, marriage, and, finally, old age. The authors come from different cultures, and several of them are historical figures. Well-known poets are among the contributors: Elizabeth Jennings, Audre Lorde, Rosemary Tonks, and Elaine Feinstein. But the emphasis is on mixing the voices of white poets with those of black poets from around the world. Many of the works are in simple, everyday language, or in the vernacular of the street; others are in more elevated speech. So this anthology, which grew out of a stage play dramatizing the experience of women through their poetry, catches the variety of voices and experiences that the poets sought to express. This is an interesting way of gaining entry into the imaginative experiences of creative women.

American Women Poets of the Nineteenth Century. *Cheryl Walker, ed.* **(1992) Rutgers University Press. 423p., pap.**

According to the editor, this anthology is "designed to introduce the contemporary reader to the range and substance of nineteenth-century women's poetry." Twenty-seven poets spanning the entire century are featured, including Julia Ward Howe, Emma Lazarus, and Helen Hunt Jackson. The editor wisely avoids including the same poetry featured in typical mainstream anthologies, such as verse by Emily Dickinson. Instead, she concentrates on the lesser-known and forgotten writers who had achieved some prominence in their time. (Unfortunately, there is no index.) Arranged chronologically, the poets are of varying talent: some good, some excellent, some mediocre. Particularly strong is Walker's introduction, where she explains the political and social changes that allowed these women to write and publish successfully. Biographical information precedes each writer's work. Recommended for all readers, this is a well-organized, exceptional collection.

An Anthology of Scottish Women Poets. *Catherine Kerrigan, ed.; Meg Bateman, tr.*

See under Scottish Poetry

A Book of Women Poets from Antiquity to Now. *Aliki Barnstone and Willis Barnstone, eds.* **(1980) Schocken Books. 613p.**

According to the editors of this anthology, the earliest known writer on earth was female, a Sumerian priestess from the third millennium B.C. Some of her poems are in this book, as are long selections from the great Greek poet Sappho, ancient Sanskrit works from India, early Persian poetry, and Chinese verses. The sampling of women's writing here is remarkable both for the length of the time period covered, and for the numbers of countries surveyed. Beginning with the Sumerian poet Enheduanna, this volume also presents anonymous Egyptian hieroglyphic texts, ancient and modern Hebrew poems, ancient Greek, Byzantine Greek, and modern Greek poets. There are also verses in several different languages of the Indian subcontinent, various traditional African poems, and extremely long selections from Chinese and Japanese writers, stretching once again from ancient to modern times. The section on Spanish poets includes old and new verses from Spain, Mexico, Puerto Rico, El Salvador, Peru, Argentina, and Chile. Finally, there is a long section of English writers from Great Britain, the United States, Canada, and Australia. For breadth, length, and excellence in translation, this volume of women's poetry is hard to surpass.

Bread and Roses; an Anthology of Nineteenth- and Twentieth-Century Poetry by Women Writers. *Diana Scott, comp.* **(1982) Virago Press. 282p., pap., o.p.**

After a general introduction, each period of women's poetry in the nineteenth and twentieth centuries is given a separate introduction, as are each of the poets. The editor states early on that she has compiled the book both for the accustomed reader of poetry and for the novice. Both should be able to enjoy the approach to these poems. The anthology is divided into four main sections. "We Who Bleed" and "A Vaster Knowledge" are devoted to British poetry of the nineteenth and the early part of the twentieth centuries. Such poets as Emily Brontë, Elizabeth Barrett Browning, Christina Rossetti, Charlotte Mew, and Alice Meynell are featured. The final two sections are "The Meeting: On Reading Contemporary Poetry 1920–80," with such writers as Frances Cornford, Stevie Smith, Elaine Feinstein, and Ruth Fainlight, and "The Renaming: Poetry Coming from the Women's Liberation Movement 1970–80," with such poets as Mary Coghill, Diana Scott, and Astra. This arrangement is effective, in that it explores the work of acknowledged, superbly talented poets alongside the efforts of a newer literary, and finally, a newer political, generation.

British Women Writers. *Dale Spender and Janet Todd, eds.* **(1989) Peter Bedrick Books. 921p., pap.**

The primary focus of this anthology is on older works by British women that have been relatively unacclaimed. Although the large print and strange design do not suggest an academic intent, the collection is interesting and informative. The editors have arranged the book chronologically by poet, each with a brief biography. The book includes a variety of poems, letters, journal entries, and fiction, and the variety gives the reader a good overview of women's voices in literary history. Indexed by author and title, this is an ambitious and competent anthology. The editors have set out to make a place for quality work by forgotten and better-known women and they have succeeded.

Chaos of the Night; Women's Poetry and Verse of the Second World War. *Catherine W. Reilly, ed.*

See under WAR POETRY

Cries of the Spirit; a Celebration of Women's Spiritualities. *Marilyn Sewell, ed.* **(1991) Beacon Press. 311p., pap.**

The editor in her introduction writes that "spirituality has too long been an exclusively male realm." The anthology attempts to redress this by featuring poetry by women for women, in which female wisdom and power are the main themes. Since feminism and New Age spirituality are popular movements today, it seems logical that a poetry collection blending the two would emerge. More than three hundred poems are featured, divided into sections subtitled, for instance, "Songs of Brokenness and Alienation" and "The Unity of All That Is." Women as diverse as Susan B. Anthony, Audre Lorde, Alta, and Anne Sexton are among the many prominent poets. Some fiction excerpts are also included. The quality of verse runs from mediocre and undistinguished to sharp and imaginative. Readers interested in New Age spirituality and feminist studies will probably appreciate this anthology most. But the constant portrayal of women as victims of male oppression diminishes the pleasure general readers might realize from the poetry. To many readers, it may render pathetic the whole concept this anthology revolves around.

Dancing the Tightrope; New Love Poems by Women. *Barbara Burford, Lindsay MacRae, and Sylvia Paskin, eds.*

See under   LOVE POETRY

The Defiant Muse; French Feminist Poems from the Middle Ages to the Present. *Domna C. Stanton, ed.* **(1986) Feminist Press. 207p.**

There are now several collections of women's poetry from different countries and different eras, but there is nothing quite like this series: feminist poems in various languages over the ages. This volume of French feminist poems reflects the editor's "determination to exclude poems that privilege *kinder, kirche, küchen,* extol conjugal bliss, passively bemoan seduction and abandonment, and seek escape into transcendent saintliness or the beauty of flora and fauna. Conversely, the decision was made to include poems that showed an awareness of the scenes and acts of 'the femininity plot' and opposed or tried to subvert them with a different script." As a result, although many of these verses were written long before any women's movement was conceived, they rebel against any marriage and the political institutions that keep women in a subservient position in society. They are bold statements against the status quo, made by courageous and imaginative poets who realized that society had dealt them cards from a marked deck. The first poets in this collection date from the twelfth and thirteenth centuries and the last are contemporary authors. All the texts are printed in both French and English. It is a brave, astonishingly relevant volume of poetry.

The Defiant Muse; German Feminist Poems from the Middle Ages to the Present. *Susan L. Cocalis, ed.* **(1986) Feminist Press. 163p.**

Another astonishing bilingual collection of virtually unknown and neglected female poets, this one features German authors from the early part of the thirteenth century to the present day. The thing that these women have in common is their purported feminist perspective on life. The editor warns that "when approaching a collection of feminist poetry

. . . the reader must suspend all previously learned and instinctively applied aesthetic criteria, as well as any preconceptions about the meaning of the term 'feminist literature' in order to reach a deeper understanding of the emancipatory nature and poetic accomplishment of the texts presented." In fact, the editor has stretched the term "feminism" to apply to any "nuances, or thematic or formal aberrations from traditional norms, or lapses that suggest a new consciousness of the poet's situation as a woman, and specifically, as a woman writer." This is a slippery definition at best, but it allows the editor to choose very interesting poetry, indeed, even if it is not always convincingly "feminist." The poets here deserve a wider audience regardless of their categorization, and they are given a fine forum here. They are a fascinating lot, and libraries should own all of these collections.

The Defiant Muse; Hispanic Feminist Poems from the Middle Ages to the Present. *Angel Flores and Kate Flores, eds.* **(1986) Feminist Press. 145p.**

This is, once again, a bilingual volume of poems written by women through the ages that can be generally categorized as feminist. These editors suggest that "to be a feminist means to be not only sensitive to the reality of women's lives, but courageous enough to do something about it, to speak out, to criticize." The poets in this collection date from thirteenth century Spain, and the poems start with anonymous ballads. The recorded poets from the next several centuries also lived in Spain, but beginning in the nineteenth century, there are poets from Ecuador, Bolivia, Uruguay, Chile, and Argentina. Twentieth-century poems come from Nicaragua, Mexico, Panama, Cuba, and Puerto Rico. This is another excellent collection in the Feminist Press series of women's poetry, featuring overlooked but highly developed artistic voices. They are sensuous, astute, and deeply conscious of their place in these Spanish-speaking countries. As usual, short biographies of the poets are placed at the end of the volume. Once again, a superior anthology.

The Defiant Muse; Italian Feminist Poems from the Middle Ages to the Present. *Beverly Allen, Muriel Kittel, and Keala Jane Jewell, eds.* **(1986) Feminist Press. 150p.**

The editors here examine the nature of feminist poetry as it occurs in a body of literature. They conclude that "whatever the historical context, the fact that these poems are written at all may itself be viewed as a feminist act." How that actually differs from the category of plain and simple "women's poetry" remains puzzling, but the collection once again is outstanding. The first poet, La Compiuta Donzella, dates from the thirteenth century with a series of sonnets. There is a rich collection from the sixteenth century, a couple from the seventeenth and eighteenth centuries, and then many diverse voices from the nineteenth and twentieth centuries. Once again, all these writers will be new to the general American reading public, and they ought to be much better known. The poems have universal appeal, and all larger libraries should own the entire collection of *The Defiant Muse.*

Early Ripening; American Women's Poetry Now. *Marge Piercy, ed.* **(1987) Pandora Press. 280p., o.p.**

This anthology offers an exciting view of the state of women's poetry writing in America today. The work of many women from various minority communities has been featured: there are Chicana writers (Barbara Brinson Curiel and Lorna Dee Cervantes), black writers (Lucille Clifton, Jayne Cortez, and Thulani Davis, among many others), and Native American poets (Linda Hogan). Many of the authors are lesbian. Each writer is represented by several poems, so it is possible to sense the flavor of her work. There is great diversity here: some of the poets are accomplished, older, and well known; others are still developing their craft; and others are simply lacking in talent. Among the well-known writers whose work is included are Denise Levertov, Mona Van Duyn, May Sarton, Adrienne Rich, Maxine Kumin, June Jordan, and Amy Clampitt. It is fascinating to see what they, and the scores of other authors, have been writing in the 1980's.

Eighteenth Century Women Poets; an Oxford Anthology. *Roger Lonsdale, ed.* **(1989) Oxford University Press. 555p.**

As we have come to expect from Oxford anthologies, this is a comprehensive, critical volume for general and more advanced readers, illuminating a group of poets whose contributions are often overlooked in English literary history. Featured here are 107 women representing many social classes and of varying degrees of ability and ambition. The poets are arranged chronologically and span the entire eighteenth century. As the century progresses, one can see a variety of themes and moods emerge, from sentimental to elegiac to feminist. The hundreds of selections illustrate a great range in style and form, showing that women's poetry of the age was not any less diverse than poetry by men. Biographical information is also provided, even in the case of many women listed simply as "Anonymous." The indexes of titles and first lines are also helpful, and Lonsdale's lengthy introduction is detailed and fascinating in its own right, explaining the social and intellectual views instilled by a society caught up in trying to determine whether women were inherently inferior to men, or merely different. Without being patronizing or revisionist, this introduction is extremely perceptive.

The Faber Book of 20th Century Women's Poetry. *Fleur Adcock, ed.* **(1987) Faber and Faber. 330p.**

Fleur Adcock, herself an eminent poet, has compiled this selection of women's verse that explores their output from the time of Charlotte Mew (1869–1928) to that of Selma Hill, who was born in 1945. The poets all write in English but hail from America, Canada, England, Australia, New Zealand, and Ireland. Most are represented by two to four poems, but several particularly prominent poets, such as Marianne Moore, Elizabeth Bishop, Stevie Smith, and Sylvia Plath, are accorded much more space. Those are the only exceptions, and this judiciousness in the selection of the best representative poems allows the editor to include the work of over sixty women. Her choices are very discerning, the poetry of the highest quality. She thus manages to introduce a select number of the best poets writing in English in the twentieth century. In a thoughtful, perceptive introduction, Adcock intelligently addresses the central questions about women's creative writing and cogently speaks about the accomplishments of the poets she has featured in this volume.

I Hear My Sisters Saying; Poems by Twentieth-Century Women. *Carol Konek and Dorothy Walters, eds.* **(1976) Thomas Y. Crowell. 295p., o.p.**

After a fairly saccharine introduction, this anthology is divided into sections that correspond to the stages of a woman's life: "It took my childhood before I could see"; "This man, this stranger in my arms"; "I am trying to think how a woman can be a rock"; "What have I made"; and so forth. The poems that follow these evocative lines are fresh and exciting. They are written by a variety of women, well known and little known: Barbara Howes, Susan Fromberg Shaeffer, Denise Levertov, Adrienne Rich, Gwendolyn Brooks, Joyce Carol Oates, and Sarah Youngblood. Many of the poems are strong, sure, and evocative, but they are mixed in with dozens of weak verses that seem to be included because they fill out the thematic scheme of the volume. Nonetheless, there are fine poems about the experiences of American women. Many of the works are by non-white women, and one section is devoted to lesbian poetry. But if one is looking for a generally higher quality of women's poetry, they might better consider *The Faber Book of 20th Century Women's Poetry, Early Ripening,* or *No More Masks!*

Kissing the Rod; an Anthology of Seventeenth-Century Women's Verse. *Germaine Greer, Susan Hastings, Jeslyn Medoff, and Melinda Sansone, eds.* **(1988) Farrar, Straus and Giroux. 477p., pap.**

Readers of this collection may be put off by the bitter tone of Germaine Greer's well-written introduction, which comes across more as a raucous criticism of the past and present male literary establishment than as a celebration of 50 interesting female poets. Once past this introduction, however, the poetry speaks for itself. Many poems confront seventeenth-century English politics, female subservience, and Anglican religious turmoil. Others are beautiful elegies written to lovers or children. Among the best are the eloquent poems of Aphra Behn and Anne Bradstreet, as well as the angry verse of "Philo-philippa." The poets are presented chronologically, with one- or two-page biographies accompanying each selection (an index would have been helpful). Unfortunately, little is known about the daily lives of most of the women. Greer's long introduction provides an historical base for the poems and details the social obstacles faced by many women writers in the seventeenth century. But ultimately the anthology suffers from the harsh feminist tone this introduction pursues. Such revisionist, historical finger-pointing overshadows the beauty of the verse. It might be well to read Greer's criticism of the English literary tradition with an open mind and hurry right to the poems, which stand as passionate testimonies of seventeenth-century life.

Looking for Home; Women Writing about Exile. *Deborah Keenan and Roseann Lloyd, eds.* **(1990) Milkweed Editions. 288p., pap.**

"Exile" here means everything from immigrant women arriving in the strange new American culture to the exile of having two or more racial heritages or the exile felt by some women living in what the editor terms a "dominant white-male" culture. This covers a lot of ground, and the anthology presents a wide range of poems written in many different forms and styles. All deal with alienation and fear, and all tend to be reflective, painful, and saddening. The 125 poems often view the woman as victim of her new surroundings, and quite a few deal with homosexuality, femininity, and the discovery of inner strength. Contemporary poets Audre Lorde, Sharon Olds, and Cynthia Olson are among the best-known writers, although most are more obscure. Many poems are translations from Hungarian, Spanish, Chinese, and other languages. The book is indexed by author and includes biographical information. The verse varies in sophistication, but it is confessional and chilling and emotionally draining.

Mother to Daughter, Daughter to Mother; Mothers on Mothering. *Tillie Olsen, ed.* **(1984) Feminist Press. 296p., pap.**

This fairly slim anthology has a dual function: it is a volume of feminist poetry, with mostly contemporary women poets, and it is a calendar or datebook. The poetry is divided into chapters based on the months, and the verse surrounds the logbook in a kind of "daily poem" arrangement. But the homey, reassuring intent of honoring motherhood quickly becomes sentimental and overdone. The 120 writers include Bradstreet, Dickinson, George Eliot, Simone de Beauvior, Zora Neale Hurston, and Gloria Steinem. Most are English speaking, and much of the modern verse was written in the 1960's and 1970's as the feminist movement grew. The chapters have subdivisions with such mawkish titles as "Anger, Chasms, Estrangements" and "Mournings, Elegies, Tributes." The quality of verse is mostly fair, generally resembling the poetry found in feminist journals and magazines. Directed at all women as a celebration of womanhood, this anthology offers bland inspiration couched in rather mediocre poetry.

Mountain Moving Day. *Elaine Gill, ed.* **(1973) Crossing Press. 126p., o.p.**

This anthology of female poets active in the 1970's is too limited in its scope to be useful to readers. In her introduction Elaine Gill writes, "I didn't have any axe to grind for or against Women's Liberation." The Japanese poet Yosano Akino opens the book with an earlier verse that has been adapted into folk song form by the Chicago Women's Liberation Rock Band; the song ends with the line, "All sleeping women now awake and move. . . ." Many of the eighty-four poems (by such authors as Margaret Atwood, Marge Piercy, and Erica Jong) are about womanhood. Here is work by twelve U.S. poets and five Canadian poets; writers more accomplished at the time of publication have been given more space than others. Each author's entry is accompanied by a photograph and a brief personal statement. The poems are arranged alphabetically by poet. There is no index.

New Poets: Women; an Anthology. *Terry Wetherby, ed.* (1976) Les Femmes Publishing. 152p., o.p.

The poems in *New Poets: Women* are mainly personal observations of women's experience, from a nun's description of a nunnery to a poet's placement of herself in a doll's body to a Vietnamese woman carrying her husband in her backpack. Very few of the forty-one poets are well known; in fact, Wetherby writes in her short introduction that she tried to collect these 133 poems without regard for establishment or critical acclaim. Works are arranged alphabetically by poet, each poet introduced by a photograph. The book has no index but is well designed and successfully evokes the tone and mood of women's poetry of the late 1970's.

New Women Poets. *Carol Rumens, ed.* (1990) Bloodaxe Books. 176p., pap.

The editor of this brief anthology tells readers that the poets here included will "help set the tone of poetry in the new decade." If you believed the introduction you might have come away a little disappointed. The 25 poets — all British and most born after 1960 — have all acquired success through literary magazines and award committees, and overall they deserve distinction. Their verse is full of lush images and strong metaphors, verse in meter and free verse of varying lengths. But as is frequent with contemporary poets, particularly young poets, there is difficulty distinguishing one from another. There is no particular arrangement, but brief biographical information precedes each poet. This volume is intended for general readers but will most likely appeal to fans of feminist poetry.

No More Masks! an Anthology of Poems by Women. *Florence Howe and Ellen Bass, eds.* (1973) Doubleday Anchor Books. 396p., o.p.

In her foreword, Florence Howe voices a sentiment that still holds true today, although to a lesser extent: "Few volumes [of poetry anthologies] have included more than a token woman — Emily Dickinson or Christina Rossetti — and fewer still, if any, their poems about women." This book set out to right the record by presenting dozens of poems by American women about both men and women. The compilers begin with Amy Lowell, who wrote in the late nineteenth and early twentieth centuries, followed by Gertrude Stein, Elinor Wylie, "H.D." (Hilda Doolittle), Marianne Moore, and Edna St. Vincent Millay. That first section of earlier poets also contains the work of Gwendolyn Brooks and May Swenson, as well as lesser-known poets. The second section begins with Mona Van Duyn, threads through the work of Denise Levertov, Maxine Kumin, Anne Sexton, Adrienne Rich, Sylvia Plath, as well as many other modern-day poets. This anthology is extremely rich. The authors are represented by approximately one to five poems, so one is often able to gain an accurate sense of their work. And the cumulative effect is startling: one wonders how anthologists could have overlooked such creativity?

The Norton Anthology of Literature by Women; the Tradition in English. *Sandra M. Gilbert and Susan Gubar, eds.* (1985) W. W. Norton. 2,457p.

Almost all students in survey classes on literature are familiar with Norton anthologies. They are meticulously prepared and indexed and are representative of great works; this volume is no exception. Beginning with fourteenth-century English prose and concluding with a modern Native-American short story, this volume is suggestive of the wealth of literature written by women. Some widely anthologized prose works had to be omitted, according to the editors. They did, however, include excerpts from many significant works: Mary Wollstonecraft's "Vindication of the Rights of Women," Virginia Woolf's "Room of One's Own," and Maya Angelou's "I Know Why the Caged Bird Sings," among others. A great diversity of poets and prose writers are featured, from Queen Elizabeth I and Anne Bradstreet to Margaret Atwood and Alice Walker; 148 women are represented by hundreds of selections, arranged chronologically and divided into six sections based on literary periods. The majority of the selections are from the twentieth century, with many of them by African-American and Native American women. The broad range of styles and themes makes this a top anthology not just for students but for all readers.

The Other Voice; Twentieth-Century Women's Poetry in Translation. *Joanna Bankier and others, eds.* (1976) W. W. Norton. 218p., pap.

This fascinating selection of women's poetry in translation begins with an introduction by the highly regarded American poet Adrienne Rich, who says of this collection, that while it "offers only a hint of the world-wide efflorescence of poetry by women in this century," still, "its strengths and richness are astonishing. It reinforces my sense that women of whatever class, nation or race share a common sensibility—a sensibility that is complex, subversive, and heterodox." The volume is organized thematically: "Being a Woman"; "Women and Men"; "Meditations"; "Speaking for Others"; and "Visions." Most of the poets will be entirely new to contemporary readers, but some familiar names surface: Anna Akhmatova and Marina Tsvetayeva, the great Russian poets, Nelly Sachs from Germany, and Dahlia Ravikovitch of Israel. Short biographical sketches and bibliographical notes can be found at the end of the book. In general, the quality of the poetry is exceptionally high, and it is fascinating to see how women from different cultures and different times have handled similar subject matter. Readers are bound to agree with Adrienne Rich that the discoveries to be made in this collection are profound.

The Penguin Book of Women Poets. *Carol Cosman, Joan Keefe, and* **Kathleen Weaver, eds.** **(1978) Penguin Books. 399p., pap.**

This comprehensive anthology of women poets begins with anonymous love poems composed in Ancient Egypt in the fifteenth century B.C., travels around the world and through the ages in Greece, Ireland, Wales, India, Japan, and many other countries, to arrive finally in the twentieth century in such countries as Russia, Finland, Denmark, Spain, Korea, the Ivory Coast, and Zaïre, as well as the United States. The scope of this volume is, therefore, vast. Each author, nonetheless, is given an ample introduction that is helpful in understanding her work. The editors have chosen a great deal of little-known poetry, much of it in translation, and have compiled an excellent and fascinating anthology that sets those obscure poets alongside the more familiar ones. Approximately half the book is allocated to pre-twentieth-century poets, and half to modern ones. Many authors are accorded space for more than one poem so that something of their range can be discerned. That there have been so many fine women poets through the ages and across the world is a revelation. It serves to balance, in a modest way, the many anthologies that lean so heavily (and sometimes even exclusively) on male creativity.

Psyche: The Feminine Poetic Consciousness; an Anthology of Modern American Women Poets. *Barbara Segnitz and Carol Rainey, eds.* **(1973) Dell. 256p., o.p.**

The introduction to this anthology proclaims: "This is an age which poetry speaks to, and this is an age which recognizes the feminine consciousness. Reason enough for an anthology of this sort." The work at hand covers a large territory — from the verse of Emily Dickinson, who often compares the poet's relationship with God to a male-female relationship, to the angry poems of Nikki Giovanni, who addresses both the struggles of women in contemporary American society and the problems currently faced by African-Americans. Can 125 poems by twenty authors adequately represent the feminine poetic consciousness? Is there such a thing as the feminine poetic consciousness? Readers will not receive any specific answers to these questions, but they might marvel at the wide range of twentieth-century women's poetry anthologized here. The poems included are those essential to an understanding of the poets' work — for example, Gwendolyn Brooks's "We Real Cool" and Marianne Moore's "Poetry." Works are arranged in chronological order by poet; the book ends with a section of short biographies; there are no indexes.

Rising Tides; 20th Century American Women Poets. *Laura Chester and Sharon Barba, eds.* **(1973) Washington Square Press. 410p., o.p.**

The 235 poems in *Rising Tides* often have very short lines. They are brief, personal, direct. The poets (among whom are Josephine Miles, Denise Levertov, and Nikki Giovanni), understandably, use much female body imagery. A short biography and a photograph accompany each poet's work, and poems are arranged chronologically by poet. Anaïs Nin's beautifully written introduction effectively describes the poetry in this anthology. She encourages us to "approach [woman] and listen to her in these condensed, in these concentrated and distilled messages, to become intimate with her." Nin's wish is granted when Anne Sexton observes that "women are born twice" or when Adrienne Rich writes, "She is the one you call sister. / Her simplest act has glamour. . . ." Here is an intimate book for repeated enjoyment.

Salt and Bitter and Good; Three Centuries of English and American Women Poets. *Cora Kaplan, ed.* **(1975) Paddington Press. 304p., o.p.**

As with many anthologies that feature exclusively women poets, this bulky volume loses ground because the editor spends so much time viewing the poetry mainly in terms of the biases against women by a male literary establishment. Kaplan spends much of her introduction condemning male critics for subordinating women and creating a "false objective standard" to hide their bias. As far as the quality of poetry goes, however, it is quite good. Some prominent writers have been omitted in favor of twenty-four other accomplished poets: Anne Bradstreet, Christina Rossetti, Elizabeth Barrett Browning, and Sylvia Plath, among others. This allows Kaplan to provide a comprehensive portrait of each poet, mixing biographical information with some critical analysis. The poets represent a variety of styles, subjects, and eras, from the English Restoration to post-Second World War America. Neatly and attractively arranged, with accompanying illustrations, this anthology offers a thorough look at a diverse group of poets. But the hard tone may alienate some readers — particularly those of the condemned sex!

Scars upon My Heart; Women's Poetry and Verse of the First World War. *Catherine W. Reilly, ed.*

See under   WAR POETRY

Shadowed Dreams; Women's Poetry of the Harlem Renaissance. *Maureen Honey, ed.*

See under   AFRICAN-AMERICAN POETRY

She Rises like the Sun; Invocations of the Goddess by Contemporary American Women Poets. *Janine Canan, ed.* **(1989) Crossing Press. 226p., pap.**

This anthology revolves around the idea that for too long a patriarchal, Western culture held back women's spiritualities and growth. The poems included are intended to address this lack of reverence and mandate a "return of the Goddess." Featured are twenty-nine female poets, some prominent, such as Audre Lorde, Denise Levertov, and Maya Angelou. Mostly they are poets who remain distinguished within the women's and minority poetry movements, but are probably not known to general readers. The verse runs the gamut from evocative and imaginative to superficial. Readers with an interest in feminist or contemporary women's poetry may enjoy this volume, but students and general readers should look also to other anthologies of modern women's verse; much of the verse here is repetitive and narrow-minded, not distinguished enough to set one poet's work apart from the rest. Brief biographical information is provided on each poet, but there is no index.

Tangled Vines; a Collection of Mother and Daughter Poems. *Lyn Lifshin, ed.* **(1978) Beacon Press, 95p., pap., o.p.**

The 50 poems in *Tangled Vines* resemble intimate conversations between mothers and daughters about menstruation, men, pregnancy, and other subjects that are pertinent to women's lives. Lifshin has chosen poems by some of today's well-known female poets (Erica Jong, Audre Lorde, Anne Sexton, Nikki Giovanni) as well as those who were popular when the book went to press. These poets pull no punches. They carefully and deliberately lay out their thoughts and emotions for our perusal, remaining honest but gentle. Lifshin suggests in her introduction that "the mother-daughter relationship has been largely ignored in literature." True or not, this anthology should bring that relationship to readers' attention. There is no index.

That's What She Said; Contemporary Poetry and Fiction by Native American Women. *Rayna Green, ed.* **(1984) Indiana University Press. 329p.**

With only eighteen writers, this anthology can be merely suggestive of the range of fiction and poetry Native American women produce. This narrow scope and the sometimes indistinguishable styles among many of the writers limit the effectiveness of the collection. There are, of course, some solid, talented writers here, writing with a unique voice and sensibility not found in most contemporary anthologies. Most of the writers will be unknown to general readers, although all have published widely with small presses and in literary magazines. Arranged alphabetically by poet, here are nearly two hundred poems and fiction pieces, lyrical and descriptive, often evoking the haunting, beautiful landscape of the Southwest desert and the Plains states. Social and political themes are common. A glossary of Native American terms and biographical notes on the writers round out this anthology, most of it in oral and poetic traditions of Native Americans.

The Virago Book of Love Poetry. *Wendy Mulford, ed., with Helen Kidd, Julia Mishkin, and Sandi Russell.*

See under LOVE POETRY

Watchers and Seekers; Creative Writing by Black Women in Britain. *Rhonda Cobham and Merle Collins, eds.* **(1988) Peter Bedrick Books. 157p., o.p.**

Written by contemporary black women in Britain, this collection presents poems written generally in open forms. Often, they represent the experiences of the writers, and deal with questions such as prejudice, male/female incompatibility, relations with children, and romantic feelings. The subject matter is very down to earth, but the treatment is not very fresh or original. Some of the strongest poems are those that one can imagine being performed, sounding a bit like strong expressions of rap music lyrics in their protest of the status quo. Many new poets are on view here, several of them very young and just beginning their careers. It is possible that as they mature their art will, too.

We Become New; Poems by Contemporary American Women. *Lucille Iverson and Kathryn Ruby, eds.* (1975) Bantam Books. 234p., o.p.

Lucille Iverson, in her well-considered preface, writes, "I found feminist poetry to be seldom oblique and seldom confused, for it speaks of the emergence from confusion, from the false stigma of 'inferiority.'" The 126 poems in this book are, indeed, refreshingly honest and clear. They speak fearlessly of such subjects as sex, identity crisis, adolescence, and death. Their authors include Denise Levertov, Adrienne Rich, Erica Jong, and Muriel Rukeyser. The editors have added a section of brief biographical notes. Kathryn Ruby's introduction employs a question-and-answer format to discuss the major issues of feminist poetry: the effect of social conditioning on the poets' work, the nature of the "women's aesthetic," and a definition of the feminist aesthetic. The channeled anger and rebellion running throughout this anthology is inspiring. There is no index.

Women on War; Essential Voices for the Nuclear Age. *Daniela Gioseffi, ed.* (1988) Simon and Schuster. 391p., pap.

Compiled during the cold war, this is a comprehensive anthology of anti-war prose and poetry written by women all over the globe, "intended to inspire empathetic feeling between differing peoples, and peacemaking action," according to the editor. The hundreds of selections are divided into four main sections by such themes as "Prophecies and Warnings" and "Hope and Survival." Women from Sappho to Simone de Beauvoir are featured; most are contemporary and many are distinguished, while several, such as Joanne Woodward and Bella Abzug, are celebrities or politicians. All offer their view of war: they are against it and condemn all fighting and all wars. Many of these condemnations, however, are just that: trite statements or opinions cloaked as a poem or an essay. Despite some fine writing and the diversity of the 182 writers included, many of the selections unfortunately just repeat the same message over and over. This is an anthology that takes itself too seriously, more concerned with its "message" than with offering consistently solid writing, not reshaped into a modern feminist ideology.

The Women Poets in English; an Anthology. *Ann Stanford, ed.* (1972)
McGraw-Hill. 374p., o.p.

One might think, given the title of this volume, that it is concerned
with women in the past two centuries. Not so. In fact, the first poem
included dates from around A.D. 800 and is written in Anglo-Saxon by
an anonymous poet who writes in a woman's voice, from a female perspective. Other very early writers in English include Marie de France,
who dates from the twelfth century, with "The Lay of the Honeysuckle,"
and a poet known only as The Lady of the Arbour, who wrote in the
middle of the fifteenth century. We are shown an excerpt from her long
poem entitled "The Flower and the Leaf." This older period also features such royal authors as Queen Elizabeth of York and Queen Anne
Boleyn, as well as Queen Elizabeth I. Later writers who achieved some
fame are included: Anne Bradstreet, Aphra Behn, and Anne Finch,
Countess of Winchilsea. They are followed by the still more famous Elizabeth Barrett Browning, Emily Brontë, Christina Rossetti, and Emily
Dickinson. Each is represented by several poems, and they are interspersed with dozens of less-well-known writers. In the modern section,
we have the work of Charlotte Mew, "H.D.," Marianne Moore, Edna St.
Vincent Millay, and scores of others, finally arriving at contemporary
writers such as Adrienne Rich, Sylvia Plath, and Margaret Atwood. This
is a balanced and exciting anthology, filling in, as it does, so many gaps
in traditional literary history.

Women Poets of Japan. *Kenneth Rexroth and Ikuko Atsumi, eds.*

See under JAPANESE POETRY

Women Poets of the West; an Anthology, 1850–1950. *A. Thomas Trusky,*
ed. (1979 (2d, rev. ed., 1979)) Ahsahta Press. 92p., o.p.

Women Poets of the West begins with an introduction that addresses each
of the poets in the book, progressing from writers active in the nineteenth century to more recent authors. Some of them, Genevieve
Taggard and Ann Stanford, for example, have published more than five
books of poetry. This does not mean, however, that readers will have
heard of them. This anthology intends to show the presence of women
poets in the western United States. Many of these 100 poems contain
images of the western landscape and depict such qualities as "loneliness,
fortitude, isolation." They range in quality from stiff and purple to observant and sensitive. This book will certainly not give the reader a full

sense of current women's poetry of the west, but it makes pleasant reading.

Women Poets of the World. *Joanna Bankier and Deirdre Lashgari, eds.* **(1983) Macmillan. 442p., o.p.**

This anthology seeks to place over two hundred female poets, from 2300 B.C. to the present day, within their particular culture. The volume is organized according to the country of origin of the poet — China, Japan, India, Iran, Sumero-Babylonia, the Arab World, Ancient Greece, Israel, Medieval Europe, Europe in the sixteenth and seventeenth centuries, Europe in the eighteenth and nineteenth centuries, Europe after 1914, Africa, Latin America, North America (which is subdivided into: Euro-American, Afro-American, Asian/Pacific American, and Chicana), and Native American poetry. Each of these sections is accompanied by an introduction to the writing by women in that culture. This is an ambitious project, and it is marked by meticulous attention to the historical aspects of women's lives and to the artistic nature of the poets' accomplishments. The editors understand that it is hopeless to comprehend fully an artist's work unless you can also understand the culture in which that artist works, and so this volume seeks to impart a sense of the culture before exposing the reader to the poems themselves. All in all, this book provides a fascinating overview of women poets of the world and through the ages.

Women Romantic Poets, 1785–1832; an Anthology. *Jennifer Breen, ed.*

See under ENGLISH POETRY: COMPREHENSIVE COLLECTIONS

The Women Troubadours. *Meg Bogin, ed.* **(1980) W. W. Norton. 192p., pap.**

Women troubadours sounds like an oxymoron: being a troubadour *means* being a man. So one might have thought before picking up this anthology. In fact, very few of these female troubadours have been translated or studied before this anthology that rides on the current wave of women's studies. Women troubadours, like their male counterparts, were serious court poets, and their poetry had a seminal relationship to subsequent European poetry: it established the convention of romantic love, it used the vernacular speech for literary purposes, and it spawned imitators wherever the songs were heard. In her introduction, Meg Bogin explores the meaning of the troubadours' work and its relation to the state of women at the time it was being composed. After lengthy essays on the historical background of these poets, about the nature of courtly love, and about the women troubadours themselves, the poems of eighteen women troubadours are printed both in ancient Provençal and in English. The context the editor provides is helpful in deciphering these verses that grew out of such an alien culture. It is fascinating to hear what women had to say about life in a culture that seems to have been defined by men.

WORLD POETRY

Ain't I a Woman! a Book of Women's Poetry from around the World.
Illona Linthwaite, ed.

See under WOMEN'S POETRY AND FEMINIST POETRY

All Kinds of Everything. *Louis Dudek, ed.* **(1973) Clarke, Irwin. 250p., o.p.**

In his introduction, Louis Dudek defines poetry as "a spontaneous happy life of the mind." The ninety-six poems in the book examine different aspects of that life. *All Kinds of Everything* is divided into such broad categories as "Poems by Young People," "Songs," "Stories," and "The Twilight Zone," each section preceded by an explanatory introduction. The collection includes such famous poems as Yeats's "Song of Wandering Aengus," Coleridge's "Kubla Khan," and Hopkins's "Pied Beauty," as well as poems from indigenous cultures, children's poetry, and concrete poetry. Little contemporary poetry has been included. Although enhanced by charming illustrations from all periods, the work suffers from the lack of an index and a haphazard layout. This anthology is not intended for the serious student; it will be more useful for the reader who has no prior knowledge of poetry and seeks an extremely broad introduction to its scope and dimensions.

Another Republic; 17 European and South American Writers. *Charles Simic and Mark Strand, eds.* **(1976) Ecco Press. 247p., pap.**

Roughly half of the seventeen poets featured in this volume are "mythological' — concerned with the unconscious and with the actual telling of the story, according to the editors in their introduction. The other poets are "historical' — concerned with the social and political events of their time. Although some of the writers seem to be a mix of the two categories, their poems are for the most part vivid and compelling. Here, then, are 127 poems by familiar and less familiar European and South American writers who, the editors explain, have had a profound influence on contemporary poets and have helped forge a distinct international style. These poems were written mainly in the first half of the twentieth century. The styles and forms vary. Some of the verse is lyrical, some comic, much of it surrealistic and fabulist, and some not even "poetry" at all in the traditional sense but free form, rhythmic prose. Arranged according to the editors' taste and judgment, the poems are all translations. This is a good anthology for readers interested in an underrepresented group of twentieth-century poets. Indeed, there is a mystical feel to the verse unlike that in most traditional English-language poetry. Biographical information is provided on the writers, although Strand and Simic, themselves distinguished poets, have left out dates for each poem that would have been helpful to the reader.

An Anthology of World Poetry. *Mark Van Doren, ed.* (Rev. and enl. ed., 1936) Reynal & Hitchcock. 1,468p.

Bulky, and chock full of familiar verse — that is a capsule summary of one of the most frequently used anthologies. It is not particularly appropriate, however, for the average reader. Not only is it too heavy, but some translations are dated, and the selection is somewhat conventional. With that said, the advantages can still be named. First, the scope is impressive, from Chinese literature to Roman and American. Second, the translations may be dated, but they remain some of the best, for example, Waddell, Waley, Pound, Dryden, and Rossetti. Third, the selection is of the first-rate, most-accepted verses, and while there are few surprises, there are even fewer omissions. There are, too, standard indexes. Everything is easy enough to find in this indispensable reference work. Van Doren was a man who knew what he was about: he devotes only four or so pages to a descriptive introduction, in this case, that is more than enough.

Being Born and Growing Older. *Bruce Vance, ed.* (1971) Van Nostrand Reinhold. 115p., o.p.

Bruce Vance has included in his collection such respected poems as Thomas's "Fern Hill," Pound's "In a Station of the Metro," and Dickinson's "Because I could not stop for Death." Most of the ninety works anthologized make pleasant reading and should appeal to an adult audience. Vance's organizing principle is unclear, however, because there is no introduction: 56 poets from various periods, such as Walter Savage Landor, John Updike, and Su T'ung Po, are mixed together under such vague categories as "Girls scream, Boys shout" and "There was a world beyond belief where anything could be something else." The table of contents lists only section titles, but the book has an index of poems and poets and many charming photographs.

Best Loved Songs and Hymns. *James Morehead and Albert Morehead, eds.*

See under BALLADS AND SONGS

The Burning Thorn. *Griselda Greaves, ed.* **(1971) Macmillan; first published in Great Britain by Hamish Hamilton Children's Books. 202p., o.p.**

Griselda Greaves, in her one-page introduction, states that "emotional accuracy" is the common denominator of the 127 poems in this anthology. The poems, while provocative, are not necessarily deserving of extensive study. Although Greaves has gathered many great poets in her collection — Donne, Dryden, Hardy, Frost, Yeats, and Eliot — the book fails to represent these poets at their best; Eliot is represented by "A Song for Simeon," Yeats by "For Anne Gregory," and Hardy by "Christmas: 1924" — all minor works by these authors. The book is indexed by poet, title, and first line, but the poems themselves are grouped into such ambiguous categories as "A Mound of Planets," "As Mirrors Live," and "A Handfulla Stars." Readers will find poems here that are often absent from other anthologies.

The Chatto Book of Nonsense Poetry. *Hugh Haughton, ed.*

See under HUMOROUS AND NONSENSE VERSE

City in All Directions; an Anthology of Modern Poems. *Arnold Adoff, ed.* **(1969) Macmillan. 128p., o.p.**

In this slim, illustrated volume, the industrial city of William Carlos Williams meets the modern ghetto of Nikki Giovanni. The result is an evocative, skillful composite of the sights, smells, and sounds common to all urban areas. Poets as seemingly different as e. e. cummings, Langston Hughes, Rainer Marie Rilke, and Federico Garcia Lorca write about the beauty, vitality, and madness of New York, Paris, Mexico City, and London. Sixty-four poets contribute to this collection of eighty-one jarring poems. The poetry is grouped in six sections, each celebrating a different aspect of city life and representing a diversity of forms and styles. Short biographies of each poet are also included. In his foreword, Adoff, a poet who has included two of his own works in this collection, writes that he compiled the volume to celebrate the energy of the city and to introduce poetry to younger readers. Indeed, the poems have a simplicity well suited to beginning readers; many lack the depth adults may be looking for.

Collected Translations. *William Jay Smith, comp.* **(1985) New Rivers Press. 152p., pap.**

One of the best-known and most highly skilled translators, William Jay Smith declares that he has gathered together "translations that I have done over the past several decades of poems in the Romance languages — Italian, French, Spanish, and Portuguese." The selection includes both major and minor poems, but they are "all poems that have delighted me in one way or another." An anonymous thirteenth-century Italian work begins the collection. There are then nine more Italian poets, ranging into the twentieth century. The chronological organization is followed in the French section, which comprises at least half the book, and in the Spanish and Portuguese sections. Among the poets one finds Eugenio Montale, Théophile Gautier, Arthur Rimbaud, Jules Laforgue (of whom Smith seems particularly fond, as he is given more space than any of the others), Paul Valéry and Federico García Lorca. In his brief introduction, Smith explains his approach to translation. "Translating poetry . . . is like converging on a flame with a series of mirrors, mirrors of technique and understanding, until the flame is reflected in upon itself in a wholly new and foreign element." The compiler's handling of mirrors is as deft as the poems themselves.

Confucius to Cummings; an Anthology of Poetry. *Ezra Pound and Marcella Spann, eds.* **(1964) New Directions. 353p., pap.**

Famous for his *Guide to Kulchur,* in which he attempted to teach poetry, Pound followed through many years later with this volume. Here, then, are the poets, from Confucius to T. S. Eliot, Basil Bunting, and e. e. cummings. This time there is no text, no guidance. As Pound explains briefly, "The active student may enjoy figuring out when and how they [i.e., earlier poets] got into the minds of later poets, if at all; and with what degree of light or muddle. . . . We assume the reader who has been able to get into a junior college will be able to put our mosaic together to her, or to his, satisfaction." The chronological arrangement is as satisfactory as the choices, many of which are truly eccentric. The imaginative selection makes this unique. Particularly interesting are the translators whom Pound chooses: Chapman for Homer, Hardy for Sappho, and himself for Sophocles, to name only a few of the early entries. The nineteenth century is fairly well represented, but there is little, indeed, from the twentieth. Pound seemed particularly fond of Browning and enjoyed Whittier's "Barbara Frietchie." Anyone who is curious about Pound should read this collection for a better understanding and appreciation of the poet.

Contemporary American & Australian Poetry. *Thomas Shapcott, ed.* **(1976) University of Queensland Press. 480p., o.p.**

Thomas Shapcott, in his lengthy introduction to *Contemporary American & Australian Poetry*, states that there are definite similarities between the culture of modern America and the culture of modern Australia, the most significant being the "New World culture" status of both countries. Although Australia and America might share certain cultural characteristics, the combination of these two literatures within one anthology nevertheless remains arbitrary. Shapcott intends to bring the literature of each culture into sharper focus but does not always succeed. Although not the most highly regarded poems by their authors, the 250 poems included here are highly readable and indicative of each poet's style. A brief biographical note precedes each author's section, in some cases too brief. There are indexes of poets, titles, and first lines. Students of either American or Australian literature should find this anthology helpful but should remember that it is not an in-depth study of either world.

Crazy to Be Alive in Such a Strange World; Poems about People. *Nancy Larrick, ed.* **(1977) M. Evans. 171p.**

Just as the title suggests, this anthology contains poems that chronicle human emotions and actions. And as one might suspect, it suffers from its innocent, saccharine tone. The sixty-six poets are fairly modern, with Walt Whitman, Edgar Lee Masters, and Edna St. Vincent Millay among the oldest. The rest are such contemporary writers as John Updike, Nikki Giovanni, David Ignatow, and Erica Jong. The anthology is divided into sections that cover different aspects of life (for example, work, familial love, and urban life) with accompanying photographs. Although never stated, it appears that this collection is planned for younger readers. The introduction has a sugar-coated feel, and many of the poems are rather amateurish and one-dimensional. Contrary to the title, which is from an included Lawrence Ferlinghetti poem, there is no "strange" world depicted here, just a smiling one. This is an adequate anthology for children and young adults, and while some of the poems are of high quality, it will probably not challenge older or more discriminating readers.

Disenchantments; an Anthology of Modern Fairy Tale Poetry. *Wolfgang Mieder, ed.* **(1985) University Press of New England. 203p.**

For readers who loved the enchanting fairy tales of childhood, this captivating collection is a gem. The ninety-seven poems take classic stories, such as Rapunzel or Cinderella, and strip them of their antiquity or innocence. The chapters are divided by fairy tale; for example, under Sleeping Beauty there are twenty-three poems, from Walter de la Mare's lovely "Sleeping Beauty" to Noelle Caskey's haunting "Ripening." Each poem varies in tone. Seventy-eight modern poets, including Galway Kinnell, Anne Sexton, and Roald Dahl, have written beautiful, joyful, and disturbing poems inspired by traditional fairy tales. In his complex, interesting introduction, Mieder analyzes the historical significance of the fairy tale: "Once adults have lost their naive understanding of the fairy tale world, they tend to read fairy tales critically rather than symbolically." The poetry in this volume is vivid and exciting, highly recommended for fairy tale enthusiasts and others looking for allegorical verse that does not always have a happy ending.

Eight Lines and Under; an Anthology of Short, Short Poems. *William Cole, ed.* **(1967) Macmillan. 164p., o.p.**

This slim, pocket-sized anthology contains an eclectic, pleasing mixture of brief verse, almost three hundred poems by such distinguished writers as William Blake, Emily Dickinson, Vachel Lindsay, John Updike, and many more lesser-known but equally skillful poets. The poems are loosely divided into such traditional poetic themes as love, aging, and death. Rather than compile just another collection of light, amusing poems, the editor presents us with verse that ranges from truly poignant and elegiac to sly and charming. Indexed by poet and title and planned to represent the tradition of short poems, this anthology includes an assortment of gems, many of which may not have appeared widely to date but which all readers will find entertaining or inspiring.

Episodes in Five Poetic Traditions: The Sonnets, the Pastoral Elegy, the Ballad, the Ode, Masks and Voices. *R. G. Barnes, ed.* **(1972) Chandler Publishing. 486p., o.p.**

The 252 poems in *Episodes in Five Poetic Traditions* are moving works comprising the traditions which form the five sections of this book: "The Sonnet," "The Pastoral Elegy," "The Ballad," "The Ode," and "Masks and Voices." Present here are world poets as ancient as Horace and Pindar and as recent as Ashbery and Snyder. Editor R. G. Barnes has included such poems as Keats's "Ode to a Nightingale" and Auden's "In Memory of W. B. Yeats." A brief explanatory introduction precedes each section; at the end of the book there are a chronological list of authors and an index of authors, titles, and first lines. This standard anthology should prove a useful reference work for students of literature.

The Faber Book of Blue Verse. *John Whitworth, ed.* **(1990) Faber and Faber. 305p.**

This is a lusty, often humorous anthology of 161 sometimes erotic, sometimes raunchy, poems. The verse is always top notch, written by such masters of English literature as Chaucer, Hardy, Shakespeare, and Swift, and carefully indexed by poet, title, and first line. But many translations of classic poets and the work of more contemporary writers are also included, from poets as diverse as Ovid, Catullus, X. J. Kennedy, e. e. cummings, and Edna St. Vincent Millay. Some are long, titillating narratives, and some are shorter, more biting verses. Arranged in twelve sections, titled, for example, "Getting Religion," "Wicked Words," and "That House of Pleasure," these are poems undoubtedly not found in the average introductory anthology. More amusing than arousing, this collection is recommended for all poetry enthusiasts.

The Faber Book of Madness. *Roy Porter, ed.* **(1991) Faber and Faber. 572p., pap.**

Using "madness" as a catch-all term for everything from true psychosis to borderline clinical depression (the blues to a nervous breakdown to being an outright lunatic), this anthology is a fascinating mixture of poetry, essay, and prose excerpts. Because a large number of the selections are letters and autobiographical prose, this volume is not quite a poetry anthology. But the amazing spectrum of old and new voices and the quality of the hundreds of selections, both poetry and prose, make this a highly recommended collection. Nineteen chapters divide the poetry into such subjects as "Delusions," "Freud and His Followers," and "Madness and Genius." The editor's commentary heads each subject, which includes both prose and poetry. The quality and range of the poetry could not be better, with hundreds of traditional English-speaking writers expounding on various states of madness. Court cases, letters, and factual writings about asylums and misusage at the hands of doctors are all here. Recommended for poetry lovers as well as those interested in the more clinical aspects of lunacy, this volume is a gold mine for any insanity enthusiast, gathering in writings from the certifiably sane and insane, with everyone from Plato to Plath included. Indexed by subject, author, and title.

The Faber Book of Useful Verse. *Simon Brett, ed.* (1981) Faber and Faber. 254p., pap., o.p.

The introduction to this volume clarifies the meaning of its title. "Groucho Marx once condemned as useless all poetry, except for the six line verse which begins 'Thirty days hath September' . . . whose usefulness was obvious." Brett soon found he would have to go a bit beyond this definition. "I have extended the field of usefulness to include verse which is instructive or functional." Given this scope, several fascinating points surfaced. First, most of the useful verse appeared in the eighteenth century. It was a time dominated by poets in quest of a meaningful topic. Second, the Romantic Movement killed, or badly wounded, useful poetry. Finally, the loss of a classical education meant the loss of verse used as a mnemonic device to learn Latin and Greek. There are twenty-five subject headings, opening with "Useful for Dates," then "Weather Forecasts," then "Lovers," etc. The chronological list of writers begins with Hesiod's eighth-century masterpiece "Book of Work and Days" and closes with the new math as explained by the satirist Tom Lehrer. "The process of selection has been an enormously enjoyable one." The same sentiment should be experienced by any reader who ventures into these pages. An exceptionally enjoyable anthology.

The Faber Book of Vernacular Verse. *Tom Paulin, ed.* (1990) Faber and Faber. 407p.

These are poems that capture the vernacular authenticity of normal speech, from Southern black dialects to Irish brogues and blue-collar American slang — hundreds of poems from obscure authors and such well-known authors as Robert Burns, e. e. cummings, Christina Rossetti, Yeats, and D. H. Lawrence. The poems are refreshingly spontaneous, usually based on the irregular meter that captures the cadence of provincial speech. They are divided among nineteen subjects, and the anthology includes a long, informative introduction about vernacular diversity in poetry. Footnotes help explain many of the provincial or historical references. Highly recommended for all readers, indexed by title and first line, this is an organized, exceptional volume of "unpolished" verse. Older and newer poets are included to produce a diversity of sounds and rhythms.

Grandfather Rock, the New Poetry and the Old. *David Morse, ed.* **(1972) Delacorte Press. 142p., o.p.**

David Morse's curious anthology strives to link poetry to musical expression by comparing the lyrics of such rock performers as Leonard Cohen, Joni Mitchell, and Paul McCartney to similar poems by Homer, Ovid, Shakespeare, and Browning. In one instance, he compares Bob Dylan's lines "Come you masters of war / You that build all the guns" to Shelley's "An old, mad, blind, despised, and dying king — / Princes, the dregs of their dull race, who flow / Through public scorn. . . ." While the two verses may both be motivated by passion, hating the men who make wars, their quality and the tone are very different. There are sixty poems in all — rock lyrics (in different type faces) paired with traditional verse, each with historical and analytical commentary. He divides the text into seven sections, e.g., "Ancient Voices," "Loneliness and Love," and "Death." The volume is indexed by author, title, performer, and first line and also suggests a few helpful books on rock music. Morse's attempt is noble, but the connections between the lyrics and the poems in *Grandfather Rock* sometimes remain unclear.

In the Midst of Winter; Selections from the Literature of Mourning. *Mary Jane Moffat, ed.*

See under   Death Poetry

Introducing Poems. *Linda W. Wagner and C. David Mead, eds.*

See under   Poetry: Study and Teaching

The Light from Another Country; Poetry from American Prisons.
Joseph Bruchac, ed. (1984) Greenfield Review Press. 326p.

These almost three hundred poems vary in sophistication and depth, but most are honest, gripping accounts of the lives of men and women in modern American prisons. The sixty writers come from a wide range of regional, social, and ethnic backgrounds. What they have in common is that at some time in the 1960's and 1970's they were in prison, where many participated in poetry workshops sponsored by state arts councils (they helped fund this anthology). Many of those in prison for violent crimes write about them in horrifying detail, but there are also tender, self-excoriating poems about family, nature, and politics. As for style, the gamut runs from the intricate and powerfully controlled verse of Daniel Berrigan, the anti-war activist, to the stark, simple, and expository. The writers are presented alphabetically, with a photograph and sometimes intimate biographical information preceding their work, which is generally unpretentious and disturbing.

Living Poets. *Michael Marpurgo and Clifford Simmons, eds.* (1974) John Murray. 115p.

Living Poets anthologizes the work of poets alive in 1974, many of whom are alive in the 90's. In the preface, the editors express their preference for accessible poetry; they later state that their anthology is intended for younger readers (but not necessarily children). Illustrated with striking black-and-white photographs, the book contains 100 poems by poets from many countries, from Miroslav Holub and Yevgeny Yevtushenko to Pablo Neruda and Philip Larkin. The works, of generally high quality, address such eternal issues as love, education, and poverty; social and political themes run throughout. The anthology is indexed by title and first line, and the average reader will find it enjoyable but perhaps too brief to be a useful reference work.

Love's Aspects; the World's Great Love Poems. *Jean Garrigue, ed.*

See under LOVE POETRY

Modern Poetry. *John Rowe Townsend, ed.* **(1971) J. B. Lippincott. 224p., o.p.**

In his vague foreword to *Modern Poetry,* Townsend describes the book's organization: "I settled in the end for a rough approximation of the order in which the poems were written, modified by a certain amount of shuffling around. . . ." He has divided the anthology into sections, but the divisions are unmarked and unclear: the black-and-white photos that occur at intervals would seem to serve as dividers. The 136 poems, dating from the 1930's to the 1970's, include Stephen Spender's "An Elementary School Classroom in a Slum" and W. H. Auden's "Musée des Beaux Arts," both well known, but while Townsend has chosen many famous poets for his collection (Dylan Thomas, Louis Simpson, Phillip Larkin, Howard Nemerov, and Thom Gunn, among others), the selections are largely obscure. Poems are indexed by author, first line, and title. This anthology is neither as extensive nor as expert as such other anthologies as *The Norton Anthology of Modern Poetry* or *Contemporary American Poetry,* edited by A. Poulin, Jr.

Moonstruck; an Anthology of Lunar Poetry. *Robert Phillips, ed.*

See under Nature Poetry

The Norton Introduction to Literature: Poetry. *J. Paul Hunter, ed.*

See under Poetry: Study and Teaching

The Now Voices; the Poetry of the Present. *Angelo Carli and Theodore Kilman, eds.* **(1971) Charles Scribner's Sons. 242p., o.p.**

Early in their introduction to *The Now Voices,* Angelo Carli and Theodore Kilman write that many students believe poetry to be "effeminate, mysterious, full of 'hidden' meanings, and consequently impossible to understand"; through study, they advise, poetry will be revealed to be "a very sensitive, very precise, and often very complete expression of the world in which one lives." This anthology will help students chiefly through its variety. Its instructional efforts oversimplify the addressed problems. The collection contains 150 poems from such poets as D. H. Lawrence, Dylan Thomas, Eliot, Poe, and a computer programmed to write poetry. The book is divided into six sections: "The Language of Poetry," "Communications," "Dissent," "Identity," "Education," and "The City." Each section has a brief introduction discussing the subject's importance in contemporary society and a list for further reading. Here are such poems as Dylan Thomas's "Fern Hill" and Robert Frost's "Mending Wall," as well as many enjoyable, lesser-known poems. Poems are indexed by author, title, and first line, and the editors have provided a glossary of literary terms.

The Oxford Book of Friendship. *D. J. Enright and David Rawlinson, eds.* **(1991) Oxford University Press. 364p.**

In an arrangement not unlike *The Oxford Book of Marriage*, this interesting anthology also collects hundreds of poems, prose excerpts, letters, and journal entries—most celebrating the virtues of friendship, but some, with a distinctly satirical tone, taking time to celebrate the downside of friendship. The selections are divided into twelve chapters based on such subjects as "The Nature of Friendship," "Between Men and Women," and "Fears, Failures, and False Friends." These headings give the anthology a slightly mawkish tone. There is a good mix of accomplished poetry and prose. Recommended as a competent collection of diverse literature, this anthology, like its Marriage counterpart, would have benefited from a first-line index or even a fuller table of contents; there is an author index.

The Oxford Book of Marriage. *Helge Rubinstein, ed.* **(1990) Oxford University Press. 383p.**

This anthology celebrates the rite of marriage by offering hundreds of poems and prose excerpts on all facets of matrimony, from the wedding ceremony to how one copes with the death of a spouse and the grief of the survivor. Twelve sections divide the writing among subjects with such titles as "With My Body I Thee Worship," "Growing Old Together," and the interesting though slightly macabre "Misery, Mayhem, and Murder." The selections come from sources as diverse as the ancient Greeks to nursery rhymes to excerpts from modern romance novels. This anthology has got to be the definitive volume on marriage literature. The moods and styles vary from page to page; Chaucer's "Wife of Bath" may be found close to a list written by Charles Darwin outlining the pros and cons of wedded life. Recommended highly for readers fond of or interested in marriage and even for readers who enjoy browsing through a fine collection of great and eclectic literature.

The Oxford Book of Verse in English Translation. *Charles Tomlinson,*
ed. **(1980) Oxford University Press. 608p., pap., o.p.**

This is a book for erudite poetry enthusiasts. The editor has organized
his material according to the chronology of the translators. One may,
therefore, read many different versions of Ancient Greek literature as it
has been translated over the ages. This is, indeed, a sophisticated pleasure for poetry lovers. The volume opens with a translation by fifteenth-
century Gavin Douglas, selections from his version of Virgil's *The Aeneid.*
Several biblical translations follow, and eventually, in the sixteenth century, such familiar names as Edmund Spenser (with translations from
French and Italian) and Christopher Marlowe (with his version of Ovid)
follow. Famous writers abound in this volume; modern ones include Ezra
Pound, Marianne Moore, Czeslaw Milosz, Robert Lowell, and Ted
Hughes. There are English versions of Navajo and Chippewa poems, as
well as Chinese, German, French, Polish, Italian, and Icelandic works,
but the emphasis seems to fall on Ancient Greek and Latin poetry. The
reader is provided with many selections from Chapman's celebrated
sixteenth-century version of Homer's *The Iliad,* and *The Odyssey;* Dryden's
translations of *The Iliad,* Virgil's *The Aeneid,* Ovid's *Metamorphoses,* and
Juvenal's *Satires;* and Pope's translations of *The Iliad* and *The Odyssey.* The
Bible is presented in several versions from the early sixteenth century,
translated by William Tyndale, Miles Coverdale, Sir Thomas Wyatt, and
Mary Herbert, Countess of Pembroke, as well as from the Authorized
Version of 1611. These are expert translations of great literary works.

P.E.N. New Poetry I. *Robert Nye, ed.* **(1986) Quartet Books. 196p., o.p.**

The compiler explains: "My brief from P.E.N. was straightforward, to
assemble in three months of early 1985 an anthology of mostly unpublished verse of which one third would be by known poets and the rest by
the little known or unknown." The result is an anthology with just over
a hundred and fifty poems by fifty-four poets. A glance at the "biographical details" at the end of the book confirms the success of the
mission. While Dannie Abse, John Ashbery, George Barker, and numerous others will be recognized immediately, the remainder are "little
known or unknown." This hardly detracts from the quality of the verse,
and some of the best entries are from this group. The majority are English, although there is a scattering of poets from other parts of the globe.
Nye, himself, is one of the best poets around, and his choices reflect an
interest in the new. Tony Harrison and Sacha Rabinovitch are among
the outstanding contributors to a fascinating overview of modern poetry.

The selections, two to four per poet, are arranged in an orderly fashion, and one poem seems to complement the next.

Poetry and Its Conventions; an Anthology Examining Poetic Forms and Themes. *John T. Shawcross and Frederick R. Lapides, eds.* (1972) Free Press. 552p., o.p.

Lapides and Shawcross explain in their introduction, "We believe that the serious student of literature needs a familiarity with his literary past. . . . a critical tool, a method, that will enable him to discuss a poem that he is examining within the perspective of this literary past." The editors present works from various historical periods. They do not, however, help readers to place these poems within a historical perspective. The anthology is divided into six large sections: "The Lyric," "Major Themes," "The Poem as Narrative," "The Poem as Drama," "Recurrent Strains and Other Occasions," and "Poetic Fusions of Form and Theme." Each section has its own introduction and is divided into smaller subsections; prefatory remarks for the major sections of the book are overly simple. The poems, by such great poets as Spenser, Marvell, Pope, Whitman, and Pound, are classics. Works are well indexed, and there is a glossary of literary terms. This anthology will make good reading.

Poetry; an Introduction and Anthology. *Edward Proffitt, ed.*

See under POETRY: STUDY AND TEACHING

The Poetry of Survival; Post-War Poets of Central and Eastern Europe. *Daniel Weissbort, ed.*

See under WAR POETRY

The Premier Book of Major Poets. *Anita Dore, ed.* (1970) Fawcett Publications. 336p., pap.

Anita Dore divides this anthology into such sections as "Stories," "Creatures," "War," "Humor," and "Commitment." She has included major poets: Yeats, Whitman, Eliot, García Lorca, Frost, MacLeish, Donne, Milton, and Keats. She has selected such great poems as Shelley's "England in 1819" and Williams's "This Is Just to Say." Also, she ends the book with a glossary of poetic terms (with a poetic example for each term), author biographies, and indexes by author, title, and first line. Some of the poets' representative works (for example, Cummings's "for prodigal read generous" and Matthew Arnold's "The Last Word") fail to "probe to the heart of our most profound and personal emotions," a quality that Dore attributes to great poetry. Perhaps those poems are less well known because they lack this probing quality. This fault aside, *The Premier Book of Major Poets* should give readers a taste of the world's great poetry.

The Rag and Bone Shop of the Heart; Poems for Men. *Robert Bly, James Hillman, and Michael Meade, eds.* **(1992) Harper Collins. 536p.**

Poetry plays a large part in the so-called "men's movement," and this anthology (its title taken from a Yeats poem) draws upon both contemporary and classic poems to emphasize male spirituality and masculine virtues. Almost 180 poets are featured, with hundreds of selections from all ages and cultures. Sixteen chapters divide the verse by subject, with such titles as "Approach to Wilderness," "The House of Fathers and Titans," and "Making a Hole in Denial." This last aptly sums up the tone of the entire book, which too often sounds like a self-help primer, rather than an intelligent collection of poems. These poems, the introduction states, are favorites at various men's movement get-togethers, presumably stirring participants to seek out some lost machismo. Poems from such distinguished writers as James Joyce and Amiri Baraka lend the volume some authenticity. But the overwrought themes of recovery and denial, together with an introduction full of trendy psychobabble, will not win over all readers. The verse is fine, the packaging pretentious, the premise ridiculous. Indexed by poet and first line.

Sappho to Valéry; Poems in Translation. *John Frederick Nims, ed.* **(Rev. and enl., 1990) University of Arkansas Press. 415p., pap.**

This is a handsome, lucid volume of new translations of major European poets of the past 2,000 years. Among them are Plato, Catullus, Dante, García Lorca, and Octavio Paz. The translations are smooth and precise, with some poems rendered into English for the very first time. They are arranged in traditional anthology style — original verse on one page and the translation facing it. A page-long biographical note introduces each poet, but of special interest is the information that details the complexities of translating each poem. This is an excellent anthology for casual readers and for those interested in the painstaking process of translating poetry. In his introduction, the editor states that he was motivated to produce this volume because of a dearth of accurate translations that would do justice to Sappho, Goethe, and Paul Valéry. Yet Nims admits that for some verse there is no fitting translation. His passion for these poems makes this a remarkable collection.

Since Feeling Is First. *James Mecklenburger and Gary Simmons, eds.* **(1971) Scott, Foresman. 190p., o.p.**

Mecklenburger and Simmons write, "We planned *Since Feeling Is First* so that nothing would intrude between the poem, picture, and reader, not even the poet." The editors, as good as their word, have omitted poets' names from the text to focus on the poems as works independent of the reputation or importance of the authors. The table of contents is at the end. Although such a device may intensify the reader's experience of each work, the outcome is still rather frustrating. The volume collects 186 poems from sources as diverse as a computer's memory bank, Swahili oral tradition, Ted Hughes, William Butler Yeats, James Tate, and Lawrence Ferlinghetti. Readers will have seen some of the poems before — Tennyson's "The Charge of the Light Brigade" and Shelley's "Ozymandias," for example — but will also be happy to discover some lesser-known works. Poems are arranged in no particular order. The book's black-and-white photographs, combined with the editors' choice of exciting and communicative poems, should make it worth more than a single glance.

Songs from Unsung Worlds; Science in Poetry. *Bonnie Bilyeu Gordon, ed.* **(1985) American Association for the Advancement of Science. 230p.**

This anthology grew out of the successful reception to poetry published in *Science 85*, a magazine sponsored by the American Association for the Advancement of Science. More than a hundred, mostly contemporary, poems are arranged by category — poems about the natural world, for example, and poetry that uses scientific terms as metaphors. Accomplished scientists and well-known writers are featured, poets as diverse as Robert Oppenheimer, William Carlos Williams, and Adrienne Rich. The poetry is intriguing and well written — verse that could very well be included in more comprehensive anthologies. The section of satirical poetry is especially appealing. Here the poets' wit comes entertainingly to life. Unfortunately, there are no indexes.

Speak Easy, Speak Free. *Antar S. K. Mberi and Cosmo Pieterse, eds.* **(1977) International Publishers. 136p., o.p.**

The eleven poets in this anthology all have present or past connections with Ohio University in Athens, Ohio. More importantly, however, they all come from Third World backgrounds and write hard, tough poems that show the wisdom and perspective gained through their experiences in America. Quincy Troupe writes, "we climb upwards / our hands gripping / the music / the stagnant / blues . . ." Antar S. K. Mberi writes an ode to W. E. B. DuBois, calling his heart "a torch firm based/ cast years before / in the smelts of Africa / before your heraldic cry. . . ." Readers won't necessarily know any of these poets by name, but the anthology is, nevertheless, worth reading. The editors have constructed the book oddly, following a brief introduction with a section entitled "Spectrum," which contains samples of work by each of the poets. The remainder of the book is an anthology whose order is identical to that of the first section, followed by an uninformative afterword. There is a section of biographies but no index. *Speak Easy, Speak Free* effectively communicates the Third World perspective, but the seventy-five poems are frustratingly few for readers searching for a significant collection of Third World poetry.

Splinters; a Book of Very Short Poems. *Michael Harrison, ed.* **(1989) Oxford University Press. 121 p.**

These 115 "short shorts" are poems of one to eight lines in length, which, the anthologist claims, "will make you smile and make you think, and which you won't be able to forget." They range from a rhyme of Tymnes (2d century B.C.) to the inscription (or perhaps the graffito) found on a sundial in Germany and admit of diverse subjects, from cats to ketchup to the color blue. Many poems are clever — here a snippet of Emily Dickinson, there an epigrammatic rhyme by Emerson — but many are forgettable and are only further endangered by the book's rather silly illustrations.

Strings; a Gathering of Family Poems. *Paul B. Janeczko, ed.* **(1984) Bradbury Press. 161p.**

The poems in this volume celebrate families — relationships between mothers, fathers, siblings, and children; family reunions; holiday gatherings. Grouped into sections according to the speaker of the poem, they are mostly eloquent and brief, capturing the joy of family; most manage to avoid sentimentality. They are the portraits and snapshots of such talented, diverse contemporary writers as John Updike, Galway Kinnell, Anne Sexton, and Naomi Shihab Nye. Janeczko provides no introduction, but a poem at the beginning of the volume, "The String of My Ancestors," by Nina Nyhart, aptly summarizes the collection. This anthology does not pretend to be intellectual or terribly complex. The verses are descriptive, echoing the personal feelings most readers identify with.

This Same Sky; a Collection of Poems from around the World. *Naomi Shihab Nye, ed.*

See under CHILDREN'S POETRY

Timeless Voices; a Poetry Anthology Celebrating the Fulfillment of Age. *Virginia Larrain, comp.* **(1978) Celestial Arts, 127p., pap.**

In her introduction, Larrain writes that her collection "speaks out against the impotence of age." Does this book shine a positive light on aging? Yes and no. Although these 59 poems constantly attempt to describe older people as vibrant survivors rather than decaying husks, many of them use a rather stereotyped or sentimental approach. The black-and-white photographs depict older people in various scenarios or scenes in nature. Among the superior poems in the volume are Yeats's "When You Are Old," Dylan Thomas's "Do Not Go Gentle into That Good Night," and Williams's "To a Poor Old Woman." Poems are indexed by author and first line. Interesting as its concept is, the book lacks depth and sophistication.

To See the World Afresh. *Lilian Moore and Judith Thurman, comps.* **(1974) Atheneum. 102p., o.p.**

The well-known poems in this book include Williams's "The Red Wheelbarrow," Stevens's "Thirteen Ways of Looking at a Blackbird," and Marianne Moore's "Poetry." Most of the selections have not, however, been heavily anthologized. Moore and Thurman would like readers to believe that their book is a collection of 65 poems that look at life in a fresh way, but it seems more a collection of the editors' favorite poems — and their taste is fairly reliable. These works, indeed, reintroduce the reader to his or her environment. Stevens depicts a blackbird from thirteen different points of view, whereas Ryojiro Yamanaka's concrete "Wind Poem" slowly breaks apart a Japanese character in the push of the wind. The seven sections of the book represent large categories, such as "The Muscle in Your Heart," "All Things Innocent," and "A Human Face." There is an index of titles and authors. This is an enjoyable short anthology.

The Touch of a Poet. *Paul C. Holmes and Harry E. Souza, eds.* **(1976) Harper & Row. 270p., o.p.**

The Touch of a Poet is an accessible, standard introduction to the study of poetry, which it classifies as "Gentle," "Harsh," Light," and "Heavy." Unfortunately, these terms are too ambiguous to constitute an authentic ordering system, and the poems in these sections do not necessarily fit their labels. Readers must use the table of contents to find entries, because there is no index. Holmes and Souza have selected 134 works whose open and direct style will encourage students toward further reading. They also aid the learning process by providing, in a separate "Handbook" section, study questions that carefully examine the works' central elements. Among the poets, who come from a wealth of backgrounds and times, are Shakespeare, Arnold, Cummings, Dylan Thomas, Gwendolyn Brooks, Kenneth Patchen, and Ferlinghetti.

A Treasury of Asian Literature. *John D. Yohannan, ed.* **(1984) Mentor Books. 432p., pap.**

This excellent anthology contains many of the great Asian works of literature — excerpts from the Koran and Confucian holy books, ancient Japanese and Chinese poetry, and Fitzgerald's translation of "The Rubaiyat." The selections are in story, drama, song, and scripture sections. Within those sections are subchapters with epics, love poems, and parables, among other genres. The range and depth of the verse is vast. Although the editor offers only a few selections in each subchapter, the selections chosen are clear, fascinating, provocative. Some translations are recent, some fairly old, but the editor assures readers of their high quality. These are hard-to-find works of literature, none of which are from the modern era, all collected in a compact little volume. The editor writes that his purpose is to offer the best examples of form and theme in literature from five national groups. He succeeds by making these beautiful works available to the general reader. There is a chronological chart at the end listing the featured works.

Twentieth Century Poetry. *Carol Marshall, ed.* **(1971) Houghton Mifflin. 180p., o.p.**

Marshall in her introduction calls the modern poet "the conscience of mankind." The five sections — "An Age of Anxiety," "The Things of This World," "Love," "My Townspeople," and "The Box Is Locked" — contain 95 poems that address the current issues considered most important by Marshall. The study questions following each group of poems will help students' comprehension of these works. The writers include Eliot, Auden, Thomas, Creeley, Yeats, and Roethke, and the poems include Yeats's "The Wild Swans at Coole," Thomas's "Fern Hill," and Eliot's "To Marina." Black-and-white photographs or reproductions of modern artwork illustrate the text. The editor has provided an index of authors and titles. While not extensive, this collection provides a clear introduction to the many voices of modernism.

Under Another Sky; an Anthology of Commonwealth Poetry Prize Winners. *Alastair Niven, ed.* **(1987) Carcanet. 106p., pap.**

Beginning in 1972, the London-based Commonwealth Institute began to offer prizes for the best, newly published poetry in a Commonwealth language. This is a collection of the poems that extends from the 1972 joint winners (Chinua Achebe and George McWhirter) and commended winners (Richard Ntiru and David Mitchell) to the joint winners and regional winners for 1986. Some thirty-five poets are found here, with two or three representative poems for each. All parts of the Commonwealth are represented, and while most of the poets are not well known, there are a few who have international status. Each of the poets is introduced by a short biographical/bibliographical paragraph. There are numerous issues raised in the poems, but one of the more surprising, for those not involved with Commonwealth affairs, is the role of English as a common language. It is a great controversy, possibly not helped by the fact that "all the poets who have won or been commended . . . write in English, either because they have no alternative or because it is the tongue best suited to their intentions. . . . A poet can use English and be true to a local culture." No matter, the poetry is well worth reading and is particularly interesting for the dominance of so-called Third World poets.

The World Comes to Iowa; Iowa International Anthology. *Paul Engle, Rowena Torrevillas, and Hualing Nieh Engle, eds.* **(1987) Iowa State University Press. 295p.**

The title is explained by the editors: "This anthology celebrates the twentieth anniversary of the International Writing Program . . . [which] brings to Iowa writers not only of many languages and countries, but also of the newest forms of the literary imagination, those about to appear in next week's book or magazine." The Engles give detailed accounts of the program in their twenty-page introduction and describe their part in insuring the success of the unique gathering of international poets, many of whom are young and not that well known. The collection of nearly a hundred poets follows a distinct format. There are individual or group photographs of most of the writers before their work. This is followed by letters, usually addressed to the compilers, in which the authors explain themselves. And while the collection is focused on poetry, a good two thirds of it is prose — criticism and memoirs. Biographical notes conclude the volume. It is difficult to find a country, East, West, South, or North, that is not represented, and the anthology is truly a world collection.

A World Treasury of Oral Poetry. *Ruth Finnegan, ed.* **(1978) Indiana University Press. 548p., o.p.**

Oral poetry from thirteen cultures is gathered here to demonstrate that "unwritten poetry can offer much that, at its best, can parallel the written poetic forms." Apart from *The Odyssey*, "Beowulf," and some individual works by English and Irish poets, the song and verse are primarily anonymous, so much a part of the culture that the original author is lost to time. Each of the thirteen sections is prefaced by a brief introductory comment, giving an outline of the background and explaining the local poetic forms and symbols. These include the epigrammatic and lyric, as well as the epic and narrative. Sometimes brief notes are given with the poem, and the translator is dutifully noted. Among the traditions represented are the Gond, Mongol, Malay, Somali (often with a credit to a specific poet), Zulu, Yoruba, Irish, Pueblo, Eskimo, Hawaiian, Maori, Australian Aborigine, and English. The epic and narrative poetry of Homer ends the volume, along with an index of titles and first lines. Anyone interested in oral poetry and its tradition should not miss the fine introduction.

YOUNG ADULT POETRY

The Cherry Tree. *Geoffrey Grigson, comp.* **(1959) Phoenix House. 518p.**

Although edited for young people, this volume is for anyone who is imaginative enough to appreciate the delights of different poetic forms and modes. What has the title to do with the twenty-nine sections of English-language poems that start with "Idle Fyno," move on to "The Cherry Fair," and end with "I Think You Stink"? Well, anyone who recognizes the name of the compiler, an English poet of no mean talent, will understand. Grigson takes a broad-minded, universal view of his art and thinks reading aloud, to yourself or to others, is just fine as long as it is poetry. Subject matter, is not important. "I have always liked — and now offer — a large book of poems of all kinds, arranged according to mood and subject; a book of so many poems that there is room inside it for endless exploration and new discovery." This journey offers many delights, and while numerous poets and poems are well known, others are new to the world of anthologies. "Idle Fyno," for example, is full of nonsense verse with a bitter, yet amusing, edge. The selection makes for fascinating bed partners: Edwin Arlington Robinson precedes Shakespeare and D. G.Rossetti — or vice versa depending on where one looks. The grab bag or cherry tree is joy for the browser and offers numerous opportunities to draw new readers to poetry.

City in All Directions; an Anthology of Modern Poems. *Arnold Adoff, ed.*

See under WORLD POETRY

Crazy to Be Alive in Such a Strange World; Poems about People. *Nancy Larrick, ed.*

See under WORLD POETRY

Eye's Delight; Poems of Art and Architecture. *Helen Plotz, comp.* **(1983) Greenwillow Books. 150p., o.p.**

In his poem "Thanksgiving for a Habitat," W. H. Auden writes; "To you, to me, / Stonehenge and Chartres Cathedral, / the Acropolis, Blenheim, the Albert Memorial / are works by the same Old Man / under different names." Under different names, the compiler brings together over one hundred poems by almost as many famous poets, writing about much the same thing — art. The poems are neatly divided into four sections — poems about pictures, poems about sculpture, and two last parts on architecture. Much of the focus is on such modern writers as Muriel Rukeyser, W. H. Auden, Richard Wilbur, Elizabeth Bishop, and others of the post-Second World War period. There are the obvious, exceptional voices from the past, such as Keats ("On Seeing the Elgin Marbles") and Melville ("Art"), but they are in the minority. The compiler is an expert at bringing together poems. She has a half dozen or more anthologies to her credit, and her skill is obvious here. The volume is a work that can be enjoyed by young people and by adults.

The Family Book of Verse. *Lewis Gannett, ed.* **(1961) Harper & Row. 351p., o.p.**

This anthology was compiled by a former book critic of *The New York Herald Tribune* and was meant to serve the purpose of helping families share poetry by reading it aloud to one another. In his warmhearted introduction, the editor describes his early morning poetry sessions with his father when he was a child. He expresses the hope that parents will continue, even in an age dominated by television, to read poetry to their children. The verses included in this volume are fine for that purpose. They are organized into sections according to major emotions or topics: ecstasy, love, mysteries, childhood. For the most part, the poets included are first rate: Keats, Emily Dickinson, Robert Browning, and Robert Frost are among those prominently featured. This would be a fine book for developing a younger person's interest in literature.

Favorite Poems Old and New. *Helen Ferris, ed.* **(1957) Doubleday. 589p., pap.**

A book of favorite poems aimed at young adults needs an organizing principle that would allow readers to locate favorite poems for themselves. Here this principle is a thematic one. The sections are labelled "Myself and I," "My Family and I," "My Almanac," "It's Fun to Play,"

"Little Things that Creep and Crawl and Swim and Sometimes Fly," "Animal Pets and Otherwise," "On the Way to Anywhere," to name a few. In each of the sections, there are dozens of poems by well-known and unknown authors: Shakespeare rubs shoulders with Hilda Conkling, Amy Lowell with Humbert Wolfe. The poems in this volume are readily accessible to the general reader and the high school student; it might provide them with some delightful moments as they locate poems about subjects that interest them. The humorous poems in the section "Almost Any Time Is Laughing Time" are particularly appealing. This could prove an effective book for introducing newcomers to poetry.

Going Over to Your Place; Poems for Each Other. *Paul B. Janeczko, comp.* **(1987) Bradbury Press. 157p.**

A teacher of high school English, and a consistent winner of American Library Association prizes for "best books for young adults," the compiler here offers over one hundred poems. They all reflect the familiar, everyday preoccupations of young adults in such poems as Stanley Kunitz's "First Love" or David Evans's "The Sound of Rain." There are almost as many poets as poems, beginning with Elizabeth Bishop and Richard Eberhart and concluding with May Swenson and John Updike. Most of the authors are not that famous or well known. Poets are chosen for what they have to say about matters relating to youth. There are no introduction, no preface, no prefatory remarks for the four sections; the compiler lets the poems speak for themselves. As the jacket copy puts it, "Listen — and be won."

The Golden Journey; Poems For Young People. *Louise Bogan and William Jay Smith, eds.* **(1990) Contemporary Books. 294p., o.p.**

This popular anthology, originally published in the 1960's, remains the same as it was more than a generation ago. The verse is divided into chapters based on theme or form and includes nonsense rhymes, reflective poems on family and nature, war poems, and some deceptively light-hearted songs. Such great poets as Blake, Yeats, Auden, William Carlos Williams, and Frost are represented by some of their best-known selections. *The Golden Journey* mercifully lacks the silliness and cloying cuteness of many children's volumes and instead presents stimulating, evocative poetry that is not too heavy for young readers. The 231 poems are arranged attractively to be read aloud or as an early book for children learning to read. The range of level of these poems ensures that this will interest any child for many years. Indexed by author and title.

Golden Numbers. *Kate Douglas Wiggin and Nora Archibald Smith, eds.* **(1902) Doubleday, Doran. 687p.**

Almost a century old, this "book of verse for youth" tells more about early American educational activities than later collections for the same group. First, it is assumed all readers are Christians. There is a final section devoted almost entirely to Christmas and "the glad evangel." Here, as elsewhere, the selection of poets is uneven. There are the well known, the "classic" voices from Herrick to Southwell and, yes, Shakespeare, but at the same time one is forced to wade through the sometimes less than felicitous verse of William Drummond of Hawthornden and Felicia Hemans. The message, then, counts considerably more than the style. Still, when style and content can be wed, the two compilers are not bashful about asking the young reader to master ballads, Emerson, Ben Jonson, Keats, Kipling, Scott, and all. In terms of coverage, Shakespeare leads, followed closely by Sir Walter Scott, James Russell Lowell, Milton, and Tennyson. And the choices are delightful reminders that several generations back, young people were expected to master the work of the classic poets, American and English. There are no "foreigners" to speak of and no translations. It is English, American, Christian, or out! The numerous headings remind one of an optimistic age, which was equally innocent: "A Garden of Girls" comes just before "New World and Old Glory" and "In Merry Mood."

Imagination's Other Place; Poems of Science and Mathematics. *Helen Plotz, comp.* **(1955) Thomas Y. Crowell. 200p.**

While this is compiled for junior high through high school readers, most of the poetry can be enjoyed by younger people and by adults. It is the subject matter that is important. Blake's "Auguries of Innocence" opens the first section, titled simply "In the Beginning." He is followed by a brief selection from T. S. Eliot's "Four Quarters." Other poets in this section, one of four, include Emily Dickinson, Shelley, Emerson, and A. E. Housman, not to mention Shakespeare and portions of the Book of Job. No one can fault the compiler here, or in numerous other works of hers, for underestimating either the taste or the skill of the average reader. Weaving the themes around mathematics, astronomy, anthropology, and aspects of general science, the collection may be used for browsing or for selecting just the appropriate poem or stanza to illustrate a scientific point. There is an index of first lines, but no subject index.

Love Is like the Lion's Tooth; an Anthology of Love Poems. *Frances McCullough, ed.*

See under LOVE POETRY

The Music of What Happens; Poems That Tell Stories. *Paul B. Janeczko, comp.* **(1988) Orchard Books. 188p.**

Story poems often appeal to teenagers, and this volume works on that safe assumption. Here one finds about fifty poets and about as many poems. As is the custom in the other compilations by this high school teacher, few of the poets are famous, and the primary emphasis is on the poem not on the name of the poet. There are no introduction and no notes. Again, this is Mr. Janeczko's custom. As the jacket copy says, one may turn here for "ghosts, lovers, dreamers, zanies, young Civil War soldiers, classroom cutups, grandchildren, stepchildren, and the childless." The opening poem, by Jared Carter, sets the stage for "The Purpose of Poetry." After that, mostly young, modern Americans tell the teenager what life is all about in poetic form. There is an index of poets, but, unfortunately, no subject index.

100 More Story Poems. *Elinor Parker, comp.* **(1960) Thomas Y. Crowell. 374p., o.p.**

The story poem is a popular kind of verse, and there are numerous collections available, all reflecting the distinctive outlook of their compilers. In this anthology, Elinor Parker is not so much concerned with content and style as with her audience. The hundred poems included here are directed to young people, and primarily those in junior high and high school. One suspects that the poems may have been selected for teachers who must try to point out the joys of poetry through the story they tell in easy to understand verse. Why else, for example, would one bother with Frederick Whittaker's "Custer's Last Charge." On the other hand there is the traditional Scottish ballad about "The Battle of Otterburn," and if Homer is not in evidence, Kipling is here in force. On balance the selection is fair, although one can see signs of a desperate effort to involve youngsters. At the same time, because it does include some downright peculiar poems, this volume is a marvelous source of hard-to-find works.

The Other Side of a Poem. *Barbara Abercrombie, ed.* **(1977) Harper & Row. 90p., o.p.**

Abercrombie begins her introduction, "When I was young I didn't like poetry at all. I hated it, as a matter of fact." She goes on to say that she later discovered poetry that dealt with familiar experiences without sacrificing profundity. Many of these eighty-eight poems were read to schoolchildren in an effort to teach them that poetry need not be dull or abstract. The poems (printed in blue and red) have been divided into such categories as "introductions," "poems like dreams," and "secret messages." They cover subjects from trains to dandelions to words themselves. The more notable authors include Kenneth Koch, Theodore Roethke, Robert Bly, and Charles Simic. Many of these enjoyable verses are actually selections from longer works. Poem titles appear at the end of poems rather than at the beginning, and the book is indexed by poet only. These quirks aside, this collection should help to change children's hesitant attitudes about poetry.

The Oxford Book of Story Poems. *Michael Harrison and Christopher Stuart-Clark, eds.*

See under   CHILDREN'S POETRY

Poems That Live Forever. *Hazel Felleman, ed.* **(1965) Doubleday. 454p., pap.**

This general anthology is the self-confessed "potpourri of favorite poems (with a few prose selections)" by one of the former editors of *The New York Times Book Review*. She divides her material into stories and ballads, love, friendship, home and family, patriotism and war, humor, nonsense and whimsy, the ages of man, death, reflection and contemplation, faith and inspiration, nature's people, and so forth. Many of the poets are little known today, while others are quite familiar. This is a disparate, unfocused collection of verse, and the quality of the poems varies widely. But many popular poems can be found here, and this volume might serve as a useful introduction for young readers, or others, who are unsure about exactly what attracts them in a poem. Here the variety is so great and the quality so diverse, that any reader is bound to find something to appeal to his or her sensibility.

Poetspeak: In Their Work, about Their Work. *Paul B. Janeczko, ed.*
(1991) Macmillan. 238p., pap.

Among other features in this carefully crafted anthology, the editor
has added four pages of headshots of many acclaimed modern poets,
William Stafford, X. J. Kennedy, Nikki Giovanni, and Joyce Carol Oates
among them. Besides seeing what these poets look like, readers are made
privy to their thoughts on the process of writing a poem. It is an interesting concept, and the editor has created an engaging format for the
poets to make their statements. Readers can learn just what contemporary poets think of the style, form, conception, and revisions of a particular poem. Most of the 154 poems are fairly accomplished to excellent
samples of modern poetry; usually, one or two poems of each poet are
followed by explanation and notes. Style and form vary widely, and the
notes are never too analytical or heavy. The poetry has no particular
arrangement. This volume seems to be intended for browsing among
favorite writers.

Postcard Poems; a Collection of Poetry for Sharing. *Paul B. Janeczko,*
ed. **(1979) Bradbury Press. 106p., o.p.**

The title comes from the fact that each of the hundred poems is brief
enough to fit on a postcard, and "each lively enough to inspire mailing
to comrades and lovers." Furthermore, according to the compiler, "the
poems in this collection are gifts from the poets, meant to be shared. . . .
If you like the poems, pass them on!" While this may be among the most
unusual justifications for an anthology, it seems to work. Most of the
authors are modern and American, a few English, and some European.
Rainer Maria Rilke opens his "Closing Piece" with a stark sentence,
"Death is great." While one might pause before sending this on a postcard, most of the other verses are at least appropriate, particularly X. J.
Kennedy's "Epitaph for a Postal Clerk" and David Ignatow's "The City,"
which has only three lines: "If flowers want to grow / right out of the
concrete sidewalk cracks / I'm going to bend down to smell them." This
may not be the most comprehensive or selective of collections, but it is
one of the more unique.

Rhythm Road; Poems to Move To. *Lillian Morrison, comp.* **(1988) Lothrop, Lee & Shepard. 148p.**

This distinguished Young Adult Services librarian knows her audience, and here she brings together poems that "sway, twist, glide, ride, rock, dive, lurch, loop, fly." The nearly one hundred poems succeed in conveying the essence of motion, and they are "an invitation to what might be called a poetry workout." The novel idea brings to the pages a great number of modern poets, although here and there one finds such earlier writers as W. S. Gilbert, Lewis Carroll, Edgar Allan Poe, and Gerard Manley Hopkins. Hilaire Belloc opens the rhythm road with "Tarantella," followed closely by Edith Sitwell's "Daisy and Lily" and Marianne Moore's "Slim dragon fly / too rapid for the eye / to cage — / contagious gem of virtuosity — make visible, mentality." The sixty-seven other poets and some anonymous verses are equally engaging. While particularly suited for young people, most of the poetry will be equally enjoyed by adults.

Room for Me and a Mountain Lion; Poetry of Open Space. *Nancy Larrick, comp.* **(1974) M. Evans. 191p.**

This differs from other collections of nature poetry in that most of the poets are modern. The entries are suitable for older children and teenagers, although all may be enjoyed by any age. Celebrating the joys of open spaces and the delights of nature are such poets as Robert Frost, Ted Hughes, Maxine Kumin, William Stafford, Theodore Roethke and D. H. Lawrence, to name only a representative few. The compiler, an imaginative teacher, was assisted in the selection by her students who chose poems they thought would be of interest to others who have "a need for freedom to breathe pure air, climb rocky trails and observe the tiniest creatures." While the focus is on poetry of the twentieth century, there are long selections from Whitman, some eighteenth-century Chinese poetry, and Native-American and Eskimo verse. There are also some indifferent photographs. For ages eleven to sixteen.

Story Poems, New and Old. *William Cole, ed.* **(1957) World Publishing. 255p., o.p.**

The remarkable thing about this collection of story poems for young people is that it eschews many of the familiar titles. What the compiler includes are the out-of-the-way poems that will have wide appeal for children and teen-agers. The selection is deliberate, as he believes that too many well-known story poems have been anthologized to the point where another similar collection is simply not needed. The ninety or so poems and ballads are literally stories in verse form, and when tried out on readers from the ages of ten to sixteen, all of them proved a great success. There is everything here from mystery and horror to love and tangled plots that would prove too unbelievable for movies, but are sure winners with poet and reader alike. The concentration is on English and American authors, and there are title and first line indexes of the poems, as well as black and white sketches by Walter Buehr that illustrate many of the narratives.

Under All Silences; Shades of Love. *Ruth Gordon, comp.*

See under Love

The Wind and the Rain; an Anthology of Poems for Young People. *John Hollander and Harold Bloom, eds.* **(1961) Doubleday. 264p.**

A distinguished poet (Hollander) and a famous critic (Bloom) collaborated to select poetry for children. The two, who became Yale professors, are relentless in their search for quality, and the result is a varied, intelligent, and always imaginative collection. The arrangement is suitable for the audience. The poems are divided by seasons, and they indicate the human moods these evoke. For children in junior high and high school this will be both a challenge and an awakening. The challenge is to grasp the meaning of some of the more difficult poems without the aid of notes from the compilers. The awakening comes from reading Shakespeare, Jonson, Rossetti, Tennyson, Blake, and others of the English school who bring pleasure and insight to verse. Unfortunately, the twentieth century is not represented, and the editors fail to say in the introduction why they drew the line at the close of the nineteenth century. No matter, what is selected is about as distinguished as anyone is likely to find in a collection for children and teenagers. The editors have a high regard for their audience and refuse to print anything which is not first rate. As a result, the collection may be enjoyed by adults as well. There is an index of first lines, authors, and titles.

See also Children's Poetry

HIGHLY RECOMMENDED ANTHOLOGIES

The following anthologies are recommended as the best by the groups that selected the basic volumes for the seventh, eighth, ninth, and tenth editions of THE COLUMBIA GRANGER'S® INDEX TO POETRY.

Anthologies in the first group are recommended for all libraries and recommended as first choices for individual readers.

Anthologies in the second group are recommended for all medium to large libraries, although, of course, small libraries will also wish to consider them.

All Libraries

An Anthology of World Poetry
The Best Loved Poems of the American People
Best Loved Songs of the American People
The Black Poets
The Harvard Book of Contemporary American Poetry
An Introduction to Poetry (X. J. Kennedy, ed.)
The New Oxford Book of American Verse
The New Oxford Book of Eighteenth Century Verse
The New Oxford Book of English Verse, 1250–1950
The New Oxford Book of Seventeenth Century Verse
The New Oxford Book of Sixteenth Century Verse
The Norton Anthology of Literature by Women
The Norton Anthology of Poetry
The Norton Book of Light Verse
The Oxford Book of American Light Verse
The Penguin Book of Women Poets
The Poetry of Black America
Poets of the English Language
The Random House Book of Poetry for Children
Sappho to Valéry
Talking to the Sun
The Top 500 Poems
Western Wind

Medium to Large Libraries

American Folk Poetry
American Hymns
American Negro Poetry
The American Poetry Anthology
Best-Loved Poems in Large Print
Black Sister
The Blues Line
The Book of Irish Verse
A Book of Love Poetry
A Book of Religious Verse
A Book of Women Poets from Antiquity to Now
Breaking Silence
Carriers of the Dream Wheel
The Cherry-Tree
Chief Modern Poets of Britain and America
Collected Black Women's Poetry
Collected Translations
The Columbia Book of Chinese Poetry
Come Hither
Contemporary Chicana Poetry
Death in Literature
Ecstatic Occasions, Expedient Forms
The Faber Book of Ballads
The Faber Book of Comic Verse
The Faber Book of Modern Verse
The Faber Book of Nonsense Verse
The Faber Book of 20th Century Women's Poetry
Fine Frenzy
Fifty Years of American Poetry
Folksinger's Wordbook
From the Country of Eight Islands
The Gambit Book of Popular Verse
Gay & Lesbian Poetry in Our Time
A Geography of Poets
The Gift Outright
Golden Treasury of the Best Songs and Lyrical Poems in the English
    Language
A Green Place
The Harper Anthology of Poetry
Harper's Anthology of 20th Century Native American Poetry

How Does a Poem Mean?
Ireland in Poetry
The Longman Anthology of Contemporary American Poetry
The Morrow Anthology of Younger American Poets
New Coasts and Strange Harbors
The New Oxford Book of Canadian Verse in English
The New Oxford Book of English Light Verse
A New Treasury of Children's Poetrty
No More Masks!
The Norton Anthology of English Literature
The Norton Anthology of Modern Poetry
The Norton Introduction to Poetry
The Open Boat
The Oxford Book of American Verse
The Oxford Book of Children's Verse in America
The Oxford Book of Light Verse
The Oxford Book of Twentieth-Century English Verse
The Oxford Book of War Poetry
The Oxford Nursery Rhyme Book
The Oxford Treasury of Children's Poems
The Poetry Anthology: 1912–1977
Popular Songs of Nineteenth-Century America
The Real Mother Goose
Shaking the Pumpkin
Sleeping on the Wing
Sound and Sense
Sounds and Silences
Speak Roughly to Your Little Boy
Sunflower Splendor
Talking like the Rain
The Treasury of American Poetry
The Treasury of English Poetry
Understanding Poetry
The Voice That Is Great within Us
Voices within the Ark
Women Poets of the World
A World Treasury of Oral Poetry

INDEX

Titles of anthologies are printed in italic type; editors, compilers, or translators are printed in roman upper and lower case type; subject categories are printed in roman capital and small capital letters.

DISCARD